A SELECT LIBRARY

OF

NICENE AND POST-NICENE FATHERS

OF

THE CHRISTIAN CHURCH

Second Series

TRANSLATED INTO ENGLISH WITH PROLEGOMENA AND EXPLANATORY NOTES

UNDER THE EDITORIAL SUPERVISION OF

PHILIP SCHAFF, D.D., LL.D., AND **HENRY WACE, D.D.,**

Professor of Church History in the Union Theological Seminary, New York.   *Principal of King's College, London.*

IN CONNECTION WITH A NUMBER OF PATRISTIC SCHOLARS OF EUROPE AND AMERICA.

VOLUME VI

ST. JEROME:

LETTERS AND SELECT WORKS:

T&T CLARK
EDINBURGH

WM. B. EERDMANS PUBLISHING COMPANY
GRAND RAPIDS, MICHIGAN

Nicene & Post-Nicene Fathers. — 2nd series
1. Fathers of the church
I. Schaff, Philip II. Mace, Henry
230'.11   BR60.A62

T&T Clark ISBN 0 567 09415 4

Eerdmans ISBN 0-8028-8120-3

Reprinted 1996

PHOTOLITHOPRINTED BY EERDMANS PRINTING COMPANY
GRAND RAPIDS, MICHIGAN, UNITED STATES OF AMERICA

THE PRINCIPAL WORKS OF ST. JEROME

TRANSLATED BY

THE HON. W. H. FREMANTLE, M.A.,

Canon of Canterbury Cathedral and Fellow and Tutor of Balliol College, Oxford,

WITH THE ASSISTANCE OF

THE REV. G. LEWIS, M.A.,

Of Balliol College, Oxford, Vicar of Dodderhill near Droitwick,

AND

THE REV. W. G. MARTLEY, M.A.,

of Balliol College, Oxford.

TRANSLATOR'S PREFACE

THE grounds on which certain works of Jerome have been selected, as most important, for translation in this edition, while others have been omitted, are given in the Prolegomena (p. xvii–xviii).

The first draught of the translation was prepared by my coadjutors and former pupils, Mr. G. Lewis and Mr. W. G. Martley, who also added most of the notes ; but I have gone minutely through every part, correcting, adding, and at times re-writing, both in the MS. and in the proof, and I have composed the Prolegomena and Indices.

I have endeavoured to make the work useful not to the theologian alone, but also to the historical student. The general reader will find interest and even entertainment in the parts of the work referred to in the Index under such headings as " Pictures of Contemporary Life," " Proverbs," "Stories" and " Quotations," or by looking at the Letters to which special atten- tion is called in the Prolegomena at p. xviii. The Table of Contents also, in which a short description is given of the purport of each Letter, will help each class of readers to select the parts suitable to them. Finally, the Life of Jerome included in the Prolegomena, though closely compressed, has been furnished with copious references, which will make it a key to the whole work. It is only to be regretted that, through the impossibility of including Jerome's work on Illustrious Men and his controversy with Rufinus in the present volume, it is necessary to send the reader for a few of the most important facts to Vol. iii of this Series.

I can hardly expect that, in a work which has been carried through amidst many pressing engagements, which has been printed two thousand miles away, and of which I have had only a single proof to correct, I have been able to avoid all mistakes. But I hope that no inaccu- racies have crept in of sufficient magnitude to mar the usefulness of the work. I have felt the responsibility of making the first translation of Jerome into English, especially as a trans- lation once made acts as a hindrance to those who might wish to attempt the same task. But I trust that the present work may be found to be not altogether an unworthy presentment of the great Latin church-writer to the English-speaking world.

W. H. FREMANTLE.

CANTERBURY, *November*, 1892.

CONTENTS

LETTERS.

TREATISES.

PREFACES.

PROLEGOMENA TO JEROME

I. INTRODUCTORY.

St. Jerome's importance lies in the facts : (1) That he was the author of the Vulgate Translation of the Bible into Latin, (2) That he bore the chief part in introducing the ascetic life into Western Europe, (3) That his writings more than those of any of the Fathers bring before us the general as well as the ecclesiastical life of his time. It was a time of special interest, the last age of the old Greco-Roman civilization, the beginning of an altered world. It included the reigns of Julian (361–63), Valens (364–78), Valentinian (364–75), Gratian (375–83), Theodosius (379–95) and his sons, the definitive establishment of orthodox Christianity in the Empire, and the sack of Rome by Alaric (410). It was the age of the great Fathers, of Ambrose and Augustine in the West, of Basil, the Gregories, and Chrysostom in the East. With several of these Jerome was brought into personal contact ; of Ambrose he often speaks in his writings (Apol. i. 2, iii. 14, in this series Vol. iii., pp. 484 and 526 ; also this Vol., pp. 74 and 496, Pref. to Origen and S. Luke ; and the Pref. to Didymus on the Holy Spirit, quoted in Rufinus' Apology, ii. 24, 43, Vol. iii. of this series, pp. 470 and 480 ; also On Illust. Men, c. 124, Vol. iii. 383 ; see also Index—Ambrose) ; with Augustin he carried on an important correspondence (see Table of Contents) ; he studied under Gregory Nazianzen (80, 93 ; see also Illust. Men, c. 117, Vol. iii. 382) at the time of the Council at Constantinople, 381 ; he was acquainted with Gregory of Nyssa (Illust. Men, c. 128, Vol. iii. 338) ; he translated the diatribe of Theophilus of Alexandria against Chrysostom (214, 215). He ranks as one of the four Doctors of the Latin Church, and his influence was the most lasting ; for, though he was not a great original thinker like Augustin, nor a champion like Ambrose, nor an organiser and spreader of Christianity like Gregory, his influence outlasted theirs. Their influence in the Middle Ages was confined to a comparatively small circle ; but the monastic institutions which he introduced, the value for relics and sacred places which he defended, the deference which he showed for Episcopal authority, especially that of the Roman Pontiff, were the chief features of the Christian system for a thousand years ; his Vulgate was the Bible of Western Christendom till the Reformation. To the theologian he is interesting rather for what he records than for any contribution of his own to the science ; but to the historian his vivid descriptions of persons and things at an important though melancholy epoch of the world are of inestimable value.

II. CONTEMPORARY HISTORY.

The references in this Section, where numbers alone are given, are to the date A. D.

It seems desirable to prefix to this Introduction some account of the times of St. Jerome. General and ecclesiastical history must not be kept too far apart.

Jerome was born in the troubled times which followed the death of Constantine (337), and before Constantius became sole Emperor (353). He was still a schoolboy during the reign of Julian (361–63), and when he heard of his death. During his student life at Rome, Jovian and Valentinian were Emperors, and at Treves, where he next sojourned, the latter Emperor held his court. His first letter refers to a scene in which Ambrose, then Prefect of Liguria, seems to have taken part (370), and his settlement at Aquileia synchronises with the law of Valentinian restraining legacies to the clergy (370). He went to the East in the year of the death of Athanasius (373), and during his stay in the desert and at Antioch (374–80) occurred the death of Valentinian, the defeat and death of his brother Valens in the battle of Adrianople, the elevation of Theodosius to the purple, and the call of Gregory Nazianzen to Constantinople. He was ordained by Paulinus, one of the three Bishops of Antioch, and studied under Apollinaris, thus touching on both the chief points for which the Council of Constantinople was called (381). At that Council he was probably present, being, as stated above, a disciple of its president, Gregory Nazianzen. He was present also at the Western Council held the next year in Rome under Pope Damasus, whose trusted counsellor he became (pp. 233, 255). His later life, spent at Bethlehem (386–420), witnessed the division of the

Empire between the sons of Theodosius, the fall of the Prefect Rufinus (p. 174), to whom Jerome had been denounced, the triumph of Stilicho and his death (at which he weakly rejoiced, p. 237), Alaric's sack of Rome (410) and his death, the revolt of Heraclian, the marriage of Alaric's successor, Adolphus, with the Emperor's sister, Galla Placidia, and the death of Arcadius (408) ; in ecclesiastical matters, it witnessed the rise of Chrysostom (398) and his exile (403) and death (407), the condemnation of Origenism (400), and the Pelagian controversy (415). It is of this period that we are now to give a sketch.

The Emperor Constantius " may be dismissed," says Gibbon, " with the remark that he inherited the defects without the abilities of his father." He died in Cilicia on November 3, 361 ; he had been stained in his youth by the blood of nine of his near relatives ; he had fallen early under the dominion of the eunuchs of his palace ; and he had done little for the defence of the empire. In ecclesiastical matters he had favoured the Arian cause, and had banished the orthodox Bishops of the principal sees, and had visited Athanasius of Alexandria with his especial displeasure. His jealousy of his cousin Julian, who had risen to fame by his just and vigorous administration and by his victories over the Germans, led him into acts which provoked the legions of Gaul and caused them to hail Julian as their Emperor. His overtures of peace were rejected by Constantius ; he marched rapidly toward Constantinople, and Constantius, leaving the Persian war in which he was engaged, turned westward to meet him. The death of Constantius saved the world from civil war.

Julian's accession was hailed by all who felt the need of a strong ruler ; and his first measures were just and tolerant. He recalled from exile the Bishops whom Constantius had banished ; his private life was virtuous, and his love of learning endeared him to some of the best of his subjects. But his contempt of Christianity made him first impatient and then a persecutor. He forbade Christians, or Galileans as he called them, to teach in the schools, or to follow the learned professions ; he restored Paganism, though it was observed that the Paganism he introduced was in many ways modified by Christian influence ; and he favoured the Jews and wished them to rebuild their temple at Jerusalem. What the result of his retrogressive policy would have been it is hard to say. He died in a skirmish in the Persian war, on June 26, 363.

Jovian, who succeeded him, was a Christian ; and his election showed that the anti-Christian policy of Julian had been without effect. He proclaimed a complete toleration, but died before reaching Constantinople, only six months after his election.

Valentinian, his successor, was an orthodox Christian, his brother Valens, whom he associated with himself, an Arian. Valentinian established his court at Treves, and successfully kept back the barbarians. Thither in 366 Jerome went for a time, and he describes the curious customs of the tribes whom he saw there (Against Jovinian, ii. 7, p. 394). The Emperors proclaimed toleration, which extended even to the celebration of the Eleusinian mysteries. But their inquisitorial and cruel treatment of all suspected of magic arts had a repressive effect upon learning. Their foundation of schools and endowment of physicians for the poorer citizens show that the hopes of social improvement were not extinguished. Yet the state of society in Rome and in other large cities, as given at this time by Ammianus Marcellinus (cxiv. 6, xxviii. 4. See Gibbon, iv. 77. Ed. Milman & Smith), reveals to us the causes of the fall of Rome.

In the reign of Valentinian many ecclesiastical events of great importance took place. The election of Damasus to the Popedom in 366, when the rival factions of Damasus and Ursinus filled the whole city with their conflict, and churches were stormed and strewed with the slain, showed how important the Bishopric of Rome had become. " If you would make me Pope, perhaps I might become a Christian," said Prætextatus, the worshipper of the old gods, to Damasus, who wished to convert him (see p. 428). The law of Valentinian forbidding legacies to be made to the clergy shows also their wealth and deterioration (p. 92). But this reign produced some of the greatest Bishops and leaders whom the Church has known. Athanasius died in 373. Ambrose became Bishop of Milan in 374. Basil was Bishop of Cæsarea in Cappadocia from 370 to 379.

Meanwhile, the reign of Valens in the East was unsuccessful, and ended in a great disaster. The Visigoths, and Ostrogoths, or Gruthungi, pressed by the Huns, implored permission to cross the Danube from their settlements in Dacia and to be allowed to cultivate the waste lands of Thrace and Asia Minor. This was conceded to them ; but they were ill treated and cajoled, and at last asserted their rights by force ; and the Emperor, who attacked them near Adrianople, was defeated and slain, and his army destroyed (378). The Goths were now a formidable force within the Empire. It was in the year before the death of Valens (377) that Stridon, the birth-place of Jerome, was destroyed.

Valentinian had died in 375, leaving two sons, Gratian, an accomplished youth of eighteen, who became Emperor of Gaul and the West, and Valentinian II., then a child, who was nominal Emperor of Italy and the central provinces, and who, with his mother Justina, had his residence at Milan. Gratian distinguished himself by his conduct of several expeditions against the German tribes beyond the Rhine, and, upon the death of his uncle Valens, nominated Theodosius to be Emperor of the East. But he afterwards yielded to idleness and frivolous pleasure, and in 383 was murdered by the agents of the usurper Maximus.

Theodosius, the son of the elder Theodosius, who had recovered Britain and Africa for the Empire, but had on a false accusation been put to death at Carthage, was called to the Empire from his retirement in Spain. He showed himself a great and capable ruler. He took the Goths in detail and gradually dispossessed them. He put down the usurper Maximus (383), and on the death of the young Valentinian (392) fought against the usurper Eugenius, and became sole Emperor (394) in the year before his death. He reformed the laws, enacting the Theodosian Code. In his reign Paganism was finally suppressed. He caused a vote to be taken in the Roman Senate for the establishment of Christian worship and the suppression of Paganism. He destroyed the temples—the destruction of the Serapeum at Alexandria in 389 being the most notable instance of this—and supported Ambrose in his vehement efforts for the suppression of Paganism. Though he loyally befriended the Empress Justina, who was an Arian, and her young son Valentinian II., he did not support their demand for the toleration of Arian worship at Milan which Ambrose had denied to them, and he suppressed Arianism throughout the Empire. To settle the doctrinal disputes raised by the teaching of Apollinaris, Bishop of the Syrian Laodicæa, who held that the Logos in Christ supplied the place of the human soul, and the disputed succession at Antioch, where the Episcopal throne was claimed by the Arian Vitalis, the Trinitarian but Arianordained Meletius, and Paulinus the champion of the uncompromising orthodoxy of the West, he summoned the Council of Constantinople, which met in 381. The President of the Council was Gregory Nazianzen, who had come to Constantinople in 379, and, partly through his own eloquence and other great powers, partly through the influence of Theodosius, had won his way from the position of minister of a single church, the Anastasis, to the Episcopal throne. The Egyptian Bishops opposed him and vainly endeavoured to foist in the Cynic Maximus into his place. The Council did not succeed in settling the dispute at Antioch, but they maintained the Nicene creed, and added to it all the articles after " I believe in the Holy Ghost." The Council held at Rome in the following year (382), to which Jerome went with Epiphanius, Bishop of Cyprus, and Paulinus of Antioch (p. 255), contradicted that of Constantinople on the subject of the succession at Antioch, but agreed with it on the creed. Gregory Nazianzen soon after the Council resigned the Bishopric of Constantinople, and Damasus, Bishop of Rome, died in 384.

Theodosius was, like Henry II. of England, liable to violent accesses of passion. When the people of Antioch rose in insurrection in 387, and destroyed the busts of the Emperor, he gave an order that the city should be razed and reduced to the rank of a village, from which sentence he was only deterred by the entreaties of the Governor of the city and its Bishop, John Chrysostom. When a similar rising took place at Thessalonica in 390, he was not similarly appeased, but ordered that the people when summoned to the theatre should be massacred by his soldiers, and seven thousand men, women and children were thus put to death. Ambrose, on Theodosius' coming to Milan, refused to admit him to the communion of the Church till he had undergone five months of penance and showed his repentance for his crime.

On the death of the young Valentinian in 391, Eugenius the rhetorician usurped the throne of the West. Justina fled to the court of Theodosius, who, after long preparations, marched against Eugenius, and defeated him at Aquileia in 394. Theodosius, however, did not long survive his rival. After this last success he gave himself up to ease and self-indulgence, and died 395.

The Empire was divided between the sons of Theodosius. Arcadius, who became Emperor of the East, was eighteen years of age, and Honorius, fourteen. Both were weak characters, ill suited to cope with the growing dangers of the Empire. Arcadius married Eudoxia, a woman of a worldly and violent disposition. Honorius married the daughter of Stilicho, the great semi-barbarian general, who was his cousin, having married Serena, the daughter of Honorius, brother to the great Theodosius. Arcadius' minister, Rufinus, became so unbearable in his rapacity (see Jerome's allusion to him, p. 447) that a tumult was raised against him and he was put to death (395). Honorius removed his court to Ravenna, among the pine forests of which he was more secure from invasion ; and, so long as he was under the guidance of Stilicho, was able to live in security.

John Chrysostom became Bishop of Constantinople in 398, and by his sermons and ascetic discipline exerted a large influence. But intrigues were raised against him by Theophilus of Alexandria on account of his reception of the Long Monks, whom Theophilus had banished in his zeal against Origenism. And the Empress Eudoxia, whom his plain speaking had offended, endeavoured to work his ruin. He was banished, after having been once brought back to the capital by the entreaties of the people, in 404, and died in 407, having continued to exercise his influence over the Church generally from his exile at Comana in Pontus. His remains were brought to Constantinople thirty years later, and were welcomed by Theodosius II. and his consort Eudocia with tears of repentance for the fault of their predecessors. Arcadius died in 408, leaving as his heir the young Theodosius, then but seven years old. His daughter Pulcheria and the Prefect Anthemius administered the Empire successfully ; the Huns, who had entered the Roman territory and encamped in Thrace, were persuaded to withdraw, and the Eastern Empire enjoyed peace during the remainder of the reign of Theodosius II.

Turning to ecclesiastical affairs, we find a certain calm settling down upon the Church after the Council of Constantinople, and an unwillingness to reopen the subjects of strife. Men used the name of heretic rather as something to frighten their opponents, and sought to identify opinions which they disliked with the Arianism of the past, which all alike condemned. There were much fewer Councils of Bishops and no General Council for fifty years (Ephesus, 431). But other subjects of dispute arose, the Christian community being saturated with Greek contentiousness. The first of these related to Origenism. The works of the great and original church teacher of Alexandria of the third century (+254) had been little studied for above a hundred years, when a new interest in them arose both in the East and the West. The earnest study of Scripture which led to the formation of the Vulgate, or translation from the original into the vulgar tongue of the Latin world, led to a wish to consult the greatest textual writer and interpreter of Scripture who had as yet appeared ; and those who learned from his Bible work to admire him were led also to study his doctrinal views. It happened to Origen, as to many modern teachers, that his name came to be identified with one or two prominent doctrines ; and, as men speak of Calvinism or Erastianism or Hegelianism, so they spoke of Origenism. The doctrines which they connected with Origen were taken from his most important work, the Περὶ Ἀρχῶν, "on First Principles." They were mainly (1) his expressions relating to the subordination of the Son to the Father, and (2) his eschatology. As to the first of these, they took isolated expressions, such as, "The Son does not see the Father," or, "the Son is darkness in comparison with the Father," and they spoke of him as the father of Arius ; as to the second, they fastened upon his speculative ideas, that the coming of men's souls into this world was a fall from a previous state of being ; that men may rise into an angelic state ; that the material body is destined to pass away ; and that in the consummation of all things all spiritual beings, including the fallen angels, will be schooled into obedience, so that the universe may be brought back into harmony. Men were incapable of entering into the general system of Origen, and still more of understanding his historical position. The Pope Anastasius who condemned him in 404 says plainly that he knows neither who Origen was nor when he lived (see Vol. iii. 433) ; and they consequently took his tenets in an absolute sense, and thought of him as denying the divinity of Christ, or the condemnation of the wicked, or the resurrection of the body. His views were most widely spread in Egypt, where the contrary tendency of Anthropomorphism, that is, the conception of God as the subject of human properties and passions, was also widely prevalent. Theophilus, Bishop of Alexandria, at first was generally favourable to Origen, as was also Jerome ; but, through various causes, not unmixed with personal feeling, he turned against Origenism in a fanatical and persecuting temper. He procured the condemnation of Origenism by the Bishops of Egypt, Syria, and Cyprus, and also by those of Rome and Italy ; and he pursued those who had fled from his persecution to Constantinople, and branded Chrysostom, who had received them, as a heretic. In all this he was aided by Jerome, who translated his missives into Latin (see Letters 86 to 100, 113 and 114). But the whole matter was transacted without any Council being called ; the Bishops were taken as speaking the general sentiment, and their decisions were reinforced by a decree of the Emperors (400).

The second controversy (which also was disposed of without any General Council) was that of Pelagianism. Pelagius and Cælestius, monks of Britain, had come to Rome in 409, and maintained the doctrine of Free Will and the possibility of a man living without sin, against the Augustinian doctrine of Grace, which asserted the helplessness of man and issued in absolute predestinarianism. They passed into Africa with the crowds who were escaping from Alaric's invasion, and there confronted the influence of Augustin. Condemned by a Council at Carthage in 413, they passed into Palestine, and procured recognition from Councils held at Jerusalem and Diospolis in 415, notwithstanding the presence of Orosius, Augustin's friend, and the accusations of the Gaulish Bishops, Heros and Lazarus. Jerome was invited to write against them (pp. 272, 279), and their followers rose against him and burnt his monasteries (p. 280, Augustin De Gest. Pel. c. 66), after which they visited Ephesus and Rome, and were at first received by the Pope Zosimus ; and several Bishops, of whom the chief was Julian of Eclana, espoused their cause. But Augustin's influence prevailed in the West, while in the East little interest was taken in a controversy which was humanistic rather than strictly theological, and men's minds were being drawn to the questions of Christology, which led to the Nestorian controversy and the Council of Ephesus (431).

The forces of the barbarians, which in the reign of Valens had threatened Constantinople, were diverted to the West in the reign of the sons of Theodosius. Those who remained within the boundaries of the Empire imbibed something of Roman civilisation, and, in many cases, became servants of Rome ; and, as the subjects of the Empire withdrew through love of luxury from military duties, the power of the barbarians enlisted as mercenaries increased. Alaric, who now rose to power, occupied an ambiguous position. He marched with his Gothic army into Greece (396), and, being a Christian, thought himself justified in plundering the historic fanes of the old religion. He was attacked by Stilicho near the Isthmus of Corinth, and defeated, but he contrived to transport his army across the gulf and to take possession of Epirus (397), and the ministers of Arcadius thought it prudent to make peace with him. In 398 he became at once Master-General of Illyricum and King of the Visigoths ; and, his rights not being respected by the Emperor of the West, he invaded the North of Italy. He was vanquished by Stilicho in the battles of Pollentia and Verona (403) ; but the conqueror, who well knew the increasing weakness of Rome, made peace with Alaric and acknowledged his official position. Alaric retreated for a time, but another barbarian invader, Radagaisus or Radaghast, with a mixed host of Vandals, Suevi, and Burgundians, forced his way to Florence. He was there met by Stilicho who gained over him his last great victory on the heights of Fiesole (406). The policy of conciliation adopted by Stilicho might have converted Alaric and his Goths into the guards of the Empire ; but his action was disowned, and he was treated as a traitor and put to death in 408. Then Alaric advanced to the attack upon Rome. He was induced by fair promises to raise the siege ; but, finding that no faith could be placed in the court of Ravenna, he renewed the siege, and took the city on August 26, 410. The only redeeming feature in the terrible destruction which ensued was the respect of the Goths for the Christian religion. They spared the clergy and the churches and those who had taken refuge in them ; and even the rich plate and ornaments of divine worship were held sacred from their rapacity. But the knell of Roman greatness had been sounded, and the end of the Empire was near at hand. Alaric on leaving Rome ravaged Italy. He marched to Rhegium, the flames of which Rufinus saw from the opposite coast while he wrote his Commentary on the Book of Numbers (Vol. iii. p. 568) ; but his attempt to cross into Sicily was frustrated by a storm, and he himself died before the year of the sack of Rome had closed. His successor, Adolphus, made peace with Rome, and dared to ask for the hand of Galla Placidia, the sister of Honorius. The King of the Goths was accepted as the brother-in-law of the Roman Emperor.

The Empire of the West might now be compared to a ship heaving to and fro in a troubled sea, encompassed by enemies and without captain or rudder. Britain had revolted in 409. From 409 to 413 Gaul was a prey to revolutions, and the usurper Constantine was with difficulty overcome by the Roman General Constantius, only to be followed by fresh usurpers, Jovinus, Sebastian, and Attalus. The Count Heraclian dared to invade Rome itself in 413, though defeat and death were the penalty. One by one the provinces of the Empire passed into the hands of the barbarians. The Goths settled in Aquitaine and in Spain ; the Vandals turned down into Africa ; the Burgundians settled in the East and North of France, and the Franks in the centre. The ruin of the Empire of the West was practically consummated at the time of Jerome's death in 419, though sixty years of disaster and disgrace intervened before its final extinction.

Meanwhile the distressed condition of Italy had driven large numbers of persons, especially of the clergy and the upper classes of society, to take refuge in the East, so as almost to justify Thierry's designation of the movement as an emigration to the Holy Land. Jerome and his friends received this tide of fugitives at Bethlehem, and corresponded with those left behind ; and thus the evils of the time made the Solitary of the East the chief Doctor of the West.

III. LIFE OF JEROME.

The figures in parentheses, when not otherwise indicated, refer to the pages in this volume.

For a full account of the Life, the translator must refer to an article (HIERONYMUS) written by him in Smith and Wace's *Dictionary of Christian Biography*. A shorter statement may suffice here, since the chief sources of information are contained in this volume, and to these reference will be continually made.

Childhood and Youth. Jerome was born at Stridon, near Aquileia, but in Pannonia, a place which was partially destroyed in the Gothic invasion of 377 (On Illustrious Men, 135, Vol. iii. p. 304). Jerome's own property, however, remained, though in a ruinous A.D. 345   state, in 397 (140). His father Eusebius (Ill. Men, as above) and his mother were Catholic Christians (492), but he was not baptised in infancy. The family was moderately wealthy, possessing houses (140) and slaves (Apol. i. 30, Vol. iii. p. 498), and was intimate with the richer family from which sprang Bonosus, Jerome's foster brother and friend (6). The parents were living in 373 when Jerome first went to the East (35), but probably died at the destruction of Stridon. He had a brother, Paulinian, twenty years his junior (140, 173), and we read of a sister (8, 9), and an aunt named Castorina (13).

He received a good education, but declares that he was an idle boy (Vol. iii. 498). He was at a grammar school when the Emperor Julian died (Comm. on Habakkuk iii. 14) and soon after went to Rome with his friend Bonosus (6), where he studied rhetoric (at that time the all-embracing pursuit) under Ælius Donatus (Vol. iii. 491), and frequented 363   the law-courts (Comm. on Gal., ii. 13). He fell into sin (9, 15, 78), but was drawn into the company of young Christians who on Sundays visited the tombs of the 366   martyrs in the Catacombs (Com. on Ezek., ch. 40, v. 5), and is believed to have been baptised by the Pope Liberius in 366 (20). He was already a keen student, though as yet having little knowledge of Greek (Rufinus Apol. ii. 9, Vol. iii. p. 464), and had begun the acquisition of a library (35).

From Rome Jerome went with Bonosus to Gaul, passing, however, through Northern Italy, where they made acquaintance with Rufinus, probably at his native place, 366–70.   Concordia (Ep. v. 2, comp. with iii. 3, pp. 7, 11). He stayed at Treves (7), and travelled in its neighbourhood (394), and copied MSS., and wrote a mystical Commentary on Obadiah (401).

Aquileia. Returning probably by Vercellæ (1) to Italy he was for three years at Aquileia, where he entered definitively upon the twin pursuits of his life, Scriptural study and the fostering of asceticism. A society of congenial minds gathered round him, comprising Rufinus, Bonosus, Heliodorus (afterwards Bishop of Altinum), Chromatius (afterwards Bishop of Aquileia), and his brother Eusebius, and the Archdeacon Jovinus, the monk Chrysogonus, the sub-deacon Niceas, Innocentius, and Hylas, the freedman 370–73.   of the wealthy but ascetic Roman lady, Melania, together with Evagrius (afterwards Bishop of Antioch), who had come to Italy with Eusebius, Bishop of Vercellæ, on his return from exile. For the mention of these in various parts of Jerome's works, the Index must be consulted. These ascetics did not form a monastery. There were as yet no Orders or Rules. The vow was merely a "purpose" (*propositum*) which each privately took on himself and the terms of which each man freely prescribed. The Greek word *Monachus* (Monk) was used, but only implied living a single or separate life. Some were hermits (5, 9, 247), some lived in cities (121, 250). Jovinian was a monk, though antiascetic (378); Heliodorus (91) and John of Jerusalem (174) were monks, though Bishops. Some members of the ascetic society at Aquileia may have resided in the same house; but there was no cenobitic discipline. Jerome visited Stridon and the neighbouring town of Æmona (12), and perhaps resided at his native place for a time, but he complains of the worldliness of the people of his native town and of the opposition of their Bishop, Lupicinus (8 n. 10). The friends at Aquileia were united in the closest friendship. Rufinus' baptism (7, Ruf. 373   Ap. i. 4, Vol. iii. 436) and the writing of Jerome's first letter on "the woman seven times struck with the axe" are the only incidents which have come down to us of this period. We only know that the society was broken up by some event which Jerome speaks of as "a sudden storm," and "a monstrous rending asunder" (5).

Jerome determined on going to the East with Evagrius and Heliodorus; Innocentius, Niceas, and Hylas accompanied him (1, 5, 6, 10). Chromatius, Eusebius, and Jovinus remained in Italy. Bonosus retired to an island in the Adriatic, where he lived the life of a hermit (5, 9). Rufinus went to Egypt and subsequently to Palestine in the company of

Melania (6, 7). Jerome and his companions travelled through Thrace, Pontus, Bithynia, Galatia, at the capital of which (Ancyra) he appears to have stayed (497), Cappadocia, and Cilicia, to Antioch, their haven of rest (5). But they did not long remain together. Helio-

374. dorus made a journey to Jerusalem, where he was the guest of Florentius (6). Jerome was in ill health, and at length, in the middle of Lent (36), fell into a fever of which he nearly died. To this illness belongs his anti-Ciceronian dream (36, Apol. ii. 6, Vol. iii. 462), which finally determined him to abandon secular learning and devote himself to sacred studies. The successive deaths of Innocentius and Hylas left Jerome alone with Evagrius, at whose country house he fell in with the ancient hermit Malchus (315), and was encouraged by him in the ascetic tendency. He hoped to see Rufinus, and wrote to him through Florentius (4, 6), but he did not come; and he determined to embrace the life of solitude. Heliodorus had some thought of accompanying him, but, to Jerome's great chagrin, felt the call to pastoral work to be the stronger, and returned to Italy (8, 13, 123).

The Desert. Jerome spent the next five years in the Desert of Chalcis, to the east of Antioch (7). It was peopled by hermits who, though living apart for most purposes, were under some kind of authority (4, 21). Jerome wrote to their head, Theodosius,

374–79. begging to be admitted into their company (4). His life while in the desert was one of rigorous penance, of tears and groans alternating with spiritual ecstasy, and of temptations from the haunting memories of Roman life (24, 25); he lived in a cell or cavern; he earned his daily bread, and was clad in sackcloth (21, 24), but he was not wholly cut off from converse with men. He saw Evagrius frequently (7, 8); he wrote and received letters and books (7, 11); he learned Hebrew from a converted Jew (Ep. xviii. 10), and copied and translated the Gospel according to the Hebrews (Ill. Men, 2, 3, Vol. iii. 362), and his brother solitaries he found only too accessible (Ep. xvii. 3). Towards the close of his sojourn he became involved in the controversies then agitating the Church at Antioch, where the Arian Vitalis, the orthodox but Arian-ordained Meletius, and the Western Paulinus disputed the possession of the bishopric (20). Jerome found himself beset with demands for a confession of faith in terms strange to his Western education (19, 20). He appealed to Pope Damasus for advice (19, 20); but he and his friends found his position intolerable. They would rather, he says, live among wild beasts than among Christians such as those about them. In the autumn of 378 he wrote to Marcus, then head of the eremite community, to say that he only begged for the "hospitality of the desert" for a few months: in the spring he would be gone (21).

Accordingly, in the spring of 379 he came to Antioch and attached himself to the party of Paulinus, the Western and orthodox Bishop, who ordained him presbyter,

379. though he then and always afterwards declined the active ministry (446). He pursued his studies under the celebrated Apollinarius of Laodicæa, though not accepting his views (176), and wrote his "Dialogue against the Luciferians" (319–334).

Constantinople. The next year Jerome went, with his Bishop, Paulinus, to Constantinople, and was there during the Second General Council, at which the views of his

380. teacher, Apollinarius, were condemned, and sentence was passed in the cause of his Bishop. He placed himself under the teaching of Gregory Nazianzen (80, 93, 357; Ill. Men, 117), and became acquainted with Gregory of Nyssa (Ill. Men, 128); he translated the Chronicle of Eusebius and dedicated it to Vincentius and Gallienus, the former of whom became henceforward his companion (483, 444–446); he imbibed his admiration for Origen, translating his Homilies on Jeremiah and Ezekiel, and writing to Damasus on the meaning given by Origen to the Seraphim in Is. vi. (22). These literary labours

381. were carried on under the disadvantage of a weakness of the eyes, from which he henceforward constantly suffered. But there is in his writings not a single refer-ence to the Council of Constantinople, and only cursory references to that held the next year at Rome, in which he was certainly called to take part (233; Ruf. Epil. to Pamph., Vol. iii. 426, 513).

Rome. He went to Rome with his Bishop, Paulinus, and with Epiphanius, Bishop of Salamis in Cyprus. At the Council which was there held he was present as a learned man whose help the Pope required. There is no ground for the notion that he became

382–5. his official secretary. But for the two main objects of Jerome's life his sojourn in Rome presented great opportunities. Damasus thoroughly appreciated his emi-nence as a biblical scholar. He constantly sent him questions, the replies to which form short exegetical treatises, such as those reckoned among Jerome's letters on the word Hosanna and the Prodigal Son. It was also for Pope Damasus that he undertook a revised version of the Psalms, a version which was used in the Roman Church for more than eleven centuries (492, 494); and also a revised version of the New Testament, the preface to which is of much critical value (487, 488 ; see also p. 357, where a whole clause in 1 Cor. vii. 35 is said to have been omitted in the old version because of the difficulty of translation). He further began the collation of the various texts of the LXX. and the other Greek versions of the Old Testament, and began to form the convictions which afterwards led to his translation direct from the Hebrew (484). These biblical studies made him acquainted with the works of Origen, and he conceived a great and almost passionate admiration for that " brazen-hearted " (Chalchenterus) worker and teacher of the Church (46), and he permitted himself to use expressions too indiscriminate in praise of him and too contemptuous towards his adversaries, which were afterwards thrown in his teeth (Ruf. Ap. ii. 14, Vol. iii. 467).

For the promotion of asceticism he found in Rome a congenial soil. Epiphanius, himself the pupil of the hermits Hesychias and Hilarion (Sozom. vi. 32, Vol. ii. 369, 370), was the guest of the noble and wealthy lady Paula, the heiress of the Æmilian race (196), who was already disposed to the ascetic life. To the circle of her family and friends Jerome was soon admitted, and she became his devoted disciple and friend during the remainder of her life (Letter cviii.). Her son, Toxotius, and her daughters, Blesilla, the young widow (47–49), Paulina, the wife of Jerome's friend, the ascetic Senator Pammachius (135), and Julia Eustochium (196), each in special ways affected the life of Jerome. Her friends, Marcella and Principia (253), Asella (42, 58), Lea (42), Furia and Titiana, Marcellina and Felicitas (60) and Fabiola, all of them belonging to the highest Roman families, formed a circle of renuntiants who sought refuge in the ascetic life from the wastefulness and immorality of those of their own quality. Marcella's house on the Aventine was their meeting place (41, 58). There they prayed and sang psalms in the Hebrew, which they had learned for the purpose (210), and read the Scriptures under the guidance of their teacher (41, 255), who wrote for them many of his expository letters, whose ascetic writings they committed to memory, and whose private letters to them (Letters xxiii.–xlvi.) reveal the various phases of the new Roman and Christian life. These are concentrated in the Treatise on the Preservation of Virginity which he addressed to Eustochium (Letter xxii.). This period also produced the first of Jerome's controversial treatises, that against Helvidius on the perpetual virginity of Mary (334–346).

This congenial scene of activity and friendship was broken up by the death of Damasus. The new Pope, Siricius, to whom many had thought of Jerome as a rival (59), was without sympathy for him : he had offended almost every class of the community by
384.   his unrestrained satire (Letters xxii., xl., liv., etc.) : he had awakened suspicion
          by his over praise of Origen (46) ; and at the funeral of Blesilla, whose end was
385.   believed to have been hastened by the hard life enjoined upon her, the fury of the
          people was excited against Jerome and the cry was raised " The monks to the
Tiber ! " (53).   He felt that he was vainly trying to " sing the Lord's song in a strange land " (60) and he resolved to leave Rome for ever and to seek a retreat in Palestine. His departure in August and the feelings excited by it are described in a passage in his Apology against Rufinus (Ap. iii. 22, Vol. iii. 530) and in his letter to Asella (Letter xlv.) written at the moment of his embarkation at Ostia.

Jerome sailed with Vincentius and with his brother Paulinian (Vol. iii. 530 as above) direct to Antioch. Paula and Eustochium, leaving the other members of their family, went to Cyprus to see Epiphanius ; and the two parties united at Antioch (198).   Thence they
          passed through Palestine and Jerusalem, on to Egypt, where they visited the
385–86. abode of the monks of Nitria (202) and became acquainted with Didymus, " the
          blind seer " of Alexandria (176); and they returned to Palestine in the autumn of
386, and settled at Bethlehem for the remainder of their lives.

Bethlehem, First Period. Jerome's life at Bethlehem lasted thirty-four years. A monastery was built, of which he was the head, and a convent for women over which Paula and
          Eustochium successively presided (206), a church where all assembled (206, 292),
386–420. and a hospice for pilgrims who came to visit the holy places from all parts of the
          world (140).   These institutions were supported by the wealth of Paula until,
through the profusion of her charities, she was so impoverished that she rather depended on Jerome and his brother, who sold the remains of their family property for their support (140). He lived in a cell, surrounded by his library, to which he constantly made additions (Ruf. Ap. ii. 8 (2), Vol. iii. 464).   He lived on bread and vegetables (165), and speaks of his life as one of repentance and prayer (446), but no special austerities are mentioned in his writings, and he did not think piety increased by the absence of cleanliness (33, 34).   He never offici-

ated in the services (83), but was much absorbed in the cares (140) and discipline (Letter cxlvii.) of the monastery, and by the crowds of monks who came from all parts of the world (64, 65, 500). Sulpicius Severus (Dial. i. 8) tells us that when he was with him towards the close of his life, he had the charge of the parish of Bethlehem ; and the presbyters associated with him certainly prepared candidates for baptism (446) ; but his call, as he often confesses, was not to the pastorate, but to the study (Letter cxii.). He had youths to whom he taught the Latin classics (Ruf. Apol. ii. 8 (2), Vol. iii. 465) ; and he expounded the Scriptures daily to the brethren in the monastery (Apol. ii. 124, Vol. iii. 515). Sulpicius speaks of him as always reading or writing, never resting day or night. Translations, commentaries, controversial works, letters dealing with important subjects, flowed constantly from his pen, while the notes passing between him and Paula and Eustochium were without number (Ill. Men, 135, Vol. iii. 384), and every thing that he wrote was caught up by friends or by enemies and published (79). He worked amidst great distractions, not merely from the cares of the monasteries and the hospice, but from the need of entertaining persons of distinction, like Fabiola (161), from all parts of the world (153, 287, 161) ; from the need of replying to the letters brought by messengers from the most distant countries for those who sought advice of the renowned teacher (Letters cxvi.–cxxx.) ; from prolonged illnesses (188, 215) ; at times from poverty (?14) ; from the panic of barbarian invasions (161, 252), and from the attacks of his enemies, who in the year 417 burned his monasteries (281, 282).

He spared no pains nor expense in the production of his works. He perfected his know-ledge of Hebrew by the aid of a Jew who came to him like Nicodemus by night (176) ; he also learned Chaldee (493) ; and for special parts of his Bible work he obtained special aid from a distance (491, 494), obtaining funds, when his own had failed, from his old friends Chromatius and Heliodorus (492).

The list of his works during the first six years of his residence at Bethlehem comprises the completion of the Commentary on Ecclesiastes, and the translation of Didymus on the Holy Spirit ; the Commentaries on Ephesians and Galatians, Titus and Philemon (498) ; a revision of the version of the New Testament begun in Rome ; a Treatise on Psalms x.–xvi., and Translation of Origen on St. Luke and the Psalms ; the Book on the Names of Hebrew Places, mainly translated from Eusebius ; the Book of Hebrew Proper Names and that of Hebrew Questions on Genesis ; the revision of his translation of the LXX., involving a comparison of Origen's Hexapla ; a considerable part of the Vulgate ; the Lives of the hermits Malchus and Hilarion ; and the Catalogue of Illustrious Church Writers. The only letter preserved to us of this period is that written in the name of Paula and Eustochium to invite Marcella to come to Palestine (60).

386–92.

Bethlehem, Second Period. The second period of Jerome's stay at Bethlehem is the period of his most conspicuous activity, which was partly employed in the salutary work of finishing the Vulgate and in writing letters which rank among the finest of his compositions, but largely also in controversies, in which the worst parts of his character and influence are brought into prominence. There were also great external hindrances to his work : the panic arising from the invasion of the Huns, on account of which the inmates of the monasteries had to leave their homes and prepare to embark at Joppa (161) ; there were long periods of ill health ; and there was the quarrel with the Bishop of Jerusalem which led to a kind of excom-munication of the monks of Bethlehem (446, 447).

392–405.

395.
398 and
404–5.
394–97.

The letters of this second period are those numbered 47 to 116. They comprise those to Nepotianus, nephew of Heliodorus, on the duties of the pastorate (89–96) ; that to Heliodorus, on the death of his nephew (123–131) ; that to Paulinus, the Roman Senator, afterwards Bishop of Nola, on his poem in praise of Theodosius, and on the study of Scripture (96–102) ; that to Furia, on the maintenance of widowhood (102–109) ; that to the Spanish noble Lucinius, who had sent scribes to copy Jerome's works (151–154), and to his widow Theodora (154, 155) ; those to Abigaus, a blind Spanish presbyter (156, 157), and to Salvina, widow of Nebridius, and closely connected with the Emperor Theodosius (163–168) ; that to Amandus, the Roman presbyter, on a difficult case of conscience (149–151) ; the letter to Oceanus, defending the second marriage of a Spanish Bishop (141–146) ; the letter to Læta, wife of Toxotius, son of Paula, on the education of her infant daughter (189–195) ; and those gems of his writings, the sketches of the lives (Epitaphia) of Fabiola (157–163) and of Paula (195–212).

391–403.

The Vulgate. The work of Jerome's life, the Vulgate version of the Scrip-tures, was completed in this period. The version which bore the name of Vul-gate, the popular or vernacular version, in his day (44, 487–488) was a loose translation of the LXX., of which almost every copy varied from every other. His first effort, therefore, was to translate, or to revise the existing translations, from a correct version of the LXX. And this revised version he used in his familiar expositions, in the monastery (Apol. ii. 24, Vol. iii. 515), though a great part of it was lost even in his lifetime (280), and all that now remains of it is Job, the Psalms, and the Preface to the Books of Solomon (494). But even the most correct text of the LXX., as he saw at once, was insufficient. In Origen's Hexapla the versions of Theodotion, Aquila, and Symmachus were given, together with two others called Quinta and Sexta, in parallel columns with the LXX. These constantly differed ; and the only mode of deciding between them was by going back to the Hebrew—"Hebraica Veritas," as he constantly terms it (80, 486, 494). Accordingly, he set himself at once, in his set-

392. tlement at Bethlehem, to the preliminary labours required for this task ; and in the sketch of his works in the Catalogue (Vol. iii. 384 ; On Ill. Men, 135) he says : "The New Testament I have restored according to the Greek original ; the Old, I

393. have translated in accordance with the Hebrew." But no portion was as yet published. In the following year he published the prophets (80) and sent other portions of his Old Testament version to Marcella at Rome, keeping the rest shut up in his closet (80), and awaiting the judgment of his friends on the portions submitted to them. He purposed from the first to publish the whole, as we see from what he calls his "helmeted preface" to the Books of Samuel and of Kings (489). But it was published in fragments, according as he had leisure to give it a final revision, or according as other circumstances were favourable. The series of Prefaces (487–494) shows that some parts were written or revised in great haste (492, 494), some parts extorted from him by the importunity of his friends (488 ; see Apol. ii. 25, in Vol. iii. 515) ; that he was subjected to severe censures and misunderstanding, as to which he was extremely sensitive ; that at times he so shrank from publicity that he wished' his friends only to read it privately ; that he was often, especially in the later portions, dependent on his friends for the provision of the copyists (492, 494). The order of publication can be traced. The Books of Samuel and of the Kings came first, then Job and the Prophets, Erza and Nehemiah, and the Book of Genesis. Thus far he had proceeded in the year 393,

395. when a break of three years occurred through external hindrances, of which the panic of the invasion of the Huns was the chief. He then, at the entreaty of Chromatius and Heliodorus (492), completed the Books of Solomon, intending to pro-

398. ceed systematically to the end. But illness intervened, after which he states that the first eight books were still wanting in the copies made for the Spaniard Lucinius

403. (153) ; nor was the publication resumed till five years later, when the remaining books from Exodus to Ruth and the Book of Esther were brought out (489, 491).

404. The whole was then collected, by others rather than by himself, and gradually superseded all other Latin versions, and, coupled with the version of the New Testament previously made, became the received, or Vulgate, edition of the Bible.

The second period of Jerome's stay at Bethlehem is the period of his great controversies. These are no less than six in number. (1) That with Jovinian on ascetic prac-

393–404. tices. (2) That with the Origenists, in which he worked with Theophilus of Alexandria and the Western Bishops. (3) That with John, Bishop of Jerusalem. (4) That with Rufinus. (5) That with Vigilantius. (6) That with Augustin. These may be described somewhat cursorily, the reader being referred for a more detailed statement of them to the Letters and Treatises themselves and to the notices prefixed to them.

(1) *Jovinian.* Jovinian was a Roman monk or, rather, solitary (for many took private monastic vows without entering any order or monastery) who had perceived the danger of degrading the ordinary Christian life which lurked in the profession of asceticism. He was not, to judge by Jerome's quotations from him (347), a man of superior ability ; but there are no apparent grounds for the imputations which Jerome throws upon his character. He put off the monastic dress, and lived like other men ; and, though he refused to marry, maintained his right as a Christian to do so. He argued that the conditions of virginity, marriage, and widowhood were equal in God's sight, provided men lived in faith and piety ; and that eating and fasting were indifferent if men gave God thanks. He seems to have had some influence, and it is stated that some who had made vows of virginity were led through his teaching to marry. Certainly his views were condemned by the Pope Siricius, by Ambrose, and by Augustin. He published a book in Rome, maintaining these opinions, and others

393. of a more speculative character, which was sent to Jerome, and was at once answered by him in his treatise "Against Jovinian" (346–416). The more speculative matters he deals with calmly ; but the anti-ascetic views he treats with violence and contempt. "These are the hissings of the old serpent ; by these the dragon expelled man

from Paradise." His intemperateness, which threw contempt upon marriage, was severely blamed by his friends at Rome, who tried to stop the publication (79 ; see also Ruf. Apol. ii. 44, Vol. iii. 480) ; but he only replied by renewed expressions of derision, and, several years later, when he has occasion to refer to Jovinian, he says, " This man, after being condemned by the authority of the Roman Church, amidst his feasts of pheasants and swine's flesh, I will not say gave up, but belched out, his life " (417).

393-403.   (2) *Origenism.* The second great controversy in which Jerome was engaged at this period relates to Origenism, about which a great controversy had arisen at Alexandria, leading to its condemnation by the Bishops of Palestine and Cyprus in the East, and by the Pope and the Bishop of Milan and others in the West.

The great church teacher of Alexandria in the third century was but little known in the West. Anastasius the Pope, in the year 399, declared that he neither knew who he was nor what he had written (Vol. iii. 433). Jerome, who had made acquaintance with his writings during his first sojourn in the East, conceived a strong admiration for him ; he did not, indeed, accept all his views, as may be seen from the first letter in which he alludes to him (22) ; but on his coming to Rome he did all in his power to make him known. He was invited by Damasus to translate some of his works (485) ; and when he found ignorant condemnations passed upon him he praised him with his usual vehemence and without discrimination, even eulogizing the Περὶ 'Αρχῶν on which the subsequent controversy mainly turned (46; Ruf. Ap. ii. 13, Vol. iii. 467). He had also quoted without blame in his Commentary on the Ephesians statements such as those relating to the pre-existence of human souls and the possible restoration of Satan (Ruf. Apol. i. 448, 454). But it was rather a literary enthusiasm and an admiration of original genius than an express consent to Origen's system. His calm judgment in later years was, that his literary services to the Church were inestimable, but that his doctrinal views were to be read with the greatest caution, and that those specially impugned were heretical (176, 177, 238, 244). It must be allowed, however, that he appears in his earlier stage as the vehement panegyrist of Origen (46, 48), and in his later stage as his equally vehement condemner ; and also that this change seems less the effect of conviction than of a fear of the imputation of heresy (Apol. iii. 33, Vol. iii. 535).

The monks in the deserts near Alexandria were divided, some holding Origenistic views, and some those of an opposite tendency and verging upon Anthropomorphism. Theophilus, the Bishop of Alexandria, at first sided with the Origenists, but afterwards turned against them, and became their relentless persecutor. During his former phase he was appealed to by John, Bishop of Jerusalem, in his controversy with Epiphanius and Jerome (427), and took his part so vehemently that he sent his confidant Isidore to Jerusalem, nominally to inquire, but really to crush out all opposition, as he stated in a letter to John (444). This letter fell into the hands of Jerome and his friends, and the intentions of Theophilus were frustrated. A period of suspicious silence followed (134) ; but when Theophilus had undergone his change he found a ready instrument in Jerome, who threw himself eagerly into the conflict (182–184), translated the encyclicals of Theophilus (185, 186, 189) which led to the condemnation of Origen in the East, and even his diatribe against St. John Chrysostom for receiving Isidore and his brethren, whom Theophilus now treated as his enemies (214). Jerome also, through his friends Pammachius, Marcella, and Eusebius (186, 256), procured the condemnation of Origen in the West.

(3) *John of Jerusalem.* The controversy with John of Jerusalem forms an episode in the more general controversy. John had been trained among the Origenistic ascetics, Epiphanius among the anti-Origenists. Jerome appears to have undergone no change in his sentiments as to Origen during the first period of his stay at Bethlehem [see his Preface to the Book of Hebrew Questions (486, 487) written in 388], and was on good terms with the Bishop of Jerusalem and with Rufinus, who was then living on the Mount of Olives. But at the beginning of the second period a certain Aterbius came to Jerusalem and spread suspicion and alarm of heresy. Jerome, herhaps weakly, " gave him satisfaction " as to his faith (Apol. iii. 33, Vol. iii. 535), while by John and Rufinus he was treated as a busybody (*id.*). This produced the first estrangement, which was greatly increased by the visit of Epiphanius in the following year. The scenes which followed may be read in Jerome's treatise " Against John of Jerusalem " (430) and in Epiphanius' letter translated by Jerome (83–85). Epiphanius was popular at Jerusalem, and after a scene in the church, in which he preached against Origenism and John against Anthropomorphism, a breach was made between the two prelates. Epiphanius came to stay at Bethlehem, and spoke of John as well nigh a heretic. John spoke of Epiphanius as " that old dotard " (430). The monks of Bethlehem took part with Epiphanius ; and he, to prevent their

393.

394.

being deprived of clerical ministration by Bishop John, ordained Jerome's brother Paulinian at his monastery of Ad in the diocese of Eleutheropolis. He was then only thirty years old, and was ordained against his will, and with the employment of force and even gagging (83). Epiphanius, returning to Cyprus, wrote to John a letter explaining his conduct (83–89), which was translated by Jerome, but which did little to allay the strife. John placed the monasteries, at least partially, under an interdict (446–447), and appealed to Rome and to Alexandria, and afterwards to Rufinus, the Pretorian Prefect at Constantinople (174, 447). Theophilus at first took John's side vehemently; but the mission of his confidant Isidore miscarried (444, 445), and after some time his views of the situation changed and he made peace with Jerome and his friends. John also was appeased; and Jerome, who 397 or 398. had written a long and bitter account of the controversy in his treatise to Pammachius "Against John of Jerusalem" (424–447), seems suddenly to have let the whole matter drop; the treatise was not finished and was not published, and we read of the strife no more.

(4) *Rufinus.* The quarrel with Jerome's early friend Rufinus did not, like that with John, 398–404. pass away. Jerome had deeply loved Rufinus (4) and highly respected Melania in early days (5, 7, 53). He had spoken of Rufinus in his Chronicle for the year 378 as "insignis monachus" (Ruf. Ap. ii. 25, 26, Vol. iii. 471) ; we do not read of any estrangement till some years after his return to Palestine. We do not, indeed, find the warm affection which we should expect in two intimate friends who meet after a 392. long separation ; and it is possible that Jerome's omission of Rufinus' name from his Catalogue of Church Writers may indicate a coolness on one side which was resented on the other. But they admit that their friendship remained (Ruf. Ap. ii. 8 (2), Vol. iii. 465), and that there was frequent intercourse between the monks of Bethlehem 393–94. and those of the Mount of Olives (*id.*). The visit of Aterbius (Ap. iii. 33, Vol. iii. 535) and that of Epiphanius mark the time of estrangement. Rufinus was with Bishop John in the scenes in the Church of the Resurrection, and is mentioned in Epiphanius' letter as a presbyter as to whose views he is paternally anxious (84–87). In the quarrel between John and Jerome Rufinus took decidedly the Bishop's side (84, 430, compared with 250). Jerome's mind grew full of suspicion, so that he even imputed to him that he had bribed some one in the monastery at Bethlehem to steal from the lodgings of Fabiola his translation of the letter of Epiphanius to John (Ap. iii. 4, Vol. iii. 521). But when Rufinus was leaving Palestine, friendship was restored. They partook together of the 397. Eucharist, and joined hands (Ap. iii. 33, Vol. iii. 535), and Jerome accompanied his friend some way upon his journey ; but the reconciliation was short-lived. When in Rome, Rufinus prefixed to a translation of Origen's Περὶ Ἀρχῶν a preface (168–170) which referred in laudatory terms to Jerome as his forerunner in this work, thus seeming to expose Jerome to the suspicions and condemnation which might be expected to fall on one who undertook such a work. This work was sent to Jerome by his friends Pammachius and Oceanus (175), together with a Preface written by Rufinus to a translation of the Apology for Origen by Pamphilus the Martyr. They spoke of the alarm excited at Rome by the translation of the Περὶ Ἀρχῶν, and their suspicions that the translation was so made as to veil the heresies contained in the original work ; they begged that Jerome would translate the work as it stood in the original, and pointed out that his own reputation for orthodoxy was at stake (175). Jerome at once complied. He sent to them a literal translation of Origen's work, together with a letter describing the relation in which he had stood and still stood to Origen : he admired him as a biblical scholar, but had never accepted him as a dogmatic teacher (176, 177). He at the same time wrote a letter to Rufinus, couched in friendly terms, but remonstrating with him for the use he had made of his name (170). This letter, having been sent to Jerome's friends at Rome, was kept back by them (Ap. i. 12, Vol. iii. 489) and not delivered to Rufinus, and thus the quarrel, which might have been allayed, became irreparable. 401–404. The further progress of the dispute is described in the notice prefixed to the Apologies of Jerome and Rufinus (Vol. iii. 434–5, 482, 518). It may suffice here to say that this disgraceful and unseemly wrangle between two well-known Christian teachers, conducted publicly before the whole Church, and breeding a hatred which Jerome continued to express even after Rufinus' death (498, 500), has only one redeeming feature to the historian, namely, that it brings to our knowledge many instructive facts which would otherwise have lain hid.

396. (5) *Vigilantius.* The controversy with Vigilantius consists only of Jerome's letter to him (131–133) and the treatise "against Vigilantius" (417–423). He had been originally introduced to Jerome by Paulinus, Bishop of Nola, who spoke of him

in high terms (123). No questions arose between them during his stay at Bethlehem. He even spoke of Jerome at times with extravagant praise (132). But he appears to have had some connection with Rufinus (Ap. iii. 19, Vol. iii. 529), and Jerome accused him afterwards of having conveyed some MSS. into the monastery at Bethlehem, probably from that on the Mount of Olives (Apol. iii. 5, 19, Vol. iii. 521, 529). Jerome afterwards heard a report that Vigilantius had written and spoken against him in various places (131), and had accused him of Origenism. To this his letter is a reply. The anti-ascetic writings of Vigilantius to which Jerome's treatise is a reply have not come down to us. Gennadius (de Script. Eccl. 35) says that he was an ignorant man, but polished in words. But, whatever his ability or literary power, he was one of the few who were able to judge rightly of the ascetic and superstitious practices by which Christianity was being overlaid; and it is on this point that Jerome is most violent and contemptuous in his treatment of him. The notices prefixed to the Letter (131) and Treatise (417) will complete this statement.

394–404. (6) *Augustin.* The remaining controversy of this period is that with St. Augustin. The two men had at an earlier time had some friendly relations, and Alypius, Augustin's friend, had stayed with Jerome at Bethlehem. But Augustin, then coadjutor Bishop of Hippo, in a letter to Jerome (112), found fault with some of his statements in his 393. Commentary on the Galatians, to which, no doubt, his attention had been called by Alypius. Jerome had maintained that the scene in Gal. ii., in which St. Paul rebukes St. Peter for inconsistent compliances with Judaism, was a merely feigned dispute, arranged between the two Apostles in order to make the truth clear to the members of the Church. Augustin objects that this is practically imputing falsehood to the Apostles. He touched upon other points, such as the translation of Scripture and the doctrine of marriage, in a manner savouring of assumption, considering the high position of Jerome, who was also eight years his senior. Through a strange series of misadventures, which illustrate the difficulty of communications at that epoch, this letter was never delivered to Jerome till nine years after it was written. It fell into the hands of persons who copied it, and became known in the West. Jerome heard casually that it had been seen among his works in an island in the Adriatic. It appeared as if Augustin had wished to gain credit by attacking a well-known man behind his back. And this suspicion was hardly allayed by a second letter from Augustin, which partially explained what had occurred (140), or by a third, in which, in answer to a letter from Jerome sending some of his works and warning his correspondent that, if it came to blows, the result might be like that described in Virgil, where the old Entellus strikes down the young Dares, Augustin criticises both severely and ignorantly Jerome's great work of translating the Hebrew Scriptures. Jerome's patience begins to fail (189). "Send me your original letter," he says, "signed by your own hand, or else cease to attack me." And he comments in his turn somewhat sharply on some of Augustin's interpretations of the Psalms. It was only on the receipt of Augustin's reply to this letter (214), couched in terms of deep respect, and deprecating any ill feeling between Christian friends, such as had arisen in the case of Rufinus, that Jerome finally answered the original letter, written ten years before, and received a letter which completely restored friendship. Henceforward they are at one. Letters pass freely between them; Augustin consults Jerome on the difficult question of the origin of souls (272, 283), and foregoes the expression of Traducianism, to which he is inclined, in deference to Jerome's objections; and he consults him on the Pelagian question, and sends Orosius to sit at his feet. Jerome recognises that each has his proper gift, and gives a plenary adherence to all that Augustin teaches. Alypius, their original link, is joined with Augustin in the address of Jerome's last letter to him (282); Paula, the granddaughter of Jerome's chief friend, is called by him the granddaughter of Augustin; and through this unity the families of Paula and Melania, which had been severed by the adherence of the one to Jerome and the other to Rufinus, are reunited by the coming of Pinianus and his wife, the younger Melania, from the church of Hippo to the convent at Bethlehem. The letters from which this episode is drawn are incorporated into the volume containing the works of Augustin, and are not reprinted here. But no life of Jerome, however limited or unpretending, would be satisfactory without some account of the relations of the two great doctors of Latin Christianity.

Bethlehem, Third Period. The last period of Jerome's life was passed in the midst of privations, the loss of friends, and frequent illnesses. Paula had died. Jerome 405–20. was poor (500, 214, 215) and often weak (498, 500). His eyesight failed (*id.*). He had enemies around him (261, 262) and in the high places of the Empire (237, 499). The barbarians were sweeping across the Empire (237, 500), some, like the Isaurians, threatening the North of Palestine (214) and even penetrating at one time to Southern Syria and Egypt (*id.*), while the main stream, after devastating Jerome's native Dalmatia, passed on under Alaric to the sack of Rome. Fugitives from Rome and Italy crowded 410. to Bethlehem, adding greatly to Jerome's labours (499, 500). It seemed as if the end of the world were at hand (260). In the sack of Rome Pammachius and Marcella died (257, 500). Eustochium followed them eight years later. The controversy with the Pelagians led to the burning of the monasteries at Bethlehem, probably also to a renewed estrangement of his Bishop, John of Jerusalem, and his successor Praylus. 417. But he continued his work with no abatement of ardour or vigour, as may be seen from the Prefaces to his later Commentaries (500, 501). He had still friends about him, Pinianus, Albina, Melania, and the younger Paula (Ep. cxliii.) ; a few survivors even in Rome, Oceanus and the younger Fabiola (252, 253) ; and men in many lands who honoured and consulted him, as is seen by his letters; and, above all, the friendship of Augustin.

The letters of this period take a wider range than those going before, Jerome's fame being now world-wide ; their addresses embrace Dalmatia (220), Gaul (215), Rome (252, 253), and Africa (260, 261). Their contents will be best estimated from the notices prefixed to them ; but we may mark as specially important the ascetic letter to Rusticus, on the solitary life (244), to Ageruchia, and those on perseverance in widowhood (230), and to Demetrias, on the preservation of virginity (260–272), which contain vivid pictures of the life (233) and events (236, 237) of the time, and of the sack of Rome (237, 257) ; the Memoir, addressed to Principia, of Marcella, who died from her ill treatment in that great day of doom (253) ; the letter to Evangelus (288) containing Jerome's view of the origin and mutual relations of the three orders of the Ministry ; and that to Sabinianus, the lapsed Deacon, who had introduced disorder into the monasteries at Bethlehem (289–295).

Pelagianism. The only great controversy of this period is the Pelagian, in which Jerome seems to have engaged rather at the instance of others than on his own initiative. He shows some mildness in dealing with the Pelagians, and wishes more to win than to condemn them (449, 499); his temperament was not such as to incline him, like Augustin, 414–18. to take an attitude of vehement hostility to the Pelagian tenets. But Orosius came from North Africa, where the Council of Carthage had lately been held ; and when, the next year, Pelagius and Cælestius came to Palestine, and Councils were held, first at Jerusalem under Bishop John, who was favourable to the reception of Pelagius, and subsequently at Diospolis, Palestine became the centre of the controversy. Augustin 416. from Africa and Ctesiphon from Rome appealed to him (272, 280); both Orosius and Pelagius quoted his words as making for them ; and at length Jerome himself felt compelled to take the pen. He resorted in this his last controversial work, as in his first against the Luciferians, to the form of dialogue. The argument must be praised for its moderation, though it must be confessed that this is gained at the expense of liveliness; it was impossible for Jerome, as a "Synergist," or believer in the co-operation of the human will with the divine, to throw himself into the fray with the eagerness of a convinced Predestinarian. But he does not scruple to brand Pelagius as a heretic ; and to a heretic he would show no mercy (449). His treatise, notwithstanding its fine drawn argument, made him at once the leader of the orthodox party in the East, and the target for the enmity 416. of their adversaries. A crowd of Pelagian monks attacked the monasteries, slew some of their inmates, and burned or threw down the buildings, the tower in which Jerome had taken refuge alone escaping (Aug. de Gestis Pelag. 66). This violence, however, was checked by a strong letter from Pope Innocentius (280, 281) to Bishop John, who died soon after ; and Jerome, to whom the Pope wrote at the same time (280), speaks of 417. Augustin's cause as triumphant (282), and of Pelagius, like another Catiline, having left the country, though Jerusalem remains in the hands of some hostile power which he speaks of under the name of Nebuchadnezzar (282). It cannot be said, however, that Jerome's arguments produced much effect in the East. He was withstood by Theodore of Mopsuestia (see Migne's Jerome, ii. 807–14) as "saying that men sin by nature, not by will " ; and from the West also a treatise opposing his views was sent to him (282) by Annianus, a deacon of Celeda, to which he was never able to reply.

His Bible work during these last fifteen years consisted entirely of Commentaries on the Prophets. Those on the Minor Prophets were finished in 406 ; that on Daniel in 407 ; that on Isaiah in 408–10 ; that on Ezekiel in 410–14. That on Jeremiah up to ch. xxxii. occupied the remaining years. The Prefaces to these Commentaries (499–501) are full of interest, recording the sack of Rome (499, 500), the death of Rufinus (498, 500), and the rise of Pelagianism, while the Commentary on Ezekiel itself (Book ix.) speaks of the occupation of Rome by Heraclian. His failing health and eyesight (498, 500), the Pelagian Controversy, the other trials above mentioned (499) and the care of the monasteries and pilgrims (500, 501), increased by the death of Eustochium in 418, shortened his time for work, and his Commentary on Jeremiah was cut short at ch. xxxii. by his last illness. Yet his last work is full of energy and of his old controversial vigour.

The last year of his life is believed to have been occupied by a long illness, in which he was tended by the younger Paula and Melania. The Chronicle of Prosper of Aquitaine gives September 20, 420, as the day of his death. Many legends sprung up around his memory. His remains are said to have been transferred from the place where they were buried beside those of Paula and Eustochium. near the grotto of the Nativity, to the Church of Santa Maria Maggiore at Rome, and miracles to have been wrought at his tomb. His descriptions of hermit life in the desert no doubt gave rise to the tradition that he was always attended by a lion, as represented in painting and sculpture, especially in the well-known etching of Albert Dürer. With such traditions a historical work must not be burdened.

IV. THE WRITINGS OF JEROME.

The following is a list of the writings arranged under various heads, and showing the date of composition and the place held by each in the Edition of Vallarsi, the eleven volumes of which will be found in Migne's Patrologia, vols. xxii. to xxx. The references are to the volumes of Jerome's works (i.–xi.) in that edition.

I. Bible translations :
(1) From the Hebrew.—The Vulgate of the Old Testament, written at Bethlehem, begun 391, finished 404, vol. ix.
(2) From the Septuagint.—The Psalms as used at Rome, written in Rome, 383, and the Psalms as used in Gaul, written at Bethlehem about 388. These two are in parallel columns in vol. x. The Gallican Psaltery is collated with the Hebrew, and shows by obeli (÷) the parts which are in the LXX. and not in the Hebrew, and by asterisks (*) the parts which are in the Hebrew and not in the Greek.
The Book of Job, forming a part of the translation of the LXX. made between 386 and 392 at Bethlehem, the rest of which was lost (Ep. 134), vol. x.
(3) From the Chaldee.—The Books of Tobit and Judith, Bethlehem, 398, vol. x.
(4) From the Greek.—The Vulgate version of the New Testament made at Rome between 382 and 385. The preface is only to the Gospels, but Jerome speaks of and quotes from his version of the other part also (De Vir. Ill. 135 ; Ep. 71 and 27), vol. x.

II. Commentaries :
(1) Original.—Ecclesiastes, vol. iii., Bethlehem, 388 ; Isaiah, vol. iv., Bethlehem, 410 ; Jeremiah i.–xxxii., 41, vol. iv., Bethlehem, 419 ; Ezekiel, vol. v., Bethlehem, 410–14 ; Daniel, vol. v., Bethlehem, 407 ; the Minor Prophets, vol. vi., Bethlehem, at various times between 391 and 406 ; Matthew, vol. vii., Bethlehem, 398 ; Galatians, Ephesians, Titus, Philemon, vol. vii., Bethlehem, 388.
(2) Translated from Origen.—Homilies on Jeremiah and Ezekiel, vol v., Bethlehem, 381 ; on Luke, vol. vii., Bethlehem, 389 ; Canticles, vol. iii., Rome and Bethlehem, 385–87.
There is also a Commentary on Job, and a specimen of one on the Psalms, attributed to Jerome, vol. vii., and the translation of Origen's Homilies on Isaiah, also attributed to him, vol. iv.

III. Books illustrative of Scripture :
(1) Book of Hebrew names, or Glossary of Proper Names in the Old Testament, Bethlehem, 388, vol. iii. 1.
(2) Book of Questions on Genesis, Bethlehem, 388, vol. iii. 301. ·
(3) A translation of Eusebius' book on the sites and names of Hebrew places, Bethlehem, 388, vol. iii. 321.
(4) Translation of Didymus on the Holy Spirit, Rome and Bethlehem, 385–87, vol. ii. 105.

IV. Books on Church History and Controversy (all in vol. ii.) :
(1) Book of Illustrious Men, or Catalogue of Ecclesiastical Writers, Bethlehem, 392.
(2) Dialogue with a Luciferian, Antioch, 379.
(3) Lives of the Hermits : Paulus, Desert, 374 ; Malchus and Hilarion, Bethlehem, 390.

(4) Translation of the Rule of Pachomius, Bethlehem, 404.

(5) Books of ascetic controversy, against Helvidius, Rome, 304; against Jovinian, Bethlehem, 393; against Vigilantius, Bethlehem, 406.

(6) Books of personal controversy, against John, Bishop of Jerusalem, Bethlehem, 397 or 398; against Rufinus, i. and ii. 402, iii. 404.

(7) Dialogue with a Pelagian, Bethlehem, 416.

V. General History:

Translation of the Chronicle of Eusebius, with Jerome's additions, vol. viii., Constantinople, 382.

VI. Personal:

The series of letters, vol. i., Ep. 1, Aquileia, 311; 2–4, Antioch, 374; 5–17, Desert, 374–79; 18, Constantinople, 381; 19–45, Rome, 382–85; 46–148, Bethlehem, 386–418.

The works attributed to Jerome, but not genuine, which are given in Vallarsi's edition are: A breviary, commentary, and preface on the Psalms, vol. vii.; some Greek fragments and a lexicon of Hebrew names; the names of places in the Acts; the ten names of God; the benedictions of the patriarchs; the ten temptations in the desert; a commentary on the Song of Deborah; Hebrew Questions in Kings and Chronicles; an exposition of Job, vol. iii.; three letters in vol. i., and fifty-one in vol. xi., together with several miscellaneous writings in vol. xi. most of which are by Pelagius.

Bibliography.—The writings of Jerome were, on the whole, well preserved, owing to the great honour in which he was held, in the Middle Ages. Considering the number of MSS., the variations are not numerous. The Editio Princeps of the Letters and a few of the Treatises appeared in Rome in 1470, and another almost contemporaneous with this in Maintz (Schöffer), after which they were reprinted in Venice (1476), Rome (1479), Parma (1480), Nürenberg (1485), and in several other places. The Editio Princeps of the Commentaries appeared in Nürenberg in 1477, and was several times reprinted in other places; that of the Translation of Origen's Homilies on St. Luke, etc., in Basle, 1475; that of the Lives of the Hermits in Nürenberg, 1476, and of the Chronicle at Milan in 1475.

But the true Editio Princeps, containing Jerome's works as a whole, is that of Erasmus (Basle, 1516–20), who bestowed on it his great critical power, aided by his strong admiration for Jerome. He was assisted by Œcolampadius and other scholars. This held its ground till 1560, when an edition appeared by Marianus Victorius, afterwards Bishop of Rieti (Rome, Paulus Manutius), which enlarged the notes and corrected the text of Erasmus, but, like him, included many spurious writings. This edition was dedicated to Pius V. and Gregory XIII., and was the favourite edition of the Roman Church. In 1684 appeared the edition of Tribbechovius of Gotha (Frankfort and Leipzig) which embodied the emendations of critics up to that date, and was published at the expense of the Protestant Frederick, Duke of Saxony. In 1693 came the Benedictine edition of Martianay and Pouget (Paris), which gave the original text of the Vulgate and a new, though still very imperfect arrangement of the Letters and Treatises. But all previous editions were thrown into the shade by that of Dominic Vallarsi the learned priest of Verona (folio ed., Verona, 1734–42; quarto, Venice, 1766–72). In this edition the Treatises are separated from the Letters, and both Letters and Treatises are arranged in order of time, the dates and the process by which they are arrived at being clearly given. I have only in one or two instances found reason to alter Vallarsi's dates. The explanatory notes, however, are not as complete as might be wished, and the references are often wrong or imperfect. This edition is reprinted by Migne, who marks the pages of it in large print in the text, and most modern writers refer to it alone, as has been done in this volume.

Literature.—Three short Lives of Jerome, composed in the Middle Ages by unknown authors (one of which was falsely attributed to Gennadius), are given by Vallarsi in his Prolegomena (vol. i. 175–214); one of these is said by Zöckler to be by Sebastian of Monte Cassino. Another, written in the fourteenth century by John Andreas of Bologna, was printed at Basle in 1514; and a work by Lasserré was published at Paris in 1530, with a curious title, "La Vie de Monseigneur Sainct Hierome," with "La Vie de Madame Saincte Paule"; and later works belonging to the uncritical region of thought were published later in Madrid by Bonadies in 1595, and by Cermellus in Ferrara (1648), the latter entirely made up of quotations from Jerome's writings.

Meanwhile the critical faculty had been aroused. Erasmus and Marianus Victorius prefixed *Lives* of Jerome to their editions of his works in 1516 and 1565; and Baronius in his Annals and Du Pin in his *Bibliothèque des Auteurs Ecclésiastiques* (1686) brought to light additional facts. Martianay at the close of his edition of Jerome's works published a *Life*, embodying many records of Jerome from the Fathers, but with many mistakes of chronology, some of which were rectified by Tillemont in his painstaking *Mémoires* (Paris, 1707) and by Ceillier in his *Histoire des Auteurs Ecclésiastiques* (Paris, 1742). The work of Sebastiano Dolci (Ancona, 1750) is entirely taken from Jerome's own writings.

But in reference to the Life as to the Writings of Jerome a new epoch was made by Vallarsi in the Preface and the Life prefixed to his Edition of Jerome. Though somewhat dry, it is thoroughly trustworthy, and in Migne's edition more accessible than any other to those who read Latin. The Bollandist Stilling (Acta Sanctorum, vol. viii., Antwerp, 1762), is less occupied with additions to our knowledge of the man and his works than with the honouring of the Saint. The work of the learned Dane, Engelstoft (1797), gives a more comprehensive estimate of Jerome's historical position than any of his predecessors. The account of Jerome in Schrökh's Ecclesiastical History (1786) and the articles of Cölln in Ersch and Grüber's Encyclopädie and of Hagenbach in Herzog's Real-Encyclopädie are excellent. In French we have the account of Jerome's ascetic influence in Montalembert's *Monks of the West* (Paris, 1861); and the *Histoire de St. Jérome* by Collombet (Paris, 1844) is useful in the appreciation of the personal and archæological part of the subject, though accepting with uncritical partisanship the polemical attitude of Jerome. We may add for English readers the articles HIERONYMUS in the *Dictionaries of Greek and Roman Biography* and *of Christian Biography*.

Our own generation has produced two excellent works : that of Dr. Otto Zöckler, *Hieronymus, Sein Leben und Werken* (Gotha, Perthes, 1865), and that of Amédée Thierry, *Saint Jérome, la Société chrétienne à Rome et l'émigration romaine en terre sainte* (Paris, 1867, originally published in the *Revue des Deux Mondes*). The former is a lucid, impartial, and comprehensive account of Jerome's Life and Writings ; the latter, a series of very vivid and interesting sketches of Jerome himself, his friends and his times, which, though generally accurate, is occasionally swayed from truth by imagination, and at times is betrayed by sympathy with the modern Roman Catholic system into mistakes of judgment. Both these writers give copious and enlightening extracts from Jerome's writings in the original ; but the value of those of Thierry is lessened by the references being to the ill-arranged edition of Martianay instead of that of Vallarsi.

It will be sufficiently obvious why it has been impossible to include all the works of Jerome in the present translation, but a few explanations may be desirable.

An exact translation of the Vulgate would serve no good purpose ; and, if made, would naturally form part of a series designed to illustrate the criticism of the Scriptures.

The Commentaries and works illustrative of the Scriptures would by themselves form two volumes of equal size with the present. Though they contain much that is interesting—the opinions of various writers, such as Origen, Apollinarius, Gregory Nazianzen, or Didymus, a few celebrated passages, such as that which caused the controversy between Jerome and Augustin, and a few remarkable allusions to historical events, such as the capture of Rome by Heraclian—the general tenour of them is hardly of sufficient importance to justify the labour of translation or the bulk and expense of the additional volumes. An exception might be made in favour of the Book on the Site and Names of Hebrew Places ; but this is a work of Eusebius rather than Jerome (see pp. 485, 486 and Prolegomena to Eusebius, Vol. i. of this series) ; and it was necessary to confine the Translation of Jerome to a single volume, with the exception of the Book *On Illustrious Men* and the *Apology against Rufinus*, which will be found in Vol. iii. of this Series.

The Chronicle of Eusebius would, if translated at all, find its place in the works of Eusebius.

The Books on Church History and Controversy are given in full.

Of the Letters, which, excepting the Vulgate, form the most important legacy of Jerome to posterity, all those which have a personal or a historical interest have been translated. The only omissions are (1) the exegetical letters, to which what has been said of the Commentaries applies ; (2) the letters to Augustin, which will be found in Vol. i. of the first series of this Library, annexed to the letters of Augustin to which they are replies ; and (3) the encyclicals and letters of Theophilus, which have been summarised.

For a separate statement of the works which are given in this volume the reader will naturally consult the table of contents ; and, for a more detailed account of the books themselves, the introductions prefixed to each.

V. ESTIMATE OF THE SCOPE AND VALUE OF JEROME'S WRITINGS.

General.   The writings of Jerome must be estimated not merely by their intrinsic merits, but by his historical position and influence.   It has already been pointed out that he stands at the close of the old Græco-Roman civilisation : the last Roman poet of any repute, Claudian, and the last Roman historian, Ammianus Marcellinus, died before him.   Augustin survived him, but the other great Fathers, both in the East and in the West, had passed away before him.   The sack of Rome by Alaric (410) and its capture by Heraclian (413) took place in his lifetime, and the Empire of the West fell in the next thirty years.   Communication between East and West had become rarer and mutual knowledge less.   Eusebius knew no Latin, Ambrose no Greek ; Rufinus, though a second-rate scholar, was welcomed in Italy on his return from the East in 397 as capable of imparting to the Latins the treasures of the Greek Church writers.   The general enfeeblement of the human mind, which remains one of the problems of history, had set in.   The new age of Christendom which was struggling to the birth was subject to the influence of Jerome more than to that of any of the Fathers.

Secular Learning.   As regards general learning, indeed, it was impossible that any legacy should descend from him.   He had systematically disparaged it (35–36, 498), though making use and even a parade of it (101, 114, 149, 178) ; and had defended himself by disingenuous pleas from the charge of acquiring it after his mature convictions were formed (Apol. i. 30, 31, Vol. iii. 498–499).   His influence, therefore, would but increase the deep ignorance of literature which now settled upon mankind till the times of the Renaissance.   His style, indeed, is excellent, correct, and well balanced, full of animation and of happy phrases (see Index—PROVERBS), and passing from one subject to another with great versatility.   It is contrasted by Erasmus with the barbarisms of the Schoolmen, as that of the Christian Cicero. But it has also Cicero's faults, especially his diffuseness.   His Latinity is remarkably pure, and, with the exception of the frequent use of the infinitive to express a purpose, and of a few words of late-Latin like *confortare,* we are hardly aware in reading him that we are 400 years away from the Augustan Age.   His mastery of style is the more remarkable because he wrote nothing but a few letters and a very poor Commentary till about his thirty-fifth year.

Letters.   His letters gain their special charm from being so personal.   He himself, his correspondents, and the scenes in which they moved, are made to live before our eyes.   See especially his descriptions of Roman life in the Epistles to Eustochium (Ep. xxii.), to Paula on the death of Blesilla (Ep. xxxix.), to Læta (Ep. cvii.) on the education of her child, and Ageruchia (Ep. cxxiii.) ; his account of the lives of Fabiola (Ep. lxxvii.), of Paula (Ep. cviii.), and of Marcella (Ep. cxxvii.) ; his description of the clerical life in his letter to Nepotian (Ep. lii.), and of the monastic life in his letters to Rusticus (Ep. cxxv.) and to Sabinian (Ep. cxlvii.) ; his letters of spiritual counsel to a mother and daughter (Ep. cxvii.), to Julianus (Ep. cxviii.), and to Rusticus (Ep. cxxii.), and of hermit life in his letter to Eustochium (Ep. xxii., pp. 24–25) ; his satirical description of Onasus (Ep. xl.), Rufinus (p. 250), and Vigilantius (p. 417) ; his enthusiastic delight in the Holy Land in the letter written by him for Paula and Eustochium inviting Marcella to join them (Ep. xlvi).   Other characteristic and celebrated letters are those to Asella (xlv.) on his leaving Rome ; to Pammachius (lvii.) on the best method of translation, which shows the liberties taken by translators in his time ; to Oceanus (lxix.) in defence of a second marriage contracted by a Spanish Bishop, the first having been before baptism ; to Magnus (lxx.), indicating his use of secular literature, and showing the great range of his knowledge ; to Lucinius (lxxi.) on the copying of his works ; to Avitus (cxxiv.) on the book of Origen, Περὶ Ἀρχῶν ; to Demetrias (cxxx.) on the maintenance of virginity ; to Ctesiphon (cxxxiii.) on the Pelagian controversy.   (See also Index, words STORIES and PICTURES OF CONTEMPORARY LIFE.)

Publication.   Two circumstances conduced to the vividness and importance of this series of letters.   One of these is the fact that no distinct line separated private documents from those designed for publication.   In the Catalogue of his works (De Vir. Ill. 135), he says : " Of the Letters to Paula and Eustochium, the number is infinite : I write them every day." And, when he became celebrated, he says (79) that whatever he wrote was at once laid hold of and published, alike by friends and enemies.   We have therefore frequently his most confidential utterances ; while on the other hand his letters frequently pass into treatises, and he turns to address others than those to whom he is writing (59, 273, 274).   But the process of publication was precarious ; so that between Letters xlvi. and xlvii. there is a gap of seven years (386–93) without any letter.   The other circumstance is the difficulty of communication, which made letters rare and induced greater care in their composition.   Both these circumstances are well illustrated by the early correspondence of Jerome with Augustin. Augustin wrote from Hippo in Africa a long and important letter to Jerome (Ep. lvi.) in the year 394, which did not reach Jerome at Bethlehem for nearly ten years. It was committed to a presbyter named Profuturus to carry to Jerome; but he, being elected to a bishopric before he started, turned back, and soon afterwards died. The letter was neither forwarded to Jerome nor returned to Augustin; but it was copied by others and became known in the West, while its somewhat severe criticisms were unknown to Jerome himself. After a time Augustin became aware by a short letter of introduction written by Jerome to a friend that his first letter had miscarried, and he wrote a second (Ep. lxvii.) much in the same strain; but Paulus, to whom it was entrusted, alleging his fear of the sea, failed to go to Bethlehem; and a copy of the letter was found a year or two afterwards by a friend of Jerome's bound up with some of Augustin's treatises in an island of the Adriatic. Jerome on hearing of this was naturally incensed; and it was not till the year 404 that he received an authentic copy of both letters direct from Augustin, and was able to return an answer. His answer, however, and a knowledge of his views are fuller than they might have been had personal communication been easier.

Knowledge. His knowledge was vast and many-sided [See especially the enumeration of Christian writers who used Pagan literature (149–151), the curious stories about marriage gathered from all ages (383–386), the descriptions of various kinds of food and medicines (392–394), and the account of Pythagoras and his doctrines (Apol. iii., 39, 40, in this Series, Vol. iii. 538)], but it was rather the curiosity of the monks of a later day than the temper of the philosopher or the historian. He was well acquainted with the history and literature of Rome and of Greece; he translated the Chronicle of Eusebius; he speaks of the various routes to India (245), of the Brahmans (97, 193, 397), of the custom of Suttee (381), and of Buddha (380). But he is quite uncritical; he makes no correction of the faults of the Chronicle, and his own additions to it reveal his credulity. He was deeply affected by the sack of Rome, and recurs to it again and again; but his reflections upon this and similar events hardly go beyond those of a mediæval chronicler. He is a recluse, and has no thought of the general interests of mankind.

Church History. This lack of criticism and of general interests combined with lack of time to prevent his making any considerable contribution to church history. That he had some faculties for this is shown by several passages in his Dialogue with a Luciferian (328–331) and his Catalogue of Ecclesiastical Writers (On Illustrious Men, Vol. iii. 361–384). But his conception of church history is shown by his declaration (315) that he intended the Lives of Malchus and Hilarion as part of a series, which when completed would have formed an ecclesiastical history. Such a history would have been nothing more than a prolix edition of Rufinus' History of the Monks. Jerome's value to the church historian is quite of another kind; it lies in the illustration of contemporary life furnished by his own life and letters and by the controversies in which he was engaged.

Theology. These controversies bring us to consider Jerome's position as a theologian. Here he is admittedly weak. He had no real interest in the subject. The first of his letters which deals with theology, that written from the Desert to Pope Damasus, points out clearly the difficulty raised by the difference of phraseology of East and West, the Eastern speaking of one Essence and three Substances, the Western, of one Substance and three Persons. But he makes no attempt to grasp the reality lying behind these expressions, and merely asks not to have the Eastern terms forced on his acceptance, while he professes in the most absolute terms his submission to the decision of the Bishop of Rome. This lack of genuine theological interest best explains his conduct in relation to Origen, his extravagant laudation of him at one time (46), his violent condemnation at another (187). He was carried away by Origen's genius and industry in the department of biblical criticism and exegesis in which he was himself absorbed, and though in his earlier discussion of the Vision of Isaiah (22), which touched the doctrine of the Trinity, he had put aside Origen's view that the Seraphim were the Son and the Spirit as wrongly expressing their relation to the Father, the doctrinal question was feebly present to his thoughts, and he repeated Origen's exposition without blame as to the pre-existence of souls and the restoration of Satan (Ruf. Apol. ii. 13, Vol. iii. 467). When the subject of Origen's orthodoxy was raised at a later time, he was unaware of any inconsistency when he fell in with the general condemnation of his doctrine. So with regard to Eusebius of Cæsarea. In the Preface to the translation of his Book on the Site and Names of Hebrew Places (485), he is "vir admirabilis"; in his controversy with Rufinus, Eusebius is nothing but a heretic. In his controversy with Augustin as to the quarrel between St. Peter and St. Paul in Gal. ii., which he interpreted as fictitious and pre-arranged with a view to bring out St. Paul's solution of the question about the Gentile converts, he was manifestly in the wrong, and eventually seems to have felt this, yet as one who was silenced rather than convinced. At a later period he says to Augustin (Ep. cxxxiv.), "If the heretics see that we hold divergent opinions they will say calumniously that this is a result of hatred, whereas it is my firm resolution to love you, to look up to you, to defer to you with admiration, and to defend your opinions as my own." His dread of heresy may be gathered from a passage in the Anti-Pelagian Dialogue (i. 28) in which he expressly declares that, while sins can be forgiven, heresy, as being impiety, is subject to the threat : " They that forsake the Lord shall be consumed." It is true that in his Catalogue he shows wider sympathies, and defends himself in writing to Augustin for the admission into it of men like Philo Judæus, and Seneca. But this, though it might have led him to the larger views of the heathen world held by Origen and Clement, did not prevent his condemning to eternal torments even the most virtuous of the heathen. He tells Marcella, a Roman lady (41–42), that one object he has in writing to her is to instruct her that the consul-elect Vettius Agorius Prætextatus, who was known as a model of public and domestic virtue, and who had then recently died, is in Tartarus, while their friend Lea, who had died the same day, is in heaven.

The lack of deep theological conviction is shown in his Dialogue against the Pelagians, where it is evident that he is far from that original and deep view of human corruption which Augustin maintained ; indeed, he appears at times to be arguing against his own side, as when he says (471) that, " Till the end we are subject to sin ; not," (as the opponent falsely imputes to him) "through the fault of our nature and constitution, but through frailty and the mutability of the human will, which varies from moment to moment"—a sentence which might be taken as expressing the doctrine of Pelagius himself. It is evident that in these cases he is swayed not so much by the force of truth as by the authority of certain powerful Bishops and the wish to maintain his orthodox reputation. In his other controversies, with Helvidius, Jovinian, John, Bishop of Jerusalem, Vigilantius, and Rufinus, his method is to take for granted the opinion current among the Christians of his day, and to support it by copious (sometimes excessive) quotations from Scripture, and by arguments sometimes well chosen and acutely maintained, as in the book against Helvidius (339), sometimes of the most frivolous character, as in that against Vigilantius (422). In the three last of these controversies the opposition is embittered by personal feeling, and Jerome hardly places any restraint on the contempt and hatred which it engenders.

In his criticisms on Scripture, however, he has a freer judgment, as when he says (337): " Whether you think that Moses wrote the Pentateuch, or that Ezra re-edited it, in either case I make no objection ; " or (349) that it was the Book of Deuteronomy which was found in the Temple in the reign of Josiah ; or contrasts "the flickering flame of the Apostles " with "the brightness of the lamp of Christ " (468). There are three points especially on which Jerome reached an independent conviction, and maintained it courageously. (1) He made a clear distinction between the Old Testament Canon and the Apocrypha (194, 491, 492, 493) and this although he records the fact that the Nicene Council had placed the Book of Judith in the Canon (494). For this he is justly commemorated in the Articles of the Church of England (Art. 6). (2) He maintains the essential identity of Bishops and Presbyters (288) and the development of the Episcopal out of the Presbyteral office (288, 289), in the face of the rapid tendency to the extreme exaltation of the Episcopate (92). (3) In the greatest work of his life, the composition of the Vulgate, he showed a clear and matured conviction, and a noble tenacity, unshaken either by popular clamour (490) or authority like that of Augustin (189).

A few words may here be said on the asceticism which Jerome so eagerly promoted. If we ask how it was that he embraced it so fervently as to read it into almost every line of the Scriptures, we can only answer that it was part of the spirit of the time. Jerome had not the elevation of mind which might have enabled him to exercise a judgment upon the current which was bearing him away, or the higher critical power which would distinguish between what was in the Scriptures and what he brought to them. His habit of mind was to accept his general principles from some kind of church authority, which was partly that of the Bishops, partly the general drift of the sentiment of the Christians of his day ; and having accepted them, to advocate them vehemently and without discrimination. Jerome could indeed exercise a certain moderation, even in matters of asceticism (246, 267). But his general attitude is that which disdained the common joys of life, which thought of eating, drinking, clothing or lodging, and most of all marriage, as physical indulgences which should be suppressed as far as possible, rather than as the means of a noble social intercourse ; and his dread of impurity haunts him to such an extent as to entirely vitiate his view of society, and to cause him to disparage, and all but forbid, the married relation (29, 384, etc.). His view of monasticism in its inner principles is seen in his treatises against Helvidius, Jovinian, and Vigilantius. The reader may be specially referred to a passage in the last-named treatise, p. 423. If we ask the further question, how the tendency arose which so completely swayed him, we can only attribute it to the state of Roman society in the fourth and fifth centuries, which laid earnest men open to influences already working in other parts of the world. Jerome knew of the Brahmans and the Gymnosophists of India (97, 193, 397), and he several times mentions Buddha (380) as an example of asceticism. But students of Buddhism have failed to trace any direct filiation between the asceticism of the East and the West.* The existence of Essenes in Palestine and the Therapeutæ in Egypt, and the unquestionable fact that Christian asceticism originated in Egypt, make some connection with the East probable; and the system of Manes, though at once repudiated, may have exerted some subtle influence. Certain states of the human mind seem all-pervasive, like the causes of diseases which spring up at once in many different places; and principles like those of asceticism may be communicated through chance conversations or commercial intercourse when the soil is prepared for their reception.

But it seems better to look to the social and political state of the world as the predisposing cause of monasticism. Even in the East it is thought that the miserable conditions of practical life have been the main cause of a religion of despair; and the decline and fall of the Roman Empire in the fourth and fifth centuries offered similar causes in abundance. The grace which is completely absent from the great Christian writers of that epoch is hope. Such hope as is found even in the Civitas Dei of Augustin is entirely that of the world to come. The world before them seemed hopelessly corrupt. The descriptions of private morals given by Jerome are borne out by Ammianus Marcellinus; the failure of public spirit and military valour was equally conspicuous; and Gratian and Stilicho appear on the scene only to be murdered. When the crash of Alaric's sack of Rome shook the existing world, no one realised that a new Christian world was coming, and the flight which Jerome witnessed of thousands of citizens from the sinking city to the mountains of Palestine was but one symptom of the despair which made them, to use Jerome's words, " quit the most frequented cities so that in the fields and solitude they might mourn for sin and draw down on themselves the compassion of Christ " (446).

As an illustrator of Scripture, Jerome did much, and in some respects excellent work. The Book of Hebrew Names was no doubt of much use in the ages in which men were ignorant of Hebrew, although it has the clumsy arrangement of a separate glossary for each book of the Bible; it is very faulty and uncritical; there is no explanation, for instance, of Lehi in Judges, or of Engedi or Ichabod in 1 Samuel, or of Bethabara or Bethany in John, and the meanings given to words are extremely uncritical and sometimes absurd. Cherubim is said to mean a multitude of knowledge; Jezebel, " flowing with blood, a litter, a dung heap "; and Laodicæa, "the tribe beloved of the Lord, or, they have been in vomiting." It is worthless now except as showing the state of knowledge of the fourth century A. D., and that of the author of the Vulgate.

The Book of the Site and Names of Hebrew Places belongs rather to Eusebius than to Jerome, being translated from Eusebius, though with some additions. An account of it is given in the Prolegomena to Eusebius. The arrangement of this book is, like the former, very inconvenient, the names under each letter being placed in separate groups in the order of the books of Scripture in which they occur: for instance, under the letter A we have first the names in Genesis, then those in Exodus, and so on. But there is less room here for what is fanciful, and the testimony of men who lived in Palestine in the fourth and fifth centuries is of great value still to the student of sacred topography. When the places are outside the writer's knowledge, credulity is apt to creep in, as when the author tells us that on Ararat portions of the ark are still to be found.

The Book of Hebrew Questions on Genesis is simply a set of notes on passages where the reference to the Hebrew text gives a different reading from that of the LXX., which was received as authoritative up to Jerome's day. For instance, in Gen. xlvi. 26, the LXX. says that Joseph's descendants born in Egypt were nine, the Hebrew, two. Jerome accounts for the discrepancy by the supposition that the LXX. added in the sons of Ephraim and Manasseh, who were subsequently born in Egypt, and who in the LXX. are enumerated just before. Jerome states in the preface his intention to compose a similar set of notes to each

---

* See a remarkable article on " The New Testament and Buddhism," by Professor Estlin Carpenter, in the *Nineteenth Century* for July, 1879.

book of the Old Testament, but he was never able to go beyond Genesis. What he gives us is of considerable interest and value, so that it is a matter of regret that he could not go further.

As a commentator, Jerome's fault is a lack of independence ; his merit lies in giving fully the opinions of others which we might otherwise not have known. This he considers, as seen in his controversy with Rufinus, the principal task of a commentator (Apol. i. 16, Vol. iii. 491). In the passages there at issue, he states the most incongruous interpretations without criticising them, and Rufinus can hardly be blamed for suggesting that he is sometimes expressing his own opinion under that of "another." In matters of ordinary interpretation his judgment is good. But fanciful ideas are apt to intrude, as when, in the Commentary on Ecclesiastes, the city delivered by the poor wise man is made to mean the individual delivered from Satan by the better man within him, or the Church delivered from the hosts of darkness by Christ. When an occasion for the introduction of asceticism occurs, Jerome never hesitates at any process, however absurd, which will draw the passage to a sanction of his peculiar views (Against Jovin. i. 30, p. 368). We should have been glad, had space permitted, to have given a specimen of his better style of exposition, but it was found necessary to suppress this.

It is as a translator of Scripture that Jerome is best known. His Vulgate was made at the right moment and by the right man. The Latin language was still living, although Latin civilisation was dying ; and Jerome was a master of it. It is only to be regretted that he did not give fuller scope to his literary power in his translation of Scripture. In his letter to Pammachius on the best method of translation (114), he advocates great freedom of treatment, even such as amounts to paraphrase, and even to the insertion of sentences congruous to the sense of the author. He takes the fact that the quotations in the New Testament from the Old often present discrepancies in words and sense as justifying similar discrepancies in a translation. He does not, however, appear in dealing with ordinary books to have used this license in any extreme way ; and his translations, without departing from correctness, read as good literary composition. But from the operation of his rules of translation he expressly excepts the Scriptures. "In other books," he says (113), "my effort is not to express word by word, but meaning by meaning ; but in the Holy Scriptures even the order of the words has a secret meaning" (et ordo verborum mysterium est). He even says (80) : "A version made for the use of the Church, even though it may possess a literary charm, ought to disguise and avoid it as far as possible." This belief in a secret meaning in the words and their order as apart from the sense goes far to injure the Vulgate translation. His principles, indeed, are excellent, namely, (1) never to swerve needlessly from the original ; (2) to avoid solecisms ; (3) even by the admission of solecisms, to give the true sense. But it is evident that they must be vitiated by the supposition of a hidden sense in the arrangement of the words ; and the result is a style which frequently deprives a passage of its proper elegance, and the pleasure which it should give to the reader, and a too frequent introduction of solecisms and abandonment of the attempt to make sense of a passage. It also gives an air of saintly unreality to many parts of the Scriptures and thus to produce confusion. The merits of the translation are also very various, as was the time which Jerome bestowed on the different parts. The Books of Solomon, for instance, he translated very rapidly (492), the Book of Tobit in a single day (494). For some parts he trusted to his own knowledge, for others he obtained aid at great cost of money and trouble (Preface to Job and to Tobit, 491, 494). But, while we thus go behind the scenes, we must not fail to look at the completed work as a whole. It was wrought out with noble perseverance and unflinching purpose amidst many discouragements. It was highly prized even in Jerome's lifetime, so that he is able to record that a large part of the Old Testament was translated into Greek from his version by his friend Sophronius, and was read in the Eastern Churches (492). After his death it won its way to become the Vulgate or common version of Western Christendom ; it was the Bible of the Middle Ages ; and in the year 1546 (eleven centuries after its author's death) was pronounced by the Council of Trent to be the only true version, and alone authorised to be printed.

A few personal details must be given to illustrate his method of composition and his surroundings. Nothing is known of his personal appearance. His health was weak, and he had several long illnesses, especially in the years 398, 404, and in the last year of his life. His eyes began to fail during his stay at Constantinople in 380–382, and he usually employed an amanuensis ; but he still wrote at times, and what he wrote was more polished than what he dictated. "In the one case I constantly turn the stylus ; in the other, whatever words come into my mouth I heap together in my rapid utterance" (Ep. lxxiv. 6). He composed with great rapidity, and dictated at times as much as one thousand lines in a day (Comm. on Ephes., Book ii. Preface). He often, especially when in weak health, lay on a couch (Ep. lxxiv. 6), taking

down one volume after another to aid in the composition of his Commentaries.   And he often
sat late into the night [his book against Vigilantius was "the lucubration of a single night "
(423)], the days being occupied in business of various kinds, as stated above—the monasteries,
the entertainment of strangers, the teaching of boys, the exposition of Scripture to his brethren
in the monastery, and, according to Sulpicius Severus, the charge of the parish of Bethlehem.
As has been mentioned above, he was interrupted again and again by illness, and on several
occasions was in alarm from the threatened invasions of the Huns and Isaurians, and at the
end of his life from the violent adherents of Pelagius.   He also suffered from poverty, and
his friends one by one were taken from him.   But he persevered against all obstacles ; and
his latest works, the Anti-Pelagian Dialogue and the Commentary on Jeremiah, show little if
any diminution of power.

VI. CHARACTER AND INFLUENCE OF JEROME.

This Introduction must be concluded with a few words on the character and influence of
Jerome, which are taken from the article upon him in the *Dictionary of Christian Biography*.
He was vain and unable to bear rivals, extremely sensitive as to the estimation in which he was
held by his contemporaries, and especially by the Bishops ; passionate and resentful, but at times
becoming suddenly placable ; scornful and violent in controversy ; kind to the weak and the
poor ; respectful in his dealings with women ; entirely without avarice ; extraordinarily diligent in work, and nobly tenacious of the main objects to which he devoted his life.   There
was, however, something of monkish cowardice in his asceticism, and his influence was not
felt by the strong.

His influence grew through his life and increased after his death.   If we may use a scriptural phrase which has sometimes been applied to such influence, " He lived and reigned for
a thousand years."   His writings contain the whole spirit of the Church of the Middle Ages,
its monasticism, its contrast of sacred things with profane, its credulity and superstition, its
value for relics, its subjection to hierarchical authority, its dread of heresy, its passion for
pilgrimages.   To the society which was thus in a great measure formed by him, his Bible was
the greatest boon which could have been given.   But he founded no school and had no
inspiring power ; there was no courage or width of view in his spiritual legacy such as could
break through the fatal circle of bondage to received authority which was closing round
mankind.   As Thierry says in the last words of his work on St. Jerome, " There is no continuation of his work ; a few more letters of Augustin and Paulinus, and night falls over
the West."

CHRONOLOGICAL TABLES OF THE LIFE

PERSONAL.	LITERARY.
345. Jerome born at Stridon (Pannonia or Dalmatia).	
360. Jerome at school. 363. To study at Rome. Baptism.	
366. To Treves.	366–69. Jerome copies works of Hilary. 369. Jerome writes a mystical Commentary on Obadiah. 370. First letter—On the woman seven times struck with the axe
370. To Aquileia. 373. Leaves Aquileia for the East.	
374. Illness at Antioch. Anti-Ciceronian dream. 374–79. In Desert of Chalcis	374. Life of Paulus, the first hermit. 374–79. Jerome copies Gospel of the Hebrews and other books. 379. Dialogue against the Luciferians.
379–80. At Antioch. 379. Ordination by Paulinus. 380. To Constantinople.	
	381. Translation of Eusebius' Chronicle. 381. Translation of Origen's Homilies on Jeremiah and Ezekiel
382–35. At Rome.	383. Translation of Psalms from LXX. and of New Testament. 383. Book against Helvidius (Perp. Virg. of B. M. V.).
385. Leaves Rome (August) ; to Antioch (December). 386. Through Palestine to Egypt, and settlement at Bethlehem.	385–87. Translation of Origen on Canticles. 386–90. Translation of LXX. into Latin. 387. Revision of version of New Testament.
	388. Commentary on Ecclesiastes. 388. Commentary on Galatians, Ephesians, Titus, Philemon. 388. Book of Hebrew Names. 388. Questions on Genesis. 388. Translation of Eusebius on Sites and Names of Hebrew Places. 388. Translation of Didymus on the Holy Spirit.
	389. Translation of Origen on St. Luke. 390. Lives of Malchus and Hilarion, hermits.
	391. Vulgate version of Old Testament begun. 392. Book of Illustrious Men. 392. Commentary on Nahum, Micah, Zephaniah, Haggai, Habakkuk. 393. Books against Jovinian.
392. Aterbius at Jerusalem. 392. Epiphanius visits Jerusalem. Schism between Jerome and John of Jerusalem, till 397.	
394. Beginning of controversy with Augustin. 395. Jerome denounced to the Emperor. 395. The Huns invade Northern Syria. 395. Oceanus and Fabiola at Bethlehem.	
397. Theophilus of Alexandria turns against Origenism. Rufinus reconciled to Jerome and returns to Italy.	397. Commentary on Jonah. 397. Book against John, Bishop of Jerusalem.
398. Jerome suffers from a long illness. 401–4. Controversy between Jerome and Rufinus.	398. Commentary on St. Matthew.
	402. Against Rufinus, Books i. and ii. 403. Commentary on Obadiah.
404. Death of Paula. 404. Close of controversy with Augustin. 404–5. Jerome ill for several months. 405. Northern Palestine invaded by Isaurians.	404. Translation of the ascetic rule of Pachomius. 404. Against Rufinus, Book iii.
	406. Commentary on Zachariah, Malachi, Hosea, Joel, Amos concluding Minor Prophets. 406. Book against Vigilantius.
	407. Commentary on Daniel. 410. Commentary on Isaiah.
410. Death of Rufinus. 412. Cœlestius condemned at Carthage. 413. Pelagius in Palestine.	
	414. Commentary on Ezekiel.
414. Orosius sent by Augustin to Jerome. 414. Pinianus and Melania at Jerusalem. 415. Synod at Jerusalem admits Pelagius. 417. Monasteries of Bethlehem burnt by adherents of Pelagius.	
	416. Dialogue against the Pelagians. 418–19. Commentary on Jeremiah.
418. Death of Eustochium. 420. Jerome dies (September 20) at Bethlehem.	

AND TIMES OF ST. JEROME, A.D. 345–420.

CONTEMPORARY HISTORY.	CONTEMPORARY HISTORY (ECCLESIASTICAL).
340. Death of Constantine.	
	341. Athanasius at Rome.
353. Constantius sole Emperor.	352. Cyril, Bishop of Jerusalem.
	356. Eusebius of Vercellæ, and other orthodox Bishops banished by Constantius.
	356. Death of Antony.
360. Julian Emperor.	359. Councils of Ariminum and Seleucia.
361. Death of Constantius.	
	362. Eusebius of Vercella and other Bishops recalled from exile.
363. Death of Julian. Jovian Emperor.	
364. Death of Jovian. Valentinian and Valens.	
366. Invasion of the Alemanni repelled by Valentinian.	365. Apollinarius, Bishop of Laodicæa.
367-69. Gothic war.	366. Damasus Pope.
367-70. Britain restored by the elder Theodosius.	370. Law of Valentinian against clerical legacies.
	371. Death of Eusebius of Vercellæ and of Lucifer.
	373. Death of Athanasius. Peter and Lucius, rival Bishops.
	374. Ambrose, Bishop of Milan.
375. Death of Valentinian. Valens and Gratian Emperors.	374. Melania and Rufinus leave Rome for the East.
376. Theodosius, after restoring Africa, executed at Carthage.	
377-80. Persian war.	
378. Battle of Adrianople. Valens killed. Gregory Nazianzen at Constantinople	378. Gregory Nazianzen at Constantinople.
379. Theodosius Emperor.	
	380. Baptism of Theodosius.
	381. Council of Constantinople.
	381. Peter, Bishop of Alexandria, succeeded by his brother Timothy.
	382. Council at Rome.
	382. Altar of Victory in Roman Senate removed.
383. Death of Gratian. Maximus Emperor.	384. Death of Damasus (December).
384. Treaty with Persia.	385. Theophilus, Bishop of Alexandria, succeeds Timothy.
	385. Siricius Pope.
	386. John succeeds Cyril as Bishop of Jerusalem.
387. Sedition of Antioch.	386. Execution of Priscillian for heresy at Treves.
388. Death of Maximus. Valentinian II. Emperor.	
390. Massacre of Thessalonica. Penance of Theodosius.	389. Temple of Serapis destroyed.
391. Death of Valentinian II. Eugenius usurper.	390. Death of Gregory Nazianzen.
	392. Laws of Theodosius against Paganism.
394. Defeat of Eugenius. Theodosius sole Emperor.	
395. Death of Theodosius. Arcadius (æt. 18) Emperor of the East; Honorius (æt. 14) of the West. Stilicho Minister and General in the West. Death of Rufinus the Prefect at Constantinople.	395. Augustin, Bishop of Hippo.
396. Alaric invades Greece.	
397. Alaric conquered by Stilicho in Arcadia.	397. Death of Ambrose. Simplicianus, Bishop of Milan.
398. Death of Gildo in Africa. Alaric Master-General of Illyricum and King of the Visigoths.	398. Chrysostom, Bishop of Constantinople.
399. Fall of Eutropius.	398. Pope Siricius dies. Anastasius Pope.
400. Gainas, conspirator, defeated and slain.	400. Origenism condemned by Bishops of Alexandria, Rome, and Milan, and by the Emperors.
	400. (August 15). Simplicianus dies. Venerius, Bishop of Millan.
	402. Pope Anastasius dies. Innocentius Pope.
	402. Death of Epiphanius.
403. Stilicho defeats Alaric at Pollentia and Verona.	
404. Triumph of Honorius. Last gladiatorial shows.	404. Exile of Chrysostom to Cucusus.
404. Emperor's seat at Ravenna.	404. Gladiatorial shows at Rome ended by the sacrifice of Telemachus, the monk.
404. Death of the Empress Eudoxia.	
406. Stilicho defeats Radagaisus at Fæsulæ, and negotiates with Alaric.	
407. Gaul overrun by barbarians.	407. Death of Chrysostom at Comana.
407. Constantine usurps power in Britain and Gaul.	
408. Rome besieged by Alaric, and ransomed.	
408. Disgrace and death of Stilicho.	
408. Death of Arcadius. Theodosius II. Emperor. Pulcheria Regent.	
409. Revolt of Britain.	409. Pelagius at Rome.
410. Sack of Rome by Alaric. Death of Alaric.	
410. Egypt, Phœnicia, etc. threatened by barbarians (Ep. cxxvi.).	
411. Death of Constantine and other usurpers. Victories of Roman General Constantius.	411. Dispute between Catholic and Donatist Bishops at Carthage. Persecution of Donatists by the Civil Power.
	412. Death of Theophilus, Bishop of Alexandria.
413. Expedition and death of Heraclian, Count of Africa.	
414. Adolphus, successor of Alaric, marries Galla Placidia.	
415. Goths established in Aquitaine and Spain.	415. Schism at Antioch healed. Alexander sole Bishop.
	415. Council of Diospolis (Lydda) accepts Pelagius.
	417. Pope Innocentius dies. Zosimus Pope.
	417. Death of John, Bishop of Jerusalem. Succeeded by Praylus.

THE LETTERS OF ST. JEROME

LETTER I.

TO INNOCENT.

Not only the first of the letters but probably the earliest extant composition of Jerome (c. 370 A.D.). Innocent, to whom it is addressed, was one of the little band of enthusiasts whom Jerome gathered round him in Aquileia. He followed his friend to Syria, where he died in 374 A.D. (See Letter III., 3.)

1. You have frequently asked me, dearest Innocent, not to pass over in silence the marvellous event which has happened in our own day. I have declined the task from modesty and, as I now feel, with justice, believing myself to be incapable of it, at once because human language is inadequate to the divine praise, and because inactivity, acting like rust upon the intellect, has dried up any little power of expression that I have ever had. You in reply urge that in the things of God we must look not at the work which we are able to accomplish, but at the spirit in which it is undertaken, and that he can never be at a loss for words who has believed on the Word.

2. What, then, must I do? The task is beyond me, and yet I dare not decline it. I am a mere unskilled passenger, and I find myself placed in charge of a freighted ship. I have not so much as handled a rowboat on a lake, and now I have to trust myself to the noise and turmoil of the Euxine. I see the shores sinking beneath the horizon, "sky and sea on every side";[1] darkness lowers over the water, the clouds are black as night, the waves only are white with foam. You urge me to hoist the swelling sails, to loosen the sheets, and to take the helm. At last I obey your commands, and as charity can do all things, I will trust in the Holy Ghost to guide my course, and I shall console myself, whatever the event. For, if our ship is wafted by the surf into the wished-for haven, I shall be content to be told that the pilotage was poor. But, if

through my unpolished diction we run aground amid the rough cross-currents of language, you may blame my lack of power, but you will at least recognize my good intentions.

3. To begin, then: Vercellæ is a Ligurian town, situated not far from the base of the Alps, once important, but now sparsely peopled and fallen into decay. When the consular[1] was holding her visitation there, a poor woman and her paramour were brought before him—the charge of adultery had been fastened upon them by the husband—and were both consigned to the penal horrors of a prison. Shortly after an attempt was made to elicit the truth by torture, and when the blood-stained hook smote the young man's livid flesh and tore furrows in his side, the unhappy wretch sought to avoid prolonged pain by a speedy death. Falsely accusing his own passions, he involved another in the charge; and it appeared that he was of all men the most miserable, and that his execution was just inasmuch as he had left to an innocent woman no means of self-defence. But the woman, stronger in virtue if weaker in sex, though her frame was stretched upon the rack, and though her hands, stained with the filth of the prison, were tied behind her, looked up to heaven with her eyes, which alone the torturer had been unable to bind, and while the tears rolled down her face, said: "Thou art witness, Lord Jesus, to whom nothing is hid, who triest the reins and the heart.[2] Thou art witness that it is not to save my life that I deny this charge. I refuse to lie because to lie is sin. And as for you, unhappy man, if you are bent on hastening your death, why must you destroy not one innocent person, but two? I also, myself, desire to die. I desire to put off this hated body, but not as an adulteress. I offer my neck; I welcome the shining sword without fear; yet I will take my innocence with me.

---

[1] Virg. A. iii. 193.

[1] I.e. the governor of the province.   [2] Ps. vii. 9.

He does not die who is slain while purposing so to live."

4. The consular, who had been feasting his eyes upon the bloody spectacle, now, like a wild beast, which after once tasting blood always thirsts for it, ordered the torture to be doubled, and cruelly gnashing his teeth, threatened the executioner with like punishment if he failed to extort from the weaker sex a confession which a man's strength had not been able to keep back.

5. Send help, Lord Jesus. For this one creature of Thine every species of torture is devised. She is bound by the hair to a stake, her whole body is fixed more firmly than ever on the rack; fire is brought and applied to her feet; her sides quiver beneath the executioner's probe; even her breasts do not escape. Still the woman remains unshaken; and, triumphing in spirit over the pain of the body, enjoys the happiness of a good conscience, round which the tortures rage in vain.[1] The cruel judge rises, overcome with passion. She still prays to God. Her limbs are wrenched from their sockets; she only turns her eyes to heaven. Another confesses what is thought their common guilt. She, for the confessor's sake, denies the confession, and, in peril of her own life, clears one who is in peril of his.

6. Meantime she has but one thing to say: "Beat me, burn me, tear me, if you will; I have not done it. If you will not believe my words, a day will come when this charge shall be carefully sifted. I have One who will judge me." Wearied out at last, the torturer sighed in response to her groans; nor could he find a spot on which to inflict a fresh wound. His cruelty overcome, he shuddered to see the body he had torn. Immediately the consular cried, in a fit of passion, "Why does it surprise you, bystanders, that a woman prefers torture to death? It takes two people, most assuredly, to commit adultery; and I think it more credible that a guilty woman should deny a sin than that an innocent young man should confess one."

7. Like sentence, accordingly, was passed on both, and the condemned pair were dragged to execution. The entire people poured out to see the sight ; indeed, so closely were the gates thronged by the outrushing crowd, that you might have fancied the city itself to be migrating. At the very first stroke of the sword the head of the hapless youth was cut off, and the headless trunk rolled over in its blood. Then came the woman's turn. She knelt down upon the ground, and the shining sword was lifted over her quivering neck. But though the headsman summoned all his strength into his bared arm, the moment it touched her flesh the fatal blade stopped short, and, lightly glancing over the skin, merely grazed it sufficiently to draw blood. The striker saw, with terror, his hand unnerved, and, amazed at his defeated skill and at his drooping sword, he whirled it aloft for another stroke. Again the blade fell forceless on the woman, sinking harmlessly on her neck, as though the steel feared to touch her. The enraged and panting officer, who had thrown open his cloak at the neck to give his full strength to the blow, shook to the ground the brooch which clasped the edges of his mantle, and not noticing this, began to poise his sword for a fresh stroke. "See," cried the woman, "a jewel has fallen from your shoulder. Pick up what you have earned by hard toil, that you may not lose it."

8. What, I ask, is the secret of such confidence as this? Death draws near, but it has no terrors for her. When smitten she exults, and the executioner turns pale. Her eyes see the brooch, they fail to see the sword. And, as if intrepidity in the presence of death were not enough, she confers a favor upon her cruel foe. And now the mysterious Power of the Trinity rendered even a third blow vain. The terrified soldier, no longer trusting the blade, proceeded to apply the point to her throat, in the idea that though it might not cut, the pressure of his hand might plunge it into her flesh. Marvel unheard of through all the ages! The sword bent back to the hilt, and in its defeat looked to its master, as if confessing its inability to slay.

9. Let me call to my aid the example of the three children,[1] who, amid the cool, encircling fire, sang hymns,[2] instead of weeping, and around whose turbans and holy hair the flames played harmlessly. Let me recall, too, the story of the blessed Daniel, in whose presence, though he was their natural prey, the lions crouched, with fawning tails and frightened mouths. Let Susannah also rise in the nobility of her faith before the thoughts of all; who, after she had been condemned by an unjust sentence, was saved through a youth inspired by the Holy Ghost. In both cases the Lord's mercy was alike shewn; for while Susannah was set free b[y]

---

[1] Text corrupt.

[1] Shadrach, Meshach and Abednego.
[2] Song of the Three Holy Children.　　[3] Dan. vi.
[4] Susannah 45; the youth spoken of is Daniel.

the judge, so as not to die by the sword, this woman, though condemned by the judge, was acquitted by the sword.

10. Now at length the populace rise in arms to defend the woman. Men and women of every age join in driving away the executioner, shouting round him in a surging crowd. Hardly a man dares trust his own eyes. The disquieting news reaches the city close at hand, and the entire force of constables is mustered. The officer who is responsible for the execution of criminals bursts from among his men, and

Staining his hoary hair with soiling dust,

exclaims: "What! citizens, do you mean to seek my life? Do you intend to make me a substitute for her? However much your minds are set on mercy, and however much you wish to save a condemned woman, yet assuredly I—I who am innocent—ought not to perish." His tearful appeal tells upon the crowd, they are all benumbed by the influence of sorrow, and an extraordinary change of feeling is manifested. Before it had seemed a duty to plead for the woman's life, now it seemed a duty to allow her to be executed.

11. Accordingly a new sword is fetched, a new headsman appointed. The victim takes her place, once more strengthened only with the favor of Christ. The first blow makes her quiver, beneath the second she sways to and fro, by the third she falls wounded to the ground. Oh, majesty of the divine power highly to be extolled! She who previously had received four strokes without injury, now, a few moments later, seems to die that an innocent man may not perish in her stead.

12. Those of the clergy whose duty it is to wrap the blood-stained corpse in a winding-sheet, dig out the earth and, heaping together stones, form the customary tomb. The sunset comes on quickly, and by God's mercy the night of nature arrives more swiftly than is its wont. Suddenly the woman's bosom heaves, her eyes seek the light, her body is quickened into new life. A moment after she sighs, she looks round, she gets up and speaks. At last she is able to cry: "The Lord is on my side; I will not fear. What can man do unto me?"[2]

13. Meantime an aged woman, supported out of the funds of the church, gave back her spirit to heaven from which it came.[3] It seemed as if the course of events had been thus purposely ordered, for her body took

the place of the other beneath the mound. In the gray dawn the devil comes on the scene in the form of a constable,[1] asks for the corpse of her who had been slain, and desires to have her grave pointed out to him. Surprised that she could have died, he fancies her to be still alive. The clergy show him the fresh turf, and meet his demands by pointing to the earth lately heaped up, taunting him with such words as these: "Yes, of course, tear up the bones which have been buried! Declare war anew against the tomb, and if even that does not satisfy you, pluck her limb from limb for birds and beasts to mangle! Mere dying is too good for one whom it took seven strokes to kill."

14. Before such opprobrious words the executioner retires in confusion, while the woman is secretly revived at home. Then, lest the frequency of the doctor's visits to the church might give occasion for suspicion, they cut her hair short and send her in the company of some virgins to a sequestered country house. There she changes her dress for that of a man, and scars form over her wounds. Yet even after the great miracles worked on her behalf, the laws still rage against her. So true is it that, where there is most law, there, there is also most injustice.[2]

15. But now see whither the progress of my story has brought me; we come upon the name of our friend Evagrius.[3] So great have his exertions been in the cause of Christ that, were I to suppose it possible adequately to describe them, I should only show my own folly; and were I minded deliberately to pass them by, I still could not prevent my voice from breaking out into cries of joy. Who can fittingly praise the vigilance which enabled him to bury, if I may so say, before his death Auxentius[4] of Milan, that curse brooding over the church? Or who can sufficiently extol the discretion with which he rescued the Roman bishop[5] from the toils of the net in which he was fairly entangled, and showed him the means at once of overcoming his opponents and of sparing them in their discomfiture? But

Such topics I must leave to other bards,
Shut out by envious straits of time and space.[6]

I am satisfied now to record the conclusion of

---

[1] Virg. A. xii. 611.
[2] Ps. cxviii. 6.
[3] Cf. Eccles. xii. 7.

[1] Lictor. [2] An allusion to the well-known proverb, summum jus, summa injuria.
[3] A presbyter of Antioch and bishop, 388 A.D. He is mentioned again in Letters III., IV., V., XV. See Jerome De Vir. iii. 125.
[4] The predecessor of Ambrose and an Arian. He was still living when Jerome wrote, but died 374.
[5] Damasus, who having successfully made good his claim to the papacy, in 369 condemned Auxentius in a council held at Rome.
[6] Virg. G. iv. 147, 148.

my tale. Evagrius seeks a special audience of the Emperor;[1] importunes him with his entreaties, wins his favor by his services, and finally gains his cause through his earnestness. The Emperor restored to liberty the woman whom God had restored to life.

LETTER II.

TO THEODOSIUS AND THE REST OF THE ANCHORITES.

Written from Antioch, 374 A.D., while Jerome was still in doubt as to his future course. Theodosius appears to have been the head of the solitaries in the Syrian Desert.

How I long to be a member of your company, and with uplifting of all my powers to embrace your admirable community! Though, indeed, these poor eyes are not worthy to look upon it. Oh! that I could behold the desert, lovelier to me than any city! Oh! that I could see those lonely spots made into a paradise by the saints that throng them! But since my sins prevent me from thrusting into your blessed company a head laden with every transgression, I adjure you (and I know that you can do it) by your prayers to deliver me from the darkness of this world. I spoke of this when I was with you, and now in writing to you I repeat anew the same request; for all the energy of my mind is devoted to this one object. It rests with you to give effect to my resolve. I have the will but not the power; this last can only come in answer to your prayers. For my part, I am like a sick sheep astray from the flock. Unless the good Shepherd shall place me on his shoulders and carry me back to the fold,[2] my steps will totter, and in the very effort of rising I shall find my feet give way. I am the prodigal son[3] who, although I have squandered all the portion entrusted to me by my father, have not yet bowed the knee in submission to him; not yet have I commenced to put away from me the allurements of my former excesses. And because it is only a little while since I have begun not so much to abandon my vices as to desire to abandon them, the devil now ensnares me in new toils, he puts new stumbling-blocks in my path, he encompasses me on every side.

　　The seas around, and all around the main.[4]

I find myself in mid-ocean, unwilling to retreat and unable to advance. It only remains that your prayers should win for me the gale of the Holy Spirit to waft me to the haven upon the desired shore.

---

[1] Valentinian I.　　　　　[2] Luke xv. 3-5.
[3] Luke xv. 11-32.　　　　[4] Virg. A. v. 9.

LETTER III.

TO RUFINUS THE MONK.[1]

Written from Antioch, 374 A.D., to Rufinus in Egypt. Jerome narrates his travels and the events which have taken place since his arrival in Syria, particularly the deaths of Innocent and Hylas (§ 3). He also describes the life of Bonosus, who was now a hermit on an island in the Adriatic (§ 4). The main object of the letter is to induce Rufinus to come to Syria.

1. That God gives more than we ask Him for,[2] and that He often grants us things which "eye hath not seen nor ear heard, neither have they entered into the heart of man,"[3] I knew indeed before from the mystic declaration of the sacred volumes; but now, dearest Rufinus, I have had proof of it in my own case. For I who fancied it too bold a wish to be allowed by an exchange of letters to counterfeit to myself your presence in the flesh, hear that you are penetrating the remotest parts of Egypt, visiting the monks and going round God's family upon earth. Oh, if only the Lord Jesus Christ would suddenly transport me to you as Philip was transported to the eunuch,[4] and Habakkuk to Daniel,[5] with what a close embrace would I clasp your neck, how fondly would I press kisses upon that mouth which has so often joined with me of old in error or in wisdom. But as I am unworthy (not that you should so come to me but) that I should so come to you, and because my poor body, weak even when well, has been shattered by frequent illnesses; I send this letter to meet you instead of coming myself, in the hope that it may bring you hither to me caught in the meshes of love's net.

2. My first joy at such unexpected good tidings was due to our brother, Heliodorus. I desired to be sure of it, but did not dare to feel sure, especially as he told me that he had only heard it from some one else, and as the strangeness of the news impaired the credit of the story. Once more my wishes hovered in uncertainty and my mind wavered, till an Alexandrian monk who had some time previously been sent over by the dutiful zeal of the people to the Egyptian confessor (in will already martyrs[6]), impelled me by his presence to believe the tidings. Even then, I must admit I still hesitated. For on

---

[1] In Jerome's day this term included all—whether hermits or cœnobites—who forsook the world and embraced an ascetic life.
[2] Cf. Eph. iii. 20.　　　　[3] 1 Cor. ii. 9.
[4] Acts, viii. 26-30.　　　　[5] Bel, 33-36.
[6] Priests, monks, and others who, because they would not declare themselves Arians, were banished by order of Valens to Heliopolis in Phenicia.

the one hand he knew nothing either of your name or country: yet on the other what he said seemed likely to be true, agreeing as it did with the hint which had already reached me. At last the truth broke upon me in all its fulness, for a constant stream of persons passing through brought the report: " Rufinus is at Nitria, and has reached the abode of the blessed Macarius."[1] At this point I cast away all that restrained my belief, and then first really grieved to find myself ill. Had it not been that my wasted and enfeebled frame fettered my movements, neither the summer heat nor the dangerous voyage should have had power to retard the rapid steps of affection. Believe me, brother, I look forward to seeing you more than the storm-tossed mariner looks for his haven, more than the thirsty fields long for the showers, more than the anxious mother sitting on the curving shore expects her son.

3. After that sudden whirlwind[2] dragged me from your side, severing with its impious wrench the bonds of affection in which we were knit together,

> The dark blue raincloud lowered o'er my head :
> On all sides were the seas, on all the sky.[3]

I wandered about, uncertain where to go. Thrace, Pontus, Bithynia, the whole of Galatia and Cappadocia, Cilicia also with its burning heat, one after another shattered my energies. At last Syria presented itself to me as a most secure harbor to a shipwrecked man. Here, after undergoing every possible kind of sickness, I lost one of my two eyes; for Innocent,[4] the half of my soul,[5] was taken away from me by a sudden attack of fever. The one eye which I now enjoy, and which is all in all to me, is our Evagrius,[6] upon whom I with my constant infirmities have come as an additional burden. We had with us also Hylas,[7] the servant of the holy Melanium,[8] who by his stainless conduct had wiped out the taint of his previous servitude. His death opened afresh the wound which had not yet healed. But as the apostle's words forbid us to mourn for those who sleep,[9] and as my excess of grief has been tempered by the joyful news that has since come to me, I recount this last, that, if you have not heard it,

you may learn it; and that, if you know it already, you may rejoice over it with me.

4. Bonosus,[1] your friend, or, to speak more truly, mine as well as yours, is now climbing the ladder foreshown in Jacob's dream.[2] He is bearing his cross, neither taking thought for the morrow[3] nor looking back at what he has left.[4] He is sowing in tears that he may reap in joy.[5] As Moses in a type so he in reality is lifting up the serpent in the wilderness.[6] This is a true story, and it may well put to shame the lying marvels described by Greek and Roman pens. For here you have a youth educated with us in the refining accomplishments of the world, with abundance of wealth, and in rank inferior to none of his associates; yet he forsakes his mother, his sisters, and his dearly loved brother, and settles like a new tiller of Eden on a dangerous island, with the sea roaring round its reefs; while its rough crags, bare rocks, and desolate aspect make it more terrible still. No peasant or monk is to be found there. Even the little Onesimus[7] you know of, in whose kisses he used to rejoice as in those of a brother, in this tremendous solitude no longer remains at his side. Alone upon the island — or rather not alone, for Christ is with him — he sees the glory of God, which even the apostles saw not save in the desert. He beholds, it is true, no embattled towns, but he has enrolled his name in the new city.[8] Garments of sackcloth disfigure his limbs, yet so clad he will be the sooner caught up to meet Christ in the clouds.[9] No watercourse pleasant to the view supplies his wants, but from the Lord's side he drinks the water of life.[10] Place all this before your eyes, dear friend, and with all the faculties of your mind picture to yourself the scene. When you realize the effort of the fighter then you will be able to praise his victory. Round the entire island roars the frenzied sea, while the beetling crags along its winding shores resound as the billows beat against them. No grass makes the ground green; there are no shady copses and no fertile fields. Precipitous cliffs surround his dreadful abode as if it were a prison. But he, careless, fearless, and armed from head to foot with the apostle's armor,[11] now listens to God by reading the

---

[1] There were two hermits of this name in Egypt, and it is not certain which is meant. One of them was a disciple of Antony.
[2] The ascetic community at Aquileia, of which Jerome and Rufinus were the leaders, had been broken up, perhaps through the efforts of Lupicinus, the bishop of Stridon.
[3] Virg. A. iii. 193, 194 : v. 9. [4] See Letter I.
[5] Hor. C. i. 3, 8. [6] See Letter I. § 15.
[7] A freedman of Melanium.
[8] A young Roman widow who had given up the world that she might adopt the ascetic life. She accompanied Rufinus to the East and settled with him on the Mount of Olives. She is mentioned again in Letters IV., XXXIX., XLV., and others.
[9] 1 Thess. iv. 13.

[1] Jerome's foster-brother who had accompanied him on his first visit to Rome. He was now living as a hermit on a small island in the neighborhood of Aquileia. See Letter VII. § 3.
[2] Gen. xxviii. 12. [3] Matt. vi. 34. [4] Luke ix. 62.
[5] Ps. cxxvi. 5. [6] Nu. xxi. 9.
[7] Of this child nothing is known.
[8] I.e. the new Jerusalem. Rev. xxi. 2. Is. iv. 3.
[9] 1 Thess. iv. 17. [10] Joh. iv. 14: xix. 34. [11] Eph. vi. 13-17.

Scriptures, now speaks to God as he prays to the Lord; and it may be that, while he lingers in the island, he sees some vision such as that once seen by John.[1]

5. What snares, think you, is the devil now weaving? What stratagems is he preparing? Perchance, mindful of his old trick,[2] he will try to tempt Bonosus with hunger. But he has been answered already: "Man shall not live by bread alone."[3] Perchance he will lay before him wealth and fame. But it shall be said to him: "They that desire to be rich fall into a trap[4] and temptations,"[5] and "For me all glorying is in Christ."[6] He will come, it may be, when the limbs are weary with fasting, and rack them with the pangs of disease; but the cry of the apostle will repel him: "When I am weak, then am I strong," and "My strength is made perfect in weakness."[7] He will hold out threats of death; but the reply will be: "I desire to depart and to be with Christ."[8] He will brandish his fiery darts, but they will be received on the shield of faith.[9] In a word, Satan will assail him, but Christ will defend. Thanks be to Thee, Lord Jesus, that in Thy day I have one able to pray to Thee for me. To Thee all hearts are open, Thou searchest the secrets of the heart,[10] Thou seest the prophet shut up in the fish's belly in the midst of the sea.[11] Thou knowest then how he and I grew up together from tender infancy to vigorous manhood, how we were fostered in the bosoms of the same nurses, and carried in the arms of the same bearers; and how after studying together at Rome we lodged in the same house and shared the same food by the half savage banks of the Rhine. Thou knowest, too, that it was I who first began to seek to serve Thee. Remember, I beseech Thee, that this warrior of Thine was once a raw recruit with me. I have before me the declaration of Thy majesty: "Whosoever shall teach and not do shall be called least in the kingdom of heaven."[12] May he enjoy the crown of virtue, and in return for his daily martyrdoms may he follow the Lamb robed in white raiment![13] For "in my Father's house are many mansions,"[14] and "one star differeth from another star in glory."[15] Give me strength to raise my head to a level with the saints' heels![16] I willed, but he performed. Do Thou therefore pardon me that I failed to keep my resolve, and reward him with the guerdon of his deserts.

I may perhaps have been tedious, and have said more than the short compass of a letter usually allows; but this, I find, is always the case with me when I have to say anything in praise of our dear Bonosus.

6. However, to return to the point from which I set out, I beseech you do not let me pass wholly out of sight and out of mind. A friend is long sought, hardly found, and with difficulty kept. Let those who will, allow gold to dazzle them and be borne along in splendor, their very baggage glittering with gold and silver. Love is not to be purchased, and affection has no price. The friendship which can cease has never been real. Farewell in Christ.

LETTER IV.

TO FLORENTIUS.

Sent to Florentius along with the preceding letter, which Jerome requests him to deliver to Rufinus. This Florentius was a rich Italian who had retired to Jerusalem to pursue the monastic life. Jerome subsequently speaks of him as "a distinguished monk so pitiful to the needy that he was generally known as the father of the poor." (Chron. ad A.D. 381.)

1. How much your name and sanctity are on the lips of the most different peoples you may gather from the fact that I commence to love you before I know you. For as, according to the apostle, "Some men's sins are evident going before unto judgment,"[1] so contrariwise the report of your charity is so widespread that it is considered not so much praiseworthy to love you as criminal to refuse to do so. I pass over the countless instances in which you have supported Christ,[2] fed, clothed, and visited Him. The aid you rendered to our brother Heliodorus[3] in his need may well loose the utterance of the dumb. With what gratitude, with what commendation, does he speak of the kindness with which you smoothed a pilgrim's path. I am, it is true, the most sluggish of men, consumed by an unendurable sickness; yet keen affection and desire have winged my feet, and I have come forward to salute and embrace you. I wish you every good thing, and pray that the Lord may establish our nascent friendship.

2. Our brother, Rufinus, is said to have come from Egypt to Jerusalem with the de-

---

[1] Rev. i. 9, 10. [2] Gen. iii. 1-6: Matt. iv. 1-4. [3] Matt. iv. 4.
[4] Literally "mousetrap." This variant is peculiar to Cyprian and Jerome. [5] 1 Tim. vi. 9. [6] 1 Cor. i. 31.
[7] 2 Cor. xii. 10, 9. [8] Philip. i. 23. [9] Eph. vi. 16.
[10] Acts i. 24: Rev. ii. 23. [11] Jon. ii. 1, 2. [12] Matt. v. 19.
[13] Rev. xiv. 4. [14] John xiv. 2. [15] 1 Cor. xv. 41.
[16] Quoted from Tert. de C. F. ii. 7.

[1] 1 Tim. v. 24, R. V. [2] Matt. xxv. 34-40.
[3] See introduction to Letter XIV.

vout lady, Melanium. He is inseparably bound to me in brotherly love; and I beg you to oblige me by delivering to him the annexed letter. You must not, however, judge of me by the virtues that you find in him. For in him you will see the clearest tokens of holiness, whilst I am but dust and vile dirt, and even now, while still living, nothing but ashes. It is enough for me if my weak eyes can bear the brightness of his excellence. He has but now washed himself[1] and is clean, yea, is made white as snow;[2] whilst I, stained with every sin, wait day and night with trembling to pay the uttermost farthing.[3] But since "the Lord looseth the prisoners,"[4] and resteth upon him who is of a contrite spirit, and that trembleth at His words,[5] perchance he may say even to me who lie in the grave of sin: "Jerome, come forth."[6]

The reverend presbyter, Evagrius, warmly salutes you. We both with united respect salute the brother, Martinianus.[7] I desire much to see him, but I am impeded by the chain of sickness. Farewell in Christ.

LETTER V.

TO FLORENTIUS.

Written a few months after the preceding (about the end of 374 A.D.) from the Syrian Desert. After dilating on his friendship for Florentius, and making a passing allusion to Rufinus, Jerome mentions certain books copies of which he desires to be sent to him. He also speaks of a runaway slave about whom Florentius had written to him.

1. Your letter, dear friend, finds me dwelling in that quarter of the desert which is nearest to Syria and the Saracens. And the reading of it rekindles in my mind so keen a desire to set out for Jerusalem that I am almost ready to violate my monastic vow in order to gratify my affection. Wishing to do the best I can, as I cannot come in person I send you a letter instead; and thus, though absent in the body, I come to you in love and in spirit.[8] For my earnest prayer is that our infant friendship, firmly cemented as it is in Christ, may never be rent asunder by time or distance. We ought rather to strengthen the bond by an interchange of letters. Let these pass between us, meet each other on the way, and converse with us. Affection will not lose much if it keeps up an intercourse of this kind.

2. You write that our brother, Rufinus,

has not yet come to you. Even if he does come it will do little to satisfy my longing, for I shall not now be able to see him. He is too far away to come hither, and the conditions of the lonely life that I have adopted forbid me to go to him. For I am no longer free to follow my own wishes. I entreat you, therefore, to ask him to allow you to have the commentaries of the reverend Rhetitius,[1] bishop of Augustodunum,[2] copied, in which he has so eloquently explained the Song of Songs. A countryman of the aforesaid brother Rufinus, the old man Paul,[3] writes that Rufinus has his copy of Tertullian, and urgently requests that this may be returned. Next I have to ask you to get written on paper by a copyist certain books which the subjoined list[4] will show you that I do not possess. I beg also that you will send me the explanation of the Psalms of David, and the copious work on Synods of the reverend Hilary,[5] which I copied for him[6] at Trêves with my own hand. Such books, you know, must be the food of the Christian soul if it is to meditate in the law of the Lord day and night.[7]

Others you welcome beneath your roof, you cherish and comfort, you help out of your own purse; but so far as I am concerned, you have given me everything when once you have granted my request. And since, through the Lord's bounty, I am rich in volumes of the sacred library,[8] you may command me in turn. I will send you what you please; and do not suppose that an order from you will give me trouble. I have pupils devoted to the art of copying. Nor do I merely promise a favor because I am asking one. Our brother, Heliodorus,[9] tells me that there are many parts of the Scriptures which you seek and cannot find. But even if you have them all, affection is sure to assert its rights and to seek for itself more than it already has.

3. As regards the present master of your slave—of whom you have done me the honor to write—I have no doubt but that he is his kidnapper. While I was still at Antioch the presbyter, Evagrius, often reproved him in my presence. To whom he made this answer: "I have nothing to fear." He declares that his master has dismissed him. If you both want him, he is here; send

---

[1] Rufinus had been baptized at Aquileia about three years previously (371 A.D.).
[2] Cf. Ps. li. 7.   [3] Matt. v. 26.   [4] Ps. cxlvi. 7.
[5] Isa. lxvi. 2.   [6] Joh. xi. 43.
[7] Acc. to Vallarsi a hermit, who at this time lived near Cæsarea.
[8] Cf. Col. ii. 5.

[1] A man of some note, as he was one of the commissioners appointed by Constantine in 313 A.D. to settle the points of issue between the Catholics and the Donatists. Jerome criticises his commentary on the Song of Songs in Letter XXXVII.
[2] Autun.   [3] See the introd. to Letter X.
[4] This list has perished.   [5] I.e. Hilary of Poitiers.
[6] Rufinus.   [7] Ps. i. 2.   [8] I.e. the Scriptures.
[9] See the introd. to Letter XIV.

him whither you will. I think I am not wrong in refusing to allow a runaway to stray farther. Here in the wilderness I cannot myself execute your orders; and therefore I have asked my dear friend Evagrius to push the affair vigorously, both for your sake and for mine. I desire your welfare in Christ.

LETTER VI.

TO JULIAN, A DEACON OF ANTIOCH.

This letter, written in 374 A.D., is chiefly interesting for its mention of Jerome's sister. It would seem that she had fallen into sin and had been restored to a life of virtue by the deacon, Julian. Jerome speaks of her again in the next letter (§ 4).

It is an old saying, "Liars are disbelieved even when they speak the truth."[1] And from the way in which you reproach me for not having written, I perceive that this has been my lot with you. Shall I say, "I wrote often, but the bearers of my letters were negligent"? You will reply, "Your excuse is the old one of all who fail to write." Shall I say, "I could not find any one to take my letters"? You will say that numbers of persons have gone from my part of the world to yours. Shall I contend that I have actually given them letters? They not having delivered them, will deny that they have received them. Moreover, so great a distance separates us that it will be hard to come at the truth. What shall I do then? Though really not to blame, I ask your forgiveness, for I think it better to fall back and make overtures for peace than to keep my ground and offer battle. The truth is that constant sickness of body and vexation of mind have so weakened me that with death so close at hand I have not been as collected as usual. And lest you should account this plea a false one, now that I have stated my case, I shall, like a pleader, call witnesses to prove it. Our reverend brother, Heliodorus, has been here; but in spite of his wish to dwell in the desert with me, he has been frightened away by my crimes. But my present wordiness will atone for my past remissness; for, as Horace says in his satire:[2]

All singers have one fault among their friends :
They never sing when asked, unasked they never cease.

Henceforth I shall overwhelm you with such bundles of letters that you will take the opposite line and beg me not to write.

I rejoice that my sister[1]—to you a daughter in Christ—remains steadfast in her purpose, a piece of news which I owe in the first instance to you. For here where I now am I am ignorant not only as to what goes on in my native land, but even as to its continued existence. Even though the Iberian viper[2] shall rend me with his baneful fangs, I will not fear men's judgment, seeing that I shall have God to judge me. As one puts it:

Shatter the world to fragments if you will :
'Twill fall upon a head which knows not fear.[3]

Bear in mind, then, I pray you, the apostle's precept[4] that we should make our work abiding; prepare for yourself a reward from the Lord in my sister's salvation; and by frequent letters increase my joy in that glory in Christ which we share together.

LETTER VII.

TO CHROMATIUS, JOVINUS, AND EUSEBIUS.[5]

This letter (written like the preceding in 374 A.D.) is addressed by Jerome to three of his former companions in the religious life. It commends Bonosus (§ 3), asks guidance for the writer's sister (§ 4), and attacks the conduct of Lupicinus, Bishop of Stridon (§ 5).

1. Those whom mutual affection has joined together, a written page ought not to sunder. I must not, therefore, distribute my words some to one and some to another. For so strong is the love that binds you together that affection unites all three of you in a bond no less close than that which naturally connects two of your number.[6] Indeed, if the conditions of writing would only admit of it, I should amalgamate your names and express them under a single symbol. The very letter which I have received from you challenges me in each of you to see all three, and in all three to recognize each. When the reverend Evagrius transmitted it to me in the corner of the desert which stretches between the Syrians and the Saracens, my joy was intense. It wholly surpassed the rejoicings felt at Rome when the defeat of Cannæ was retrieved, and Marcellus at Nola cut to pieces the forces of Hannibal. Evagrius frequently comes to see me, and cherishes me in Christ as his own bowels.[7] Yet as he is separated from me by a long distance, his departure has gener-

---

[1] Aristotle is the author of this remark. [2] Hor. S. i. 3, 1-3.

[1] Mentioned again in Letter VII., § 4.
[2] The person meant is uncertain. Probably it was Lupicinus, bishop of Stridon, for whom see the next letter.
[3] Horace, C. iii. 3, 7, 8. [4] 1 Cor. iii. 14.
[5] Jovinus was archdeacon of Aquileia. All three became bishops—Chromatius of Aquileia, the others of unknown sees.
[6] Chromatius and Eusebius were brothers. [7] Philem. 12.

ally left me as much regret as his arrival has brought me joy.

2. I converse with your letter, I embrace it, it talks to me; it alone of those here speaks Latin. For hereabout you must either learn a barbarous jargon or else hold your tongue. As often as the lines—traced in a well-known hand—bring back to me the faces which I hold so dear, either I am no longer here, or else you are here with me. If you will credit the sincerity of affection, I seem to see you all as I write this.

Now at the outset I should like to ask you one petulant question. Why is it that, when we are separated by so great an interval of land and sea, you have sent me so short a letter? Is it that I have deserved no better treatment, not having first written to you? I cannot believe that paper can have failed you while Egypt continues to supply its wares. Even if a Ptolemy had closed the seas, King Attalus would still have sent you parchments from Pergamum, and so by his skins you could have made up for the want of paper. The very name parchment is derived from a historical incident of the kind which occurred generations ago.[1] What then? Am I to suppose the messenger to have been in haste? No matter how long a letter may be, it can be written in the course of a night. Or had you some business to attend to which prevented you from writing? No claim is prior to that of affection. Two suppositions remain, either that you felt disinclined to write or else that I did not deserve a letter. Of the two I prefer to charge you with sloth than to condemn myself as undeserving. For it is easier to mend neglect than to quicken love.

3. You tell me that Bonosus, like a true son of the Fish, has taken to the water.[2] As for me who am still foul with my old stains, like the basilisk and the scorpion I haunt the dry places.[3] Bonosus has his heel already on the serpent's head, whilst I am still as food to the same serpent which by divine appointment devours the earth.[4] He can scale already that ladder of which the psalms of degrees[5] are a type; whilst I, still weeping on its first step, hardly know whether I shall ever be able to say: "I will lift up mine eyes unto the hills, from whence

cometh my help."[1] Amid the threatening billows of the world he is sitting in the safe shelter of his island,[2] that is, of the church's pale, and it may be that even now, like John, he is being called to eat God's book;[3] whilst I, still lying in the sepulchre of my sins and bound with the chains of my iniquities, wait for the Lord's command in the Gospel: "Jerome, come forth."[4] But Bonosus has done more than this. Like the prophet[5] he has carried his girdle across the Euphrates (for all the devil's strength is in the loins[6]), and has hidden it there in a hole of the rock. Then, afterwards finding it rent, he has sung: "O Lord, thou hast possessed my reins.[7] Thou hast broken my bonds in sunder. I will offer to thee the sacrifice of thanksgiving."[8] But as for me, Nebuchadnezzar has brought me in chains to Babylon, to the babel that is of a distracted mind. There he has laid upon me the yoke of captivity; there inserting in my nostrils a ring of iron,[9] he has commanded me to sing one of the songs of Zion. To whom I have said, "The Lord looseth the prisoners; the Lord openeth the eyes of the blind."[10] To complete my contrast in a single sentence, whilst I pray for mercy Bonosus looks for a crown.

4. My sister's conversion is the fruit of the efforts of the saintly Julian. He has planted, it is for you to water, and the Lord will give the increase.[11] Jesus Christ has given her to me to console me for the wound which the devil has inflicted on her. He has restored her from death to life. But in the words of the pagan poet, for her

There is no safety that I do not fear.[12]

You know yourselves how slippery is the path of youth—a path on which I have myself fallen,[13] and which you are now traversing not without fear. She, as she enters upon it, must have the advice and the encouragement of all, she must be aided by frequent letters from you, my reverend brothers. And—for "charity endureth all things,"[14]—I beg you to get from Pope[15] Valerian[16] a letter to confirm her resolution. A girl's courage, as you know, is strength-

---

1 See Pliny, H. N. xiii. 21.
2 The Greek word ΙΧΘΥΣ represented to the early Christians the sentence Ἰησοῦς Χριστὸς Θεοῦ Ὑιὸς Σωτήρ. Hence the fish became a favorite emblem of Christ. Tertullian connects the symbol with the water of baptism, saying: "We little fishes are born by our Fish, Jesus Christ, in water and can thrive only by continuing in the water." The allusion in the text is to the baptism of Bonosus. See Schaff, "Ante-Nicene Christianity," p. 279.
3 Deut. viii. 15.   4 Gen. iii. 14.
5 Viz., Pss. cxx.–cxxxiv.

1 Ps. cxxi. 1.   2 See Letter III.
3 Rev. x. 9, 10.   4 John xi. 43.   5 Jer. xiii. 4, 5.
6 Job xl. 16 (said of Behemoth); cf. Letter XXII. § 11.
7 Ps. cxxxix. 13.   8 Ps. cxvi. 14, 15, P.B.V.
9 Cf. 2 K. xix. 28.   10 Pss. cxxxvii. 3; cxlvi. 7, 8.
11 1 Cor. iii. 6.   12 Virg. A. iv. 298.
13 Jerome again refers to his own frailty in Letters XIV. § 6, XVIII. § 11, and XLVIII. § 20.   14 1 Cor. xiii. 7.
15 Papa. The word "pope" was at this time used as a name of respect ("father in God") for bishops generally. Only by degrees did it come to be restricted to the bishop of Rome. Similarly the word "imperator," originally applied to any Roman general, came to be used of the Emperor alone.
16 Bishop of Aquileia.

ened when she realizes that persons in high place are interested in her.

5. The fact is that my native land is a prey to barbarism, that in it men's only God is their belly,[1] that they live only for the present, and that the richer a man is the holier he is held to be. Moreover, to use a well-worn proverb, the dish has a cover worthy of it; for Lupicinus is their priest.[2] Like lips like lettuce, as the saying goes— the only one, as Lucilius tells us,[3] at which Crassus ever laughed—the reference being to a donkey eating thistles. What I mean is that an unstable pilot steers a leaking ship, and that the blind is leading the blind straight to the pit. The ruler is like the ruled.

6. I salute your mother and mine with the respect which, as you know, I feel towards her. Associated with you as she is in a holy life, she has the start of you, her holy children, in that she is your mother. Her womb may thus be truly called golden. With her I salute your sisters, who ought all to be welcomed wherever they go, for they have triumphed over their sex and the world, and await the Bridegroom's coming,[4] their lamps replenished with oil. O happy the house which is a home of a widowed Anna, of virgins that are prophetesses, and of twin Samuels bred in the Temple![5] Fortunate the roof which shelters the martyr-mother of the Maccabees, with her sons around her, each and all wearing the martyr's crown![6] For although you confess Christ every day by keeping His commandments, yet to this private glory you have added the public one of an open confession; for it was through you that the poison of the Arian heresy was formerly banished from your city.

You are surprised perhaps at my thus making a fresh beginning quite at the close of my letter. But what am I to do? I cannot refuse expression to my feelings. The brief limits of a letter compel me to be silent; my affection for you urges me to speak. I write in haste, my language is confused and ill-arranged; but love knows nothing of order.

LETTER VIII.

TO NICEAS, SUB-DEACON OF AQUILEIA.

Niceas, the sub-deacon, had accompanied Jerome to the East but had now returned home. In after-years

he became bishop of Aquileia in succession to Chromatius. The date of the letter is 374 A.D.

The comic poet Turpilius[1] says of the exchange of letters that it alone makes the absent present. The remark, though occurring in a work of fiction, is not untrue. For what more real presence—if I may so speak— can there be between absent friends than speaking to those whom they love in letters, and in letters hearing their reply? Even those Italian savages, the Cascans of Ennius, who—as Cicero tells us in his books on rhetoric—hunted their food like beasts of prey, were wont, before paper and parchment came into use, to exchange letters written on tablets of wood roughly planed, or on strips of bark torn from the trees. For this reason men called letter-carriers tablet-bearers,[2] and letter-writers bark-users,[3] because they used the bark of trees. How much more then are we, who live in a civilized age, bound not to omit a social duty performed by men who lived in a state of gross savagery, and were in some respects entirely ignorant of the refinements of life. The saintly Chromatius, look you, and the reverend Eusebius, brothers as much by compatibility of disposition as by the ties of nature, have challenged me to diligence by the letters which they have showered upon me. You, however, who have but just left me, have not merely unknit our new-made friendship; you have torn it asunder—a process which Lælius, in Cicero's treatise,[4] wisely forbids. Can it be that the East is so hateful to you that you dread the thought of even your letters coming hither? Wake up, wake up, arouse yourself from sleep, give to affection at least one sheet of paper. Amid the pleasures of life at home sometimes heave a sigh over the journeys which we have made together. If you love me, write in answer to my prayer. If you are angry with me, though angry still write. I find my longing soul much comforted when I receive a letter from a friend, even though that friend be out of temper with me.

LETTER IX.

TO CHRYSOGONUS, A MONK OF AQUILEIA.

A bantering letter to an indifferent correspondent. Of the same date as the preceding.

Heliodorus,[5] who is so dear to us both, and who loves you with an affection no less

---

[1] Phi. iii. 19.
[2] Sacerdos. In the letters this word generally denotes a bishop. Lupicinus held the see of Stridon.   [3] Cic. de Fin. v. 30.
[4] Matt. xxv. 4.   [5] Luke ii. 36: Acts xxi. 9: 1 Sam. ii. 18.
[6] 2 Macc. vii.

[1] Turpilius, who appears to have been a dramatist of some note, died in 101 B.C. He is mentioned by Jerome in his edition of the Eusebian Chronicle.
[2] Tabellarii, from tabella, a small tablet.
[3] Librarii, from liber, bark.
[4] Cic. Lælius, 76.   [5] See introd. to Letter XIV.

deep than my own, may have given you a faithful account of my feelings towards you; how your name is always on my lips, and how in every conversation which I have with him I begin by recalling my pleasant intercourse with you, and go on to marvel at your lowliness, to extol your virtue, and to proclaim your holy love.

Lynxes, they say, when they look behind them, forget what they have just seen, and lose all thought of what their eyes have ceased to behold. And so it seems to be with you. For so entirely have you forgotten our joint attachment that you have not merely blurred but erased the writing of that epistle which, as the apostle tells us,[1] is written in the hearts of Christians. The creatures that I have mentioned lurk on branches of leafy trees and pounce on fleet roes or frightened stags. In vain their victims fly, for they carry their tormentors with them, and these rend their flesh as they run. Lynxes, however, only hunt when an empty belly makes their mouths dry. When they have satisfied their thirst for blood, and have filled their stomachs with food, satiety induces forgetfulness, and they bestow no thought on future prey till hunger recalls them to a sense of their need.

Now in your case it cannot be that you have already had enough of me. Why then do you bring to a premature close a friendship which is but just begun? Why do you let slip what you have hardly as yet fully grasped? But as such remissness as yours is never at a loss for an excuse, you will perhaps declare that you had nothing to write. Had this been so, you should still have written to inform me of the fact.

LETTER X.

TO PAUL, AN OLD MAN OF CONCORDIA.

Jerome writes to Paul of Concordia, a centenarian (§ 2), and the owner of a good theological library (§ 3), to lend him some commentaries. In return he sends him his life (newly written) of Paul the hermit.[2] The date of the letter is 374 A.D.

1. The shortness of man's life is the punishment for man's sin; and the fact that even on the very threshold of the light death constantly overtakes the new-born child proves that the times are continually sinking into deeper depravity. For when the first tiller of paradise had been entangled by the serpent in his snaky coils, and had been forced in consequence to migrate earthwards, although his deathless state was changed for a mortal one, yet the sentence[1] of man's curse was put off for nine hundred years, or even more, a period so long that it may be called a second immortality. Afterwards sin gradually grew more and more virulent, till the ungodliness of the giants[2] brought in its train the shipwreck of the whole world. Then when the world had been cleansed by the baptism—if I may so call it—of the deluge, human life was contracted to a short span. Yet even this we have almost altogether wasted, so continually do our iniquities fight against the divine purposes. For how few there are, either who go beyond their hundredth year, or who, going beyond it, do not regret that they have done so; according to that which the Scripture witnesses in the book of Psalms: "the days of our years are threescore years and ten; and if by reason of strength they be fourscore years, yet is their strength labor and sorrow."[3]

2. Why, say you, these opening reflections so remote and so far fetched that one might use against them the Horatian witticism:

> Back to the eggs which Leda laid for Zeus,
> The bard is fain to trace the war of Troy?[4]

Simply that I may describe in fitting terms your great age and hoary head as white as Christ's.[5] For see, the hundredth circling year is already passing over you, and yet, always keeping the commandments of the Lord, amid the circumstances of your present life you think over the blessedness of that which is to come. Your eyes are bright and keen, your steps steady, your hearing good, your teeth are white, your voice musical, your flesh firm and full of sap; your ruddy cheeks belie your white hairs, your strength is not that of your age. Advancing years have not, as we too often see them do, impaired the tenacity of your memory; the coldness of your blood has not blunted an intellect at once warm and wary.[6] Your face is not wrinkled nor your brow furrowed. Lastly, no tremors palsy your hand or cause it to travel in crooked pathways over the wax on which you write. The Lord shows us in you the bloom of the resurrection that is to be ours; so that whereas in others who die by inches whilst yet living, we recognize the results of sin, in your case we ascribe it

---

[1] Elogium. [2] Gen. vi. 4. [3] Ps. xc. 10.
[4] Hor. A. P. 147. Zeus having visited Leda in the form of a swan, she produced two eggs, from one of which came Castor and Pollux, and from the other Helen, who was the cause of the Trojan war.
[5] Rev. i. 14. [6] A play on words: callidus, "wary," is indistinguishable in sound from calidus, "warm."

to righteousness that you still simulate youth at an age to which it is foreign. And although we see the like haleness of body in many even of those who are sinners, in their case it is a grant of the devil to lead them into sin, whilst in yours it is a gift of God to make you rejoice.

3. Tully in his brilliant speech on behalf of Flaccus[1] describes the learning of the Greeks as "innate frivolity and accomplished vanity."

Certainly their ablest literary men used to receive money for pronouncing eulogies upon their kings or princes. Following their example, I set a price upon my praise. Nor must you suppose my demand a small one. You are asked to give me the pearl of the Gospel,[2] "the words of the Lord," "pure words, even as the silver which from the earth is tried, and purified seven times in the fire,"[3] I mean the commentaries of Fortunatian[4] and—for its account of the persecutors—the History of Aurelius Victor,[5] and with these the Letters of Novatian;[6] so that, learning the poison set forth by this schismatic, we may the more gladly drink of the antidote supplied by the holy martyr Cyprian. In the mean time I have sent to you, that is to say, to Paul the aged, a Paul that is older still.[7] I have taken great pains to bring my language down to the level of the simpler sort. But, somehow or other, though you fill it with water, the jar retains the odor which it acquired when first used.[8] If my little gift should please you, I have others also in store which (if the Holy Spirit shall breathe favorably), shall sail across the sea to you with all kinds of eastern merchandise.

LETTER XI.

TO THE VIRGINS OF ÆMONA.

Æmona was a Roman colony not far from Stridon, Jerome's birthplace. The virgins to whom the note is addressed had omitted to answer his letters, and he now writes to upbraid them for their remissness. The date of the letter is 374 A.D.

This scanty sheet of paper shows in what a wilderness I live, and because of it I have to say much in few words. For, desirous though I am to speak to you more fully, this miserable scrap compels me to leave much unsaid. Still ingenuity makes up for lack of means, and by writing small I can say a great deal. Observe, I beseech you, how I love you, even in the midst of my difficulties, since even the want of materials does not stop me from writing to you.

Pardon, I beseech you, an aggrieved man: if I speak in tears and in anger it is because I have been injured. For in return for my regular letters you have not sent me a single syllable. Light, I know, has no communion with darkness,[1] and God's handmaidens no fellowship with a sinner, yet a harlot was allowed to wash the Lord's feet with her tears,[2] and dogs are permitted to eat of their masters' crumbs.[3] It was the Saviour's mission to call sinners and not the righteous; for, as He said Himself, "they that be whole need not a physician.[4] He wills the repentance of a sinner rather than his death,[5] and carries home the poor stray sheep on His own shoulders.[6] So, too, when the prodigal son returns, his father receives him with joy.[7] Nay more, the apostle says: "Judge nothing before the time."[8] For "who art thou that judgest another man's servant? To his own master he standeth or falleth."[9] And "let him that standeth take heed lest he fall."[10] "Bear ye one another's burdens."[11]

Dear sisters, man's envy judges in one way, Christ in another; and the whisper of a corner is not the same as the sentence of His tribunal. Many ways seem right to men which are afterwards found to be wrong.[12] And a treasure is often stowed in earthen vessels.[13] Peter thrice denied his Lord, yet his bitter tears restored him to his place. "To whom much is forgiven, the same loveth much."[14] No word is said of the flock as a whole, yet the angels joy in heaven over the safety of one sick ewe.[15] And if any one demurs to this reasoning, the Lord Himself has said: "Friend, is thine eye evil because I am good?"[16]

LETTER XII.

TO ANTONY, MONK.

The subject of this letter is similar to that of the preceding. Of Antony nothing is known except that some MSS. describe him as "of Æmona." The date of the letter is 374 A.D.

While the disciples were disputing concerning precedence our Lord, the teacher of

---

[1] The words quoted do not occur in the extant portion of Cicero's speech.   [2] Matt. xiii. 46.   [3] Ps. xii. 7, P. B. V.
[4] For some account of this writer see Jerome, De V. iii. c. xcvii.
[5] A Roman annalist some of whose works are still extant. He was contemporary with but probably older than Jerome.
[6] A puritan of the third century who seceded from the Roman church because of the laxity of its discipline.
[7] I.e. the life of Paul the Hermit, translated in this vol.
[8] Hor. Ep. I. ii. 69 ; cf. T. Moore :
    "You may break, you may shatter the vase if you will :
      The scent of the roses will hang round it still."

[1] 2 Cor. vi. 14.   [2] Luke vii. 37 sqq.   [3] Matt. xv. 27.
[4] Matt. ix. 12, 13.   [5] Ezek. xxxiii. 11.   [6] Luke xv. 5.
[7] Luke xv. 20.   [8] 1 Cor. iv. 5.   [9] Rom. xiv. 4.
[10] 1 Cor. x. 12.   [11] Gal. vi. 2.   [12] Cf. Prov. xiv. 12.
[13] 2 Cor. iv. 7.   [14] Luke vii. 47.   [15] Luke xv. 7, 10.
[16] Matt. xx. 15.

humility, took a little child and said: "Except ye be converted and become as little children ye cannot enter the kingdom of heaven." [1] And lest He should seem to preach more than he practised, He fulfilled His own precept in His life. For He washed His disciples' feet, [2] he received the traitor with a kiss, [3] He conversed with the woman of Samaria, [4] He spoke of the kingdom of heaven with Mary at His feet, [5] and when He rose again from the dead He showed Himself first to some poor women. [6] Pride is opposed to humility, and through it Satan lost his eminence as an archangel. The Jewish people perished in their pride, for while they claimed the chief seats and salutations in the market place, [7] they were superseded by the Gentiles, who had before been counted as "a drop of a bucket." [8] Two poor fishermen, Peter and James, were sent to confute the sophists and the wise men of the world. As the Scripture says: "God resisteth the proud and giveth grace to the humble." [9] Think, brother, what a sin it must be which has God for its opponent. In the Gospel the Pharisee is rejected because of his pride, and the publican is accepted because of his humility. [10]

Now, unless I am mistaken, I have already sent you ten letters, affectionate and earnest, whilst you have not deigned to give me even a single line. The Lord speaks to His servants, but you, my brother servant, refuse to speak to me. Believe me, if reserve did not check my pen, I could show my annoyance in such invective that you would have to reply—even though it might be in anger. But since anger is human, and a Christian must not act injuriously, I fall back once more on entreaty, and beg you to love one who loves you, and to write to him as a servant should to his fellow-servant. Farewell in the Lord.

LETTER XIII.

TO CASTORINA, HIS MATERNAL AUNT.

An interesting letter, as throwing some light on Jerome's family relations. Castorina, his maternal aunt, had, for some reason, become estranged from him, and he now writes to her to effect a reconciliation. Whether he succeeded in doing so, we do not know. The date of the letter is 374 A.D.

The apostle and evangelist John rightly says, in his first epistle, that "whosoever

hateth his brother is a murderer." [1] For, since murder often springs from hate, the hater, even though he has not yet slain his victim, is at heart a murderer. Why, you ask, do I begin in this style? Simply that you and I may both lay aside past ill feeling and cleanse our hearts to be a habitation for God. "Be ye angry," David says, "and sin not," or, as the apostle more fully expresses it, "let not the sun go down upon your wrath." [2] What then shall *we* do in the day of judgment, upon whose wrath the sun has gone down not one day but many years? The Lord says in the Gospel: "If thou bring thy gift to the altar, and there rememberest that thy brother hath aught against thee; leave there thy gift before the altar, and go thy way; first be reconciled to thy brother, and then come and offer thy gift." [3] Woe to me, wretch that I am; woe, I had almost said, to you also. This long time past we have either offered no gift at the altar or have offered it whilst cherishing anger "without a cause." How have we been able in our daily prayers to say "Forgive us our debts as we forgive our debtors," [4] whilst our feelings have been at variance with our words, and our petition inconsistent with our conduct? Therefore I renew the prayer which I made a year ago in a previous letter, [5] that the Lord's legacy of peace [6] may be indeed ours, and that my desires and your feelings may find favor in His sight. Soon we shall stand before His judgment seat to receive the reward of harmony restored or to pay the penalty for harmony broken. In case you shall prove unwilling—I hope that it may not be so—to accept my advances, I for my part shall be free. For this letter, when it is read, will insure my acquittal.

LETTER XIV.

TO HELIODORUS, MONK.

Heliodorus, originally a soldier, but now a presbyter of the Church, had accompanied Jerome to the East, but, not feeling called to the solitary life of the desert, had returned to Aquileia. Here he resumed his clerical duties, and in course of time was raised to the episcopate as bishop of Altinum.

The letter was written in the first bitterness of separation and reproaches Heliodorus for having gone back from the perfect way of the ascetic life. The description given of this is highly colored and seems to have produced a great impression in the West. Fabiola was so much enchanted by it that she learned the letter by heart. [7] The date is 373 or 374 A.D.

1. So conscious are you of the affection which exists between us that you cannot but

---

1 Matt. xviii. 3.   2 Joh. xiii. 5.
3 Luke xxii. 47.   4 Joh. iv. 7.
5 Luke vii. 40 *sqq.*: the heroine of this story is identified by Jerome with Mary Magdalene.
6 Matt. xxviii. 1, 9.   7 Matt. xxiii. 6, 7.   8 Isa. xl. 15.
9 1 Pet. v. 5.   10 Luke xviii. 9 *sqq.*

1 1 Joh. iii. 15.   2 Ps. iv. 4, LXX.: Eph. iv. 26.
3 Matt. v. 23, 24.   4 Matt. vi. 12.   5 This is no longer extant.
6 John xiv. 27.   7 See Ep. lxxvii. 9.

recognize the love and passion with which I strove to prolong our common sojourn in the desert. This very letter — blotted, as you see, with tears—gives evidence of the lamentation and weeping with which I accompanied your departure. With the pretty ways of a child you then softened your refusal by soothing words, and I, being off my guard, knew not what to do. Was I to hold my peace? I could not conceal my eagerness by a show of indifference. Or was I to entreat you yet more earnestly? You would have refused to listen, for your love was not like mine. Despised affection has taken the one course open to it. Unable to keep you when present, it goes in search of you when absent. You asked me yourself, when you were going away, to invite you to the desert when I took up my quarters there, and I for my part promised to do so. Accordingly I invite you now; come, and come quickly. Do not call to mind old ties; the desert is for those who have left all. Nor let the hardships of our former travels deter you. You believe in Christ, believe also in His words: "Seek ye first the kingdom of God and all these things shall be added unto you."[1] Take neither scrip nor staff. He is rich enough who is poor—with Christ.

2. But what is this, and why do I foolishly importune you again? Away with entreaties, an end to coaxing words. Offended love does well to be angry. You have spurned my petition; perhaps you will listen to my remonstrance. What keeps you, effeminate soldier, in your father's house? Where are your ramparts and trenches? When have you spent a winter in the field? Lo, the trumpet sounds from heaven! Lo, the Leader comes with clouds![2] He is armed to subdue the world, and out of His mouth proceeds a two-edged sword[3] to mow down all that encounters it. But as for you, what will you do? Pass straight from your chamber to the battle-field, and from the cool shade into the burning sun? Nay, a body used to a tunic cannot endure a buckler; a head that has worn a cap refuses a helmet; a hand made tender by disuse is galled by a sword-hilt.[4] Hear the proclamation of your King: "He that is not with me is against me, and he that gathereth not with me scattereth."[5] Remember the day on which you enlisted, when, buried with Christ in baptism, you swore fealty to Him, declaring that for His sake you would spare neither father nor mother. Lo, the enemy

is striving to slay Christ in your breast. Lo, the ranks of the foe sigh over that bounty which you received when you entered His service. Should your little nephew[1] hang on your neck, pay no regard to him; should your mother with ashes on her hair and garments rent show you the breasts at which she nursed you, heed her not; should your father prostrate himself on the threshold, trample him under foot and go your way. With dry eyes fly to the standard of the cross. In such cases cruelty is the only true affection.

3. Hereafter there shall come—yes, there shall come—a day when you will return a victor to your true country, and will walk through the heavenly Jerusalem crowned with the crown of valor. Then will you receive the citizenship thereof with Paul.[2] Then will you seek the like privilege for your parents. Then will you intercede for me who have urged you forward on the path of victory.

I am not ignorant of the fetters which you may plead as hindrances. My breast is not of iron nor my heart of stone. I was not born of flint or suckled by a tigress.[3] I have passed through troubles like yours myself. Now it is a widowed sister who throws her caressing arms around you. Now it is the slaves, your foster-brothers, who cry, "To what master are you leaving us?" Now it is a nurse bowed with age, and a body-servant loved only less than a father, who exclaim: "Only wait till we die and follow us to our graves." Perhaps, too, an aged mother, with sunken bosom and furrowed brow, recalling the lullaby[4] with which she once soothed you, adds her entreaties to theirs. The learned may call you, if they please,

The sole support and pillar of your house.[5]

The love of God and the fear of hell will easily break such bonds.

Scripture, you will argue, bids us obey our parents.[6] Yes, but whoso loves them more than Christ loses his own soul.[7] The enemy takes sword in hand to slay me, and shall I think of a mother's tears? Or shall I desert the service of Christ for the sake of a father to whom, if I am Christ's servant, I owe no rites of burial,[8] albeit if I am Christ's true servant I owe these to all? Peter with his cowardly advice was an offence to the Lord on the eve of His passion;[9] and to the breth-

[1] Matt. vi. 33.   [2] Rev. i. 7.   [3] Rev. i. 16.   [4] A reminiscence of Tertullian.   [5] Matt. xii. 30.

[1] Nepotian, afterwards famous as the recipient of Letter LII., and the subject of Letter LX.
[2] Phi. iii. 20, R.V.   [3] Virg. A. iv. 367.   [4] Pers. iii. 18.
[5] Virg. A. xii. 59.   [6] Eph. vi. 1.   [7] Matt. x. 37.
[8] Luke ix. 59, 60.   [9] Matt. xvi. 23.

ren who strove to restrain him from going up to Jerusalem, Paul's one answer was: "What mean ye to weep and to break my heart? For I am ready not to be bound only, but also to die at Jerusalem for the name of the Lord Jesus."[1] The battering-ram of natural affection which so often shatters faith must recoil powerless from the wall of the Gospel. "My mother and my brethren are these whosoever do the will of my Father which is in heaven."[2] If they believe in Christ let them bid me God-speed, for I go to fight in His name. And if they do not believe, "let the dead bury their dead."[3]

4. But all this, you argue, only touches the case of martyrs. Ah! my brother, you are mistaken, you are mistaken, if you suppose that there is ever a time when the Christian does not suffer persecution. Then are you most hardly beset when you know not that you are beset at all. "Our adversary as a roaring lion walketh about seeking whom he may devour,"[4] and do you think of peace? "He sitteth in the lurking-places of the villages: in the secret places doth he murder the innocent; his eyes are privily set against the poor. He lieth in wait secretly as a lion in his den; he lieth in wait to catch the poor;"[5] and do you slumber under a shady tree, so as to fall an easy prey? On one side self-indulgence presses me hard; on another covetousness strives to make an inroad; my belly wishes to be a God to me, in place of Christ,[6] and lust would fain drive away the Holy Spirit that dwells in me and defile His temple.[7] I am pursued, I say, by an enemy

Whose name is Legion and his wiles untold ;[8]

and, hapless wretch that I am, how shall I hold myself a victor when I am being led away a captive?

5. My dear brother, weigh well the various forms of transgression, and think not that the sins which I have mentioned are less flagrant than that of idolatry. Nay, hear the apostle's view of the matter. "For this ye know," he writes, "that no whoremonger or unclean person, nor covetous man, who is an idolater, hath any inheritance in the kingdom of Christ and of God."[9] In a general way all that is of the devil savors of enmity to God, and what is of the devil is idolatry, since all idols are subject to him. Yet Paul elsewhere lays down the law in express and unmistakable terms, saying: "Mortify your members, which are upon the earth, laying aside fornication, uncleanness, evil concupiscence and covetousness, which are[1] idolatry, for which things' sake the wrath of God cometh."[2]

Idolatry is not confined to casting incense upon an altar with finger and thumb, or to pouring libations of wine out of a cup into a bowl. Covetousness is idolatry, or else the selling of the Lord for thirty pieces of silver was a righteous act.[3] Lust involves profanation, or else men may defile with common harlots[4] those members of Christ which should be "a living sacrifice acceptable to God."[5] Fraud is idolatry, or else they are worthy of imitation who, in the Acts of the Apostles, sold their inheritance, and because they kept back part of the price, perished by an instant doom.[6] Consider well, my brother; nothing is yours to keep. "Whosoever he be of you," the Lord says, "that forsaketh not all that he hath, he cannot be my disciple."[7] Why are you such a half-hearted Christian?

6. See how Peter left his net;[8] see how the publican rose from the receipt of custom.[9] In a moment he became an apostle. "The Son of man hath not where to lay his head,"[10] and do you plan wide porticos and spacious halls? If you look to inherit the good things of the world you can no longer be a joint-heir with Christ.[11] You are called a monk, and has the name no meaning? What brings you, a solitary, into the throng of men? The advice that I give is that of no inexperienced mariner who has never lost either ship or cargo, and has never known a gale. Lately shipwrecked as I have been myself, my warnings to other voyagers spring from my own fears. On one side, like Charybdis, self-indulgence sucks into its vortex the soul's salvation. On the other, like Scylla, lust, with a smile on her girl's face, lures it on to wreck its chastity. The coast is savage, and the devil with a crew of pirates carries irons to fetter his captives. Be not credulous, be not over-confident. The sea may be as smooth and smiling as a pond, its quiet surface may be scarcely ruffled by a breath of air, yet sometimes its waves are as high as mountains. There is danger in its depths, the foe is lurking there. Ease your sheets, spread

---

[1] Acts xxi. 13.
[2] Luke viii. 21 : Matt. xii. 50.
[3] Matt. viii. 22.
[4] 1 Pet. v. 8.
[5] Ps. x. 8, 9.
[6] Phi. iii. 19.
[7] 1 Cor. iii. 17.
[8] Virg. A. vii. 337.
[9] Eph. v. 5.

[1] So Jerome, although the Vulg. has "is."
[2] Col. iii. 5, 6.
[3] Matt. xxvi. 15.
[4] Publicarum libidinum victimæ; words borrowed from Tertullian, de C. F. II. 12.
[5] Rom. xii. 1.
[6] Acts v., Ananias and Sapphira.
[7] Luke xiv. 33.
[8] Matt. iv. 18-20.
[9] Matt. ix. 9.
[10] Matt. viii. 20.
[11] Rom. viii. 17.

your sails, fasten the cross as an ensign on your prow. The calm that you speak of is itself a tempest. "Why so?" you will perhaps argue; "are not all my fellow-townsmen Christians?" Your case, I reply, is not that of others. Listen to the words of the Lord: "If thou wilt be perfect go and sell that thou hast, and give to the poor, and come and follow me."[1] You have already promised to be perfect. For when you forsook the army and made yourself an eunuch for the kingdom of heaven's sake,[2] you did so that you might follow the perfect life. Now the perfect servant of Christ has nothing beside Christ. Or if he have anything beside Christ he is not perfect. And if he be not perfect when he has promised God to be so, his profession is a lie. But "the mouth that lieth slayeth the soul."[3] To conclude, then, if you are perfect you will not set your heart on your father's goods; and if you are not perfect you have deceived the Lord. The Gospel thunders forth its divine warning: "Ye cannot serve two masters,"[4] and does any one dare to make Christ a liar by serving at once both God and Mammon? Repeatedly does He proclaim, "If any one will come after me let him deny himself and take up his cross and follow me."[5] If I load myself with gold can I think that I am following Christ? Surely not. "He that saith he abideth in Him ought himself also so to walk even as He walked."[6]

7. I know you will rejoin that you possess nothing. Why, then, if you are so well prepared for battle, do you not take the field? Perhaps you think that *you* can wage war in your own country, although the Lord could do no signs in His?[7] Why not? you ask. Take the answer which comes to you with his authority: "No prophet is accepted in his own country."[8] But, you will say, I do not seek honor; the approval of my conscience is enough for me. Neither did the Lord seek it; for when the multitudes would have made Him a king he fled from them.[9] But where there is no honor there is contempt; and where there is contempt there is frequent rudeness; and where there is rudeness there is vexation; and where there is vexation there is no rest; and where there is no rest the mind is apt to be diverted from its purpose. Again, where, through restlessness, earnestness loses any of its force, it is lessened by what it loses, and that

which is lessened cannot be called perfect. The upshot of all which is that a monk cannot be perfect in his own country. Now, not to aim at perfection is itself a sin.

8. Driven from this line of defence you will appeal to the example of the clergy. These, you will say, remain in their cities, and yet they are surely above criticism. Far be it from me to censure the successors of the apostles, who with holy words consecrate the body of Christ, and who make us Christians.[1] Having the keys of the kingdom of heaven, they judge men to some extent before the day of judgment, and guard the chastity of the bride of Christ. But, as I have before hinted, the case of monks is different from that of the clergy. The clergy feed Christ's sheep; I as a monk am fed by them. They live of the altar:[2] I, if I bring no gift to it, have the axe laid to my root as to that of a barren tree.[3] Nor can I plead poverty as an excuse, for the Lord in the gospel has praised an aged widow for casting into the treasury the last two coins that she had.[4] I may not sit in the presence of a presbyter;[5] he, if I sin, may deliver me to Satan, "for the destruction of the flesh that the spirit may be saved."[6] Under the old law he who disobeyed the priests was put outside the camp and stoned by the people, or else he was beheaded and expiated his contempt with his blood.[7] But now the disobedient person is cut down with the spiritual sword, or he is expelled from the church and torn to pieces by ravening demons. Should the entreaties of your brethren induce you to take orders, I shall rejoice that you are lifted up, and fear lest you may be cast down. You will say: "If a man desire the office of a bishop, he desireth a good work."[8] I know that; but you should add what follows: such an one "must be blameless, the husband of one wife, vigilant, sober, chaste, of good behavior, given to hospitality, apt to teach, not given to wine, no striker but patient."[9] After fully explaining the qualifications of a bishop the apostle speaks of ministers of the third degree with equal care. "Likewise must the deacons be grave," he writes, "not double-tongued, not given to much wine, not greedy of filthy lucre, holding the mystery of the faith in a pure conscience. And let these also first be proved; then, let them minister, being found blameless."[10] Woe to the man who goes in to the supper without a wedding garment. Nothing remains for

[1] Matt. xix. 21. [2] Matt. xix. 12. [3] Wisd. i. 11.
[4] Luke xvi. 13. [5] Luke ix. 23. [6] 1 Joh. ii. 6.
[7] Matt. xiii. 58. [8] Luke iv. 24. [9] Joh. vi. 15.

[1] In the sacrament of baptism.
[2] 1 Cor. ix. 13, 14. [3] Matt. iii. 10. [4] Luke xxi. 1–4.
[5] Cf. Letter CXLVI. § 2. [6] 1 Cor. v. 5. [7] Deut. xvii. 5, 12.
[8] 1 Tim. iii. 1. [9] 1 Tim. iii. 2, 3. [10] 1 Tim. iii. 8–10.

him but the stern question, "Friend, how camest thou in hither?" And when he is speechless the order will be given, "Bind him hand and foot, and take him away, and cast him into outer darkness; there shall be weeping and gnashing of teeth."[1] Woe to him who, when he has received a talent, has bound it in a napkin; and, whilst others make profits, only preserves what he has received. His angry lord shall rebuke him in a moment. "Thou wicked servant," he will say, "wherefore gavest thou not my money into the bank that at my coming I might have required mine own with usury?"[2] That is to say, you should have laid before the altar what you were not able to bear. For whilst you, a slothful trader, keep a penny in your hands, you occupy the place of another who might double the money. Wherefore, as he who ministers well purchases to himself a good degree,[3] so he who approaches the cup of the Lord unworthily shall be guilty of the body and blood of the Lord.[4]

9. Not all bishops are bishops indeed. You consider Peter; mark Judas as well. You notice Stephen; look also on Nicolas, sentenced in the Apocalypse by the Lord's own lips,[5] whose shameful imaginations gave rise to the heresy of the Nicolaitans. "Let a man examine himself and so let him come."[6] For it is not ecclesiastical rank that makes a man a Christian. The centurion Cornelius was still a heathen when he was cleansed by the gift of the Holy Spirit. Daniel was but a child when he judged the elders.[7] Amos was stripping mulberry bushes when, in a moment, he was made a prophet.[8] David was only a shepherd when he was chosen to be king.[9] And the least of His disciples was the one whom Jesus loved the most. My brother, sit down in the lower room, that when one less honorable comes you may be bidden to go up higher.[10] Upon whom does the Lord rest but upon him that is lowly and of a contrite spirit, and that trembleth at His word?[11] To whom God has committed much, of him He will ask the more.[12] "Mighty men shall be mightily tormented."[13] No man need pride himself in the day of judgment on merely physical chastity, for then shall men give account for every idle word,[14] and the reviling of a brother shall be counted as the sin of murder.[15] Paul and Peter now reign

with Christ, and it is not easy to take the place of the one or to hold the office of the other. There may come an angel to rend the veil of your temple,[1] and to remove your candlestick out of its place.[2] If you intend to build the tower, first count the cost.[3] Salt that has lost its savor is good for nothing but to be cast out and to be trodden under foot of swine.[4] If a monk fall, a priest shall intercede for him; but who shall intercede for a fallen priest?

10. At last my discourse is clear of the reefs; at last this frail bark has passed from the breakers into deep water. I may now spread my sails to the breeze; and, as I leave the rocks of controversy astern, my epilogue will be like the joyful shout of mariners. O desert, bright with the flowers of Christ! O solitude whence come the stones of which, in the Apocalypse, the city of the great king is built![5] O wilderness, gladdened with God's especial presence! What keeps you in the world, my brother, you who are above the world?[6] How long shall gloomy roofs oppress you? How long shall smoky cities immure you? Believe me, I have more light than you. Sweet it is to lay aside the weight of the body and to soar into the pure bright ether. Do you dread poverty? Christ calls the poor blessed.[7] Does toil frighten you? No athlete is crowned but in the sweat of his brow. Are you anxious as regards food? Faith fears no famine. Do you dread the bare ground for limbs wasted with fasting? The Lord lies there beside you. Do you recoil from an unwashed head and uncombed hair? Christ is your true head.[8] Does the boundless solitude of the desert terrify you? In the spirit you may walk always in paradise. Do but turn your thoughts thither and you will be no more in the desert. Is your skin rough and scaly because you no longer bathe? He that is once washed in Christ needeth not to wash again.[9] To all your objections the apostle gives this one brief answer: "The sufferings of this present time are not worthy to be compared with the glory" which shall come after them, "which shall be revealed in us."[10] You are too greedy of enjoyment, my brother, if you wish to rejoice with the world here, and to reign with Christ hereafter.

11. It shall come, it shall come, that day when this corruptible shall put on incorrup-

---

1 Matt. xxii. 11-13.   2 Luke xix. 23.   3 1 Tim. iii. 13.
4 1 Cor. xi. 27.   5 Rev. ii. 6.   6 1 Cor. xi. 28.
7 Susannah 45 sqq.   8 Amos vii. 14.   9 1 Sam. xvi. 11-13.
10 Luke xiv. 10.   11 Isa. lxvi. 2.   12 Luke xii. 48.
13 Wisd. vi. 6.   14 Matt. xii. 36.   15 Matt. v. 21, 22.

1 Matt. xxvii. 51.   2 Rev. ii. 5.   3 Luke xiv. 28.
4 Matt. v. 13.   5 Rev. xxi. 19, 20.
6 From Cyprian, Letter I. 14 (to Donatus).   7 Luke vi. 20.
8 From Cyprian, Letter LXXVII. 2 (to Nemesianus).
9 Joh. xiii. 10.   10 Rom. viii. 18.

tion, and this mortal shall put on immortality.[1] Then shall that servant be blessed whom the Lord shall find watching.[2] Then at the sound of the trumpet[3] the earth and its peoples shall tremble, but you shall rejoice. The world shall howl at the Lord who comes to judge it, and the tribes of the earth shall smite the breast. Once mighty kings shall tremble in their nakedness. Venus shall be exposed, and her son too. Jupiter with his fiery bolts will be brought to trial; and Plato, with his disciples, will be but a fool. Aristotle's arguments shall be of no avail. You may seem a poor man and country bred, but then you shall exult and laugh, and say: Behold my crucified Lord, behold my judge. This is He who was once an infant wrapped in swaddling clothes and crying in a manger.[4] This is He whose parents were a workingman and a workingwoman.[5] This is He, who, carried into Egypt in His mother's bosom, though He was God, fled before the face of man. This is He who was clothed in a scarlet robe and crowned with thorns.[6] This is He who was called a sorcerer and a man with a devil and a Samaritan.[7] Jew, behold the hands which you nailed to the cross. Roman, behold the side which you pierced with the spear. See both of you whether it was this body that the disciples stole secretly and by night.[8] For this you profess to believe.

My brother, it is affection which has urged me to speak thus; that you who now find the Christian life so hard may have your reward in that day.

LETTER XV.

TO POPE DAMASUS.

This letter, written in 376 or 377 A.D., illustrates Jerome's attitude towards the see of Rome at this time held by Damasus, afterwards his warm friend and admirer. Referring to Rome as the scene of his own baptism and as a church where the true faith has remained unimpaired (§ 1), and laying down the strict doctrine of salvation only within the pale of the church (§ 2), Jerome asks "the successor of the fisherman" two questions, viz.: (1) who is the true bishop of the three claimants of the see of Antioch, and (2) which is the correct terminology, to speak of three "hypostases" in the Godhead, or of one? On the latter question he expresses fully his own opinion.

1. Since the East, shattered as it is by the long-standing feuds, subsisting between its peoples, is bit by bit tearing into shreds the seamless vest of the Lord, "woven from the top throughout,"[1] since the foxes are destroying the vineyard of Christ,[2] and since among the broken cisterns that hold no water it is hard to discover "the sealed fountain" and "the garden inclosed,"[3] I think it my duty to consult the chair of Peter, and to turn to a church whose faith has been praised by Paul.[4] I appeal for spiritual food to the church whence I have received the garb of Christ.[5] The wide space of sea and land that lies between us cannot deter me from searching for "the pearl of great price."[6] "Wheresoever the body is, there will the eagles be gathered together."[7] Evil children have squandered their patrimony; you alone keep your heritage intact. The fruitful soil of Rome, when it receives the pure seed of the Lord, bears fruit an hundredfold; but here the seed corn is choked in the furrows and nothing grows but darnel or oats.[8] In the West the Sun of righteousness[9] is even now rising; in the East, Lucifer, who fell from heaven,[10] has once more set his throne above the stars.[11] "Ye are the light of the world,"[12] "ye are the salt of the earth,"[13] ye are "vessels of gold and of silver." Here are vessels of wood or of earth,[14] which wait for the rod of iron,[15] and eternal fire.

2. Yet, though your greatness terrifies me, your kindness attracts me. From the priest I demand the safe-keeping of the victim, from the shepherd the protection due to the sheep. Away with all that is overweening; let the state of Roman majesty withdraw. My words are spoken to the successor of the fisherman, to the disciple of the cross. As I follow no leader save Christ, so I communicate with none but your blessedness, that is with the chair of Peter. For this, I know, is the rock on which the church is built![16] This is the house where alone the paschal lamb can be rightly eaten.[17] This is the ark of Noah, and he who is not found in it shall perish when the flood prevails.[18] But since by reason of my sins I have betaken myself to this desert which lies between Syria and the uncivilized waste, I cannot, owing to the great distance between us, always ask of your sanctity the holy thing of the Lord.[19] Con-

---

[1] 1 Cor. xv. 53. [2] Matt. xxiv. 46. [3] 1 Thess. iv. 16.
[4] Luke ii. 7. [5] From Tertullian, de Spect. xxx.
[6] Matt. xxvii. 28, 29. [7] Joh. viii. 48. [8] Matt. xxvii. 64.

[1] Joh. xix. 23. [2] Cant. ii. 15. [3] Cant. iv. 12.
[4] Rom. i. 8: I thank my God through Jesus Christ for you all that your faith is spoken of throughout the whole world.
[5] I.e. holy baptism; cf. Gal. iii. 27. [6] Matt. xiii. 46.
[7] Matt. xxiv. 28. [8] Matt. xiii. 22, 23. [9] Mal. iv. 2.
[10] Luke x. 18. [11] Isa. xiv. 12. [12] Matt. v. 14.
[13] Matt. v. 13. [14] 2 Tim. ii. 20. [15] Rev. ii. 27.
[16] Matt. xvi. 18. [17] Ex. xii. 22. [18] Gen. vii. 23.
[19] I.e. the bread of the Eucharist, at this time sent by one bishop to another in token of communion; or possibly the allusion is different, and what Jerome means to say is: "You are the oracle of God, but owing to my present situation I cannot consult you."

sequently I here follow the Egyptian confessors[1] who share your faith, and anchor my frail craft under the shadow of their great argosies. I know nothing of Vitalis; I reject Meletius; I have nothing to do with Paulinus.[2] He that gathers not with you scatters;[3] he that is not of Christ is of Antichrist.

3. Just now, I am sorry to say, those Arians, the Campenses,[4] are trying to extort from me, a Roman Christian, their unheard-of formula of three hypostases.[5] And this, too, after the definition of Nicæa[6] and the decree of Alexandria,[7] in which the West has joined. Where, I should like to know, are the apostles of these doctrines? Where is their Paul, their new doctor of the Gentiles? I ask them what three hypostases are supposed to mean. They reply three persons subsisting. I rejoin that this is my belief. They are not satisfied with the meaning, they demand the term. Surely some secret venom lurks in the words. "If any man refuse," I cry, "to acknowledge three hypostases in the sense of three things hypostatized, that is three persons subsisting, let him be anathema." Yet, because I do not learn their words, I am counted a heretic. "But, if any one, understanding by hypostasis essence,[8] deny that in the three persons there is one hypostasis, he has no part in Christ." Because this is my confession I, like you, am branded with the stigma of Sabellianism.[9]

4. If you think fit enact a decree; and then I shall not hesitate to speak of three hypostases. Order a new creed to supersede the Nicene; and then, whether we are Arians or orthodox, one confession will do for us all. In the whole range of secular learning hypostasis never means anything but essence. And can any one, I ask, be so profane as to speak of three essences or substances in the Godhead? There is one nature of God and one only; and this, and this alone, truly *is*. For absolute being is derived from no other source but is all its own. All things besides, that is all things created, although they appear to be, are not. For there was a time when they were not, and that which once was not may again cease to be. God alone who is eternal, that is to say, who has no beginning, really deserves to be called an essence. Therefore also He says to Moses from the bush, "I am that I am," and Moses says of Him, "I am hath sent me."[1] As the angels, the sky, the earth, the seas, all existed at the time, it must have been as the absolute being that God claimed for himself that name of essence, which apparently was common to all. But because His nature alone is perfect, and because in the three persons there subsists but one Godhead, which truly is and is one nature; whosoever in the name of religion declares that there are in the Godhead three elements, three hypostases, that is, or essences, is striving really to predicate three natures of God. And if this is true, why are we severed by walls from Arius, when in dishonesty we are one with him? Let Ursicinus be made the colleague of your blessedness; let Auxentius be associated with Ambrose.[2] But may the faith of Rome never come to such a pass! May the devout hearts of your people never be infected with such unholy doctrines! Let us be satisfied to speak of one substance and of three subsisting persons—perfect, equal, coeternal. Let us keep to one hypostasis, if such be your pleasure, and say nothing of three. It is a bad sign when those who mean the same thing use different words. Let us be satisfied with the form of creed which we have hitherto used. Or, if you think it right that I should speak of three hypostases, explaining what I mean by them, I am ready to submit. But, believe me, there is poison hidden under their honey; the angel of Satan has transformed himself into an angel of light.[3] They give a plausible explanation of the term hypostasis; yet when I profess to hold it in the same sense they count me a heretic. Why are they so tenacious of a word? Why do they shelter themselves under ambiguous language? If their belief corresponds to their explanation of it, I do not condemn them for keeping it. On the other hand, if

---

[1] Certain bishops banished from their sees by Valens. See Letter III. § 2.
[2] The three rival claimants of the see of Antioch. See note on Letter XVI. § 2. [3] Matt. xii. 30.
[4] *I.e.* the field party. The Meletians were so called because, denied access to the churches of the city, they had to worship in the open air outside the walls.
[5] ὑπόστασις=substantia. It is the word used in Heb. i. 3, "The express image of his person [R. V. substance]." Except at Alexandria it was usual to speak of one *hypostasis* as of one *ousia* in the Divine Nature. But at Alexandria from Origen downwards three hypostases had been ascribed to the Deity. Two explanations are given of the latter formula: (1) That at Alexandria ὑπόστασις was taken in the sense of πρόσωπον, so that by "three hypostases" was meant only "three persons." (2) That "three hypostases" was an inexact expression standing for "three hypostatic persons" or "a threefold hypostasis." This latter seems to be the true account of the matter. See an interesting note in Newman, Arians of the Fourth Century, Appendix IV.
[6] In the Nicene Creed the Son is declared to be "of one substance [οὐσία] with the Father."
[7] This decree allowed the formula of "three hypostases" to be susceptible of an orthodox interpretation. It did not, however, encourage its use. [8] οὐσία.
[9] Cauterio unionis inurimur. Sabellius recognized three "aspects" in the Godhead but denied "three persons," at least in the Catholic sense.

---

[1] Ex. iii. 14.
[2] Ursicinus, at this time anti-pope; Auxentius, Arian bishop of Milan. [3] 2 Cor. xi. 14.

my belief corresponds to their expressed opinions, they should allow me to set forth their meaning in my own words.

5. I implore your blessedness, therefore, by the crucified Saviour of the world, and by the consubstantial trinity, to authorize me by letter either to use or to refuse this formula of three hypostases. And lest the obscurity of my present abode may baffle the bearers of your letter, I pray you to address it to Evagrius, the presbyter, with whom you are well acquainted. I beg you also to signify with whom I am to communicate at Antioch. Not, I hope, with the Campenses;[1] for they—with their allies the heretics of Tarsus[2]—only desire communion with you to preach with greater authority their traditional doctrine of three hypostases.

LETTER XVI.

TO POPE DAMASUS.

This letter, written a few months after the preceding, is another appeal to Damasus to solve the writer's doubts. Jerome once more refers to his baptism at Rome, and declares that his one answer to the factions at Antioch is, "He who clings to the chair of Peter is accepted by me." Written from the desert in the year 377 or 378.

1. By her importunity the widow in the gospel at last gained a hearing,[3] and by the same means one friend induced another to give him bread at midnight, when his door was shut and his servants were in bed.[4] The publican's prayers overcame God,[5] although God is invincible. Nineveh was saved by its tears from the impending ruin caused by its sin.[6] To what end, you ask, these far-fetched references? To this end, I make answer; that you in your greatness should look upon me in my littleness; that you, the rich shepherd, should not despise me, the ailing sheep. Christ Himself brought the robber from the cross to paradise,[7] and, to show that repentance is never too late, He turned a murderer's death into a martyrdom. Gladly does Christ embrace the prodigal son when he returns to Him;[8] and, leaving the ninety and nine, the good shepherd carries home on His shoulders the one poor sheep that is left.[9] From a persecutor Paul becomes a preacher. His bodily eyes are blinded to clear the eyes of his soul,[10] and he who once haled Christ's servants in chains

before the council of the Jews,[1] lives afterwards to glory in the bonds of Christ.[2]

2. As I have already written to you,[3] I, who have received Christ's garb in Rome, am now detained in the waste that borders Syria. No sentence of banishment, however, has been passed upon me; the punishment which I am undergoing is self-inflicted. But, as the heathen poet says:

They change not mind but sky who cross the sea.[4]

The untiring foe follows me closely, and the assaults that I suffer in the desert are severer than ever. For the Arian frenzy raves, and the powers of the world support it. The church is rent into three factions, and each of these is eager to seize me for its own. The influence of the monks is of long standing, and it is directed against me. I meantime keep crying: "He who clings to the chair of Peter is accepted by me." Meletius, Vitalis, and Paulinus[5] all profess to cleave to you, and I could believe the assertion if it were made by one of them only. As it is, either two of them or else all three are guilty of falsehood. Therefore I implore your blessedness, by our Lord's cross and passion, those necessary glories of our faith, as you hold an apostolic office, to give an apostolic decision. Only tell me by letter with whom I am to communicate in Syria, and I will pray for you that you may sit in judgment enthroned with the twelve;[6] that when you grow old, like Peter, you may be girded not by yourself but by another,[7] and that, like Paul, you may be made a citizen of the heavenly kingdom.[8] Do not despise a soul for which Christ died.

LETTER XVII.

TO THE PRESBYTER MARCUS.

In this letter, addressed to one who seems to have had some pre-eminence among the monks of the Chalcidian desert, Jerome complains of the hard treatment meted out to him because of his refusal to take any part in the great theological dispute then raging in Syria. He protests his own orthodoxy, and begs permission to remain where he is until the return of spring, when he will retire from "the inhospitable desert." Written in A.D. 378 or 379.

1. I had made up my mind to use the words of the psalmist: "While the wicked

---

[1] *I.e.* the followers of the orthodox Bishop Meletius, who, as they had no church in Antioch, were compelled to meet for worship outside the city.
[2] These appear to have been semi-Arians or Macedonians. Silvanus of Tarsus was their recognized leader.
[3] Matt. xv. 28.   [4] Luke xi. 7, 8.   [5] Luke xviii. 10-14.
[6] Jon. iii. 5, 10.   [7] Luke xxiii. 43.   [8] Luke xv. 20.
[9] Luke xv. 5.   [10] Acts ix. 8.

[1] Acts viii. 3.   [2] 2 Cor. xii. 10.
[3] See Letter XV.   [4] Hor. Epist. i. 11, 27.
[5] The three rival claimants of the see of Antioch. Paulinus and Meletius were both orthodox, but Meletius derived his orders from the Arians and was consequently not recognized in the West. In the East, however, he was so highly esteemed that some years after this he was chosen to preside over the Council of Constantinople (A.D. 391). Vitalis, the remaining claimant, was a follower of Apollinaris, but much respected by the orthodox on account of his high character.
[6] Matt. xix. 28.   [7] Joh. xxi. 18.   [8] Phi. iii. 20, R.V.

was before me I was dumb with silence; I was humbled, and I held my peace even from good:"[1] and "I, as a deaf man, heard not; and I was as a dumb man that openeth not his mouth. Thus I was as a man that heareth not."[2] But charity overcomes all things,[3] and my regard for you defeats my determination. I am, indeed, less careful to retaliate upon my assailants than to comply with your request. For among Christians, as one has said,[4] not he who endures an outrage is unhappy, but he who commits it.

2. And first, before I speak to you of my belief (which you know full well), I am forced to cry out against the inhumanity of this country. A hackneyed quotation best expresses my meaning:

What savages are these who will not grant
A rest to strangers, even on their sands!
They threaten war and drive us from their coasts.[5]

I take this from a Gentile poet that one who disregards the peace of Christ may at least learn its meaning from a heathen. I am called a heretic, although I preach the consubstantial trinity. I am accused of the Sabellian impiety, although I proclaim with unwearied voice that in the Godhead there are three distinct,[6] real, whole, and perfect persons. The Arians do right to accuse me, but the orthodox forfeit their orthodoxy when they assail a faith like mine. They may, if they like, condemn me as a heretic; but if they do they must also condemn Egypt and the West, Damasus and Peter.[7] Why do they fasten the guilt on one and leave his companions uncensured? If there is but little water in the stream, it is the fault, not of the channel, but of the source. I blush to say it, but from the caves which serve us for cells we monks of the desert condemn the world. Rolling in sack-cloth and ashes,[8] we pass sentence on bishops. What use is the robe of a penitent if it covers the pride of a king? Chains, squalor, and long hair are by right tokens of sorrow, and not ensigns of royalty. I merely ask leave to remain silent. Why do they torment a man who does not deserve their ill-will? I am a heretic, you say. What is it to you if I am? Stay quiet, and all is said. You are afraid, I suppose, that, with my

fluent knowledge of Syriac and Greek, I shall make a tour of the churches, lead the people into error, and form a schism! I have robbed no man of anything; neither have I taken what I have not earned. With my own hand[1] daily and in the sweat of my brow[2] I labor for my food, knowing that it is written by the apostle: "If any will not work, neither shall he eat."[3]

3. Reverend and holy father, Jesus is my witness with what groans and tears I have written all this. "I have kept silence, saith the Lord, but shall I always keep silence? Surely not."[4] I cannot have so much as a corner of the desert. Every day I am asked for my confession of faith, as though when I was regenerated in baptism I had made none. I accept their formulas, but they are still dissatisfied. I sign my name to them, but they still refuse to believe me. One thing only will content them, that I should leave the country. I am on the point of departure. They have already torn away from me my dear brothers, who are a part of my very life. They are, as you see, anxious to depart—nay, they are actually departing; it is preferable, they say, to live among wild beasts rather than with Christians such as these. I myself, too, would be at this moment a fugitive were I not withheld by physical infirmity and by the severity of the winter. I ask to be allowed the shelter of the desert for a few months till spring returns; or if this seems too long a delay, I am ready to depart now. "The earth is the Lord's and the fulness thereof."[5] Let them climb up to heaven alone;[6] for them alone Christ died; they possess all things and glory in all. Be it so. "But God forbid that I should glory save in the cross of our Lord Jesus Christ, by whom the world is crucified unto me and I unto the world."[7]

4. As regards the questions which you have thought fit to put to me concerning the faith, I have given to the reverend Cyril[8] a written confession which sufficiently answers them. He who does not so believe has no part in Christ. My faith is attested both by your ears and by those of your blessed brother, Zenobius, to whom, as well as to yourself, we all of us here send our best greeting.

---

[1] Ps. xxxix. 1, 2, Vulg.   [2] Ps. xxxviii. 13, 14.
[3] Cf. 1 Cor. xiii. 7.
[4] Cyprian, Letter LV. Cf. Cic. T. Q. v. accipere quam facere praestat injuriam.
[5] Virg. A. i. 539–541.   [6] Subsistentes.
[7] The contemporary bishops of Rome and Alexandria.
[8] Tert. Apol. 40, s. f.

[1] 1 Cor. iv. 12.   [2] Gen. iii. 19.
[3] 2 Thess. iii. 10.   [4] Isa. xlii. 14, LXX.
[5] Ps. xxiv. 1.
[6] Was Jerome thinking of Constantine's rebuke to the Novatian bishop at Nicæa, "Plant a ladder for thyself, Acesius, and mount alone to heaven"?
[7] Gal. vi. 14.
[8] Who this was is unknown. The extant document purporting to contain this confession is not genuine.

LETTER XVIII.

TO POPE DAMASUS.

This (written from Constantinople in A.D. 381) is the earliest of Jerome's expository letters. In it he explains at length the vision recorded in the sixth chapter of Isaiah, and enlarges upon its mystical meaning. "Some of my predecessors," he writes, "make 'the Lord sitting upon a throne' God the Father, and suppose the seraphim to represent the Son and the Holy Spirit. I do not agree with them, for John expressly tells us [1] that it was Christ and not the Father whom the prophet saw." And again, "The word seraphim means either 'glow' or 'beginning of speech,' and the two seraphim thus stand for the Old and New Testaments.[2] 'Did not our heart burn within us,' said the disciples, 'while he opened to us the Scriptures?'[3] Moreover, the Old Testament is written in Hebrew, and this unquestionably was man's original language." Jerome then speaks of the unity of the sacred books. "Whatever," he asserts, "we read in the Old Testament we find also in the Gospel; and what we read in the Gospel is deduced from the Old Testament.[4] There is no discord between them, no disagreement. In both Testaments the Trinity is preached."

The letter is noticeable for the evidence it affords of the thoroughness of Jerome's studies. Not only does he cite the several Greek versions of Isaiah in support of his argument, but he also reverts to the Hebrew original. So far as the West was concerned he may be said to have discovered this anew. Even educated men like Augustine had ceased to look beyond the LXX., and were more or less aghast at the boldness with which Jerome rejected its time-honored but inaccurate renderings [5]

The letter also shows that independence of judgment which always marked Jerome's work. At the time when he wrote it he was much under the sway of Origen. But great as was his admiration for the master, he was not afraid to discard his exegesis when, as in the case of the seraphim, he believed it to be erroneous.

LETTER XIX.

FROM POPE DAMASUS.

A letter from Damasus to Jerome, in which he asks for an explanation of the word "Hosanna" (A.D. 383).

LETTER XX.

TO POPE DAMASUS.

Jerome's reply to the foregoing. Exposing the error of Hilary of Poitiers, who supposed the expression to signify "redemption of the house of David," he goes on to show that in the gospels it is a quotation from Ps. cxviii. 25 and that its true meaning is "save now" (so A.V.). "Let us," he writes, "leave the streamlets of conjecture and return to the fountain-head. It is from the Hebrew writings that the truth is to be drawn." Written at Rome A.D. 383.

LETTER XXI.

TO DAMASUS.

In this letter Jerome, at the request of Damasus, gives a minutely detailed explanation of the parable of the prodigal son.

[1] John xii. 41.
[2] Jerome greatly prides himself on this explanation, and frequently reverts to it.
[3] Luke xxiv. 32.
[4] Cf. Augustine's dictum: "The New Testament is latent in the Old; the Old Testament is patent in the New."
[5] See Augustine's letters to Jerome, *passim*.

LETTER XXII.

TO EUSTOCHIUM.

Perhaps the most famous of all the letters. In it Jerome lays down at great length (1) the motives which ought to actuate those who devote themselves to a life of virginity, and (2) the rules by which they ought to regulate their daily conduct. The letter contains a vivid picture of Roman society as it then was—the luxury, profligacy, and hypocrisy prevalent among both men and women, besides some graphic autobiographical details (§§ 7, 30), and concludes with a full account of the three kinds of monasticism then practised in Egypt (§§ 34–36). Thirty years later Jerome wrote a similar letter to Demetrias (CXXX.), with which this ought to be compared. Written at Rome 384 A.D.

1. "Hear, O daughter, and consider, and incline thine ear; forget also thine own people and thy father's house, and the king shall desire thy beauty."[1] In this forty-fourth[2] psalm God speaks to the human soul that, following the example of Abraham,[3] it should go out from its own land and from its kindred, and should leave the Chaldeans, that is the demons, and should dwell in the country of the living, for which elsewhere the prophet sighs: "I think to see the good things of the Lord in the land of the living."[4] But it is not enough for you to go out from your own land unless you forget your people and your father's house; unless you scorn the flesh and cling to the bridegroom in a close embrace. "Look not behind thee," he says, "neither stay thou in all the plain; escape to the mountain lest thou be consumed."[5] He who has grasped the plough must not look behind him [6] or return home from the field, or having Christ's garment, descend from the roof to fetch other raiment.[7] Truly a marvellous thing, a father charges his daughter not to remember her father. "Ye are of your father the devil, and the lusts of your father it is your will to do."[8] So it was said to the Jews. And in another place, "He that committeth sin is of the devil."[9] Born, in the first instance, of such parentage we are naturally black, and even when we have repented, so long as we have not scaled the heights of virtue, we may still say: "I am black but comely, O ye daughters of Jerusalem."[10] But you will say to me, "I have left the home of my childhood; I have forgotten my father, I am born anew in Christ. What reward do I receive for this?" The context shows—"The king shall desire thy beauty." This, then, is the great mystery. "For this cause shall

[1] Ps. xlv. 10, 11.   [2] According to the Vulgate.
[3] Gen. xi. 31; xii. 1.   [4] Ps. xxvii. 13.   [5] Gen. xix. 17.
[6] Luke ix. 62.   [7] Matt. xxiv. 17, 18.   [8] Joh. viii. 44, R.V.
[9] 1 Joh. iii. 8.   [10] Cant. i. 5.

a man leave his father and his mother and shall be joined unto his wife, and they two shall be" not as is there said, "of one flesh,"[1] but "of one spirit." Your bridegroom is not haughty or disdainful; He has "married an Ethiopian woman."[2] When once you desire the wisdom of the true Solomon and come to Him, He will avow all His knowledge to you; He will lead you into His chamber with His royal hand;[3] He will miraculously change your complexion so that it shall be said of you, "Who is this that goeth up and hath been made white?"[4]

2. I write to you thus, Lady Eustochium (I am bound to call my Lord's bride "lady"), to show you by my opening words that my object is not to praise the virginity which you follow, and of which you have proved the value, or yet to recount the drawbacks of marriage, such as pregnancy, the crying of infants, the torture caused by a rival, the cares of household management, and all those fancied blessings which death at last cuts short. Not that married women are as such outside the pale; they have their own place, the marriage that is honorable and the bed undefiled.[5] My purpose is to show you that you are fleeing from Sodom and should take warning by Lot's wife.[6] There is no flattery, I can tell you, in these pages. A flatterer's words are fair, but for all that he is an enemy. You need expect no rhetorical flourishes setting you among the angels, and while they extol virginity as blessed, putting the world at your feet.

3. I would have you draw from your monastic vow not pride but fear.[7] You walk laden with gold; you must keep out of the robber's way. To us men this life is a race-course: we contend here, we are crowned elsewhere. No man can lay aside fear while serpents and scorpions beset his path. The Lord says: "My sword hath drunk its fill in heaven,"[8] and do you expect to find peace on the earth? No, the earth yields only thorns and thistles, and its dust is food for the serpent.[9] "For our wrestling is not against flesh and blood, but against the principalities, against the powers, against the world-rulers of this darkness, against the spiritual hosts of wickedness in the heavenly places."[10] We are hemmed in by hosts of foes, our enemies are upon every side. The weak flesh will soon be ashes: one against many, it fights against tremendous odds. Not till it has been dissolved, not till the

Prince of this world has come and found no sin therein,[1] not till then may you safely listen to the prophet's words: "Thou shalt not be afraid for the terror by night nor for the arrow that flieth by day; nor for the trouble which haunteth thee in darkness; nor for the demon and his attacks at noonday. A thousand shall fall at thy side and ten thousand at thy right hand; but it shall not come nigh thee."[2] When the hosts of the enemy distress you, when your frame is fevered and your passions roused, when you say in your heart, "What shall I do?" Elisha's words shall give you your answer, "Fear not, for they that be with us are more than they that be with them."[3] He shall pray, "Lord, open the eyes of thine handmaid that she may see." And then when your eyes have been opened you shall see a fiery chariot like Elijah's waiting to carry you to heaven,[4] and shall joyfully sing: "Our soul is escaped as a bird out of the snare of the fowlers: the snare is broken and we are escaped."[5]

4. So long as we are held down by this frail body, so long as we have our treasure in earthen vessels;[6] so long as the flesh lusteth against the spirit and the spirit against the flesh,[7] there can be no sure victory. "Our adversary the devil goeth about as a roaring lion seeking whom he may devour."[8] "Thou makest darkness," David says, "and it is night: wherein all the beasts of the forest do creep forth. The young lions roar after their prey and seek their meat from God."[9] The devil looks not for unbelievers, for those who are without, whose flesh the Assyrian king roasted in the furnace.[10] It is the church of Christ that he "makes haste to spoil."[11] According to Habakkuk, "His food is of the choicest."[12] A Job is the victim of his machinations, and after devouring Judas he seeks power to sift the [other] apostles.[13] The Saviour came not to send peace upon the earth but a sword.[14] Lucifer fell, Lucifer who used to rise at dawn;[15] and he who was bred up in a paradise of delight had the well-earned sentence passed upon him, "Though thou exalt thyself as the eagle, and though thou set thy nest among the stars, thence will I bring thee down, saith the Lord."[16] For he had said in his heart, "I will exalt my throne above the stars of God," and "I will be like the Most High."[17] Wherefore God says

---

1 Eph. v. 31, 32.   2 Nu. xii. 1.   3 Cant. i. 4.
4 Cant. viii. 5, LXX.   5 Heb. xiii. 4.   6 Gen. xix. 26.
7 Rom. xi. 20.   8 Isa. xxxiv. 5, R.V.
9 Gen. iii. 14, 18.   10 Eph. vi. 12, R.V.

1 Joh. xiv. 30. The variant is difficult to explain and may be only a slip.   2 Ps. xci. 5–7, Vulg.   3 2 K. vi. 16.
4 2 K. ii. 11; vi. 17.   5 Ps. cxxiv. 7.   6 2 Cor. iv. 7.
7 Gal. v. 17.   8 1 Pet. v. 8.   9 Ps. civ. 20, 21.   10 Jer. xxix. 22.
11 An allusion to "Maher-shalal-hash-baz," Isa. viii. 1.
12 Hab. i. 16, LXX.   13 Luke xxii. 31.   14 Matt. x. 34.
15 Isa. xiv. 12.   16 Obad. 4.   17 Isa. xiv. 13, 14.

every day to the angels, as they descend the ladder that Jacob saw in his dream,[1] "I have said ye are Gods and all of you are children of the Most High. But ye shall die like men and fall like one of the princes."[2] The devil fell first, and since "God standeth in the congregation of the Gods and judgeth among the Gods,"[3] the apostle writes to those who are ceasing to be Gods—"Whereas there is among you envying and strife, are ye not carnal and walk as men?"[4]

5. If, then, the apostle, who was a chosen vessel[5] separated unto the gospel of Christ,[6] by reason of the pricks of the flesh and the allurements of vice keeps under his body and brings it into subjection, lest when he has preached to others he may himself be a castaway;[7] and yet, for all that, sees another law in his members warring against the law of his mind, and bringing him into captivity to the law of sin;[8] if after nakedness, fasting, hunger, imprisonment, scourging and other torments, he turns back to himself and cries: "Oh, wretched man that I am, who shall deliver me from the body of this death?"[9] do you fancy that you ought to lay aside apprehension? See to it that God say not some day of you: "The virgin of Israel is fallen and there is none to raise her up."[10] I will say it boldly, though God can do all things He cannot raise up a virgin when once she has fallen. He may indeed relieve one who is defiled from the penalty of her sin, but He will not give her a crown. Let us fear lest in us also the prophecy be fulfilled, "Good virgins shall faint."[11] Notice that it is good virgins who are spoken of, for there are bad ones as well. "Whosoever looketh on a woman," the Lord says, "to lust after her hath committed adultery with her already in his heart."[12] So that virginity may be lost even by a thought. Such are evil virgins, virgins in the flesh, not in the spirit; foolish virgins, who, having no oil, are shut out by the Bridegroom.[13]

6. But if even real virgins, when they have other failings, are not saved by their physical virginity, what shall become of those who have prostituted the members of Christ, and have changed the temple of the Holy Ghost into a brothel? Straightway shall they hear the words: "Come down and sit in the dust, O virgin daughter of Babylon, sit on the ground; there is no throne, O daughter of the Chaldæans: for thou shalt no more be called tender and delicate. Take the mill-

stone and grind meal; uncover thy locks, make bare the legs, pass over the rivers; thy nakedness shall be uncovered, yea, thy shame shall be seen."[1] And shall she come to this after the bridal-chamber of God the Son, after the kisses of Him who is to her both kinsman and spouse?[2] Yes, she of whom the prophetic utterance once sang, "Upon thy right hand did stand the queen in a vesture of gold wrought about with divers colours,"[3] shall be made naked, and her skirts shall be discovered upon her face.[4] She shall sit by the waters of loneliness, her pitcher laid aside; and shall open her feet to every one that passeth by, and shall be polluted to the crown of her head.[5] Better had it been for her to have submitted to the yoke of marriage, to have walked in level places, than thus, aspiring to loftier heights, to fall into the deep of hell. I pray you, let not Zion the faithful city become a harlot:[6] let it not be that where the Trinity has been entertained, there demons shall dance and owls make their nests, and jackals build.[7] Let us not loose the belt that binds the breast. When lust tickles the sense and the soft fire of sensual pleasure sheds over us its pleasing glow, let us immediately break forth and cry: "The Lord is on my side: I will not fear what the flesh can do unto me."[8] When the inner man shows signs for a time of wavering between vice and virtue, say: "Why art thou cast down, O my soul, and why art thou disquieted within me? Hope thou in God, for I shall yet praise Him who is the health of my countenance and my God."[9] You must never let suggestions of evil grow on you, or a babel of disorder win strength in your breast. Slay the enemy while he is small; and, that you may not have a crop of tares, nip the evil in the bud. Bear in mind the warning words of the Psalmist: "Hapless daughter of Babylon, happy shall he be that rewardeth thee as thou hast served us. Happy shall he be that taketh and dasheth thy little ones against the stones."[10] Because natural heat inevitably kindles in a man sensual passion, he is praised and accounted happy who, when foul suggestions arise in his mind, gives them no quarter, but dashes them instantly against the rock. "Now the Rock is Christ."[11]

7. How often, when I was living in the desert, in the vast solitude which gives to hermits a savage dwelling-place, parched by a burning sun, how often did I fancy myself

[1] Gen. xxviii. 12. [2] Ps. lxxxii. 6, 7. [3] Ps. lxxxii. 1.
[4] 1 Cor. iii. 3. [5] Acts ix. 15. [6] Gal. i. 15. [7] 1 Cor. ix. 27.
[8] Rom. vii. 23. [9] Rom. vii. 24. [10] Am. v. 2.
[11] Am. viii. 13. [12] Matt. v. 28. [13] Matt. xxv. 3, 10.

[1] Isa. xlvii. 1–3. [2] Cant. v. 2, LXX. [3] Ps. xlv. 10, P.B.V.
[4] Jer. xiii. 26. [5] Ezek. xvi. 25. [6] Isa. i. 21.
[7] Isa. xxxiv. 15 ; xiii. 22, R.V. [8] Pss. cxviii. 6 ; lvi. 4.
[9] Ps. xlii. 11. [10] Ps. cxxxvii. 9. [11] 1 Cor. x. 4.

among the pleasures of Rome! I used to sit alone because I was filled with bitterness. Sackcloth disfigured my unshapely limbs and my skin from long neglect had become as black as an Ethiopian's. Tears and groans were every day my portion; and if drowsiness chanced to overcome my struggles against it, my bare bones, which hardly held together, clashed against the ground. Of my food and drink I say nothing: for, even in sickness, the solitaries have nothing but cold water, and to eat one's food cooked is looked upon as self-indulgence. Now, although in my fear of hell I had consigned myself to this prison, where I had no companions but scorpions and wild beasts, I often found myself amid bevies of girls. My face was pale and my frame chilled with fasting; yet my mind was burning with desire, and the fires of lust kept bubbling up before me when my flesh was as good as dead. Helpless, I cast myself at the feet of Jesus, I watered them with my tears, I wiped them with my hair: and then I subdued my rebellious body with weeks of abstinence. I do not blush to avow my abject misery; rather I lament that I am not now what once I was. I remember how I often cried aloud all night till the break of day and ceased not from beating my breast till tranquillity returned at the chiding of the Lord. I used to dread my very cell as though it knew my thoughts; and, stern and angry with myself, I used to make my way alone into the desert. Wherever I saw hollow valleys, craggy mountains, steep cliffs, there I made my oratory, there the house of correction for my unhappy flesh. There, also—the Lord Himself is my witness —when I had shed copious tears and had strained my eyes towards heaven, I sometimes felt myself among angelic hosts, and for joy and gladness sang: "because of the savour of thy good ointments we will run after thee." [1]

8. Now, if such are the temptations of men who, since their bodies are emaciated with fasting, have only evil thoughts to fear, how must it fare with a girl whose surroundings are those of luxury and ease? Surely, to use the apostle's words, "She is dead while she liveth." [2] Therefore, if experience gives me a right to advise, or clothes my words with credit, I would begin by urging you and warning you as Christ's spouse to avoid wine as you would avoid poison. For wine is the first weapon used by demons against the young. Greed does not shake, nor pride puff up, nor ambition infatuate so much as this. Other vices we easily escape, but this enemy is shut up within us, and wherever we go we carry him with us. Wine and youth between them kindle the fire of sensual pleasure. Why do we throw oil on the flame—why do we add fresh fuel to a miserable body which is already ablaze. Paul, it is true, says to Timothy "drink no longer water, but use a little wine for thy stomach's sake, and for thine often infirmities." [1] But notice the reasons for which the permission is given, to cure an aching stomach and a frequent infirmity. And lest we should indulge ourselves too much on the score of our ailments, he commands that but little shall be taken; advising rather as a physician than as an apostle (though, indeed, an apostle is a spiritual physician). He evidently feared that Timothy might succumb to weakness, and might prove unequal to the constant moving to and fro involved in preaching the Gospel. Besides, he remembered that he had spoken of "wine wherein is excess," [2] and had said, "it is good neither to eat flesh nor to drink wine." [3] Noah drank wine and became intoxicated; but living as he did in the rude age after the flood, when the vine was first planted, perhaps he did not know its power of inebriation. And to let you see the hidden meaning of Scripture in all its fulness (for the word of God is a pearl and may be pierced on every side) after his drunkenness came the uncovering of his body; self-indulgence culminated in lust. [4] First the belly is crammed; then the other members are roused. Similarly, at a later period, "The people sat down to eat and to drink and rose up to play." [5] Lot also, God's friend, whom He saved upon the mountain, who was the only one found righteous out of so many thousands, was intoxicated by his daughters. And, although they may have acted as they did more from a desire of offspring than from love of sinful pleasure—for the human race seemed in danger of extinction—yet they were well aware that the righteous man would not abet their design unless intoxicated. In fact he did not know what he was doing, and his sin was not wilful. Still his error was a grave one, for it made him the father of Moab and Ammon, [6] Israel's enemies, of whom it is said: "Even to the fourteenth generation they shall not enter into the congregation of the Lord forever." [7]

9. When Elijah, in his flight from Jezebel,

---

[1] Cant. i. 3, 4.   [2] 1 Tim. v. 6.

[1] 1 Tim. v. 23.   [2] Eph. v. 18.   [3] Rom. xiv. 21.
[4] Gen. ix. 20, 21.   [5] Ex. xxxii. 6.   [6] Gen. xix. 30–38.
[7] Deut. xxiii. 3: Jerome substitutes "fourteenth" for "tenth."

lay weary and desolate beneath the oak, there came an angel who raised him up and said, "Arise and eat." And he looked, and behold there was a cake and a cruse of water at his head.[1] Had God willed it, might He not have sent His prophet spiced wines and dainty dishes and flesh basted into tenderness? When Elisha invited the sons of the prophets to dinner, he only gave them field-herbs to eat; and when all cried out with one voice: "There is death in the pot," the man of God did not storm at the cooks (for he was not used to very sumptuous fare), but caused meal to be brought, and casting it in, sweetened the bitter mess[2] with spiritual strength as Moses had once sweetened the waters of Mara.[3] Again, when men were sent to arrest the prophet, and were smitten with physical and mental blindness, that he might bring them without their own knowledge to Samaria, notice the food with which Elisha ordered them to be refreshed. "Set bread and water," he said, "before them, that they may eat and drink and go to their master."[4] And Daniel, who might have had rich food from the king's table,[5] preferred the mower's breakfast, brought to him by Habakkuk,[6] which must have been but country fare. He was called "a man of desires,"[7] because he would not eat the bread of desire or drink the wine of concupiscence.

10. There are, in the Scriptures, countless divine answers condemning gluttony and approving simple food. But as fasting is not my present theme and an adequate discussion of it would require a treatise to itself, these few observations must suffice of the many which the subject suggests. By them you will understand why the first man, obeying his belly and not God, was cast down from paradise into this vale of tears;[8] and why Satan used hunger to tempt the Lord Himself in the wilderness;[9] and why the apostle cries: "Meats for the belly and the belly for meats, but God shall destroy both it and them;"[10] and why he speaks of the self-indulgent as men "whose God is their belly."[11] For men invariably worship what they like best. Care must be taken, therefore, that abstinence may bring back to Paradise those whom satiety once drove out.

11. You will tell me, perhaps, that, high-born as you are, reared in luxury and used to lie softly, you cannot do without wine and dainties, and would find a stricter rule of life unendurable. If so, I can only say: "Live,

then, by your own rule, since God's rule is too hard for you." Not that the Creator and Lord of all takes pleasure in a rumbling and empty stomach, or in fevered lungs; but that these are indispensable as means to the preservation of chastity. Job was dear to God, perfect and upright before Him;[1] yet hear what he says of the devil: "His strength is in the loins, and his force is in the navel."[2] The terms are chosen for decency's sake, but the reproductive organs of the two sexes are meant. Thus, the descendant of David, who, according to the promise is to sit upon his throne, is said to come from his loins.[3] And the seventy-five souls descended from Jacob who entered Egypt are said to come out of his thigh.[4] So, also, when his thigh shrank after the Lord had wrestled with him,[5] he ceased to beget children. The Israelites, again, are told to celebrate the passover with loins girded and mortified.[6] God says to Job: "Gird up thy loins as a man."[7] John wears a leathern girdle.[8] The apostles must gird their loins to carry the lamps of the Gospel.[9] When Ezekiel tells us how Jerusalem is found in the plain of wandering, covered with blood, he uses the words: "Thy navel has not been cut."[10] In his assaults on men, therefore, the devil's strength is in the loins; in his attacks on women his force is in the navel.

12. Do you wish for proof of my assertions? Take examples. Sampson was braver than a lion and tougher than a rock; alone and unprotected he pursued a thousand armed men; and yet, in Delilah's embrace, his resolution melted away. David was a man after God's own heart, and his lips had often sung of the Holy One, the future Christ; and yet as he walked upon his housetop he was fascinated by Bathsheba's nudity, and added murder to adultery.[11] Notice here how, even in his own house, a man cannot use his eyes without danger. Then repenting, he says to the Lord: "Against thee, thee only, have I sinned and done this evil in Thy sight."[12] Being a king he feared no one else. So, too, with Solomon. Wisdom used him to sing her praise,[13] and he treated of all plants "from the cedar tree that is in Lebanon even unto the hyssop that springeth out of the wall;"[14] and yet he went back from God because he was a lover of women.[15] And, as if to show that near relationship is no safe-

---

[1] K. xix. 4–6.　　[2] 2 K. iv. 38–41.　　[3] Exod. xv. 23–25.
[4] 2 K. vi. 18–23.　　[5] Dan. i. 8.　　[6] Bel. 33–39.
[7] Dan. ix. 23, A.V. marg.　　[8] Ps. lxxxiv. 6, R.V.
[9] Matt. iv. 2, 3.　　[10] 1 Cor. vi. 13.　　[11] Phil. iii. 19.

[1] Job ii. 3.　　[2] Job xl. 16, of behemoth.　　[3] Ps. cxxxii. 11.
[4] Gen. xlvi. 26.　　[5] Gen. xxxii. 24, 25.　　[6] Exod. xii. 11.
[7] Job. xxxviii. 3.　　[8] Matt. iii. 4.　　[9] Luke xii. 35.
[10] Ezek. xvi. 4–6.　　[11] 2 Sam. xi.　　[12] Ps. li. 4.
[13] Solomon was the reputed author of the Book of Wisdom.
[14] 1 K. iv. 33.　　[15] 1 K. xi 1–4.

guard, Amnon burned with illicit passion for his sister Tamar.[1]

13. I cannot bring myself to speak of the many virgins who daily fall and are lost to the bosom of the church, their mother: stars over which the proud foe sets up his throne,[2] and rocks hollowed by the serpent that he may dwell in their fissures. You may see many women widows before wedded, who try to conceal their miserable fall by a lying garb. Unless they are betrayed by swelling wombs or by the crying of their infants, they walk abroad with tripping feet and heads in the air. Some go so far as to take potions, that they may insure barrenness, and thus murder human beings almost before their conception. Some, when they find themselves with child through their sin, use drugs to procure abortion, and when (as often happens) they die with their offspring, they enter the lower world laden with the guilt not only of adultery against Christ but also of suicide and child murder. Yet it is these who say: "'Unto the pure all things are pure;'[3] my conscience is sufficient guide for me. A pure heart is what God looks for. Why should I abstain from meats which God has created to be received with thanksgiving?"[4] And when they wish to appear agreeable and entertaining they first drench themselves with wine, and then joining the grossest profanity to intoxication, they say: "Far be it from me to abstain from the blood of Christ." And when they see another pale or sad they call her "wretch" or "manichæan;"[5] quite logically, indeed, for on their principles fasting involves heresy. When they go out they do their best to attract notice, and with nods and winks encourage troops of young fellows to follow them. Of each and all of these the prophet's words are true: "Thou hast a whore's forehead; thou refusest to be ashamed."[6] Their robes have but a narrow purple stripe,[7] it is true; and their head-dress is somewhat loose, so as to leave the hair free. From their shoulders flutters the lilac mantle which they call "maforte;" they have their feet in cheap slippers and their arms tucked up tight-fitting sleeves. Add to these marks of their profession an easy gait, and you have all the virginity that they possess. Such may have eulogizers of their own, and may fetch a higher price in the market of perdition, merely because they are called virgins. But to such virgins as these I prefer to be displeasing.

14. I blush to speak of it, it is so shocking; yet though sad, it is true. How comes this plague of the agapetæ[1] to be in the church? Whence come these unwedded wives, these novel concubines, these harlots, so I will call them, though they cling to a single partner? One house holds them and one chamber. They often occupy the same bed, and yet they call us suspicious if we fancy anything amiss. A brother leaves his virgin sister; a virgin, slighting her unmarried brother, seeks a brother in a stranger. Both alike profess to have but one object, to find spiritual consolation from those not of their kin; but their real aim is to indulge in sexual intercourse. It is on such that Solomon in the book of proverbs heaps his scorn. "Can a man take fire in his bosom," he says, "and his clothes not be burned? Can one go upon hot coals and his feet not be burned?"[2]

15. We cast out, then, and banish from our sight those who only wish to seem and not to be virgins. Henceforward I may bring all my speech to bear upon you who, as it is your lot to be the first virgin of noble birth in Rome, have to labor the more diligently not to lose good things to come, as well as those that are present. You have at least learned from a case in your own family the troubles of wedded life and the uncertainties of marriage. Your sister, Blæsilla, before you in age but behind you in declining the vow of virginity, has become a widow but seven months after she has taken a husband. Hapless plight of us mortals who know not what is before us! She has lost, at once, the crown of virginity and the pleasures of wedlock. And, although, as a widow, the second degree of chastity is hers, still can you not imagine the continual crosses which she has to bear, daily seeing in her sister what she has lost herself; and, while she finds it hard to go without the pleasures of wedlock, having a less reward for her present continence? Still she, too, may take heart and rejoice. The fruit which is an hundredfold and that which is sixtyfold both spring from one seed, and that seed is chastity.[3]

16. Do not court the company of married ladies or visit the houses of the high-born. Do not look too often on the life which you despised to become a virgin. Women of the world, you know, plume themselves because their husbands are on the bench or in other

---

[1] 2 Sam. xiii.   [2] Isa. xiv. 13.   [3] Tit. i. 15.   [4] 1 Tim. iv. 3.
[5] The Manichæans believed evil to be inseparable from matter. Hence they inculcated a rigid asceticism.   [6] Jer. iii. 3.
[7] Plebeians wore a narrow stripe, patricians a broad one.

[1] Beloved ones, viz., women who lived with the unmarried clergy professedly as spiritual sisters, but really (in too many cases) as mistresses. The evil custom was widely prevalent and called forth many protests. The councils of Elvira, Ancyra, and Nicæa passed canons against it.   [2] Prov. vi. 27, 28.   [3] Matt. xiii. 8.

high positions. And the wife of the emperor always has an eager throng of visitors at her door. Why do you, then, wrong your husband? Why do you, God's bride, hasten to visit the wife of a mere man? Learn in this respect a holy pride; know that you are better than they. And not only must you avoid intercourse with those who are puffed up by their husbands' honors, who are hedged in with troops of eunuchs, and who wear robes inwrought with threads of gold. You must also shun those who are widows from necessity and not from choice. Not that they ought to have desired the death of their husbands; but that they have not welcomed the opportunity of continence when it has come. As it is, they only change their garb; their old self-seeking remains unchanged. To see them in their capacious litters, with red cloaks and plump bodies, a row of eunuchs walking in front of them, you would fancy them not to have lost husbands but to be seeking them. Their houses are filled with flatterers and with guests. The very clergy, who ought to inspire them with respect by their teaching and authority, kiss these ladies on the forehead, and putting forth their hands (so that, if you knew no better, you might suppose them in the act of blessing), take wages for their visits. They, meanwhile, seeing that priests cannot do without them, are lifted up into pride; and as, having had experience of both, they prefer the license of widowhood to the restraints of marriage, they call themselves chaste livers and nuns. After an immoderate supper they retire to rest to dream of the apostles.[1]

17. Let your companions be women pale and thin with fasting, and approved by their years and conduct; such as daily sing in their hearts: "Tell me where thou feedest thy flock, where thou makest it to rest at noon,"[2] and say, with true earnestness, "I have a desire to depart and to be with Christ."[3] Be subject to your parents, imitating the example of your spouse.[4] Rarely go abroad, and if you wish to seek the aid of the martyrs seek it in your own chamber. For you will never need a pretext for going out if you always go out when there is need. Take food in moderation, and never overload your stomach. For many women, while temperate as regards wine, are intemperate in the use of food. When you rise at night to pray, let your breath be that of an empty and not that of an overfull

stomach. Read often, learn all that you can. Let sleep overcome you, the roll still in your hands; when your head falls, let it be on the sacred page. Let your fasts be of daily occurrence and your refreshment such as avoids satiety. It is idle to carry an empty stomach if, in two or three days' time, the fast is to be made up for by repletion. When cloyed the mind immediately grows sluggish, and when the ground is watered it puts forth the thorns of lust. If ever you feel the outward man sighing for the flower of youth, and if, as you lie on your couch after a meal, you are excited by the alluring train of sensual desires; then seize the shield of faith, for it alone can quench the fiery darts of the devil.[1] "They are all adulterers," says the prophet; "they have made ready their heart like an oven."[2] But do you keep close to the footsteps of Christ, and, intent upon His words, say: "Did not our heart burn within us by the way while Jesus opened to us the Scriptures?"[3] and again: "Thy word is tried to the uttermost, and thy servant loveth it."[4] It is hard for the human soul to avoid loving something, and our mind must of necessity give way to affection of one kind or another. The love of the flesh is overcome by the love of the spirit. Desire is quenched by desire. What is taken from the one increases the other. Therefore, as you lie on your couch, say again and again: "By night have I sought Him whom my soul loveth."[5] "Mortify, therefore," says the apostle, "your members which are upon the earth."[6] Because he himself did so, he could afterwards say with confidence: "I live, yet not I, but Christ, liveth in me."[7] He who mortifies his members, and feels that he is walking in a vain show,[8] is not afraid to say: "I am become like a bottle in the frost.[9] Whatever there was in me of the moisture of lust has been dried out of me." And again: "My knees are weak through fasting; I forget to eat my bread. By reason of the voice of my groaning my bones cleave to my skin."[10]

18. Be like the grasshopper and make night musical. Nightly wash your bed and water your couch with your tears.[11] Watch and be like the sparrow alone upon the housetop.[12] Sing with the spirit, but sing with the understanding also.[13] And let your song be that of the psalmist: "Bless the

---

[1] Cena dubia. The allusion is to Terence, Phormio, 342.
[2] Cant. i. 7, R.V.   [3] Phil. i. 23.   [4] Luke ii. 51.

[1] Eph. vi. 16.   [2] Hos. vii. 4, 6, R. V.   [3] Luke xxiv. 32.
[4] Ps. cxix. 140, P.B.V.   [5] Cant. iii. 1.   [6] Col. iii. 5.
[7] Gal. ii. 20.   [8] Ps. xxxix. 6, Vulg. That is, who knows that the world is vanity.   [9] Ps. cxix. 83, Vulg.   [10] Ps. cix. 24; cii. 5.
[11] Ps. vi. 6, P.B.V.   [12] Ps. cii. 7.   [13] 1 Cor. xiv. 15.

Lord, O my soul; and forget not all his benefits; who forgiveth all thine iniquities; who healeth all thy diseases; who redeemeth thy life from destruction."[1] Can we, any of us, honestly make his words our own: "I have eaten ashes like bread and mingled my drink with weeping?"[2] Yet, should we not weep and groan when the serpent invites us, as he invited our first parents, to eat forbidden fruit, and when after expelling us from the paradise of virginity he desires to clothe us with mantles of skins such as that which Elijah, on his return to paradise, left behind him on earth?[3] Say to yourself: "What have I to do with the pleasures of sense that so soon come to an end? What have I to do with the song of the sirens so sweet and so fatal to those who hear it?" I would not have you subject to that sentence whereby condemnation has been passed upon mankind. When God says to Eve, "In pain and in sorrow thou shalt bring forth children," say to yourself, "That is a law for a married woman, not for me." And when He continues, "Thy desire shall be to thy husband,"[4] say again: "Let her desire be to her husband who has not Christ for her spouse." And when, last of all, He says, "Thou shalt surely die,"[5] once more, say, "Marriage indeed must end in death; but the life on which I have resolved is independent of sex. Let those who are wives keep the place and the time that properly belong to them. For me, virginity is consecrated in the persons of Mary and of Christ."

19. Some one may say, "Do you dare detract from wedlock, which is a state blessed by God?" I do not detract from wedlock when I set virginity before it. No one compares a bad thing with a good. Wedded women may congratulate themselves that they come next to virgins. "Be fruitful," God says, "and multiply, and replenish the earth."[6] He who desires to replenish the earth may increase and multiply if he will. But the train to which you belong is not on earth, but in heaven. The command to increase and multiply first finds fulfilment after the expulsion from paradise, after the nakedness and the fig-leaves which speak of sexual passion. Let them marry and be given in marriage who eat their bread in the sweat of their brow; whose land brings forth to them thorns and thistles,[7] and whose crops are choked with briars. My seed produces fruit hundredfold.[8] "All men cannot receive

God's saying, but they to whom it is given."

Some people may be eunuchs from necessity; I am one of free will.[1] "There is a time to embrace and a time to refrain from embracing. There is a time to cast away stones, and a time to gather stones together."[2] Now that out of the hard stones of the Gentiles God has raised up children unto Abraham,[3] they begin to be "holy stones rolling upon the earth."[4] They pass through the whirlwinds of the world, and roll on in God's chariot on rapid wheels. Let those stitch coats to themselves who have lost the coat woven from the top throughout;[5] who delight in the cries of infants which, as soon as they see the light, lament that they are born. In paradise Eve was a virgin, and it was only after the coats of skins that she began her married life. Now paradise is your home too. Keep therefore your birthright and say: "Return unto thy rest, O my soul."[6] To show that virginity is natural while wedlock only follows guilt, what is born of wedlock is virgin flesh, and it gives back in fruit what in root it has lost. "There shall come forth a rod out of the stem of Jesse, and a flower shall grow out of his roots."[7] The rod[8] is the mother of the Lord—simple, pure, unsullied; drawing no germ of life from without but fruitful in singleness like God Himself. The flower of the rod is Christ, who says of Himself: "I am the rose of Sharon and the lily of the valleys."[9] In another place He is foretold to be "a stone cut out of the mountain without hands,"[10] a figure by which the prophet signifies that He is to be born a virgin of a virgin. For the hands are here a figure of wedlock as in the passage: "His left hand is under my head and his right hand doth embrace me."[11] It agrees, also, with this interpretation that the unclean animals are led into Noah's ark in pairs, while of the clean an uneven number is taken.[12] Similarly, when Moses and Joshua were bidden to remove their shoes because the ground on which they stood was holy,[13] the command had a mystical meaning. So, too, when the disciples were appointed to preach the gospel they were told to take with them neither shoe nor shoe-latchet;[14] and when the soldiers came to cast lots for the garments of Jesus[15] they found no boots that they could take away.

---

[1] Matt. xix. 11, 12.   [2] Eccles. iii. 5.   [3] Matt. iii. 9.
[4] Zech. ix. 16, LXX.   [5] Joh. xix. 23.
[6] Ps. cxvi. 7.   [7] Isa. xi. 1, LXX.
[8] In the Latin there is a play on words here between virga and virgo.   [9] Cant. ii. 1.   [10] Dan. ii. 45.
[11] Cant. ii. 6.   [12] Gen. vii. 2.   [13] Ex. iii. 5; Josh. v. 15.
[14] Matt. x. 10.   According to Letter XXIII. § 4, these typify dead works.   [15] Joh. xix. 23, 24.

[1] Ps. ciii. 2–4.   [2] Ps. cii. 9.   [3] 2 K. ii. 13.
[4] Gen. iii. 16.   [5] Gen. ii. 17.   [6] Gen. i. 28.
[7] Gen. iii. 18, 19.   [8] See Letter XLVIII. §§ 2, 3.

For the Lord could not Himself possess what He had forbidden to His servants.

20. I praise wedlock, I praise marriage, but it is because they give me virgins. I gather the rose from the thorns, the gold from the earth, the pearl from the shell. "Doth the plowman plow all day to sow?"[1] Shall he not also enjoy the fruit of his labor? Wedlock is the more honored, the more what is born of it is loved. Why, mother, do you grudge your daughter her virginity? She has been reared on your milk, she has come from your womb, she has grown up in your bosom. Your watchful affection has kept her a virgin. Are you angry with her because she chooses to be a king's wife and not a soldier's? She has conferred on you a high privilege; you are now the mother-in-law of God. "Concerning virgins," says the apostle, "I have no commandment of the Lord."[2] Why was this? Because his own virginity was due, not to a command, but to his free choice. For they are not to be heard who feign him to have had a wife; for, when he is discussing continence and commending perpetual chastity, he uses the words, "I would that all men were even as I myself." And farther on, "I say, therefore, to the unmarried and widows, it is good for them if they abide even as I."[3] And in another place, "have we not power to lead about wives even as the rest of the apostles?"[4] Why then has he no commandment from the Lord concerning virginity? Because what is freely offered is worth more than what is extorted by force, and to command virginity would have been to abrogate wedlock. It would have been a hard enactment to compel opposition to nature and to extort from men the angelic life; and not only so, it would have been to condemn what is a divine ordinance.

21. The old law had a different ideal of blessedness, for therein it is said: "Blessed is he who hath seed in Zion and a family in Jerusalem:"[5] and "Cursed is the barren who beareth not:"[6] and "Thy children shall be like olive-plants round about thy table."[7] Riches too are promised to the faithful and we are told that "there was not one feeble person among their tribes."[8] But now even to eunuchs it is said, "Say not, behold I am a dry tree,"[9] for instead of sons and daughters you have a place forever in heaven. Now the poor are blessed, now Lazarus is set before Dives in his purple.[10] Now he who is weak is counted strong. But in those days

the world was still unpeopled: accordingly, to pass over instances of childlessness meant only to serve as types, those only were considered happy who could boast of children. It was for this reason that Abraham in his old age married Keturah;[1] that Leah hired Jacob with her son's mandrakes,[2] and that fair Rachel—a type of the church—complained of the closing of her womb.[3] But gradually the crop grew up and then the reaper was sent forth with his sickle. Elijah lived a virgin life, so also did Elisha and many of the sons of the prophets. To Jeremiah the command came: "Thou shalt not take thee a wife."[4] He had been sanctified in his mother's womb,[5] and now he was forbidden to take a wife because the captivity was near. The apostle gives the same counsel in different words. "I think, therefore, that this is good by reason of the present distress, namely that it is good for a man to be as he is."[6] What is this distress which does away with the joys of wedlock? The apostle tells us, in a later verse: "The time is short: it remaineth that those who have wives be as though they had none."[7] Nebuchadnezzar is hard at hand. The lion is bestirring himself from his lair. What good will marriage be to me if it is to end in slavery to the haughtiest of kings? What good will little ones be to me if their lot is to be that which the prophet sadly describes: "The tongue of the sucking child cleaveth to the roof of his mouth for thirst the young children ask for bread and no man breaketh it unto them"?[8] In those days, as I have said, the virtue of continence was found only in men: Eve still continued to travail with children. But now that a virgin has conceived[9] in the womb and has borne to us a child of which the prophet says that "Government shall be upon his shoulder, and his name shall be called the mighty God, the everlasting Father,"[10] now the chain of the curse is broken. Death came through Eve, but life has come through Mary. And thus the gift of virginity has been bestowed most richly upon women, seeing that it has had its beginning from a woman. As soon as the Son of God set foot upon the earth He formed for Himself a new household there; that, as He was adored by angels in heaven, angels might serve Him also on earth. Then chaste Judith once more cut off the head of Holofernes.[11] Then Haman—whose name means iniquity—was once

[1] Isa. xxviii. 24.   [2] 1 Cor. vii. 25.
[3] 1 Cor. vii. 7, 8.   [4] 1 Cor. ix. 5.   [5] Isa. xxxi. 9, LXX.
[6] Isa. liv. 1, LXX. (?)   [7] Ps. cxxviii. 3.   [8] Ps. cv. 37.
[9] Isa. lvi. 3.   [10] Cf. Luke xvi. 19 sqq.

[1] Gen. xxv. 1.   [2] Gen. xxx. 14–16.
[3] Gen. xxx. 1, 2.   [4] Jer. xvi. 2.
[5] Jer. i. 5.   [6] 1 Cor. vii. 26, R.V.   [7] 1 Cor. vii. 29.
[8] Lam. iv. 4.   [9] Isa. vii. 14.   [10] Isa. ix. 6.   [11] Judith xiii.

more burned in fire of his own kindling.[1] Then James and John forsook father and net and ship and followed the Saviour: neither kinship nor the world's ties, nor the care of their home could hold them back. Then were the words heard: "Whosoever will come after me, let him deny himself and take up his cross and follow me."[2] For no soldier goes with a wife to battle. Even when a disciple would have buried his father, the Lord forbade him, and said: "Foxes have holes and the birds of the air have nests, but the Son of Man hath not where to lay His head."[3] So you must not complain if you have but scanty house-room. In the same strain, the apostle writes: "He that is unmarried careth for the things that belong to the Lord, how he may please the Lord: but he that is married careth for the things that are of the world how he may please his wife. There is difference also between a wife and a virgin. The unmarried woman careth for the things of the Lord that she may be holy both in body and in spirit. But she that is married careth for the things of the world how she may please her husband."[4]

22. How great inconveniences are involved in wedlock and how many anxieties encompass it I have, I think, described shortly in my treatise—published against Helvidius[5]— on the perpetual virginity of the blessed Mary. It would be tedious to go over the same ground now; and any one who pleases may draw from that fountain. But lest I should seem wholly to have passed over the matter, I will just say now that the apostle bids us pray without ceasing,[6] and that he who in the married state renders his wife her due[7] cannot so pray. Either we pray always and are virgins, or we cease to pray that we may fulfil the claims of marriage. Still he says: "If a virgin marry she hath not sinned. Nevertheless such shall have trouble in the flesh."[8] At the outset I promised that I should say little or nothing of the embarrassments of wedlock, and now I give you notice to the same effect. If you want to know from how many vexations a virgin is free and by how many a wife is fettered you should read Tertullian "to a philosophic friend,"[9] and his other treatises on virginity, the blessed Cyprian's noble volume, the writings of Pope Damasus[10] in prose and verse, and the treatises recently written for his sister by our own Ambrose.[1] In these he has poured forth his soul with such a flood of eloquence that he has sought out, set forth, and put in order all that bears on the praise of virgins.

23. We must proceed by a different path, for our purpose is not the praise of virginity but its preservation. To know that it is a good thing is not enough: when we have chosen it we must guard it with jealous care. The first only requires judgment, and we share it with many; the second calls for toil, and few compete with us in it. "He that shall endure unto the end," the Lord says, "the same shall be saved,"[2] and "many are called but few are chosen."[3] Therefore I conjure you before God and Jesus Christ and His elect angels to guard that which you have received, not readily exposing to the public gaze the vessels of the Lord's temple (which only the priests are by right allowed to see), that no profane person may look upon God's sanctuary. Uzzah, when he touched the ark which it was not lawful to touch, was struck down suddenly by death.[4] And assuredly no gold or silver vessel was ever so dear to God as is the temple of a virgin's body. The shadow went before, but now the reality is come. You indeed may speak in all simplicity, and from motives of amiability may treat with courtesy the veriest strangers, but unchaste eyes see nothing aright. They fail to appreciate the beauty of the soul, and only value that of the body. Hezekiah showed God's treasure to the Assyrians,[5] who ought never to have seen what they were sure to covet. The consequence was that Judæa was torn by continual wars, and that the very first things carried away to Babylon were these vessels of the Lord. We find Belshazzar at his feast and among his concubines (vice always glories in defiling what is noble) drinking out of these sacred cups.[6]

24. Never incline your ear to words of mischief. For men often say an improper word to make trial of a virgin's steadfastness, to see if she hears it with pleasure, and if she is ready to unbend at every silly jest. Such persons applaud whatever you affirm and deny whatever you deny; they speak of you as not only holy but accomplished, and say that in you there is no guile. "Behold," say they, "a true handmaid of Christ; behold entire singleness of heart. How different from that rough, un-

---

[1] Esther vii. 10.   [2] Mark viii. 34.   [3] Matt. viii. 20-22.
[4] 1 Cor. vii. 32-34.   [5] See the treatise "Against Helvidius," in his volume.   [6] 1 Thess. v. 17.   [7] 1 Cor. vii. 3, R.V.   [8] 1 Cor. vii. 28.
[9] Not extant.   Jerome alludes to it again in his treatise against Jovinian.   [10] See Migne's "Patrologia," xiii., col. 347-418.

[1] Ambrose de Virg.   Migne's "Patrologia," xvi., col. 187.
[2] Matt. xxiv. 13.   [3] Matt. xx. 16; xxii. 14.   [4] 2 Sam. vi. 6, 7.
[5] 2 Kings xx. 12, 13.   [6] Dan. v. 1-3.

sightly, countrified fright, who most likely never married because she could never find a husband." Our natural weakness induces us readily to listen to such flatterers; but, though we may blush and reply that such praise is more than our due, the soul within us rejoices to hear itself praised.

Like the ark of the covenant Christ's spouse should be overlaid with gold within and without;[1] she should be the guardian of the law of the Lord. Just as the ark contained nothing but the tables of the covenant,[2] so in you there should be no thought of anything that is outside. For it pleases the Lord to sit in your mind as He once sat on the mercy-seat and the cherubims.[3] As He sent His disciples to loose Him the foal of an ass that he might ride on it, so He sends them to release you from the cares of the world, that leaving the bricks and straw of Egypt, you may follow Him, the true Moses, through the wilderness and may enter the land of promise. Let no one dare to forbid you, neither mother nor sister nor kinswoman nor brother: "The Lord hath need of you."[4] Should they seek to hinder you, let them fear the scourges that fell on Pharaoh, who, because he would not let God's people go that they might serve Him,[5] suffered the plagues described in Scripture. Jesus entering into the temple cast out those things which belonged not to the temple. For God is jealous and will not allow the father's house to be made a den of robbers.[6] Where money is counted, where doves are sold, where simplicity is stifled, where, that is, a virgin's breast glows with cares of this world; straightway the veil of the temple is rent,[7] the bridegroom rises in anger, he says: "Your house is left unto you desolate."[8] Read the gospel and see how Mary sitting at the feet of the Lord is set before the zealous Martha. In her anxiety to be hospitable Martha was preparing a meal for the Lord and His disciples; yet Jesus said to her: "Martha, Martha, thou art careful and troubled about many things. But few things are needful or one.[9] And Mary hath chosen that good part which shall not be taken away from her."[10] Be then like Mary; prefer the food of the soul to that of the body. Leave it to your sisters to run to and fro and to seek how they may fitly welcome Christ. But do you, having once for all cast away the burden of the world, sit at the Lord's feet and say: "I have found him

whom my soul loveth; I will hold him, I will not let him go."[1] And He will answer: "My dove, my undefiled is but one; she is the only one of her mother, she is the choice one of her that bare her."[2] Now the mother of whom this is said is the heavenly Jerusalem.[3]

25. Ever let the privacy of your chamber guard you; ever let the Bridegroom sport with you within.[4] Do you pray? You speak to the Bridegroom. Do you read? He speaks to you. When sleep overtakes you He will come behind and put His hand through the hole of the door, and your heart[5] shall be moved for Him; and you will awake and rise up and say: "I am sick of love."[6] Then He will reply: "A garden inclosed is my sister, my spouse; a spring shut up, a fountain sealed."[7]

Go not from home nor visit the daughters of a strange land, though you have patriarchs for brothers and Israel for a father. Dinah went out and was seduced.[8] Do not seek the Bridegroom in the streets; do not go round the corners of the city. For though you may say: "I will rise now and go about the city: in the streets and in the broad ways I will seek Him whom my soul loveth," and though you may ask the watchmen: "Saw ye Him whom my soul loveth?"[9] no one will deign to answer you. The Bridegroom cannot be found in the streets: "Strait and narrow is the way which leadeth unto life."[10] So the Song goes on: "I sought him but I could not find him: I called him but he gave me no answer."[11] And would that failure to find Him were all. You will be wounded and stripped, you will lament and say: "The watchmen that went about the city found me: they smote me, they wounded me, they took away my veil from me."[12] Now if one who could say: "I sleep but my heart waketh,"[13] and "A bundle of myrrh is my well beloved unto me; he shall lie all night betwixt my breasts";[14] if one who could speak thus suffered so much because she went abroad, what shall become of us who are but young girls; of us who, when the bride goes in with the Bridegroom, still remain without? Jesus is jealous. He does not choose that your face should be seen of others. You may excuse yourself and say: "I have drawn close my veil, I have covered my face and I have sought Thee there and have said: 'Tell me, O Thou whom my soul

[1] Ex. xxv. 11.　　　　[2] 1 K. viii. 9.
[3] Ex. xxv. 22.　　　　[4] Matt. xxi. 1-3.
[5] Ex. vii. 16.　[6] Matt. xxi. 12, 13, R.V.　[7] Matt. xxvii. 51.
[6] Matt. xxiii. 38.　[9] R.V. marg.　[10] Luke x. 41, 42.

[1] Cant. iii. 4.　　[2] Cant. vi. 9.　　[3] Gal. iv. 26.
[4] Cf. Gen. xxvi. 8.　[5] R.V.　　[6] Cant. v. 2, 4, 8.
[7] Cant. iv. 12.　[8] Gen. xxxiv.　[9] Cant. iii. 2, 3.
[10] Matt. vii. 14.　[11] Cant. iii. 2 ; v. 6.　[12] Cant. v. 7.
[13] Cant. v. 2.　[14] Cant. i. 13.

loveth, where Thou feedest Thy flock, where Thou makest it to rest at noon. For why should I be as one that is veiled beside the flocks of Thy companions?' " [1] Yet in spite of your excuses He will be wroth, He will swell with anger and say: "If thou know not thyself, O thou fairest among women, go thy way forth by the footsteps of the flock and feed thy goats beside the shepherd's tents." [2] You may be fair, and of all faces yours may be the dearest to the Bridegroom; yet, unless you know yourself, and keep your heart with all diligence, [3] unless also you avoid the eyes of the young men, you will be turned out of My bride-chamber to feed the goats, which shall be set on the left hand. [4]

26. These things being so, my Eustochium, daughter, lady, fellow-servant, sister —these names refer the first to your age, the second to your rank, the third to your religious vocation, the last to the place which you hold in my affection—hear the words of Isaiah: "Come, my people, enter thou into thy chambers, and shut thy doors about thee: hide thyself as it were for a little moment, until the indignation" of the Lord "be overpast." [5] Let foolish virgins stray abroad, but for your part stay at home with the Bridegroom; for if you shut your door, and, according to the precept of the Gospel, [6] pray to your Father in secret, He will come and knock, saying: "Behold, I stand at the door and knock; if any man . . . open the door, I will come in to him, and will sup with him, and he with me." [7] Then straightway you will eagerly reply: "It is the voice of my beloved that knocketh, saying, Open to me, my sister, my love, my dove, my undefiled." It is impossible that you should refuse, and say: "I have put off my coat; how shall I put it on? I have washed my feet; how shall I defile them?" [8] Arise forthwith and open. Otherwise while you linger He may pass on and you may have mournfully to say: "I opened to my beloved, but my beloved was gone." [9] Why need the doors of your heart be closed to the Bridegroom? Let them be open to Christ but closed to the devil according to the saying: "If the spirit of him who hath power rise up against thee, leave not thy place." [10] Daniel, in that upper story to which he withdrew when he could no longer continue below, had his windows open toward Jerusalem. [11] Do you too keep your windows open, but only on the side where light may enter and whence you may see the eye of the Lord. Open not those other windows of which the prophet says: "Death is come up into our windows." [1]

27. You must also be careful to avoid the snare of a passion for vainglory. "How," Jesus says, "can ye believe which receive glory one from another?" [2] What an evil that must be the victim of which cannot believe! Let us rather say: "Thou art my glorying," [3] and "He that glorieth, let him glory in the Lord," [4] and "If I yet pleased men I should not be the servant of Christ," [5] and "Far be it from me to glory save in the cross of our Lord Jesus Christ, through whom the world hath been crucified unto me and I unto the world;" [6] and once more: "In God we boast all the day long; my soul shall make her boast in the Lord." [7] When you do alms, let God alone see you. When you fast, be of a cheerful countenance. [8] Let your dress be neither too neat nor too slovenly; neither let it be so remarkable as to draw the attention of passers-by, and to make men point their fingers at you. Is a brother dead? Has the body of a sister to be carried to its burial? Take care lest in too often performing such offices you die yourself. Do not wish to seem very devout nor more humble than need be, lest you seek glory by shunning it. For many, who screen from all men's sight their poverty, charity, and fasting, desire to excite admiration by their very disdain of it, and strangely seek for praise while they profess to keep out of its way. From the other disturbing influences which make men rejoice, despond, hope, and fear I find many free; but this is a defect which few are without, and he is best whose character, like a fair skin, is disfigured by the fewest blemishes. I do not think it necessary to warn you against boasting of your riches, or against priding yourself on your birth, or against setting yourself up as superior to others. I know your humility; I know that you can say with sincerity: "Lord, my heart is not haughty nor mine eyes lofty;" [9] I know that in your breast as in that of your mother the pride through which the devil fell has no place. It would be time wasted to write to you about it; for there is no greater folly than to teach a pupil what he knows already. But now that you have despised the boastfulness of the world, do not let the fact inspire you with new boastfulness. Harbor

---

1 Cant. i. 7, R.V.   2 Cant. i. 8, LXX.   3 Prov. iv. 23.
4 Matt. xxv. 33.   5 Isa. xxvi. 20.   6 Matt. vi. 6.
7 Rev. iii. 20.   8 Cant. v. 2, 3.   9 Cant. v. 6.
10 Eccles. x. 4, A.V., "the spirit of the ruler."
11 Dan. vi. 10, LXX.

1 Jer. ix. 21.   2 Joh. v. 44, R.V.
3 Jer. ix. 24.   4 1 Cor. i. 31.   5 Gal. i. 10.
6 Gal. vi. 14, R.V. marg.   7 Pss. xliv. 8 ; xxxiv. 2.
8 Matt. vi. 3, 16-18.   9 Ps. cxxxi. 1.

not the secret thought that having ceased to court attention in garments of gold you may begin to do so in mean attire. And when you come into a room full of brothers and sisters, do not sit in too low a place or plead that you are unworthy of a footstool. Do not deliberately lower your voice as though worn out with fasting; nor, leaning on the shoulder of another, mimic the tottering gait of one who is faint. Some women, it is true, disfigure their faces, that they may appear unto men to fast.[1] As soon as they catch sight of any one they groan, they look down; they cover up their faces, all but one eye, which they keep free to see with. Their dress is sombre, their girdles are of sackcloth, their hands and feet are dirty; only their stomachs—which cannot be seen—are hot with food. Of these the psalm is sung daily: "The Lord will scatter the bones of them that please themselves."[2] Others change their garb and assume the mien of men, being ashamed of being what they were born to be—women. They cut off their hair and are not ashamed to look like eunuchs. Some clothe themselves in goat's hair, and, putting on hoods, think to become children again by making themselves look like so many owls.[3]

28. But I will not speak only of women. Avoid men, also, when you see them loaded with chains and wearing their hair long like women, contrary to the apostle's precept,[4] not to speak of beards like those of goats, black cloaks, and bare feet braving the cold. All these things are tokens of the devil. Such an one Rome groaned over some time back in Antimus; and Sophronius is a still more recent instance. Such persons, when they have once gained admission to the houses of the high-born, and have deceived "silly women laden with sins, ever learning and never able to come to the knowledge of the truth,"[5] feign a sad mien and pretend to make long fasts while at night they feast in secret. Shame forbids me to say more, for my language might appear more like invective than admonition. There are others—I speak of those of my own order—who seek the presbyterate and the diaconate simply that they may be able to see women with less restraint. Such men think of nothing but their dress; they use perfumes freely, and see that there are no creases in their leather shoes. Their curling hair shows traces of the tongs; their fingers glisten with rings; they walk on tiptoe across a damp road, not to splash their feet. When you see men acting in this way, think of them rather as bridegrooms than as clergymen. Certain persons have devoted the whole of their energies and life to the single object of knowing the names, houses, and characters of married ladies. I will here briefly describe the head of the profession, that from the master's likeness you may recognize the disciples. He rises and goes forth with the sun; he has the order of his visits duly arranged; he takes the shortest road; and, troublesome old man that he is, forces his way almost into the bedchambers of ladies yet asleep. If he sees a pillow that takes his fancy or an elegant table-cover—or indeed any article of household furniture—he praises it, looks admiringly at it, takes it into his hand, and, complaining that he has nothing of the kind, begs or rather extorts it from the owner. All the women, in fact, fear to cross the news-carrier of the town. Chastity and fasting are alike distasteful to him. What he likes is a savory breakfast—say off a plump young crane such as is commonly called a cheeper. In speech he is rude and forward, and is always ready to bandy reproaches. Wherever you turn he is the first man that you see before you. Whatever news is noised abroad he is either the originator of the rumor or its magnifier. He changes his horses every hour; and they are so sleek and spirited that you would take him for a brother of the Thracian king.[1]

29. Many are the stratagems which the wily enemy employs against us. "The serpent," we are told, "was more subtile than any beast of the field which the Lord God had made."[2] And the apostle says: "We are not ignorant of his devices."[3] Neither an affected shabbiness nor a stylish smartness becomes a Christian. If there is anything of which you are ignorant, if you have any doubt about Scripture, ask one whose life commends him, whose age puts him above suspicion, whose reputation does not belie him; one who may be able to say: "I have espoused you to one husband that I may present you as a chaste virgin to Christ." Or if there should be none such able to explain, it is better to avoid danger at the price of ignorance than to court it for the sake of learning. Remember that you walk in the midst of snares, and that many veteran virgins, of a chastity never called in question, have, on the very threshold of death, let their crowns fall from their hands.

---

[1] Matt. vi. 16.　[2] Ps. liii. 5, according to the Roman Psalter.
[3] Cucullis fabrefactis, ut ad infantiam redeant, imitantur noctuas et bubones.　[4] 1 Cor. xi. 14.　[5] 2 Tim. iii. 6, 7.

[1] Diomede. See Lucretius, v. 31, and Virgil, A. i. 752.
[2] Gen. iii. 1.　[3] 2 Cor. ii. 11.

If any of your handmaids share your vocation, do not lift up yourself against them or pride yourself because you are their mistress. You have all chosen one Bridegroom; you all sing the same psalms; together you receive the Body of Christ. Why then should your thoughts be different?[1] You must try to win others, and that you may attract the more readily you must treat the virgins in your train with the greatest respect. If you find one of them weak in the faith, be attentive to her, comfort her, caress her, and make her chastity your treasure. But if a girl pretends to have a vocation simply because she desires to escape from service, read aloud to her the words of the apostle: "It is better to marry than to burn."[2]

Idle persons and busybodies, whether virgins or widows; such as go from house to house calling on married women and displaying an unblushing effrontery greater than that of a stage parasite, cast from you as you would the plague. For "evil communications corrupt good manners,"[3] and women like these care for nothing but their lowest appetites. They will often urge you, saying, "My dear creature, make the best of your advantages, and live while life is yours," and "Surely you are not laying up money for your children." Given to wine and wantonness, they instill all manner of mischief into people's minds, and induce even the most austere to indulge in enervating pleasures. And "when they have begun to wax wanton against Christ they will marry, having condemnation because they have rejected their first faith."[4]

Do not seek to appear over-eloquent, nor trifle with verse, nor make yourself gay with lyric songs. And do not, out of affectation, follow the sickly taste[5] of married ladies who, now pressing their teeth together, now keeping their lips wide apart, speak with a lisp, and purposely clip their words, because they fancy that to pronounce them naturally is a mark of country breeding. Accordingly they find pleasure in what I may call an adultery of the tongue. For "what communion hath light with darkness? And what concord hath Christ with Belial?"[6] How can Horace go with the psalter, Virgil with the gospels, Cicero with the apostle?[7] Is not a brother made to stumble if he sees you sitting at meat in an idol's temple?[8] Although "unto the pure all things are pure,"[1] and "nothing is to be refused if it be received with thanksgiving,"[2] still we ought not to drink the cup of Christ, and, at the same time, the cup of devils.[3] Let me relate to you the story of my own miserable experience.

30. Many years ago, when for the kingdom of heaven's sake I had cut myself off from home, parents, sister, relations, and—harder still—from the dainty food to which I had been accustomed; and when I was on my way to Jerusalem to wage my warfare, I still could not bring myself to forego the library which I had formed for myself at Rome with great care and toil. And so, miserable man that I was, I would fast only that I might afterwards read Cicero. After many nights spent in vigil, after floods of tears called from my inmost heart, after the recollection of my past sins, I would once more take up Plautus. And when at times I returned to my right mind, and began to read the prophets, their style seemed rude and repellent. I failed to see the light with my blinded eyes; but I attributed the fault not to them, but to the sun. While the old serpent was thus making me his plaything, about the middle of Lent a deep-seated fever fell upon my weakened body, and while it destroyed my rest completely—the story seems hardly credible—it so wasted my unhappy frame that scarcely anything was left of me but skin and bone. Meantime preparations for my funeral went on; my body grew gradually colder, and the warmth of life lingered only in my throbbing breast. Suddenly I was caught up in the spirit and dragged before the judgment seat of the Judge; and here the light was so bright, and those who stood around were so radiant, that I cast myself upon the ground and did not dare to look up. Asked who and what I was I replied: "I am a Christian." But He who presided said: "Thou liest, thou art a follower of Cicero and not of Christ. For 'where thy treasure is, there will thy heart be also.'"[4] Instantly I became dumb, and amid the strokes of the lash—for He had ordered me to be scourged—I was tortured more severely still by the fire of conscience, considering with myself that verse, "In the grave who shall give thee thanks?"[5] Yet for all that I began to cry and to bewail myself, saying: "Have mercy upon me, O Lord: have mercy upon me." Amid the sound of the scourges this cry still made itself heard. At last the bystanders, falling

---

[1] Cur mens diversa sit. The ordinary text has " menda."
[2] I Cor. vii. 9.   [3] I Cor. xv. 33.   [4] I Tim. v. 11, 12.
[5] Persius i. 104.   [6] 2 Cor. vi. 14, 15.
[7] Viz., the epistles of St. Paul. In like manner the Psalter was often called David.   [8] I Cor. viii. 10.

[1] Tit. i. 15.   [2] I Tim. iv. 4.   [3] I Cor. x. 21.
[4] Matt. vi. 21.   [5] Ps. vi. 5.

down before the knees of Him who presided, prayed that He would have pity on my youth, and that He would give me space to repent of my error. He might still, they urged, inflict torture on me, should I ever again read the works of the Gentiles. Under the stress of that awful moment I should have been ready to make even still larger promises than these. Accordingly I made oath and called upon His name, saying: "Lord, if ever again I possess worldly books, or if ever again I read such, I have denied Thee." Dismissed, then, on taking this oath, I returned to the upper world, and, to the surprise of all, I opened upon them eyes so drenched with tears that my distress served to convince even the incredulous. And that this was no sleep nor idle dream, such as those by which we are often mocked, I call to witness the tribunal before which I lay, and the terrible judgment which I feared. May it never, hereafter, be my lot to fall under such an inquisition! I profess that my shoulders were black and blue, that I felt the bruises long after I awoke from my sleep, and that thenceforth I read the books of God with a zeal greater than I had previously given to the books of men.

31. You must also avoid the sin of covetousness, and this not merely by refusing to seize upon what belongs to others, for that is punished by the laws of the state, but also by not keeping your own property, which has now become no longer yours. "If ye have not been faithful," the Lord says, "in that which is another man's, who shall give you that which is your own?"[1] "That which is another man's" is a quantity of gold or of silver, while "that which is our own" is the spiritual heritage of which it is elsewhere said: "The ransom of a man's life is his riches."[2] "No man can serve two masters, for either he will hate the one and love the other; or else he will hold to the one and despise the other. Ye cannot serve God and Mammon."[3] Riches, that is; for in the heathen tongue of the Syrians riches are called mammon. The "thorns" which choke our faith[4] are the taking thought for our life.[5] Care for the things which the Gentiles seek after[6] is the root of covetousness. But you will say: "I am a girl delicately reared, and I cannot labor with my hands. Suppose that I live to old age and then fall sick, who will take pity on me?" Hear Jesus speaking to the apostles: "Take no thought what ye shall eat; nor yet for your

body what ye shall put on. Is not the life more than meat, and the body than raiment? Behold the fowls of the air: for they sow not, neither do they reap nor gather into barns; yet your heavenly Father feedeth them."[1] Should clothing fail you, set the lilies before your eyes. Should hunger seize you, think of the words in which the poor and hungry are blessed. Should pain afflict you, read "Therefore I take pleasure in infirmities," and "There was given to me a thorn in the flesh, the messenger of Satan to buffet me, lest I should be exalted above measure."[2] Rejoice in all God's judgments; for does not the psalmist say: "The daughters of Judah rejoiced because of thy judgments, O Lord"?[3] Let the words be ever on your lips: "Naked came I out of my mother's womb, and naked shall I return thither;"[4] and "We brought nothing into this world, and it is certain we can carry nothing out."[5]

32. To-day you may see women cramming their wardrobes with dresses, changing their gowns from day to day, and for all that unable to vanquish the moths. Now and then one more scrupulous wears out a single dress; yet, while she appears in rags, her boxes are full. Parchments are dyed purple, gold is melted into lettering, manuscripts are decked with jewels, while Christ lies at the door naked and dying. When they hold out a hand to the needy they sound a trumpet;[6] when they invite to a love-feast[7] they engage a crier. I lately saw the noblest lady in Rome—I suppress her name, for I am no satirist—with a band of eunuchs before her in the basilica of the blessed Peter. She was giving money to the poor, a coin apiece; and this with her own hand, that she might be accounted more religious. Hereupon a by no means uncommon incident occurred. An old woman, "full of years and rags,"[8] ran forward to get a second coin, but when her turn came she received not a penny but a blow hard enough to draw blood from her guilty veins.

"The love of money is the root of all evil,"[9] and the apostle speaks of covetousness as being idolatry.[10] "Seek ye first the kingdom of God and all these things shall be added unto you."[11] The Lord will never allow a righteous soul to perish of hunger.

---

[1] Luke xvi. 12.   [2] Prov. xiii. 8, R.V.   [3] Matt. vi. 24.
[4] Matt. xiii. 7, 22.   [5] Matt. vi. 25.   [6] Matt. vi. 32.

[1] Matt. vi. 25, 26.   [2] 2 Cor. xii. 10, 7.   [3] Ps. xcvii. 8.
[4] Job i. 21.   [5] 1 Tim. vi. 7.   [6] Matt. vi. 2.   [8]Terence, Eun. 236.
[7] "The eucharist was at first preceded, but at a later date was more usually followed, by the *agape* or love-feast. The materials of this were contributed by the members of the congregation, of whatever station sat down to it as equals, and the meal was concluded with psalmody and prayer." (Robertson, C. H., i. p. 235.) Scandals arose in connection with the practice, and it gradually fell into disuse, though even at a later date allusions to it are not infrequent.   [9] 1 Tim. vi. 10.   [10] Col. iii. 5.   [11] Matt. vi. 33.

"I have been young," the psalmist says, "and now am old, yet have I not seen the righteous forsaken nor his seed begging bread."[1] Elijah is fed by ministering ravens.[2] The widow of Zarephath, who with her sons expected to die the same night, went without food herself that she might feed the prophet. He who had come to be fed then turned feeder, for, by a miracle, he filled the empty barrel.[3] The apostle Peter says: "Silver and gold have I none, but such as I have give I thee. In the name of Jesus Christ rise up and walk."[4] But now many, while they do not say it in words, by their deeds declare: "Faith and pity have I none; but such as I have, silver and gold, these I will not give thee." "Having food and raiment let us be therewith content."[5] Hear the prayer of Jacob: "If God will be with me and will keep me in this way that I go, and will give me bread to eat and raiment to put on, then shall the Lord be my God."[6] He prayed only for things necessary; yet, twenty years afterwards, he returned to the land of Canaan rich in substance and richer still in children.[7] Numberless are the instances in Scripture which teach men to "Beware of covetousness."[8]

33. As I have been led to touch on the subject—it shall have a treatise to itself if Christ permit—I will relate what took place not very many years ago at Nitria. A brother, more thrifty than covetous, and ignorant that the Lord had been sold for thirty pieces of silver,[9] left behind him at his death a hundred pieces of money which he had earned by weaving linen. As there were about five thousand monks in the neighborhood, living in as many separate cells, a council was held as to what should be done. Some said that the coins should be distributed among the poor; others that they should be given to the church, while others were for sending them back to the relatives of the deceased. However, Macarius, Pambo, Isidore and the rest of those called fathers, speaking by the Spirit, decided that they should be interred with their owner, with the words: "Thy money perish with thee."[10] Nor was this too harsh a decision; for so great fear has fallen upon all throughout Egypt, that it is now a crime to leave after one a single shilling.

34. As I have mentioned the monks, and know that you like to hear about holy things, lend an ear to me for a few moments.

There are in Egypt three classes of monks. First, there are the cœnobites,[1] called in their Gentile language Sauses,[2] or, as we should say, men living in a community.[3] Secondly, there are the anchorites,[4] who live in the desert, each man by himself, and are so called because they have withdrawn from human society. Thirdly, there is the class called Remoboth,[5] a very inferior and little regarded type, peculiar to my own province,[6] or, at least, originating there. These live together in twos and threes, but seldom in larger numbers, and are bound by no rule; but do exactly as they choose. A portion of their earnings they contribute to a common fund, out of which food is provided for all. In most cases they reside in cities and strongholds; and, as though it were their workmanship which is holy, and not their life, all that they sell is extremely dear. They often quarrel because they are unwilling, while supplying their own food, to be subordinate to others. It is true that they compete with each other in fasting; they make what should be a private concern an occasion for a triumph. In everything they study effect: their sleeves are loose, their boots bulge, their garb is of the coarsest. They are always sighing, or visiting virgins, or sneering at the clergy; yet when a holiday comes, they make themselves sick—they eat so much.

35. Having then rid ourselves of these as of so many plagues, let us come to that more numerous class who live together, and who are, as we have said, called Cœnobites. Among these the first principle of union is to obey superiors and to do whatever they command. They are divided into bodies of ten and of a hundred, so that each tenth man has authority over nine others, while the hundredth has ten of these officers under him. They live apart from each other, in separate cells. According to their rule, no monk may visit another before the ninth hour;[7] except the deans[8] above mentioned, whose office is to comfort, with soothing words, those whose thoughts disquiet them. After the ninth hour they meet together to sing psalms and read the Scriptures according to usage. Then when the prayers have ended and all have sat down, one called the

---

[1] Ps. xxxvii. 25.   [2] 1 Kings xvii. 4, 6.
[3] 1 Kings xvii. 9-16.   [4] Acts iii. 6.   [5] 1 Tim. vi. 8.
[6] Gen. xxviii. 20, 21.   [7] Gen. xxxii. 5, 10.   [8] Luke xii. 15.
[9] Matt. xxvi. 15.   [10] Acts viii. 20.

[1] From κοινὸς βίος (koinos bios), a common life.
[2] Apparently an Egyptian word. It does not occur elsewhere.
[3] In commune viventes.
[4] From ἀναχωρεῖν (anachorein), to withdraw.
[5] These were monks who lived under no settled rule, but collected in little groups of two and three, generally in some populous place. They seem to have practised all the arts whereby a reputation for sanctity may be won, while they disparaged those who led more regular lives. Cassian (Collat. xviii. 7) draws an unfavorable picture of them. See Bingham, Antiquities, vii. ii. 4, and Dict. Xt. Ant., s. v. Sarabaitæ.   [6] Pannonia.
[7] I.e. three o'clock.   [8] Decani, "leaders of ten."

father stands up among them and begins to expound the portion of the day. While he is speaking the silence is profound; no man ventures to look at his neighbor or to clear his throat. The speaker's praise is in the weeping of his hearers.[1] Silent tears roll down their cheeks, but not a sob escapes from their lips. Yet when he begins to speak of Christ's kingdom, and of future bliss, and of the glory which is to come, every one may be noticed saying to himself, with a gentle sigh and uplifted eyes: "Oh, that I had wings like a dove! For then would I fly away and be at rest."[2] After this the meeting breaks up and each company of ten goes with its father to its own table. This they take in turns to serve, each for a week at a time. No noise is made over the food; no one talks while eating. Bread, pulse and greens form their fare, and the only seasoning that they use is salt. Wine is given only to the old, who with the children often have a special meal prepared for them to repair the ravages of age and to save the young from premature decay. When the meal is over they all rise together, and, after singing a hymn, return to their dwellings. There each one talks till evening with his comrade thus: "Have you noticed so-and-so? What grace he has! How silent he is! How soberly he walks!" If any one is weak they comfort him; or if he is fervent in love to God, they encourage him to fresh earnestness. And because at night, besides the public prayers, each man keeps vigil in his own chamber, they go round all the cells one by one, and putting their ears to the doors, carefully ascertain what their occupants are doing. If they find a monk slothful, they do not scold him; but, dissembling what they know, they visit him more frequently, and at first exhort rather than compel him to pray more. Each day has its allotted task, and this being given in to the dean, is by him brought to the steward. This latter, once a month, gives a scrupulous account to their common father. He also tastes the dishes when they are cooked, and, as no one is allowed to say, "I am without a tunic or a cloak or a couch of rushes," he so arranges that no one need ask for or go without what he wants. In case a monk falls ill, he is moved to a more spacious chamber, and there so attentively nursed by the old men, that he misses neither the luxury of cities nor a mother's kindness. Every Lord's day they spend their whole time in prayer and reading; in-

deed, when they have finished their tasks, these are their usual occupations. Every day they learn by heart a portion of Scripture. They keep the same fasts all the year round, but in Lent they are allowed to live more strictly. After Whitsuntide they exchange their evening meal for a midday one; both to satisfy the tradition of the church and to avoid overloading their stomachs with a double supply of food. A similar description is given of the Essenes by Philo,[1] Plato's imitator; also by Josephus,[2] the Greek Livy, in his narrative of the Jewish captivity.

36. As my present subject is virgins, I have said rather too much about monks. I will pass on, therefore, to the third class, called anchorites, who go from the monasteries into the deserts, with nothing but bread and salt. Paul[3] introduced this way of life; Antony made it famous, and—to go farther back still—John the Baptist set the first example of it. The prophet Jeremiah describes one such in the words: "It is good for a man that he bear the yoke in his youth. He sitteth alone and keepeth silence, because he hath borne it upon him. He giveth his cheek to him that smiteth him, he is filled full with reproach. For the Lord will not cast off forever."[4] The struggle of the anchorites and their life—in the flesh, yet not of the flesh—I will, if you wish, explain to you at some other time. I must now return to the subject of covetousness, which I left to speak of the monks. With them before your eyes you will despise, not only gold and silver in general, but earth itself and heaven. United to Christ, you will sing, "The Lord is my portion."[5]

37. Farther, although the apostle bids us to "pray without ceasing,"[6] and although to the saints their very sleep is a supplication, we ought to have fixed hours of prayer, that if we are detained by work, the time may remind us of our duty. Prayers, as every one knows, ought to be said at the third, sixth and ninth hours, at dawn and at evening.[7] No meal should be begun without prayer, and before leaving table thanks should be returned to the Creator. We should rise two or three times in the night, and go over the parts of Scripture which we know by heart. When we leave the roof which shelters us, prayer should be our armor; and

---

[1] Cf. Letter LII. § 8. [2] Ps. lv. 6.

[1] See Letter LXX. § 3, De Vir. LII. xi.
[2] Josephus, The Jewish War, ii. 8. [3] I.e. the hermit of that name. See his Life in vol. iii. of this series.
[4] Lam. iii. 27, 28, 30, 31. [5] Lam. iii. 24. [6] 1 Thess. v. 17
[7] In Jerome's time the seven canonical hours of prayer had not yet been finally fixed. He mentions, however, six which correspond to the later, Mattins, Terce, Sext, None, Vespers, and Nocturns. Cp. Letters CVII. § 9, CVIII. § 20, and CXXX. § 15.

when we return from the street we should pray before we sit down, and not give the frail body rest until the soul is fed. In every act we do, in every step we take, let our hand trace the Lord's cross. Speak against nobody, and do not slander your mother's son.[1] "Who art thou that judgest the servant of another? To his own lord he standeth or falleth; yea, he shall be made to stand, for the Lord hath power to make him stand."[2] If you have fasted two or three days, do not think yourself better than others who do not fast. You fast and are angry; another eats and wears a smiling face. You work off your irritation and hunger in quarrels. He uses food in moderation and gives God thanks.[3] Daily Isaiah cries: "Is it such a fast that I have chosen, saith the Lord?"[4] and again: "In the day of your fast ye find your own pleasure, and oppress all your laborers. Behold ye fast for strife and contention, and to smite with the fist of wickedness. How fast ye unto me?"[5] What kind of fast can his be whose wrath is such that not only does the night go down upon it, but that even the moon's changes leave it unchanged?

38. Look to yourself and glory in your own success and not in others' failure. Some women care for the flesh and reckon up their income and daily expenditure: such are no fit models for you. Judas was a traitor, but the eleven apostles did not waver. Phygellus and Alexander made shipwreck; but the rest continued to run the race of faith.[6] Say not: "So-and-so enjoys her own property, she is honored of men, her brothers and sisters come to see her. Has she then ceased to be a virgin?" In the first place, it is doubtful if she is a virgin. For "the Lord seeth not as man seeth; for man looketh upon the outward appearance, but the Lord looketh on the heart."[7] Again, she may be a virgin in body and not in spirit. According to the apostle, a true virgin is "holy both in body and in spirit."[8] Lastly, let her glory in her own way. Let her override Paul's opinion and live in the enjoyment of her good things But you and I must follow better examples.

Set before you the blessed Mary, whose surpassing purity made her meet to be the mother of the Lord. When the angel Gabriel came down to her, in the form of a man, and said: "Hail, thou that art highly favored; the Lord is with thee,"[9] she was terror-stricken and unable to reply, for she had never been saluted by a man before. But, on learning who he was, she spoke, and one who had been afraid of a man conversed fearlessly with an angel. Now you, too, may be the Lord's mother. "Take thee a great roll and write in it with a man's pen Maher-shalal-hash-baz."[1] And when you have gone to the prophetess, and have conceived in the womb, and have brought forth a son,[2] say: "Lord, we have been with child by thy fear, we have been in pain, we have brought forth the spirit of thy salvation, which we have wrought upon the earth."[3] Then shall your Son reply: "Behold my mother and my brethren."[4] And He whose name you have so recently inscribed upon the table of your heart, and have written with a pen upon its renewed surface[5]—He, after He has recovered the spoil from the enemy, and has spoiled principalities and powers, nailing them to His cross[6]—having been miraculously conceived, grows up to manhood; and, as He becomes older, regards you no longer as His mother, but as His bride. To be as the martyrs, or as the apostles, or as Christ, involves a hard struggle, but brings with it a great reward.

All such efforts are only of use when they are made within the church's pale;[7] we must celebrate the passover in the one house,[8] we must enter the ark with Noah,[9] we must take refuge from the fall of Jericho with the justified harlot, Rahab.[10] Such virgins as there are said to be among the heretics and among the followers of the infamous Manes[11] must be considered, not virgins, but prostitutes. For if—as they allege—the devil is the author of the body, how can they honor that which is fashioned by their foe? No; it is because they know that the name virgin brings glory with it, that they go about as wolves in sheep's clothing.[12] As antichrist pretends to be Christ, such virgins assume an honorable name, that they may the better cloak a discreditable life. Rejoice, my sister; rejoice, my daughter; rejoice, my virgin; for you have resolved to be, in reality, that which others insincerely feign.

---

[1] Ps. l. 20. [2] Rom. xiv. 4, R.V. [3] Rom. xiv. 6, R.V.
[4] Isa. lviii. 5. [5] Isaiah lviii. 3, 4, R.V. marg.
[6] 1 Tim. i. 19, 20; 2 Tim. i. 15. [7] 1 Sam. xvi. 7.
[8] 1 Cor. vii. 34. [9] Luke i. 28.

[1] Isa. viii. 1, i.e. "the spoil speedeth, the prey hasteth;" or, in Jerome's rendering, "quickly carry away the spoils."
[2] Isa. viii. 3. Jerome should have substituted "prophet" for "prophetess." As it stands the quotation is meaningless.
[3] Isa. xxvi. 18, Vulg. [4] Matt. xii. 49.
[5] Prov. vii. 3; Jer. xxxi. 33. [6] Col. ii. 14, 15.
[7] Cp. the maxim of Cyprian: Extra ecclesiam nulla salus, "Outside the church there is no salvation."
[8] Exod. xii. 46. [9] 1 Peter iii. 20, 21. [10] James ii. 25.
[11] Founder of the widely prevalent sect of Manichæans, which at one time numbered Augustine among its adherents. One of its leading tenets was that matter as such was essentially evil.
[12] Matt. vii. 15.

39. The things that I have here set forth will seem hard to her who loves not Christ. But one who has come to regard all the splendor of the world as off-scourings, and to hold all things under the sun as vain, that he may win Christ;[1] one who has died with his Lord and risen again, and has crucified the flesh with its affections and lusts;[2] he will boldly cry out: "Who shall separate us from the love of Christ? Shall tribulation, or distress, or persecution, or famine, or nakedness, or peril, or sword?" and again: "I am persuaded that neither death nor life, nor angels, nor principalities nor powers, nor things present, nor things to come, nor height, nor depth, nor any other creature shall be able to separate us from the love of God which is in Christ Jesus, our Lord."[3]

For our salvation the Son of God is made the Son of Man.[4] Nine months He awaits His birth in the womb, undergoes the most revolting conditions,[5] and comes forth covered with blood, to be swathed in rags and covered with caresses. He who shuts up the world in His fist[6] is contained in the narrow limits of a manger. I say nothing of the thirty years during which he lives in obscurity, satisfied with the poverty of his parents.[7] When He is scourged He holds His peace; when He is crucified, He prays for His crucifiers. "What shall I render unto the Lord for all His benefits towards me? I will take the cup of salvation and call upon the name of the Lord. Precious in the sight of the Lord is the death of His saints."[8] The only fitting return that we can make to Him is to give blood for blood; and, as we are redeemed by the blood of Christ, gladly to lay down our lives for our Redeemer. What saint has ever won his crown without first contending for it? Righteous Abel is murdered. Abraham is in danger of losing his wife. And, as I must not enlarge my book unduly, seek for yourself: you will find that all holy men have suffered adversity. Solomon alone lived in luxury and perhaps it was for this reason that he fell. For "whom the Lord loveth, He chasteneth, and scourgeth every son whom He receiveth."[9] Which is best—for a short time to do battle, to carry stakes for the palisades, to bear arms, to faint under heavy bucklers, that ever afterwards we may rejoice as victors? or to become slaves forever, just because we cannot endure for a single hour?[10]

40. Love finds nothing hard; no task is difficult to the eager. Think of all that Jacob bore for Rachel, the wife who had been promised to him. "Jacob," the Scripture says, "served seven years for Rachel. And they seemed unto him but a few days for the love he had to her."[1] Afterwards he himself tells us what he had to undergo. "In the day the drought consumed me and the frost by night."[2] So we must love Christ and always seek His embraces. Then everything difficult will seem easy; all things long we shall account short; and smitten with His arrows,[3] we shall say every moment: "Woe is me that I have prolonged my pilgrimage."[4] For "the sufferings of this present time are not worthy to be compared with the glory which shall be revealed in us."[5] For "tribulation worketh patience, and patience experience, and experience hope; and hope maketh not ashamed."[6] When your lot seems hard to bear read Paul's second epistle to the Corinthians: "In labors more abundant; in stripes above measure; in prisons more frequent; in deaths oft. Of the Jews five times received I forty stripes save one; thrice was I beaten with rods; once was I stoned; thrice I suffered shipwreck; a night and a day I have been in the deep; in journeyings often, in perils of waters, in perils of robbers, in perils by mine own countrymen, in perils by the heathen, in perils in the city, in perils in the wilderness, in perils in the sea, in perils among false brethren, in weariness and painfulness, in watchings often, in hunger and thirst, in fastings often, in cold and nakedness."[7] Which of us can claim the veriest fraction of the virtues here enumerated? Yet it was these which afterwards made him bold to say: "I have finished my course, I have kept the faith. Henceforth there is laid up for me a crown of righteousness which the Lord, the righteous Judge, shall give me at that day."[8]

But we, if our food is less appetizing than usual, get sullen, and fancy that we do God a favor by drinking watered wine. And if the water brought to us is a trifle too warm, we break the cup and overturn the table and scourge the servant in fault until blood comes. "The kingdom of heaven suffereth violence and the violent take it by force."[9] Still, unless you use force you will never seize the kingdom of heaven. Unless you knock importunately you will never receive the sacramental bread.[10] Is it not truly violence,

---

[1] Phil. iii. 8.   [2] Rom. vi. 4; Gal. v. 24.
[3] Rom. viii. 35, 38, 39.   [4] An echo of the Nicene Creed.
[5] Cp. Virgil, Ecl. iv. 61.   [6] Cp. Ps. xcv. 4, 5; Isa. xl. 12.
[7] Luke ii. 51, 52.   [8] Ps. cxvi. 12, 13, 15.
[9] Heb. xii. 6.   [10] Cp. Matt. xxvi. 40.

[1] Gen. xxix. 20.   [2] Gen. xxxi. 40.
[3] Ps. xxxviii. 2.   [4] Ps. cxx. 5, Vulg.
[5] Rom. viii. 18.   [6] Rom. v. 3-5.   [7] 2 Cor. xi. 23-27.
[8] 2 Tim. iv. 7, 8.   [9] Matt. xi. 12.   [10] Luke xi. 5-8.

think you, when the flesh desires to be as God and ascends to the place whence angels have fallen [1] to judge angels?

41. Emerge, I pray you, for a while from your prison-house, and paint before your eyes the reward of your present toil, a reward which "eye hath not seen, nor ear heard, neither hath it entered into the heart of man." [2] What will be the glory of that day when Mary, the mother of the Lord, shall come to meet you, accompanied by her virgin choirs! When, the Red Sea past and Pharaoh drowned with his host, Miriam, Aaron's sister, her timbrel in her hand, shall chant to the answering women: "Sing ye unto the Lord, for he hath triumphed gloriously; the horse and his rider hath he thrown into the sea." [3] Then shall Thecla [4] fly with joy to embrace you. Then shall your Spouse himself come forward and say: "Rise up, my love, my fair one, and come away, for lo! the winter is past, the rain is over and gone." [5] Then shall the angels say with wonder: "Who is she that looketh forth as the morning, fair as the moon, clear as the sun?" [6] "The daughters shall see you and bless you; yea, the queens shall proclaim and the concubines shall praise you." [7] And, after these, yet another company of chaste women will meet you. Sarah will come with the wedded; Anna, the daughter of Phanuel, with the widows. In the one band you will find your natural mother and in the other your spiritual. [8] The one will rejoice in having borne, the other will exult in having taught you. Then truly will the Lord ride upon his ass, [9] and thus enter the heavenly Jerusalem. Then the little ones (of whom, in Isaiah, the Saviour says: "Behold, I and the children whom the Lord hath given me" [10]) shall lift up palms of victory and shall sing with one voice: "Hosanna in the highest, blessed is he that cometh in the name of the Lord, hosanna in the highest." [11] Then shall the "hundred and forty and four thousand" hold their harps before the throne and before the elders and shall sing the new song. And no man shall have power to learn that song save those for whom it is appointed. "These are they which were not defiled with women; for they are virgins. These are they which follow the Lamb whithersoever he goeth." [12] As often as this life's idle show tries to charm you; as often as you see in the world some vain

pomp, transport yourself in mind to Paradise, essay to be now what you will be hereafter, and you will hear your Spouse say: "Set me as a sunshade in thine heart and as a seal upon thine arm." [1] And then, strengthened in body as well as in mind, you, too, will cry aloud and say: "Many waters cannot quench love, neither can the floods drown it." [2]

LETTER XXIII.

TO MARCELLA.

Jerome writes to Marcella to console her for the loss of a friend who, like herself, was the head of a religious society at Rome. The news of Lea's death had first reached Marcella when she was engaged with Jerome in the study of the 73d psalm. Later in the day he writes this letter in which, after extolling Lea, he contrasts her end with that of the consul-elect, Vettius Agorius Prætextatus, a man of great ability and integrity, whom he declares to be now "in Tartarus." Written at Rome in 384 A.D.

1. To-day, about the third hour, just as I was beginning to read with you the seventy-second psalm [3]—the first, that is, of the third book—and to explain that its title belonged partly to the second book and partly to the third—the previous book, I mean, concluding with the words "the prayers of David the son of Jesse are ended," [4] and the next commencing with the words "a psalm of Asaph" [5]—and just as I had come on the passage in which the righteous man declares: "If I say, I will speak thus; behold I should offend against the generation of thy children," [6] a verse which is differently rendered in our Latin version: [7]—suddenly the news came that our most saintly friend Lea had departed from the body. As was only natural, you turned deadly pale; for there are few persons, if any, who do not burst into tears when the earthen vessel breaks. [8] But if you wept it was not from doubt as to her future lot, but only because you had not rendered to her the last sad offices which are due to the dead. Finally, as we were still conversing together, a second message informed us that her remains had been already conveyed to Ostia.

2. You may ask what is the use of repeating all this. I will reply in the apostle's words, "much every way." [9] First, it shows that all must hail with joy the release of a soul which has trampled Satan under foot, and won for itself, at last, a crown of

---

[1] Is. xiv. 12, 13.   [2] 1 Cor. ii. 9.   [3] Ex. xv. 20, 21.
[4] A legendary virgin of Iconium said to have been converted by Paul.   [5] Cant. ii. 10, 11.   [6] Cant. vi. 10.   [7] Cant. vi. 9.
[8] Viz. Paula, for whom see Letter CVIII., and Marcella, for whom see Letter CXXVII.
[9] Matt. xxi. 1–9, literally "she-ass."
[10] Isa. viii. 18.   [11] Matt. xxi. 9.   [12] Rev. xiv. 1–4.

[1] Cant. viii. 6; the variant is peculiar to Jerome.
[2] Cant. viii. 7.   [3] In the English Version Ps. lxxiii.
[4] Ps. lxxii. 20.   [5] Ps. lxxiii. title.   [6] Ps. lxxiii. 15.
[7] I.e. the Old Latin Version superseded by Jerome's Vulgate.
[8] 2 Cor. iv. 7.
[9] Rom. iii. 2.

tranquillity. Secondly, it gives me an opportunity of briefly describing her life. Thirdly, it enables me to assure you that the consul-elect,[1] that detractor of his age,[2] is now in Tartarus.[3]

Who can sufficiently eulogize our dear Lea's mode of living? So complete was her conversion to the Lord that, becoming the head of a monastery, she showed herself a true mother[4] to the virgins in it, wore coarse sack-cloth instead of soft raiment, passed sleep-less nights in prayer, and instructed her companions even more by example than by precept. So great was her humility that she, who had once been the mistress of many, was accounted the servant of all; and certainly, the less she was reckoned an earthly mistress the more she became a servant of Christ. She was careless of her dress, neglected her hair, and ate only the coarsest food. Still, in all that she did, she avoided ostentation that she might not have her reward in this world.[5]

3. Now, therefore, in return for her short toil, Lea enjoys everlasting felicity; she is welcomed into the choirs of the angels; she is comforted in Abraham's bosom. And, as once the beggar Lazarus saw the rich man, for all his purple, lying in torment, so does Lea see the consul, not now in his triumphal robe but clothed in mourning, and asking for a drop of water from her little finger.[6] How great a change have we here! A few days ago the highest dignitaries of the city walked before him as he ascended the ramparts of the capitol like a general celebrating a tri-umph; the Roman people leapt up to welcome and applaud him, and at the news of his death the whole city was moved. Now he is desolate and naked, a prisoner in the foulest darkness, and not, as his unhappy wife[7] falsely asserts, set in the royal abode of the milky way.[8] On the other hand Lea, who was al-ways shut up in her one closet, who seemed poor and of little worth, and whose life was accounted madness,[9] now follows Christ and sings, "Like as we have heard, so have we seen in the city of our God."[10]

4. And now for the moral of all this, which, with tears and groans, I conjure you to re-member. While we run the way of this world, we must not clothe ourselves with two coats, that is, with a twofold faith, or burthen our-selves with leathern shoes, that is, with dead works; we must not allow scrips filled with money to weigh us down, or lean upon the staff of worldly power.[1] We must not seek to possess both Christ and the world. No; things eternal must take the place of things transitory;[2] and since, physically speaking, we daily anticipate death, if we wish for im-mortality we must realize that we are but mortal.

LETTER XXIV.

TO MARCELLA.

Concerning the virgin Asella. Dedicated to God before her birth, Marcella's sister had been made a church-virgin at the age of ten. From that time she had lived a life of the severest asceticism, first as a member and then as the head of Marcella's com-munity upon the Aventine. Jerome, who subse-quently wrote her a letter (XLV.) on his departure from Rome, now holds her up as a model to be ad-mired and imitated. Written at Rome A.D. 384.

1. Let no one blame my letters for the eu-logies and censures which are contained in them. To arraign sinners is to admonish those in like case, and to praise the virtuous is to quicken the zeal of those who wish to do right. The day before yesterday I spoke to you concerning Lea of blessed memory,[3] and I had hardly done so, when I was pricked in my conscience. It would be wrong for me, I thought, to ignore a virgin after speaking of one who, as a widow, held a lower place. Accordingly, in my present letter, I mean to give you a brief sketch of the life of our dear Asella. Please do not read it to her; for she is sure to be displeased with eulogies of which she is herself the object. Show it rather to the young girls of your acquaint-ance, that they may guide themselves by her example, and may take her behavior as the pattern of a perfect life.

2. I pass over the facts that, before her birth, she was blessed while still in her mother's womb, and that, virgin-like, she was delivered to her father in a dream in a bowl of shining glass brighter than a mirror. And I say nothing of her consecration to the blessed life of virginity, a ceremony which took place when she was hardly more than ten years old, a mere babe still wrapped in swad-dling clothes. For all that comes before works should be counted of grace;[4] although, doubt-less, God foreknew the future when He sanc-

---

[1] One of the most distinguished men of his day, Prætextatus, had filled the high position of Prefect of Rome. As such he ironically assured Damasus that, if he could hope to obtain the papacy, he would immediately embrace the Christian religion (Jerome, "Against John of Jerusalem," § 8).
[2] De suis sæculis detrahentem. The text is clearly corrupt, and no satisfactory emendation has yet been suggested.
[3] So the author of II. Peter speaks of God "*tartarizing* the angels that sinned " (ii. 4).
[4] *I.e.* her conduct justified her official title.   [5] Cf. Matt. vi. 2.
[6] Luke xvi. 19–24.   [7] Paulina, chief priestess of Ceres.
[8] In the Roman mythology the abode of gods and heroes. Cf. Ovid, M. i. 175, 176.   [9] Wisd. v. 4.   [10] Ps. xlviii. 8.

[1] Matt. x. 10.   [2] 2 Cor. iv. 18.
[3] *Vide* the preceding Letter.   [4] Rom. xi. 6.

tified Jeremiah as yet unborn,[1] when He made John to leap in his mother's womb,[2] and when, before the foundation of the world, He set apart Paul to preach the gospel of His son.[3]

3. I come now to the life which after her twelfth year she, by her own exertion, chose, laid hold of, held fast to, entered upon, and fulfilled. Shut up in her narrow cell she roamed through paradise. Fasting was her recreation and hunger her refreshment. If she took food it was not from love of eating, but because of bodily exhaustion; and the bread and salt and cold water to which she restricted herself sharpened her appetite more than they appeased it.

But I have almost forgotten to mention that of which I should have spoken first. When her resolution was still fresh she took her gold necklace made in the lamprey pattern (so called because bars of metal are linked together so as to form a flexible chain), and sold it without her parents' knowledge. Then putting on a dark dress such as her mother had never been willing that she should wear, she concluded her pious enterprise by consecrating herself forthwith to the Lord. She thus showed her relatives that they need hope to wring no farther concessions from one who, by her very dress, had condemned the world.

4. To go on with my story, her ways were quiet and she lived in great privacy. In fact, she rarely went abroad or spoke to a man. More wonderful still, much as she loved her virgin sister,[4] she did not care to see her. She worked with her own hands, for she knew that it was written: "If any will not work neither shall he eat."[5] To the Bridegroom she spoke constantly in prayer and psalmody. She hurried to the martyrs' shrines unnoticed. Such visits gave her pleasure, and the more so because she was never recognized. All the year round she observed a continual fast, remaining without food for two or three days at a time; but when Lent came she hoisted— if I may so speak—every stitch of canvas and fasted well-nigh from week's end to week's end with "a cheerful countenance."[6] What would perhaps be incredible, were it not that "with God all things are possible,"[7] is that she lived this life until her fiftieth year without weakening her digestion or bringing on herself the pain of colic. Lying on the dry ground did not affect her limbs, and the rough sackcloth that she wore failed to make her skin either foul or rough. With a sound body and a still sounder soul[1] she sought all her delight in solitude, and found for herself a monkish hermitage in the centre of busy Rome.

5. You are better acquainted with all this than I am, and the few details that I have given I have learned from you. So intimate are you with Asella that you have seen, with your own eyes, her holy knees hardened like those of a camel from the frequency of her prayers. I merely set forth what I can glean from you. She is alike pleasant in her serious moods and serious in her pleasant ones: her manner, while winning, is always grave, and while grave is always winning. Her pale face indicates continence but does not betoken ostentation. Her speech is silent and her silence is speech. Her pace is neither too fast nor too slow. Her demeanor is always the same. She disregards refinement and is careless about her dress. When she does attend to it it is without attending. So entirely consistent has her life been that here in Rome, the centre of vain shows, wanton license, and idle pleasure, where to be humble is to be held spiritless, the good praise her conduct and the bad do not venture to impugn it. Let widows and virgins imitate her, let wedded wives make much of her, let sinful women fear her, and let bishops[2] look up to her.

LETTER XXV.

TO MARCELLA.

An explanation of the ten names given to God in the Hebrew Scriptures. 'The ten names are El, Elohim, Sabaôth, Eliôn, Asher yeheyeh (Ex. iii. 14), Adonai, Jah, the tetragram JHVH, and Shaddai. Written at Rome 384 A.D.

LETTER XXVI.

TO MARCELLA.

An explanation of certain Hebrew words which have been left untranslated in the versions. The words are Alleluia, Amen, Maran atha. Written at Rome 384 A.D.

LETTER XXVII.

TO MARCELLA.

In this letter Jerome defends himself against the charge of having altered the text of Scripture, and shows that he has merely brought the Latin Version of the N.T. into agreement with the Greek original. Written at Rome 384 A.D.

1. After I had written my former letter,[3] containing a few remarks on some Hebrew words, a report suddenly reached me that

---

1 Jer. i. 5.　　2 Luke i. 41.　　3 Eph. i. 4.
4 Probably Marcella before she was married.
5 2 Thess. iii. 10.　　6 Matt. vi. 17.　　7 Matt. xix. 26.

1 Cf. Juvenal, Sat. x. 356.　　2 Sacerdotes.　　3 XXVI.

certain contemptible creatures were deliberately assailing me with the charge that I had endeavored to correct passages in the gospels, against the authority of the ancients and the opinion of the whole world. Now, though I might—as far as strict right goes—treat these persons with contempt (it is idle to play the lyre for an ass[1]), yet, lest they should follow their usual habit and reproach me with superciliousness, let them take my answer as follows: I am not so dull-witted nor so coarsely ignorant (qualities which they take for holiness, calling themselves the disciples of fishermen as if men were made holy by knowing nothing)—I am not, I repeat, so ignorant as to suppose that any of the Lord's words is either in need of correction or is not divinely inspired; but the Latin manuscripts of the Scriptures are proved to be faulty by the variations which all of them exhibit, and my object has been to restore them to the form of the Greek original, from which my detractors do not deny that they have been translated. If they dislike water drawn from the clear spring, let them drink of the muddy streamlet, and when they come to read the Scriptures let them lay aside[2] the keen eye which they turn on woods frequented by game-birds and waters abounding in shellfish. Easily satisfied in this instance alone, let them, if they will, regard the words of Christ as rude sayings, albeit that over these so many great intellects have labored for so many ages rather to divine than to expound the meaning of each single word. Let them charge the great apostle with want of literary skill, although it is said of him that much learning made him mad.[3]

2. I know that as you read these words you will knit your brows, and fear that my freedom of speech is sowing the seeds of fresh quarrels; and that, if you could, you would gladly put your finger on my mouth to prevent me from even speaking of things which others do not blush to do. But, I ask you, wherein have I used too great license? Have I ever embellished my dinner plates with engravings of idols? Have I ever, at a Christian banquet, set before the eyes of virgins the polluting spectacle of Satyrs embracing bacchanals? or have I ever assailed any one in too bitter terms? Have I ever complained of beggars turned millionaires? Have I ever censured heirs for the funerals which they have given to their benefactors?[4] The one thing that I have unfortunately said has been

that virgins ought to live more in the company of women than of men,[1] and by this I have made the whole city look scandalized and caused every one to point at me the finger of scorn. "They that hate me without a cause are more than the hairs of mine head,"[2] and I am become "a proverb to them."[3] Do you suppose after this that I will now say anything rash?

3. But "when I set the wheel rolling I began to form a wine flagon; how comes it that a waterpot is the result?"[4] Lest Horace laugh at me I come back to my two-legged asses, and din into their ears, not the music of the lute, but the blare of the trumpet.[5] They may say if they will, "rejoicing in hope; serving *the time*," but we will say "rejoicing in hope; serving *the Lord*."[6] They may see fit to receive an accusation against a presbyter unconditionally; but we will say in the words of Scripture, "Against an elder[7] receive not an accusation, *but before two or three witnesses*. Them that sin rebuke before all."[8] They may choose to read, "It is *a man's* saying, and worthy of all acceptation;" we are content to err with the Greeks, that is to say with the apostle himself, who spoke Greek. Our version, therefore, is, it is "a *faithful* saying, and worthy of all acceptation."[9] Lastly, let them take as much pleasure as they please in their Gallican "geldings;"[10] we will be satisfied with the simple "ass" of Zechariah, loosed from its halter and made ready for the Saviour's service, which received the Lord on its back, and so fulfilled Isaiah's prediction: "Blessed is he that soweth beside all waters, where the ox and the ass tread under foot."[11]

LETTER XXVIII.
TO MARCELLA.

An explanation of the Hebrew word Selah. This word, rendered by the LXX. διάψαλμα and by Aquila ἀεί, was as much a crux in Jerome's day as it is in ours. "Some," he writes, "make it a 'change of metre,' others 'a pause for breath,' others 'the beginning of a new subject.' According to yet others it has something to do with rhythm or marks a burst of instrumental music." Jerome himself inclines to follow Aquila and Origen, who make the word mean "forever," and suggests that it betokens completion, like the "explicit" or "feliciter" in contemporary Latin MSS. Written at Rome A.D. 384.

---

1 'Όνῳ λύρα was a Greek proverb.
2 Reading *nec diligentiam* instead of *et*.
3 Acts xxvi. 24.   4 Hæreditarias sepulturas.

1 The reference is to Letter XXII.   2 Ps. lxix. 4.   3 Ps. lxix. 11.
4 Hor. A. P. 21, 22.   5 Perhaps an allusion to the Greek proverb, ὄνος λύρας ἤκουσε καὶ σάλπιγγος ὗς. "The ass listened to the lyre, and the pig to the trumpet."
6 Rom. xii. 11, 12.   The reading κυρίῳ "Lord" is probably correct. The R.V. says, "Some ancient authorities read the opportunity," (καιρῷ).
7 *I.e.* a "presbyter."   8 1 Tim. v. 19, 20.   9 1 Tim. i. 15.
10 Jerome's detractors suggested this word instead of the simpler "ass" in Zech. ix. 9 and Matt. xxi. 2–5. The phrase "Gallican geldings" appears to be a quotation from Plaut. Aul. iii. 5, 21.
11 Isa. xxxii. 20, LXX.

LETTER XXIX.

TO MARCELLA.

An explanation of the Hebrew words *Ephod bad* (1 Sam. ii. 18) and *Teraphim* (Judges xvii. 5). Written at Rome to Marcella, also at Rome A.D. 384.

LETTER XXX.

TO PAULA.

Some account of the so-called alphabetical psalms (XXXVII., CXI., CXII., CXIX., CXLV.). After explaining the mystical meaning of the alphabet, Jerome goes on thus: "What honey is sweeter than to know the wisdom of God? others, if they will, may possess riches, drink from a jewelled cup, shine in silks, and try in vain to exhaust their wealth in the most varied pleasures. Our riches are to meditate in the law of the Lord day and night,[1] to knock at the closed door,[2] to receive the 'three loaves' of the Trinity,[3] and, when the Lord goes before us, to walk upon the water of the world."[4] Written at Rome A.D. 384.

LETTER XXXI.

TO EUSTOCHIUM.

Jerome writes to thank Eustochium for some presents sent to him by her on the festival of St. Peter. He also moralizes on the mystical meaning of the articles sent. The letter should be compared with Letter XLIV., of which the theme is similar. Written at Rome in 384 A.D. (on St. Peter's Day).

1. Doves, bracelets, and a letter are outwardly but small gifts to receive from a virgin, but the action which has prompted them enhances their value. And since honey may not be offered in sacrifice to God,[5] you have shown skill in taking off their overmuch sweetness and making them pungent—if I may so say—with a dash of pepper. For nothing that is simply pleasurable or merely sweet can please God. Everything must have in it a sharp seasoning of truth. Christ's passover must be eaten with bitter herbs.[6]

2. It is true that a festival such as the birthday[7] of Saint Peter should be seasoned with more gladness than usual; still our merriment must not forget the limit set by Scripture, and we must not stray too far from the boundary of our wrestling-ground. Your presents, indeed, remind me of the sacred volume, for in it Ezekiel decks Jerusalem with bracelets,[8] Baruch receives letters from Jeremiah,[9] and the Holy Spirit descends in the form of a dove at the baptism of Christ.[10] But to give you, too, a sprinkling of pepper and to remind you of my former letter,[11] I send you to-day this three-fold warning. Cease not to adorn yourself with good works—the true bracelets of a Christian woman.[1] Rend not the letter written on your heart[2] as the profane king cut with his penknife that delivered to him by Baruch.[3] Let not Hosea say to you as to Ephraim, "Thou art like a silly dove."[4]

My words are too harsh, you will say, and hardly suitable to a festival like the present. If so, you have provoked me to it by the nature of your own gifts. So long as you put bitter with sweet, you must expect the same from me, sharp words that is, as well as praise.

3. However, I do not wish to make light of your gifts, least of all the basket of fine cherries, blushing with such a virgin modesty that I can fancy them freshly gathered by Lucullus[5] himself. For it was he who first introduced the fruit at Rome after his conquest of Pontus and Armenia; and the cherry tree is so called because he brought it from Cerasus. Now as the Scriptures do not mention cherries, but do speak of a basket of figs,[6] I will use these instead to point my moral. May you be made of fruits such as those which grow before God's temple and of which He says, "Behold they are good, very good."[7] The Saviour likes nothing that is half and half, and, while he welcomes the hot and does not shun the cold, he tells us in the Apocalypse that he will spew the lukewarm out of his mouth.[8] Wherefore we must be careful to celebrate our holy day not so much with abundance of food as with exultation of spirit. For it is altogether unreasonable to wish to honor a martyr by excess who himself, as you know, pleased God by fasting. When you take food always recollect that eating should be followed by reading, and also by prayer. And if, by taking this course, you displease some, repeat to yourself the words of the Apostle: "If I yet pleased men I should not be the servant of Christ"[9]

LETTER XXXII.

TO MARCELLA.

Jerome writes that he is busy collating Aquila's Greek version of the Old Testament with the Hebrew, inquires after Marcella's mother, and forwards the two preceding letters (XXX., XXXI.). Written at Rome in 384 A.D.

1. There are two reasons for the shortness of this letter, one that its bearer is impatient

---

[1] Ps. i. 2.   [2] Matt. vii. 7.   [3] Luke xi. 5–8.
[4] Matt. xiv. 25–33.   [5] Lev. ii. 11.   [6] Ex. xii. 8.
[7] *I.e.* the day of his martyrdom, his heavenly nativity.
[8] Ezek. xvi. 11.   [9] Jer. xxxvi.; Baruch vi.
[10] Matt. iii. 16.   [11] Letter XXII.

[1] Tim. ii. 10.   [2] 2 Cor. iii. 2.   [3] Jer. xxxvi. 23.   [4] Hos. vii. 11.
[5] Celebrated for his campaigns against Mithridates, and also as a prince of epicures.
[6] Jer. xxiv. 1–3.   [7] Jer. xxiv. 3.
[8] Rev. iii. 15, 16.   [9] Gal. i. 10.

to start, and the other that I am too busy to waste time on trifles. You ask what business can be so urgent as to stop me from a chat on paper. Let me tell you, then, that for some time past I have been comparing Aquila's version[1] of the Old Testament with the scrolls of the Hebrew, to see if from hatred to Christ the synagogue has changed the text; and—to speak frankly to a friend—I have found several variations which confirm our faith. After having exactly revised the prophets, Solomon,[2] the psalter, and the books of Kings, I am now engaged on Exodus (called by the Jews, from its opening words, Eleh shemôth[3]), and when I have finished this I shall go on to Leviticus. Now you see why I can let no claim for a letter withdraw me from my work. However, as I do not wish my friend Currentius[4] to run altogether in vain, I have tacked on to this little talk two letters[5] which I am sending to your sister Paula, and to her dear child Eustochium. Read these, and if you find them instructive or pleasant, take what I have said to them as meant for you also.

2. I hope that Albina, your mother and mine, is well. In bodily health, I mean, for I doubt not of her spiritual welfare. Pray salute her for me, and cherish her with double affection, both as a Christian and as a mother.

LETTER XXXIII.

TO PAULA.

A fragment of a letter in which Jerome institutes a comparison between the industry as writers of M. T. Varro and Origen. It is noteworthy as passing an unqualified eulogium upon Origen, which contrasts strongly with the tone adopted by the writer in subsequent years (see, *e.g.*, Letter LXXXIV.). Its date is probably 384 A.D.

1. Antiquity marvels at Marcus Terentius Varro,[6] because of the countless books which he wrote for Latin readers; and Greek writers are extravagant in their praise of their man of brass,[7] because he has written more works than one of us could so much as copy. But since Latin ears would find a list of Greek writings tiresome, I shall confine myself to the Latin Varro. I shall try to show that we of to-day are sleeping the sleep of Epimenides,[1] and devoting to the amassing of riches the energy which our predecessors gave to sound, if secular, learning.

2. Varro's writings include forty-five books of antiquities, four concerning the life of the Roman people.

* * * * * * *

3. But why, you ask me, have I thus mentioned Varro and the man of brass? Simply to bring to your notice our Christian man of brass, or, rather, man of adamant[2]—Origen, I mean—whose zeal for the study of Scripture has fairly earned for him this latter name. Would you learn what monuments of his genius he has left us? The following list exhibits them. His writings comprise thirteen books on Genesis, two books of Mystical Homilies, notes on Exodus, notes on Leviticus, * * * * also single books,[3] four books on First Principles, two books on the Resurrection, two dialogues on the same subject.[4]

* * * * * * *

4. So, you see, the labors of this one man have surpassed those of all previous writers, Greek and Latin. Who has ever managed to read all that he has written? Yet what reward have his exertions brought him? He stands condemned by his bishop, Demetrius,[5] only the bishops of Palestine, Arabia, Phenicia, and Achaia dissenting. Imperial Rome consents to his condemnation, and even convenes a senate to censure him,[6] not—as the rabid hounds who now pursue him cry—because of the novelty or heterodoxy of his doctrines, but because men could not tolerate the incomparable eloquence and knowledge which, when once he opened his lips, made others seem dumb.

5. I have written the above quickly and incautiously, by the light of a poor lantern. You will see why, if you think of those who to-day represent Epicurus and Aristippus.[7]

---

[1] This version, made in the reign of Hadrian by a Jewish proselyte who is said to have been a renegade Christian, was marked by an exaggerated literalism and a close following of the Hebrew original. By the Church it was regarded with suspicion as being designedly anti-Christian. Jerome, however, here acquits Aquila of the charge brought against him.
[2] *I.e.* all the sapiential books, viz. Proverbs, Ecclesiastes, Ecclesiasticus, Wisdom. אלה שמות, A.V., "these are the names."
[3] Exod. i. 1, אלה שמות, A.V., "these are the names."
[4] The name means *runner*. Hence the allusion to Gal. ii. 2.
[5] XXX., XXXI.
[6] Of the 490 books composed by this voluminous writer only two are extant, a treatise on husbandry and an essay on the Latin language.
[7] The epithet χαλκέντερος, "heart of brass," is applied by Suidas to the grammarian Didymus, who, according to Athenæus, wrote 3,500 books. Of these not one is extant.

[1] Which lasted 57 years.
[2] Ἀδαμάντιος—Origen is so called by Eusebius (H. E. vi. 14, 10). It appears to have been his proper name.
[3] "They may have been detached essays on particular subjects."—Westcott.
[4] All the works mentioned have perished except the treatise on First Principles, and this in its completeness is extant only in the Latin version of Rufinus. The version made by Jerome has perished.
[5] Origen left Alexandria for good in 231 A.D., and it was in that or the following year that Demetrius convoked the synod which condemned not so much his writings as his conduct. He appears to have been excommunicated as a heretic.
[6] For Origen's condemnation in a synod held at Rome this passage is the principal authority. It is more than doubtful whether such a synod ever met; if it did it must have been when Pontianus was pope, in 231 or 232 A.D. Jerome may only mean that the great men of Rome all agreed in this condemnation.
[7] Both these philosophers were hedonists, and the latter was a sensualist as well. Jerome is probably satirizing the worldly clergy of Rome, just as in after-years he nicknames his opponent Jovinian "the Christian Epicurus."

LETTER XXXIV.

TO MARCELLA.

In reply to a request from Marcella for information concerning two phrases in Ps. cxxvii. ("bread of sorrow," v. 2, and "children of the shaken off," A.V. "of the youth," v. 4). Jerome, after lamenting that Origen's notes on the psalm are no longer extant, gives the following explanations:

The Hebrew phrase " bread of sorrow " is rendered by the LXX. " bread of idols"; by Aquila, " bread of troubles"; by Symmachus, "bread of misery." Theodotion follows the LXX. So does Origen's Fifth Version. The Sixth renders "bread of error." In support of the LXX. the word used here is in Ps. cxv. 4, translated "idols." Either the troubles of life are meant or else the tenets of heresy.

With the second phrase he deals at greater length. After showing that Hilary of Poitiers's view (viz. that the persons meant are the apostles, who were told to shake the dust off their feet, Matt. x. 14) is untenable and would require "shakers off " to be substituted for "shaken off," Jerome reverts to the Hebrew as before and declares that the true rendering is that of Symmachus and Theodotion, viz. "children of youth." He points out that the LXX. (by whom the Latin translators had been misled) fall into the same mistake at Neh. iv. 16. Finally he corrects a slip of Hilary as to Ps. cxxviii. 2, where, through a misunderstanding of the LXX., the latter had substituted "the labors of thy fruits " for " the labors of thy hands." He speaks throughout with high respect of Hilary, and says that it was not the bishop's fault that he was ignorant of Hebrew. The date of the letter is probably A.D. 384.

LETTER XXXV.

FROM POPE DAMASUS.

Damasus addresses five questions to Jerome with a request for information concerning them. They are:

1. What is the meaning of the words "Whosoever slayeth Cain vengeance shall be taken on him sevenfold"? (Gen. iv. 15.)

2. If God has made all things good, how comes it that He gives charge to Noah concerning unclean animals, and says to Peter, "What God hath cleansed that call not thou common"? (Acts x. 15.)

3. How is Gen. xv. 16, " in the fourth generation they shall come hither again," to be reconciled with Ex. xiii. 18, LXX., " in the fifth generation the children of Israel went up out of the land of Egypt"?

4. Why did Abraham receive circumcision as a seal of his faith? (Rom. iv. 11.)

5. Why was Isaac, a righteous man and dear to God, allowed by God to become the dupe of Jacob? (Gen. xxvii.) Written at Rome 384 A.D.

LETTER XXXVI.

TO POPE DAMASUS.

Jerome's reply to the foregoing. For the second and fourth questions he refers Damasus to the writings of Tertullian, Novatian, and Origen. The remaining three he deals with in detail.

Gen. iv. 15, he understands to mean "the slayer of Cain shall complete the sevenfold vengeance which is to be wreaked upon him."

Exodus xiii. 18, he proposes to reconcile with Gen.

xv. 16, by supposing that in the one place the tribe of Levi is referred to, in the other the tribe of Judah. He suggests, however, that the words rendered by the LXX. "in the fifth generation" more probably mean "harnessed" (so A.V.) or "laden." In reply to the question about Isaac he says: "No man save Him who for our salvation has deigned to put on flesh has full knowledge and a complete grasp of the truth. Paul, Samuel, David, Elisha, all make mistakes, and holy men only know what God reveals to them." He then goes on to give a mystical interpretation of the passage suggested by the martyr Hippolytus. Written the day after the previous letter.

LETTER XXXVII.

TO MARCELLA.

Marcella had asked Jerome to lend her a copy of a commentary by Rhetitius, bishop of Augustodunum (Autun), on the Song of Songs. He now refuses to do so on the ground that the work abounds with errors, of which the two following are samples: (1) Rhetitius identifies Tharshish with Tarsus, and (2) he supposes that Uphaz (in the phrase "gold of Uphaz") is the same as Cephas. Written at Rome A.D. 384.

LETTER XXXVIII.

TO MARCELLA.

Blaesilla, the daughter of Paula and sister of Eustochium, had lost her husband seven months after her marriage. A dangerous illness had then led to her conversion, and she was now famous throughout Rome for the length to which she carried her austerities. Many censured her for what they deemed her fanaticism, and Jerome, as her spiritual adviser, came in for some of the blame. In the present letter he defends her conduct, and declares that persons who cavil at lives like hers have no claim to be considered Christians. Written at Rome in 385 A.D.

1. When Abraham is tempted to slay his son the trial only serves to strengthen his faith.[1] When Joseph is sold into Egypt, his sojourn there enables him to support his father and his brothers.[2] When Hezekiah is panic-stricken at the near approach of death, his tears and prayers obtain for him a respite of fifteen years.[3] If the faith of the apostle, Peter, is shaken by his Lord's passion, it is that, weeping bitterly, he may hear the soothing words: " Feed my sheep."[4] If Paul, that ravening wolf,[5] that little Benjamin,[6] is blinded in a trance, it is that he may receive his sight, and may be led, by the sudden horror of surrounding darkness, to call Him Lord Whom before he persecuted as man.[7]

2. So is it now, my dear Marcella, with our beloved Blaesilla. The burning fever from which we have seen her suffering unceasingly for nearly thirty days has been

---

1 Gen. xxii. 2 Gen. xxxvii., xlvi. 3 2 K xx.; Isa. xxxviii.
4 Luke xxii. 54-62 ; Joh. xxi. 16. 5 Gen. xlix. 27.
6 Ps. lxviii. 27. 7 Acts ix. 3-18.

sent to teach her to renounce her over-great attention to that body which the worms must shortly devour. The Lord Jesus has come to her in her sickness, and has taken her by the hand, and behold, she arises and ministers unto Him.[1] Formerly her life savored somewhat of carelessness; and, fast bound in the bands of wealth, she lay as one dead in the tomb of the world. But Jesus was moved with indignation,[2] and was troubled in spirit, and cried aloud and said, Blaesilla, come forth.[3] She, at His call, has arisen and has come forth, and sits at meat with the Lord.[4] The Jews, if they will, may threaten her in their wrath; they may seek to slay her, because Christ has raised her up.[5] It is enough that the apostles give God the glory. Blaesilla knows that her life is due to Him who has given it back to her. She knows that now she can clasp the feet of Him whom but a little while ago she dreaded as her judge.[6] Then life had all but forsaken her body, and the approach of death made her gasp and shiver. What succour did she obtain in that hour from her kinsfolk? What comfort was there in their words lighter than smoke? She owes no debt to you, ye unkindly kindred, now that she is dead to the world and alive unto Christ.[7] The Christian must rejoice that it is so, and he that is vexed must admit that he has no claim to be called a Christian.

3. A widow who is "loosed from the law of her husband"[8] has, for her one duty, to continue a widow. But, you will say, a sombre dress vexes the world. In that case, John the Baptist would vex it, too; and yet, among those that are born of women, there has not been a greater than he.[9] He was called an angel;[10] he baptized the Lord Himself, and yet he was clothed in raiment of camel's hair, and girded with a leathern girdle.[11] Is the world displeased because a widow's food is coarse? Nothing can be coarser than locusts, and yet these were the food of John. The women who ought to scandalize Christians are those who paint their eyes and lips with rouge and cosmetics; whose chalked faces, unnaturally white, are like those of idols; upon whose cheeks every chance tear leaves a furrow; who fail to realize that years make them old; who heap their heads with hair not their own; who smooth their faces, and rub out the

wrinkles of age; and who, in the presence of their grandsons, behave like trembling school-girls. A Christian woman should blush to do violence to nature, or to stimulate desire by bestowing care upon the flesh. "They that are in the flesh," the apostle tells us, "cannot please God."[1]

4. In days gone by our dear widow was extremely fastidious in her dress, and spent whole days before her mirror to correct its deficiencies. Now she boldly says: "We all with unveiled face, beholding as in a glass the glory of the Lord, are changed into the same image, from glory to glory, even as by the spirit of the Lord."[2] In those days maids arranged her hair, and her head, which had done no harm, was forced into a waving head-dress. Now she leaves her hair alone, and her only head-dress is a veil. In those days the softest feather-bed seemed hard to her, and she could scarcely find rest on a pile of mattresses. Now she rises eager for prayer, her shrill voice cries Alleluia before every other, she is the first to praise her Lord. She kneels upon the bare ground, and with frequent tears cleanses a face once defiled with white lead. After prayer comes the singing of psalms, and it is only when her neck aches and her knees totter, and her eyes begin to close with weariness, that she gives them leave reluctantly to rest. As her dress is dark, lying on the ground does not soil it. Cheap shoes permit her to give to the poor the price of gilded ones. No gold and jewels adorn her girdle; it is made of wool, plain and scrupulously clean. It is intended to keep her clothes right, and not to cut her waist in two. Therefore, if the scorpion looks askance upon her purpose, and with alluring words tempts her once more to eat of the forbidden tree, she must crush him beneath her feet with a curse, and say, as he lies dying in his allotted dust:[3] "Get thee behind me, Satan."[4] Satan means adversary,[5] and one who dislikes Christ's commandments, is more than Christ's adversary; he is anti-christ.

5. But what, I ask you, have we ever done that men should be offended at us? Have we ever imitated the apostles? We are told of the first disciples that they forsook their boat and their nets, and even their aged father.[6] The publican stood up from the receipt of custom and followed the Saviour once for all.[7] And when a disciple

---

[1] Cf. Mark i. 30, 31. [2] John xi. 38, R.V. marg.
[3] Joh. xi. 38–44. [4] Joh. xii. 2.
[5] Joh. xii. 10. [6] Luke vii. 38. [7] Rom. vi. 11.
[8] Rom. vii. 2. [9] Luke vii. 28.
[10] Luke vii. 27. The word " angel " means " messenger."
[11] Matt. iii. 4.

[1] Rom. viii. 8. [2] 2 Cor. iii. 18, R.V.
[3] Gen. iii. 14. [4] Matt. xvi. 23. [5] 1 Pet. v. 8.
[6] Matt. iv. 18–22. [7] Matt. ix. 9.

wished to return home, that he might take leave of his kinsfolk, the Master's voice refused consent.[1] A son was even forbidden to bury his father,[2] as if to show that it is sometimes a religious duty to be undutiful for the Lord's sake.[3] With us it is different. We are held to be monks if we refuse to dress in silk. We are called sour and severe if we keep sober and refrain from excessive laughter. The mob salutes us as Greeks and impostors[4] if our tunics are fresh and clean. They may deal in still severer witticisms if they please; they may parade every fat paunch[5] they can lay hold of, to turn us into ridicule. Our Blaesilla will laugh at their efforts, and will bear with patience the taunts of all such croaking frogs, for she will remember that men called her Lord, Beelzebub.[6]

LETTER XXXIX.

TO PAULA.

Blaesilla died within three months of her conversion, and Jerome now writes to Paula to offer her his sympathy and, if possible, to moderate her grief. He asks her to remember that Blaesilla is now in paradise, and so far to control herself as to prevent enemies of the faith from cavilling at her conduct. Then he concludes with the prophecy (since more than fulfilled) that in his writings Blaesilla's name shall never die. Written at Rome in 389 A.D.

1. "Oh that my head were waters and mine eyes a fountain of tears: that I might weep," not as Jeremiah says, "For the slain of my people,"[7] nor as Jesus, for the miserable fate of Jerusalem,[8] but for holiness, mercy, innocence, chastity, and all the virtues, for all are gone now that Blaesilla is dead. For her sake I do not grieve, but for myself I must; my loss is too great to be borne with resignation. Who can recall with dry eyes the glowing faith which induced a girl of twenty to raise the standard of the Cross, and to mourn the loss of her virginity more than the death of her husband? Who can recall without a sigh the earnestness of her prayers, the brilliancy of her conversation, the tenacity of her memory, and the quickness of her intellect? Had you heard her speak Greek you would have deemed her ignorant of Latin; yet when she used the tongue of Rome her words were free from a foreign accent. She even rivalled the great Origen in those acquirements which won for him the admiration of Greece. For in a few months, or rather

days, she so completely mastered the difficulties of Hebrew as to emulate her mother's zeal in learning and singing the psalms. Her attire was plain, but this plainness was not, as it often is, a mark of pride. Indeed, her self-abasement was so perfect that she dressed no better than her maids, and was only distinguished from them by the greater ease of her walk. Her steps tottered with weakness, her face was pale and quivering, her slender neck scarcely upheld her head. Still she always had in her hand a prophet or a gospel. As I think of her my eyes fill with tears, sobs impede my voice, and such is my emotion that my tongue cleaves to the roof of my mouth. As she lay there dying, her poor frame parched with burning fever, and her relatives gathered round her bed, her last words were: "Pray to the Lord Jesus, that He may pardon me, because what I would have done I have not been able to do." Be at peace, dear Blaesilla, in full assurance that your garments are always white.[1] For yours is the purity of an everlasting virginity. I feel confident that my words are true: conversion can never be too late. The words to the dying robber are a pledge of this: "Verily I say unto thee, to-day shalt thou be with me in paradise."[2] When at last her spirit was delivered from the burden of the flesh, and had returned to Him who gave it;[3] when, too, after her long pilgrimage, she had ascended up into her ancient heritage, her obsequies were celebrated with customary splendor. People of rank headed the procession, a pall made of cloth of gold covered her bier. But I seemed to hear a voice from heaven, saying: "I do not recognize these trappings; such is not the garb I used to wear; this magnificence is strange to me."

2. But what is this? I wish to check a mother's weeping, and I groan myself. I make no secret of my feelings; this entire letter is written in tears. Even Jesus wept for Lazarus because He loved him.[4] But he is a poor comforter who is overcome by his own sighs, and from whose afflicted heart tears are wrung as well as words. Dear Paula, my agony is as great as yours. Jesus knows it, whom Blaesilla now follows; the holy angels know it, whose company she now enjoys. I was her father in the spirit, her foster-father in affection. Sometimes I say: "Let the day perish wherein I was born,"[5] and again, "Woe is me, my mother,

---

1 Luke ix. 61, 62.   2 Matt. viii. 21.
3 Luke xiv. 26.   4 Cf. Letter LIV. § 5.
5 Pinguis aqualiculus—Pers. i. 57.   6 Matt. x. 25.
7 Jer. ix. 1.   8 Luke xix. 41.

1 Eccles. ix. 8.   2 Luke xxiii. 43.
3 Cf. Eccles. xii. 7.   4 John xi. 35, 36.
5 Job iii. 3: cf. Jer. xx. 14.

that thou hast borne me a man of strife and
a man of contention to the whole earth."[1]
I cry: "Righteous art thou, O Lord . . . yet
let me talk with thee of thy judgments.
Wherefore doth the way of the wicked prosper?"[2] and "as for me, my feet were almost
gone, my steps had well-nigh slipped. For
I was envious at the foolish when I saw the
prosperity of the wicked, and I said: How
doth God know? and is there knowledge in
the most high? Behold these are the ungodly who prosper in the world; they increase in riches."[3] But again I recall other
words, "If I say I will speak thus, behold I
should offend against the generation of thy
children."[4] Do not great waves of doubt
surge up over my soul as over yours? How
comes it, I ask, that godless men live to old
age in the enjoyment of this world's riches?
How comes it that untutored youth and innocent childhood are cut down while still in
the bud? Why is it that children three
years old or two, and even unweaned infants, are possessed with devils, covered
with leprosy, and eaten up with jaundice,
while godless men and profane, adulterers
and murderers, have health and strength to
blaspheme God? Are we not told that the
unrighteousness of the father does not fall
upon the son,[5] and that "the soul that sinneth
it shall die?"[6] Or if the old doctrine holds
good that the sins of the fathers must be
visited upon the children,[7] an old man's
countless sins cannot fairly be avenged upon
a harmless infant. And I have said: "Verily, I have cleansed my heart in vain, and
washed my hands in innocency. For all the
day long have I been plagued."[8] Yet when
I have thought of these things, like the
prophet I have learned to say: "When I
thought to know this, it was too painful for
me; until I went into the sanctuary of God;
then understood I their end."[9] Truly the
judgments of the Lord are a great deep.[10]
"O the depth of the riches both of the wisdom and knowledge of God! How unsearchable are His judgments, and His ways
past finding out!"[11] God is good, and all
that He does must be good also. Does He
decree that I must lose my husband? I
mourn my loss, but because it is His will I
bear it with resignation. Is an only son
snatched from me? The blow is hard, yet
it can be borne, for He who has taken away
is He who gave.[12] If I become blind a

friend's reading will console me. If I become deaf I shall escape from sinful words,
and my thoughts shall be of God alone.
And if, besides such trials as these, poverty,
cold, sickness, and nakedness oppress me, I
shall wait for death, and regard them as
passing evils, soon to give way to a better
issue. Let us reflect on the words of the
sapiential psalm: "Righteous art thou, O
Lord, and upright are thy judgments."[1]
Only he can speak thus who in all his
troubles magnifies the Lord, and, putting
down his sufferings to his sins, thanks God
for his clemency.

The daughters of Judah, we are told, rejoiced, because of all the judgments of the
Lord.[2] Therefore, since Judah means confession, and since every believing soul confesses its faith,[3] he who claims to believe in
Christ must rejoice in all Christ's judgments. Am I in health? I thank my Creator. Am I sick? In this case, too, I
praise God's will. For "when I am weak,
then am I strong;" and the strength of the
spirit is made perfect in the weakness of the
flesh. Even an apostle must bear what he
dislikes, that ailment for the removal of
which he besought the Lord thrice. God's
reply was: "My grace is sufficient for thee;
for my strength is made perfect in weakness."[4] Lest he should be unduly elated by
his revelations, a reminder of his human
weakness was given to him, just as in the
triumphal car of the victorious general there
was always a slave to whisper constantly,
amid the cheerings of the multitude, "Remember that thou art but man."[5]

3. But why should that be hard to bear
which we must one day ourselves endure?
And why do we grieve for the dead? We are
not born to live forever. Abraham, Moses,
and Isaiah, Peter, James, and John, Paul,
the "chosen vessel,"[6] and even the Son of
God Himself have all died; and are we vexed
when a soul leaves its earthly tenement?
Perhaps he is taken away, "lest that wickedness should alter his understanding . . . for
his soul pleased the Lord: therefore hasted
he to take him away from the people"[7]
—lest in life's long journey he should lose
his way in some trackless maze. We should
indeed mourn for the dead, but only for him
whom Gehenna receives, whom Tartarus devours, and for whose punishment the eternal
fire burns. But we who, in departing, are accompanied by an escort of angels, and met

---

[1] Jer. xv. 10.   [2] Jer. xii. 1.
[3] Ps. lxxiii. 2, 3, 11, 12, Vulg.   [4] Ps. lxxiii. 15.
[5] Ezek. xviii. 20.   [6] Ezek. xviii. 4.
[7] Ex. xx. 5.   [8] Ps. lxxiii. 13, 14.   [9] Ps. lxxiii. 16, 17.
[10] Ps. xxxvi. 6.   [11] Rom. xi. 33.   [12] Job i. 21.

[1] Ps. cxix. 137.   [2] Ps. xcvii. 8.   [3] Rom. x. 10.
[4] 2 Cor. xii. 8, 9, 10.   [5] Cf. Tertullian, Apol. 33.
[6] Acts ix. 15.   [7] Wisd. iv. 11, 14.

by Christ Himself, should rather grieve that we have to tarry yet longer in this tabernacle of death.[1] For "whilst we are at home in the body, we are absent from the Lord."[2] Our one longing should be that expressed by the psalmist: "Woe is me that my pilgrimage is prolonged, that I have dwelt with them that dwell in Kedar, that my soul hath made a far pilgrimage."[3] Kedar means darkness, and darkness stands for this present world (for, we are told, "the light shineth in darkness; and the darkness comprehendeth it not"[4]). Therefore we should congratulate our dear Blaesilla that she has passed from darkness to light,[5] and has in the first flush of her dawning faith received the crown of her completed work. Had she been cut off (as I pray that none may be) while her thoughts were full of worldly desires and passing pleasures, then mourning would indeed have been her due, and no tears shed for her would have been too many. As it is, by the mercy of Christ she, four months ago, renewed her baptism in her vow of widowhood, and for the rest of her days spurned the world, and thought only of the religious life. Have you no fear, then, lest the Saviour may say to you: "Are you angry, Paula, that your daughter has become my daughter? Are you vexed at my decree, and do you, with rebellious tears, grudge me the possession of Blaesilla? You ought to know what my purpose is both for you and for yours. You deny yourself food, not to fast but to gratify your grief; and such abstinence is displeasing to me. Such fasts are my enemies. I receive no soul which forsakes the body against my will. A foolish philosophy may boast of martyrs of this kind; it may boast of a Zeno,[6] a Cleombrotus,[7] or a Cato.[8] My spirit rests only upon him "that is poor and of a contrite spirit, and that trembleth at my word.[9] Is this the meaning of your vow to me that you would lead a religious life? Is it for this that you dress yourself differently from other matrons, and array yourself in the garb of a nun? Mourning is for those who wear silk dresses. In the midst of your tears the call will come, and you, too, must die; yet you flee from me as from a cruel judge, and fancy that you can avoid falling into my hands. Jonah, that headstrong prophet,

once fled from me, yet in the depths of the sea he was still mine.[1] If you really believed your daughter to be alive, you would not grieve that she had passed to a better world. This is the commandment that I have given you through my apostle, that you sorrow not for them that sleep, even as the Gentiles, which have no hope.[2] Blush, for you are put to shame by the example of a heathen. The devil's handmaid[3] is better than mine. For, while she imagines that her unbelieving husband has been translated to heaven, you either do not or will not believe that your daughter is at rest with me."

4. Why should I not mourn, you say? Jacob put on sackcloth for Joseph, and when all his family gathered round him, refused to be comforted. "I will go down," he said, "into the grave unto my son mourning."[4] David also mourned for Absalom, covering his face, and crying: "O my son, Absalom . . . my son, Absalom! Would God I had died for thee, O Absalom, my son!"[5] Moses,[6] too, and Aaron,[7] and the rest of the saints were mourned for with a solemn mourning. The answer to your reasoning is simple. Jacob, it is true, mourned for Joseph, whom he fancied slain, and thought to meet only in the grave (his words were: "I will go down into the grave unto my son mourning"), but he only did so because Christ had not yet broken open the door of paradise, nor quenched with his blood the flaming sword and the whirling of the guardian cherubim.[8] (Hence in the story of Dives and Lazarus, Abraham and the beggar, though really in a place of refreshment, are described as being in hell.[9]) And David, who, after interceding in vain for the life of his infant child, refused to weep for it, knowing that it had not sinned, did well to weep for a son who had been a parricide —in will, if not in deed.[10] And when we read that, for Moses and Aaron, lamentation was made after ancient custom, this ought not to surprise us, for even in the Acts of the Apostles, in the full blaze of the gospel, we see that the brethren at Jerusalem made great lamentation for Stephen.[11] This great lamentation, however, refers not to the mourners, but to the funeral procession and to the crowds which accompanied it. This

---

[1] 2 Cor. v. 4. [2] 2 Cor. v. 6. [3] Ps. cxx. 5, 6, Vulg.
[4] Joh. i. 5. [5] Eph. v. 8.
[6] A famous stoic who committed suicide in extreme old age. See Diogenes Laertius (vii. 1) for an account of his death.
[7] An academic philosopher of Ambracia, who is said to have killed himself after reading the Phædo of Plato.
[8] Cato of Utica, who, after the battle of Thapsus (46 B.C.), committed suicide to avoid falling into the hands of Cæsar.
[9] Isa. lxvi. 2.

[1] Jon. ii. 2–7. [2] 1 Thess. iv. 13.
[3] Viz. Paulina, wife of Prætextatus and priestess of Ceres. See Letter XXIII. § 3. [4] Gen. xxxvii. 35.
[5] 2 Sam. xviii. 33. [6] Deut. xxxiv. 8. [7] Nu. xx. 29.
[8] Gen. iii. 24: cf. Ezek. i. 15–20. Here as in his Comm. on Eccles. iii. 16–22, Jerome follows Origen, who, in his homily de Engastrimytho, lays down that until Christ came to set them free the patriarchs, prophets, and saints of the Old Testament were all in hell. [9] Apud inferos—Luke xvi. 23.
[10] 2 Sam. xvii. 1–4. [11] Acts viii. 2.

is what the Scripture says of Jacob: "Joseph went up to bury his father: and with him went up all the servants of Pharaoh, the elders of his house, and all the elders of the land of Egypt, and all the house of Joseph and his brethren"; and a few lines farther on: "And there went up with him both chariots and horsemen: and it was a great company." Finally, "they mourned with a great and very sore lamentation." [1] This solemn lamentation does not impose prolonged weeping upon the Egyptians, but simply describes the funeral ceremony. In like manner, when we read of weeping made for Moses and Aaron, [2] this is all that is meant.

I cannot adequately extol the mysteries of Scripture, nor sufficiently admire the spiritual meaning conveyed in its most simple words. We are told, for instance, that lamentation was made for Moses; yet when the funeral of Joshua is described [3] no mention at all is made of weeping. The reason, of course, is that under Moses—that is under the old Law—all men were bound by the sentence passed on Adam's sin, and when they descended into hell [4] were rightly accompanied with tears. For, as the apostle says, "death reigned from Adam to Moses, even over them that had not sinned." [5] But under Jesus, [6] that is, under the Gospel of Christ, who has unlocked for us the gate of paradise, death is accompanied, not with sorrow, but with joy. The Jews go on weeping to this day; they make bare their feet, they crouch in sackcloth, they roll in ashes. And to make their superstition complete, they follow a foolish custom of the Pharisees, and eat lentils, [7] to show, it would seem, for what poor fare they have lost their birthright. [8] Of course they are right to weep, for as they do not believe in the Lord's resurrection they are being made ready for the advent of antichrist. But we who have put on Christ [9] and according to the apostle are a royal and priestly race, [10] we ought not to grieve for the dead. "Moses," the Scripture tells us, "said unto Aaron and unto Eleazar, and unto Ithamar, his sons that were left: Uncover not your heads, neither rend your clothes; lest ye die, and lest wrath come upon all the people." [11] Rend not your clothes, he says, neither mourn as pagans, lest you die. For, for us

sin is death. In this same book, Leviticus, there is a provision which may perhaps strike some as cruel, yet is necessary to faith: the high priest is forbidden to approach the dead bodies of his father and mother, of his brothers and of his children; [1] to the end, that no grief may distract a soul engaged in offering sacrifice to God, and wholly devoted to the Divine mysteries. Are we not taught the same lesson in the Gospel in other words? Is not the disciple forbidden to say farewell to his home or to bury his dead father? [2] Of the high priest, again, it is said: "He shall not go out of the sanctuary, and the sanctification of his God shall not be contaminated, for the anointing oil of his God is upon him." [3] Certainly, now that we have believed in Christ, and bear Him within us, by reason of the oil of His anointing which we have received, [4] we ought not to depart from His temple—that is, from our Christian profession—we ought not to go forth to mingle with the unbelieving Gentiles, but always to remain within, as servants obedient to the will of the Lord.

5. I have spoken plainly, lest you might ignorantly suppose that Scripture sanctions your grief; and that, if you err, you have reason on your side. And, so far, my words have been addressed to the average Christian woman. But now it will not be so. For in your case, as I well know, renunciation of the world has been complete; you have rejected and trampled on the delights of life, and you give yourself daily to fasting, to reading, and to prayer. Like Abraham, [5] you desire to leave your country and kindred, to forsake Mesopotamia and the Chaldæans, to enter into the promised land. Dead to the world before your death, you have spent all your mere worldly substance upon the poor, or have bestowed it upon your children. I am the more surprised, therefore, that you should act in a manner which in others would justly call for reprehension. You call to mind Blaesilla's companionship, her conversation, and her endearing ways; and you cannot endure the thought that you have lost them all. I pardon you the tears of a mother, but I ask you to restrain your grief. When I think of the parent I cannot blame you for weeping; but when I think of the Christian and the recluse, the mother disappears from my view. Your wound is still fresh, and any touch of mine, however gentle, is more

---

[1] Gen. l. 7-10.
[2] Nu. xx. 29; Deut. xxxiv. 6-8.   [3] Josh. xxiv. 30.
[4] Ad inferos. Hades is meant, not Gehenna.   [5] Rom. v. 14.
[6] The Greek form of Joshua. Cf. Acts vii. 45, A. V.
[7] I learn from Dr. Neubauer, of Oxford, that this is still a practice during mourning among the Jews of the East. He refers to Tur Joreh Deah. § 378.   [8] Gen. xxv. 34.   [9] Gal. iii. 27.
[10] 1 Pet. ii. 9.   [11] Lev. x. 6, 12.

[1] Lev. xxi. 10-12.   [2] Luke ix. 59-62.
[3] Lev. xxi. 12, Vulg.   [4] 1 Joh. ii. 27.   [5] Gen. xii. 1-4.

likely to inflame than to heal it. Yet why do you not try to overcome by reason a grief which time must inevitably assuage? Naomi, fleeing because of famine to the land of Moab, there lost her husband and her sons. Yet when she was thus deprived of her natural protectors, Ruth, a stranger, never left her side.[1] And see what a great thing it is to comfort a lonely woman! Ruth, for her reward, is made an ancestress of Christ.[2] Consider the great trials which Job endured, and you will see that you are over-delicate. Amid the ruins of his house, the pains of his sores, his countless bereavements, and, last of all, the snares laid for him by his wife, he still lifted up his eyes to heaven, and maintained his patience unbroken. I know what you are going to say: "All this befell him as a righteous man, to try his righteousness." Well, choose which alternative you please. Either you are holy, in which case God is putting your holiness to the proof; or else you are a sinner, in which case you have no right to complain. For if so, you endure far less than your deserts.

Why should I repeat old stories? Listen to a modern instance. The holy Melanium,[3] eminent among Christians for her true nobility (may the Lord grant that you and I may have part with her in His day!), while the dead body of her husband was still unburied, still warm, had the misfortune to lose at one stroke two of her sons. The sequel seems incredible, but Christ is my witness that my words are true. Would you not suppose that in her frenzy she would have unbound her hair, and rent her clothes, and torn her breast? Yet not a tear fell from her eyes. Motionless she stood there; then casting herself at the feet of Christ, she smiled, as though she held Him with her hands. "Henceforth, Lord," she said, "I will serve Thee more readily, for Thou hast freed me from a great burden." But perhaps her remaining children overcame her determination. No, indeed; she set so little store by them that she gave up all that she had to her only son, and then, in spite of the approaching winter, took ship for Jerusalem.

6. Spare yourself, I beseech you, spare Blaesilla, who now reigns with Christ; at least spare Eustochium, whose tender years and inexperience depend on you for guidance and instruction. Now does the devil rage and complain that he is set at naught, because he sees one of your children exalted in triumph. The victory which he failed to win over her that is gone he hopes to obtain over her who still remains. Too great affection towards one's children is disaffection towards God. Abraham gladly prepares to slay his only son, and do you complain if one child out of several has received her crown? I cannot say what I am going to say without a groan. When you were carried fainting out of the funeral procession, whispers such as these were audible in the crowd. "Is not this what we have often said. She weeps for her daughter, killed with fasting. She wanted her to marry again, that she might have grandchildren. How long must we refrain from driving these detestable monks out of Rome? Why do we not stone them or hurl them into the Tiber? They have misled this unhappy lady; that she is not a nun from choice is clear. No heathen mother ever wept for her children as she does for Blaesilla." What sorrow, think you, must not Christ have endured when He listened to such words as these! And how triumphantly must Satan have exulted, eager as he is to snatch your soul! Luring you with the claims of a grief which seems natural and right, and always keeping before you the image of Blaesilla, his aim is to slay the mother of the victress, and then to fall upon her forsaken sister. I do not speak thus to terrify you. The Lord is my witness that I address you now as though I were standing at His judgment seat. Tears which have no meaning are an object of abhorrence. Yours are detestable tears, sacrilegious tears, unbelieving tears; for they know no limits, and bring you to the verge of death. You shriek and cry out as though on fire within, and do your best to put an end to yourself. But to you and others like you Jesus comes in His mercy and says: "Why weepest thou? the damsel is not dead, but sleepeth."[1] The bystanders may laugh him to scorn; such unbelief is worthy of the Jews. If you prostrate yourself in grief at your daughter's tomb you too will hear the chiding of the angel, "Why seek ye the living among the dead?"[2] It was because Mary Magdalene had done this that when she recognized the Lord's voice calling her and fell at His feet, He said to her: "Touch me not, for I am not yet ascended to my Father;"[3] that is to say, you are not worthy to touch, as risen, one whom you suppose still in the tomb.

7. What crosses and tortures, think you, must not our Blaesilla endure to see Christ

---

[1] Ruth i. [2] Matt. i. 5. [3] Or Melania. She went with Rufinus to the East, and settled with him on the Mt. of Olives; and incurred Jerome's resentment as Rufinus' friend. See Ep. cxxxiii. 3. "She whose name of blackness attests the darkness of her perfidy."

[1] Mark v. 39. [2] Luke xxiv. 5. [3] Joh. xx. 17.

angry with you, though it be but a little! At this moment she cries to you as you weep: "If ever you loved me, mother, if I was nourished at your breast, if I was taught by your precepts, do not grudge me my exaltation, do not so act that we shall be separated forever. Do you fancy that I am alone? In place of you I now have Mary the mother of the Lord. Here I see many whom before I have not known. My companions are infinitely better than any that I had on earth. Here I have the company of Anna, the prophetess of the Gospel;[1] and—what should kindle in you more fervent joy—I have gained in three short months what cost her the labor of many years to win. Both of us widows indeed, we have been both rewarded with the palm of chastity. Do you pity me because I have left the world behind me? It is I who should, and do, pity you who, still immured in its prison, daily fight with anger, with covetousness, with lust, with this or that temptation leading the soul to ruin. If you wish to be indeed my mother, you must please Christ. She is not my mother who displeases my Lord." Many other things does she say which here I pass over; she prays also to God for you. For me, too, I feel sure, she makes intercession, and asks God to pardon my sins in return for the warnings and advice that I bestowed on her, when to secure her salvation I braved the ill will of her family.

8. Therefore, so long as breath animates my body, so long as I continue in the enjoyment of life, I engage, declare, and promise that Blaesilla's name shall be forever on my tongue, that my labors shall be dedicated to her honor, and that my talents shall be devoted to her praise. No page will I write in which Blaesilla's name shall not occur. Wherever the records of my utterance shall find their way, thither she, too, will travel with my poor writings. Virgins, widows, monks and priests, as they read, will see how deeply her image is impressed upon my mind. Everlasting remembrance will make up for the shortness of her life. Living as she does with Christ in heaven, she will live also on the lips of men. The present will soon pass away and give place to the future, and that future will judge her without partiality and without prejudice. As a childless widow she will occupy a middle place between Paula, the mother of children, and Eustochium the virgin. In my writings she will never die. She will hear

me conversing of her always, either with her sister or with her mother.

LETTER XL.

TO MARCELLA.

Onasus, of Segesta, the subject of this letter, was among Jerome's Roman opponents. He is here held up to ridicule in a manner which reflects little credit on the writer's urbanity. The date of the letter is 385 A.D.

1. The medical men called surgeons pass for being cruel, but really deserve pity. For is it not pitiful to cut away the dead flesh of another man with merciless knives without being moved by his pangs? Is it not pitiful that the man who is curing the patient is callous to his sufferings, and has to appear as his enemy? Yet such is the order of nature. While truth is always bitter, pleasantness waits upon evil-doing. Isaiah goes naked without blushing as a type of captivity to come.[1] Jeremiah is sent from Jerusalem to the Euphrates (a river in Mesopotamia), and leaves his girdle to be marred in the Chaldæan camp, among the Assyrians hostile to his people.[2] Ezekiel is told to eat bread made of mingled seeds and sprinkled with the dung of men and cattle.[3] He has to see his wife die without shedding a tear.[4] Amos is driven from Samaria.[5] Why is he driven from it? Surely in this case as in the others, because he was a spiritual surgeon, who cut away the parts diseased by sin and urged men to repentance. The apostle Paul says: "Am I therefore become your enemy because I tell you the truth?"[6] And so the Saviour Himself found it, from whom many of the disciples went back because His sayings seemed hard.[7]

2. It is not surprising, then, that by exposing their faults I have offended many. I have arranged to operate on a cancerous nose;[8] let him who suffers from wens tremble. I wish to rebuke a chattering daw; let the crow realize that she is offensive.[9] Yet, after all, is there but one person in Rome

"Whose nostrils are disfigured by a scar?"[10]

Is Onasus of Segesta alone in puffing out his cheeks like bladders and balancing hollow phrases on his tongue?

I say that certain persons have, by crime, perjury, and false pretences, attained to this or that high position. How does it hurt you who know that the charge does not touch you? I laugh at a pleader who has no

---

[1] Luke ii. 36, 37.

[1] Isa. xx. 2.   [2] Jer. xiii. 6, 7.   [3] Ezek. iv. 9–16.
[4] Ezek. xxiv. 15–18.   [5] Amos vii. 12, 13.   [6] Gal. iv. 16.
[7] John vi. 60, 66.   [8] Nasus. A play on the name Onasus.
[9] Cf. Persius, l. 33.   [10] Virg. A. vi. 497.

clients, and sneer at a penny-a-liner's eloquence. What does it matter to you who are such a refined speaker? It is my whim to inveigh against mercenary priests. You are rich already, why should you be angry? I wish to shut up Vulcan and burn him in his own flames. Are you his guest or his neighbor that you try to save an idol's shrine from the fire? I choose to make merry over ghosts and owls and monsters of the Nile; and whatever I say, you take it as aimed at you. At whatever fault I point my pen, you cry out that you are meant. You collar me and drag me into court and absurdly charge me with writing satires when I only write plain prose!

So you really think yourself a pretty fellow just because you have a lucky name![1] Why it does not follow at all. A brake is called a brake just because the light does not break through it.[2] The Fates are called "sparers,"[3] just because they never spare. The Furies are spoken of as gracious,[4] because they show no grace. And in common speech Ethiopians go by the name of silverlings. Still, if the showing up of faults always angers you, I will soothe you now with the words of Persius: "May you be a catch for my lord and lady's daughter! May the pretty ladies scramble for you! May the ground you walk on turn to a rose-bed!"[5]

3. All the same, I will give you a hint what features to hide if you want to look your best. Show no nose upon your face and keep your mouth shut. You will then stand some chance of being counted both handsome and eloquent.

LETTER XLI.

TO MARCELLA.

An effort having been made to convert Marcella to Montanism,[6] Jerome here summarizes for her its leading doctrines, which he contrasts with those of the Church. Written at Rome in 385 A.D.

1. As regards the passages brought together from the gospel of John with which a certain votary of Montanus has assailed you, passages in which our Saviour promises that He will go to the Father, and that He will send the Paraclete[7]—as regards these, the Acts of the Apostles inform us both for what time the promises were made, and at what time

they were actually fulfilled. Ten days had elapsed, we are told, from the Lord's ascension and fifty from His resurrection, when the Holy Spirit came down, and the tongues of the believers were cloven, so that each spoke every language. Then it was that, when certain persons of those who as yet believed not declared that the disciples were drunk with new wine, Peter standing in the midst of the apostles, and of all the concourse said: "Ye men of Judæa and all ye that dwell at Jerusalem, be this known unto you and hearken to my words: for these are not drunken as ye suppose, seeing it is but the third hour of the day. But this is that which was spoken of by the prophet Joel. And it shall come to pass in the last days, saith God, I will pour out of my spirit upon all flesh: and your sons and daughters shall prophesy, and your young men shall see visions, and your old men shall dream dreams: and on my servants, and on my handmaidens I will pour out . . . of my spirit."[1]

2. If, then, the apostle Peter, upon whom the Lord has founded the Church,[2] has expressly said that the prophecy and promise of the Lord were then and there fulfilled, how can we claim another fulfilment for ourselves? If the Montanists reply that Philip's four daughters prophesied[3] at a later date, and that a prophet is mentioned named Agabus,[4] and that in the partition of the spirit, prophets are spoken of as well as apostles, teachers and others,[5] and that Paul himself prophesied many things concerning heresies still future, and the end of the world; we tell them that we do not so much reject prophecy —for this is attested by the passion of the Lord—as refuse to receive prophets whose utterances fail to accord with the Scriptures old and new.

3. In the first place we differ from the Montanists regarding the rule of faith. We distinguish the Father, the Son, and the Holy Spirit as three persons, but unite them as one substance. They, on the other hand, following the doctrine of Sabellius,[6] force the Trinity into the narrow limits of a single personality. We, while we do not encourage them, yet allow second marriages, since Paul bids the younger widows to marry.[7] They suppose a repetition of marriage a sin so awful that he who has committed it is to be regarded as an adulterer. We, according

---

[1] Onasus means "lucky" or "profitable;" it is another form of Onesimus.
[2] Quoted from Quintilian i. 6, 34 (lucus a non lucendo).
[3] Parcæ, from parcere, to spare.
[4] Eumenides, the Greek name for the Furies. [5] Pers. ii. 37, 38.
[6] Montanus lived at Ardaban, in Phrygia, in the second half of the second century, and founded a sect of prophetic enthusiasts and ascetics, which was afterward joined by Tertullian.
[7] Joh. xiv. 28; xv. 26.

[1] Acts ii. 14–18.   [2] Matt. xvi. 18.   [3] Acts xxi. 9.
[4] Acts xi. 28; xxi. 10, 11.   [5] 1 Cor. xii. 28; cf. Eph. iv. 11.
[6] A presbyter of the Libyan Pentapolis who taught at Rome in the early years of the third century. He "confounded the persons" of the Trinity and was subsequently accounted a heretic. Cf. Letter XV.   [7] 1 Tim. v. 14.

to the apostolic tradition (in which the whole world is at one with us), fast through one Lent yearly; whereas they keep three in the year as though three saviours had suffered. I do not mean, of course, that it is unlawful to fast at other times through the year—always excepting Pentecost[1]—only that while in Lent it is a duty of obligation, at other seasons it is a matter of choice. With us, again, the bishops occupy the place of the apostles, but with them a bishop ranks not first but third. For while they put first the patriarchs of Pepusa[2] in Phrygia, and place next to these the ministers called stewards,[3] the bishops are relegated to the third or almost the lowest rank. No doubt their object is to make their religion more pretentious by putting that last which we put first. Again they close the doors of the Church to almost every fault, whilst we read daily, "I desire the repentance of a sinner rather than his death,"[4] and "Shall they fall and not arise, saith the Lord,"[5] and once more "Return ye backsliding children and I will heal your backslidings."[6] Their strictness does not prevent them from themselves committing grave sins, far from it; but there is this difference between us and them, that, whereas they in their self-righteousness blush to confess their faults, we do penance for ours, and so more readily gain pardon for them.

4. I pass over their sacraments[7] of sin, made up as they are said to be, of sucking children subjected to a triumphant martyrdom.[8] I prefer, I say, not to credit these; accusations of blood-shedding may well be false. But I must confute the open blasphemy of men who say that God first determined in the Old Testament to save the world by Moses and the prophets, but that finding Himself unable to fulfil His purpose He took to Himself a body of the Virgin, and preaching under the form of the Son in Christ, underwent death for our salvation. Moreover that, when by these two steps He was unable to save the world, He last of all descended by the Holy Spirit upon Montanus and those demented women Prisca and Maximilla; and that thus the mutilated and emasculate[9] Montanus possessed a fulness of knowledge such as was never claimed by Paul; for he was content to say, "We know in part, and

we prophesy in part," and again, "Now we see through a glass darkly."[1]

These are statements which require no refutation. To expose the infidelity of the Montanists is to triumph over it. Nor is it necessary that in so short a letter as this I should overthrow the several absurdities which they bring forward. You are well acquainted with the Scriptures; and, as I take it, you have written, not because you have been disturbed by their cavils, but only to learn my opinion about them.

LETTER XLII.

TO MARCELLA.

At Marcella's request Jerome explains to her what is "the sin against the Holy Ghost" spoken of by Christ, and shows Novatian's[2] explanation of it to be untenable. Written at Rome in 385 A.D.

1. The question you send is short and the answer is clear. There is this passage in the gospel: "Whosoever speaketh a word against the Son of Man, it shall be forgiven him; but whosoever speaketh against the Holy Ghost, it shall not be forgiven him neither in this world nor in the world to come."[3] Now if Novatian affirms that none but Christian renegades can sin against the Holy Ghost, it is plain that the Jews who blasphemed Christ were not guilty of this sin. Yet they were wicked husbandmen, they had slain the prophets, they were then compassing the death of the Lord;[4] and so utterly lost were they that the Son of God told them that it was they whom he had come to save.[5] It must be proved to Novatian, therefore, that the sin which shall never be forgiven is not the blasphemy of men disembowelled by torture who in their agony deny their Lord, but is the captious clamor of those who, while they see that God's works are the fruit of virtue, ascribe the virtue to a demon and declare the signs wrought to belong not to the divine excellence but to the devil. And this is the whole gist of our Saviour's argument, when He teaches that Satan cannot be cast out by Satan, and that his kingdom is not divided against itself.[6] If it is the devil's object to injure God's creation, how can he wish to cure the sick and to expel himself from the bodies possessed by him? Let Novatian prove that of those who have been compelled to sacrifice before a judge's tribu

---

1 Viz. the period between Easter Day and Whitsunday.
2 Called by the Montanists the New Jerusalem.
3 Oeconomos—according to a probable emendation. The text has cenonas. 4 Ezek. xviii. 23. 5 Jer. viii. 4.
6 Jer. iii. 22. 7 Mysteria.
8 Victuro martyre confarrata. The precise meaning of the words is obscure.
9 Some suppose him to have been a priest of Cybele, but it would be a mistake to lay too much stress on Jerome's words.

1 1 Cor. xiii. 9, 12.
2 Novatian, a Roman presbyter in the middle of the third century, held that the "lapsed," who had failed during the persecutions, could not be readmitted to the church. His sect upheld an extreme moral puritanism, as is shown in the speech of Constantine to their bishop at the Council of Nicæa: "Acesius, you should set up a ladder to heaven, and go up by yourself alone."
3 Matt. xii. 32. 4 Matt. xxi. 33.
5 Matt. xviii. 11. 6 Matt. xii. 25, 26.

nal any has declared of the things written in the gospel that they were wrought not by the Son of God but by Beelzebub, the prince of the devils;[1] and then he will be able to make good his contention that this[2] is the blasphemy against the Holy Ghost which shall never be forgiven.

2. But to put a more searching question still: let Novatian tell us how he distinguishes speaking against the Son of Man from blasphemy against the Holy Ghost. For I maintain that on his principles men who have denied Christ under persecution have only spoken against the Son of Man, and have not blasphemed the Holy Ghost. For when a man is asked if he is a Christian, and declares that he is not; obviously in denying Christ, that is the Son of Man, he does no despite to the Holy Ghost. But if his denial of Christ involves a denial of the Holy Ghost, this heretic can perhaps tell us how the Son of Man can be denied without sinning against the Holy Ghost. If he thinks that we are here intended by the term Holy Ghost to understand the Father, no mention at all of the Father is made by the denier in his denial. When the apostle Peter, taken aback by a maid's question, denied the Lord, did he sin against the Son of Man or against the Holy Ghost? If Novatian absurdly twists Peter's words, "I know not the man,"[3] to mean a denial not of Christ's Messiahship but of His humanity, he will make the Saviour a liar, for He foretold[4] that He Himself, that is His divine Sonship, must be denied. Now, when Peter denied the Son of God, he wept bitterly and effaced his threefold denial by a threefold confession.[5] His sin, therefore, was not the sin against the Holy Ghost which can never be forgiven. It is obvious, then, that this sin involves blasphemy, calling one Beelzebub for his actions, whose virtues prove him to be God. If Novatian can bring an instance of a renegade who has called Christ Beelzebub, I will at once give up my position and admit that after such a fall the denier can win no forgiveness. To give way under torture and to deny oneself to be a Christian is one thing, to say that Christ is the devil is another. And this you will yourself see if you read the passage[6] attentively.

3. I ought to have discussed the matter more fully, but some friends have visited my humble abode, and I cannot refuse to give myself up to them. Still, as it might seem arrogant not to answer you at once, I have compressed a wide subject into a few words, and have sent you not a letter but an explanatory note.[1]

LETTER XLIII.

TO MARCELLA.

Jerome draws a contrast between his daily life and that of Origen, and sorrowfully admits his own shortcomings. He then suggests to Marcella the advantages which life in the country offers over life in town, and hints that he is himself disposed to make trial of it. Written at Rome in 385 A.D.

1. Ambrose who supplied Origen, true man of adamant and of brass,[2] with money, materials and amanuenses to bring out his countless books—Ambrose, in a letter to his friend from Athens, states that they never took a meal together without something being read, and never went to bed till some portion of Scripture had been brought home to them by a brother's voice. Night and day, in fact, were so ordered that prayer only gave place to reading and reading to prayer.

2. Have we, brute beasts that we are, ever done the like? Why, we yawn if we read for over an hour; we rub our foreheads and vainly try to suppress our languor. And then, after this great feat, we plunge for relief into worldly business once more. I say nothing of the meals with which we dull our faculties, and I would rather not estimate the time that we spend in paying and receiving visits. Next we fall into conversation; we waste our words, we attack people behind their backs, we detail their way of living, we carp at them and are carped at by them in turn. Such is the fare that engages our attention at dinner and afterwards. Then, when our guests have retired, we make up our accounts, and these are sure to cause us either anger or anxiety. The first makes us like raging lions, and the second seeks vainly to make provision for years to come. We do not recollect the words of the Gospel: "Thou fool, this night thy soul shall be required of thee: then whose shall those things be which thou hast provided?"[3] The clothing which we buy is designed not merely for use but for display. Where there is a chance of saving money we quicken our pace, speak promptly, and keep our ears open. If we hear of household losses—such as often occur—our looks become dejected and gloomy. The gain of a penny[4] fills us with joy; the loss of a halfpenny[5] plunges us into sorrow. One man

---

1 Matt. xii. 24. 2 Viz. denial of Christ by Christians.
3 Matt. xxvi. 74. 4 Matt. xxvi. 33–35 ; Joh. xiii. 38.
5 Joh. xxi. 15–17. 6 Viz. Matt. xii. 32, quoted above.

1 Commentariolum.
2 For the meaning of these epithets as applied to Origen see Letter XXXIII. § 1. 3 Luke xii. 20.
4 Nummus. Sc. Sestertius = 4 cents = 2 pence.
5 Obolus = 3 1-2 cents = 1 penny 3 farthings.

is of so many minds that the prophet's prayer is: "Lord, in thy city scatter their image."[1] For created as we are in the image of God and after His likeness,[2] it is our own wickedness which makes us assume masks.[3] Just as on the stage the same actor now figures as a brawny Hercules, now softens into a tender Venus, now shivers in the role of Cybele; so we—who, if we were not of the world, would be hated by the world[4]—for every sin that we commit have a corresponding mask.

3. Wherefore, seeing that we have journeyed for much of our life through a troubled sea, and that our vessel has been in turn shaken by raging blasts and shattered upon treacherous reefs, let us, as soon as may be, make for the haven of rural quietude. There such country dainties as milk and household bread, and greens watered by our own hands, will supply us with coarse but harmless fare. So living, sleep will not call us away from prayer, nor satiety from reading. In summer the shade of a tree will afford us privacy. In autumn the quality of the air and the leaves strewn under foot will invite us to stop and rest. In springtime the fields will be bright with flowers, and our psalms will sound the sweeter for the twittering of the birds. When winter comes, with its frost and snow, I shall not have to buy fuel, and, whether I sleep or keep vigil, shall be warmer than in town. At least, so far as I know, I shall keep off the cold at less expense. Let Rome keep to itself its noise and bustle, let the cruel shows of the arena go on, let the crowd rave at the circus, let the playgoers revel in the theatres and—for I must not altogether pass over our Christian friends—let the House of Ladies[5] hold its daily sittings. It is good for us to cleave to the Lord,[6] and to put our hope in the Lord God, so that when we have exchanged our present poverty for the kingdom of heaven, we may be able to exclaim: "Whom have I in heaven but thee? and there is none upon earth that I desire beside thee."[7] Surely if we can find such blessedness in heaven we may well grieve to have sought after pleasures poor and passing here upon earth. Farewell.

LETTER XLIV.

TO MARCELLA.

Marcella had sent some small articles as a present (probably to Paula and Eustochium) and Jerome now

writes in their name to thank her for them. He notices the appropriateness of the gifts, not only to the ladies, but also to himself. Written at Rome in 385 A.D.

When absent in body we are wont to converse together in spirit.[1] Each of us does what he or she can. You send us gifts, we send you back letters of thanks. And as we are virgins who have taken the veil,[2] it is our duty to show that hidden meanings lurk under your nice presents. Sackcloth, then, is a token of prayer and fasting, the chairs remind us that a virgin should never stir abroad, and the wax tapers that we should look for the bridegroom's coming with our lights burning.[3] The cups also warn us to mortify the flesh and always to be ready for martyrdom. "How bright," says the psalmist, "is the cup of the Lord, intoxicating them that drink it!"[4] Moreover, when you offer to matrons little fly-flaps to brush away mosquitoes, it is a charming way of hinting that they should at once check voluptuous feelings, for "dying flies," we are told, "spoil sweet ointment."[5] In such presents, then, as these, virgins can find a model, and matrons a pattern. To me, too, your gifts convey a lesson, although one of an opposite kind. For chairs suit idlers, sackcloth does for penitents, and cups are wanted for the thirsty. And I shall be glad to light your tapers, if only to banish the terrors of the night and the fears of an evil conscience.

LETTER XLV.

TO ASELLA.

After leaving Rome for the East, Jerome writes to Asella to refute the calumnies by which he had been assailed, especially as regards his intimacy with Paula and Eustochium. Written on board ship at Ostia, in August, 385 A.D.

1. Were I to think myself able to requite your kindness I should be foolish. God is able in my stead to reward a soul which is consecrated to Him. So unworthy, indeed, am I of your regard that I have never ventured to estimate its value or even to wish that it might be given me for Christ's sake. Some consider me a wicked man, laden with iniquity; and such language is more than justified by my actual sins. Yet in dealing with the bad you do well to account them good. It is dangerous to judge another man's servant;[8] and to speak evil of the righteous is a sin not easily pardoned. The day will surely come

---

[1] Ps. lxxiii. 20, Vulg.   [2] Gen. i. 26.   [3] These were worn by both Greek and Roman actors.   [4] Joh. xv. 19.   [5] Ps. lxxiii. 28.   [6] Senatus Matronarum. Comp. Letter XXXIII. 4: "Rome calls together its senate to condemn him."   [7] Ps. lxxiii. 25.

[1] Cf. Col. ii. 5.   [2] Cf. Letter CXXX. § 2.   [3] Matt. xxv. 1.   [4] Ps. xxiii. 5, according to the Gallican psalter.   [5] Eccles. x. 1, Vulg.   [6] Rom. xiv. 4.

when you and I shall mourn for others; for not a few will be in the flames

2. I am said to be an infamous turncoat, a slippery knave, one who lies and deceives others by Satanic arts. Which is the safer course, I should like to know, to invent or credit these charges against innocent persons, or to refuse to believe them, even of the guilty? Some kissed my hands, yet attacked me with the tongues of vipers; sympathy was on their lips, but malignant joy in their hearts. The Lord saw them and had them in derision,[1] reserving my poor self and them for judgment to come. One would attack my gait or my way of laughing; another would find something amiss in my looks; another would suspect the simplicity of my manner. Such is the company in which I have lived for almost three years.

It often happened that I found myself surrounded with virgins, and to some of these I expounded the divine books as best I could. Our studies brought about constant intercourse, this soon ripened into intimacy, and this, in turn, produced mutual confidence. If they have ever seen anything in my conduct unbecoming a Christian let them say so. Have I taken any one's money? Have I not disdained all gifts, whether small or great? Has the chink of any one's coin been heard in my hand?[2] Has my language been equivocal, or my eye wanton? No; my sex is my one crime, and even on this score I am not assailed, save when there is a talk of Paula going to Jerusalem. Very well, then. They believed my accuser when he lied; why do they not believe him when he retracts? He is the same man now that he was then, and yet he who before declared me guilty now confesses that I am innocent. Surely a man's words under torture are more trustworthy than in moments of gayety, except, indeed, that people are prone to believe falsehoods designed to gratify their ears, or, worse still, stories which, till then uninvented, they have urged others to invent.

3. Before I became acquainted with the family of the saintly Paula, all Rome resounded with my praises. Almost every one concurred in judging me worthy of the episcopate. Damasus, of blessed memory, spoke no words but mine.[3] Men called me holy, humble, eloquent.

Did I ever cross the threshold of a light woman? Was I ever fascinated by silk dresses, or glowing gems, or rouged faces, or display of gold? Of all the ladies in Rome but one had power to subdue me, and that one was Paula. She mourned and fasted, she was squalid with dirt, her eyes were dim from weeping. For whole nights she would pray to the Lord for mercy, and often the rising sun found her still at her prayers. The psalms were her only songs, the Gospel her whole speech, continence her one indulgence, fasting the staple of her life. The only woman who took my fancy was one whom I had not so much as seen at table. But when I began to revere, respect, and venerate her as her conspicuous chastity deserved, all my former virtues forsook me on the spot.

4. Oh! envy, that dost begin by tearing thyself! Oh! cunning malignity of Satan, that dost always persecute things holy! Of all the ladies in Rome, the only ones that caused scandal were Paula and Melanium, who, despising their wealth and deserting their children, uplifted the cross of the Lord as·a standard of religion. Had they frequented the baths, or chosen to use perfumes, or taken advantage of their wealth and position as widows to enjoy life and to be independent, they would have been saluted as ladies of high rank and saintliness. As it is, of course, it is in order to appear beautiful that they put on sackcloth and ashes, and they endure fasting and filth merely to go down into the Gehenna of fire! As if they could not perish with the crowd whom the mob applauds![1] If it were Gentiles or Jews who thus assailed their mode of life, they would at least have the consolation of failing to please only those whom Christ Himself has failed to please. But, shameful to say, it is Christians who thus neglect the care of their own households, and, disregarding the beams in their own eyes, look for motes in those of their neighbors.[2] They pull to pieces every profession of religion, and think that they have found a remedy for their own doom, if they can disprove the holiness of others, if they can detract from every one, if they can show that those who perish are many, and sinners, a great multitude.

5. You bathe daily; another regards such over-niceness as defilement. You surfeit yourself on wild fowl and pride yourself on eating sturgeon; I, on the contrary, fill my belly with beans. You find pleasure in troops of laughing girls; I prefer Paula and Melanium who weep. You covet what belongs to others; they disdain what is their own. You like wines flavored with honey; they drink cold water, more delicious still. You count as lost what you cannot have, eat up,

---

[1] Ps. ii. 4.   [2] Cf. 1 Sam. xii. 3.
[3] Damasus meus sermo erat, or "spoke of none but me."

[1] Ironical.   [2] Matt. vii. 3.

and devour on the moment; they believe in the Scriptures, and look for good things to come. And if they are wrong, and if the resurrection of the body on which they rely is a foolish delusion, what does it matter to you? We, on our side, look with disfavor on such a life as yours. You can fatten yourself on your good things as much as you please; I for my part prefer paleness and emaciation. You suppose that men like me are unhappy; we regard you as more unhappy still. Thus we reciprocate each other's thoughts, and appear to each other mutually insane.

6. I write this in haste, dear Lady Asella, as I go on board, overwhelmed with grief and tears; yet I thank my God that I am counted worthy of the world's hatred.[1] Pray for me that, after Babylon, I may see Jerusalem once more; that Joshua, the son of Josedech, may have dominion over me,[2] and not Nebuchadnezzar, that Ezra, whose name means helper, may come and restore me to my own country. I was a fool in wishing to sing the Lord's song in a strange land,[3] and in leaving Mount Sinai, to seek the help of Egypt. I forgot that the Gospel warns us[4] that he who goes down from Jerusalem immediately falls among robbers, is spoiled, is wounded, is left for dead. But, although priest and Levite may disregard me, there is still the good Samaritan who, when men said to him, "Thou art a Samaritan and hast a devil,"[5] disclaimed having a devil, but did not disclaim being a Samaritan,[6] this being the Hebrew equivalent for our word guardian. Men call me a mischief-maker, and I take the title as a recognition of my faith. For I am but a servant, and the Jews still call my master a magician. The apostle,[7] likewise, is spoken of as a deceiver. There hath no temptation taken me but such as is common to man.[8] How few distresses have I endured, I who am yet a soldier of the cross! Men have laid to my charge a crime of which I am not guilty;[9] but I know that I must enter the kingdom of heaven through evil report as well as through good.[10]

7. Salute Paula and Eustochium, who, whatever the world may think, are always mine in Christ. Salute Albina, your mother, and Marcella, your sister; Marcellina also, and the holy Felicitas; and say to them all: "We must all stand before the judgment seat of Christ,"[11] and there shall be revealed the principle by which each has lived."

And now, illustrious model of chastity and virginity, remember me, I beseech you, in your prayers, and by your intercessions calm the waves of the sea.

LETTER XLVI.

PAULA AND EUSTOCHIUM TO MARCELLA.

Jerome writes to Marcella in the name of Paula and Eustochium, describing the charms of the Holy Land, and urging her to leave Rome and to join her old companions at Bethlehem. Much of the letter is devoted to disposing of the objection that since the Passion of Christ the Holy Land has been under a curse. The date of the letter is A.D. 386. It is written from Bethlehem, which now becomes Jerome's home for the remainder of his life.

1. Love cannot be measured, impatience knows no bounds, and eagerness can brook no delay. Wherefore we, oblivious of our weakness, and relying more on our will than our capacity, desire—pupils though we be—to instruct our mistress. We are like the sow in the proverb,[1] which sets up to teach the goddess of invention. You were the first to set our tinder alight; the first, by precept and example, to urge us to adopt our present life. As a hen gathers her chickens, so did you take us under your wing.[2] And will you now let us fly about at random with no mother near us? Will you leave us to dread the swoop of the hawk and the shadow of each passing bird of prey? Separated from you, we do what we can: we utter our mournful plaint, and more by sobs than by tears we adjure you to give back to us the Marcella whom we love. She is mild, she is suave, she is sweeter than the sweetest honey. She must not, therefore, be stern and morose to us, whom her winning ways have roused to adopt a life like her own.

2. Assuming that what we ask is for the best, our eagerness to obtain it is nothing to be ashamed of. And if all the Scriptures agree with our view, we are not too bold in urging you to a course to which you have yourself often urged us.

What are God's first words to Abraham? "Get thee out of thy country and from thy kindred unto a land that I will show thee."[3] The patriarch—the first to receive a promise of Christ—is here told to leave the Chaldees, to leave the city of confusion[4] and its *rehoboth*[5] or broad places; to leave also the plain of Shinar, where the tower of pride had been raised to heaven.[6] He has to pass through the waves of this world, and to ford its rivers;

---

[1] Joh. xv. 18. [2] Haggai i. 1. [3] Ps. cxxxvii. 4.
[4] Luke x. 30–35. [5] Joh. viii. 48. [6] Joh. viii. 49.
[7] *I.e.* Paul. See 2. Cor. vi. 9. [8] 1 Cor. x. 13.
[9] He means the sin of incontinence. [10] 2 Cor. vi. 8.
[11] Rom. xiv. 10.

[1] Sus Minervam. [2] 2 Esdras. i. 30; Matt. xxiii. 37.
[3] Gen. xii. 1. [4] *I.e.* Babel—Gen. xi. 9.
[5] Gen. x. 11. [6] Gen. xi. 2, 4.

hose by which the saints sat down and wept vhen they remembered Zion,[1] and Chebar's .ood, whence Ezekiel was carried to Jeru-alem by the hair of his head.[2] All this \braham undergoes that he may dwell in a .and of promise watered from above, and .ot like Egypt, from below,[3] no producer of .erbs for the weak and ailing,[4] but a land .hat looks for the early and the latter rain .rom heaven.[5] It is a land of hills and val-eys,[6] and stands high above the sea. The .ttractions of the world it entirely wants, .ut its spiritual attractions are for this all .he greater. Mary, the mother of the Lord, .eft the lowlands and made her way to the .ill country, when, after receiving the an-.el's message, she realized that she bore vithin her womb the Son of God.[7] When of .ld the Philistines had been overcome, when .heir devilish audacity had been smitten, vhen their champion had fallen on his face .o the earth,[8] it was from this city that there vent forth a procession of jubilant souls, a .armonious choir to sing our David's victory .ver tens of thousands.[9] Here, too, it was .hat the angel grasped his sword, and while .e laid waste the whole of the ungodly city, .narked out the temple of the Lord in the .hreshing floor of Ornan, king of the Jebus-.tes.[10] Thus early was it made plain that Christ's church would grow up, not in Israel, .ut among the Gentiles. Turn back to Gen-.sis,[11] and you will find that this was the city .ver which Melchizedek held sway,, that .ing of Salem who, as a type of Christ, .ffered to Abraham bread and wine, and even .hen consecrated the mystery which Chris-.ians consecrate in the body and blood of the .aviour.[12]

3. Perhaps you will tacitly reprove us for .leserting the order of Scripture, and letting .ur confused account ramble this way and .hat, as one thing or another strikes us. If .o, we say once more what we said at the .utset: love has no logic, and impatience .nows no rule. In the Song of Songs the .recept is given as a hard one: "Regulate .our love towards me."[13] And so we plead .hat, if we err, we do so not from ignorance .ut from feeling.

Well, then, to bring forward something .till more out of place, we must go back to .et remoter times. Tradition has it that in .his city, nay, more, on this very spot, Adam

lived and died. The place where our Lord was crucified is called Calvary,[1] because the skull of the primitive man was buried there. So it came to pass that the second Adam, that is the blood[2] of Christ, as it dropped from the cross, washed away the sins of the buried protoplast,[3] the first Adam, and thus the words of the apostle were fulfilled: "Awake, thou that sleepest, and arise from the dead, and Christ shall give thee light."[4]

It would be tedious to enumerate all the prophets and holy men who have been sent forth from this place. All that is strange and mysterious to us is familiar and natural to this city and country. By its very names, three in number, it proves the doctrine of the trinity. For it is called first Jebus, then Salem, then Jerusalem: names of which the first means "down-trodden," the second "peace," and the third "vision of peace."[5] For it is only by slow stages that we reach our goal; it is only after we have been trod-den down that we are lifted up to see the vision of peace. Because of this peace Sol-omon,[6] the man of peace, was born there, and "in peace was his place made."[7] King of kings, and lord of lords, his name and that of the city show him to be a type of Christ. Need we speak of David and his descendants, all of whom reigned here? As Judæa is exalted above all other provinces, so is this city exalted above all Judæa. To speak more tersely, the glory of the province is derived from its capital; and whatever fame the members possess is in every case due to the head.

4. You have long been anxious to break forth into speech; the very letters we have formed perceive it, and our paper already un-derstands the question you are going to put. You will reply to us by saying: it was so of old, when "the Lord loved the gates of Zion more than all the dwellings of Jacob," and when her foundations were in the holy moun-tains.[8] Even these verses, however, are sus-ceptible of a deeper interpretation. But things are changed since then. The risen Lord has proclaimed in tones of thunder: "Your house is left unto you desolate." With tears He has prophesied its downfall: "O Jerusalem, Jerusalem, thou that killest the prophets, and stonest them which are sent un-

---

[1] Ps. cxxxvii. 1.   [2] Ezek. viii. 3.
[3] Deut. xi. 10.   [4] Rom. xiv. 2.   [5] Deut. xi. 14.
[6] Dt. xi. 11.   [7] Luke i. 26–31, 39.   [8] 1 Sam. xvii. 49.
[9] 1 Sam. xviii. 6, 7.   [10] 1 Chron. xxi. 15, 18 ; 2 Chron. iii. 1.
[11] Gen. xiv. 18.
[12] Mysterium christianum in salvatoris sanguine et corpore .edicavit.   [13] Cant. ii. 4 b, Vulg. Hebrew = A.V.

---

[1] I.e. the place of a skull (Latin, Calvaria).
[2] One of Jerome's fanciful ideas. Haddam דדם is the Hebrew for "the blood."
[3] ὁ πρωτόπλαστος = "the first-formed." The word is ap-plied to Adam in Wisd. vii. 1.   [4] Eph. v. 14.
[5] Cf. Hymns Ancient and Modern, No. 235.
    "Truly Jerusalem name we that shore
        Vision of peace that brings joy evermore."
[6] Hebrew, Shelomoh, connected with shalem, peace.
[7] Ps. lxxvi. 2, LXX.   [8] Ps. lxxxvii. 1, 2.

to thee; how often would I have gathered thy children together even as a hen gathereth her chickens under her wings, and ye would not. Behold your house is left unto you desolate."[1] The veil of the temple has been rent;[2] an army has encompassed Jerusalem, it has been stained by the blood of the Lord. Now, therefore, its guardian angels have forsaken it and the grace of Christ has been withdrawn. Josephus, himself a Jewish writer, asserts[3] that at the Lord's crucifixion there broke from the temple voices of heavenly powers, saying: "Let us depart hence." These and other considerations show that where grace abounded there did sin much more abound.[4] Again, when the apostles received the command: "Go ye and teach all nations,"[5] and when they said themselves: "It was necessary that the word of God should first have been spoken to you, but seeing ye put it from you ... lo we turn to the Gentiles,"[6] then all the spiritual importance[7] of Judæa and its old intimacy with God were transferred by the apostles to the nations.

5. The difficulty is strongly stated, and may well puzzle even those proficient in Scripture; but for all that, it admits of an easy solution. The Lord wept for the fall of Jerusalem,[8] and He would not have done so if He did not love it. He wept for Lazarus because He loved him.[9] The truth is that it was the people who sinned and not the place. The capture of a city is involved in the slaying of its inhabitants. If Jerusalem was destroyed, it was that its people might be punished; if the temple was overthrown, it was that its figurative sacrifices might be abolished. As regards its site, lapse of time has but invested it with fresh grandeur. The Jews of old reverenced the Holy of Holies, because of the things contained in it—the cherubim, the mercy-seat, the ark of the covenant, the manna, Aaron's rod, and the golden altar.[10] Does the Lord's sepulchre seem less worthy of veneration? As often as we enter it we see the Saviour in His grave clothes, and if we linger we see again the angel sitting at His feet, and the napkin folded at His head.[11] Long before this sepulchre was hewn out by Joseph,[12] its glory was foretold in Isaiah's prediction, "his rest shall be glorious,"[13] meaning that the place of the Lord's burial should be held in universal honor.

6. How, then, you will say, do we read in the apocalypse written by John: "The beast that ascendeth out of the bottomless pit shall . . . kill them [that is, obviously, the prophets], and their dead bodies shall lie in the street of the great city which spiritually is called Sodom and Egypt, where also their Lord was crucified?"[1] If the great city where the Lord was crucified is Jerusalem, and if the place of His crucifixion is spiritually called Sodom and Egypt then as the Lord was crucified at Jerusalem, Jerusalem must be Sodom and Egypt. Holy Scripture, I reply first of all, cannot contradict itself. One book cannot invalidate the drift of the whole. A single verse cannot annul the meaning of a book. Ten lines earlier in the apocalypse it is written: "Rise and measure the temple of God, and the altar, and them that worship therein. But the court which is without the temple leave out and measure it not; for it is given unto the Gentiles; and the holy city shall they tread under foot forty and two months."[2] The apocalypse was written by John long after the Lord's passion, yet in it he speaks of Jerusalem as the holy city. But if so, how can he spiritually call it Sodom and Egypt? It is no answer to say that the Jerusalem which is called holy is the heavenly one which is to be, while that which is called Sodom is the earthly one tottering to its downfall. For it is the Jerusalem to come that is referred to in the description of the beast, "which shall ascend out of the bottomless pit, and shall make war against the two prophets, and shall overcome them and kill them, and their dead bodies shall lie in the street of the great city."[3] At the close of the book it is farther described thus: "And the city lieth four-square, and the length of it and the breadth are the same as the height and he measured the city with the golden reed twelve thousand furlongs. The length and the breadth and the height of it are equal. And he measured the walls thereof an hundred and forty and four cubits, according to the measure of a man, that is, of the angel. And the building of the wall of it was of jasper; and the city was pure gold"—and so on. Now where there is a square there can be neither length nor breadth. And what kind of measurement is that which makes length and breadth equal to height And how can there be walls of jasper, or a whole city of pure gold; its foundations and its streets of precious stones, and its twelve gates each glowing with pearls?

---

[1] Matt. xxiii. 37, 38.   [2] Matt. xxvii. 51.
[3] Bellum Judaicum, vi. 5.   [4] Rom. v. 20.
[5] Matt. xxviii. 19.   [6] Acts xiii. 46.   [7] Sacramentum.
[8] Luke xix. 41.   [9] Joh. xi. 35, 36.   [10] Heb. ix. 3-5.
[11] John xx. 6, 7, 12.
[12] *I.e.* Joseph of Arimathæa.—Joh. xix. 38 *sqq.*   [13] Isa. xi. 10.

[1] Rev. xi. 7, 8, R.V.   [2] Rev. xi. 2.
[3] Rev. xi. 7, 8.   [4] Rev. xxi. 16-18.

7. Evidently this description cannot be taken literally (in fact, it is absurd to suppose a city the length, breadth and height of which are all twelve thousand furlongs), and therefore the details of it must be mystically understood. The great city which Cain first built and called after his son[1] must be taken to represent this world, which the devil, that accuser of his brethren, that fratricide who is doomed to perish, has built of vice, cemented with crime, and filled with iniquity. Therefore it is spiritually called Sodom and Egypt. Thus it is written, "Sodom shall return to her former estate,"[2] that is to say, the world must be restored as it has been before. For we cannot believe that Sodom and Gomorrah, Admah and Zeboim[3] are to be built again: they must be left to lie in ashes forever. We never read of Egypt as put for Jerusalem: it always stands for this world. To collect from Scripture the countless proofs of this would be tedious: I shall adduce but one passage, a passage in which this world is most clearly called Egypt. The apostle Jude, the brother of James, writes thus in his catholic epistle: "I will, therefore, put you in remembrance, though ye once knew this, now that Jesus,[4] having saved the people out of the land of Egypt, afterward destroyed them that believed not."[5] And, lest you should fancy Joshua the son of Nun to be meant, the passage goes on thus: "And the angels which kept not their first estate, but left their own habitation, he hath reserved in everlasting chains, under darkness, unto the judgment of the great day."[6] Moreover, to convince you that in every place where Egypt, Sodom and Gomorrah are named together it is not these spots, but the present world, which is meant, he mentions them immediately in this sense. "Even as Sodom and Gomorrah," he writes, "and the cities about them, in like manner giving themselves over to fornication and going after strange flesh, are set forth for an example, suffering the vengeance of eternal fire."[7] But what need is there to collect more proofs when, after the passion and the resurrection of the Lord, the evangelist Matthew tells us: "The rocks rent, and the graves were opened; and many bodies of the saints which slept arose and came out of the graves after his resurrection, and went into the holy city and appeared unto many"?[8] We must not interpret this passage straight off, as many people[9]

absurdly do, of the heavenly Jerusalem: the apparition there of the bodies of the saints could be no sign to men of the Lord's rising. Since, therefore, the evangelists and all the Scriptures speak of Jerusalem as the holy city, and since the psalmist commands us to worship the Lord "at his footstool;"[1] allow no one to call it Sodom and Egypt, for by it the Lord forbids men to swear because "it is the city of the great king."[2]

8. The land is accursed, you say, because it has drunk in the blood of the Lord. On what grounds, then, do men regard as blessed those spots where Peter and Paul, the leaders of the Christian host, have shed their blood for Christ? If the confession of men and servants is glorious, must there not be glory likewise in the confession of their Lord and God? Everywhere we venerate the tombs of the martyrs; we apply their holy ashes to our eyes; we even touch them, if we may, with our lips. And yet some think that we should neglect the tomb in which the Lord Himself is buried. If we refuse to believe human testimony, let us at least credit the devil and his angels.[3] For when in front of the Holy Sepulchre they are driven out of those bodies which they have possessed, they moan and tremble as if they stood before Christ's judgment-seat, and grieve, too late that they have crucified Him in whose presence they now cower. If—as a wicked theory maintains—this holy place has, since the Lord's passion, become an abomination, why was Paul in such haste to reach Jerusalem to keep Pentecost in it?[4] Yet to those who held him back he said: "What mean ye to weep and to break my heart? For I am ready not to be bound only, but also to die at Jerusalem, for the name of the Lord Jesus."[5] Need I speak of those other holy and illustrious men who, after the preaching of Christ, brought their votive gifts and offerings to the brethren who were at Jerusalem?

9. Time forbids me to survey the period which has passed since the Lord's ascension, or to recount the bishops, the martyrs, the divines, who have come to Jerusalem from a feeling that their devotion and knowledge would be incomplete and their virtue without the finishing touch, unless they adored Christ in the very spot where the gospel first flashed from the gibbet. If a famous orator[6] blames a man for having learned Greek at Lilybæum instead of at Athens, and Latin in Sicily instead of at Rome (on the ground,

---

[1] Gen. iv. 17. [2] Ezek. xvi. 55."
[3] Deut. xxix. 23. [4] A.V. "the Lord." [5] Jude 5.
[6] Jude 6. [7] Jude 7. [8] Matt. xxvii. 51, 53.
[9] *E.g.* Origen in his commentary on the passage.

[1] Ps. cxxxii. 7. [2] Matt. v. 35. [3] Matt. xxv. 41.
[4] Acts xx. 16. [5] Acts xxi. 13.
[6] Cicero of Cæcilius (in Q. Cæc. xii.).

obviously, that each province has its own characteristics), can we suppose a Christian's education complete who has not visited the Christian Athens?

10. In speaking thus we do not mean to deny that the kingdom of God is within us,[1] or to say that there are no holy men elsewhere; we merely assert in the strongest manner that those who stand first throughout the world are here gathered side by side. We ourselves are among the last, not the first; yet we have come hither to see the first of all nations. Of all the ornaments of the Church our company of monks and virgins is one of the finest; it is like a fair flower or a priceless gem. Every man of note in Gaul hastens hither. The Briton, "sundered from our world,"[2] no sooner makes progress in religion than he leaves the setting sun in quest of a spot of which he knows only through Scripture and common report. Need we recall the Armenians, the Persians, the peoples of India and Arabia? Or those of our neighbor, Egypt, so rich in monks; of Pontus and Cappadocia; of Cæle-Syria and Mesopotamia and the teeming east? In fulfilment of the Saviour's words, "Wherever the body is, thither will the eagles be gathered together,"[3] they all assemble here and exhibit in this one city the most varied virtues. Differing in speech, they are one in religion, and almost every nation has a choir of its own. Yet amid this great concourse there is no arrogance, no disdain of self-restraint; all strive after humility, that greatest of Christian virtues. Whosoever is last is here regarded as first.[4] Their dress neither provokes remark nor calls for admiration. In whatever guise a man shows himself he is neither censured nor flattered. Long fasts help no one here. Starvation wins no deference, and the taking of food in moderation is not condemned. "To his own master" each one "standeth or falleth."[5] No man judges another lest he be judged of the Lord.[6] Backbiting, so common in other parts, is wholly unknown here. Sensuality and excess are far removed from us. And in the city there are so many places of prayer that a day would not be sufficient to go round them all.

11. But, as every one praises most what is within his reach, let us pass now to the cottage-inn which sheltered Christ and Mary.[7] With what expressions and what language can we set before you the cave of the Saviour? The stall where he cried as a babe can be best honored by silence; for words are inadequate to speak its praise. Where are the spacious porticoes? Where are the gilded ceilings? Where are the mansions furnished by the miserable toil of doomed wretches? Where are the costly halls raised by untitled opulence for man's vile body to walk in? Where are the roofs that intercept the sky, as if anything could be finer than the expanse of heaven? Behold, in this poor crevice of the earth the Creator of the heavens was born; here He was wrapped in swaddling clothes; here He was seen by the shepherds; here He was pointed out by the star; here He was adored by the wise men. This spot is holier, methinks, than that Tarpeian rock[1] which has shown itself displeasing to God by the frequency with which it has been struck by lightning.

12. Read the apocalypse of John, and consider what is sung therein of the woman arrayed in purple, and of the blasphemy written upon her brow, of the seven mountains, of the many waters, and of the end of Babylon.[2] "Come out of her, my people," so the Lord says, "that ye be not partakers of her sins, and that ye receive not of her plagues."[3] Turn back also to Jeremiah and pay heed to what he has written of like import: "Flee out of the midst of Babylon, and deliver every man his soul."[4] For "Babylon the great is fallen, is fallen, and is become the habitation of devils, and the hold of every foul spirit."[5] It is true that Rome has a holy church, trophies of apostles and martyrs, a true confession of Christ. The faith has been preached there by an apostle, heathenism has been trodden down, the name of Christian is daily exalted higher and higher. But the display, power, and size of the city, the seeing and the being seen, the paying and the receiving of visits, the alternate flattery and detraction, talking and listening as well as the necessity of facing so great a throng even when one is least in the mood to do so—all these things are alike foreign to the principles and fatal to the repose of the monastic life. For when people come in our way we either see them coming and are compelled to speak, or we do not see them and lay ourselves open to the charge of haughtiness. Sometimes, also, in returning visits we are obliged to pass through proud portals and gilded doors and to face the clamor of carping lackeys. But, as we have

---

1 Luke xvii. 21.   2 Virgil, E. i. 67.   3 Luke xvii. 37.
4 Cf. Matt. xix. 30. 5 Rom. xiv. 4. 6 Matt. vii. 1. 7 Luke ii. 7.

1 Otherwise called the capitol. Here stood the great temple of Jupiter, which was to the religion of Rome what the Parthenon was to that of Athens.   2 Rev. xvii. 4, 5, 9; i. 15; xvii.; xviii.
3 Rev. xviii. 4.   4 Jer. li. 6.   5 Rev. xviii. 2.

said above, in the cottage of Christ all is simple and rustic: and except for the chanting of psalms there is complete silence. Wherever one turns the laborer at his plough sings alleluia, the toiling mower cheers himself with psalms, and the vine-dresser while he prunes his vine sings one of the lays of David. These are the songs of the country; these, in popular phrase, its love ditties; these the shepherd whistles; these the tiller uses to aid his toil.

13. But what are we doing? Forgetting what is required of us, we are taken up with what we wish. Will the time never come when a breathless messenger shall bring the news that our dear Marcella has reached the shores of Palestine, and when every band of monks and every troop of virgins shall unite in a song of welcome? In our excitement we are already hurrying to meet you: without waiting for a vehicle, we hasten off at once on foot. We shall clasp you by the hand, we shall look upon your face; and when, after long waiting, we at last embrace you, we shall find it hard to tear ourselves away. Will the day never come when we shall together enter the Saviour's cave, and together weep in the sepulchre of the Lord with His sister and with His mother?[1] Then shall we touch with our lips the wood of the cross, and rise in prayer and resolve upon the Mount of Olives with the ascending Lord.[2] We shall see Lazarus come forth bound with grave clothes,[3] we shall look upon the waters of Jordan purified for the washing of the Lord.[4] Thence we shall pass to the folds of the shepherds,[5] we shall pray together in the mausoleum of David.[6] We shall see the prophet, Amos,[7] upon his crag blowing his shepherd's horn. We shall hasten, if not to the tents, to the monuments of Abraham, Isaac and Jacob, and of their three illustrious wives.[8] We shall see the fountain in which the eunuch was immersed by Philip.[9] We shall make a pilgrimage to Samaria, and side by side venerate the ashes of John the Baptist, of Elisha,[10] and of Obadiah. We shall enter the very caves where in the time of persecution and famine the companies of the prophets were fed.[11] If only you will come, we shall go to see Nazareth, as its name denotes, the flower[12] of Galilee. Not far off Cana will be visible, where the water was turned into wine.[13] We shall make our way to Tabor,[14] and see the tabernacles there

which the Saviour shares, not, as Peter once wished, with Moses and Elijah, but with the Father and with the Holy Ghost. Thence we shall come to the Sea of Gennesaret, and when there we shall see the spots where the five thousand were filled with five loaves,[1] and the four thousand with seven.[2] The town of Nain will meet our eyes, at the gate of which the widow's son was raised to life.[3] Hermon too will be visible, and the torrent of Endor, at which Sisera was vanquished.[4] Our eyes will look also on Capernaum, the scene of so many of our Lord's signs—yes, and on all Galilee besides. And when, accompanied by Christ, we shall have made our way back to our cave through Shiloh and Bethel, and those other places where churches are set up like standards to commemorate the Lord's victories, then we shall sing heartily, we shall weep copiously, we shall pray unceasingly. Wounded with the Saviour's shaft, we shall say one to another: "I have found Him whom my soul loveth; I will hold Him and will not let Him go."[5]

LETTER XLVII.

TO DESIDERIUS.

Jerome invites two of his old friends at Rome, Desiderius and his sister (or wife) Serenilla, to join him at Bethlehem. It is possible but not probable that this Desiderius is the same with Desiderius of Aquitaine, who afterwards induced Jerome to write against Vigilantius.

An interval of seven years separates this letter (of which the date is 393 A.D.) from the preceding, and all the letters written during this period have wholly perished.

1. Surprised as I have been, my excellent friend, to read the language which your kindness has prompted you to hold concerning me, I have rejoiced that I possess the testimony of one both eloquent and sincere; but when I turn from you to myself I feel vexed that, owing to my unworthiness, your words of praise and eulogy rather weigh me down than lift me up. You know, of course, that I make it a principle to raise the standard of humility, and to prepare for scaling the heights by walking for the present in the lowest places. For what am I or what is my significance that I should have the voice of learning raised to bear witness of me, or that the palm of eloquence should be laid at my feet by one whose style is so charming that it has almost deterred me from writing a letter at all? I must, however, make the attempt in order that charity which seeks not

---

[1] Joh. xix. 25. [2] Acts i. 9, 12. [3] Joh. xi. 43, 44. [4] Matt. iii. 13. [5] Luke ii. 8. [6] 1 K. ii. 10. [7] "Who was among the herdsmen of Tekoa"—Am. i. 1. [8] Sarah, Rebekah, Leah—Gen. xlix. 31. [9] Acts viii. 36. [10] 2 K. xiii. 21. [11] 1 K. xviii. 3, 4. [12] Lit. "sprout." In Isa. xi. 1 it is rendered by A.V. "branch." [13] Joh. ii. 1–11. [14] Matt. xvii. 1–9.

[1] Matt. xiv. 15, *sqq.* [2] Matt. xv. 32, *sqq.* [3] Luke vii. 11, *sqq.* [4] Ps. lxxxiii. 9, 10. [5] Cant. iii. 4, Vulg.

her own[1] but always her neighbor's good, may at least return a compliment, since it cannot convey a lesson.

2. I offer my congratulations to you and to your holy and revered sister,[2] Serenilla, who, true to her name,[3] has trodden down the troubled waves of the world, and has passed to Christ's calm haven: a happiness which—if we may trust the augury of your name—is in store for you also. For we read that the holy Daniel was called "a man of desires,"[4] and the friend of God, because he desired to know His mysteries. Therefore, I do with pleasure what the revered Paula has asked of me. I urge and implore you both by the charity of the Lord that you will give your presence to us, and that a visit to the holy places may induce you to enrich us with this great gift. Even supposing that you do not care for our society, it is still your duty as believers to worship on the spot where the Lord's feet once stood, and to see for yourselves the still fresh traces of His birth, His cross, and His passion.

3. Several of my little pieces have flown away out of their nest, and have rashly sought for themselves the honor of publication. I have not sent you any lest I should send works which you already have. But if you care to borrow copies of them, you can do so either from our holy sister, Marcella, who has her abode upon the Aventine, or from that holy man, Domnio, who is the Lot of our times.[5] Meantime, I look for your arrival, and will give you all I have when you once come; or, if any hindrances prevent you from joining us, I will gladly send you such treatises as you shall desire. Following the example of Tranquillus[6] and of Apollonius the Greek,[7] I have written a book concerning illustrious men[8] from the apostles' time to our own; and after enumerating a great number I have put myself down on the last page as one born out of due time, and the least of all Christians.[9] Here I have found it necessary to give a short account of my writings down to the fourteenth year[10] of the Emperor Theodosius. If you find, on procuring this treatise from the persons mentioned above, that there are any pieces mentioned which you have not already got, I will have them copied for you by degrees, if you wish it.

---

[1] 1 Cor. xiii. 5. [2] *I.e.* his wife. Cf. 1 Cor. ix. 5.
[3] Serenilla, "calm."
[4] Dan. ix. 23, A.V. marg. Desiderius means "one who is an object of desire." [5] Cf. 2 Peter ii. 7, 8.
[6] *I.e.* the historian Suetonius.
[7] Probably Apollonius of Tyre, who appears to have written an account of the principal philosophers who followed Zeno.
[8] See this work in Vol. III. of this series. [9] Cf. 1 Cor. xv. 8, 9.
[10] A.D. 392–3.

LETTER XLVIII.

TO PAMMACHIUS.

An "apology" for the two books "against Jovinian" which Jerome had written a short time previously, and of which he had sent copies to Rome. These Pammachius and his other friends had withheld from publication, thinking that Jerome had unduly exalted virginity at the expense of marriage. He now writes to make good his position, and to do this makes copious extracts from the obnoxious treatise. The date of the letter is 393 or 394 A.D.

1. Your own silence is my reason for not having written hitherto. For I feared that, if I were to write to you without first hearing from you, you would consider me not so much a conscientious as a troublesome correspondent. But, now that I have been challenged by your most delightful letter, a letter which calls upon me to defend my views by an appeal to first principles, I receive my old fellow-learner, companion, and friend with open arms, as the saying goes; and I look forward to having in you a champion of my poor writings; if, that is to say, I can first conciliate your judgment to give sentence in my favor, and can instruct my advocate in all those points on which I am assailed. For both your favorite, Cicero, and before him—in his one short treatise—Antonius,[1] write to this effect, that the chief requisite for victory is to acquaint one's self carefully with the case which one has to plead.

2. Certain persons find fault with me because in the books which I have written against Jovinian I have been excessive (so they say) in praise of virginity and in depreciation of marriage; and they affirm that to preach up chastity till no comparison is left between a wife and a virgin is equivalent to a condemnation of matrimony. If I remember aright the point of the dispute, the question at issue between myself and Jovinian is that he puts marriage on a level with virginity, while I make it inferior; he declares that there is little or no difference between the two states, I assert that there is a great deal. Finally—a result due under God to your agency—he has been condemned because he has dared to set matrimony on an equality with perpetual chastity. Or, if a virgin and a wife are to be looked on as the same, how comes it that Rome has refused to listen to this impious doctrine? A virgin owes her being to a man, but a man does not owe his to a virgin. There can be no middle course. Either my view of the matter must be embraced, or else that of Jovinian. If I am blamed for putting wed-

---

[1] Marcus Antonius, a Roman orator spoken of by Cicero. Orator c. 5, De Oratore i. c. 21, 47, 48. His treatise "De ratione dicendi" is lost. See Quintal iii. 1, 192.

lock below virginity, he must be praised for putting the two states on a level. If, on the other hand, he is condemned for supposing them equal, his condemnation must be taken as testimony in favor of my treatise. If men of the world chafe under the notion that they occupy a position inferior to that of virgins, I wonder that clergymen and monks—who both live celibate lives—refrain from praising what they consistently practise. They cut themselves off from their wives to imitate the chastity of virgins, and yet they will have it that married women are as good as these. They should either be joined again to their wives whom they have renounced, or, if they persist in living apart from them, they will have to confess—by their lives if not by their words —that, in preferring virginity to marriage, they have chosen the better course. Am I then a mere novice in the Scriptures, reading the sacred volumes for the first time? And is the line there drawn between virginity and marriage so fine that I have been unable to observe it? I could know nothing, forsooth, of the saying, " Be not righteous overmuch!" [1] Thus, while I try to protect myself on one side, I am wounded on the other; to speak more plainly still, while I close with Jovinian in hand-to-hand combat, Manichæus stabs me in the back. Have I not, I would ask, in the very forefront of my work set the following preface: [2] " We are no disciples of Marcion [3] or of Manichæus, [4] to detract from marriage. Nor are we deceived by the error of Tatian, [5] the chief of the Encratites, [6] into supposing all cohabitation unclean. For he condemns and reprobates not marriage only, but foods also which God has created for us to enjoy. [7] We know that in a large house there are vessels not only of silver and of gold, but of wood also and of earth. [8] We know, too, that on the foundation of Christ which Paul the master builder has laid, some build up gold, silver, and precious stones; others, on the contrary, hay, wood, and stubble. [9] We are not ignorant that 'marriage is honorable . . . and the bed undefiled.' [10] We have read the first decree of God: 'Be fruitful and multiply and replenish the earth.' [11] But while we allow marriage, we prefer the virginity which springs from it. Gold is more precious than silver, but is silver on that account the less silver? Is it an insult to a tree to prefer its apples to its roots or its leaves? Is it an injury to corn to put the ear before the stalk and the blade? As apples come from the tree and grain from the straw, so virginity comes from wedlock. Yields of one hundredfold, of sixtyfold, and of thirtyfold [1] may all come from one soil and from one sowing, yet they will differ widely in quantity. The yield thirtyfold signifies wedlock, for the joining together of the fingers to express that number, suggestive as it is of a loving gentle kiss or embracing, aptly represents the relation of husband and wife. The yield sixtyfold refers to widows who are placed in a position of distress and tribulation. Accordingly, they are typified by that finger which is placed under the other to express the number sixty; for, as it is extremely trying when one has once tasted pleasure to abstain from its enticements, so the reward of doing this is proportionately great. Moreover, a hundred—I ask the reader to give me his best attention —necessitates a change from the left hand to the right; but while the hand is different the fingers are the same as those which on the left hand signify married women and widows; only in this instance the circle formed by them indicates the crown of virginity." [2]

3. Does a man who speaks thus, I would ask you, condemn marriage? If I have called virginity gold, I have spoken of marriage as silver. I have set forth that the yields an hundredfold, sixtyfold, and thirtyfold—all spring from one soil and from one sowing, although in amount they differ widely. Will any of my readers be so unfair as to judge me, not by my words, but by his own opinion? At any rate, I have dealt much more gently with marriage than most Latin and Greek writers; [3] who, by referring the hundredfold yield to martyrs, the sixtyfold to virgins, and the thirtyfold to widows, show that in their opinion married persons are excluded from the good ground and from the seed of the great Father. [4] But, lest it might be supposed that, though cautious at the outset, I was imprudent in the remainder of my work, have I not, after

---

[1] Eccl. vii. 16: see Ag. Jov. i. 14.   [2] Against Jov. i. 3.
[3] A Gnostic presbyter of the second century who rejected the Old Testament.
[4] An Eastern teacher of the third century, A.D., the main feature of whose system was its uncompromising dualism.
[5] A Syrian rhetorician converted to Christianity by Justin Martyr. He wrote a harmony of the Gospels called Diatessaron.
[6] *I.e.* "the abstainers," or "the continent," a Gnostic sect in the second century.   [7] 1 Tim. iv. 3.   [8] 2 Tim. ii. 20.
[9] 1 Cor. iii. 10–12.   [10] Heb. xiii. 4.   [11] Gen. i. 28.

[1] Matt. xiii. 8.   [2] From this passage compared with Ep. cxxiii. 9, and Bede De Temporum Ratione, c. 1. (De Loquelâ Digitorum), it appears that the number thirty was indicated by joining the tips of the thumb and forefinger of the left hand, sixty was indicated by curling up the forefinger of the same hand and then doubling the thumb over it, while one hundred was expressed by joining the tips of the thumb and forefinger of the right hand. See Prof. Mayor's learned note on Juv. x. 249.
[3] *E.g.* Cyprian and Origen (Hom. i. in Jos.).
[4] Paterfamilias. *Vide* Cypr. de Hab. Virg. 21.

marking out the divisions of it, on coming to the actual questions immediately introduced the following:[1] "I ask all of you of both sexes, at once those who are virgins and continent and those who are married or twice married, to aid my efforts with your prayers." Jovinian is the foe of all indiscriminately, but can I condemn as Manichæan heretics persons whose prayers I need and whose assistance I entreat to help me in my work?

4. As the brief compass of a letter does not suffer us to delay too long on a single point, let us now pass to those which remain. In explaining the testimony of the apostle, "The wife hath not power of her own body, but the husband; and likewise, also, the husband hath not power of his own body, but the wife,"[2] we have subjoined the following:[3] "The entire question relates to those who are living in wedlock, whether it is lawful for them to put away their wives, a thing which the Lord also has forbidden in the Gospel.[4] Hence, also, the apostle says: 'It is good for a man not to touch' a wife or 'a woman,'[5] as if there were danger in the contact which he who should so touch one could not escape. Accordingly, when the Egyptian woman desired to touch Joseph he flung away his cloak and fled from her hands.[6] But as he who has once married a wife cannot, except by consent, abstain from intercourse with her or repudiate her, so long as she does not sin, he must render unto his wife her due,[7] because he has of his own free will bound himself to render it under compulsion." Can one who declares that it is a precept of the Lord that wives should not be put away, and that what God has joined together man must not, without consent, put asunder[8]—can such an one be said to condemn marriage? Again, in the verses which follow, the apostle says: "But every man hath his proper gift of God, one after this manner, and another after that."[9] In explanation of this saying we made the following remarks:[10] "What I myself would wish, he says, is clear. But since there are diversities of gifts in the church,[11] I allow marriage as well, that I may not appear to condemn nature. Reflect, too, that the gift of virginity is one thing, that of marriage another. For had there been one reward for married women and for virgins he would never, after giving the counsel of conti-

nence, have gone on to say: 'But every man hath his proper gift of God, one after this manner and another after that.' Where each class has its proper gift, there must be some distinction between the classes. I allow that marriage, as well as virginity, is the gift of God, but there is a great difference between gift and gift. Finally, the apostle himself says of one who had lived in incest and afterwards repented: 'Contrariwise ye ought rather to forgive him and comfort him,'[1] and 'To whom ye forgive anything, I forgive also.'[2] And, lest we might suppose a man's gift to be but a small thing, he has added: 'For if I forgave anything, to whom I forgave it, for your sakes forgave I it in the sight[3] of Christ.'[4] The gifts of Christ are different. Hence Joseph as a type of Him had a coat of many colors.[5] So in the forty-fourth psalm[6] we read of the Church: 'Upon thy right hand did stand the queen in a vesture of gold, wrought about with divers colors.'[7] The apostle Peter, too, speaks (of husbands and wives) 'as being heirs together of the manifold grace of God.'[8] In Greek the expression is still more striking, the word used being ποικίλη, that is, 'many-colored.'"

5. I ask, then, what is the meaning of men's obstinate determination to shut their eyes and to refuse to look on what is as clear as day? I have said that there are diversities of gifts in the Church, and that virginity is one gift and wedlock another. And shortly after I have used the words: "I allow marriage also to be a gift of God, but there is a great difference between gift and gift." Can it be said that I condemn that which in the clearest terms I declare to be the gift of God? Moreover, if Joseph is taken as a type of the Lord, his coat of many colors is a type of virgins and widows, celibates and wedded. Can any one who has any part in Christ's tunic be regarded as an alien? Have we not spoken of the very queen herself—that is, the Church of the Saviour—as wearing a vesture of gold wrought about with divers colors? Moreover, when I came to discuss marriage in connection with the following verses,[9] I still adhered to the same view.[10] "This passage," I said, "has indeed no relation to the present controversy; for, following the decision of the Lord, the apostle teaches that a wife must not be put away saving for fornication, and

---

[1] Ag. Jov. i. 4.　　　　[2] 1 Cor. vii. 4.
[3] Ag. Jov. i. 7.　　　　[4] Matt. xix. 9.
[5] 1 Cor. vii. 1.　　[6] Gen. xxxix. 12, 13.　　[7] 1 Cor. vii. 3, R.V.
[8] Matt. xix. 6.　　　　[9] 1 Cor. vii. 7.
[10] Ag. Jov. i. 8.　　　[11] 1 Cor. xii. 4.

[1] 2 Cor. ii. 7.　　　　　　[2] 2 Cor. ii. 10.
[3] A.V. marg.　[4] 2 Cor. ii. 10.　[5] Gen. xxxvii. 23.
[6] Acc. to the Vulgate.　In A.V. it is the 45th.
[7] Ps. xlv. 10, P.B.V.　[8] 1 Pet. iii. 7; iv. 10.
[9] 1 Cor. vii. 8-10.　　　[10] Ag. Jov. i. 10.

that, if she has been put away, she cannot during the lifetime of her husband marry another man, or, at any rate, that she ought, if possible, to be reconciled to her husband. In another verse he speaks to the same effect: ' The wife is bound . . . as long as her husband liveth; but if her husband be dead, she is loosed from the law of her husband;[1] she is at liberty to be married to whom she will; only in the Lord,'[2] that is, to a Christian. Thus the apostle, while he allows a second or a third marriage in the Lord, forbids even a first with a heathen."

6. I ask my detractors to open their ears and to realize the fact that I have allowed second and third marriages " in the Lord." If, then, I have not condemned second and third marriages, how can I have proscribed a first? Moreover, in the passage where I interpret the words of the apostle, " Is any man called being circumcised? Let him not become uncircumcised. Is any called in uncircumcision? let him not be circumcised"[3] (a passage, it is true, which some most careful interpreters of Scripture refer to the circumcision and slavery of the Law), do I not in the clearest terms stand up for the marriage-tie? My words are these:[4] " ' If any man is called in uncircumcision, let him not be circumcised.' You had a wife, the apostle says, when you believed. Do not fancy your faith in Christ to be a reason for parting from her. For 'God hath called us in peace.'[5] 'Circumcision is nothing and uncircumcision is nothing but the keeping of the commandments of God.'[6] Neither celibacy nor wedlock is of the slightest use without works, since even faith, the distinguishing mark of Christians, if it have not works, is said to be dead,[7] and on such terms as these the virgins of Vesta or of Juno, who was constant to one[8] husband, might claim to be numbered among the saints. And a little further on he says: 'Art thou called being a servant, care not for it; but, if thou mayest be made free, use it rather;'[9] that is to say, if you have a wife, and are bound to her, and render her her due, and have not power of your own body—or, to speak yet more plainly—if you are the slave of a wife, do not allow this to cause you sorrow, do not sigh over the loss of your virginity. Even if you can find pretexts for parting from her to enjoy the freedom of chastity, do not seek your own welfare at the price of another's ruin. Keep your wife for a little, and do not try too hastily to overcome her reluctance. Wait till she follows your example. If you only have patience, your wife will some day become your sister."

7. In another passage we have discussed the reasons which led Paul to say: " Now concerning virgins, I have no commandment of the Lord: yet I give my judgment, as one that hath obtained mercy of the Lord to be faithful."[1] Here also, while we have extolled virginity, we have been careful to give marriage its due.[2] " Had the Lord commanded virginity," we said, " He would have seemed to condemn marriage and to do away with that seed-plot of humanity from which virginity itself springs. Had He cut away the root how could He have looked for fruit? Unless He had first laid the foundations, how could He have built the edifice or crowned it with a roof made to cover its whole extent?" If we have spoken of marriage as the root whose fruit is virginity, and if we have made wedlock the foundation on which the building or the roof of perpetual chastity is raised, which of my detractors can be so captious or so blind as to ignore the foundation on which the fabric and its roof are built, while he has before his eyes both the fabric and the roof themselves? Once more, in another place, we have brought forward the testimony of the apostle to this effect: " Art thou bound unto a wife? Seek not to be loosed. Art thou loosed from a wife? Seek not a wife."[3] To this we have appended the following remarks:[4] " Each of us has his own sphere allotted to him. Let me have mine, and do you keep yours. If you are bound to a wife, do not put her away. If I am loosed from a wife, let me not seek a wife. Just as I do not loose marriage-ties when they are once made, so do you refrain from binding together what at present is loosed from such ties." Yet another passage bears unmistakable testimony to the view which we have taken of virginity and of wedlock:[5] " The apostle casts no snare upon us,[6] nor does he compel us to be what we do not wish. He only urges us to what is honorable and seemly, inciting us earnestly to serve the Lord, to be anxious always to please Him, and to look for His will which He has prepared for us to do. We are to be like alert and armed soldiers, who immediately execute the orders given to them and perform them without that travail of mind[7] which,

---

[1] Rom. vii. 2. [2] 1 Cor. vii. 39.
[3] 1 Cor. vii. 18. [4] Ag. Jov. i. 11.
[5] 1 Cor. vii. 15, R.V. [6] 1 Cor. vii. 19. [7] Jas. ii. 17.
[8] Univira. [9] 1 Cor. vii. 21.

[1] 1 Cor. vii. 25. [2] Ag. Jov. i. 12. [3] 1 Cor. vii. 21.
[4] Ag. Jov. i. 12. [5] Ag. Jov. i. 13. [6] 1 Cor. vii. 35.
[7] Jerome here explains the word ἀπερισπαστῶς (A.V. " without distraction ") in 1 Cor. vii. 35.

according to the preacher, is given to the men of this world 'to be exercised therewith.'"[1] At the end, also, of our comparison of virgins and married women we have summed up the discussion thus:[2] "When one thing is good and another thing is better; when that which is good has a different reward from that which is better; and when there are more rewards than one, then, obviously, there exists a diversity of gifts. The difference between marriage and virginity is as great as that between not doing evil and doing good—or, to speak more favorably still, as that between what is good and what is still better."

8. In the sequel we go on to speak thus:[3] "The apostle, in concluding his discussion of marriage and of virginity, is careful to observe a mean course in discriminating between them, and, turning neither to the right hand nor to the left, he keeps to the King's highway,[4] and thus fulfils the injunction, 'Be not righteous overmuch.'[5] Moreover, when he goes on to compare monogamy with digamy, he puts digamy after monogamy, just as before he subordinated marriage to virginity." Do we not clearly show by this language what is typified in the Holy Scriptures by the terms right and left, and also what we take to be the meaning of the words "Be not righteous overmuch"? We turn to the left if, following the lust of Jews and Gentiles, we burn for sexual intercourse; we turn to the right if, following the error of the Manichæans, we under a pretence of chastity entangle ourselves in the meshes of unchastity. But we keep to the King's highway if we aspire to virginity yet refrain from condemning marriage. Can any one, moreover, be so unfair in his criticism of my poor treatise as to allege that I condemn first marriages, when he reads my opinion on second ones as follows:[6] "The apostle, it is true, allows second marriages, but only to such women as are bent upon them, to such as cannot contain,[7] lest 'when they have begun to wax wanton against Christ they marry, having condemnation because they have rejected their first faith,'[8] and he makes this concession because many 'are turned aside after Satan.'[9] But they will be happier if they abide as widows. To this he immediately adds his apostolical authority, 'after my judgment.' Moreover, lest any should consider that authority, being human, to be of small weight, he goes

on to say, 'and I think also that I have the spirit of God.'[1] Thus, where he urges men to continence he appeals not to human authority, but to the Spirit of God; but when he gives them permission to marry he does not mention the Spirit of God, but allows prudential considerations to turn the balance, relaxing the strictness of his code in favor of individuals according to their several needs." Having thus brought forward proofs that second marriages are allowed by the apostle, we at once added the remarks which follow:[2] "As marriage is permitted to virgins by reason of the danger of fornication, and as what in itself is not desirable is thus made excusable, so by reason of the same danger widows are permitted to marry a second time. For it is better that a woman should know one man (though he should be a second husband or a third) than that she should know several. In other words, it is preferable that she should prostitute herself to one rather than to many." Calumny may do its worst. We have spoken here not of a first marriage, but of a second, of a third, or (if you like) of a fourth. But lest any one should apply my words (that it is better for a woman to prostitute herself to one man than to several) to a first marriage when my whole argument dealt with digamy and trigamy, I marked my own view of these practices with the words:[3] "'All things are lawful, but all things are not expedient.'[4] I do not condemn digamists nor yet trigamists, nor even, to put an extreme case, octogamists. I will make a still greater concession: I am ready to receive even a whoremonger, if penitent. In every case where fairness is possible, fair consideration must be shown."

9. My calumniator should blush at his assertion that I condemn first marriages when he reads my words just now quoted: "I do not condemn digamists or trigamists, or even, to put an extreme case, octogamists." Not to condemn is one thing, to commend is another. I may concede a practice as allowable and yet not praise it as meritorious. But if I seem severe in saying, "In every case where fairness is possible, fair consideration must be shown," no one, I fancy, will judge me either cruel or stern who reads that the places prepared for virgins and for wedded persons are different from those prepared for trigamists, octogamists, and penitents. That Christ Himself, although in the flesh a virgin, was in the spirit a monogamist,

---

[1] Eccles. i. 13; iii. 10.   [2] Ag. Jov. i. 13.   [3] Ag. Jov. i. 14.
[4] Nu. xx. 17.   [5] Eccles. vii. 16.   [6] Ag. Jov. i. 14.
[7] 1 Cor. vii. 9.   [8] 1 Tim. v. 11, 12, R.V.   [9] 1 Tim. v. 15.

[1] 1 Cor. vii. 40.   [2] Ag. Jov. i. 14.
[3] Ag. Jov. i. 15.   [4] 1 Cor. vi. 12.

having one wife, even the Church,[1] I have shown in the latter part of my argument.[2] And yet I am supposed to condemn marriage! I am said to condemn it, although I use such words as these:[3] "It is an undoubted fact that the levitical priests were descended from the stock of Aaron, Eleazar, and Phinehas; and, as all these were married men, we might well be confronted with them if, led away by the error of the Encratites, we were to contend that marriage is in itself deserving of condemnation." Here I blame Tatian, the chief of the Encratites, for his rejection of marriage, and yet I myself am said to condemn it! Once more, when I contrast virgins with widows, my own words show what my view is concerning wedlock, and set forth the threefold gradation which I propose of virgins, widows—whether in practice or in fact[4]—and wedded wives. "I do not deny"—these are my words[5]—"the blessedness of widows who continue such after their baptism, nor do I undervalue the merit of wives who live in chastity with their husbands; but, just as widows receive a greater reward from God than wives obedient to their husbands, they, too, must be content to see virgins preferred before themselves."

10. Again, when explaining the witness of the apostle to the Galatians, "By the works of the law shall no flesh be justified," I have spoken to the following effect: "Marriages also are works of the law. And for this reason there is a curse upon such as do not produce offspring. They are permitted, it is true, even under the Gospel; but it is one thing to concede an indulgence to what is a weakness and quite another to promise a reward to what is a virtue." See my express declaration that marriage is allowed in the Gospel, yet that those who are married cannot receive the rewards of chastity so long as they render their due one to another. If married men feel indignant at this statement, let them vent their anger not on me but on the Holy Scriptures; nay, more, upon all bishops, presbyters, and deacons, and the whole company of priests and levites, who know that they cannot offer sacrifices if they fulfil the obligations of marriage. Again, when I adduce evidence from the Apocalypse,[6] is it not clear what view I take concerning virgins, widows, and wives? "These are they who sing a new song[7] which no man can sing except he be a virgin. These are 'the first fruits unto God

and unto the Lamb," and they are without spot. If virgins are the first fruits unto God, then widows and wives who live in continence must come after the first fruits— that is to say, in the second place and in the third." We place widows, then, and wives in the second place and in the third, and for this we are charged by the frenzy of a heretic with condemning marriage altogether.

11. Throughout the book I have made many remarks in a tone of great moderation on virginity, widowhood, and marriage. But for the sake of brevity, I will here adduce but one passage, and that of such a kind that no one, I think, will be found to gainsay it save some one who wishes to prove himself malicious or mad. In describing our Lord's visit to the marriage at Cana in Galilee,[2] after some other remarks I have added these:[3] "He who went but once to a marriage has taught us that a woman should marry but once; and this fact might tell against virginity if we failed to give marriage its due place—after virginity that is, and chaste widowhood. But, as it is only heretics who condemn marriage and tread under foot the ordinance of God, we listen with gladness to every word said by our Lord in praise of marriage. For the Church does not condemn marriage, but only subordinates it. It does not reject it altogether, but regulates it, knowing (as I have said above) that 'in a great house there are not only vessels of gold and of silver, but also of wood and of earth; and some to honor and some to dishonor. If a man, therefore, purge himself . . . he shall be a vessel unto honor meet . . . and prepared unto every good work.'"[4] I listen with gladness, I say here, to every word said by the apostle in praise of marriage. Do I listen with gladness to the praise of marriage, and do I yet condemn marriage? The Church, I say, does not condemn wedlock, but subordinates it. Whether you like it or not, marriage is subordinated to virginity and widowhood. Even when marriage continues to fulfil its function, the Church does not condemn it, but only subordinates it; it does not reject it, but only regulates it. It is in your power, if you will, to mount the second step of chastity.[5] Why are you angry if, standing on the third and lowest step, you will not make haste to go up higher?

12. Since, then, I have so often reminded my reader of my views; and since I have picked

---

[1] Eph. v. 23, 24.   [2] Ag. Jov. i. 9.   [3] Ag. Jov. i. 23.
[4] Viduitas vel continentia.   [5] Ag. Jov. i. 33.
[6] Ag. Jov. i. 40.   [7] Rev. xiv. 3.

[1] Rev. xiv. 4.   [2] Joh. ii. 1, 2.   [3] Ag. Jov. i. 40.
[4] 2 Tim. ii. 20, 21.   [5] I.e. continence in marriage.

my way like a prudent traveller over every inch of the road, stating repeatedly that, while I receive marriage as a thing in itself admissible, I yet prefer continence, widowhood, and virginity, the wise and generous reader ought to have judged what seemed hard sayings by my general drift, and not to have charged me with putting forward inconsistent opinions in one and the same book. For who is so dull or so inexperienced in writing as to praise and to condemn one and the same object, as to destroy what he has built up, and to build up what he has destroyed; and when he has vanquished his opponent, to turn his sword, last of all, against himself? Were my detractors country bred or unacquainted with the arts of rhetoric or of logic, I should pardon their want of insight; nor should I censure them for accusing me if I saw that their ignorance was in fault and not their will. As it is, men of intellect who have enjoyed a liberal education make it their object less to understand me than to wound me, and for such I have this short answer, that they should correct my faults and not merely censure me for them. The lists are open, I cry; your enemy has marshalled his forces, his position is plain, and (if I may quote Virgil[1])—

The foeman calls you: meet him face to face.

Such men should answer their opponent. They ought to keep within the limits of debate, and not to wield the schoolmaster's rod. Their books should aim at showing in what my statements have fallen short of the truth, and in what they have exceeded it. For, although I will not listen to faultfinders, I will follow the advice of teachers. To direct the fighter how to fight when you yourself occupy a post of vantage on the wall is a kind of teaching that does not commend itself; and when you are yourself bathed in perfumes, it is unworthy to charge a bleeding soldier with cowardice. Nor in saying this do I lay myself open to a charge of boasting that while others have slept I only have entered the lists. My meaning simply is that men who have seen me wounded in this warfare may possibly be a little too cautious in their methods of fighting. I would not have you engage in an encounter in which you will have nothing to do but to protect yourself, your right hand remaining motionless while your left manages your shield. You must either strike or fall. I cannot account you a victor unless I see your opponent put to the sword.

13. You are, no doubt, men of vast acquirements; but we too have studied in the schools, and, like you, we have learned from the precepts of Aristotle—or, rather, from those which he has derived from Gorgias— that there are different ways of speaking; and we know, among other things, that he who writes for display uses one style, and he who writes to convince, another.[1] In the former case the debate is desultory; to confute the opposer, now this argument is adduced and now that. One argues as one pleases, saying one thing while one means another. To quote the proverb, "With one hand one offers bread, in the other one holds a stone."[2] In the latter case a certain frankness and openness of countenance are necessary. For it is one thing to start a problem and another to expound what is already proved. The first calls for a disputant, the second for a teacher. I stand in the thick of the fray, my life in constant danger: you who profess to teach me are a man of books. "Do not," you say, "attack unexpectedly or wound by a sidethrust. Strike straight at your opponent. You should be ashamed to resort to feints instead of force." As if it were not the perfection of fighting to menace one part and to strike another. Read, I beg of you, Demosthenes or Cicero, or (if you do not care for pleaders whose aim is to speak plausibly rather than truly) read Plato, Theophrastus, Xenophon, Aristotle, and the rest of those who draw their respective rills of wisdom from the Socratic fountain-head. Do they show any openness? Are they devoid of artifice? Is not every word they say filled with meaning? And does not this meaning always make for victory? Origen, Methodius, Eusebius, and Apollinaris[3] write at great length against Celsus and Porphyry.[4] Consider how subtle are the arguments, how insidious the engines with which they overthrow what the spirit of the devil has wrought. Sometimes, it is true, they are compelled to say not what they think but what is needful; and for this reason they employ against their opponents the assertions of the Gentiles themselves. I say nothing of the Latin authors, of Tertullian, Cyprian, Minutius, Victorinus, Lactantius, Hilary, lest I should appear not so much to be defending myself as to be assailing

---

[1] Virg. A. xi. 374, 5.

[1] Aliud esse γυμναστικῶς scribere, aliud δογματικῶς. The words do not appear to be used in this sense in the extant works of Aristotle. [2] Plaut. Aul. ii. 2, 18.
[3] The reply of Origen to Celsus is still extant ; those of Methodius, Eusebius and Apollinaris to Porphyry have perished. Cf. Letter LXX. § 3.
[4] Two philosophic opponents of Christianity who flourished, the first in the second, the second in the third, century of our era.

others. I will only mention the Apostle Paul, whose words seem to me, as often as I hear them, to be not words, but peals of thunder. Read his epistles, and especially those addressed to the Romans, to the Galatians, and to the Ephesians, in all of which he stands in the thick of the battle, and you will see how skilful and how careful he is in the proofs which he draws from the Old Testament, and how warily he cloaks the object which he has in view. His words seem simplicity itself: the expressions of a guileless and unsophisticated person—one who has no skill either to plan a dilemma or to avoid it. Still, whichever way you look, they are thunderbolts. His pleading halts, yet he carries every point which he takes up. He turns his back upon his foe only to overcome him; he simulates flight, but only that he may slay. He, then, if any one, ought to be calumniated; we should speak thus to him: "The proofs which you have used against the Jews or against other heretics bear a different meaning in their own contexts to that which they bear in your epistles. We see passages taken captive by your pen and pressed into service to win you a victory which in the volumes from which they are taken have no controversial bearing at all." May he not reply to us in the words of the Saviour: "I have one mode of speech for those that are without and another for those that are within; the crowds hear my parables, but their interpretation is for my disciples alone"?[1] The Lord puts questions to the Pharisees, but does not elucidate them. To teach a disciple is one thing; to vanquish an opponent, another. "My mystery is for me," says the prophet; "my mystery is for me and for them that are mine."[2]

14. You are indignant with me because I have merely silenced Jovinian and not instructed him. You, do I say? Nay, rather, they who grieve to hear him anathematized, and who impeach their own pretended orthodoxy by eulogizing in another the heresy which they hold themselves. I should have asked him, forsooth, to surrender peaceably! I had no right to disregard his struggles and to drag him against his will into the bonds of truth! I might use such language had the desire of victory induced me to say anything counter to the rule laid down in Scripture, and had I taken the line—so often adopted by strong men in controversy—of justifying the means by the result. As it is, however, I have been an exponent of the

apostle rather than a dogmatist on my own account; and my function has been simply that of a commentator. Anything, therefore, which seems a hard saying should be imputed to the writer expounded by me rather than to me the expounder; unless, indeed, he spoke otherwise than he is represented to have done, and I have by an unfair interpretation wrested the plain meaning of his words. If any one charges me with this disingenuousness let him prove his charge from the Scriptures themselves.

I have said in my book,[1] "If 'it is good for a man not to touch a woman,' then it is bad for him to touch one, for bad, and bad only, is the opposite of good. But, if though bad it is made venial, then it is allowed to prevent something which would be worse than bad," and so on down to the commencement of the next chapter. The above is my comment upon the apostle's words: "It is good for a man not to touch a woman. Nevertheless, to avoid fornication, let every man have his own wife, and let every woman have her own husband."[2] In what way does my meaning differ from that intended by the apostle? Except that where he speaks decidedly I do so with hesitation. He defines a dogma, I hazard an inquiry. He openly says: "It is good for a man not to touch a woman." I timidly ask if it is good for a man not to touch one. If I thus waver, I cannot be said to speak positively. He says: "It is good not to touch." I add what is a possible antithesis to "good." And immediately afterwards I speak thus:[3] "Notice the apostle's carefulness. He does not say: 'It is good for a man not to have a wife,' but, 'It is good for a man not to touch a woman'; as if there is danger in the very touching of one—danger which he who touches cannot escape." You see, therefore, that I am not expounding the law as to husbands and wives, but simply discussing the general question of sexual intercourse—how in comparison with chastity and virginity, the life of angels, "It is good for a man not to touch a woman."

"Vanity of vanities," says the Preacher, "all is vanity."[4] But if all created things are good,[5] as being the handiwork of a good Creator, how comes it that all things are vanity? If the earth is vanity, are the heavens vanity too?—and the angels, the thrones, the dominations, the powers, and the rest of the virtues?[6] No; if things which are

---

[1] Matt. xiii. 10-17. [2] Isa. xxiv. 16, Vulg.

[1] Ag. Jov. i. 7. [2] 1 Cor. vii. 1, 2. [3] Ag. Jov. i. 7.
[4] Eccles. i. 2. [5] Gen. i. 31; 1 Tim. iv. 4.
[6] Col. i. 16. Cf. Milton, P. L. v. 601.

good in themselves as being the handiwork of a good Creator are called vanity, it is because they are compared with things which are better still. For example, compared with a lamp, a lantern is good for nothing; compared with a star, a lamp does not shine at all; the brightest star pales before the moon; put the moon beside the sun, and it no longer looks bright; ·compare the sun with Christ, and it is darkness. "I am that I am," God says;[1] and if you compare all created things with Him they have no existence. "Give not thy sceptre," says Esther, "unto them that be nothing"[2]—that is to say, to idols and demons. And certainly they were idols and demons to whom she prayed that she and hers might not be given over. In Job also we read how Bildad says of the wicked man: "His confidence shall be rooted out of his tabernacle, and destruction as a king shall trample upon him. The companions also of him who is not shall abide in his tabernacle."[3] This evidently relates to the devil, who must be in existence, otherwise he could not be said to have companions. Still, because he is lost to God, he is said not to be.

Now it was in a similar sense that I declared it to be a bad thing to touch a woman —I did not say a wife—because it is a good thing not to touch one. And I added:[4] "I call virginity fine corn, wedlock barley, and fornication cow-dung." Surely both corn and barley are creatures of God. But of the two multitudes miraculously supplied in the Gospel the larger was fed upon barley loaves, and the smaller on corn bread.[5] "Thou, Lord," says the psalmist, "shalt save both man and beast."[6] I have myself said the same thing in other words, when I have spoken of virginity as gold and of wedlock as silver.[7] Again, in discussing[8] the one hundred and forty-four thousand sealed virgins who were not defiled with women,[9] I have tried to show that all who have not remained virgins are reckoned as defiled when compared with the perfect chastity of the angels and of our Lord Jesus Christ. But if any one thinks it hard or reprehensible that I have placed the same interval between virginity and wedlock as there is between fine corn and barley, let him read the book of the holy Ambrose "On Widows," and he will find, among other statements concerning virginity and marriage, the following:[10]

"The apostle has not expressed his preference for marriage so unreservedly as to quench in men the aspiration after virginity; he commences with a recommendation of continence, and it is only subsequently that he stoops to mention the remedies for its opposite. And although to the strong he has pointed out the prize of their high calling,[1] yet he suffers none to faint by the way;[2] whilst he applauds those who lead the van, he does not despise those who bring up the rear. For he had himself learned that the Lord Jesus gave to some barley bread, lest they should faint by the way, but offered to others His own body, that they should strive to attain His kingdom;"[3] and immediately afterwards: "The nuptial tie, then, is not to be avoided as a crime, but to be refused as a hard burden. For the law binds the wife to bring forth children in labor and in sorrow. Her desire is to be to her husband that he should rule over her.[4] It is not the widow, then, but the bride, who is handed over to labor and sorrow in childbearing. It is not the virgin, but the married woman, who is subjected to the sway of a husband." And in another place, "Ye are bought," says the apostle, "with a price;[5] be not therefore the servants of men."[6] You see how clearly he defines the servitude which attends the married state. And a little farther on: "If, then, even a good marriage is servitude, what must a bad one be, in which husband and wife cannot sanctify, but only mutually destroy each other?" What I have said about virginity and marriage diffusely, Ambrose has stated tersely and pointedly, compressing much meaning into a few words. Virginity is described by him as a means of recommending continence, marriage as a remedy for incontinence. And when he descends from broad principles to particular details, he significantly holds out to virgins the prize of the high calling, yet comforts the married, that they may not faint by the way. While eulogizing the one class, he does not despise the other. Marriage he compares to the barley bread set before the multitude, virginity to the body of Christ given to the disciples. There is much less difference, it seems to me, between barley and fine corn than between barley and the body of Christ. Finally, he speaks of marriage as a hard burden, to be avoided if possible, and as a badge of the most unmistakable servi-

---

[1] Ex. iii. 14. [2] Esth. xiv. 11. [3] Job xviii. 14, 15, Vulg.
[4] Ag. Jov. i. 7. [5] Matt. xiv. 15-21 ; xv. 32-38. Cf. Joh. vi. 5-13.
[6] Ps. xxxvi. 7, P.B.V. [7] Ag. Jov. i. 3.
[8] Ag. Jov. i. 40. [9] Rev. xiv. 1, 4.
[10] Ambrose, On Widowhood, xiii. 79 ; xiii. 81 ; xi. 69.

[1] Phil. iii. 14. [2] Matt. xv. 32.
[3] Matt. xxvi. 26, 29. [4] Gen. iii. 16.
[5] 1 Cor. vi. 20; vii. 23. [6] Cf. Eph. vi. 6.

tude. He makes, also, many other statements, which he has followed up at length in his three books " On Virgins."

15. From all which considerations it is clear that I have said nothing at all new concerning virginity and marriage, but have followed in all respects the judgment of older writers—of Ambrose, that is to say, and others who have discussed the doctrines of the Church. "And I would sooner follow them in their faults than copy the dull pedantry of the writers of to-day." [1] Let married men, if they please, swell with rage because I have said, [2] "I ask you, what kind of good thing is that which forbids a man to pray, and which prevents him from receiving the body of Christ?" When I do my duty as a husband, I cannot fulfil the requirements of continence. The same apostle, in another place, commands us to pray always. [3] "But if we are always to pray we must never yield to the claims of wedlock, for, as often as I render her due to my wife, I incapacitate myself for prayer." When I spoke thus it is clear that I relied on the words of the apostle: "Defraud ye not one the other, except it be with consent for a time, that ye may give yourselves to . . . prayer." [4] The Apostle Paul tells us that when we have intercourse with our wives we cannot pray. If, then, sexual intercourse prevents what is less important—that is, prayer—how much more does it prevent what is more important—that is, the reception of the body of Christ? Peter, too, exhorts us to continence, that our "prayers be not hindered." [5] How, I should like to know, have I sinned in all this? What have I done? How have I been in fault? If the waters of a stream are thick and muddy, it is not the river-bed which is to blame, but the source. Am I attacked because I have ventured to add to the words of the apostle these words of my own: "What kind of good thing is that which prevents a man from receiving the body of Christ?" If so, I will make answer briefly thus: Which is the more important, to pray or to receive Christ's body? Surely to receive Christ's body. If, then, sexual intercourse hinders the less important thing, much more does it hinder that which is the more important.

I have said in the same treatise[6] that David and they that were with him could not have lawfully eaten the shew-bread had they not made answer that for three days

they had not been defiled with women[1]— not, of course, with harlots, intercourse with whom was forbidden by the law, but with their own wives, to whom they were lawfully united. Moreover, when the people were about to receive the law on Mount Sinai they were commanded to keep away from their wives for three days.[2] I know that at Rome it is customary for the faithful always to receive the body of Christ, a custom which I neither censure nor indorse. "Let every man be fully persuaded in his own mind."[3] But I appeal to the consciences of those persons who after indulging in sexual intercourse on the same day receive the communion—having first, as Persius puts it, "washed off the night in a flowing stream,"[4] and I ask such why they do not presume to approach the martyrs or to enter the churches.[5] Is Christ of one mind abroad and of another at home? What is unlawful in church cannot be lawful at home. Nothing is hidden from God. "The night shineth as the day" before Him.[6] Let each man examine himself, and so let him approach the body of Christ.[7] Not, of course, that the deferring of communion for one day or for two makes a Christian any the holier or that what I have not deserved to-day I shall deserve to-morrow or the day after. But if I grieve that I have not shared in Christ's body it does help me to avoid for a little while my wife's embraces, and to prefer to wedded love the love of Christ. A hard discipline, you will say, and one not to be borne. What man of the world could bear it? He that can bear it, I reply, let him bear it;[8] he that cannot must look to himself. It is my business to say, not what each man can do or will do, but what the Scriptures inculcate.

16. Again, objection has been taken to my comments on the apostle in the following passage:[9] "But lest any should suppose from the context of the words before quoted (namely, 'that ye may give yourselves . . . to prayer and come together again') that

---

[1] 1 Sam. xxi. 4, 5.   [2] Ex. xix. 15.
[3] Rom. xiv. 5.   [4] Pers. ii. 16.
[5] That what is now known as reservation of the elements was practised in the early church there is abundant evidence to show. Justin Martyr (Apol. I. 65) writes: " The deacons communicate each of those present and carry away to the absent of the blest bread and wine and water." And those to whom the eucharist was thus taken were not bound to consume it immediately, or all at once, but might reserve a part or all for future occasions. According to Basil (Ep. 93), "in Egypt the laity for the most part had every one the communion in their own houses "—and " all those who dwell alone in the desert, when there is no priest, keep the communion at home and receive it at their own hands." So Jerome speaks (Letter CXXV. 20) of Exuperius as "carrying the Lord's body in a wicker basket, His blood in a vessel of glass." See the article "Reservation" in Smith and Cheetham's Dict. of Christian Antiquities.
[6] Ps. cxxxix. 11, 12.   [7] Cf. 1 Cor. xi. 28.
[8] Cf. Matt. xix. 12.   [9] Against Jov. i. 8.

---

[1] Ter. Andria Prol. 20, 21.   [2] Ag. Jov. i. 7.
[3] 1 Th. v. 17.   [4] 1 Cor. vii. 5.
[5] 1 Pet. iii. 7.   [6] Ag. Jov. i. 20.

the apostle desires this consummation, and does not merely concede it to obviate a worse downfall, he immediately adds, 'that Satan tempt you not for your incontinency.'[1] 'And come together again.' What a noble indulgence the words convey! One which he blushes to speak of in plainer words, which he prefers only to Satan's temptation, and which has its root in incontinence. Do we labor to expound this as a dark saying when the writer has himself explained his meaning? 'I speak this,' he says, 'by way of permission, and not as a command.'[2] Do we still hesitate to speak of wedlock as a thing permitted instead of as a thing enjoined? or are we afraid that such permission will exclude second or third marriages or some other case?" What have I said here which the apostle has not said? The phrase, I suppose, "which he blushes to speak of in plainer words." I imagine that when he says "come together," and does not mention for what, he takes a modest way of indicating what he does not like to name openly—that is, sexual intercourse. Or is the objection to the words which follow— "which he prefers only to Satan's temptation, and which has its root in incontinence"? Are they not the very words of the apostle, only differently arranged—"that Satan tempt you not for your incontinency"? Or do people cavil because I said, "Do we still hesitate to speak of wedlock as a thing permitted instead of as a thing enjoined?" If this seems a hard saying, it should be ascribed to the apostle, who says, "But I speak this by way of permission, and not as a command," and not to me, who, except that I have rearranged their order, have changed neither the words nor their meaning.

17. The shortness of a letter compels me to hasten on. I pass, accordingly, to the points which remain. "I say," remarks the apostle, "to the unmarried and widows, It is good for them if they abide even as I. But if they cannot contain, let them marry; for it is better to marry than to burn."[3] This section I have interpreted thus:[4] "When he has granted to those who are married the use of wedlock, and has made clear his own wishes and concessions, he passes on to those who are unmarried or widows, and sets before them his own example. He calls them happy if they abide even as he,[5] but he goes on, 'if they cannot contain, let them marry.' He thus repeats his former language, 'but only to avoid fornication,' and 'that Satan tempt you not for your incontinence.' And when he says, 'If they cannot contain, let them marry,' he gives as a reason for his words that 'it is better to marry than to burn.' It is only good to marry, because it is bad to burn. But take away the fire of lust, and he will not say 'it is better to marry.' For a thing is said to be better in antithesis to something which is worse, and not simply in contrast with what is admittedly good. It is as though he said, 'It is better to have one eye than none.'" Shortly afterwards, apostrophizing the apostle, I spoke thus:[1] "If marriage is good in itself, do not compare it with a conflagration, but simply say, 'It is good to marry.' I must suspect the goodness of a thing which only becomes a lesser evil in the presence of a greater one. I, for my part, would have it not a lighter evil but a downright good." The apostle wishes unmarried women and widows to abstain from sexual intercourse, incites them to follow his own example, and calls them happy if they abide even as he. But if they cannot contain, and are tempted to quench the fire of lust by fornication rather than by continence, it is better, he tells them, to marry than to burn. Upon which precept I have made this comment: "It is good to marry, simply because it is bad to burn," not putting forward a view of my own, but only explaining the apostle's precept, "It is better to marry than to burn;" that is, it is better to take a husband than to commit fornication. If, then, you teach that burning or fornication is good, the good will still be surpassed by what is still better.[2] But if marriage is only a degree better than the evil to which it is preferred, it cannot be of that unblemished perfection and blessedness which suggest a comparison with the life of angels. Suppose I say, "It is better to be a virgin than a married woman;" in this case I have preferred to what is good what is still better. But suppose I go a step further and say, "It is better to marry than to commit fornication;" in that case I have preferred, not a better thing to a good thing, but a good thing to a bad one. There is a wide difference between the two cases; for, while virginity is related to marriage as better is to good, marriage is related to fornication as good is to bad. How, I should like to know, have I sinned in this explanation? My fixed purpose was not to bend the Scriptures to my own wishes, but simply to

---

[1] 1 Cor. vii. 5. [2] 1 Cor. vii. 6, Vulg.
[3] 1 Cor. vii. 8, 9. [4] Ag. Jov. i. 9. [5] 1 Cor. vii. 8.

[1] Ag. Jov. i. 9.
[2] Fornication must still be subordinated to marriage.

say what I took to be their meaning. A commentator has no business to dilate on his own views; his duty is to make plain the meaning of the author whom he professes to interpret. For, if he contradicts the writer whom he is trying to expound, he will prove to be his opponent rather than his interpreter. When I am freely expressing my own opinion, and not commenting upon the Scriptures, then any one that pleases may charge me with having spoken hardly of marriage. But if he can find no ground for such a charge, he should attribute such passages in my commentaries as appear severe or harsh to the author commented on, and not to me, who am only his interpreter.

18. Another charge brought against me is simply intolerable! It is urged that in explaining the apostle's words concerning husbands and wives, "Such shall have trouble in the flesh," I have said:[1] "We in our ignorance had supposed that in the flesh at least wedlock would have rejoicing. But if married persons are to have trouble in the flesh, the only thing in which they seemed likely to have pleasure, what motive will be left to make women marry? for, besides having trouble in spirit and soul, they will also have it even in the flesh."[2] Do I condemn marriage if I enumerate its troubles, such as the crying of infants, the death of children, the chance of abortion, domestic losses, and so forth? Whilst Damasus of holy memory was still living, I wrote a book against Helvidius "On the Perpetual Virginity of the Blessed Mary," in which, duly to extol the bliss of virginity, I was forced to say much of the troubles of marriage. Did that excellent man—versed in Scripture as he was, and a virgin doctor of the virgin Church—find anything to censure in my discourse? Moreover, in the treatise which I addressed to Eustochium[3] I used much harsher language regarding marriage, and yet no one was offended at it. Nay, every lover of chastity strained his ears to catch my eulogy of continence. Read Tertullian, read Cyprian, read Ambrose, and either accuse me with them or acquit me with them. My critics resemble the characters of Plautus. Their only wit lies in detraction; and they try to make themselves out men of learning by assailing all parties in turn. Thus they bestow their censure impartially upon myself and upon my opponent, and maintain that we are both beaten, although one or other of us must have succeeded.

Moreover, when in discussing digamy and trigamy I have said,[1] "It is better for a woman to know one man, even though he be a second husband or a third, than several; it is more tolerable for her to prostitute herself to one man than to many," have I not immediately subjoined my reason for so saying? "The Samaritan woman in the Gospel, when she declares that her present husband is her sixth, is rebuked by the Lord on the ground that he is not her husband."[2] For my own part, I now once more freely proclaim that digamy is not condemned in the Church—no, nor yet trigamy—and that a woman may marry a fifth husband, or a sixth, or a greater number still just as lawfully as she may marry a second; but that, while such marriages are not condemned, neither are they commended. They are meant as alleviations of an unhappy lot, and in no way redound to the glory of continence. I have spoken to the same effect elsewhere.[3] "When a woman marries more than once—whether she does so twice or three times matters little—she ceases to be a monogamist. 'All things are lawful . . . but all things are not expedient.'[4] I do not condemn digamists or trigamists, or even, to put an impossible case, octogamists. Let a woman have an eighth husband if she must; only let her cease to prostitute herself."

19. I will come now to the passage in which I am accused of saying that—at least according to the true Hebrew text—the words "God saw that it was good"[5] are not inserted after the second day of the creation, as they are after the first, third, and remaining ones, and of adding immediately the following comment:[6] "We are meant to understand that there is something not good in the number two, separating us as it does from unity, and prefiguring the marriage-tie. Just as in the account of Noah's ark all the animals that enter by twos are unclean, but those of which an uneven number is taken are clean."[7] In this statement a passing objection is made to what I have said concerning the second day, whether on the ground that the words mentioned really occur in the passage, although I say that they do not occur, or because, assuming them to occur, I have understood them in a sense different from that which the context evidently requires. As regards the non-occurrence of the words in question (viz., "God saw that it was good"), let them take not my evidence, but that of all the Jew-

---

[1] Ag. Jov. i. 13.   [2] 1 Th. v. 23.   [3] Letter XXII.

[1] Ag. Jov. i. 14.
[2] Joh. iv. 16–18.   Jerome's version of the story is inaccurate.
[3] Ag. Jov. i. 15.   [4] 1 Cor. vi. 12.   [5] Gen. i. 10.
[6] Ag. Jov. i. 16.   [7] Gen. vii. 2.

ish and other translators—Aquila[1] namely, Symmachus,[2] and Theodotion.[3] But if the words, although occurring in the account of the other days, do not occur in the account of this, either let them give a more plausible reason than I have done for their non-occurrence, or, failing such, let them, whether they like it or not, accept the suggestion which I have made. Furthermore, if in Noah's ark all the animals that enter by twos are unclean, whilst those of which an uneven number is taken are clean, and if there is no dispute about the accuracy of the text, let them explain if they can why it is so written. But if they cannot explain it, then, whether they will or not, they must embrace my explanation of the matter. Either produce better fare and ask me to be your guest, or else rest content with the meal that I offer you, however poor it may be.[4]

I must now mention the ecclesiastical writers who have dealt with this question of the odd number. They are, among the Greeks, Clement, Hippolytus, Origen, Dionysius, Eusebius, Didymus; and, among ourselves, Tertullian, Cyprian, Victorinus, Lactantius, Hilary. What Cyprian said to Fortunatus about the number seven is clear from the letter which he sent to him.[5] Or perhaps I ought to bring forward the reasonings of Pythagoras, Archytas of Tarentum, and Publius Scipio in (Cicero's) sixth book "Concerning the Common Weal." If my detractors will not listen to any of these I will make the grammar schools shout in their ears the words of Virgil:

Uneven numbers are the joy of God.[6]

20. To say, as I have done, that virginity is cleaner than wedlock, that the even numbers must give way to the odd, that the types of the Old Testament establish the truth of the Gospel: this, it appears, is a great sin subversive of the churches and intolerable to the world. The remaining points which are censured in my treatise are, I take it, of less importance, or else resolve themselves into this. I have, therefore, refrained from answering them, both that I may not exceed the limit at my disposal, and that I may not seem to distrust your intelligence, knowing as I do that you are ready to be my champion even before I ask you. With my last breath, then, I protest that neither now nor at any former time have I condemned marriage. I have merely answered an opponent without any fear that they of my own party would lay snares for me. I extol virginity to the skies, not because I myself possess it, but because, not possessing it, I admire it all the more. Surely it is a modest and ingenuous confession to praise in others that which you lack yourself. The weight of my body keeps me fixed to the ground, but do I fail to admire the flying birds or to praise the dove because, in the words of Virgil,[1] it

Glides on its liquid path with motionless swift wings?

Let no man deceive himself, let no man, giving ear to the voice of flattery, rush upon ruin. The first virginity man derives from his birth, the second from his second birth.[2] The words are not mine; it is an old saying, "No man can serve two masters;"[3] that is, the flesh and the spirit. For "the flesh lusteth against the spirit, and the spirit against the flesh; and these are contrary the one to the other," so that we cannot do the things that we would.[4] When, then, anything in my little work seems to you harsh, have regard not to my words, but to the Scripture, whence they are taken.

21. Christ Himself is a virgin;[5] and His mother is also a virgin; yea, though she is His mother, she is a virgin still. For Jesus has entered in through the closed doors,[6] and in His sepulchre—a new one hewn out of the hardest rock—no man is laid either before Him or after Him.[7] Mary is "a garden enclosed . . . a fountain sealed,"[8] and from that fountain flows, according to Joel,[9] the river which waters the torrent bed either[10] of cords or of thorns;[11] the cords being those of the sins by which we were beforetime bound,[12] the thorns those which choked the seed the goodman of the house had sown.[13] She is the east gate, spoken of by the prophet Ezekiel,[14] always shut and always shining, and either concealing or revealing the Holy of Holies; and through her "the Sun of Righteousness,"[15] our "high priest after the order of Melchizedek,"[16] goes in and out. Let my critics explain to me how Jesus can have entered in through closed doors when He allowed His hands and His side to be handled, and showed that He had bones and flesh,[17] thus proving that His was a true body and no

---

[1] The author of a literal Greek version of the O. T. made in the second century.
[2] An ebionitic translator, free, not literal, in style.
[3] A careful reviser of the LXX. whose work was welcomed by the Church. His version of Daniel completely superseded the older one. [4] Cf. Hor. Ep. i. 6, 67, 68.
[5] Cyprian, Letter to Fortunatus, xiii. 11. [6] Virg. E. viii. 75.

[1] Virg. A. v. 217. [2] Tert. de Exh. Cast. I.
[3] Matt. vi. 24. [4] Gal. v. 17. [5] Ag. Jov. i. 31.
[6] Joh. xx. 19. [7] Joh. xix. 41. [8] Cant. iv. 12.
[9] Joel, iii. 18; according to the LXX. and Hebrew. A.V. has "vale of Shittim" (thorns). [10] LXX. [11] Hebrew.
[12] Cf. Prov. v. 22. [13] Matt. xiii. 7. [14] Ezek. xliv. 2, 3.
[15] Mal. iv. 2. [16] Heb. v. 10. [17] Joh. xx. 19, 27.

mere phantom of one, and I will explain how the holy Mary can be at once a mother and a virgin. A mother before she was wedded, she remained a virgin after bearing her son. Therefore, as I was going to say, the virgin Christ and the virgin Mary have dedicated in themselves the first fruits of virginity for both sexes.[1] The apostles have either been virgins or, though married, have lived celibate lives. Those persons who are chosen to be bishops, priests, and deacons are either virgins or widowers; or at least, when once they have received the priesthood, are vowed to perpetual chastity. Why do we delude ourselves and feel vexed if, while we are continually straining after sexual indulgence, we find the palm of chastity denied to us? We wish to fare sumptuously, and to enjoy the embraces of our wives, yet at the same time we desire to reign with Christ among virgins and widows. Shall there be but one reward, then, for hunger and for excess, for filth and for finery, for sackcloth and for silk? Lazarus,[2] in his lifetime, received evil things, and the rich man, clothed in purple, fat and sleek, while he lived enjoyed the good things of the flesh; but, now that they are dead, they occupy different positions. Misery has given place to satisfaction, and satisfaction to misery. And it rests with us whether we will follow Lazarus or the rich man.

LETTER XLIX.

TO PAMMACHIUS.

Jerome encloses the preceding letter, thanks Pammachius for his efforts to suppress his treatise " against Jovinian," but declares these to be useless, and exhorts him, if he still has any hesitation in his mind, to turn to the Scriptures and the commentaries made upon them by Origen and others. Written at the same time as the preceding letter.

1. Christian modesty sometimes requires us to be silent even to our friends, and to nurse our humility in peace, where the renewal of an old friendship would expose us to the charge of self-seeking. Thus, when you have kept silence I have kept silence too, and have not cared to remonstrate with you, lest I should be thought more anxious to conciliate a person of influence than to cultivate a friend. But, now that it has become a duty to reply to your letter, I will endeavor always to be beforehand with you, and not so much to answer your queries as to write independently of them. Thus, if I have shown my modesty hitherto by silence,

I will henceforth show it still more by coming forward to speak.

2. I quite recognize the kindness and forethought which have induced you to withdraw from circulation some copies of my work against Jovinian. Your diligence, however, has been of no avail, for several people coming from the city have repeatedly read aloud to me passages which they have come across in Rome. In this province, also, the books have already been circulated; and, as you have read yourself in Horace, " Words once uttered cannot be recalled." [1] I am not so fortunate as are most of the writers of the day—able, that is, to correct my trifles whenever I like. When once I have written anything, either my admirers or my ill-wishers—from different motives, but with equal zeal—sow my work broadcast among the public; and their language, whether it is that of eulogy or of criticism, is apt to run to excess.[2] They are guided not by the merits of the piece, but by their own angry feelings. Accordingly, I have done what I could. I have dedicated to you a defence of the work in question, feeling sure that when you have read it you will yourself satisfy the doubts of others on my behalf; or else, if you too turn up your nose at the task, you will have to explain in some new manner that section of the apostle[3] in which he discusses virginity and marriage.

3. I do not speak thus that I may provoke you to write on the subject yourself— although I know your zeal in the study of the sacred writings to be greater than my own— but that you may compel my tormentors to do so. They are educated; in their own eyes no mean scholars; competent not merely to censure but to instruct me. If they write on the subject, my view will be the sooner neglected when it is compared with theirs. Read, I pray you, and diligently consider the words of the apostle, and you will then see that—with a view to avoid misrepresentation—I have been much more gentle towards married persons than he was disposed to be. Origen, Dionysius, Pierius, Eusebius of Cæsarea, Didymus, Apollinaris, have used great latitude in the interpretation of this epistle.[4] When Pierius, sifting and expounding the apostle's meaning, comes to the words, " I would that all men were even as I myself," [5] he makes this comment upon them: " In saying this Paul plainly preaches abstinence from mar-

---

[1] Cf. Letter XXII. § 18.   [2] Luke xvi. 19–25.

[1] Hor. AP. 390.
[2] See the Preface to Jerome's Comm. on Daniel.
[3] 1 Cor. vii.   [4] 1 Corinthians.   [5] 1 Cor. vii. 7.

riage." Is the fault here mine, or am I responsible for harshness? Compared with this sentence of Pierius,[1] all that I have ever written is mild indeed. Consult the commentaries of the above-named writers and take advantage of the Church libraries; you will then more speedily finish as you would wish the enterprise which you have so happily begun.[2]

4. I hear that the hopes of the entire city are centred in you, and that bishop[3] and people are agreed in wishing for your exaltation. To be a bishop[4] is much, to deserve to be one is more.

If you read the books of the sixteen prophets[5] which I have rendered into Latin from the Hebrew; and if, when you have done so, you express satisfaction with my labors, the news will encourage me to take out of my desk some other works now shut up in it. I have lately translated Job into our mother tongue: you will be able to borrow a copy of it from your cousin, the saintly Marcella. Read it both in Greek and in Latin, and compare the old version with my rendering. You will then clearly see that the difference between them is that between truth and falsehood. Some of my commentaries upon the twelve prophets I have sent to the reverend father Domnio, also the four books of Kings—that is, the two called Samuel and the two called Malâchim.[6] If you care to read these you will learn for yourself how difficult it is to understand the Holy Scriptures, and particularly the prophets; and how through the fault of the translators passages which for the Jews flow clearly on for us abound with mistakes. Once more, you must not in my small writings look for any such eloquence as that which for Christ's sake you disregard in Cicero. A version made for the use of the Church, even though it may possess a literary charm, ought to disguise and avoid it as far as possible; in order that it may not speak to the idle schools and few disciples of the philosophers, but may address itself rather to the entire human race.

LETTER L.

TO DOMNIO.

Domnio, a Roman (called in Letter XLV. "the Lot of our time"), had written to Jerome to tell him that an ignorant monk had been traducing his books

"against Jovinian." Jerome, in reply, sharply rebukes the folly of his critic and comments on the want of straightforwardness in his conduct. He concludes the letter with an emphatic restatement of his original position. Written in 394 A.D.

1. Your letter is full at once of affection and of complaining. The affection is your own, which prompts you unceasingly to warn me of impending danger, and which makes you on my behalf

Of safest things distrustful and afraid.[1]

The complaining is of those who have no love for me, and seek an occasion against me in my sins. They speak against their brother, they slander their own mother's son.[2] You write to me of these—nay, of one in particular—a lounger who is to be seen in the streets, at crossings, and in public places; a monk who is a noisy newsmonger, clever only in detraction, and eager, in spite of the beam in his own eye, to remove the mote in his neighbor's.[3] And you tell me that he preaches publicly against me, gnawing, rending, and tearing asunder with his fangs the books that I have written against Jovinian. You inform me, moreover, that this home-grown dialectician, this mainstay of the Plautine company, has read neither the "Categories" of Aristotle nor his treatise "On Interpretation," nor his "Analytics," nor yet the "Topics" of Cicero, but that, moving as he does only in uneducated circles, and frequenting no society but that of weak women, he ventures to construct illogical syllogisms and to unravel by subtle arguments what he is pleased to call my sophisms. How foolish I have been to suppose that without philosophy there can be no knowledge of these subjects; and to account it a more important part of composition to erase than to write! In vain have I perused the commentaries of Alexander; to no purpose has a skilled teacher used the "Introduction" of Porphyry to instruct me in logic; and—to make light of human learning—I have gained nothing at all by having Gregory of Nazianzum and Didymus as my catechists in the Holy Scriptures. My acquisition of Hebrew has been wasted labor; and so also has been the daily study which from my youth I have bestowed upon the Law and the Prophets, the Gospels and the Apostles.

2. Here we have a man who has reached perfection without a teacher, so as to be a vehicle of the spirit and a self-taught genius. He surpasses Cicero in eloquence, Aristotle in argument, Plato in discretion, Aristarchus

---

[1] Master of the catechetical school of Alexandria, 265 A.D. His writings have perished. His name occurs again in Letter LXX. § 4. [2] Ad optata cæptaque pervenies.
[3] Pontifex. [4] Sacerdos. [5] Thus including Daniel.
[6] The Hebrew word for "Kings."

[1] Virg. A. iv. 298. [2] Ps. l. 20. [3] Matt. vii. 3–5.

n learning, Didymus, that man of brass, in he number of his books; and not only Didymus, but all the writers of his time in his knowledge of the Scriptures. It is reported that you have only to give him a theme and he is always ready—like Carneales[1]—to argue on this side or on that, for justice or against it. The world escaped a great danger, and civil actions and suits concerning succession were saved from a yawning gulf on the day when, despising the bar, he transferred himself to the Church. For, had he been unwilling, who could ever have been proved innocent? And, if he once began to reckon the points of the case upon his fingers, and to spread his syllogistic nets, what criminal would his pleading have failed to save? Had he but stamped his foot, or fixed his eyes, or knitted his brow, or moved his hand, or twirled his beard, he would at once have thrown dust in the eyes of the jury. No wonder that such a complete Latinist and so profound a master of eloquence overcomes poor me, who—as I have been some time[2] away (from Rome), and without opportunities for speaking Latin—am half a Greek if not altogether a barbarian. No wonder, I say, that he overcomes me when his eloquence has crushed Jovinian in person. Good Jesus! what! even Jovinian that great and clever man! So clever, indeed, that no one can understand his writings, and that when he sings it is only for himself—and for the muses!

3. Pray, my dear father, warn this man not to hold language contrary to his profession, and not to undo with his words the chastity which he professes by his garb. Whether he elects to be a virgin or a married celibate—and the choice must rest with himself—he must not compare wives with virgins, for that would be to have striven in vain against Jovinian's eloquence. He likes, I am told, to visit the cells of widows and virgins, and to lecture them with his brows knit on sacred literature. What is it that he teaches these poor women in the privacy of their own chambers? Is it to feel assured that virgins are no better than wives? Is it to make the most of the flower of their age, to eat and drink, to frequent the baths, to live in luxury, and not to disdain the use of perfumes? Or does he preach to them chastity, fasting, and neglect of their persons? No doubt the precepts that he inculcates are full of virtue. But

if so, let him admit publicly what he says privately. Or, if his private teaching is the same as his public, he should keep aloof altogether from the society of girls. He is a young man—a monk, and in his own eyes an eloquent one (do not pearls fall from his lips, and are not his elegant phrases sprinkled with comic salt and humor?)—I am surprised, therefore, that he can without a blush frequent noblemen's houses, pay constant visits to married ladies, make our religion a subject of contention, distort the faith of Christ by misapplying words, and—in addition to all this—detract from one who is his brother in the Lord. He may, however, have supposed me to be in error (for "in many things we offend all," and "if any man offend not in word he is a perfect man"[1]). In that case he should have written to convict me or to question me, the course taken by Pammachius, a man of high attainments and position. To this latter I defended myself as best I could, and in a lengthy letter explained the exact sense of my words. He might at least have copied the diffidence which led you to extract and arrange such passages as seemed to give offence; asking me for corrections or explanations, and not supposing me so mad that in one and the same book I should write for marriage and against it.

4. Let him spare himself, let him spare me, let him spare the Christian name. Let him realize his position as a monk, not by talking and arguing, but by holding his peace and sitting still. Let him read the words of Jeremiah: "It is good for a man that he bear the yoke in his youth. He sitteth alone and keepeth silence, because he hath borne it upon him."[2] Or if he has really the right to apply the censor's rod to all writers, and fancies himself a man of learning because he alone understands Jovinian (you know the proverb: Balbus best knows what Balbus means); yet, as Atilius[3] reminds us, "we are not all writers." Jovinian himself—an unlettered man of letters if ever there was one—will with most justice proclaim the fact to him. "That the bishops condemn me," he says, "is not reason but treason. I want no answers from nobodies, who, while they have authority to put me down, have not the wit to teach me. Let one write against me who has a tongue that I can understand, and whom to vanquish will be to vanquish all.

---

[1] A philosopher of the Academy noted for his opposition to stoicism. [2] Eight years.

[1] Jas. iii. 2. [2] Lam. iii. 27, 28. [3] An early Roman dramatist of whose works only a few fragments remain. He is said to have translated the Electra of Sophocles, but for the most part to have preferred comedy to tragedy.

> " ' I know full well : believe me, I have felt
> The hero's force when rising o'er his shield
> He hurls his whizzing spear.' [1]

He is strong in argument, intricate and tenacious, one to fight with his head down. Often has he cried out against me in the streets from late one night till early the next. He is a well-built man, and his thews are those of an athlete. Secretly I believe him to be a follower of my teaching. He never blushes or stops to weigh his words: his only aim is to speak as loud as possible. So famous is he for his eloquence that his sayings are held up as models to our curly-headed youngsters. [2] How often, when I have met him at meetings, has he aroused my wrath and put me into a passion! How often has he spat upon me, and then departed spat upon! But these are vulgar methods, and any of my followers can use them. I appeal to books, to those memorials which must be handed down to posterity. Let us speak by our writings, that the silent reader may judge between us; and that, as I have a flock of disciples, he may have one also—flatterers and parasites worthy of the Gnatho and Phormio [3] who is their master."

5. It is no difficult matter, my dear Domnio, to chatter at street corners or in apothecaries' shops and to pass judgment on the world. "So-and-so has made a good speech, so-and-so a bad one; this man knows the Scriptures, that one is crazy; this man talks glibly, that never says a word at all." But who considers him worthy thus to judge every one? To make an outcry against a man in every street, and to heap, not definite charges, but vague imputations, on his head, is nothing. Any buffoon or litigiously disposed person can do as much. Let him put forth his hand, put pen to paper, and bestir himself; let him write books and prove in them all he can. Let him give me a chance of replying to his eloquence. I can return bite for bite, if I like; when hurt myself, I can fix my teeth in my opponent. I too have had a liberal education. As Juvenal says, "I also have often withdrawn my hand from the ferule." [4] Of me, too, it may be said in the words of Horace, "Flee from him; he has hay on his horn." [5] But I prefer to be a disciple of Him who says, " I gave my back to the smiters . . . I hid not my face from shame and spitting." [6] When He was reviled He reviled not again. [7] After the buffeting, the cross, the scourge, the blasphemies, at the very last He prayed for His crucifiers, saying, " Father, forgive them, for they know not what they do." [1] I, too, pardon the error of a brother. He has been deceived, I feel sure, by the art of the devil. Among the women he was held clever and eloquent; but, when my poor writings reached Rome, dreading me as a rival, he tried to rob me of my laurels. No man on earth, he resolved, should please his eloquent self, unless such as commanded respect rather than sought it, and showed themselves men to be feared more than favored. A man of consummate address, he desired, like an old soldier, with one stroke of the sword to strike down both his enemies, [2] and to make clear to every one that, whatever view he might take, Scripture was always with him. Well, he must condescend to send me his account of the matter, and to correct my indiscreet language, not by censure but by instruction. If he tries to do this, he will find that what seems forcible on a lounge is not equally forcible in court; and that it is one thing to discuss the doctrines of the divine law amid the spindles and work-baskets of girls and another to argue concerning them among men of education. As it is, without hesitation or shame, he raises again and again the noisy shout, " Jerome condemns marriage," and, whilst he constantly moves among women with child, crying infants, and marriage-beds, he suppresses the words of the apostle just to cover me—poor me—with odium. However, when he comes by and by to write books and to grapple with me at close quarters, then he will feel it, then he will stick fast; Epicurus and Aristippus [3] will not be near him then; the swineherds [4] will not come to his aid; the prolific sow [5] will not so much as grunt. For I also may say, with Turnus:

> Father, I too can launch a forceful spear,
> And when I strike blood follows from the wound. [6]

But if he refuses to write, and fancies that abuse is as effective as criticism, then, in spite of all the lands and seas and peoples which lie between us, he must hear at least the echo of my cry, " I do not condemn marriage," " I do not condemn wedlock." Indeed—and this I say to make my meaning quite clear to him—I should like every one to take a wife who, because they get frightened in the night, cannot manage to sleep alone. [7]

---

1 Virgil, Æn. xi. 283, 284.   2 Persius i. 29.
1 Virgil, Æn. xi. 283, 284.   2 Persius i. 29.
3 Characters in the Eunuchus and Phormio of Terence.
4 Juv. i. 15.   5 Hor. S. i. iv. 34.   6 Isa. l. 6.   7 1 Pet. ii. 23.

1 Luke xxiii. 34.   2 Viz. Jerome and Jovinian.
3 According to both these philosophers pleasure is the highest good.
4 The followers of Jovinian.   5 Jovinian himself.
6 Virg. A. xii. 50, 51.   7 Cic. pro Cælio xv.

LETTER LI.

FROM EPIPHANIUS, BISHOP OF SALAMIS, IN
CYPRUS, TO JOHN, BISHOP OF JERUSALEM.

A coolness had arisen between these two bishops in
connection with the Origenistic controversy, which at
this time was at its height. Epiphanius had openly
charged John with being an Origenist, and had also
uncanonically conferred priests' orders on Jerome's
brother Paulinian, in order that the monastery at Bethlehem might henceforth be entirely independent of John.
Naturally, John resented this conduct and showed his
resentment. The present letter is a kind of half-apology
made by Epiphanius for what he had done, and like all
such, it only seems to have made matters worse. The
controversy is fully detailed in the treatise "Against
John of Jerusalem" in this volume, esp. § 11–14.
An interesting paragraph (§ 9) narrates how Epiphanius destroyed at Anablatha a church-curtain on
which was depicted "a likeness of Christ or of some
saint"—an early instance of the iconoclastic spirit.
Originally written in Greek, the letter was (by the
writer's request) rendered into Latin by Jerome. Its
date is 394 A.D.

To the lord bishop and dearly beloved brother, John, Epiphanius sends greeting.

1. It surely becomes us, dearly beloved,
not to abuse our rank as clergy, so as to
make it an occasion of pride, but by diligently keeping and observing God's commandments, to be in reality what in name
we profess to be. For, if the Holy Scriptures say, "Their lots shall not profit
them,"[1] what pride in our clerical position[2]
will be able to avail us who sin not only in
thought and feeling, but in speech? I have
heard, of course, that you are incensed
against me, that you are angry, and that you
threaten to write about me—not merely to
particular places and provinces, but to the
uttermost ends of the earth. Where is that
fear of God which should make us tremble
with the trembling spoken of by the Lord—
"Whosoever is angry with his brother without a cause shall be in danger of the judgment"?[3] Not that I greatly care for your
writing what you please. For Isaiah tells
us[4] of letters written on papyrus and cast
upon the waters—missives soon carried away
by time and tide. I have done you no
harm, I have inflicted no injury upon you, I
have extorted nothing from you by violence.
My action concerned a monastery whose inmates were foreigners in no way subject
to your provincial jurisdiction. Moreover,
their regard for my insignificance and for
the letters which I frequently addressed to
them had commenced to produce a feeling
of dislike to communion with you. Feeling, therefore, that too great strictness or
scrupulosity on my part might have the

effect of alienating them from the Church
with its ancient faith, I ordained one of the
brothers deacon, and after he had ministered
as such, admitted him to the priesthood.
You should, I think, have been grateful to
me for this, knowing, as you surely must,
that it is the fear of God which has compelled me to act in this way, and particularly when you recollect that God's priesthood is everywhere the same, and that I
have simply made provision for the wants of
the Church. For, although each individual
bishop of the Church has under him churches
which are placed in his charge, and although
no man may stretch himself beyond his
measure,[1] yet the love of Christ, which is
without dissimulation,[2] is set up as an example to us all; and we must consider not
so much the thing done as the time and
place, the mode and motive, of doing it. I
saw that the monastery contained a large
number of reverend brothers, and that the
reverend presbyters, Jerome and Vincent,
through modesty and humility, were unwilling to offer the sacrifices permitted to their
rank, and to labor in that part of their calling which ministers more than any other to
the salvation of Christians. I knew, moreover, that you could not find or lay hands
on this servant of God[3] who had several
times fled from you simply because he was
reluctant to undertake the onerous duties of
the priesthood, and that no other bishop
could easily find him. Accordingly, I was a
good deal surprised when, by the ordering
of God, he came to me with the deacons of
the monastery and others of the brethren, to
make satisfaction to me for some grievance
or other which I had against them. While,
therefore, the Collect[4] was being celebrated
in the church of the villa which adjoins our
monastery—he being quite ignorant and
wholly unsuspicious of my purpose—I gave
orders to a number of deacons to seize him
and to stop his mouth, lest in his eagerness
to free himself he might adjure me in the
name of Christ. First of all, then, I ordained him deacon, setting before him the
fear of God, and forcing him to minister;
for he made a hard struggle against it, crying out that he was unworthy, and protest-
ing that this heavy burden was beyond his
strength. It was with difficulty, then, that
I overcame his reluctance, persuading him
as well as I could with passages from Scripture, and setting before him the command-

---

[1] Jer. xii. 13, LXX.   [2] A play on words. Clericatus ("clerical
position") is a derivative of clerus (κλῆρος), the word used in the
LXX. for "lot."   [3] Matt. v. 22.   [4] Isa. xviii. 2, LXX.

[1] Cf. 2 Cor. x. 14.   [2] Rom. xii. 9.   [3] Paulinian, Jerome's
brother, at this time about 28 years of age.   [4] I.e. the short service
which preceded the eucharist. The words might, however, be rendered, "When the congregation was gathered together."

ments of God. And when he had ministered in the offering of the holy sacrifices, once more with great difficulty I closed his mouth and ordained him presbyter. Then, using the same arguments as before, I induced him to sit in the place set apart for the presbyters. After this I wrote to the reverend presbyters and other brothers of the monastery, chiding them for not having written to me about him. For a year before I had heard many of them complain that they had no one to celebrate for them the sacraments of the Lord. All then agreed in asking him to undertake the duty, pointing out how great his usefulness would be to the community of the monastery. I blamed them for omitting to write to me and to propose that I should ordain him, when the opportunity was given to them to do so.

2. All this I have done, as I said just now, relying on that Christian love which you, I feel sure, cherish towards my insignificance; not to mention the fact that I held the ordination in a monastery, and not within the limits of your jurisdiction. How truly blessed is the mildness and complacency of the bishops of (my own) Cyprus, as well as their simplicity, though to your refinement and discrimination it appears deserving only of God's pity! For many bishops in communion with me have ordained presbyters in my province whom I had been unable to capture, and have sent to me deacons and subdeacons[1] whom I have been glad to receive. I myself, too, have urged the bishop Philo of blessed memory, and the reverend Theoprepus, to make provision for the Church of Christ by ordaining presbyters in those churches of Cyprus which, although they were accounted to belong to my see, happened to be close to them, and this for the reason that my province was large and straggling. But for my part I have never ordained deaconesses nor sent them into the provinces of others,[2] nor have I done anything to rend the Church. Why, then, have you thought fit to be so angry and indignant with me for that work of God which I have wrought for the edification of the brethren, and not for their destruction?[3] Moreover, I have been much surprised at the assertion which you have made to my clergy, that you sent me a message by that reverend presbyter, the abbot Gregory, that I was to ordain no one, and that I promised to comply, saying, "Am I

a stripling, or do I not know the canons?" By God's word I am telling you the truth when I say that I know and have heard nothing of all this, and that I have not the slightest recollection of using any language of the sort. As, however, I have had misgivings, lest possibly, being only a man, I may have forgotten this among so many other matters, I have made inquiry of the reverend Gregory, and of the presbyter Zeno, who is with him. Of these, the abbot Gregory replies that he knows nothing whatever about the matter, while Zeno says that the presbyter Rufinus, in the course of some desultory remarks, spoke these words, "Will the reverend bishop, think you, venture to ordain any persons?" but that the conversation went no further. I, Epiphanius, however, have never either received the message or answered it. Do not, then, dearly beloved, allow your anger to overcome you or your indignation to get the better of you, lest, you should disquiet yourself in vain; and lest you should be thought to be putting forward this grievance only to get scope for tendencies of another kind,[1] and thus to have sought out an occasion of sinning. It is to avoid this that the prophet prays to the Lord, saying: "Turn not aside my heart to words of wickedness, to making excuses for my sins."[2]

3. This also I have been surprised to hear, that certain persons who are in the habit of carrying tales backwards and forwards, and of always adding something fresh to what they have heard, to stir up grievances and disputes between brothers, have succeeded in disquieting you by saying that, when I offer sacrifices to God, I am wont to say this prayer on your behalf: "Grant, O Lord, to John grace to believe aright." Do not suppose me so untutored as to be capable of saying this so openly. To tell you the simple truth, my dearest brother, although I continually use this prayer mentally, I have never confided it to the ears of others, lest I should seem to dishonor you. But when I repeat the prayers required by the ritual of the mysteries, then I say on behalf of all and of you as well as others, "Guard him, that he may preach the truth," or at least this, "Do Thou, O Lord, grant him Thine aid, and guard him, that he may preach the word of truth," as occasion offers itself for the words, and as the turn comes for the particular prayer. Wherefore I beseech you, dearly beloved, and, casting myself down at your feet, I entreat you to

---

[1] Subdeacons cannot be traced back earlier than the third century. At first their province seems to have been to keep the church doors during divine service.
[2] It seems to be implied that John had done so.   [3] 2 Cor. x. 8.

[1] That is, Origenistic heresies.   [2] Ps. cxli. 4, acc. to the Gallican Psalter.

grant to me and to yourself this one prayer, that you would save yourself, as it is written, "from an untoward generation."[1] Withdraw, dearly beloved, from the heresy of Origen and from all heresies. For I see that all your indignation has been roused against me simply because I have told you that you ought not to eulogize one who is the spiritual father of Arius, and the root and parent of all heresies. And when I appealed to you not to go astray, and warned you of the consequences, you traversed my words, and reduced me to tears and sadness; and not me only, but many other Catholics who were present.[2] This I take to be the origin of your indignation and of your passion on the present occasion. On this account you threaten to send out letters against me, and to circulate your version of the matter in all directions;[3] and thus, while with a view to defending your heresy you kindle men's passions against me, you break through the charity which I have shown towards you, and act with so little discretion that you make me regret that I have held communion with you, and that I have by so doing upheld the erroneous opinions of Origen.

4. I speak plainly. To use the language of Scripture, I do not spare to pluck out my own eye if it cause me to offend, nor to cut off my hand and my foot if they cause me to do so.[4] And you must be treated in the same way whether you are my eyes, or my hands, or my feet. For what Catholic, what Christian who adorns his faith with good works, can hear with calmness Origen's teaching and counsel, or believe in his extraordinary preaching? "The Son," he tells us, "cannot see the Father, and the Holy Spirit cannot see the Son." These words occur in his book "On First Principles;" thus we read, and thus Origen has spoken. "For as it is unsuitable to say that the Son can see the Father, it is consequently unsuitable to suppose that the Spirit can see the Son."[5] Can any one, moreover, brook Origen's assertion that men's souls were once angels in heaven, and that having sinned in the upper world, they have been cast down into this, and have been confined in bodies as in barrows or tombs, to pay the penalty for their former sins; and that the bodies of believers are not temples of Christ,[6] but prisons of the condemned? Again, he

tampers with the true meaning of the narrative by a false use of allegory, multiplying words without limit; and undermines the faith of the simple by the most varied arguments. Now he maintains that souls, in Greek the "cool things," from a word meaning to be cool,[1] are so called because in coming down from the heavenly places to the lower world they have lost their former heat;[2] and now, that our bodies are called by the Greeks chains, from a word meaning chain,[3] or else (on the analogy of our own Latin word) "things fallen,"[4] because our souls have fallen from heaven; and that the other word for body which the abundance of the Greek idiom supplies[5] is by many taken to mean a funeral monument,[6] because the soul is shut up within it in the same way as the corpses of the dead are shut up in tombs and barrows. If this doctrine is true what becomes of our faith? Where is the preaching of the resurrection? Where is the teaching of the apostles, which lasts on to this day in the churches of Christ? Where is the blessing to Adam, and to his seed, and to Noah and his sons? "Be fruitful, and multiply, and replenish the earth."[7] According to Origen, these words must be a curse and not a blessing; for he turns angels into human souls, compelling them to leave the place of highest rank and to come down lower, as though God were unable through the action of His blessing to grant souls to the human race, had the angels not sinned, and as though for every birth on earth there must be a fall in heaven. We are to give up, then, the teaching of apostles and prophets, of the law, and of our Lord and Saviour Himself, in spite of His language loud as thunder in the gospel. Origen, on the other hand, commands and urges—not to say binds—his disciples not to pray to ascend into heaven, lest sinning once more worse than they had sinned on earth they should be hurled down into the world again. Such foolish and insane notions he generally confirms by distorting the sense of the Scriptures and making them mean what they do not mean at all. He quotes this passage from the Psalms: "Before thou didst humble me by reason of my wickedness, I went wrong;"[8] and this, "Return unto thy rest, O my soul;"[9] this also, "Bring my soul out of prison;"[10] and this, "I will make confession

---

[1] Acts ii. 40.
[2] Epiphanius, on a visit to Jerusalem, had preached against Origenism in the presence of John. See "Ag. John of Jerus.," § 11.
[3] John actually did write to Theophilus of Alexandria giving a full account of the controversy from his (John's) point of view. (Ag. J. of Jerus., § 37.) [4] Matt. xviii. 8, 9.
[5] First Principles, i. 1; ii. 4. [6] 1 Cor. vi. 15, 19.

[1] ψυχαὶ ἀπὸ τοῦ ψύχεσθαι. The etymology is right, but the explanation of it wrong. [2] First Principles ii. 8.
[3] δέμας as if from δέω, "I bind."
[4] πτῶμα, from πίπτειν: cadaver, from cado.
[5] σῶμα. [6] σῆμα. [7] Gen. i. 28; ix. 7.
[8] Ps. cxix. 67. From memory, or perhaps from the old Latin version. [9] Ps. cxvi. 7. [10] Ps. cxlii. 7.

unto the Lord in the land of the living," [1] although there can be no doubt that the meaning of the divine Scripture is different from the interpretation by which he unfairly wrests it to the support of his own heresy. This way of acting is common to the Manichæans, the Gnostics, the Ebionites, the Marcionites, and the votaries of the other eighty heresies, [2] all of whom draw their proofs from the pure well of the Scriptures, not, however, interpreting it in the sense in which it is written, but trying to make the simple language of the Church's writers accord with their own wishes.

5. Of one position which he strives to maintain I hardly know whether it calls for my tears or my laughter. This wonderful doctor presumes to teach that the devil will once more be what he at one time was, that he will return to his former dignity and rise again to the kingdom of heaven. Oh horror! that a man should be so frantic and foolish as to hold that John the Baptist, Peter, the apostle and evangelist John, Isaiah, Jeremiah, and the rest of the prophets, are made co-heirs of the devil in the kingdom of heaven! I pass over his idle explanation of the coats of skins, [3] and say nothing of the efforts and arguments he has used to induce us to believe that these coats of skins represent human bodies. Among many other things, he says this: "Was God a tanner or a saddler, that He should prepare the hides of animals, and should stitch from them coats of skins for Adam and Eve?" "It is clear," he goes on, "that he is speaking of human bodies." If this is so, how is it that before the coats of skins, and the disobedience, and the fall from paradise, Adam speaks not in an allegory, but literally, thus: "This is now bone of my bones and flesh of my flesh;" [4] or what is the ground of the divine narrative, "And the Lord God caused a deep sleep to fall upon Adam, and he slept; and he took one of his ribs, and closed up the flesh instead thereof; and the rib which the Lord God had taken from man, made He a woman" [5] for him? Or what bodies can Adam and Eve have covered with fig-leaves after eating of the forbidden tree? [6] Who can patiently listen to the perilous arguments of Origen when he denies the resurrection of this flesh, as he most clearly does in his book of explanations of the first psalm and in many other places? Or who can tolerate

him when he gives us a paradise in the third heaven, and transfers that which the Scripture mentions from earth to the heavenly places, and when he explains allegorically all the trees which are mentioned in Genesis, saying in effect that the trees are angelic potencies, a sense which the true drift of the passage does not admit? For the divine Scripture has not said, "God put down Adam and Eve upon the earth," but "He drove them out of the paradise, and made them dwell over against the paradise." [1] He does not say "under the paradise." "He placed . . . cherubims and a flaming sword . . . to keep the way of [2] the tree of life." [3] He says nothing about an ascent to it. "And a river went out of Eden." [4] He does not say "went down from Eden." "It was parted and became into four heads. The name of the first is Pison . . . and the name of the second is Gihon." [5] I myself have seen the waters of Gihon, have seen them with my bodily eyes. It is this Gihon to which Jeremiah points when he says, "What hast thou to do in the way of Egypt to drink the muddy water of Gihon?" [6] I have drunk also from the great river Euphrates, not spiritual but actual water, such as you can touch with your hand and imbibe with your mouth. But where there are rivers which admit of being seen and of being drunk, it follows that there also there will be fig-trees and other trees; and it is of these that the Lord says, "Of every tree of the garden thou mayest freely eat." [7] They are like other trees and timber, just as the rivers are like other rivers and waters. But if the water is visible and real, then the fig-tree and the rest of the timber must be real also, and Adam and Eve must have been originally formed with real and not phantasmal bodies, and not, as Origen would have us believe, have afterwards received them on account of their sin. But, you say, "we read that Saint Paul was caught up to the third heaven, into paradise." [8] You explain the words rightly: "When he mentions the third heaven, and then adds the word paradise, he shows that heaven is in one place and paradise in another." Must not every one reject and despise such special pleading as that by which Origen says of the waters that are above the firmament [9] that they are not waters, but heroic beings of angelic power, [10] and again of the waters

[1] Ps. cxvi. 9. This form of the verse is peculiar to Jerome.
[2] Epiphanius had written a book "against all the heresies."
[3] In his note on Gen. iii. 21.　　　[4] Gen. ii. 23.
[5] Gen. ii. 21, 22.　　　[6] Gen. iii. 7.

[1] Gen. iii. 23, LXX.　[2] Introitus.　[3] Gen. iii. 24.
[4] Gen. ii. 10.　　[5] Gen. ii. 10, 11, 13.
[6] Jer. ii. 18, LXX. and Vulg.　[7] Gen. ii. 16.
[8] 2 Cor. xii 2, 4.　　[9] In his note on Gen. i. 7.
[10] Fortitudines angelicæ potestatis.

that are over the earth—that is, below the firmament—that they are potencies[1] of the contrary sort—that is, demons? If so, why do we read in the account of the deluge that the windows of heaven were opened, and that the waters of the deluge prevailed? In consequence of which the fountains of the deep were opened, and the whole earth was covered with the waters.[2]

6. Oh! the madness and folly of those who have forsaken the teaching of the book of Proverbs, "My son, keep thy father's commandment, and forsake not the law of thy mother,"[3] and have turned to error, and say to the fool that he shall be their leader, and do not despise the foolish things which are said by the foolish man, even as the scripture bears witness, "The foolish man speaketh foolishly, and his heart understandeth vanity."[4] I beseech you, dearly beloved, and by the love which I feel towards you, I implore you—as though it were my own members on which I would have pity[5]—by word and letter to fulfil that which is written, "Do not I hate them, O Lord, that hate thee? and am not I grieved with those that rise up against thee?"[6] Origen's words are the words of an enemy, hateful and repugnant to God and to His saints; and not only those which I have quoted, but countless others. For it is not now my intention to argue against all his opinions. Origen has not lived in my day, nor has he robbed me. I have not conceived a dislike to him nor quarrelled with him because of an inheritance or of any worldly matter; but—to speak plainly—I grieve, and grieve bitterly, to see numbers of my brothers, and of those in particular who show the most promise, and have reached the highest rank in the sacred ministry,[7] deceived by his persuasive arguments, and made by his most perverse teaching the food of the devil, whereby the saying is fulfilled: " He derides every stronghold, and his fare is choice, and he hath gathered captives as the sand."[8] But may God free you, my brother, and the holy people of Christ which is intrusted to you, and all the brothers who are with you, and especially the presbyter Rufinus, from the heresy of Origen, and other heresies, and from the perdition to which they lead. For, if for one word or for two opposed to the faith many heresies have been rejected by the Church, how much more shall he be held a heretic who has contrived such perverse

interpretations and such mischievous doctrines to destroy the faith, and has in fact declared himself the enemy of the Church! For, among other wicked things, he has presumed to say this, too, that Adam lost the image of God, although Scripture nowhere declares that he did. Were it so, never would all the creatures in the world be subject to Adam's seed—that is, to the entire human race; yet, in the words of the apostle, everything " is tamed and hath been tamed of mankind."[1] For never would all things be subjected to men if men had not—together with their authority over all—the image of God. But the divine Scripture conjoins and associates with this the grace of the blessing which was conferred upon Adam and upon the generations which descended from him. No one can by twisting the meaning of words presume to say that this grace of God was given to one only, and that he alone was made in the image of God (he and his wife, that is, for while he was formed of clay she was made of one of his ribs), but that those who were subsequently conceived in the womb and not born as was Adam did not possess God's image, for the Scripture immediately subjoins the following statement: "And Adam lived two hundred and thirty years,[2] and knew Eve his wife, and she bare him a son in his image and after his likeness, and called his name Seth."[3] And again, in the tenth generation, two thousand two hundred and forty-two years afterwards,[4] God, to vindicate His own image and to show that the grace which He had given to men still continued in them, gives the following commandment: "Flesh . . . with the blood thereof shall ye not eat. And surely your blood will I require at the hand of every man that sheddeth it; for in the image of God have I made man."[5] From Noah to Abraham ten generations passed away,[6] and from Abraham's time to David's, fourteen more,[7] and these twenty-four generations make up, taken together, two thousand one hundred and seventeen years.[8] Yet the Holy Spirit in the thirty-ninth[9] psalm, while lamenting that all men walk in a vain show, and that they are subject to sins, speaks thus: "For all that every man walk-

---

[1] Virtues.   [2] Gen. vii. 11.   [3] Prov. vi. 20.
[4] Isa. xxxii. 6, Vulg.   [5] Cf. Philem. 12.   [6] Ps. cxxxix. 21.
[7] Sacerdotium.   [8] Hab. i. 10, 16, 9, LXX.

[1] Jas. iii. 7.
[2] LXX. The Heb. text which A.V. follows gives " an hundred and thirty years."   [3] Gen. iv. 25 ; v. 3 ; i. 26.
[4] According to the LXX. The chronology of the Hebrew text gives a period of 1656 years (Gen. v.).
[5] Gen. ix. 4–6 ; substantially as in A.V.
[6] Gen. xi. 10–26.   [7] Matt. i. 17.
[8] This calculation appears to be based on the LXX.
[9] Acc. to the Vulg., which Jerome here follows, the thirty-eighth.

eth in the image."[1] Also after David's time, in the reign of Solomon his son, we read a somewhat similar reference to the divine likeness. For in the book of Wisdom, which is inscribed with his name, Solomon says: "God created man to be immortal, and made him to be an image of His own eternity."[2] And again, about eleven hundred and eleven years afterwards, we read in the New Testament that men have not lost the image of God. For James, an apostle and brother of the Lord, whom I have mentioned above—that we may not be entangled in the snares of Origen—teaches us that man does possess God's image and likeness. For, after a somewhat discursive account of the human tongue, he has gone on to say of it: "It is an unruly evil . . . therewith bless we God, even the Father; and therewith curse we men, which are made after the similitude of God."[3] Paul, too, the "chosen vessel,"[4] who in his preaching has fully maintained the doctrine of the gospel, instructs us that man is made in the image and after the likeness of God. "A man," he says, "ought not to wear long hair, forasmuch as he is the image and glory of God."[5] He speaks of "the image" simply, but explains the nature of the likeness by the word "glory."

7. Instead of the three proofs from Holy Scripture which you said would satisfy you if I could produce them, behold I have given you seven. Who, then, will put up with the follies of Origen? I will not use a severer word and so make myself like him or his followers, who presume at the peril of their soul to assert dogmatically whatever first comes into their head, and to dictate to God, whereas they ought either to pray to Him or to learn the truth from Him. For some of them say that the image of God which Adam had previously received was lost when he sinned. Others surmise that the body which the Son of God was destined to take of Mary was the image of the Creator. Some identify this image with the soul, others with sensation, others with virtue. These make it baptism, those assert that it is in virtue of God's image that man exercises universal sway. Like drunkards in their cups, they ejaculate now this, now that, when they ought rather to have avoided so serious a risk, and to have obtained salvation by simple faith, not denying the words of God. To God they ought to have left the sure and exact knowledge of His

own gift, and of the particular way in which He has created men in His image and after His likeness. Forsaking this course, they have involved themselves in many subtle questions, and through these they have been plunged into the mire of sin. But we, dearly beloved, believe the words of the Lord, and know that God's image remains in all men, and we leave it to Him to know in what respect man is created in His image. And let no one be deceived by that passage in the epistle of John, which some readers fail to understand, where he says: "Now are we the sons of God, and it doth not yet appear what we shall be: but we know that, when He shall appear, we shall be like Him; for we shall see Him as He is."[1] For this refers to the glory which is then to be revealed[2] to His saints; just as also in another place we read the words "from glory to glory,"[3] of which glory the saints have even in this world received an earnest and a small portion. At their head stand Moses, whose face shone exceedingly, and was bright with the brightness of the sun. Next to him comes Elijah, who was caught up into heaven in a chariot of fire,[5] and did not feel the effects of the flame. Stephen too, when he was being stoned, had the face of an angel visible to all.[6] And this which we have verified in a few cases is to be understood of all, that what is written may be fulfilled. "Every one that sanctifieth himself shall be numbered among the blessed." For, "blessed are the pure in heart, for they shall see God."[7]

8. These things being so, dearly beloved, keep watch over your own soul and cease to murmur against me. For the divine Scripture says: "Neither murmur ye [one against another[8]] as some of them also murmured and were destroyed of serpents."[9] Rather give way to the truth and love me who love both you and the truth. And may the God of peace, according to His mercy, grant to us that Satan may be bruised under the feet of Christians,[10] and that every occasion of evil may be shunned, so that the bond of love and peace may not be rent asunder between us, or the preaching of the right faith be anywise hindered.

9. Moreover, I have heard that certain persons have this grievance against me. When I accompanied you to the holy place called Bethel, there to join you in celebrating the Collect,[11] after the use of the

---

[1] Ps. 39, 6. "In a vain show," R.V.   [2] Wisd. ii. 23.
[3] Jas. iii. 8, 9.   [4] Acts. ix. 15.   [5] 1 Cor. xi. 7.

[1] 1 Joh. iii. 2.   [2] 1 Pet. v. 1.   [3] 2 Cor. iii. 18.
[4] Exod. xxxiv. 29 *sqq.*; 2 Cor. iii. 7.   [5] 2 Kings ii. 11.
[6] Acts vi. 15.   [7] Matt. v. 8.   [8] Words added by this writer.
[9] 1 Cor. x. 10.   [10] Rom. xvi. 20.   [11] See note on § 1 above.

Church, I came to a villa called Anablatha, and, as I was passing, saw a lamp burning there. Asking what place it was, and learning it to be a church, I went in to pray, and found there a curtain hanging on the doors of the said church, dyed and embroidered.[1] It bore an image either of Christ or of one of the saints; I do not rightly remember whose the image was. Seeing this, and being loth that an image of a man should be hung up in Christ's church contrary to the teaching of the Scriptures, I tore it asunder and advised the custodians of the place to use it as a winding sheet for some poor person. They, however, murmured, and said that if I made up my mind to tear it, it was only fair that I should give them another curtain in its place. As soon as I heard this, I promised that I would give one, and said that I would send it at once. Since then there has been some little delay, due to the fact that I have been seeking a curtain of the best quality to give to them instead of the former one, and thought it right to send to Cyprus for one. I have now sent the best that I could find, and I beg that you will order the presbyter of the place to take the curtain which I have sent from the hands of the Reader, and that you will afterwards give directions that curtains of the other sort—opposed as they are to our religion—shall not be hung up in any church of Christ. A man of your uprightness should be careful to remove an occasion of offence[2] unworthy alike of the Church of Christ and of those Christians who are committed to your charge. Beware of Palladius of Galatia—a man once dear to me, but who now sorely needs God's pity—for he preaches and teaches the heresy of Origen; and see to it that he does not seduce any of those who are intrusted to your keeping into the perverse ways of his erroneous doctrine. I pray that you may fare well in the Lord.

LETTER LII.

TO NEPOTIAN.

Nepotian, the nephew of Heliodorus (for whom see Letter XIV.), had, like his uncle, abandoned the military for the clerical calling, and was now a presbyter at Altinum, where Heliodorus was bishop. The letter is a systematic treatise on the duties of the clergy and on the rule of life which they ought to adopt. It had a great vogue, and called forth much indignation against Jerome. Its date is 394 A.D.

1. Again and again you ask me, my dear Nepotian, in your letters from over the sea, to draw for you a few rules of life, showing how one who has renounced the service of the world to become a monk or a clergyman may keep the straight path of Christ, and not be drawn aside into the haunts of vice. As a young man, or rather as a boy, and while I was curbing by the hard life of the desert the first onslaughts of youthful passion, I sent a letter of remonstrance[1] to your reverend uncle, Heliodorus, which, by the tears and complainings with which it was filled, showed him the feelings of the friend whom he had deserted. In it I acted the part suited to my age, and as I was still aglow with the methods and maxims of the rhetoricians, I decked it out a good deal with the flourishes of the schools. Now, however, my head is gray, my brow is furrowed, a dewlap like that of an ox hangs from my chin, and, as Virgil says,

> The chilly blood stands still around my heart.[2]

Elsewhere he sings:

> Old age bears all, even the mind, away.

And a little further on:

> So many of my songs are gone from me,
> And even my very voice has left me now.[3]

2. But that I may not seem to quote only profane literature, listen to the mystical teaching of the sacred writings. Once David had been a man of war, but at seventy age had chilled him so that nothing would make him warm. A girl is accordingly sought from the coasts of Israel—Abishag the Shunamite—to sleep with the king and warm his aged frame.[4] Does it not seem to you—if you keep to the letter that killeth[5]—like some farcical story or some broad jest from an Atellan play?[6] A chilly old man is wrapped up in blankets, and only grows warm in a girl's embrace. Bathsheba was still living, Abigail was still left, and the remainder of those wives and concubines whose names the Scripture mentions. Yet they are all rejected as cold, and only in the one young girl's embrace does the old man become warm. Abraham was far older than David; still, so long as Sarah lived he sought no other wife. Isaac counted twice the years of David, yet never felt cold with Rebekah, old though she was. I say nothing of the antediluvians, who, although after nine hundred years their limbs must have been not old merely, but decayed with age, had no recourse to girls' embraces. Moses, the leader of the Israelites, counted

---

1 Velum . . . tinctum atque depictum.　2 Scrupulositas.

1 Letter XIV. 9 v.　2 Virgil, G. ii. 484.
3 Virgil, Ec. ix. 51, 54, 55.　4 1 K. i. 1–4.　5 2 Cor. iii. 6.
6 So called because first devised in the Oscan town of Atella.

one hundred and twenty years, yet sought no change from Zipporah.

3. Who, then, is this Shunamite, this wife and maid, so glowing as to warm the cold, yet so holy as not to arouse passion in him whom she warmed?[1] Let Solomon, wisest of men, tell us of his father's favorite; let the man of peace[2] recount to us the embraces of the man of war.[3] "Get wisdom," he writes, "get understanding: forget it not; neither decline from the words of my mouth. Forsake her not and she shall preserve thee: love her and she shall keep thee. Wisdom is the principal thing, therefore get wisdom, and with all thy getting get understanding. Exalt her and she shall promote thee. She shall bring thee to honor when thou dost embrace her. She shall give to thine head an ornament of grace: a crown of glory shall she deliver to thee."[4]

Almost all bodily excellences alter with age, and while wisdom alone increases all things else decay. Fasts and vigils and almsdeeds become harder. So also do sleeping on the ground, moving from place to place, hospitality to travellers, pleading for the poor, earnestness and steadfastness in prayer, the visitation of the sick, manual labor to supply money for almsgiving. All acts, in short, of which the body is the medium decrease with its decay.

Now, there are young men still full of life and vigor who, by toil and burning zeal, as well as by holiness of life and constant prayer to the Lord Jesus, have obtained knowledge. I do not speak of these, or say that in them the love of wisdom is cold, for this withers in many of the old by reason of age. What I mean is that youth, as such, has to cope with the assaults of passion, and amid the allurements of vice and the tinglings of the flesh is stifled like a fire among green boughs, and cannot develop its proper brightness. But when men have employed their youth in commendable pursuits and have meditated on the law of the Lord day and night,[5] they learn with the lapse of time, fresh experience and wisdom come as the years go by, and so from the pursuits of the past their old age reaps a harvest of delight. Hence that wise man of Greece, Themistocles,[6] perceiving, after the expiration of one hundred and seven years, that he was on the verge of the grave, is reported to have said that he regretted extremely having to leave life just when he was beginning to grow wise. Plato died in his eighty-first year, his pen still in his hand. Isocrates completed ninety years and nine in the midst of literary and scholastic work.[1] I say nothing of other philosophers, such as Pythagoras, Democritus, Xenocrates, Zeno, and Cleanthes, who in extreme old age displayed the vigor of youth in the pursuit of wisdom. I pass on to the poets, Homer, Hesiod, Simonides, Stesichorus, who all lived to a great age, yet at the approach of death sang each of them a swan song sweeter than their wont.[2] Sophocles, when charged by his sons with dotage on account of his advanced years and his neglect of his property, read out to his judges his recently composed play of Œdipus, and made so great a display of wisdom—in spite of the inroads of time—that he changed the decorous silence of the law court into the applause of the theatre.[3] And no wonder, when Cato the censor, that most eloquent of Romans, in his old age neither blushed at the thought of learning Greek nor despaired of succeeding.[4] Homer, for his part, relates that from the tongue of Nestor, even when quite aged and helpless, there flowed speech sweeter than honey.[5]

Even the very name Abishag in its mystic meaning points to the greater wisdom of old men. For the translation of it is, "My father is over and above," or "my father's roaring." The term "over and above" is obscure, but in this passage is indicative of excellence, and implies that the old have a larger stock of wisdom, and that it even overflows by reason of its abundance. In another passage "over and above" forms an antithesis to "necessary." Moreover, Abishag, that is, "roaring," is properly used of the sound which the waves make, and of the murmur which we hear coming from the sea. From which it is plain that the thunder of the divine voice dwells in old men's ears with a volume of sound beyond the voices of men. Again, in our tongue Shunamite means "scarlet," a hint that the love of wisdom becomes warm and glowing through religious study. For though the color may point to the mystery of the Lord's blood, it also sets forth the warm glow of wisdom. Hence it is a scarlet thread that in Genesis the midwife binds upon the hand of Pharez—Pharez "the divider," so called because he divided the partition which had before separated two peoples.[6] So, too, with a

---

[1] 1 K. i. 4. [2] The name Solomon means "man of peace."
[3] 1 Chr. xxviii. 3. [4] Prov. iv. 5-9. [5] Ps. i. 2.
[6] A slip of the pen for Theophrastus.

[1] Cicero, de Sen. v. [2] Cicero, de Sen. vii.
[3] Id. ibid. [4] Cic. de Sen. viii.
[5] Homer, Il. i. 249 ; Cic. de Sen. x. [6] Gen. xxxviii. 28, 29.

mystic reference to the shedding of blood, it was a scarlet cord which the harlot Rahab (a type of the church) hung in her window to preserve her house in the destruction of Jericho.[1] Hence, in another place Scripture says of holy men: "These are they which came from the warmth of the house of the father of Rechab."[2] And in the gospel the Lord says: "I am come to cast fire upon the earth, and fain am I to see it kindled."[3] This was the fire which, when it was kindled in the disciples' hearts, constrained them to say: "Did not our heart burn within us while He talked with us by the way, and while He opened to us the Scriptures?"[4]

4. To what end, you ask, these recondite references? To show that you need not expect from me boyish declamation, flowery sentiments, a meretricious style, and at the close of every paragraph the terse and pointed aphorisms which call forth approving shouts from those who hear them. Let Wisdom alone embrace me; let her nestle in my bosom, my Abishag who grows not old. Undefiled truly is she, and a virgin forever; for although she daily conceives and unceasingly brings to the birth, like Mary she remains undeflowered. When the apostle says "be fervent in spirit,"[5] he means "be true to wisdom." And when our Lord in the gospel declares that in the end of the world—when the shepherd shall grow foolish, according to the prophecy of Zechariah[6]— "the love of many shall wax cold,"[7] He means that wisdom shall decay. Hear, therefore—to quote the sainted Cyprian— "words forcible rather than elegant."[8] Hear one who, though he is your brother in orders, is in years your father; who can conduct you from the cradle of faith to spiritual manhood; and who, while he builds up stage by stage the rules of holy living, can instruct others in instructing you. I know, of course, that from your reverend uncle, Heliodorus, now a bishop of Christ, you have learned and are daily learning all that is holy; and that in him you have before you a rule of life and a pattern of virtue. Take, then, my suggestions for what they are worth, and compare my precepts with his. He will teach you the perfection of a monk, and I shall show you the whole duty of a clergyman.

5. A clergyman, then, as he serves Christ's church, must first understand what his name

means; and then, when he realizes this, must endeavor to be that which he is called. For since the Greek word κλῆρος means "lot," or "inheritance," the clergy are so called either because they are the lot of the Lord, or else because the Lord Himself is their lot and portion. Now, he who in his own person is the Lord's portion, or has the Lord for his portion, must so bear himself as to possess the Lord and to be possessed by Him. He who possesses the Lord, and who says with the prophet, "The Lord is my portion,"[1] can hold to nothing beside the Lord. For if he hold to something beside the Lord, the Lord will not be his portion. Suppose, for instance, that he holds to gold or silver, or possessions or inlaid furniture; with such portions as these the Lord will not deign to be his portion. I, if I am the portion of the Lord, and the line of His heritage,[2] receive no portion among the remaining tribes; but, like the Priest and the Levite, I live on the tithe,[3] and serving the altar, am supported by its offerings.[4] Having food and raiment, I shall be content with these,[5] and as a disciple of the Cross shall share its poverty. I beseech you, therefore, and

Again and yet again admonish you ;[6]

do not look to your military experience for a standard of clerical obligation. Under Christ's banner seek for no worldly gain, lest having more than when you first became a clergyman, you hear men say, to your shame, "Their portion shall not profit them."[7] Welcome poor men and strangers to your homely board, that with them Christ may be your guest. A clergyman who engages in business, and who rises from poverty to wealth, and from obscurity to a high position, avoid as you would the plague. For "evil communications corrupt good manners."[8] You despise gold; he loves it. You spurn wealth; he eagerly pursues it. You love silence, meekness, privacy; he takes delight in talking and effrontery, in squares, and streets, and apothecaries' shops. What unity of feeling can there be where there is so wide a divergency of manners?

A woman's foot should seldom, if ever, cross the threshold of your home. To all who are Christ's virgins show the same regard or the same disregard. Do not linger under the same roof with them, and do not

---

1 Josh. ii. 18.   2 1 Chron. ii. 55, Vulg.   3 Luke xii. 49.
4 Luke xxiv. 32.   5 Rom. xii. 11.   6 Zech. xi. 15.
7 Matt. xxiv. 12.   8 Cyprian, Ep. ad Donatum.

1 Pss. xvi. 5 ; lxxiii. 26.   2 Ps. xvi. 5, 6.   3 Nu. xviii. 24.
4 1 Cor. ix. 13.   5 1 Tim. vi. 8.   6 Virgil, Æn. iii. 436.
7 Jer. xii. 13, LXX. There is a play on the word κλῆρος, which means (1) portion, (2) clergy.   8 1 Cor. xv. 33.

rely on your past continence. You cannot be holier than David or wiser than Solomon. Always bear in mind that it was a woman who expelled the tiller of paradise from his heritage.[1] In case you are sick one of the brethren may attend you; your sister also or your mother or some woman whose faith is approved with all. But if you have no persons so connected with you or so marked out by chaste behaviour, the Church maintains many elderly women who by their ministrations may oblige you and benefit themselves so that even your sickness may bear fruit in the shape of almsdeeds. I know of cases where the recovery of the body has but preluded the sickness of the soul. There is danger for you in the service of one for whose face you constantly watch. If in the course of your clerical duty you have to visit a widow or a virgin, never enter the house alone. Let your companions be persons association with whom will not disgrace you. If you take a reader with you or an acolyte or a psalm-singer, let their character not their garb be their adornment; let them use no tongs to curl their hair; rather let their mien be an index of their chastity. You must not sit alone with a woman or see one without witnesses. If she has anything confidential to disclose, she is sure to have some nurse or housekeeper,[2] some virgin, some widow, some married woman. She cannot be so friendless as to have none save you to whom she can venture to confide her secret. Beware of all that gives occasion for suspicion; and, to avoid scandal, shun every act that may give colour to it. Frequent gifts of handkerchiefs and garters, of face-cloths and dishes first tasted by the giver —to say nothing of notes full of fond expressions—of such things as these a holy love knows nothing. Such endearing and alluring expressions as 'my honey' and 'my darling,' 'you who are all my charm and my delight' the ridiculous courtesies of lovers and their foolish doings, we blush for on the stage and abhor in men of the world. How much more do we loathe them in monks and clergymen who adorn the priesthood by their vows[3] while their vows are adorned by the priesthood. I speak thus not because I dread such evils for you or for men of saintly life, but because in all ranks and callings and among both men and women there are found both good and bad and in condemning the bad I commend the good.

6. Shameful to say, idol-priests, play-actors, jockeys, and prostitutes can inherit property: clergymen and monks alone lie under a legal disability, a disability enacted not by perse-cutors but by Christian emperors.[1] I do not complain of the law, but I grieve that we have deserved a statute so harsh. Cauterizing is a good thing, no doubt; but how is it that I have a wound which makes me need it? The law is strict and far-seeing, yet even so rapacity goes on unchecked. By a fiction of trusteeship we set the statute at defiance; and, as if imperial decrees outweigh the mandates of Christ, we fear the laws and despise the Gospels. If heir there must be, the mother has first claim upon her children, the Church upon her flock—the members of which she has borne and reared and nourished. Why do we thrust ourselves in between mother and children?

It is the glory of a bishop to make provision for the wants of the poor; but it is the shame of all priests to amass private fortunes. I who was born (suppose) in a poor man's house, in a country cottage, and who could scarcely get of common millet and household bread enough to fill an empty stomach, am now come to disdain the finest wheat flour and honey. I know the several kinds of fish by name. I can tell unerringly on what coast a mussel has been picked. I can distinguish by the flavour the province from which a bird comes. Dainty dishes delight me because their ingredients are scarce and I end by finding pleasure in their ruinous cost.

I hear also of servile attention shewn by some towards old men and women when these are childless. They fetch the basin, beset the bed and perform with their own hands the most revolting offices. They anxiously await the advent of the doctor and with trembling lips they ask whether the patient is better. If for a little while the old fellow shews signs of returning vigour, they are in agonies. They pretend to be delighted, but their covetous hearts undergo secret torture. For they are afraid that their labours may go for nothing and compare an old man with a clinging to life to the patriarch Methuselah. How great a reward might they have with God if their hearts were not set on a temporal prize! With what great exertions do they pursue an empty heritage! Less labour might have purchased for them the pearl of Christ.

7. Read the divine scriptures constantly; never, indeed, let the sacred volume be out of your hand. Learn what you have to teach. "Hold fast the faithful word as you have been taught that you may be able by sound doctrine to exhort and convince the gainsayers. Continue thou in the things that thou hast learned and hast been assured of, knowing of whom thou hast learned them;"[2] and

---

[1] Another allusion to the word κλῆρος. [2] Major domus.
[3] The vow of celibacy is probably intended.

[1] The disability alluded to was enacted by Valentinian.
[1] Titus, i. 9; 2 Tim. iii. 14.

be ready always to give an answer to every man that asketh you a reason of the hope and faith that are in you." [1] Do not let your deeds belie your words ; lest when you speak in church someone may mentally reply " Why do you not practise what you profess ? Here is a lover of dainties turned censor ! his stomach is full and he reads us a homily on fasting. As well might a robber accuse others of covetousness." In a priest of Christ mouth, mind, and hand should be at one.

Be obedient to your bishop and welcome him as the parent of your soul. Sons love their fathers and slaves fear their masters. " If I be a father," He says, " where is mine honour ? And if I am a master where is my fear ? " [2] In your case the bishop combines in himself many titles to your respect. He is at once a monk, a prelate, and an uncle who has before now instructed you in all holy things. This also I say that the bishops should know themselves to be priests not lords. Let them render to the clergy the honour which is their due that the clergy may offer to them the respect which belongs to bishops. There is a witty saying of the orator Domitius which is here to the point : " Why am I to recognize you as leader of the Senate when you will not recognize my rights as a private member ? " [3] We should realize that a bishop and his presbyters are like Aaron and his sons. As there is but one Lord and one Temple ; so also should there be but one ministry. Let us ever bear in mind the charge which the apostle Peter gives to priests : " feed the flock of God which is among you, taking the oversight thereof not by constraint but willingly as God would have you ; [4] not for filthy lucre but of a ready mind ; neither as being lords over God's heritage but being ensamples to the flock," and that gladly ; that " when the chief-shepherd shall appear ye may receive a crown of glory that fadeth not away." [5] It is a bad custom which prevails in certain churches for presbyters to be silent when bishops are present on the ground that they would be jealous or impatient hearers. " If anything," writes the apostle Paul, " be revealed to another that sitteth by, let the first hold his peace. For ye may all prophesy one by one that all may learn and all may be comforted ; and the spirits of the prophets are subject to the prophets. For God is not the author of confusion but of peace." [6] " A wise son maketh a glad father ; " [7] and a bishop should rejoice in the discrimination which has led him to choose such for the priests of Christ.

8. When teaching in church seek to call forth not plaudits but groans. Let the tears of your hearers be your glory. A presbyter's words ought to be seasoned by his reading of scripture. Be not a declaimer or a ranter, one who gabbles without rhyme or reason; but shew yourself skilled in the deep things and versed in the mysteries of God. To mouth your words and by your quickness of utterance astonish the unlettered crowd is a mark of ignorance. Assurance often explains that of which it knows nothing ; and when it has convinced others imposes on itself. My teacher, Gregory of Nazianzus, when I once asked him to explain Luke's phrase σάββατον δευτερόπρωτον, that is "the second-first Sabbath," playfully evaded my request saying : " I will tell you about it in church, and there, when all the people applaud me, you will be forced against your will to know what you do not know at all. For, if you alone remain silent, every one will put you down for a fool." There is nothing so easy as by sheer volubility to deceive a common crowd or an uneducated congregation : such most admire what they fail to understand. Hear Marcus Tullius, the subject of that noble eulogy: " You would have been the first of orators but for Demosthenes: he would have been the only one but for you." Hear what in his speech for Quintus Gallius [1] he has to say about unskilled speakers and popular applause and then you will not be the sport of such illusions. " What I am telling you," said he, "is a recent experience of my own. One who has the name of a poet and a man of culture has written a book entitled *Conversations of Poets and Philosophers*. In this he represents Euripides as conversing with Menander and Socrates with Epicurus—men whose lives we know to be separated not by years but by centuries. Nevertheless he calls forth limitless applause and endless acclamations. For the theatre contains many who belong to the same school as he: like him they have never learned letters."

9. In dress avoid sombre colours as much as bright ones. Showiness and slovenliness are alike to be shunned ; for the one savours of vanity and the other of pride. To go about without a linen scarf on is nothing: what is praiseworthy is to be without money to buy one. It is disgraceful and absurd to boast of having neither napkin nor handkerchief and yet to carry a well-filled purse.

Some bestow a trifle on the poor to receive a larger sum themselves and under the cloak of almsgiving do but seek for riches. Such are almshunters rather than almsgivers. Their methods are those by which birds, beasts, and

---

[1] 1 Pet. iii. 15. [2] Mal. i. 6. [3] Cicero, de Orat. iii. 1.
[4] So the Vulgate. [5] 1 Pet. v. 4. [6] 1 Cor. xiv. 30–33.
[7] Prov. x. 1.

[1] This is not extant.

fishes are taken. A morsel of bait is put on the hook—to land a married lady's purse! The church is committed to the bishop; let him take heed whom he appoints to be his almoner. It is better for me to have no money to give away than shamelessly to beg what I mean to hoard. It is arrogance too to wish to seem more liberal than he who is Christ's bishop. "All things are not open to us all." [1] In the church one is the eye, another is the tongue, another the hand, another the foot, others ears, belly, and so on. Read Paul's epistle to the Corinthians and learn how the one body is made up of different members. [2] The rude and simple brother must not suppose himself a saint just because he knows nothing; and he who is educated and eloquent must not measure his saintliness merely by his fluency. Of two imperfect things holy rusticity is better than sinful eloquence.

10. Many build churches nowadays; their walls and pillars of glowing marble, their ceilings glittering with gold, their altars studded with jewels. Yet to the choice of Christ's ministers no heed is paid. And let no one allege against me the wealth of the temple in Judæa, its table, its lamps, its censers, its dishes, its cups, its spoons, [3] and the rest of its golden vessels. If these were approved by the Lord it was at a time when the priests had to offer victims and when the blood of sheep was the redemption of sins. They were figures typifying things still future and were "written for our admonition upon whom the ends of the world are come." [4] But now our Lord by His poverty has consecrated the poverty of His house. Let us, therefore, think of His cross and count riches to be but dirt. Why do we admire what Christ calls "the mammon of unrighteousness"? [5] Why do we cherish and love what it is Peter's boast not to possess? [6] Or if we insist on keeping to the letter and find the mention of gold and wealth so pleasing, let us keep to everything else as well as the gold. Let the bishops of Christ be bound to marry wives, who must be virgins. [7] Let the best-intentioned priest be deprived of his office if he bear a scar and be disfigured. [8] Let bodily leprosy be counted worse than spots upon the soul. Let us be fruitful and multiply and replenish the earth, [9] but let us slay no lamb and celebrate no mystic passover, for where there is no temple, [10] the law forbids these acts. Let us pitch tents in the seventh month [11] and noise abroad a solemn fast with the sound of a horn. [12] But

if we compare all these things as spiritual with things which are spiritual; [1] and if we allow with Paul that "the Law is spiritual" [2] and call to mind David's words: "open thou mine eyes that I may behold wondrous things out of thy law;" [3] and if on these grounds we interpret it as our Lord interprets it—He has explained the Sabbath in this way: [4] then rejecting the superstitions of the Jews, we must also reject the gold; or, approving the gold, we must approve the Jews as well. For we must either accept them with the gold or condemn them with it.

11. Avoid entertaining men of the world especially those whose honours make them swell with pride. You are the priest of Christ —one poor and crucified who lived on the bread of strangers. It is a disgrace to you if the consul's lictors or soldiers keep watch before your door, and if the Judge of the province has a better dinner with you than in his own palace. If you plead as an excuse you wish to intercede for the unhappy and the oppressed, I reply that a worldly judge will defer more to a clergyman who is self-denying than to one who is rich; he will pay more regard to your holiness than to your wealth. Or if he is a man who will not hear the clergy on behalf of the distressed except over the bowl, I will readily forego his aid and will appeal to Christ who can help more effectively and speedily than any judge. Truly "it is better to trust in the Lord than to put confidence in man. It is better to trust in the Lord than to put confidence in princes." [5]

Let your breath never smell of wine lest the philosopher's words be said to you: "instead of offering me a kiss you are giving me a taste of wine." Priests given to wine are both condemned by the apostle [6] and forbidden by the old Law. Those who serve the altar, we are told, must drink neither wine nor *shechar*. Now every intoxicating drink is in Hebrew called *shechar* whether it is made of corn or of the juice of apples, whether you distil from the honeycomb a rude kind of mead or make a liquor by squeezing dates or strain a thick syrup from a decoction of corn. Whatever intoxicates and disturbs the balance of the mind avoid as you would wine. I do not say that we are to condemn what is a creature of God. The Lord Himself was called a "wine bibber" and wine in moderation was allowed to Timothy because of his weak stomach. only require that drinkers should observe that limit which their age, their health, or their constitution requires. But if without drink

[1] Virgil. Ec. viii. 63.   [2] 1 Cor. xii. 12-27.
[3] Mortariola. See Nu. vii. 24, Vulg.   [4] 1 Cor. X. 11.
[5] Luke xvi. 9.   [6] Acts iii. 6.   [7] Levit. xxi. 14.
[8] Levit. xxi. 17-23.   [9] Gen. i. 28.   [10] Deut. xvi. 5.
[11] Levit. xxiii. 40-42.   [12] Joel ii. 15.

[1] 1 Cor. ii. 13.   [2] Rom. vii. 14.   [3] Ps. cxix. 18.
[4] Matt. xii. 1-9.   [5] Ps. cxviii. 8, 9.   [6] 1 Tim. iii. 3.
[7] Levit. x. 9; the word *shechar* occurs in the Greek text of Luke i. 15.

g wine at all I am aglow with youth and am inflamed by the heat of my blood and am of a strong and lusty habit of body, I will readily forego the cup in which I cannot but suspect poison. The Greeks have an excellent saying which will perhaps bear translation,

Fat bellies have no sentiments refined.[1]

12. Lay upon yourself only as much fasting as you can bear, and let your fasts be pure, chaste, simple, moderate, and not superstitious. What good is it to use no oil if you seek after the most troublesome and out-of-the-way kinds of food, dried figs, pepper, nuts, dates, fine flour, honey, pistachios? All the resources of gardening are strained to save us from eating household bread; and to pursue dainties we turn our backs on the kingdom of heaven. There are some, I am told, who reverse the laws of nature and the race; for they neither eat bread nor drink water but imbibe thin decoctions of crushed herbs and beet-juice—not from a cup but from a shell. Shame on us that we have no blushes for such follies and that we feel no disgust at such superstition! To crown all, in the midst of our dainties we seek a reputation for abstinence. The strictest fast is bread and water. But because it brings with it no glory and because we all of us live on bread and water, it is reckoned no fast at all but an ordinary and common matter.

13. Do not angle for compliments, lest, while you win the popular applause, you do despite to God. "If I yet pleased men," says the apostle, "I should not be the servant of Christ."[2] He ceased to please men when he became Christ's servant Christ's soldier marches on through good report and evil report,[3] the one on the right hand and the other on the left. No praise elates him, no reproaches crush him. He is not puffed up by riches, nor does he shrink into himself because of poverty. Joy and sorrow he alike despises. The sun does not burn him by day nor the moon by night.[4] Do not pray at the corners of the streets,[5] lest the applause of men interrupt the straight course of your prayers. Do not broaden your fringes and for show wear phylacteries,[6] or, despite of conscience, wrap yourself in the self-seeking of the Pharisee.[7] Would you know what mode of apparel the Lord requires? Have prudence, justice, temperance, fortitude.[8] Let these be the four quarters of your horizon, let them be a four-

horse team to bear you, Christ's charioteer, at full speed to your goal. No necklace can be more precious than these; no gems can form a brighter galaxy. By them you are decorated, you are girt about, you are protected on every side. They are your defence as well as your glory; for every gem is turned into a shield.

14. Beware also of a blabbing tongue and of itching ears. Neither detract from others nor listen to detractors. "Thou sittest," says the psalmist, "and speakest against thy brother; thou slanderest thine own mother's son. These things hast thou done and I kept silence; thou thoughtest wickedly that I was such an one as thyself, but I will reprove thee and set them[1] in order before thine eyes."[2] Keep your tongue from cavilling and watch over your words. Know that in judging others you are passing sentence on yourself and that you are yourself guilty of the faults which you blame in them. It is no excuse to say: "if others tell me things I cannot be rude to them." No one cares to speak to an unwilling listener. An arrow never lodges in a stone: often it recoils upon the shooter of it. Let the detractor learn from your unwillingness to listen not to be so ready to detract. Solomon says:—"meddle not with them that are given to detraction: for their calamity shall rise suddenly; and who knoweth the destruction of them both?"[3]—of the detractor, that is, and of the person who lends an ear to his detraction.

15. It is your duty to visit the sick, to know the homes and children of ladies who are married, and to guard the secrets of noblemen. Make it your object, therefore, to keep your tongue chaste as well as your eyes. Never discuss a woman's figure nor let one house know what is going on in another. Hippocrates,[4] before he will teach his pupils, makes them take an oath and compels them to swear fealty to him. He binds them over to silence, and prescribes for them their language, their gait, their dress, their manners. How much more reason have we to whom the medicine of the soul has been committed to love the houses of all Christians as our own homes. Let them know us as comforters in sorrow rather than as guests in time of mirth. That clergyman soon becomes an object of contempt who being often asked out to dinner never refuses to go.

16. Let us never seek for presents and rarely accept them when we are asked to do so. For "it is more blessed to give than to

---

[1] Cf. Shakespere:—
  Fat paunches have lean pates, and dainty bits
  Make rich the ribs, but bankrupt quite the wits.
[2] Gal. i. 10.   [3] 2 Cor. vi. 8.
[4] Ps. cxxi. 6.   [5] Matt. vi. 5.   [6] Matt. xxiii. 5.
[7] Some irrelevant sentences are found here in the ordinary text which are obviously an interpolation.
[8] Wisd. viii. 7, the cardinal virtues of Greek philosophy.

[1] Viz. thy misdeeds.   [2] Ps. l. 20, 21.
[3] Prov. xxiv. 21, 22, Vulg.
[4] The principal physician of this name flourished in the fifth century, B. C.

receive."[1] Somehow or other the very man who begs leave to offer you a gift holds you the cheaper for your acceptance of it ; while, if you refuse it, it is wonderful how much more he will come to respect you. The preacher of continence must not be a maker of marriages. Why does he who reads the apostle's words "it remaineth that they that have wives be as though they had none"[2]— why does he press a virgin to marry ? Why does a priest, who must be a monogamist,[3] urge a widow to marry again ? How can the clergy be managers and stewards of other men's households, when they are bidden to disregard even their own interests ? To wrest a thing from a friend is theft but to cheat the Church is sacrilege. When you have received money to be doled out to the poor, to be cautious or to hesitate while crowds are starving is to be worse than a robber ; and to subtract a portion for yourself is to commit a crime of the deepest dye. I am tortured with hunger and are you to judge what will satisfy my cravings ? Either divide immediately what you have received, or, if you are a timid almoner, send the donor to distribute his own gifts. Your purse ought not to remain full while I am in need. No one can look after what is mine better than I can. He is the best almoner who keeps nothing for himself.

17. You have compelled me, my dear Nepotian, in spite of the castigation which my treatise on *Virginity* has had to endure—the one which I wrote for the saintly Eustochium at Rome :[4]—you have compelled me after ten years have passed once more to open my mouth at Bethlehem and to expose myself to the stabs of every tongue. For I could only escape from criticism by writing nothing—a course made impossible by your request ; and I knew when I took up my pen that the shafts of all gainsayers would be launched against me. I beg such to hold their peace and to desist from gainsaying : for I have written to them not as to opponents but as to friends. I have not inveighed against those who sin : I have but warned them to sin no more. My judgment of myself has been as strict as my judgment of them. When I have wished to remove the mote from my neighbour's eye, I have first cast out the beam in my own.[5] I have calumniated no one. Not a name has been hinted at. My words have not been aimed at individuals and my criticism of shortcomings has been quite general. If any one wishes to be angry with me he will have first to own that he himself suits my description.

LETTER LIII.

TO PAULINUS.

Jerome urges Paulinus, bishop of Nola, (for whom see Letter LVIII.) to make a diligent study of the Scriptures and to this end reminds him of the zeal fo learning displayed not only by the wisest of the pagan but also by the apostle Paul. Then going through the two Testaments in detail he describes the contents o the several books and the lessons which may be learne from them. He concludes with an appeal to Paulinu to divest himself wholly of his earthly wealth and t devote himself altogether to God. Written in 394 A.D

1. Our brother Ambrose along with you little gifts has delivered to me a most charm ing letter which, though it comes at the be ginning of our friendship, gives assurance o tried fidelity and of long continued attach ment. A true intimacy cemented by Chris Himself is not one which depends upon ma terial considerations, or upon the presence o the persons, or upon an insincere and exag gerated flattery ; but one such as ours wrought by a common fear of God and a join study of the divine scriptures.

We read in old tales that men traverse provinces, crossed seas, and visited strang peoples, simply to see face to face person whom they only knew from books. Thu Pythagoras visited the prophets of Memphis and Plato, besides visiting Egypt and Ar chytas of Tarentum, most carefully explore that part of the coast of Italy which wa formerly called Great Greece. In this wa the influential Athenian master with whos lessons the schools[1] of the Academy resounde became at once a pilgrim and a pupil choos ing modestly to learn what others had t teach rather than over confidently to pro pound views of his own. Indeed his pursui of learning—which seemed to fly before hin all the world over—finally led to his captur by pirates who sold him into slavery to a crue tyrant.[2] Thus he became a prisoner, a bond man, and a slave ; yet, as he was always philosopher, he was greater still than the ma who purchased him. Again we read tha certain noblemen journeyed from the mos remote parts of Spain and Gaul to visit Titu Livius,[3] and listen to his eloquence whic flowed like a fountain of milk. Thus th fame of an individual had more power t draw men to Rome than the attractions of th city itself ; and the age displayed an unhear of and noteworthy portent in the shape o men who, entering the great city, bestowe their attention not upon it but upon somethin else. Apollonius[4] too was a traveller—the on

---

[1] Acts xx. 35.   [2] 1 Cor. vii. 29.   [3] 1 Tim. iii. 2.
[4] Viz. Letter XXII.   [5] Matt. vii. 3-5.

[1] Gymnasia. [2] Dionysius of Syracuse. [3] Cf. Quint. X. i. 3
[4] Apollonius of Tyana, whose strange life and adventure have been written for us by Philostratus.

I mean who is called the sorcerer[1] by ordinary people and the philosopher by such as follow Pythagoras. He entered Persia, traversed the Caucasus and made his way through the Albanians, the Scythians, the Massagetæ, and the richest districts of India. At last, after crossing that wide river the Pison,[2] he came to the Brahmans. There he saw Hiarcas[3] sitting upon his golden throne and drinking from his Tantalus-fountain, and heard him instructing a few disciples upon the nature, motions, and orbits of the heavenly bodies. After this he travelled among the Elamites, the Babylonians, the Chaldeans, the Medes, the Assyrians, the Parthians, the Syrians, the Phenicians, the Arabians, and the Philistines.[4] Then returning to Alexandria he made his way to Ethiopia to see the gymnosophists and the famous table of the sun spread in the sands of the desert.[5] Everywhere he found something to learn, and as he was always going to new places, he became constantly wiser and better. Philostratus has written the story of his life at length in eight books.

2. But why should I confine my allusions to the men of this world, when the Apostle Paul, the chosen vessel[6] the doctor[7] of the Gentiles, who could boldly say : " Do ye seek a proof of Christ speaking in me ? "[8] knowing that he really had within him that greatest of guests—when even he after visiting Damascus and Arabia " went up to Jerusalem to see Peter and abode with him fifteen days." [9] For he who was to be a preacher to the Gentiles had to be instructed in the mystical numbers seven and eight. And again fourteen years after he took Barnabas and Titus and communicated his gospel to the apostles lest by any means he should have run or had run in vain.[10] Spoken words possess an indefinable hidden power, and teaching that passed directly from the mouth of the speaker into the ears of the disciples is more impressive than any other. When the speech of Demosthenes against Æschines was recited before the latter during his exile at Rhodes, amid all the admiration and applause he sighed " if you could but have heard the brute deliver his own periods ! "[11]

3. I do not adduce these instances because I have anything in me from which you either can or will learn a lesson, but to show you that your zeal and eagerness to learn—even though you cannot rely on help from me—are in themselves worthy of praise. A mind willing to learn deserves commendation even when it has no teacher. What is of importance to me is not what you find but what you seek to find. Wax is soft and easy to mould even where the hands of craftsman and modeller are wanting to work it. It is already potentially all that it can be made. The apostle Paul learned the Law of Moses and the prophets at the feet of Gamaliel and was glad that he had done so, for armed with this spiritual armour, he was able to say boldly " the weapons of our warfare are not carnal, but mighty through God to the pulling down of strongholds ; " armed with these we war " casting down imaginations and every high thing that exalteth itself against the knowledge of God, and bringing into captivity every thought to the obedience of Christ ; and being in a readiness to revenge all disobedience." [1] He writes to Timothy who had been trained in the holy writings from a child exhorting him to study them diligently[2] and not to neglect the gift which was given him with the laying on of the hands of the presbytery.[3] To Titus he gives commandment that among a bishop's other virtues (which he briefly describes) he should be careful to seek a knowledge of the scriptures : A bishop, he says, must hold fast " the faithful word as he hath been taught that he may be able by sound doctrine both to exhort and to convince the gainsayers." [4] In fact want of education in a clergyman[5] prevents him from doing good to any one but himself and much as the virtue of his life may build up Christ's church, he does it an injury as great by failing to resist those who are trying to pull it down. The prophet Haggai says—or rather the Lord says it by the mouth of Haggai—"Ask now the priests concerning the law." [6] For such is the important function of the priesthood to give answers to those who question them concerning the law. And in Deuteronomy we read " Ask thy father and he will shew thee ; thy elders and they will tell thee." [7] Also in the one hundred and nineteenth psalm " thy statutes have been my songs in the house of my pilgrimage." David too, in the description of the righteous man whom he compares to the tree of life in paradise, amongst his other excellences speaks of this, " His delight is in the law of the Lord ; and in his law doth he meditate day and night." [9] In the close of his most solemn vision Daniel declares that " the righteous shall shine as the stars ; and the wise, that is the learned, as the firmament." [10] You can see, therefore, how great is the difference between righteous ignorance and instructed righteous-

---

[1] Magus. [2] Gen. ii. 11. [3] Philostratus iii. 7.
[4] i. e. dwellers in Palestine. [5] Herod. iii. 17, 18. [6] Acts ix. 15.
[7] A favourite title for theologians in the Middle Ages.
[8] 2 Cor. xiii. 3. [9] Gal. i. 17, 18. [10] Gal. ii. 1, 2.
[11] Cic. de Orat. iii. 56, the word 'brute' is inserted by Jerome.

[1] 2 Cor. x. 4-6. [2] 2 Tim. iii. 14, 15. [3] 1 Tim. iv. 14.
[4] Tit. i. 9. [5] Sancta rusticitas. [6] Hag. ii. 11.
[7] Deut. xxxii. 7. [8] v. 54. In the Vulg. this psalm is the 118th.
[9] Ps. i. 2. [10] Dan. xii. 3.

ness. Those who have the first are compared with the stars, those who have the second with the heavens. Yet, according to the exact sense of the Hebrew, both statements may be understood of the learned, for it is to be read in this way :—" They that be wise shall shine as the brightness of the firmament ; and they that turn many to righteousness as the stars forever and ever." Why is the apostle Paul called a chosen vessel ?[1] Assuredly because he is a repertory of the Law and of the holy scriptures. The learned teaching of our Lord strikes the Pharisees dumb with amazement, and they are filled with astonishment to find that Peter and John know the Law although they have not learned letters. For to these the Holy Ghost immediately suggested what comes to others by daily study and meditatión ; and, as it is written,[2] they were " taught of God." The Saviour had only accomplished his twelfth year when the scene in the temple took place ;[3] but when he interrogated the elders concerning the Law His wise questions conveyed rather than sought information.

4. But perhaps we ought to call Peter and John ignorant, both of whom could say of themselves, " though I be rude in speech, yet not in knowledge."[4] Was John a mere fisherman, rude and untaught? If so, whence did he get the words " In the beginning was the word, and the word was with God and the word was God."[5] *Logos* in Greek has many meanings. It signifies word and reason and reckoning and the cause of individual things by which those which are subsist. All of which things we rightly predicate of Christ. This truth Plato with all his learning did not know, of this Demosthenes with all his eloquence was ignorant. " I will destroy," it is said, " the wisdom of the wise, and will bring to nothing the understanding of the prudent."[6] The true wisdom must destroy the false, and, although the foolishness of preaching[7] is inseparable from the Cross, Paul speaks " wisdom among them that are perfect, yet not the wisdom of this world, nor of the princes of this world that come to nought," but he speaks " the wisdom of God in a mystery, even the hidden wisdom, which God ordained before the world."[8] God's wisdom is Christ, for Christ, we are told, is " the power of God and the wisdom of God."[9] He is the wisdom which is hidden in a mystery, of which also we read in the heading of the ninth psalm " for the hidden things of the son."[10] In Him are hidden all the treasures of wisdom and knowledge. He also who was hidden in a

mystery is the same that was foreordained before the world. Now it was in the Law and in the Prophets that he was foreordained and prefigured. For this reason too the prophets were called seers,[1] because they saw Him whom others did not see. Abraham saw His day and was glad.[2] The heavens which were sealed to a rebellious people were opened to Ezekiel. " Open thou mine eyes," saith David, " that I may behold wonderful things out of thy Law."[3] For " the law is spiritual "[4] and a revelation is needed to enable us to comprehend it and, when God uncovers His face, to behold His glory.

5. In the apocalypse a book is shewn sealed with seven seals,[5] which if you deliver to one that is learned saying, Read this, he will answer you, I cannot, for it is sealed.[6] How many there are to-day who fancy themselves learned, yet the scriptures are a sealed book to them, and one which they cannot open save through Him who has the key of David, " he that openeth and no man shutteth ; and shutteth and no man openeth."[7] In the Acts of the Apostles the holy eunuch (or rather " man " for so the scripture calls him[8]) when reading Isaiah he is asked by Philip " Understandest thou what thou readest ?", makes answer :—" How can I except some man should guide me ? "[9] To digress for a moment to myself, I am neither holier nor more diligent than this eunuch, who came from Ethiopia, that is from the ends of the world, to the Temple leaving behind him a queen's palace, and was so great a lover of the Law and of divine knowledge that he read the holy scriptures even in his chariot. Yet although he had the book in his hand and took into his mind the words of the Lord, nay even had them on his tongue and uttered them with his lips, he still knew not Him, whom—not knowing—he worshipped in the book. Then Philip came and shewed him Jesus, who was concealed beneath the letter. Wondrous excellence of the teacher ! In the same hour the eunuch believed and was baptized ; he became one of the faithful and a saint. He was no longer a pupil but a master ; and he found more in the church's font there in the wilderness than he had ever done in the gilded temple of the synagogue.

6. These instances have been just touched upon by me (the limits of a letter forbid a more discursive treatment of them) to convince you that in the holy scriptures you can make no progress unless you have a guide to shew you the way. I say nothing of the knowledge of grammarians, rhetoricians, philoso-

[1] Acts ix. 15.　　　[2] 1 Thess. iv. 9.　　　[3] Luke ii. 46.
[4] 2 Cor. xi. 6.　　　[5] Joh. i. 1.　　　[6] 1 Cor. i. 19.
[7] 1 Cor. i. 21.　　　[8] 1 Cor. ii. 6, 7.　　　[9] 1 Cor. i. 24.
[10] " Upon Muthlabben " AV. See Perowne on the words.

[1] 1 Sam. ix. 9.　　　[2] Joh. viii. 56.　　　[3] Ps. cxix. 18.
[4] Rom. vii. 14.　　　[5] Rev. v. 1.　　　[6] Isa. xxix. 11.
[7] Rev. iii. 7.　　　[8] Acts viii. 27.　　　[9] Acts viii. 30, 31.

phers, geometers, logicians, musicians, astrono-
mers, astrologers, physicians, whose several
kinds of skill are most useful to mankind, and
may be ranged under the three heads of
teaching, method, and proficiency. I will pass
to the less important crafts which require
manual dexterity more than mental ability.
Husbandmen, masons, carpenters, workers in
wood and metal, wool-dressers and fullers, as
well as those artisans who make furniture and
cheap utensils, cannot attain the ends they
seek without instruction from qualified persons. As Horace says [1]

Doctors alone profess the healing art
And none but joiners ever try to join.

7. The art of interpreting the scriptures is
the only one of which all men everywhere
claim to be masters. To quote Horace again

Taught or untaught we all write poetry. [2]

The chatty old woman, the doting old man,
and the wordy sophist, one and all take in
hand the Scriptures, rend them in pieces and
teach them before they have learned them.
Some with brows knit and bombastic words,
balanced one against the other philosophize
concerning the sacred writings among weak
women. Others—I blush to say it—learn of
women what they are to teach men; and as
if even this were not enough, they boldly explain to others what they themselves by no
means understand. I say nothing of persons
who, like myself have been familiar with secular literature before they have come to the
study of the holy scriptures. Such men
when they charm the popular ear by the finish
of their style suppose every word they say to
be a law of God. They do not deign to
notice what Prophets and apostles have intended but they adapt conflicting passages to
suit their own meaning, as if it were a grand
way of teaching—and not rather the faultiest
of all—to misrepresent a writer's views and to
force the scriptures reluctantly to do their
will. They forget that we have read centos
from Homer and Virgil; but we never think
of calling the Christless Maro [3] a Christian because of his lines :—

Now comes the Virgin back and Saturn's reign,
Now from high heaven comes a Child newborn. [4]

Another line might be addressed by the
Father to the Son :—

Hail, only Son, my Might and Majesty. [5]

And yet another might follow the Saviour's
words on the cross :—

Such words he spake and there transfixed remained. [6]

But all this is puerile, and resembles the
sleight-of-hand of a mountebank. It is idle
to try to teach what you do not know, and—
if I may speak with some warmth—it is worse
still to be ignorant of your ignorance.

8. Genesis, we shall be told, needs no explanation; its topics are too simple—the birth
of the world, the origin of the human race,[1]
the division of the earth,[2] the confusion of
tongues,[3] and the descent of the Hebrews into
Egypt![4] Exodus, no doubt, is equally plain,
containing as it does merely an account of the
ten plagues,[5] the decalogue,[6] and sundry mysterious and divine precepts! The meaning of
Leviticus is of course self-evident, although
every sacrifice that it describes, nay more
every word that it contains, the description
of Aaron's vestments,[7] and all the regula-
tions connected with the Levites are symbols
of things heavenly! The book of Numbers
too—are not its very figures,[8] and Balaam's
prophecy,[9] and the forty-two camping places
in the wilderness [10] so many mysteries? Deuteronomy also, that is the second law or the
foreshadowing of the law of the gospel,—does
it not, while exhibiting things known before,
put old truths in a new light? So far the
'five words' of the Pentateuch, with which
the apostle boasts his wish to speak in the
Church.[11] Then, as for Job,[12] that pattern of
patience, what mysteries are there not contained in his discourses? Commencing in
prose the book soon glides into verse and at
the end once more reverts to prose. By the
way in which it lays down propositions, assumes postulates, adduces proofs, and draws
inferences, it illustrates all the laws of logic.
Single words occurring in the book are full of
meaning. To say nothing of other topics, it
prophesies the resurrection of men's bodies at
once with more clearness and with more caution than any one has yet shewn. "I know,"
Job says, "that my redeemer liveth, and that
at the last day I shall rise again from the
earth; and I shall be clothed again with my
skin, and in my flesh shall I see God. Whom
I shall see for myself, and mine eyes shall behold, and not another. This my hope is stored
up in my own bosom." [13] I will pass on to
Jesus the son of Nave [14]—a type of the Lord
in name as well as in deed—who crossed over
Jordan, subdued hostile kingdoms, divided
the land among the conquering people and

---

[1] Cc. 1–2.   [2] C. x.   [3] C. xi.   [4] C. xlvi.
[5] Cc. vii.–xii.   [6] C. xx.   [7] C. viii.   [8] C. xxvi.
[9] Cc. xxiii., xxiv.
[10] C. xxxiii. See Letter lxxviii.
[11] 1 Cor. xiv. 19.
[12] The mention of Job at this point is curious: it would seem
that in Jerome's opinion he was coæval with or very little later
than Moses.
[13] Job xix. 25–27, Vulg.
[14] I.e., Joshua the son of Nun whose name is so rendered by the
LXX. Cf. Ecclus. xlvi. 1, AV.

---

[1] Hor. Ep. II. 1. 115, 116.   [2] Hor. Ep. II. 1. 117.
[3] Virgil's full name was Publius Vergilius Maro.
[4] Virg. E. iv. 6, 7.   [5] Virg. A. i. 664.   [6] Virg. A. ii. 650.

who, in every city, village, mountain, river, hill-torrent, and boundary which he dealt with, marked out the spiritual realms of the heavenly Jerusalem, that is, of the church.[1] In the book of Judges every one of the popular leaders is a type. Ruth the Moabitess fulfils the prophecy of Isaiah :—"Send thou a lamb, O Lord, as ruler of the land from the rock of the wilderness to the mount of the daughter of Zion."[2] Under the figures of Eli's death and the slaying of Saul Samuel shews the abolition of the old law. Again in Zadok and in David he bears witness to the mysteries of the new priesthood and of the new royalty. The third and fourth books of Kings called in Hebrew *Malâchim* give the history of the kingdom of Judah from Solomon to Jeconiah,[3] and of that of Israel from Jeroboam the son of Nebat to Hoshea who was carried away into Assyria. If you merely regard the narrative, the words are simple enough, but if you look beneath the surface at the hidden meaning of it, you find a description of the small numbers of the church and of the wars which the heretics wage against it. The twelve prophets whose writings are compressed within the narrow limits of a single volume,[4] have typical meanings far different from their literal ones. Hosea speaks many times of Ephraim, of Samaria, of Joseph, of Jezreel, of a wife of whoredoms and of children of whoredoms,[5] of an adulteress shut up within the chamber of her husband, sitting for a long time in widowhood and in the garb of mourning, awaiting the time when her husband will return to her.[6] Joel the son of Pethuel describes the land of the twelve tribes as spoiled and devastated by the palmerworm, the canker-worm, the locust, and the blight,[7] and predicts that after the overthrow of the former people the Holy Spirit shall be poured out upon God's servants and handmaids ;[8] the same spirit, that is, which was to be poured out in the upper chamber at Zion upon the one hundred and twenty believers.[9] These believers rising by gradual and regular gradations from one to fifteen form the steps to which there is a mystical allusion in the "psalms of degrees."[10] Amos, although he is only "an herdman" from the country, "a gatherer of sycomore fruit,"[11] cannot be explained in a few words. For who can adequately speak of the three transgressions and the four of Damascus, of Gaza, of Tyre, of Idumæa, of Moab, of the children of Ammon, and in the seventh and eighth place of Judah and of Israel? He speaks to the fat kine that are in the mountain of Samaria,[1] and bears witness that the great house and the little house shall fall.[2] He sees now the maker of the grasshopper,[3] now the Lord, standing upon a wall[4] daubed[5] or made of adamant,[6] now a basket of apples[7] that brings doom to the transgressors, and now a famine upon the earth, "not a famine of bread, nor a thirst for water, but of hearing the words of the Lord."[8] Obadiah, whose name means the servant of God, thunders against Edom red with blood and against the creature born of earth.[9] He smites him with the spear of the spirit because of his continual rivalry with his brother Jacob. Jonah, fairest of doves, whose shipwreck shews in a figure the passion of the Lord, recalls the world to penitence, and while he preaches to Nineveh, announces salvation to all the heathen. Micah the Morasthite a joint heir with Christ[10] announces the spoiling of the daughter of the robber and lays siege against her, because she has smitten the jawbone of the judge of Israel.[11] Nahum, the consoler of the world, rebukes "the bloody city"[12] and when it is overthrown cries :— "Behold upon the mountains the feet of him that bringeth good tidings."[13] Habakkuk, like a strong and unyielding wrestler,[14] stands upon his watch and sets his foot upon the tower[15] that he may contemplate Christ upon the cross and say "His glory covered the heavens and the earth was full of his praise. And his brightness was as the light ; he had horns coming out of his hand : and there was the hiding of his power."[16] Zephaniah, that is the bodyguard and knower of the secrets of the Lord,[17] hears "a cry from the fishgate, and an howling from the second, and a great crashing from the hills."[18] He proclaims "howling to the inhabitants of the mortar ;[19] for all the people of Canaan are undone ; all they that were laden with silver are cut off."[20] Haggai, that is he who is glad or joyful, who has sown in tears to reap in joy,[21] is occupied with the rebuilding of the temple. He represents the Lord (the Father, that is) as saying "Yet once, it is a little while, and I will shake the heavens, and the earth, and the sea, and the dry land ; and I will shake all nations

---

[1] Gal. iv. 26.
[2] Isa. xvi. 1, Vulg. 'the rock of the wilderness'=Moab.
[3] Also called Coniah and Jehoiachin.
[4] They are reckoned as forming one book in the Hebrew Bible.
[5] Hos. i. 2.　[6] Hos. iii. 1, 3, 4.　[7] Joel i. 4.　[8] Joel ii. 29.
[9] Acts i. 13, 15.
[10] The allusion is to Psalms cxx.–cxxxiv. One hundred and twenty is the sum of the numerals one to fifteen.
[11] Amos vii. 14.

[1] Amos iv. 1.　[2] Amos vi. 11.　[3] Amos vii. 1.　[4] Amos vii. 7.
[5] So the Vulgate.　[6] So the LXX.　[7] Amos viii. 1.
[8] Amos viii. 11.
[9] 'Edom' means 'red' and is connected with 'Adâmâh'= 'the earth.'
[10] Jerome interprets the Hebrew word 'Morasthite' to mean 'my possession.'　[11] Mic. v. 1, Vulg.
[12] *i.e.*, Nineveh—Nahum iii. 1.　[13] Nahum i. 15.
[14] The name strictly means 'embrace.'　[15] Hab. ii. 1.
[16] Hab. iii. 3, 4.　[17] Strictly 'the Lord guards' or 'hides.'
[18] Zeph. i. 10.　[19] So RV. marg. Probably a place in Jerusalem.　[20] Zeph. i. 11, RV.　[21] Ps. cxxvi. 5.

and he who is desired [1] of all nations shall come' [2] Zechariah, he that is mindful of his Lord,[3] gives us many prophecies. He sees Jesus,[4] "clothed with filthy garments," [5] a stone with seven eyes,[6] a candle-stick all of gold with lamps as many as the eyes, and two olivetrees on the right side of the bowl [7] and on the left. After he has described the horses, red, black, white, and grisled,[8] and the cutting off of the chariot from Ephraim and of the horse from Jerusalem [9] he goes on to prophesy and predict a king who shall be a poor man and who shall sit "upon a colt the foal of an ass." [10] Malachi, the last of all the prophets, speaks openly of the rejection of Israel and the calling of the nations. "I have no pleasure in you, saith the Lord of hosts, neither will I accept an offering at your hand. For from the rising of the sun even unto the going down of the same, my name is great among the Gentiles : and in every place incense[11] is offered unto my name, and a pure offering." [12] As for Isaiah, Jeremiah, Ezekiel, and Daniel, who can fully understand or adequately explain them ? The first of them seems to compose not a prophecy but a gospel. The second speaks of a rod of an almond tree [13] and of a seething pot with its face toward the north,[14] and of a leopard which has changed its spots.[15] He also goes four times through the alphabet in different metres.[16] The beginning and ending of Ezekiel, the third of the four, are involved in so great obscurity that like the commencement of Genesis they are not studied by the Hebrews until they are thirty years old. Daniel, the fourth and last of the four prophets, having knowledge of the times and being interested in the whole world, in clear language proclaims the stone cut out of the mountain without hands that overthrows all kingdoms.[17] David, who is our Simonides, Pindar, and Alcæus, our Horace, our Catullus, and our Serenus all in one, sings of Christ to his lyre ; and on a psaltery with ten strings calls him from the lower world to rise again. Solomon, a lover of peace [18] and of the Lord, corrects morals, teaches nature, unites Christ and the church, and sings a sweet marriage song [19] to celebrate that holy bridal. Esther, a type of the church, frees her people from danger and, after having slain Haman whose name means iniquity, hands down to posterity a memorable day and a great feast. [1] The book of things omitted [2] or epitome of the old dispensation [3] is of such importance and value that without it any one who should claim to himself a knowledge of the scriptures would make himself a laughing stock in his own eyes. Every name used in it, nay even the conjunction of the words, serves to throw light on narratives passed over in the books of Kings and upon questions suggested by the gospel. Ezra and Nehemiah, that is the Lord's helper and His consoler, are united in a single book. They restore the Temple and build up the walls of the city. In their pages we see the throng of the Israelites returning to their native land, we read of priests and Levites, of Israel proper and of proselytes ; and we are even told the several families to which the task of building the walls and towers was assigned. These references convey one meaning upon the surface, but another below it.

9. [In Migne, 8.] You see how, carried away by my love of the scriptures, I have exceeded the limits of a letter yet have not fully accomplished my object. We have heard only what it is that we ought to know and to desire, so that we too may be able to say with the psalmist :—" My soul breaketh out for the very fervent desire that it hath alway unto thy judgments." [4] But the saying of Socrates about himself—" this only I know that I know nothing " [5]—is fulfilled in our case also. The New Testament I will briefly deal with. Matthew, Mark, Luke and John are the Lord's team of four,[6] the true cherubim or store of knowledge.[7] With them the whole body is full of eyes,[8] they glitter as sparks,[9] they run and return like lightning,[10] their feet are straight feet,[11] and lifted up, their backs also are winged, ready to fly in all directions. They hold together each by each and are interwoven one with another : [12] like wheels within wheels they roll along [13] and go whithersoever the breath of the Holy Spirit wafts them.[14] The apostle Paul writes to seven churches [15] (for the eighth epistle—that to the Hebrews—is not generally counted in with the others). He instructs Timothy and Titus ; he intercedes with Philemon for his runaway slave.[16] Of him I think it better to say nothing than to write inadequately. The Acts of the Apostles seem to relate a mere unvarnished narrative descrip-

---

[1] So Vulg. 'the desire ' AV.   [2] Hag. ii. 6, 7.
[3] Strictly 'the Lord is mindful.'
[4] *i.e.*, Joshua the High Priest.   [5] Zech. iii. 3.
[6] Zech. iii. 9.   [7] Zech. iv. 2, 3.   [8] Zech. vi. 1-3.
[9] Zech. ix. 10.   [10] Zech. ix. 9.
[11] This word is not in the Vulg.   [12] Mal. i. 1c, 11, RV.
[13] Jer. i. 11.   [14] Jer. i. 13.   [15] Jer. xiii. 23.
[16] Lamentations cc. I.–IV., each verse in which begins with a different letter of the alphabet.
[17] Dan. ii. 45.
[18] See note on LII. 3, p.   [19] The Song of Songs.

[1] *i.e.* the feast of Purim—Esth. ix. 20-32.
[2] Paraleipomena, the name given in the LXX. to the books of Chronicles.   [3] Veteris instrumenti 'ἐπιτομή.
[4] Ps. cxix. 20, PBV.   [5] Plato, Ap. Soc. 21, 22.
[6] Quadriga. cf Irenæus, Adv. Hær. III. ii. 8.
[7] Clement of Alexandria, following Philo, makes cherub mean wisdom.
[8] Ezek. i. 18, Vulg.   [9] Ezek. i. 7.   [10] Ezek. i. 14.
[11] Ezek. i. 7.   [12] Ezek. i. 11.   [13] Ezek. i. 16.   [14] Ezek. i. 20.
[15] *i.e.* those of Rome, Corinth, Galatia, Ephesus, Philippi, Colosse, Thessalonica.   [16] Onesimus.

tive of the infancy of the newly born church; but when once we realize that their author is Luke the physician whose praise is in the gospel,[1] we shall see that all his words are medicine for the sick soul. The apostles James, Peter, John, and Jude, have published seven epistles at once spiritual and to the point, short and long, short that is in words but lengthy in substance so that there are few indeed who do not find themselves in the dark when they read them. The apocalypse of John has as many mysteries as words. In saying this I have said less than the book deserves. All praise of it is inadequate; manifold meanings lie hid in its every word.

10. [In Migne, 9.] I beg of you, my dear brother, to live among these books, to meditate upon them, to know nothing else, to seek nothing else. Does not such a life seem to you a foretaste of heaven here on earth? Let not the simplicity of the scripture or the poorness of its vocabulary offend you; for these are due either to the faults of translators or else to deliberate purpose: for in this way it is better fitted for the instruction of an unlettered congregation as the educated person can take one meaning and the uneducated another from one and the same sentence. I am not so dull or so forward as to profess that I myself know it, or that I can pluck upon the earth the fruit which has its root in heaven, but I confess that I should like to do so. I put myself before the man who sits idle and, while I lay no claim to be a master, I readily pledge myself to be a fellow-student. "Every one that asketh receiveth; and he that seeketh findeth; and to him that knocketh it shall be opened."[2] Let us learn upon earth that knowledge which will continue with us in heaven.

11. [In Migne, 10.] I will receive you with open hands and—if I may boast and speak foolishly like Hermagoras[3]—I will strive to learn with you whatever you desire to study. Eusebius who is here regards you with the affection of a brother; he[4] has made your letter twice as precious by telling me of your sincerity of character, your contempt for the world, your constancy in friendship, and your love to Christ. The letter bears on its face (without any aid from him) your prudence and the charm of your style. Make haste then, I beseech you, and cut instead of loosing the hawser which prevents your vessel from moving in the sea. The man who sells his goods because he despises them and means to renounce the world can have no desire to sell them

dear. Count as money gained the sum that you must expend upon your outfit. There is an old saying that a miser lacks as much what he has as what he has not. The believer has a whole world of wealth; the unbeliever has not a single farthing. Let us always live "as having nothing and yet possessing all things."[1] Food and raiment, these are the Christian's wealth.[2] If your property is in your own power,[3] sell it: if not, cast it from you. "If any man . . . will take away thy coat, let him have thy cloke also."[4] You are all for delay, you wish to defer action: unless—so you argue—unless I sell my goods piecemeal and with caution, Christ will be at a loss to feed his poor. Nay, he who has offered himself to God, has given Him everything once for all. The apostles did but forsake ships and nets.[5] The widow cast but two brass coins into the treasury[6] and yet she shall be preferred before Croesus[7] with all his wealth. He readily despises all things who reflects always that he must die.

LETTER LIV.

TO FURIA.

A letter of guidance to a widow on the best means of preserving her widowhood (according to Jerome 'the second of the three degrees of chastity'). Furia had at one time thought of marrying again but eventually abandoned her intention and devoted herself to the care of her young children and her aged father. Jerome draws a vivid picture of the dangers to which she is exposed at Rome, lays down rules of conduct for her guidance, and commends her to the care of the presbyter Exuperius (afterwards bishop of Toulouse). The date of the letter is 394 A.D.

1. You beg and implore me in your letter to write to you—or rather write back to you —what mode of life you ought to adopt to preserve the crown of widowhood and to keep your reputation for chastity unsullied. My mind rejoices, my reins exult, and my heart is glad that you desire to be after marriage what your mother Titiana of holy memory for a long time in marriage.[8] Her prayers and supplications are heard. She has succeeded in winning afresh in her only daughter that which she herself when living possessed. It is a high privilege of your family that from the time of Camillus[9] few or none of your house are described as contracting second marriages. Therefore it will not redound so much to your praise if you continue a widow as to your shame if being a Christian you fail

---

[1] Col. iv. 14; 2 Cor. viii. 18.   [2] Matt. vii. 8.
[3] A verbose rhetorician mentioned by Cic. de Inv. i. 6.
[4] Eusebius of Cremona, who for the next five years remained with Jerome, and afterwards corresponded with him from Italy. See Letter LVII. §2. Rufinus, Apol. i. 19. Jerome, Apol. iii. 4, 5, etc.

[1] 2 Cor. vi. 10.   [2] 1 Tim. vi. 8.   [3] Cf. Acts v. 4.
[4] Matt. v. 40.   [5] Matt. iv. 18-22.   [6] Mark xii. 41-44.
[7] The last king of Lydia, celebrated for his riches.
[8] i.e. a celibate.
[9] Lucius Furius Camillus, the hero who conquered Veii and freed Rome from the Gauls.

to keep what heathen women have jealously guarded for so many centuries.

2. I say nothing of Paula and Eustochium, the fairest flowers of your stock ; for, as my object is to exhort you, I do not wish it to appear that I am praising them. Blaesilla too I pass over who following her husband—your brother—to the grave, fulfilled in a short time of life a long time of virtue.[1] Would that men would imitate the laudable examples of women, and that wrinkled old age would pay at last what youth gladly offers at first ! In saying this I am putting my hand into the fire deliberately and with my eyes open. Men will knit their brows and shake their clenched fists at me ;

In swelling tones will angry Chremes rave.[2]

The leaders will rise as one man against my epistle ; the mob of patricians will thunder at me. They will cry out that I am a sorcerer and a seducer ; and that I should be transported to the ends of the earth. They may add, if they will, the title of Samaritan ; for in it I shall but recognize a name given to my Lord. But one thing is certain. I do not sever the daughter from the mother, I do not use the words of the gospel : "let the dead bury their dead."[3] For whosoever believes in Christ is alive ; and he who believes in Him " ought himself also so to walk even as He walked."[4]

3. A truce to the calumnies which the malice of backbiters continually fastens upon all who call themselves Christians to keep them through fear of shame from aspiring to virtue. Except by letter we have no knowledge of each other ; and where there is no knowledge after the flesh, there can be no motive for intercourse save a religious one. " Honour thy father,"[5] the commandment says, but only if he does not separate you from your true Father. Recognize the tie of blood but only so long as your parent recognizes his Creator. Should he fail to do so, David will sing to you : " hearken, O daughter, and consider, and incline thine ear ; forget also thine own people and thy father's house. So shall the king greatly desire thy beauty, for he is thy Lord."[6] Great is the prize offered for the forgetting of a parent, " the king shall desire thy beauty." You have heard, you have considered, you have inclined your ear, you have forgotten your people and your father's house ; therefore the king shall desire your beauty and shall say to you :—"thou art all fair, my love ; there is no spot in thee."[7] What can

be fairer than a soul which is called the daughter of God,[1] and which seeks for herself no outward adorning.[2] She believes in Christ, and, dowered with this hope of greatness[3] makes her way to her spouse ; for Christ is at once her bridegroom and her Lord.

4. What troubles matrimony involves you have learned in the marriage state itself ; you have been surfeited with quails' flesh[4] even to loathing ; your mouth has been filled with the gall of bitterness ; you have expelled the indigestible and unwholesome food ; you have relieved a heaving stomach. Why will you again swallow what has disagreed with you ? " The dog is turned to his own vomit again and the sow that was washed to her wallowing in the mire."[5] Even brute beasts and flying birds do not fall into the same snares twice. Do you fear extinction for the line of Camillus if you do not present your father with some little fellow to crawl upon his breast and slobber his neck ? As if all who marry have children ! and as if when they do come, they always resemble their forefathers ! Did Cicero's son exhibit his father's eloquence ? Had your own Cornelia,[6] pattern at once of chastity and of fruitfulness, cause to rejoice that she was mother of her Gracchi ? It is ridiculous to expect as certain the offspring which many, as you can see, have not got, while others who have had it have lost it again. To whom then are you to leave your great riches ? To Christ who cannot die. Whom shall you make your heir ? The same who is already your Lord. Your father will be sorry but Christ will be glad ; your family will grieve but the angels will rejoice with you. Let your father do what he likes with what is his own. You are not his to whom you have been born, but His to whom you have been born again, and who has purchased you at a great price with His own blood.[7]

5. Beware of nurses and waiting maids and similar venomous creatures who try to satisfy their greed by sucking your blood. They advise you to do not what is best for you but what is best for them. They are for ever dinning into your ears Virgil's lines :—

Will you waste all your youth in lonely grief
And children sweet, the gifts of love, forswear ?[8]

Wherever there is holy chastity, there is also frugal living ; and wherever there is frugal living, servants lose by it. What they do not get is in their minds so much taken from them. The actual sum received is what they look to, and not its relative amount. The

[1] Wisdom iv. 13.
[2] Horace, A. P. 94 : the allusion is to a scene in the Heauton Timorumenus of Terence.
[3] Matt. viii. 22.   [4] 1 Joh. ii. 6.
[5] Ex. xx. 12.   [6] Ps. xlv. 10, 11.   [7] Cant. iv. 7.

[1] Ps. xlv. 10.   [2] Cf. 1 Pet. iii. 3.   [3] Hac ambitione ditata.
[4] Numb. xi. 20, 31-4.   [5] Pet. ii. 22.
[6] Furia's sister-in-law Blaesilla was through her mother Paula descended from the Gracchi. See Letter CVIII. § 33.
[7] Acts xx. 28.   [8] Virg. A. iv. 32.

moment they see a Christian they at once repeat the hackneyed saying :—" The Greek ! The impostor ! " [1] They spread the most scandalous reports and, when any such emanates from themselves, they pretend that they have heard it from others, managing thus at once to originate the story and to exaggerate it. A lying rumour goes forth ; and this, when it has reached the married ladies and has been fanned by their tongues, spreads through the provinces. You may see numbers of these— their faces painted, their eyes like those of vipers, their teeth rubbed with pumice-stone— raving and carping at Christians with insane fury. One of these ladies,

A violet mantle round her shoulders thrown,
Drawls out some mawkish stuff, speaks through her nose,
And minces half her words with tripping tongue. [2]

Hereupon the rest chime in and every bench expresses hoarse approval. They are backed up by men of my own order who, finding themselves assailed, assail others. Always fluent in attacking me, they are dumb in their own defence ; just as though they were not monks themselves, and as though every word said against monks did not tell also against their spiritual progenitors the clergy. Harm done to the flock brings discredit on the shepherd. On the other hand we cannot but praise the life of a monk who holds up to veneration the priests of Christ and refuses to detract from that order to which he owes it that he is a Christian.

6. I have spoken thus, my daughter in Christ, not because I doubt that you will be faithful to your vows, [3] (you would never have asked for a letter of advice had you been uncertain as to the blessedness of monogamy): but that you may realize the wickedness of servants who merely wish to sell you for their own advantage, the snares which relations may set for you and the well meant but mistaken suggestions of a father. While I allow that this latter feels love toward you, I cannot admit that it is love according to knowledge. I must say with the apostle : " I bear them record that they have a zeal of God, but not according to knowledge." [4] Imitate rather—I cannot say it too often— your holy mother [5] whose zeal for Christ comes into my mind as often as I remember her, and not her zeal only but the paleness induced in her by fasting, the alms given by her to the poor, the courtesy shewn by her to the servants of God, the lowliness of her garb and heart, and the constant moderation of her language. Of your father too I

speak with respect, not because he is a patrician and of consular rank but because he is a Christian. Let him be true to his profession as such. Let him rejoice that he has begotten a daughter for Christ and not for the world. Nay rather let him grieve that you have in vain lost your virginity as the fruits of matrimony have not been yours. Where is the husband whom he gave to you ? Even had he been lovable and good, death would still have snatched all away, and his decease would have terminated the fleshly bond between you. Seize the opportunity, I beg of you, and make a virtue of necessity. In the lives of Christians we look not to the beginnings but to the endings. Paul began badly but ended well. The start of Judas wins praise ; his end is condemned because of his treachery. Read Ezekiel, " The righteousness of the righteous shall not deliver him in the day of his transgression ; as for the wickedness of the wicked he shall not fall thereby in the day that he turneth from his wickedness." [1] The Christian life is the true Jacob's ladder on which the angels ascend and descend, [2] while the Lord stands above it holding out His hand to those who slip and sustaining by the vision of Himself the weary steps of those who ascend. But while He does not wish the death of a sinner, but only that he should be converted and live, He hates the lukewarm [3] and they quickly cause him loathing. To whom much is forgiven, the same loveth much. [4]

7. In the gospel a harlot wins salvation. How ? She is baptized in her tears and wipes the Lord's feet with that same hair with which she had before deceived many. She does not wear a waving headdress or creaking boots, she does not darken her eyes with antimony. Yet in her squalor she is lovelier than ever. What place have rouge and white lead on the face of a Christian woman ? The one simulates the natural red of the cheeks and of the lips ; the other the whiteness of the face and of the neck. They serve only to inflame young men's passions, to stimulate lust, and to indicate an unchaste mind. How can a woman weep for her sins whose tears lay bare her true complexion and mark furrows on her cheeks ? Such adorning is not of the Lord ; a mask of this kind belongs to Antichrist. With what confidence can a woman raise features to heaven which her Creator must fail to recognize ? It is idle to allege in excuse for such practices girlishness and youthful vanity. A widow who has ceased to have a husband to please, and who in the apostle's language is a widow indeed, [5] needs nothing more but

---

[1] See Letter XXXVIII. § 5.   [2] Persius i. 32 sqq.
[3] Propositum. The word was passing from the meaning of a purpose into that of a formal vow.
[4] Rom. x. 2.   [5] Titiana.

[1] Ezek. xxxiii. 12.   [2] Gen. xxviii. 12.   [3] Rev. iii. 16.
[4] Luke vii. 47.   [5] 1 Tim. v. 5.

perseverance only. She is mindful of past enjoyments, she knows what gave her pleasure and what she has now lost. By rigid fast and vigil she must quench the fiery darts of the devil.[1] If we are widows, we must either speak as we are dressed, or else dress as we speak. Why do we profess one thing, and practise another? The tongue talks of chastity, but the rest of the body reveals incontinence.

8. So much for dress and adornment. But a widow "that liveth in pleasure"—the words are not mine but those of the apostle—"is dead while she liveth."[2] What does that mean—"is dead while she liveth"? To those who know no better she seems to be alive and not, as she is, dead in sin; yes, and in another sense dead to Christ, from whom no secrets are hid. "The soul that sinneth it shall die."[3] "Some men's sins are open . . . going before to judgment: and some they follow after. Likewise also good works are manifest, and they that are otherwise cannot be hid.[4] The words mean this:—Certain persons sin so deliberately and flagrantly that you no sooner see them than you know them at once to be sinners. But the defects of others are so cunningly concealed that we only learn them from subsequent information. Similarly the good deeds of some people are public property, while those of others we come to know only through long intimacy with them. Why then must we needs boast of our chastity, a thing which cannot prove itself to be genuine without its companions and attendants, continence and plain living? The apostle macerates his body and brings it into subjection to the soul lest what he has preached to others he should himself fail to keep;[5] and can a mere girl whose passions are kindled by abundance of food, can a mere girl afford to be confident of her own chastity?

9. In saying this, I do not of course condemn food which God created to be enjoyed with thanksgiving,[6] but I seek to remove from youths and girls what are incentives to sensual pleasure. Neither the fiery Etna nor the country of Vulcan,[7] nor Vesuvius, nor Olympus, burns with such violent heat as the youthful marrow of those who are flushed with wine and filled with food. Many trample covetousness under foot, and lay it down as readily as they lay down their purse. An enforced silence serves to make amends for a railing tongue. The outward appearance and the mode of dress can be changed in a single hour. All other sins are external, and what is external

can easily be cast away. Desire alone, implanted in men by God to lead them to procreate children, is internal; and this, if it once oversteps its own bounds, becomes a sin, and by a law of nature cries out for sexual intercourse. It is therefore a work of great merit, and one which requires unremitting diligence to overcome that which is innate in you; while living in the flesh not to live after the flesh; to strive with yourself day by day and to watch the foe shut up within you with the hundred eyes of the fabled Argus.[1] This is what the apostle says in other words: "Every sin that a man doeth is without the body; but he that committeth fornication sinneth against his own body."[2] Physicians and others who have written on the nature of the human body, and particularly Galen in his books entitled *On matters of health*, say that the bodies of boys and of young men and of full grown men and women glow with an interior heat and consequently that for persons of these ages all food is injurious which tends to promote this heat: while on the other hand it is highly conducive to health in eating and in drinking to take things cold and cooling. Contrariwise they tell us that warm food and old wine are good for the old who suffer from humours and from chilliness. Hence it is that the Saviour says "Take heed to yourselves lest at any time your hearts be overcharged with surfeiting and drunkenness, and cares of this life."[3] So too speaks the apostle: "Be not drunk with wine, wherein is excess."[4] No wonder that the potter spoke thus of the vessel which He had made when even the comic poet whose only object is to know and to describe the ways of men tells us that

Where Ceres fails and Liber, Venus droops.[5]

10. In the first place then, till you have passed the years of early womanhood, take only water to drink, for this is by nature of all drinks the most cooling. This, if your stomach is strong enough to bear it; but if your digestion is weak, hear what the apostle says to Timothy: "use a little wine for thy stomach's sake and thine often infirmities."[6] Then as regards your food you must avoid all heating dishes. I do not speak of flesh dishes only (although of these the chosen vessel declares his mind thus: "it is good neither to eat flesh nor to drink wine"[7]) but of vegetables as well. Everything provocative or indigestible is to be refused. Be assured that nothing is so good for young Christians as

---

[1] Eph. vi. 16.   [2] 1 Tim. v. 6.   [3] Ezek. xviii. 20.
[4] 1 Tim. v. 24, 25.   [5] 1 Cor. ix. 27.   [6] 1 Tim. iv. 4.
[7] The island of Lemnos in the Ægean Sea.

[1] The hundred-eyed son of Inachus appointed by Hera to be the guardian of Io.
[2] 1 Cor. vi. 18.   [3] Luke xxi. 34.   [4] Eph. v. 18.
[5] Ter. Enn. iv. 5, 6.   [6] 1 Tim. v. 23.   [7] Rom. xiv. 21.

the eating of herbs. Accordingly in another place he says : "another who is weak eateth herbs."[1] Thus the heat of the body must be tempered with cold food. Daniel and the three children lived on pulse.[2] They were still boys and had not come yet to that frying-pan on which the King of Babylon fried the elders[3] who were judges. Moreover, by an express privilege of God's own giving their bodily condition was improved by their regimen. We do not expect that it will be so with us, but we look for increased vigour of soul which becomes stronger as the flesh grows weaker. Some persons who aspire to the life of chastity fall midway in their journey from supposing that they need only abstain from flesh. They load their stomachs with vegetables which are only harmless when taken sparingly and in moderation. If I am to say what I think, there is nothing which so much heats the body and inflames the passions as undigested food and breathing broken up with hiccoughs. As for you, my daughter, I would rather wound your modesty than endanger my case by understatement. Regard everything as poison which bears within it the seeds of sensual pleasure. A meagre diet which leaves the appetite always unsatisfied is to be preferred to fasts three days long. It is much better to take a little every day than some days to abstain wholly and on others to surfeit oneself. That rain is best which falls slowly to the ground. Showers that come down suddenly and with violence wash away the soil.

11. When you eat your meals, reflect that you must immediately afterwards pray and read. Have a fixed number of lines of holy scripture, and render it as your task to your Lord. On no account resign yourself to sleep until you have filled the basket of your breast with a woof of this weaving. After the holy scriptures you should read the writings of learned men ; of those at any rate whose faith is well known. You need not go into the mire to seek for gold ; you have many pearls, buy the one pearl with these.[4] Stand, as Jeremiah says, in more ways than one that so you may come on the true way that leads to the Father.[5] Exchange your love of necklaces and of gems and of silk dresses for earnestness in studying the scriptures. Enter the land of promise that flows with milk and honey.[6] Eat fine flour and oil. Let your clothing be, like Joseph's, of many colors.[7] Let your ears like those of Jerusalem[8] be pierced by the word of God that the precious grains of new corn may hang from them. In that reverend man Exuperius[1] you have a man of tried years and faith ready to give you constant support with his advice.

12. Make to yourself friends of the mammon of unrighteousness that they may receive you into everlasting habitations.[2] Give your riches not to those who feed on pheasants but to those who have none but common bread to eat, such as stays hunger while it does not stimulate lust. Consider the poor and needy.[3] Give to everyone that asks of you,[4] but especially unto them who are of the household of faith.[5] Clothe the naked, feed the hungry, visit the sick.[6] Every time that you hold out your hand, think of Christ. See to it that you do not, when the Lord your God asks an alms of you, increase riches which are none of His.

13. Avoid the company of young men. Let long haired youths dandified and wanton never be seen under your roof. Repel a singer as you would some bane. Hurry from your house women who live by playing and singing, the devil's choir whose songs are the fatal ones of sirens. Do not arrogate to yourself a widow's license and appear in public preceded by a host of eunuchs. It is a most mischievous thing for those who are weak owing to their sex and youth to misuse their own discretion and to suppose that things are lawful because they are pleasant. "All things are lawful, but all things are not expedient."[7] No frizzled steward nor shapely foster brother nor fair and ruddy footman must dangle at your heels. Sometimes the tone of the mistress is inferred from the dress of the maid. Seek the society of holy virgins and widows ; and, if need arises for holding converse with men, do not shun having witnesses, and let your conversation be marked with such confidence that the entry of a third person shall neither startle you nor make you blush. The face is the mirror of the mind and a woman's eyes without a word betray the secrets of her heart. I have lately seen a most miserable scandal traverse the entire East. The lady's age and style, her dress and mien, the indiscriminate company she kept, her dainty table and her regal appointments bespoke her the bride of a Nero or of a Sardanapallus. The scars of others should teach us caution. 'When he that causeth trouble is scourged the fool will be wiser.'[8] A holy love knows no impatience. A false rumor is quickly crushed and the after life passes judgment on that which has gone

---

[1] Rom. xiv. 2.　　　　　　[2] Dan. i. 16.
[3] *i.e.* Ahab and Zedekiah whose fate is recorded Jer. xxix. 20–23. According to Jerome tradition identified them with the elders who tempted Susannah. although these latter are said to have been stoned and not burned.　　[4] Matt. xiii. 45, 46.
[5] Jer. vi. 16. 'The ways.' Vulg. VA V. 'More than one' is Jerome's Gloss.
[6] Ex. xxxiii. 3.　　[7] Gen. xxxvii. 23.　　[8] Ezek. xvi. 12.

[1] Afterwards Bishop of Tolosa (Toulouse). He is mentioned again in Letters CXXIII. and CXXV.
[2] Luke xvi. 9.　　[3] Ps. xli. i, PBV.　　[4] Matt. v. 42.
[5] Gal. vi. 10.　　　　[6] Cf. Matt. xxv. 35, 36.
[7] 1 Cor. vi. 12.　　[8] Prov. xix. 25, Vulg.

before. It is not indeed possible that any one should come to the end of life's race without suffering from calumny; the wicked find it a consolation to carp at the good, supposing the guilt of sin to be less, in proportion as the number of those who commit it is greater. Still a fire of straw quickly dies out and a spreading flame soon expires if fuel to it be wanting. Whether the report which prevailed a year ago was true or false, when once the sin ceases, the scandal also will cease. I do not say this because I fear anything wrong in your case but because, owing to my deep affection for you, there is no safety that I do not fear.[1] Oh! that you could see your sister[2] and that it might be yours to hear the eloquence of her holy lips and to behold the mighty spirit which animates her diminutive frame. You might hear the whole contents of the old and new testaments come bubbling up out of her heart. Fasting is her sport, and prayer she makes her pastime. Like Miriam after the drowning Pharaoh she takes up her timbrel and sings to the virgin choir, "Let us sing to the Lord for He hath triumphed gloriously; the horse and his rider hath he thrown into the sea."[3] She teaches her companions to be music girls but music girls for Christ, to be luteplayers but luteplayers for the Saviour. In this occupation she passes both day and night and with oil ready to put in the lamps she waits the coming of the Bridegroom.[4] Do you therefore imitate your kinswoman. Let Rome have in you what a grander city than Rome, I mean Bethlehem, has in her.

14. You have wealth and can easily therefore supply food to those who want it. Let virtue consume what was provided for self-indulgence; one who means to despise matrimony need fear no degree of want. Have about you troops of virgins whom you may lead into the king's chamber. Support widows that you may mingle them as a kind of violets with the virgins' lilies and the martyrs' roses. Such are the garlands you must weave for Christ in place of that crown of thorns[5] in which he bore the sins of the world. Let your most noble father thus find in you his joy and support, let him learn from his daughter the lessons he used to learn from his wife. His hair is already gray, his knees tremble, his teeth fall out, his brow is furrowed through years, death is nigh even at the doors, the pyre is all but laid out hard by. Whether we like it or not, we grow old. Let him provide for himself the provision which is needful for his long journey. Let him take with him what otherwise he must unwillingly leave behind, nay let him send before him to heaven what if he declines it, will be appropriated by earth.

15. Young widows, of whom some "are already turned aside after Satan, when they have begun to wax wanton against Christ"[1] and wish to marry, generally make such excuses as these. "My little patrimony is daily decreasing, the property which I have inherited is being squandered, a servant has spoken insultingly to me, a maid has neglected my orders. Who will appear for me before the authorities? Who will be responsible for the rents of my estates?[2] Who will see to the education of my children, and to the bringing up of my slaves?" Thus, shameful to say, they put that forward as a reason for marrying again, which alone should deter them from doing so. For by marrying again a mother places over her sons not a guardian but a foe, not a father but a tyrant. Inflamed by her passions she forgets the fruit of her womb, and among the children who know nothing of their sad fate the lately weeping widow dresses herself once more as a bride. Why these excuses about your property and the insolence of slaves? Confess the shameful truth. No woman marries to avoid cohabiting with a husband. At least, if passion is not your motive, it is mere madness to play the harlot just to increase wealth. You do but purchase a paltry and passing gain at the price of a grace which is precious and eternal! If you have children already, why do you want to marry? If you have none, why do you not fear a recurrence of your former sterility? Why do you put an uncertain gain before a certain loss of self-respect?

A marriage-settlement is made in your favour to-day but in a short time you will be constrained to make your will. Your husband will feign sickness and will do for you what he wants you to do for him. Yet he is sure to live and you are sure to die. Or if it happens that you have sons by the second husband, domestic strife is certain to result and intestine disputes. You will not be allowed to love your first children, nor to look kindly on those to whom you have yourself given birth. You will have to give them their food secretly; yet even so your present husband will bear a grudge against your previous one and, unless you hate your sons, he will think that you still love their father. But your husband have may issue by a former wife. If so when he takes you to his home, though you should be the kindest person in the world,

1 Cf. Virg. A. iv. 298.
2 Her cousin Eustochium seems to be meant.
3 Ex. xv. 21.   4 Matt. xxv. 4.   5 Matt. xxvii. 29. | 1 1 Tim. v. 15, 11.   2 Agrorum tributa.

all the commonplaces of rhetoricians and dec-
lamations of comic poets and writers of mimes
will be hurled at you as a cruel stepmother.
If your stepson fall sick or have a headache
you will be calumniated as a poisoner. If you
refuse him food, you will be cruel, while if
you give it, you will be held to have bewitched
him. I ask you what benefit has a second
marriage to confer great enough to compen-
sate for these evils?

16. Do we wish to know what widows
ought to be? Let us read the gospel according to Luke. "There was one Anna," he
says, "a prophetess, the daughter of Phanuel
of the tribe of Aser."[1] The meaning of the
name Anna is grace. Phanuel is in our
tongue the face of God. Aser may be translated either as blessedness or as wealth.
From her youth up to the age of fourscore
and four years she had borne the burden of
widowhood, not departing from the temple
and giving herself to fastings and prayers
night and day; therefore she earned spiritual
grace, received the title 'daughter of the
face of God,'[2] and obtained a share in the
'blessedness and wealth'[3] which belonged to
her ancestry. Let us recall to mind the widow
of Zarephath[4] who thought more of satisfying
Elijah's hunger than of preserving her own life
and that of her son. Though she believed
that she and he must die that very night unless they had food, she determined that her
guest should survive. She preferred to sacrifice her life rather than to neglect the duty of
almsgiving. In her handful of meal she
found the seed from which she was to reap a
harvest sent her by the Lord. She sows her
meal and lo! a cruse of oil comes from it. In
the land of Judah grain was scarce for the
corn of wheat had died there;[5] but in the
house of a heathen widow oil flowed in
streams. In the book of Judith—if any one
is of opinion that it should be received as
canonical—we read of a widow wasted with
fasting and wearing the sombre garb of a
mourner, whose outward squalor indicated
not so much the regret which she felt for her
dead husband as the temper[6] in which she
looked forward to the coming of the Bridegroom. I see her hand armed with the sword
and stained with blood. I recognize the head
of Holofernes which she has carried away
from the camp of the enemy. Here a woman
vanquishes men, and chastity beheads lust.
Quickly changing her garb, she puts on once
more in the hour of victory her own mean dress
finer than all the splendours of the world.[7]

17. Some from a misapprehension number
Deborah among the widows, and suppose that
Barak the leader of the army is her son,
though the scripture tells a different story.
I will mention her here because she was a
prophetess and is reckoned among the judges,
and again because she might have said with
the psalmist:—"How sweet are thy words
unto my taste! yea sweeter than honey to
my mouth."[1] Well was she called the bee[2]
for she fed on the flowers of scripture, was
enveloped with the fragrance of the Holy
Spirit, and gathered into one with prophetic
lips the sweet juices of the nectar. Then
there is Naomi, in Greek παρακεκλημένη[3]
or she who is consoled, who, when her husband and her children died abroad, carried
her chastity back home and, being supported
on the road by its aid, kept with her her Moab-
itish daughter-in-law, that in her the prophecy of Isaiah[4] might find a fulfilment. "Send
out the lamb, O Lord, to rule over the land
from the rock of the desert to the mount of
the daughter of Zion."[5] I pass on to the
widow in the gospel who, though she was but
a poor widow was yet richer than all the
people of Israel.[6] She had but a grain of
mustard seed, but she put her leaven in three
measures of flour; and, combining her confession of the Father and of the Son with the
grace of the Holy Spirit, she cast her two
mites into the treasury. All the substance
that she had, her entire possessions, she
offered in the two testaments of her faith.
These are the two seraphim which glorify
the Trinity with threefold song[7] and are
stored among the treasures of the church.
They also form the legs of the tongs by
which the live coal is caught up to purge the
sinner's lips.[8]

18. But why should I recall instances from
history and bring from books types of saintly
women, when in your own city you have many
before your eyes whose example you may well
imitate? I shall not recount their merits here
lest I should seem to flatter them. It will
suffice to mention the saintly Marcella[9] who,
while she is true to the claims of her birth and
station, has set before us a life which is worthy
of the gospel. Anna "lived with an husband
seven years from her virginity";[10] Marcella
lived with one for seven months. Anna looked
for the coming of Christ; Marcella holds fast
the Lord whom Anna received in her arms.
Anna sang His praise when He was still a

---

[1] Luke ii. 36.
[2] Penuel (AV. Phanuel) means 'face of God' cf. Gen. xxxii.
30.
[3] Asher = 'blessedness or wealth.'   [4] 1 K. xvii.
[5] Joh. xii. 24.   [6] i.e., that of penitence.   [7] Judith xiii.

[1] Ps. cxix. 103.   [2] The meaning of Deborah.
[3] Jerome appears to have read נתמי for נעמי. The latter
means 'my pleasantness.'
[4] Made long afterwards.
[5] Isa. xvi. 1 Vulg. 'the rock of the desert' is a poetical name
for Moab.   [6] Mark xii. 43.
[7] Isa. vi. 2, 3. See Letter, XVIII. ante.   [8] Isa. vi. 6.
[9] See Letters XXIII., LXXVII., etc.   [10] Luke ii. 36.

wailing infant ; Marcella proclaims His glory now that He has won His triumph. Anna spoke of Him to all those who waited for the redemption of Israel ; Marcella cries out with the nations of the redeemed : " A brother redeemeth not, yet a man shall redeem," [1] and from another psalm : " A man was born in her, and the Highest Himself hath established her." [2]

About two years ago, as I well remember, I published a book against Jovinian in which by the authority of scripture I crushed the objections raised on the other side on account of the apostle's concession of second marriages. It is unnecessary that I should repeat my arguments afresh here, as you can find them all in this treatise. That I may not exceed the limits of a letter, I will only give you this one last piece of advice. Think every day that you must die, and you will then never think of marrying again.

LETTER LV.

TO AMANDUS.

A very interesting letter. Amandus a presbyter of Burdigala (Bourdeaux) had written to Jerome for an explanation of three passages of scripture, viz. Matt. vi. 34, 1 Cor. vi. 18, 1 Cor. xv. 25, 26, and had in the same letter on behalf of a 'sister' (supposd by Thierry to have been Fabiola) put the following question : ' Can a woman who has divorced her first husband on account of his vices and who has during his lifetime under compulsion married again, communicate with the Church without first doing penance ? Jerome in his reply gives the explanations asked for but answers the farther question, that concerning the 'sister,' with an emphatic negative. Written about the year 394 A. D.

1. A short letter does not admit of long explanations ; compressing much matter into a small space it can only give a few words to topics which suggest many thoughts. You ask me what is the meaning of the passage in the gospel according to Matthew, " take no thought for the morrow. Sufficient unto the day is the evil thereof." [3] In the holy scriptures " the morrow " signifies the time to come. Thus in Genesis Jacob says : " So shall my righteousness answer for me to-morrow." [4] Again when the two tribes of Reuben and Gad and the half tribe of Manasseh had built an altar and when all Israel had sent to them an embassy, they made answer to Phinehas the high priest that they had built the altar lest " to-morrow " it might be said to their children, " ye have no part in the Lord." [5] You may find many similar passages in the old

instrument.[1] While then Christ forbids us to take thought for things future, He has allowed us to do so for things present, knowing as He does the frailty of our mortal condition. His remaining words " sufficient unto the day is the evil thereof" are to be understood as meaning that it is sufficient for us to think of the present troubles of this life. Why need we extend our thoughts to contingencies, to objects which we either cannot obtain or else having obtained must soon relinquish? The Greek word κακία rendered in the Latin version " wickedness " has two distinct meanings, wickedness and tribulation, which latter the Greek call κακωσίν and in this passage " tribulation " would be a better rendering than " wickedness." But if any one demurs to this and insists that the word κακία must mean " wickedness " and not " tribulation " or " trouble," the meaning must be the same as in the words "the whole world lieth in wickedness " [2] and as in the Lord's prayer in the clause, " deliver us from evil : " [3] the purport of the passage will then be that our present conflict with the wickedness of this world should be enough for us.

2. Secondly, you ask me concerning the passage in the first epistle of the blessed apostle Paul to the Corinthians where he says : ' every sin that a man doeth is without the body ; but he that committeth fornication sinneth against his own body." [4] Let us go back a little farther and read on until we come to these words, for we must not seek to learn the whole meaning of the section, from the concluding parts of it, or, if I may so say, from the tail of the chapter.[5] " The body is not for fornication but for the Lord ; and the Lord for the body. And God hath both raised up the Lord and will also raise up us [with Him] by his own power. Know ye not that your bodies are the members of Christ ? Shall I then take the members of Christ, and make them the members of an harlot ? God forbid. What ! Know ye not that he which is joined to an harlot is one body ? For two, saith he, shall be one flesh. But he that is joined unto the Lord is one spirit. Flee fornication. Every sin that a man doeth is without the body ; but he that committeth fornication sinneth against his own body," [6] and so on. The holy apostle has been arguing against excess and has just before said " meats for the belly and the belly for meats : but God shall destroy

---

[1] Instrumentum—a legal term introduced by Tertullian. He uses it both of the Christian dispensation and of its written record.
[2] 1 Joh. v. 19. Where, however, the word is ἐντῷ πονηῳῷ.
[3] Matt. vi. 13. ἀπὸ τοῦ πονηροῦ.   [4] 1 Cor. vi. 18.
[5] Capitulum, " Passage." The present division of the Bible into chapters did not exist in Jerome's time. It is ascribed by some to Abp. Stephen Langton and by others to Card. Hugh de St. Cher.   [6] 1 Cor. vi. 13–18.

---

[1] Ps. xlix. 7. Vulg.   [2] Ps. lxxxvii. 5.
[3] Matt. vi. 34.   [4] Gen. xxx. 33, AV. marg.
[5] Josh. xxii. 27 : AV. and RV. have " in time to come."

both it and them." [1] Now he comes to treat of fornication. For excess in eating is the mother of lust ; a belly that is distended with food and saturated with draughts of wine is sure to lead to sensual passion. As has been elsewhere said "the arrangement of man's organs suggests the course of his vices." [2] Accordingly all such sins as theft, manslaughter, pillage, perjury, and the like can be repented of after they have been committed ; and, however much interest may tempt him, conscience always smites the offender. It is only lust and sensual pleasure that in the very hour of penitence undergo once more the temptations of the past, the itch of the flesh, and the allurements of sin ; so that the very thought which we bestow on the correction of such transgressions becomes in itself a new source of sin. Or to put the matter in a different light : other sins are outside of us ; and whatever we do we do against others. But fornication defiles the fornicator both in conscience and body ; and in accordance with the words of the Lord, "for this cause shall a man leave father and mother, and shall cleave to his wife ; and they twain shall be one flesh," [3] he too becomes one body with a harlot and sins against his own body by making what is the temple of Christ the body of a harlot. Not to pass over any suggestion of the Greek commentators, I shall give you one more explanation. It is one thing, they say, to sin with the body, and another to sin in the body. Theft, manslaughter, and all other sins except fornication we commit with our hands outside ourselves. Fornication alone we commit inside ourselves in our bodies and not with our bodies upon others. The preposition ' with ' denotes the instrument used in sinning, while the preposition ' in ' signifies the sphere of the passion is ourselves. Some again give this explanation that according to the scripture a man's body is his wife and that when a man commits fornication, he is said to sin against his own body that is against his wife inasmuch as he defiles her by his own fornication and causes her though herself free from sin to become a sinner through her intercourse with him.

3. I find joined to your letter of inquiries a short paper containing the following words : " ask him, (that is me,) whether a woman who has left her husband on the ground that he is an adulterer and sodomite and has found herself compelled to take another may in the lifetime of him whom she first left be in communion with the church without doing penance for her fault." As I read the case put I recall the verse "they make excuses for their sins." [1] We are all human and all indulgent to our own faults ; and what our own will leads us to do we attribute to a necessity of nature. It is as though a young man were to say, "I am overborne by my body, the glow of nature kindles my passions, the structure of my frame and its reproductive organs call for sexual intercourse." Or again a murderer might say, "I was in want, I stood in need of food, I had nothing to cover me. If I shed the blood of another, it was to save myself from dying of cold and hunger." Tell the sister, therefore, who thus enquires of me concerning her condition, not my sentence but that of the apostle. "Know ye not, brethren (for I speak to them that know the law,) how that the law hath dominion over a man as long as he liveth ? For the woman which hath an husband is bound by the law to her husband, so long as he liveth ; but if the husband be dead, she is loosed from the law of her husband. So then, if, while her husband liveth, she be married to another man, she shall be called an adulteress." [2] And in another place : "the wife is bound by the law as long as her husband liveth ; but if her husband be dead, she is at liberty to be married to whom she will ; only in the Lord." [3] The apostle has thus cut away every plea and has clearly declared that, if a woman marries again while her husband is living, she is an adulteress. You must not speak to me of the violence of a ravisher, a mother's pleading, a father's bidding, the influence of relatives, the insolence and the intrigues of servants, household losses. A husband may be an adulterer or a sodomite, he may be stained with every crime and may have been left by his wife because of his sins ; yet he is still her husband and, so long as he lives, she may not marry another. The apostle does not promulgate this decree on his own authority but on that of Christ who speaks in him. For he has followed the words of Christ in the gospel : "whosoever shall put away his wife, saving for the cause of fornication, causeth her to commit adultery : and whosoever shall marry her that is divorced, committeth adultery." [4] Mark what he says : "whosoever shall marry her that is divorced committeth adultery." Whether she has put away her husband or her husband her, the man who marries her is still an adulterer. Wherefore the apostles seeing how heavy the yoke of marriage was thus made said to Him : "if the case of the man be so with his wife, it is not good to marry," and the Lord replied, "he that is able to receive it, let him receive it."

---

[1] 1 Cor. vi. 13.   [2] Tertullian, on Fasting, I.
[3] Matt. xix. 5 ; 1 Cor. vi. 16.

[1] Ps. clxi. 4, Vulg.   [2] Rom. vii. 1–3.
[3] 1 Cor. vii. 39.   [4] Matt. v. 32.

And immediately by the instance of the three eunuchs he shows the blessedness of virginity which is bound by no carnal tie.[1]

4. I have not been able quite to determine what it is that she means by the words " has found herself compelled " to marry again. What is this compulsion of which she speaks? Was she overborne by a crowd and ravished against her will? If so, why has she not, thus victimized, subsequently put away her ravisher? Let her read the books of Moses and she will find that if violence is offered to a betrothed virgin in a city and she does not cry out, she is punished as an adulteress: but if she is forced in the field, she is innocent of sin and her ravisher alone is amenable to the laws.[2] Therefore if your sister, who, as she says, has been forced into a second union, wishes to receive the body of Christ and not to be accounted an adulteress, let her do penance; so far at least as from the time she begins to repent to have no farther intercourse with that second husband who ought to be called not a husband but an adulterer. If this seems hard to her and if she cannot leave one whom she has once loved and will not prefer the Lord to sensual pleasure, let her hear the declaration of the apostle: " ye cannot drink the cup of the Lord and the cup of devils: ye cannot be partakers of the Lord's table and of the table of devils,"[3] and in another place: " what communion hath light with darkness? and what concord hath Christ with Belial?"[4] What I am about to say may sound novel but after all it is not new but old for it is supported by the witness of the old testament. If she leaves her second husband and desires to be reconciled with her first, she cannot be so now; for it is written in Deuteronomy: " When a man hath taken a wife, and married her, and it come to pass that she find no favour in his eyes, because he hath found some uncleanness in her; then let him write her a bill of divorcement, and give it in her hand, and send her out of his house. And when she is departed out of his house, she may go and be another man's wife. And if the latter husband hate her, and write her a bill of divorcement and giveth it in her hand, and sendeth her out of his house; or if the latter husband die which took her to be his wife; her former husband, which sent her away may not take her again to be his wife, after that she is defiled; for that is abomination before the Lord: and thou shalt not cause the land to sin, which the Lord thy God giveth thee for an inheritance."[5] Wherefore, I beseech you, do your best to comfort her and to urge her to seek

salvation. Diseased flesh calls for the knife and the searing-iron. The wound is to blame and not the healing art, if with a cruelty that is really kindness a physician to spare does not spare, and to be merciful is cruel.[1]

5. Your third and last question relates to the passage in the same epistle where the apostle in discussing the resurrection, comes to the words: " for he must reign, till he hath put all things under his feet. The last enemy that shall be destroyed is death. For he hath put all things under his feet. But when he saith, all things are put under him, it is manifest that he is excepted, which did put all things under him. And when all things shall be subdued unto him, then shall the Son also himself be subject unto him that put all things under him that God may be all in all."[2] I am surprised that you have resolved to question me about this passage when that reverend man, Hilary, bishop of Poictiers, has occupied the eleventh book of his treatise against the Arians with a full examination and explanation of it. Yet I may at least say a few words. The chief stumbling-block in the passage is that the Son is said to be subject to the Father. Now which is the more shameful and humiliating, to be subject to the Father (often a mark of loving devotion as in the psalm " truly my soul is subject unto God "[3]) or to be crucified and made the curse of the cross? For " cursed is everyone that hangeth on a tree."[4] If Christ then for our sakes was made a curse that He might deliver us from the curse of the law, are you surprised that He is also for our sakes subject to the Father to make us too subject to Him as He says in the gospel: " No man cometh unto the Father but by me,"[5] and " I, if I be lifted up from the earth, will draw all men unto me."[6] Christ then is subject to the Father in the faithful; for all believers, nay the whole human race, are accounted members of His body. But in unbelievers, that is in Jews, heathens, and heretics, He is said to be not subject; for these members of His body are not subject to the faith. But in the end of the world when all His members shall see Christ, that is their own body, reigning, they also shall be made subject to Christ, that is to their own body, that the whole of Christ's body may be subject unto God and the Father, and that God may be all in all. He does not say " that the Father may be all in all " but that " God " may be, a title which properly belongs to the Trinity and may be referred not only to the Father but also to the Son and to the Holy Ghost.

---

[1] Matt. xix. 10-12. [2] Deut. xxii. 23-27. [3] 1 Cor. x. 21.
[4] 2 Cor. vi. 14, 15. [5] Deut. xxiv. 1-4.

[1] Cf. Letter XL. §1. [2] 1 Cor. xv. 25-28. [3] Ps. lxii. 1, Vulg.
[4] Gal. iii. 13. [5] Joh. xiv. 6. [6] Joh. xii. 32.

His meaning therefore is "that humanity may be subject to the Godhead." By humanity we here intend not that gentleness and kindness which the Greeks call philanthropy but the whole human race. Moreover when he says "that God may be all in all," it is to be taken in this sense. At present our Lord and Saviour is not all in all, but only a part in each of us. For instance He is wisdom in Solomon, generosity in David, patience in Job, knowledge of things to come in Daniel, faith in Peter, zeal in Phinehas and Paul, virginity in John, and other virtues in others. But when the end of all things shall come, then shall He be all in all, for then the saints shall severally possess all the virtues and all will possess Christ in His entirety.

LETTER LVI.

FROM AUGUSTINE.

Augustine's first letter to Jerome (printed in his correspondence in this Library as Letter XXVIII.): through a series of accidents it was not delivered until nine years after it had been written. In it Augustine comments on Jerome's new Latin version of the O. T. and advises him in his future labours to adhere more closely to the text of the LXX. He also discusses Jerome's account (in his commentary on the epistle to the Galatians) of the quarrel between Paul and Peter at Antioch. This according to Jerome was not a real misunderstanding but only one artificially 'got up' to put clearly before the Church the mischief of Christians conforming to the now obsolete Mosaic Law. Augustine strongly controverts this view and maintains that it is fatal to the veracity and authority claimed for scripture. Written from Hippo about the year 394 A. D.

LETTER LVII.

TO PAMMACHIUS ON THE BEST METHOD OF TRANSLATING.

Written to Pammachius (for whom see Letter LXVI.) in A. D. 395. In the previous year Jerome had rendered into Latin Letter LI. (from Epiphanius to John of Jerusalem) under circumstances which he here describes (§2). His version soon became public and incurred severe criticism from some person not named by Jerome but supposed by him to have been instigated by Rufinus (§12). Charged with having falsified his original he now repudiates the charge and defends his method of translation ("to give sense for sense and not word for word" §5) by an appeal to the practice of classical (§5), ecclesiastical (§6), and N. T. (§§7–10) writers.

When at a subsequent period Rufinus gave to the world what was in Jerome's opinion a misleading version of Origen's *First Principles*, he appealed to this letter as giving him ample warranty for what he had done. See Letters LXXX. and LXXXI, and Rufinus' Preface to the πεεὶ ᾽Αεχῶν in Vol. iii. of this series.

1. The apostle Paul when he appeared before King Agrippa to answer the charges which were brought against him, wishing to use language intelligible to his hearers and confident of the success of his cause, began by congratulating himself in these words : " I think myself happy, King Agrippa, because I shall answer for myself this day before thee touching all the things whereof I am accused by the Jews : especially because thou art expert in all customs and questions which are among the Jews."[1] He had read the saying of Jesus :[2] " Well is him that speaketh in the ears of them that will hear ; "[3] and he knew that a pleader only succeeds in proportion as he impresses his judge. On this occasion I too think myself happy that learned ears will hear my defence. For a rash tongue charges me with ignorance or falsehood ; it alleges that in translating another man's letter I have made mistakes through incapacity or carelessness ; it convicts me of either an involuntary error or a deliberate offence. And lest it should happen that my accuser—encouraged by a volubility which stops at nothing and by an impunity which arrogates to itself an unlimited license—should accuse me as he has already done our father (Pope) Epiphanius ; I send this letter to inform you— and through you others who think me worthy of their regard—of the true order of the facts.

2. About two years ago the aforesaid Pope Epiphanius sent a letter[4] to Bishop John, first finding fault with him as regarded some of his opinions and then mildly calling him to penitence. Such was the repute of the writer or else the elegance of the letter that all Palestine fought for copies of it. Now there was in our monastery a man of no small estimation in his country, Eusebius of Cremona, who, when he found that this letter was in everybody's mouth and that the ignorant and the educated alike admired it for its teaching and for the purity of its style, set to work to beg me to translate it for him into Latin and at the same time to simplify the argument so that he might more readily understand it ; for he was himself altogether unacquainted with the Greek language. I consented to his request and calling to my aid a secretary speedily dictated my version, briefly marking on the side of the page the contents of the several chapters. The fact is that he asked me to do this merely for himself, and I requested of him in return to keep his copy private and not too readily to circulate it. A year and six months went by, and then the aforesaid translation found its way by a novel stratagem from his desk to Jerusalem. For a pretended monk—either bribed as there is much reason to believe or actuated by malice of his own as his tempter vainly tries to convince us— shewed himself a second Judas by robbing

---

[1] Acts xxvi. 2, 3.
[2] *i.e.*, the son of Sirach.
[3] Ecclus. xxv. 9.
[4] Letter LI. to John Bp. of Jerusalem.

Eusebius of his literary property and gave to the adversary an occasion of railing[1] against me. They tell the unlearned that I have falsified the original, that I have not rendered word for word, that I have put 'dear friend' in place of ' honourable sir,' and more shameful still ! that I have cut down my translation by omitting the words αἰδεσιμῶτατε Πάππα.[2] These and similar trifles form the substance of the charges brought against me.

3. At the outset before I defend my version I wish to ask those persons who confound wisdom with cunning, some few questions. Where did you get your copy of the letter ? Who gave it to you ? How have you the effrontery to bring forward what you have procured by fraud ? What place of safety will be left us if we cannot conceal our secrets even within our own walls and our own writing-desks ? Were I to press such a charge against you before a legal tribunal, I could make you amenable to the laws which even in fiscal cases appoint penalties for meddlesome informers and condemn the traitor even while they accept his treachery. For though they welcome the profit which the information gives them, they disapprove the motive which actuates the informer. A little while ago a man of consular rank named Hesychius (against whom the patriarch Gamaliel waged an implacable war) was condemned to death by the emperor Theodosius simply because he had laid hold of imperial papers through a secretary whom he had tempted. We read also in old histories[3] that the schoolmaster who betrayed the children of the Faliscans was sent back to his boys and handed over to them in bonds, the Roman people refusing to accept a dishonourable victory. When Pyrrhus king of Epirus was lying in his camp ill from the effects of a wound, his physician offered to poison him, but Fabricius thinking it shame that the king should die by treachery sent the traitor back in chains to his master, refusing to sanction crime even when its victim was an enemy.[4] A principle which the laws uphold, which is maintained by enemies, which warfare and the sword fail to violate, has hitherto been held unquestioned among the monks and priests of Christ. And can any one of them presume now, knitting his brow and snapping his fingers,[5] to spend his breath in saying : " What if he did use bribes or other inducements ! he did what suited his purpose." A strange plea truly to defend a fraud as though robbers, thieves, and pirates did not do the same. Certainly, when Annas and Caiaphas led hapless Judas astray, they only did what they believed to be expedient for themselves.

4. Suppose that I wish to write down in my note books this or that silly trifle, or to make comments upon the scriptures, to retort upon my calumniators, to digest my wrath, to practise myself in the use of commonplaces and to stow away sharp shafts for the day of battle. So long as I do not publish my thoughts, they are only unkind words not matter for a charge of libel ; in fact they are not even unkind words for the public ear never hears them. You[1] may bribe my slaves and tamper with my clients. You may, as the fable has it, penetrate by means of your gold to the chamber of Danaë ;[2] and then, dissembling what you have done, you may call me a falsifier ; but, if you do so, you will have to plead guilty yourself to a worse charge than any that you can bring against me. One man inveighs against you as a heretic, another as a perverter of doctrine. You are silent yourself ; you do not venture to answer ; you assail the translator ; you cavil about syllables and you fancy your defence complete if your calumnies provoke no reply. Suppose that I have made a mistake or an omission in my rendering. Your whole case turns upon this ; this is the defence which you offer to your accusers. Are you no heretic because I am a bad translator ? Mind, I do not say that I know you to be a heretic ; I leave such knowledge to your accuser, to him who wrote the letter :[3] what I do say is that it is the height of folly for you when you are accused by one man to attack another, and when you are covered with wounds yourself to seek comfort by wounding one who is still quiescent and unaggressive.

5. In the above remarks I have assumed that I have made alterations in the letter and that a simple translation may contain errors though not wilful ones. As, however the letter itself shews that no changes have been made in the sense, that nothing has been added, and that no doctrine has been foisted into it, " obviously their object is understanding to understand nothing ; "[4] and while they desire to arraign another's want of skill, they betray their own. For I myself not only admit but freely proclaim that in translating from the Greek (except in the case of the holy scriptures where even the order of the words is a mystery) I render sense for sense and not word for word. For this course I have the

---

[1] Cf. Jude 9.
[2] i.e., 'most reverend pope.' This title at first given to all bishops was in Jerome's time becoming restricted to metropolitans and patriarchs. Jerome, however, still uses it in the wider sense. The omission of the title here may well have seemed deliberate, as Jerome was known to entertain very bitter feelings towards John of Jerusalem.
[3] Livy v. 27.   [4] Plutarch, Life of Pyrrhus.
[5] Jerome constantly speaks of Rufinus in this way. See Letter CXXV. 18 and Apol. c. Ruf. I. 13, 32.

[1] Rufinus is meant.
[2] Danaë, the daughter of Acrisius, was confined by her father in a brazen tower to which Zeus obtained access in the shape of a shower of gold.
[3] Epiphanius.   [4] Ter. And. prol. 17.

authority of Tully who has so translated the Protagoras of Plato, the Oeconomicus of Xenophon, and the two beautiful orations[1] which Æschines and Demosthenes delivered one against the other. What omissions, additions, and alterations he has made substituting the idioms of his own for those of another tongue, this is not the time to say. I am satisfied to quote the authority of the translator who has spoken as follows in a prologue[2] prefixed to the orations. "I have thought it right to embrace a labour which though not necessary for myself will prove useful to those who study. I have translated the noblest speeches of the two most eloquent of the Attic orators, the speeches which Æschines and Demosthenes delivered one against the other; but I have rendered them not as a translator but as an orator, keeping the sense but altering the form by adapting both the metaphors and the words to suit our own idiom. I have not deemed it necessary to render word for word but I have reproduced the general style and emphasis. I have not supposed myself bound to pay the words out one by one to the reader but only to give him an equivalent in value." Again at the close of his task he says, "I shall be well satisfied if my rendering is found, as I trust it will be, true to this standard. In making it I have utilized all the excellences of the originals, I mean the sentiments, the forms of expression and the arrangement of the topics, while I have followed the actual wording only so far as I could do so without offending our notions of taste. If all that I have written is not to be found in the Greek, I have at any rate striven to make it correspond with it." Horace too, an acute and learned writer, in his Art of Poetry gives the same advice to the skilled translator:—

> And care not thou with over anxious thought
> To render word for word.[3]

Terence has translated Menander; Plautus and Cæcilius the old comic poets.[4] Do they ever stick at words? Do they not rather in their versions think first of preserving the beauty and charm of their originals? What men like you call fidelity in transcription, the learned term pestilent minuteness.[5] Such were my teachers about twenty years ago; and even then[6] I was the victim of a similar error to that which is now imputed to me, though indeed I never imagined that *you* would charge me with it. In translating the Chronicle of Eusebius of Cæsarea into Latin, I made among others the following prefatory observations: "It is

difficult in following lines laid down by other not sometimes to diverge from them, and it i hard to preserve in a translation the charm o expressions which in another language ar most felicitous. Each particular word con veys a meaning of its own, and possibly I hav no equivalent by which to render it, and if make a circuit to reach my goal, I have to g many miles to cover a short distance.[1] T these difficulties must be added the winding of hyperbata, differences in the use of cases divergencies of metaphor; and last of all th peculiar and if I may so call it, inbred charac ter of the language. If I render word fo word, the result will sound uncouth, and i compelled by necessity I alter anything in th order or wording, I shall seem to have depart ed from the function of a translator."[2] An after a long discussion which it would be te dious to follow out here, I added what follows —"If any one imagines that translation doe not impair the charm of style, let him rende Homer word for word into Latin, nay I wil go farther still and say, let him render it int Latin prose, and the result will be that th order of the words will seem ridiculous and th most eloquent of poets scarcely articulate."[3]

6. In quoting my own writings my only object has been to prove that from my youth u I at least have always aimed at rendering sense not words, but if such authority as the supply is deemed insufficient, read and consider the short preface dealing with this matter which occurs in a book narrating the lif of the blessed Antony.[4] "A literal translation from one language into another obscures the sense; the exuberance of the growth lessens the yield. For while one's diction is enslaved to cases and metaphors, it has to explain by tedious circumlocutions what a few words would otherwise have sufficed to make plain. I have tried to avoid this error in the translation which at your request I have made of the story of the blessed Antony. My version always preserves the sense although it does not invariably keep the words of the original. Leave others to catch at syllables and letters, do you for your part look for the meaning." Time would fail me were I to unfold the testimonies of all who have translated only according to the sense. It is sufficient for the present to name Hilary the confessor[5] who has turned some homilies on Job and several treatises on the Psalms from Greek into Latin; yet has not bound himself to the drowsiness of the letter or fettered himself by the

---

[1] The two speeches on the Crown.
[2] Only a small part of this is extant.   [3] Hor. A. P. 133.
[4] *i.e* the poets of the so called New Comedy.   [5] κακοζηλίαν.
[6] That is, five years later. Jerome translated the Chronicle of Eusebius at Constantinople in 381-2.

[1] Vix brevis viæ spatia consummo.
[2] Preface, translated in this Volume, § 1.   [3] Preface § 2.
[4] This life long supposed to have been the work of Athanasius was originally composed in Greek but had been rendered into Latin by Evagrius bishop of Antioch.
[5] *i.e.*, Hilary of Poitiers.

stale literalism of inadequate culture. Like a conqueror he has led away captive into his own tongue the meaning of his originals.

7. That secular and church writers should have adopted this line need not surprise us when we consider that the translators of the Septuagint,[1] the evangelists, and the apostles, have done the same in dealing with the sacred writings. We read in Mark[2] of the Lord saying *Talitha cumi* and it is immediately added "which is interpreted, Damsel, I say unto thee, arise." The evangelist may be charged with falsehood for having added the words "I say unto thee" for the Hebrew is only "Damsel arise." To emphasize this and to give the impression of one calling and commanding he has added "I say unto thee." Again in Matthew[3] when the thirty pieces of silver are returned by the traitor Judas and the potter's field is purchased with them, it is written :—" Then was fulfilled that which was spoken of by Jeremy the prophet, saying, "And they took the thirty pieces of silver the price of him that was valued which[4] they of the children of Israel did value, and gave them for the potter's field, as the Lord appointed me." This passage is not found in Jeremiah at all but in Zechariah, in quite different words and an altogether different order. In fact the Vulgate renders it as follows :—"And I will say unto them, If it is good in your sight, give ye me a price or refuse it : So they weighed for my price thirty pieces of silver. And the Lord said unto me, Put them into the melting furnace and consider if it is tried as I have been tried by them. And I took the thirty pieces of silver and cast them into the house of the Lord."[5] It is evident that the rendering of the Septuagint differs widely from the quotation of the evangelist. In the Hebrew also, though the sense is the same, the words are quite different and differently arranged. It says : "And I said unto them, If ye think good, give me my price ; and, if not, forbear. So they weighed for my price thirty pieces of silver. And the Lord said unto me, Cast it unto the potter ;[6] a goodly price that I was priced at of them. And I took the thirty pieces of silver and cast them to the potter in the house of the Lord."[7] They may accuse the apostle of falsifying his version seeing that it agrees neither with the Hebrew nor with the translators of the Septuagint : and worse than this, they may say that he has mistaken the author's name putting down Jeremiah when it should be Zechariah. Far be it from us to speak thus of a follower[8] of Christ, who made it his care to formulate

dogmas rather than to hunt for words and syllables. To take another instance from Zechariah, the evangelist John quotes from the Hebrew, "They shall look on him whom they pierced,"[1] for which we read in the Septuagint, "And they shall look upon me because they have mocked me," and in the Latin version, "And they shall look upon me for the things which they have mocked or insulted." Here the evangelist, the Septuagint, and our own version[2] all differ ; yet the divergence of language is atoned by oneness of spirit. In Matthew again we read of the Lord preaching flight to the apostles and confirming His counsel with a passage from Zechariah. "It is written," he says, "I will smite the shepherd, and the sheep of the flock shall be scattered abroad."[3] But in the Septuagint and in the Hebrew it reads differently, for it is not God who speaks, as the evangelist makes out, but the prophet who appeals to God the Father saying :—" Smite the shepherd, and the sheep shall be scattered." In this instance according to my judgment—and I have some careful critics with me—the evangelist is guilty of a fault in presuming to ascribe to God what are the words of the prophet. Again the same evangelist writes that at the warning of an angel Joseph took the young child and his mother and went into Egypt and remained there till the death of Herod ; "that it might be fulfilled which was spoken of the Lord by the prophet saying, Out of Egypt have I called my son."[4] The Latin manuscripts do not so give the passage, but in Hosea[5] the true Hebrew text has the following :—"When Israel was a child then I loved him, and called my son out of Egypt." Which the Septuagint renders thus :—"When Israel was a child then I loved him, and called his sons out of Egypt." Are they[6] altogether to be rejected because they have given another turn to a passage which refers primarily to the mystery of Christ ? Or should we not rather pardon the shortcomings of the translators on the score of their human frailty according to the saying of James, "In many things we offend all. If any man offend not in word the same is a perfect man and able also to bridle the whole body."[7] Once more it is written in the pages of the same evangelist, "And he came and dwelt in a city called Nazareth : that it might be fulfilled which was spoken by the prophets, He shall be called a Nazarene."[8] Let these word fanciers and nice critics of all composition tell us where they have read the words ;

---

[1] Lit. the seventy translators.   [2] Mark v. 41.
[3] xxvii. 9, 10.   [4] Quod. AV. has 'whom.'
[5] Zech. xi. 12, 13, Vulg.   [6] Statuarius.
[7] Zech. xi. 12, 13, AV.   [8] Pedissequus.

[1] Joh. xix. 37: Zech. xii. 10.
[2] *i.e.*, the Italic, for the Vulgate, which was not then published, accurately represents the Hebrew.
[3] Matt. xxvi. 31: Zech. xiii. 7.   [4] Matt. ii. 13-15.
[5] Hos. xi. 1.   [6] *i.e.*, the Septuagint and Vulgate versions.
[7] James iii. 2.   [8] Matt. ii. 23.

and if they cannot, let me tell them that they are in Isaiah.[1] For in the place where we read and translate, "There shall come forth a rod out of the stem of Jesse, and a branch shall grow out of his roots,"[2] in the Hebrew idiom it is written thus, "There shall come forth a rod out of the root of Jesse and a Nazarene shall grow from his root." How can the Septuagint leave out the word 'Nazarene,' if it is unlawful to substitute one word for another? It is sacrilege either to conceal or to set at naught a mystery.

8. Let us pass on to other passages, for the brief limits of a letter do not suffer us to dwell too long on any one point. The same Matthew says :—"Now all this was done that it might be fulfilled which was spoken of the Lord by the prophet saying, Behold a virgin shall be with child and shall bring forth a son and they shall call his name Emmanuel."[3] The rendering of the Septuagint is, "Behold a virgin shall receive seed and shall bring forth a son, and ye shall call his name Emmanuel." If people cavil at words, obviously 'to receive seed' is not the exact equivalent of 'to be with child,' and 'ye shall call' differs from 'they shall call.' Moreover in the Hebrew we read thus, "Behold a virgin shall conceive and bear a son and shall call his name Immanuel."[4] Ahaz shall not call him so for he was convicted of want of faith, nor the Jews for they were destined to deny him, but she who is to conceive him, and bear him, the virgin herself. In the same evangelist we read that Herod was troubled at the coming of the Magi and that gathering together the scribes and the priests he demanded of them where Christ should be born and that they answered him, "In Bethlehem of Judæa : for thus it is written by the prophet ; And thou Bethlehem in the land of Judah art not the least among the princes of Judah, for out of thee shall come a governour that shall rule my people Israel."[5] In the Vulgate[6] this passage appears as follows :—"And thou Bethlehem, the house of Ephratah, art small to be among the thousands of Judah, yet one shall come out of thee for me to be a prince in Israel." You will be more surprised still at the difference in words and order between Matthew and the Septuagint if you look at the Hebrew which runs thus :—"But thou Bethlehem Ephratah, though thou be little among the thousands of Judah, yet out of thee shall he come forth unto me that is to be ruler in Israel."[7] Consider one by one the words of the evangelist :— "And thou Bethlehem in the land of Judah."

For "the land of Judah" the Hebrew has "Ephratah" while the Septuagint gives "the house of Ephratah." The evangelist writes, "art not the least among the princes of Judah." In the Septuagint this is, "art small to be among the thousands of Judah," while the Hebrew gives, "though thou be little among the thousands of Judah." There is a contradiction here—and that not merely verbal —between the evangelist and the prophet ; for in this place at any rate both Septuagint and Hebrew agree. The evangelist says that he is not little among the princes of Judah, while the passage from which he quotes says exactly the opposite of this, " Thou art small indeed and little; but yet out of thee, small and little as thou art, there shall come forth for me a leader in Israel," a sentiment in harmony with that of the apostle, "God hath chosen the weak things of the world to confound the things which are mighty."[1] Moreover the last clause "to rule" or "to feed my people Israel" clearly runs differently in the original.

9. I refer to these passages, not to convict the evangelists of falsification—a charge worthy only of impious men like Celsus, Porphyry, and Julian—but to bring home to my critics their own want of knowledge, and to gain from them such consideration that they may concede to me in the case of a simple letter what, whether they like it or not, they will have to concede to the Apostles in the Holy Scriptures. Mark, the disciple of Peter, begins his gospel thus :—"The beginning of the gospel of Jesus Christ, as it is written in the prophet Isaiah : Behold I send my messenger before thy face which shall prepare thy way before thee. The voice of one crying in the wilderness, Prepare ye the way of the Lord, make his paths straight."[2] This quotation is made up from two prophets, Malachi that is to say and Isaiah. For the first part : " Behold I send my messenger before thy face which shall prepare thy way before thee," occurs at the close of Malachi.[3] But the second part: " The voice of one crying, etc.," we read in Isaiah.[4] On what grounds then has Mark in the very beginning of his book set the words : "As it is written in the prophet Isaiah, Behold I send my messenger," when, as we have said, it is not written in Isaiah at all, but in Malachi the last of the twelve prophets ? Let ignorant presumption solve this nice question if it can, and I will ask pardon for being in the wrong. The same Mark brings before us the Saviour thus addressing the Pharisees : " Have ye never read what David did when he had need and was an

---

[1] Isa. xi. 1.   [2] So AV. the Vulg. varies slightly.
[3] Matt. i. 22, 23 : Isa. vii. 14.   [4] AV.   [5] Matt. ii. 5, 6.
[6] i.e. the Versio Itala which was vulgata or ' commonly used ' at this time as Jerome's Version was afterwards.
[7] Mic. v. 2'

[1] 1 Cor. i. 27.   [2] Mark i. 1-3; see RV.
[3] Mal. iii. 1.   [4] Isa. xl. 3.

hungred, he and they that were with him, how he went into the house of God in the days of Abiathar the highpriest, and did eat the shewbread which is not lawful to eat but for the priests?"[1] Now let us turn to the books of Samuel, or, as they are commonly called, of Kings, and we shall find there that the highpriest's name was not Abiathar but Ahimelech,[2] the same that was afterwards put to death with the rest of the priests by Doeg at the command of Saul.[3] Let us pass on now to the apostle Paul who writes thus to the Corinthians: "For had they known it, they would not have crucified the Lord of glory. But, as it is written, Eye hath not seen nor ear heard, neither have entered into the heart of man, the things which God hath prepared for them that love Him."[4] Some writers on this passage betake themselves to the ravings of the apocryphal books and assert that the quotation comes from the Revelation of Elijah;[5] whereas the truth is that it is found in Isaiah according to the Hebrew text: "Since the beginning of the world men have not heard nor perceived by the ear, neither hath the eye seen, O God, beside thee what thou hast prepared for them that wait for thee."[6] The Septuagint has rendered the words quite differently: "Since the beginning of the world we have not heard, neither have our eyes seen any God beside thee and thy true works, and thou wilt shew mercy to them that wait for thee." We see then from what place the quotation is taken and yet the apostle has not rendered his original word for word, but, using a paraphrase, he has given the sense in different terms. In his epistle to the Romans the same apostle quotes these words from Isaiah: "Behold I lay in Sion a stumblingstone and rock of offence,"[7] a rendering which is at variance with the Greek version[8] yet agrees with the original Hebrew. The Septuagint gives an opposite meaning, "that you fall not òn a stumblingstone nor on a rock of offence." The apostle Peter agrees with Paul and the Hebrew, writing: "but to them that do not believe, a stone of stumbling and a rock of offence."[9] From all these passages it is clear that the apostles and evangelists in translating the old testament scriptures have sought to give the meaning rather than the words, and that they have not greatly cared to preserve forms or constructions, so long as they could make clear the subject to the understanding.

10. Luke the evangelist and companion of apostles describes Christ's first martyr Stephen as relating what follows in a Jewish assembly. "With threescore and fifteen souls Jacob went down into Egypt, and died himself, and our fathers were carried over[1] into Sychem, and laid in the sepulchre that Abraham bought for a sum of money of the sons of Emmor[2] the father of Sychem."[3] In Genesis this passage is quite differently given, for it is Abraham that buys of Ephron the Hittite, the son of Zohar, near Hebron, for four hundred shekels[4] of silver, a double cave,[5] and the field that is about it, and that buries in it Sarah his wife. And in the same book we read that, after his return from Mesopotamia with his wives and his sons, Jacob pitched his tent before Salem, a city of Shechem which is in the land of Canaan, and that he dwelt there and "bought a parcel of a field where he had spread his tent at the hand of Hamor, the father of Sychem, for an hundred lambs,"[6] and that "he erected there an altar and called there upon the God of Israel."[7] Abraham does not buy the cave from Hamor the father of Sychem, but from Ephron the son of Zohar, and he is not buried in Sychem but in Hebron which is corruptly called Arboch. Whereas the twelve patriarchs are not buried in Arboch but in Sychem, in the field purchased not by Abraham but by Jacob. I postpone the solution of this delicate problem to enable those who cavil at me to search and see that in dealing with the scriptures it is the sense we have to look to and not the words. In the Hebrew the twenty-second psalm begins with the exact words which the Lord uttered on the cross: *Eli Eli lama azabthani*, which means, "My God, my God, why hast thou forsaken me?"[8] Let my critics tell me why the Septuagint introduces here the words "look thou upon me." For its rendering is as follows: "My God, my God, look thou upon me, why hast thou forsaken me?" They will answer no doubt that no harm is done to the sense by the addition of a couple of words. Let them acknowledge then that, if in the haste of dictation I have omitted a few, I have not by so doing endangered the position of the churches.

11. It would be tedious now to enumerate, what great additions and omissions the Septuagint has made, and all the passages which in church-copies are marked with daggers and asterisks. The Jews generally laugh when they hear our version of this passage of Isaiah, "Blessed is he that hath seed in Zion and servants in Jerusalem."[9] In Amos also[10] after a

---

[1] Mark ii. 25, 26.   [2] 1 Sam. xxi. 1.
[3] 1 Sam. xxii. 16–18.   [4] 1 Cor. ii. 8, 9.
[5] This book is no longer extant. It belonged to the same class as the Book of Enoch.
[6] Isa. lxiv. 4, lxx. AV. has 'what he hath prepared for him that waiteth for him.'
[7] Rom. ix. 33.   [8] Lit. 'with the old version.'
[9] 1 Pet. ii. 8. AV. is different.

[1] So the Vulg.: AV. punctuates differently.   [2] *i.e.* Hamor.
[3] Acts vii. 15–16.   [4] Drachmæ.   [5] Spelunca duplex.
[6] AV. marg.   [7] Gen. xxxiii. 18–20. AV. varies slightly.
[8] Ps. xxii. 1.   [9] Isa. xxxi. 9, LXX.   [10] According to the LXX.

description of self-indulgence[1] there come these words : "They have thought of these things as halting and not likely to fly," a very rhetorical sentence quite worthy of Tully. But how shall we deal with the Hebrew originals in which these passages and others like them are omitted, passages so numerous that to reproduce them all would require books without number ? The number of the omissions is shown alike by the asterisks mentioned above and by my own version when compared by a careful reader with the old translation.[2] Yet the Septuagint has rightly kept its place in the churches, either because it is the first of all the versions in time, made before the coming of Christ, or else because it has been used by the apostles (only however in places where it does not disagree with the Hebrew[3]). On the other hand we do right to reject Aquila, the proselyte and controversial translator, who has striven to translate not words only but their etymologies as well. Who could accept as renderings of "corn and wine and oil"[4] such words as χεῖμα ὀπωρισμός, στιλπνότης, or, as we might say, 'pouring,' and 'fruitgathering,' and 'shining'? or, because Hebrew has in addition to the article other prefixes[5] as well, he must with an unhappy pedantry translate syllable by syllable and letter by letter thus : σὺν τὸν οὐρανὸν καὶ σὺν τὴν γήν, a construction which neither Greek nor Latin admits of,[6] as many passages in our own writers shew. How many are the phrases charming in Greek which, if rendered word for word, do not sound well in Latin, and again how many there are that are pleasing to us in Latin, but which—assuming the order of the words not to be altered—would not please in Greek.

12. But to pass by this limitless field of discussion and to shew you, most Christian of nobles, and most noble of Christians, what is the kind of falsification which is censured in my translation, I will set before you the opening words of the letter in the Greek original and as rendered by me, that from one count in the indictment you may form an opinion of all. The letter begins Ἔδει ἡμᾶς, ἀγάπητε, μὴ τῇ οἰήσει τῶν κλήρων φέρεσθαι which I remember to have rendered as follows : "Dearly beloved, we ought not to misuse our position as ministers to gratify our pride." See there, they cry, what a number of falsehoods in a single line ! In the first place ἀγαπητός means 'loved,' not 'dearly beloved.' Then οἴησις means 'estimate,' not 'pride,' for this and not οἴδημα is the word used. Οἴδημα signifies 'a swelling' but οἴησις means 'judgment.' All the rest, say they : "not to misuse our position to gratify our pride" is your own. What is this you are saying, O pillar of learning[1] and latter day Aristarchus,[2] who are so ready to pass judgment upon all writers ? It is all for nothing then that I have studied so long ; that, as Juvenal says,[3] "I have so often withdrawn my hand from the ferule." The moment I leave the harbour I run aground. Well, to err is human and to confess one's error wise. Do you therefore, who are so ready to criticise and to instruct me, set me right and give me a word for word rendering of the passage. You tell me I should have said : "Beloved, we ought not to be carried away by the estimation of the clergy." Here, indeed we have eloquence worthy of Plautus, here we have Attic grace, the true style of the Muses. The common proverb is true of me : "He who trains an ox for athletics loses both oil and money."[4] Still he is not to blame who merely puts on the mask and plays the tragedy for another : his teachers[5] are the real culprits ; since they for a great price have taught him —to know nothing. I do not think the worse of any Christian because he lacks skill to express himself ; and I heartily wish that we could all say with Socrates "I know that I know nothing ;"[6] and carry out the precept of another wise man, "Know thyself."[7] I have always held in esteem a holy simplicity but not a wordy rudeness. He who declares that he imitates the style of apostles should first imitate the virtue of their lives ; the great holiness of which made up for much plainness of speech. They confuted the syllogisms of Aristotle and the perverse ingenuities of Chrysippus by raising the dead. Still it would be absurd for one of us—living as we do amid the riches of Croesus and the luxuries of Sardanapalus—to make his boast of mere ignorance. We might as well say that all robbers and criminals would be men of culture if they were to hide their blood-stained swords in books of philosophy and not in trunks of trees.

13. I have exceeded the limits of a letter, but I have not exceeded in the expression of my chagrin. For, though I am called a falsifier, and have my reputation torn to shreds, wherever there are shuttles and looms and women to

---

[1] Amos vi. 4-6.
[2] Jerome's Vulgate version supplied from the Hebrew the omissions and removed the redundancies of the old Latin version. These were due to the uncertain text of the LXX., on which alone the old Latin version was founded.
[3] This statement is not borne out by the facts.
[4] Cf. Deut. vii. 13.   [5] πρόαρθρα.
[6] Lit. 'with the heaven and with the earth' (Gen. i. 1). In Hebrew the preposition 'with' is identical in form with the sign of the accus. Hence Aquila's rendering.

[1] Jerome apostrophises his critic.
[2] The famous grammarian and critic of Homer.
[3] Juv. i. 15.
[4] Oleum perdit et impensas qui bovem mittit ad ceroma.
[5] Rufinus and Melania, who were believed by Jerome to have instigated the theft. Their names are inserted in some copies.
[6] Plato, Apol. Soc. 21, 22.
[7] This saying is variously attributed to Chilon and others of the seven wise men of Greece.

work them; I am content to repudiate the charge without retaliating in kind. I leave everything to your discretion. You can read the letter of Epiphanius both in Greek and in Latin; and, if you do so, you will see at once the value of my accusers' lamentations and insulting complaints. For the rest, I am satisfied to have instructed one of my dearest friends and am content simply to stay quiet in my cell and to wait for the day of judgment. If it may be so, and if my enemies allow it, I hope to write for you, not philippics like those of Demosthenes or Tully, but commentaries upon the scriptures.

LETTER LVIII.

TO PAULINUS.

In this his second letter to Paulinus of Nola Jerome dissuades him from making a pilgrimage to the Holy Places, and describes Jerusalem not as it ought to be but as it is. He then gives his friend counsels for his life similar to those which he has previously addressed to Nepotian, praises Paulinus for his Panegyric (now no longer extant) on the Emperor Theodosius, compares his style with those of the great writers of the Latin Church, and concludes with a commendation of his messenger, that Vigilantius who was soon to become the object of his bitterest contempt. Written about the year 395 A.D.

1. "A good man out of the good treasure of the heart bringeth forth good things,"[1] and "every tree is known by his fruit."[2] You measure me by the scale of your own virtues and because of your own greatness magnify my littleness. You take the lowest room at the banquet that the goodman of the house may bid you to go up higher.[3] For what is there in me or what qualities do I possess that should merit praise from a man of learning? that I, small and lowly as I am, should be eulogized by lips which have pleaded on behalf of our most religious sovereign? Do not, my dearest brother, estimate my worth by the number of my years. Gray hairs are not wisdom; it is wisdom which is as good as gray hairs. At least that is what Solomon says: "wisdom is the gray hair unto men."[4] Moses too in choosing the seventy elders is told to take those whom he knows to be elders indeed, and to select them not for their years but for their discretion.[5] And, as a boy, Daniel judges old men and in the flower of youth condemns the incontinence of age.[6] Do not, I repeat, weigh faith by years, nor suppose me better than yourself merely because I have enlisted under Christ's banner earlier than you. The apostle Paul, that chosen vessel framed out of a perse-

cutor,[1] though last in the apostolic order is first in merit. For though last he has laboured more than they all.[2] To Judas it was once said: "thou art a man who didst take sweet food with me, my guide and mine acquaintance; we walked in the house of God with company:"[3] yet the Saviour accuses him of betraying his friend and master. A line of Virgil well describes his end:

From a high beam he knots a hideous death.[4]

The dying robber, on the contrary, exchanges the cross for paradise and turns to martyrdom the penalty of murder. How many there are nowadays who have lived so long that they bear corpses rather than bodies and are like whited sepulchres filled with dead men's bones![5] A newly kindled heat is more effective than a long continued lukewarmness.

2. As for you, when you hear the Saviour's counsel: "if thou wilt be perfect, go and sell that thou hast, and give to the poor, and come follow me,"[6] you translate his words into action; and baring yourself to follow the bare cross[7] you mount Jacob's ladder the easier for carrying nothing. Your dress changes with the change in your convictions, and you aim at no showy shabbiness which leaves your purse as full as before. No, with pure hands and a clear conscience you make it your glory that you are poor both in spirit and in deed. There is nothing great in wearing a sad or a disfigured face, in simulating and in showing off fasts, or in wearing a cheap cloak while you retain a large income. When Crates the Theban—a millionaire of days gone by—was on his way to Athens to study philosophy, he cast away untold gold in the belief that wealth could not be compatible with virtue. What a contrast he offers to us, the disciples of a poor Christ, who cram our pockets with gold and cling under pretext of almsgiving to our old riches. How can we faithfully distribute what belongs to another when we thus timidly keep back what is our own?[8] When the stomach is full, it is easy to talk of fasting. What is praiseworthy is not to have been at Jerusalem but to have lived a good life while there.[9] The city which we are to praise and to seek is not that which has slain the prophets[10] and shed the blood of Christ, but that which is made glad by the streams of the river,[11] which is set upon a mountain and so cannot be hid,[12] which the apostle declares to be a mother of the saints,[13] and in which he rejoices to have his citizenship with the righteous.[14]

---

[1] Acts ix. 15.   [2] 1 Cor. xv. 10.
[3] Ps. lv. 13: *Consessu* substituted for *consensu* of the Vulgate.
[4] Virgil, Æn. xii. 603.   [5] Matt. xxiii. 27.   [6] Matt. xix. 21.
[7] Compare Letter LII. § 5.   [8] Cf. Luke xvi. 12.
[9] Cicero, pro Murena, V.   [10] Matt. xxiii. 37.   [11] Ps. xlvi. 4.
[12] Matt. v. 14.   [13] Gal. iv. 26.   [14] Phil. iii. 20., RV.

---

[1] Matt. xii. 35.   [2] Luke vi. 44.   [3] Luke xiv. 10.
[4] Wisd. iv. 9.   [5] Nu. xi. 16.   [6] Story of Susannah.

3. In speaking thus I am not laying myself open to a charge of inconsistency or condemning the course which I have myself taken. It is not, I believe, for nothing that I, like Abraham, have left my home and people. But I do not presume to limit God's omnipotence or to restrict to a narrow strip of earth Him whom the heaven cannot contain. Each believer is judged not by his residence in this place or in that but according to the deserts of his faith. The true worshippers worship the Father neither at Jerusalem nor on mount Gerizim ; for "God is a spirit, and they that worship Him must worship Him in spirit and in truth." [1] "Now the spirit bloweth where it listeth," [2] and "the earth is the Lord's and the fulness thereof." [3] When the fleece of Judæa was made dry although the whole world was wet with the dew of heaven,[4] and when many came from the East and from the West [5] and sat in Abraham's bosom : [6] then God ceased to be known in Judah only and His name to be great in Israel alone ; [7] the sound of the apostles went out into all the earth and their words into the ends of the world.[8] The Saviour Himself speaking to His disciples in the temple [9] said : "arise, let us go hence," [10] and to the Jews : "your house is left unto you desolate." [11] If heaven and earth must pass away,[12] obviously all things that are earthly must pass away also. Therefore the spots which witnessed the crucifixion and the resurrection profit those only who bear their several crosses, who day by day rise again with Christ, and who thus shew themselves worthy of an abode so holy. Those who say "the temple of the Lord, the temple of the Lord," [13] should give ear to the words of the apostle : "ye are the temple of the Lord," [14] and the Holy Ghost "dwelleth in you." [15] Access to the courts of heaven is as easy from Britain as it is from Jerusalem ; for "the kingdom of God is within you." [16] Antony and the hosts of monks who are in Egypt, Mesopotamia, Pontus, Cappadocia, and Armenia, have never seen Jerusalem : and the door of Paradise is opened for them at a distance from it. The blessed Hilarion, though a native of and a dweller in Palestine, only set eyes on Jerusalem for a single day, not wishing on the one hand when he was so near to neglect the holy places, nor yet on the other to appear to confine God within local limits. From the time of Hadrian to the reign of Constantine—a period of about one hundred and eighty years [1]—the spot which had witnessed the resurrection was occupied by a figure of Jupiter ; while on the rock where the cross had stood, a marble statue of Venus was set up by the heathen and became an object of worship. The original persecutors indeed, supposed that by polluting our holy places they would deprive us of our faith in the passion and in the resurrection. Even my own Bethlehem, as it now is, that most venerable spot in the whole world of which the psalmist sings : "the truth hath sprung out of the earth," [2] was overshadowed by a grove of Tammuz,[3] that is of Adonis ; and in the very cave [4] where the infant Christ had uttered His earliest cry lamentation was made for the paramour of Venus.[5]

4. Why, you will say, do I make these remote allusions ? To assure you that nothing is lacking to your faith although you have not seen Jerusalem and that I am none the better for living where I do. Be assured that whether you dwell here or elsewhere, a like recompense is in store for your good works with our Lord. Indeed, if I am frankly to express my own feelings, when I take into consideration your vows and the earnestness with which you have renounced the world, I hold that as long as you live in the country one place is as good as another. Forsake cities and their crowds, live on a small patch of ground, seek Christ in solitude, pray on the mount alone with Jesus,[6] keep near to holy places : keep out of cities, I say, and you will never lose your vocation. My advice concerns not bishops, presbyters, or the clergy for these have a different duty. I am speaking only to a monk who having been a man of note in the world has laid the price of his possessions at the apostles' feet,[7] to shew men that they must trample on their money, and has resolved to live a life of loneliness and seclusion and always to continue to reject what he has once rejected. Had the scenes of the Passion and of the Resurrection been elsewhere than in a populous city with court and garrison, with prostitutes, playactors, and buffoons, and with the medley of persons usually found in such centres ; or had the crowds which thronged it been composed of monks ; then a city would be a desirable abode for those who have embraced the monastic life. But, as things are, it would be the height of folly first to renounce the world, to

---

[1] Joh. iv. 24.   [2] Joh. iii. 8, RV. marg.
[3] Ps. xxiv. 1.   [4] Judg. vi. 36-40.   [5] Luke xiii. 29.
[6] Luke xvi. 22.   [7] Ps. lxxvi. 1.   [8] Ps. xix. 4.
[9] Only the second sentence was spoken in the temple : the first was uttered in the chamber of the last supper.
[10] Joh. xiv. 31.   [11] Matt. xxiii. 38.   [12] Luke xxi. 33.
[13] Jer. vii. 4.   [14] 2 Cor. vi. 16.
[15] Rom. viii. 11.   [16] Luke xvii. 21.

[1] Hadrian died in 138 A. D.; Constantine became Emperor in 306 A. D.
[2] Ps. lxxxv. 11, Vulg.   [3] Ezek. viii. 14.
[4] For the tradition that Christ was born in a cave Justin Martyr is the earliest authority (dial. c. Try. 78).
[5] Adonis, killed by a boar and spending half his time in the upper, half in the lower world, is a type of summer overcome and overcome by winter.
[6] Cf. Luke, vi.   [7] Acts iv. 37.

forswear one's country, to forsake cities, to profess one's self a monk ; and then to live among still greater numbers the same kind of life that you would have lived in your own country. Men rush here from all quarters of the world, the city is filled with people of every race, and so great is the throng of men and women that here you will have to tolerate in its full dimensions an evil from which you desired to flee when you found it partially developed elsewhere.

5. Since you ask me as a brother in what path you should walk, I will be open with you. If you wish to take duty as a presbyter, and are attracted by the work or dignity which falls to the lot of a bishop, live in cities and walled towns,[1] and by so doing turn the salvation of others into the profit of your own soul. But if you desire to be in deed what you are in name—a monk,[2] that is, one who lives alone, what have you to do with cities which are the homes not of solitaries but of crowds ? Every mode of life has its own exponents. For instance, let Roman generals imitate men like Camillus, Fabricius, Regulus, and Scipio. Let philosophers take for models Pythagoras, Socrates, Plato, and Aristotle. Let poets strive to rival Homer, Virgil, Menander, and Terence. Let writers of history follow Thucydides, Sallust, Herodotus and Livy. Let orators find masters in Lysias, the Gracchi, Demosthenes, and Tully. And, to come to our own case, let bishops and presbyters take for their examples the apostles or their companions ; and as they hold the rank which these once held, let them endeavour to exhibit the same excellence. And last of all let us monks take as the patterns which we are to follow the lives of Paul, of Antony, of Julian, of Hilarion, of the Macarii. And to go back to the authority of scripture, we have our masters in Elijah and Elisha, and our leaders in the sons of the prophets ; who lived in fields and solitary places and made themselves tents by the waters of Jordan.[3] The sons of Rechab too are of the number who drank neither wine nor strong drink and who abode in tents ; men whom God's voice praises through Jeremiah,[4] and to whom a promise is made that there shall never be wanting a man of their stock to stand before God.[5] This is probably what is meant by the title of the seventy-first psalm : " of the sons of Jonadab and of those who were first led into captivity." [6] The person intended is Jonadab the son of Rechab who is described in the book of Kings [7] as having gone up into the chariot of Jehu. His sons having always

lived in tents until at last (owing to the inroads made by the Chaldean army) they were forced to come into Jerusalem, are described [1] as being the first to undergo captivity ; because after the freedom of their lonely life they found confinement in a city as bad as imprisonment.

6. Since you are not wholly independent but are bound to a wife who is your sister in the Lord, I entreat you—whether here or there —that you will avoid large gatherings, visits official and complimentary, and social parties, indulgences all of which tend to enchain the soul. Let your food be coarse—say cabbage and pulse—and do not take it until evening. Sometimes as a great delicacy you may have some small fish. He who longs for Christ and feeds upon the true bread cares little for dainties which must be transmuted into ordure. Food that you cannot taste when once it has passed your gullet might as well be—so far as you are concerned—bread and pulse. You have my books against Jovinian which speak yet more largely of despising the appetite and the palate. Let some holy volume be ever in your hand. Pray constantly, and bowing down your body lift up your mind to the Lord. Keep frequent vigils and sleep often on an empty stomach. Avoid tittle-tattle and all self-laudation. Flee from wheedling flatterers as from open enemies. Distribute with your own hand provisions to alleviate the miseries of the poor and of the brethren. With your own hands, I say, for good faith is rare among men. You do not believe what I say ? Think of Judas and his bag. Seek not a lowly garb for a swelling soul. Avoid the society of men of the world, especially if they are in power. Why need you look again on things contempt for which has made you a monk ? Above all let your sister [2] hold aloof from married ladies. And, if women round her wear silk dresses and gems while she is meanly attired, let her neither fret nor congratulate herself. For by so doing she will either regret her resolution or sow the seeds of pride. If you are already famed as a faithful steward of your own substance, do not take other people's money to give away. You understand what I mean, for the Lord has given you understanding in all things. Be simple as a dove and lay snares for no man : but be cunning as a serpent and let no man lay snares for you.[3] For a Christian who allows others to deceive him is almost at much at fault as one who tries to deceive others. If a man talks to you always or nearly always about money (except it be about almsgiving, a topic which is open to all) treat him as a broker rather than a monk. Besides food and clothing and things manifestly neces-

---

[1] Castella.
[2] Monachus, lit. "a solitary." Men frequently at this time made vows, especially those of celibacy, without entering a monastery. [3] 2 Kings vi. 1, 2. [4] Jer. xxxv. [5] Jer. xxxv. 19. [6] This title occurs only in the LXX. [7] 2 Kings, x. 15, 16.

---

[1] Jer. xxxv. 11. [2] Therasia, the wife of Paulinus is meant.
[3] Matt. x. 16.

sary give no man anything; for dogs must not eat the children's bread.[1]

7. The true temple of Christ is the believer's soul; adorn this, clothe it, offer gifts to it, welcome Christ in it. What use are walls blazing with jewels when Christ in His poor[2] is in danger of perishing from hunger? Your possessions are no longer your own but a stewardship is entrusted to you. Remember Ananias and Sapphira who from fear of the future kept what was their own, and be careful for your part not rashly to squander what is Christ's. Do not, that is, by an error of judgment give the property of the poor to those who are not poor; lest, as a wise man has told us,[3] charity prove the death of charity. Look not upon

> Gay trappings or a Cato's empty name.[4]

In the words of Persius, God says :—

> I know thy thoughts and read thine inmost soul.[5]

To be a Christian is the great thing, not merely to seem one. And somehow or other those please the world most who please Christ least. In speaking thus I am not like the sow lecturing Minerva; but, as a friend warns a friend, so I warn you before you embark on your new course. I would rather fail in ability than in will to serve you; for my wish is that where I have fallen you may keep your footing.

8. It is with much pleasure that I have read the book which you have sent to me containing your wise and eloquent defence of the emperor Theodosius; and your arrangement of the subject has particularly pleased me. While in the earlier chapters you surpass others, in the latter you surpass yourself. Your style is terse and neat; it has all the purity of Tully, and yet it is packed with meaning. For, as someone has said,[6] that speech is a failure of which men only praise the diction. You have been successful in preserving both sequence of subjects and logical connexion. Whatever sentence one takes, it is always a conclusion to what goes before or an introduction to what follows. Theodosius is fortunate in having a Christian orator like you to plead his cause. You have made his purple illustrious and have consecrated for future ages his useful laws. Go on and prosper, for, if such be your first ventures in the field, what will you not do when you become a trained soldier? Oh! that it were mine to conduct a genius like you, not (as the poets sing) through the Aonian mountains and the peaks of Helicon but through Zion and Tabor and the high places of Sinai. If I might teach you what I have learned myself and might pass on to you the mystic rolls of the prophets, then might we give birth to something such as Greece with all her learning could not shew.

9. Hear me, therefore, my fellow-servant, my friend, my brother; give ear for a moment that I may tell you how you are to walk in the holy scriptures. All that we read in the divine books, while glistening and shining without, is yet far sweeter within. "He who desires to eat the kernel must first break the nut."[1] "Open thou mine eyes," says David, "that I may behold wondrous things out of thy law."[2] Now, if so great a prophet confesses that he is in the darkness of ignorance; how deep, think you, must be the night of misapprehension with which we, mere babes and unweaned infants, are enveloped! Now this veil rests not only on the face of Moses,[3] but on the evangelists and the apostles as well.[4] To the multitudes the Saviour spoke only in parables and, to make it clear that His words had a mystical meaning, said :—"he that hath ears to hear, let him hear."[5] Unless all things that are written are opened by Him "who hath the key of David, who openeth and no man shutteth, and shutteth and no man openeth,"[6] no one can undo the lock or set them before you. If only you had the foundation which He alone can give; nay, if even His fingers were but passed over your work; there would be nothing finer than your volumes, nothing more learned, nothing more attractive, nothing more Latin.

10. Tertullian is packed with meaning but his style is rugged and uncouth. The blessed Cyprian like a fountain of pure water flows softly and sweetly but, as he is taken up with exhortations to virtue and with the troubles consequent on persecution, he has nowhere discussed the divine scriptures. Victorinus, although he has the glory of a martyr's crown, yet cannot express what he knows. Lactantius has a flow of eloquence worthy of Tully: would that he had been as ready to teach our doctrines as he was to pull down those of others! Arnobius is lengthy and unequal, and often confused from not making a proper division of his subject. That reverend man Hilary gains in height from his Gallic buskin; yet, adorned as he is with the flowers of Greek rhetoric, he sometimes entangles himself in long periods and offers by no means easy reading to the less learned brethren. I say

---

[1] Matt. xv. 26.　[2] Matt. xxv. 40.　[3] Cicero, de Off. II. xv.
[4] Probably a quotation from memory incorrectly made up from Lucan's ' Nomina vana Catonis ' (i. 313).
[5] Persius, iii. 30.　[6] Quintilian, Inst. Or. viii. Proem.

[1] Plautus, Curc. I. i. 55.　[2] Ps. cxix. 18.　[3] 2 Cor. iii. 14. 15.
[4] i.e., the new testament as well as the old may have its true meaning concealed from some.
[5] Luke viii. 8, 10.　[6] Rev. iii. 7.

nothing of other writers whether dead or living; others will hereafter judge them both for good and for evil.[1]

11. I will come to yourself, my fellow-mystic, my companion, and my friend; my friend, I say, though not yet personally known: and I will ask you not to suspect a flatterer in one so intimate. Better that you should think me mistaken or led astray by affection than that you should hold me capable of fawning on a friend. You have a great intellect and an inexhaustible store of language, your diction is fluent and pure, your fluency and purity are mingled with wisdom. Your head is clear and all your senses keen. Were you to add to this wisdom and eloquence a careful study and knowledge of scripture, I should soon see you holding our citadel against all comers; you would go up with Joab upon the roof of Zion,[2] and sing upon the housetops what you had learned in the secret chambers.[3] Gird up, I pray you, gird up your loins. As Horace says:—

Life hath no gifts for men except they toil.[4]

Shew yourself as much a man of note in the church, as you were before in the senate. Provide for yourself riches which you may spend daily yet they will not fail. Provide them while you are still strong and while as yet your head has no gray hairs: before, in the words of Virgil,

Diseases creep on you, and gloomy age,
And pain, and cruel death's inclemency.[5]

I am not content with mediocrity for you: I desire all that you do to be of the highest excellence.

How heartily I have welcomed the reverend presbyter Vigilantius,[6] his own lips will tell you better than this letter. Why he has so soon left us and started afresh I cannot say; and, indeed, I do not wish to hurt anyone's feelings.[7] Still, mere passer-by as he was, in haste to continue his journey, I managed to keep him back until I had given him a taste of my friendship for you. Thus you can learn from him what you want to know about me. Kindly salute your reverend sister[8] and fellow-servant, who with you fights the good fight in the Lord.

---

[1] Cf. Letter LXX. 5.
[2] I Chron. xi. 5, 6.
[3] Cf. Luke xii. 3.
[4] Horace, Sat. I. ix. 59, 60.
[5] Virgil, Georg. iii. 67, 68.
[6] Afterwards noted as an assailant of Jerome's ascetic doctrines. See the introduction to Letter LXI.
[7] The allusion seems to be to the behaviour of Vigilantius during an earthquake which occurred when he was at Bethlehem. His fright on the occasion exposed him to the ridicule of the community there. (Against Vig., i. 11.)
[8] As before, Therasia, the wife of Paulinus is meant.

LETTER LIX.

TO MARCELLA.

An answer to five questions put to Jerome by Marcella in a letter not preserved. The questions are as follows.

(1) What are the things which eye hath not seen nor ear heard (I Cor. ii. 9)? Jerome answers that they are spiritual things which as such can only be spiritually discerned.

(2) Is it not a mistake to identify the sheep and the goats of Christ's parable (Matt. xxv. 31 sqq.) with Christians and heathens? Are they not rather the good and the bad? For an answer to this question Jerome refers Marcella to his treatise against Jovinian (II. §§ 18–23).

(3) Paul says that some shall be "alive and remain unto the coming of the Lord;" and that they shall be "caught up to meet the Lord in the air" (I Thess. iv. 15, 17). Are we to suppose this assumption to be corporeal and that those assumed will escape death? Yes, Jerome answers, but their bodies will be glorified.

(4) How is John xx. 17, "touch me not," to be reconciled with Matt. xxviii. 9, "they came and held him by the feet"? In the one case, Jerome replies, Mary Magdalen failed to recognize the divinity of Jesus; in the other the women recognized it. Accordingly they were admitted to a privilege which was denied to her.

(5) Was the risen Christ before His ascension present only with the disciples, or was He in heaven and elsewhere as well? The latter according to Jerome is the true doctrine. "The Divine Nature," he writes, "exists everywhere in its entirety. Christ, therefore, was at one and the same time with the apostles and with the angels; in the Father and in the uttermost parts of the sea. So afterwards he was with Thomas in India, with Peter at Rome, with Paul in Illyricum, with Titus in Crete, with Andrew in Achaia." The date of the letter is A. D. 395 or A. D. 396.

LETTER LX.

TO HELIODORUS.

One of Jerome's finest letters, written to console his old friend, Heliodorus, now Bp. of Altinum, for the loss of his nephew Nepotian who had died of fever a short time previously. Jerome tries to soothe his friend's grief (1) by contrasting pagan despair or resignation with Christian hope, (2) by an eulogy of the departed both as man and presbyter, and (3) by a review of the evils which then beset the Empire and from which, as he contended, Nepotian had been removed. The letter is marked throughout with deep and sincere feeling. Its date is 396 A. D.

1. Small wits cannot grapple large themes but venturing beyond their strength fail in the very attempt; and, the greater a subject is, the more completely is he overwhelmed who cannot find words to unfold its grandeur. Nepotian who was mine and yours and ours—or rather who was Christ's and because Christ's all the more ours—has forsaken us his elders so that we are smitten with pangs of regret and overcome with a grief which is past bearing. We supposed him our heir, yet now his corpse is all that is ours. For whom shall my intellect now labour? Whom shall my poor

letters desire to please? Where is he, the impeller of my work, whose voice was sweeter than a swan's last song? My mind is dazed, my hand trembles, a mist covers my eyes, stammering seizes my tongue. Whatever my words, they seem as good as unspoken seeing that he no longer hears them. My very pen seems to feel his loss, my very wax tablet looks dull and sad; the one is covered with rust, the other with mould. As often as I try to express myself in words and to scatter the flowers of this encomium upon his tomb, my eyes fill with tears, my grief returns, and I can think of nothing but his death. It was a custom in former days for children over the dead bodies of their parents publicly to proclaim their praises and (as when pathetic songs are sung) to draw tears from the eyes and sighs from the breasts of those who heard them. But in our case, behold, the order of things is changed: to deal us this blow nature has forfeited her rights. For the respect which the young man should have paid to his elders, we his elders are paying to him.

2. What shall I do then? Shall I join my tears to yours? The apostle forbids me for he speaks of dead Christians as "them which are asleep."[1] So too in the gospel the Lord says, "the damsel is not dead but sleepeth,"[2] and Lazarus when he is raised from the dead is said to have been asleep.[3] No, I will be glad and rejoice that "speedily he was taken away lest that wickedness should alter his understanding" for "his soul pleased the Lord."[4] But though I am loth to give way and combat my feelings, tears flow down my cheeks, and in spite of the teachings of virtue and the hope of the resurrection a passion of regret crushes my too yielding mind. O death that dividest brothers knit together in love, how cruel, how ruthless thou art so to sunder them! "The Lord hath fetched a burning wind that cometh up from the wilderness: which hath dried thy veins and hath made thy well spring desolate."[5] Thou didst swallow up our Jonah, but even in thy belly He still lived. Thou didst carry Him as one dead, that the world's storm might be stilled and our Nineveh saved by His preaching. He, yes He, conquered thee, He slew thee, that fugitive prophet who left His home, gave up His inheritance and surrendered his dear life into the hands of those who sought it. He it was who of old threatened thee in Hosea: "O death, I will be thy plagues; O grave, I will be thy destruction."[6] By His death thou art dead; by His death we live. Thou hast swallowed up and thou art swallowed up. Whilst thou art smitten with a longing for the

body assumed by Him, and whilst thy greedy jaws fancy it a prey, thy inward parts are wounded with hooked fangs.

3. To Thee, O Saviour Christ, do we Thy creatures offer thanks that, when Thou wast slain, Thou didst slay our mighty adversary. Before Thy coming was there any being more miserable than man who cowering at the dread prospect of eternal death did but receive life that he might perish! For "death reigned from Adam to Moses even over them that had not sinned after the similitude of Adam's transgression."[1] If Abraham, Isaac, and Jacob be in hell, who can be in the kingdom of heaven? If Thy friends—even those who had not sinned themselves—were yet for the sins of another liable to the punishment of offending Adam, what must we think of those who have said in their hearts "There is no God;" who "are corrupt and abominable"[2] in their self-will, and of whom it is said "they are gone out of the way, they are become unprofitable; there is none that doeth good, no not one"?[3] Even if Lazarus is seen in Abraham's bosom and in a place of refreshment, still the lower regions cannot be compared with the kingdom of heaven. Before Christ's coming Abraham is in the lower regions: after Christ's coming the robber is in paradise. And therefore at His rising again "many bodies of the saints which slept arose, and were seen in the heavenly Jerusalem."[4] Then was fulfilled the saying: "Awake thou that sleepest, and arise from the dead, and Christ shall give thee light."[5] John the Baptist cries in the desert: "repent ye; for the kingdom of heaven is at hand."[6] For "from the days of John the Baptist the kingdom of heaven suffereth violence and the violent take it by force."[7] The flaming sword that keeps the way of paradise and the cherubim that are stationed at its doors[8] are alike quenched and unloosed by the blood of Christ.[9] It is not surprising that this should be promised us in the resurrection: for as many of us as living in the flesh do not live after the flesh,[10] have our citizenship in heaven,[11] and while we are still here on earth we are told that "the kingdom of heaven is within us."[12]

4. Moreover before the resurrection of Christ God was "known in Judah" only and "His name was great in Israel" alone.[13] And they who knew Him were despite their knowledge dragged down to hell. Where in those days were the inhabitants of the globe from India to Britain, from the frozen zone of the North to the burning heat of the Atlantic ocean?

---

[1] 1 Thess. iv. 13. [2] Mark v. 39. [3] Joh. xi. 11.
[4] Wisd. iv. 11, 14. [5] Hos. xiii. 15, LXX. [6] Hos. xiii. 14.

[1] Rom. v. 14. [2] Ps. xiv. 1. [3] Rom. iii. 12.
[4] Matt. xxvii. 52, 53. [5] Eph. v. 14.
[6] Matt. iii. 2. [7] Matt. xi. 12. [8] Gen. iii. 24.
[9] Cf. Letter XXXIX. § 4. [10] 2 Cor. x 3.
[11] Phi. iii. 20. [12] Luke xvii. 21. [13] Ps. lxxvi. 1.

Where were the countless peoples of the world? Where the great multitudes

Unlike in tongue, unlike in dress and arms?[1]

They were crushed like fishes and locusts, like flies and gnats. For apart from knowledge of his Creator every man is but a brute. But now the voices and writings of all nations proclaim the passion and the resurrection of Christ. I say nothing of the Jews, the Greeks, and the Romans, peoples which the Lord has dedicated to His faith by the title written on His cross.[2] The immortality of the soul and its continuance after the dissolution of the body—truths of which Pythagoras dreamed, which Democritus refused to believe, and which Socrates discussed in prison to console himself for the sentence passed upon him—are now the familiar themes of Indian and of Persian, of Goth and of Egyptian. The fierce Bessians[3] and the throng of skinclad savages who used to offer human sacrifices in honour of the dead have broken out of their harsh discord into the sweet music of the cross and Christ is the one cry of the whole world.

5. What can we do, my soul? Whither must we turn? What must we take up first? What must we pass over? Have you forgotten the precepts of the rhetoricians? Are you so preoccupied with grief, so overcome with tears, so hindered with sobs, that you forget all logical sequence? Where are the studies you have pursued from your childhood? Where is that saying of Anaxagoras and Telamon (which you have always commended) "I knew myself to have begotten a mortal"?[4] I have read the books of Crantor which he wrote to soothe his grief and which Cicero has imitated.[5] I have read the consolatory writings of Plato, Diogenes, Clitomachus, Carneades, Posidonius, who at different times strove by book or letter to lessen the grief of various persons. Consequently, were my own wit to dry up, it could be watered anew from the fountains which these have opened. They set before us examples without number; and particularly those of Pericles and of Socrates's pupil Xenophon. The former of these after the loss of his two sons put on a garland and delivered a harangue;[6] while the latter, on hearing when he was offering sacrifice that his son had been slain in war, is said to have laid down his garland; and then, on learning that he had fallen fighting bravely, is said to have put it on his head again. What shall I say of those

Roman generals whose heroic virtues glitter like stars on the pages of Latin history? Pulvillus was dedicating the capitol[1] when receiving the news of his son's sudden death, he gave orders that the funeral should take place without him. Lucius Paullus[2] entered the city in triumph in the week which intervened between the funerals of his two sons. I pass over the Maximi, the Catos, the Galli, the Pisos, the Bruti, the Scævolas, the Metelli, the Scauri, the Marii, the Crassi, the Marcelli, the Aufidii, men who shewed equal fortitude in sorrow and war, and whose bereavements Tully has set forth in his book *Of consolation*. I pass them over lest I should seem to have chosen the words and woes of others in preference to my own. Yet even these instances may suffice to ensure us mortification if our faith fails to surpass the achievements of unbelief.

6. Let me come then to my proper subject. I will not beat my breast with Jacob and with David for sons dying in the Law, but I will receive them rising again with Christ in the Gospel. The Jew's mourning is the Christian's joy. "Weeping may endure for a night but joy cometh in the morning."[3] "The night is far spent, the day is at hand."[4] Accordingly when Moses dies, mourning is made for him,[5] but when Joshua is buried, it is without tears or funeral pomp.[6] All that can be drawn from scripture on the subject of lamentation I have briefly set forth in the letter of consolation which I addressed to Paula at Rome.[7] Now I must take another path to arrive at the same goal. Otherwise I shall seem to be walking anew in a track once beaten but now long disused.

7. We know indeed that our Nepotian is with Christ and that he has joined the choirs of the saints. What here with us he groped after on earth afar off and sought for to the best of his judgment, there he sees nigh at hand, so that he can say: "as we have heard so have we seen in the city of the Lord of hosts, in the city of our God."[8] Still we cannot bear the feeling of his absence, and grieve, if not for him, for ourselves. The greater the happiness which he enjoys, the deeper the sorrow in which the loss of a blessing so great plunges us. The sisters of Lazarus could not help weeping for him, although they knew that he would rise again. And the Saviour himself—to shew that he possessed true human feeling—mourned for him whom He was about to raise.[9] His apostle also, though he says: "I desire to depart and to be with Christ,"[10] and elsewhere "to

[1] Virg. A. viii. 723.   [2] Luke xxiii. 38.
[3] A Thracian tribe.
[4] The words are quoted by Cicero (T. Q. iii. 13) apparently from the Telamon of Ennius. They are ascribed to Anaxagoras by Diog. Laert.
[5] In his *De consolatione* of which only a few fragments remain.
[6] Val. Max. v. 10.

[1] In the first year of the Republic. Acc. to Livy (ii. 8) his son was not really dead.
[2] The conqueror of Macedonia. He celebrated his triumph 167 B.C.
[3] Ps. xxx. 5.   [4] Rom. xiii. 12.   [5] Deut. xxxiv. 8.
[6] Josh. xxiv. 30.   [7] Letter XXXIX.
[8] Ps. xlviii. 8.   [9] Joh. xi. 35.   [10] Phi. i. 23.

me to live is Christ and to die is gain,"[1] thanks God that Epaphras[2] (who had been "sick nigh unto death") has been given back to him that he might not have sorrow upon sorrow.[3] Words prompted not by the fear that springs of unbelief but by the passionate regret that comes of true affection. How much more deeply must you who were to Nepotian both uncle and bishop, (that is, a father both in the flesh and in the spirit), deplore the loss of one so dear, as though your heart were torn from you. Set a limit, I pray you, to your sorrow and remember the saying "in nothing overmuch."[4] Bind up for a little while your wound and listen to the praises of one in whose virtue you have always delighted. Do not grieve that you have lost such a paragon : rejoice rather that he has once been yours. As on a small tablet men depict the configuration of the earth, so in this little scroll of mine you may see his virtues if not fully depicted at least sketched in outline. I beg that you will take the will for the performance.

8. The advice of the rhetoricians in such cases is that you should first search out the remote ancestors of the person to be eulogized and recount their exploits, and then come gradually to your hero ; so as to make him more illustrious by the virtues of his forefathers, and to shew either that he is a worthy successor of good men, or that he has conferred lustre upon a lineage in itself obscure. But as my duty is to sing the praises of the soul, I will not dwell upon those fleshly advantages which Nepotian for his part always despised. Nor will I boast of his family, that is of the good points belonging not to him but to others ; for even those holy men Abraham and Isaac had for sons the sinners Ishmael and Esau. And on the other hand Jephthah who is reckoned by the apostle in the roll of the righteous[5] is the son of a harlot.[6] It is said "the soul that sinneth, it shall die."[7] The soul therefore that has not sinned shall live. Neither the virtues nor the vices of parents are imputed to their children. God takes account of us only from the time when we are born anew in Christ. Paul, the persecutor of the church, who is in the morning the ravening wolf of Benjamin,[8] in the evening "gave food,"[9] that is yields himself up to the sheep Ananias.[10] Let us likewise reckon our Nepotian a crying babe and an untutored child who has been born to us in a moment fresh from the waters of Jordan.

9. Another would perhaps describe how for his salvation you left the east and the desert and how you soothed me your dearest comrade by holding out hopes of a return : and all this that you might save, if possible, both your sister, then a widow with one little child, or, should she reject your counsels, at any rate your sweet little nephew. It was of him that I once used the prophetic words : "though your little nephew cling to your neck."[1] Another, I say, would relate how while Nepotian was still in the service of the court, beneath his uniform and his brilliantly white linen,[2] his skin was chafed with sackcloth ; how, while standing before the powers of this world, his lips were discoloured with fasting ; how still in the uniform of one master he served another ; and how he wore the sword-belt only that he might succour widows and wards, the afflicted and the unhappy. For my part I dislike men to delay the complete dedication of themselves to God. When I read of the centurion Cornelius[3] that he was a just man I immediately hear of his baptism.

10. Still we may approve these things as the swathing bands of an infant faith. He who has been a loyal soldier under a strange banner is sure to deserve the laurel when he comes to serve his own king. When Nepotian laid aside his baldrick and changed his dress, he bestowed upon the poor all the pay that he had received. For he had read the words : "if thou wilt be perfect, sell that thou hast, and give to the poor and follow me,"[4] and again : "ye cannot serve two masters God and Mammon."[5] He kept nothing for himself but a common tunic and cloak to cover him and to keep out the cold. Made in the fashion of his province his attire was not remarkable either for elegance or for squalor. He burned daily to make his way to the monasteries of Egypt, or to visit the communities of Mesopotamia, or at least to live a lonely life in the Dalmatian islands,[6] separated from the mainland only by the strait of Altinum. But he had not the heart to forsake his episcopal uncle in whom he beheld a pattern of many virtues and from whom he could take lessons without going abroad. In one and the same person he both found a monk to imitate and a bishop to revere. What so often happens did not happen here. Constant intimacy did not produce familiarity, nor did familiarity breed contempt. He revered him as a father and every day admired him for some new virtue. To be brief, he became a clergyman, and after passing through the usual stages was ordained a presbyter. Good

[1] Phi. i. 21.   [2] i.e. Epaphroditus.   [3] Phi. ii. 27.
[4] μηδέν ἄγαν, ne quid nimis. A saying of one of the Seven Wise Men of Greece, 6th cent. B.C. See Grote iv. 127.
[5] Heb. xi. 32. [6] Judg. xi. 1. [7] Ezek. xviii. 4. [8] Gen. xlix. 27.
[9] Dedit escam. This is the reading of the LXX. The Vulgate, like the A.V., has "shall divide the spoil." Compare Letter LXIX 6.
[10] Acts ix. 17. (Cf. Letter LXIX. § 6.)

[1] Letter XIV. § 2.
[2] For other allusions to a Roman officer's uniform see Letters LXXIX. § 2 and CXVIII. § 1.
[3] Acts x.   [4] Matt. xix. 21.   [5] Matt. vi. 24.
[6] Like Bonosus (Letter III. 4).

Jesus ! how he sighed and groaned ! how he fasted and fled the eyes of all ! For the first and only time he was angry with his uncle, complaining that the burthen laid upon him was too heavy for him and that his youth unfitted him for the priesthood. But the more he struggled against it, the more he drew to himself the hearts of all : his refusal did but prove him worthy of an office which he was reluctant to assume, and all the more worthy because he declared himself unworthy. We too in our day have our Timothy ; we too have seen that wisdom which is as good as gray hairs ;[1] our Moses has chosen an elder whom he has known to be an elder indeed.[2] Nepotian regarded the clerical state less as an honour than a burthen. He made it his first care to silence envy by humility, and his next to give no cause for scandal that such as assailed his youth might marvel at his continence. He helped the poor, visited the sick, stirred men up to hospitality, soothed them with soft words, rejoiced with those who rejoiced and wept with those who wept.[3] He was a staff to the blind, food to the hungry, hope to the dejected, consolation to the bereaved. Each single virtue was as conspicuous in him as if he possessed no other. Among his fellow-presbyters while ever foremost in work, he was ever satisfied with the lowest place. Any good that he did he ascribed to his uncle : but if the result did not correspond to his expectations, he would say that his uncle knew nothing of it, that it was his own mistake. In public he recognized him as a bishop ; at home he looked upon him as a father. The seriousness of his disposition was mitigated by a cheerful expression. But while his laughter was joyous it was never loud. Christ's virgins and widows he honoured as mothers and exhorted as sisters " with all purity."[4] When he returned home he used to leave the clergyman outside and to give himself over to the hard rule of a monk. Frequent in supplication and watchful in prayer he would offer his tears not to man but to God. His fasts he regulated—as a driver does the pace of his horses—according to the weariness or vigour of his body. When at his uncle's table he would just taste what was set before him, so as to avoid superstition and yet to preserve self-control. In conversing at entertainments his habit was to propose some topic from scripture, to listen modestly, to answer diffidently, to support the right, to refute the wrong, but both without bitterness ; to instruct his opponent rather than to vanquish him. Such was the ingenuous modesty which adorned his youth that he would frankly confess from what sources his several arguments came ; and in this way, while disclaiming a reputation for learning, he came to be held most learned. This he would say is the opinion of Tertullian, that of Cyprian ; this of Lactantius, that of Hilary ; to this effect speaks Minucius Felix, thus Victorinus, after this manner Arnobius. Myself too he would sometimes quote, for he loved me because of my intimacy with his uncle. Indeed by constant reading and long-continued meditation he had made his breast a library of Christ.

11. How often in letters from beyond the sea he urged me to write something to him ! How often he reminded me of the man in the gospel who sought help by night [1] and of the widow who importuned the cruel judge ![2] And when I silently ignored his request and made my petitioner blush by blushing to reply, he put forward his uncle to enforce his suit, knowing that as the boon was for another he would more readily ask it, and that as I held his episcopal office in respect he would more easily obtain it. Accordingly I did what he wished and in a brief essay [3] dedicated our mutual friendship to everlasting remembrance. On receiving this Nepotian boasted that he was richer than Crœsus and wealthier than Darius. He held it in his hands, devoured it with his eyes, kept it in his bosom, repeated it with his lips. And often when he unrolled it upon his couch, he fell asleep with the cherished page upon his breast. When a stranger came or a friend, he rejoiced to let them know my witness to him. The deficiencies of my little book he made good by careful punctuation and varied emphasis, so that when it was read aloud it was always he not I who seemed to please or to displease. Whence came such zeal, if not from the love of God ? Whence came such untiring study of Christ's law, if not from a yearning for Him who gave it ? Let others add coin to coin till their purses are chock-full ; let others demean themselves to sponge on married ladies ; let them be richer as monks than they were as men of the world ; let them possess wealth in the service of a poor Christ such as they never had in the service of a rich devil ; let the church lose breath at the opulence of men who in the world were beggars. Our Nepotian spurns gold and begs only for written books. But while he despises himself in the flesh and walks abroad more splendid than ever in his poverty, he still seeks out everything that may adorn the church.

12. In comparison with what has gone before what I am now about to say may appear trivial,

[1] Wisd. iv. 9.
[2] Nu. xi. 16. Presbyterum. This name (afterwards contracted into Priest) is taken from that of the Elders of Israel.
[3] Rom. xii. 15.   [4] 1 Tim. v. 2.

[1] Luke xi. 5, 8.   [2] Luke xviii. 1, 5.   [3] Letter LII.

but even in trifles the same spirit makes itself manifest. For as we admire the Creator not only as the framer of heaven and earth, of sun and ocean, of elephants, camels, horses, oxen, pards, bears, and lions ; but also as the maker of the most tiny creatures, ants, gnats, flies, worms, and the like, whose shapes we know better than their names, and as in all alike we revere the same creative skill; so the mind that is given to Christ shews the same earnestness in things of small as of great importance, knowing that it must render an account of every idle word.[1] Nepotian took pains to keep the altar bright, the church walls free from soot and the pavement duly swept. He saw that the doorkeeper was constantly at his post, that the doorhangings were in their places, the sanctuary clean and the vessels shining. The careful reverence that he shewed to every rite led him to neglect no duty small or great. Whenever you looked for him in church you found him there.

In Quintus Fabius[2] antiquity admired a nobleman and the author of a history of Rome, yet his paintings gained him more renown than his writings. Our own Bezaleel[3] also and Hiram, the son of a Tyrian woman,[4] are spoken of in scripture as filled with wisdom and the spirit of God because they framed, the one the furniture of the tabernacle, the other that of the temple. For, as it is with fertile tillage-fields and rich plough-lands which at times go out into redundant growths of stalk or ear, so is it with distinguished talents and a mind filled with virtue. They are sure to overflow into elegant and varied accomplishments. Accordingly among the Greeks we hear of a philosopher[5] who used to boast that everything he wore down to his cloak and ring was made by himself. We may pass the same eulogy on our friend, for he adorned both the basilicas of the church and the halls[6] of the martyrs with sketches of flowers, foliage, and vine-tendrils, so that everything attractive in the church, whether made so by its position or by its appearance, bore witness to the labour and zeal of the presbyter set over it.

13. Go on blessed in thy goodness ! What kind of ending should we expect after such a beginning ! Ah ! hapless plight of mortal men and vanity of all life that is not lived in Christ ! Why, O my words, do you shrink back ? Why do you shift and turn ? I fear to come to the end, as if I could put off his death or make his life longer. " All flesh is as grass and all the glory of man as the flower of grass." [1] Where now are that handsome face and dignified figure with which as with a fair garment his beautiful soul was clothed ? The lily began to wither, alas ! when the south wind blew, and the purple violet slowly faded into paleness. Yet while he burned with fever and while the fire of sickness was drying up the fountains of his veins, gasping and weary he still tried to comfort his sorrowing uncle. His countenance shone with gladness, and while all around him wept he and he only smiled. He flung aside his cloak, put out his hand, saw what others failed to see, and even tried to rise that he might welcome new comers. You would have thought that he was starting on a journey instead of dying and that in place of leaving all his friends behind him he was merely passing from some to others. Tears roll down my cheeks and, however much I steel my mind, I cannot disguise the grief that I feel. Who could suppose that at such an hour he would remember his intimacy with me, and that while he struggled for life he would recall the sweetness of study ? Yet grasping his uncle's hand he said to him : " Send this tunic that I wore in the service of Christ to my dear friend, my father in age, but my brother in office, and transfer the affection hitherto claimed by your nephew to one who is as dear to you as he is to me." With these words he passed away holding his uncle's hand and with my name upon his lips.

14. I know how unwilling you were to prove the affection of your people at such a cost, and that you would have preferred to win your countrymen's love while retaining your happiness. Such expressions of feeling, pleasant as they are when all goes well, are doubly welcome in time of sorrow. All Altinum, all Italy mourned Nepotian. The earth received his body ; his soul was given back to Christ. You lost a nephew, the church a priest. He who should have followed you went before you. To the office which you held, he in the judgment of all deserved to succeed. And so one family has had the honour of producing two bishops, the first to be congratulated because he has held the office, the second to be lamented because he has been taken away too soon to hold it. Plato thinks that a wise man's whole life ought to be a meditation of death ;[2] and philosophers praise the sentiment and extol it to the skies. But much more full of power are the words of the apostle : " I die daily through your glory." [4] For to have an ideal is one thing, to realize it another. It is one thing to live so as to die, another to die

---

[1] Matt. xii. 36.
[2] Jerome here confounds two distinct persons : C. Fabius Pictor was the painter ; his grandson Q. Fabius the historian.
[3] Ex. xxxi. 2, 3.
[4] 1 K. vii. 14. A mistake of Jerome. It was Hiram's father who was a Tyrian.
[5] Hippias of Elis. See Cic. Or. iii. 32.   [6] Conciliabula.

[1] 1 Pet. i. 24.
[2] A similar phrase occurs in Letter CXVIII. § 4.
[3] Plato, Phædo xii. Cic. T. Q. 1. 31.   [4] 1 Cor. xv. 31, Vulgate.

so as to live. The sage and Christian must both of them die : but the one always dies out of his glory, the other into it. Therefore we also should consider beforehand the end which must one day overtake us and which, whether we wish it or not, cannot be very far distant. For though we should live nine hundred years or more, as men did before the deluge, and though the days of Methuselah[1] should be granted us, yet that long space of time, when once it should have passed away and come to an end, would be as nothing. For to the man who has lived ten years and to him who has lived a thousand, when once the end of life comes and death's inexorable doom, all the past whether long or short is just the same ; except that the older a man is, the heavier is the load of sin that he has to take with him.

> First hapless mortals lose from out their life
> The fairest days : disease and age come next ;
> And lastly cruel death doth claim his prey.[2]

The poet Nævius too says that

> Mortals must many woes perforce endure.

Accordingly antiquity has feigned that Niobe because of her much weeping was turned to stone and that other women were metamorphosed into beasts. Hesiod also bewails men's birthdays and rejoices in their deaths, and Ennius wisely says :

> The mob has one advantage o'er its king :
> For it may weep while tears for him are shame.

If a king may not weep, neither may a bishop ; indeed a bishop has still less license than a king. For the king rules over unwilling subjects, the bishop over willing ones. The king compels submission by terror ; the bishop exercises lordship by becoming a servant. The king guards men's bodies till they die ; the bishop saves their souls for life eternal. The eyes of all are turned upon you. Your house is set on a watchtower ; your life fixes for others the limits of their self-control. Whatever you do, all think that they may do the same. Do not so commit yourself that those who seek ground for cavil may be thought to have rightly assailed you, or that those who are eager to imitate you may be forced to do wrong. Overcome as much as you can—nay even more than you can—the sensitiveness of your mind and check the copious flow of your tears. Else your deep affection for your nephew may be construed by unbelievers as indicating despair of God. You must regret him not as dead but as absent. You must seem to be looking for him rather than have lost him.

15. But why do I try to heal a sorrow which has already, I suppose, been assuaged by time and reason ? Why do I not rather unfold to you—they are not far to seek—the miseries of our rulers and the calamities of our time ? He who has lost the light of life is not so much to be pitied as he is to be congratulated who has escaped from such great evils. Constantius,[1] the patron of the Arian heresy, was hurrying to do battle with his enemy[2] when he died at the village of Mopsus and to his great vexation left the empire to his foe. Julian[3], the betrayer of his own soul, the murderer of a Christian army, felt in Media the hand of the Christ whom he had previously denied in Gaul. Desiring to annex new territories to Rome, he did but lose annexations previously made. Jovian[4] had but just tasted the sweets of sovereignty when a coal-fire suffocated him : a good instance of the transitoriness of human power. Valentinian[5] died of a broken blood vessel, the land of his birth laid waste, and his country unavenged. His brother Valens[6] defeated in Thrace by the Goths, was buried where he died. Gratian, betrayed by his army and refused admittance by the cities on his line of march, became the laughing-stock of his foe ; and your walls, Lyons, still bear the marks of that bloody hand.[7] Valentinian was yet a youth—I may say, a mere boy—when, after flight and exile and the recovery of his power by bloodshed, he was put to death[8] not far from the city which had witnessed his brother's end. And not only so but his lifeless body was gibbeted to do him shame. What shall I say of Procopius, of Maximus, of Eugenius,[9] who while they held sovereign sway were a terror to the nations, yet stood one and all as prisoners in the presence of their conquerors, and —cruellest wound of all to the great and powerful—felt the pang of an ignominious slavery before they fell by the edge of the sword.

16. Some one may say : such is the lot of kings :

> The lightning ever smites the mountain-tops.[10]

I will come therefore to persons of private position, and in speaking of these I will not go farther back than the last two years. In fact I will content myself—omitting all others— with recounting the respective fates of three recent consulars. Abundantius is a beggared exile at Pityus.[11] The head of Rufinus has

---

[1] Gen. v. 27.   [2] Virg. G. iii. 66-68.

[1] Died 361 A.D.   [2] Julian.   [3] Died 363 A.D.
[4] Died 364 A.D.   [5] Died 375 A.D.
[6] Burned to death in a hut after the battle of Adrianople, 378 A.D.
[7] Died 383 A.D. by the hand of Andragathius.
[8] Strangled by Arbogastes at Vienne, 392 A.D.
[9] Aspirants to the purple who were put to death, the first by Valens, the second and third by Theodosius.
[10] Hor. C. II. x. 11, 12.
[11] Banished by Eutropius who had owed his advancement to him.

been carried on a pike to Constantinople, and his severed hand has begged alms from door to door to shame his insatiable greed.[1] Timasius,[2] hurled suddenly from a position of the highest rank thinks it an escape that he is allowed to live in obscurity at Assa. I am describing not the misfortunes of an unhappy few but the thread upon which human fortunes as a whole depend. I shudder when I think of the catastrophes of our time. For twenty years and more the blood of Romans has been shed daily between Constantinople and the Julian Alps. Scythia, Thrace, Macedonia, Dardania, Dacia, Thessaly, Achaia, Epirus, Dalmatia, the Pannonias—each and all of these have been sacked and pillaged and plundered by Goths and Sarmatians, Quades and Alans, Huns and Vandals and Marchmen. How many of God's matrons and virgins, virtuous and noble ladies, have been made the sport of these brutes! Bishops have been made captive, priests and those in minor orders have been put to death. Churches have been overthrown, horses have been stalled by the altars of Christ, the relics of martyrs have been dug up.

> Mourning and fear abound on every side
> And death appears in countless shapes and forms.[3]

The Roman world is falling: yet we hold up our heads instead of bowing them. What courage, think you, have the Corinthians now, or the Athenians or the Lacedæmonians or the Arcadians, or any of the Greeks over whom the barbarians bear sway? I have mentioned only a few cities, but these once the capitals of no mean states. The East, it is true, seemed to be safe from all such evils: and if men were panic-stricken here, it was only because of bad news from other parts. But lo! in the year just gone by the wolves (no longer of Arabia but of the whole North[4]) were let loose upon us from the remotest fastnesses of Caucasus and in a short time overran these great provinces. What a number of monasteries they captured! What many rivers they caused to run red with blood! They laid siege to Antioch and invested other cities on the Halys, the Cydnus, the Orontes, and the Euphrates. They carried off troops of captives. Arabia, Phenicia, Palestine and Egypt, in their terror fancied themselves already enslaved.

> Had I a hundred tongues, a hundred lips,
> A throat of iron and a chest of brass,
> I could not tell men's countless sufferings.[5]

And indeed it is not my purpose to write a history: I only wish to shed a few tears over your sorrows and mine. For the rest, to treat such themes as they deserve, Thucydides and Sallust would be as good as dumb.

17. Nepotian is happy who neither sees these things nor hears them. We are unhappy, for either we suffer ourselves or we see our brethren suffer. Yet we desire to live, and regard those beyond the reach of these evils as miserable rather than blessed. We have long felt that God is angry, yet we do not try to appease Him. It is our sins which make the barbarians strong, it is our vices which vanquish Rome's soldiers: and, as if there were here too little material for carnage, civil wars have made almost greater havoc among us than the swords of foreign foes. Miserable must those Israelites have been compared with whom Nebuchadnezzar was called God's servant.[1] Unhappy too are we who are so displeasing to God that He uses the fury of the barbarians to execute His wrath against us. Still when Hezekiah repented, one hundred and eighty-five thousand Assyrians were destroyed in one night by a single angel.[2] When Jehosaphat sang the praises of the Lord, the Lord gave His worshipper the victory.[3] Again when Moses fought against Amalek, it was not with the sword but with prayer that he prevailed.[4] Therefore, if we wish to be lifted up, we must first prostrate ourselves. Alas! for our shame and folly reaching even to unbelief! Rome's army, once victor and lord of the world, now trembles with terror at the sight of the foe and accepts defeat from men who cannot walk afoot and fancy themselves dead if once they are unhorsed.[5] We do not understand the prophet's words: "One thousand shall flee at the rebuke of one."[6] We do not cut away the causes of the disease, as we must do to remove the disease itself. Else we should soon see the enemies' arrows give way to our javelins, their caps to our helmets, their palfreys to our chargers.

18. But I have gone beyond the office of a consoler, and while forbidding you to weep for one dead man I have myself mourned the dead of the whole world. Xerxes the mighty king who rased mountains and filled up seas, looking from high ground upon the untold host, the countless army before him is said[7] to have wept at the thought that in a hundred years not one of those whom he then saw would be alive. Oh! if we could but get up into a watch-tower so high that from it we might behold the whole earth spread out under our feet, then I would shew you the

---

[1] The prime minister of Theodosius I. Shortly after the accession of Arcadius Gainas the Goth procured his assassination.
[2] One of the generals of Theodosius I., banished to the Oasis at the instigation of Eutropius.
[3] Virg. A. ii. 369.
[4] i.e. the Huns have taken the place of the Chaldæans described in Hab. i. 8, LXX.   [5] Virg. A. vi. 625-7.

[1] Jer. xxvii. 6.   [2] 2 K. xix. 35.
[3] 2 Chr. xx. 5-25.   [4] Ex. xvii. 11.
[5] Jornandes corroborates the account of the Huns here given by Jerome.
[6] Isa. xxx. 17.   [7] Herod. vii. cc. 45, 46.

wreck of a world, nation warring against nation and kingdom in collision with kingdom ; some men tortured, others put to the sword, others swallowed up by the waves, some dragged away into slavery ; here a wedding, there a funeral ; men born here, men dying there ; some living in affluence, others begging their bread ; and not the army of Xerxes, great as that was, but all the inhabitants of the world, alive now but destined soon to pass away. Language is inadequate to a theme so vast and all that I can say must fall short of the reality.

19. Let us return then to ourselves and coming down from the skies let us look for a few moments upon what more nearly concerns us. Are you conscious, I would ask, of the stages of your growth ? Can you fix the time when you became a babe, a boy, a youth, an adult, an old man ? Every day we are changing, every day we are dying, and yet we fancy ourselves eternal. The very moments that I spend in dictation, in writing, in reading over what I write, and in correcting it, are so much taken from my life. Every dot that my secretary makes is so much gone from my allotted time. We write letters and reply to those of others, our missives cross the sea, and, as the vessel ploughs its furrow through wave after wave, the moments which we have to live vanish one by one. Our only gain is that we are thus knit together in the love of Christ. " Charity suffereth long and is kind ; charity envieth not ; charity vaunteth not itself, is not puffed up ; beareth all things, believeth all things, hopeth all things, endureth all things. Charity never faileth." [1] It lives always in the heart, and thus our Nepotian though absent is still present, and widely sundered though we are has a hand to offer to each. Yes, in him we have a hostage for mutual charity. Let us then be joined together in spirit, let us bind ourselves each to each in affection and let us who have lost a son shew the same fortitude with which the blessed pope Chromatius[2] bore the loss of a brother. Let every page that we write echo his name, let all our letters ring with it. If we can no longer clasp him to our hearts, let us hold him fast in memory ; and if we can no longer speak with him, let us never cease to speak of him.

LETTER LXI.

TO VIGILANTIUS.

Vigilantius on his return to the West after his visit to Jerusalem (whither he had gone as the bearer of letters from Paulinus of Nola—see Letter LVIII. § 11.) had openly accused Jerome of a leaning to the heresy of Origen. Jerome now writes to him in the most severe

tone repudiating the charge of Origenism and fastening upon his opponent those of ignorance and blasphemy. He singles out for especial reprobation Vigilantius's explanation of 'the stone cut out without hands' in Daniel and urges him to repent of his sins in which case he will have as much chance of forgiveness as the devil has according to Origen ! The letter is often referred to as showing Jerome's way of dealing with Origen's works. Jerome subsequently wrote a refutation of Vigilantius's work, of all his controversial writings the most violent and the least reasonable. See the translation of it in this volume. See also Letter CIX. The date of this letter is 396 A.D.

1. Since you have refused to believe your own ears, I might justly decline to satisfy you by a letter ; for, if you have failed to credit the living voice, it is not likely that you will give way to a written paper. But, since Christ has shewn us in Himself a pattern of perfect humility, bestowing a kiss upon His betrayer and receiving the robber's repentance upon the cross, I tell you now when absent as I have told you already when present, that I read and have read Origen only as I read Apollinaris, or other writers whose books in some things the Church does not receive. I by no means say that everything contained in such books is to be condemned, but I admit that there are things in them deserving of censure. Still, as it is my task and study by reading many authors to cull different flowers from as large a number as possible, not so much making it an object to prove all things as to choose what are good, I take up many writers that from the many I may learn many things ; according to that which is written " reading all things, holding fast those that are good." [1] Hence I am much surprised that you have tried to fasten upon me the doctrines of Origen, of whose mistaken teaching on many points you are up to the present altogether unaware. Am I a heretic ? Why pray then do heretics dislike me so ? And are you orthodox, you who either against your convictions and the words of your own mouth signed [2] unwillingly and are consequently a prevaricator, or else signed deliberately and are consequently a heretic ? You have taken no account of Egypt ; you have relinquished all those provinces where numbers plead freely and openly for your sect ; and you have singled out me for assault, me who not only censure but publicly condemn all doctrines that are contrary to the church.

2. Origen is a heretic, true ; but what does that take from me who do not deny that on very many points he is heretical ? He has erred concerning the resurrection of the body, he has erred concerning the condition of souls, he

---

[1] 1 Cor. xiii. 4, 7, 8.
[2] Bishop of Aquileia. His brother Eusebius was also a bishop.

[1] 1 Th. v. 21. " Prove all things," Vulg. and A. V.
[2] Probably Aterbius (for whom see Jerome Apol. iii. 33, and note on Letter LXXXVI.) had brought with him some test-formula of orthodoxy which he called upon all anti-Origenists to sign.

has erred by supposing it possible that the devil may repent, and—an error more important than these—he has declared in his commentary upon Isaiah that the Seraphim mentioned by the prophet [1] are the divine Son and the Holy Ghost. If I did not allow that he has erred or if I did not daily anathematize his errors, I should be partaker of his fault. For while we receive what is good in his writings we must on no account bind ourselves to accept also what is evil. Still in many passages he has interpreted the scriptures well, has explained obscure places in the prophets, and has brought to light very great mysteries, both in the old and in the new testament. If then I have taken over what is good in him and have either cut away or altered or ignored what is evil, am I to be regarded as guilty on the score that through my agency those who read Latin receive the good in his writings without knowing anything of the bad? If this be a crime the confessor Hilary must be convicted; for he has rendered from Greek into Latin Origen's *Explanation* of the Psalms and his *Homilies* on Job. Eusebius of Vercellæ, who witnessed a like confession, must also be held in fault; for he has translated into our tongue the *Commentaries* upon all the Psalms of his heretical namesake, omitting however the unsound portions and rendering only those parts which are profitable. I say nothing of Victorinus of Petavium and others who have merely followed and expanded Origen in their explanation of the scriptures. Were I to do so, I might seem less anxious to defend myself than to find for myself companions in guilt. I will come to your own case: Why do you keep copies of his treatises on Job? In these, while arguing against the devil and concerning the stars and heavens, he has said certain things which the Church does not receive. Is it for you alone, with that very wise head of yours, to pass sentence upon all writers Greek and Latin, with a wave of your censor's wand to eject some from our libraries and to admit others, and as the whim takes you to pronounce me either a Catholic or a heretic? And am I to be forbidden to reject things which are wrong and to condemn what I have often condemned already? Read what I have written upon the epistle to the Ephesians, read my other works, particularly my commentary upon Ecclesiastes, and you will clearly see that from my youth up I have never been terrified by any man's influence into acquiescence in heretical pravity.

3. It is no small gain to know your own ignorance. It is a man's wisdom to know his own measure, that he may not be led away at the instigation of the devil to make the whole world a witness of his incapacity. You are bent, I suppose, on magnifying yourself and boast in your own country that I found myself unable to answer your eloquence and that I dreaded in you the sharp satire of a Chrysippus.[1] Christian modesty holds me back and I do not wish to lay open the retirement of my poor cell with biting words. Otherwise I should soon shew up all your bravery and your parade of triumph.[2] But these I leave to others either to talk of or to laugh at; while for my own part as a Christian speaking to a Christian I beseech you my brother not to pretend to know more than you do, lest your pen may proclaim your innocence and simplicity, or at any rate those qualities of which I say nothing but which, though you do not see them in yourself others see in you. For then you will give everyone reason to laugh at your folly. From your earliest childhood you have been taught other lessons and have been used to a different kind of schooling. One and the same person can hardly be a tester both of gold coins on the counter and also of the scriptures, or be a connoisseur of wines and an adept in expounding prophets or apostles.[3] As for me, you tear me limb from limb, our reverend brother Oceanus you charge with heresy, you dislike the judgment of the presbyters Vincent and Paulinian, and our brother Eusebius also displeases you. You alone are to be our Cato, the most eloquent of the Roman race, and you wish us to accept what you say as the words of prudence herself. Pray call to mind the day when I preached on the resurrection and on the reality of the risen body, and when you jumped up beside me and clapped your hands and stamped your feet and applauded my orthodoxy. Now, however, that you have taken to sea travelling the stench of the bilge water has affected your head, and you have called me to mind only as a heretic. What can I do for you? I believed the letters of the reverend presbyter Paulinus, and it did not occur to me that his judgment concerning you could be wrong. And although, the moment that you handed me the letter, I noticed a certain incoherency in your language, yet I fancied this due to want of culture and knowledge in you and not to an unsettled brain. I do not censure the reverend writer who preferred, no doubt, in writing to me to keep back what he knew rather than to accuse in his missive one who was both under his patronage and entrusted with his letter; but I find fault with myself that I have

---

[1] Isa. vi. 2. See Letter XVIII.   [2] Sacramenta.
[3] This expression is given in Greek.

[1] A disciple of Cleanthes and Zeno, and after them the leading teacher of the Stoic school at Athens. He was born in 280 A.D.
[2] This expression is given in Greek.
[3] The father of Vigilantius is said by Jerome to have been an inn-keeper.

rested in another's judgment rather than my own, and that, while my eyes saw one thing, I believed on the evidence of a scrap of paper something else than what I saw.

4. Wherefore cease to worry me and to overwhelm me with your scrolls. Spare at least your money with which you hire secretaries and copyists, employing the same persons to write for you and to applaud you. Possibly their praise is due to the fact that they make a profit out of writing for you. If you wish to exercise your mind, hand yourself over to the teachers of grammar and rhetoric, learn logic, have yourself instructed in the schools of the philosophers ; and when you have learned all these things you will perhaps begin to hold your tongue. And yet I am acting foolishly in seeking teachers for one who is competent to teach everyone, and in trying to limit the utterance of one who does not know how to speak yet cannot remain silent. The old Greek proverb is quite true " A lyre is of no use to an ass." [1] For my part I imagine that even your name was given you out of contrariety.[2] For your whole mind slumbers and you actually snore, so profound is the sleep—or rather the lethargy—in which you are plunged. In fact amongst the other blasphemies which with sacrilegious lips you have uttered you have dared to say that the mountain in Daniel [3] out of which the stone was cut without hands is the devil, and that the stone is Christ, who having taken a body from Adam (whose sins had before connected him with the devil) is born of a virgin to separate mankind from the mountain, that is, from the devil. Your tongue deserves to be cut out and torn into fragments. Can any true Christian explain this image of the devil instead of referring it to God the Father Almighty, or defile the ears of the whole world with so frightful an enormity ? If your explanation has ever been accepted by any—I will not say Catholic but —heretic or heathen, let your words be regarded as pious. If on the other hand the Church of Christ has never yet heard of such an impiety, and if yours has been the first mouth through which he who once said " I will be like the Most High " [4] has declared that he is the mountain spoken of by Daniel, then repent, put on sackcloth and ashes, and with fast-flowing tears wash away your awful guilt ; if so be that this impiety may be forgiven you, and, supposing Origen's heresy to be true, that you may obtain pardon when the devil himself shall obtain it, the devil who has never been convicted of greater blasphemy

than that which he has uttered through you. Your insult offered to myself I bear with patience : your impiety towards God I cannot bear. Accordingly I may seem to have been somewhat more acrid in this latter part of my letter than I declared I would be at the outset. Yet having once before repented and asked pardon of me, it is extremely foolish in you again to commit a sin for which you must anew do penance. May Christ give you grace to hear and to hold your peace, to understand and so to speak.

LETTER LXII.

TO TRANQUILLINUS.

Tranquillinus, one of Jerome's Roman friends, had written (1) to tell him of the stand that Oceanus was making against the Origenists at Rome, and (2) to ask whether any parts of Origen's works might be studied with safety and profit. Jerome welcomes the tidings about Oceanus and answers the question of Tranquillinus in the affirmative. He classes Origen with Tertullian, Apollinaris and others whose works continued to be read in spite of their heresies. Written in 396 or 397 A. D.

1. Though I formerly doubted the fact, I have now proved that the links which bind spirit to spirit are stronger than any physical bond. For you, my reverend friend, cling to me with all your soul, and I am united to you by the love of Christ. I speak simply and sincerely to your spotless heart : the very paper on which you write, the very letters which you have formed—voiceless though they are—inspire in me a sense of your affection.

2. You tell me that many have been deceived by the mistaken teaching of Origen, and that that saintly man, my son Oceanus, is doing battle with their madness. I grieve to think that simple folk have been thrown off their balance, but I am rejoiced to know that one so learned as Oceanus is doing his best to set them right again. Moreover you ask me, insignificant though I am, for an opinion as to the advisability of reading Origen's works. Are we, you say, to reject him altogether with our brother Faustinus, or are we, as others tell us, to read him in part ? My opinion is that we should sometimes read him for his learning just as we read Tertullian, Novatus, Arnobius, Apollinarius and some other church writers both Greek and Latin, and that we should select what is good and avoid what is bad in their writings according to the words of the Apostle, " Prove all things : hold fast that which is good." [1] Those, however, who are led by some perversity in their dispositions to conceive for him too much fondness or too much aversion seem to me to lie under the

---

[1] ὄνῳ λύρα
[2] Jerome subsequently (Letter CIX.) nicknamed his opponent Dormitantius ('the Sleepy One'), his own name Vigilantius meaning 'the Wakeful.'
[3] Dan. ii. 34, 45.   [4] Isa. xiv. 14.

[1] 1 Th. v. 21.

curse of the Prophet :—" Woe unto them that call evil good and good evil ; that put bitter for sweet and sweet for bitter !"[1] For while the ability of his teaching must not lead us to embrace his wrong opinions, the wrongness of his opinions should not cause us altogether to reject the useful commentaries which he has published on the holy scriptures. But if his admirers and his detractors are bent on having a tug of war one against the other, and if, seeking no mean and observing no moderation, they must either approve or disapprove his works indiscriminately, I would choose rather to be a pious boor than a learned blasphemer. Our reverend brother, Tatian the deacon, heartily salutes you.

LETTER LXIII.

TO THEOPHILUS.

When the dispute arose between Jerome and Epiphanius on the one side and Rufinus and John of Jerusalem on the other (see Letter LI.), Theophilus bishop of Alexandria, being appealed to by the latter sent the presbyter Isidore to report to him on the matter. Isidore reported against Jerome and consequently Theophilus refused to answer several of his letters. Finally he wrote counselling him to obey the canons of the church. Jerome replies that to do this has always been his first object. He then remonstrates with Theophilus on his too great leniency towards the Origenists and declares it to be productive of the worst results. The date of the letter is probably 397 A.D.

Jerome to the most blessed pope[2] Theophilus.

1. Your holiness will remember that at the time when you kept silence towards me, I never ceased to do my duty by writing to you, not taking so much into account what you in the exercise of your discretion were then doing as what it became me to do. And now that I have received a letter from your grace, I see that my reading of the gospel has not been without fruit. For if the frequent prayers of a woman changed the determination of an unyielding judge,[3] how much more must my constant appeals have softened a fatherly heart like yours?

2. I thank you for your reminder concerning the canons of the Church. Truly, " whom the Lord loveth he chasteneth, and scourgeth every son whom he receiveth."[4] Still I would assure you that nothing is more my aim than to maintain the rights of Christ, to keep to the lines laid down by the fathers, and always to remember the faith of Rome ; that faith which is praised by the lips of an

apostle,[1] and of which the Alexandrian church boasts to be a sharer.

3. Many religious persons are displeased that you are so long-suffering in regard to that shocking heresy,[2] and that you suppose yourself able by such lenity to amend those who are attacking the Church's vitals. They believe that, while you are waiting for the penitence of a few, your action is fostering the boldness of abandoned men and making their party stronger. Farewell in Christ.

LETTER LXIV.

TO FABIOLA.

Fabiola's visit to Bethlehem had been shortened by the threatened invasion of the Huns which compelled Jerome and his friends to take refuge for a time on the seaboard of Palestine. Fabiola here took leave of her companions and set sail for Italy, but not until Jerome had completed this letter for her use (§ 22). It contains a mystical account of the vestments of the High Priest worked out with Jerome's usual ingenuity and learning. Similar treatises are ascribed to Tertullian and to Hosius bishop of Cordova, but these have long since perished. Its date is 396 or 397 A.D.

LETTER LXV.

TO PRINCIPIA.

A commentary on Ps. XLV. addressed to Marcella's friend and companion Principia (see Letter CXXVII.). Jerome prefaces what he has to say by a defence of his practice of writing for women, a practice which had exposed him to many foolish sneers. He deals with the same subject in his dedication of the Commentary of Sophronius. The date of the letter is 397 A.D.

LETTER LXVI.

TO PAMMACHIUS.

Pammachius a Roman senator, had lost his wife Paulina one of Paula's daughters, while she was still in the flower of her youth. It was not till two years had elapsed that Jerome ventured to write to him; and when he did so he dwelt but little on the life and virtues of Paulina. Probably there was but little to tell. The greater part of the letter is taken up with commendation of Pammachius himself who, in spite of his high rank and position, had become a monk and was now living a life of severe self-denial. Jerome speaks approvingly of the Hospice for Strangers which, in conjunction with Fabiola, Pammachius had set up at Portus, and describes his own somewhat similar institutions at Bethlehem. He also mentions Paula, Eustochium, and the dead Blæsilla, all in terms of the highest praise. The date of the letter is 397 A.D.

1. Supposing a wound to be healed and a scar to have been formed upon the skin, any course of treatment designed to remove the

[1] Is. v. 20.   [2] See note on Letter LVIII.
[3] Luke xviii. 2-5.   [4] Heb. xii. 6.

[1] Rom. i. 8.   [5] That of the Origenists.

mark must in its effort to improve the appearance renew the smart of the original wound. After two years of inopportune silence my condolence now comes rather late ; yet even so I am afraid that my present speech may be still more inopportune. I fear lest in touching the sore spot in your heart I may by my words inflame afresh a wound which time and reflection have availed to cure. For who can have ears so dull or hearts so flinty as to hear the name of your Paulina without weeping? Even though reared on the milk of Hyrcanian tigresses [1] they must still shed tears. Who can with dry eyes see thus untimely cut down and withered an opening rose, an undeveloped bud,[2] which has not yet formed itself into a cup nor spread forth the proud display of its crimson petals? In her a most priceless pearl is broken. In her a vivid emerald is shattered. Sickness alone shews us the blessedness of health. We realize better what we have had when we cease to have it.

2. The good ground of which we read in the parable brought forth fruit, some an hundredfold, some sixtyfold, and some thirtyfold.[3] In this threefold yield I recognize an emblem of the three different rewards of Christ which have fallen to three women [4] closely united in blood and moral excellence. Eustochium culls the flowers of virginity. Paula sweeps the toilsome threshing floor of widowhood. Paulina keeps the bed undefiled of marriage. A mother with such daughters wins for herself on earth all that Christ has promised to give in heaven. Then to complete the team—if I may so call it—of four saints turned out by a single family, and to match the women's virtues by those of a man, the three have a fit companion in Pammachius who is a cherub such as Ezekiel describes,[5] brother-in-law to the first, son-in-law to the second, husband to the third. Husband did I say? Nay, rather a most devoted brother ; for the language of marriage is inadequate to describe the holy bonds of the Spirit. Of this team Jesus holds the reins, and it is of steeds like these that Habakkuk sings : "ride upon thy horses and let thy riding be salvation." [6] With like resolve if with unlike speed they strain after the victor's palm. Their colours are different ; their object is the same. They are harnessed in one yoke, they obey one driver, not waiting for the lash but answering the call of his voice with fresh efforts.

3. Let me use for a moment the language of philosophy. According to the Stoics there are four virtues so closely related and mutually coherent that he who lacks one lacks all. They are prudence, justice, fortitude, and temperance.[1] While all of you possess the four, yet each is remarkable for one. You have prudence, your mother has justice, your virgin sister has fortitude, your wedded wife has temperance. I speak of you as wise, for who can be wiser than one who, despising the folly of the world, has followed Christ " the power of God and the wisdom of God "?[2] Or what better instance can there be of justice than your mother, who having divided her substance among her offspring has taught them by her own contempt of riches the true object on which to fix their affections? Who has set a better example of courage than Eustochium, who by resolving to be a virgin has breached the gates of the nobility and broken down the pride of a consular house? The first of Roman ladies, she has brought under the yoke the first of Roman families. Has there ever been temperance greater than that of Paulina, who, reading the words of the apostle : " marriage is honourable in all and the bed undefiled," [3] and not presuming to aspire to the happiness of her virgin sister or the continence of her widowed mother, has preferred to keep to the safe track of a lower path rather than treading on air to lose herself in the clouds? When once she had entered upon the married state, her one thought day and night was that, as soon as her union should be blessed with offspring, she would live thenceforth in the second degree of chastity,[4] and

Though woman, foremost in the high emprise,[5]

would induce her husband to follow a like course. She would not forsake him but looked for the day when he would become a companion in salvation. Finding by several miscarriages that her womb was not barren, she could not give up all hope of having children and had to allow her own reluctance to give way to the eagerness of her mother-in-law and the chagrin of her husband. Thus she suffered much as Rachel suffered,[6] although instead of bringing forth like her a son of pangs and of the right hand,[7] the heir she had longed for was no other than her husband. I have learned on good authority that her wish in submitting herself to her husband was not to take advantage of God's primitive command " Be faithful and multiply and replenish the earth " [8] but that she only desired children that she might bring forth virgins to Christ.

4. We read that the wife of Phinehas the priest, on hearing that the ark of the Lord

---

[1] Virgil, Æn. iv. 367.
[2] Quoted from a poet in the Latin Anthology.
[3] Matt. xiii. 8.
[4] Paula and her two daughters. Paulina and Eustochium.
[5] Ezek. x. 8–22.   [6] Hab. iii. 8, LXX.

[1] Cf. Wisdom, viii. 7.   [2] 1 Cor. i. 24.
[3] Heb. xiii. 4.   [4] i.e., continence in marriage.
[5] Virg. A. i. 494.   [6] Gen. xxxv. 16.
[7] The respective meanings of Benoni and Benjamin.
[8] Gen. i. 28.

had been taken, was seized suddenly with the pains of travail and that she brought forth a son Ichabod and died a mother in the hands of the women who nursed her.[1] Rachel's son is called Benjamin, that is 'son of excellence' or 'of the right hand'; but the son of the other, afterwards to be a distinguished priest of God, derives his name from the ark.[2] The same thing has come to pass in our own day, for since Paulina fell asleep the Church has posthumously borne the monk Pammachius, a patrician by his parentage and marriage, rich in alms, and lofty in lowliness. The apostle writes to the Corinthians, " Ye see your calling, brethren, how that not many wise men, not many noble are called."[3] The conditions of the nascent church required this to be so that the grain of mustard seed might grow up little by little into a tree,[4] and that the leaven of the gospel might gradually raise more and more the whole lump of the church.[5] In our day Rome possesses what the world in days gone by knew not of. Then few of the wise or mighty or noble were Christians ; now many wise powerful and noble are not Christians only but even monks. And among them all my Pammachius is the wisest, the mightiest, and the noblest ; great among the great, a leader among leaders, he is the commander in chief of all monks. He and others like him are the offspring which Paulina desired to have in her life time and which she has given us in her death. " Sing, O barren, thou that didst not bear ; break forth into singing and cry aloud, thou that didst not travail with child";[6] for in a moment thou hast brought forth as many sons as there are poor men in Rome.

5. The glowing gems which in old days adorned the neck and face of Paulina now purchase food for the needy. Her silk dresses and gold brocades are exchanged for soft woollen garments intended to keep out the cold and not to expose the body to vain admiration. All that formerly ministered to luxury is now at the service of virtue. That blind man holding out his hand, and often crying aloud when there is none to hear, is the heir of Paulina, is co-heir with Pammachius. That poor cripple who can scarcely drag himself along, owes his support to the help of a tender girl. Those doors which of old poured forth crowds of visitors, are now beset only by the wretched. One suffers from a dropsy, big with death ; another mute and without the means of begging, begs the more appealingly because he cannot beg ; another maimed

from his childhood implores an alms which he may not himself enjoy. Still another has his limbs rotted with jaundice and lives on after his body has become a corpse. To use the language of Virgil :

Had I a hundred tongues, a hundred lips, I could not tell men's countless sufferings.[1]

Such is the bodyguard which accompanies Pammachius wherever he walks ; in the persons of such he ministers to Christ Himself ; and their squalor serves to whiten his soul. Thus he speeds on his way to heaven, beneficent as a giver of games to the poor, and kind as a provider of shows for the needy. Other husbands scatter on the graves of their wives violets, roses, lilies, and purple flowers ; and assuage the grief of their hearts by fulfilling this tender duty. Our dear Pammachius also waters the holy ashes and the revered bones of Paulina, but it is with the balm of almsgiving. These are the confections and the perfumes with which he cherishes the dead embers of his wife knowing that it is written : " Water will quench a flaming fire ; and alms maketh an atonement for sins."[2] What great power compassion has and what high rewards it is destined to win, the blessed Cyprian sets forth in an extensive work.[3] It is proved also by the counsel of Daniel who desired the most impious of kings—had he been willing to hear him—to be saved by shewing mercy to the poor.[4] Paulina's mother may well be glad of Paulina's heir. She cannot regret that her daughter's wealth has passed into new hands when she sees it still spent upon the objects she had at heart. Nay, rather she must congratulate herself that without any exertion of her own her wishes are being carried out. The sum available for distribution is the same as before : only the distributor is changed.

6. Who can credit the fact that one, who is the glory of the Furian stock and whose grandfathers and great grandfathers have been consuls, moves amid the senators in their purple clothed in sombre garb, and that, so far from blushing when he meets the eyes of his companions, he actually derides those who deride him ! " There is a shame that leadeth to death and there is a shame that leadeth to life."[5] It is a monk's first virtue to despise the judgments of men and always to remember the apostle's words :—" If I yet pleased men, I should not be the servant of Christ."[6] In the same sense the Lord says to the prophets that He has made their face a brazen city and

---

[1] 1 Sam. iv. 19-22.
[2] Ichabod means 'there is no glory' ; glory being (apparently) a synonym for the ark.
[3] 1 Cor. i 26.   [4] Matt. xiii. 31.
[5] Matt. xiii. 33.   [·] Isa. liv. 1.

[1] Virg. A. vi. 625, 627.   [2] Ecclus. iii. 30.
[3] Viz. the treatise entitled Of Work and Alms.
[4] Dan. iv. 27.
[5] Ecclus. iv. 25. Est confusio adducens peccatum : et est confusio adducens gloriam et gratiam, Vulg. Jerome probably quotes from memory. AV. follows the Greek and the Vulg.
[6] Gal. i. 10.

a stone of adamant and an iron pillar,[1] to the end that they shall not be afraid of the insults of the people but shall by the sternness of their looks discompose the effrontery of those who sneered at them. A finely strung mind is more readily overcome by contumely than by terror. And men whom no tortures can overawe are sometimes prevailed over by the fear of shame. Surely it is no small thing for a man of birth, eloquence, and wealth to avoid the company of the powerful in the streets, to mingle with the crowd, to cleave to the poor, to associate on equal terms with the untaught, to cease to be a leader and to become one of the people. The more he humbles himself, the more he is exalted.[2]

7. A pearl will shine in the midst of squalor and a gem of the first water will sparkle in the mire. This is what the Lord promised when He said : "Them that honour me I will honour."[3] Others may understand this of the future when sorrow shall be turned into joy and when, although the world shall pass away, the saints shall receive a crown which shall never pass. But I for my part see that the promises made to the saints are fulfilled even in this present life. Before he began to serve Christ with his whole heart, Pammachius was a well known person in the senate. Still there were many other senators who wore the badges of proconsular rank. The whole world is filled with similar decorations. He was in the first rank it is true, but there were others in it besides him. Whilst he took precedence of some, others took precedence of him. The most distinguished privilege loses its prestige when lavished on a crowd, and dignities themselves become less dignified in the eyes of good men when held by persons who have no dignity. Thus Tully finely says of Cæsar, when he wished to advance some of his adherents, "he did not so much honour them as dishonour the honourable positions in which he placed them."[4] To-day all the churches of Christ are talking of Pammachius. The whole world admires as a poor man one whom heretofore it ignored as rich. Can anything be more splendid than the consulate ? Yet the honour lasts only for a year and when another has succeeded to the post its former occupant gives way. Each man's laurels are lost in the crowd and sometimes triumphs themselves are marred by the shortcomings of those who celebrate them. An office which was once handed down from patrician to patrician, which only men of noble birth could hold, of which the consul Marius — victor

though he was over Numidia and the Teutons and the Cimbri—was held unworthy on account of the obscurity of his family, and which Scipio won before his time as the reward of valour,—this great office is now obtained by merely belonging to the army ; and the shining robe of victory[1] now envelops men who a little while ago were country boors. Thus we have received more than we have given. The things we have renounced are small ; the things we possess are great. All that Christ promises is duly performed and for what we have given up we have received an hundredfold.[2] This was the ground in which Isaac sowed his seed,[3] Isaac who in his readiness to die[4] bore the cross of the Gospel before the Gospel came.

8. "If thou wilt be perfect," the Lord says, "go and sell that thou hast and give to the poor . . . and come and follow me."[5] If thou wilt be perfect. Great enterprises are always left to the free choice of those who hear of them. Thus the apostle refrains from making virginity a positive duty, because the Lord in speaking of eunuchs who had made themselves such for the kingdom of heaven's sake finally said : "He that is able to receive it, let him receive it."[6] For, to quote the apostle, "it is not of him that willeth, nor of him that runneth, but of God that sheweth mercy."[7] If thou wilt be perfect. There is no compulsion laid upon you : if you are to win the prize it must be by the exercise of your own free will. If therefore you will to be perfect and desire to be as the prophets, as the apostles, as Christ Himself, sell not a part of your substance (lest the fear of want become an occasion of unfaithfulness, and so you perish with Ananias and Sapphira[8]) but all that you have. And when you have sold all, give the proceeds not to the wealthy or to the highminded but to the poor. Give each man enough for his immediate need but do not give money to swell what a man has already. "Thou shalt not muzzle the mouth of the ox that treadeth out the corn,"[9] and "the labourer is worthy of his reward."[10] Again "they which wait at the altar are partakers with the altar."[11] Remember also these words : "having, food and raiment let us be therewith content."[12] Where you see smoking dishes, steaming pheasants, massive silver plate, spirited nags, long-haired boy-slaves, expensive clothing, and embroidered hangings, give nothing there. For he to whom you would give is richer than you the giver. It is moreover a kind of sacrilege to give what belongs to the poor to those who are not poor. Yet to be a

1 Cf. Jer. i. 18.   Ezek. iii. 8, 9.
2 Cf. Luke xiv. 11.   3 1 S. ii. 30.
4 Cf. the remark of Æneas Silvius that " men should be given to places not places, to men."

1 Palma, i.e. tunica palmata.   2 Cf. Matt. xix. 29.
3 Gen. xxvi. 12.   4 Gen. xxii.   5 Matt. xix. 21.
6 Matt. xix. 12.   7 Rom. ix. 16   8 Acts v.   9 1 Cor. ix. 9.
10 1 Tim. v. 18.   11 1 Cor. ix. 13.   12 1 Tim. vi. 8.

perfect and complete Christian it is not enough
to despise wealth or to squander and fling away
one's money, a thing which can be lost and
found in a single moment.   Crates the Theban[1]
did this, so did Antisthenes and several others,
whose lives shew them to have had many
faults.   The disciple of Christ must do more
for the attainment of spiritual glory than the
philosopher of the world, than the venal slave
of flying rumours and of the people's breath.
It is not enough for you to despise wealth
unless you follow Christ as well.   And only
he follows Christ who forsakes his sins and
walks hand in hand with virtue.   We know
that Christ is wisdom.   He is the treasure
which in the scriptures a man finds in his
field.[2]   He is the peerless gem which is bought
by selling many pearls.[3]   But if you love a
captive woman, that is, worldly wisdom, and
if no beauty but hers attracts you, make her
bald and cut off her alluring hair, that is to
say, the graces of style, and pare away her
dead nails.[4]   Wash her with the nitre of which
the prophet speaks,[5] and then take your ease
with her and say " Her left hand is under my
head, and her right hand doth embrace me."[6]
Then shall the captive bring to you many
children; from a Moabitess[7] she shall become
an Israelitish woman.   Christ is that sanctification without which no man shall see the face of
God.   Christ is our redemption, for He is at
once our Redeemer and our Ransom.[8]   Christ
is all, that he who has left all for Christ may
find One in place of all, and may be able to
proclaim freely.   " The Lord is my portion."[9]

9, I see clearly that you have a warm
affection for divine learning and that far from
trying—like some rash persons—to teach that
of which you are yourself ignorant you make
it your first object to learn what you are going
to teach.   Your letters in their simplicity are
redolent of the prophets and savour strongly
of the apostles.   You do not affect a stilted
eloquence, nor boylike balance shallow sentences in clauses neatly-turned.   The quickly
frothing foam disappears with equal quickness; and a tumour though it enlarges the
size of the body is injurious to health.   It
is moreover a shrewd maxim, this of Cato,
" Fast enough if well enough."   Long ago it
is true in the days of our youth we laughed
outright at this dictum when the finished
orator[10] used it in his exordium.   I fancy you
remember the mistake[11] shared by the speaker
in our Athenæum and how the whole room
resounded with the cry taken up by the stu-

dents " Fast enough if well enough."   According to Fabius[1] crafts would be sure to prosper if none but craftsmen were allowed to
criticise them.   No man can adequately estimate a poet unless he is competent himself
to write verse   No man can comprehend
philosophers, unless he is acquainted with the
various theories that they have held.   Material
and visible products are best appraised by
those who make them.   To what a cruel lot
we men of letters are exposed you may gather
from the fact that we are forced to rely on
the judgment of the public ; and many a man is
in company a formidable opponent who would
certainly be despised could he be seen alone.
I have touched on this in passing to make you
content, if possible, with the ear of the learned.
Disregard the remarks which uneducated persons make concerning your ability ; but day
by day imbibe the marrow of the prophets, that
you may know the mystery of Christ and share
this mystery with the patriarchs.

10. Whether you read or write, whether
you wake or sleep, let the herdsman's horn of
Amos[2] always ring in your ears.   Let the
sound of the clarion arouse your soul, let the
divine love carry you out of yourself ; and
then seek upon your bed him whom your soul
loveth,[3] and boldly say : " I sleep, but my
heart waketh."[4]   And when you have found
him and taken hold of him, let him not go.
And if you fall asleep for a moment and He
escapes from your hands, do not forthwith
despair.   Go out into the streets and charge
the daughters of Jerusalem : then shall you
find him lying down in the noontide weary
and drunk with passion, or wet with the dew
of night by the flocks of his companions, or
fragrant with many kinds of spices, amid the
apples of the garden.[5]   There give to him
your breasts, let him suck your learned bosom,
let him rest in the midst of his heritage,[6] his
feathers as those of a dove overlaid with silver and his inward parts with the brightness
of gold.   This young child, this mere boy, who
is fed on butter and honey,[7] and who is reared
among curdled mountains,[8] quickly grows up
to manhood, speedily spoils all[9] that is opposed to him in you, and when the time is ripe
plunders [the spiritual] Damascus and puts
in chains the king of [the spiritual] Assyria.

11. I hear that you have erected a hospice
for strangers at Portus and that you have
planted a twig from the tree of Abraham[10]

1 Cf. Letter LVIII. § 2.   2 Matt. xiii. 44.
3 Matt. xiii. 45.   4 Cf. Dt. xxi. 11, 12.
5 Jer. ii. 22.   6 Cant. ii. 6. AV." his ' for ' her.'
7 Jerome is thinking of Ruth.   8 1 Cor. i. 30 : Heb. xii. 14.
9 Ps. lxxiii. 26.   10 Quintilian.
11 What was the mistake ? Did the orator say, " Well enough
if fast enough " ? The text seems obscure.

1 Fabius Pietor.   2 Cf. Letter XLVI. § 12.
3 Cant. iii. 1.   4 Cant. v. 2.   5 Cf. Cant. i. 7, ii. 5, v. 2.
6 Ps. lxviii. 13.   7 Isa. vii. 14, 15.
8 Ps. lxviii. 14, Vulg. (acc. to some MSS.). Intermedios cleros—
the lot or inheritance—with an allusion perhaps to the word
clergy formed from clerus.
9 Perhaps an allusion to Isa. viii. 1. Mahershalal-hash-baz
' Spoil speedeth, prey hasteth.'
10 i.e. the oak of Mamre under which he entertained the
three angels (Gen. xviii. 1-8).

upon the Ausonian shore. Like Æneas you are tracing the outlines of a new encampment; only that, whereas he, when he reached the waters of the Tiber, under pressure of want had to eat the square flat cakes which formed the tables spoken of by the oracle,[1] you are able to build a house of bread to rival this little village of Bethlehem[2] wherein I am staying ; and here after their long privations you propose to satisfy travellers with sudden plenty. Well done. You have surpassed my poor beginning.[3] You have reached the highest point. You have made your way from the root to the top of the tree. You are the first of monks in the first city of the world: you do right therefore to follow the first of the patriarchs. Let Lot, whose name means 'one who turns aside' choose the plain[4] and let him follow the left and easy branch of the famous letter of Pythagoras.[5] But do you make ready for yourself a monument like Sarah's[6] on steep and rocky heights. Let the City of Books be near ;[7] and when you have destroyed the giants, the sons of Anak,[8] make over your heritage to joy and merriment.[9] Abraham was rich in gold and silver and cattle, in substance and in raiment: his household was so large that on an emergency he could bring a picked body of young men into the field, and could pursue as far as Dan and then slay four kings who had already put five kings to flight.[10] Frequently exercising hospitality and never turning any man away from his door, he was accounted worthy at last to entertain God himself. He was not satisfied with giving orders to his servants and handmaids to attend to his guests, nor did he lessen the favour he conferred by leaving others to care for them ; but as though he had found a prize, he and Sarah his wife gave themselves to the duties of hospitality. With his own hands he washed the feet of his guests, upon his own shoulders he brought home a fat calf from the herd. While the strangers dined he stood by to serve them, and set before them the dishes cooked by Sarah's hands—though meaning to fast himself.

12. The regard which I feel for you, my dear brother, makes me remind you of these things; for you must offer to Christ not only your money but yourself, to be a "living sacrifice, holy, acceptable unto God, which is your reasonable service,"[11] and you must imitate the son of man who "came not to be ministered unto but to minister."[1] What the patriarch did for strangers that our Lord and Master did for His servants and disciples. " Skin for skin, yea, all that a man hath will he give for his life. But," says the devil, " touch his flesh and he will curse thee to thy face."[2] The old enemy knows that the battle with impurity is a harder one than that with covetousness. It is easy to cast off what clings to us from without, but a war within our borders involves far greater peril. We have to unfasten things joined together, we have to sunder things firmly united. Zacchæus was rich while the apostles were poor. He restored fourfold all that he had taken and gave to the poor the half of his remaining substance. He welcomed Christ as his guest, and salvation came unto his house.[3] And yet because he was little of stature and could not reach the apostolic standard of height, he was not numbered with the twelve apostles. Now as regards wealth the apostles gave up nothing at all, but as regards will they one and all gave up the whole world. If we offer to Christ our souls as well as our riches, he will gladly receive our offering. But if we give to God only those things which are without while we give to the devil those things which are within, the division is not fair, and the divine voice says : " Hast thou not sinned in offering aright, and yet not dividing aright ? "[4]

13. That you, the leader of the patrician order, first set the example of turning monk should not be to you an occasion of boasting but rather one of humility, knowing as you do that the Son of God became the Son of man. However low you may abase yourself, you cannot be more lowly than Christ. Even supposing that you walk barefooted, that you dress in sombre garb, that you rank yourself with the poor, that you condescend to enter the tenements of the needy, that you are eyes to the blind, hands to the weak, feet to the lame, that you carry water and hew wood and make fires—even supposing that you do all this, where are the chains, the buffets, the spittings, the scourgings, the gibbet, the death which the Lord endured ? And even when you have done all the things I have mentioned, you are still surpassed by your sister Eustochium as well as by Paula : for considering the weakness of their sex they have done more work relatively if less absolutely, than you. I myself was not at Rome but in the desert— would that I had continued there—at the time when your father-in-law Toxotius was still alive and his daughters were still given up to the world. But I have heard that they were too dainty to walk in the muddy streets, that

---

1 Virg. Æn. vii. 112–129.
2 Beth-lehem means ' house of bread.'
3 v. § 14 below.   4 Gen. xiii. 5–11.
5 The letter Y. Cf. Pers. iii. 56, 57 and Conington's note.
6 Gen. xxiii. 19.
7 i.e. Kirjathsepher close to Hebron (Josh. xv. 13–15) where Sarah was buried.   8 Cf. Jos. xv. 14.
9 An allusion to the name of Abraham's heir, Isaac or ' laughter' (Gen. xxi. 3, 6).
10 Gen. xiv. 13–16.   11 Rom. xii. 1.

1 Matt. xx. 28.   2 Job ii. 4, 5.
3 Luke xix. 2–9.   4 Gen. iv. 7, LXX.

they were carried about in the arms of eunuchs, that they disliked crossing uneven ground, that they found a silk dress a burthen and felt sunshine too scorching. But now, squalid and sombre in their dress, they are positive heroines in comparison with what they used to be. They trim lamps, light fires, sweep floors, clean vegetables, put heads of cabbage in the pot to boil, lay tables, hand cups, help dishes and run to and fro to wait on others. And yet there is no lack of virgins under the same roof with them. Is it then that they have no servants upon whom they can lay these duties? Surely not. They are unwilling that others should surpass them in physical toil whom they themselves surpass in vigour of mind. I say all this not because I doubt your mental ardour but that I may quicken the pace at which you are running, and in the heat of battle may add warmth to your warmth.

14. I for my part am building in this province a monastery and a hospice close by; so that, if Joseph and Mary chance to come to Bethlehem, they may not fail to find shelter and welcome. Indeed, the number of monks who flock here from all quarters of the world is so overwhelming that I can neither desist from my enterprise nor bear so great a burthen. The warning of the gospel has been all but fulfilled in me, for I did not sufficiently count the cost of the tower I was about to build;[1] accordingly I have been constrained to send my brother Paulinian[2] to Italy to sell some ruinous villas which have escaped the hands of the barbarians, and also the property inherited from our common parents. For I am loth, now that I have begun it, to give up ministering to the saints, lest I incur the ridicule of carping and envious persons.

15. Now that I have come to the conclusion of my letter I recall my metaphor of the four-horse team, and recollect that Blæsilla would have made a fifth, had she been spared to share your resolve. I had almost forgotten to mention her, the first of you all to go to meet the Lord. You who once were five I now see to be two and three. Blæsilla and her sister Paulina rest in sweet sleep: you with the two others on either side of you will fly upward to Christ more easily.

LETTER LXVII.

FROM AUGUSTINE.

Jerome having written him a short letter (no longer extant) Augustine now replies. He speaks with approval of Jerome's treatise *On Famous Men*, incorrectly called the *Epitaph* (see Letter CXII. § 3). He also re-

peats his objections to Jerome's account of the quarrel between Paul and Peter at Antioch and then concludes with a request that he will draw up a short notice of the principal heresies condemned by the Church.

Like the preceding letter of Augustine (Letter LVI.) this also failed to reach Jerome. It was however published in the West, but without Augustine's knowledge and by degrees its contents found their way to Bethlehem where they caused much annoyance and pain. The date of the letter is 397 A.D. In Augustine's correspondence in this Library it is printed in full as Letter XL.

LETTER LXVIII.

TO CASTRUTIUS.

Castrutius, a blind man of Pannonia, had set out for Bethlehem to visit Jerome. However, on reaching Cissa (whether that in Thrace or that on the Adriatic is uncertain) he was induced by his friends to turn back. Jerome writes to thank him for his intention and to console him for his inability to carry it out. He then tries to comfort him in his blindness (1) by referring to Christ's words concerning the man born blind (Joh. ix. 3) and (2) by telling him the story of Antony and Didymus. The date of the letter is 397 A.D.

1. My reverend son Heraclius the deacon has reported to me that in your eagerness to see me you came as far as Cissa, and that, though a Pannonian and consequently a land animal, you did not quail before the surges of the Adriatic and the dangers of the Ægean and Ionian seas. He tells me that you would have actually accomplished your purpose, had not our brethren with affectionate care held you back. I thank you all the same and regard it as a kindness shewn. For in the case of friends one must accept the will for the deed. Enemies often give us the latter, but only sincere attachment can bring us the former. And now that I am writing to you I beseech you do not regard the bodily affliction which has befallen you as due to sin. When the Apostles speculated concerning the man that was born blind from the womb and asked our Lord and Saviour: "Who did sin, this man or his parents, that he was born blind?" they were told "Neither hath this man sinned nor his parents, but that the works of God should be made manifest in him."[1] Do we not see numbers of heathens, Jews, heretics and men of various opinions rolling in the mire of lust, bathed in blood, surpassing wolves in ferocity and kites in rapacity, and for all this the plague does not come nigh their dwellings?[2] They are not smitten as other men, and accordingly they wax insolent against God and lift up their faces even to heaven. We know on the other hand that holy men are afflicted with sicknesses, miseries, and want, and perhaps they are tempted

---

[1] Luke xiv. 28.   [2] See Letter LXI § 31.   [1] Joh. ix. 2, 3.   [2] Ps. xci. 10.

to say " Verily I have cleansed my heart in vain, and washed my hands in innocency." Yet immediately they go on to reprove themselves, " If I say, I will speak thus ; behold I should offend against the generation of thy children." [1] If you suppose that your blindness is caused by sin, and that a disease which physicians are often able to cure is an evidence of God's anger, you will think Isaac a sinner because he was so wholly sightless that he was deceived into blessing one whom he did not mean to bless.[2] You will charge Jacob with sin, whose vision became so dim that he could not see Ephraim and Manasseh,[3] although with the inner eye and the prophetic spirit he could foresee the distant future and the Christ that was to come of his royal line.[4] Were any of the kings holier than Josiah? Yet he was slain by the sword of the Egyptians.[5] Were there ever loftier saints than Peter and Paul? Yet their blood stained the blade of Nero. And to say no more of men, did not the Son of God endure the shame of the cross? And yet you fancy those blessed who enjoy in this world happiness and pleasure? God's hottest anger against sinners is when he shews no anger. Wherefore in Ezekiel he says to Jerusalem : " My jealousy will depart from thee and I will be quiet and will be no more angry." [6] For " whom the Lord loveth He chasteneth, and scourgeth every son whom He receiveth." [7] The father does not instruct his son unless he loves him. The master does not correct his disciple unless he sees in him signs of promise. When once the doctor gives over caring for the patient, it is a sign that he despairs. You should answer thus : " as Lazarus in his lifetime [8] received evil things so will I now gladly suffer torments that future glory may be laid up for me." For " affliction shall not rise up the second time." [9] If Job, a man holy and spotless and righteous in his generation, suffered terrible afflictions, his own book explains the reason why.

2. That I may not make myself tedious or exceed the due limits of a letter by repeating old stories, I will briefly relate to you an incident which happened in my childhood. The saintly Athanasius bishop of Alexandria had summoned the blessed Antony to that city to confute the heretics there. Hereupon Didymus, a man of great learning who had lost his eyes, came to visit the hermit and, the conversation turning upon the holy scriptures, Antony could not help admiring his ability and eulogizing his insight. At last he said : You do not regret, do you, the loss of your eyes? At first Didymus was ashamed to answer, but when the question had been repeated a second time and a third, he frankly confessed that his blindness was a great grief to him. Whereupon Antony said : " I am surprised that a wise man should grieve at the loss of a faculty which he shares with ants and flies and gnats, and not rejoice rather in having one of which only saints and apostles have been thought worthy." From this story you may perceive how much better it is to have spiritual than carnal vision and to possess eyes into which the mote of sin cannot fall.[1]

Though you have failed to come this year, I do not yet despair of your coming. If the reverend deacon [2] who is the bearer of this letter is again caught in the toils of your affection, and if you come hither in his company I shall be delighted to welcome you and shall readily acknowledge that the delay in payment is made up for by the largeness of the interest.

LETTER LXIX.

TO OCEANUS.

Oceanus, a Roman nobleman zealous for the faith, had asked Jerome to back him in a protest against Carterius a Spanish bishop who contrary to the apostolic rule that a bishop is to be "the husband of one wife" had married a second time. Jerome refuses to take the line suggested on the ground that Carterius's first marriage having preceded his baptism cannot be taken into account. He therefore advises Oceanus to let the matter drop. The date of the letter is 397 A.D.

1. I never supposed, son Oceanus, that the clemency of the Emperor would be assailed by criminals, or that persons just released from prison would after their own experience of its filth and fetters complain of relaxations allowed to others. In the gospel he who envies another's salvation is thus addressed : "Friend, is thine eye evil because I am good?" [3] "God hath concluded them all in sin [4] that he might have mercy upon all." [5] "When sin abounded grace did much more abound." [6] The first born of Egypt are slain and not even a beast belonging to Israel is left behind in Egypt.[7] The heresy of the Cainites rises before me and the once slain viper lifts up its shattered head, destroying not partially as most often hitherto but altogether the mystery of Christ.[8] This

---

[1] Ps. lxxiii. 13, 15. [2] Gen. xxvii. [3] Gen. xlviii. 10.
[4] Gen. xlix. 10. [5] 2 K. xxiii. 29.
[6] Ezek. xvi. 42. In the Vulgate the tenses are different, but the sense is substantially the same.
[7] Heb. xii. 6. [8] Luke xvi. 25. [9] Nahum i. 9.

[1] Luke vi. 42.
[2] Heraclius, a deacon of Pannonia, who had been sent to Bethlehem by his bishop Amabilis to procure from Jerome a long promised commentary on the Visions of Isaiah. This, which Jerome subsequently incorporated as book V. in his complete work on the prophet, Heraclius succeeded in obtaining from him. See the Preface to the Commentary.
[3] Matt. xx. 15. [4] AV. ' unbelief.' [5] Rom. xi. 32.
[6] Rom. v. 20. [7] Ex. xii. 29, 30, 38.
[8] The Cainites appear to have denied the efficacy of the atonement.

heresy declares that there are some sins which Christ cannot cleanse with His blood, and that the scars left by old transgressions on the body and the soul are sometimes so deep that they cannot be effaced by the remedy which He supplies. What else is this but to say that Christ has died in vain ? He has indeed died in vain if there are any whom He cannot make alive. When John the Baptist points to Christ and says : " Behold the lamb of God which taketh away the sins [1] of the world " [2] he utters a falsehood if after all there are persons living whose sins Christ has not taken away. For either it must be shewn that they are not of the world whom the grace of Christ thus ignores : or, if it be admitted that they are of the world, we have to choose between the horns of a dilemma. Either they have been delivered from their sins, in which case the power of Christ to save all men is proved; or they remain undelivered and as it were still under the charge of misdoing, in which case Christ is proved to be powerless. But far be it from us to believe of the Almighty that He is powerless in aught. For "what things soever the Father doeth, these also doeth the Son likewise." [3] To ascribe weakness to the Son is to ascribe it to the Father also. The shepherd carries the whole sheep and not only this or that part of it : all the epistles of the apostle [4] speak continually of the grace of Christ. And, lest a single announcement of this grace might seem a little thing, Peter says : " Grace unto you and peace be multiplied." [5] The Scripture promises abundance ; yet we affirm scarcity.

2. To what does all this tend, you ask. I reply ; you remember the question that you proposed. It was this. A Spanish bishop named Carterius, old in years and in the priesthood has married two wives, one before he was baptized, and, she having died, another since he has passed through the laver ; and you are of opinion that he has violated the precept of the apostle, who in his list of episcopal qualifications commands that a bishop shall be "the husband of one wife." [6] I am surprised that you have pilloried an individual when the whole world is filled with persons ordained in similar circumstances; I do not mean presbyters or clergy of lower rank, but speak only of bishops of whom if I were to enumerate them all one by one I should gather a sufficient number to surpass the crowd which attended the synod of Ariminum. [7] Still it does not become me to de-

fend one by incriminating many ; nor if reason condemns a sin, to make the number of those who commit it an excuse for it. At Rome an eloquent pleader caught me, as the phrase goes, between the horns of a dilemma : whichever way I turned I was held fast. Is it sinful, said he, to marry a wife, or is it not sinful? I in my simplicity, not being wary enough to avoid the snare laid for me, replied that it was not sinful. Then he propounded another question : Is it good deeds which are done away with in baptism or is it evil ? Here again my simplicity induced me to say that it was sins which were forgiven. At this point, just as I began to fancy myself secure, the horns of the dilemma commenced to close in on me from this side and from that and their points hidden before began to shew themselves. If, said he, to marry a wife is not sinful, and if baptism forgives sins, all that is not done away with is held over. On the instant a dark mist rose before my eyes as though I had been struck by a strong boxer. Yet recalling the sophism attributed to Chrysippus : [1] "Whether you lie or whether you speak the truth, in either case you lie," I came to myself again and turned upon my opponent with a dilemma of my own. Pray tell me, I said, does baptism make a new man or does it not? He grudgingly admitted that it did. I pursued my advantage by saying, Does it make him wholly new or only partially so ? He replied, Wholly. Then I asked, Is there nothing then of the old man held over in baptism? He assented. Hereupon I propounded the argument ; If baptism makes a man new and creates a wholly new being, and if there is nothing of the old man held over in the new, that which once was in the old cannot be imputed to the new. At first my thorny friend held his tongue ; afterwards however, making Piso's mistake, [2] though he had nothing to say he could not remain silent. Sweat stood upon his brow, his cheeks turned pale, his lips trembled, his tongue clove to his mouth, his throat became dry ; and fear (not age) made him cower. At last he broke out in these words, Have you not read how the apostle permits none to be ordained priest save the husband of one wife, and that what he lays stress upon is the fact of the marriage and not the time at which it is contracted ? Now as the fellow had challenged me with syllogisms, and as I saw that he was feeling his way towards some intricate and awkward questions, I proceeded to turn his own weapons against him. I said therefore, Whom did the apostle select for the episcopate, baptized persons or catechumens ? He refused

---

[1] AV. 'sin.'   [2] Joh. i. 29.   [3] Joh. v. 19.
[4] *i.e.* Paul.   [5] 1 Pet. i. 2.   [6] 1 Tim. iii. 2.
[7] This synod held in 359 A.D. was attended by about 450 bishops. It put forth an Arian formula which caused general consternation. "The whole world," says Jerome, "groaned and was astonished to find itself Arian."

[1] See note on Letter LXI. 3.   [2] Cf. Cic. In Pis. 1.

to reply. I however made a fresh onslaught repeating my question a second time and a third. You would have taken him for Niobe changed to stone by excessive weeping. I turned to the audience and said : It is all the same to me, good people, whether I bind my opponent awake or sleeping ; but it is easier to fetter a man who offers no resistance. If those whom the apostle admits into the ranks of the clergy are not catechumens but the faithful, and if he who is ordained bishop is always one of the faithful, being one of the faithful he cannot have the faults of a catechumen imputed to him. Such were the darts I hurled at my paralysed opponent. Such the quivering spears I cast at him. At last his mouth opened and he vomited forth the contents of his mind. Certainly, he blurted out, that is the doctrine of the apostle Paul.

3. Accordingly I bring out two epistles of the apostle, the first to Timothy, and the second to Titus. In the first is the following passage : " If a man desire the office of a bishop he desireth a good work. A bishop then must be blameless, the husband of one wife, vigilant, sober, of good behaviour, given to hospitality, apt to teach, not given to wine, no striker . . . but patient, not a brawler, not covetous ; one that ruleth well his own house, having his children in subjection with all gravity. (For if a man know not how to rule his own house, how shall he take care of the church of God ?) Not a novice lest being lifted up with pride he fall into the condemnation of the devil. Moreover he must have a good report of them which are without ; lest he fall into reproach and the snare of the devil." [1] While immediately at the commencement of the epistle to Titus the following behests are laid down : " For this cause left I thee in Crete that thou shouldest set in order the things that are wanting, and ordain elders in every city, as I had appointed thee : if any be blameless, the husband of one wife, having faithful children not accused of riot or unruly. For a bishop must be blameless as the steward of God ; not self-willed, not soon angry, not given to wine, no striker, not given to filthy lucre ; but a lover of hospitality, a lover of good men, sober, just, holy, temperate ; holding fast the faithful word as he hath been taught, that he may be able by sound doctrine both to exhort and to convince the gainsayers." [2] In both epistles commandment is given that only monogamists should be chosen for the clerical office whether as bishops or as presbyters. [3] Indeed with the ancients these names were synonymous, one alluding to the office, the other to the age of the clergy. No one at any rate can doubt that

the apostle is speaking only of those who have been baptized. If therefore it in no wise prejudices the case of one who is to be ordained bishop that before his baptism he has not possessed all the requisite qualifications (for it is asked what he is and not what he has been), why should a previous marriage—the one thing which is in itself not sinful—prove a hindrance to his ordination ? You argue that as his marriage was not a sin it was not done away with at his baptism. This is news to me indeed, that what in itself was not a sin is to be reckoned as such. All fornication and contamination with open vice, impiety towards God, parricide and incest, the change of the natural use of the sexes into that which is against nature [1] and all extraordinary lusts are washed away in the fountain of Christ. Can it be possible that the stains of marriage are indelible, and that harlotry is judged more leniently than honourable wedlock ? I do not, Carterius might say, hold you to blame for the hosts of mistresses and the troops of favourites [2] that you have kept ; I do not charge you with your bloodshedding and sow-like wallowings in the mire of uncleanness : yet you are ready to drag from her grave for my confusion my poor wife, who has been dead long years, and whom I married that I might be kept from those sins into which you have fallen. Tell this to the heathen who form the church's harvest with which she stores her granaries ; tell this to the catechumens who seek admission to the number of the faithful ; tell them, I say, not to contract marriages before their baptism, not to enter upon honourable wedlock, but like the Scots and the Atacotti [3] and the people of Plato's republic [4] to have community of wives and no discrimination of children, nay more, to beware of any semblance even of matrimony ; lest, after they have come to believe in Christ, He shall tell them that those whom they have had have not been concubines or mistresses but wedded wives.

4. Let every man examine his own conscience and let him deplore the violence he has done to it at every period of his life ; and then when he has brought himself to deliver a true judgment on his own former misdeeds, let him give ear to the chiding of Jesus : " Thou hypocrite, first cast out the beam out of thine own eye ; and then shalt thou see clearly to cast out the mote out of thy brother's eye." [5] Truly like the scribes and pharisees we strain out the gnat and swallow the camel, we pay tithe of mint and anise, and we omit the just judgment which God requires. [6] What parallel can be drawn between a wife

---

[1] 1 Tim. iii. 1-7.   [2] Tit. i. 5-9.
[3] Rendered 'elders' in AV.

[1] Cf. Rom. i. 26, 27.   [2] Exoleti.
[3] A Scottish tribe, cannibals according to Jerome (Against Jov. ii. 7.)
[4] Bk. V. 457.   [5] Matt. vii. 5.   [6] Matt. xxiii. 23, 24, RV.

and a prostitute? Is it fair to make a marriage now dissolved by death a ground of accusation, while dissolute living wins for itself a garland of praise? He, had his former wife lived, would not have married another; but as for you, how can you defend the bestial unions you indiscriminately make? Perhaps indeed you will say that you feared to contract marriage lest by so doing you might disqualify yourself for ordination. He took a wife that he might have children by her; you by taking a harlot have lost the hope of children. He withdrew into the privacy of his own chamber when he sought to obey nature and to win God's blessing: "Be fruitful and multiply and replenish the earth."[1] You on the contrary outraged public decency in the hot eagerness of your lust. He covered a lawful indulgence beneath a veil of modesty; you pursued an unlawful one shamelessly before the eyes of all. For him it is written "Marriage is honourable . . . and the bed undefiled," while to you the words are read, "but whoremongers and adulterers God will judge,"[2] and "if any man destroyeth the temple of God, him shall God destroy."[3] All iniquities, we are told, are forgiven us at our baptism, and when once we have received God's mercy we need not afterwards dread from Him the severity of a judge. The apostle says:—"And such were some of you: but ye are washed, but ye are sanctified, but ye are justified in the name of the Lord Jesus, and by the Spirit of our God."[4] All sins then are forgiven; it is an honest and faithful saying. But I ask you, how comes it that, while your uncleanness is washed away, my cleanness is made unclean? You reply, "No, it is not made unclean, it remains just what it was. Had it been uncleanness, it would have been washed away like mine." I want to know what you mean by this shuffling. Your remarks seem to have no more point in them than the round end of a pestle. Is a thing sin because it is not sin? or is a thing unclean because it is not unclean? The Lord, you say, has not forgiven because He had nothing to forgive; yet because He has not forgiven, that which has not been forgiven still remains.

5. What the true effect of baptism is, and what is the real grace conveyed by water hallowed in Christ, I will presently tell you; meantime I will deal with this argument as it deserves. 'An ill knot,' says the common proverb, 'requires but an ill wedge to split it.' The text quoted by the objector, "a bishop must be the husband of one wife," admits of quite another explanation. The apostle came of the Jews and the primitive Christian

church was gathered out of the remnants of Israel. Paul knew that the Law allowed men to have children by several wives,[1] and was aware that the example of the patriarchs had made polygamy familiar to the people. Even the very priests might at their own discretion enjoy the same license.[2] He gave commandment therefore that the priests of the church should not claim this liberty, that they should not take two wives or three together, but that they should each have but one wife at one time. Perhaps you may say that this explanation which I have given is disputed; in that case listen to another. You must not have a monopoly of bending the Law to suit your will instead of bending your will to suit the Law. Some by a strained interpretation say that wives are in this passage to be taken for churches and husbands for their bishops. A decree was made by the fathers assembled at the council of Nicæa[3] that no bishop should be translated from one church to another, lest scorning the society of a poor yet virgin see he should seek the embraces of a wealthy and adulterous one. For as the word λογισμόι, that is, "disputings," refers to the fault and misdoing of sons in the faith,[4] and as the precept concerning the management of a house refers to the right direction of body and of soul,[5] so by the wives of the bishops we are to understand their churches. Concerning whom it is written in Isaiah, "Make haste ye women and come from the show, for it is a people of no understanding."[6] And again "Rise up, ye women that are wealthy,[7] and hear my voice."[8] And in the Book of Proverbs, "Who can find a virtuous woman? for her price is far above rubies. The heart of her husband doth safely trust in her."[9] In the same book too it is written, "Every wise woman buildeth her house: but the foolish plucketh it down with her hands."[10] Nor does this, say they, derogate from the dignity of the episcopate; for the same figure is used in relation to God. Jeremiah writes: "As a wife treacherously departeth from her husband, so have ye dealt treacherously with me, O house of Israel."[11] And the apostle employs the same comparison: "I have espoused you," he says to his converts, "to one husband, that I may present you as a chaste virgin to Christ."[12] The word woman is in the Greek ambiguous and should in all these places be understood as meaning wife. You will say that this interpretation is harsh and does violence to the sense. In that case give back to the scripture its simple

---

[1] Gen. i. 28.   [2] Heb. xiii. 4.
[3] 1 Cor. iii. 17, RV.   [4] 1 Cor. vi. 11.

[1] Ex. xxi. 10.   [2] Lev. xxi. 7, 13.   [3] Canon xv.
[4] Cf. Ph. ii. 14, 15.   [5] 1 Tim. iii. 4.
[6] Isa. xxvii. 11, LXX. AV. follows the Hebrew.
[7] AV. that are at ease.   [8] Isa. xxxii. 9.
[9] Prov. xxxi. 10, 11.   [10] Prov. xiv. 1.
[11] Jer. iii. 20.   [12] 2 Cor. xi. 2.

meaning and save me from the necessity of fighting you on your own ground.[1] I will ask you the following question, Can a man who before his baptism has kept a concubine, and after her death has received baptism and has taken a wife, become a clergyman or not? You will answer me that he can, because his first partner was a concubine and not a wife. What the apostle condemns then, it would seem, is not mere sexual intercourse but marriage contracts and conjugal rights. Many persons, we see, because of narrow circumstances refuse to take upon them the burthen of matrimony. Instead of taking wives they live with their maid-servants and bring up as their own the children which these bear to them. Thus, if through the bounty of the Emperor they gain for their mistresses the right of wearing a matron's robes,[2] they will at once come beneath the yoke of the apostle and sorely against their will will have to receive their partners as their wedded wives. But, if their poverty prevents them from obtaining an imperial rescript such as I have mentioned, the decrees of the Church will vary with the laws of Rome. Be careful therefore not to interpret the words "the husband of one wife," that is, of one woman, as approving indiscriminate intercourse and condemning only contracts of marriage.

I bring forward all these explanations not for the purpose of resisting the true and simple sense of the words in question but to shew you that you must take the holy scriptures as they are written, and that you must not empty of its efficacy the baptismal rite ordained by the Saviour, or render vain the whole mystery of the cross.

6. Let me now fulfil the promise I made a little while ago and with all the skill of a rhetorician sing the praises of water and of baptism. In the beginning the earth was without form and void, there was no dazzling sun or pale moon, there were no glittering stars. There was nothing but matter inorganic and invisible, and even this was lost in abysmal depths and shrouded in a distorting gloom. The Spirit of God above moved, as a charioteer, over the face of the waters,[3] and produced from them the infant world, a type of the Christian child that is drawn from the laver of baptism. A firmament is constructed between heaven and earth, and to this is allotted the name heaven,—in the Hebrew *Shamayim* or 'what comes out of the waters,'—[4] and the waters which are above the heavens are parted from the others to the praise of God. Wherefore also in the vision of the prophet Ezekiel there is seen above the cherubim a crystal stretched forth,[1] that is, the compressed and denser waters. The first living beings come out of the waters; and believers soar out of the laver with wings to heaven. Man is formed out of clay[2] and God holds the mystic waters in the hollow of his hand.[3] In Eden a garden[4] is planted, and a fountain in the midst of it parts into four heads.[5] This is the same fountain which Ezekiel later on describes as issuing out of the temple and flowing towards the rising of the sun, until it heals the bitter waters and quickens those that are dead.[6] When the world falls into sin nothing but a flood of waters can cleanse it again. But as soon as the foul bird of wickedness is driven away, the dove of the Holy Spirit comes to Noah[7] as it came afterwards to Christ in the Jordan,[8] and, carrying in its beak a branch betokening restoration and light, brings tidings of peace to the whole world. Pharaoh and his host, loth to allow God's people to leave Egypt, are overwhelmed in the Red Sea figuring thereby our baptism. His destruction is thus described in the book of Psalms: "Thou didst endow the sea with virtue through thy power: thou brakest the heads of the dragons in the waters: thou brakest the heads of leviathan in pieces."[9] For this reason adders and scorpions haunt dry places[10] and whenever they come near water behave as if rabid or insane.[11] As wood sweetens Marah so that seventy palm-trees are watered by its streams, so the cross makes the waters of the law lifegiving to the seventy who are Christ's apostles.[12] It is Abraham and Isaac who dig wells, the Philistines who try to prevent them.[13] Beersheba too, the city of the oath,[14] and [Gihon], the scene of Solomon's coronation,[15] derive their names from springs. It is beside a well that Eliezer finds Rebekah.[16] Rachel too is a drawer of water and wins a kiss thereby[17] from the supplanter[18] Jacob. When the daughters of the priests of Midian are in a strait to reach the well, Moses opens a way for them and delivers them from outrage.[19] The Lord's forerunner at Salem (a name which means peace or perfection) makes ready the people for Christ with spring-water.[20] The Saviour Himself does not preach the kingdom of heaven until by His baptismal immersion He has cleansed the Jordan.[21]

---

[1] *i.e.* that of strained interpretations.
[2] V. Dict. Ant. s. v. stola and cf. Cic. Phil. ii. 18, 44.
[3] Gen. i. 2.
[4] It is hardly necessary to remark that this derivation is purely fanciful and has no foundation in fact.

[1] Ezek. i. 22. [2] Gen. ii. 7.
[3] Query a reference to Isa. xl. 12: the Latin is obscure.
[4] Paradisus. [5] Gen. ii. 8, 10.
[6] Ezek. xlvii. 1, 8. [7] Gen. viii. 8, 11.
[8] Matt. iii. 16. [9] Ps. lxxiv. 13, 14, LXX.
[10] Deut. viii. 15. [11] ὑδροφόβους et lymphaticos faciunt.
[12] Exod. xv. 23-27; Luke x. i. [13] Gen. xxvi. 15, 18.
[14] Gen. xxi. 31. [15] 1 Kings i. 38; 2 Chron. xxxii. 30.
[16] Gen. xxiv. 15, 16. [17] Gen. xxix. 10, 11.
[18] Gen. xxvii. 36. [19] Exod. ii. 16, 17.
[20] Joh. iii. 23. [21] Matt. iii. 13, 17.

Water is the matter of His first miracle [1] and it is from a well that the Samaritan woman is bidden to slake her thirst.[2] To Nicodemus He secretly says:—"Except a man be born of water and of the Spirit, he cannot enter into the Kingdom of God."[3] As His earthly course began with water, so it ended with it. His side is pierced by the spear, and blood and water flow forth, twin emblems of baptism and of martyrdom.[4] After His resurrection also, when sending His apostles to the Gentiles, He commands them to baptize these in the mystery of the Trinity.[5] The Jewish people repenting of their misdoing are sent forthwith by Peter to be baptized.[6] Before Sion travails she brings forth children, and a nation is born at once.[7] Paul the persecutor of the church, that ravening wolf out of Benjamin,[8] bows his head before Ananias one of Christ's sheep, and only recovers his sight when he applies the remedy of baptism.[9] By the reading of the prophet the eunuch of Candace the queen of Ethiopia is made ready for the baptism of Christ.[10] Though it is against nature the Ethiopian does change his skin and the leopard his spots.[11] Those who have received only John's baptism and have no knowledge of the Holy Spirit are baptized again, lest any should suppose that water unsanctified thereby could suffice for the salvation of either Jew or Gentile.[12] "The voice of the Lord is upon the waters . . . The Lord is upon many waters . . . the Lord maketh the flood to inhabit it."[13] His "teeth are like a flock of sheep that are even shorn which came up from the washing; whereof everyone bear twins, and none is barren among them."[14] If none is barren among them, all of them must have udders filled with milk and be able to say with the apostle: "Ye are my little children, of whom I travail in birth again until Christ be formed in you;"[15] and "I have fed you with milk and not with meat."[16] And it is to the grace of baptism that the prophecy of Micah refers: "He will turn again, he will have compassion upon us: he will subdue our iniquities, and will cast all our sins[17] into the depths of the sea."[18]

7. How then can you say that all sins are drowned in the baptismal laver if a man's wife is still to swim on the surface as evidence against him? The psalmist says:—"Blessed is he whose transgression is forgiven, whose sin is covered. Blessed is the man unto whom the Lord imputeth not iniquity."[1] It would seem that we must add something to this song and say "Blessed is the man to whom the Lord imputeth not a wife." Let us hear also the declaration which Ezekiel the so called "son of man"[2] makes concerning the virtue of him who is to be the true son of man, the Christian: "I will take you," he says, "from among the heathen . . . then will I sprinkle clean water upon you, and ye shall be clean from all your filthiness . . . a new heart also will I give you and a new spirit."[3] "From all your filthiness," he says, "will I cleanse you." If all is taken away nothing can be left. If filthiness is cleansed, how much more is cleanness kept from defilement. "A new heart also will I give you and a new spirit." Yes, for "in Christ Jesus neither circumcision availeth anything nor uncircumcision but a new nature."[4] Wherefore the song also which we sing is a new song,[5] and putting off the old man[6] we walk not in the oldness of the letter but in the newness of the spirit.[7] This is the new stone wherein the new name is written, "which no man knoweth saving he that receiveth it."[8] "Know ye not," says the apostle, "that so many of us as were baptized into Jesus Christ were baptized into his death? Therefore we are buried with him by baptism into death: that like as Christ was raised up from the dead by the glory of the Father, even so we also should walk in newness of life."[9] Do we read so often of newness and of making new and yet can no renewing efface the stain which the word wife brings with it? We are buried with Christ by baptism and we have risen again by faith in the working of God who hath called Him from the dead. And "when we were dead in our sins and in the uncircumcision of our flesh, God hath quickened us together with Him, having forgiven us all trespasses; blotting out the handwriting of ordinances that was against us, which was contrary to us, and took it out of the way nailing it to His cross."[10] Can it be that when our whole being is dead with Christ and when all the sins noted down in the old "handwriting" are blotted out, the one word "wife" alone lives on? Time would fail me were I to try to lay before you in order all the passages in the Holy Scriptures which relate to the efficacy of baptism or to explain the mysterious doctrine of that second birth which though it is our second is yet our first in Christ.

8. Before I make an end of dictating (for I

---

[1] The turning of the water into wine at Cana (Joh. ii. 1, 11).
[2] Joh. iv. 13, 14.   [3] Joh. iii. 5.
[4] Joh. xix. 34: Jerome here follows Tertullian and Cyril of Jerusalem.
[5] Matt. xxviii. 19.   [6] Acts ii. 38.   [7] Isa. lxvi. 7, 8.
[8] Gen. xlix. 27.   [9] Acts ix. 17, 18. Comp. Letter LX. 8.
[10] Acts viii. 27-38.   [11] Jer. xiii. 23.   [12] Acts xix. 1-7.
[13] Ps. xxix. 3, 10. AV. 'the Lord sitteth upon the flood.'
[14] Cant. iv. 2.   [15] Gal. iv. 19.   [16] 1 Cor. iii. 2.
[17] AV. "thou wilt cast all their sins."   [18] Mic. vii. 19.

[1] Ps. xxxii. 1-2   [2] Ezek. ii. 1.
[3] Ezek. xxxvi. 24-26. AV. punctuates differently.
[4] Gal. vi. 15, 'nature for 'creature,' a slip of memory.
[5] Rev. xiv. 3.   [6] Eph. iv. 22.   [7] Rom. vii. 6.
[8] Rev. ii. 17.   [9] Rom. vi. 3, 4.   [10] Col. ii. 13, 14.

perceive that I have already exceeded the just limits of a letter) I wish to give a brief explanation of the previous verses of the epistle in which the apostle describes the life of him that is to be made a bishop. We shall thus recognize him as Doctor of the Nations [1] not only for his praise of monogamy but also for all his precepts. At the same time I beg that no one will suppose that in what I write my design is to blacken the priests of the present day. My one object is to promote the interest of the church. Just as orators and philosophers in giving their notions of the perfect orator and the perfect philosopher do not detract from Demosthenes and Plato but merely set forth abstract ideals; so, when I describe a bishop and explain the qualifications laid down for the episcopate, I am but supplying a mirror for priests. Every man's conscience will tell him that it rests with himself what image he will see reflected there, whether one that will grieve him by its deformity or one that will gladden him by its beauty. I turn now to the passage in question. [2] "If a man desire the office of a bishop, he desireth a good work." Work, you see, not rank; toil not pleasure; work that he may increase in lowliness, not grow proud by reason of elevation. "A bishop then must be blameless." The same thing that he says to Titus, "if any be blameless." [3] All the virtues are comprehended in this one word; thus he seems to require an impossible perfection. For if every sin, even every idle word, is deserving of blame, who is there in this world that is sinless and blameless? Still he who is chosen to be shepherd of the church must be one compared with whom other men are rightly regarded as but a flock of sheep. Rhetoricians define an orator as a good man able to speak. To be worthy of so high an honour he must be blameless in life and lip. For a teacher loses all his influence whose words are rendered null by his deeds. "The husband of one wife." Concerning this requirement I have spoken above. I will now only warn you that if monogamy is insisted on before baptism the other conditions laid down must be insisted on before baptism too. For it is impossible to regard the remaining obligations as binding only on the baptized and this alone as binding also on the unbaptized. "Vigilant (or "temperate" for νηφαλιος means both) wise, [4] of good behaviour, given to hospitality, apt to teach." The priests who minister in God's temple are forbidden to drink wine and strong drink, [5] to keep their wits from being stupefied with drunkenness and to enable their understanding to do its duty in God's service.

By the word 'wise' those are excluded who plead simplicity as an excuse for a priest's folly. For if the brain be not sound, all the members will be amiss. The phrase "of good behaviour" is an extension of the previous epithet "blameless." One who has no faults is called "blameless;" one who is rich in virtues is said to be "of good behaviour." Or the words may be differently explained in accord with Tully's maxim, [1] 'the main thing is that what you do you should do gracefully.' For some persons are so ignorant of their own measure [2] and so stupid and foolish that they make themselves laughing stocks to those who see them because of their gesture or gait or dress or conversation. Fancying that they know what is and what is not good taste they deck themselves out with finery and bodily adornments and give banquets which profess to be elegant: but all such attempts at dress and display are nastier than a beggar's rags. As regards the obligation of priests to be teachers we have the precepts of the old Law [3] and the fuller instructions given on the subject to Titus. [4] For an innocent and unobtrusive conversation does as much harm by its silence as it does good by its example. If the ravening wolves are to be frightened away it must be by the barking of dogs and by the staff of the shepherd. "Not given to wine, no striker." With the virtues they are to aim at he contrasts the vices they are to avoid.

9. We have learned what we ought to be: let us now learn what priests ought not to be. Indulgence in wine is the fault of diners out and revellers. When the body is heated with drink it soon boils over with lust. Wine drinking means self-indulgence, self-indulgence means sensual gratification, sensual gratification means a breach of chastity. He that lives in pleasure is dead while he lives, [5] and he that drinks himself drunk is not only dead but buried. One hour's debauch makes Noah uncover his nakedness which through sixty years of sobriety he had kept covered. [6] Lot in a fit of intoxication unwittingly adds incest to incontinence, and wine overcomes the man whom Sodom failed to conquer. [7] A bishop that is a striker is condemned by Him who gave His back to the smiters, [8] and when He was reviled reviled not again. [9] "But moderate": [10] one good thing is set over against two evil things. Drunkenness and passion are to be held in check by moderation. "Not a brawler, not covetous." Nothing is more overweening than the assurance of the ignorant who fancy that incessant chatter will carry

---

[1] Doctor Gentium. [2] 1 Tim. iii. 1–7. [3] Tit. i. 6.
[4] AV. 'sober.' [5] Lev. x. 9.

[1] Cic. de Or. i 29. [2] Cf. 2 Cor. x. 14.
[3] Cf. Dt. xvii. 9–11. [4] Tit. i. 9–14.
[5] Cf. 1 Tim. v. 6. [6] Gen. ix. 20. 21. [7] Gen. xix. 30–38.
[8] Isa. l. 6. [9] 1 Pet. ii. 23. [10] AV. 'patient.'

conviction with it and are always ready for a dispute that they may thunder with turgid eloquence against the flock committed to their charge. That a priest must avoid covetousness even Samuel teaches when he proves before all the people that he has taken nothing from any man.[1] And the same lesson is taught by the poverty of the apostles who used to receive sustenance and refreshment from their brethren and to boast that they neither had nor wished to have anything besides food and raiment.[2] What the epistle to Timothy calls covetousness, that to Titus openly censures as the desire for filthy lucre.[3] "One that ruleth well his own house." Not by increasing riches, not by providing regal banquets, not by having a pile of finely-wrought plates, not by slowly steaming pheasants so that the heat may reach the bones without melting the flesh upon them; no, but by first requiring of his own household the conduct which he has to inculcate in others. "Having his children in subjection with all gravity." They must not, that is, follow the example of the sons of Eli who lay with the women in the vestibule of the Temple and, supposing religion to consist in plunder, diverted to the gratification of their own appetites all the best parts of the victims.[4] "Not a novice lest being lifted up with pride he fall into the condemnation of the devil." I cannot sufficiently express my amazement at the great blindness which makes men discuss such questions as that of marriage before baptism and causes them to charge people with a transaction which is dead in baptism, nay even quickened into a new life with Christ, while no one regards a commandment so clear and unmistakable as this about bishops not being novices. One who was yesterday a catechumen is to-day a bishop[5]; one who was yesterday in the amphitheatre is to-day in the church; one who spent the evening in the circus stands in the morning at the altar: one who a little while ago was a patron of actors is now a dedicator of virgins. Was the apostle ignorant of our shifts and subterfuges? did he know nothing of our foolish arguments? He not only says that a bishop must be the husband of one wife, but he has given commandment that he must be blameless, vigilant, sober, of good behaviour, given to hospitality, apt to teach, moderate,[6] not given to wine, no striker, not a brawler, not covetous, not a novice. Yet to all these requirements we shut our eyes and notice nothing but the wives of the aspirants. Who cannot give instances to shew the need of the warning: "lest being lifted up with pride he fall into

the condemnation of the devil?" A priest[1] who is made such in a moment knows nothing of the lowliness and meekness which mark the meanest of the faithful, he knows nothing of Christian courtesy, he is not wise enough to think little of himself. He passes from one dignity to another, yet he has not fasted, he has not wept, he has not taken himself to task for his life, he has not striven by constant meditation to amend it, he has not given his substance to the poor. Yet he is moved from one see[2] to another, he passes, that is, from pride to pride. There can be no doubt that arrogance is what the Apostle means when he speaks of the condemnation and downfall of the devil. And all men fall into this who are in a moment made masters, actually before they are disciples. "Moreover he must have a good report of them which are without." The last requirement is like the first. One who is really "blameless" obtains the unanimous approval not only of his own household but of outsiders as well. By aliens and persons outside the church we are to understand Jews, heretics and Gentiles. A Christian bishop then must be such that they who cavil at his religion may not venture to cavil at his life. At present however we see but too many bishops who are willing, like the charioteers in the horse races, to bid money for the popular applause; while there are some so universally hated that they can wring no money from their people, a feat which clowns accomplish by means of a few gestures.

10. Such are the conditions, son Oceanus, which the master-teachers of the church ought with anxiety and fear to require of others and to observe themselves. Such too are the canons which they should follow in the choice of persons for the priesthood; for they must not interpret the law of Christ to suit private animosities and feuds or to gratify ill-feeling which is sure to recoil on the man who cherishes it. Consider how unimpeachable is the character of Carterius in whose life his ill-wishers can find nothing to censure except a marriage contracted before baptism. "He that said, Do not commit adultery, said also, Do not kill. If we commit no adultery yet if we kill, we are become transgressors of the law."[3] "Whosoever shall keep the whole law and yet offend in one point, he is guilty of all."[4] Accordingly when they cast in our teeth a marriage entered into before baptism, we must require of them compliance with all the precepts which are given to the baptized. For they pass over much that is not allowable while they censure much that is allowed.

---

[1] 1 Sam. xii. 3-5.   [2] Cf. 1 Tim. vi. 8.   [3] Tit. i. 7.
[4] 1 Sam. ii. 12-17, 22.   [5] The case of Ambrose.
[6] AV. 'patient.'

[1] Sacerdos: as usual a bishop is meant.
[2] Lit. 'chair.'   [3] Jas. ii. 11.   [4] Jas. ii. 10.

LETTER LXX.

TO MAGNUS AN ORATOR OF ROME.

Jerome thanks Magnus, a Roman orator, for his services in bringing a young man named Sebesius to apologize to him for some fault that he had committed. He then replies to a criticism of Magnus on his fondness for making quotations from profane writers, a practice which he defends by the example of the fathers of the church and of the inspired penmen of scripture. He ends by hinting that the objection really comes not from Magnus himself but from Rufinus (here nicknamed Calpurnius Lanarius). The date of the letter is 397 A.D.

1. That our friend Sebesius has profited by your advice I have learned less from your letter than from his own penitence. And strange to say the pleasure which he has given me since his rebuke is greater than the pain he caused me from his previous waywardness. There has been indeed a conflict between indulgence in the father, and affection in the son ; while the former is anxious to forget the past, the latter is eager to promise dutiful behaviour in the future. Accordingly you and I must equally rejoice, you because you have successfully put a pupil to the test, I because I have received a son again.

2. You ask me at the close of your letter why it is that sometimes in my writings I quote examples from secular literature and thus defile the whiteness of the church with the foulness of heathenism. I will now briefly answer your question. You would never have asked it, had not your mind been wholly taken up with Tully ; you would never have asked it had you made it a practice instead of studying Volcatius[1] to read the holy scriptures and the commentators upon them. For who is there who does not know that both in Moses and in the prophets there are passages cited from Gentile books and that Solomon proposed questions to the philosophers of Tyre and answered others put to him by them.[2] In the commencement of the book of Proverbs he charges us to understand prudent maxims and shrewd adages, parables and obscure discourse, the words of the wise and their dark sayings ;[3] all of which belong by right to the sphere of the dialectician and the philosopher. The Apostle Paul also, in writing to Titus, has used a line of the poet Epimenides : " The Cretians are always liars, evil beasts, slow bellies."[4] Half of which line was afterwards adopted by Callimachus. It is not surprising that a literal rendering of the words into Latin should fail to preserve the metre, seeing that Homer when translated into

the same language is scarcely intelligible even in prose. In another epistle Paul quotes a line of Menander : " Evil communications corrupt good manners."[1] And when he is arguing with the Athenians upon the Areopagus he calls Aratus as a witness citing from him the words " For we are also his offspring ; "[2] in Greek τοῦ γὰρ καὶ γένος ἐσμέν, the close of a heroic verse. And as if this were not enough, that leader of the Christian army, that unvanquished pleader for the cause of Christ, skilfully turns a chance inscription into a proof of the faith.[3] For he had learned from the true David to wrench the sword of the enemy out of his hand and with his own blade to cut off the head of the arrogant Goliath.[4] He had read in Deuteronomy the command given by the voice of the Lord that when a captive woman had had her head shaved, her eyebrows and all her hair cut off, and her nails pared, she might then be taken to wife.[5] Is it surprising that I too, admiring the fairness of her form and the grace of her eloquence, desire to make that secular wisdom which is my captive and my handmaid, a matron of the true Israel ? Or that shaving off and cutting away all in her that is dead whether this be idolatry, pleasure, error, or lust, I take her to myself clean and pure and beget by her servants for the Lord of Sabaoth ? My efforts promote the advantage of Christ's family, my so-called defilement with an alien increases the number of my fellow-servants. Hosea took a wife of whoredoms, Gomer the daughter of Diblaim, and this harlot bore him a son called Jezreel or the seed of God.[6] Isaiah speaks of a sharp razor which shaves " the head of sinners and the hair of their feet ; "[7] and Ezekiel shaves his head as a type of that Jerusalem which has been an harlot,[8] in sign that whatever in her is devoid of sense 'and life must be removed.

3. Cyprian, a man renowned both for his eloquence and for his martyr's death, was assailed—so Firmian tells us[9]—for having used in his treatise against Demetrius passages from the Prophets and the Apostles which the latter declared to be fabricated and made up, instead of passages from the philosophers and poets whose authority he, as a heathen, could not well gainsay. Celsus[10] and Porphyry[11] have written against us and have been ably answered, the former by Origen, the latter by Methodius, Eusebius, and Apollinaris.[12] Origen wrote a treatise in eight books, the work of

---

[1] Either a teacher of civil law mentioned by Pliny (viii. 40), or else one of the writers of the Augustan History.
[2] The authority for this is Josephus.
[3] Prov. i. 1-6. [4] Tit. i. 12.

[1] 1 Cor. xv. 33. The line is also attributed to Euripides.
[2] Acts xvii. 28. [3] Acts xvii. 22. [4] Cf. 1 Sam. xvii. 50, 51.
[5] Deut. xxi. 10-13. [6] Hos. i. 2-4. [7] Isa. vii. 20.
[8] Ezek. v. 1-5. [9] i.e. Lactantius, vide Inst. v. 4.
[10] The author of a polemical treatise against Christianity, fragments of which are still preserved in Origen's reply. He was a Platonist.
[11] A neoplatonist writer who flourished in the third century.
[12] See note on Letter XLVIII. § 13.

Methodius[1] extended to ten thousand lines, while Eusebius[2] and Apollinaris[3] composed twenty-five and thirty volumes respectively. Read these and you will find that compared with them I am a mere tyro in learning, and that, as my wits have long lain fallow, I can barely recall as in a dream what I have learned as a boy. The emperor Julian[4] found time during his Parthian campaign to vomit forth seven books against Christ and, as so often happens in poetic legends, only wounded himself with his own sword. Were I to try to confute him with the doctrines of philosophers and stoics you would doubtless forbid me to strike a mad dog with the club of Hercules. It is true that he presently felt in battle the hand of our Nazarene or, as he used to call him, the Galilæan,[5] and that a spear-thrust in the vitals paid him due recompense for his foul calumnies. To prove the antiquity of the Jewish people Josephus[6] has written two books against Appio a grammarian of Alexandria; and in these he brings forward so many quotations from secular writers as to make me marvel how a Hebrew brought up from his childhood to read the sacred scriptures could also have perused the whole library of the Greeks. Need I speak of Philo[7] whom critics call the second or the Jewish Plato?

4. Let me now run through the list of our own writers. Did not Quadratus[8] a disciple of the apostles and bishop of the Athenian church deliver to the Emperor Hadrian (on the occasion of his visit to the Eleusinian mysteries) a treatise in defence of our religion. And so great was the admiration caused in everyone by his eminent ability that it stilled a most severe persecution. The philosopher Aristides,[9] a man of great eloquence, presented to the same Emperor an apology for the Christians composed of extracts from philosophic writers. His example was afterwards followed by Justin[10] another philosopher who delivered to Antoninus Pius and his sons[11] and to the senate a treatise Against the Gentiles, in which

he defended the ignominy of the cross and preached the resurrection of Christ with all freedom. Need I speak of Melito[1] bishop of Sardis, of Apollinaris[2] chief-priest of the Church of Hierapolis, of Dionysius[3] bishop of the Corinthians, of Tatian,[4] of Bardesanes,[5] of Irenæus[6] successor to the martyr Pothinus;[7] all of whom have in many volumes explained the uprisings of the several heresies and tracked them back, each to the philosophic source from which it flows. Pantænus,[8] a philosopher of the Stoic school, was on account of his great reputation for learning sent by Demetrius bishop of Alexandria to India, to preach Christ to the Brahmans and philosophers there. Clement,[9] a presbyter of Alexandria, in my judgment the most learned of men, wrote eight books of *Miscellanies*[10] and as many of *Outline Sketches*,[11] a treatise against the Gentiles, and three volumes called the *Pedagogue*. Is there any want of learning in these, or are they not rather drawn from the very heart of philosophy? Imitating his example Origen[12] wrote ten books of *Miscellanies*, in which he compares together the opinions held respectively by Christians and by philosophers, and confirms all the dogmas of our religion by quotations from Plato and Aristotle, from Numenius[13] and Cornutus.[14] Miltiades[15] also wrote an excellent treatise against the Gentiles. Moreover Hippolytus[16] and a Roman senator named Apollonius[17] have each compiled apologetic works. The books of Julius Africanus[18] who wrote a history of his own times are still extant, as also are those of Theodore who was afterwards called Gregory,[19]

---

[1] Fl. A.D. 170. He composed an Apology addressed to the Emperor Marcus Aurelius.
[2] A highly esteemed writer, from 171 A.D. onwards, who wrote many treatises, amongst which were an apology addressed to Marcus Aurelius, and several works against Montanism.
[3] Fl. A.D. 171, the writer of several pastoral letters to other churches famous in their day but no longer extant.
[4] See note on Letter XLVIII. § 3.
[5] Born at Edessa c. 155 A.D. died 223 A.D. A mystical theologian of a gnostic type who held a high position at the court of the Abgars. His writings have perished.
[6] Bishop of Lyons in the latter half of the second century. He was a native of Asia Minor and in his younger days had known Polycarp.
[7] Bishop of Lyons, suffered martyrdom under Marcus Aurelius.
[8] A convert from stoicism to Christianity in the latter part of the second century who as the head of the catechetical school at Alexandria was the instructor of Clement.
[9] Head of the catechetical school at Alexandria A.D. 190-203.
[10] στρωματεῖς.   [11] ὑποτυπώσεις.
[12] See Letter XXXIII. Of Origen's Miscellanies only a few fragments remain. 'They appear to have discussed various topics in the light of ancient philosophy and scripture.'—Westcott.
[13] A neoplatonic and neopythagorean philosopher who flourished in the age of the Antonines.
[14] A Stoic philosopher, the friend and teacher of the poet Persius. Having criticised Nero's literary style too freely he was banished by that emperor.
[15] An active Christian writer of the reign of Commodus.
[16] Fl. A.D. 200-225, the first antipope. His *Refutation of All Heresies* is of great interest and value.
[17] Fl. A.D. 186. Accused of being a Christian, he delivered in the senate an apology for the faith.
[18] A writer of the third century who compiled a Chronicle of the world's history from the creation to his own day. It has long since perished.
[19] Surnamed Thaumaturgus or the Wonderworker. One of Origen's pupils, he wrote a Panegyric (extant) on his master. Fl. 233-270.

---

[1] Contemporary with Eusebius the historian. His *Symposium* still extant proves him to have been a warm admirer of Plato.
[2] The learned bishop of Cæsarea (A.D. 260-340). His Church History and other works are translated or described in Vol. i. of this series.
[3] Probably the learned Bishop of Laodicea, whose views were condemned at Constantinople in 381.
[4] Julian was emperor from A.D. 261 to A.D. 263. He reverted from Christianity to paganism and did all in his power to harass the Church.
[5] According to Theodoret (H. E. iii. 25) Julian's last words were "Thou hast conquered, O Galilæan."
[6] A Jew born at Jerusalem A.D. 37. His historical works, still extant, are of great value.
[7] See note on Letter XXII. § 35.
[8] The author of an apology for the Christians presented to the Emperor Hadrian. Only small fragments of the work are now extant. See for him and Aristides Jerome's *Book on Famous Men*, in Vol. iii. of this series, c. xix. xx.
[9] Another Athenian apologist contemporary with Quadratus. His Apology has lately been published. Cambridge, Eng., 1891.
[10] Commonly called Justin Martyr. Born in Samaria of Greek parents, he is said to have undergone martyrdom at Rome. Fl. A.D. 140-150.
[11] Marcus Aurelius and Lucius Verus.

a man endowed with apostolic miracles as well as with apostolic virtues. We still have the works of Dionysius [1] bishop of Alexandria, of Anatolius [2] chief priest of the church of Laodicea, of the presbyters Pamphilus,[3] Pierius,[4] Lucian,[5] Malchion ; [6] of Eusebius [7] bishop of Cæsarea, Eustathius [8] of Antioch and Athanasius [9] of Alexandria ; of Eusebius [10] of Emisa, of Triphyllius [11] of Cyprus, of Asterius [12] of Scythopolis, of the confessor Serapion,[13] of Titus [14] bishop of Bostra ; and of the Cappadocians Basil,[15] Gregory,[16] and Amphilochius.[17] All these writers so frequently interweave in their books the doctrines and maxims of the philosophers that you might easily be at a loss which to admire most, their secular erudition or their knowledge of the scriptures.

5. I will pass on to Latin writers. Can anything be more learned or more pointed than the style of Tertullian ? [18] His *Apology* and his books *Against the Gentiles* contain all the wisdom of the world. Minucius Felix [19] a pleader in the Roman courts has ransacked all heathen literature to adorn the pages of his *Octavius* and of his treatise *Against the astrologers* (unless indeed this latter is falsely ascribed to him). Arnobius [20] has published seven books against the Gentiles, and his pupil Lactantius [21] as many, besides two volumes, one *on Anger* and the other *on the creative activity of God.* If you read any of these you will find in them an epitome of Cicero's dialogues. The Martyr Victorinus [1] though as a writer deficient in learning is not deficient in the wish to use what learning he has. Then there is Cyprian.[2] With what terseness, with what knowledge of all history, with what splendid rhetoric and argument has he touched the theme that idols are no Gods ! Hilary [3] too, a confessor and bishop of my own day, has imitated Quintilian's twelve books both in number and in style, and has also shewn his ability as a writer in his short treatise against Dioscorus the physician. In the reign of Constantine the presbyter Juvencus [4] set forth in verse the story of our Lord and Saviour, and did not shrink from forcing into metre the majestic phrases of the Gospel. Of other writers dead and living I say nothing. Their aim and their ability are evident to all who read them.[5]

6. You must not adopt the mistaken opinion, that while in dealing with the Gentiles one may appeal to their literature in all other discussions one ought to ignore it ; for almost all the books of all these writers—except those who like Epicurus [6] are no scholars—are extremely full of erudition and philosophy. I incline indeed to fancy—the thought comes into my head as I dictate—that you yourself know quite well what has always been the practice of the learned in this matter. I believe that in putting this question to me you are only the mouthpiece of another who by reason of his love for the histories of Sallust might well be called Calpurnius Lanarius.[7] Please beg of him not to envy eaters their teeth because he is toothless himself, and not to make light of the eyes of gazelles because he is himself a mole. Here as you see there is abundant material for discussion, but I have already filled the limits at my disposal.

LETTER LXXI.

TO LUCINIUS.

Lucinius was a wealthy Spaniard of Bætica who in conformity with the ascetic ideas of his time had made a vow of continence with his wife Theodora. Being much interested in the study of scripture he pro-

---

[1] Head of the catechetical school, and afterwards bishop, of Alexandria. He died A.D. 265.
[2] Trained in the school of Alexandria and praised by Eusebius for his great learning.
[3] The intimate friend of Eusebius of Cæsarea and founder of the famous library in that city.
[4] See note on Letter XLVIII. § 3.
[5] A presbyter of Antioch and apparently a pupil of Malchion. He suffered martyrdom at Nicomedia A.D. 311.
[6] A presbyter of Antioch in the reign of Aurelian. He took part in the proceedings against Paul of Samosata.
[7] See note on § 3 above.
[8] Bishop of Antioch at the time of the Nicene Council. One of the earliest and most vigorous opponents of Arianism.
[9] Bishop of Alexandria from A.D. 326 to A.D. 373. The great champion of the divinity of Christ against Arius and his followers.
[10] Flor. A.D. 341-359. After studying at Alexandria he lived for some time at Antioch where he took part in an Arian council.
[11] A famous lawyer of Berytus converted to Christianity by Spyridon a bishop in Cyprus.
[12] Bishop of Amasea in Pontus, a constant student of Demosthenes and himself no mean orator.
[13] An Egyptian bishop the friend of Antony and Athanasius. Some of his writings are still extant.
[14] This bishop is best known through the Emperor Julian's vain attempt to expel him from his see.
[15] A.D. 329-379. Bishop of Cæsarea in Cappadocia and a strenuous champion of orthodoxy. His works are still extant.
[16] Gregory of Nazianzus, Bishop of Sasima and for a short time of Constantinople (A.D. 379-381).
[17] Flor. A.D. 350-400. Archbishop of Iconium. A friend of Basil and of Gregory Nazianzen.
[18] An African writer who in his last days became a Montanist. Flor. A.D. 175-225.
[19] A Roman lawyer of the second century. His Apology—a Dialogue entitled Octavius—is extant.
[20] Fl. A.D. 300. A professor of rhetoric at Sicca in Africa and a heathen. He composed his apology to prove the reality of his conversion.
[21] An African rhetorician and apologist of the fourth century. His works are extant.

[1] A celebrated man of letters at Rome in the middle of the fourth century, the story of whose conversion is told in Augustine's *Confessions* (viii. 2-5).
[2] Bishop of Carthage. He suffered martyrdom A.D. 358. His works are extant.
[3] Bishop of Poitiers (died A.D. 368). A champion of the orthodox faith against Arianism.
[4] A Spanish Christian of the fourth century. His "Story of the Gospels," a life of Christ in hexameter verse, still exists.
[5] For most of the writers mentioned in this section see also Jerome's *Book of Famous Men* translated in Vol. iii. of this series.
[6] For an account of Epicurus see Letter V. § 5, note. He professed to have read but little.
[7] That Rufinus is the person meant is plain from a reference made to this passage in Apol. adv. Rufinum, i. 30 and also from Letter CII. § 3. Jerome is however mistaken in connecting this Calpurnius with Sallust. He is mentioned by Plutarch as a treacherous friend. Sallust does mention a certain Calpurnius Bestia, and Jerome has probably confounded the two.

posed to visit Bethlehem, and in A.D. 397 sent several scribes thither to transcribe for him Jerome's principal writings. To these on their return home Jerome now entrusts the following letter. In it he encourages Lucinius to fulfil his purpose of coming to Bethlehem, describes the books which he is sending to him, and answers two questions relating to ecclesiastical usage. He also sends him some trifling presents.

Shortly after receiving the letter (written in 398 A.D.) Lucinius died and Jerome wrote to Theodora to console her for her loss (Letter LXXV.).

1. Your letter which has suddenly arrived was not expected by me, and coming in an unlooked for way it has helped to rouse me from my torpor by the glad tidings which it conveys. I hasten to embrace with the arms of love one whom my eyes have never seen, and silently say to myself:—'"oh that I had wings like a dove! for then would I flee away and be at rest."[1] Then would I find him "whom my soul loveth."[2] In you the Lord's words are now truly fulfilled: "many shall come from the east and west and shall sit down with Abraham."[3] In those days the faith of my Lucinius was foreshadowed in Cornelius, "centurion of the band called the Italian band."[4] And when the apostle Paul writes to the Romans: "whensoever I take my journey into Spain I will come to you: for I trust to see you in my journey, and to be brought on my way thitherward by you;"[5] he shews by the tale of his previous successes what he looked to gain from that province.[6] Laying in a short time the foundation of the gospel "from Jerusalem and round about unto Illyricum,"[7] he enters Rome in bonds, that he may free those who are in the bonds of error and superstition. Two years he dwells in his own hired house[8] that he may give to us the house eternal which is spoken of in both the testaments.[9] The apostle, the fisher of men,[10] has cast forth his net, and, among countless kinds of fish, has landed you like a magnificent gilt-bream. You have left behind you the bitter waves, the salt tides, the mountain-fissures; you have despised Leviathan who reigns in the waters.[11] Your aim is to seek the wilderness with Jesus and to sing the prophet's song: "my soul thirsteth for thee, my flesh longeth for thee in a dry and thirsty land where no water is; to see thy power and thy glory, so as I have seen thee in the sanctuary,"[12] or, as he sings in another place, "lo, then would I wander far off and remain in the wilderness. I would hasten my escape from the windy storm and tempest."[13]

Since you have left Sodom and are hastening to the mountains, I beseech you with a father's affection not to look behind you. Your hands have grasped the handle of the plough,[1] the hem of the Saviour's garment,[2] and His locks wet with the dew of night;[3] do not let them go. Do not come down from the housetop of virtue to seek for the clothes which you wore of old, nor return home from the field.[4] Do not like Lot set your heart on the plain or upon the pleasant gardens;[5] for these are watered not, as the holy land, from heaven but by Jordan's muddy stream made salt by contact with the Dead Sea.

2. Many begin but few persevere to the end. "They which run in a race run all, but one receiveth the crown."[6] But of us on the other hand it is said: "So run that ye may obtain."[7] Our master of the games is not grudging; he does not give the palm to one and disgrace another. His wish is that all his athletes may alike win garlands. My soul rejoices, yet the very greatness of my joy makes me feel sad. Like Ruth[8] when I try to speak I burst into tears. Zacchæus, the convert of an hour, is accounted worthy to receive the Saviour as his guest.[9] Martha and Mary make ready a feast and then welcome the Lord to it.[10] A harlot washes His feet with her tears and against His burial anoints His body with the ointment of good works.[11] Simon the leper invites the Master with His disciples and is not refused.[12] To Abraham it is said: "Get thee out of thy country and from thy kindred and from thy father's house, unto a land that I will shew thee."[13] He leaves Chaldæa, he leaves Mesopotamia; he seeks what he knows not, not to lose Him whom he has found. He does not deem it possible to keep both his country and his Lord; even at that early day he is already fulfilling the prophet David's words: "I am a stranger with thee and a sojourner, as all my fathers were."[14] He is called "a Hebrew," in Greek περάτης, a passer-over, for not content with present excellence but forgetting those things which are behind he reaches forth to that which is before.[15] He makes his own the words of the psalmist: "they shall go from strength to strength."[16] Thus his name has a mystic meaning and he has opened for you a way to seek not your own things but those of another. You too must leave your home as he did, and must take for your parents, brothers, and relations only those

---

[1] Ps. lv. 6. PBV. [2] Cant. iii. 1. [3] Matt. viii. 11.
[4] Acts x. 1. [5] Rom. xv. 24. [6] Italy.
[7] Rom. xv. 19. [8] Acts xxviii. 30.
[9] Utriusque instrumenti æternam domum. The 'twofold record' is that of the old and new testaments both of which speak of the church under the figure of a house. For the term "instrument" see note on Letter
[10] Matt. iv. 19. [11] Cf. Ps. civ. 26.
[12] Ps. lxiii. 1, 2. [13] Ps. lv. 7, 8.

[1] Luke ix. 62. [2] Matt. ix. 20. [3] Cant. v. 2.
[4] Matt. xxiv. 17, 18. [5] Gen. xiii. 10.
[6] Jerome quoting from memory substitutes 'crown' for 'prize.'
[7] 1 Cor. ix. 24. [8] Ruth i. 14. [9] Luke xix. 5.
[10] Joh. xii. 2. [11] Mark xiv. 8. [12] Matt. xxvi. 6.
[13] Gen. xii. 1. [14] Ps. xxxix. 12.
[15] Phil. iii. 13. [16] Ps. lxxxiv. 7.

who are linked to you in Christ. "Whosoever," He says, "shall do the will of my father . . . the same is my brother and sister and mother."[1]

3. You have with you one who was once your partner in the flesh but is now your partner in the spirit ; once your wife but now your sister ; once a woman but now a man ; once an inferior but now an equal.[2] Under the same yoke as you she hastens toward the same heavenly kingdom.

A too careful management of one's income, a too near calculation of one's expenses—these are habits not easily laid aside. Yet to escape the Egyptian woman Joseph had to leave his garment with her.[3] And the young man who followed Jesus having a linen cloth cast about him, when he was assailed by the servants had to throw away his earthly covering and to flee naked.[4] Elijah also when he was carried up in a chariot of fire to heaven left his mantle of sheepskin on earth.[5] Elisha used for sacrifice the oxen and the yokes which hitherto he had employed in his work.[6] We read in Ecclesiasticus : "he that toucheth pitch shall be defiled therewith."[7] As long as we are occupied with the things of the world, as long as our soul is fettered with possessions and revenues, we cannot think freely of God. "For what fellowship hath righteousness with unrighteousness? And what communion hath light with darkness? And what concord hath Christ with Belial? Or what part hath he that believeth with an infidel?"[8] "Ye cannot," the Lord says, "serve God and Mammon."[9] Now the laying aside of money is for those who are beginners in the way, not for those who are made perfect. Heathens like Antisthenes[10] and Crates[11] the Theban have done as much before now. But to offer one's self to God, this is the mark of Christians and apostles. These like the widow out of their penury cast their two mites into the treasury, and giving all that they have to the Lord are counted worthy to hear his words : "ye also shall sit upon twelve thrones judging the twelve tribes of Israel."[12]

4. You can see for yourself why I mention these things ; without expressly saying it I am inviting you to take up your abode at the holy places. Your abundance has supported the want of many that some day their riches may abound to supply your want ;[13] you have made to yourself " friends of the mammon of unrighteousness that they may receive you into everlasting habitations."[1] Such conduct deserves praise and merits to be compared with the virtue of apostolic times. Then, as you know, believers sold their possessions and brought the prices of them and laid them down at the apostles' feet :[2] a symbolic act designed to shew that men must trample on covetousness. But the Lord yearns for believers' souls more than for their riches. We read in the Proverbs : "the ransom of a man's soul are his own riches."[3] We may, indeed, take a man's own riches to be those which do not come from some one else, or from plunder ; according to the precept : "honour God with thy just labours."[4] But the sense is better if we understand a man's " own riches " to be those hidden treasures which no thief can steal and no robber wrest from him.[5]

5. As for my poor works which from no merits of theirs but simply from your own kindness you say that you desire to have ; I have given them to your servants to transcribe, I have seen the paper-copies made by them, and I have repeatedly ordered them to correct them by a diligent comparison with the originals. For so many are the pilgrims passing to and fro that I have been unable to read so many volumes. They have found me also troubled by a long illness from which this Lent I am slowly recovering as they are leaving me. If then you find errors or omissions which interfere with the sense, these you must impute not to me but to your own servants ; they are due to the ignorance or carelessness of the copyists, who write down not what they find but what they take to be the meaning, and do but expose their own mistakes when they try to correct those of others. It is a false rumour which has reached you to the effect that I have translated the books of Josephus[6] and the volumes of the holy men Papias[7] and Polycarp.[8] I have neither the leisure nor the ability to preserve the charm of these masterpieces in another tongue. Of Origen[9] and Didymus[10] I have translated a few things, to set before my countrymen some specimens of Greek teaching. The canon of the Hebrew verity[11] —except the octoteuch[12] which I have at present in hand—I have placed at the disposal of your slaves and copyists. Doubtless you already possess the version from the septuagint[13]

---

[1] Matt. xii. 50.   [2] His wife Theodora.
[3] Gen. xxxix. 12.   [4] Mark xiv. 51, 52.
[5] 2 Kings ii. 11, 13.   [6] 1 Kings xix. 21.
[7] Ecclus. xiii. 1.   [8] 2 Cor. vi. 14, 15.   [9] Matt. vi. 24.
[10] A disciple of Socrates, subsequently the founder of the Cynic School. Fl. 366 B.C.
[11] See note on Letter LXVI. § 8.
[12] Matt. xix. 28.   [13] 2 Cor. viii. 14.

[1] Luke xvi. 9.   [2] Acts iv. 34, 35.
[3] Prov. xiii. 8, LXX.   [4] Prov. iii. 9, LXX.
[5] Cf. Matt. vi. 20.   [6] See note on Letter XXII. § 35.
[7] A writer of the sub-apostolic age who had been a disciple of the apostle John. He was bishop of Hierapolis in Phrygia.
[8] Another sub-apostolic writer who was also a disciple of John. He became bishop of Smyrna and underwent martyrdom at the age of 86.
[9] See note on Letter XXXIII.
[10] The blind theologian of Alexandria by whose teaching Jerome had himself profited. See Letter XXXIV. § 3.
[11] The old testament as translated direct from the Hebrew.
[12] The first eight books.
[13] This work Jerome accomplished between the years 383 and 390 A.D. Only the Psalter and Job are extant.

which many years ago I diligently revised for the use of students. The new testament I have restored to the authoritative form of the Greek original.[1] For as the true text of the old testament can only be tested by a reference to the Hebrew, so the true text of the new requires for its decision an appeal to the Greek.

6. You ask me whether you ought to fast on the Sabbath[2] and to receive the eucharist daily according to the custom—as currently reported—of the churches of Rome and Spain.[3] Both these points have been treated by the eloquent Hippolytus,[4] and several writers have collected passages from different authors bearing upon them. The best advice that I can give you is this. Church-traditions—especially when they do not run counter to the faith— are to be observed in the form in which previous generations have handed them down; and the use of one church is not to be annulled because it is contrary to that of another.[5] As regards fasting, I wish that we could practise it without intermission as—according to the Acts of the Apostles[6]—Paul did and the believers with him even in the season of Pentecost and on the Lord's Day. They are not to be accused of manichæism, for carnal food ought not to be preferred before spiritual. As regards the holy eucharist you may receive it at all times[7] without qualm of conscience or disapproval from me. You may listen to the psalmist's words:—" O taste and see that the Lord is good;"[8] you may sing as he does: —" my heart poureth forth a good word."[9] But do not mistake my meaning. You are not to fast on feast-days, neither are you to abstain on the week days in Pentecost.[10] In such matters each province may follow its own inclinations, and the traditions which have been handed down should be regarded as apostolic laws.

7. You send me two small cloaks and a sheepskin mantle from your wardrobe and ask me to wear them myself or to give them to the poor. In return I send to you and your sister[11] in the Lord four small haircloths suitable to your religious profession and to your daily needs, for they are the mark of poverty and the outward witness of a continual penitence. To these I have added a manuscript containing Isaiah's ten most obscure visions which I have lately elucidated with a critical commentary. When you look upon these trifles call to mind the friend in whom you delight and hasten the voyage which you have for a time deferred. And because " the way of man is not in himself" but it is the Lord that " directeth his steps;"[1] if any hindrance should interfere—I hope none may—to prevent you from coming, I pray that distance may not sever those united in affection and that I may find my Lucinius present in absence through an interchange of letters.

LETTER LXXII.

TO VITALIS.

Vitalis had asked Jerome " Is Scripture credible when it tells us that Solomon and Ahaz became fathers at the age of eleven?" The difficulty had previously occurred to Jerome himself (Letter XXXVI. 10, whence perhaps Vitalis took it) and in this letter he suggests several ways in which it may be met. He is quite prepared, if necessary, to accept the alleged fact on the grounds that "there are many things in Scripture which sound incredible and yet are true" and that "nature cannot resist the Lord of nature" (§ 2). He is disposed, however, to regard the question as trivial and of no importance. The date of the letter is 398 A.D.

LETTER LXXIII.

TO EVANGELUS.

Evangelus had sent Jerome an anonymous treatise in which Melchisedek was indentified with the Holy Ghost, and had asked him what he thought of the theory. Jerome in his reply repudiates the idea as absurd and insists that Melchisedek was a real man, possibly, as the Jews said, Shem the eldest son of Noah. The date of the letter is 398 A.D.

LETTER LXXIV.

TO RUFINUS OF ROME.

Rufinus, a Roman Presbyter (to be carefully distinguished from Rufinus of Aquileia and Rufinus the Syrian), had written to Jerome for an explanation of the judgment of Solomon (1 Kings iii. 16–28). This Jerome gives at length, treating the narrative as a parable and making the false and true mothers types of the Synagogue and the Church. The date of the letter is 398 A.D.

LETTER LXXV.

TO THEODORA.

Theodora the wife of the learned Spaniard Lucinius (for whom see Letter LXXI.) had recently lost her husband,

---

[1] This task he undertook at the request of pope Damasus in 383 A.D. See Letter XXVII.
[2] i.e. on Saturday.
[3] At this time the communion was celebrated daily at Constantinople, in Africa, and in Spain. At Rome it was celebrated on every day of the week except Saturday (the Sabbath). See Socrates, H. E. v. 22.
[4] A leading Roman churchman, bishop of Portus, in the early part of the third century, the rival and enemy of pope Callistus and author of many theological treatises, one of which—the Refutation of all Heresies—has recently become famous.
[5] Compare the similar advice given by Gregory the Great to Augustine of Canterbury (Bede, H. E. i. 27).
[6] Nothing in the book of Acts bears out this statement. Fasting at the times mentioned was forbidden in Jerome's day.
[7] Daily if you will and on fast days as well as on feast days.
[8] Ps. xxxiv. 8.　　　　[9] Ps. xlv. 1, Vulg.
[10] i.e. the period of fifty days between Easterday and Whitsunday. See Letter XLI. § 3.
[11] i.e. his wife Theodora.

[1] Jer. x. 23.

a bereavement which suggested the present letter. In it Jerome recounts the many virtues of Lucinius and especially his zeal in resisting the gnostic heresy of Marcus which during his life was prevalent in Spain. The date of the letter is 399 A.D.

1. So overpowered am I by the sad intelligence of the falling asleep of the holy and by me deeply revered Lucinius that I am scarcely able to dictate even a short letter. I do not, it is true, lament his fate, for I know that he has passed to better things : like Moses he can say : "I will now turn aside and see this great sight,"[1] but I am tormented with regret that I was not allowed to look upon the face of one, who was likely, as I believed, in a short time to come hither. True indeed is the prophetic warning concerning the doom of death that it divides brothers,[2] and with harsh and cruel hand sunders those whose names are linked together in the bonds of love. But we have this consolation that it is slain by the word of the Lord. For it is said : "O death, I will be thy plagues ; O grave, I will be thy destruction," and in the next verse : "An east wind shall come, the wind of the Lord shall come up from the wilderness, and his spring shall become dry, and his fountain shall be dried up."[3] For, as Isaiah says, "there shall come forth a rod out of the stem of Jesse, and a branch shall grow out of his roots":[4] and He says Himself in the Song of Songs, "I am the rose of Sharon and the lily of the valley."[5] Our rose is the destruction of death, and died that death itself might die in His dying. But, when it is said that He is to be brought "from the wilderness," the virgin's womb is indicated, which without sexual intercourse or impregnation has given to us God in the form of an infant able to quench by the glow of the Holy Spirit the fountains of lust and to sing in the words of the psalm : "as in a dry and pathless and waterless land, so have I appeared unto thee in the sanctuary."[6] Thus when we have to face the hard and cruel necessity of death, we are upheld by this consolation, that we shall shortly see again those whose absence we now mourn. For their end is not called death but a slumber and a falling asleep. Wherefore also the blessed apostle forbids us to sorrow concerning them which are asleep,[7] telling us to believe that those whom we know to sleep now may hereafter be roused from their sleep, and when their slumber is ended may watch once more with the saints and sing with the angels :— "Glory to God in the highest and on earth peace among men of good will."[8] In heaven

where there is no sin, there is glory and perpetual praise and unwearied singing ; but on earth where sedition reigns, and war and discord hold sway, peace must be gained by prayer, and it is to be found not among all but only among men of good will, who pay heed to the apostolic salutation : "Grace to you and peace from God our Father and the Lord Jesus Christ."[1] For "His abode is in peace and His dwelling place is in Zion,"[2] that is, on a watch-tower,[3] on a height of doctrines and of virtues, in the soul of the believer ; for the angel of this latter daily beholds the face of God,[4] and contemplates with unveiled face the glory of God.

2. Wherefore, though you are already running in the way, I urge a willing horse, as the saying goes, and implore you, while you regret in your Lucinius a true brother, to rejoice as well that he now reigns with Christ. For, as it is written in the book of Wisdom, he was "taken away lest that wickedness should alter his understanding . . . for his soul pleased the Lord . . . and he . . . in a short time fulfilled a long time."[5] We may with more right weep for ourselves that we stand daily in conflict with our sins, that we are stained with vices, that we receive wounds, and that we must give account for every idle word.[6] Victorious now and free from care he looks down upon you from on high and supports you in your struggle, nay more, he prepares for you a place near to himself ; for his love and affection towards you are still the same as when, disregarding his claim on you as a husband, he resolved to treat you even on earth as a sister, or indeed I may say as a brother, for difference of sex while essential to marriage is not so to a continent tie. And since even in the flesh, if we are born again in Christ, we are no longer Greek and Barbarian, bond and free, male and female, but are all one in Him,[7] how much more true will this be when this corruptible has put on incorruption and when this mortal has put on immortality.[8] "In the resurrection," the Lord tells us, "they neither marry nor are given in marriage but are as the angels . . . in heaven."[9] Now when it is said that they neither marry nor are given in marriage but are as the angels in heaven, there is no taking away of a natural and real body but only an indication of the greatness of the glory to come. For the words are not "they shall be angels" but "they shall be as the angels" : thus while likeness to the angels is promised

1 Exod. iii. 3.
2 Hos. xiii. 15, Vulg. Quia ipse inter fratres dividet. AV. follows the Hebrew.
3 Hos. xiii. 14, 15.   4 Isa. xi. 1, Vulg.   5 Cant. ii. 1.
6 Ps. lxiii. 1, 2, Vulg.   7 1 Thess. iv. 13.   8 Luke ii. 14, Vulg.

1 Rom. i. 7.
2 Ps. lxxvi. 2. "Salem" (A.V.), the Hebrew word for peace.
3 See Jerome's Book of Hebrew Names § 5. Cf. also Letter CVIII. §9.
4 Matt. xviii. 10.   5 Wisd. iv. 11-14.   6 Matt. xii. 36.
7 Gal. iii. 28.   8 1 Cor. xv. 53.   9 Matt. xxii. 30.

identity with them is refused. "They shall be," Christ tells us, "as the angels," that is like the angels; therefore they will not cease to be human. Glorious indeed they shall be, and graced with angelic splendour, but they will still be human; the apostle Paul will still be Paul, Mary will still be Mary. Then shall confusion overtake that heresy [1] which holds out great but vague promises only that it may take away hopes which are at once modest and certain.

3. And now that I have once mentioned the word "heresy," where can I find a trumpet loud enough to proclaim the eloquence of our dear Lucinius, who, when the filthy heresy of Basilides [2] raged in Spain and like a pestilence ravaged the provinces between the Pyrenees and the ocean, upheld in all its purity the faith of the church and altogether refused to embrace Armagil, Barbelon, Abraxas, Balsamum, and the absurd Leusibora. Such are the portentous names which, to excite the minds of unlearned men and weak women, they pretend to draw from Hebrew sources, terrifying the simple by barbarous combinations which they admire the more the less they understand them. [3] The growth of this heresy is described for us by Irenæus, bishop of the church of Lyons, a man of the apostolic times, who was a disciple of Papias the hearer of the evangelist John. He informs us that a certain Mark, [4] of the stock of the gnostic Basilides, came in the first instance to Gaul, that he contaminated with his teaching those parts of the country which are watered by the Rhone and the Garonne, and that in particular he misled by his errors high-born women; to whom he promised certain secret mysteries and whose affection he enlisted by magic arts and hidden indulgence in unlawful intercourse. Irenæus goes on to say that subsequently Mark crossed the Pyrenees and occupied Spain, making it his object to seek out the houses of the wealthy, and in these especially the women, concerning whom we are told that they are "led away with divers lusts, ever learning and never able to come to the knowledge of the truth." [5] All this he wrote about three hundred years ago [6] in the extremely learned and eloquent books which he composed under the title *Against all heresies*.

4. From these facts you in your wisdom will realize how worthy of praise our dear Lucinius shewed himself when he shut his ears that he might not have to hear the judgement passed upon bloodshedders, [1] and dispersed all his substance and gave to the poor that his righteousness might endure for ever. [2] And not satisfied with bestowing his bounty upon his own country, he sent to the churches of Jerusalem and Alexandria gold enough to alleviate the want of large numbers. But while many will admire and extol in him this liberality, I for my part will rather praise him for his zeal and diligence in the study of the scriptures. With what eagerness he asked for my poor works! He actually sent six copyists (for in this province there is a dearth of scribes who understand Latin) to copy for him all that I have ever dictated from my youth until the present time. The honour was not of course paid to me who am but a little child, the least of all Christians, living in the rocks near Bethlehem because I know myself a sinner; but to Christ who is honoured in his servants [3] and who makes this promise to them, "He that receiveth you receiveth me, and he that receiveth me receiveth him that sent me." [4]

5. Therefore, my beloved daughter, regard this letter as the epitaph which love prompts me to write upon your husband, and if there is any spiritual work of which you think me to be capable, boldly command me to undertake it: that so ages to come may know that He who says of Himself in Isaiah, "He hath made me a polished shaft; in his quiver hath he hid me," [5] has with His sharp arrow so wounded two men severed by an immense interval of sea and land, that, although they know each other not in the flesh, they are knit together in love in the spirit.

May you be kept holy both in body and spirit by the Samaritan—that is, saviour and keeper—of whom it is said in the psalm, "He that keepeth Israel shall neither slumber nor sleep." [6] May the watcher and the holy one who came down to Daniel [7] come also to you, that you too may be able to say, "I sleep but my heart waketh." [8]

LETTER LXXVI.

TO ABIGAUS.

Abigaus the recipient of this letter was a blind presbyter of Bætica in Spain. He had asked the help of Jerome's prayers in his struggles with evil and Jerome now writes to cheer and to console him. He concludes his remarks by commending to his especial care the widow Theodora. The letter should be compared with that addressed to Castrutius (LXVIII.). It was written at the same time with the preceding.

---

[1] Origenism.
[2] Probably as revived by Priscillian, who was put to death 385. See Jerome *On Illustrious Men*, c. 121.
[3] These terms, the meanings of which are very uncertain, are either the names of æons or magical formulæ used by the Marcosians in the celebration of their mysteries.
[4] A gnostic of the school of Valentinus, who taught in the middle of the second century. Jerome is in error when he describes him as a disciple of Basilides.
[5] 2 Tim. iii. 6, 7.   [6] An error for 'two hundred years ago.'

[1] Is. xxxiii. 15. Jerome's allusion may be to the execution of Priscillian in 385. Lucinius may have shared the views of Ambrose and Martin against the shedding of blood.
[2] Ps. cxii. 9.   [3] Luke ix. 48.   [4] Matt. x. 40.
[5] Isa. xlix. 2.   [6] Ps. cxxi. 4.
[7] Dan. iv. 13. Lit. May *Hir*, that is the watcher, *Hir* being the Hebrew word.
[8] Cant. v. 2.

1. Although I am conscious of many sins and every day pray on bended knees, " Remember not the sins of my youth nor my transgressions,[1] yet because I know that it has been said by the Apostle " let a man not be lifted up with pride lest he fall into the condemnation of the devil,"[2] and that it is written in another passage, " God resisteth the proud but giveth grace to the humble,"[3] there is nothing I have striven so much to avoid from my boyhood up as a swelling mind and a stiff neck,[4] things which always provoke against themselves the wrath of God. For I know that my master and Lord and God has said in the lowliness of His flesh : " Learn of me ; for I am meek and lowly in heart,"[5] and that before this He has sung by the mouth of David : " Lord, remember David and all his gentleness.[6] Again we read in another passage, " Before destruction the heart of man is haughty ; and before honour is humility."[7] Do not, then, I implore you, suppose that I have received your letter and have passed it over in silence. Do not, I beseech you, lay to my charge the dishonesty and negligence of which others have been guilty. For why should I, when called on to respond to your kind advances, continue dumb and repel by my silence the friendship which you offer ? I who am always forward to seek intimate relations with the good and even to thrust myself upon their affection. " Two," we read, " are better than one . . . . for if they fall, the one will lift up his fellow . . . . a three fold cord is not quickly broken, and a brother that helps his brother shall be exalted."[8] Write to me, therefore, boldly, and overcome the effect of absence by frequent colloquies.

2. You should not grieve that you are destitute of those bodily eyes which ants, flies, and creeping things have as well as men ; rather you should rejoice that you possess that eye of which it is said in the Song of Songs, " Thou hast ravished my heart, my sister, my spouse; thou hast ravished my heart with one of thine eyes."[9] This is the eye with which God is seen and to which Moses refers when he says :—" I will now turn aside and see this great sight."[10] We even read of some philosophers of this world[11] that they have plucked out their eyes in order to turn all their thoughts upon the pure depths of the mind. And a prophet has said " Death has entered through our windows."[12] Our Lord too tells the Apostles : " Whosoever looketh upon a woman to lust after her hath committed adultery with her already in his heart."[1] Consequently they are commanded to lift up their eyes and to look on the fields, for these are white and ready for harvest.[2]

3. You request me by my exhortations to slay in you Nebuchadnezzar and Rabshakeh and Nebuzar-adan and Holofernes.[3] Were they alive in you, you would never have sought my aid. No, they are dead within you, and you have begun to build up the ruins of Jerusalem with the help of Zerubbabel and of Joshua the son of Josedech the high priest, of Ezra and of Nehemiah. You do not put your wages into a bag with holes,[4] but you lay up for yourselves treasures in heaven,[5] and if you seek my friendship, it is because you believe me to be a servant of Christ.

I commend to you—although she needs no commendation but her own—my holy daughter Theodora, formerly the wife or rather the sister of Lucinius of blessed memory. Tell her that she must not grow weary of the path upon which she has entered, and that she can only reach the Holy Land by toiling through the wilderness. Warn her against supposing that the work of virtue is perfected when she has made her exodus from Egypt. Remind her that she must pass through snares innumerable to arrive at mount Nebo and the River Jordan,[6] that she must receive circumcision anew at Gilgal,[7] that Jericho must fall before her, overthrown by the blasts of priestly trumpets,[8] that Adoni-zedec must be slain,[9] that Ai and Hazor, once fairest of cities, must both fall.[10]

The brothers who are with me in the monastery salute you, and I through you earnestly salute those reverend persons who deign to bestow upon me their regard.

LETTER LXXVII.

TO OCEANUS.

The eulogy of Fabiola whose restless life had come to an end in 399 A.D. Jerome tells the story of her sin and of her penitence (for which see Letter LV.), of the hospital established by her at Portus, of her visit to Bethlehem, and of her earnestness in the study of scripture. He relates how he wrote for her his account of the vestments of the high priest (Letter LXIV.) and how at the time of her death he was at her request engaged upon a commentary on the forty-two halting-places of the Israelites in the wilderness (Letter LXXIX.). This last he now sends along with this letter to Oceanus. Jerome also bestows praise upon Pammachius as the companion of all Fabiola's labours. The date of the letter is 399 A.D.

---

[1] Ps. xxv. 7.   [2] 1 Tim. iii. 6. AV. adapted.
[3] James iv. 6.   [4] Cf. Ps. lxxv. 5.   [5] Matt. xi. 29.
[6] Ps. cxxxii. 1, Vulg. AV. has ' afflictions.'
[7] Prov. xviii. 12.
[8] Eccl. iv. 9–12. The last clause is Jerome's own.
[9] Cant. iv. 9.   [10] Ex. iii. 3.
[11] Cicero ascribes this piece of fanaticism to Democritus and Metrodorus.
[12] Jer. ix. 21. LXX.

[1] Matt. v. 28.   [2] Joh. iv. 35.
[3] The legendary oppressor of the Jews, whose fate is described in the Book of Judith.
[4] Hagg. i. 6.   [5] Matt. vi. 20.   [6] Nu. xxxiii. 47, 48.
[7] Josh. v. 2, 9.   [8] Josh. vi. 20.
[9] Josh. x. 1, 26.   [10] Josh. viii., xi. 10.

1. Several years since I consoled the venerated Paula, whilst her affliction was still recent, for the falling asleep of Blæsilla.[1] Four summers ago I wrote for the bishop Heliodorus the epitaph of Nepotian, and expended what ability I possessed in giving expression to my grief at his loss.[2] Only two years have elapsed since I sent a brief letter to my dear Pammachius on the sudden flitting of his Paulina.[3] I blushed to say more to one so learned or to give him back his own thoughts : lest I should seem less the consoler of a friend than the officious instructor of one already perfect. But now, Oceanus my son, the duty that you lay upon me is one that I gladly accept and would even seek unasked. For when new virtues have to be dealt with, an old subject itself becomes new. In previous cases I have had to soften and restrain a mother's affection, an uncle's grief, and a husband's yearning ; according to the different requirements of each I have had to apply from scripture different remedies.

2. To-day you give me as my theme Fabiola, the praise of the Christians, the marvel of the gentiles, the sorrow of the poor, and the consolation of the monks. Whatever point in her character I choose to treat of first, pales into insignificance compared with those which follow after. Shall I praise her fasts ? Her alms are greater still. Shall I commend her lowliness ? The glow of her faith is yet brighter. Shall I mention her studied plainness in dress, her voluntary choice of plebeian costume and the garb of a slave that she might put to shame silken robes ? To change one's disposition is a greater achievement than to change one's dress. It is harder for us to part with arrogance than with gold and gems. For, even though we throw away these, we plume ourselves sometimes on a meanness that is really ostentatious, and we make a bid with a saleable poverty for the popular applause. But a virtue that seeks concealment and is cherished in the inner consciousness appeals to no judgement but that of God. Thus the eulogies which I have to bestow upon Fabiola will be altogether new : I must neglect the order of the rhetoricians and begin all I have to say only from the cradle of her conversion and of her penitence. Another writer, mindful of the school, would perhaps bring forward Quintus Maximus, "the man who by delaying rescued Rome,"[4] and the whole Fabian family ; he would describe their struggles and battles and would exult that Fabiola had come to us through a line so noble, shewing that qualities not apparent in the branch still existed in the root. But as I am a lover of the inn at Beth-

lehem and of the Lord's stable in which th virgin travailed with and gave birth to an in fant God, I shall deduce the lineage of Christ handmaid not from a stock famous in histor but from the lowliness of the church.

3. And because at the very outset there a rock in the path and she is overwhelmed b a storm of censure, for having forsaken he first husband and having taken a second, will not praise her for her conversion till have first cleared her of this charge. So te rible then were the faults imputed to her fo mer husband that not even a prostitute or common slave could have put up with them If I were to recount them, I should undo th heroism of the wife who chose to bear th blame of a separation rather than to blacke the character and expose the stains of hir who was one body with her. I will onl urge this one plea which is sufficient to exor erate a chaste matron and a Christian woma The Lord has given commandment that a wif must not be put away "except it be for forn cation, and that, if put away, she must rema unmarried."[1] Now a commandment whic is given to men logically applies to wome also. For it cannot be that, while an adulte ous wife is to be put away, an incontinen husband is to be retained. The apostle says "he which is joined to an harlot is one body." Therefore she also who is joined to a whor monger and unchaste person is made one bod with him. The laws of Cæsar are different, is true, from the laws of Christ : Papinianus commands one thing ; our own Paul anothe Earthly laws give a free rein to the unchastit of men, merely condemning seduction an adultery ; lust is allowed to range unrestraine among brothels and slave girls, as if the gui were constituted by the rank of the perso assailed and not by the purpose of the assai ant. But with us Christians what is unlawft for women is equally unlawful for men, an as both serve the same God both are boun by the same obligations. Fabiola then ha put away—they are quite right—a husban that was a sinner, guilty of this and that crim sins—I have almost mentioned their names— with which the whole neighbourhood resounde but which the wife alone refused to disclos If however it is made a charge against he that after repudiating her husband she di not continue unmarried, I readily admit th to have been a fault, but at the same time d clare that it may have been a case of necessit " It is better," the apostle tells us, "to marr than to burn."[4] She was quite a youn

[1] Letter XXXIX.   [2] Letter LX.
[3] Letter LXVI.   [4] Ennius.

[1] Matt. xix. 9. 1 Cor. vii. 11.   [2] 1 Cor. vi. 16.
[3] A Roman jurist of great renown who held high legal offi
first under Marcus Aurelius and afterwards under Severus. H
was put to death by Caracalla.
[4] 1 Cor. vii. 9.

woman, she was not able to continue in wid-whood. In the words of the apostle she saw another law in her members warring against the law of her mind ;[1] she felt herself dragged in chains as a captive towards the indulgences of wedlock. Therefore she thought it better openly to confess her weakness and to accept the semblance of an unhappy marriage than, with the name of a monogamist, to ply the trade of a courtesan. The same apostle wills that the younger widows should marry, bear children, and give no occasion to the adversary to speak reproachfully.[2] And he at once goes on to explain his wish : " for some are already turned aside after Satan."[3] Fabiola therefore was fully persuaded in her own mind : she thought she had acted legitimately in putting away her husband, and that when she had done so she was free to marry again. She did not know that the rigour of the gospel takes away from women all pretexts for re-marriage so long as their former husbands are alive ; and not knowing this, though she contrived to evade other assaults of the devil, she at this point unwittingly exposed herself to a wound from him.

4. But why do I linger over old and forgotten matters, seeking to excuse a fault for which Fabiola has herself confessed her penitence ? Who would believe that, after the death of her second husband at a time when most widows, having shaken off the yoke of servitude, grow careless and allow themselves more liberty than ever, frequenting the baths, flitting through the streets, shewing their harlot faces everywhere ; that at this time Fabiola came to herself ? Yet it was then that she put on sackcloth to make public confession of her error. It was then that in the presence of all Rome (in the basilica which formerly belonged to that Lateranus who perished by the sword of Cæsar[4]) she stood in the ranks of the penitents and exposed before bishop, presbyters, and people—all of whom wept when they saw her weep—her dishevelled hair, pale features, soiled hands and unwashed neck. What sins would such penance fail to purge away ? What ingrained stains would such tears be unable to wash out ? By a threefold confession Peter blotted out his threefold denial.[5] If Aaron committed sacrilege by fashioning molten gold into the head of a calf, his brother's prayers made amends for his transgressions.[6] If holy David, meekest of men, committed the double sin of murder and adultery, he atoned for it by a fast of seven days. He

lay upon the earth, he rolled in the ashes, he forgot his royal power, he sought for light in the darkness.[1] And then, turning his eyes to that God whom he had so deeply offended, he cried with a lamentable voice : " Against thee, thee only, have I sinned, and done this evil in thy sight," and " Restore unto me the joy of thy salvation and uphold me with thy free spirit."[2] He who by his virtues teaches me how to stand and not to fall, by his penitence teaches me how, if I fall, I may rise again. Among the kings do we read of any so wicked as Ahab, of whom the scripture says : "there was none like unto Ahab which did sell himself to work wickedness in the sight of the Lord " ?[3] For shedding Naboth's blood Elijah rebuked him, and the prophet denounced God's wrath against him : " Hast thou killed and also taken possession ? . . . behold I will bring evil upon thee and will take away thy posterity "[4] and so on. Yet when Ahab heard these words " he rent his clothes, and put sackcloth upon his flesh, and fasted . . . in sackcloth, and went softly."[5] Then came the word of God to Elijah the Tishbite saying : " Seest thou how Ahab humbleth himself before me ? Because he humbleth himself before me, I will not bring the evil in his days."[6] O happy penitence which has drawn down upon itself the eyes of God, and which has by confessing its error changed the sentence of God's anger ! The same conduct is in the Chronicles[7] attributed to Manasseh, and in the book of the prophet Jonah[8] to Nineveh, and in the gospel to the publican.[9] The first of these not only was allowed to obtain forgiveness but also recovered his kingdom, the second broke the force of God's impending wrath, while the third, smiting his breast with his hands, " would not lift up so much as his eyes to heaven." Yet for all that the publican with his humble confession of his faults went back justified far more than the Pharisee with his arrogant boasting of his virtues. This is not however the place to preach penitence, neither am I writing against Montanus and Novatus.[10] Else would I say of it that it is "a sacrifice . . . well pleasing to God,"[11] I would cite the words of the psalmist : " the sacrifices of God are a broken spirit,"[12] and those of Ezekiel " I prefer the repentance of a sinner rather than his death,"[13] and those of Baruch, " Arise, arise, O Jerusalem,"[14] and many other proclamations made by the trumpets of the prophets.

---

[1] Rom. vii. 23.   [2] 1 Tim. v. 14.   [3] 1 Tim. v. 15.
[4] A senator who having conspired against Nero was by that emperor put to death. His palace on the Ælian Hill was long afterwards bestowed by Constantine upon pope Silvester who made it a church which it has ever since remained.
[5] Joh. xviii. 15-27 : xxi. 15-17.   [6] Ex. xxxii. 30-35.

[1] 2 Sam. xii. 16.   [2] Ps. li. 4, 12.   [3] 1 Kings xxi. 25.
[4] 1 K. xxi. 19, 21.   [5] 1 K. xxi. 27.
[6] 1 K. xxi. 28, 29.   [7] 2 Chr. xxxiii. 12, 13.
[8] Jon. iii. 5-10.   [9] Luke xviii. 13.
[10] Rigourists who denied the power of the Church to absolve persons who had fallen into sin.
[11] Ph. iv. 18.   [12] Ps. li. 17.
[13] Cf. Ezek. xviii. 23.   [14] Bar. v. 5, cf. Isa. lx. 1.

5. But this one thing I will say, for it is at once useful to my readers and pertinent to my present theme. As Fabiola was not ashamed of the Lord on earth, so He shall not be ashamed of her in heaven.[1] She laid bare her wound to the gaze of all, and Rome beheld with tears the disfiguring scar which marred her beauty. She uncovered her limbs, bared her head, and closed her mouth. She no longer entered the church of God but, like Miriam the sister of Moses,[2] she sat apart without the camp, till the priest who had cast her out should himself call her back. She came down like the daughter of Babylon from the throne of her daintiness, she took the millstones and ground meal, she passed barefooted through rivers of tears.[3] She sat upon the coals of fire, and these became her aid.[4] That face by which she had once pleased her second husband she now smote with blows; she hated jewels, shunned ornaments and could not bear to look upon fine linen.[5] In fact she bewailed the sin she had committed as bitterly as if it had been adultery, and went to the expense of many remedies in her eagerness to cure her one wound.

6. Having found myself aground in the shallows of Fabiola's sin, I have dwelt thus long upon her penitence in order that I might open up a larger and quite unimpeded space for the description of her praises. Restored to communion before the eyes of the whole church, what did she do? In the day of prosperity she was not forgetful of affliction;[6] and, having once suffered shipwreck she was unwilling again to face the risks of the sea. Instead therefore of re-embarking on her old life, she broke up[7] and sold all that she could lay hands on of her property (it was large and suitable to her rank), and turning it into money she laid out this for the benefit of the poor. She was the first person to found a hospital, into which she might gather sufferers out of the streets, and where she might nurse the unfortunate victims of sickness and want. Need I now recount the various ailments of human beings? Need I speak of noses slit, eyes put out, feet half burnt, hands covered with sores? Or of limbs dropsical and atrophied? Or of diseased flesh alive with worms? Often did she carry on her own shoulders persons infected with jaundice or with filth. Often too did she wash away the matter discharged from wounds which others, even though men, could not bear to look at. She gave food to her patients with her own hand, and moistened the scarce breathing lips of the dying with sips of liquid. I know of many wealthy and devout persons who, unable to overcome their natural repugnance to such sights, perform this work of mercy by the agency of others, giving money instead of personal aid. I do not blame them and am far from construing their weakness of resolution into a want of faith. While however I pardon such squeamishness, I extol to the skies the enthusiastic zeal of a mind that is above it. A great faith makes little of such trifles. But I know how terrible was the retribution which fell upon the proud mind of the rich man clothed in purple for not having helped Lazarus.[1] The poor wretch whom we despise, whom we cannot so much as look at, and the very sight of whom turns our stomachs, is human like ourselves, is made of the same clay as we are, is formed out of the same elements. All that he suffers we too may suffer. Let us then regard his wounds as though they were our own, and then all our insensibility to another's suffering will give way before our pity for ourselves.

Not with a hundred tongues or throat of bronze
Could I exhaust the forms of fell disease [2]

which Fabiola so wonderfully alleviated in the suffering poor that many of the healthy fell to envying the sick. However she showed the same liberality towards the clergy and monks and virgins. Was there a monastery which was not supported by Fabiola's wealth? Was there a naked or bedridden person who was not clothed with garments supplied by her? Were there ever any in want to whom she failed to give a quick and unhesitating supply? Even Rome was not wide enough for her pity. Either in her own person or else through the agency of reverend and trustworthy men she went from island to island and carried her bounty not only round the Etruscan Sea, but throughout the district of the Volscians, as it stands along those secluded and winding shores where communities of monks are to be found.

7. Suddenly she made up her mind, against the advice of all her friends, to take ship and to come to Jerusalem. Here she was welcomed by a large concourse of people and for a short time took advantage of my hospitality. Indeed, when I call to mind our meeting, I seem to see her here now instead of in the past. Blessed Jesus, what zeal, what earnestness she bestowed upon the sacred volumes! In her eagerness to satisfy what was a veritable craving she would run through Prophets, Gospels, and Psalms: she would suggest questions and treasure up the answers in the desk of her own bosom. And yet this eager

---

[1] Luke ix. 26.   [2] Nu. xii. 14.   [3] Isa. xlvii. 1, 2.
[4] Isa. xlvii. 14, Vulg.   [5] Linteamina.   [6] Ecclus. xi. 25.
[7] Dilapidare, vendre pierre à pierre—Goelzer.

[1] Luke xvi. 19-24.   [2] Virg. Æn. vi. 625-627.

ess to hear did not bring with it any feeling of satiety : increasing her knowledge she also increased her sorrow,[1] and by casting oil upon the flame she did but supply fuel for a still more burning zeal. One day we had before us the book of *Numbers* written by Moses, and she modestly questioned me as to the meaning of the great mass of names there to be found. Why was it, she inquired, that single tribes were differently associated in this passage and in that, how came it that the soothsayer Balaam in prophesying of the future mysteries of Christ[2] spoke more plainly of Him than almost any other prophet ? I replied as best I could and tried to satisfy her enquiries. Then unrolling the book still farther she came to the passage[3] in which is given the list of all the halting-places by which the people after leaving Egypt made its way to the waters of Jordan. And when she asked me the meaning and reason of each of these, I spoke doubtfully about some, dealt with others in a tone of assurance, and in several instances simply confessed my ignorance. Hereupon she began to press me harder still, expostulating with me as though it were a thing unallowable that I should be ignorant of what I did not know, yet at the same time affirming her own unworthiness to understand mysteries so deep. In a word I was ashamed to refuse her request and allowed her to extort from me a promise that I would devote a special work to this subject for her use. Till the present time I have had to defer the fulfilment of my promise : as I now perceive, by the Will of God in order that it should be consecrated to her memory. As in a previous work[4] I clothed her with the priestly vestments, so in the pages of the present[5] she may rejoice that she has passed through the wilderness of this world and has come at last to the land of promise.

8. But let me continue the task which I have begun. Whilst I was in search of a suitable dwelling for so great a lady, whose only conception of the solitary life included a place of resort like Mary's inn ; suddenly messengers flew this way and that and the whole East was terror-struck. For news came that the hordes of the Huns had poured forth all the way from Mæotis[6] (they had their haunts between the icy Tanais[7] and the rude Massagetæ[8] where the gates of Alexander keep back the wild peoples behind the Caucasus) ; and that, speeding hither and thither on their nimble-footed horses, they were filling all the world with panic and bloodshed. The Roman army was absent at the time, being de-

tained in Italy on account of the civil wars. Of these Huns Herodotus[1] tells us that under Darius King of the Medes they held the East in bondage for twenty years and that from the Egyptians and Ethiopians they exacted a yearly tribute. May Jesus avert from the Roman world the farther assaults of these wild beasts ! Everywhere their approach was unexpected, they outstripped rumour in speed, and, when they came, they spared neither religion nor rank nor age, even for wailing infants they had no pity. Children were forced to die before it could be said that they had begun to live ; and little ones not realizing their miserable fate might be seen smiling in the hands and at the weapons of their enemies. It was generally agreed that the goal of the invaders was Jerusalem and that it was their excessive desire for gold which made them hasten to this particular city. Its walls uncared for in time of peace were accordingly put in repair. Antioch was in a state of siege. Tyre, desirous of cutting itself off from the land, sought once more its ancient island. We too were compelled to man our ships and to lie off the shore as a precaution against the arrival of our foes. No matter how hard the winds might blow, we could not but dread the barbarians more than shipwreck. It was not, however, so much for our own safety that we were anxious as for the chastity of the virgins who were with us. Just at that time also there was dissension among us,[2] and our intestine struggles threw into the shade our battle with the barbarians. I myself clung to my long-settled abode in the East and gave way to my deep-seated love for the holy places. Fabiola, used as she was to moving from city to city and having no other property but what her baggage contained, returned to her native land ; to live in poverty where she had once been rich, to lodge in the house of another, she who in old days had lodged many guests in her own, and—not unduly to prolong my account—to bestow upon the poor before the eyes of Rome the proceeds of that property which Rome knew her to have sold.

9. This only do I lament that in her the holy places lost a necklace of the loveliest. Rome recovered what it had previously parted with, and the wanton and slanderous tongues of the heathen were confuted by the testimony of their own eyes. Others may commend her pity, her humility, her faith : I will rather praise her ardour of soul. The letter[3] in which as a young man I once urged Heliodorus to the life of a hermit she knew by heart,

---

[1] Eccl. i. 18
[2] Nu. xxiv. 15-19.
[3] Nu. xxxiii.
[4] Letter LXIV.
[5] Letter LXXVIII. on the Mansions or Halting-places of Israel in the Desert.
[6] The Sea of Azov.
[7] The Don.
[8] An Asiatic tribe to the East of the Caspian Sea.

[1] Hdt. i. 106. (of the Scythians).
[2] The Origenistic controversy in which Jerome, Paula and Epiphanius took one side, John bishop of Jerusalem, Rufinus, and Melania the other.
[3] Letter XIV.

and whenever she looked upon the walls of Rome she complained that she was in a prison. Forgetful of her sex, unmindful of her frailty, and only desiring to be alone she was in fact there [1] where her soul lingered. The counsels of her friends could not hold her back ; so eager was she to burst from the city as from a place of bondage. Nor did she leave the distribution of her alms to others ; she distributed them herself. Her wish was that, after equitably dispensing her money to the poor, she might herself find support from others for the sake of Christ. In such haste was she and so impatient of delay that you would fancy her on the eve of her departure. As she was always ready, death could not find her unprepared.

10. As I pen her praises, my dear Pammachius seems suddenly to rise before me. His wife Paulina sleeps that he may keep vigil; she has gone before her husband that he remaining behind may be Christ's servant. Although he was his wife's heir, others—I mean the poor—are now in possession of his inheritance. He and Fabiola contended for the privilege of setting up a tent like that of Abraham [2] at Portus. The contest which arose between them was for the supremacy in shewing kindness. Each conquered and each was overcome. Both admitted themselves to be at once victors and vanquished ; for what each had desired to effect alone both accomplished together. They united their resources and combined their plans that harmony might forward what rivalry must have brought to nought. No sooner was the scheme broached than it was carried out. A house was purchased to serve as a shelter, and a crowd flocked into it. " There was no more travail in Jacob nor distress in Israel." [3] The seas carried voyagers to find a welcome here on landing. Travellers left Rome in haste to take advantage of the mild coast before setting sail. What Publius once did in the island of Malta for one apostle and—not to leave room for gainsaying—for a single ship's crew, [4] Fabiola and Pammachius have done over and over again for large numbers ; and not only have they supplied the wants of the destitute, but so universal has been their munificence that they have provided additional means for those who have something already. The whole world knows that a home for strangers has been established at Portus ; and Britain has learned in the summer what Egypt and Parthia knew in the spring.

11. In the death of this noble lady we have seen a fulfilment of the apostle's words :—
" All things work together for good to them

that fear God." [1]   Having a presentiment of what would happen, she had written to several monks to come and release her from the burthen under which she laboured ; [2] for she wished to make to herself friends of the mammon of unrighteousness that they might receive her into everlasting habitations. [3]   They came to her and she made them her friends; she fell asleep in the way that she had wished, and having at last laid aside her burthen she soared more lightly up to heaven. How great a marvel Fabiola had been to Rome while she lived came out in the behaviour of the people now that she was dead. Hardly had she breathed her last breath, hardly had she given back her soul to Christ whose it was when

Flying Rumour heralding the woe [4]

gathered the entire city to attend her obsequies. Psalms were chaunted and the gilded ceilings of the temples were shaken with uplifted shouts of Alleluia.

The choirs of young and old extolled her deeds
And sang the praises of her holy soul. [5]

Her triumph was more glorious far than those won by Furius over the Gauls, by Papirius over the Samnites, by Scipio over Numantia, by Pompey over Pontus. They had conquered physical force, she had mastered spiritual iniquities. [6]   I seem to hear even now the squadrons which led the van of the procession and the sound of the feet of the multitude which thronged in thousands to attend her funeral. The streets, porches, and roofs from which a view could be obtained were inadequate to accommodate the spectators. On that day Rome saw all her peoples gathered together in one, and each person present flattered himself that he had some part in the glory of her penitence. No wonder indeed that men should thus exult in the salvation of one at whose conversion there was joy among the angels in heaven. [7]

12. I give you this, Fabiola, [8] the best gift of my aged powers, to be as it were a funeral offering. Oftentimes have I praised virgins and widows and married women who have kept their garments always white [9] and who follow the Lamb whithersoever He goeth. [10] Happy indeed is she in her encomium who throughout her life has been stained by no defilement. But let envy depart and censoriousness be silent. If the father of the house is good why should our eye be evil ? [11] The soul which fell among thieves has been

---

[1] i.e. in the desert where many women lived as solitaries.
[2] Like that in which Abraham entertained the angels. See Letter LXVI. 11.
[3] Num. xxiii. 21. LXX.   [4] Acts xxviii. 7.

[1] Rom. viii. 28: note that Jerome substitutes 'fear' for 'love.'
[2] The remnant of her fortune.   [3] Luke xvi. 9.
[4] Virg. A. xi. 139.   [5] Virg. A. viii. 287, 288.
[6] Eph. vi. 12.   [7] Luke xv. 7, 10.
[8] i.e. Letter LXXVIII. q. v.   [9] Eccl. ix. 8 ; Rev. iii. 4.
[10] Rev. xiv. 4.   [11] Matt. xx. 15.

arried home upon the shoulders of Christ.[1] n our father's house are many mansions.[2] Where sin hath abounded, grace hath much nore abounded.[3] To whom more is forgiven he same loveth more.[4]

LETTER LXXVIII.

TO FABIOLA.

A treatise on the Forty-two Mansions or Halting-laces of the Israelites, originally intended for Fabiola ut not completed until after her death. Sent to Oceanus long with the preceding letter. These Mansions are lade an emblem of the Christian's pilgrimage, the true Iebrew hastening to pass from earth to heaven.

LETTER LXXIX.

TO SALVINA.

A letter of consolation addressed by Jerome to Sal-ina (a lady of the imperial court) on the death of her usband Nebridius. After excusing his temerity in ddressing a complete stranger Jerome eulogizes the irtues of Nebridius, particularly his chastity and his ounty to the poor. He next warns Salvina (in no ourtier-like terms) of the dangers that will beset her s a widow and recommends her to devote all her nergies to the careful training of the son and daughter rho are now her principal charge. The tone of the etter is somewhat arrogant and it can hardly be re-arded as one of Jerome's happiest efforts. Salvina, how-ver, consecrated her life to deeds of piety, and became ne of Chrysostom's deaconesses. Its date is 400 A.D.

1. My desire to do my duty may, I fear, xpose me to a charge of self-seeking ; and lthough I do but follow the example of Him vho said: "learn of me for I am meek and owly of heart,"[5] the course that I am taking nay be attributed to a desire for notoriety. Men may say that I am not so much trying o console a widow in affliction as endeavouring o creep into the imperial court ; and that, vhile I make a pretext of offering comfort, I m really seeking the friendship of the great. Clearly this will not be the opinion of any one vho knows the commandment: "thou shalt not espect the person of the poor,"[6] a precept given est under pretext of shewing pity we should udge unjust judgment. For each individual s to be judged not by his personal importance out by the merits of his case. His wealth need not stand in the way of the rich man, if ne makes a good use of it ; and poverty can oe no recommendation to the poor if in the nidst of squalor and want he fails to keep clear of wrong doing. Proofs of these things ire not wanting either in scriptural times or our own ; for Abraham, in spite of his im-mense wealth, was "the friend of God"[7] and poor men are daily arrested and punished for heir crimes by law. She whom I now ad-dress is both rich and poor so that she cannot say what she actually has. For it is not of her purse that I am speaking but of the pur-ity of her soul. I do not know her face but I am well acquainted with her virtues ; for report speaks well of her and her youth makes her chastity all the more commendable. By her grief for her young husband she has set an example to all wives ; and by her resignation she has proved that she believes him not lost but gone before. The greatness of her bereave-ment has brought out the reality of her religion. For while she forgets her lost Nebridius, she knows that in Christ he is with her still.

But why do I write to one who is a stranger to me ? For three reasons. First, because (as a priest is bound to do) I love all Chris-tians as my children and find my glory in pro-moting their welfare. Secondly because the father of Nebridius was bound to me by the closest ties.[1] Lastly—and this is a stronger reason than the others—because I have failed to say no to my son Avitus.[2] With an impor-tunacy surpassing that of the widow towards the unjust judge[3] he wrote to me so frequently and put before me so many instances in which I had previously dealt with a similar theme, that he overcame my modest reluctance and made me resolve to do not what would best become me but what would most nearly meet his wishes.

2. As the mother of Nebridius was sister to the empress[4] and as he was brought up in the bosom of his aunt, another might perhaps praise him for having so much endeared himself to the unvanquished emperor. Theodosius, indeed, procured him from Africa a wife of the highest rank,[5] who, as her native land at this time was distracted by civil wars, became a kind of host-age for its loyalty. I ought to say at the very outset that Nebridius seems to have had a pre-sentiment that he would die early. For amid the splendour of the palace and in the high positions to which his rank and not his years entitled him he lived always as one who be-lieved that he must soon go to meet Christ. Of Cornelius, the centurion of the Italian band, the sacred narrative tells us that God so fully accepted him as to send to him an angel ; and that this angel told him that to his merit was due the mystery whereby Peter from the nar-row limits of the circumcision was conveyed to the wide field of the uncircumcision. He was the first Gentile baptized by the apostle, and in him the Gentiles were set apart to sal-vation. Now of this man it is written : "there

---

[1] Luke x. 30 ; xv. 5.   [2] Joh. xiv. 2.
[3] Rom. v. 20.   [4] Luke vii. 47.   [5] Matt. xi. 29.
[6] Lev. xix. 15.   [7] Isa. xli. 8; Jas. ii. 23.

[1] Also named Nebridius, Prefect of Gaul, then of the East.
[2] See letter CXXIV.   [3] Luke xviii. 1-5.
[4] Ælia Flaccilla, the wife of Theodosius who is here called "the unvanquished emperor."
[5] Salvina was the daughter of Gildo who at the time was trib-utary king of Mauritania.

was a certain man in Cæsarea called Cornelius, a centurion of the band called the Italian band, a devout man and one that feared God with all his house, which gave much alms to the people, and prayed to God alway." [1] All this that is said of him I claim—with a change of name only—for my dear Nebridius. So "devout" was this latter and so enamoured of chastity that at his marriage he was still pure. So truly did he "fear God with all his house" that forgetting his high position he spent all his time with monks and clergymen. So profuse were the alms which he gave to the people that his doors were continually beset with swarms of sick and poor. And assuredly he "prayed to God alway" that what was for the best might happen to him. Therefore "speedily was he taken away lest that wickedness should alter his understanding . . . for his soul pleased the Lord." [2] Thus I may truthfully apply to him the apostle's words: " Of a truth I perceive that God is no respecter of persons : but in every nation he that feareth Him and worketh righteousness, is accepted with Him." [3] As a soldier Nebridius took no harm from his cloak and sword-belt and troops of orderlies ; for while he wore the uniform of the emperor he was enlisted in the service of God. On the other hand nothing is gained by men who while they affect coarse mantles, sombre tunics, dirt, and poverty, belie by their deeds their lofty pretensions. Of another centurion we find in the gospel this testimony from our Lord :—" I have not found so great faith, no not in Israel." [4] And, to go back to earlier times, we read of Joseph who gave proof of his integrity both when he was in want and when he was rich, and who inculcated freedom of soul both as slave and as lord. He was made next to Pharaoh and invested with the emblems of royalty ; [5] yet so dear was he to God that, alone of all the patriarchs, he became the father of two tribes. [6] Daniel and the three children were set over the affairs of Babylon and were numbered among the princes of the state ; yet although they wore the dress of Nebuchadnezzar, in their hearts they served God. Mordecai also and Esther amid purple and silk and jewels overcame pride with humility ; and although captives were so highly esteemed as to be able to impose commands upon their conquerors.

3. These remarks are intended to shew that the youth of whom I speak used his kinship to the royal family, his abundant wealth, and the outward tokens of power, as helps to virtue. For, as the preacher says, "wisdom is a defence and money is a defence " [7] also. We

must not hastily conclude that this statement conflicts with that of the Lord : "verily I say unto you that a rich man shall hardly enter into the kingdom of heaven ; and again I say unto you, It is easier for a camel to go through the eye of a needle than for a rich man to enter into the kingdom of heaven." [1] Were it so the salvation of Zacchæus the publican, described in scripture as a man of great wealth would contradict the Lord's declaration. But that what is impossible with men is possible with God [2] we are taught by the counsel of the apostle who thus writes to Timothy :—" charge them that are rich in this world that they be not highminded, nor trust in uncertain riches but in the living God who giveth us richly all things to enjoy, that they do good, that they be rich in good works, ready to distribute willing to communicate, laying up in store for themselves a good foundation against the time to come that they may lay hold on the true life." [3] We have learned how a camel can pass through a needle's eye, how an animal with a hump on its back,[4] when it has laid down its packs, can take to itself the wings of a dove [5] and rest in the branches of the tree which has grown from a grain of mustard seed.[6] In Isaiah we read of camels, the dromedaries of Midian and Ephah and Sheba which carry gold and incense to the city of the Lord.[7] On like typical camels the Ishmaelitish merchantmen [8] bring down to the Egyptians perfume and incense and balm (of the kind that grows in Gilead good for the healing of wounds [9]) ; and so fortunate are they that in the purchase and sale of Joseph they have for their merchandise the Saviour of the world.[10] And Æsop's fable tells us of a mouse which after eating its fill can no longer creep out as before it crept in.[11]

4. Daily did my dear Nebridius revolve the words : "they that will be rich fall into temptation and a snare " of the devil " and into many lusts." [12] All the money that the Emperor's bounty gave him or that his badge of office procured him he laid out for the benefit of the poor. For he knew the commandment of the Lord : " If thou wilt be perfect go and sell that thou hast, and give to the poor and come and follow me." [13] And because he could not literally fulfil these directions, having a wife and little children and a large household, he made to himself friends of the mammon of unrighteousness that they might receive him into everlasting habitations.[14] H

---

[1] Matt. xix. 23, 24.   [2] Mark x. 27.
[3] 1 Tim. vi. 17-19 : AV. has "eternal life " in the last verse.
[4] Animal tortuosum. The epithet recurs in Letter CVII. §
[5] Ps. lv. 6.   [6] Matt. xiii. 31, 32.   [7] Isa. lx. 6.
[8] Gen. xxxvii. 25.   [9] Jer. viii. 22.
[10] So the Vulgate renders Zaphnath-Paaneah the name given to Joseph by Pharaoh. (Gen. xli. 45).
[11] Horace, Epist. I. vii. 30, 31.   [12] 1 Tim. vi. 9.
[13] Matt. xix . 21.   [14] Luke xvi. 9.

---

[1] Acts x. 1, 2.   [2] Wisdom iv. 11, 14.   [3] Acts x. 34, 35.
[4] Matt. viii. 10.   [5] Gen. xli. 42-44.
[6] Gen. xli. 50-52.   [7] Eccl. vii. 12.

did not once for all cast away his brethren, as did the apostles who forsook father and nets and ship,[1] but by an equality he ministered to the want of others out of his own abundance that afterwards their wealth might be a supply for his own want.[2] The lady to whom this letter is addressed knows that what I narrate is only known to me by hearsay, but she is aware also that I am no Greek writer repaying with flattery some benefit conferred upon me. Far be such an imputation from all Christians. Having food and raiment we are therewith content.[3] Where there is cheap cabbage and household bread, a sufficiency to eat and a sufficiency to drink, these riches are superfluous and no place is left for flattery with its sordid calculations. You may conclude therefore that, where there is no motive to tell a falsehood, the testimony given is true.

5. It must not, however, be supposed that I praise Nebridius only for his liberality in almsgiving, although we are taught the great importance of this in the words: "water will quench a flaming fire; and alms maketh an atonement for sins."[4] I will pass on now to his other virtues each one of which is to be found but in few men. Who ever entered the furnace of the King of Babylon without being burned?[5] Was there ever a young man whose garment his Egyptian mistress did not seize?[6] Was there ever a eunuch's[7] wife contented with a childless marriage bed? Is there any man who is not appalled by the struggle of which the apostle says: "I see another law in my members warring against the law of my mind, and bringing me into captivity to the law of sin which is in my members?"[8] But wonderful to say Nebridius, though bred up in a palace as a companion and fellow pupil of the Augusti[9] (whose table is supplied by the whole world and ministered to by land and sea); Nebridius, I say, though in the midst of abundance and in the flower of his age, shewed himself more modest than a girl and never gave occasion, even the slightest, for scandalous rumours. Again though he was the friend, companion, and cousin of princes and had been educated along with them—a thing which makes even strangers intimate—he did not allow pride to inflate him or frown with contempt upon others who were less fortunate than he: no, he was kind to all, and while he loved the princes as brothers he revered them as sovereigns. He used to avow that his own health and safety were dependent upon theirs. Their attendants and all those officers of the palace who by their numbers

add to the grandeur of the imperial court he had so well conciliated by shewing his regard for them, that men who were in reality inferior to him were led by his attention to believe themselves his peers. It is no easy task to throw one's rank into the shade by one's virtue, or to gain the affection of men who are forced to yield you precedence. What widow was not supported by his help? What ward did not find in him a father? To him the bishops of the entire East used to bring the prayers of the unfortunate and the petitions of the distressed. Whenever he asked the Emperor for a boon, he sought either alms for the poor or ransom for captives or clemency for the afflicted. Accordingly the princes also used gladly to accede to his requests, for they knew well that their bounty would benefit not one man but many.

6. Why do I farther postpone the end? "All flesh is grass and all the goodliness thereof is as the flower of the field."[1] The dust has returned to the dust.[2] He has fallen asleep in the Lord and has been laid with his fathers, full of days and of light and fostered in a good old age. For "wisdom is the grey hair unto men."[3] "In a short time he" has "fulfilled a long time."[4] In his place we now have his charming children. His wife is the heir of his chastity. To those who miss his father the tiny Nebridius shews him once more, for

Such were the eyes and hands and looks he bore.[5]

A spark of the parent's excellence shines in the son: the child's face betrays like a mirror a resemblance in character.

That narrow frame contains a hero's heart.[6]

And with him there is his sister, a basket of roses and lilies, a mixture of ivory and purple. Her face though it takes after that of her father inclines to be still more attractive; and, while her complexion is that of her mother, she is so like both her parents that the lineaments of each are reflected in her features. So sweet and honied is she that she is the pride of all her kinsfolk. The Emperor[7] does not disdain to hold her in his arms, and the Empress[8] likes nothing better than to nurse her on her lap. Everyone runs to be the first to catch her up. Now she clings to the neck of one, and now she is fondled in the arms of another. She prattles and stammers, and is all the sweeter for her faltering tongue.

7. You have, therefore, Salvina, those to

---

[1] Matt. iv. 18-22.   [2] 2 Cor. viii. 14.   [3] 1 Tim. vi. 8.
[4] Ecclus. iii. 30.   [5] Cf. Dan. iii. 25.   [6] Gen. xxxix. 12.
[7] The allusion is to the word "officer" in Gen. xxxvii. 36. See AV. margin.
[8] Rom. vii. 23.   [9] Arcadius and Honorius.

[1] Isa. xl. 6.   [2] Gen. iii. 19.   [3] Wisd. iv. 9.
[4] Wisd. iv. 13.   [5] Virg. A. iii. 490.
[6] Virg. G. iv. 82.   [7] Arcadius.   [8] Eudoxia.

nurse who may well represent to you your absent husband : " Lo, children are an heritage of the Lord ; and the fruit of the womb is his reward." [1] In the place of one husband you have received two children, and thus your affection has more objects than before. All that was due to him you can give to them. Temper grief with love, for if he is gone they are still with you. It is no small merit in God's eyes to bring up children well. Hear the apostle's counsel : " Let not a widow be taken into the number under threescore years old, having been the wife of one man, well reported of for good works ; if she have brought up children, if she have lodged strangers, if she have washed the saints' feet, if she have relieved the afflicted, if she have diligently followed every good work." [2] Here you learn the roll of the virtues which God requires of you, what is due to the name of widow which you bear, and by what good deeds you can attain to that second degree of chastity [3] which is still open to you. Do not be disturbed because the apostle allows none to be chosen as a widow under threescore years old, neither suppose that he intends to reject those who are still young. Believe that you are indeed chosen by him who said to his disciple, " Let no man despise thy youth," [4] your want of age that is, not your want of continence. If this be not his meaning, all who become widows under threescore years will have to take husbands. He is training a church still untaught in Christ, and making provision for people of all stations but especially for the poor, the charge of whom had been committed to himself and Barnabas. [5] Thus he wishes only those to be supported by the exertions of the church who cannot labour with their own hands, and who are widows indeed, [6] approved by their years and by their lives. The faults of his children made Eli the priest an offence to God. On the other hand He is appeased by the virtues of such as " continue in faith and charity and holiness with chastity." [7] " O Timothy," cries the apostle, " keep thyself pure." [8] Far be it from me to suspect you capable of doing anything wrong ; still it is only a kindness to admonish one whose youth and opulence lead her into temptation. You must take what I am going to say as addressed not to you but to your girlish years. A widow " that liveth in pleasure is dead while she liveth." [9] So speaks the " chosen vessel " [10] and the words are brought out from his treasure who could boldly say : " Do ye seek a proof of Christ speaking in me ? " [1] Yet they are the words of one who in his own person admitted the weakness of the human body saying : " 'The good that I would I do not but the evil which I would not that I do." And again : Therefore " I keep under my body and bring it into subjection lest that by any means when I have preached to others I myself should be a castaway." [3] If Paul is afraid, which of us can venture to be confident ? If David the friend of God and Solomon who loved God [4] were overcome like other men, if their fall is meant to warn us and their penitence to lead us to salvation, who in this slippery life can be sure of not falling Never let pheasants be seen upon your table or plump turtledoves or black cock from Ionia or any of those birds so expensive that they fly away with the largest properties. And do not fancy that you eschew meat diet when you reject pork, hare, and venison and the savoury flesh of other quadrupeds. [5] It is not the number of feet that makes the difference but delicacy of flavour. I know that the apostle has said : " every creature of God is good and nothing to be refused if it be received with thanksgiving." [6] But the same apostle says " it is good neither to eat flesh nor to drink wine," [7] and in another place : " be not drunk with wine wherein is excess." [8] " Every creature of God is good "—the precept is intended for those who are careful how they may please their husbands. [9] Let those feed on flesh who serve the flesh, whose bodies boil with desire, who are tied to husbands, and who set their hearts on having offspring. Let those whose wombs are burthened cram their stomachs with flesh. But you have buried every indulgence in your husband's tomb : over his bier you have cleansed with tears a face stained with rouge and whitelead ; you have exchanged a white robe and gilded buskins for a sombre tunic and black shoes ; and only one thing more is needed, perseverance in fasting. Let paleness and squalor be henceforth your jewels. Do not pamper your youthful limbs with a bed of down or kindle your young blood with hot baths. Hear what words a heathen poet [10] puts into the mouth of a chaste widow : [11]

He, my first spouse, has robbed me of my loves.
So be it : let him keep them in the tomb.

If common glass is worth so much, what must be the value of a pearl of price ? [12] If in def-

---

[1] Ps. cxxvii. 3.   [2] 1 Tim. v. 9, 10.
[3] The three degrees of chastity are those of a virgin, a widow, and a wife.
[4] 1 Tim. iv. 12.   [5] Gal. ii. 9, 10.   [6] Cf. 1 Tim. v. 3.
[7] 1 Tim. ii. 15. AV. has ' sobriety ' for ' chastity.'
[8] 1 Tim. v. 22.   [9] 1 Tim. v. 6.   [10] Acts ix. 15.

[1] 2 Cor. xiii. 3, Vulg.   [2] Rom. vii. 19.
[3] 1 Cor. ix. 27.   [4] 1 K. iii. 3.
[5] Many drew a distinction between the flesh of quadrupeds and that of birds, abstaining from the former but using the latter.
[6] 1 Tim. iv. 4.   [7] Rom. xiv. 21.   [8] Eph. v. 18.
[9] 1 Cor. vii. 34.   [10] Virgil, Æn. iv. 28, 29.
[11] Dido, queen of Carthage.
[12] Quoted from Tertullian (ad Mart. IV.). The same words recur in Letters CVII. § 8 and CXXX. § 9.

erence to a law of nature a Gentile widow can condemn all sensual indulgence, what must we expect from a Christian widow who owes her chastity not to one who is dead but to one with whom she shall reign in heaven?

8. Do not, I pray you, regard these general remarks—applying as they do to all young women—as intended to insult you or to take you to task. I write in a spirit of apprehension, yet pray that you may never know the nature of my fears. A woman's reputation is a tender plant; it is like a fair flower which withers at the slightest blast and fades away at the first breath of wind. Especially is this so when she is of an age to fall into temptation and the authority of a husband is wanting to her. For the very shadow of a husband is a wife's safeguard. What has a widow to do with a large household or with troops of retainers? As servants, it is true, she must not despise them, but as men she ought to blush before them. If a grand establishment requires such domestics, let her at least set over them an old man of spotless morals whose dignity may guard the honour of his mistress. I know of many widows who, although they live with closed doors, have not escaped the imputation of too great intimacy with their servants. These latter become objects of suspicion when they dress above their degree, or when they are stout and sleek, or when they are of an age inclined to passion, or when knowledge of the favour in which they are secretly held betrays itself in a too confident demeanour. For such pride, however carefully concealed, is sure to break out in a contempt for fellow-servants as servants. I make these seemingly superfluous remarks that you may keep your heart with all diligence[1] and guard against every scandal that may be broached concerning you.

9. Take no well-curled steward to walk with you, no effeminate actor, no devilish singer of poisoned sweetness, no spruce and smooth-shorn youth. Let no theatrical compliments, no obsequious adulation be associated with you. Keep with you bands of widows and virgins; and let your consolers be of your own sex. The character of the mistress is judged by that of the maid. So long as you have with you a holy mother, so long as an aunt vowed to virginity is at your side, you ought not to neglect them and at your own risk to seek the company of strangers. Let the divine scripture be always in your hands, and give yourself so frequently to prayer that such shafts of evil thoughts as ever assail the young may thereby find a shield to repel them. It is difficult, nay more it is impossible, to escape the beginnings of those internal mo-

tions which the Greeks with much significance call προπάθειαι, that is 'predispositions to passion.' The fact is that suggestions of sin tickle all our minds, and the decision rests with our own hearts either to admit or to reject the thoughts which come. The Lord of nature Himself says in the gospel:—"out of the heart proceed evil thoughts, murders, adulteries, fornications, thefts, false witness, blasphemies."[1] It is clear from the testimony of another book that "the imagination of man's heart is evil from his youth,"[2] and that the soul wavers between the works of the flesh and of the spirit enumerated by the apostle,[3] desiring now the former and now the latter. For

> From faults no mortal man is wholly free;
> The best is he who has but few of them.[4]

And, to quote the same poet,

> At moles men cavil when they mark fair skins.[5]

To the same effect in different words the prophet says:—"I am so troubled that I cannot speak,"[6] and in the same book, "Be ye angry and sin not."[7] So Archytas of Tarentum[8] once said to a careless steward: "I should have flogged you to death had I not been in a passion." For "the wrath of man worketh not the righteousness of God."[9] Now what is here said of one form of perturbation may be applied to all. Just as anger is human and the repression of it Christian, so it is with other passions. The flesh always lusts after the things of the flesh, and by its allurements draws the soul to partake of deadly pleasures; but it is for us Christians to restrain the desire for sensual indulgence by an intenser love for Christ. It is for us to break in the mettlesome brute within us by fasting, in order that it may desire not lust but food and amble easily and steadily forward having for its rider the Holy Spirit.

10. Why do I write thus? To shew you that you are but human and subject, unless you guard against them, to human passions. We are all of us made of the same clay and formed of the same elements. Whether we wear silk or rags we are all at the mercy of the same desire. It does not fear the royal purple; it does not disdain the squalor of the mendicant. It is better then to suffer in stomach than in soul to rule the body than to serve it, to lose one's balance than to lose one's chastity. Let us not lull ourselves with the delusion that we can always fall back on penitence. For this is at best but a remedy

---

[1] Prov. iv. 23.

[1] Matt. xv. 19.   [2] Gen. viii. 21.   [3] Gal. v. 19-23.
[4] Horace, Sat. I iii. 68, 69.   [5] Horace, Sat. I. vi. 66.
[6] Ps. lxxvii. 4.   [7] Ps. iv. 4, LXX. Quoted Eph. iv. 26.
[8] A pythagorean philosopher, mathematician, general, and statesman. He was a contemporary of Plato.
[9] Jas. i. 20.

for misery. Let us shrink from incurring a wound which must be painful to cure. For it is one thing to enter the haven of salvation with ship safe and merchandise uninjured, and another to cling naked to a plank and, as the waves toss you this way and that, to be dashed again and again on the sharp rocks. A widow should be ignorant that second marriage is permitted ; she should know nothing of the apostle's words : — "It is better to marry than to burn." [1] Remove what is said to be worse, the risk of burning, and marriage will cease to be regarded as good. Of course I repudiate the slanders of the heretics ; I know that "marriage is honourable . . . and the bed undefiled." [2] Yet Adam even after he was expelled from paradise had but one wife. The accursed and blood-stained Lamech, descended from the stock of Cain, was the first to make out of one rib two wives ; and the seedling of digamy then planted was altogether destroyed by the doom of the deluge. It is true that in writing to Timothy the apostle from fear of fornication is forced to countenance second marriage. His words are these : —"I will therefore that the younger women marry, bear children, guide the house, give none occasion to the adversary to speak reproachfully." But he immediately adds as a reason for this concession ; "for some are already turned aside after Satan." [3] Thus we see that he is offering not a crown to those who stand but a helping hand to those who are down. What must a second marriage be if it is looked on merely as an alternative to the brothel ! "For some," he writes, "are already turned aside after Satan." The upshot of the whole matter is that, if a young widow cannot or will not contain herself, she had better take a husband to her bed than the devil.

A noble alternative truly which is only to be embraced in preference to Satan ! In old days even Jerusalem went a-whoring and opened her feet to every one that passed by. [4] It was in Egypt that she was first deflowered and there that her teats were bruised. [5] And afterwards when she had come to the wilderness and, impatient of the delays of her leader Moses, had said when maddened by the stings of lust : "these be thy gods, O Israel, which brought thee up out of the land of Egypt," [6] she received statutes that were not good and commandments that were altogether evil whereby she should not live [7] but should be punished through them. Is it surprising then that when the apostle had said in another place of young widows : "when they have begun to wax wanton against Christ they

will marry, having damnation because they have cast off their first faith," [1] he granted to such as should wax wanton statutes of digamy that were not good and commandments that were altogether evil ? For the reason which he gives for allowing a second husband would justify a woman in marrying a third or even, if she liked, a twentieth. He evidently wished to shew them that he was not so much anxious that they should take husbands as that they should avoid paramours. These things, dearest daughter in Christ, I impress upon you and frequently repeat, that you may forget those things which are behind and reach forth unto those things which are before. [2] You have widows like yourself worthy to be your models, Judith renowned in Hebrew story and Anna the daughter of Phanuel famous in the gospel. Both these lived day and night in the temple and preserved the treasure of their chastity by prayer and by fasting. One was a type of the Church which cuts off the head of the devil [3] and the other first received in her arms the saviour of the world and had revealed to her the holy mysteries which were to come. [4] In conclusion I beg you to attribute the shortness of my letter not to want of language or scarcity of matter but to a deep sense of modesty which makes me fear to force myself too long upon the ears of a stranger, and causes me to dread the secret verdict of those who read my words.

LETTER LXXX.

FROM RUFINUS TO MACARIUS.

Rufinus on his return from Bethlehem to Rome published a Latin version of Origen's treatise περὶ Ἀρχῶν, *On First Principles*. To this he prefixed the preface which is here printed among Jerome's letters. Professing to take as his model Jerome's own translations of Origen's commentaries which he greatly praises, he declares that, following his example, he has paraphrased the obscure passages of the treatise and has omitted as due to interpolators such parts as seem heretical. This preface with its insincere praise of Jerome (whose name, however, is not mentioned) and its avowed manipulation of Origen's text caused much perplexity at Rome (see Letters LXXXI., LXXXIII., and LXXXIV.), and gave rise to the controversy between Rufinus and Jerome described in the Prolegomena, and given at length in vol. iii. of this Series. The date is 398 A.D.

1. Large numbers of the brethren have, I know, in their zeal for the knowledge of the scriptures begged learned men skilled in Greek literature to make Origen a Roman by bringing home his teaching to Latin ears. One of these scholars, a dear brother and associate, [5] at the request of bishop Damasus

---

[1] 1 Cor. vii. 9.   [2] Heb. xiii. 4.   [3] 1 Tim. v. 14, 15.
[4] Ezek. xvi. 25.   [5] Ezek. xxiii. 3.
[6] Exod. xxxii. 4.   [7] Ezek. xx. 25.

[1] 1 Tim. v. 11, 12.   [2] Phil. iii. 13.
[3] As Judith cut off the head of Holofernes (Judith xiii.).
[4] Luke ii. 36–38.   [5] *i.e.* Jerome.

translated from Greek into Latin his two homilies on the Song of Songs and prefaced the work with an eloquent and eulogistic introduction such as could not fail to arouse in all an ardent desire to read and to study Origen. To the soul of that just man—so he declared —the words of the Song were applicable : "the king hath brought me into his chambers;"[1] and he went on to speak thus : "while in his other books Origen surpasses all former writers, in dealing with the Song of Songs he surpasses himself." In his preface he pledges himself to give to Roman ears these homilies of Origen and as many of his other works as he can. His style is certainly attractive but I can see that he aims at a more ambitious task than that of a mere translator. Not content with rendering the words of Origen he desires to be himself the teacher.[2] I for my part do but follow up an enterprise which he has sanctioned and commenced, but I lack his vigorous eloquence with which to adorn the sayings of this great man. I am even afraid lest my deficiencies and inadequate command of Latin may detract seriously from the reputation of one whom this writer has deservedly termed second only to the apostles as a teacher of the Church in knowledge and in wisdom.

2. Often turning this over in my mind I held my peace and refused to listen to the brethren when—as frequently happened—they urged me to undertake the work. But your persistence, most faithful brother Macarius, is so great that even want of ability cannot resist it. Thus, to escape the constant importunings to which you subject me, I have given way contrary to my resolution ; yet only on these terms that, so far as is possible, I am to be free to follow the rules of translation laid down by my predecessors, and particularly those acted upon by the writer whom I have just mentioned. He has rendered into Latin more than seventy of Origen's homiletical treatises and a few also of his commentaries upon the apostle ;[3] and in these wherever the Greek text presents a stumbling block, he has smoothed it down in his version and has so emended the language used that a Latin writer can find no word that is at variance with our faith. In his steps, therefore, I propose to walk, if not displaying the same vigorous eloquence at least observing the same rules. I shall not reproduce passages in Origen's books which disagree with or contradict his own statements elsewhere. The reason of these inconsistencies I have put more fully before you in the defence of Origen's writings composed by Pamphilianus[1] which I have supplemented by a short treatise of my own. I have given what I consider plain proofs that his books have been corrupted in numbers of places by heretics and ill-disposed persons, and particularly those which you now urge me to translate. The books περὶ Ἀρχῶν, that is of Principles or of Powers, are in fact in other respects extremely obscure and difficult. For they treat of subjects on which the philosophers have spent all their days and yet have been able to discover nothing. In dealing with these themes Origen has done his best to make belief in a Creator and a rational account of things created subservient to religion and not, as with the philosophers, to irreligion. Wherever then in his books I have found a statement concerning the Trinity contrary to those which in other places he has faithfully made on the same subject, I have either omitted the passage as garbled and misleading or have substituted that view of the matter which I find him to have frequently asserted. Again, wherever—in haste to get on with his theme—he is brief or obscure relying on the skill and intelligence of his readers, I, to make the passage clearer, have sought to explain it by adding any plainer statements that I have read on the point in his other books. But I have added nothing of my own. The words used may be found in other parts of his writings : they are his, not mine. I mention this here to take from cavillers all pretext for once more[2] finding fault. But let such perverse and contentious persons look well to what they are themselves doing.

3. Meantime I have taken up this great task—if so be that God will grant your prayers —not to stop the mouths of slanderers (an impossible feat except perhaps to God) but to give to those who desire it the means of making progress in knowledge.

In the sight of God, the Father, the Son, and the Holy Ghost,[3] I adjure and require everyone who shall either read or copy these books of mine, by his belief in a kingdom to come, by the mystery of the resurrection from the dead, by the eternal fire which is " prepared for the devil and his angels ;"[4] as he hopes not to inherit eternally that place where "there is weeping and gnashing of teeth,"[5] and where " their worm dieth not and the fire is not quenched,"[6] let him add nothing to what is written, let him subtract nothing, let him insert nothing, let him alter nothing, but let him

---

[1] Cant. i. 4. See the Preface to Origen on the Canticles translated in this volume.
[2] Rem maioris gloriæ sequitur ut pater verbi sit potius quam interpres.
[3] *i.e.* St. Paul.

[1] Or Pamphilus.
[2] See this treatise in vol. iii. of this series. Rufinus with John of Jerusalem had been already accused of Origenism. See Letter LI. 6.
[3] For this adjuration comp. Rev. xxii. 18, 19, and Stieren's Irenæus i. 821.
[4] Matt. xxv. 41.   [5] Matt. xxii. 13.   [6] Mark ix. 44.

compare his transcript with the copies from which it is made, let him correct it to the letter, and let him punctuate it aright. Every manuscript that is not properly corrected and punctuated he must reject: for otherwise the difficulties in the text arising from the want of punctuation will make obscure arguments still more obscure to those who read them.

LETTER LXXXI.

TO RUFINUS.

A friendly letter of remonstrance written by Jerome to Rufinus on receipt of his version of the περὶ Ἀρχῶν see the preceding letter). Being sent in the first instance to Pammachius this latter treacherously suppressed it and thus put an end to all hope of the reconciliation of the two friends. The date of the letter is 399 A.D.

1. That you have lingered some time at Rome your own language shews. Yet I feel sure that a yearning to see your spiritual parents [1] would have drawn you to your native country,[2] had not grief for your mother deterred you lest a sorrow scarce bearable away might have proved unbearable at home.

As to your complaint that men listen only to the dictates of passion and refuse to acquiesce in your judgement and mine ; the Lord is witness to my conscience that since our reconciliation I have harboured no rancour in my breast to injure anyone ; on the contrary I have taken the utmost pains to prevent any chance occurrence being set down to ill-will. But what can I do so long as everyone supposes that he has a right to do as he does and thinks that in publishing a slander he is requiting not originating a calumny? True friendship ought never to conceal what it thinks.

The short preface to the books περὶ Ἀρχῶν which has been sent to me I recognize as yours by the style. You know best with what intention it was written ; but even a fool can see how it must necessarily be understood. Covertly or rather openly I am the person aimed at. I have often myself feigned a controversy to practise declamation.[3] Thus I might now recall this well-worn artifice and praise you in your own method.[4] But far be it from me to imitate what I blame in you. In fact I have so far restrained my feelings that I make no charge against you, and, although injured, decline for my part to injure a friend. But another time, if you wish to follow any one, pray be satisfied with your own judgement. The objects which we seek are either good or bad. If they are good, they need no help from another ; and if they are bad, the fact that

many sin together is no excuse. I prefer thus to expostulate with you as a friend rather than to give public vent to my indignation at the wrong I have suffered. I want you to see that when I am reconciled to anyone I become his sincere friend and do not—to borrow a figure from Plautus [1]—while offering him bread with one hand, hold a stone in the other.

2. My brother Paulinian has not yet returned from home and I fancy that you will see him at Aquileia at the house of the reverend pope Chromatius.[2] I am also sending the reverend presbyter Rufinus [3] on business to Milan by way of Rome, and have requested him to communicate to you my feelings and respects. I am sending the same message to the rest of my friends ; lest, as the apostle says, ye bite and devour one another, ye be consumed one of another.[4] It only remains for you and your friends to shew your moderation by giving no offence to those who are disinclined to put up with it. For you will hardly find everyone like me. There are few who can be pleased with pretended eulogies.

LETTER LXXXII.

TO THEOPHILUS BISHOP OF ALEXANDRIA.

Two years after his former attempt (see Letter LXIII.) Theophilus again wrote to Jerome urging him to be reconciled with John of Jerusalem. Jerome replies that there is nothing he desires more earnestly than peace but that this must be real and not a hollow truce. He speaks very bitterly of John who has, he alleges, intrigued to procure his banishment from Palestine. He also deals with the ordination of his brother Paulinian (for which see Letter LI.) and defends himself for having translated Origen's commentaries by adducing the example of Hilary of Poitiers. This letter should be compared with the Treatise "Against John of Jerusalem" in this volume. Its date is 399 A.D.

1. Your letter shews you to possess that heritage of the Lord of which when going to the Father he said to the apostles, "peace I leave with you, my peace I give unto you,"[5] and to own the happiness described in the words, "blessed are the peace-makers."[6] You coax as a father, you teach as a master, you enjoin as a bishop. You come to me not with a rod and severity but in a spirit of kindness, gentleness, and meekness.[7] Your opening words echo the humility of Christ who saved men not with thunder and lightning [8] but as a wailing babe in the manger and as a silent sufferer upon the cross. You

---

[1] Chromatius and Eusebius of Aquileia.
[2] Concordia. near Aquileia.
[3] See the introduction to Letter CXVII.   [4] i.e. insincerely.

[1] Plautus, Aul. ii. 2. 18.
[2] Paulinian (of whose ordination an account is given in Letter LI.) had been sent to Italy by Jerome in A.D. 398 partly to counteract the proceedings of Rufinus and partly to sell the family property at Stridon (see Letter LXVI. § 14).
[3] Rufinus the Syrian, to be carefully distinguished from his more famous namesake (to whom this letter is addressed) of Aquileia. He was a monk in Jerome's monastery at Bethlehem.
[4] Gal. v. 15.   [5] Joh. xiv. 27.   [6] Matt. v. 9.
[7] 1 Cor. iv. 21.   [8] Cf. Heb. xii. 18.

have read the prediction made in one who was a type of Him, "Lord, remember David and all his meekness,"[1] and you know how it was fulfilled afterwards in Himself. "Learn of me," He said, "for I am meek and lowly in heart."[2] You have quoted many passages from the sacred books in praise of peace, you have flitted like a bee over the flowery fields of scripture, you have culled with cunning eloquence all that is sweet and conducive to concord. I was already running after peace, but you have made me quicken my pace : my sails were set for the voyage but your exhortation has filled them with a stronger breeze. I drink in the sweet streams of peace not reluctantly and with aversion but eagerly and with open mouth.

2. But what can I do, I who can only wish for peace and have no power to bring it about? Even though the wish may win its recompense with God, its futility must still sadden him who cherishes it. When the apostle said, "as much as lieth in you, live peaceably with all men,"[3] he knew quite well that the realisation of peace depends upon the consent of two parties. The prophet truly cries "They say Peace, peace : and yet there is no peace."[4] To overthrow peace by actions while professing it in words is not hard. To point out its advantages is one thing and to strive for it another. Men's speeches may be all for unity but their actions may enforce bondage. I wish for peace as much as others; and not only do I wish for it, I ask for it. But the peace which I want is the peace of Christ; a true peace, a peace without rancour, a peace which does not involve war, a peace which will not reduce opponents but will unite friends. How can I term domination peace? I must call things by their right names. Where there is hatred there let men talk of feuds; and where there is mutual esteem, there only let peace be spoken of. For my part I neither rend the church nor separate myself from the communion of the fathers. From my very cradle, I may say, I have been reared on Catholic milk; and no one can be a better churchman than one who has never been a heretic. But I know nothing of a peace that is without love or of a communion that is without peace. In the gospel I read :—"if thou bring thy gift to the altar and there rememberest that thy brother hath aught against thee; leave there thy gift before the altar and go thy way; first be reconciled to thy brother, and then come and offer thy gift."[5] If then we may not offer gifts that are our own unless we are at peace with our brothers; how much

less can we receive the body of Christ if we cherish enmity in our hearts? How can I conscientiously approach Christ's eucharist and answer the Amen[1] if I doubt the charity of him who ministers it?

3. Hear me, I beg you with patience and do not take truthfulness for flattery. Is any man reluctant to communicate with you? Does any turn his face away when you hold out your hand? Does any at the holy banquet offer you the kiss of Judas?[2] At your approach the monks instead of trembling rejoice. They race to meet you and leaving their dens in the desert are fain to master you by their humility. What compels them to come forth? Is it not their love for you? What draws together the scattered dwellers in the desert? Is it not the esteem in which they hold you? A parent ought to love his children; and not only a parent but a bishop ought to be loved by his children. Neither ought to be feared. There is an old saying :[3] "whom a man fears he hates; and whom he hates, he would fain see dead." Accordingly, while for the young the holy scripture makes fear the beginning of knowledge,[4] it also tells us that "perfect love casteth out fear."[5] You exact no obedience from them; therefore the monks obey you. You offer them a kiss; therefore they bow the neck. You shew yourself a common soldier; therefore they make you their general. Thus from being one among many you become one above many. Freedom is easily roused if attempts are made to crush it. No one gets more from a free man than he who does not force him to be a slave. I know the canons of the church; I know what rank her ministers hold; and from men and books I have daily up to the present learned and gathered many things. The kingdom of the mild David was quickly dismembered by one who chastised his people with scorpions and fancied that his fingers were thicker than his father's loins.[6] The Roman people refused to brook insolence even in a king.[7] Moses was leader of the host of Israel; he brought ten plagues upon Egypt; sky, earth, and sea alike obeyed his commands : yet he is spoken of as "very meek above all the men which were" at that time "upon the face of the earth."[8] He maintained his forty-years' supremacy because he tempered the insolence of office with gentleness and meekness. When he was being stoned by the people he

---

[1] Ps. cxxxii. 1, LXX. [2] Matt. xi 29.
[3] Rom. xii. 18. [4] Jer. xi. 14, LXX. [5] Matt. v. 23, 24.

[1] 1 Cor. xiv. 16, where in the Greek 'giving of thanks' is 'eucharist.'
[2] Matt. xxvi. 48, 49 : the kiss of peace formed an integral part of the eucharistic office from primitive till mediæval times.
[3] Attributed by Cicero to Ennius. [4] Prov. i. 7.
[5] 1 Joh. iv. 18. [6] 1 K. xii. 10.
[7] Tarquin the Proud the last king of Rome was driven into exile because of his many acts of tyranny.
[8] Nu. xii. 3.

made intercession for them ;[1] nay more he wished to be blotted out of God's book sooner than that the flock committed to him should perish.[2] He sought to imitate the Shepherd who would, he knew, carry on his shoulders even the wandering sheep. "The good Shepherd"—they are the Lord's own words—"layeth down his life for the sheep."[3] One of his disciples can wish to be anathema from Christ for his brethren's sake, his kinsmen according to the flesh who were Israelites.[4] If then Paul can desire to perish that the lost may not be lost, how much should good parents not provoke their children to wrath[5] or by too great severity embitter those who are naturally mild.

4. The limits of a letter compel me to restrain myself ; otherwise, indignation would make me diffuse. In an epistle which its writer regards as conciliatory but which to me appears full of malice my opponent[6] admits that I have never calumniated him or accused him of heresy. Why then does he calumniate me by spreading a rumour that I am infected with that awful malady and am in revolt against the Church ? Why is he so ready to spare his real assailants and so eager to injure me who have done nothing to injure him ? Before my brother's ordination he said nothing of any dogmatic difference between himself and pope Epiphanius. What then can have "forced" him—I use his own word—publicly to argue a point which no one had yet raised ? One so full of wisdom as you knows well the danger of such discussions and that silence is in such cases the safest course ; except, indeed, on some occasion which renders it imperative to deal with great matters. What ability and eloquence it must have needed to compress into a single sermon—as he boasts to have done[7]—all the topics which the most learned writers have treated in detail in voluminous treatises ! But this is nothing to me : it is for the hearers of the sermon to notice and for the writer of the letter to realize. But as for me he ought of his own accord to acquit me of bringing the charge against him. I was not present and did not hear the sermon. I was only one of the many, indeed hardly one of them ; for while others were crying out I held my peace. Let us confront the accused and the accuser, and let us give credit to him whose services, life, and doctrine are seen to be the best.

5. You see, do you not, that I shut my eyes

to many things and touch upon others only in the most cursory manner, hinting at what I suppose rather than saying out what I think.

I understand and approve your manœuvres ;[1] how in the interests of the peace of the Church you stop your ears when you come within range of the Sirens. Moreover, trained as you have been from childhood in sacred studies, you know exactly what is meant by each expression which you use. You knowingly employ ambiguous terms and carefully balanced sentences so as not to condemn others[2] or repudiate us.[3] But it is not a pure faith and a frank confession which look for quibbles or circumlocutions. What is simply believed must be professed with equal simplicity. For my part I could cry out—though it were amid the swords and fires of Babylon, "why does the answer evade the question ? why is there no frank, straightforward declaration ?" From beginning to end all is shrinking, compromise, ambiguity : as though he were trying to walk on spikes of corn. His blood boils with eagerness for peace ; yet he will not give a straightforward answer ! others are free to insult him ; for, when he is insulted, he does not venture to retaliate. I meantime hold my peace : for the present I shall let it be thought that I am too busy, or ignorant, or afraid ; for how would he treat me were I to accuse him, if when I praise him—as he admits himself that I do—he secretly traduces me ?

6. His whole letter is less an exposition of his faith than a mass of calumnies aimed at myself. Without any of those mutual courtesies which men may use towards each other without flattery, he takes up my name again and again, flouts it, and bandies it about as though I were blotted out of the book of the living. He thinks that he has beaten me black and blue with his letter ; and that I live for the trifles at which he aims, I who from my boyhood have been shut up in a monastic cell, and have always made it my aim to be rather than to seem a good man. Some of us, it is true, he mentions with respect, but only that he may afterwards wound us more deeply. As if, forsooth, we too have no open secrets to reveal ! One of his charges is that we have allowed a slave to be ordained. Yet he himself has clergymen of the same class, and he must have read of Onesimus who, being made regenerate by Paul in prison,[4] from a slave became a deacon. Then he throws out that the slave in question was a common informer ; and, lest he should be compelled to prove the charge, declares he has it from hearsay only ! Why,

[1] Exod. xvii. 4.   [2] Exod. xxxii. 31, 32.
[3] Joh. x. 11, RV.; Luke xv. 4, 5.
[4] Rom. ix. 3, 4, RV.   [5] Eph. vi. 4.
[6] John, Bishop of Jerusalem, who had accused Jerome of Origenism, a charge which was brought against himself by Epiphanius (see Letter LI.).
[7] Jerome represents John as saying that he took advantage of a verse in the lesson " to preach on faith and all the dogmas of the Church (c. Joh. Jer. ii.).

[1] Jerome now addresses John of Jerusalem.
[2] The Origenists.   [3] The orthodox.   [4] Philemon, 10.

if I had chosen to repeat the talk of the crowd and to listen to scandal-mongers, he would have learned before now that I too know what all the world knows and have heard the same stories as other people. He declares farther that ordination has been given to this slave as a reward for a slander spread abroad by him. Does not such cunning and subtlety appal one? And is there any answer to eloquence so overwhelming? Which is best, to spread a calumny or to suffer from one? To accuse a man whose love you may afterwards wish for, or to pardon a sinner? And is it more tolerable that a common informer should be made a consul than that he should be made an ædile?[1] He knows what I pass over in silence and what I say; what I myself have heard and what—from the fear of Christ—I perhaps refuse to believe.

7. He charges me with having translated Origen into Latin. In this I do not stand alone for the confessor Hilary has done the same, and we are both at one in this that while we have rendered all that is useful, we have cut away all that was harmful. Let him read our versions for himself, if he knows how (and as he constantly converses and daily associates with Italians,[2] I think he cannot be ignorant of Latin); or else, if he cannot quite take it in, let him use his interpreters and then he will come to know that I deserve nothing but praise for the work on which he grounds a charge against me. For, while I have always allowed to Origen his great merit as an interpreter and critic of the scriptures, I have invariably denied the truth of his doctrines. Is it I then that let him loose upon the crowd? Is it I that act sponsor to other preachers like him? No, for I know that a difference must be made between the apostles and all other preachers. The former always speak the truth; but the latter being men sometimes go astray. It would be a strange defence of Origen surely to admit his faults and then to excuse them by saying that other men have been guilty of similar ones! As if, when you cannot venture to defend a man openly, you may hope to shield him by imputing his mistake to a number of others! As for the six thousand volumes of Origen of which he speaks, it is impossible that any one should have read books which have never been written: and I for my part find it easier to suppose that this falsehood is due to the man who professes to have heard it rather than to him who is said to have told it.[3]

8. Again he avers that my brother[1] is the cause of the disagreement which has arisen, a man who is content to stay in a monastic cell and who regards the clerical office as onerous rather than honourable. And although up to this very day he has spoon-fed us with insincere protestations of peace, he has caused commotion in the minds of the western bishops[2] by telling them that a mere youth, hardly more than a boy, has been ordained[3] presbyter of Bethlehem in his own diocese. If this is the truth, all the bishops of Palestine must be aware of it. For the monastery of the reverend pope Epiphanius—called the old monastery—where my brother was ordained presbyter is situated in the district of Eleutheropolis[4] and not in that of Ælia.[5] Furthermore his age is well known to your Holiness; and as he has now attained to thirty years I apprehend that no blame can attach to him on that score. Indeed this particular age is stamped as full and complete by the mystery of Christ's assumed manhood. Let him call to mind the ancient law, and he will see that after his twenty-fifth year a Levite might be chosen to the priesthood;[6] or if in this passage he prefers to follow the Hebrew he will find that candidates for the priesthood must be thirty years old. And that he may not venture to say that "old things are passed away; and, behold, all things are become new,"[7] let him hear the apostle's words to Timothy, "Let no man despise thy youth."[8] Certainly when my opponent was himself ordained bishop, he was not much older than my brother is now. And if he argues that youth is no hindrance to a bishop but that it is to a presbyter because a young elder[9] is a contradiction in terms, I ask him this question: Why has he himself ordained a presbyter of this age or younger still, and that too to minister in another man's church? But if he cannot be at peace with my brother unless he consents to submit and to renounce the bishop who has ordained him, he shews plainly that his object is not peace but revenge, and that he will not rest satisfied with the quietude of repose and peace unless he is able to inflict to the full every penalty that he now threatens. Had he himself ordained my brother, it would have made no difference to this latter. So dearly does he love seclusion that he would even then have continued to live

---

[1] The highest and lowest offices in the Roman magistracy. Jerome insinuates that if the ordained slave was a common informer so also was John of Jerusalem.   [2] A hit at Rufinus.
[3] The statement that he had read 6000 volumes of Origen was attributed to Epiphanius by Rufinus and John of Jerusalem. Cf. Apol. c. Ruf. ii. c. 13.

[1] Paulinian, who had been ordained by Epiphanius.
[2] Sacerdotes; lit. 'sacrificing priests.'
[3] Not by himself but by Epiphanius.
[4] Otherwise Lydda, a town in the south of Judah at this time the seat of a bishopric.
[5] Ælia Capitolina was the name given by Hadrian to the colony established by him on the site of Jerusalem.
[6] Nu. iv. 3, LXX. AV. follows the Hebrew.
[7] 2 Cor. v. 17.   [8] 1 Tim. iv. 12.
[9] The word 'presbyter' means elder.

quietly and would not have exercised his office. And should the bishop have seen fit to rend the church on that score, he would then have owed him nothing save the respect which is due to all who offer sacrifice.[1]

9. So much for his prolix defence of himself or I should rather say his attack on me. In this letter I have only answered him briefly and cursorily that from what I have said he may perceive what I do not say, and may know that as I am a human being I am a rational animal and well able to understand his shrewdness, and that I am not so obtuse or brutish as to catch only the sound of his words and not their meaning. I now ask of you to pardon my chagrin and to allow that if it is arrogant to answer back, it is yet more arrogant to bring baseless charges. Yet my answer has indicated what I might have said rather than has actually said it. Why do men look for peace at a distance? and why do they wish to have it enforced by word of command? Let them shew themselves peacemakers, and peace will follow at once. Why do they use the name of your holiness to terrorize us, when your letter—strange contrast to their harsh and menacing words—breathes only peace and meekness? For that the letter which Isidore the presbyter has brought for me from you does make for peace and harmony I know by this, that these insincere professors of a wish for peace have refused to deliver it to me. Let them choose whichever alternative they please. Either I am a good man or I am a bad one. If I am a good one let them leave me in quiet: if I am a bad one, why do they desire to be in bad company? Surely my opponent has learnt by experience the value of humility. He who now tears asunder things which, formerly separate, he of his own will put together, proves that in severing now what he then joined, he is acting at the instigation of another.[2]

10. Recently he sought and obtained a decree of exile against me, and I only wish that he had been able to carry it out,[3] so that, as the will is imputed to him for the deed, so I too not in will only but in deed might wear the crown of exile. The church of Christ has been founded by shedding its own blood not that of others, by enduring outrage not by inflicting it. Persecutions have made it grow; martyrdoms have crowned it. Or if the Christians among whom I live are unique in their love of severity and know only how to perse-

cute and not how to undergo persecution, there are Jews here, there are heretics professing various false doctrines, and in particular the foulest of all, I mean, Manichæism. Why is it that they do not venture to say a word against them? Why am I the only person they wish to drive into exile? Am I who communicate with the church the only person of whom it can be said that he rends the church? I put it to you, is it not a fair demand either that they should expel these others as well as myself, or that, if they keep them, they should keep me too? All the same they honour men by sending them into exile, for by so doing they separate them from the company of heretics. It is a monk,[1] shame to say, who menaces monks and obtains decrees of exile against them; and that too a monk who boasts that he holds an apostolic chair. But the monastic tribe does not succumb to terrorism: it prefers to expose its neck to the impending sword rather than to allow its hands to be tied. Is not every monk an exile from his country? Is he not an exile from the whole world? Where is the need for the public authority, the cost of a rescript, the journeyings up and down the earth to obtain one? Let him but touch me with his little finger, and I will go into exile of myself. "The earth is the Lord's and the fulness thereof."[2] Christ is not shut up in any one spot.

11. Moreover when he writes that, though I seem to be separated from communion with him, I in reality hold communion with him through you and through the church of Rome: he need not go so far afield, for I am connected with him in the same way also here in Palestine. And lest even this should appear distant, in this village of Bethlehem I hold communion with his presbyters as much as I can. Thus it is clear that a private chagrin is not to be taken for the cause of the church, and that one man's choler, or even that of several stirred up by him, ought not to be styled the displeasure of the church. Accordingly I now repeat what I said at the beginning of my letter that I for my part am desirous of Christ's peace, that I pray for harmony, and that I request you to admonish him not to exact peace but to purpose it. Let him be satisfied with the pain which he has caused by the insults that he has inflicted upon me in the past. Let him efface old wounds by a little new charity. Let him shew himself what he was before, when of his own choice he bestowed upon me his esteem. Let his words no longer be tinged with a gall that flows from the heart of another. Let him do what he wishes himself, and not what others

---

[1] Here as frequently in Jerome the word 'sacerdos' is used to denote a bishop.
[2] Probably Isidore, who had taken a view hostile to Jerome, and who at this time fell under the displeasure of Theophilus.
[3] The execution of the decree was stopped by the sudden death of the imperial minister Rufinus.

[1] John of Jerusalem.   [2] Ps. xxiv. 1.

force him to wish. Either as a pontiff, let him exercise authority over all alike, or as a follower of the apostle, let him serve all for the salvation of all.[1] If he will shew himself such, I am ready freely to yield and to hold out my arms ; he will find me a friend and a kinsman, and will perceive that in Christ I am submissive to him as to all the saints. "Charity," writes the apostle, "suffereth long and is kind ; charity envieth not ; . . . is not puffed up . . . beareth all things, believeth all things."[2] Charity is the mother of all virtues, and the apostle's words about faith hope and charity[3] are like that threefold cord which is not quickly broken.[4] We believe, we hope, and through our faith and hope we are joined together in the bond of charity.[5] It is for these virtues that I and others have left our homes, it is for these that we would live peaceably without any contention in the fields and alone ; paying all due veneration to Christ's pontiffs—so long as they preach the right faith—not because we fear them as lords but because we honour them as fathers ; deferring also to bishops as bishops, but refusing to serve under compulsion, beneath the shadow of episcopal authority, men whom we do not choose to obey. I am not so much puffed up in mind as not to know what is due to the priests of Christ. For he who receives them, receives not them but Him, whose bishops they are.[6] But let them be content with the honour which is theirs. Let them know that they are fathers and not lords, especially in relation to those who scorn the ambitions of the world and count peace and repose the best of all things. And may Christ who is Almighty God grant to your prayers that I and my opponent may be united not in a feigned and hollow peace but in true and sincere mutual esteem, lest biting and devouring one another we be consumed one of another.[7]

LETTER LXXXIII.

FROM PAMMACHIUS AND OCEANUS.

A letter from Pammachius and Oceanus in which they express the perplexity into which they have been thrown by Rufinus's version of Origen's treatise, *On First Principles* (see Letter LXXX.) and request Jerome to make for them a literal translation of the work. Written in 399 or 400 A.D.

1. Pammachius and Oceanus to the presbyter Jerome, health.

A reverend brother has brought to us sheets containing a certain person's translation into Latin of a treatise by Origen—entitled περὶ ἀρχῶν. These contain many things

which disturb our poor wits and which appear to us to be uncatholic. We suspect also that with a view of clearing the author many passages of his books have been removed which had they been left would have plainly proved the irreligious character of his teaching. We therefore request your excellency to be so good as to bestow upon this particular matter an attention which will benefit not only ourselves but all who reside in the city ; we ask you to publish in your own language the abovementioned book of Origen exactly as it was brought out by the author himself ; and we desire you to make evident the interpolations which his defender has introduced. You will also confute and overthrow all statements in the sheets which we have sent to your holiness that are ignorantly made or contradict the Catholic faith. The writer in the preface to his work has, with much subtlety but without mentioning your holiness's name, implied that he has done no more than complete a work which you had yourself promised, thus indirectly suggesting that you agree with him. Remove then the suspicions men cannot help feeling and confute your assailant ; for, if you ignore his implications, people will say that you admit their truth.

LETTER LXXXIV.

TO PAMMACHIUS AND OCEANUS.

A calm letter in which Jerome defines and justifies his own attitude towards Origen, but unduly minimizes his early enthusiasm for him. He admires him in the same way that Cyprian admired Tertullian but does not in any way adopt his errors. He then describes his own studies and recounts his obligations to Apollinaris, Didymus, and a Jew named Bar-anina. The rest of the letter deals with the errors of Origen, the state of the text of his writings, and the eulogy of him composed by the martyr Pamphilus (the authenticity of which Jerome assails without any sufficient reason). The date of the letter is 400 A.D.

Jerome to the brothers Pammachius and Oceanus, with all good wishes.

1. The sheets that you send me[1] cover me at once with compliments and confusion ; for, while they praise my ability, they take away my sincerity in the faith. But as both at Alexandria and at Rome and, I may say, throughout the whole world good men have made it a habit to take the same liberties with my name, esteeming me only so far that they cannot bear to be heretics without having me of the number, I will leave aside personalities and only answer specific charges. For it is of no benefit to a cause to

1 Cf. 1 Cor. ix. 19.　　2 1 Cor. xiii. 4–7.
3 1 Cor. xiii. 13.　　4 Eccl. iv. 12.
5 Cf. Col. iii. 14.　　6 Cf. Joh. xiii. 20.　　7 Gal. v. 15.

1 *i.e.* Rufinus's version of Origen's treatise, *On First Principles*, with the Preface, translated in vol. iii. of this series. See also Letters LXXX. and LXXXI.

encounter railing with railing and to retaliate for attacks upon oneself by attacks upon one's opponents. We are commanded not to return evil for evil[1] but to overcome evil with good,[2] to take our fill of insults, and to turn the other cheek to the smiter.[3]

2. It is charged against me that I have sometimes praised Origen. If I am not mistaken I have only done so in two places, in the short preface (addressed to Damasus) to his homilies on the Song of Songs and in the prologue to my book of Hebrew Names. In these passages do the dogmas of the church come into question? Is anything said of the Father, the Son, and the Holy Ghost? or of the resurrection of the flesh? or of the condition and material of the soul? I have merely praised the simplicity of his rendering and commentary and neither the faith nor the dogmas of the Church come in at all. Ethics only are dealt with and the mist of allegory is dispelled by a clear explanation. I have praised the commentator but not the theologian, the man of intellect but not the believer, the philosopher but not the apostle. But if men wish to know my real judgement upon Origen; let them read my commentaries upon Ecclesiastes, let them go through my three books upon the epistle to the Ephesians: they will then see that I have always opposed his doctrines. How foolish it would be to eulogize a system so far as to endorse its blasphemy! The blessed Cyprian takes Tertullian for his master, as his writings prove; yet, delighted as he is with the ability of this learned and zealous writer, he does not join him in following Montanus and Maximilla.[4] Apollinaris is the author of a most weighty book against Porphyry, and Eusebius has composed a fine history of the Church; yet of these the former has mutilated Christ's incarnate humanity,[5] while the latter is the most open champion of the Arian impiety.[6] "Woe," says Isaiah, "unto them that call evil good and good evil; that put bitter for sweet and sweet for bitter."[7] We must not detract from the virtues of our opponents—if they have any praiseworthy qualities—but neither must we praise the defects of our friends. Each several case must be judged on its own merits and not by a reference to the persons concerned. While Lucilius is rightly assailed by Horace[1] for the unevenness of his verses, he is equally rightly praised for his wit and his charming style.

3. In my younger days I was carried away with a great passion for learning, yet I was not like some presumptuous enough to teach myself. At Antioch I frequently listened to Apollinaris of Laodicea, and attended his lectures; yet, although he instructed me in the holy scriptures, I never embraced his disputable doctrine as to their meaning. At length my head became sprinkled with gray hairs so that I looked more like a master than a disciple. Yet I went on to Alexandria and heard Didymus.[2] And I have much to thank him for: for what I did not know I learned from him, and what I knew already I did not forget. So excellent was his teaching. Men fancied that I had now made an end of learning. Yet once more I came to Jerusalem and to Bethlehem. What trouble and expense it cost me to get Baraninas[3] to teach me under cover of night. For by his fear of the Jews he presented to me in his own person a second edition of Nicodemus.[4] Of all of these I have frequently made mention in my works. The doctrines of Apollinaris and of Didymus are mutually contradictory. The squadrons of the two leaders must drag me in different directions, for I acknowledge both as my masters. If it is expedient to hate any men and to loath any race, I have a strange dislike to those of the circumcision. For up to the present day they persecute our Lord Jesus Christ in the synagogues of Satan.[5] Yet can anyone find fault with me for having had a Jew as a teacher? Does a certain person dare to bring forward against me the letter I wrote to Didymus calling him my master? It is a great crime, it would seem, for me a disciple to give to one both old and learned the name of master. And yet when I ask leave to look at the letter which has been held over so long to discredit me at last, there is nothing in it but courteous language and a few words of greeting. Such charges are both foolish and frivolous. It would be more to the point to exhibit a passage in which I have defended heresy or praised some wicked doctrine of Origen. In the portion of Isaiah which describes the crying of the two seraphim[6] he explains these to be the Son and the Holy Ghost; but have not I altered this hateful explanation into a reference to the two testaments?[7]

---

[1] 1 Thess. v. 15.   [2] Rom. xii. 21.   [3] Matt. v. 39.
[4] Of these the two founders of Montanism the first was a Phrygian of the second century who professed to be the special organ of the Holy Ghost while the second was a female disciple who claimed to exercise the gift of prophecy in furtherance of his aims.
[5] Dimidiatam Christi introduxit œconomiam. Apollinaris taught that in Christ the divine personality supplied the place of a human soul. In his view, therefore, Christ ceased to be "very man."
[6] Eusebius, although he sided with the Arians, always claimed to be orthodox. However, as Newman says, "his acts are his confession."
[7] Isa. v. 20.

[1] Hor. S. i. x. 1-4.   [2] See Letter L. § 2.
[3] From this Jew Jerome took lessons in Hebrew during the earlier years of his life at Bethlehem. From time to time he also consulted other Jewish scholars.
[4] Joh. iii. 2.   [5] Cf. Rev. ii. 0.
[6] Isa. vi. 2.   [7] Cf. Letter XVIII. § 14.

I have the book in my hand as it was published twenty years ago. In numbers of my works and especially in my commentaries I have, as occasion has offered, mangled this heathen school. And if my opponents allege that I have done more than anyone else to form a collection of Origen's books, I answer that I only wish I could have the works of all theological writers that by diligent study of them, I might make up for the slowness of my own wits. I have made a collection of his books, I admit ; but because I know everything that he has written I do not follow his errors. I speak as a Christian to Christians : believe one who has tried him. His doctrines are poisonous, they are unknown to the Holy Scriptures, nay more, they do them violence. I have read Origen, I repeat, I have read him; and if it is a crime to read him, I admit my guilt: indeed, these Alexandrian writings have emptied my purse. If you will believe me, I have never been an Origenist: if you will not believe me, I have now ceased to be one. But if even this fails to convince you, you will compel me in self-defence to write against your favourite, so that, if you will not believe me when I disclaim him, you will have to believe me when I attack him. But I find readier credence when I go wrong than when I shew amendment. And this is not surprising, for my would-be friends suppose me a fellow-disciple with them in the arcana of their system. I am loath, they fancy, to profess esoteric doctrines before persons who according to them are brute-like and made of clay. For it is an axiom with them that pearls ought not to be lightly cast before swine, nor that which is holy given to the dogs.[1] They agree with David when he says: "Thy word have I hid in mine heart that I might not sin against thee;"[2] and when in another place he describes the righteous man as one "who speaketh truth with his neighbour,"[3] that is with those who "are of the household of faith."[4] From these passages they conclude that those of us who as yet are uninitiated ought to be told falsehoods, lest, being still unweaned babes, we should be choked by too solid food. Now that perjury and lying enter into their mysteries and form a bond between them appears most clearly from the sixth book of Origen's Miscellanies,[5] in which he harmonizes the Christian doctrine[6] with the conceptions of Plato.

4. What must I do then? deny that I am of Origen's opinion? They will not believe me. Swear that I am not? They will laugh and say that I deal in lies. I will do the one thing which they dread. I will bring forward their sacred rites and mysteries, and will expose the cunning whereby they delude simple folk like myself. Perhaps, although they refuse credence to my voice when I deny, they may believe my pen when I accuse. Of one thing they are particularly apprehensive, and that is that their writings may some day be taken as evidence against their master. They are ready to make statements on oath and to disclaim them afterwards with an oath as false as the first. When asked for their signatures they use shifts and seek excuses. One says : "I cannot condemn what no one else has condemned." Another says : "No decision was arrived at on the point by the Fathers."[1] It is thus that they appeal to the judgment of the world to put off the necessity of assenting to a condemnation. Another says with yet more assurance : "how am I to condemn men whom the council of Nicæa has left untouched? For the council which condemned Arius would surely have condemned Origen too, had it disapproved of his doctrines." They were bound in other words to cure all the diseases of the church at once and with one remedy ; and by parity of reasoning we must deny the majesty of the Holy Ghost because nothing was said of his nature in that council. But the question was of Arius, not of Origen ; of the Son, not of the Holy Ghost. The bishops at the council proclaimed their adherence to a dogma which was at the time denied ; they said nothing about a difficulty which no one had raised. And yet they covertly struck at Origen as the source of the Arian heresy : for, in condemning those who deny the Son to be of the substance of the Father, they have condemned Origen as much as Arius. On the ground taken by these persons we have no right to condemn Valentine,[2] or Marcion,[3] or the Cataphrygians,[4] or Manichæus, none of whom are named by the council of Nicæa, and yet there is no doubt that in time they were prior to it. But when they find themselves pressed either to subscribe or to leave the Church, you may see some strange twisting. They qualify their words, they arrange them anew, they use vague expressions ; so as, if possible, to hold both our confession and that of our opponents, to be called indifferently heretics and Catholics. As if it were not in the same spirit that the Delphian Apollo (or, as he is sometimes called, Loxias) gave his oracles

---

[1] Matt. vii. 6.
[2] Ps. cxix. 11.
[3] Ps. xv. 2, 3 from memory.
[4] Gal. vi. 10.
[5] στρωμάτεις, lit. = 'tapestries.' See note on Letter LXX. § 4.
[6] The doctrine alluded to is probably that of the Trinity.

[1] *i. e.* the Bishops present at Nicæa.
[2] The founder of a Gnostic sect in the second century. He taught first in Egypt and afterwards in Rome.
[3] See note on Letter XLVIII. § 2.
[4] The Montanists were so called because the headquarters of their sect were at Pepuza a small village in Phrygia.

to Crœsus and to Pyrrhus; cheating with a similar device two men widely separated in time.[1] To make my meaning clear I will give a few examples.

5. We believe, say they, in the resurrection of the body. This confession, if only it be sincere, is free from objection. But as there are bodies celestial and bodies terrestrial[2] and as thin air and the æther are both according to their natures called bodies, they use the word body instead of the word flesh in order that an orthodox person hearing them say body may take them to mean flesh while a heretic will understand that they mean spirit. This is their first piece of craft, and if this is found out, they devise fresh wiles, and, pretending innocence themselves, accuse us of malice. As though they were frank believers they say, " We believe in the resurrection of the flesh." Now when they have said this, the ignorant crowd thinks it ought to be satisfied, particularly because these exact words are found in the creed.[3] If you go on to question them farther, a buzz of disapproval is heard in the ring and their backers cry out : " You have heard them say that they believe in the resurrection of the flesh; what more do you want?" the popular favour is transferred from our side to theirs, and while they are called honest, we are looked on as false accusers. But if you set your face steadily and keeping a firm hold of their admission about the flesh, proceed to press them as to whether they assert the resurrection of that flesh which is visible and tangible, which walks and speaks, they first laugh and then signify their assent. And when we inquire whether the resurrection will exhibit anew the hair and the teeth, the chest and the stomach, the hands and the feet, and all the other members of the body, then no longer able to contain their mirth they burst out laughing and tell us that in that case we shall need barbers, and cakes, and doctors, and cobblers. Do we, they ask us in turn, believe that after the resurrection men's cheeks will still be rough and those of women smooth, and that sex will differentiate their bodies as it does at present? Then if we admit this, they at once deduce from our admission conclusions involving the grossest materialism. Thus, while they maintain the resurrection of the body as a whole, they deny the resurrection of its separate members.

6. The present is not a time to speak rhetorically against a perverse doctrine. Neither the rich vocabulary of Cicero nor the fervid eloquence of Demosthenes could adequately convey the warmth of my feeling, were I to attempt to expose the quibbles by which these heretics, while verbally professing a belief in the resurrection, in their hearts deny it. For their women finger their breasts, slap their chests, pinch their legs and arms, and say, "What will a resurrection profit us if these frail bodies are to rise again? No, if we are to be like angels,[1] we shall have the bodies of angels." That is to say they scorn to rise again with the flesh and bones wherewith even Christ rose.[2] Now suppose for a moment that in my youth I went astray and that, trained as I was in the schools of heathen philosophy, I was ignorant, in the beginning of my faith, of the dogmas of Christianity, and fancied that what I had read in Pythagoras and Plato and Empedocles was also contained in the writings of the apostle : Supposing, I say, that I believed all this, why do you yet follow the error of a mere babe and sucking child in Christ? Why do you learn irreligion of one who as yet knew not religion? After shipwreck one has still a plank to cling to ;[3] and one may atone for sin by a frank confession. You have followed me when I have gone astray; follow me also now that I have been brought back. In youth we have wandered; now that we are old let us mend our ways. Let us unite our tears and our groans; let us weep together, and return to the Lord our Maker.[4] Let us not wait for the repentance of the devil; for this is a vain anticipation and one that will drag us into the deep of hell. Life must be sought or lost here. If I have never followed Origen, it is in vain that you seek to discredit me : if I have been his disciple, imitate my penitence. You have believed my confession ; credit also my denial.

7. But it will be said, "If you knew these things, why did you praise him in your works?" I should praise him today but that you and men like you praise his errors. I should still find his talent attractive, but that some people have been attracted by his impiety. " Read[5] all things," says the apostle, " hold fast that which is good." [6] Lactantius in his books and particularly in his letters to Demetrian altogether denies the subsistence of the Holy Spirit, and following the error of the Jews says that the passages in which he is spoken of refer to the Father or to the Son and that the words ' holy spirit ' merely prove

---

[1] Crœsus when he asked whether he should resist Cyrus was told that, if he did so, he would overthrow a mighty kingdom, a prophecy fulfilled in his own destruction ; while Pyrrhus long afterwards received an equally evasive answer in the words, " Pyrrhus the Sons of Rome may well defeat."
[2] 1 Cor. xv. 40.
[3] Article XI. of the Apostles' Creed speaks in the original forms of the resurrection not of " the body " but of " the flesh :" and it is still found in this shape in the Anglican office for the visitation of the sick.

[1] Cf. Matt. xxii. 30.   [2] Cf. Luke xxiv. 39.
[3] A favourite metaphor with Jerome to describe the nature of Christian penitence.
[4] Ps. xcv. 6, Vulg.   [5] AV. ' prove.'   [6] 1 Thess. v. 21.

the holiness of these two persons in the Godhead. But who can forbid me to read his *Institutes*—in which he has written against the Gentiles with much ability—simply because this opinion of his is to be abhorred? Apollinaris[1] has written excellent treatises against Porphyry, and I approve of his labours, although I despise his doctrine in many points because of its foolishness. If you too for your parts will but admit that Origen errs in certain things I will not say another syllable. Acknowledge that he thought amiss concerning the Son, and still more amiss concerning the Holy Spirit, point out the impiety of which he has been guilty in speaking of men's souls as having fallen from heaven, and shew that, while in word he asserts the resurrection of the flesh, he destroys the force of this language by other assertions. As, for instance, that, after many ages and one "restitution of all things,"[2] it will be the same for Gabriel as for the devil, for Paul as for Caiaphas, for virgins as for prostitutes. When once you have rejected these misstatements and have parted them with your censor's wand from the faith of the Church, I may read what is left with safety, and having first taken the antidote need no longer dread the poison. For instance it will do me no harm to say as I have said, "Whereas in his other books Origen has surpassed all other writers, in commenting on the Song of Songs he has surpassed himself"; nor will I fear to face the words with which formerly in my younger days I spoke of him as a doctor of the churches.[3] Will it be pretended, that I was bound to accuse a man whose works I was translating by special request? that I was bound to say in my preface, "This writer whose books I translate is a heretic: beware of him, reader, read him not, flee from the viper: or, if you are bent on reading him, know that the treatises which I have translated have been garbled by heretics and wicked men; yet you need not fear, for I have corrected all the places which they have corrupted," that in other words I ought to have said: "the writer that I translate is a heretic, but I, his translator, am a Catholic." The fact is that you and your party in your anxiety to be straightforward, ingenuous, and honest, have paid too little regard to the precepts of rhetoric and to the devices of oratory. For in admitting that his books *On First Principles* are heretical and in trying to lay the blame of this upon others, you raise difficulties for your readers; you induce them to examine the whole life of the author and

to form a judgment on the question from the remainder of his writings. I on the other hand have been wise enough to emend silently what I wished to emend: thus by ignoring the crime I have averted prejudice from the criminal. Doctors tell us that serious maladies ought not to be subjected to treatment, but should be left to nature, lest the remedies applied should intensify the disease. It is now almost one hundred and fifty years since Origen died at Tyre.[1] Yet what Latin writer has ever ventured to translate his books *On the Resurrection* and *On First Principles*, his *Miscellanies*[2] and his *Commentaries* or as he himself calls them his *Tomes?*[3] Who has ever cared by so infamous a work to cover himself with infamy? I am not more eloquent than Hilary or truer to the faith than Victorinus who both have rendered his *Homilies*[4] not in exact versions but in independent paraphrases. Recently also Ambrose appropriated his *Six Days' Work*,[5] but in such a way that it expressed the views of Hippolytus and Basil rather than of Origen. You profess to take me for your model, and blind as moles in relation to others you scan me with the eyes of gazelles. Well, had I been ill-disposed towards Origen, I might have translated these very books so as to make his worst writings known to Latin readers; but this I have never done; and, though many have asked me, I have always refused. For it has never been my habit to crow over the mistakes of men whose talents I admire. Origen himself, were he still alive, would soon fall out with you his would-be patrons and would say with Jacob: "Ye have troubled me to make me to stink among the inhabitants of the land."[6]

8. Does any one wish to praise Origen? Let him praise him as I do. From his childhood he was a great man, and truly a martyr's son.[7] At Alexandria he presided over the school of the church, succeeding a man of great learning the presbyter Clement. So greatly did he abhor sensuality that, out of a zeal for God but yet one not according to knowledge,[9] he castrated himself with a knife. Covetousness he trampled under foot. He knew the scriptures by heart and laboured hard day and night to explain their meaning. He delivered in church more than a thousand sermons, and published innumerable commentaries which he called tomes. These I now pass over, for it is not my purpose to catalogue his writings. Which of us can read all that he has written? and who can fail to ad-

---

[1] See note on § 2 above.   [2] Acts iii. 21.
[3] See Jerome's preface to his version of Origen's Homilies on Ezekiel: and his preface to his own Treatise on Hebrew Names. See also Letter XXXIII.

[1] Origen died at Tyre about the year 255 A.D.
[2] See note on Letter LXX. § 4.   [3] τόμοι.   [4] Tractatus.
[5] Hexaëmeron: an account of the creation is meant.
[6] Gen. xxxiv. 30.
[7] His father Leonides suffered martyrdom in the persecution of Severus.
[8] See note on Letter LXX. § 4.   [9] Rom. x. 2.

mire his enthusiasm for the scriptures? If some one in the spirit of Judas the Zealot[1] brings up to me his mistakes, he shall have his answer in the words of Horace:

'Tis true that sometimes Homer sleeps, but then
He's not without excuse:
The fault is venial, for his work is long.[2]

Let us not imitate the faults of one whose virtues we cannot equal. Other men have erred concerning the faith, both Greeks and Latins, but I must not mention their names lest I should be supposed to defend Origen not by his own merits but by the errors of others. This, you will say, is to accuse them and not to excuse him. You would be right, if I had declared him not to have erred, or if I had professed a belief that the apostle Paul or an angel from heaven[3] ought to be listened to in a depravation of the faith. But as it is, seeing I frankly admit him to be wrong, I may read him on the same terms as I read others, because if he is wrong so also are they. But you may say, If error is common to many, why do you assail him alone? I answer, because he alone is praised by you as an apostle. Take away your exaggerated love for him, and I am ready to take away the greatness of my dislike. While you gather other men's faulty statements out of their books merely to defend Origen in his error, you extol this latter to the sky and will not allow that he has erred at all. Whosoever you are who are thus preaching new doctrines, I beseech you, spare the ears of the Romans, spare the faith of a church which an apostle has praised.[4] Why after four hundred years do you try to teach us Romans doctrines of which until now we have known nothing? Why do you publicly proclaim opinions which Peter and Paul[5] refused to profess? Until now no such teaching has been heard of, and yet the world has become christian. For my part I will hold fast in my old age the faith wherein I was born again in my boyhood.[6] They speak of us as claytowners,[7] made out of dirt, brutish and carnal, because, say they, we refuse to receive the things of the spirit; but of course they themselves are citizens of Jerusalem and their mother is in heaven.[8] I do not despise the flesh in which Christ was born and rose again, or scorn the mud which, baked into a clean vessel, reigns in heaven. And yet I wonder why they who detract from the flesh live after the flesh,[9] and cherish and delicately nurture that which is their enemy. Perhaps indeed they wish to fulfil the words of scripture: "love your enemies and bless them that persecute you."[1] I love the flesh, but I love it only when it is chaste, when it is virginal, when it is mortified by fasting: I love not its works but itself, that flesh which knows that it must be judged, and therefore dies as a martyr for Christ, which is scourged and torn asunder and burned with fire.

9. The folly also of their contention that certain heretics and ill-disposed persons have tampered with Origen's writings may be shewn thus. Could any person be more wise, more learned, or more eloquent than were Eusebius and Didymus, Origen's supporters? Of these the former in the six volumes of his *Apology*[2] asserts that Origen is of the same mind with himself; while the latter, though he tries to excuse his errors, admits that he has made them. Not being able to deny what he finds written, he endeavours to explain it away. It is one thing to say that additions have been made by heretics, but another to maintain that heretical statements are commendable. Origen's case would be unique if his writings were falsified all over the world and if in one day by an edict like that of Mithridates[3] all the truth were shorn from his volumes. Even supposing that some one treatise of his has been tampered with, can it be possible that all his works, published as they were at different times and places, have been corrupted? Origen himself in a letter written to Fabian, bishop of Rome,[4] expresses penitence for having made erroneous statements, and charges Ambrose[5] with over haste in making public what was meant only for private circulation. And yet to this day his disciples search for shifts to prove that all that excites disapprobation in his writings is due not to him but to others.

10. Moreover, when they speak of Pamphilus as one who praised Origen, I am personally much obliged to them for accounting me worthy to be calumniated with that martyr. For if, sirs, you tell me that Origen's books have been tampered with by his enemies to bring them into discredit; why may not I in my turn allege that his friends and followers have attributed to Pamphilus a volume composed by themselves to vindicate their master from disrepute by the testimony of a martyr? Lo and behold, you yourselves

---

[1] *i.e.* Judas the Gaulonite whose fanatical rising against the Romans is mentioned in Acts v. 37.
[2] Hor. A. P. 359, 360. [3] Cf. Gal. i. 8. [4] Rom. i. 8.
[5] The (traditional) founders of the Roman Church.
[6] Jerome was baptized at Rome about the year 367 A.D.
[7] Pelusiotæ, men of Pelusium, supposed to be derived from πηλός, "clay." See Jerome's Comm. on Jer. xxix. 14-20.
[8] Gal. iv. 26.
[9] See the description of Rufinus in Letter CXXV. 18.

[1] Matt v. 44 from memory.
[2] This treatise the joint work of Eusebius and his friend Pamphilus has perished. Part of the Latin version of Rufinus still remains. Jerome at this time erroneously supposed that the two friends had written separate works in defence of Origen. (See De VV. Ill. c. 75, 81, in vol. iii. of this series.)
[3] In accordance with this edict (promulgated in 88 B.C.) all the Romans in Pontus were massacred in one day.
[4] This letter is no longer extant.
[5] A wealthy Alexandrian, who employed shorthand writers to take down Origen's lectures. Euseb. Eccl. Hist. B. vi. c. 23.

correct in Origen's books passages which (according to you) he never wrote : and yet you are surprised if a man is said to have published a book which as a matter of fact he did not publish. But while your statements can easily be brought to the test by an appeal to Origen's published works ; as Pamphilus has published nothing else, it is easier for calumny to fix a book upon him. For shew me any other work of Pamphilus ; you will nowhere find any, this is his only one. How then can I know that it is by Pamphilus? You will tell me, that the style and tone ought to inform me. Well, I shall never believe that a man so learned has dedicated the first fruits of his talent to defend doubtful and discredited positions. The very name of an apology which the treatise bears implies a previous charge made ; for nothing is defended that is not first attacked. I will now bring forward but a single argument, one, however, the force of which only folly and effrontery can deny. The treatise attributed to Pamphilus contains nearly the first thousand lines of Eusebius's sixth book in defence of Origen.[1] Yet in the remaining parts of his work the writer brings forward passages by which he seeks to prove that Origen was a Catholic. Now Eusebius and Pamphilus were in such thorough harmony with each other that they seemed to have but one soul between them, and one even went so far as to adopt the other's name.[2] How then could they have disagreed so fundamentally on this point, Eusebius in all his works proving Origen to be an Arian, and Pamphilus describing him as a supporter of the Nicene council, which had not yet been held? It is evident from this consideration that the book belongs not to Pamphilus but to Didymus or somebody else, who having cut off the head of Eusebius's sixth book supplied the other members himself. But I am willing to be generous and to allow that the book is written by Pamphilus, only by Pamphilus not yet a martyr. For he must have written the book before he underwent martyrdom. And why, you will say, was he accounted worthy of martyrdom? Surely that he might efface his error by a martyr's death, and wash away his one fault by shedding his blood. How many martyrs there have been all the world over who before their deaths have been the slaves of sins ! Are we then to palliate the sins because those who committed them have afterwards become martyrs?

11. This reply to your letter, my most loving brothers, I have dictated in all haste; and, overcoming my scruples, I have taken up my pen against a man whose ability I once eulogized. I would sooner, indeed, risk my reputation than my faith. My friends have placed me in the awkward dilemma that if I say nothing I shall be held guilty, and if I offer a defence I shall be accounted an enemy. Both alternatives are hard; but of the two I will choose that which is the least so. A quarrel can be made up, but blasphemy can find no forgiveness. I leave to your judgment to discover how much labour I have expended in translating the books *On First Principles ;* for on the one hand if one alters anything from the Greek the work becomes less a version than a perversion ; and on the other hand a literal adherence to the original by no means tends to preserve the charm of its eloquence.

LETTER LXXXV.

TO PAULINUS.

Paulinus had asked Jerome two questions, (1) how can certain passages of scripture (Exod. vii. 13 : Rom. ix. 16) be reconciled with Free Will ? and (2) Why are the children of believers said to be holy (1 Cor. vii. 14) apart from baptismal grace ? For the first of these questions Jerome refers Paulinus to his version (newly made) of Origen's treatise, *On First Principles.* For the second he quotes the explanation of Tertullian. Written in 400 A.D.

1. Your words urge me to write to you but your eloquence deters me from doing so. For as a letter-writer you are almost as good as Tully. You complain that my letters are short and unpolished : this is not due to carelessness but to fear of you, lest writing to you at greater length I should but send you more sentences to find fault with. Moreover, to make a clean breast of it to a good man like you, just about the time the vessels sail for the west, so many letters are demanded of me at once that, if I were to reply to all my correspondents, I should be unable to accomplish my task. Hence it happens that, neglecting the niceties of composition and not revising the work of my secretaries, I dictate whatever first comes into my head. Thus when I write to you I regard you as a friend and not as a critic.

2. Your letter propounds two questions, the first, why God hardened Pharaoh's heart, and why the apostle said : " So then it is not of him that willeth, nor of him that runneth, but of God that sheweth mercy ; "[1] and other things which appear to do away with free will : the second, how those are holy who are born of believing, that is, of baptized parents,[2] seeing that without the gift of grace

---

[1] If the text is sound here Jerome is again misled by supposing that Eusebius and Pamphilus had written separate books in defence of Origen.
[2] Eusebius calls himself Eusebius Pamphili, that is, 'the friend of Pamphilus.'

[1] Rom. ix. 16.   [2] 1 Cor. vii. 14.

afterwards received and kept they cannot be saved.

3. Your first question is most ably answered by Origen in his treatise *on First Principles* which, at the request of my friend Pammachius, I have recently translated. This task has occupied me so fully that I am unable to keep my word with you and must again postpone the sending my commentary on Daniel. Indeed, distinguished and devoted to me as Pammachius is, had he been alone in his request, I should have deferred it to another time, but, as it was, almost all our brothers at Rome urged the same demand declaring that many persons were in danger, and that some even accepted Origen's heretical teaching. I have found myself forced therefore to translate a book in which there is more of bad than of good, and to keep to this rule that I should neither add nor subtract but should preserve in Latin in its integrity the true sense of the Greek. You will be able to borrow a copy of my version from the aforesaid brother, though in your case the Greek will serve quite as well; neither should you, who can drink from the fountain head, turn to the muddy streamlets supplied by my poor wits.

4. Moreover, as I am speaking to an educated man, well versed both in the sacred scriptures and in secular literature, I desire to give your excellency this note of warning. Do not suppose that I am a clumsy buffoon [1] who condemn everything that Origen has written,—as his injudicious friends falsely assert—or that I have changed my mind as suddenly as the philosopher Dionysius. [2] The fact is that I repudiate merely his objectionable dogmas. For I know that one curse hangs over those who call evil good and over those who call good evil, over those who put bitter for sweet, and over those who put sweet for bitter. [3] Who would go so far in praise of another man's teaching as to acquiesce in blasphemy?

5. Your second question is discussed by Tertullian in his books *on Monogamy* [4] where he declares that the children of believers are called holy because they are as it were candidates for the faith and have suffered no pollution from idolatry. Consider also that the vessels of which we read in the tabernacle are called holy and everything else required for the ceremonial worship : although in strictness of speech there can be nothing holy except creatures which know of and worship God. But it is a scriptural usage sometimes to give the name of holy to those

who are clean, or who have been purified, or who have made expiation. For instance, it is written of Bathsheba that she was made holy [1] from her uncleanness, [2] and the temple itself is called the holy place.

6. I beg that you will not silently in your mind accuse me either of vanity or of insincerity. God bears me witness in my conscience that the unavoidable circumstances mentioned above drew me back when I was just going to grapple with my commentary ; and you know that what is done when the mind is pre-occupied is never well done. I gladly accept the cap that you have sent me, a mark, though small, of no small affection and just the thing to keep an old man's head warm. I am delighted alike with the gift and with the giver.

LETTER LXXXVI.

TO THEOPHILUS.

Jerome congratulates Theophilus on the success of his crusade against Origenism, and speaks of the good work done in Palestine by his emissaries Priscus and Eubulus. He then (by a singular change in his sentiments) asks Theophilus to forgive John of Jerusalem for having unwittingly received an excommunicated Egyptian. The date of the Letter is 400 A.D.

Jerome to the most blessed Pope Theophilus. I have recently received despatches from your blessedness setting right your long silence and summoning me to return to my duty. So, though the reverend brothers Priscus and Eubulus have been slow in bringing me your letters, yet, as they are now hastening in the ardour of faith from end to end of Palestine and scattering and driving into their holes the basilisks of heresy, I write a few lines to congratulate you on your success. The whole world glories in your victories. An exultant crowd of all nations gazes on the standard of the cross raised by you at Alexandria and upon the shining trophies which mark your triumph over heresy. Blessings on your courage ! blessings on your zeal ! You have shewn that your long silence has been due to policy and not to inclination. I speak quite openly to your reverence. I grieved to find you too forbearing, and, knowing nothing of the course shaped by the pilot, I yearned for the destruction of those abandoned men. But, as I now see, you have had your hand raised and, if you have delayed to strike, it has only been that you might strike harder. As regards the welcome given to a certain person, [3] you have no reason to be vexed with

---

[1] Cf. Hor. S. II. viii. 21.
[2] Dionysius of Heraclea called the renegade because he abandoned the Stoic for the Cyrenaic school.
[3] Isa. v. 20.   [4] Ad. Ux. ii. 2.

[1] AV. 'purified.'   [2] 2 Sam. xi. 4.
[3] Doubtless some Egyptian monk or ecclesiastic placed under ban by Theophilus on account of Origenism.

the prelate of this city;[1] for as you gave no instructions on the point in your letter, it would have been rash in him to decide a case of which he knew nothing. Still I think that he would neither wish nor venture to annoy you in any way.

LETTER LXXXVII.

FROM THEOPHILUS TO JEROME.

Theophilus informs Jerome that he has expelled the Origenists from the monasteries of Nitria, and urges him to shew his zeal for the faith by writing against the prevalent heresy. The date of the letter is 400 A.D.

Theophilus, bishop, to the well-beloved and most loving brother, the presbyter Jerome. The reverend bishop Agatho with the well-beloved deacon Athanasius is accredited to you with tidings relating to the church. When you learn their import I feel no doubt but that you will approve my resolution and will exult in the church's victory. For we have cut down with the prophet's sickle[2] certain wicked fanatics who were eager to sow broadcast in the monasteries of Nitria the heresy of Origen. We have remembered the warning words of the apostle, "rebuke with all authority."[3] Do you therefore on your part, as you hope to receive a share in this reward, make haste to bring back with scriptural discourses those who have been deceived. It is our desire, if possible, to guard in our days not only the Catholic faith and the rules of the church, but the people committed to our charge, and to give a quietus to all strange doctrines.

LETTER LXXXVIII.

TO THEOPHILUS.

Replying to the preceding letter Jerome again congratulates Theophilus on the success of his efforts to put down Origenism, and informs him that they have already borne fruit as far west as Italy. He then asks him for the decrees of his council (held recently at Alexandria). The date of the letter is 400 A.D.

Jerome to the most blessed pope Theophilus. The letter of your holiness has given me a twofold pleasure, partly because it has had for its bearers those reverend and estimable men, the bishop Agatho and the deacon Athanasius, and partly because it has shewn your zeal for the faith against a most wicked heresy. The voice of your holiness has rung throughout the world, and to the joy of all Christ's churches the poisonous suggestions of the devil have been silenced. The old serpent[1] hisses no longer, but, writhing and disembowelled, lurks in dark caverns unable to bear the shining of the sun. I have already, before the writing of your letter, sent missives to the West pointing out to those of my own language some of the quibbles employed by the heretics. I hold it due to the special providence of God that you should have written to the pope Anastasius[2] at the same time as myself, and should thus without knowing it have been the means of confirming my testimony. Now that you have directly urged me to do so, I shall shew myself more zealous than ever to recall from their error simple souls both near and far. Nor shall I hesitate, if needful, to incur odium with some, for we ought to please God rather than men:[3] although indeed they have been much more forward to defend their heresy than I and others have been to attack it. At the same time I beg that if you have any synodical decrees bearing upon the subject you will forward them to me, that, strengthened with the authority of so great a prelate, I may open my mouth for Christ with more freedom and confidence. The presbyter Vincent has arrived from Rome two days ago and humbly salutes you. He tells me again and again that Rome and almost the whole of Italy owe their deliverance after Christ to your letters. Shew diligence therefore, most loving and most blessed pope, and whenever opportunity offers write to the bishops of the West not to hesitate—in your own words[4]— to cut down with a sharp sickle the sprouts of evil.

LETTER LXXXIX.

FROM THEOPHILUS TO JEROME.

This letter (probably earlier in date than the three preceding) commends to Jerome the monk Theodore, who, having come from Rome to declare the condemnation of Origenism by the church there, had visited the monasteries of Nitria now purged of heresy, and wished before returning to the West to see the Holy Places as well. The date of the letter is 400 A.D.

Theophilus, bishop, to the well-beloved lord and most loving brother the presbyter Jerome. I have learned the project of the monk Theodore—which will be known also to your holiness—and I approve of it. Having to leave us on a voyage for Rome, he has been unwilling to set out without first visiting and embracing as his own flesh and

---

[1] John of Jerusalem. He had probably, like Rufinus, been reconciled to Jerome, and seems to have taken no part in the subsequent quarrel between Jerome and Rufinus.
[2] Joel iii. 13. [3] Tit. ii. 15.

[1] Rev. xii. 9. [2] Bishop of Rome, A.D. 398–402.
[3] Acts v. 29. [4] See the preceding letter.

blood you and the reverend brothers who are with you in the monastery. You will, I am sure, rejoice in the news with which he will meet your welcome, that quiet has been restored to the church here. He has seen all the monasteries of Nitria and can tell you of the continence and meekness of the monks in them ; as also how the Origenists have been put down and scattered, how peace has been restored to the church, and how the discipline of the Lord is being upheld. How gladly would I see the mask of hypocrisy laid aside by those also who near you are said to be undermining the truth. I feel obliged to write thus because the brothers in your neighbourhood[1] are mistaken concerning them. Wherefore take heed to yourselves and shun men of this type ; even as it is written :—"if any man bring not to you the faith of the church, bid him not God speed."[2] It may, indeed, be superfluous to write thus to you who can recall the erring from their error, yet no harm is done when those careful for the faith admonish even the wise and learned. Kindly salute in my name all the brothers who are with you.

LETTER XC.

FROM THEOPHILUS TO EPIPHANIUS.

Theophilus writes to Epiphanius to convoke a council in Cyprus for the condemnation of Origenism and asks him to transmit to Constantinople by a trustworthy messenger a copy of its decrees together with the synodical letter of Theophilus himself. His anxiety about this last point is caused by the news that certain of the excommunicated monks have set sail for Constantinople to lay their case before the bishop, John Chrysostom. The date of the letter is 400 A.D.

Theophilus to his well-beloved lord, brother, and fellow-bishop Epiphanius.

The Lord has said to his prophet, " See, I have this day set thee over the nations and over the kingdoms to root out and to pull down and to destroy and . . . to build and to plant."[3] In every age he bestows the same grace upon his church, that His Body[4] may be preserved intact and that the poison of heretical opinions may nowhere prevail over it. And now also do we see the words fulfilled. For the church of Christ " not having spot or wrinkle or any such thing "[5] has with the sword of the gospel cut down the Origenist serpents crawling out of their caves, and has delivered from their deadly contagion the fruitful host of the monks of Nitria. I have compressed a short account of my proceedings (it was all that

time would allow) into the general letter[1] which I have addressed indiscriminately to all. As your excellency has often fought in contests of the kind before me, it is your present duty to strengthen the hands of those who are in the field and to gather together to this end the bishops of your entire island.[2] A synodical letter should be sent to myself and the bishop of Constantinople[3] and to any others whom you think fit ; that by universal consent Origen himself may be expressly condemned and also the infamous heresy of which he was the author. I have learned that certain calumniators of the true faith, named Ammonius, Eusebius, and Euthymius, filled with a fresh access of enthusiasm in behalf of the heresy, have taken ship for Constantinople, to ensnare with their deceits as many new converts as they can and to confer anew with the old companions of their impiety. Let it be your care, therefore, to set forth the course of the matter to all the bishops throughout Isauria and Pamphylia and the rest of the neighbouring provinces : moreover, if you think fit, you can add my letter, so that all of us gathered together in one spirit with the power of our Lord Jesus Christ may deliver these men unto Satan for the destruction of the impiety which possesses them.[4] And to ensure the speedy arrival of my despatches at Constantinople, send a diligent messenger, one of the clergy (as I send fathers from the monasteries of Nitria with others also of the monks, learned men and continent) that when they arrive they may be able themselves to relate what has been done. Above all I beg of you to offer up earnest prayers to the Lord that we may be able in this contest also to gain the victory ; for no small joy has filled the hearts of the people both in Alexandria and throughout all Egypt, because a few men have been expelled from the Church that the body of it might be kept pure. Salute the brothers who are with you. The people[5] with us salute you in the Lord.

LETTER XCI.

FROM EPIPHANIUS TO JEROME.

An exultant letter from Epiphanius in which he describes the success of his council (convened at the suggestion of Theophilus), sends Jerome a copy of its synodical letter, and urges him to go on with his work of translating into Latin documents bearing on the Origenistic controversy. Written in 400 A.D.

To his most loving lord, son, and brother,

---

[1] The bishops of Palestine are meant.　See Letter XCII.
[2] 2 John 10, inexactly quoted.　　[3] Jer. i. 10.
[4] Eph. i. 23.　　　　　　[5] Eph. v. 27.

[1] Letter XCII.　　　　　　[2] Cyprus.
[3] i.e. John Chrysostom who had been raised to the patriarchate in 398 A.D.
[4] Cf. 1 Cor. v. 4, 5.　　　　[5] Plebs.

the presbyter Jerome, Epiphanius sends greeting in the Lord. The general epistle written[1] to all Catholics belongs particularly to you ; for you, having a zeal for the faith against all heresies, particularly oppose the disciples of Origen and of Apollinaris ; whose poisoned roots and deeply planted impiety almighty God has dragged forth into our midst, that having been unearthed at Alexandria they might wither throughout the world. For know, my beloved son, that Amalek has been destroyed root and branch and that the trophy of the cross has been set up on the hill of Rephidim.[2] For as when the hands of Moses were held up on high Israel prevailed, so the Lord has strengthened His servant Theophilus to plant His standard against Origen on the altar of the church of Alexandria ; that in him might be fulfilled the words : "Write this for a memorial, for I will utterly put out Origen's heresy from under heaven together with that Amalek himself." And that I may not appear to be repeating the same things over and over and thus to be making my letter tedious, I send you the actual missive written to me that you may know what Theophilus has said to me, and what a great blessing the Lord has granted to my last days in approving the principles which I have always proclaimed by the testimony of so great a prelate. I fancy that by this time you also have published something and that, as I suggested in my former letter to you on this subject, you have elaborated a treatise for readers of your own language. For I hear that certain of those who have made shipwreck[3] have come also to the West, and that, not content with their own destruction, they desire to involve others in death with them ; as if they thought that the multitude of sinners lessens the guilt of sin and the flames of Gehenna do not grow in size in proportion as more logs are heaped upon them. With you and by you we send our best greetings to the reverend brothers who are with you in the monastery serving God.

LETTER XCII.

THE SYNODICAL LETTER OF THEOPHILUS TO THE BISHOPS OF PALESTINE AND OF CYPRUS.

The synodical letter of the council held at Alexandria in 400 A.D. to condemn Origenism. Written originally in Greek it was translated into Latin by Jerome.

This letter has been sent in identical terms to the Bishops of Palestine and to those of Cyprus. We reproduce the headings of both copies. That to the Bishops of Palestine commences thus : To the well-be-

loved lords, brothers, and fellow-bishops, Eulogius, John, Zebianus, Auxentius, Dionysius, Gennadius, Zeno, Theodosius, Dicterius, Porphyry, Saturninus, Alan, Paul, Ammonius, Helianus, Eusebius, the other Paul, and to all the Catholic bishops gathered together at the dedication festival of Ælid,[1] Theophilus [sends] greeting in the Lord.

The Cyprians he addresses thus : To the well-beloved lords, brothers, and fellow-bishops, Epiphanius, Marcianus, Agapetus, Boethius, Helpidius, Entasius, Norbanus, Macedonius, Aristo, Zeno, Asiaticus, Heraclides, the other Zeno, Cyriacus, and Aphroditus, Theophilus [sends] greeting in the Lord.

The scope of the letter is as follows :

We have personally visited the monasteries of Nitria and find that the Origenistic heresy has made great ravages among them. It is accompanied by a strange fanaticism : men even maim themselves or cut out their tongues[2] to show how they despise the body. I find that some men of this kind have gone from Egypt into Syria and other countries[3] where they speak against us and the truth.

The books of Origen have been read before a council of bishops and unanimously condemned. The following are his chief errors, mainly found in the $\pi\epsilon\rho\grave{\iota}$ $\grave{A}\rho\chi\grave{\omega}\nu$.

1. The Son compared with us is truth, but compared with the Father he is falsehood.

2. Christ's kingdom will one day come to an end.

3. We ought to pray to the Father alone, not to the Son.

4. Our bodies after the resurrection will be corruptible and mortal.

5. There is nothing perfect even in heaven ; the angels themselves are faulty, and some of them feed on the Jewish sacrifices.

6. The stars are conscious of their own movements, and the demons know the future by their courses.

7. Magic, if real, is not evil.

8. Christ suffered once for men ; he will suffer again for the demons.

The Origenists have tried to coerce me ; they have even stirred up the heathen by denouncing the destruction of the Serapeum ; and have sought to withdraw from the ecclesiastical jurisdiction two persons accused of grave crimes. One of these is the woman[4]

---

[1] In Æliæ encæniis. Ælia was the name given by the emperor Hadrian to the Roman colony founded by him on the site of Jerusalem.

[2] The monk Ammonius is said to have done this and similar things.

[3] Some fifty, led by Ammonius and his three brothers (called the Long or Tall Monks) went first to Syria and then to Constantinople.

[4] This woman is said to have brought a charge of immorality against Isidore and then suppressed it on being placed by him on the list of widows who received the church's bounty. Isidore was now eighty years old, and there were many causes for the quarrel. Palladius, Socrates and Sozomen intimate that the real cause of Theophilus' enmity to his old confidant Isidore was that Isidore knew secrets unfavorable to Theophilus. He afterwards went with the Long Monks to Constantinople, where Chrysostom by his reception of them incurred the hatred of Theophilus. See Jerome Letter CXIII.

---

[1] By Theophilus. [2] Cf. Exod. xvii. 8–14. [3] 1 Tim. i. 19.

who was wrongly placed on the list of widows by Isidore, the other Isidore himself. He is the standard-bearer of the heretical faction, and his wealth supplies them with unbounded resources for their violent enterprises. They have tried to murder me ; they seized the monastery church at Nitria, and for a time prevented the bishops from entering and the offices from being performed. Now, like Zebul (Beelzebub) they go to and fro on the earth.

I have done them no harm ; I have even protected them. But I would not let an old friendship (with Isidore) impair our faith and discipline. I implore you to oppose them wherever they come, and to prevent them from unsettling the brethren committed to you.

LETTER XCIII.

FROM THE BISHOPS OF PALESTINE TO THEOPHILUS.

The synodical letter of the council of Jerusalem sent to Theophilus in reply to the preceding. The translation as before is due to Jerome.

The following is an epitome : We have done all that you wished, and Palestine is almost wholly free from the taint of heresy. We wish that not only the Origenists, but Jews, Samaritans and heathen also, could be put down. Origenism does not exit among us. ·The doctrines you describe are never heard here. We anathematize those who hold such doctrines, and also those of Apollinaris, and shall not receive anyone whom you excommunicate.

LETTER XCIV.

FROM DIONYSIUS TO THEOPHILUS.

In this letter (translated into Latin by Jerome) Dionysius, bishop of Lydda, praises Theophilus for his signal victories over Origenism and urges him to continue his efforts against that heresy. Written in 400 A.D.

LETTER XCV.

FROM POPE ANASTASIUS TO SIMPLICIANUS.

At the request of Theophilus Anastasius, bishop of Rome, writes to Simplicianus, bishop of Milan, to inform him that he, like Theophilus, has condemned Origen whose blasphemies have been brought under his notice by Eusebius of Cremona. This latter had shewn him a copy of the version by Rufinus of the treatise On First Principles. *The date of the letter is 400 A.D.*

To his lord and brother Simplicianus, Anastasius.

1. It is felt right that a shepherd should bestow great care and watchfulness upon his flock. In like manner too from his lofty tower the careful watchman keeps a lookout day and night on behalf of the city. So also in the hour of tempest when the sea is dangerous the shipmaster suffers keen anxiety [1] lest the gale and the violence of the waves shall dash his vessel upon the rocks. It is with similar feelings that the reverend and honourable Theophilus our brother and fellow-bishop, ceases not to watch over the things that make for salvation, that God's people in the different churches may not by reading Origen run into awful blasphemies.

2. Being informed, then, by a letter of the aforesaid bishop, we inform your holiness that we in like manner who are set in the city of Rome in which the prince of the apostles, the glorious Peter, first founded the church and then by his faith strengthened it ; to the end that no man may contrary to the commandment read these books which we have mentioned, have condemned the same ; and have with earnest prayers urged the strict observance of the precepts which God and Christ have inspired the evangelists to teach. We have charged men to remember the words of the venerable apostle Paul, prophetic and full of warning :—" if any man preach any other gospel unto you than that which we have preached unto you, let him be accursed." [2] Holding fast, therefore, this precept, we have intimated that everything written in days gone by by Origen that is contrary to our faith is even by us rejected and condemned.

3. I send this letter to your holiness by the hand of the presbyter Eusebius, [3] a man filled with a glowing faith and love for the Lord. He has shewn to me some blasphemous chapters which made me shudder as I passed judgement on them. If Origen has put forth any other writings, you are to know that they and their author are alike condemned by me. The Lord have you in safe keeping, my lord and brother deservedly held in honour.

LETTER XCVI.

FROM THEOPHILUS.

A translation by Jerome of Theophilus's paschal letter for the year 401 A.D. In it Theophilus refutes at length the heresies of Apollinaris and Origen.

LETTER XCVII.

TO PAMMACHIUS AND MARCELLA.

With this letter Jerome sends to Pammachius and Marcella a translation of the paschal letter issued by

---

[1] Magister hactenus navis hora tempestatis æquoris et periculo magnam patitur animi jactationem.
[2] Gal. i. 8.
[3] See the account of the meeting of Eusebius with Rufinus in the presence of Simplicianus. Ruf. Apol. i. 19.

Theophilus for the year 402 A.D. together with the Greek original. He takes the precaution of sending this latter because in the preceding year complaints have been made that his translation was not accurate. Written in 402 A.D.

1. Once more with the return of spring I enrich you with the wares of the east and send the treasures of Alexandria to Rome: as it is written, "God shall come from the south and the Holy One from Mount Paran, even a thick shadow."[1] (Hence in the Song of Songs the joyous cry of the bride: "I sat down under his shadow with great delight and his fruit was sweet to my taste."[2]) Now truly is Isaiah's prophecy fulfilled: "In that day shall there be an altar to the Lord in the land of Egypt."[3] "Where sin hath abounded, grace doth much more abound."[4] They who fostered the infant Christ now with glowing faith defend Him in His manhood; and they who once saved Him from the hands of Herod are ready to save Him again from this blasphemer and heretic. Demetrius expelled Origen from the city of Alexander; but he is now thanks to Theophilus outlawed from the whole world. Like him to whom Luke has dedicated the *Acts of the Apostles*[5] this bishop derives his name from his love to God. Where now is the wriggling serpent?[6] In what plight does the venomous viper find himself? His is

A human face with wolfish body joined.[7]

Where now is that heresy which crawled hissing through the world and boasted that both the bishop Theophilus and I were partisans of its errors? Where now is the yelping of those shameless hounds who, to win over the simple minded, falsely proclaimed our adherence to their cause? Crushed by the authority and eloquence of Theophilus they are now like demon-spirits only able to mutter and that from out of the earth.[8] For they know nothing of Him who, as He comes from above,[9] speaks only of the things that are above.

2. Would that this generation of vipers[10] would either honestly accept our doctrines, or else consistently defend its own; that we might know whom we are to esteem and whom we are to shun. As it is they have invented a new kind of penitence, hating us as enemies though they dare not deny our faith. What, I ask, is this chagrin of theirs which neither time nor reason seems able to cure? When swords flash in battle and men fall and blood flows in streams, hostile hands are often clasped in amity and the fury of war is exchanged for an unexpected peace. The partisans of this heresy alone can make no terms with churchmen; for they repudiate mentally the verbal assent that is extorted from them. When their open blasphemy is made plain to the public ear, and when they perceive their hearers clamouring against them; then they assume an air of simplicity, declaring that they hear such doctrines for the first time and that they have no previous knowledge of them as taught by their master. And when you hold their writings in your hand, they deny with their lips what their hands have written. Why, sirs, need you beset the Propontis,[1] shift your abode, wander through different countries, and rend with foaming mouths a distinguished prelate of Christ and his followers? If your recantations are sincere, you should replace your former zeal for error with an equal zeal for the faith. Why do you patch together from this quarter and from that these rags of cursing? And why do you rail at the lives of men whose faith you cannot resist? Do you cease to be heretics because according to you sundry persons believe us to be sinners? And does impiety cease to disfigure your lips because you can point to scars on our ears? So long as you have a leopard's spots and an Ethiopian's skin,[2] how can it help your perfidy to know that I too am marked by moles? See, Pope Theophilus is freely allowed to prove Origen a heretic; and the disciples do not defend the master's words. They merely pretend that they have been altered by heretics and tampered with, like the works of many other writers. Thus they seek to maintain his cause not by their own belief but by other people's errors. So much I would say against heretics who in the fury of their unjust hostility to us betray the secret feelings of their minds and prove the incurable nature of the wound that rankles in their breasts.

3. But you are Christians and the lights of the senate: accept therefore from me the letter which I append.[3] This year I send it both in Greek and Latin that the heretics may not again lyingly assert that I have made many changes in and additions to the original. I have laboured hard, I must confess, to preserve the charm of the diction by a like elegance in my version: and keeping within fixed lines and never allowing myself to deviate from these I have done my best to maintain the smooth flow of the writer's

---

[1] Hab. iii. 3, LXX. [2] Cant. ii. 3. [3] Isa. xix. 19.
[4] Rom. v. 20. [5] Acts i. 1. [6] The allusion is to Rufinus.
[7] Virg. A. iii. 426. [8] Cf. I. Sam. xxviii. 13.
[9] Joh. viii. 23. [10] Matt. iii. 7.

[1] Many of the Egyptian Origenists had fled to Constantinople and thrown themselves on the kindness of the patriarch John Chrysostom.
[2] Jer. xiii. 23. [3] Letter XCVIII.

eloquence and to render his remarks in the tone in which they are made. Whether I have succeeded in these two objects or not I must leave to your judgement to determine. As for the letter itself you are to know that it is divided into four parts. In the first Theophilus exhorts believers to celebrate the Lord's passover; in the second he slays Apollinarius; in the third he demolishes Origen; while in the fourth and last he exhorts the heretics to penitence. If the polemic against Origen should seem to you to be inadequate, you are to remember that Origenism was fully treated in last year's letter;[1] and that this which I have just translated, as it aims at brevity, was not bound to dwell farther upon the subject. Besides, its terse and clear confession of faith directed against Apollinarius is not lacking in dialectical subtlety. Theophilus first wrests the dagger from his opponent's hand, and then stabs him to the heart.

4. Entreat the Lord, therefore, that a composition which has won favour in Greek may not fail to win it also in Latin, and that what the whole East admires and praises Rome may gladly take to her heart. And may the chair of the apostle Peter by its preaching confirm the preaching of the chair of the evangelist Mark. Popular rumour, indeed, has it that the blessed pope Anastasius is of like zeal and spirit with Theophilus and that he has pursued the heretics even to the dens in which they lurk. Moreover his own letters inform us that he condemns in the West what is already condemned in the East. May he live for many years[2] so that the reviving sprouts of heresy may in course of time by his efforts be made to wither and to die.

LETTER XCVIII.

FROM THEOPHILUS.

A translation by Jerome of Theophilus's paschal letter for the year 402 A.D. Like that of the previous year (Letter XCVI.) it deals mainly with the heresies of Apollinarius and Origen.

LETTER XCIX.

TO THEOPHILUS.

Jerome forwards to Theophilus a translation of the latter's paschal letter for 404 A.D. and apologizes for his delay in sending it, on the ground that ill-health and grief for the death of Paula have prevented him from doing literary work. The date of the letter is 404 A.D.

To the most blessed pope Theophilus, Jerome.

1. From the time that I received the letters of your holiness together with the paschal

treatise[1] until the present day I have been so harassed with sorrow and mourning, with anxiety, and with the different reports which have come from all quarters concerning the condition of the church, that I have hardly been able to turn your volume into Latin. You know the truth of the old saying, grief chokes utterance; and it is more than ever true when to sickness of the mind is added sickness of the body. I have now been five days in bed in a burning fever: consequently it is only by using the greatest haste that I can dictate this very letter. But I wish to shew your holiness in a few words what pains I have taken, in translating your treatise, to transfer the charm of diction which marks every sentence in the original, and to make the style of the Latin correspond in some degree with that of the Greek.

2. At the outset you use the language of philosophy; and, without appearing to particularize, you slay one[2] while you instruct all. In the remaining sections—a task most difficult of accomplishment—you combine philosophy and rhetoric and draw together for us Demosthenes and Plato. What diatribes you have launched against self-indulgence! What eulogies you have bestowed upon the virtue of continence! With what secret stores of wisdom you have spoken of the interchange of day and night, the course of the moon, the laws of the sun, the nature of our world; always appealing to the authority of scripture lest in a paschal treatise you should appear to have borrowed anything from secular sources! To be brief, I am afraid to praise you for these things lest I should be charged with offering flattery. The book is excellent both in the philosophical portions and where, without making personal attacks, you plead the cause which you have espoused. Wherefore, I beseech you, pardon me my backwardness: I have been so completely overcome by the falling asleep of the holy and venerable Paula[3] that except my translation of this book I have hitherto written nothing bearing on sacred subjects. As you yourself know, I have suddenly lost the comforter whom I have led about with me, not—the Lord is my witness—to minister to my own needs, but for the relief and refreshment of the saints upon whom she has waited with all diligence. Your holy and estimable daughter Eustochium (who refuses to be comforted for the loss of her mother), and with her all the brotherhood humbly salute you. Kindly send me the books which you say that you have lately written that I may translate them or, if not that, at least read them. Farewell in Christ.

---

[1] Letter XCVI.
[2] He was already dead when these words were written.

[1] Letter C.   [2] Origen.   [3] See Letter CVIII.

LETTER C.

FROM THEOPHILUS.

A translation by Jerome of Theophilus's paschal letter
or 404 A.D. In it Theophilus inculcates penitence for
nners, recommends the practice of fasting and con-
emns the errors of Origen.

LETTER CI.

FROM AUGUSTINE.

A letter from Augustine in which he denies that he
as written a book against Jerome and sent it to Rome
ut confesses that he has criticized him although with-
ut giving details. Written in 402 A.D. This and the
ollowing letters are to be found in the First Volume of
e First Series of this Library. Letter LXVII.

LETTER CII.

TO AUGUSTINE.

Jerome's reply to the foregoing in which, it has been
aid, friendship struggles with suspicion and resentment.
e warns Augustine not to provoke him, lest old as he
he may prove a dangerous opponent; and encloses
art of his reply to the apology of Rufinus. Written in
02 A.D. See Augustine, vol. i., Letter LXVIII.

LETTER CIII.

TO AUGUSTINE.

A letter of introduction in which Jerome commends
e deacon Praesidius to the kind offices of Augustine.
ritten in 403 A.D. See Augustine, vol. i., Letter
XXIX.

LETTER CIV.

FROM AUGUSTINE.

In this letter Augustine (1) commends to Jerome the
eacon Cyprian, (2) explains how it is that his first let-
r (Letter LVI.) has miscarried, and (3) urges Jerome
base his scriptural labours not on the Hebrew text
ut on the version of the LXX. The date of the letter
403 A.D. See Augustine, vol. i., Letter LXXI.

LETTER CV.

TO AUGUSTINE.

Jerome's answer to the foregoing. He complains that
en now he has not received Augustine's letter and
ks him to send him a copy of it. Popular rumour, he
clares, credits Augustine with a deliberate suppression
the letter in order that he may seem to win an easy
ctory over his opponent. Jerome next deals with
ugustine's denial of having made a written attack upon
m and concludes by refusing for the present all dis-
ssion of points of criticism. The date of the letter is
3 A.D. See Augustine, vol. i., Letter LXXII.

LETTER CVI.

TO SUNNIAS AND FRETELA.

A long letter in which Jerome answers a number of
estions put to him by two sojourners in Getica,
nnias and Fretela. Diligent students of scripture,
ese men were at a loss to understand the frequent
fferences between Jerome's Latin psalter of 383 A.D.
he so-called Roman psalter) and the LXX. and ac-
rdingly sent him a long list of passages with a

request for explanation. Jerome in his reply deals
fully with all these and points out to his correspondents that they have been misled by their edition of the LXX. (the "common" edition) which
differs widely from the critical text of Origen as
given in the Hexapla and used by himself. He also
expresses his joy to find that even among the Getæ
the scriptures are now diligently studied. The date of
the letter is about 403 A.D.

LETTER CVII.

TO LAETA.

Laeta, the daughter-in-law of Paula, having written
from Rome to ask Jerome how she ought to bring up
her infant daughter (also called Paula) as a virgin consecrated to Christ, Jerome now instructs her in detail as
to the child's training and education. Feeling some
doubt, however, as to whether the scheme proposed by
him will be practicable at Rome, he advises Laeta in
case of difficulty to send Paula to Bethlehem where she
will be under the care of her grandmother and aunt,
the elder Paula and Eustochium. Laeta subsequently
accepted Jerome's advice and sent the child to Bethlehem where she eventually succeeded Eustochium as
head of the nunnery founded by her grandmother. The
date of the letter is 403 A.D.

1. The apostle Paul writing to the Corinthians and instructing in sacred discipline a
church still untaught in Christ has among
other commandments laid down also this:
"The woman which hath an husband that
believeth not, and if he be pleased to dwell
with her, let her not leave him. For the unbelieving husband is sanctified by the believing wife, and the unbelieving wife is sanctified by the believing husband; else were
your children unclean but now are they
holy." [1] Should any person have supposed
hitherto that the bonds of discipline are too
far relaxed and that too great indulgence is
conceded by the teacher, let him look at the
house of your father, a man of the highest
distinction and learning, but one still walking
in darkness; and he will perceive as the result of the apostle's counsel sweet fruit growing from a bitter stock and precious balsams
exhaled from common canes. You yourself
are the offspring of a mixed marriage; but
the parents of Paula—you and my friend
Toxotius—are both Christians. Who could
have believed that to the heathen pontiff
Albinus should be born — in answer to a
mother's vows—a Christian granddaughter;
that a delighted grandfather should hear from
the little one's faltering lips Christ's Alleluia,
and that in his old age he should nurse in his
bosom one of God's own virgins? Our expectations have been fully gratified. The one
unbeliever is sanctified by his holy and believing family. For, when a man is surrounded
by a believing crowd of children and grand-

---

[1] 1 Cor. vii. 13, 14, the word 'believing' is twice inserted by
Jerome.

children, he is as good as a candidate for the faith. I for my part think that, had he possessed so many Christian kinsfolk when he was a young man, he might then have been brought to believe in Christ. For though he may spit upon my letter and laugh at it, and though he may call me a fool or a madman, his son-in-law did the same before he came to believe. Christians are not born but made. For all its gilding the Capitol is beginning to look dingy. Every temple in Rome is covered with soot and cobwebs. The city is stirred to its depths and the people pour past their half-ruined shrines to visit the tombs of the martyrs. The belief which has not been accorded to conviction may come to be extorted by very shame.

2. I speak thus to you, Laeta my most devout daughter in Christ, to teach you not to despair of your father's salvation. My hope is that the same faith which has gained you your daughter may win your father too, and that so you may be able to rejoice over blessings bestowed upon your entire family. You know the Lord's promise: "The things which are impossible with men are possible with God." [1] It is never too late to mend. The robber passed even from the cross to paradise. [2] Nebuchadnezzar also, the king of Babylon, recovered his reason, even after he had been made like the beasts in body and in heart and had been compelled to live with the brutes in the wilderness. [3] And to pass over such old stories which to unbelievers may well seem incredible, did not your own kinsman Gracchus whose name betokens his patrician origin, when a few years back he held the prefecture of the City, overthrow, break in pieces, and shake to pieces the grotto of Mithras [4] and all the dreadful images therein? Those I mean by which the worshippers were initiated as Raven, Bridegroom, Soldier, Lion, Perseus, Sun, Crab, and Father? Did he not, I repeat, destroy these and then, sending them before him as hostages, obtain for himself Christian baptism?

Even in Rome itself paganism is left in solitude. They who once were the gods of the nations remain under their lonely roofs with horned-owls and birds of night. The standards of the military are emblazoned with the sign of the Cross. The emperor's robes of purple and his diadem sparkling with jewels are ornamented with representations of the shameful yet saving gibbet. Already the Egyptian Serapis has been made a Christian ; [5] while at

Gaza Marnas [1] mourns in confinement an every moment expects to see his temple ove turned. From India, from Persia, from Eth opia we daily welcome monks in crowd The Armenian bowman has laid aside h quiver, the Huns learn the psalter, the chil Scythians are warmed with the glow of th faith. The Getæ, [2] ruddy and yellow-haire carry tent-churches about with their armies and perhaps their success in fighting again us may be due to the fact that they believe the same religion.

3. I have nearly wandered into a new sub ject, and while I have kept my wheel goin, my hands have been moulding a flagon whe it has been my object to frame an ewer For, in answer to your prayers and those the saintly Marcella, I wish to address you a a mother and to instruct you how to bring u our dear Paula, who has been consecrated Christ before her birth and vowed to H service before her conception. Thus in ou own day we have seen repeated the story tol us in the Prophets, [4] of Hannah, who thoug at first barren afterwards became fruitfu You have exchanged a fertility bound up wit sorrow for offspring which shall never di For I am confident that having given to th Lord your first-born you will be the mother o sons. It is the first-born that is offered und the Law. [5] Samuel and Samson are both in stances of this, as is also John the Bapti who when Mary came in leaped for joy For he heard the Lord speaking by the mout of the Virgin and desired to break from h mother's womb to meet Him. As then Pau has been born in answer to a promise, he parents should give her a training suitable t her birth. Samuel, as you know, was nu tured in the Temple, and John was traine in the wilderness. The first as a Nazarit wore his hair long, drank neither wine no strong drink, and even in his childhood talke with God. The second shunned cities, wore leathern girdle, and had for his meat locust and wild honey. [7] Moreover, to typify that pen itence which he was to preach, he was clothe in the spoils of the hump-backed camel. [8]

4. Thus must a soul be educated which is t be a temple of God. It must learn to hea nothing and to say nothing but what belong to the fear of God. It must have no unde

---

[1] Luke xviii. 27.   [2] Cf. Luke xxiii. 42, 43.   [3] Dan. iv. 33-37.
[4] The Persian sun-god, at this time one of the most popular deities of the Roman pantheon. Gracchus appears to have done this as Urban Prætor, A. C. 378.
[5] In the year 389 A.D. the temple of Serapis at Alexandria had been pulled down and a Christian church built upon its site.

[1] Elsewhere (Life of Hilarion § 20) Jerome relâtes an extraor dinary story about the discomfiture of this ' demon.'
[2] A well-known Thracian tribe not to be confounded with t' Goths.
[3] Cf. Hor. A. P., 21, 22. Amphora caepit Institui : curren rota cur urceus exit ?
[4] The books of Joshua, Judges, Samuel, and Kings are call in the Hebrew Bible the Former Prophets.
[5] Ex. xiii. 2.   [6] Luke i. 41.   [7] Matt. iii. 4.
[8] Cf. Letter LXXIX. § 3. Apparently Jerome means that t difficulty of penitence is as great as that of the camel passi through the eye of a needle. John, he implies, by wearing t camel's hair shows that he has surmounted this.

tanding of unclean words, and no knowledge of the world's songs. Its tongue must be steeped while still tender in the sweetness of the psalms. Boys with their wanton thoughts must be kept from Paula : even her maids and female attendants must be separated from worldly associates. For if they have learned some mischief they may teach more. Get for her a set of letters made of boxwood or of ivory and called each by its proper name. Let her play with these, so that even her play may teach her something. And not only make her grasp the right order of the letters and see that she forms their names into a rhyme, but constantly disarrange their order and put the last letters in the middle and the middle ones at the beginning that she may know them all by sight as well as by sound. Moreover, so soon as she begins to use the style upon the wax, and her hand is still faltering, either guide her soft fingers by laying your hand upon hers, or else have simple copies cut upon a tablet ; so that her efforts confined within these limits may keep to the lines traced out for her and not stray outside of these. Offer prizes for good spelling and draw her onwards with little gifts such as children of her age delight in. And let her have companions in her lessons to excite emulation in her, that she may be stimulated when she sees them praised. You must not scold her if she is slow to learn but must employ praise to excite her mind, so that she may be glad when she excels others and sorry when she is excelled by them. Above all you must take care not to make her lessons distasteful to her lest a dislike for them conceived in childhood may continue into her maturer years. The very words which she tries bit by bit to put together and to pronounce ought not to be chance ones, but names specially fixed upon and heaped together for the purpose, those for example of the prophets or the apostles or the list of patriarchs from Adam downwards as it is given by Matthew and Luke. In this way while her tongue will be well-trained, her memory will be likewise developed. Again, you must choose for her a master of approved years, life, and learning. A man of culture will not, I think, blush to do for a kinswoman or a highborn virgin what Aristotle did for Philip's son when, descending to the level of an usher, he consented to teach him his letters.[1] Things must not be despised as of small account in the absence of which great results cannot be achieved. The very rudiments and first beginnings of knowledge sound differently in the mouth of an educated man and of an uneducated. Accordingly you must see that the child is not led away by the silly coaxing of women to form a habit of shortening long words or of decking herself with gold and purple. Of these habits one will spoil her conversation and the other her character. She must not therefore learn as a child what afterwards she will have to unlearn. The eloquence of the Gracchi is said to have been largely due to the way in which from their earliest years their mother spoke to them.[1] Hortensius [2] became an orator while still on his father's lap. Early impressions are hard to eradicate from the mind. When once wool has been dyed purple who can restore it to its previous whiteness ? An unused jar long retains the taste and smell of that with which it is first filled.[3] Grecian history tells us that the imperious Alexander who was lord of the whole world could not rid himself of the tricks of manner and gait which in his childhood he had caught from his governor Leonides.[4] We are always ready to imitate what is evil ; and faults are quickly copied where virtues appear inattainable. Paula's nurse must not be intemperate, or loose, or given to gossip. Her bearer must be respectable, and her foster-father of grave demeanour. When she sees her grandfather, she must leap upon his breast, put her arms round his neck, and, whether he likes it or not, sing Alleluia in his ears. She may be fondled by her grandmother, may smile at her father to shew that she recognizes him, and may so endear herself to everyone, as to make the whole family rejoice in the possession of such a rosebud. She should be told at once whom she has for her other grandmother and whom for her aunt ; and she ought also to learn in what army it is that she is enrolled as a recruit, and what Captain it is under whose banner she is called to serve. Let her long to be with the absent ones and encourage her to make playful threats of leaving you for them.

5. Let her very dress and garb remind her to Whom she is promised. Do not pierce her ears or paint her face consecrated to Christ with white lead or rouge. Do not hang gold or pearls about her neck or load her head with jewels, or by reddening her hair make it suggest the fires of gehenna. Let her pearls be of another kind and such that she may sell them hereafter and buy in their place the pearl that is " of great price." [5] In days gone by a lady of rank, Praetextata by name, at the bidding of her husband Hymettius, the uncle of Eustochium, altered that virgin's dress and appearance and arranged her neglected hair after the manner of the world, desiring to overcome the resolution of the virgin herself and the expressed wishes of her mother. But

---

[1] Quintilian, Inst. I. 1.

[1] Quint. Inst. I. 1.　[2] The contemporary and rival of Cicero.
[3] Horace, Epist. I. ii. 69.　[4] Quint. Inst. I. 1.　[5] Matt. xiii. 46.

lo in the same night it befell her that an angel came to her in her dreams. With terrible looks he menaced punishment and broke silence with these words, ' Have you presumed to put your husband's commands before those of Christ? Have you presumed to lay sacrilegious hands upon the head of one who is God's virgin? Those hands shall forthwith wither that you may know by torment what you have done, and at the end of five months you shall be carried off to hell.[1] And farther, if you persist still in your wickedness, you shall be bereaved both of your husband and of your children.' All of which came to pass in due time, a speedy death marking the penitence too long delayed of the unhappy woman. So terribly does Christ punish those who violate His temple,[2] and so jealously does He defend His precious jewels. I have related this story here not from any desire to exult over the misfortunes of the unhappy, but to warn you that you must with much fear and carefulness keep the vow which you have made to God.

6. We read of Eli the priest that he became displeasing to God on account of the sins of his children;[3] and we are told that a man may not be made a bishop if his sons are loose and disorderly.[4] On the other hand it is written of the woman that " she shall be saved in childbearing, if they continue in faith and charity and holiness with chastity."[5] If then parents are responsible for their children when these are of ripe age and independent; how much more must they be responsible for them when, still unweaned and weak, they cannot, in the Lord's words, " discern between their right hand and their left: "[6]—when, that is to say, they cannot yet distinguish good from evil? If you take precautions to save your daughter from the bite of a viper, why are you not equally careful to shield her from " the hammer of the whole earth "?[7] to prevent her from drinking of the golden cup of Babylon? to keep her from going out with Dinah to see the daughters of a strange land?[8] to save her from the tripping dance and from the trailing robe? No one administers drugs till he has rubbed the rim of the cup with honey;[9] so, the better to deceive us, vice puts on the mien and the semblance of virtue. Why then, you will say, do we read :—" the son shall not bear the iniquity of the father, neither shall the father bear the iniquity of the son," but " the soul that sinneth it shall die "?[10] The passage, I answer, refers to those who have dis-

cretion, such as he of whom his parents said in the gospel :—" he is of age . . . h shall speak for himself."[1] While the son is child and thinks as a child and until he come to years of discretion to choose between th two roads to which the letter of Pythagora points,[2] his parents are responsible for hi actions whether these be good or bad. Bu perhaps you imagine that, if they are not bap tized, the children of Christians are liable fc their own sins ; and that no guilt attaches t parents who withhold from baptism those wh by reason of their tender age can offer n objection to it. The truth is that, as baptisr ensures the salvation of the child, this in tur brings advantage to the parents. Whethe you would offer your child or not lay withi your choice, but now that you have offere her, you neglect her at your peril. I spea generally for in your case you have no discre tion, having offered your child even befor her conception. He who offers a victim tha is lame or maimed or marked with any blemis is held guilty of sacrilege.[3] How much mor then shall she be punished who makes read for the embraces of the king a portion of he own body and the purity of a stainless sou and then proves negligent of this her offer ing?

7. When Paula comes to be a little olde and to increase like her Spouse in wisdom an stature and in favour with God and man,[4] le her go with her parents to the temple of he true Father but let her not come out of th temple with them. Let them seek her upo the world's highway amid the crowds and th throng of their kinsfolk, and let them find he nowhere but in the shrine of the scriptures questioning the prophets and the apostles o the meaning of that spiritual marriage t which she is vowed. Let her imitate the re tirement of Mary whom Gabriel found alon in her chamber and who was frightened,[6] would appear, by seeing a man there. Let th child emulate her of whom it is written tha " the king's daughter is all glorious within." Wounded with love's arrow let her say to he beloved, " the king hath brought me into hi chambers."[8] At no time let her go abroad lest the watchmen find her that go about th city, and lest they smite and wound her an take away from her the veil of her chastity, and leave her naked in her blood.[10] Nay rathe when one knocketh at her door[11] let her say " I am a wall and my breasts like towers."[12]

[1] Inferna. [2] Cf. 1 Cor. iii. 17.
[3] 1 Sam. ii. 27-36. [4] 1 Tim. iii. 4.
[5] 1 Tim. ii. 15 A.V. has 'sobriety' for 'chastity' but Jerome deliberately prefers the latter word.
[6] Jon. iv. 11. [7] Babylon, the world-power. Jer. l. 23.
[8] Gen. xxxiv. [9] Lucretius, I. 936, sqq.
[10] Ezek. xviii. 20.

[1] John ix. 21.
[2] The letter Y used by Pythagoras to symbolize the diverg ing paths of good and evil. Cf. Persius. iii. 56.
[3] Deut. xv. 21. [4] Luke ii. 52.
[5] Cf. Luke ii. 43-46. [6] Luke i. 29.
[7] Ps. xlv. 13. [8] Cant. i. 4. [9] Cant. v. 7.
[10] Cf. Ezek. xvi. 1-10. [11] Cant. v. 2. [12] Cant. viii. 10.

ave washed my feet ; how shall I defile hem ? " [1]

8. Let her not take her food with others, hat is, at her parents' table ; lest she see lishes she may long for. Some, I know, hold t a greater virtue to disdain a pleasure which s actually before them, but I think it a safer elf-restraint to shun what must needs attract ou. Once as a boy at school I met the words : It is ill blaming what you allow to become a abit.' [2] Let her learn even now not to drink vine "wherein is excess." [3] But as, before :hildren come to a robust age, abstinence is langerous and trying to their tender frames, et her have baths if she require them, and let ier take a little wine for her stomach's sake. [4] Let her also be supported on a flesh diet, lest ier feet fail her before they commence to run heir course. But I say this by way of con- :ession not by way of command ; because I ear to weaken her, not because I wish to each her self-indulgence. Besides why should lot a Christian virgin do wholly what others lo in part ? The superstitious Jews reject :ertain animals and products as articles of ood, while among the Indians the Brahmans ind among the Egyptians the Gymnosophists iubsist altogether on porridge, rice, and apples. f mere glass repays so much labour, must not i pearl be worth more labour still ? [5] Paula ias been born in response to a vow. Let her ife be as the lives of those who were born inder the same conditions. If the grace ac- :orded is in both cases the same, the pains)estowed ought to be so too. Let her be deaf o the sound of the organ, and not know even he uses of the pipe, the lyre, and the cithern.

9. And let it be her task daily to bring to ou the flowers which she has culled from icripture. Let her learn by heart so many verses in the Greek, but let her be instructed n the Latin also. For, if the tender lips are lot from the first shaped to this, the tongue is ipoiled by a foreign accent and its native ipeech debased by alien elements. You must ourself be her mistress, a model on which she nay form her childish conduct. Never either n you nor in her father let her see what she :annot imitate without sin. Remember both if you that you are the parents of a conse- rated virgin, and that your example will teach ier more than your precepts. Flowers are juick to fade and a baleful wind soon withers he violet, the lily, and the crocus. Let her lever appear in public unless accompanied by ou. Let her never visit a church or a martyr's hrine unless with her mother. Let no young nan greet her with smiles ; no dandy with curled hair pay compliments to her. If our little virgin goes to keep solemn eves and all- night vigils, let her not stir a hair's breadth from her mother's side. She must not single out one of her maids to make her a special fa- vourite or a confidante. What she says to one all ought to know. Let her choose for a com- panion not a handsome well-dressed girl, able to warble a song with liquid notes but one pale and serious, sombrely attired and with the hue of melancholy. Let her take as her model some aged virgin of approved faith, character, and chastity, apt to instruct her by word and by example. She ought to rise at night to recite prayers and psalms ; to sing hymns in the morning ; at the third, sixth, and ninth hours to take her place in the line to do battle for Christ ; and, lastly, to kindle her lamp and to offer her evening sacrifice. [1] In these occupa- tions let her pass the day, and when night comes let it find her still engaged in them. Let read- ing follow prayer with her, and prayer again succeed to reading. Time will seem short when employed on tasks so many and so varied.

10. Let her learn too how to spin wool, to hold the distaff, to put the basket in her lap, to turn the spinning wheel and to shape the yarn with her thumb. Let her put away with disdain silken fabrics, Chinese fleeces, [2] and gold brocades : the clothing which she makes for herself should keep out the cold and not expose the body which it professes to cover. Let her food be herbs and wheaten bread [3] with now and then one or two small fishes. And that I may not waste more time in giving precepts for the regulation of appetite (a sub- ject I have treated more at length elsewhere) [4] let her meals always leave her hungry and able on the moment to begin reading or chanting. I strongly disapprove—especially for those of tender years—of long and immoderate fasts in which week is added to week and even oil and apples are forbidden as food. I have learned by experience that the ass toiling along the high way makes for an inn when it is weary. [5] Our abstinence may turn to glutting, like that of the worshippers of Isis and of Cy- bele who gobble up pheasants and turtle-doves piping hot that their teeth may not violate the gifts of Ceres. [6] If perpetual fasting is allowed, it must be so regulated that those who have a long journey before them may hold out all through ; and we must take care that we do not, after starting well, fall halfway. However in Lent, as I have written before now, those who

---

[1] Cant. v. 3.   [2] Again quoted in Letter CXXVIII. § 4.
[3] Eph. v. 18.   [4] 1 Tim. v. 23.
[5] Cp. Letter LXXIX, § 7. The heathen sage is glass, the ?hristian virgin the pearl.

[1] See note on Letter XXII. § 37.
[2] A Virgilian expression, 9, II., 121.
[3] *Simila*, but as elsewhere (L. 52, 6) this is spoken of as a lux- ury, perhaps we should read *similia* = ' and such like.'
[4] Jerome refers to his second book against Jovinian.
[5] Cf. the dying words of S. Francis (which have a similar reference) ' I have sinned against my brother the ass.'
[6] *i.e.* having vowed to abstain from bread, they indemnify themselves with flesh.

practise self-denial should spread every stitch of canvas, and the charioteer should for once slacken the reins and increase the speed of his horses. Yet there will be one rule for those who live in the world and another for virgins and monks. The layman in Lent consumes the coats of his stomach, and living like a snail on his own juices makes ready a paunch for rich foods and feasting to come. But with the virgin and the monk the case is different ; for, when these give the rein to their steeds, they have to remember that for them the race knows of no intermission. An effort made only for a limited time may well be severe, but one that has no such limit must be more moderate. For whereas in the first case we can recover our breath when the race is over, in the last we have to go on continually and without stopping.

11. When you go a short way into the country, do not leave your daughter behind you. Leave her no power or capacity of living without you, and let her feel frightened when she is left to herself. Let her not converse with people of the world or associate with virgins indifferent to their vows. Let her not be present at the weddings of your slaves and let her take no part in the noisy games of the household. As 'regards the use of the bath, I know that some are content with saying that a Christian virgin should not bathe along with eunuchs or with married women, with the former because they are still men at all events in mind, and with the latter because women with child offer a revolting spectacle. For myself, however, I wholly disapprove of baths for a virgin of full age. Such an one should blush and feel overcome at the idea of seeing herself undressed. By vigils and fasts she mortifies her body and brings it into subjection. By a cold chastity she seeks to put out the flame of lust and to quench the hot desires of youth. And by a deliberate squalor she makes haste to spoil her natural good looks. Why, then, should she add fuel to a sleeping fire by taking baths ?

12. Let her treasures be not silks or gems but manuscripts of the holy scriptures ; and in these let her think less of gilding, and Babylonian parchment, and arabesque patterns,[1] than of correctness and accurate punctuation. Let her begin by learning the psalter, and then let her gather rules of life out of the proverbs of Solomon. From the Preacher let her gain the habit of despising the world and its vanities.[2] Let her follow the example set in Job of virtue and of patience. Then let her pass on to the gospels never to be laid aside when once they have been taken in hand. Let her also drink in with a willing heart the Acts of the Apostles and the Epistles. As soon as she has enriched the storehouse of her mind with these treasures let her commit to memory the prophets, the heptateuch,[1] the books of Kings and of Chronicles, the rolls also of Ezra and Esther. When she has done all these she may safely read the Song of Songs but not before : for, were she to read it at the beginning, she would fail to perceive that, though it is written in fleshly words, it is a marriage song of a spiritual bridal. And not understanding this she would suffer hurt from it. Let her avoid all apocryphal writings, and if she is led to read such not by the truth of the doctrines which they contain but out of respect for the miracles contained in them ; let her understand that they are not really written by those to whom they are ascribed, that many faulty elements have been introduced into them, and that it requires infinite discretion to look for gold in the midst of dirt. Cyprian's writings let her have always in her hands. The letters of Athanasius[2] and the treatises of Hilary[3] she may go through without fear of stumbling. Let her take pleasure in the works and wits of all in whose books a due regard for the faith is not neglected. But if she reads the works of others let it be rather to judge them than to follow them.

13. You will answer, 'How shall I, a woman of the world, living at Rome, surrounded by a crowd, be able to observe all these injunctions ?' In that case do not undertake a burthen to which you are not equal. When you have weaned Paula as Isaac was weaned and when you have clothed her as Samuel was clothed, send her to her grandmother and aunt ; give up this most precious of gems, to be placed in Mary's chamber and to rest in the cradle where the infant Jesus cried. Let her be brought up in a monastery, let her be one amid companies of virgins, let her learn to avoid swearing, let her regard lying as sacrilege, let her be ignorant of the world, let her live the angelic life, while in the flesh let her be without the flesh, and let her suppose that all human beings are like herself. To say nothing of its other advantages this course will free you from the difficult task of minding her, and from the responsibility of guardianship. It is better to regret her absence than to be for ever trembling for her. For you cannot but tremble as you watch what she

---

[1] Vermiculata pictura.
[2] Jerome tells us that he read the book with Blaesilla for this purpose.

[1] i.e. Genesis, Exodus, Leviticus, Numbers, Deuteronomy, Joshua, Judges.
[2] Of these a large number are still extant. Over twenty of them are " festal epistles " announcing to the churches the correct day on which to celebrate Easter.
[3] These include commentaries on many parts of Scripture and a work on the Trinity.

ays and to whom she says it, to whom she bows and whom she likes best to see. Hand her over to Eustochium while she is still but an infant and her every cry is a prayer for you. She will thus become her companion in holiness now as well as her successor hereafter. Let her gaze upon and love, let her "from her earliest years admire"[1] one whose language and gait and dress are an education in virtue.[2] Let her sit in the lap of her grandmother, and let this latter repeat to her granddaughter the lessons that she once bestowed upon her own child. Long experience as shewn Paula how to rear, to preserve, and to instruct virgins ; and daily inwoven in her gown is the mystic century which betokens the highest chastity.[3] O happy virgin ! happy Paula, daughter of Toxotius, who through the virtues of her grandmother and aunt is nobler in holiness than she is in lineage ! Yes, Laeta : were it possible for you with your own eyes to see your mother-in-law and your sister, and to realize the mighty souls which animate their small bodies ; such is your innate thirst for chastity that I cannot doubt but that you would go to them even before your daughter, and would emancipate yourself from God's first decree of the Law[4] to put yourself under His second dispensation of the Gospel.[5] You would count as nothing your desire for other offspring and would offer up yourself to the service of God. But because "there is a time to embrace, and a time to refrain from embracing,"[6] and because "the wife hath not power of her own body,"[7] and because the apostle says "Let every man abide in the same calling wherein he was called"[8] in the Lord, and because he that is under the yoke ought to to run as not to leave his companion in the mire, I counsel you to pay back to the full in your offspring what meantime you defer paying in your own person. When Hannah had once offered in the tabernacle the son whom she had vowed to God she never took him back ; for she thought it unbecoming that one who was to be a prophet should grow up in the same house with her who still desired to have other children. Accordingly after she had conceived him and given him birth, she did not venture to come to the temple alone or to appear before the Lord empty, but first paid to Him what she owed ; and then, when she had offered up that great sacrifice, she returned home and because she had borne her firstborn for God, she was given five children for herself.[9] Do you marvel at the happiness of that holy woman ? Imitate her faith. More-

over, if you will only send Paula, I promise to be myself both a tutor and a fosterfather to her. Old as I am I will carry her on my shoulders and train her stammering lips ; and my charge will be a far grander one than that of the worldly philosopher ;[1] for while he only taught a King of Macedon who was one day to die of Babylonian poison, I shall instruct the handmaid and spouse of Christ who must one day be offered to her Lord in heaven.

LETTER CVIII.

TO EUSTOCHIUM.

This, one of the longest of Jerome's letters, was written to console Eustochium for the loss of her mother who had recently died. Jerome relates the story of Paula in detail ; speaking first of her high birth, marriage, and social success at Rome, and then narrating her conversion and subsequent life as a Christian ascetic. Much space is devoted to an account of her journey to the East which included a visit to Egypt and to the monasteries of Nitria as well as a tour of the most sacred spots in the Holy Land. The remainder of the letter describes her daily routine and studies at Bethlehem, and recounts the many virtues for which she was distinguished. It then concludes with a touching description of her death and burial and gives the epitaph placed upon her grave. The date of the letter is 404 A.D.

1. If all the members of my body were to be converted into tongues, and if each of my limbs were to be gifted with a human voice, I could still do no justice to the virtues of the holy and venerable Paula. Noble in family, she was nobler still in holiness ; rich formerly in this world's goods, she is now more distinguished by the poverty that she has embraced for Christ. Of the stock of the Gracchi and descended from the Scipios, the heir and representative of that Paulus whose name she bore, the true and legitimate daughter of that Martia Papyria who was mother to Africanus, she yet preferred Bethlehem to Rome, and left her palace glittering with gold to dwell in a mud cabin. We do not grieve that we have lost this perfect woman ; rather we thank God that we have had her, nay that we have her still. For "all live unto" God,[2] and they who return unto the Lord are still to be reckoned members of his family. We have lost her, it is true, but the heavenly mansions have gained her ; for as long as she was in the body she was absent from the Lord[3] and would constantly complain with tears :—"Woe is me that I sojourn in Mesech, that I dwell in the tents of Kedar ; my soul hath been this long time a pilgrim."[4] It was no wonder that she

---

[1] Virgil, A. viii. 507.   [2] Comp. Ecclus. xix. 30.
[3] The number 100 denotes virginity to which in her own person Paula could have no claim. See note on Letter XLVIII. § 2.
[4] Gen. i. 28.   [5] 1 Cor. vii. 1.   [6] Eccl. iii. 5.
[7] 1 Cor. vii. 4.   [8] 1 Cor. vii. 20.   [9] 1 Sam. ii. 21.

---

[1] The allusion is to Aristotle who was tutor to Alexander, King of Macedon.
[2] Luke xx. 38.   [3] 2 Cor. v. 6.
[4] Ps. cxx. 5, 6 acc. to Jerome's latest version.

sobbed out that even she was in darkness (for this is the meaning of the word Kedar) seeing that, according to the apostle, "the world lieth in the evil one ; " [1] and that, "as its darkness is, so is its light ; " [2] and that "the light shineth in darkness and the darkness comprehended it not." [3] She would frequently exclaim : "I am a stranger with thee and a sojourner with all my fathers were," [4] and again, I desire "to depart and to be with Christ." [5] As often too as she was troubled with bodily weakness (brought on by incredible abstinence and by redoubled fastings), she would be heard to say : "I keep under my body and bring it into subjection ; lest that by any means, when I have preached to others, I myself should be a castaway ; " [6] and "It is good neither to eat flesh nor to drink wine ; " [7] and "I humbled my soul with fasting ; " [8] and "thou wilt make all" my "bed in" my "sickness ; " [9] and "Thy hand was heavy upon me : my moisture is turned into the drought of summer." [10] And when the pain which she bore with such wonderful patience darted through her, as if she saw the heavens opened [11] she would say : "Oh that I had wings like a dove ! for then would I fly away and be at rest." [12]

2. I call Jesus and his saints, yes and the particular angel who was the guardian and the companion of this admirable woman to bear witness that these are no words of adulation and flattery but sworn testimony every one of them borne to her character. They are, indeed, inadequate to the virtues of one whose praises are sung by the whole world, who is admired by bishops, [13] regretted by bands of virgins, and wept for by crowds of monks and poor. Would you know all her virtues, reader, in short ? She has left those dependent on her poor, but not so poor as she was herself. In dealing thus with her relatives and the men and women of her small household—her brothers and sisters rather than her servants—she has done nothing strange ; for she has left her daughter Eustochium—a virgin consecrated to Christ for whose comfort this sketch is made—far from her noble family and rich only in faith and grace.

3. Let me then begin my narrative. Others may go back a long way even to Paula's cradle and, if I may say so, to her swaddling-clothes, and may speak of her mother Blaesilla and her father Rogatus. Of these the former was a descendant of the Scipios and the Gracchi ; whilst the latter came of a line distinguished in Greece down to the present day. He was said, indeed, to have in his

veins the blood of Agamemnon who destroye[d] Troy after a ten years' siege. But I sha[ll] praise only what belongs to herself, wha[t] wells forth from the pure spring of her hol[y] mind. When in the gospel the apostles as[k] their Lord and Saviour what He will give t[o] those who have left all for His sake, He tell[s] them that they shall receive an hundredfol[d] now in this time and in the world to com[e] eternal life. [1] From which we see that it is n[ot] the possession of riches that is praiseworth[y] but the rejection of them for Christ's sake[;] that, instead of glorying in our privileges, w[e] should make them of small account as com[-] pared with God's faith. Truly the Saviou[r] has now in this present time made good H[is] promise to His servants and handmaiden[s.] For one who despised the glory of a singl[e] city is to-day famous throughout the world[;] and one who while she lived at Rome wa[s] known by no one outside it has by hiding her[-] self at Bethlehem become the admiration [of] all lands Roman and barbarian. For wha[t] race of men is there which does not send pi[l-] grims to the holy places ? And who coul[d] there find a greater marvel than Paula ? A[s] among many jewels the most precious shine[s] most brightly, and as the sun with its beam[s] obscures and puts out the paler fires of th[e] stars ; so by her lowliness she surpassed a[ll] others in virtue and influence and, while sh[e] was least among all, was greater than al[l.] The more she cast herself down, the more sh[e] was lifted up by Christ. She was hidden an[d] yet she was not hidden. By shunning glor[y] she earned glory ; for glory follows virtue a[s] its shadow ; and deserting those who seek i[t] it seeks those who despise it. But I must n[ot] neglect to proceed with my narrative or dwe[ll] too long on a single point forgetful of th[e] rules of writing.

4. Being then of such parentage, Paula mar[-] ried Toxotius in whose veins ran the nobl[e] blood of Æneas and the Julii. Accordingl[y] his daughter, Christ's virgin Eustochium, [is] called Julia, as he Julius.

A name from great Iulus handed down. [2]

I speak of these things not as of importanc[e] to those who have them, but as worthy o[f] remark in those who despise them. Men o[f] the world look up to persons who are rich i[n] such privileges. We on the other hand prais[e] those who for the Saviour's sake despis[e] them ; and strangely depreciating all wh[o] keep them, we eulogize those who are unwill[-] ing to do so. Thus nobly born, Paula throug[h] her fruitfulness and her chastity won approv[al] from all, from her husband first, then fro[m]

[1] 1 Joh. v. 19. [2] Ps. cxxxix. 12, A.V. marg.
[3] Joh. i. 5. [4] Ps. xxxix. 12. [5] Phil. i. 23.
[6] 1 Cor. ix. 27. [7] Rom. xiv. 21. [8] Ps. xxxv. 13.
[9] Ps. xli. 3. [10] Ps. xxxii. 4. [11] Cf. Acts vii. 56.
[12] Ps. lv. 6. [13] Sacerdotes.

[1] Mark x. 28–30. [2] Virg. A. i. 292.

er relatives, and lastly from the whole city.
he bore five children; Blaesilla, for whose
eath I consoled her while at Rome;[1] Pau-
na, who has left the reverend and admirable
ammachius to inherit both her vows[2] and
roperty, to whom also I addressed a little
ook on her death; Eustochium, who is now
1 the holy places, a precious necklace of
irginity and of the church; Rufina, whose
ntimely end overcame the affectionate heart
f her mother; and Toxotius, after whom she
ad no more children. You can thus see that
was not her wish to fulfil a wife's duty, but
hat she only complied with her husband's
onging to have male offspring.

5. When he died, her grief was so great
hat she nearly died herself: yet so com-
letely did she then give herself to the service
f the Lord, that it might have seemed that
he had desired his death.

In what terms shall I speak of her dis-
nguished, and noble, and formerly wealthy
ouse; all the riches of which she spent upon
he poor? How can I describe the great con-
ideration she shewed to all and her far reach-
ng kindness even to those whom she had
ever seen? What poor man, as he lay dying,
vas not wrapped in blankets given by her?
Vhat bedridden person was not supported
vith money from her purse? She would seek
out such with the greatest diligence throughout the city, and would think it a misfortune
vere any hungry or sick person to be supported
by another's food. So lavish was her charity
hat she robbed her children; and, when her relatives remonstrated with her for doing so, she
leclared that she was leaving to them a better
nheritance in the mercy of Christ.

6. Nor was she long able to endure the
visits and crowded receptions, which her high
position in the world and her exalted family
entailed upon her. She received the homage
paid to her sadly, and made all the speed she
could to shun and to escape those who wished
to pay her compliments. It so happened that
at that time[3] the bishops of the East and
West had been summoned to Rome by letter
from the emperors[4] to deal with certain dis-
sensions between the churches, and in this way
she saw two most admirable men and Christian
prelates, Paulinus bishop of Antioch and Epiphanius, bishop of Salamis or, as it is now
called, Constantia, in Cyprus. Epiphanius,
indeed, she received as her guest; and, although Paulinus was staying in another person's house, in the warmth of her heart she
treated him as if he too were lodged with her.
Inflamed by their virtues she thought more
and more each moment of forsaking her

home. Disregarding her house, her children,
her servants, her property, and in a word
everything connected with the world, she was
eager—alone and unaccompanied (if ever it
could be said that she was so)—to go to the
desert made famous by its Pauls and by its
Antonies. And at last when the winter was
over and the sea was open, and when the
bishops were returning to their churches, she
also sailed with them in her prayers and desires. Not to prolong the story, she went
down to Portus accompanied by her brother,
her kinsfolk and above all her own children
eager by their demonstrations of affection to
overcome their loving mother. At last the
sails were set and the strokes of the rowers
carried the vessel into the deep. On the shore
the little Toxotius stretched forth his hands
in entreaty, while Rufina, now grown up, with
silent sobs besought her mother to wait till
she should be married. But still Paula's eyes
were dry as she turned them heavenwards;
and she overcame her love for her children by
her love for God. She knew herself no more
as a mother, that she might approve herself a
handmaid of Christ. Yet her heart was rent
within her, and she wrestled with her grief,
as though she were being forcibly separated
from parts of herself. The greatness of the
affection she had to overcome made all admire
her victory the more. Among the cruel hardships which attend prisoners of war in the
hands of their enemies, there is none severer
than the separation of parents from their
children. Though it is against the laws of
nature, she endured this trial with unabated
faith; nay more she sought it with a joyful
heart: and overcoming her love for her children by her greater love for God, she concentrated herself quietly upon Eustochium alone,
the partner alike of her vows and of her
voyage. Meantime the vessel ploughed onwards and all her fellow-passengers looked
back to the shore. But she turned away her
eyes that she might not see what she could not
behold without agony. No mother, it must be
confessed, ever loved her children so dearly.
Before setting out she gave them all that she
had, disinheriting herself upon earth that she
might find an inheritance in heaven.

7. The vessel touched at the island of
Pontia ennobled long since as the place of
exile of the illustrious lady Flavia Domitilla
who under the Emperor Domitian was banished because she confessed herself a Christian;[1] and Paula, when she saw the cells in
which this lady passed the period of her long
martyrdom, taking to herself the wings of
faith, more than ever desired to see Jerusalem

---

and the holy places. The strongest winds seemed weak and the greatest speed slow. After passing between Scylla and Charybdis [1] she committed herself to the Adriatic sea and had a calm passage to Methone.[2] Stopping here for a short time to recruit her wearied frame

> She stretched her dripping limbs upon the shore :
> Then sailed past Malea and Cythera's isle,
> The scattered Cyclades, and all the lands
> That narrow in the seas on every side.[3]

Then leaving Rhodes and Lycia behind her, she at last came in sight of Cyprus, where falling at the feet of the holy and venerable Epiphanius, she was by him detained ten days ; though this was not, as he supposed, to restore her strength but, as the facts prove, that she might do God's work. For she visited all the monasteries in the island, and left, so far as her means allowed, substantial relief for the brothers in them whom love of the holy man had brought thither from all parts of the world. Then crossing the narrow sea she landed at Seleucia, and going up thence to Antioch allowed herself to be detained for a little time by the affection of the reverend confessor Paulinus.[4] Then, such was the ardour of her faith that she, a noble lady who had always previously been carried by eunuchs, went her way—and that in midwinter—riding upon an ass.

8. I say nothing of her journey through Cœle-Syria and Phœnicia (for it is not my purpose to give you a complete itinerary of her wanderings) ; I shall only name such places as are mentioned in the sacred books. After leaving the Roman colony of Berytus and the ancient city of Zidon she entered Elijah's town on the shore at Zarephath and therein adored her Lord and Saviour. Next passing over the sands of Tyre on which Paul had once knelt [5] she came to Acco or, as it is now called, Ptolemais, rode over the plains of Megiddo which had once witnessed the slaying of Josiah,[6] and entered the land of the Philistines. Here she could not fail to admire the ruins of Dor, once a most powerful city ; and Strato's Tower, which though at one time insignificant was rebuilt by Herod king of Judæa and named Cæsarea in honour of Cæsar Augustus.[7] Here she saw the house of Cornelius now turned into a Christian church ; and the humble abode of Philip ; and the chambers of his daughters the

four virgins "which did prophesy." [1] She arrived next at Antipatris, a small town half in ruins, named by Herod after his father Antipater, and at Lydda, now become Diospolis, a place made famous by the raising again of Dorcas [2] and the restoration to health of Æneas.[3] Not far from this are Arimathæa the village of Joseph who buried the Lord, and Nob, once a city of priests but now the tomb in which their slain bodies rest.[5] Joppa too is hard by, the port of Jonah's flight ; which also—if I may introduce a poetic fable—saw Andromeda bound to the rock. Again resuming her journey, she came to Nicopolis, once called Emmaus, where the Lord became known in the breaking of bread ; [8] an action by which He dedicated the house of Cleopas as a church. Starting thence she made her way up lower and higher Bethhoron, cities founded by Solomon [9] but subsequently destroyed by several devastating wars ; seeing on her right Ajalon and Gibeon where Joshua the son of Nun when fighting against the five kings gave commandments to the sun and moon,[10] where also he condemned the Gibeonites (who by a crafty stratagem had obtained a treaty) to be hewers of wood and drawers of water.[11] At Gibeah also, now a complete ruin, she stopped for a little while remembering its sin, and the cutting of the concubine into pieces, and how in spite of all this three hundred men of the tribe of Benjamin were saved [12] that in after days Paul might be called a Benjamite.

9. To make a long story short, leaving on her left the mausoleum of Helena queen of Adiabene [13] who in time of famine had sent corn to the Jewish people, Paula entered Jerusalem, Jebus, or Salem, that city of three names which after it had sunk to ashes and decay was by Ælius Hadrianus restored once more as Ælia.[14] And although the proconsul of Palestine, who was an intimate friend of her house, sent forward his apparitors and gave orders to have his official residence placed at her disposal, she chose a humble cell in preference to it. Moreover, in visiting the holy places so great was the passion and the enthusiasm she exhibited for each, that she could never have torn herself away from one had she not been eager to visit the rest. Before the Cross she threw herself down in

---

[1] *i.e.* the straits of Messina.
[2] A port on the S.W. coast of the Peloponnese.
[3] Virg. A. iii. 126-8.
[4] At this time one of the three bishops who claimed the see of Antioch. See Ep. xv. 2.
[5] Acts xxi. 5.   [6] 2 K. xxiii. 29.
[7] A maritime city of Palestine which subsequently to its restoration by Herod became first the civil, and then the ecclesiastical, capital of Palestine.

[1] Acts xxi. 8,9.   [2] Acts ix. 36-41.   [3] Acts ix. 32-34.
[4] John xix. 38.   [5] 1 Sam. xxii. 17-19.   [6] Jon. i. 3.
[7] Andromeda had been chained to a rock by her father to assuage the wrath of Poseidon who had sent a sea monster to ravage the country. Here she was found by Perseus who slew the monster and effected her rescue. See Josephus B. J. iii. ix. 3.
[8] Luke xxiv. 13, 28-31.   [9] 2 Chr. viii. 5.
[10] Josh. x. 12-14.   [11] Josh. ix.
[12] Judges xix. xx. According to xx. 47 the number of Benjamites who escaped was *six* hundred.
[13] Josephus, A.J. xx. ii. 6.
[14] Or more fully Ælia Capitolina, a Roman colony from which all Jews were expelled.
[15] Prætorium. The word occurs in John xviii. 28.

adoration as though she beheld the Lord hanging upon it : and when she entered the tomb which was the scene of the Resurrection she kissed the stone which the angel had rolled away from the door of the sepulchre.[1] Indeed so ardent was her faith that she even licked with her mouth the very spot on which the Lord's body had lain, like one athirst for the river which he has longed for. What tears she shed there, what groans she uttered, and what grief she poured forth, all Jerusalem knows ; the Lord also to whom she prayed knows. Going out thence she made the ascent of Zion ; a name which signifies either " citadel " or " watch-tower." This formed the city which David formerly stormed and afterwards rebuilt.[2] Of its storming it is written, " Woe to Ariel, to Ariel "—that is, God's lion, (and indeed in those days it was extremely strong)—" the city which David stormed : "[3] and of its rebuilding it is said, " His foundation is in the holy mountains : the Lord loveth the gates of Zion more than all the dwellings of Jacob."[4] He does not mean the gates which we see to-day in dust and ashes ; the gates he means are those against which hell prevails not[5] and through which the multitude of those who believe in Christ enter in.[6] There was shewn to her upholding the portico of a church the blood-stained column to which our Lord is said to have been bound when He suffered His scourging. There was shewn to her also the spot where the Holy Spirit came down upon the souls of the one hundred and twenty believers, thus fulfilling the prophecy of Joel.[7]

10. Then, after distributing money to the poor and her fellow-servants so far as her means allowed, she proceeded to Bethlehem stopping only on the right side of the road to visit Rachel's tomb. (Here it was that she gave birth to her son destined to be not what his dying mother called him, Benoni, that is the " Son of my pangs " but as his father in the spirit prophetically named him Benjamin, that is " the Son of the right hand)."[8] After this she came to Bethlehem and entered into the cave where the Saviour was born.[9] Here, when she looked upon the inn made sacred by the virgin and the stall where the ox knew his owner and the ass his master's crib,[10] and where the words of the same prophet had been fulfilled " Blessed is he that soweth beside the waters where the ox and the ass trample the seed under their feet : "[11] when she looked upon these things I say, she protested in my hearing that she could behold

with the eyes of faith the infant Lord wrapped in swaddling clothes and crying in the manger, the wise men worshipping Him, the star shining overhead, the virgin mother, the attentive foster-father, the shepherds coming by night to see " the word that was come to pass " [1] and thus even then to consecrate those opening phrases of the evangelist John " In the beginning was the word " and " the word was made flesh." [2] She declared that she could see the slaughtered innocents, the raging Herod, Joseph and Mary fleeing into Egypt ; and with a mixture of tears and joy she cried : ' Hail Bethlehem, house of bread,[3] wherein was born that Bread that came down from heaven.[4] Hail Ephratah, land of fruitfulness[3] and of fertility, whose fruit is the Lord Himself. Concerning thee has Micah prophesied of old, " Thou Bethlehem Ephratah art not[5] the least among the thousands of Judah, for out of thee shall he come forth unto me that is to be ruler in Israel ; whose goings forth have been from of old, from everlasting. Therefore wilt thou[6] give them up, until the time that she which travaileth hath brought forth : then the remnant of his brethren shall return unto the children of Israel." [7] For in thee was born the prince begotten before Lucifer.[8] Whose birth from the Father is before all time : and the cradle of David's race continued in thee, until the virgin brought forth her son and the remnant of the people that believed in Christ returned unto the children of Israel and preached freely to them in words like these : " It was necessary that the word of God should first have been spoken to you ; but seeing ye put it from you and judge yourselves unworthy of everlasting life, lo, we turn to the Gentiles." [9] For the Lord hath said : " I am not sent but unto the lost sheep of the house of Israel." [10] At that time also the words of Jacob were fulfilled concerning Him, " A prince shall not depart from Judah nor a lawgiver from between his feet, until He come for whom it is laid up,[11] and He shall be for the expectation of the nations." [12] Well did David swear, well did he make a vow saying : " Surely I will not come into the tabernacle of my house nor go up into my bed : I will not give sleep to mine eyes, or slumber to my eyelids, or rest to the temples of my head,[13] until I find out a place for the Lord, an habitation for the . . God of Jacob." [14] And immediately he

---

1 Matt. xxviii. 2.   2 2 Sam. v. 7, 9.   3 Isa. xxix. 1. Vulg.
4 Ps. lxxxvii. 1, 2.   5 Matt. xvi. 18.   6 Rev. xxii. 14.
7 Acts ii. 16-21.   8 Gen. xxxv. 18, 19.
9 This legend of the cave dates back to Justin Martyr.
10 Isa. i. 3.   11 Isa. xxxii. 20, LXX.

1 Luke ii. 15, ῥῆμα.
2 Joh. i. 1, 14 λόγος the Vulg. has 'verbum' both here and in Luke.
3 The name means this in Hebrew.   4 Joh. vi. 51.
5 The word 'not' is inserted by Paula from Matt. ii. 6.
6 ' Will he ' A.V. following the Hebrew.
7 Mic. v. 2, 3 : Cf. Matt. ii. 6.   8 Ps. cx. 3, Vulg.
9 Acts xiii. 46.   10 Matt. xv. 24.
11 LXX. acc. to one reading.   12 Gen. xlix. 10, LXX.
13 This clause comes from the LXX.   14 Ps. cxxxii. 2-5.

explained the object of his desire, seeing with prophetic eyes that He would come whom we now believe to have come. " Lo we heard of Him at Ephratah : we found Him in the fields of the wood." [1] The Hebrew word *Zo* as I have learned from your lessons [2] means not *her*, that is Mary the Lord's mother, but *him* that is the Lord Himself. Therefore he says boldly : " We will go into His tabernacle : we will worship at His footstool." [3] I too, miserable sinner though I am, have been accounted worthy to kiss the manger in which the Lord cried as a babe, and to pray in the cave in which the travailing virgin gave birth to the infant Lord. " This is my rest " for it is my Lord's native place ; " here will I dwell " [4] for this spot has my Saviour chosen. " I have prepared a lamp for my Christ " [5] " My soul shall live unto Him and my seed shall serve Him." [6]

After this Paula went a short distance down the hill to the tower of Edar, [7] that is 'of the flock,' near which Jacob fed his flocks, and where the shepherds keeping watch by night were privileged to hear the words : " Glory to God in the highest and on earth peace, good-will toward men." [8] While they were keeping their sheep they found the Lamb of God ; whose fleece bright and clean was made wet with the dew of heaven when it was dry upon all the earth beside, [9] and whose blood when sprinkled on the doorposts drove off the destroyer of Egypt [10] and took away the sins of the world. [11]

11. Then immediately quickening her pace she began to move along the old road which leads to Gaza, that is to the 'power' or 'wealth' of God, silently meditating on that type of the Gentiles, the Ethiopian eunuch, who in spite of the prophet changed his skin [12] and whilst he read the old testament found the fountain of the gospel. [13] Next turning to the right she passed from Beth-zur [14] to Eshcol which means " a cluster of grapes." It was hence that the spies brought back that marvellous cluster which was the proof of the fertility of the land [15] and a type of Him who says of Himself : " I have trodden the wine press alone ; and of the people there was none with me." [16] Shortly afterwards she entered the home [17] of Sarah and beheld the birthplace of Isaac and the traces of Abraham's oak under which he saw Christ's day and was glad. [18] And rising up from thence she went up to Hebron, that is Kirjath-Arba, or the City of the Four Men. These are Abraham, Isaac, Jacob, and the great Adam whom the Hebrews suppose (from the book of Joshua the son of Nun) to be buried there. [1] But many are of opinion that Caleb is the fourth and a monument at one side is pointed out as his. After seeing these places she did not care to go on to Kirjath-sepher, that is " the village of letters ; " because despising the letter that killeth she had found the spirit that giveth life. [2] She admired more the upper springs and the nether springs which Othniel the son of Kenaz the son of Jephunneh received in place of a south land and a waterless possession, [3] and by the conducting of which he watered the dry fields of the old covenant. For thus did he typify the redemption which the sinner finds for his old sins in the waters of baptism. On the next day soon after sunrise she stood upon the brow of Caphar-barucha, [4] that is, "the house of blessing," the point to which Abraham pursued the Lord when he made intercession with Him. [5] And here, as she looked down upon the wide solitude and upon the country once belonging to Sodom and Gomorrah, to Admah and Zeboim, she beheld the balsam vines of Engedi and Zoar. By Zoar I mean that " heifer of three years old " [6] which was formerly called Bela [7] and in Syriac is rendered Zoar that is ' little.' She called to mind the cave in which Lot found refuge, and with tears in her eyes warned the virgins her companions to beware of " wine wherein is excess ; " [8] for it was to this that the Moabites and Ammonites owe their origin. [9]

12. I linger long in the land of the midday sun for it was there and then that the spouse found her bridegroom at rest [10] and Joseph drank wine with his brothers once more. [11] I will return to Jerusalem and, passing through Tekoa the home of Amos, [12] I will look upon the glistening cross of Mount Olivet from which the Saviour made His ascension to the Father. [13] Here year by year a red heifer was burned as a holocaust to the Lord and its ashes were used to purify the children of Israel. [14] Here also according to Ezekiel the Cherubim after leaving the temple founded the church of the Lord. [15]

After this Paula visited the tomb of Lazarus and beheld the hospitable roof of Mary and Martha, as well as Bethphage, 'the town of the

---

[1] Ps. cxxxii. 6, Vulg. [2] Jerome taught Paula Hebrew.
[3] Ps. cxxxii. 7. [4] Ps. cxxxii. 14.
[5] Ps. cxxxii. 17, Vulg. [6] Ps. xxii. 29, 30, LXX.
[7] Gen. xxxv. 21 : Mic. iv. 8. [8] Luke ii. 14.
[9] Jud. vi. 37. [10] Ex. xii. 21-23. [11] Joh. i. 29.
[12] Jer. xiii. 23. [13] Acts viii. 27-39.
[14] This town played an important part in the wars of the Maccabees.
[15] Nu. xiii. 23, 24. [16] Isa. lxiii. 3.
[17] Cellulæ, lit. 'little cells.'
[18] Joh. viii. 56 : cf. Gen. xviii. 1, R.V. —q.v.

[1] Josh. xiv. 15. In Hebrew 'Adam' and 'man' are the same word. Hence the mistake.
[2] 2 Cor. iii. 6. [3] Jud. i. 13-15.
[4] Perhaps identical with "the valley of Berachah" mentioned in 2 Chr. xx. 26.
[5] Gen. xviii. 23-33. [6] Isa. xv. 5. [7] Gen. xiv. 2.
[8] Eph. v. 18. [9] Gen. xix. 30-38. [10] Cant. i. 7.
[11] Gen. xliii. 16. [12] Amos i. 1.
[13] Luke xxiv. 50, 51 : Acts i. 9-12.
[14] Nu. xix. 1-10. [15] Ezek. x. 18, 19.

priestly jaws.'[1] Here it was that a restive foal typical of the Gentiles received the bridle of God, and covered with the garments of the apostles[2] offered its lowly back[3] for Him to sit on. From this she went straight on down the hill to Jericho thinking of the wounded man in the gospel, of the savagery of the priests and Levites who passed him by, and of the kindness of the Samaritan, that is, the guardian, who placed the half-dead man upon his own beast and brought him down to the inn of the church.[4] She noticed the place called Adomim[5] or the Place of Blood, so-called because much blood was shed there in the frequent incursions of marauders. She beheld also the sycamore tree[6] of Zacchaeus, by which is signified the good works of repentance whereby he trod under foot his former sins of bloodshed and rapine, and from which he saw the Most High as from a pinnacle of virtue. She was shewn too the spot by the wayside where the blind men sat who, receiving their sight from the Lord,[7] became types of the two peoples[8] who should believe upon Him. Then entering Jericho she saw the city which Hiel founded in Abiram his firstborn and of which he set up the gates in his youngest son Segub.[9] She looked upon the camp of Gilgal and the hill of the foreskins[10] suggestive of the mystery of the second circumcision;[11] and she gazed at the twelve stones brought thither out of the bed of Jordan[12] to be symbols of those twelve foundations on which are written the names of the twelve apostles.[13] She saw also that fountain of the Law most bitter and barren which the true Elisha healed by his wisdom changing it into a well sweet and fertilising.[14] Scarcely had the night passed away when burning with eagerness she hastened to the Jordan, stood by the brink of the river, and as the sun rose recalled to mind the rising of the sun of righteousness ;[15] how the priest's feet stood firm in the middle of the river-bed ;[16] how afterwards at the command of Elijah and Elisha the waters were divided hither and thither and made way for them to pass ; and again how the Lord had cleansed by His baptism waters which the deluge had polluted and the destruction of mankind had defiled.

13. It would be tedious were I tell of the valley of Achor, that is, of 'trouble and crowds,' where theft and covetousness were condemned ;[17] and of Bethel, 'the house of God,' where Jacob poor and destitute slept upon the bare ground. Here it was that, having set beneath his head a stone which in Zechariah is described as having seven eyes[1] and in Isaiah is spoken of as a corner-stone,[2] he beheld a ladder reaching up to heaven ; yes, and the Lord standing high above it[3] holding out His hand to such as were ascending and hurling from on high such as were careless. Also when she was in Mount Ephraim she made pilgrimages to the tombs of Joshua the son of Nun and of Eleazar the son of Aaron the priest, exactly opposite the one to the other ; that of Joshua being built at Timnath-serah "on the north side of the hill of Gaash,"[4] and that of Eleazar "in a hill that pertained to Phinehas his son."[5] She was somewhat surprised to find that he who had had the distribution of the land in his own hands had selected for himself portions uneven and rocky. What shall I say about Shiloh where a ruined altar[6] is still shewn to-day, and where the tribe of Benjamin anticipated Romulus in the rape of the Sabine women?[7] Passing by Shechem (not Sychar as many wrongly read[8]) or as it is now called Neapolis, she entered the church built upon the side of Mount Gerizim around Jacob's well ; that well where the Lord was sitting when hungry and thirsty He was refreshed by the faith of the woman of Samaria. Forsaking her five husbands by whom are intended the five books of Moses, and that sixth not a husband of whom she boasted, to wit the false teacher Dositheus,[9] she found the true Messiah and the true Saviour. Turning away thence Paula saw the tombs of the twelve patriarchs, and Samaria which in honour of Augustus Herod renamed Augusta or in Greek Sebaste. There lie the prophets Elisha and Obadiah and John the Baptist than whom there is not a greater among those that are born of women.[10] And here she was filled with terror by the marvels she beheld ; for she saw demons screaming under different tortures before the tombs of the saints, and men howling like wolves, baying like dogs, roaring like lions, hissing like serpents and bellowing like bulls. They twisted their heads and bent them backwards until they touched the ground ; women too were suspended head downward and their clothes did not fall off.[11] Paula pitied them all, and shedding tears over them prayed Christ to have mercy on them. And weak as she was she climbed the mountain on foot ; for in two of its caves Obadiah in a time of persecution

---

[1] The jaw was the priest's portion and hence the epithet "priestly": or else Bethphage belonged to the priests.
[2] Matt. xxi. 1-7. [3] Humilia. [4] Luke x. 30-35.
[5] Strictly Dâmim. [6] Luke xix. 4. [7] Matt. xx. 30-34.
[8] *i.e.* the Jews and the Gentiles. [9] 1 Kings xvi. 34.
[10] Josh. v. 3. [11] Rom. ii. 28, 29.
[12] Josh. iv. 3, 20. [13] Rev. xxi. 14.
[14] 2 K. ii. 19-22, type and antitype are, as often, here confounded.
[15] Mal. iv. 2. [16] Josh. iii. 17. [17] Josh. vii. 24-26.

[1] Zech. iii. 9. [2] Isa. xxviii. 16. [3] Gen. xxviii. 12, 13.
[4] Josh. xxiv. 30. [5] Josh. xxiv. 33. [6] Cf. 1 Sam. i. 3.
[7] Judg. xxi. 19-23 : cf. Liv. i. 9. [8] From Joh. iv. 5.
[9] The founder of a Samaritan sect akin to the Essenes.
[10] Luke vii. 28.
[11] Other authorities for these strange phenomena are Hilary, Sulpicius, and Paulinus.

and famine had fed a hundred prophets with bread and water.[1] Then she passed quickly through Nazareth the nursery of the Lord ; Cana and Capernaum familiar with the signs wrought by Him ; the lake of Tiberias sanctified by His voyages upon it ; the wilderness where countless Gentiles were satisfied with a few loaves while the twelve baskets of the tribes of Israel were filled with the fragments left by them that had eaten.[2] She made the ascent of mount Tabor whereon the Lord was transfigured.[3] In the distance she beheld the range of Hermon ;[4] and the wide stretching plains of Galilee where Sisera and all his host had once been overcome by Barak ; and the torrent[5] Kishon separating the level ground into two parts. Hard by also the town of Nain was pointed out to her, where the widow's son was raised.[6] Time would fail me sooner than speech were I to recount all the places to which the revered Paula was carried by her incredible faith.

14. I will now pass on to Egypt, pausing for a while on the way at Socoh, and at Samson's well which he clave in the hollow place that was in the jaw.[7] Here I will lave my parched lips and refresh myself before visiting Moresheth ; in old days famed for the tomb of the prophet Micah,[8] and now for its church. Then skirting the country of the Horites and Gittites, Mareshah, Edom, and Lachish, and traversing the lonely wastes of the desert where the tracks of the traveller are lost in the yielding sand, I will come to the river of Egypt called Sihor,[9] that is "the muddy river," and go through the five cities of Egypt which speak the language of Canaan,[10] and through the land of Goshen and the plains of Zoan[11] on which God wrought his marvellous works. And I will visit the city of No, which has since become Alexandria ;[12] and Nitria, the town of the Lord, where day by day the filth of multitudes is washed away with the pure nitre of virtue. No sooner did Paula come in sight of it than there came to meet her the reverend and estimable bishop, the confessor Isidore, accompanied by countless multitudes of monks many of whom were of priestly or of Levitical rank.[13] On seeing these Paula rejoiced to behold the Lord's glory manifested in them ; but protested that she had no claim to be received with such honour. Need I speak of the Macarii, Arsenius, Serapion,[14] or other pillars of Christ ! Was there

any cell that she did not enter ? Or any man at whose feet she did not throw herself ? In each of His saints she believed that she saw Christ Himself ; and whatever she bestowed upon them she rejoiced to feel that she had bestowed it upon the Lord. Her enthusiasm was wonderful and her endurance scarcely credible in a woman. Forgetful of her sex and of her weakness she even desired to make her abode, together with the girls who accompanied her, among these thousands of monks. And, as they were all willing to welcome her, she might perhaps have sought and obtained permission to do so ; had she not been drawn away by a still greater passion for the holy places. Coming by sea from Pelusium to Maioma on account of the great heat, she returned so rapidly that you would have thought her a bird. Not long afterwards, making up her mind to dwell permanently in holy Bethlehem, she took up her abode for three years in a miserable hostelry ; till she could build the requisite cells and monastic buildings, to say nothing of a guest house for passing travellers where they might find the welcome which Mary and Joseph had missed. At this point I conclude my narrative of the journeys that she made accompanied by Eustochium and many other virgins.

15. I am now free to describe at greater length the virtue which was her peculiar charm ; and in setting forth this I call God to witness that I am no flatterer. I add nothing. I exaggerate nothing. On the contrary I tone down much that I may not appear to relate incredibilities. My carping critics must not insinuate that I am drawing on my imagination or decking Paula, like Æsop's crow, with the fine feathers of other birds. Humility is the first of Christian graces, and hers was so pronounced that one who had never seen her, and who on account of her celebrity had desired to see her, would have believed that he saw not her but the lowest of her maids. When she was surrounded by companies of virgins she was always the least remarkable in dress, in speech, in gesture, and in gait. From the time that her husband died until she fell asleep herself she never sat at meat with a man, even though she might know him to stand upon the pinnacle of the episcopate. She never entered a bath except when dangerously ill. Even in the severest fever she rested not on an ordinary bed but on the hard ground covered only with a mat of goat's hair ; if that can be called rest which made day and night alike a time of almost unbroken prayer. Well did she fulfil the words of the psalter : "All the night make I my bed to swim ; I water my couch with my tears " ![1]

---

[1] 1 Kings xviii. 4.   [2] Matt. xiv. 13-21.
[3] According to the common tradition, but Hermon is more likely to have been the place.
[4] In the original 'Hermon and the Hermons' ; an allusion to the Hebrew text of Ps. xlii. 6.
[5] Jud. v. 21, Vulg.   [6] Luke vii. 11-15.   [7] Jud. xv. 17-19, R.V.
[8] Micah i. 1, 14.   [9] Jer. ii. 18.   [10] Isa. xix. 18.
[11] Ps. lxxviii. 12.   [12] A mistake : No is Thebes.
[13] i.e. presbyters and deacons. Cf. § 29, infra.
[14] At that time the most famous of the Egyptian hermits.

[1] Ps. vi. 6.

Her tears welled forth as it were from fountains, and she lamented her slightest faults as if they were sins of the deepest dye. Constantly did I warn her to spare her eyes and to keep them for the reading of the gospel; but she only said: 'I must disfigure that face which contrary to God's commandment I have painted with rouge, white lead, and antimony. I must mortify that body which has been given up to many pleasures. I must 'make up for my long laughter by constant weeping. I must exchange my soft linen and costly silks for rough goat's hair. I who have pleased my husband and the world in the past, desire now to please Christ.' Were I among her great and signal virtues to select her chastity as a subject of praise, my words would seem superfluous; for, even when she was still in the world, she set an example to all the matrons of Rome, and bore herself so admirably that the most slanderous never ventured to couple scandal with her name.[1] No mind could be more considerate than hers, or none kinder towards the lowly. She did not court the powerful; at the same time, if the proud and the vainglorious sought her, she did not turn from them with disdain. If she saw a poor man, she supported him: and if she saw a rich one, she urged him to do good. Her liberality alone knew no bounds. Indeed, so anxious was she to turn no needy person away that she borrowed money at interest and often contracted new loans to pay off old ones. I was wrong, I admit; but when I saw her so profuse in giving, I reproved her alleging the apostle's words: "I mean not that other men be eased and ye burthened; but by an equality that now at this time your abundance may be a supply for their want, that their abundance also may be a supply for your want."[2] I quoted from the gospel the Saviour's words: "he that hath two coats, let him impart one of them to him that hath none";[3] and I warned her that she might not always have means to do as she would wish. Other arguments I adduced to the same purpose; but with admirable modesty and brevity she overruled them all. "God is my witness," she said, "that what I do I do for His sake. My prayer is that I may die a beggar not leaving a penny to my daughter and indebted to strangers for my winding sheet." She then concluded with these words: "I, if I beg, shall find many to give to me; but if this beggar does not obtain help from me who by borrowing can give it to him, he will die; and if he

dies, of whom will his soul be required?" I wished her to be more careful in managing her concerns, but she with a faith more glowing than mine clave to the Saviour with her whole heart and poor in spirit followed the Lord in His poverty, giving back to Him what she had received and becoming poor for His sake. She obtained her wish at last and died leaving her daughter overwhelmed with a mass of debt. This Eustochium still owes and indeed cannot hope to pay off by her own exertions; only the mercy of Christ can free her from it.

16. Many married ladies make it a habit to confer gifts upon their own trumpeters, and while they are extremely profuse to a few, withhold all help from the many. From this fault Paula was altogether free. She gave her money to each according as each had need, not ministering to self-indulgence but relieving want. No poor person went away from her empty handed. And all this she was enabled to do not by the greatness of her wealth but by her careful management of it. She constantly had on her lips such phrases as these: "Blessed are the merciful for they shall obtain mercy:"[1] and "water will quench a flaming fire; and alms maketh an atonement for sins;"[2] and "make to yourselves friends of the mammon of unrighteousness that . . . they may receive you into everlasting habitations;"[3] and "give alms . . . and behold all things are clean unto you;"[4] and Daniel's words to King Nebuchadnezzar in which he admonished him to redeem his sins by almsgiving.[5] She wished to spend her money not upon these stones, that shall pass away with the earth and the world, but upon those living stones, which roll over the earth;[6] of which in the apocalypse of John the city of the great king is built;[7] of which also the scripture tells us that they shall be changed into sapphire and emerald and jasper and other gems.[8]

17. But these qualities she may well share with a few others and the devil knows that it is not in these that the highest virtue consists. For, when Job has lost his substance and when his house and children have been destroyed, Satan says to the Lord: "Skin for skin, yea all that a man hath, will he give for his life. But put forth thine hand now and touch his bone and his flesh, and he will curse thee to thy face."[9] We know that many persons while they have given alms have yet given nothing which touches their bodily comfort; and while they have held out a helping hand to those in need are themselves overcome with sensual indulgences; they white-

---

[1] Jerome's own name had been coupled with Paula's when they both lived at Rome, but he was able to shew that his relations with her were wholly innocent.
[2] 2 Cor. viii. 13, 14.
[3] Luke iii. 11. The word alteram, one of two (therefore, Jerome means, retaining the second) is found in the Syriac Version of Cureton. It is not found in the Vulgate.

[1] Matt. v. 7.   [2] Ecclus. iii. 30.   [3] Luke xvi. 9.
[4] Luke xi. 41.   [5] Dan. iv. 27, LXX.   [6] Zech. ix. 16, LXX.
[7] Rev. xxi. 14.   [8] Rev. xxi. 19-21.   [9] Job ii. 4, 5.

wash the outside but within they are "full of dead men's bones."[1] Paula was not one of these. Her self-restraint was so great as to be almost immoderate; and her fasts and labours were so severe as almost to weaken her constitution. Except on feast days she would scarcely ever take oil with her food; a fact from which may be judged what she thought of wine, sauce, fish, honey, milk, eggs, and other things agreeable to the palate. Some persons believe that in taking these they are extremely frugal; and, even if they surfeit themselves with them, they still fancy their chastity safe.

18. Envy always follows in the track of virtue: as Horace says, it is ever the mountain top that is smitten by the lightning.[2] It is not surprising that I declare this of men and women, when the jealousy of the Pharisees succeeded in crucifying our Lord Himself. All the saints have had illwishers, and even Paradise was not free from the serpent through whose malice death came into the world.[3] So the Lord stirred up against Paula Hadad the Edomite[4] to buffet her that she might not be exalted, and warned her frequently by the thorn in her flesh[5] not to be elated by the greatness of her own virtues or to fancy that, compared with other women, she had attained the summit of perfection. For my part I used to say that it was best to give in to rancour and to retire before passion. So Jacob dealt with his brother Esau; so David met the unrelenting persecution of Saul. I reminded her how the first of these fled into Mesopotamia;[6] and how the second surrendered himself to the Philistines,[7] and chose to submit to foreign foes rather than to enemies at home. She however replied as follows:—'Your suggestion would be a wise one if the devil did not everywhere fight against God's servants and handmaidens, and did he not always precede the fugitives to their chosen refuges. Moreover, I am deterred from accepting it by my love for the holy places; and I cannot find another Bethlehem elsewhere. Why may I not by my patience conquer this ill will? Why may I not by my humility break down this pride, and when I am smitten on the one cheek offer to the smiter the other?[8] Surely the apostle Paul says "Overcome evil with good."[9] Did not the apostles glory when they suffered reproach for the Lord's sake? Did not even the Saviour humble Himself, taking the form of a servant and being made obedient to the Father unto death, even the death of the cross,[10] that He might save us by His passion?

If Job had not fought the battle and won the victory, he would never have received the crown of righteousness, or have heard the Lord say: "Thinkest thou that I have spoken unto thee for aught else than this, that thou mightest appear righteous."[1] In the gospel those only are said to be blessed who suffer persecution for righteousness' sake.[2] My conscience is at rest, and I know that it is not from any fault of mine that I am suffering: moreover affliction in this world is a ground for expecting a reward hereafter.' When the enemy was more than usually forward and ventured to reproach her to her face, she used to chant the words of the psalter: "While the wicked was before me, I was dumb with silence; I held my peace even from good:"[3] and again, "I as a deaf man heard not; and I was as a dumb man that openeth not his mouth:"[4] and "I was as a man that heareth not, and in whose mouth are no reproofs."[5] When she felt herself tempted, she dwelt upon the words in Deuteronomy: "The Lord your God proveth you, to know whether ye love the Lord your God with all your heart and with all your soul."[6] In tribulations and afflictions she turned to the splendid language of Isaiah: "Ye that are weaned from the milk and drawn from the breasts, look for tribulation upon tribulation, for hope also upon hope: yet a little while must these things be by reason of the malice of the lips and by reason of a spiteful tongue."[7] This passage of scripture she explained for her own consolation as meaning that the weaned, that is, those who have come to full age, must endure tribulation upon tribulation that they may be accounted worthy to receive hope upon hope. She recalled to mind also the words of the apostle, "we glory in tribulations also: knowing that tribulation worketh patience, and patience experience, and experience hope: and hope maketh not ashamed"[8] and "though our outward man perish, yet the inward man is renewed day by day":[9] and "our light affliction which is but for a moment worketh in us[10] an eternal weight of glory; while we look not at the things which are seen but at the things which are not seen: for the things which are seen are temporal but the things which are not seen are eternal."[11] She used to say that, although to human impatience the time might seem slow in coming, yet that it would not be long but that presently help would come from God who says: "In an acceptable time have I heard thee, and in a day of salvation have I helped

---

[1] Matt. xxiii. 27.   [2] Hor. C. ii. x. ii.   [3] Wisd. ii. 24.
[4] The enemy of Solomon—1 K. xi. 14. Who Paula's enemy may have been we do not know.
[5] 2 Cor. xii. 7.   [6] Gen. xxvii. 41-46: xxviii. 1-5.
[7] 1 Sam. xxi. 10.   [8] Matt. v. 39.   [9] Rom. xii. 21.   [10] Phil. ii. 7, 8.

[1] Job xl. 8, LXX.   [2] Matt. v. 10.
[3] Ps. xxxix. 1, 2, acc. to the Gallican psalter.
[4] Ps. xxxviii. 13.   [5] Ps. xxxviii. 14.   [6] Deut. xiii. 3.
[7] Isa. xxviii. 9-11, LXX.   [8] Rom. v. 3-5.   [9] 2 Cor. iv. 16.
[10] Vulg.   [11] 2 Cor. iv. 17, 18.

thee."[1] We ought not, she declared, to dread the deceitful lips and tongues of the wicked, for we rejoice in the aid of the Lord who warns us by His prophet: "fear ye not the reproach of men, neither be ye afraid of their revilings ; for the moth shall eat them up like a garment, and the worm shall eat them like wool":[2] and she quoted His own words, "In your patience ye shall win your souls " :[3] as well as those of the apostle, "the sufferings of this present time are not worthy to be compared with the glory which shall be revealed in us":[4] and in another place, "we are to suffer affliction "[5] that we may be patient in all things that befall us, for "he that is slow to wrath is of great understanding : but he that is hasty of spirit exalteth folly."[6]

19. In her frequent sicknesses and infirmities she used to say, "when I am weak, then am I strong: "[7] "we have our treasure in earthen vessels "[8] until "this corruptible shall have put on incorruption and this mortal shall have put on immortality "[9] and again "as the sufferings of Christ abound in us, so our consolation also aboundeth by Christ:"[10] and then "as ye are partakers of the sufferings, so shall ye be also of the consolation.[11] In sorrow she used to sing: "Why art thou cast down, O my soul ? and why art thou disquieted within me ? hope thou in God for I shall yet praise him who is the health of my countenance and my God."[12] In the hour of danger she used to say : " If any man will come after me, let him deny himself and take up his cross and follow me : "[13] and again " whosoever will save his life shall lose it," and " whosoever will lose his life for my sake the same shall save it."[14] When the exhaustion of her substance and the ruin of her property were announced to her she only said : " What is a man profited, if he shall gain the whole world and lose his own soul ? or what shall a man give in exchange for his soul : "[15] and " naked came I out of my mother's womb, and naked shall I return thither. The Lord gave, and the Lord hath taken away: blessed be the name of the Lord : "[16] and Saint John's words, " Love not the world neither the things that are in the world. For all that is in the world, the lust of the flesh, and the lust of the eyes and the pride of life, is not of the Father but is of the world. And the world passeth away and the lust thereof."[17] I know that when word was sent to her of the serious illnesses of her children and particularly of Toxotius whom she dearly loved, she first by her self-control fulfilled the saying : " I was troubled and I did not speak,"[18]

and then cried out in the words of scripture, " He that loveth son or daughter more than me is not worthy of me."[1] And she prayed to the Lord and said : Lord "preserve thou the children of those that are appointed to die,"[2] that is, of those who for thy sake every day die bodily. I am aware that a talebearer —a class of persons who do a great deal of harm—once told her as a kindness that owing to her great fervour in virtue some people thought her mad and declared that something should be done for her head. She replied in the words of the apostle, "we are made a spectacle unto the world and to angels and to men,"[3] and " we are fools for Christ's sake "[4] but "the foolishness of God is wiser than men."[5] It is for this reason she said that even the Saviour says to the Father, " Thou knowest my foolishness,"[6] and again " I am as a wonder unto many, but thou art my strong refuge."[7] "I was as a beast before thee ; nevertheless I am continually with thee."[8] In the gospel we read that even His kinsfolk desired to bind Him as one of weak mind.[9] His opponents also reviled him saying "thou art a Samaritan and hast a devil,"[10] and another time "he casteth out devils through Beelzebub the chief of the devils."[11] But let us, she continued, listen to the exhortation of the apostle, "Our rejoicing is this, the testimony of our conscience that in simplicity and sincerity . . . by the grace of God we have had our conversation in the world."[12] And let us hear the Lord when He says to His apostles, "If ye were of the world the world would love his own ; but because ye are not of the world . . . therefore the world hateth you."[13] And then she turned to the Lord Himself, saying, "Thou knowest the secrets of the heart,"[14] and "all this is come upon us ; yet have we not forgotten thee, neither have we dealt falsely in thy covenant; our heart is not turned back."[15] " Yea for thy sake are we killed all the day long ; we are counted as sheep for the slaughter."[16] But " the Lord is on my side : I will not fear what man doeth unto me."[17] She had read the words of Solomon, " My son, honour the Lord and thou shalt be made strong ; and beside the Lord fear thou no man."[18] These passages and others like them she used as God's armour against the assaults of wickedness, and particularly to defend herself against the furious onslaughts of envy ; and thus by patiently enduring wrongs she soothed the violence of the most savage breasts. Down to the very

---

1 Isa. xlix. 8.   2 Isa. li. 7. 8.   3 Luke xxi. 19, R.V.
4 Rom. viii. 18.   5 1 Th. iii. 4, R.V.   6 Prov. xiv. 29.
7 2 Cor. xii. 10.   8 2 Cor. iv. 7.   9 1 Cor. xv. 54.
10 2 Cor. i. 5.   11 2 Cor. i. 7.   12 Ps. xlii. 11.
13 Luke ix. 23.   14 Luke ix. 24.   15 Matt. xvi. 26.
16 Job i. 21.   17 1 Joh. ii. 15-17.   18 Ps. lxxvii. 4, Vulg.

1 Matt. x. 37.   2 Ps. lxxix. 11, LXX.   3 1 Cor. iv. 9.
4 1 Cor. iv. 10.   5 1 Cor. i. 25.   6 Ps. lxix. 5.
7 Ps. lxxi. 7.   8 Ps. lxxiii. 22, 23.   9 Mark iii. 21.
10 Joh. viii. 48.   11 Luke xi. 15.   12 2 Cor. i. 12.
13 Joh. xv. 19.   14 Cf. Ps. xliv. 21.   15 Ps. xliv. 17, 18.
16 Ps. xliv. 22.   17 Ps. cxviii. 6, P.B.V.
18 Prov. vii. 2, LXX.

day of her death two things were conspicuous in her life, one her great patience and the other the jealousy which was manifested towards her. Now jealousy gnaws the heart of him who harbours it : and while it strives to injure its rival raves with all the force of its fury against itself.

20. I shall now describe the order of her monastery and the method by which she turned the continence of saintly souls to her own profit. She sowed carnal things that she might reap spiritual things ;[1] she gave earthly things that she might receive heavenly things ; she forewent things temporal that she might in their stead obtain things eternal. Besides establishing a monastery for men, the charge of which she left to men, she divided into three companies and monasteries the numerous virgins whom she had gathered out of different provinces, some of whom are of noble birth while others belonged to the middle or lower classes. But, although they worked and had their meals separately from each other, these three companies met together for psalm-singing and prayer. After the chanting of the Alleluia—the signal by which they were summoned to the Collect[2]— no one was permitted to remain behind. But either first or among the first Paula used to await the arrival of the rest, urging them to diligence rather by her own modest example than by motives of fear. At dawn, at the third, sixth, and ninth hours, at evening, and at midnight they recited the psalter each in turn.[3] No sister was allowed to be ignorant of the psalms, and all had every day to learn a certain portion of the holy scriptures. On the Lord's day only they proceeded to the church beside which they lived, each company following its own mother-superior. Returning home in the same order, they then devoted themselves to their allotted tasks, and made garments either for themselves or else for others. If a virgin was of noble birth, she was not allowed to have an attendant belonging to her own household lest her maid having her mind full of the doings of old days and of the license of childhood might by constant converse open old wounds and renew former errors. All the sisters were clothed alike. Linen was not used except for drying the hands. So strictly did Paula separate them from men that she would not allow even eunuchs to approach them ; lest she should give occasion to slanderous tongues (always ready to cavil at the religious) to console themselves for their own misdoing. When a

sister was backward in coming to the recitation of the psalms or shewed herself remiss in her work, Paula used to approach her in different ways. Was she quick-tempered ? Paula coaxed her. Was she phlegmatic ? Paula chid her, copying the example of the apostle who said : "What will ye ? Shall I come to you with a rod or in love and in the spirit of meekness ? "[1] Apart from food and raiment she allowed no one to have anything she could call her own, for Paul had said, "Having food and raiment let us be therewith content."[2] She was afraid lest the custom of having more should breed covetousness in them ; an appetite which no wealth can satisfy, for the more it has the more it requires, and neither opulence nor indigence is able to diminish it.[3] When the sisters quarrelled one with another she reconciled them with soothing words. If the younger ones were troubled with fleshly desires, she broke their force by imposing redoubled fasts ; for she wished her virgins to be ill in body rather than to suffer in soul. If she chanced to notice any sister too attentive to her dress, she reproved her for her error with knitted brows and severe looks, saying ; "a clean body and a clean dress mean an unclean soul. A virgin's lips should never utter an improper or an impure word, for such indicate a lascivious mind and by the outward man the faults of the inward are made manifest." When she saw a sister verbose and talkative or forward and taking pleasure in quarrels, and when she found after frequent admonitions that the offender shewed no signs of improvement ; she placed her among the lowest of the sisters and outside their society, ordering her to pray at the door of the refectory instead of with the rest, and commanding her to take her food by herself, in the hope that where rebuke had failed shame might bring about a reformation. The sin of theft she loathed as if it were sacrilege ; and that which among men of the world is counted little or nothing she declared to be in a monastery a crime of the deepest dye. How shall I describe her kindness and attention towards the sick or the wonderful care and devotion with which she nursed them ? Yet, although when others were sick she freely gave them every indulgence, and even allowed them to eat meat ; when she fell ill herself, she made no concessions to her own weakness, and seemed unfairly to change in her own case to harshness the kindness which she was always ready to shew to others.

21. No young girl of sound and vigorous constitution could have delivered herself up to a regimen so rigid as that imposed upon

---

[1] Cf. 1 Cor. ix. 11.
[2] The Gathering ; perhaps used, like the Greek σύνοδος, for the Communion. The opening prayer came thus to be called The Collect. See note on Letter LI. § 1.
[3] For the canonical hours see note on Letter XXII. § 37.

[1] 1 Cor. iv. 21.   [2] 1 Tim. vi. 8.   [3] Cf. Sall. Cat. xi.

herself by Paula whose physical powers age had impaired and enfeebled. I admit that in this she was too determined, refusing to spare herself or to listen to advice. I will relate what I know to be a fact. In the extreme heat of the month of July she was once attacked by a violent fever and we despaired of her life. However by God's mercy she rallied, and the doctors urged upon her the necessity of taking a little light wine to accelerate her recovery; saying that if she continued to drink water they feared that she might become dropsical. I on my side secretly appealed to the blessed pope Epiphanius to admonish, nay even to compel her, to take the wine. But she with her usual sagacity and quickness at once perceived the stratagem, and with a smile let him see that the advice he was giving her was after all not his but mine. Not to waste more words, the blessed prelate after many exhortations left her chamber; and, when I asked him what he had accomplished, replied, "Only this that old as I am I have been almost persuaded to drink no more wine." I relate this story not because I approve of persons rashly taking upon themselves burthens beyond their strength (for does not the scripture say : "Burden not thyself above thy power"?[1]) but because I wish from this quality of perseverance in her to shew the passion of her mind and the yearning of her believing soul ; both of which made her sing in David's words, "My soul thirsteth for thee, my flesh longeth after thee."[2] Difficult as it is always to avoid extremes, the philosophers[3] are quite right in their opinion that virtue is a mean and vice an excess, or as we may express it in one short sentence "In nothing too much."[4] While thus unyielding in her contempt for food Paula was easily moved to sorrow and felt crushed by the deaths of her kinsfolk, especially those of her children. When one after another her husband and her daughters fell asleep, on each occasion the shock of their loss endangered her life. And although she signed her mouth and her breast with the sign of the cross, and endeavoured thus to alleviate a mother's grief ; her feelings overpowered her and her maternal instincts were too much for her confiding mind. Thus while her intellect retained its mastery she was overcome by sheer physical weakness. On one occasion a sickness seized her and clung to her so long that it brought anxiety to us and danger to herself. Yet even then she was full of joy and repeated every moment the apostle's words : "O wretched man that I am ! who shall deliver me from the body of this death?"[5]

The careful reader may say that my words are an invective rather than an eulogy. I call that Jesus whom she served and whom I desire to serve to be my witness that so far from unduly eulogizing her or depreciating her I tell the truth about her as one Christian writing of another ; that I am writing a memoir and not a panegyric, and that what were faults in her might well be virtues in others less saintly. I speak thus of her faults to satisfy my own feelings and the passionate regret of us her brothers and sisters, who all of us love her still and all of us deplore her loss.

22. However, she has finished her course, she has kept the faith, and now she enjoys the crown of righteousness.[1] She follows the Lamb whithersoever he goes.[2] She is filled now because she was hungry.[3] With joy does she sing : "as we have heard, so have we seen in the city of the Lord of hosts, in the city of our God."[4] O blessed change ! Once she wept but now laughs for evermore. Once she despised the broken cisterns of which the prophet speaks ;[5] but now she has found in the Lord a fountain of life.[6] Once she wore haircloth but now she is clothed in white raiment, and can say : "thou hast put off my sackcloth, and girded me with gladness."[7] Once she ate ashes like bread and mingled her drink with weeping ;[8] saying "my tears have been my meat day and night ;"[9] but now for all time she eats the bread of angels[10] and sings : "O taste and see that the Lord is good ;"[11] and "my heart is overflowing with a goodly matter ; I speak the things which I have made touching the king."[12] She now sees fulfilled Isaiah's words, or rather those of the Lord speaking through Isaiah : "Behold, my servants shall eat but ye shall be hungry : behold, my servants shall drink but ye shall be thirsty : behold, my servants shall rejoice, but ye shall be ashamed : behold, my servants shall sing for joy of heart, but ye shall cry for sorrow of heart, and shall howl for vexation of spirit."[13] I have said that she always shunned the broken cisterns : she did so that she might find in the Lord a fountain of life, and that she might rejoice and sing : "as the hart panteth after the waterbrooks, so panteth my soul after Thee, O God. When shall I come and appear before God?"[14]

23. I must briefly mention the manner in which she avoided the foul cisterns of the heretics whom she regarded as no better than heathen. A certain cunning knave, in his own estimation both learned and clever, began with-

---

[1] Ecclus. xiii. 2.   [2] Ps. lxiii. 1.   [3] e.g. Aristotle, E.N. ii. 6.
[4] Ne quid nimis, in Greek Μηδὲν ἄγαν.   [5] Rom. vii. 24.

[1] 2 Tim. iv. 7, 8.   [2] Rev. xiv. 4.   [3] Cf. Luke vi. 21.
[4] Ps. xlviii. 8.   [5] Jer. ii. 13.   [6] Joh. iv. 14.
[7] Ps. xxx. 11.   [8] Ps. cii. 9.   [9] Ps. xlii. 3.
[10] Cf. Ps. lxxviii. 25.   [11] Ps. xxxiv. 8.
[12] Ps. xlv. 1, R.V.   [13] Isa. lxv. 13, 14.   [14] Ps. xlii. 1, 2.

out my knowledge to put to her such questions as these : What sin has an infant committed that it should be seized by the devil? Shall we be young or old when we rise again? If we die young and rise young, we shall after the resurrection require to have nurses. If however we die young and rise old, the dead will not rise again at all : they will be transformed into new beings. Will there be a distinction of sexes in the next world? Or will there be no such distinction? If the distinction continues, there will be wedlock and sexual intercourse and procreation of children. If however it does not continue, the bodies that rise again will not be the same. For, he argued, "the earthy tabernacle weigheth down the mind that museth upon many things,"[1] but the bodies that we shall have in heaven will be subtle and spiritual according to the words of the apostle : "it is sown a natural body : it is raised a spiritual body."[2] From all of which considerations he sought to prove that rational creatures have been for their faults and previous sins subjected to bodily conditions ; and that according to the nature and guilt of their transgression they are born in this or that state of life. Some, he said, rejoice in sound bodies and wealthy and noble parents ; others have for their portion diseased frames and poverty stricken homes ; and by imprisonment in the present world and in bodies pay the penalty of their former sins. Paula listened and reported what she heard to me, at the same time pointing out the man. Thus upon me was laid the task of opposing this most noxious viper and deadly pest. It is of such that the Psalmist speaks when he writes : "deliver not the soul of thy turtle dove unto the wild beast,"[3] and "Rebuke the wild beast of the reeds ;"[4] creatures who write iniquity and speak lies against the Lord and lift up their mouths against the Most High. As the fellow had tried to deceive Paula, I at her request went to him, and by asking him a few questions involved him in a dilemma. Do you believe, said I, that there will be a resurrection of the dead or do you disbelieve? He replied, I believe. I went on : Will the bodies that rise again be the same or different? He said, The same. Then I asked : What of their sex? Will that remain unaltered or will it be changed? At this question he became silent and swayed his head this way and that as a serpent does to avoid being struck. Accordingly I continued, As you have nothing to say I will answer for you and will draw the conclusion from your premises. If the woman shall not rise again as a woman nor the man as a man, there will be no resurrection of the

dead. For the body is made up of sex and members. But if there shall be no sex and no members what will become of the resurrection of the body, which cannot exist without sex and members? And if there shall be no resurrection of the body, there can be no resurrection of the dead. But as to your objection taken from marriage, that, if the members shall remain the same, marriage must inevitably be allowed ; it is disposed of by the Saviour's words : "ye do err not knowing the scriptures nor the power of God. For in the resurrection they neither marry nor are given in marriage but are as the angels."[1] When it is said that they neither marry nor are given in marriage, the distinction of sex is shewn to persist. For no one says of things which have no capacity for marriage such as a stick or a stone that they neither marry nor are given in marriage ; but this may well be said of those who while they can marry yet abstain from doing so by their own virtue and by the grace of Christ. But if you cavil at this and say, how shall we in that case be like the angels with whom there is neither male nor female, hear my answer in brief as follows. What the Lord promises to us is not the nature of angels but their mode of life and their bliss. And therefore John the Baptist is called an angel[2] even before he is beheaded, and all God's holy men and virgins manifest in themselves even in this world the life of angels. When it is said "ye shall be like the angels," likeness only is promised and not a change of nature.

24. And now do you in your turn answer me these questions. How do you explain the fact that Thomas felt the hands of the risen Lord and beheld His side pierced by the spear?[3] And the fact that Peter saw the Lord standing on the shore[4] and eating a piece of a roasted fish and a honeycomb.[5] If He stood, He must certainly have had feet. If He pointed to His wounded side He must have also had chest and belly for to these the sides are attached and without them they cannot be. If He spoke, He must have used a tongue and palate and teeth. For as the bow strikes the strings, so to produce vocal sound does the tongue come in contact with the teeth. If His hands were felt, it follows that He must have had arms as well. Since therefore it is admitted that He had all the members which go to make up the body, He must have also had the whole body formed of them, and that not a woman's but a man's ; that is to say, He rose again in the sex in which He died. And if you cavil farther and say : We shall eat

---

[1] Wisd. ix. 15.　　[2] 1 Cor. xv. 44.
[3] Ps. lxxiv. 19, R.V.　　[4] Ps. lxviii. 30, R.V.

[1] Matt. xxii. 29, 30.
[2] Luke vii. 27. 'Angel' is a Greek word and means 'messenger.'
[3] Joh. xx. 26–28.　　[4] Joh. xxi. 4.　　[5] Luke xxiv. 42, 43.

then, I suppose, after the resurrection ; or How can a solid and material body enter in contrary to its nature through closed doors ? you shall receive from me this reply. Do not for this matter of food find fault with belief in the resurrection : for our Lord after raising the daughter of the ruler of the synagogue commanded food to be given her.[1] And Lazarus who had been dead four days is described as sitting at meat with Him,[2] the object in both cases being to shew that the resurrection was real and not merely apparent. And if from our Lord's entering in through closed doors[3] you strive to prove that His body was spiritual and aerial, He must have had this spiritual body even before He suffered ; since —contrary to the nature of heavy bodies—He was able to walk upon the sea.[4] The apostle Peter also must be believed to have had a spiritual body for he also walked upon the waters with buoyant step.[5] The true explanation is that when anything is done against nature, it is a manifestation of God's might and power. And to shew plainly that in these great signs our attention is asked not to a change in nature but to the almighty power of God, he who by faith had walked on water began to sink for the want of it and would have done so, had not the Lord lifted him up with the reproving words, " O thou of little faith wherefore didst thou doubt ? "[6] I wonder that you can display such effrontery when the Lord Himself said, "reach hither thy finger, and behold my hands ; and reach hither thy hand and thrust it into my side : and be not faithless but believing."[7] and in another place, "behold my hands and my feet that it is I myself : handle me and see ; for a spirit hath not flesh and bones as ye see me have. And when he had thus spoken he shewed them his hands and his feet."[8] You hear Him speak of bones and flesh, of feet and hands ; and yet you want to palm off on me the bubbles and airy nothings of which the stoics rave ![9]

25. Moreover, if you ask how it is that a mere infant which has never sinned is seized by the devil, or at what age we shall rise again seeing that we die at different ages ; my only answer—an unwelcome one, I fancy—will be in the words of scripture : " The judgments of God are a great deep," [10] and " O the depth of the riches both of the wisdom and knowledge of God ! how unsearchable are his judgments, and his ways past finding out ! For who hath known the mind of the Lord ? or who hath been his counsellor ? " [11] No difference of age can affect the reality of the body. Although

our frames are in a perpetual flux and lose or gain daily, these changes do not make us different individuals. I was not one person at ten years old, another at thirty and another at fifty ; nor am I another now when all my head is gray.[1] According to the traditions of the church and the teaching of the apostle Paul, the answer must be this ; that we shall rise as perfect men in the measure of the stature of the fulness of Christ.[2] At this age the Jews suppose Adam to have been created and at this age we read that the Lord and Saviour rose again. Many other arguments did I adduce from both testaments to stifle the outcry of this heretic.

26. From that day forward so profoundly did Paula commence to loathe the man—and all who agreed with him in his doctrines—that she publicly proclaimed them as enemies of the Lord. I have related this incident less with the design of confuting in a few words a heresy which would require volumes to confute it, than with the object of shewing the great faith of this saintly woman who preferred to subject herself to perpetual hostility from men rather than by friendships hurtful to herself to provoke or to offend God.

27. To revert then to that description of her character which I began a little time ago ; no mind was ever more docile than was hers. She was slow to speak and swift to hear,[3] remembering the precept, "Keep silence and hearken, O Israel."[4] The holy scriptures she knew by heart, and said of the history contained in them that it was the foundation of the truth ; but, though she loved even this, she still preferred to seek for the underlying spiritual meaning and made this the keystone of the spiritual building raised within her soul. She asked leave that she and her daughter might read over the old and new testaments[5] under my guidance. Out of modesty I at first refused compliance, but as she persisted in her demand and frequently urged me to consent to it, I at last did so and taught her what I had learned not from myself —for self-confidence is the worst of teachers— but from the church's most famous writers. Wherever I stuck fast and honestly confessed myself at fault she would by no means rest content but would force me by fresh questions to point out to her which of many different solutions seemed to me the most probable. I will mention here another fact which to those who are envious may well seem incredible. While I myself beginning as a young man have with much toil and effort partially acquired the Hebrew tongue and study it now unceas-

---

[1] Mark v. 43.   [2] Joh. xii. 2.   [3] Joh. xx. 19.
[4] Matt. xiv. 25.   [5] Matt. xiv. 29.   [6] Matt. xiv. 31.
[7] Joh. xx. 27.   [8] Luke xxiv. 39, 40.
[9] Globos stoicorum atque aëria quædam deliramenta.
[10] Ps. xxxvi. 6.   [11] Rom. xi. 33, 34.

---

[1] Jerome was at this time about 60 years old.
[2] Eph. iv. 13.   [3] Jas. i. 19.   [4] Deut. xxvii. 9, R.V.
[5] Vetus et novum instrumentum.

ingly lest if I leave it, it also may leave me ;
Paula, on making up her mind that she too
would learn it, succeeded so well that she
could chant the psalms in Hebrew and could
speak the language without a trace of the pro-
nunciation peculiar to Latin.   The same accomplishment can be seen to this day in her
daughter Eustochium, who always kept close
to her mother's side, obeyed all her commands, never slept apart from her, never
walked abroad or took a meal without her,
never had a penny that she could call her
own, rejoiced when her mother gave to the
poor her little patrimony, and fully believed
that in filial affection she had the best heritage and the truest riches.   I must not pass
over in silence the joy which Paula felt when
she heard her little granddaughter and namesake, the child of Laeta and Toxotius—who
was born and I may even say conceived in
answer to a vow of her parents dedicating her
to virginity—when, I say, she heard the little
one in her cradle sing "alleluia" and falter
out the words "grandmother" and "aunt."
One wish alone made her long to see her
native land again ; that she might know her
son and his wife and child [1] to have renounced
the world and to be serving Christ.   And it
has been granted to her in part.   For while
her granddaughter is destined to take the
veil, her daughter-in-law has vowed herself to
perpetual chastity, and by faith and alms
emulates the example that her mother has set
her.   She strives to exhibit at Rome the
virtues which Paula set forth in all their fulness at Jerusalem.

28. What ails thee, my soul ? Why dost
thou shudder to approach her death ? I have
made my letter longer than it should be
already ; dreading to come to the end and
vainly supposing that by saying nothing of it
and by occupying myself with her praises I
could postpone the evil day.   Hitherto the
wind has been all in my favour and my keel
has smoothly ploughed through the heaving
waves.   But now my speech is running upon
the rocks, the billows are mountains high, and
imminent shipwreck awaits both you and me.
We must needs cry out : " Master, save us,
we perish :" [2] and "awake, why sleepest thou,
O Lord ?" [3]   For who could tell the tale of
Paula's dying with dry eyes ? She fell into a
most serious illness and thus gained what she
most desired, power to leave us and to be
joined more fully to the Lord.   Eustochium's
affection for her mother, always true and
tried, in this time of sickness approved itself
still more to all.   She sat by Paula's bedside,
she fanned her, she supported her head, she

arranged her pillows, she chafed her feet, she
rubbed her stomach, she smoothed down the
bedclothes, she heated hot water, she brought
towels.   In fact she anticipated the servants
in all their duties, and when one of them did
anything she regarded it as so much taken
away from her own gain.   How unceasingly
she prayed, how copiously she wept, how constantly she ran to and fro between her prostrate mother and the cave of the Lord !
imploring God that she might not be deprived
of a companion so dear, that if Paula was to
die she might herself no longer live, and that
one bier might carry to burial her and her
mother.   Alas for the frailty and perishable-
ness of human nature ! Except that our belief in Christ raises us up to heaven and
promises eternity to our souls, the physical
conditions of life are the same for us as for the
brutes.   "There is one event to the righteous
and to the wicked ; to the good and to the
evil ; to the clean and to the unclean ; to him
that sacrificeth and to him that sacrificeth
not : as is the good so is the sinner ; and he
that sweareth as he that feareth an oath." [1]
Man and beast alike are dissolved into dust
and ashes.

29. Why do I still linger, and prolong my
suffering by postponing it ? Paula's intelligence shewed her that her death was near.
Her body and limbs grew cold and only in her
holy breast did the warm beat of the living
soul continue.   Yet, as though she were leaving strangers to go home to her own people,
she whispered the verses of the psalmist :
"Lord, I have loved the habitation of thy
house and the place where thine honour
dwelleth," [2] and "How amiable are thy tabernacles, O Lord of hosts ! My soul longeth
yea even fainteth for the courts of the Lord," [3]
and "I had rather be an outcast in the house
of my God than to dwell in the tents of
wickedness." [4]   When I asked her why she
remained silent refusing to answer my call, [5]
and whether she was in pain, she replied in
Greek that she had no suffering and that all
things were to her eyes calm and tranquil.
After this she said no more but closed her
eyes as though she already despised all mortal things, and kept repeating the verses just
quoted down to the moment in which she
breathed out her soul, but in a tone so low
that we could scarcely hear what she said.
Raising her finger also to her mouth she made
the sign of the cross upon her lips.   Then her
breath failed her and she gasped for death ;
yet even when her soul was eager to break
free, she turned the death-rattle (which comes

---

[1] Eccles. ix. 2.   [2] Ps. xxvi. 8.
[3] Ps. lxxxiv. 1, 2.   [4] Ps. lxxxiv. 10, Vulg.
[5] For the technical meaning of *inclamatio* vide Virg. A. i.
219, with Conington's note.

---

[1] Toxotius, Laeta, the younger Paula.   Comp. Letter CVII.
[2] Matt. viii. 25 : Luke viii. 24.   [3] Ps. xliv. 23.

at last to all) into the praise of the Lord. The bishop of Jerusalem and some from other cities were present, also a great number of the inferior clergy, both priests and levites.[1] The entire monastery was filled with bodies of virgins and monks. As soon as Paula heard the bridegroom saying: "Rise up my love my fair one, my dove, and come away: for, lo, the winter is past, the rain is over and gone," she answered joyfully "the flowers appear on the earth; the time to cut them has come"[2] and "I believe that I shall see the good things of the Lord in the land of the living."[3]

30. No weeping or lamentation followed her death, such as are the custom of the world; but all present united in chanting the psalms in their several tongues. The bishops lifted up the dead woman with their own hands, placed her upon a bier, and carrying her on their shoulders to the church in the cave of the Saviour, laid her down in the centre of it. Other bishops meantime carried torches and tapers in the procession, and yet others led the singing of the choirs. The whole population of the cities of Palestine came to her funeral. Not a single monk lurked in the desert or lingered in his cell. Not a single virgin remained shut up in the seclusion of her chamber. To each and all it would have seemed sacrilege to have withheld the last tokens of respect from a woman so saintly. As in the case of Dorcas,[4] the widows and the poor shewed the garments Paula had given them; while the destitute cried aloud that they had lost in her a mother and a nurse. Strange to say, the paleness of death had not altered her expression; only a certain solemnity and seriousness had overspread her features. You would have thought her not dead but asleep.

One after another they chanted the psalms, now in Greek, now in Latin, now in Syriac; and this not merely for the three days which elapsed before she was buried beneath the church and close to the cave of the Lord, but throughout the remainder of the week. All who were assembled felt that it was their own funeral at which they were assisting, and shed tears as if they themselves had died. Paula's daughter, the revered virgin Eustochium, "as a child that is weaned of his mother,"[5] could not be torn away from her parent. She kissed her eyes, pressed her lips upon her brow, embraced her frame, and wished for nothing better than to be buried with her.

31. Jesus is witness that Paula has left not a single penny to her daughter but, as I said before, on the contrary a large mass of debt;

and, worse even than this, a crowd of brothers and sisters whom it is hard for her to support but whom it would be undutiful to cast off. Could there be a more splendid instance of self-renunciation than that of this noble lady who in the fervour of her faith gave away so much of her wealth that she reduced herself to the last degree of poverty? Others may boast, if they will, of money spent in charity, of large sums heaped up in God's treasury,[1] of votive offerings hung up with cords of gold. None of them has given more to the poor than Paula, for Paula has kept nothing for herself. But now she enjoys the true riches and those good things which eye hath not seen nor ear heard, neither have they entered into the heart of man.[2] If we mourn, it is for ourselves and not for her; yet even so, if we persist in weeping for one who reigns with Christ, we shall seem to envy her her glory.

32. Be not fearful, Eustochium: you are endowed with a splendid heritage. The Lord is your portion; and, to increase your joy, your mother has now after a long martyrdom won her crown. It is not only the shedding of blood that is accounted a confession: the spotless service of a devout mind is itself a daily martyrdom. Both alike are crowned; with roses and violets in the one case, with lilies in the other. Thus in the Song of Songs it is written: "my beloved is white and ruddy;"[3] for, whether the victory be won in peace or in war, God gives the same guerdon to those who win it. Like Abraham your mother heard the words: "get thee out of thy country, and from thy kindred, unto a land that I will shew thee;"[4] and not only that but the Lord's command given through Jeremiah: "flee out of the midst of Babylon, and deliver every man his soul."[5] To the day of her death she never returned to Chaldæa, or regretted the fleshpots of Egypt or its strong-smelling meats. Accompanied by her virgin bands she became a fellow-citizen of the Saviour; and now that she has ascended from her little Bethlehem to the heavenly realms she can say to the true Naomi: "thy people shall be my people and thy God my God."[6]

33. I have spent the labour of two nights in dictating for you this treatise; and in doing so I have felt a grief as deep as your own. I say in 'dictating' for I have not been able to write it myself. As often as I have taken up my pen[7] and have tried to fulfil my promise; my fingers have stiffened, my hand has fallen, and my power over it has vanished. The rudeness of the diction, devoid as it is of all

---

[1] i.e. presbyters and deacons—see § 14 above.
[2] Cant. ii. 10-12, Vulg.   [3] Ps. xxvii. 13.
[4] Acts ix. 39.   [5] Ps. cxxxi. 2.

[1] Corbona. See Matt. xxvii. 6, Vulg.
[2] 1 Cor. ii. 9.   [3] Cant. v. 10.   [4] Gen. xii. 1.
[5] Jer. li. 6.   [6] Ruth i. 16.   [7] Stilus.

elegance or charm, bears witness to the feeling of the writer.

34. And now, Paula, farewell, and aid with your prayers the old age of your votary. Your faith and your works unite you to Christ ; thus standing in His presence you will the more readily gain what you ask. In this letter " I have built " to your memory " a monument more lasting than bronze," [1] which no lapse of time will be able to destroy. And I have cut an inscription on your tomb, which I here subjoin ; that, wherever my narrative may go, the reader may learn that you are buried at Bethlehem and not uncommemorated there.

THE INSCRIPTION ON PAULA'S TOMB.

Within this tomb a child of Scipio lies,
A daughter of the farfamed Pauline house,
A scion of the Gracchi, of the stock
Of Agamemnon's self, illustrious :
Here rests the lady Paula, well-beloved
Of both her parents, with Eustochium
For daughter ; she the first of Roman dames
Who hardship chose and Bethlehem for Christ.

In front of the cavern there is another inscription as follows :—

Seest thou here hollowed in the rock a grave,
'Tis Paula's tomb ; high heaven has her soul.
Who Rome and friends, riches and home forsook
Here in this lonely spot to find her rest.
For here Christ's manger was, and here the kings
To Him, both God and man, their off'rings made.

35. The holy and blessed Paula fell asleep on the seventh day before the Kalends of February, on the third day of the week, after the sun had set. She was buried on the fifth day before the same Kalends, in the sixth consulship of the Emperor Honorius and the first of Aristænetus. She lived in the vows of religion five years at Rome and twenty years at Bethlehem. The whole duration of her life was fifty-six years eight months and twenty-one days.

LETTER CIX.

TO RIPARIUS.

Riparius, a presbyter of Aquitaine had written to inform Jerome that Vigilantius (for whom see Letter LXI.) was preaching in southern Gaul against the worship of relics and the keeping of night vigils ; and this apparently with the consent of his bishop. Jerome now replies in a letter more noteworthy for its bitterness than for its logic. Nevertheless he offers to write a full confutation of Vigilantius if Riparius will send him the book containing his heresies. This Riparius subsequently did and then Jerome wrote his treatise *Against Vigilantius*, the most extreme and least convincing of all his works.

The date of the letter is 404 A.D.

1. Now that I have received a letter from you, if I do not answer it I shall be guilty of pride, and if I do I shall be guilty of rashness. For the matters concerning which you ask my opinion are such that they cannot either be spoken of or listened to without profanity. You tell me that Vigilantius (whose very name *Wakeful* is a contradiction : he ought rather to be described as *Sleepy*) has again opened his fetid lips and is pouring forth a torrent of filthy venom upon the relics of the holy martyrs ; and that he calls us who cherish them ashmongers and idolaters who pay homage to dead men's bones. Unhappy wretch ! to be wept over by all Christian men, who sees not that in speaking thus he makes himself one with the Samaritans and the Jews who hold dead bodies unclean and regard as defiled even vessels which have been in the same house with them, following the letter that killeth and not the spirit that giveth life. [1] We, it is true, refuse to worship or adore, I say not the relics of the martyrs, but even the sun and moon, the angels and archangels, the Cherubim and Seraphim and "every name that is named, not only in this world but also in that which is to come." [2] For we may not "serve the creature rather than the Creator, who is blessed for ever. [3] Still we honour the relics of the martyrs, that we may adore Him whose martyrs they are. We honour the servants that their honour may be reflected upon their Lord who Himself says : —"he that receiveth you receiveth me." [4] I ask Vigilantius, Are the relics of Peter and of Paul unclean ? Was the body of Moses unclean, of which we are told (according to the correct Hebrew text) that it was buried by the Lord Himself ? [5] And do we, every time that we enter the basilicas of apostles and prophets and martyrs, pay homage to the shrines of idols ? Are the tapers which burn before their tombs only the tokens of idolatry ? I will go farther still and ask a question which will make this theory recoil upon the head of its inventor and which will either kill or cure that frenzied brain of his, so that simple souls shall be no more subverted by his sacrilegious reasonings. Let him answer me this, Was the Lord's body unclean when it was placed in the sepulchre ? And did the angels clothed in white raiment merely watch over a corpse dead and defiled, that ages afterwards this sleepy fellow might indulge in dreams and vomit forth his filthy surfeit, so as, like the persecutor Julian, either to destroy the basilicas of the saints or to convert them into heathen temples ?

2. I am surprised that the reverend bishop [6]

---

[1] 2 Cor. iii. 6.   [2] Eph. i. 21.   [3] Rom. i. 25.
[4] Matt. x. 40.   [5] Deut. xxxiv. 6.
[6] Probably Exuperius of Toulouse.

in whose diocese he is said to be a presbyter acquiesces in this his mad preaching, and that he does not rather with apostolic rod, nay with a rod of iron, shatter this useless vessel [1] and deliver him for the destruction of the flesh that the spirit may be saved. [2] He should remember the words that are said : " When thou sawest a thief, then thou consentedst unto him ; and hast been partaker with adulterers ; " [3] and in another place, " I will early destroy all the wicked of the land ; that I may cut off all wicked doers from the city of the Lord ; " [4] and again " Do not I hate them, O Lord, that hate thee ? and am not I grieved with those that rise up against thee ? I hate them with perfect hatred." [5] If the relics of the martyrs are not worthy of honour, how comes it that we read " Precious in the sight of the Lord is the death of his saints ? " [6] If dead men's bones defile those that touch them, how came it that the dead Elisha raised another man also dead, and that life came to this latter from the body of the prophet which according to Vigilantius must have been unclean ? In that case every encampment of the host of Israel and the people of God was unclean ; for they carried the bodies of Joseph and of the patriarchs with them in the wilderness, and carried their unclean ashes even into the holy land. In that case Joseph, who was a type of our Lord and Saviour, was a wicked man ; for he carried up Jacob's bones with great pomp to Hebron merely to put his unclean father beside his unclean grandfather and great grandfather, that is, one dead body along with others. The wretch's tongue should be cut out, or he should be put under treatment for insanity. As he does not know how to speak, he should learn to be silent. I have myself before now seen the monster, and have done my best to bind the maniac with texts of scripture, as Hippocrates binds his patients with chains ; but " he went away, he departed, he escaped, he broke out," [7] and taking refuge between the Adriatic and the Alps of King Cotius [8] declaimed in his turn against me. For all that a fool says must be regarded as mere noise and mouthing.

3. You may perhaps in your secret thoughts find fault with me for thus assailing a man behind his back. I will frankly admit that my indignation overpowers me ; I cannot listen with patience to such sacrilegious opinions. I have read of the javelin of Phinehas, [9] of the harshness of Elijah, [10] of the jealous anger of Simon the zealot, [11] of the severity of Peter

in putting to death Ananias and Sapphira, [1] and of the firmness of Paul who, when Elymas the sorcerer withstood the ways of the Lord, doomed him to lifelong blindness. [2] There is no cruelty in regard for God's honour. Wherefore also in the Law it is said : " If thy brother or thy friend or the wife of thy bosom entice thee from the truth, thine hand shall be upon them and thou shalt shed their blood, [3] and so shalt thou put the evil away from the midst of Israel." [4] Once more I ask, Are the relics of the martyrs unclean ? If so, why did the apostles allow themselves to walk in that funeral procession before the body—the unclean body—of Stephen? Why did they make great lamentation over him, [5] that their grief might be turned into our joy ?

You tell me farther that Vigilantius execrates vigils. In this surely he goes contrary to his name. The Wakeful one wishes to sleep and will not hearken to the Saviour's words, " What, could ye not watch with me one hour ? Watch and pray that ye enter not into temptation : the spirit indeed is willing but the flesh is weak." [6] And in another place a prophet sings : " At midnight I will rise to give thanks unto thee because of thy righteous judgments." [7] We read also in the gospel how the Lord spent whole nights in prayer [8] and how the apostles when they were shut up in prison kept vigil all night long, singing their psalms until the earth quaked, and the keeper of the prison believed, and the magistrates and citizens were filled with terror. [9] Paul says: "continue in prayer and *watch* in the same," [10] and in another place he speaks of himself as " in watchings often." [11] Vigilantius may sleep if he pleases and may choke in his sleep, destroyed by the destroyer of Egypt and of the Egyptians. But let us say with David : " Behold, he that keepeth Israel shall neither slumber nor sleep." [12] So will the Holy One and the Watcher come to us. [13] And if ever by reason of our sins He fall asleep, let us say to Him : " Awake, why sleepest thou, O Lord ; " [14] and when our ship is tossed by the waves let us rouse Him and say, " Master, save us : we perish." [15]

4. I would dictate more were it not that the limits of a letter impose upon me a modest silence. I might have gone on, had you sent me the books which contain this man's rhapsodies, for in that case I should have known what points I had to refute. As it is I am only beating the air [16] and revealing not so

---

[1] Ps. ii. 9.   [2] 1 Cor. v. 5.   [3] Ps. l. 18.
[4] Ps. ci. 8.   [5] Ps. cxxxix. 21, 22.
[6] Ps. cxvi. 15.   [7] Cic. Cat. ii. 1, of Catiline.
[8] A contemporary and ally of Augustus.
[9] Nu. xxv. 7, 8.   [10] 1 K. xviii. 40.
[11] Luke vi. 15 : so called probably because he came from the most fanatical party among the Pharisees.

[1] Acts v. 1-10.   [2] Acts xiii. 8-11.   [3] Deut. xiii. 6-9.
[4] Deut. xiii. 5.   [5] Acts viii. 2.   [6] Matt. xxvi. 40, 41.
[7] Ps. cxix. 62.   [8] Luke vi. 12.   [9] Acts xvi. 25-38.
[10] Col. iv. 2.   [11] 2 Cor. xi. 27.   [12] Ps. cxxi. 4.
[13] Dan. iv. 13. Jerome gives the Hebrew word for watcher, viz. עִיר.
[14] Ps. xliv. 23.
[15] Matt. viii. 25 : Luke viii. 24.   [16] Cf. 1 Cor. ix. 26.

much his infidelity—for this is patent to all—as my own faith. But if you wish me to write against him at greater length, send me those wretched dronings of his and in my answer he shall hear an echo of John the Baptist's words : " Now also the axe is laid unto the root of the trees ; therefore every tree which bringeth not forth good fruit is hewn down and cast into the fire." [1]

LETTER CX.

FROM AUGUSTINE.

Augustine's answer to Letter CII. He now tries to soothe Jerome's wounded feelings, begs him to overlook the offence that he has committed, and implores him not to break off the friendly relations hitherto maintained between them. He touches on the quarrel between Jerome and Rufinus and sincerely hopes that no such breach may ever separate Jerome from himself. The tone of the letter is throughout conciliatory and is marked in places with deep feeling. More than once Augustine dwells on Jerome's words (" would that I could embrace you and that by mutual converse we might learn one from the other," Letter CII. § 2) and speaks of the comfort which they have brought to him. The date of the letter is 404 A.D.

LETTER CXI.

FROM AUGUSTINE TO PRÆSIDIUS.

Augustine asks Præsidius to forward the preceding letter to Jerome and also to write himself to urge him to forgive Augustine.

LETTER CXII.

TO AUGUSTINE.

On receiving Letter CIV. together with duly authenticated copies of Letters LVI. and LXVII. Jerome in three days completes an exhaustive reply to all the questions which Augustine had raised. He explains what is the true title of his book On Illustrious Men, deals at great length with the dispute between Paul and Peter, expounds his views with regard to the Septuagint, and shews by the story of " the gourd " how close and accurate his translations are. His language throughout is kind but rather patronising : indeed in this whole correspondence Jerome seldom sufficiently recognizes the greatness of Augustine. The date of the letter is 404 A.D.

LETTER CXIII.

FROM THEOPHILUS TO JEROME.

Theophilus, bishop of Alexandria, had compiled an invective against John Chrysostom, bishop of Constantinople who was now (largely through his efforts) an exile from his see. This he now sends to Jerome with a request that the latter will render it into Latin for dissemination in the West. The invective (of which only a few fragments remain) is of the most violent kind. Nevertheless Jerome translated it along with this letter, the date of which is 405 A.D. The latter part of the letter has perished.

To the well-beloved and most loving brother Jerome, Theophilus sends greeting in the Lord.

1. At the outset the verdict which is in accordance with the truth satisfies but few. But the Lord speaking by the prophet says : " my judgment goeth forth as the light : " [1] and they who are surrounded with a horror of darkness and do not with clear comprehension perceive the nature of things, are covered with eternal shame and know by the issues of their acts that their efforts have been in vain. Wherefore we also have always desired for John who has for a time ruled the church of Constantinople grace that he might please God, and we have been slow to attribute to him the rash acts which have caused his downfall. But, not to speak of his other misdeeds, he has taken the Origenists into his confidence, has advanced many of them to the priesthood, and by committing this crime has saddened with no slight grief that man of God, Epiphanius of blessed memory, who has shone throughout all the world a bright star among bishops. And therefore he has rightly come to hear the words of doom : " Babylon is fallen, is fallen." [2]

2. Knowing then that the Saviour has said : " judge not according to the appearance but judge righteous judgment." [3]   . . .

LETTER CXIV.

TO THEOPHILUS.

Jerome writes to Theophilus to apologize for his delay in sending Latin versions of the latter's letter (CXIII.) and invective against John Chrysostom. Possibly, however, the allusion may be not to these but to some other work of Theophilus (e.g. a paschal letter.) This delay he attributes to the disturbed state of Palestine, the severity of the winter, the prevalent famine, and his own ill-health. He now sends the translations that he has made and, while he deprecates criticism on his own work, praises that of Theophilus, quoting with particular approval the directions given by this latter for the reverent care of the vessels used in celebrating the holy communion. The date of the letter is 405 A.D.

To the most blessed pope Theophilus, Jerome.

1. My delay in sending back to your holiness your treatise translated into Latin is accounted for by the many interruptions and obstacles that I have met with. There has been a sudden raid of the Isaurians ; Phœnicia and Galilee have been laid waste ; Palestine has been panic-stricken, and particularly Jerusalem ; we have all been engaged in making not books but walls. There has also been a severe winter and an almost unbearable famine ; and these have told heavily upon me who have the charge of many brothers. Amid

---

[1] Matt. iii. 10.   [1] Hos. vi. 5, LXX.   [2] Isa. xxi. 9.   [3] Joh. vii. 24.

these difficulties the work of translation went on by night, as I could save or snatch time to give to it. At last I got it done and by Lent nothing remained but to collate the fair copy with the original. However, just then a severe illness seized me and I was brought to the threshold of death, from which I have only been saved by God's mercy and your prayers; perhaps for this very purpose that I might fulfil your behest and render with its writer's elegance the charming volume which you have adorned with the scripture's fairest flowers. But bodily weakness and sorrow of heart have, I need hardly say, dulled the edge of my intellect and obstructed the free flow of my language.

2. I admire in your work its practical aim, designed as it is to instruct by the authority of scripture ignorant persons in all the churches concerning the reverence with which they must handle holy things and minister at Christ's altar; and to impress upon them that the sacred chalices, veils,[1] and other accessories used in the celebration of the Lord's passion are not mere lifeless and senseless objects devoid of holiness, but that rather, from their association with the body and blood of the Lord, they are to be venerated with the same awe as the body and the blood themselves.

3. Take back then your book, nay mine or better still ours; for when you flatter me you will but flatter yourself. It is for you that my brain has toiled; it is for you that I have striven with the poor resources of the Latin tongue to find an equivalent for the eloquence of the Greek. I have not indeed given a word-for-word rendering, as skilled translators do, nor have I counted out the money you have given to me coin by coin; but I have given you full weight. Some words may be missing but none of the sense is lost. Moreover I have translated into Latin and prefixed to this volume the letter that you sent to me, so that all who read it may know that I have acted under the commands of your holiness, and have not rashly and over-confidently undertaken a task that is beyond my powers. Whether I have succeeded in it I must leave to your judgment. Even though you may blame my weakness, you will at least give me credit for my good intention.

LETTER CXV.

TO AUGUSTINE.

A short but most friendly letter in which Jerome excuses himself for the freedom with which he has dealt with Augustine's questions (the allusion is to Letter CXII.) and hopes that henceforth they may be able to avoid controversy and to labour like brothers in the field of scripture.

Written probably in 405 A.D.

LETTER CXVI.

FROM AUGUSTINE.

A long letter in which Augustine for the third time (see Letters LVI., LXVII.) restates his opinion about Jerome's theory of the dispute between Peter and Paul at Antioch. In doing so, however, he disclaims all desire to hurt Jerome's feelings, apologizes for the tone of his previous letters, and again explains that it is not his fault that they have failed so long to reach Jerome.

Written shortly after the preceding.

LETTER CXVII.

TO A MOTHER AND DAUGHTER LIVING IN GAUL.

A monk of Gaul had during a visit to Bethlehem asked Jerome for advice under the following circumstances. His mother was a church-widow and his sister a religious virgin but the two could not agree. They were accordingly living apart but neither by herself. For each had taken into her house a monk ostensibly to act as steward but really to be a paramour. At the request of his visitor Jerome now writes to both mother and daughter urging them to dismiss their companions; or at any rate to live together: and pointing out the grave scandal that must otherwise be caused.

From the treatise *against Vigilantius* (§ 3) we learn that ill-natured critics maintained that the persons and circumstances described in the letter were alike fictitious and that Jerome in writing it was but exercising his ingenuity on a congenial theme.

The date is A. D. 405.

INTRODUCTION.

1. A certain brother from Gaul has told me that his virgin-sister and widowed mother, though living in the same city, have separate abodes and have taken to themselves clerical protectors either as guests or stewards; and that by thus associating with strangers they have caused more scandal than by living apart. When I groaned and expressed what I felt more by silence than words; "I beseech you," said he, "rebuke them in a letter and recall them to mutual harmony; make them once more mother and daughter." To whom I replied, "a nice task this that you lay upon me, for me a stranger to reconcile two women whom you, a son and brother, have failed to influence. You speak as though I occupied the chair of a bishop instead of being shut up in a monastic cell where, far removed from the world's turmoil, I lament the sins of the past and try to avoid the temptations of the present. Moreover, it is surely inconsistent, while one buries oneself out of sight, to allow one's tongue free course through the world." "You are too fearful," he replied; "where is

---

[1] So the embroidered cloths used in Catholic Churches to cover the sacramental elements are still called.

that old hardihood of yours which made you 'scour the world with copious salt,' as Horace says of Lucilius?"[1] "It is this," I rejoined, "that makes me shy and forbids me to open my lips. For through accusing crime I have been myself made out a criminal. Men have disputed and denied my assertions until, as the proverb goes, I hardly know whether I have ears or feeling left. The very walls have resounded with curses levelled at me, and 'I was the song of drunkards.'[2] Under the compulsion of an unhappy experience I have learned to be silent, thinking it better to set a watch before my mouth and to keep the door of my lips than to incline my heart to any evil thing,[3] or, while censuring the faults of others, myself to fall into that of detraction." In answer to this he said : "Speaking the truth is not detraction. Nor will you lecture the world by administering a particular rebuke ; for there are few persons, if any, open to this special charge. I beg of you, therefore, as I have put myself to the trouble of this long journey, that you will not suffer me to have come for nothing. The Lord knows that, after the sight of the holy places, my principal object in coming has been to heal by a letter from you the division between my sister and my mother." "Well," I replied, "I will do as you wish, for after all the letters will be to persons beyond the sea and words written with reference to definite persons can seldom offend other people. But I must ask you to keep what I say secret. You will take my advice with you to encourage you by the way ; if it is listened to, I will rejoice as much as you ; while if, as I rather think, it is rejected, I shall have wasted my words and you will have made a long journey for nothing."

The Letter.

2. In the first place my sister and my daughter, I wish you to know that I am not writing to you because I suspect anything evil of you. On the contrary I implore you to live in harmony, so as to give no ground for any such suspicions. Moreover had I supposed you fast bound in sin—far be this from you—I should never have written, for I should have known that my words would be addressed to deaf ears. Again, if I write to you somewhat sharply, I beg of you to ascribe this not to any harshness on my part but to the nature of the ailment which I attempt to treat. Cautery and the knife are the only remedies when mortification has once set in ; poison is the only antidote known for poison ; great pain can only be relieved by inflicting greater pain.

Lastly I must say this that even if your own consciences acquit you of misdoing, yet the very rumour of such brings disgrace upon you. Mother and daughter are names of affection ; they imply natural ties and reciprocal duties ; they form the closest of human relations after that which binds the soul to God. If you love each other, your conduct calls for no praise : but if you hate each other, you have committed a crime. The Lord Jesus was subject to His parents.[1] He reverenced that mother of whom He was Himself the parent ; He respected the foster-father whom He had Himself fostered ; for He remembered that He had been carried in the womb of the one and in the arms of the other. Wherefore also when He hung upon the cross He commended to His disciple[2] the mother whom He had never before His passion parted from Himself.

3. Well, I shall say no more to the mother, for perhaps age, weakness, and loneliness make sufficient excuses for her ; but to you the daughter I say : "Is a mother's house too small for you whose womb was not too small? When you have lived with her for ten months in the one, can you not bear to live with her for one day in the other? or are you unable to meet her gaze? Can it be that one who has borne you and reared you, who has brought you up and knows you, is dreaded by you as a witness of your home-life? If you are a true virgin, why do you fear her careful guardianship ; and, if you have fallen, why do you not openly marry? Wedlock is like a plank offered to a shipwrecked man and by its means you may remedy what previously you have done amiss. I do not mean that you are not to repent of your sin or that you are to continue in evil courses ; but, when a tie of the kind has been formed, I despair of breaking it altogether. However, a return to your mother will make it easier for you to bewail the virginity which you have lost through leaving her. Or if you are still unspotted and have not lost your chastity, be careful of it for you may lose it. Why must you live in a house where you must daily struggle for life and death? Can any one sleep soundly with a viper near him? No ; for, though it may not attack him it is sure to frighten him. It is better to be where there is no danger, than to be in danger and to escape. In the one case we have a calm ; in the other careful steering is necessary. In the one case we are filled with joy ; in the other we do but avoid sorrow.

4. But you will perhaps reply : "my mother is not well-behaved, she desires the things of the world, she loves riches, she disregards

[1] Hor. Sat. I. x. 3, 4.   [2] Ps. lxix. 12.   [3] Ps. cxli. 3, 4.   [1] Luke ii. 51.   [2] Joh. xix. 26, 27.

fasting, she stains her eyes with antimony, she likes to walk abroad in gay attire, she hinders me from the monastic vow, and so I cannot live with her." But first of all, even though she is as you say, you will have the greater reward for refusing to forsake her with all her faults. She has carried you in her womb, she has reared you; with gentle affection she has borne with the troublesome ways of your childhood. She has washed your linen, she has tended you when sick, and the sickness of maternity was not only borne for you but caused by you. She has brought you up to womanhood, she has taught you to love Christ. You ought not to be displeased with the behaviour of a mother who has consecrated you as a virgin to the service of your spouse. Still if you cannot put up with her dainty ways and feel obliged to shun them, and if your mother really is, as people so often say, a woman of the world, you have others, virgins like yourself, the holy company of chastity. Why, when you forsake your mother, do you choose for companion a man who perhaps has left behind him a sister and mother of his own? You tell me that she is hard to get on with and that he is easy; that she is quarrelsome and that he is amiable. I will ask you one question : Did you go straight from your home to the man, or did you fall in with him afterwards? If you went straight to him, the reason why you left your mother is plain. If you fell in with him afterwards, you shew by your choice what you missed under your mother's roof.[1] The pain that I inflict is severe and I feel the knife as much as you. "He that walketh uprightly walketh surely."[2] Only that my conscience would smite me, I should keep silence and be slow to blame others where I am not guiltless myself. Having a beam in my own eye I should be reluctant to see the mote in my neighbour's. But as it is I live far away among Christian brothers; my life with them is honourable as eyewitnesses of it can testify; I rarely see, or am seen by, others. It is most shameless, therefore, in you to refuse to copy me in respect of self-restraint, when you profess to take me as your model. If you say : "my conscience is enough for me too. God is my judge who is witness of my life. I care not what men may say;" let me urge upon you the apostle's words : "provide things honest" not only in the sight of God but also "in the sight of all men."[3] If any one carps at you for being a Christian and a virgin, mind it not; you have left your mother it may be said to live in a monastery among virgins, but censure on this score is your glory. When men blame a maid of God

not for self-indulgence but only for insensibility to affection, what they condemn as callous disregard of a parent is really a lively devotion towards God. For you prefer to your mother Him whom you are bidden to prefer to your own soul.[1] And if the day ever comes that she also shall so prefer Him, she will find in you not a daughter only but a sister as well.

5. "What then?" you will say, "is it a crime to have a man of religion in the house with me?" You seize me by the collar and drag me into court either to sanction what I disapprove or else to incur the dislike of many. A man of religion never separates a daughter from her mother. He welcomes both and respects both. A daughter may be as religious as she pleases; still a mother who is a widow is a guaranty for her chastity. If this person whoever he is is of the same age with yourself, he should honour your mother as though she were his own; and, if he is older, he should love you as a daughter and subject you to a mother's discipline. It is not good either for your reputation or for his that he should like you more than your mother; for his affection might appear to be less for you than for your youth. This is what I should say if a monk were not your brother and if you had no relatives able to protect you. But what excuse has a stranger for thrusting himself in where there are both a mother and a brother, the one a widow and the other a monk? It is good for you to feel that you are a daughter and a sister. However, if you cannot manage both, and if your mother is too hard a morsel to swallow, your brother at any rate should satisfy you. Or, if he is too harsh, she that bore you may prove more gentle. Why do you turn pale? Why do you get excited? Why do you blush, and with trembling lips betray the restlessness of your mind? One thing only can surpass a woman's love for her mother and brother; and that is her passion for her husband.

6. I am told, moreover, that you frequent suburban villas and their pleasant gardens in the company of relatives and intimate friends. I have no doubt that it is some female cousin or connexion who for her own satisfaction carries you about with her as a novel kind of attendant. Far be it from me to suspect that you would desire men's society; even though they should be those of your own family. But pray, maiden, answer me this; do you appear alone in your kinsfolk's society? or do you bring your favourite with you? Shameless as you may be, you will hardly venture to flaunt him in the eyes of the world. If you ever do so, your whole circle will cry out about both you

---

and him; every one's finger will be pointed at you; and your cousins who in your presence to please you call him a monk and a man of religion, will laugh at you behind your back for having such an unnatural husband. If on the other hand you go out alone—which I rather suppose to be the case—you will find yourself clothed in sober garb among slave youths, women married or soon to be so, wanton girls, and dandies with long hair and tight-fitting vests.[1] Some bearded fop will offer you his hand he will hold you up if you feel tired, and the pressure of his fingers will either be a temptation to you, or will shew that you are a temptation to him. Again when you sit down to table with married men and women, you will have to see kisses in which you have no part, and dishes partaken of which are not for you. Moreover it cannot but do you harm to see other women attired in silk dresses and gold brocades. At table also whether you like it or not, you will be forced to eat flesh and that of different kinds. To make you drink wine they will praise it as a creature of God. To induce you to take baths they will speak of dirt with disgust; and, when on second thoughts you do as you are bid, they will with one voice salute you as spotless and open, a thorough lady. Meantime some singer will give to the company a selection of softly flowing airs; and as he will not venture to look at other men's wives, he will constantly fix his eyes on you who have no protector. He will speak by nods and convey by his tone what he is afraid to put into words. Amid inducements to sensuality so marked as these, even iron wills are apt to be overcome with desire; an appetite which is the more imperious in virgins because they suppose that sweetest of which they have no experience. Heathen legends tell us that sailors actually ran their ships on the rocks that they might listen to the songs of the Sirens; and that the lyre of Orpheus had power to draw to itself trees and animals and to soften flints. In the banquet-hall chastity is hard to keep. A shining skin shews a sin-stained soul.

7. As a schoolboy I have read of one—and have seen his effigy true to the life in the streets—who continued to cherish an unlawful passion even when his flesh scarcely clung to his bones, and whose malady remained uncured until death cured it. What then will become of you a young girl physically sound, dainty, stout, and ruddy, if you allow yourself free range among flesh-dishes, wines, and baths, not to mention married men and bachelors? Even if when solicited you refuse to consent, you will take the fact of your being asked as evidence that you are considered handsome. A sensual mind pursues dishonourable objects with greater zest than honourable ones; and when a thing is forbidden hankers after it with greater pleasure. Your very dress, cheap and sombre as it is, is an index of your secret feelings. For it has no creases and trails along the ground to make you appear taller than you are. Your vest is purposely ripped asunder to shew what is beneath and while hiding what is repulsive, to reveal what is fair. As you walk, the very creaking of your black and shiny shoes attracts the notice of the young men. You wear stays to keep your breasts in place, and a heaving girdle closely confines your chest. Your hair covers either your forehead or your ears. Sometimes too you let your shawl drop so as to lay bare your white shoulders; and, as if unwilling that they should be seen, you quickly conceal what you have purposely disclosed. And when in public you for modesty's sake cover your face, like a practised harlot you only shew what is likely to please.

8. You will exclaim "How do you know what I am like, or how, when you are so far away, can you see what I am doing?" Your own brother's tears and sobs have told me, his frequent and scarcely endurable bursts of grief. Would that he had lied or that his words had been words of apprehension only and not of accusation. But, believe me, liars do not shed tears. He is indignant that you prefer to himself a young man, not it is true clothed in silk or wearing his hair long but muscular and dainty in the midst of his squalor; and that this fellow holds the purse-strings, looks after the weaving, allots the servants their tasks, rules the household, and buys from the market all that is needed. He is at once steward and master, and, as he anticipates the slaves in their duties,[1] he is carped at by all the domestics. Everything that their mistress has not given them they declare that he has stolen from them. Servants as a class are full of complaints; and no matter what you give them, it is always too little. For they do not consider how much you have but only how much you give; and they make up for their chagrin in the only way they can, that is, by grumbling. One calls him a parasite, another an impostor, another a money-seeker, another by some novel appellation that hits his fancy. They noise it abroad that he is constantly at your bed-side, that when you are sick he runs to fetch nurses, that he holds basins, airs sheets, and folds bandages for you. The world is only too ready to believe scandal, and stories invented at home soon get afloat

---

[1] Lineatos juvenes. The linea appears to have been a close-fitting jerkin.

[1] To ingratiate himself with their mistress. Cf. 108.

abroad. Nor need you be surprised if your servantmen and servantmaids get up such tales about you, when even your mother and your brother complain of your conduct.

9. Do, therefore, what I advise you and entreat you to do : if possible, be reconciled with your mother ; or, if this may not be, at least come to terms with your brother. Or if you are filled with an implacable hatred of relationships usually so dear, separate at all events from the man, whom you are said to prefer to your own flesh and blood, and, if even this is impossible for you, (for, if you could leave him, you would certainly return to your own) pay more regard to appearances in harbouring him as your companion. Live in a separate building and take your meals apart ; for if you remain under one roof with him slanderers will say that you share with him your bed. You may thus easily get help from him when you feel you need it, and yet to a considerable degree escape public discredit. Yet you must take care not to contract the stain of which Jeremiah tells us that no nitre or fuller's soap can wash it out.[1] When you wish him to come to see you, always have witnesses present ; either friends, or freedmen, or slaves. A good conscience is afraid of no man's eyes. Let him come in unembarrassed and go out at his ease. Let his silent looks, his unspoken words and his whole carriage, though at times they may imply embarrassment, yet indicate peace of mind. Pray, open your ears and listen to the outcry of the whole city. You have already both of you lost your own names and are known each by that of the other. You are spoken of as his, and he is said to be yours. Your mother and your brother have heard this and are ready to take you in between them. They implore you to consent to this arrangement, so that the scandal of your intimacy with this man which is confined to yourself may give place to a glory common to all. You can live with your mother and he with your brother. You can more boldly shew your regard for one who is your brother's comrade ; and your mother will more properly esteem one who is the friend of her son and not of her daughter. But if you frown and refuse to accept my advice, this letter will openly expostulate with you. 'Why,' it will say, ' do you beset another man's servant ? Why do you make Christ's minister your slave ? Look at the people and scan each face as it comes under your view. When he reads in the church all eyes are fixed upon you ; and you, using the licence of a wife, glory in your shame. Secret infamy no longer contents you ; you call boldness freedom ; " you have a whore's forehead and refuse to be ashamed." [2]

10. Once more you exclaim that I am over-suspicious, a thinker of evil, too ready to follow rumours. What ? I suspicious ? I ill-natured ? I, who as I said in the beginning have taken up my pen because I have no suspicions ? Or is it you that are careless, loose, disdainful ? You who at the age of twenty-five have netted in your embrace a youth whose beard has scarcely grown ? An excellent instructor he must be, able no doubt by his severe looks both to warn and frighten you ! No age is safe from lust, yet gray hairs are some security for decent conduct. A day will surely come (for time glides by imperceptibly) when your handsome young favourite will find a wealthier or more youthful mistress. For women soon age and particularly if they live with men. You will be sorry for your decision and regret your obstinacy in a day when your means and reputation shall be alike gone, and when this unhappy intimacy shall be happily broken off. But perhaps you feel sure of your ground and see no reason to fear a breach where affection has had so long a time to develop and grow.

11. To you also, her mother, I must say a word. Your years put you beyond the reach of scandal ; do not take advantage of this to indulge in sin. It is more fitting that your daughter should learn from you how to part from a companion than that you should learn from her how to give up a paramour. You have a son, a daughter, and a son-in-law, or at least one who is your daughter's partner.[1] Why then should you seek other society than theirs, or wish to kindle anew expiring flames ? It would be more becoming in you to screen your daughter's fault than to make it an excuse for your own misdoing. Your son is a monk, and, if he were to live with you, he would strengthen you in your religious profession and in your vow of widowhood. Why should you take in a complete stranger, especially in a house not large enough to hold a son and a daughter ? You are old enough to have grand-children. Invite the pair home then. Your daughter went away by herself ; let her return with this man. I say 'man' and not 'husband' that none may cavil. The word describes his sex and not his relation to her. Or if she blushes to accept your offer or finds the house in which she was born too narrow for her, then move both of you to her abode. However limited may be its accommodation, it can take in a mother and a brother better than a stranger. In fact, if she lives in the same house and occupies the same room with a man, she cannot long preserve her chastity. It is different when two women and two men live together. If the third person concerned

---

[1] Jer. ii. 22.   [2] From Jer. iii. 3.   [1] Contubernalis.

—he, I mean, who fosters your old age—will not make one of the party and causes only dissension and confusion, the pair of you[1] can do without him. But if the three of you remain together, then your brother and son[2] will offer him a sister and a mother. Others may speak of the two strangers as step-father and son-in-law ; but your son must speak of them as his foster-father and his brother.

NOTE.

12. Working quickly I have completed this letter in a single night anxious alike to gratify a friend and to try my hand on a rhetorical theme. Then early in the morning he has knocked at my door on the point of starting. I wish also to shew my detractors that like them I too can say the first thing that comes into my head. I have, therefore, introduced few quotations from the scriptures and have not, as in most of my books, interwoven its flowers in my discourse. The letter has been, in fact, dictated off-hand and poured forth by lamp-light so fast that my tongue has outstripped my secretaries' pens and that my volubility has baffled the expedients of shorthand. I have said this much that those who make no allowances for want of ability may make some for want of time.

LETTER CXVIII.

TO JULIAN.

Jerome writes to Julian, a wealthy nobleman apparently of Dalmatia (§ 5), to console him for the loss of his wife and two daughters all of whom had recently died. He reminds Julian of the trials of Job and recommends him to imitate the patience of the patriarch. He also urges him to follow the example set by Pammachius and Paulinus, that is, to give up his riches and to become a monk for the sake of Christ. The date of the letter is 406 A.D.

1. At the very instant of his departure Ausonius, a son to me as he is a brother to you, gave me a late glimpse of himself but quickly hurried away again, saying good-morning and good-bye together. Yet he thought that he would return empty-handed unless he could bring you some trifle from me however hastily written. Clothed in scarlet as befitted his rank, he had already strapped on his sword-belt[3] and sent down a requisition to have a stage-horse saddled. Still he made me send for my secretary and dictate a letter to him. This I did with such rapidity that his nimble hand could hardly keep pace with my words or manage to put down my hurried

sentences. Thus hasty dictation has taken the place of careful writing ; and, if I break my long silence, it is but to offer you an expression of good will. This is an impromptu letter without logical order or charm of style. You must look on me for once as a friend only ; you will find, I assure you, nothing of the orator here. Bear in mind that it has been dashed off on the spur of the moment and given as a provision for the way to one in a hurry to depart.

Holy scripture says : "a tale out of season is as musick in mourning."[1] Accordingly I have disdained the graces of rhetoric and those charms of eloquence which boys find so captivating, and have fallen back on the serious tone of the sacred writings. For in these are to be found true medicines for wounds and sure remedies for sorrow. In these a mother receives back her only son even on the bier.[2] In these a crowd of mourners hears the words : "the maid is not dead but sleepeth."[3] In these one that is four days dead comes forth bound at the call of the Lord."[4]

2. I hear that in a short space of time you have suffered several bereavements, that you have buried in quick succession two young unmarried daughters, and that Faustina, most chaste and loyal of wives, your sister in the fervour of her faith and your one comfort in the loss of your children, has suddenly fallen asleep and been taken from you. You have been like a shipwrecked man who has no sooner reached the shore than he falls into the hands of brigands, or in the eloquent language of the prophet like one "who did flee from a lion, and a bear met him ; or went into the house, and leaned his hand on the wall, and a serpent bit him."[5] Pecuniary losses have followed your bereavements ; the entire province has been overrun by a barbarian enemy, and in the general devastation your private property has been destroyed, your flocks and herds have been driven off, and your poor slaves either made prisoners or else slain. To crown all, your only daughter, made all the more dear to you by the loss of the others, has for her husband a young nobleman who, to say nothing worse of him, has given you more occasion for sorrow than for rejoicing. Such is the list of the trials that have been laid upon you ; such is the conflict waged by the old enemy against Julian a raw recruit to Christ's standard. If you look only to yourself your troubles are indeed great but if you look to the strong Warrior,[6] they are but child's play and the conflict is only the semblance of one. After

1 Viz. the mother and daughter.
2 Viz. the monk who was son of the widow and brother of the virgin.
3 Cf. Letter LX. § 9.

1 Ecclus. xxii. 6.　　　2 Luke vii. 11-15.
3 Matt. ix. 24.　　　4 Joh. xi. 39, 43, 44.
5 Amos v. 19.　　　6 Cf. Rev. xix. 11-16.

untold trials a wicked wife was still left to the blessed Job, the devil hoping that he might learn from her to blaspheme God. You on the other hand have been deprived of an excellent one that you might learn to go without consolation in the hour of misfortune. Yet it is far harder to put up with a wife whom you dislike than it is to mourn for one whom you dearly love. Moreover when Job's children died they found a common tomb beneath the ruins of his house, and all he could do to shew his parental affection was to rend his garments to fall upon the ground and to worship, saying: "Naked came I out of my mother's womb, and naked shall I return thither: the Lord gave and the Lord hath taken away: it has been as the Lord pleased: blessed be the name of the Lord."[1] But you, to put the matter briefly, have been allowed to perform the obsequies of your dear ones; and those obsequies have been attended by many respectful kinsmen and comforting friends. Again Job lost all his wealth at once; and, as, one after another, the messengers of woe unfolded new calamities, he flinched as little as the sage of whom Horace writes:[2]—

Shatter the world to atoms if you will.
Fearless will be the man on whom it falls.

But with you the case is different. The greater part of your substance has been left to you, and your trials have not been greater than you can bear. For you have not yet attained to such perfection that the devil has to marshal all his forces against you.

3. Long ago this wealthy proprietor and still wealthier father was made by a sudden stroke destitute and bereaved. But as, in spite of all that befel him, he had not sinned before God or spoken foolishly, the Lord—exulting in the victory of his servant and regarding Job's patience as His own triumph—said to the devil: "Hast thou considered my servant Job, that there is none like him in the earth, a perfect and an upright man, one that feareth God and escheweth evil? and still he holdeth fast his integrity?"[3] He finely adds the last clause because it is difficult for innocence to refrain from murmuring when it is overborne by misfortune; and to avoid making a shipwreck of faith when it sees that its sufferings are unjustly inflicted. The devil answered the Lord and said: "Skin for skin, yea, all that a man hath will he give for his life. But put forth thine hand now, and touch his bone and his flesh, and he will curse thee to thy face."[4] See how crafty the adversary is, and how hardened in sin his evil ways have made him! He knows the difference between things external and internal. He knows that even the philosophers of the world call the former ἀδιάφορα, that is indifferent, and that the perfection of virtue does not consist in losing or disdaining them. It is the latter, those that are internal and objects of preference,[1] the loss of which inevitably causes chagrin. Wherefore he boldly contradicts what God has said and declares that Job deserves no praise at all; since he has yielded up no part of himself but only what is outside himself, since he has given for his own skin the skins of his children, and since he has but laid down his purse to secure the health of his body. From this your sagacity may perceive that your trials have so far only reached the point at which you give hide for hide, skin for skin, and are ready to give all that you have for your life. The Lord has not yet stretched forth His hand upon you, or touched your flesh, or broken your bones. Yet it is when such afflictions as these are laid upon you that it is hard not to groan and not to 'bless' God to His face, that is to curse Him. The word 'bless' is used in the same way in the books of Kings where it is said of Naboth that he 'blessed' God and the king and was therefore stoned by the people.[2] But the Lord knew His champion and felt sure that this great hero would even in this last and severest conflict prove unconquerable. Therefore He said: "Behold he is in thine hand; but save his life."[3] The holy man's flesh is placed at the devil's disposal, but his vital powers are withheld. For if the devil had smitten that on which sensation and mental judgment depend, the guilt arising from a misuse of these faculties I would have lain at the door not of him who committed the sin but of him who had overthrown the balance of his mind.

4. Others may praise you if they will, and celebrate your victories over the devil. They may eulogize you for the smiling face with which you bore the loss of your daughters, or for the resolution with which, forty days after they fell asleep, you exchanged your mourning for a white robe to attend the dedication of a martyr's bones; unconcerned for a bereavement which was the concern of the whole city, and anxious only to share in a martyr's triumph. Nay, say they, when you bore your wife to burial, it was not as one dead but as one setting forth on a journey. But I shall not deceive you with flattering words or take the ground from under your feet with slippery praises. Rather will I say what it is good for you to hear: "My son, if thou come to serve

---

[1] Job i. 20, 21, LXX.　[2] Horace, C. III. iii. 7, 8.
[3] Job ii. 3.　[4] Job ii. 4, 5.

[1] He alludes to the προηγμένα of the Stoics.
[2] 1 K. xxi. 10, Vulg. (which mistranslates the neutral verb of the Hebrew).
[3] Job ii. 6.

the Lord, prepare thy soul for temptation,"[1] and "when thou shalt have done all those things which are commanded thee, say, I am an unprofitable servant; I have done that which was my duty to do."[2] Say to God: "the children that thou hast taken from me were Thine own gift. The hand-maiden that Thou hast taken to Thyself Thou also didst lend to me for a season to be my solace. I am not aggrieved that Thou hast taken her back, but thankful rather that Thou hast previously given her to me."

Once upon a time a rich young man boasted that he had fulfilled all the requirements of the law, but the Lord said to him (as we read in the gospel): "One thing thou lackest: if thou wilt be perfect, go thy way, sell whatsoever thou hast, and give to the poor; and come and follow me."[3] He who declared that he had done all things gave way at the first onset to the power of riches. Wherefore they who are rich find it hard to enter the kingdom of heaven, a kingdom which desires for its citizens souls that soar aloft free from all ties and hindrances. "Go thy way," the Lord says, "and sell" not a part of thy substance but "all that thou hast, and give to the poor;" not to thy friends or kinsfolk or relatives, not to thy wife or to thy children. I will even go farther and say: keep back nothing for yourself because you fear to be some day poor, lest by so doing you share the condemnation of Ananias and Sapphira;[4] but give everything to the poor and make to yourself friends of the mammon of unrighteousness that they may receive you into everlasting habitations.[5] Obey the Master's injunction "follow me,"[6] and take the Lord of the world for your possession; that you may be able to sing with the prophet, "The Lord is my portion,"[7] and like a true Levite[8] may possess no earthly inheritance. I cannot but advise you thus if you wish to be perfect, if you desire to attain the pinnacle of the apostles' glory, if you wish to take up your cross and to follow Christ. When once you have put your hand to the plough you must not look back;[9] when once you stand on the housetop you must think no more of your clothes within; to escape your Egyptian mistress[10] you must abandon the cloak that belongs to this world. Even Elijah, in his quick translation to heaven could not take his mantle with him, but left in the world the garments of the world.[11] Such conduct, you will object, is for him who would emulate the apostles, for the man who aspires to be perfect. But why should not you aspire to be perfect? Why should not you who hold a foremost place in the world hold a foremost place also in Christ's household? Is it because you have been married? Peter was married too, but when he forsook his ship and his nets he forsook his wife also.[1] The Lord who wills that all men shall be saved and prefers the repentance of a sinner to his death[2] has, in His almighty providence removed from you this excuse. Your wife can no longer draw you earthwards, but you can follow her as she draws you heavenwards. Provide good things for your children who have gone home before you to the Lord. Do not let their portions go to swell their sister's fortune, but use them to ransom your own soul and to give sustenance to the needy. These are the necklaces your daughters expect from you; these are the jewels they wish to see sparkle on their foreheads. The money which they would have wasted in buying silks may well be considered saved when it provides cheap clothing for the poor. They ask you for their portions. Now that they are united to their spouse they are loth to appear poor and undistinguished: they desire to have the ornaments that befit their rank.

5. Nor may you excuse yourself on the score of your noble station and the responsibilities of wealth. Look at Pammachius and at Paulinus that presbyter of glowing faith both of whom have offered to the Lord not only their riches but themselves. In spite of the devil and his shuffling they have by no means given skin for skin, but have consecrated their own flesh and bones, yea and their very souls unto the Lord. Surely these may lead you to higher things both by their example and by their preaching, that is, by their deeds and words. You are of noble birth so are they: but in Christ they are made noble still. You are rich and held in repute, so once were they: but now instead of being rich and held in repute they are poor and obscure, yet because it is for Christ's sake, they are really richer and more famous than ever. You too it is true, shew yourself beneficent, you are said to minister to the wants of the saints, to entertain monks, and to present large sums of money to churches. This however is only the a b c of your soldiership. You despise money the world's philosophers have done the same. One of these[3]—to say nothing of the rest— cast the price of many possessions into the sea saying as he did so "To the bottom with you ye provokers of evil lusts. I shall drown you in the sea that you may never drown me in sin." If then a philosopher—a creature o

[1] Ecclus. ii. 1.   [2] Luke xvii. 10 (adapted).
[3] Mark x. 21.   [4] Acts v. 1-10.
[5] Luke xvi. 9.   [6] Matt. ix. 9.   [7] Ps. xvi. 5.
[8] Nu. xviii. 20-24.   [9] Luke ix. 62.
[10] Gen. xxxix. 12.   [11] 2 K. ii. 11, 13.

[1] But see 1 Cor. ix. 5.   [2] 1 Tim. ii. 4; 2 Pet. iii. 9.
[3] Crates the Theban.

anity whom popular applause can buy and sell—laid down all his burthen at once, how can you think that you have reached virtue's crowning height when you have yielded up but a portion of yours? It is you yourself that the Lord wishes for, "a living sacrifice . . . acceptable unto God."[1] Yourself, I say, and not what you have. And therefore, as he trained Israel by subjecting it to many plagues and afflictions, so does He now admonish you by sending you trials of different kinds. "For whom the Lord loveth he chasteneth, and scourgeth every son whom he receiveth."[2] The poor widow did but cast two mites into the treasury; yet because she cast in all that she had it is said of her that she surpassed all the rich in offering gifts to God.[3] Such gifts are valued not by their weight but by the good-will with which they are made. You may have spent your substance upon numbers of people, and a portion of your fellows may have reason to rejoice in your bounty; yet those who have received nothing at your hands are still more numerous. Neither the wealth of Darius nor the riches of Crœsus would suffice to satisfy the wants of the world's poor. But if you once give yourself to the Lord and resolve to follow the Saviour in the perfection of apostolic virtue, then you will come to see what your place has hitherto been, and how you have lagged in the rear of Christ's army. Hardly had you begun to mourn for your dead daughters when the fear of Christ dried the tears of paternal affection upon your cheeks. It was a great triumph of faith, true. But how much greater was that won by Abraham who was content to lay his only son, of whom he had been told that he was to inherit the world, yet did not cease to hope that after death Isaac would live again.[4] Jephthah too offered up his virgin daughter, and for this is placed by the apostle in the roll of the saints.[5] I would not therefore have you offer to the Lord only what a thief may steal from you or an enemy fall upon, or a proscription confiscate, what is liable to fluctuations in value now going up and now down, what belongs to a succession of masters who follow each other as fast as in the sea wave follows wave, and—to say everything in a word—what, whether you like it or not, you must leave behind you when you die. Rather offer to God that which no enemy can carry off and no tyrant take from you, which will go down with you into the grave, nay on to the kingdom of heaven and the enchantments of paradise. You already build monasteries and support in the various islands of Dalmatia a large number of holy men. But you would do better still if you were to live among these holy men as a holy man yourself. "Be ye holy, saith the Lord, for I am holy."[1] The apostles boasted that they had left all things and had followed the Saviour."[2] We do not read that they left anything except their ship and their nets; yet they were crowned with the approval of Him who was to be their judge. Why? Because in offering up themselves they had indeed left all that they had.

6. I say all this not in disparagement of your good works or because I wish to underrate your generosity in almsgiving, but because I do not wish you to be a monk among men of the world and a man of the world among monks. I shall require every sacrifice of you for I hear that your mind is devoted to the service of God. If some friend, or follower, or kinsman tries to combat this counsel of mine and to recall you to the pleasures of a handsome table, be sure that he is thinking less of your soul than of his own belly, and remember that death in a moment terminates both elegant entertainments and all other pleasures provided by wealth. Within the short space of twenty days you have lost two daughters, the one eight years old and the other six; and do you suppose that one so old as you are yourself can live much longer? David tells you how long a time you can look for: "the days of our years are threescore years and ten; and if by reason of strength they be fourscore years, yet is their strength labour and sorrow."[3] Happy is he and to be held worthy of the highest bliss whom old age shall find a servant of Christ and whom the last day shall discover fighting for the Saviour's cause. "He shall not be ashamed when he speaketh with his enemies in the gate."[4] On his entrance into paradise it shall be said to him: "thou in thy lifetime receivedst evil things but now here thou art comforted."[5] The Lord will not avenge the same sin twice. Lazarus, formerly poor and full of ulcers, whose sores the dogs licked and who barely managed to live, poor wretch, on the crumbs that fell from the rich man's table, is now welcomed into Abraham's bosom and has the joy of finding a father in the great patriarch. It is difficult nay impossible for a man to enjoy both the good things of the present and those of the future, to satisfy his belly here and his mind yonder, to pass from the pleasures of this life to the pleasures of that, to be first in both worlds, and to be held in honour both on earth and in heaven.

7. And if in your secret thoughts you are troubled because I who give you this advice am not myself what I desire you to be, and

[1] Rom. xii. 1.   [2] Heb. xii. 6.   [3] Mark xii. 43, 44.
[4] Cf. Heb. xi. 17–19.   [5] Judg. xi. 34–40; Heb. xi. 32.

[1] Lev. xix. 2; 1 Pet. i. 16.   [2] Luke xviii. 28.   [3] Ps. xc. 10.
[4] Ps. cxxvii. 5 (adapted from R.V.S.)   [5] Luke xvi. 25 (adapted).

because you have seen some after beginning well fall midway on their journey ; I shall briefly plead in reply that the words which I speak are not mine but those of the Lord and Saviour, and that I urge upon you not the standard which is possible to myself but the ideal which every true servant of Christ must wish for and realize. Athletes as a rule are stronger than their backers ; yet the weaker presses the stronger to put forth all his efforts. Look not upon Judas denying his Lord but upon Paul confessing Him. Jacob's father was a man of great wealth ; yet, when Jacob went to Mesopotamia, he went alone and destitute leaning upon his staff. When he felt weary he had to lie down by the wayside and, delicately nurtured as he had been by his mother Rebekah, was forced to content himself with a stone for a pillow. Yet it was then [1] that he saw the ladder set up from earth to heaven, and the angels ascending and descending on it, and the Lord above it holding out a helping hand to such as fall and encouraging the climbers to fresh efforts by the vision of Himself. Therefore is the spot called Bethel or the house of God ; for there day by day there is ascending and descending. When they are careless, even holy men lose their footing ; and sinners, if they wash away their stains with tears regain their place. I say this not that those coming down may frighten you but that those going up may stimulate you. For evil can never supply a model and even in worldly affairs incentives to virtue come always from the brighter side.

But I have forgotten my purpose and the limits set to my letter. I should have liked to say a great deal more. Indeed all that I can say is inadequate alike to satisfy the seriousness of the subject and the claims of your rank. But here is our Ausonius beginning to be impatient for the sheets, hurrying the secretaries, and in his impatience at the neighing of his horse, accusing my poor wits of slowness. Remember me, then, and prosper in Christ. And one thing more ; follow the example set you at home by the holy Vera,[2] who like a true follower of Christ does not fear to endure the hardships of pilgrimage. Find in a woman your ' leader in this high emprise.' [3]

LETTER CXIX.

TO MINERVIUS AND ALEXANDER.

Minervius and Alexander two monks of Toulouse had written to Jerome asking him to explain for them a large number of passages in scripture. Jerome in his

---

[1] Gen. xxviii. 12, 13. Cp. Letters CVIII. § 13, and CXXIII. § 15.
[2] Of this lady nothing is known.
[3] Words of Virg. A. i. 364, relating to Dido.

reply postpones most of these to a future time but deals with two in detail viz. (1) " we shall not all sleep but we shall all be changed," 1 Cor. xv. 51 ; and (2) " we shall be caught up in the clouds," 1 Th. iv. 17. With regard to (1) Jerome prefers the reading " we shall all sleep but we shall not all be changed," and with regard to (2) he looks upon the language as metaphorical and interprets it to mean that believers will be ' assumed' into the company of the apostles and prophets. The date of the letter is 406 A.D.

LETTER CXX.

TO HEDIBIA.[1]

At the request of Hedibia, a lady of Gaul much interested in the study of scripture, Jerome deals with the following twelve questions. It will be noticed that several of them belong to the historical criticism of our own day.

(1) How can anyone be perfect ? and How ought a widow without children to live to God ?
(2) What is the meaning of Matt. xxvi. 29 ?
(3) How are the discrepancies in the evangelical narratives to be accounted for ? How can Matt. xxviii. be reconciled with Mark xvi. 1, 2 ?
(4) How can Matt. xxviii. 9 (Saturday evening) be reconciled with John xx. 1–18 (Sunday morning) ?
(5) How can Matt. xxviii. 9 be reconciled with John xx. 17 ?
(6) How was it that, if there was a guard of soldiers at the sepulchre, Peter and John were allowed to go freely ? (Matt. xxvii. 66 : John xx. 1–8.)
(7) How is the statement of Matthew and Mark that the apostles were ordered to go into Galilee to see Jesus there to be reconciled with that of Luke and John who make Him appear to them in Jerusalem ?
(8) What is the meaning of Matt. xxvii. 50, 51 ?
(9) How is the statement of John xx. 22 that Jesus breathed on his apostles the Holy Ghost to be reconciled with that of Luke (Luke xxiv. 49 : Acts i. 4) that He would send it to them after His ascension ?
(10) What is the meaning of the passage, Rom. ix. 14–29 ?
(11) What is the meaning of 2 Cor. ii. 16 ?
(12) What is the meaning of 1 Th. v. 23 ?
The date of the letter is 406 or 407 A.D.

LETTER CXXI.

TO ALGASIA.

Jerome writes to a lady of Gaul named Algasia to answer eleven questions which she had submitted to him. They were as follows :—
(1) How is Luke vii. 18, 19, to be reconciled with John i. 36 ?
(2) What is the meaning of Matt. xii. 20 ?
(3) And of Matt. xvi. 24 ?
(4) And of Matt. xxiv. 19, 20 ?
(5) And of Luke ix. 53 ?
(6) What is the meaning of the parable of the unjust steward ?
(7) What is the meaning of Rom. v. 7 ?
(8) And of Rom. vii. 8 ?
(9) And of Rom. ix. 3 ?
(10) And of Col. ii. 18 ?
(11) And of 2 Th. ii. 3 ?
The date of the letter is 406 A.D.

---

[1] For Hedibia and her family, see an article in Dict. of Chris. Biog.

LETTER CXXII.

TO RUSTICUS.

Rusticus and Artemia his wife having made a vow of continence broke it. Artemia proceeded to Palestine to do penance for her sin and Rusticus promised to follow her. However he failed to do so, and Jerome was asked to write this letter in the hope that it might induce him to fulfil his promise. The date is about 408 A.D.

1. I am induced to write to you, a stranger to a stranger, by the entreaties of that holy servant of Christ Hedibia[1] and of my daughter in the faith Artemia, once your wife but now no longer your wife but your sister and fellow-servant. Not content with assuring her own salvation she has sought yours also, in former days at home and now in the holy places. She is anxious to emulate the thoughtfulness of the apostles Andrew and Philip; who after Christ had found them, desired in their turn to find, the one his brother Simon and the other his friend Nathanael.[2] To the former of these it was said "Thou art Simon, the son of Jona : thou shalt be called Cephas which is by interpretation a stone ;"[3] while the latter, whose name Nathanael means the gift of God, was comforted by Christ's witness to him : "behold an Israelite indeed in whom is no guile."[4] So of old Lot[5] desired to rescue his wife as well as his two daughters, and refusing to leave blazing Sodom and Gomorrah until he was himself half-on-fire, tried to lead forth one who was tied and bound by her past sins. But in her despair she lost her composure, and looking back became a monument of an unbelieving soul.[6] Yet, as if to make up for the loss of a single woman, Lot's glowing faith set free the whole city of Zoar. In fact when he left the dark valleys in which Sodom lay and came to the mountains, the sun rose upon him as he entered Zoar or the little City ; so-called because the little faith that Lot possessed, though unable to save greater places, was at least able to preserve smaller ones. For one who had gone so far astray as to live in Gomorrah could not all at once reach the noonland where Abraham, the friend of God,[7] entertained God and His angels.[8] (For it was in Egypt that Joseph fed his brothers, and when the bride speaks to the Bridegroom her cry is : "tell me where thou feedest, where thou makest thy flock to rest at noon."[9]) Good men have always sorrowed for the sins of others. Samuel of old lamented for Saul[10] because he neglected to treat the ulcers of pride with the balm of penitence. And Paul

wept for the Corinthians[1] who refused to wash out with their tears the stains of fornication. For the same reason Ezekiel swallowed the book where were written within and without song, and lamentation and woe ;[2] the song in praise of the righteous, the lamentation over the penitent, and the woe for those of whom it is written, "When the wicked man falleth into the depths of evil, then is he filled with scorn."[3] It is to these that Isaiah alludes when he says : "in that day did the Lord God of hosts call to weeping and to mourning and to baldness and to girding with sackcloth : and behold joy and gladness, slaying oxen, and killing sheep, eating flesh" and saying, "let us eat and drink, for tomorrow we die."[4] Yet of such persons Ezekiel is bidden to speak thus : "O thou son of man, speak unto the house of Israel ; Thus ye speak, saying, If our transgressions and our sins be upon us, and we pine away in them, how should we then live ? Say unto them, As I live, saith the Lord God, I have no pleasure in the death of the wicked ; but that the wicked turn from his way and live," and again, "turn ye, turn ye from your evil ways; for why will ye die, O house of Israel?"[5] Nothing makes God so angry as when men from despair of better things cleave to those which are worse ; and indeed this despair in itself is a sign of unbelief. One who despairs of salvation can have no expectation of a judgment to come. For if he dreaded such, he would by doing good works prepare to meet his Judge. Let us hear what God says through Jeremiah, "withhold thy foot from a rough way and thy throat from thirst,"[6] and again "shall they fall, and not arise ? Shall he turn away, and not return ?"[7] Let us hear also what God says by Isaiah : "When thou shalt turn and bewail thyself, then shalt thou be saved, and then shalt thou know where thou hast hitherto been."[8] We do not realize the miseries of sickness till returning health reveals them to us. So sins serve as a foil to the blessedness of virtue ; and light shines more brightly when it is relieved against darkness. Ezekiel uses language like that of the other prophets because he is animated by a similar spirit. "Repent," he cries, "and turn yourselves from all your transgressions; so iniquity shall not be your ruin. Cast away from you all your transgressions whereby ye have transgressed ; and make you a new heart and a new spirit : for why will ye die, O house of Israel? For I have no pleasure in the death of him that dieth, saith the Lord."[9] Wherefore in a subsequent passage

---

[1] This lady lived in Gaul and was a diligent student of scripture. Letter CXX. is addressed to her.
[2] Joh. i. 41, 45.   [3] Joh. i. 42.   [4] Joh. i. 47.
[5] Gen. xix. 15–26.   [6] Cf. Wisdom, x. 7.   [7] Jas. ii. 23.
[8] Gen. xviii. 1.   [9] Cant. i. 7.   [10] 1 Sam. xv. 35.

[1] 2 Cor. ii. 4.   [2] Ezek. ii. 10, LXX.
[3] Prov. xviii. 3, LXX.   [4] Isa. xxii. 12, 13.
[5] Ezek. xxxiii. 10, 11.   [6] Jer. ii. 25, LXX.
[7] Jer. viii. 4.   [8] Isa. xxx. 15, LXX.
[9] Ezek. xviii. 30–32.

he says: "As I live, saith the Lord God, I have no pleasure in the death of the wicked: but that the wicked turn from his way and live."[1] These words shew us that the mind must not through disbelief in the promised blessings give way to despair; and that the soul once marked out for perdition must not refuse to apply remedies on the ground that its wounds are past curing. Ezekiel describes God as swearing, that if we refuse to believe His promise in regard to our salvation we may at least believe His oath. It is with full confidence that the righteous man prays and says, "Turn us, O God of our salvation, and cause thine anger toward us to cease,"[2] and again, "Lord, by thy favour thou hast made my mountain to stand strong: thou didst hide thy face and I was troubled."[3] He means to say, "when I forsook the foulness of my faults for the beauty of virtue, God strengthened my weakness with His grace." Lo, I hear His promise: "I will pursue mine enemies and overtake them: neither will I turn again till they are consumed,"[4] so that I who was once thine enemy and a fugitive from thee, shall be laid hold of by thine hand. Cease not from pursuing me till my wickedness is consumed, and I return to my old husband who will give me my wool and my flax, my oil and my fine flour and will feed me with the richest foods.[5] He it was who hedged up and enclosed my evil ways[6] that I might find Him the true way, who says in the gospel, "I am the way, the truth, and the life."[7] Hear the words of the prophet: "they that sow in tears shall reap in joy. He that goeth forth and weepeth, bearing precious seed, shall doubtless come again with rejoicing, bringing his sheaves with him."[8] Say also with him: "All the night make I my bed to swim; I water my couch with my tears"[9]: and again, "As the hart panteth after the water brooks, so panteth my soul after thee, O God. My soul thirsteth for God, for the living God: when shall I come and appear before God? My tears have been my meat day and night,"[10] and in another place, "O God, thou art my God; early will I seek thee: my soul thirsteth for thee, my flesh longeth for thee in a dry and weary land where no water is. So have I looked upon thee in the sanctuary."[11] For although my soul has thirsted after thee, yet much more have I sought thee by the labour of my flesh and have not been able to look upon thee in thy sanctuary; not at any rate till I have first dwelt in a land barren of sin, where the weary wayfarer is no more assailed by the adversary, and where there are no pools or rivers of lust.

The Saviour also wept over the city of Jerusalem because its inhabitants had not repented;[1] and Peter washed out his triple denial with bitter tears,[2] thus fulfilling the words of the prophet: "rivers of waters run down mine eyes."[3] Jeremiah too laments over his impenitent people, saying: "Oh that my head were waters and mine eyes a fountain of tears, that I might weep day and night for . . . my people!"[4] And farther on he gives a reason for his lamentation: "weep ye not for the dead," he writes, "neither bemoan him: but weep sore for him that goeth away: for he shall return no more."[5] The Jew and the Gentile therefore are not to be bemoaned, for they have never been in the Church and have died once for all (it is of these that the Saviour says: "let the dead bury their dead"[6]); weep rather for those who by reason of their crimes and sins go away from the Church, and who suffering condemnation for their faults shall no more return to it. It is in this sense that the prophet speaks to ministers of the Church, calling them its walls and towers, and saying to each in turn, "O wall, let tears run down."[7] In this way, it is prophetically implied, you will fulfil the apostolic precept: "rejoice with them that do rejoice and weep with them that weep,"[8] and by your tears you will melt the hard hearts of sinners till they too weep; whereas, if they persist in evil doing they will find these words applied to them, "I . . . planted thee a noble vine, wholly a right seed: how then art thou turned into the degenerate plant of a strange vine unto me?"[9] and again "saying to a stock, Thou art my father; and to a stone, Thou hast brought me forth: for they have turned their back unto me, and not their face."[10] He means, they would not turn towards God in penitence; but in the hardness of their hearts turned their backs upon Him to insult Him. Wherefore also the Lord says to Jeremiah: "hast thou seen that which backsliding Israel hath done? She is gone up upon every high mountain and under every green tree, and there hath played the harlot. And I said after she" had played the harlot and "had done all these things, Turn thou unto me. But she returned not."[11]

2. How hard hearted we are and how merciful God is! who even after our many sins urges us to seek salvation. Yet not even so are we willing to turn to better things. Hear the words of the Lord: "If a man put away his wife, and she go from him, and become another man's and shall afterwards desire to

---

[1] Ezek. xxxiii. 11.   [2] Ps. lxxxv. 4.   [3] Ps. xxx. 7.
[4] Ps. xviii. 37, R.V.   [5] Hos. ii. 7-9.   [6] Hos. ii. 6.
[7] Joh. xiv. 6.   [8] Ps. cxxvi. 5, 6.   [9] Ps. vi. 6.
[10] Ps. xlii. 1-3.   [11] Ps. lxiii. 1-3 R.V.

[1] Luke xix. 41.   [2] Luke xxii. 62.   [3] Ps. cxix. 136.
[4] Jer. ix. 1.   [5] Jer. xxii. 10.   [6] Matt. viii. 22.
[7] Lam. ii. 18.   [8] Rom. xii. 15.   [9] Jer. ii. 21.
[10] Jer. ii. 27.   [11] Jer. iii. 6, 7.

eturn to him, will he at all receive her ? Will
e not loathe her rather ? But thou hast
layed the harlot with many lovers : yet
eturn again to me, saith the Lord." In place
f the last clause the true Hebrew text (which
not preserved in the Greek and Latin
ersions) gives the following : "thou hast
rsaken me, yet return, and I will receive
ee, saith the Lord." [1] Isaiah also speaking
the same sense uses almost the same words :
Return," he cries, " O children of Israel, ye
ho think deep counsel and wicked.[2] Return
ou unto me and I will redeem thee. I am
od, and there is no God else beside me ; a
st God and a Saviour ; there is none beside
e. Look unto me, and be ye saved, all the
ds of the earth.[3] Remember this and shew
urselves men : bring it again to mind, O ye
ansgressors. Return in heart and remember
e former things of old : for I am God and
ere is none else." [4] Joel also writes : "turn
e even to me with all your heart, and with
sting and with weeping and with mourning :
d rend your heart and not your garments
d turn unto the Lord your God ; for he is
acious and merciful . . . and repenteth
m of the evil." [5] How great His mercy is
d how excessive—if I may so say—and
speakable is His pitifulness, the prophet
osea tells us when he speaks in the Lord's
me : "how shall I give thee up, Ephraim ?
w shall I deliver thee, Israel ? how shall I
ake thee as Admah ? How shall I set thee
Zeboim ? Mine heart is turned within me,
y repentings are kindled together. I will
t execute the fierceness of mine anger." [6]
avid also says in a psalm : "in death there
no remembrance of thee ; in the grave who
all give thee thanks ?" [7] and in another
ace : " I acknowledged my sin unto thee,
d mine iniquity have I not hid. I said, I
ll confess my transgressions unto the Lord ;
d thou forgavest the iniquity of my sin.
r this shall every one that is godly pray
to thee in a time when thou mayest be
und : surely in the floods of great waters
ey shall not come nigh unto him." [8]
3. Think how great that weeping must be
hich deserves to be compared to a flood of
aters. Whosoever so weeps and says with
e prophet Jeremiah "let not the apple of
ine eye cease " [9] shall straightway find the
ords fulfilled of him : "mercy and truth are
et together : righteousness and peace have
ssed each other ;" [10] so that, if righteousness
d truth terrify him, mercy and peace may
courage him to seek salvation.

The whole repentance of a sinner is exhibited to us in the fifty-first [1] psalm written by
David after he had gone in unto Bathsheba the
wife of Uriah the Hittite,[2] and when, to the rebuke of the prophet Nathan he had replied, " I
have sinned." Immediately that he confessed
his fault he was comforted by the words :
"the Lord also hath put away thy sin." [3]
He had added murder to adultery ; yet bursting into tears he says : " Have mercy upon
me, O God, according to thy loving kindness :
according unto the multitude of thy tender
mercies blot out my transgressions." [4] A sin
so great needed to find great mercy. Accordingly he goes on to say : " Wash me
throughly from mine iniquity, and cleanse me
from my sin. For I acknowledge my transgressions : and my sin is ever before me.
Against thee, thee only have I sinned "—as a
king he had no one to fear but God—" and
done this evil in thy sight ; that thou mightest
be justified when thou speakest and be clear
when thou judgest." [5] For "God hath concluded all in unbelief, that he might have
mercy upon all." [6] And such was the progress that David made that he who had once
been a sinner and a penitent afterwards became a master able to say : " I will teach
transgressors thy ways ; and sinners shall be
converted unto thee." [7] For as "confession
and beauty are before God," [8] so a sinner who
confesses his sins and says : "my wounds
stink and are corrupt because of my foolishness " [9] loses his foul wounds and is made
whole and clean. But "he that covereth his
sins shall not prosper." [10]
The ungodly king Ahab, who shed the
blood of Naboth to gain his vineyard, was with
Jezebel, the partner less of his bed than of his
cruelty, severely rebuked by Elijah. "Thus
saith the Lord, hast thou killed and also taken
possession ?" and again, " in the place where
dogs licked the blood of Naboth, shall dogs
lick thy blood, even thine ;" and " the dogs
shall eat Jezebel by the wall of Jezreel." [11]
"And it came to pass "—the passage goes on
—" when Ahab heard those words that he rent
his clothes, and put sackcloth upon his flesh,
and fasted, and lay in sackcloth . . . and
the word of the Lord came to Elijah saying, Because Ahab humbleth himself before
me, I will not bring the evil in his days." [12]
Ahab's sin and Jezebel's were the same ; yet
because Ahab repented, his punishment was
postponed so as to fall upon his sons, while
Jezebel persisting in her wickedness met her
doom then and there.

Jer. iii. 1, Vulg. The Hebrew contains nothing correspond-
g to the words " and I will receive thee." The Latin Version
ntioned in the text is of course the old Latin.
[2] Isa. xxxi. 6, LXX. [3] Isa. xlv. 21, 22. [4] Isa. xlvi. 8, 9, LXX.
[5] Joel ii. 12, 13. [6] Hos. xi. 8, 9. [7] Ps. vi. 5.
Ps. xxxii. 5, 6. [9] Lam. ii. 18. [10] Ps. lxxxv. 10.

[1] In the Vulg. the fiftieth.
[2] Cf. the heading of the psalm in A.V.
[3] 2 Sam. xii. 13. [4] Ps. li. 1. [5] Ps. li. 2-4.
[6] Rom. xi. 32. [7] Ps. li. 13. [8] Ps. xcvi. 6, Vulg.
[9] Ps. xxxviii. 5. [10] Prov. xxviii. 13.
[11] 1 Kings xxi. 19, 23. [12] 1 Kings xxi. 27-29.

Moreover the Lord tells us in the gospel, "the men of Nineveh shall rise in judgment with this generation and shall condemn it : because they repented at the preaching of Jonas;"[1] and again He says "I am not come to call the righteous but sinners to repentance."[2] The lost piece of silver is sought for until it is found in the mire.[3] So also the ninety and nine sheep are left in the wilderness, while the shepherd carries home on his shoulders the one sheep which has gone astray.[4] Wherefore also "there is joy in the presence of the angels over one sinner that repenteth."[5] What a blessed thought it is that heavenly beings rejoice in our salvation! For it is of us that the words are said : "Repent ye : for the kingdom of heaven is at hand."[6] Death and life are contrary the one to the other ; there is no middle term. Yet penitence can knit death to life. The prodigal son, we are told, wasted all his substance, and in the far country away from his father "would fain have filled his belly with the husks that the swine did eat." Yet, when he comes back to his father, the fatted calf is killed, a robe and a ring are given to him.[7] That is to say, he receives again Christ's robe which he had before defiled, and hears to his comfort the injunction : "let thy garments be always white."[8] He receives the signet of God and cries to the Lord : "Father, I have sinned against heaven and before thee ;" and receiving the kiss of reconciliation, he says to Him : "Now is the light of thy countenance sealed upon us, O Lord."[9]

Hear the words of Ezekiel : "as for the wickedness of the wicked, he shall not fall thereby in the day that he turneth from his wickedness ; neither shall the righteous be able to live for his righteousness in the day that he sinneth."[10] The Lord judges every man according as he finds him. It is not the past that He looks upon but the present. Bygone sins there may be, but renewal and conversion remove them. "A just man," we read, "falleth seven times and riseth up again."[11] If he falls, how is he just? and if he is just, how does he fall? The answer is that a sinner does not lose the name of just if he always repents of his sins and rises again. If a sinner repents, his sins are forgiven him not only till seven times but till seventy times seven.[12] To whom much is forgiven, the same loveth much.[13] The harlot washed with her tears the Saviour's feet and wiped them with her hair ;

and to her, as a type of the Church gathered from the nations, was the declaration made " Thy sins are forgiven."[1] The self-righteous Pharisee perished in his pride, while the humble publican was saved by his confession.[2]

God makes asseveration by the mouth of the prophet Jeremiah : "At what instant I shall speak concerning a nation and concerning a kingdom, to pluck up to pull down and to destroy it : if that nation, against whom I have pronounced, turn from their evil, I will repent of the evil that I thought to do unto them. And at what instant I shall speak concerning a nation, and concerning a kingdom to build and to plant it ; if it do evil in my sight that it obey not my voice, then I will repent of the good wherewith I said I would benefit them." And immediately he adds : "Behold I frame evil against you, and devise a device against you : return ye now every one from his evil way, and make your ways and your doings good. And they said, there is no hope but we will walk after our own devices, and we will every one do the imagination of his evil heart."[3] The righteous Simeon says in the gospel : "Behold, this child is set for the fall and rising again of many,"[4] for the fall that is, of sinners and for the rising again of the penitent. So the apostle writes to the Corinthians : "it is reported commonly that there is fornication among you, and such fornication as is not so much as named among the Gentiles that one should have his father's wife. And ye are puffed up and have not rather mourned that he that hath done this deed might be taken away from among you."[5] And in his second epistle to the same, "lest such a one should be swallowed up with overmuch sorrow,"[6] he calls him back, and begs them to confirm their love towards him, so that he who had been destroyed by incest might be saved by penitence.

"There is no man clean from sin ; even though he has lived but for one day."[7] And the years of man's life are many in number. "The stars are not pure in his sight,[8] and his angels he charged with folly."[9] If there is sin in heaven, how much more must there be sin on earth? If they are stained with guilt who have no bodily temptations, how much more must we be, enveloped as we are in frail flesh and forced to cry each one of us with the apostle : "O wretched man that I am ! who shall deliver me from the body of this death ? For in my flesh there dwelleth no good thing."[11] For we do not what we would but what we would not ; the soul desires to do one

[1] Matt. xii. 41.   [2] Matt. ix. 13.   [3] Luke xv. 8–10.
[4] Luke xv. 4, 5.   [5] Luke xv. 10.   [6] Matt. iii. 2.
[7] Luke xv. 11–24.   [8] Eccles. ix. 8.
[9] Ps. iv. 6, acc. to the Gallican and Roman psalters. The allusions throughout are to the ritual practised in Jerome's day in connection with the reception of penitents.
[10] Ezek. xxxiii. 12.   [11] Prov. xxiv. 16.
[12] Cf. Matt. xviii. 21, 22.   [13] Cf. Luke vii. 47.

[1] Luke vii. 48.   [2] Cf. Luke xviii. 14.
[3] Jer. xviii. 7–12.   [4] Luke ii. 34.   [5] 1 Cor. v. 1, 2.
[6] 2 Cor. ii. 7.   [7] Job xiv. 4, 5, LXX.   [8] Job xxv. 5.
[9] Job iv. 18.   [10] Rom. vii. 24.   [11] Rom. vii. 18.

ning, the flesh is compelled to do another. If any persons are called righteous in scripture, and not only righteous but righteous in the sight of God, they are called righteous according to that righteousness mentioned in the passage I have quoted : " A just man falleth seven times and riseth up again," [1] and on the principle laid down that the wickedness of the wicked shall not hurt him in the day that he turns to repentance.[2] In fact Zachariah the father of John who is described as a righteous man sinned in disbelieving the message sent to him and was at once punished with dumbness.[3] Even Job, who at the outset of his history is spoken of as perfect and upright and uncomplaining, is afterwards proved to be a sinner both by God's words and by his own confession. If Abraham, Isaac, and Jacob, the prophets also and the apostles were by no means free from sin and if the finest wheat had chaff mixed with it, what can be said of us of whom it is written : " What is the chaff to the wheat, saith the Lord ? " [4] Yet the chaff is reserved for future burning ; as also are the tares which at present are mingled with the growing corn. 'For one shall come whose fan is in His hand, and shall purge His floor, and shall gather His wheat into the garner, and shall burn the chaff in the fire of hell.[5]

4. Roaming thus through the fairest fields of scripture I have culled its loveliest flowers to weave for your brows a garland of penitence ; for my aim is that, flying on the wings of a dove, you may find rest [6] and make your peace with the Father of mercy. Your former wife, who is now your sister and fellow-servant, has told me that, acting on the apostolic precept, [7] you and she lived apart by consent that you might give yourselves to prayer ; but that after a time your feet sank beneath you as if resting on water and indeed—to speak plainly—gave way altogether. For her part she heard the Lord saying to her as to Moses : " as for thee stand thou here by me ; " [8] and with the psalmist she said of Him : " He hath set my feet upon a rock." [9] But your house —she went on—having no sure foundation of faith fell before a whirlwind of the devil. [10] Hers however still stands in the Lord, and does not refuse its shelter to you ; you can still be joined in spirit to her to whom you were once joined in body. For, as the apostle says, " he that is joined unto the Lord is one spirit " with him.[11] Moreover, when the fury of the barbarians and the risk of captivity separated you again, you promised with a solemn oath that, if she made her way to the holy

places, you would follow her either immediately or later, and that you would try to save your soul now that by your carelessness you had seemed to lose it. Perform, now, the vow which you then made in the presence of God. Human life is uncertain. Therefore, lest you may be snatched away before you have fulfilled your promise, imitate her whose teacher you ought to have been. For shame ! the weaker vessel overcomes the world, and yet the stronger is overcome by it !

A woman leadeth in the high emprise ; [1]

and yet you will not follow her when her salvation leads you to the threshold of the faith ! Perhaps, however, you desire to save the remnants of your property and to see the last of your friends and fellow-citizens and of their cities and villas. If so, amid the horrors of captivity, in the presence of exulting foes, and in the shipwreck of the province, at least hold fast to the plank of penitence ; [2] and remember your fellow-servant [3] who daily sighs for your salvation and never despairs of it. While you are wandering about your own country (though, indeed, you no longer have a country ; that which you once had, you have lost) she is interceding for you in the venerable spots which witnessed the nativity, crucifixion and resurrection of our Lord and Saviour, and in the first of which He uttered His infant-cry. She draws you to her by her prayers that you may be saved, if not by your own exertions, at any rate by her faith. Of old one lay upon his bed sick of the palsy, so powerless in all his joints that he could neither move his feet to walk nor his hands to pray ; yet when he was carried to our Lord by others, he was by Him so completely restored to health as to carry the bed which a little before had carried him.[4] You too—absent in the body but present to her faith—your fellow-servant offers to her Lord and Saviour ; and with the Canaanite woman she says of you : " my daughter is grievously vexed with a devil." [5] Souls are of no sex ; therefore I may fairly call your soul the daughter of hers. For as a mother coaxes her unweaned child which is as yet unable to take solid food ; so does she call you to the milk suitable for babes and offer to you the sustenance that a nursing mother gives. Thus shall you be able to say with the prophet : " I have gone astray like a lost sheep ; seek thy servant ; for I do not forget thy commandments." [6]

[1] Prov. xxiv. 16. [2] Cf. Ezek. xxxiii. 12.
[3] Luke i. 20-22. [4] Jer. xxiii. 28.
[5] Matt. iii. 12. [6] Ps. lv. 6. [7] 1 Cor. vii. 5.
[8] Deut. v. 31. [9] Ps. xl. 2.
[10] Cf. Matt. vii. 24-27. [11] 1 Cor. vi. 17.

[1] Virgil, Æneid, i. 364.
[2] A favourite phrase with Jerome. See Letter CXVII. § 3.
[3] Viz. Artemia.
[4] Matt. ix. 1-7.
[5] Matt. xv. 22.
[6] Ps. cxix. 176.

LETTER CXXIII.

TO AGERUCHIA.

An appeal to the widow Ageruchia, a highborn lady of Gaul, not to marry again. It should be compared with the letters to Furia (LIV.) and to Salvina (LXXIX.) The allusion to Stilicho's treaty with Alaric fixes the date to 409 A.D.

1. I must look for a new track on the old road and devise a natural treatment, the same yet not the same, for a hackneyed and well-worn theme.[1] It is true that there is but one road; yet one can often reach one's goal by striking across country. I have several times written letters to widows[2] in which for their instruction I have sought out examples from scripture, weaving its varied flowers into a single garland of chastity. On the present occasion I address myself to Ageruchia; whose very name[3] (allotted to her by the divine guidance) has proved a prophecy of her after-life. Around her stand her grandmother, her mother, and her aunt; a noble band of tried Christian women. Her grandmother, Metronia, now a widow for forty years, reminds us of Anna the daughter of Phanuel in the gospel.[4] Her mother, Benigna, now in the fourteenth year of her widowhood, is surrounded by virgins whose chastity bears fruit a hundredfold.[5] The sister of Celerinus, Ageruchia's father, has nursed her niece from infancy and indeed took her into her lap the moment that she was born. Deprived of the solace of her husband she has for twenty years trained her brother's child, teaching her the lessons which she has learned from her own mother.

2. I make these brief remarks to shew my young friend that in resolving not to marry again she does but perform a duty to her family; and that, while she will deserve no praise for fulfilling it, she will be justly blamed if she fails to do so. The more so that she has a posthumous son named after his father Simplicius and thus cannot plead loneliness or the want of an heir. For the lust of many shelters itself under such excuses as though the promptings of incontinence were only a desire for offspring. But why do I speak as to one who wavers when I hear that Ageruchia seeks the church's protection against the many suitors whom she meets in the palace? For the devil inflames men to vie with one another in proving the chastity of our beloved widow; and rank and beauty, youth and riches cause her to be sought after by all. But the greater the assaults that are made upon her continence, the greater will be the rewards that will follow her victory.

3. But no sooner do I clear the harbour than I find my way to the sea barred by rock.[1] I am confronted with the authority of the apostle Paul who in writing to Timothy thus speaks concerning widows: "I will therefore that the younger women marry, bear children, guide the house, give none occasion to the adversary to speak reproachfully. For some are already turned aside after Satan." I must accordingly begin by considering the meaning of this pronouncement and examining the context of the whole passage. I must then plant my feet in the steps of the apostle and, as the saying goes, not deviate a hair's breadth from them either to this side or to that. He had previously described his ideal widow as one who had been the wife of one man, who had brought up children, who was well reported of for good works, who had relieved the afflicted with her substance,[3] whose trust had been in God, and who had continued in prayer day and night.[4] With her he contrasted her opposite, saying: "She that liveth in pleasure is dead while she liveth." And that he might warn his disciple Timothy with all needful admonition, he immediately added these words: "the younger widows refuse for when they have begun to wax wanton against Christ they will marry; having damnation because they have cast off their first faith."[5] It is then for these who have outraged Christ their Spouse by committing fornication against Him (for this is the sense of the Greek word καταστρηνιάσωσι)—it is for these that the apostle wishes a second marriage, thinking digamy preferable to fornication; but this second marriage is a concession and not a command.

4. We must also take the passage clause by clause. "I will," he says, "that the younger women marry." Why, pray? because I would not have young women commit fornication. "That they bear children;"[6] for what reason? That they may not be induced by fear of the consequences to kill children whom they have conceived in adultery. "That they be the heads of households."[7] Wherefore, pray? Because it is much more tolerable that a woman should marry again than that she should be a prostitute, and better that she should have a second husband than several paramours. The first alternative brings relief in a miserable plight, but the second involves sin and its punishment. He continues: "that they give none occasion to the adversary to speak reproachfully," a brief and comprehen

---

[1] Cf. Letter LX. § 6.
[2] Letters LIV., LXXV., LXXIX., and others.
[3] Ageruchia = Greatheart.   [4] Luke ii. 36, 37.
[5] See Letter XLVIII., § 2; also § 9 infra.

[1] Cf. Letter LXXVII. § 3.   [2] 1 Tim. v. 14, 15.
[3] 1 Tim. v. 9, 10.   [4] 1 Tim. v. 5.
[5] 1 Tim. v. 11, 12.   [6] 1 Tim. v. 14, 15.
[7] So Vulg.

sive precept in which many admonitions are summed up. As for instance these : that a woman must not bring discredit upon her profession of widowhood by too great attention to her dress, that she must not draw troops of young men after her by gay smiles or expressive glances, that she must not profess one thing by her words and another by her behaviour, that she must give no ground for the application to herself of the well known line :

She gave a meaning look and slyly smiled.[1]

Lastly, that Paul may compress into a few words all the reasons for such marriages, he shews the motive of his command by saying : "for some are already turned aside after Satan." Thus he allows to the incontinent a second marriage, or in case of need a third, simply that he may rescue them from Satan, preferring that a woman should be joined to the worst of husbands rather than to the devil. To the Corinthians he uses somewhat similar language : " I say therefore to the unmarried and widows, It is good for them if they abide even as I. But if they cannot contain, let them marry : for it is better to marry than to burn."[2] Why, O apostle, is it better to marry ? He answers immediately : because it is worse to burn.[3]

5. Apart from these considerations, that which is absolutely good and not merely relatively so is to be as the apostle, that is, loose, not bound ; free, not enslaved ; caring for the things of God, not for the things of a wife. Immediately afterwards he adds : " The wife is bound by the law to her husband as long as her husband liveth, but if her husband be fallen asleep,[4] she is at liberty to be married to whom she will ; only in the Lord. But she is happier if she so abide, after my judgment : and I think also that I have the spirit of God."[5] This passage corresponds with the former in meaning, because the spirit of the two is the same. For though the epistles are different, they are the work of one author. While her husband lives the woman is bound, and when he is dead, she is loosed. Marriage then is a bond, and widowhood is the loosing of it. The wife is bound to the husband and the husband to the wife ; and so close is the tie that they have no power over their own bodies, but each stands indebted to the other. They who are under the yoke of wedlock have not the option of choosing continence. When the apostle adds the words " only in the Lord," he excludes heathen marriages of which he had spoken in another place thus : " be ye not unequally yoked together with unbelievers : for

what fellowship hath righteousness with unrighteousness ? and what communion hath light with darkness ? and what concord hath Christ with Belial ? or what part hath he that believeth with an infidel ? and what agreement hath the temple of God with idols ? "[1] We must not plough with an ox and an ass together ;[2] nor weave our wedding garment of different colours. He at once takes back the concession he made, and, as if repenting of his opinion, withdraws it by saying : " She is happier if she so abide," that is, unmarried ; and declares that in his judgment this course is preferable. And that this may not be made light of as a merely human utterance, he claims for it the authority of the Holy Spirit, so that we are listening not to a fellowman making concessions to the weakness of the flesh but to the Holy Spirit using the apostle for his mouthpiece.

6. Again, no widow of youthful age must quiet her qualms of conscience by the plea that he gives commandment that no widow is to be taken into the number under three-score years old.[3] He does not by this arrangement urge unmarried girls or youthful widows to marry, seeing that even of the married he says : " the time is short : it remaineth that they that have wives be as though they had none."[4] No, he is speaking of widows who have relations able to support them, who have sons and grandsons to be responsible for their maintenance. The apostle commands these latter to shew piety at home and to requite their parents and to relieve them adequately ; that the church may not be charged, but may be free to relieve those that are widows indeed. " Honour widows," he writes, " that are widows indeed," that is, such as are desolate and have no relations to help them, who cannot labour with their hands, who are weakened by poverty and overcome by years, whose trust is in God and their only work prayer.[5] From which it is easy to infer that the younger widows, unless they are excused by ill health, are either left to their own exertions or else are consigned to the care of their children or relations. The word ' honour ' in this passage implies either alms or a gift, as also in the verse immediately following : " Let the elders . . . be counted worthy of double honour, especially they who labour in the word and doctrine."[6] So also in the gospel when the Lord discusses that commandment of the Law which says : " Honour thy father and thy mother,"[7] He declares that it is to be interpreted not of mere words which while offering an empty shew of regard may still leave a parent's wants unrelieved, but of the actual provision of the necessaries

---

[1] Ovid, Am. iii. 2, 83.   [2] 1 Cor. vii. 8, 9.
[3] Cf. Letters XLVIII. § 19. and LXXIX. § 10.
[4] So R.V. marg.   [5] 1 Cor. vii. 39, 40, cf. Rom. vii. 2.

[1] 2 Cor. vi. 14-16.   [2] Dt. xxii. 10.   [3] 1 Tim. v. 9.
[4] 1 Cor. vii. 29. [5] 1 Tim. v. 3-5, 16. [6] 1 Tim. v. 17. [7] Ex. xx. 12.

of life. The Lord commanded that poor parents should be supported by their children and that these should pay them back when old those benefits which they had themselves received in their childhood. The scribes and pharisees on the other hand taught the children to answer their parents by saying : "It is Corban, that is to say, a gift[1] which I have promised to the altar and engaged to present to the temple : it will relieve you as much there, as if I were to give it you directly to buy food."[2] So it frequently happened that while father and mother were destitute their children were offering sacrifices for the priests and scribes to consume. If then the apostle compels poor widows—yet only those who are young and not broken down by sickness—to labour with their hands that the church, not charged with their maintenance, may be able to support such widows as are old, what plea can be urged by one who has abundance of this world's goods, both for her own wants and those of others, and who can make to herself friends of the mammon of unrighteousness able to receive her into everlasting habitations?[3]

Consider too that no one is to be elected a widow, except she has been the wife of one husband. We sometimes fancy it to be the distinctive mark of the priesthood that none but monogamists shall be admitted to the altar. But not only are the twice-married excluded from the priestly office, they are debarred from receiving the alms of the church. A woman who has resorted to a second marriage is held unworthy to be supported by the faithful. And even the layman is bound by the law of the priest, for his conduct must be such as to admit of his election to the priesthood. If he has been twice married, he cannot be so elected. Therefore, as priests are chosen from the ranks of laymen, the layman also is bound by the commandment, fulfilment of which is indispensable for the attainment of the priesthood.[4]

7. We must distinguish between what the apostle himself desires and what he is compelled to acquiesce in. If he allows me to marry again, this is due to my own incontinence and not to his wish. For he wishes all men to be as he is, and to think the things of God, and when once they are loosed no more to seek to be bound. But when he sees unstable men in danger through their incontinence of falling into the abyss of lust, he extends to them the offer of a second marriage ; that, if they must wallow in the mire, it may be with

one and not with many. The husband of a second wife must not consider this a harsh saying or one that conflicts with the rule laid down by the apostle. The apostle is of two minds : first, he proclaims a command, " I say therefore to the unmarried and widows, It is good for them if they abide even as I." Next, he makes a concession, " But if they cannot contain, let them marry : for it is better to marry than to burn."[1] He first shews what he himself desires, then that in which he is forced to acquiesce. He wishes us—after one marriage—to abide even as he, that is, unmarried, and sets before us in his own apostolic example an instance of the blessedness of which he speaks. If however he finds that we are unwilling to do as he wishes, he makes a concession to our incontinence. Which then of the two alternatives do we choose for ourselves ? The one which he prefers and which is in itself good ? Or the one which in comparison with evil is tolerable, yet as it is only a substitute for evil is not altogether good ? Suppose that we choose that course which the apostle does not wish but to which he only consents against his will, allowing those who seek lower ends to have their own way ; in this case we carry out not the apostle's wish but our own. We read in the old testament that the daughters of the priests who have been married once and have become widows are to eat of the priests' food and that when they die they are to be buried with the same ceremonies as their father and mother.[2] If on the other hand they take other husbands they are to be kept apart both from their father and from the sacrifices and are to be counted as strangers.[3]

8. These restraints on marriage are observed even among the heathen ; and it is our condemnation if the true faith cannot do for Christ what false ones do for the devil, who has substituted for the saving chastity of the gospel a damning chastity of his own.[4] The Athenian hierophant disowns his manhood and weakens his passions by a perpetual restraint.[5] The holy office of the flamen is limited to those who have been once married, and the attendants of the flamens' wives must also have had but one husband.[6] Only monogamists are allowed to share in the sacred rites connected with the Egyptian bull.[7] I need say nothing of the vestal virgins and those of Apollo, the Achivan Juno, Diana, and Minerva, all of whom waste away in the perpetual virginity required by their vocation. I will just glance at the queen of Carthage[8] who was willing to burn herself

---

[1] Mark vii. 11.
[2] Text corrupt : probably 'quasi' should be substituted for 'si.'
[3] Cf. Luke xvi. 9.
[4] A reminiscence of Tert. de Exh. Cast. vii.

[1] 1 Cor. vii. 8, 9.
[2] Jerome seems to be here relying on tradition.
[3] Lev. xxii. 12, 13.   [4] From Tert. de Exh. Cast. xiii.
[5] Julian, Orat. v.   [6] See Dict. Antiq. s.v. flamen.
[7] The sacred bull of Memphis, generally called Apis.
[8] Dido.

ther than marry king Iarbas ; at the wife of Hasdrubal [1] who taking her two children one in each hand cast herself into the flames beneath her rather than surrender her honour ; and at Lucretia [2] who having lost the prize of her chastity refused to survive the defilement of her soul. I will not lengthen my letter by quoting the many instances of the like virtue which you can read to your profit in my first book against Jovinian.[3] I will merely relate one which took place in your own country and which will shew you that chastity is held in high honour even among wild and barbarous and cruel peoples. Once the Teutons who came from the remote shores of the German Ocean overran all parts of Gaul, and it was only when they had cut to pieces several Roman armies that Marius at last defeated them in an encounter at Aquæ Sextiæ.[4] By the conditions of the surrender three hundred of their married women were to be handed over to the Romans. When the Teuton matrons heard of this stipulation they first begged the consul that they might be set apart to minister in the temples of Ceres and Venus ;[5] and then when they failed to obtain their request and were removed by the lictors, they slew their little children and next morning were all found dead in each other's arms having strangled themselves in the night.[6]

9. Shall then a highborn lady do what these barbarian women refused to do even as prisoners of war ? After losing a first husband, good or bad as the case may be, shall she make trial of a second, and thus run counter to the judgment of God? And in case that she immediately loses this second, shall she take a third ? And if he too is called to his rest, shall she go on to a fourth and a fifth, and by so doing identify herself with the harlots ? No, a widow must take every precaution not to overstep by an inch the bounds of chastity. For if she once oversteps them and breaks through the modesty which becomes a matron, she will soon riot in every kind of excess ; so much so that the prophet's words shall be true of her "Thou hast a whore's forehead, thou refusest to be ashamed." [7]

What then? do I condemn second marriages? not at all ; but I commend first ones. Do I expel twice-married persons from the church? Far from it ; but I urge those who have been once married to lives of continence. The Ark of Noah contained unclean animals as well as clean. It contained both creeping things and human beings. In a great house there are vessels of different kinds, some to honour and

some to dishonour.[1] In the gospel parable the seed sown in the good ground brings forth fruit, some an hundredfold, some sixtyfold, some thirtyfold.[2] The hundredfold which comes first betokens the crown of virginity ; the sixtyfold which comes next refers to the work of widows ; while the thirtyfold—indicated by joining together the points of the thumb and forefinger [3]—denotes the marriage-tie. What room is left for double marriages ? None. They are not counted. Such weeds do not grow in good ground but among briers and thorns, the favourite haunts of those foxes to whom the Lord compares the impious Herod.[4] A woman who marries more than once fancies herself worthy of praise because she is not so bad as the prostitutes, because she compares favourably with these victims of indiscriminate lust by surrendering herself to one alone and not to a number.

10. The story which I am about to relate is an incredible one ; yet it is vouched for by many witnesses. A great many years ago when I was helping Damasus bishop of Rome with his ecclesiastical correspondence, and writing his answers to the questions referred to him by the councils of the east and west, I saw a married couple, both of whom were sprung from the very dregs of the people. The man had already buried twenty wives, and the woman had had twenty-two husbands. Now they were united to each other as each believed for the last time. The greatest curiosity prevailed both among men and women to see which of these two veterans would live to bury the other. The husband triumphed and walked before the bier of his often-married wife, amid a great concourse of people from all quarters, with garland and palm-branch, scattering spelt as he went along among an approving crowd. What shall we say to such a woman as that? Surely just what the Lord said to the woman of Samaria : "Thou hast had twenty-two husbands, and he by whom you are now buried is not your husband." [5]

11. I beseech you therefore, my devout daughter in Christ, not to dwell on those passages which offer succour to the incontinent and the unhappy but rather to read those in which chastity is crowned. It is enough for you that you have lost the first and highest kind, that of virginity, and that you have passed through the third to the second ; that is to say, having formerly fulfilled the obligations of a wife, that you now live in continence as a widow. Think not of the

---

[1] Who refused to survive the fall of Carthage. The story is told by Polybius.
[2] See Livy, I. cc. 57, 58.   [3] Against Jov. i. 20.
[4] The battle of Aix was fought in 102 B.C.
[5] The priestesses in these temples seem to have been vowed to chastity.
[6] Val. Max. vi. 1.   [7] Jer. iii. 3.

[1] 2 Tim. ii. 20.
[2] Matt. xiii. 8 : for this explanation of the parable see Letter XLVIII. § 2.
[3] See Letter XLVIII. § 2 and note there.
[4] Luke xiii. 32.   [5] Cf. Joh. iv. 18.

lowest grade, nay of that which does not count at all, I mean, second marriage ; and do not seek for far fetched precedents to justify you in marrying again. You cannot too closely imitate your grandmother, your mother, and your aunt ; whose teaching and advice as to life will form for you a rule of virtue. For if many wives in the lifetime of their husbands come to realize the truth of the apostle's words : "all things are lawful unto me but all things are not expedient," [1] and make eunuchs of themselves for the kingdom of heaven's sake [2] either by consent after their regeneration through the baptismal laver, or else in the ardour of their faith immediately after their marriage ; why should not a widow, who by God's decree has ceased to have a husband, joyfully cry again and again with Job : "the Lord gave, and the Lord hath taken away," [3] and seize the opportunity offered to her of having power over her own body instead of again becoming the servant of a man. Assuredly it is much harder to abstain from enjoying what you have than it is to regret what you have lost. Virginity is the easier because virgins know nothing of the promptings of the flesh, and widowhood is the harder because widows cannot help thinking of the license they have enjoyed in the past. And it is harder still if they suppose their husbands to be lost and not gone before ; for while the former alternative brings pain, the latter causes joy.

12. The creation of the first man should teach us to reject more marriages than one. There was but one Adam and but one Eve ; in fact the woman was fashioned from a rib of Adam.[4] Thus divided they were subsequently joined together in marriage ; in the words of scripture "the twain shall be one flesh," not two or three. "Therefore shall a man leave his father and his mother, and shall cleave unto his wife." [5] Certainly it is not said "to his wives." Paul in explaining the passage refers it to Christ and the church ; [6] making the first Adam a monogamist in the flesh and the second a monogamist in the spirit. As there is one Eve who is "the mother of all living," [7] so is there one church which is the parent of all Christians. And as the accursed Lamech made of the first Eve two separate wives,[8] so also the heretics sever the second into several churches which, according to the apocalypse of John, ought rather to be called synagogues of the devil than congregations of Christ.[9] In the Book of Songs we read as follows :—"there are threescore queens, and fourscore concubines, and virgins without

number. My dove, my undefiled is but one , she is the only one of her mother, she is the choice one of her that bare her." [1] It is to this choice one that the same John addresses an epistle in these words, "the elder unto the elect lady and her children." [2] So too in the case of the ark which the apostle Peter interprets as a type of the church,[3] Noah brings in for his three sons one wife apiece and not two.[4] Likewise of the unclean animals pairs only are taken, male and female, to shew that digamy has no place even among brutes, creeping things, crocodiles and lizards. And if of the clean animals there are seven taken of each kind,[5] that is, an uneven number ; this points to the palm which awaits virginal chastity. For on leaving the ark Noah sacrificed victims to God [6] not of course of the animals taken by twos for these were kept to multiply their species, but of those taken by sevens some of which had been set apart for sacrifice.

13. It is true that the patriarchs had each of them more wives than one and that they had numerous concubines besides. And as if their example was not enough, David had many wives and Solomon a countless number. Judah went in to Tamar thinking her to be a harlot ; [7] and according to the letter that killeth the prophet Hosea married not only a whore but an adulteress.[8] If these instances are to justify us let us neigh after every woman that we meet ; [9] like the people of Sodom and Gomorrah let us be found by the last day buying and selling, marrying and giving in marriage ; [10] and let us only end our marrying with the close of our lives. And if both before and after the deluge the maxim held good : "be fruitful and multiply and replenish the earth :" [11] what has that to do with us upon whom the ends of the ages are come,[12] unto whom it is said, "the time is short," [13] and "now the axe is laid unto the root of the trees ;" [14] that is to say, the forests of marriage and of the law must be cut down by the chastity of the gospel. There is "a time to embrace, and a time to refrain from embracing." [15] Owing to the near approach of the captivity Jeremiah is forbidden to take a wife.[16] In Babylon Ezekiel says : "my wife is dead and my mouth is opened." [17] Neither he who wished to marry nor he who had married could in wedlock prophesy freely. In days gone by men rejoiced to hear it said of them : "thy children shall be like olive plants

---

[1] 1 Cor. vi. 12. [2] Matt. xix. 12. [3] Job i. 21.
[4] Gen. ii. 21, 22. [5] Gen. ii. 24, LXX. [6] Eph. v. 31, 32.
[7] Gen. iii. 20. [8] Gen. iv. 19. [9] Rev. ii. 9.

[1] Cant. vi. 8, 9.
[2] 2 Joh. i. In Latin ' choice ' and ' elect ' are one word.
[3] 1 Pet. iii. 20, 21. [4] Gen. vii. 13. [5] Gen. vii. 2.
[6] Gen. viii. 20. [7] Gen. xxxviii. 12–18.
[8] Hos. i. 2, 3. [9] Cf Jer. v. 8. [10] Luke xvii. 27–29.
[11] Gen. i. 28, ix. 7. [12] 1 Cor. x. 11, R.V.
[13] 1 Cor. vii. 29. [14] Matt. iii. 10.
[15] Eccles. iii. 5. [16] Jer. xvi. 2. [17] Cf. Ezek. xxiv. 16–18, 27.

round about thy table," and "thou shalt see thy children's children." [1] But now it is said of those who live in continence: "he that is joined unto the Lord is one spirit;" [2] and "my soul followeth hard after thee: thy right hand upholdeth me." [3] Then it was said "an eye for an eye;" now the commandment is: "whosoever shall smite thee on thy right cheek, turn to him the other also." [4] In those days men said to the warrior: "gird thy sword upon thy thigh, O most mighty;" [5] now it is said to Peter: "put up again thy sword into his place: for all they that take the sword shall perish with the sword." [6]

In speaking thus I do not mean to sever the law from the gospel, as Marcion [7] falsely does. No, I receive one and the same God in both who, as the time and the object vary, is both the Beginning and the End, who sows that He may reap, who plants that He may have somewhat to cut down, and who lays the foundation that in the fulness of time He may crown the edifice. Besides, if we are to deal with symbols and types of things to come, we must judge of them not by our own opinions but in the light of the apostle's explanations. Hagar and Sarah, or Sinai and Zion, are typical of the two testaments. [8] Leah who was tender-eyed and Rachel whom Jacob loved [9] signify the synagogue and the church. So likewise do Hannah and Peninnah of whom the former, at first barren, afterwards exceeded the latter in fruitfulness. In Isaac and Rebekah we see an early example of monogamy: it was only to Rebekah that the Lord revealed Himself in the hour of childbirth and she alone went of herself to enquire of the Lord. [10] What shall I say of Tamar who bore twin sons, Pharez and Zarah? [11] At their birth was broken down that middle wall of partition which typified the division existing between the two peoples; [12] while the binding of Zarah's hand with the scarlet thread even then marked the conscience of the Jews with the stain of Christ's blood. And how shall I speak of the whore married by the prophet [13] who is a figure either of the church as gathered in from the Gentiles or—an interpretation which better suits the passage—of the synagogue? First adopted from among the idolaters by Abraham and Moses, this has now denied the Saviour and proved unfaithful to Him. Therefore it has long been deprived of its altar, priests, and prophets and has to abide many days for its first husband. [14] For

when the fulness of the Gentiles shall have come in, all Israel shall be saved. [1]

14. I have tried to compress a great deal into a limited space as a draughtsman does when he delineates a large country in a small map. For I wish to deal with other questions, the first of which I shall give in Anna's words to her sister Dido:

> Why waste your youth alone in ceaseless grief
> Unblest with offspring, sweetest gift of love?
> Think you the buried dead require this?

To whom the sufferer thus briefly replies:

> 'Twas you, my sister, you, who were the first
> To plunge my frenzied soul into this woe.
> Why could I not have lived a virgin life
> Like some wild creature innocent of care?
> Alas! I pledged my soul unto the dead:
> I vowed a vow and I have broken it. [2]

You set before me the joys of wedlock. I for my part will remind you of Dido's sword and pyre and funeral flames. In marriage there is not so much good to be hoped for as there is evil which may happen and must be feared. Passion when indulged always brings repentance with it; it is never satisfied, and once quenched it is soon kindled anew. Its growth or decay is a matter of habit; led like a captive by impulse it refuses to obey reason. But you will argue, 'the management of wealth and property requires the superintendence of a husband.' Do you mean to say that the affairs of those who live single are ruined; and that, unless you make yourself as much a slave as your own servants, you will not be able to govern your household? Do not your grandmother, your mother and your aunt enjoy even more than their old influence and respect, looked up to as they are by the whole province and by the leaders of the churches? Do not soldiers and travellers manage their domestic affairs and give entertainments to one another with no wives to help them? [3] Why can you not have grave and elderly servants or freedmen, such as those who have nursed you in your childhood, to preside over your house, to answer public calls, to pay taxes; men who will look up to you as a patroness, who will love you as a nursling, who will revere you as a saint? "Seek first the kingdom of God, and all these things shall be added unto you." [4] If you are careful for raiment the gospel bids you "consider the lilies;" and, if for food, to go back to the fowls which "sow not neither do they reap; yet your heavenly father feedeth them." [5] How many virgins and widows there are who have looked after their property for

---

[1] Ps. cxxviii. 3, 6. [2] 1 Cor. vi. 17.
[3] Ps. lxiii. 8. [4] Matt. v. 38, 39.
[5] Ps. xlv. 3. [6] Matt. xxvi. 52.
[7] A gnostic of the second century who rejected the whole of the old testament as incompatible with the new.
[8] Gal. iv. 22–26. [9] Gen. xxix. 17, 18.
[10] Gen. xxv. 22, 23. [11] Gen. xxxviii. 27–30.
[12] Eph. ii. 14. [13] Gomer the wife of Hosea.
[14] Hos. ii. 7, iii. 3.

[1] Rom. xi. 25, 26. [2] Virg. A. iv. 32–34: 548, 552.
[3] From Tert. de Exh. Cast. xii.
[4] Matt. vi. 33. [5] Matt. vi. 26, 28.

themselves without thereby incurring any stain of scandal !

15. Do not associate with young women or cleave to them, for it is on account of such that the apostle makes his concession of second marriage, and so you may be shipwrecked in what appears to be calm water. If Paul can say to Timothy, "the younger widows refuse,"[1] and again "love the elder women as mothers ; the younger as sisters, with all purity,"[2] what plea can you urge for refusing to hear my admonitions? Avoid all persons to whom a suspicion of evil living may attach itself, and do not content yourself with the trite answer. 'my own conscience is enough for me ; I do not care what people say of me.' That was not the principle on which the apostle acted. He provided things honest not only in the sight of God but in the sight of all men ;[3] that the name of God might not be blasphemed among the Gentiles.[4] Though he had power to lead about a sister, a wife,[5] he would not do so, for he did not wish to be judged by an unbeliever's conscience.[6] And, though he might have lived by the gospel,[7] he laboured day and night with his own hands, that he might not be burdensome to the believers.[8] "If meat," he says, "make my brother to offend, I will eat no flesh while the world standeth."[9] Let us then say, if a sister or a brother causes not one or two but the whole church to offend, 'I will not see that sister or that brother.' It is better to lose a portion of one's substance than to imperil the salvation of one's soul. It is better to lose that which some day, whether we like it or not, must be lost to us and to give it up freely, than to lose that for which we should sacrifice all that we have. Which of us can add—I will not say a cubit for that would be an immense addition—but the tenth part of a single inch to his stature? Why are we careful what we shall eat or what we shall drink? Let us "take no thought for the morrow : sufficient unto the day is the evil thereof."[10]

Jacob in his flight from his brother left behind in his father's house great riches and made his way with nothing into Mesopotamia. Moreover, to prove to us his powers of endurance, he took a stone for his pillow. Yet as he lay there he beheld a ladder set up on the earth reaching to heaven and behold the Lord stood above it, and the angels ascended and descended on it ;[11] the lesson being thus taught that the sinner must not despair of salvation nor the righteous man rest secure in his virtue.[12]

To pass over much of the story (for there is no time to explain all the points in the narrative) after twenty years he who before had passed over Jordan with his staff returned into his native land with three droves of cattle, rich in flocks and herds and richer still in children.[1] The apostles likewise travelled throughout the world without either money in their purses, or staves in their hands, or shoes on their feet ;[2] and yet they could speak of themselves as "having nothing and yet possessing all things."[3] "Silver and gold," say they, "have we none, but such as we have give we thee : in the name of Jesus Christ of Nazareth rise up and walk."[4] For they were not weighed down with the burthen of riches. Therefore they could stand, as Elijah, in the crevice of the rock, they could pass through the needle's eye, and behold the back parts of the Lord.[5]

But as for us we burn with covetousness and, even while we declaim against the love of money, we hold out our skirts to catch gold and never have enough.[6] There is a common saying about the Megarians which may rightly be applied to all who suffer from this passion : "They build as if they are to live forever ; they live as if they are to die to-morrow." We do the same, for we do not believe the Lord's words. When we attain the age which all desire we forget the nearness of that death which as human beings we owe to nature and with futile hope promise to ourselves a long length of years. No old man is so weak and decrepit as to suppose that he will not live for one year more. A forgetfulness of his true condition gradually creeps upon him ; so that—earthly creature that he is and close to dissolution as he stands—he is lifted up into pride, and in imagination seats himself in heaven.

16. But what am I doing? Whilst I talk about the cargo, the vessel itself founders. He that letteth[7] is taken out of the way, and yet we do not realize that Antichrist is near. Yes, Antichrist is near whom the Lord Jesus Christ "shall consume with the spirit of his mouth."[8] "Woe unto them," he cries, "that are with child, and to them that give suck in those days."[9] Now these things are both the fruits of marriage.

I shall now say a few words of our present miseries. A few of us have hitherto survived them, but this is due not to anything we have done ourselves but to the mercy of the Lord. Savage tribes in countless numbers have over-

---

[1] 1 Tim. v. 11.
[2] 1 Tim. v. 2. Jerome substitutes 'love' for 'rebuke.'
[3] Rom. xii. 17, cf. Letter cxvii. §4. [4] Rom. ii. 24.
[5] 1 Cor. ix. 5. [6] 1 Cor. x. 29. [7] 1 Cor. ix. 14.
[8] 1 Cor. iv. 12 : 1 Thess. ii. 9 : 2 Cor. xii. 14. [9] 1 Cor. viii. 13.
[10] Matt. vi. 25, 27, 34. [11] Gen. xxviii. 11-13.
[12] Cf. Letters cviii. §13 and cxviii. §7.

[1] Gen. xxxii. 7, 10. [2] Matt. x. 9, 10.
[3] 2 Cor. vi. 10. [4] Acts iii. 6.
[5] 1 K. xix. 11-13, cf. Exod. xxxiii. 21-23. [6] Cf. Juv. i. 88.
[7] Jerome follows Tertullian, Irenæus, and the majority of the fathers in supposing the apostle to allude to the Roman Empire. See Letter CXXI. §11, Comm. in Hierem. xxv. 26, Comm. in Dan. vii. 7, 8.
[8] 2 Thess. ii. 7, 8. [9] Matt. xxiv. 19.

run all parts of Gaul. The whole country between the Alps and the Pyrenees, between the Rhine and the Ocean, has been laid waste by hordes of Quadi, Vandals, Sarmatians, Alans, Gepids, Herules, Saxons, Burgundians, Allemanni and—alas ! for the commonweal !—even Pannonians. For "Assur also is joined with them." [1] The once noble city of Moguntiacum [2] has been captured and destroyed. In its church many thousands have been massacred. The people of Vangium [3] after standing a long siege have been extirpated. The powerful city of Rheims, the Ambiani, the Altrebatæ, [4] the Belgians on the skirts of the world, Tournay, Spires, and Strasburg have fallen to Germany : while the provinces of Aquitaine and of the Nine Nations, of Lyons and of Narbonne are with the exception of a few cities one universal scene of desolation. And those which the sword spares without, famine ravages within. I cannot speak without tears of Toulouse which has been kept from falling hitherto by the merits of its reverend bishop Exuperius. [5] Even the Spains are on the brink of ruin and tremble daily as they recall the invasion of the Cymry ; and, while others suffer misfortunes once in actual fact, they suffer them continually in anticipation.

17. I say nothing of other places that I may not seem to despair of God's mercy. All that is ours now from the Pontic Sea to the Julian Alps in days gone by once ceased to be ours. For thirty years the barbarians burst the barrier of the Danube and fought in the heart of the Roman Empire. Long use dried our tears. For all but a few old people had been born either in captivity or during a blockade, and consequently they did not miss a liberty which they had never known. Yet who will hereafter credit the fact or what histories will seriously discuss it, that Rome has to fight within her own borders not for glory but for bare life ; and that she does not even fight but buys the right to exist by giving gold and sacrificing all her substance ? This humiliation has been brought upon her not by the fault of her Emperors [6] who are both most religious men, but by the crime of a half-barbarian traitor [7] who with our money has armed our foes against us. [8] Of old the Roman Empire was branded with eternal shame because after ravaging the country and routing the Romans at the Allia, Brennus with his Gauls entered Rome itself. [9] Nor could this ancient stain be wiped out until Gaul, the birth-place of the Gauls, and Gaulish Greece, [1] wherein they had settled after triumphing over East and West, were subjugated to her sway. Even Hannibal [2] who swept like a devastating storm from Spain into Italy, although he came within sight of the city, did not dare to lay siege to it. Even Pyrrhus [3] was so completely bound by the spell of the Roman name that destroying everything that came in his way, he yet withdrew from its vicinity and, victor though he was, did not presume to gaze upon what he had learned to be a city of kings. Yet in return for such insults—not to say such haughty pride—as theirs which ended thus happily for Rome, one [4] banished from all the world found death at last by poison in Bithynia ; while the other [5] returning to his native land was slain in his own dominions. The countries of both became tributary to the Roman people. But now, even if complete success attends our arms, we can wrest nothing from our vanquished foes but what we have already lost to them. The poet Lucan describing the power of the city in a glowing passage says : [6]

If Rome be weak, where shall we look for strength ?

we may vary his words and say :

If Rome be lost, where shall we look for help ?

or quote the language of Virgil :

Had I a hundred tongues and throat of bronze
The woes of captives I could not relate
Or ev'n recount the names of all the slain. [7]

Even what I have said is fraught with danger both to me who say it and to all who hear it ; for we are no longer free even to lament our fate, and are unwilling, nay, I may even say, afraid to weep for our sufferings.

Dearest daughter in Christ, answer me this question : will you marry amid such scenes as these ? Tell me, what kind of husband will you take ? One that will run or one that will fight ? In either case you know what the result will be. Instead of the Fescennine song, [8] the hoarse blare of the terrible trumpet will deafen your ears and your very brides-women may be turned into mourners. In what pleasures can you hope to revel now that you have lost the proceeds of all your possessions, now that you see your small retinue under close blockade and a prey to the inroads of pestilence and famine ? But far be it from me to think so meanly of you or to harbour any suspicions of one who has dedicated her soul to the Lord. Though nomin-

[1] Ps. lxxxiii. 8. [2] Now Maintz. [3] Now Worms.
[4] Tribes whose memories linger in the names Amiens and Arras.
[5] See note on Letter LIV. § 11. [6] Arcadius and Honorius.
[7] Stilicho who induced the senate to grant a subsidy to the Gothic King Alaric. See Gibbon, C. xxx.
[8] This, one of Jerome's few criticisms on the public policy of his day, shows him to have taken a narrow and inadequate view of the issues involved.
[9] In the year 390 B.C.

[1] i.e. Galatia.
[2] The great Carthaginian general in the second Punic war.
[3] King of Epirus who invaded Italy in the years 280, 279, 276, 275 B.C.
[4] Hannibal. [5] Pyrrhus. [6] Lucan, Phars. v. 274.
[7] Virg. A. vi. 625-627. [8] See note on Letter CXXX. § 5.

ally addressed to you my words are really meant for others such as are idle, inquisitive and given to gossip. These wander from house to house and from one married lady to another,[1] their god is their belly and their glory is in their shame,[2] of the scriptures they know nothing except the texts which favour second marriages, but they love to quote the example of others to justify their own self-indulgence, and flatter themselves that they are no worse than their fellow-sinners. When you have confounded the shameless proposals of such women by explaining the true drift of the apostle's meaning; then to show you by what mode of life you can best preserve your widowhood, you may read with advantage what I have written. I mean my treatise on the preservation of virginity addressed to Eustochium[3] and my two letters to Furia[4] and Salvina.[5] Of these two latter you may like to know that the first is daughter-in-law to Probus some time consul, and the second daughter to Gildo formerly governour of Africa. This tract on monogamy I shall call by your name.

LETTER CXXIV.

TO AVITUS.

Avitus to whom this letter is addressed is probably the same person who induced Jerome to write to Salvina (see Letter LXXIX., § 1, ante). The occasion of writing is as follows. Ten years previously (that is to say in A.D. 399 or 400) Pammachius had asked Jerome to supply him with a correct version of Origen's *First Principles* to enable him to detect the variations introduced by Rufinus into his rendering. This Jerome willingly did (see Letters LXXXIII. and LXXXIV.) but when the work in its integrity was perused by Pammachius he thought it so erroneous in doctrine that he determined not to circulate it. However, "a certain brother" induced him to lend the MS. to him for a short time; and then, when he had got it into his hands, had a hasty and incorrect transcript made, which he forthwith published much to the chagrin of Pammachius. Falling into the hands of Avitus a copy of this much perplexed him and he seems to have appealed to Jerome for an explanation. This the latter now gives forwarding at the same time an authentic edition of his version of the *First Principles*. The date of the letter is A.D. 409 or 410.

1. About ten years ago that saintly man Pammachius sent me a copy of a certain person's rendering,[6] or rather misrendering, of Origen's *First Principles;* with a request that in a Latin version I should give the true sense of the Greek and should set down the writer's words for good or for evil without bias in either direction.[7] When I did as he wished and sent him the book,[8] he was shocked to read it and locked it up in his desk lest being circulated it might wound the souls of many. However, a certain brother, who had "a zeal for God but not according to knowledge,"[1] asked for a loan of the manuscript that he might read it; and, as he promised to return it without delay, Pammachius, thinking no harm could happen in so short a time, unsuspectingly consented. Hereupon he who had borrowed the book to read, with the aid of scribes copied the whole of it and gave it back much sooner than he had promised. Then with the same rashness or—to use a less severe term—thoughtlessness he made bad worse by confiding to others what he had thus stolen. Moreover, since a bulky treatise on an abstruse subject is difficult to reproduce with accuracy, especially if it has to be taken down surreptitiously and in a hurry, order and sense were sacrificed in several passages. Whence it comes, my dear Avitus, that you ask me to send you a copy of my version as made for Pammachius and not for the public, a garbled edition of which has been published by the aforesaid brother.

2. Take then what you have asked for; but know that there are countless things in the book to be abhorred, and that, as the Lord says, you will have to walk among scorpions and serpents.[2] It begins by saying that Christ was made God's son not born;[3] that God the Father, as He is by nature invisible, is invisible even to the Son;[4] that the Son, who is the likeness of the invisible Father, compared with the Father is not the truth but compared with us who cannot receive the truth of the almighty Father seems a figure of the truth so that we perceive the majesty and magnitude of the greater in the less, the Father's glory limited in the Son;[5] that God the Father is a light incomprehensible and that Christ compared with him is but a minute brightness, although by reason of our incapacity to us he appears a great one.[6] The Father and the Son are compared to two statues, a larger one and a small; the first filling the world and being somehow invisible through its size, the second cognisable by the eyes of men.[7] God the Father omnipotent the writer terms good and of perfect goodness; but of the Son he says: "He is not good but an emanation and likeness of goodness; not good absolutely but only with a qualification, as 'the good shepherd' and the like."[8] The Holy Spirit he places after the Father and the Son as third in dignity and honour. And while he de-

---

[1] 1 Tim. v. 13.　　[2] Phil. iii. 19.　　[3] Letter XXII.
[4] Letter LIV.　　[5] Letter LXXIX.
[6] The 'certain person' is of course Rufinus.
[7] See Letter LXXXIII.　　[8] See Letter LXXXIV.

[1] Rom. x. 2, R.V.　　[2] Cf. Luke x. 19: Ezek. ii. 6.
[3] This statement is not borne out by the existing fragments of the treatise. In fact Origen declares Christ's divinity in unambiguous language. "Being God he was made man" First Principles, I. Preface.
[4] F. P., I. 1, 8.　　[5] F. P., I. 2, 6.　　[6] F. P., I. 2, 7.
[7] F. P., I. 2, 8.
[8] F. P., I. 2, 9, 13. The last words are omitted by Rufinus.

clares that he does not know whether the Holy Spirit is created or uncreated,[1] he has later on given his own opinion that except God the Father alone there is nothing uncreated. " The Son," he states, " is inferior to the Father, inasmuch as He is second and the Father first ; and the Holy Spirit which dwells in all the saints is inferior to the Son. In the same way the power of the Father is greater than that of the Son and of the Holy Spirit. Likewise the power of the Son is greater than that of the Holy Spirit, and as a consequence the Holy Spirit in its turn has greater virtue than other things called holy." [2]

3. Then, when he comes to deal with rational creatures and to describe their lapse into earthly bodies as due to their own negligence, he goes on to say : " Surely it argues great negligence and sloth for a soul so far to empty itself as to fall into sin and allow itself to be tied to the material body of an unreasoning brute ; " and in a subsequent passage : " These reasonings induce me to suppose that it is by their own free act that some are numbered with God's saints and servants, and that it was through their own fault that others fell from holiness into such negligence that they were changed into forces of an opposite kind." [3] He maintains that after every end a fresh beginning springs forth and an end from each beginning, and that wholesale variation is possible ; so that one who is now a human being may in another world become a demon, while one who by reason of his negligence is now a demon may hereafter be placed in a more material body and thus become a human being.[4] So far does he carry this transforming process that on his theory an archangel may become the devil and the devil in turn be changed back into an archangel. " Such as have wavered or faltered but have not altogether fallen shall be made subject, for rule and government and guidance, to better things—to principalities and powers, to thrones and dominations ; and of these perhaps another human race will be formed, when in the words of Isaiah there shall be ' new heavens and a new earth.' [5] But such as have not deserved to return through humanity to their former estate shall become the devil and his angels, demons of the worst sort ; and according to what they have done shall have special duties assigned to them in particular worlds." Moreover, the very demons and rulers of darkness in any world or worlds, if they are willing to turn to better things, may become human beings and so come back to their first beginning. That is to say, after

they have borne the discipline of punishment and torture for a longer or a shorter time in human bodies, they may again reach the angelic pinnacles from which they have fallen. Hence it may be shewn that we men may change into any other reasonable beings, and that not once only or on emergency but time after time ; we and angels shall become demons if we neglect our duty ; and demons, if they will take to themselves virtues, may attain to the rank of angels.

4. Bodily substances too are to pass away utterly or else at the end of all things will become highly rarified like the sky and æther and other subtle bodies. It is clear that these principles must affect the writer's view of the resurrection. The sun also and the moon and the rest of the constellations are alive. Nay more ; as we men by reason of our sins are enveloped in bodies material and sluggish ; so the lights of heaven have for like reasons received bodies more or less luminous, and demons have been for more serious faults clothed with starry frames. This, he argues, is the view of the apostle who writes :—" the creation has been subjected to vanity and shall be delivered for the revealing of the sons of God." [1] That it may not be supposed that I am imputing to him ideas of my own I shall give his actual words. " At the end and consummation of the world," he writes, " when souls and beings endowed with reason shall be released from prison by the Lord, they will move slowly or fly quickly according as they have previously been slothful or energetic. And as all of them have free will and are free to choose virtue or vice, those who choose the latter will be much worse off than they now are. But those who choose the former will improve their condition. Their movements and decisions in this direction or in that will determine their various futures ; whether, that is, angels are to become men or demons, and whether demons are to become men or angels." Then after adducing various arguments in support of his thesis and maintaining that while not incapable of virtue the devil has yet not chosen to be virtuous, he has finally reasoned with much diffuseness that an angel, a human soul, and a demon—all according to him of one nature but of different wills—may in punishment for great negligence or folly be transformed into brutes. Moreover, to avoid the agony of punishment and the burning flame the more sensitive may choose to become low organisms, to dwell in water, to assume the shape of this or that animal ; so that we have reason to fear a metamorphosis not only into four-footed things but even into fishes. Then,

---

[1] F. P., I. Preface, 4.
[2] F. P., I. 3,5. The words are omitted by Rufinus.
[3] F. P., I. 5, 5.   [4] F. P., I. 6, 2.   [5] Isa. lxv. 17.

[1] Rom. viii. 19-21, R.V.

lest he should be held guilty of maintaining with Pythagoras the transmigration of souls, he winds up the wicked reasoning with which he has wounded his reader by saying : "I must not be taken to make dogmas of these things ; they are only thrown out as conjectures to shew that they are not altogether overlooked."

5. In his second book he maintains a plurality of worlds ; not, however, as Epicurus taught, many like ones existing at once, but a new one beginning each time that the old comes to an end. There was a world before this world of ours, and after it there will be first one and then another and so on in regular succession. He is in doubt whether one world shall be so completely similar to another as to leave no room for any difference between them, or whether one world shall never wholly be indistinguishable from another. And again a little farther on he writes : "if, as the course of the discussion makes necessary, all things can live without body, all bodily existence shall be swallowed up and that which once has been made out of nothing shall again be reduced to nothing. And yet a time will come when its use will be once more necessary." And in the same context : "but if, as reason and the authority of scripture shew, this corruptible shall put on incorruption and this mortal shall put on immortality, death shall be swallowed up in victory and corruption in incorruption.[1] And it may be that all bodily existence shall be removed, for it is only in this that death can operate." And a little farther on : "if these things are not contrary to the faith, it may be that we shall some day live in a disembodied state. Moreover, if only he is fully subject to Christ who is disembodied, and if all must be made subject to Him, we too shall lose our bodies when we become fully subject to Him." And in the same passage : "if all are to be made subject to God, all shall lay aside their bodies ; and then all bodily existence shall be brought to nought. But if through the fall of reasonable beings it is a second time required it will reappear. For God has left souls to strive and struggle, to teach them that full and complete victory is to be attained not by their own efforts but by His grace. And so to my mind worlds vary with the sins which cause them, and those are exploded theories which maintain that all worlds are alike." And again : "three conjectures occur to me with regard to the end ; it is for the reader to determine which is nearest to the truth. For either we shall be bodiless when being made subject to Christ we shall be made subject to God and He shall be all in all ; or as things

made subject to Christ shall be with Christ Himself made subject to God and brought under one law, so all substance shall be refined into its most perfect form and rarified into æther which is a pure and uncompounded essence ; or else the sphere which I have called motionless and all that it contains will be dissolved into nothing, and the sphere in which the antizone[1] itself is contained shall be called 'good ground,'[2] and that other sphere which in its revolution surrounds the earth and goes by the name of heaven shall be reserved for the abode of the saints."

6. In speaking thus does he not most clearly follow the error of the heathen and foist upon the simple faith of Christians the ravings of philosophy ? In the same book he writes : "it remains that God is invisible. But if He is by nature invisible, He must be so even to the Saviour." And lower down : "no soul which has descended into a human body has borne upon it so true an impress of its previous character as Christ's soul of which He says : 'no man taketh it from me, but I lay it down of myself.'"[3] And in another place : "we must carefully consider whether souls, when they have won salvation and have attained to the blessed life, may not cease to be souls. For as the Lord and Saviour came to seek and to save that which was lost[4] that it might cease to be lost ; so the lost soul which the Lord came to save, when saved, will cease to be a soul. We must ask ourselves whether, as the lost was not lost once and again will not be, the soul likewise may have been and again may be not a soul."[5] And after a good many remarks upon the soul he brings in the following, "νοῦς or" intelligence by falling becomes a soul ; and by acquiring virtue this will become intelligence again. This at least is a fair inference from the case of Esau who for his old sins is condemned to lead a lower life. And concerning the heavenly bodies we must make a similar acknowledgment. The soul of the sun—or whatever else you like to call it—does not date its existence from the creation of the world ; it already existed before it entered its shining and glowing body. So also with the moon and stars. From antecedent causes they have been made subject to vanity not willingly but for future reward,[6] and are forced to do not their own will but the creator's who has assigned to them their several spheres."

7. Hellfire, moreover, and the torments with

---

[1] This word is doubtful.   [2] Matt. xiii. 8.
[3] Joh. x. 18.   [4] Luke xix. 10.
[5] The paralogism in this reasoning—so obvious to modern minds—is due to the confusion of the copula with the verb substantive.
[6] Rom. viii. 20.

which holy scripture threatens sinners he explains not as external punishments but as the pangs of guilty consciences when by God's power the memory of our transgressions is set before our eyes. " The whole crop of our sins grows up afresh from seeds which remain in the soul, and all our dishonourable and undutiful acts are again pictured before our gaze. Thus it is the fire of conscience and the stings of remorse which torture the mind as it looks back on former self-indulgence." And again : " but perhaps this coarse and earthly body ought to be described as mist and darkness ; for at the end of this world and when it becomes necessary to pass into another, the like darkness will lead to the like physical birth." In speaking thus he clearly pleads for the transmigration of souls as taught by Pythagoras and Plato.[1] And at the end of the second book in dealing with our perfection he has said : " when we shall have made such progress as not only to cease to be flesh or body but perhaps also to cease to be souls our perfect intelligence and perception, undimmed with any mist of passion, will discern reasonable and intelligible substances face to face.

8. In the third book the following faulty statements are contained. " If we once admit that, when one vessel is made to honour and another to dishonour,[2] this is due to antecedent causes ; why may we not revert to the mystery of the soul and allow that it is loved in one and hated in another because of its past actions, before in Jacob it becomes a supplanter and before in Esau it is supplanted ? "[3] And again: " the fact that souls are made some to honour and some to dishonour is to be explained by their previous history." And in the same place : " on this hypothesis of mine a vessel made to honour which fails to fulfil its object will in another world become a vessel made to dishonour ; and contrariwise a vessel which has from a previous fault been condemned to dishonour will, if it accepts correction in this present life, become in the new creation a vessel ' sanctified and meet for the Master's use and prepared unto every good work.' "[4] And he immediately goes on to say : " I believe that men who begin with small faults may become so hardened in wickedness that, if they do not repent and turn to better things, they must become inhuman energies ;[5] and contrariwise that hostile and demonic beings may in course of time so far heal their wounds and check the current of their former sins that they may attain to the abode of the perfect. As I have often said, in those countless and unceasing worlds in which the soul lives and has its being some grow worse and worse until they reach the lowest depths of degradation ; while others in those lowest depths grow better and better until they reach the perfection of virtue." Thus he tries to shew that men, or rather their souls, may become demons ; and that demons in turn may be restored to the rank of angels. In the same book he writes : " this too must be considered ; why the human soul is diversely acted upon now by influences of one kind and now by influences of another." And he surmises that this is due to conduct which has preceded birth. It is for this, he argues, that John leaps in his mother's womb when at Mary's salutation Elizabeth declares herself unworthy of her notice.[1] And he immediately subjoins : " on the other hand infants that are hardly weaned are possessed with evil spirits and become diviners and soothsayers ;[2] indeed, some are indwelt from their earliest years with the spirit of a python. Now as they have done nothing to bring upon themselves these visitations, one who holds that nothing happens without God's permission, and that all things are governed by His justice, cannot suppose that God's providence has abandoned them without good reason.

9. Again, of the world he writes thus : " The belief commends itself to me that there was a world before this world and that after it there will be another. Do you wish to know that after the decay of this world there will be a new one ? Hear the words of Isaiah : 'the new heavens and the new earth which I will make shall remain before me.'[3] Do you wish to know that before the making of this world there have previously been others ? Listen to the Preacher who says : 'the thing which hath been, it is that which shall be ; and that which is done is that which shall be done : and there is no new thing under the sun. Is there anything whereof it may be said, See, this is new ? It hath been already of old time, which was before us.'[4] A passage which proves not only that other worlds have been but that other worlds shall be ; not, however, simultaneously and side by side but one after another." And he immediately adds : " I hold that heaven is the abode of the deity, the true place of rest ; and that it was there that reasonable creatures enjoyed their ancient bliss, before coming down to a lower plane and exchanging the invisible for the visible, they fell to the earth and came to need material bodies. Now that they have fallen, God the creator has made for them bodies suitable to their surroundings ; and has fashioned this visible world, and has sent into it ministers to ensure the salva-

---

1 Phædo, 70-77.   2 2 Tim. ii. 20.   3 Mal. i. 2, 3.   1 Luke i. 41.   2 Cf. Acts xvi. 16, A.V. margin.
4 2 Tim. ii. 21.   5 i.e. demons.   3 Isa. lxvi. 22.   4 Eccles. i. 9, 10.

tion and correction of the fallen. Of these ministers some have held assigned positions and have been subject to the world's necessary laws; while others have intelligently performed duties laid upon them in times and seasons determined by God's plan. To the former class belong the sun, moon, and stars called by the apostle 'the creation;' and these have had allotted to them the heights of heaven. Now the creation is subjected to vanity[1] because it is encased in material bodies and visible to the eye. And yet it is 'made subject to vanity not willingly but by reason of him who hath subjected the same in hope.' Others again of the second class, at particular places and times known to their Maker only, we believe to be His angels sent to steer the world." A little farther on he says: "the affairs of the world are so ordered by Providence that while some angels fall from heaven others freely glide down to earth. The former are hurled down against their will; the latter descend from choice alone. The former are forced to continue in a distasteful service for a fixed period; the latter spontaneously embrace the task of lending a hand to those who fall." Again he writes: "whence it follows that these different movements result in the creation of different worlds; and that this world of ours will be succeeded by one quite unlike it. Now, as regards this falling and rising, this rewarding of virtue and punishment of vice, whether they take place in the past, present, or future, God, the creator, can alone apportion desert and make all things converge to one end. For He only knows why He allows some to follow their own inclination and to descend from the higher planes to the lowest; and why He visits others and giving them His hand draws them back to their former state and places them once more in heaven."

10. In discussing the end of the world he has made use of the following language. "Since, as I have often said, a new beginning springs from the end, it may be asked whether bodies will then continue to exist, or whether, when they have been annihilated, we shall live without bodies and be incorporeal as we know God to be. Now there can be no doubt but that, if bodies or, as the apostle calls them, visible things, belong only to our sensible world, the life of the disembodied will be incorporeal." And a little farther on: "when the apostle writes, 'the creation shall be delivered from the bondage of corruption into the liberty of the glory of the children of God,'[2] I explain his words thus. Reasonable and incorporeal beings are the highest of

God's creatures, for not being clothed with bodies they are not the slaves of corruption. Since where there are bodies, there corruption is sure to be found. But hereafter 'the creation shall be delivered from the bondage of corruption,' and then men shall receive the glory of the children of God and God shall be all in all." And in the same passage he writes: "that the final state will be an incorporeal one is rendered credible by the words of our Saviour's prayer: 'as thou, Father, art in me and I in thee, that they also may be one in us.'[1] For we ought to realize what God is and what the Saviour will finally be, and how the likeness to the Father and the Son here promised to the Saints consists in this that as They are one in Themselves so we shall be one in Them. For if in the end the life of the Saints is to be assimilated to the life of God, we must either admit that the Lord of the universe is clothed with a body and that he is enveloped in matter as we are in flesh; or, if it is unbecoming to suppose this, especially in persons who have but small clues from which to infer God's majesty and to guess at the glory of His innate and transcendent nature, we are reduced to the following dilemma. Either we shall always have bodies and in that case must despair of ever being like God; or, if the blessedness of the life of God is really promised to us, the conditions of His life must be the conditions of ours."

11. These passages prove what his view is regarding the resurrection. For he evidently maintains that all bodies will perish and that we shall be incorporeal as according to him we were before we received our present bodies. Again when he comes to argue for a variety of worlds and to maintain that angels will become demons, demons either angels or men, and men in their turn demons; in a word that everything will be turned into something else, he thus sums up his own opinion: "no doubt, after an interval matter will exist afresh and bodies will be formed and a different world will be created to meet the varying wills of reasonable beings who, having forfeited the perfect bliss which continues to the end, have gradually fallen into so great wickedness as to change their nature and refuse to keep their first estate of unalloyed blessedness. Many reasonable beings, it is right to say, keep it until a second, a third, and a fourth world, and give God no ground for changing their condition. Others deteriorate so little that they seem to have lost hardly anything, and others again have to be hurled headlong into the abyss. God who orders all things alone knows how to use each class according to its

---

[1] Rom. viii. 20, R.V.   [2] Rom. viii. 21, R.V.   [1] Joh. xvii. 21.

deserts in a suitable sphere; for He only understands opportunities and motives and the course in which the world must be steered. Thus one who has borne away the palm for wickedness and has sunk into the lowest degradation will in the world which is hereafter to be fashioned be made a devil, a kind of first fruits of the Lord's handiwork, to be a laughing stock to the angels who have lost their first virtue." What is this but to argue that the sinful men of this world may become a devil and demons in another; and contrariwise that those who are now demons may hereafter become either men or angels? And after a lengthy discussion in which he maintains that all corporeal creatures must exchange their material for subtle and spiritual bodies and that all substance must become one pure and inconceivably bright body, of which the human mind can at present form no conception, he winds up thus:—"'God shall be all in all;' that is to say, all bodily existence shall be made as perfect as possible; it shall be brought into the divine essence, than which there is none better."

12. In the fourth and last book of his work the following passages deserve the church's condemnation. "It may be that as, when men die in this world by the separation of soul and body, they are allotted different positions in hell according to the difference in their works; so when angels die, out of the system of the heavenly Jerusalem, they come down to this world as a hell and are placed on earth according to their deserts." And again: "as we have compared the souls which pass from this world to hell with those which as they come from heaven to us are in a manner dead; so we must carefully inquire whether this is true of all souls without exception. For in that case souls born on earth when they desire better things rise out of hell and assume human bodies or when they desire worse things come down to us from better worlds; and in the firmament above us likewise there are souls on their way from our world to higher ones, and others who, while they have fallen from heaven, have not sinned so grievously as to be thrust down to earth." He thus tries to prove that the firmament, that is the sky, is hell compared with heaven; and that this earth is hell compared with the firmament; and again that our world is heaven to hell. Or in other words what is hell to some is heaven to others. And not content with saying this he goes on: "at the end of all things when we shall return to the heavenly Jerusalem the hostile powers shall declare war[1] against the people of God to breathe and exercise their valour and strengthen their resolve. For this they cannot have until they have faced and foiled their foes; of whom we read in the book of Numbers[1] that they are overcome by reason, discipline, and tactical skill."

13. After saying that according to the apocalypse of John "the everlasting gospel" which shall be revealed in heaven[2] as much surpasses our gospel as Christ's preaching does the sacraments[3] of the ancient law, he has asserted what it is sacrilegious even to think; that Christ will once more suffer in the sky for the salvation of demons. And although he has not expressly said it, it is yet implied in his words that as for men God became man to set men free, so for the salvation of demons' when He comes to deliver them He will become a demon. To shew that this is no gloss of mine, I must give his own words: "As Christ," he writes, "has fulfilled the shadow of the law by the shadow of the gospel, and as all law is a pattern and shadow of things done in heaven, we must inquire whether we are justified in supposing that even the heavenly law and the rites of the celestial worship are still incomplete and need the true gospel which in the apocalypse of John is called everlasting to distinguish it from ours which is only temporal, set forth in a world that shall pass away. Now if we extend our inquiry to the passion of our Lord and Saviour, it may indeed be overbold to suppose that He will suffer in heaven; yet if there is spiritual wickedness in heavenly places[4] and if we confess without a blush that the Lord has once been crucified to destroy those things which He has destroyed by His passion; why need we fear to imagine a like occurrence in the upper world in the fulness of time, so that the nations of all realms shall be saved by a passion of Christ?"

14. Here is another blasphemy which he has spoken of the Son. "Assuming that the Son knows the Father, it would seem that by this knowledge He can comprehend Him as much as a craftsman can comprehend the rules of his art. And, doubtless, if the Father is in the Son, He is also comprehended by Him in whom He is. But if we mean by comprehension not merely that the knower takes a thing in by perception and insight but that he contains it within himself by virtue of a special faculty; in this sense we cannot say that the Son comprehends the Father. For the Father comprehends all things, and of these the Son is one; therefore, He comprehends the Son." And to shew us reasons why, while the Father

---

[1] Reading adversariorum fortitudinum . . . bella consurgere.

[1] Passim.   [2] Rev. xiv. 6.
[3] This term had not in Jerome's time become restricted to its later sense. Anything mysterious or sacred was called a sacrament. Here it refers to the mystic teaching of the O.T.
[4] Eph. vi. 12.

comprehends the Son, the Son cannot comprehend the Father, he adds : " the curious reader may inquire whether the Father knows Himself in the same way that the Son knows Him. But if he recalls the words : 'the Father who sent me is greater than I,'[1] he will allow that they must be universally true and will admit that, in knowledge as in everything else, the Father is greater than the Son, and knows Himself more perfectly and immediately than the Son can do."

15. The following passage is a convincing proof that he holds the transmigration of souls and annihilation of bodies. "If it can be shewn that an incorporeal and reasonable being has life in itself independently of the body and that it is worse off in the body than out of it ; then beyond a doubt bodies are only of secondary importance and arise from time to time to meet the varying conditions of reasonable creatures. Those who require bodies are clothed with them, and contrariwise, when fallen souls have lifted themselves up to better things, their bodies are once more annihilated. They are thus ever vanishing and ever reappearing." And to prevent us from minimizing the impiety of his previous utterances he ends his work by maintaining that all reasonable beings, that is, the Father, the Son, and the Holy Ghost, angels, powers, dominations, and virtues, and even man by right of his soul's dignity, are of one and the same essence. "God," he writes, "and His only-begotten Son and the Holy Spirit are conscious of an intellectual and reasonable nature. But so also are the angels, the powers, and the virtues, as well as the inward man who is created in the image and after the likeness of God.[2] From which I conclude that God and they are in some sort of one essence." He adds "in some sort" to escape the charge of blasphemy ; and while in another place he will not allow the Son and the Holy Spirit to be of one substance with the Father lest by so doing he should appear to make the divine essence divisible, he here bestows the nature of God almighty upon angels and men.

16. This being the nature of Origen's book, is it anything short of madness to change a few blasphemous passages regarding the Son and the Holy Spirit and then to publish the rest unchanged with an unprincipled eulogy when the parts unaltered as well as the parts altered flow from the same fountain head of gross impiety ? This is not the time to confute all the statements made in detail ; and indeed those who have written against Arius, Eunomius, Manichæus, and various other heretics must be supposed to have answered these blasphemies as well. If anyone, therefore, wishes to read the work let him walk with his feet shod towards the land of promise ; let him guard against the jaws of the serpent and the crooked jaws of the scorpion ; let him read this treatise first and before he enters upon the path let him know the dangers which he will have to avoid.

LETTER CXXV.

TO RUSTICUS.

Rusticus, a young monk of Toulouse, (to be carefully distinguished from the recipient of Letter CXXII.) is advised by Jerome not to become an anchorite but to continue in a community. Rules are suggested for the monastic life and a vivid picture is drawn of the difference between a good monk and a bad. Incidentally Jerome indulges his spleen against his dead opponent Rufinus (§18). The date of the letter is 411 A.D.

1. No man is happier than the Christian, for to him is promised the kingdom of heaven. No man struggles harder than he, for he goes daily in danger of his life. No man is stronger, for he overcomes the Devil. No man is weaker, for he is overcome by the flesh. Both pairs of statements can be proved by many examples. For instance, the robber believes upon the cross and immediately hears the assuring words : " verily I say unto thee, To-day shalt thou be with me in paradise :"[1] while Judas falls from the pinnacle of the apostolate into the abyss of perdition. Neither the close intercourse of the banquet nor the dipping of the sop[2] nor the Lord's gracious kiss[3] can save him from betraying as man Him whom he had known as the Son of God. Could any one have been viler than the woman of Samaria ? Yet not only did she herself believe, and after her six husbands find one Lord, not only did she recognize that Messiah by the well, whom the Jews failed to recognize in the temple ; she brought salvation to many and, while the apostles were away buying food, refreshed the Saviour's hunger and relieved His weariness.[4] Was ever man wiser than Solomon ? Yet love for women made even him foolish. Salt is good, and every offering must be sprinkled with it.[5] Wherefore also the apostle has given commandment : "let your speech be alway with grace, seasoned with salt."[6] But "if the salt have lost his savour," it is cast out.[7] And so utterly does it lose its value that it is not even fit for the dunghill,[8] whence believers fetch manure to enrich the barren soil of their souls.

I begin thus, Rusticus my son, to teach you

---

[1] Joh. xiv. 28. [2] 2 Cor. iv. 16 : Gen. i. 27.

[1] Luke xxiii. 43. [2] Joh. xiii. 26. [3] Matt. xxvi. 49.
[4] Joh. iv. [5] Lev. ii. 13. [6] Col. iv. 6.
[7] Matt. v. 13. [8] Luke xiv. 35.

the greatness of your enterprise and the loftiness of your ideal ; and to shew you that only by trampling under foot youthful lusts can you hope to climb the heights of true maturity. For the path along which you walk is a slippery one and the glory of success is less than the shame of failure.

2. I need not now conduct the stream of my discourse through the meadows of virtue, nor exert myself to shew to you the beauty of its several flowers. I need not dilate on the purity of the lily, the modest blush of the rose, the royal purple of the violet, or the promise of glowing gems which their various colours hold out. For through the mercy of God you have already put your hand to the plough ; [1] you have already gone up upon the housetop like the apostle Peter.[2] Who when he became hungry among the Jews had his hunger satisfied by the faith of Cornelius, and stilled the craving caused by their unbelief through the conversion of the centurion and other Gentiles. By the vessel let down from heaven to earth, the four corners of which typified the four gospels, he was taught that all men can be saved. Once more, this fair white sheet which in his vision was taken up again was a symbol of the church which carries believers from earth to heaven, an assurance that the Lord's promise should be fulfilled : " blessed are the pure in heart, for they shall see God." [3]

All this means that I take you by the hand and do my best to impress certain facts upon your mind ; that, like a skilled sailor who has been through many shipwrecks, I am anxious to caution an inexperienced passenger of the risks before him. For on one side is the Charybdis of covetousness, " the root of all evil ; " [4] and on the other lurks the Scylla of detraction girt with the railing hounds of which the apostle says : " if ye bite and devour one another, take heed that ye be not consumed one of another." [5] Sometimes, you must know, the quicksands of vice [6] suck us down as we sail at ease through the calm water ; and the desert of this world is not untenanted by venomous reptiles.

3. Those who navigate the Red Sea—where we must pray that the true Pharaoh may be drowned with all his host—have to encounter many difficulties and dangers before they reach the city of Auxuma.[7] Nomad savages and ferocious wild beasts haunt the shores on either side. Thus travellers must be always armed and on the alert, and they must carry with them a whole year's provisions. Moreover, so full are the waters of hidden reefs and

impassable shoals that a look-out has constantly to be kept from the masthead to direct the helmsman how to shape his course. They may count themselves fortunate if after six months they make the port of the above-mentioned city. At this point the ocean begins, to cross which a whole year hardly suffices. Then India is reached and the river Ganges—called in holy scripture Pison—" which compasseth the whole land of Havilah " [1] and is said to carry down with it—from its source in paradise—various dyes and pigments. Here are found rubies and emeralds, glowing pearls and gems of the first water, such as high born ladies passionately desire. There are also mountains of gold which however men cannot approach by reason of the griffins, dragons, and huge monsters which haunt them ; for such are the guardians which avarice needs for its treasures.

4. What, you ask, is the drift of all this ? Surely it is clear enough. For if the merchants of the world undergo such hardships to win a doubtful and passing gain, and if after seeking it through many dangers they only keep it at risk of their lives ; what should Christ's merchant do who " selleth all that he hath " that he may acquire the " one pearl of great price ; " who with his whole substance buys a field that he may find therein a treasure which neither thief can dig up nor robber carry away ? [2]

5. I know that I must offend large numbers who will be angry with my criticisms as aimed at their own deficiencies. Yet such anger does but shew an uneasy conscience and they will pass a far severer sentence on themselves than on me. For I shall not mention names ; or copy the licence of the old comedy [3] which criticized individuals. Wise men and wise women will try to hide or rather to correct whatever they perceive to be amiss in them ; they will be more angry with themselves than with me, and will not be disposed to heap curses upon the head of their monitor. For he, although he is liable to the same charges, is certainly superior in this that he is discontented with his own faults.

6. I am told that your mother is a religious woman, a widow of many years' standing ; and that when you were a child she reared and taught you herself. Afterwards when you had spent some time in the flourishing schools of Gaul she sent you to Rome, sparing no expense and consoling herself for your absence by the thought of the future that lay before you. She hoped to see the exuberance and

---

[1] Luke ix. 62.　　　　[2] Acts x. 3-16.
[3] Matt. v. 8.　　　　[4] 1 Tim. vi. 10.
[5] Gal. v. 15.　　　　[6] Lybicæ Syrtes.
[7] An important city of Abyssinia in Jerome's day, 120 miles from the Red Sea. It is now in ruins.

[1] Gen. ii. 11.　　　　[2] Matt. xiii. 45-46 : vi. 19, 20.
[3] The Old Comedy at Athens ridiculed citizens by name. Most of the extant plays of Aristophanes belong to it.

glitter of your Gallic eloquence toned down by Roman sobriety, for she saw that you required the rein more than the spur. So we are told of the greatest orators of Greece that they seasoned the bombast of Asia with the salt of Athens and pruned their vines when they grew too fast. For they wished to fill the wine-press of eloquence not with the tendrils of mere words but with the rich grape-juice of good sense. Your mother has done the same thing for you ; you should, therefore, look up to her as a parent, love her as a tender nurse, and venerate her as a saint. You must not imitate those who leave their own relations and pay court to strange women. Their infamy is apparent to all, for what they aim at under the pretence of pure affection [1] is simply illicit intercourse. I know some women of riper years, indeed a good many, who, finding pleasure in their young freedmen, make them their spiritual children and thus, pretending to be mothers to them, gradually overcome their own sense of shame and allow themselves in the licence of marriage. Other women desert their maiden sisters and unite themselves to strange widows. There are some who hate their parents and have no affection for their kin. Their state of mind is indicated by a restlessness which disdains excuses ; they rend the veil of chastity and put it aside like a cobweb. Such are the ways of women ; not, indeed, that men are any better. For there are persons to be seen who (for all their girded loins, sombre garb, and long beards) are inseparable from women, live under one roof with them, dine in their company, have young girls to wait upon them, and, save that they do not claim to be called husbands, are as good as married. Still it is no fault of Christianity that a hypocrite falls into sin ; rather, it is the confusion of the Gentiles that the churches condemn what is condemned by all good men.

7. But if for your part you desire to be a monk and not merely to seem one, be more careful of your soul than of your property ; for in adopting a religious profession you have renounced this once for all. Let your garments be squalid to shew that your mind is white ; and your tunic coarse to prove that you despise the world. But give not way to pride lest your dress and language be found at variance. Baths stimulate the senses and must, therefore, be avoided ; for to quench natural heat is the aim of chilling fasts. Yet even these must be moderate, for, if they are carried to excess, they weaken the stomach and by making more food necessary to it promote indigestion, that fruitful parent of unclean desires. A frugal and temperate diet is good for both body and soul.

See your mother as often as you please but not with other women, for their faces may dwell in your thoughts and so

A secret wound may fester in your breast. [1]

The maidservants who attend upon her you must regard as so many snares laid to entrap you ; for the lower their condition is the more easy is it for you to effect their ruin. John the Baptist had a religious mother and his father was a priest. [2] Yet neither his mother's affection nor his father's wealth could induce him to live in his parents' house at the risk of his chastity. He lived in the desert, and seeking Christ with his eyes refused to look at anything else. His rough garb, his girdle made of skins, his diet of locusts and wild honey [3] were all alike designed to encourage virtue and continence. The sons of the prophets, who were the monks of the Old Testament, built for themselves huts by the waters of Jordan and forsaking the crowded cities lived in these on pottage and wild herbs. [4] As long as you are at home make your cell your paradise, [5] gather there the varied fruits of scripture, let this be your favourite companion, and take its precepts to your heart. If your eye offend you or your foot or your hand, cast them from you. [6] To spare your soul spare nothing else. The Lord says : "whosoever looketh on a woman to lust after her hath committed adultery with her already in his heart." [7] "Who can say," writes the wise man, "I have made my heart clean ?" [8] The stars are not pure in the Lord's sight ; how much less men whose whole life is one long temptation. [9] Woe be to us who commit fornication every time that we cherish lust. "My sword," God says, "hath drunk its fill in heaven ;" [10] much more then upon the earth with its crop of thorns and thistles. [11] The chosen vessel [12] who had Christ's name ever on his lips kept under his body and brought it into subjection. [13] Yet even he was hindered by carnal desire and had to do what he would not. As one suffering violence he cries : "O wretched man that I am ! who shall deliver me from the body of this death ?" [14] Is it likely then that you can pass without fall or wound, unless you keep your heart with all diligence, [15] and say with the Saviour : "my mother and my brethren are these which hear the word of God and do it." [16] This may seem cruelty, but it is really affection. What

1 Pietas.

1 Virgil, Æn. iv. 67.   2 Pontifex.
3 Mark i. 6.   4 2 Kings iv. 38, 39 : vi. 1, 2.
5 i. e. 'garden.'   6 Matt. xviii. 8, 9.   7 Matt. v. 28.
8 Prov. xx. 9.   9 Job xxv. 5, 6.   10 Isa. xxxiv. 5, R.V.
11 Gen. iii. 18.   12 Acts ix. 15.   13 1 Cor. ix. 27.
14 Rom. vii. 24.   15 Prov. iv. 23.   16 Luke viii. 21.

greater proof, indeed, can there be of affection than to guard for a holy mother a holy son? She too desired your eternal welfare and is content to forego seeing you for a time that she may see you for ever with Christ. She is like Hannah who brought forth Samuel not for her own solace but for the service of the tabernacle.[1]

The sons of Jonadab, we are told, drank neither wine nor strong drink and dwelt in tents pitched wherever night overtook them.[2] According to the psalter they were the first to undergo captivity; for, when the Chaldæans began to ravage Judah they were compelled to take refuge in cities.[3]

8. Others may think what they like and follow each his own bent. But to me a town is a prison and solitude paradise. Why do we long for the bustle of cities, we whose very name speaks of loneliness?[4] To fit him for the leadership of the Jewish people Moses was trained for forty years in the wilderness;[5] and it was not till after these that the shepherd of sheep became a shepherd of men. The apostles were fishers on lake Gennesaret before they became "fishers of men."[6] But at the Lord's call they forsook all that they had, father, net, and ship, and bore their cross daily without so much as a rod in their hands.

I say these things that, in case you desire to enter the ranks of the clergy, you may learn what you must afterwards teach, that you may offer a reasonable sacrifice[7] to Christ, that you may not think yourself a finished soldier while still a raw recruit, or suppose yourself a master while you are as yet only a learner. It does not become one of my humble abilities to pass judgment upon the clergy or to speak to the discredit of those who are ministers in the churches. They have their own rank and station and must keep it. If ever you become one of them my published letter to Nepotian[8] will teach you the mode of life suitable to you in that vocation. At present I am dealing with the forming and training of a monk; of one too who has put the yoke of Christ upon his neck after receiving a liberal education in his younger days.

9. The first point to be considered is whether you ought to live by yourself or in a monastery with others.[9] For my part I should like you to have the society of holy men so as not to be thrown altogether on your own resources. For if you set out upon a road that is new to you without a guide, you are sure to turn aside immediately either to the right or to the left, to lay yourself open to the assaults of error, to go too far or else not far enough, to weary yourself with running too fast or to loiter by the way and to fall asleep. In loneliness pride quickly creeps upon a man: if he has fasted for a little while and has seen no one, he fancies himself a person of some note; forgetting who he is, whence he comes, and whither he goes, he lets his thoughts riot within and outwardly indulges in rash speech. Contrary to the apostle's wish he judges another man's servants,[1] puts forth his hand to grasp whatever his appetite desires, sleeps as long he pleases, fears nobody, does what he likes, fancies everyone inferior to himself, spends more of his time in cities than in his cell, and, while with the brothers he affects to be retiring, rubs shoulders with the crowd in the streets. What then, you will say? Do I condemn a solitary life? By no means: in fact I have often commended it. But I wish to see the monastic schools turn out soldiers who have no fear of the rough training of the desert, who have exhibited the spectacle of a holy life for a considerable time, who have made themselves last that they might be first, who have not been overcome by hunger or satiety, whose joy is in poverty, who teach virtue by their garb and mien, and who are too conscientious to invent—as some silly men do—monstrous stories of struggles with demons, designed to magnify their heroes in the eyes of the crowd and before all to extort money from it.

10. Quite recently we have seen to our sorrow a fortune worthy of Crœsus brought to light by a monk's death, and a city's alms, collected for the poor, left by will to his sons and successors. After sinking to the bottom the iron has once more floated upon the surface,[2] and men have again seen among the palmtrees the bitter waters of Marah.[3] In this there is, however, nothing strange, for the man had for his companion and teacher one who turned the hunger of the needy into a source of wealth for himself and kept back sums left to the miserable to his own subsequent misery. Yet their cry came up to heaven and entering God's ears overcame His patience. Wherefore, He sent an angel of woe to say to this new Carmelite, this second Nabal,[4] "Thou fool, this night thy soul shall be required of thee: then whose shall those things be which thou hast provided?"[5]

11. If I wish you then not to live with your mother, it is for the reasons given above, and above all for the two following. If she offers you delicacies to eat, you will grieve her by refusing them; and if you take them, you will add fuel to the flame that already burns within

---

[1] 1 Sam. i. 27, 28.   [2] Jer. xxxv. 6. 7.
[3] See Letter LVIII. § 5 and note there.
[4] An allusion to the word 'monachus,' 'solitary' or 'monk.'
[5] Acts vii. 29, 30.   [6] Matt. iv. 19.   [7] Rom. xii. 1.
[8] Letter LII.   [9] Cf. Letter CXXX. § 17.

[1] Rom. xiv. 4.   [2] 2 K. vi. 5, 6.   [3] Ex. xv. 23, 27.
[4] 1 Sam. xxv. 38.   [5] Luke xii. 20.

you. Again in a house where there are so many girls you will see in the daytime sights that will tempt you at night. Never take your hand or your eyes off your book; learn the psalms word for word, pray without ceasing,[1] be always on the alert, and let no vain thoughts lay hold upon you. Direct both body and mind to the Lord, overcome wrath by patience, love the knowledge of scripture, and you will no longer love the sins of the flesh. Do not let your mind become a prey to excitement, for if this effects a lodgment in your breast it will have dominion over you and will lead you into the great transgression.[2] Always have some work on hand, that the devil may find you busy. If apostles who had the right to live of the Gospel[3] laboured with their own hands that they might be chargeable to no man,[4] and bestowed relief upon others whose carnal things they had a claim to reap as having sown unto them spiritual things;[5] why do you not provide a supply to meet your needs? Make creels of reeds or weave baskets out of pliant osiers. Hoe your ground; mark out your garden into even plots; and when you have sown your cabbages or set your plants convey water to them in conduits; that you may see with your own eyes the lovely vision of the poet:

Art draws fresh water from the hilltop near
Till the stream plashing down among the rocks
Cools the parched meadows and allays their thirst.[6]

Graft unfruitful stocks with buds and slips that you may shortly be rewarded for your toil by plucking sweet apples from them. Construct also hives for bees, for to these the proverbs of Solomon send you,[7] and you may learn from the tiny creatures how to order a monastery and to discipline a kingdom. Twist lines too for catching fish, and copy books; that your hand may earn your food and your mind may be satisfied with reading. For "every one that is idle is a prey to vain desires."[8] In Egypt the monasteries make it a rule to receive none who are not willing to work; for they regard labour as necessary not only for the support of the body but also for the salvation of the soul. Do not let your mind stray into harmful thoughts, or, like Jerusalem in her whoredoms, open its feet to every chance comer.[9]

12. In my youth when the desert walled me in with its solitude I was still unable to endure the promptings of sin and the natural heat of my blood; and, although I tried by frequent fasts to break the force of both, my mind still surged with [evil] thoughts.[10] To subdue its

turbulence I betook myself to a brother[1] who before his conversion had been a Jew and asked him to teach me Hebrew. Thus, after having familiarised myself with the pointedness of Quintilian, the fluency of Cicero, the seriousness of Fronto and the gentleness of Pliny, I began to learn my letters anew and to study to pronounce words both harsh and guttural. What labour I spent upon this task, what difficulties I went through, how often I despaired, how often I gave over and then in my eagerness to learn commenced again, can be attested both by myself the subject of this misery and by those who then lived with me. But I thank the Lord that from this seed of learning sown in bitterness I now cull sweet fruits.

13. I will recount also another thing that I saw in Egypt. There was in a community a young Greek the flame of whose desire neither continual fasting nor the severest labour could avail to quench. He was in great danger of falling, when the father of the monastery saved him by the following device. He gave orders to one of the older brothers to pursue him with objurgations and reproaches, and then after having thus wronged him to be beforehand with him in laying a complaint against him. When witnesses were called they spoke always on behalf of the aggressor. On hearing such falsehoods he used to weep that no one gave credit to the truth; the father alone used cleverly to put in a word for him that he might not be "swallowed up with overmuch sorrow."[2] To make the story short, a year passed in this way and at the expiration of it the young man was asked concerning his former evil thoughts and whether they still troubled him. "Good gracious," he replied "how can I find pleasure in fornication when I am not allowed so much as to live?" Had he been a solitary hermit, by whose aid could he have overcome the temptations that assailed him?

14. The world's philosophers drive out an old passion by instilling a new one; they hammer out one nail by hammering in another. It was on this principle that the seven princes of Persia acted towards king Ahasuerus, for they subdued his regret for queen Vashti by inducing him to love other maidens.[4] But whereas they cured one fault by another fault and one sin by another sin, we must overcome our faults by learning to love the opposite virtues. "Depart from evil," says the psalmist, "and do good; seek peace and pursue it."[5] For if we do not hate evil we cannot love

[1] 1 Thess. v. 17.　　　　　[2] Ps. xix. 13.
[3] 1 Cor. ix. 14.　　　　　　[4] 1 Thess. ii. 9.: 1 Cor. iv. 12.
[5] 1 Cor. ix. 11.　　[6] Virg., G. i. 108-10.　　[7] Prov. vi. 8, LXX.
[8] Prov. xiii. 4, LXX.　　[9] Ezek. xvi. 25.　　[10] Cf. Letter XXII. § 7.

[1] In Letter XVIII. § 10 Jerome speaks of his teacher as one so learned in the Hebrew language that the very scribes regarded him as a Chaldæan (i.e., as a graduate of the Babylonian school of Rabbinic learning).
[2] 2 Cor. ii. 7.　　　　　　[3] Cic., T. Q. iv. 35.
[4] Esth. ii. 1-4.　　　　　　[5] Ps. xxxiv. 14.

good. Nay more, we must do good if we are to depart from evil. We must seek peace if we are to avoid war. And it is not enough merely to seek it; when we have found it and when it flees before us we must pursue it with all our energies. For "it passeth all understanding;"[1] it is the habitation of God. As the psalmist says, "in peace also is his habitation."[2] The pursuing of peace is a fine metaphor and may be compared with the apostle's words, "pursuing hospitality."[3] It is not enough, he means, for us to invite guests with our lips; we should be as eager to detain them as though they were robbers carrying off our savings.

15. No art is ever learned without a master. Even dumb animals and wild herds follow leaders of their own. Bees have princes, and cranes fly after one of their number in the shape of a Y.[4] There is but one emperor and each province has but one judge. Rome was founded by two brothers,[5] but, as it could not have two kings at once, was inaugurated by an act of fratricide. So too Esau and Jacob strove in Rebekah's womb.[6] Each church has a single bishop, a single archpresbyter, a single archdeacon;[7] and every ecclesiastical order is subjected to its own rulers. A ship has but one pilot, a house but one master, and the largest army moves at the command of one man. That I may not tire you by heaping up instances, my drift is simply this. Do not rely on your own discretion, but live in a monastery. For there, while you will be under the control of one father, you will have many companions; and these will teach you, one humility, another patience, a third silence, and a fourth meekness. You will do as others wish; you will eat what you are told to eat; you will wear what clothes are given you; you will perform the task allotted to you; you will obey one whom you do not like, you will come to bed tired out; you will go to sleep on your feet and you will be forced to rise before you have had sufficient rest. When your turn comes, you will recite the psalms, a task which requires not a well modulated voice but genuine emotion. The apostle says: "I will pray with the spirit and I will pray with the understanding also,"[8] and to the Ephesians, "make melody in your hearts to the Lord."[9] For he had read the precept of the psalmist: "Sing ye praises with understanding."[10] You will serve the brothers, you will wash the guests'

feet; if you suffer wrong you will bear it in silence; the superior of the community you will fear as a master and love as a father. Whatever he may order you to do you will believe to be wholesome for you. You will not pass judgment upon those who are placed over you, for your duty will be to obey them and to do what you are told, according to the words spoken by Moses: "keep silence and hearken, O Israel."[1] You will have so many tasks to occupy you that you will have no time for [evil] thoughts; and while you pass from one thing to another and fresh work follows work done, you will only be able to think of what you have it in charge at the moment to do.

16. But I myself have seen monks of quite a different stamp from this, men whose renunciation of the world has consisted in a change of clothes and a verbal profession, while their real life and their former habits have remained unchanged. Their property has increased rather than diminished. They still have the same servants and keep the same table. Out of cheap glasses and common earthenware they swallow gold. With servants about them in swarms they claim for themselves the name of hermits. Others who though poor think themselves discerning, walk as solemnly as pageants[2] through the streets and do nothing but snarl[3] at every one whom they meet. Others shrug their shoulders and croak out what is best known to themselves. While they keep their eyes fixed upon the earth, they balance swelling words upon their tongues.[4] Only a crier is wanted to persuade you that it is his excellency the prefect who is coming along. Some too there are who from the dampness of their cells and from the severity of their fasts, from their weariness of solitude and from excessive study have a singing in their ears day and night and turn melancholy mad so as to need the poultices of Hippocrates[5] more than exhortations from me. Great numbers are unable to break free from the crafts and trades they have previously practised. They no longer call themselves dealers but they carry on the same traffic as before; seeking for themselves not "food and raiment"[6] as the apostle directs, but money-profits and these greater than are looked for by men of the world. In former days the greed of sellers was kept within bounds by the action of the Ædiles or as the Greeks call them market-inspectors,[7] and men could not then cheat with impunity. But now persons who profess religion are not ashamed to seek unjust profits and the good name of Christianity is more

---

[1] Phil. iv. 7. [2] Ps. lxxvi. 2, LXX.
[3] Rom. xii. 13, R.V. marg. [4] Pliny, N. H. x. 32.
[5] Romulus and Remus, the first of whom slew the second.
[6] Gen. xxv. 22.
[7] When Jerome wrote, these terms had but recently come into use in the West; no doubt, however, the offices described by them were of older date. Archpresbyters seem to have been the forerunners of those who are now called "rural deans."
[8] 1 Cor. xiv. 15. [9] Eph. v. 19. [10] Ps. xlvii. 7.

[1] Deut. xxvii. 9, R.V. [2] Cic., Off. i. 36.
[3] Caninam exercent facundiam. The phrase recurs in Letter CXXXIV. § 1. [4] See also Lactantius, vi. 18.
[5] The most celebrated physician of antiquity.
[6] 1 Tim. vi. 8. [7] ἀγορόνμοι.

often a cloak for fraud than a victim to it.
I am ashamed to say it, yet it must be said—
we are at least bound to blush for our infamy
—while in public we hold out our hands for
alms we conceal gold beneath our rags; and
to the amazement of every one after living as
poor men we die rich and with our purses
well-filled.

But you, since you will not be alone but
one of a community, will have no temptation
to act thus. Things at first compulsory will
become habitual. You will set to work un-
bidden and will find pleasure in your toil. You
will forget things which are behind and will
reach forth to those which are before.[1] You
will think less of the evil that others do than
of the good you ought to do.

17. Be not led by the multitude of those
who sin, neither let the host of those who perish tempt you to say secretly : " What ? must
all be lost who live in cities? Behold, they
continue to enjoy their property, they serve
churches, they frequent baths, they do not disdain cosmetics, and yet they are universally
well-spoken of." To this kind of remark I
have before replied and now shortly reply
again that the object of this little work is not
to discuss the clergy but to lay down rules for
a monk. The clergy are holy men and their
lives are always worthy of praise. Rouse
yourself then and so live in your monastery
that you may deserve to be a clergyman, that
you may preserve your youth from defilement,
that you may go to Christ's altar as a virgin
out of her chamber. See that you are well-
reported of without and that women are familiar with your reputation but not with your
appearance. When you come to mature years,
if, that is, you live so long, and when you
have been chosen into the ranks of the clergy
either by the people of the city or by its
bishop, act in a way that befits a clergyman,
and choose for your models the best of your
brothers. For in every rank and condition of
life the bad are mingled with the good.

18. Do not be carried away by some mad
caprice and rush into authorship. Learn long
and carefully what you propose to teach. Do
not credit all that flatterers say to you, or, I
should rather say, do not lend too ready an
ear to those who mean to mock you. They
will fawn upon you with fulsome praise and
do their best to blind your judgment ; yet if
you suddenly look behind you, you will find
that they are making gestures of derision with
their hands, either a stork's neck or the flap-
ping ears of a donkey or a thirsty dog's pro-
truding tongue.[2]

Never speak evil of anyone or suppose that

you make yourself better by assailing the repu-
tations of others. The charges we bring
against them often come home to ourselves ;
we inveigh against faults which are as much
ours as theirs ; and so our eloquence ends by
telling against ourselves. It is as though
dumb persons were to criticize orators. When
the grunter[1] wished to speak he used to come
forward at a snail's pace[2] and to utter a word
now and again with such long pauses between
that he seemed less making a speech than
gasping for breath. Then, when he had placed
his table and arranged on it his pile of books,
he used to knit his brow, to draw in his nostrils, to wrinkle his forehead and to snap his
fingers, signs meant to engage the attention
of his pupils. Then he would pour forth a
torrent of nonsense and declaim so vehemently against every one that you would take him
for a critic like Longinus[3] or fancy him a second Cato the Censor[4] passing judgment on
Roman eloquence and excluding whom he
pleased from the senate of the learned. As
he had plenty of money he made himself
still more popular by giving entertainments.
Numbers of persons shared in his hospitality ;
and thus it was not surprising that when he
went out he was surrounded always by a
buzzing throng. At home he was a monster
like Nero, abroad a paragon like Cato. Made
up of different and opposing natures, as a
whole he baffled description. You would say
that he was formed of jarring elements like
that unnatural and unheard of monster of
which the poet tells us that it was ' in front a
lion, behind a dragon, in the middle the goat
whose name it bears.'[5]

19. Men such as these you must never look
at or associate with. Nor must you turn aside
your heart unto words of evil[6] lest the psalmist say to you : " Thou sittest and speakest
against thy brother ; thou slanderest thine
own mother's son,"[7] and lest you become as
" the sons of men whose teeth are spears and
arrows,"[8] and as the man whose " words were
softer than oil yet were they drawn swords."[9]
The Preacher expresses this more clearly still
when he says : " Surely the serpent will bite
where there is no enchantment, and the slan-

[1] i.e., Rufinus who was now dead. The nickname is taken
from a burlesque very popular in Jerome's day entitled " The
Porker's Last Will and Testament." In this the testator's full
name is set down as Marcus Grunnius Corocotta, i.e., Mark
Grunter Hog. In the beginning of the twelfth book of his
commentary on Isaiah Jerome mentions the " Testament " as
being then a popular school book.
[2] Plautus, Aulularia, I. i. 10.
[3] A Platonist of the third century after Christ, much celebrated for his learning and critical skill. " To judge like
Longinus " became a synonym for accurate discrimination.
[4] A martinet of the old school, who did his utmost to oppose
what he considered the luxury of his age. He was censor in
184 B.C.
[5] Lucr. V. 905, Munro. The words come first from Homer, Il.
vi. 181.
[6] Ps. cxli. 4, Vulg.   [7] Ps. l. 20.
[8] Ps. lvii. 4.   [9] Ps. lv. 21.

[1] Phil. iii. 13,   [2] Imitated from Persius (I. 58-60).

derer is no better." [1] But you will say, ' I am not given to detraction, but how can I check others who are ?' If we put forward such a plea as this it can only be that we may " practise wicked works with men that work iniquity." [2] Yet Christ is not deceived by this device. It is not I but an apostle who says : " Be not deceived ; God is not mocked." [3] " Man looketh upon the outward appearance but the Lord looketh upon the heart." [4] And in the proverbs Solomon tells us that as " the north wind driveth away rain, so doth an angry countenance a backbiting tongue." [5] It sometimes happens that an arrow when it is aimed at a hard object rebounds upon the bowman, wounding the would-be wounder, and thus, the words are fulfilled, " they were turned aside like a deceitful bow," [6] and in another passage : " whoso casteth a stone on high casteth it on his own head." [7] So when a slanderer sees anger in the countenance of his hearer who will not hear him but stops his ears that he may not hear of blood, [8] he becomes silent on the moment, his face turns pale, his lips stick fast, his mouth becomes parched. Wherefore the same wise man says : " meddle not with them that are given to detraction : for their calamity shall rise suddenly ; and who knoweth the ruin of them both ? " [9] of him who speaks, that is, and of him who hears. Truth does not love corners or seek whisperers. To Timothy it is said, " Against an elder receive not an accusation suddenly ; but him that sinneth rebuke before all, that others also may fear." [10] When a man is advanced in years you must not be too ready to believe evil of him ; his past life is itself a defence, and so also is his rank as an elder. Still, since we are but human and sometimes in spite of the ripeness of our years fall into the sins of youth, if I do wrong and you wish to correct me, accuse me openly of my fault : do not backbite me secretly. " Let the righteous smite me, it shall be a kindness, and let him reprove me ; but let not the oil of the sinner enrich my head. " [11] For what says the apostle ? " Whom the Lord loveth, he chasteneth, and scourgeth every son whom he receiveth." [12] By the mouth of Isaiah the Lord speaks thus : "O my people, they who call you happy cause you to err and destroy the way of your paths." [13] How do you help me by telling my misdeeds to others ? You may, without my knowing of it, wound some one else by the narration of my sins or rather of those which you slanderously attribute to me ;

and while you are eager to spread the news in all quarters, you may pretend to confide in each individual as though you had spoken to no one else. Such a course has for its object not my correction but the indulgence of your own failing. The Lord gives commandment that those who sin against us are to be arraigned privately or else in the presence of a witness, and that if they refuse to hear reason, the matter is to be laid before the church, and those who persist in their wickedness are to be regarded as heathen men and publicans. [1]

20. I lay great emphasis on these points that I may deliver a young man who is dear to me from the itching both of the tongue and of the ears : that, since he has been born again in Christ, I may present him without spot or wrinkle [2] as a chaste virgin, [3] chaste in mind as well as in body ; that the virginity of which he boasts may be more than nominal and that he may not be shut out by the bridegroom because being unprovided with the oil of good works his lamp has gone out. [4] In Proculus you have a reverend and most learned prelate, [5] able by the sound of his voice to do more for you than I with my written sheets and sure to direct you on your path by daily homilies. He will not suffer you to turn to the right hand or to the left or to leave the king's highway ; for to this Israel pledges itself to keep in its hasty passage to the land of promise. [6] May God hear the voice of the church's supplication. " Lord, ordain peace for us, for thou hast also wrought all our works for us." [7] May our renunciation of the world be made freely and not under compulsion ! May we seek poverty gladly to win its glory and not suffer anguish because others lay it upon us ! For the rest amid our present miseries with the sword making havoc around us, he is rich enough who has bread sufficient for his need, and he is abundantly powerful who is not reduced to be a slave. Exuperius, [8] the reverend bishop of Toulouse, imitating the widow of Zarephath, [9] feeds others though hungry himself. His face is pale with fasting, yet it is the cravings of others that torment him most. In fact he has bestowed his whole substance to meet the needs of Christ's poor. Yet none is richer than he, for his wicker basket contains the body of the Lord, and his plain glass-cup the precious blood. Like his Master he has banished greed out of the temple ; and without either scourge of cords or words of chiding he has overthrown the chairs of them that sell doves, that is, the gifts of the

---

[1] Eccl. x. 11, R.V. marg.   [2] Ps. cxli. 4.
[3] Gal. vi. 7.   [4] 1 Sam. xvi. 7.   [5] Prov. xxv. 23.
[6] Ps. lxxviii. 57.   [7] Ecclus. xxvii. 25.   [8] Isa. xxxiii. 15.
[9] Prov. xxiv. 21, 22 Vulg.   [10] 1 Tim. v. 19, 20 (inexact).
[11] Ps. cxli. 5. LXX.   [12] Heb. xii. 6.
[13] Isa. iii. 12. LXX.

[1] Matt. xviii. 15-17.   [2] Eph. v. 27.   [3] 2 Cor. xi. 2.
[4] Matt. xxv. 1-10.   [5] He was bishop of Massilia (Marseilles).
[6] Num. xx. 17.   [7] Isa. xxvi. 12. LXX.
[8] Bishop of Toulouse. See Letter LIV. 11, and Pref. to Comm. on Zech.
[9] 1 Kings xvii. 8-16.

Holy Spirit. He has upset the tables of Mammon and has scattered the money of the money-changers; zealous that the house of God may be called a house of prayer and not a den of robbers.[1] In his steps follow closely and in those of others like him in virtue, whom the priesthood makes poor men and more than ever humble. Or if you will be perfect, go out with Abraham from your country and from your kindred, and go whither you know not.[2] If you have substance, sell it and give to the poor. If you have none, then are you free from a great burthen. Destitute yourself, follow a destitute Christ. The task is a hard one, it is great and difficult; but the reward is also great.

LETTER CXXVI.

TO MARCELLINUS AND ANAPSYCHIA.

Marcellinus, a Roman official of high rank, and Anapsychia his wife had written to Jerome from Africa to ask him his opinion on the vexed question of the origin of the soul. Jerome in his reply briefly enumerates the several views that have been held on the subject. For fuller information he refers his questioners to his treatise against Rufinus and also to their bishop Augustin who will, he says, explain the matter to them by word of mouth. Although it hardly appears in this letter Jerome is a decided creationist (see his Comm. on Eccles. xii. 7). But, though he vehemently condemns Rufinus (Ap. ii. 10) for professing ignorance on the subject, he assents (Letter CXXXIV.) to Augustin (Letter CXXXI.) who similarly professes ignorance but seems to lean to traducianism. The date of writing is A.D. 412.

To his truly holy lord and lady, his children worthy of the highest respect and affection, Marcellinus and Anapsychia, Jerome sends greeting.

1. I have at last received from Africa your joint letter and no longer regret the effrontery which led me, in spite of your silence to ply you both with so many missives. I hoped, indeed, by so doing to gain a reply and to learn of your welfare not indirectly from others but directly from yourselves.

I well remember your little problem about the nature of the soul; although I ought not to call it little, seeing that it is one of the greatest with which the church has to deal. You ask whether it has fallen from heaven, as Pythagoras, all Platonists, and Origen suppose; or whether it is part of God's essence as the Stoics, Manes, and the Spanish Priscillianists hint. Whether souls created long since are kept in God's storehouse as some ecclesiastical writers[3] foolishly imagine; or whether they are formed by God and introduced into bodies day by day according to that saying in the Gospel: "my Father worketh hitherto and I work;"[4] or

whether, lastly, they are transmitted by propagation. This is the view of Tertullian, Apollinaris, and most western writers who hold that soul is derived from soul as body is from body and that the conditions of life are the same for men and brutes. I have given my opinion on the matter in my reply to the treatise which Rufinus presented to Anastasius, bishop of Rome, of holy memory. He strives in this by an evasive and crafty but sufficiently foolish confession to play with the simplicity of his hearers, but only succeeds in playing with his own faith or rather want of it. My book,[1] which has been published a good while, contains an answer to the calumnies which in his various writings Rufinus has directed against me. Your reverend father Oceanus[2] has, I think, a copy of it. But if you cannot procure it your bishop Augustine is both learned and holy. He will teach you by word of mouth and will give you his opinion, or rather mine, in his own words.

2. I have long wished to attack the prophecies of Ezekiel and to make good the promises which I have so often given to curious readers. When, however, I began to dictate I was so confounded by the havoc wrought in the West and above all by the sack of Rome that, as the common saying has it, I forgot even my own name. Long did I remain silent knowing that it was a time to weep.[3] This year I began again and had written three books of commentary when a sudden incursion of those barbarians of whom your Virgil speaks[4] as the "far-wandering men of Barce" (and to whom may be applied what holy scripture says of Ishmael: "he shall dwell over against all his brethren"[5]) overran the borders of Egypt, Palestine, Phenicia, and Syria, and like a raging torrent carried everything before them. It was with difficulty and only through Christ's mercy that we were able to escape from their hands. But if, as the great orator says, "amid the clash of arms law ceases to be heard;"[6] how much more truly may it be said that war puts an end to the study of holy scripture. For this requires plenty of books and silence and careful copyists and above all freedom from alarm and a sense of security. I have accordingly only been able to complete two books and these I have sent to my daughter, Fabiola,[7] from

---

[1] John ii. 14-16: Matt. xxi. 12, 13.   [2] Gen. xii. 1: Heb. xi. 8.
[3] The allusion is probably to Clement of Alexandria.
[4] John v. 17.

[1] *Against Rufinus*, ii. §§ 8-10; iii. § 30; in neither place, however, does Jerome clearly state his own view.
[2] See Letter LXIX. introduction. It is doubtful whether Oceanus was in holy orders although the title 'father' seems to imply it.
[3] Eccl. iii. 4.
[4] Virg., A. iv. 43. It does not appear who these barbarians were. Barce is near Cyrene in Africa.
[5] Gen. xvi. 12. R.V. marg.   [6] Cicero, pro Milon. 4.
[7] This Fabiola (who must be carefully distinguished from the lady so often mentioned by Jerome) is probably the person to whom Augustine addressed a letter on communion with the spiritual world.

vhom you can if you like borrow them. For vant of time I have not been able as yet to ranscribe the rest. But when you have read hese you will have seen the ante-chamber nd will easily form from this a notion of the vhole edifice. I trust in God's mercy and velieve that, as he has helped me in the diffiult opening chapters of the prophecy, so he vill help me in the chapters towards the close. These describe the wars of Gog and Magog, nd set forth the mode of building, the plan, nd the dimensions of the holy and mysteriius temple.

3. Our reverend brother Oceanus to whom ou desire an introduction is a great and good nan and so learned in the law of the Lord hat no words of mine are needed to make iim able and willing to instruct you both and o explain to you in conformity with the rules vhich govern our common studies, my opinon and his on all questions arising out of the criptures. In conclusion, my truly holy lord nd lady, may Christ our God by his almighty ower have you in his safekeeping and cause ou to live long and happily.

LETTER CXXVII.

TO PRINCIPIA.

This letter is really a memoir of Marcella (for whom ee note on Letter XXIII.) addressed to her greatest iend. After describing her history, character, and vourite studies, Jerome goes on to recount her emient services in the cause of orthodoxy at a time when, rough the efforts of Rufinus, it seemed likely that rigenism would prevail at Rome (§§ 9, 10). He iefly relates the fall of the city and the horrors conseuent upon it (§§ 12, 13) which appear to have been ie immediate cause of Marcella's death (§ 14). The ite of the letter is 412 A.D.

1. You have besought me often and earestly, Principia,[1] virgin of Christ, to dedicate letter to the memory of that holy woman Iarcella,[2] and to set forth the goodness long njoyed by us for others to know and to imiite. I am so anxious myself to do justice to er merits that it grieves me that you should pur me on and fancy that your entreaties re needed when I do not yield even to you I love of her. In putting upon record her gnal virtues I shall receive far more benet myself than I can possibly confer upon thers. If I have hitherto remained silent nd have allowed two years to go over without iaking any sign, this has not been owing to a ish to ignore her as you wrongly suppose, ut to an incredible sorrow which so overcame iy mind that I judged it better to remain lent for a while than to praise her virtues

in inadequate language. Neither will I now follow the rules of rhetoric in eulogizing one so dear to both of us and to all the saints, Marcella the glory of her native Rome. I will not set forth her illustrious family and lofty lineage, nor will I trace her pedigree through a line of consuls and prætorian prefects. I will praise her for nothing but the virtue which is her own and which is the more noble, because forsaking both wealth and rank she has sought the true nobility of poverty and lowliness.

2. Her father's death left her an orphan, and she had been married less than seven months when her husband was taken from her. Then as she was young, and highborn, as well as distinguished for her beauty—always an attraction to men—and her self-control, an illustrious consular named Cerealis paid court to her with great assiduity. Being an old man he offered to make over to her his fortune so that she might consider herself less his wife than his daughter. Her mother Albina went out of her way to secure for the young widow so exalted a protector. But Marcella answered : "had I a wish to marry and not rather to dedicate myself to perpetual chastity, I should look for a husband and not for an inheritance ; " and when her suitor argued that sometimes old men live long while young men die early, she cleverly retorted : "a young man may indeed die early, but an old man cannot live long." This decided rejection of Cerealis convinced others that they had no hope of winning her hand.

In the gospel according to Luke we read the following passage : "there was one Anna, a prophetess, the daughter of Phanuel, of the tribe of Aser : she was of great age, and had lived with an husband seven years from her virginity ; and she was a widow of about fourscore and four years, which departed not from the temple but served God with fastings and prayers night and day."[1] It was no marvel that she won the vision of the Saviour, whom she sought so earnestly. Let us then compare her case with that of Marcella and we shall see that the latter has every way the advantage. Anna lived with her husband seven years ; Marcella seven months. Anna only hoped for Christ ; Marcella held Him fast. Anna confessed him at His birth ; Marcella believed in Him crucified. Anna did not deny the Child ; Marcella rejoiced in the Man as king. I do not wish to draw distinctions between holy women on the score of their merits, as some persons have made it a custom to do as regards holy men and leaders of churches ; the conclusion at which I aim is that, as both have one task, so both have one reward.

---

[1] This Roman lady, like her friend Marcella, took a great inrest in the study of scripture. In Letter LXV. Jerome gives er an explanation of the 45th Psalm.
[2] See Letter XXIII.

[1] Luke ii. 36, 37.

3. In a slander-loving community such as Rome, filled as it formerly was with people from all parts and bearing the palm for wickedness of all kinds, detraction assailed the upright and strove to defile even the pure and the clean. In such an atmosphere it is hard to escape from the breath of calumny. A stainless reputation is difficult nay almost impossible to attain ; the prophet yearns for it but hardly hopes to win it : "Blessed," he says, "are the undefiled in the way who walk in the law of the Lord."[1] The undefiled in the way of this world are those whose fair fame no breath of scandal has ever sullied, and who have earned no reproach at the hands of their neighbours. It is this which makes the Saviour say in the gospel : "agree with," or be complaisant to, "thine adversary whilst thou art in the way with him."[2] Who ever heard a slander of Marcella that deserved the least credit ? Or who ever credited such without making himself guilty of malice and defamation ? No ; she put the Gentiles to confusion by shewing them the nature of that Christian widowhood which her conscience and mien alike set forth. For women of the world are wont to paint their faces with rouge and whitelead, to wear robes of shining silk, to adorn themselves with jewels, to put gold chains round their necks, to pierce their ears and hang in them the costliest pearls of the Red Sea,[3] and to scent themselves with musk. While they mourn for the husbands they have lost they rejoice at their own deliverance and freedom to choose fresh partners—not, as God wills, to obey these[4] but to rule over them.

With this object in view they select for their partners poor men who contented with the mere name of husbands are the more ready to put up with rivals as they know that, if they so much as murmur, they will be cast off at once. Our widow's clothing was meant to keep out the cold and not to shew her figure. Of gold she would not wear so much as a seal-ring, choosing to store her money in the stomachs of the poor rather than to keep it at her own disposal. She went nowhere without her mother, and would never see without witnesses such monks and clergy as the needs of a large house required her to interview. Her train was always composed of virgins and widows, and these women serious and staid ; for, as she well knew, the levity of the maids speaks ill for the mistress and a woman's character is shewn by her choice of companions.[5]

4. Her delight in the divine scriptures was incredible. She was for ever singing, "Thy words have I hid in mine heart that I might

not sin against thee,"[1] as well as the word which describe the perfect man, "his deligh is in the law of the Lord ; and in his la doth he meditate day and night."[2] Thi meditation in the law she understood not o a review of the written words as among th Jews the Pharisees think, but of action accord ing to that saying of the apostle, "whether therefore, ye eat or drink or what soever y do, do all to the glory of God."[3] She remem bered also the prophet's words, "through th precepts I get understanding,"[4] and felt sur that only when she had fulfilled these woul she be permitted to understand the scriptures In this sense we read elsewhere that "Jesu began both to do and teach."[5] For teachin is put to the blush when a man's conscienc rebukes him ; and it is in vain that his tongu preaches poverty or teaches alms-giving if h is rolling in the riches of Crœsus and if, i spite of his threadbare cloak, he has silke robes at home to save from the moth.

Marcella practised fasting, but in modera tion. She abstained from eating flesh, an she knew rather the scent of wine than it taste ; touching it only for her stomach's sak and for her often infirmities.[6] She seldor appeared in public and took care to avoid th houses of great ladies, that she might not b forced to look upon what she had once fo all renounced. She frequented the basilica of apostles and martyrs that she might escap from the throng and give herself to privat prayer. So obedient was she to her mothe that for her sake she did things of which sh herself disapproved. For example, when he mother, careless of her own offspring, was fo transferring all her property from her childre and grandchildren to her brother's family Marcella wished the money to be given to th poor instead, and yet could not bring hersel to thwart her parent. Therefore she mad over her ornaments and other effects to per sons already rich, content to throw away he money rather than to sadden her mother heart.

5. In those days no highborn lady at Rom had made profession of the monastic lif or had ventured—so strange and ignominiou and degrading did it then seem—publicly t call herself a nun. It was from some priests o Alexandria, and from pope Athanasius, an subsequently from Peter,[7] who, to escape th persecution of the Arian heretics, had all fle for refuge to Rome as the safest haven i which they could find communion—it wa from these that Marcella heard of the life o the blessed Antony, then still alive, and of th

[1] Ps. cxix. 1.   [2] Matt. v. 25.
[3] *i.e.* the Indian Ocean.   [4] Eph. v. 22.
[5] Cf. Letter LXXIX. § 9.

[1] Ps. cxix. 11.   [2] Ps. i. 2.   [3] 1 Cor. x. 31.
[4] Ps. cxix. 104.   [5] Acts i. 1.   [6] 1 Tim. v. 23.
[7] The successor of Athanasius in the see of Alexandria.

monasteries in the Thebaid founded by Pachomius, and of the discipline laid down for virgins and for widows. Nor was she ashamed to profess a life which she had thus learned to be pleasing to Christ. Many years after her example was followed first by Sophronia and then by others, of whom it may be well said in the words of Ennius: [1]

> Would that ne'er in Pelion's woods
> Had the axe these pinetrees felled.

My revered friend Paula was blessed with Marcella's friendship, and it was in Marcella's cell that Eustochium, that paragon of virgins, was gradually trained. Thus it is easy to see of what type the mistress was who found such pupils.

The unbelieving reader may perhaps laugh at me for dwelling so long on the praises of mere women; yet if he will but remember how holy women followed our Lord and Saviour and ministered to Him of their substance, and how the three Marys stood before the cross and especially how Mary Magdalen—called the tower[2] from the earnestness and glow of her faith—was privileged to see the rising Christ first of all before the very apostles, he will convict himself of pride sooner than me of folly. For we judge of people's virtue not by their sex but by their character, and hold those to be worthy of the highest glory who have renounced both rank and wealth. It was for this reason that Jesus loved the evangelist John more than the other disciples. For John was of noble birth[3] and known to the high priest, yet was so little appalled by the plottings of the Jews that he introduced Peter into his court,[4] and was the only one of the apostles bold enough to take his stand before the cross. For it was he who took the Saviour's parent to his own home;[5] it was the virgin son[6] who received the virgin mother as a legacy from the Lord.

6. Marcella then lived the ascetic life for many years, and found herself old before she bethought herself that she had once been young. She often quoted with approval Plato's saying that philosophy consists in meditating on death.[7] A truth which our own apostle indorses when he says: "for your salvation I die daily."[8] Indeed according to the old copies our Lord himself says:

"whosoever doth not bear His cross daily and come after me cannot be my disciple."[1] Ages before, the Holy Spirit had said by the prophet: "for thy sake are we killed all the day long: we are counted as sheep for the slaughter."[2] Many generations afterwards the words were spoken: "remember the end and thou shalt never do amiss,"[3] as well as that precept of the eloquent satirist: "live with death in your mind; time flies; this say of mine is so much taken from it."[4] Well then, as I was saying, she passed her days and lived always in the thought that she must die. Her very clothing was such as to remind her of the tomb, and she presented herself as a living sacrifice, reasonable and acceptable, unto God.[5]

7. When the needs of the Church at length brought me to Rome[6] in company with the reverend pontiffs, Paulinus and Epiphanius—the first of whom ruled the church of the Syrian Antioch while the second presided over that of Salamis in Cyprus,—I in my modesty was for avoiding the eyes of highborn ladies, yet she pleaded so earnestly, "both in season and out of season"[7] as the apostle says, that at last her perseverance overcame my reluctance. And, as in those days my name was held in some renown as that of a student of the scriptures, she never came to see me that she did not ask me some question concerning them, nor would she at once acquiesce in my explanations but on the contrary would dispute them; not, however, for argument's sake but to learn the answers to those objections which might, as she saw, be made to my statements. How much virtue and ability, how much holiness and purity I found in her I am afraid to say; both lest I may exceed the bounds of men's belief and lest I may increase your sorrow by reminding you of the blessings that you have lost. This much only will I say, that whatever in me was the fruit of long study and as such made by constant meditation a part of my nature, this she tasted, this she learned and made her own. Consequently after my departure from Rome, in case of a dispute arising as to the testimony of scripture on any subject, recourse was had to her to settle it. And so wise was she and so well did she understand what philosphers call τό πρέπον, that is, the becoming, in what she did, that when she answered questions she gave her own opinion not as her own but as from me or some one else, thus admitting that what she taught she had herself learned from others. For she knew that the apostle had said: "I suffer not a

---

[1] A fragment from the Medea of Ennius relating to the unlucky ship Argo which had brought Jason to Colchis. Here however the words seem altogether out of place. Unless, indeed, they are supposed to be spoken by pagans.
[2] Magdala means 'tower.'   [3] So Ewald.
[4] Joh. xviii. 15, 16, R.V.   [5] Joh. xix. 26, 27.
[6] Tertullian goes so far as to call him 'Christ's eunuch' (de Monog. c. xvii.).
[7] Tota philosophorum vita commentatio mortis est—Cicero, T. Q. i. 30, 74 (summarizing Plato's doctrine as given in his Phædo, p. 64).
[8] 1 Cor. xv. 31 (apparently quoted from memory).

---

[1] Luke xiv. 27: cf. ix. 23.   [2] Ps. xliv. 22.
[3] Ecclus. vii. 36.   [4] Pers. v. 153 Corvington.
[5] Rom. xii. 1.   [6] In 382 A.D.   [7] 2 Tim. iv. 2.

woman to teach," [1] and she would not seem to inflict a wrong upon the male sex many of whom (including sometimes priests) questioned her concerning obscure and doubtful points.

8. I am told that my place with her was immediately taken by you, that you attached yourself to her, and that, as the saying goes, you never let even a hair's-breadth [2] come between her and you. You both lived in the same house and occupied the same room so that every one in the city knew for certain that you had found a mother in her and she a daughter in you. In the suburbs you found for yourselves a monastic seclusion, and chose the country instead of the town because of its loneliness. For a long time you lived together, and as many ladies shaped their conduct by your examples, I had the joy of seeing Rome transformed into another Jerusalem. Monastic establishments for virgins became numerous, and of hermits there were countless numbers. In fact so many were the servants of God that monasticism which had before been a term of reproach became subsequently one of honour. Meantime we consoled each other for our separation by words of mutual encouragement, and discharged in the spirit the debt which in the flesh we could not pay. We always went to meet each other's letters, tried to outdo each other in attentions, and anticipated each other in courteous inquiries. Not much was lost by a separation thus effectually bridged by a constant correspondence.

9. While Marcella was thus serving the Lord in holy tranquillity, there arose in these provinces a tornado of heresy which threw everything into confusion; indeed so great was the fury into which it lashed itself that it spared neither itself nor anything that was good. And as if it were too little to have disturbed everything here, it introduced a ship [3] freighted with blasphemies into the port of Rome itself. The dish soon found itself a cover; [4] and the muddy feet of heretics fouled the clear waters [5] of the faith of Rome. No wonder that in the streets and in the market places a soothsayer can strike fools on the back or, catching up his cudgel, shatter the teeth of such as carp at him; when such venomous and filthy teaching as this has found at Rome dupes whom it can lead astray. Next came the scandalous version [6] of Origen's book *On First Principles*, and that 'fortunate' disciple [7] who would have

been indeed fortunate had he never fallen in with such a master. Next followed the confutation set forth by my supporters, which destroyed the case of the Pharisees [1] and threw them into confusion. It was then that the holy Marcella, who had long held back lest she should be thought to act from party motives, threw herself into the breach. Conscious that the faith of Rome—once praised by an apostle [2]—was now in danger, and that this new heresy was drawing to itself not only priests and monks but also many of the laity besides imposing on the bishop [3] who fancied others as guileless as he was himself, she publicly withstood its teachers choosing to please God rather than men.

10. In the gospel the Saviour commends the unjust steward because, although he defrauded his master, he acted wisely for his own interests. [4] The heretics in this instance pursue the same course; for, seeing how great a matter a little fire had kindled, [5] and that the flame applied by them to the foundations had by this time reached the housetops, and that the deception practised on many could no longer be hid, they asked for and obtained letters of commendation from the church, [6] so that they might appear that till the day of their departure they had continued in full communion with it. Shortly afterwards [7] the distinguished Anastasius succeeded to the pontificate; but he was soon taken away, for it was not fitting that the head of the world should be struck off [8] during the episcopate of one so great. He was removed, no doubt, that he might not seek to turn away by his prayers the sentence of God passed once for all. For the words of the Lord to Jeremiah concerning Israel applied equally to Rome: "pray not for this people for their good. When they fast I will not hear their cry; and when they offer burnt offering and oblation, I will not accept them; but I will consume them by the sword and by the famine and by the pestilence." [9] You will say, what has this to do with the praises of Marcella? I reply, She it was who originated the condemnation of the heretics. She it was who furnished witnesses first taught by them and then carried away by their heretical teaching. She it was who showed how large a number they had deceived and who brought up against them the impious books *On First Principles*, books which were passing from hand to hand after being 'improved' by the hand of the scorpion.

---

[1] 1 Tim. ii. 12.   [2] Literally "thickness of a nail."
[3] The movement connected with Rufinus' translation of Origen's Περὶ Ἀρχῶν. His coming was likened, in the dream of his friend Macarius (Ruf. Apol. i. 11), to that of a ship laden with Eastern wares.
[4] The same proverb occurs in Letter VII. § 5.
[5] Cf. Ezek. xxxiv. 18.
[6] *i.e.* That published by Rufinus. See Letter LXXX.
[7] 'ὄλβιος, *i.e.* Macarius, a Roman Christian who wrote a book on the providence of God. To him Rufinus dedicated his version of Origen's treatise.

[1] Apparently the Roman clergy who sided with Rufinus.
[2] Rom. i. 8.
[3] Siricius, the successor of Damasus. He died A.D. 398.
[4] Luke xvi. 8.   [5] James iii. 5.
[6] Rufinus obtained such letters from Pope Siricius when he left Rome for Aquileia. See Jer. Apol. iii. 21.   [7] 398 A.D.
[8] The allusion is to the capture of Rome by Alaric in 410 A.D.
[9] Jer. xiv. 11, 12.
[10] Emendata manu scorpii. The scorpion is Rufinus whom Jerome accused of suppressing the worst statements of Origen so that the subtler heresy might be accepted.

She it was lastly who called on the heretics in letter after letter to appear in their own defence. They did not indeed venture to come, for they were so conscience-stricken that they let the case go against them by default rather than face their accusers and be convicted by them. This glorious victory originated with Marcella, she was the source and cause of this great blessing. You who shared the honour with her know that I speak the truth. You know too that out of many incidents I only mention a few, not to tire out the reader by a wearisome recapitulation. Were I to say more, ill natured persons might fancy me, under pretext of commending a woman's virtues, to be giving vent to my own rancour. I will pass now to the remainder of my story.

11. The whirlwind[1] passed from the West into the East and threatened in its passage to shipwreck many a noble craft. Then were the words of Jesus fulfilled : " when the son of man cometh, shall he find faith on the earth?"[2] The love of many waxed cold.[3] Yet the few who still loved the true faith rallied to my side. Men openly sought to take their lives and every expedient was employed against them. So hotly indeed did the persecution rage that " Barnabas also was carried away with their dissimulation ; "[4] nay more he committed murder, if not in actual violence at least in will. Then behold God blew and the tempest passed away ; so that the prediction of the prophet was fulfilled, "thou takest away their breath, they die, and return to their dust.[5] In that very day his thoughts perish, "[6] as also the gospel-saying, "Thou fool, this night thy soul shall be required of thee : then whose shall those things be, which thou hast provided ?"[7]

12. Whilst these things were happening in Jebus[8] a dreadful rumour came from the West. Rome had been besieged[9] and its citizens had been forced to buy their lives with gold. Then thus despoiled they had been besieged again so as to lose not their substance only but their lives. My voice sticks in my throat ; and, as I dictate, sobs choke my utterance. The City which had taken the whole world was itself taken ;[10] nay more famine was beforehand with the sword and but few citizens were left to be made captives. In their frenzy the starving people had recourse to hideous food ; and tore each other limb from limb that they might have flesh to eat. Even the mother did not spare the babe at her breast.

In the night was Moab taken, in the night did her wall fall down.[1] "O God, the heathen have come into thine inheritance ; thy holy temple have they defiled ; they have made Jerusalem an orchard.[2] The dead bodies of thy servants have they given to be meat unto the fowls of the heaven, the flesh of thy saints unto the beasts of the earth. Their blood have they shed like water round about Jerusalem ; and there was none to bury them."[3]

> Who can set forth the carnage of that night?
> What tears are equal to its agony ?
> Of ancient date a sovran city falls ;
> And lifeless in its streets and houses lie
> Unnumbered bodies of its citizens.
> In many a ghastly shape doth death appear.[4]

13. Meantime, as was natural in a scene of such confusion, one of the bloodstained victors found his way into Marcella's house. Now be it mine to say what I have heard,[5] to relate what holy men have seen ; for there were some such present and they say that you too were with her in the hour of danger. When the soldiers entered she is said to have received them without any look of alarm ; and when they asked her for gold she pointed to her coarse dress to shew them that she had no buried treasure. However they would not believe in her self-chosen poverty, but scourged her and beat her with cudgels. She is said to have felt no pain but to have thrown herself at their feet and to have pleaded with tears for you, that you might not be taken from her, or owing to your youth have to endure what she as an old woma had no occasion to fear. Christ softened their hard hearts and even among bloodstained swords natural affection asserted its rights. The barbarians conveyed both you and her to the basilica of the apostle Paul, that you might find there either a place of safety or, if not that, at least a tomb. Hereupon Marcella is said to have burst into great joy and to have thanked God for having kept you unharmed in answer to her prayer. She said she was thankful too that the taking of the city had found her poor, not made her so, that she was now in want of daily bread, that Christ satisfied her needs so that she no longer felt hunger, that she was able to say in word and in deed : " naked came I out of my mother's womb, and naked shall I return thither : the Lord gave and the Lord hath taken away ; blessed be the name of the Lord."[6]

14. After a few days she fell asleep in the Lord ; but to the last her powers remained unimpaired. You she made the heir of her

---

[1] i.e. the Origenistic heresy.
[2] Luke xviii. 8.   [3] Matt. xxiv. 12.
[4] Gal. ii. 13.   The allusion is perhaps to John of Jerusalem ; possibly to Chrysostom.
[5] Ps. civ. 29.   [6] Ps. cxlvi. 4.
[7] Luke xii. 20.   [8] The Canaanite name for Jerusalem.
[9] By Alaric the Goth, 408 A.D.   [10] By Alaric, 410 A.D.

[1] Isa. xv. 1.   [2] Ps. lxxix. 1. LXX.
[3] Ps. lxxix. 1–3.   [4] Virg. A. ii. 361.
[5] Virg. A. vi. 266.   [6] Job i. 21, LXX.

poverty, or rather the poor through you. When she closed her eyes, it was in your arms ; when she breathed her last breath, your lips received it ; you shed tears but she smiled, conscious of having led a good life and hoping for her reward hereafter.

In one short night I have dictated this letter in honour of you, revered Marcella, and of you, my daughter Principia ; not to shew off my own eloquence but to express my heart-felt gratitude to you both ; my one desire has been to please both God and my readers.

LETTER CXXVIII.

TO GAUDENTIUS.

Gaudentius had written from Rome to ask Jerome's advice as to the bringing up of his infant daughter ; whom after the religious fashion of the day he had dedi-cated to a life of virginity. Jerome's reply may be compared with his advice to Læta (Letter CVII.) which it closely resembles. It is noticeable also for the vivid account which it gives of the sack of Rome by Alaric in A.D. 410. The date of the letter is A.D. 413.

1. It is hard to write to a little girl who cannot understand what you say, of whose mind you know nothing, and of whose inclina-tions it would be rash to prophesy. In the words of a famous orator "she is to be praised more for what she will be than for what she is." [1] For how can you speak of self-control to a child who is eager for cakes, who babbles on her mother's knee, and to whom honey is sweeter than any words ? Will she hear the deep things of the apostle when all her de-light is in nursery tales ? Will she heed the dark sayings of the prophets when her nurse can frighten her by a frowning face ? Or will she comprehend the majesty of the gospel, when its splendour dazzles the keenest intellect ? Shall I urge her to obey her parents when with her chubby hand she beats her smiling mother? For such reasons as these my dear Pacatula must read some other time the letter that I send her now. Meanwhile let her learn the alphabet, spelling, grammar, and syntax. To induce her to repeat her lessons with her little shrill voice, hold out to her as rewards cakes and mead and sweetmeats. [2] She will make haste to perform her task if she hopes after-wards to get some bright bunch of flowers, some glittering bauble, some enchanting doll. She must also learn to spin, shaping the yarn with her tender thumb ; for, even if she con-stantly breaks the threads, a day will come when she will no longer break them. Then when she has finished her lessons she ought to have some recreation. At such times she may

hang round her mother's neck, or snatch kisses from her relations. Reward her for singing psalms that she may love what she has to learn. Her task will then become a pleas-ure to her and no compulsion will be neces-sary.

2. Some mothers when they have vowed a daughter to virginity clothe her in sombre gar-ments, wrap her up in a dark cloak, and let her have neither linen nor gold ornaments. They wisely refuse to accustom her to what she will afterwards have to lay aside. Others act on the opposite principle. "What is the use," say they, "of keeping such things from her ? Will she not see them with others ? Women are fond of finery and many whose chastity is be-yond question dress not for men but for them-selves. Give her what she asks for, but she her that those are most praised who ask for nothing. It is better that she should enjoy things to the full and so learn to despise them than that from not having them she should wish to have them." "This," they continue "was the plan which the Lord adopted with the children of Israel. When they longed for the fleshpots of Egypt He sent them flights of quails and allowed them to gorge themselves until they were sick. [1] Those who have once lived worldly lives more readily forego the pleasures of sense than such as from the youth up have known nothing of desire." For while the former—so they argue—trample on what they know, the latter are attracted by what is to them unknown. While the former penitently shun the insidious advances which pleasure makes, the latter coquet with the al-lurements of sense and fancying them to be as sweet as honey find them to be deadly poison. They quote the passage which says that "the lips of a strange woman drop as an honey-comb ; " [2] which is sweet indeed in the eater's mouth but is afterwards found more bitter than gall. [3] This they argue, is the reason that neither honey nor wax is offered in the sacri-fices of the Lord, [4] and that oil the product of the bitter olive is burned in His temple. Moreover it is with bitter herbs that the pass-over is eaten, [6] and "with the unleavened bread of sincerity and truth." [7] He that re-ceives these shall suffer persecution in the world. Wherefore the prophet symbolically sings : "I sat alone because I was filled with bitterness." [8]

3. What then, I reply ? Is youth to run riot that self-indulgence may afterwards be more resolutely rejected ? Far from it, they rejoin "let every man, wherein he is called, therein abide. [9] Is any called being circumcised,"—

---

[1] Spes in ea magis laudanda est quam res. Cic. de Rep. Jerome again quotes the words in Letter CXXX. § 1.
[2] cf. Hor. 1 S. i. 25, 26.

[1] Numb. xi. 4, 20, 31.　[2] Prov. v. 3.　[3] Rev. x. 9.
[4] Lev. ii. 11.　[5] Ex. xxvii. 20.　[6] Ex. xii. 8.
[7] 1 Cor. v. 8.　[8] Jer. xv. 17, LXX.　[9] 1 Cor. vii. 2

at is, as a virgin ?—"let him not become un-rcumcised " [1]—that is, let him not seek the at of marriage given to Adam on his expulsion from the paradise of virginity.[2] "Is any lled in uncircumcision,"—that is, having a fe and enveloped in the skin of matrimony? c him not seek the nakedness of virginity [3] d of that eternal chastity which he has lost ce for all. No, let him "possess his vessel sanctification and honour," [4] let him drink his own wells not out of the dissolute cisrns [5] of the harlots which cannot hold within em the pure waters of chastity.[6] The same aul also in the same chapter, when discussg the subjects of virginity and marriage, lls those who are married slaves of the flesh, t those not under the yoke of wedlock freeen who serve the Lord in all freedom.[7] What I say I do not say as universally applicable ; my treatment of the subject is only artial. I speak of some only, not of all. However my words are addressed to those of both xes, and not only to "the weaker vessel." [8] re you a virgin? Why then do you find easure in the society of a woman? Why do u commit to the high seas your frail patched at, why do you so confidently face the great eril of a dangerous voyage? You know not hat you desire, and yet you cling to her as ough you had either desired her before or, put it as leniently as possible, as though u would hereafter desire her. Women, you ill say, make better servants than men. In at case choose a misshapen old woman, oose one whose continence is approved in e Lord. Why should you find pleasure in young girl, pretty, and voluptuous? You equent the baths, walk abroad sleek and ddy, eat flesh, abound in riches, and wear e most expensive clothes ; and yet you ncy that you can sleep safely beside a deathealing serpent. You tell me perhaps that u do not live in the same house with her. his is only true at night. But you spend hole days in conversing with her. Why o you sit alone with her? Why do you disense with witnesses? By so doing if you o not actually sin you appear to do so, and o important is your influence) you embolden nhappy men by your example to do what is rong. You too, whether virgin or widow, hy do you allow a man to detain you in onversation so long? Why are you not fraid to be left alone with him? At least go ut of doors to satisfy the wants of nature, and r this at any rate leave the man with whom u have given yourself more liberty than you ould with your brother, and have behaved

more immodestly than you would with your husband. You have some question, you say, to ask concerning the holy scriptures. If so, ask it publicly ; let your maids and your attendants hear it. "Everything that is made manifest is light." [1] He who says only what he ought does not look for a corner to say it in ; he is glad to have hearers for he likes to be praised. He must be a fine teacher, on the other hand, who thinks little of men, does not care for the brothers, and labours in secret merely to instruct just one weak woman !

3a. I have wandered for a little from my immediate subject to discuss the procedure of others in such a case as yours ; and while it is my object to train, nay rather to nurse, the infant Pacatula, I have in a moment drawn upon myself the hostility of many women who are by no means daughters of peace.[2] But I shall now return to my proper theme.

A girl should associate only with girls, she should know nothing of boys and should dread even playing with them. She should never hear an unclean word, and if amid the bustle of the household she should chance to hear one, she should not understand it. Her mother's nod should be to her as much a command as a spoken injunction. She should love her as her parent, obey her as her mistress, and reverence her as her teacher. She is now a child without teeth and without ideas, but, as soon as she is seven years old, a blushing girl knowing what she ought not to say and hesitating as to what she ought, she should until she is grown up commit to memory the psalter and the books of Solomon ; the gospels, the apostles and the prophets should be the treasure of her heart. She should not appear in public too freely or too frequently attend crowded churches. All her pleasure should be in her chamber. She must never look at young men or turn her eyes upon curled fops ; and the wanton songs of sweet voiced girls which wound the soul through the ears must be kept from her. The more freedom of access such persons possess, the harder is it to avoid them when they come ; and what they have once learned themselves they will secretly teach her and will thus contaminate our secluded Danaë by the talk of the crowd. Give her for guardian and companion a mistress and a governess, one not given to much wine or in the apostle's words idle and a tattler, but sober, grave, industrious in spinning wool [3] and one whose words will form her childish mind to the practice of virtue. For, as water follows a finger drawn

---

[1] 1 Cor. vii. 18.   [2] Gen. iii. 21.   [3] Gen. iii. 25.
[4] Thess. iv. 4.   [5] Jer. ii. 13, Cisternas dissipates.
[6] Prov. v. 15.   [7] 1 Cor. vii. 21, 22.   [8] 1 Pet. iii. 7.

[1] Eph. v. 13, R. V..
[2] *Male pacatæ,* a pun on Pacatula, which means 'Little Peaceful.'
[3] Lanifica. Cf. the well-known epitaph on a Roman matron : " She stayed at home and spun wool."

through the sand, so one of soft and tender years is pliable for good or evil; she can be drawn in whatever direction you choose to guide her. Moreover spruce and gay young men often seek access for themselves by paying court to nurses or dependants or even by bribing them, and when they have thus gently effected their approach they blow up the first spark of passion until it bursts into flame and little by little advance to the most shameless requests. And it is quite impossible to check them then, for the verse is proved true in their case : " It is ill rebuking what you have once allowed to become ingrained." ¹ I am ashamed to say it and yet I must ; high born ladies who have rejected more high born suitors cohabit with men of the lowest grade and even with slaves. Sometimes in the name of religion and under the cloak of a desire for celibacy they actually desert their husbands in favour of such paramours. You may often see a Helen following her Paris without the smallest dread of Menelaus. Such persons we see and mourn for but we cannot punish, for the multitude of sinners procures tolerance for the sin.

4. The world sinks into ruin : yes ! but shameful to say our sins still live and flourish. The renowned city, the capital of the Roman Empire, is swallowed up in one tremendous fire ; and there is no part of the earth where Romans are not in exile. Churches once held sacred are now but heaps of dust and ashes ; and yet we have our minds set on the desire of gain. We live as though we are going to die tomorrow ; yet we build as though we are going to live always in this world.² Our walls shine with gold, our ceilings also and the capitals of our pillars ; yet Christ dies before our doors naked and hungry in the persons of His poor. The pontiff Aaron, we read, faced the raging flames, and by putting fire in his censer checked the wrath of God. The High Priest stood between the dead and the living, and the fire dared not pass his feet.³ On another occasion God said to Moses, " Let me alone . . . that I may consume this people," ⁴ shewing by the words " let me alone " that he can be withheld from doing what he threatens. The prayers of His servant hindered His power. Who, think you, is there now under heaven able to stay God's wrath, to face the flame of His judgment, and to say with the apostle, " I could wish that I myself were accursed for my brethren " ? ⁵ Flocks and shepherds perish together, because as it is with the people, so is it with the priest.⁶ Of old it was not so. Then Moses spoke in a

passion of pity, " yet now if thou wilt forgive their sin— ; and if not, blot me, I pray thee, out of thy book." ¹ He is not satisfied to secure his own salvation, he desires to perish with those that perish. And he is right, for " in the multitude of people is the king's honour." ²

Such are the times in which our little Pacatula is born. Such are the swaddling clothes in which she draws her first breath ; she is destined to know of tears before laughter and to feel sorrow sooner than joy. And hardly does she come upon the stage when she is called on to make her exit. Let her then suppose that the world has always been what it is now. Let her know nothing of the past, let her shun the present, and let her long for the future.

These thoughts of mine are but hastily mustered. For my grief for lost friends has known no intermission and only recently have I recovered sufficient composure to write an old man's letter to a little child. My affection for you, brother Gaudentius, has induced me to make the attempt and I have thought it better to say a few words than to say nothing at all. The grief that paralyses my will will excuse my brevity ; whereas, were I to say nothing, the sincerity of my friendship might well be doubted.

LETTER CXXIX.

TO DARDANUS.

In answer to a question put by Dardanus, prefect of Gaul, Jerome writes concerning the Promised Land which he identifies not with Canaan but with heaven. He then points out that the present sufferings of the Jews are due altogether to the crime of which they have been guilty in the crucifixion of Christ. The date of the letter is 414 A.D.

LETTER CXXX.

TO DEMETRIAS.

Jerome writes to Demetrias, a highborn lady of Rome who had recently embraced the vocation of a virgin. After narrating her life's history first at Rome and then in Africa, he goes on to lay down rules and principles to guide her in her new life. These which cover the whole field of ascetic practice and include the duties of study, of prayer, of fasting, of obedience, of giving up money for Christ, and of constant industry, are in substance similar to those which thirty years before Jerome had suggested to Eustochium (Letter XXII.). The tone of the letter is however milder and less fanatical ; the asceticism recommended is not so severe ; there is less of rhapsody and more of common sense. This letter should also be compared with the letter addressed to Demetrias by Pelagius, which is given in Vol. xi. of Jerome's works (Migne's Patr. Lat. xxx. ed. 15). The date is 414 A.D.

1. Of all the subjects that I have treated from my youth up until now, either with my

¹ Already quoted in Letter CVII. § 8.
² cf. Letter CXXIII. 15.   ³ Nu. xvi. 46–48, Vulg.
⁴ Ex. xxxii. 10.   ⁵ Rom. ix. 3.   ⁶ Isa. xxiv. 2.

¹ Ex. xxxii. 32.   ² Prov. xiv. 28.

wn pen or that of my secretaries I have dealt
ith none more difficult than that which now
ccupies me. I am going to write to Demetrias
 virgin of Christ and a lady whose birth and
ches make her second to none in the Roman
orld. If, therefore, I employ language ade-
uate to describe her virtue, I shall be thought
 flatter her ; and if I suppress some details
n the score that they might appear incred-
le, my reserve will not do justice to her un-
oubted merits. What am I to do then ? I
m unequal to the task before me, yet I cannot
enture to decline it. Her grandmother and
er mother are both women of mark, and they
ave alike authority to command, faith to seek
nd perseverance to obtain that which they
equire. It is not indeed anything very new
r special that they ask of me ; my wits have
ften been exercised upon similar themes.
Vhat they wish for is that I should raise my
oice and bear witness as strongly as I can to
ne virtues of one who—in the words of the
mous orator [1]—is to be praised less for what
he is than for what she gives promise of
eing. Yet, girl though she is, she has a
lowing faith beyond her years, and has
tarted from a point at which others think it a
nark of signal virtue to leave off.

2. Let detraction stand aloof and envy
ive way ; let no charge of self seeking be
rought against me. I write as a stranger to
 stranger, at least so far as the personal ap-
earance is concerned. For the inner man
nds itself well known by that knowledge
vhereby the apostle Paul knew the Colos-
ians and many other believers whom he had
ever seen. How high an esteem I entertain
or this virgin, nay more what a miracle of
irtue I think her, you may judge by the fact
hat being occupied in the explanation of
zekiel's description of the temple—the hard-
st piece in the whole range of scripture—
nd finding myself in that part of the sacred
difice wherein is the Holy of Holies and the
ltar of incense, I have chosen by way of a
rief rest to pass from that altar to this, that
pon it I might consecrate to eternal chastity
 living offering acceptable to God [2] and free
rom all stain. I am aware that the bishop [3]
as with words of prayer covered her holy
read with the virgin's bridal-veil, reciting the
vhile the solemn sentence of the apostle : " I
vish to present you all as a chaste virgin to
Christ." [4] She stood as a queen at his right
and, her clothing of wrought gold and her
aiment of needlework.[5] Such was the coat
f many colours, that is, formed of many different virtues, which Joseph wore ; and simi-

lar ones were of old the ordinary dress of
king's daughters. Thereupon [1] the bride
herself rejoices and says : " the king hath
brought me into his chambers," [2] and the
choir of her companions responds : " the
king's daughter is all glorious within." [3]
Thus she is a professed virgin. Still these
words of mine will not be without their use.
The speed of racehorses is quickened by the
applause of spectators ; prize fighters are
urged to greater efforts by the cries of their
backers ; and when armies are drawn up for
battle and swords are drawn, the general's
speech does much to fire his soldiers' valour.
So also is it on the present occasion. The
grandmother and the mother have planted,
but it is I that water and the Lord that giveth
the increase.[4]

3. It is the practice of the rhetoricians to
exalt him who is the subject of their praises
by referring to his forefathers and the past
nobility of his race, so that a fertile root may
make up for barren branches and that you
may admire in the stem what you have not
got in the fruit. Thus I ought now to recall
the distinguished names of the Probi and of
the Olybrii, and that illustrious Anician house,
the representatives of which have seldom or
never been unworthy of the consulship. Or
I ought to bring forward Olybrius our virgin's
father, whose untimely loss Rome has had to
mourn. I fear to say more of him, lest I should
intensify the pain of your saintly mother,
and lest the commemoration of his virtues
should become a renewing of her grief. He
was a dutiful son, a loveable husband, a kind
master, a popular citizen. He was made
consul while still a boy ; [5] but the goodness of his character made him more illustrious as a senator. He was happy in his death [6]
for it saved him from seeing the ruin of
his country ; and happier still in his offspring, for the distinguished name of his
great grandmother Demetrias has become yet
more distinguished now that his daughter
Demetrias has vowed herself to perpetual
chastity.

4. But what am I doing ? Forgetful of
my purpose and filled with admiration for
this young man, I have spoken in terms of
praise of mere worldly advantages ; whereas
I should rather have commended our virgin
for having rejected all these, and for having
determined to regard herself not as a wealthy
or a high born lady, but simply as a woman
like other women. Her strength of mind almost passes belief. Though she had silks
and jewels freely at her disposal, and though

---

[1] Cicero in his Dialogue on the Republic. Cf. Or. xxx.
[2] Rom. xii. 1.   [3] Pontifex.
[4] 2 Cor. xi. 2.   [5] Ps. xlv. 9, 13, 14.

[1] i.e. After receiving the veil.   [2] Cant. i. 4.
[3] Ps. xlv. 13.   [4] 1 Cor. iii. 6.   [5] In the year 395 A.D.
[6] Which took place before the fall of Rome in 410 A D.

she was surrounded by crowds of eunuchs and serving-women, a bustling household of flattering and attentive domestics, and though the daintiest feasts that the abundance of a large house could supply were daily set before her ; she preferred to all these severe fasting, rough clothing, and frugal living. For she had read the words of the Lord : " they that wear soft clothing are in kings' houses." [1] She was filled with admiration for the manner of life followed by Elijah and by John the Baptist ; both of whom confined and mortified their loins with girdles of skin,[2] while the second of them is said to have come in the spirit and power of Elijah as the forerunner of the Lord.[3] As such he prophesied while still in his mother's womb,[4] and before the day of judgment won the commendation of the Judge.[5] She admired also the zeal of Anna the daughter of Phanuel, who continued even to extreme old age to serve the Lord in the temple with prayers and fastings.[6] When she thought of the four virgins who were the daughters of Philip,[7] she longed to join their band and to be numbered with those who by their virginal purity have attained the grace of prophecy. With these and similar meditations she fed her mind, dreading nothing so much as to offend her grandmother and her mother. Although she was encouraged by their example, she was discouraged by their expressed wish and desire ; not indeed that they disapproved of her holy purpose, but that the prize was so great that they did not venture to hope for it, or to aspire to it. Thus this poor novice in Christ's service was sorely perplexed. She came to hate all her fine apparel and cried like Esther to the Lord : " Thou knowest that I abhor the sign of my high estate "—that is to say, the diadem which she wore as queen—" and that I abhor it as a menstruous rag." [8] Among the holy and highborn ladies who have seen and known her some have been driven by the tempest which has swept over Africa, from the shores of Gaul to a refuge in the holy places. These tell me that secretly night after night, though no one knew of it but the virgins dedicated to God in her mother's and grandmother's retinue, Demetrias, refusing sheets of linen and beds of down, spread a rug of goat's hair upon the ground and watered her face with ceaseless tears. Night after night she cast herself in thought at the Saviour's knees and implored him to accept her choice, to fulfil her aspiration, and to soften the hearts of her grandmother and of her mother.

5. Why do I still delay to relate the sequel? When her wedding day was now close at hand and when a marriage chamber was being got ready for the bride and bridegroom secretly without any witnesses and with only the night to comfort her, she is said to have nerved herself with such considerations as these: "What ails you, Demetrias ? Why are you so fearful of defending your chastity? What you need is freedom and courage. If you are so panic-stricken in time of peace what would you do if you were called on to undergo martyrdom ? If you cannot bear so much as a frown from your own, how would you steel yourself to face the tribunals of persecutors ? If men's examples leave you unmoved, at least gather courage and confidence from the blessed martyr Agnes [1] who vanquished the temptations both of youth and of a despot and by her martyrdom hallowed the very name of chastity. Unhappy girl ! you know not, you know not to whom your virginity is due. It is not long since you have trembled in the hands of the barbarians and clung to your grandmother and your mother cowering under their cloaks for safety. You have seen yourself a prisoner and your chastity not in your own power. You have shuddered at the fierce looks of your enemies ; you have seen with secret agony the virgins of God ravished. Your city, once the capital of the world, is now the grave of the Roman people ; and will you on the shores of Libya, yourself an exile, accept an exile for a husband ? Where will you find a matron to be present at your bridal ?[3] Whom will you get to escort you home ? No tongue but a harsh Punic one will sing for you the wanton Fescennine verses.[4] Away with all hesitations ! ' Perfect love' of God ' casteth out fear.' [5] Take to yourself the shield of faith, the breastplate of righteousness, the helmet of salvation,[6] and sally forth to battle. The preservation of your chastity involves a martyrdom of its own. Why do you fear your grandmother ? Why do you dread your mother ? Perhaps they may themselves wish for you a course which they do not think you wish for yourself." When by these and other arguments she had wrought herself to the necessary pitch of resolution, she cast from her as so many hindrances all her ornaments and worldly attire

[1] A virgin 13 years old beheaded at Rome under Diocletian after vain efforts first made to overcome her faith by subjecting her to assault and outrage.
[2] See § 7 for the cruelties of the Count Heraelian.
[3] Quam habitura pronubam ?
[4] Wedding songs so called from the place of their origin Fescennia in Etruria. See Catullus LXI. for the several customs here mentioned.
[5] 1 John iv. 18.   [6] Eph. vi. 14-17.

[1] Matt. xi. 8.   [2] 2 Kings i. 8 : Matt. iii. 4.
[3] Matt. xi, 14 : Luke i. 17.   [4] Luke i. 41.
[5] Matt. xi. 7-14. Jerome here borrows a phrase from Cyprian, de Op. et El. xv.
[6] Luke ii. 36, 37.   [7] Acts xxi. 9.   [8] Esther xiv. 16.

Ier precious necklaces, costly pearls, and lowing gems she put back in their cases. 'hen dressing herself in a coarse tunic and hrowing over herself a still coarser cloak she ame in at an unlooked for moment, threw erself down suddenly at her grandmother's nees, and with tears and sobs shewed her rhat she really was. That staid and holy roman was amazed when she beheld her randdaughter in so strange a dress. Her 1other was completely overcome for joy. 3oth women could hardly believe that true rhich they had longed to be true. Their oices stuck in their throats,[1] and, what with lushing and turning pale, with fright and rith joy, they were a prey to many conflict-1g emotions.

6. I must needs give way here and not ttempt to describe what defies description. n the effort to explain the greatness of that oy past all belief, the flow of Tully's elouence would run dry and the bolts poised nd hurled by Demosthenes would become pent and fall short. Whatever mind can onceive or speech can interpret of human ladness was seen then. Mother and child, randmother and granddaughter kissed each ther again and again. The two elder women rept copiously for joy, they raised the prosrate girl, they embraced her trembling form. n her purpose they recognized their own nind, and congratulated each other that now virgin was to make a noble house more 1oble still by her virginity. She had found, hey said, a way to benefit her family and to essen the calamity of the ruin of Rome. 3ood Jesus! What exultation there was all hrough the house! Many virgins sprouted ut at once as shoots from a fruitful stem, and he example set by their patroness and lady vas followed by a host both of clients and ervants. Virginity was warmly espoused n every house and although those who made rofession of it were as regards the flesh of ower rank than Demetrias they sought one eward with her, the reward of chastity. My vords are too weak. Every church in Africa lanced for joy. The news reached not only he cities, towns, and villages but even the cattered huts. Every island between Africa nd Italy was full of it, the glad tidings an far and wide, disliked by none. Then taly put off her mourning and the ruined valls of Rome resumed in part their olden plendour; for they believed the full conver-ion of their fosterchild to be a sign of God's avour towards them. You would fancy that he Goths had been annihilated and that that concourse of deserters and slaves had fallen

by a thunderbolt from the Lord on high. There was less elation in Rome when Marcellus won his first success at Nola[1] after thousands of Romans had fallen at the Trebia, Lake Thrasymenus, and Cannæ. There was less joy among the nobles cooped up in the capitol, on whom the future of Rome depended, when after buying their lives with gold they heard that the Gauls had at length been routed.[2] The news penetrated to the coasts of the East, and this triumph of Christian glory was heard of in the remote cities of the interior. What Christian virgin was not proud to have Demetrias as a companion? What mother did not call Juliana's womb blessed? Unbelievers may scoff at the doubtfulness of rewards to come. Meantime, in becoming a virgin you have gained more than you have sacrificed. Had you become a man's bride but one province would have known of you; while as a Christian virgin you are known to the whole world. Mothers who have but little faith in Christ are unhappily wont to dedicate to virginity only deformed and crippled daughters for whom they can find no suitable husbands. Glass beads, as the saying goes, are thought equal to pearls.[3] Men who pride themselves on their religion give to their virgin daughters sums scarcely sufficient for their maintenance, and bestow the bulk of their property upon sons and daughters living in the world. Quite recently in this city a rich presbyter left two of his daughters who were professed virgins with a mere pittance, while he provided his other children with ample means for selfindulgence and pleasure. The same thing has been done, I am sorry to say, by many women who have adopted the ascetic life. Would that such instances were rare, but unfortunately they are not. Yet the more frequent they are the more blessed are those who refuse to follow an example which is set them by so many.

7. All Christians are loud in their praises of Christ's holy yokefellows,[4] because they gave to Demetrias when she professed herself a virgin the money which had been set apart as a dowry for her marriage. They would not wrong her heavenly bridegroom; in fact they wished her to come to Him with all her previous riches, that these might not be wasted on the things of the world, but might relieve the distress of God's servants. Who would believe it? That Proba, who of all persons of high rank and birth in the

---

[1] Virg., A. ii. 774.

[1] Over Hannibal, B.C. 216. Jerome is quoting from Cicero, Brutus, III.
[2] The reference is to the siege of the Capitol by Brennus and the Gauls, B.C. 390.
[3] See note on Letter LXXIX. § 7.
[4] i.e. Juliana and Proba, the mother and grandmother of Demetrias.

Roman world bears the most illustrious name, whose holy life and universal charity have won for her esteem even among the barbarians, who has made nothing of the regular consulships enjoyed by her three sons, Probinus, Olybrius, and Probus,—that Proba, I say, now that Rome has been taken and its contents burned or carried off, is said to be selling what property she has and to be making for herself friends of the mammon of unrighteousness, that these may receive her into everlasting habitations![1] Well may the church's ministers, whatever their degree, and those monks who are only monks in name, blush for shame that they are buying estates, when this noble lady is selling them.

Hardly had she escaped from the hands of the barbarians, hardly had she ceased weeping for the virgins whom they had torn from her arms, when she was overwhelmed by a sudden and unbearable bereavement, one too which she had had no cause to fear, the death of her loving son.[2] Yet as one who was to be grandmother to a Christian virgin, she bore up against this death-dealing stroke, strong in hope of the future and proving true of herself the words of the lyric:

"Should the round world in fragments burst, its fall
May strike the just, may slay, but not appal."[3]

We read in the book of Job how, while the first messenger of evil was yet speaking, there came also another;[4] and in the same book it is written: "is there not a temptation"—or as the Hebrew better gives it—"a warfare to man upon earth?"[5] It is for this end that we labour, it is for this end that we risk our lives in the warfare of this world, that we may be crowned in the world to come. That we should believe this to be true of men is nothing wonderful, for even the Lord Himself was tempted,[6] and of Abraham the scripture bears witness that God tempted him.[7] It is for this reason also that the apostle says: "we glory in tribulations . . . knowing that tribulation worketh patience; and patience experience; and experience hope; and hope maketh not ashamed;"[8] and in another passage: "Who shall separate us from the love of Christ? Shall tribulation or distress or persecution or famine or nakedness or peril or sword? As it is written, For thy sake we are killed all the day long; we are accounted as sheep for the slaughter."[9] The prophet Isaiah comforts those in like case in these words: "ye that

are weaned from the milk, ye that are drawn from the breasts, look for tribulation upon tribulation, but also for hope upon hope."[1] For, as the apostle puts it "the sufferings of this present time are not worthy to be compared with the glory which shall be revealed in us."[2] Why I have here brought together all these passages the sequel will make plain.

Proba who had seen from the sea the smoke of her native city and had committed her own safety and that of those dear to her to a fragile boat, found the shores of Africa even more cruel than those which she had left. For one[3] lay in wait for her of whom it would be hard to say whether he was more covetous or heartless, one who cared for nothing but wine and money, one who under pretence of serving the mildest of emperors[4] stood forth as the most savage of all despots. If I may be allowed to quote a fable of the poets, he was like Orcus[5] in Tartarus. Like him too he had with him a Cerberus,[6] not three headed but many headed, ready to seize and rend everything within his reach. He tore betrothed daughters from their mothers' arms[7] and sold high-born maidens in marriage to those greediest of men, the merchants of Syria. No plea of poverty induced him to spare either ward or widow or virgin dedicated to Christ. Indeed he looked more at the hands than at the faces of those who appealed to him. Such was the dread Charybdis and such the hound-girt Scylla which this lady encountered in fleeing from the barbarians; monsters who neither spared the shipwrecked nor heeded the cry of those made captive. Cruel wretch![8] at least imitate the enemy of the Roman Empire. The Brennus of our day[9] took only what he found, but you seek what you cannot find.

Virtue, indeed, is always exposed to envy, and cavillers may marvel at the secret agreement by which Proba purchased the chastity of her numerous companions. They may allege that the count who could have taken all would not have been satisfied[10] with a part; and that she could not have questioned his claim since in spite of her rank she was but a slave in his despotic hands. I perceive also that I am laying myself open to the attacks of enemies and that I may seem to be flattering a lady of the highest birth and distinction. Yet these men will not be able to accuse me when

---

[1] Luke xvi. 9. [2] *i.e.* Olybrius, the father of Demetrias.
[3] Horace, Carm. iii. 3. 7, 8. [4] Job i. 16. [5] Job vii. 1.
[6] Matt. iv. 1, sqq. [7] Gen. xxii. 1.
[8] Rom. v. 3-5. [9] Rom. viii. 35, 36.

[1] Isa. xxviii. 9, 10, LXX. [2] Rom. viii. 18.
[3] Heraclian, Count of Africa. [4] Honorius.
[5] *i.e.* Pluto, king of the lower world.
[6] Sabinus, the son-in-law of Heraclian. [7] Virg., A. x. 79.
[8] Jerome here apostrophizes Heraclian.
[9] Alaric the Goth. [10] Reading *dedignatus* for *dignatus.*

hey learn that hitherto I have said nothing about her. I have never either in the lifeime of her husband or since his decease praised her for the antiquity of her family or or the extent of her wealth and power, subects which others might perhaps have improved in mercenary speeches. My purpose s to praise the grandmother of my virgin in a style befitting the church, and to thank her or having aided with her goodwill the desire vhich Demetrias has formed. For the rest my cell, my food and clothing, my advanced years, and my narrow circumstances sufficiently refute the charge of flattery. In what remains of my letter I shall direct all ny words to Demetrias herself, whose holiness ennobles her as much as her rank, and of whom it may be said that the higher she climbs the more terrible will be her fall.

For the rest
This one thing, child of God, I lay on thee ;
Yea before all, and urge it many times : [1]

Love to occupy your mind with the reading of scripture. Do not in the good ground of your breast gather only a crop of darnel and wild oats. Do not let an enemy sow tares among the wheat when the householder is asleep [2] (that is, when the mind which ever cleaves to God is off its guard) ; but say always with the bride in the song of songs : " By night I sought him whom my soul loveth. Tell me where thou feedest, where thou makest thy flock to rest at noon ; " [3] and with the psalmist : " my soul followeth hard after thee : thy right hand upholdeth me ; " [4] and with Jeremiah : " I have not found it hard . . . to follow thee," [5] for " there is no grief in Jacob neither is there travail in Israel." [6] When you were in the world you loved the things of the world. You rubbed your cheeks with rouge and used whitelead to improve your complexion. You dressed your hair and built up a tower on your head with tresses not your own. I shall say nothing of your costly earrings, your glistening pearls from the depths of the Red Sea, [7] your bright green emeralds, your flashing onyxes, your liquid sapphires,—stones which turn the heads of matrons, and make them eager to possess the like. For you have relinquished the world and besides your baptismal vow have taken a new one ; you have entered into a compact with your adversary and have said : " I renounce thee, O devil, and thy world and thy pomp and thy works." Observe, therefore, the treaty that you have made, and keep

terms with your adversary while you are in the way of this world. Otherwise he may some day deliver you to the judge and prove that you have taken what is his ; and then the judge will deliver you to the officer—at once your foe and your avenger—and you will be cast into prison ; into that outer darkness [1] which surrounds us with the greater horror as it severs us from Christ the one true light. [2] And you shall by no means come out thence till you have paid the uttermost farthing, [3] that is, till you have expiated your most trifling sins ; for we shall give account of every idle word in the day of judgment. [4]

8. In speaking thus I do not wish to utter an ill-omened prophecy against you but only to warn you as an apprehensive and prudent monitor who in your case fears even what is safe. What says the scripture ? " If the spirit of the ruler rise up against thee, leave not thy place." [5] We must always stand under arms and in battle array, ready to engage the foe. When he tries to dislodge us from our position and to make us fall back, we must plant our feet firmly down, and say with the psalmist, " he hath set my feet upon a rock " [6] and " the rocks are a refuge for the conies." [7] In this latter passage for ' conies ' many read ' hedgehogs.' Now the hedgehog is a small animal, very shy, and covered over with thorny bristles. When Jesus was crowned with thorns and bore our sins and suffered for us, it was to make the roses of virginity and the lilies of chastity grow for us out of the brambles and briers which have formed the lot of women since the day when it was said to Eve, " in sorrow thou shalt bring forth children ; and thy desire shall be to thy husband and he shall rule over thee." [8] We are told that the bridegroom feeds among the lilies, [9] that is, among those who have not defiled their garments, for they have remained virgins [10] and have hearkened to the precept of the Preacher : " let thy garments be always white." [11] As the author and prince of virginity He says boldly of Himself : " I am the rose of Sharon and the lily of the valleys." [12] " The rocks " then " are a refuge for the conies " who when they are persecuted in one city flee into another [13] and have no fear that the prophetic words " refuge failed me " [14] will be fulfilled in their case. " The high hills are a refuge for the wildgoats," [15] and their food are the serpents which a little child draws out of their holes. Meanwhile the leopard lies down with the kid and the

---

[1] Virg., A. iii. 435. [2] Matt. xiii. 25. [3] Cant. iii. 1: i. 7.
[4] Ps. lxiii. 8. [5] Jer. xvii. 16, LXX.
[6] Nu. xxiii. 21, LXX. [7] *i. e.* The Indian Ocean.

[1] Matt. viii. 12. [2] Joh. viii. 12.
[3] Matt. v. 25, 26. [4] Matt. xii. 36.
[5] Eccles. x. 4. Jerome takes ' the ruler ' to be the devil.
[6] Ps. xl. 2. [7] Ps. civ. 18. [8] Gen. iii. 16.
[9] Cant. ii. 16. [10] Rev. xiv. 4. [11] Eccles. ix. 8.
[12] Cant. ii. 1. [13] Matt. x. 23.
[14] Ps. cxlii. 4. [15] Ps. civ. 18.

lion eats straw like the ox ; [1] not of course that the ox may learn ferocity from the lion but that the lion may learn docility from the ox.

But let us turn back to the passage first quoted, " If the spirit of the ruler rise up against thee, leave not thy place," a sentence which is followed by these words : " for yielding pacifieth great offences." [2] The meaning is, that if the serpent finds his way into your thoughts you must " keep your heart with all diligence " [3] and sing with David, " cleanse thou me from secret faults : keep back thy servant also from presumptuous sins," and come not to " the great transgression " [4] which is sin in act. Rather slay the allurements to vice while they are still only thoughts ; and dash the little ones of the daughter of Babylon against the stones [5] where the serpent can leave no trail. Be wary and vow a vow unto the Lord : " let them not have dominion over me : then shall I be upright and I shall be innocent from the great transgression." [6] For elsewhere also the scripture testifies, " I will visit the iniquity of the fathers upon the children unto the third and fourth generation." [7] That is to say, God will not punish us at once for our thoughts and resolves but will send retribution upon their offspring, that is, upon the evil deeds and habits of sin which arise out of them. As He says by the mouth of Amos : " for three transgressions of such and such a city and for four I will not turn away the punishment thereof." [8]

9. I cull these few flowers in passing from the fair field of the holy scriptures. They will suffice to warn you that you must shut the door of your breast and fortify your brow by often making the sign of the cross. Thus alone will the destroyer of Egypt find no place to attack you ; thus alone will the first-born of your soul escape the fate of the first-born of the Egyptians ; [9] thus alone will you be able with the prophet to say : " my heart is fixed, O God, my heart is fixed ; I will sing and give praise. Awake up, my glory ; awake, psaltery and harp." [10] For, sin stricken as she is, even Tyre is bidden to take up her harp [11] and to do penance ; like Peter she is told to wash away the stains of her former foulness with bitter tears. Howbeit, let us know nothing of penitence, lest the thought of it lead us into sin. It is a plank for those who have had the misfortune to be shipwrecked ; [12] but an inviolate virgin may hope to save the ship itself. For it is one thing to look for what you have cast away, and another to keep what you have never lost. Even the apostle kept under his body and brought it into subjection, lest having preached to others he might himself become a castaway. [1] Heated with the violence of sensual passion he made himself the spokesman of the human race : " O wretched man that I am ! who shall deliver me from the body of this death ? " and again, " I know that in me, that is in my flesh, dwelleth no good thing : for to will is present with me ; but how to perform that which is good, I find not. For the good that I would, I do not : but the evil which I would not, that I do ; " [2] and once more : " they that are in the flesh cannot please God. But ye are not in the flesh, but in the spirit, if so be that the spirit of God dwell in you." [3]

10. After you have paid the most careful attention to your thoughts, you must then put on the armour of fasting and sing with David : " I chastened my soul with fasting," [4] and " I have eaten ashes like bread," [5] and " as for me when they troubled me my clothing was sackcloth." [6] Eve was expelled from paradise because she had eaten of the forbidden fruit. Elijah on the other hand after forty days of fasting was carried in a fiery chariot into heaven. For forty days and forty nights Moses lived by the intimate converse which he had with God, thus proving in his own case the complete truth of the saying, " man doth not live by bread only but by every word that proceedeth out of the mouth of the Lord." [7] The Saviour of the world, who in His virtues and His mode of life has left us an example to follow, [8] was, immediately after His baptism, taken up by the spirit that He might contend with the devil, [9] and after crushing him and overthrowing him might deliver him to his disciples to trample under foot. For what says the apostle ? " God shall bruise Satan under your feet shortly." [10] And yet after the Saviour had fasted forty days, it was through food that the old enemy laid a snare for him, saying, " If thou be the Son of God, command that these stones be made bread." [11] Under the law, in the seventh month after the blowing of trumpets and on the tenth day of the month, a fast was proclaimed for the whole Jewish people, and that soul was cut off from among his people which on that day preferred self-indulgence to self-denial. [12] In Job it is written of behemoth that " his strength is in his loins, and his force is in the navel of his

---

[1] Isa. xi. 6-8.   [2] Eccles. x. 4.   [3] Prov. iv. 23.
[4] Ps. xix. 12-14.   [5] Ps. cxxxvii. 9.   [6] Ps. xix. 13.
[7] Nu. xiv. 18.   [8] Amos i. 3.   [9] Exod. xii. 23, 29.
[10] Ps. lvii. 7, 8.   [11] Isa. xxiii. 15, 16.   [12] See Letter CXXII. §4.

[1] 1 Cor. ix. 27.   [2] Rom. vii. 24, 18, 19.   [3] Rom. viii. 8, 9.
[4] Ps. lxix. 10.   [5] Ps. cii. 9.   [6] Ps. xxxv. 13. Vulg.
[7] Deut. viii. 3.   [8] Joh. xiii. 15: 1 Pet. ii. 21.   [9] Matt. iv. 1.
[10] Rom. xvi. 20.   [11] Matt. iv. 3.   [12] Lev. xxiii. 27, 29.

belly."[1] Our foe uses the heat of youthful passion to tempt young men and maidens and "sets on fire the wheel of our birth."[2] He thus fulfils the words of Hosea, "they are all adulterers, their heart is like an oven;"[3] an oven which only God's mercy and severe fasting can extinguish. These are "the fiery darts"[4] with which the devil wounds men and sets them on fire, and it was these which the king of Babylon used against the three children. But when he made his fire forty-nine cubits high[5] he did but turn to his own ruin[6] the seven weeks which the Lord had appointed for a time of salvation.[7] And as then a fourth bearing a form like the son of God slackened the terrible heat[8] and cooled the flames of the blazing fiery furnace, until, menacing as they looked, they became quite harmless, so is it now with the virgin soul. The dew of heaven and severe fasting quench in a girl the flame of passion and enable her soul even in its earthly tenement to live the angelic life. Therefore the chosen vessel[9] declares that concerning virgins he has no commandment of the Lord.[10] For you must act against nature or rather above nature if you are to forswear your natural function, to cut off your own root, to cull no fruit but that of virginity, to abjure the marriage-bed, to shun intercourse with men, and while in the body to live as though out of it.

11. I do not, however, lay on you as an obligation any extreme fasting or abnormal abstinence from food. Such practices soon break down weak constitutions and cause bodily sickness before they lay the foundations of a holy life. It is a maxim of the philosophers that virtues are means, and that all extremes are of the nature of vice;[11] and it is in this sense that one of the seven wise men propounds the famous saw quoted in the comedy, "In nothing too much."[12] You must not go on fasting until your heart begins to throb and your breath to fail and you have to be supported or carried by others. No; while curbing the desires of the flesh, you must keep sufficient strength to read scripture, to sing psalms, and to observe vigils. For fasting is not a complete virtue in itself but only a foundation on which other virtues may be built. The same may be said of sanctification and of that chastity without which no man shall see the Lord.[13] Each of these is a step on the upward way, yet none of them by itself will avail to win the virgin's crown.

The gospel teaches us this in the parable of the wise and foolish virgins; the former of whom enter into the bridechamber of the bridegroom, while the latter are shut out from it because not having the oil of good works[1] they allow their lamps to fail.[2] This subject of fasting opens up a wide field in which I have often wandered myself,[3] and many writers have devoted treatises to the subject. I must refer you to these if you wish to learn the advantages of self-restraint and on the other hand the evils of over-feeding.

12. Follow the example of your Spouse:[4] be subject to your grandmother and to your mother. Never look upon a man, especially upon a young man, except in their company. Never know a man whom they do not know. It is a maxim of the world that the only sure friendship is one based on an identity of likes and dislikes.[5] You have been taught by their example as well as instructed by the holy life of your home to aspire to virginity, to recognize the commandments of Christ, to know what is expedient for you and what course you ought to choose. But do not regard what is your own as absolutely your own. Remember that part of it belongs to those who have communicated their chastity to you and from whose honourable marriages and beds undefiled[6] you have sprung up like a choice flower. For you are destined to produce perfect fruit if only you will humble yourself under the mighty hand of God,[7] always remembering that it is written: "God resisteth the proud and giveth grace to the humble."[8] Now where there is grace, this is not given in return for works but is the free gift of the giver, so that the apostles' words are fulfilled: "it is not of him that willeth nor of him that runneth, but of God that sheweth mercy."[9] And yet it is ours to will and not to will; and all the while the very liberty that is ours is only ours by the mercy of God.

13. Again in selecting for yourself eunuchs and maids and servingmen look rather to their characters than to their good looks; for, whatever their age or sex, and even if mutilation ensures in them a compulsory chastity, you must take account of their dispositions, for these cannot be operated on save by the fear of Christ. When you are present buffoonery and loose talk must find no place. You should never hear an improper word; if you do hear one, you must not be carried away by it. Abandoned men often make use of a single light expression to

---

[1] Job xl. 16. Cf. Letter XXII. §11.   [2] Jas. iii. 6, R.V. marg.
[3] Hos. vii. 4, Vulg.   [4] Eph. vi. 16.
[5] Song of the Three Holy Children, 24.
[6] Dan. iv. 16, 25, 32.   [7] Lev. xxv. 8.
[8] Dan. iii. 25.   [9] Acts ix. 15.
[10] 1 Cor. vii. 25.   [11] See Letter CVIII. §20.
[12] Μηδὲν 'ἄγαν quoted by Terence (Andria, 61).
[13] Heb. xii. 14, R.V.

[1] See Jerome's commentary on the parable.
[2] Matt. xxv. 1–12.   [3] See Letters XXII., LII., etc.
[4] Luke ii. 51.   [5] Sall. Cat. i. 20.   [6] Heb. xiii. 4.
[7] 1 Pet. v. 6.   [8] 1 Pet. v. 5.   [9] Rom. ix. 16.

try the gates of chastity.[1] Leave to world-lings the privileges of laughing and being laughed at. One who is in your position ought to be serious. Cato the Censor, in old time a leading man in your city, (the same who in his last days turned his attention to Greek literature without either blushing for himself as censor or despairing of success on account of his age) is said by Lucilius[2] to have laughed only once in his life, and the same remark is made about Marcus Crassus. These men may have affected that austere mien to gain for themselves reputation and notoriety. For so long as we dwell in the tabernacle of this body and are envel-oped with this fragile flesh, we can but restrain and regulate our affections and pas-sions; we cannot wholly extirpate them. Knowing this the psalmist says: "be ye angry and sin not;"[3] which the apostle ex-plains thus: "let not the sun go down upon your wrath."[4] For, if to be angry is human, to put an end to one's anger is Christian.

14. I think it unnecessary to warn you against covetousness since it is the way of your family both to have riches and to de-spise them. The apostle too tells us that covetousness is idolatry,[5] and to one who asked the Lord the question: "Good Master, what good thing shall I do that I may have eternal life?" He thus replied: "If thou wilt be perfect, go and sell that thou hast and give to the poor, and thou shalt have treas-ure in heaven; and come and follow me."[6] Such is the climax of complete and apostolic virtue—to sell all that one has and to dis-tribute to the poor,[7] and thus freed from all earthly encumbrance to fly up to the heav-enly realms with Christ. To us, or I should rather say to you, a careful stewardship is entrusted, although in such matters full free-dom of choice is left to every individual, whether old or young. Christ's words are "if thou wilt be perfect." I do not compel you, He seems to say, I do not command you, but I set the palm before you, I shew you the prize; it is for you to choose whether you will enter the arena and win the crown. Let us consider how wisely Wisdom has spoken. "Sell that thou hast." To whom is the command given? Why, to him to whom it was said, "if thou wilt be per-fect." Sell not a part of thy goods but "all that thou hast." And when you have sold them, what then? "Give to the poor." Not to the rich, not to your kinsfolk, not to

minister to self indulgence; but to relieve need. It does not matter whether a man is a priest or a relation or a connexion, you must think of nothing but his poverty. Let your praises come from the stomachs of the hungry and not from the rich banquets of the overfed. We read in the Acts of the Apostles how, while the blood of the Lord was still warm and believers were in the fer-vour of their first faith, they all sold their possessions and laid the price of them at the apostles' feet (to shew that money ought to be trampled underfoot) and "distribution was made unto every man according as he had need."[1] But Ananias and Sapphira proved timid stewards, and what is more, deceit-ful ones; therefore they brought on them-selves condemnation. For having made a vow they offered their money to God as if it were their own and not His to whom they had vowed it; and keeping back for their own use a part of that which belonged to another, through fear of famine which true faith never fears, they drew down on them-selves suddenly the avenging stroke, which was meant not in cruelty towards them but as a warning to others.[2] In fact the apostle Peter by no means called down death upon them as Porphyry[3] foolishly says. He merely announced God's judg-ment by the spirit of prophecy, that the doom of two persons might be a lesson to many. From the time of your dedication to perpetual virginity your property is yours no longer; or rather is now first truly yours because it has come to be Christ's. Yet while your grandmother and mother are liv-ing you must deal with it according to their wishes. If, however, they die and rest in the sleep of the saints (and I know that they desire that you should survive them); when your years are riper, and your will steadier, and your resolution stronger, you will do with your money what seems best to you, or rather what the Lord shall command, know-ing as you will that hereafter you will have nothing save that which you have here spent on good works. Others may build churches, may adorn their walls when built with mar-bles, may procure massive columns, may deck the unconscious capitals with gold and precious ornaments, may cover church doors with silver and adorn the altars with gold and gems. I do not blame those who do these things; I do not repudiate them.[4] Everyone must follow his own judgment. And it is better to spend one's money thus than to hoard it up and brood over it. However

---

[1] Cf. Letter XXII. §24.
[2] The fragment of Lucilius (preserved by Cic. de Fin. V. 30) says nothing of Cato: possibly therefore the text is here corrupt. See for Cato Letter LII. §3.
[3] Ps. iv. 4, LXX.   [4] Eph. iv. 26.   [5] Eph. v. 5.
[6] Matt. xix. 16, 21.   [7] Luke xviii. 22. Cf. Letter CXIX. §4.

[1] Acts iv. 34, 35.   [2] Acts v. 1-10.
[3] A philosopher of the Neoplatonic school (fl. 232-300 A.D.). Of his books against Christianity only small fragments remain.
[4] But see Letter LII. § 10.

your duty is of a different kind. It is yours to clothe Christ in the poor, to visit Him in the sick, to feed Him in the hungry, to shelter Him in the homeless, particularly such as are of the household of faith,[1] to support communities of virgins, to take care of God's servants, of those who are poor in spirit, who serve the same Lord as you day and night, who while they are on earth live the angelic life and speak only of the praises of God. Having food and raiment they rejoice and count themselves rich. They seek for nothing more, contented if only they can persevere in their design. For as soon as they begin to seek more they are shewn to be undeserving even of those things that are needful. The preceding counsels have been addressed to a virgin who is wealthy and a lady of rank.

15. But what I am now going to say will be addressed to the virgin alone. I shall take into consideration, that is, not your circumstances but yourself. In addition to the rule of psalmody and prayer which you must always observe at the third, sixth, and ninth hours, at evening, at midnight, and at dawn,[2] you should determine how much time you will bind yourself to give to the learning and reading of scripture, aiming to please and instruct the soul rather than to lay a burthen upon it. When you have spent your allotted time in these studies, often kneeling down to pray as care for your soul will impel you to do ; have some wool always at hand, shape the threads into yarn with your thumb, attach them to the shuttle, and then throw this to weave a web, or roll up the yarn which others have spun or lay it out for the weavers. Examine their work when it is done, find fault with its defects, and arrange how much they are to do. If you busy yourself with these numerous occupations, you will never find your days long ; however late the summer sun may be in setting, a day will always seem too short on which something remains undone. By observing such rules as these you will save yourself and others, you will set a good example as a mistress, and you will place to your credit the chastity of many. For the scripture says : "the soul of every idler is filled with desires."[3] Nor may you excuse yourself from toil on the plea that God's bounty has left you in want of nothing. No ; you must labour with the rest, that being always busy you may think only of the service of the Lord. I shall speak quite plainly. Even supposing that you give all your property to the poor, Christ will value nothing more highly than what you have wrought with your own hands. You may work for

yourself or to set an example to your virgins ; or you may make presents to your mother and grandmother to draw from them larger sums for the relief of the poor.

16. I have all but passed over the most important point of all. While you were still quite small, bishop Anastasius of holy and blessed memory ruled the Roman church.[1] In his days a terrible storm of heresy[2] came from the East and strove first to corrupt and then to undermine that simple faith which an apostle has praised.[3] However the bishop, rich in poverty and as careful of his flock as an apostle, at once smote the noxious thing on the head, and stayed the hydra's hissing. Now I have reason to fear—in fact a report has reached me to this effect—that the poisonous germs of this heresy still live and sprout in the minds of some to this day. I think, therefore, that I ought to warn you, in all kindness and affection, to hold fast the faith of the saintly Innocent, the spiritual son of Anastasius and his successor in the apostolic see ; and not to receive any foreign doctrine, however wise and discerning you may take yourself to be. Men of this type whisper in corners and pretend to inquire into the justice of God. Why, they ask, was a particular soul born in a particular province ? What is the reason that some are born of Christian parents, others among wild beasts and savage tribes who have no knowledge of God ? Wherever they can strike the simple with their scorpion-sting and form an ulcer fitted to their purpose, there they diffuse their venom. "Is it for nothing, think you,"— thus they argue—"that a little child scarcely able to recognize its mother by a laugh or a look of joy,[4] which has done nothing either good or evil, is seized by a devil or overwhelmed with jaundice or doomed to bear afflictions which godless men escape, while God's servants have to bear them?" Now if God's judgments, they say, are "true and righteous altogether,"[5] and if "there is no unrighteousness in Him,"[6] we are compelled by reason to believe that our souls have pre-existed in heaven, that they are condemned to and, if I may so say, buried in human bodies because of some ancient sins, and that we are punished in this valley of weeping[7] for old misdeeds. This according to them is the prophet's reason for saying : "Before I was afflicted I went astray,"[8] and again, "Bring my soul out of prison."[9] They explain in the same way the question of the disciples in the gospel : "Who did sin, this

---

1 Gal. vi. 10.   2 See note on Letter XXII. § 37.
3 Prov. xiii. 4, LXX. comp. Letter CXXV. § 11.

1 Anastasius was pope from 398 to 402 A. D.
2 That of the Origenists.   3 Rom. i. 8.
4 Virg. Ecl. iv. 60.   5 Ps. xix. 9.   6 Ps. xcii. 15.
7 Ps. lxxxiv. 6, R.V.   8 Ps. cxix. 67.   9 Ps. cxlii. 7.

man or his parents, that he was born blind?"[1] and other similar passages.

This godless and wicked teaching was formerly ripe in Egypt and the East; and now it lurks secretly like a viper in its hole among many persons in those parts, defiling the purity of the faith and gradually creeping on like an inherited disease till it assails a large number. But I am sure that if you hear it you will not accept it. For you have preceptresses under God whose faith is a rule of sound doctrine. You will understand what I mean, for God will give you understanding in all things. You must not ask me on the spot to give you a refutation of this dreadful heresy and of others worse still; for were I to do so I should "criticize where I ought to forbid,"[2] and my present object is not to refute heretics but to instruct a virgin. However, I have defeated their wiles and counterworked their efforts to undermine the truth in a treatise[3] which by God's help I have written; and if you desire to have this, I shall send it to you promptly and with pleasure. I say, if you desire to have it, for as the proverb says, wares proffered unasked are little esteemed, and a plentiful supply brings down prices, which are always highest where scarcity prevails.

17. Men often discuss the comparative merits of life in solitude and life in a community; and the preference is usually given to the first over the second. Still even for men there is always the risk that, being withdrawn from the society of their fellows, they may become exposed to unclean and godless imaginations, and in the fulness of their arrogance and disdain may look down upon everyone but themselves, and may arm their tongues to detract from the clergy or from those who like themselves are bound by the vows of a solitary life.[4] Of such it is well said by the psalmist, "as for the children of men their teeth are spears and arrows and their tongue a sharp sword."[5] Now if all this is true of men, how much more does it apply to women whose fickle and vacillating minds, if left to their own devices, soon degenerate. I am myself acquainted with anchorites of both sexes who by excessive fasting have so impaired their faculties that they do not know what to do or where to turn, when to speak or when to be silent. Most frequently those who have been so affected have lived in solitary cells, cold and damp. Moreover if persons untrained in secular learning read

the works of able church writers, they only acquire from them a wordy fluency and not, as they might do, a fuller knowledge of the scriptures. The old saying is found true of them, although they have not the wit to speak, they cannot remain silent. They teach to others the scriptures that they do not understand themselves; and if they are fortunate enough to convince them, they take upon themselves airs as men of learning.[1] In fact, they set up as instructors of the ignorant before they have gone to school themselves. It is a good thing therefore to defer to one's betters, to obey those set over one, to learn not only from the scriptures but from the example of others how one ought to order one's life, and not to follow that worst of teachers, one's own self-confidence. Of women who are thus presumptuous the apostle says that they "are carried about with every wind of doctrine,[2] ever learning and never able to come to the knowledge of the truth."[3]

18. Avoid the company of married women who are devoted to their husbands and to the world, that your mind may not become unsettled by hearing what a husband says to his wife, or a wife to her husband. Such conversations are filled with deadly venom. To express his condemnation of them the apostle has taken a verse of a profane writer and has pressed it into the service of the church. It may be literally rendered at the expense of the metre: "evil communications corrupt good manners."[4] No; you should choose for your companions staid and serious women, particularly widows and virgins, persons of approved conversation, of few words, and of a holy modesty. Shun gay and thoughtless girls, who deck their heads and wear their hair in fringes, who use cosmetics to improve their skins and affect tight sleeves, dresses without a crease, and dainty buskins; and by pretending to be virgins more easily sell themselves into destruction. Moreover, the character and tastes of a mistress are often inferred from the behaviour of her attendants. Regard as fair and lovable and a fitting companion one who is unconscious of her good looks and careless of her appearance; who does not expose her breast out of doors or throw back her cloak to reveal her neck; who veils all of her face except her eyes, and only uses these to find her way.

19. I hesitate about what I am going to say but, as often happens, whether I like it or not, it must be said; not that I have

---

[1] John ix. 2.
[2] A phrase borrowed from Cicero (p. Sext. Rosc.).
[3] Apparently Letter CXXIV. concerning Origen's book on *First Principles.*
[4] Cf. Letter CXXV. §9.   [5] Ps. lvii. 4.

[1] Cf. Letters LIII. §7, and LXVI. §9.
[2] Eph. iv. 14.   [3] 2 Tim. iii. 7.
[4] 1 Cor. xv. 33; the words are quoted from a lost comedy of Menander.

reason to fear anything of the kind in your case, for probably you know nothing of such things and have never even heard of them, but that in advising you I may warn others. A virgin should avoid as so many plagues and banes of chastity all ringletted youths who curl their hair and scent themselves with musk; to whom may well be applied the words of Petronius Arbiter, "too much perfume makes an ill perfume."[1] I need not speak of those who by their pertinacious visits to virgins bring discredit both on themselves and on these; for, even if nothing wrong is done by them, no wrong can be imagined greater than to find oneself exposed to the calumnies and attacks of the heathen. I do not here speak of all, but only of those whom the church itself rebukes, whom sometimes it expels, and against whom the censure of bishops and presbyters is not seldom directed. For, as it is, it is almost more dangerous for giddy girls to shew themselves in the abodes of religion than even to walk abroad. Virgins who live in communities and of whom large numbers are assembled together, should never go out by themselves or unaccompanied by their mother.[2] A hawk often singles out one of a flight of doves, pounces on it and tears it open till it is gorged with its flesh and blood. Sick sheep stray from the flock and fall into the jaws of wolves. I know some saintly virgins who on holy days keep at home to avoid the crowds and refuse to go out when they must either take a strong escort, or altogether avoid all public places.

It is about thirty years since I published a treatise *on the preservation of virginity*,[3] in which I felt constrained to oppose certain vices and to lay bare the wiles of the devil for the instruction of the virgin to whom it was addressed. My language then gave offence to a great many, for everyone applied what I said to himself and instead of welcoming my admonitions turned away from me as an accuser of his deeds. Was it any use, do you ask, thus to arm a host of remonstrants and to show by my complaints the wounds which my conscience received? Yes, I answer, for, while they have passed away, my book still remains. I have also written short exhortations to several virgins and widows, and in these smaller works I have gathered together all that there is to be said on the subject. So that I am reduced to the alternative of repeating exhortations which seem superfluous or of omitting them to the serious injury of this treatise. The blessed Cyprian

has left a noble work on virginity;[1] and many other writers, both Greek and Latin, have done the same. Indeed the virginal life has been praised both with tongue and pen among all nations and particularly among the churches. Most, however, of those who have written on the subject have addressed themselves to such as have not yet chosen virginity, and who need help to enable them to choose aright. But I and those to whom I write have made our choice; and our one object is to remain constant to it. Therefore, as our way lies among scorpions and adders, among snares and banes, let us go forward staff in hand, our loins girded and our feet shod;[2] that so we may come to the sweet waters of the true Jordan, and enter the land of promise and go up to the house of God. Then shall we sing with the prophet: "Lord, I have loved the habitation of thy house and the place where thine honour dwelleth;"[3] and again: "one thing have I desired of the Lord, that will I seek after; that I may dwell in the house of the Lord all the days of my life."[4]

Happy is the soul, happy is the virgin in whose heart there is room for no other love than the love of Christ. For in Himself He is wisdom and chastity, patience and justice and every other virtue. Happy too is she who can recall a man's face without the least sigh of regret, and who has no desire to set eyes on one whom, after she has seen him, she may find herself unwilling to give up. Some there are, however, who by their ill-behaviour bring discredit on the holy profession of virginity and upon the glory of the heavenly and angelic company who have made it. These must be frankly told either to marry if they cannot contain, or to contain if they will not marry. It is also a matter for laughter or rather for tears, that when mistresses walk abroad they are preceded by maids better dressed than themselves; indeed so usual has this become that, if of two women you see one less neat than the other, you take her for the mistress as a matter of course. And yet these maids are professed virgins. Again not a few virgins choose sequestered dwellings where they will not be under the eyes of others, in order that they may live more freely than they otherwise could do. They take baths, do what they please, and try as much as they can to escape notice. We see these things and yet we put up with them; in fact, if we catch sight of the glitter of gold, we are ready to account of them as good works.

20. I end as I began, not content to have

---

[1] The words are not extant in Petronius but occur in Martial ii. 12. 4.
[2] *i.e.* the head of the community.
[3] Letter XXII. to Eustochium.

[1] See Letter XXII. § 22 *ante*.
[2] Exod. xii. 11.
[3] Ps. xxvi. 8.
[4] Ps. xxvii. 4.

given you but a single warning. Love the holy scriptures, and wisdom will love you. Love wisdom, and it will keep you safe. Honour wisdom, and it will embrace you round about.[1] Let the jewels on your breast and in your ears be the gems of wisdom. Let your tongue know no theme but Christ, let no sound pass your lips that is not holy, and let your words always reproduce that sweetness of which your grandmother and your mother set you the example. Imitate them, for they are models of virtue.

LETTER CXXXI.

FROM AUGUSTINE.

At the suggestion of Jerome, Marcellinus (for whom see Letter CXXVI.) had consulted Augustine on the difficult question of the origin of the soul but had failed to get any definite opinion from this latter. Augustine now writes to Jerome confessing his inability to decide the question and asking for advice upon it. He begins by reciting—and justifying—his own belief that the soul is immortal and incorporeal and that its fall into sin is due not to God but to its own free choice. He then goes on to say that he is quite ready to accept creationism as a solution of the difficulty if Jerome will shew him how this theory is reconcilable with the church's condemnation of Pelagius and its assertion of the doctrine of original sin. The damnation of unbaptized infants is assumed throughout.

The date of the letter is 415 A.D. Its number in the Letters of Augustine is CLXVI.

LETTER CXXXII.

FROM AUGUSTINE.

In this letter Augustine deals with the statement of James ii. 10 ("whosoever shall keep the whole law and yet offend in one point, he is guilty of all") and explains it by saying that every breach of the law is a breach of love. He also takes occasion to criticise two doctrines of the schools then prevalent, (1) that all sins are equal and (2) that he who has one virtue has all and that all virtues are wanting to him who lacks one.

The date of the letter is 415 A.D. Its number in the Letters of Augustine is CLXVII.

LETTER CXXXIII.

TO CTESIPHON.

Ctesiphon had written to Jerome for his opinion on two points in the teaching of Pelagius, (1) his quietism and (2) his denial of original sin. Jerome now refutes these two doctrines and points out that Pelagius has drawn them partly from the philosophers and partly from the heretics. He censures Rufinus, who had died 5 years before, for attributing to Sixtus bishop of Rome a book which is really the work of Xystus a Pythagorean, and for passing off as the composition of the martyr Pamphilus a panegyric of Origen really due to his friend Eusebius. In both these assertions, however, Jerome is more wrong than right. (See Prolegomena to the works of Rufinus.) The letter concludes with a promise to deal more fully with the heresy of Pelagius at some future time, a promise afterwards redeemed by the publication of a 'dialogue against the Pelagians.' The date of the letter is 415 A.D.

1. In acquainting me with the new controversy which has taken the place of the old you are wrong in thinking that you have acted rashly, for your conduct has been prompted by zeal and friendship. Already before the arrival of your letter many in the East have been deceived into a pride which apes humility and have said with the devil: "I will ascend into heaven, I will exalt my throne above the stars of God ; I will be like the Most High."[1] Can there be greater presumption than to claim not likeness to God but equality with Him, and so to compress into a few words the poisonous doctrines of all the heretics which in their turn flow from the statements of the philosophers, particularly of Pythagoras and Zeno the founder of the Stoic school? For those states of feeling which the Greeks call πάθη and which we may describe as "passions," relating to the present or the future such as vexation and gladness, hope and fear,—these, they tell us, it is possible to root out of our minds ; in fact all vice may be destroyed root and branch in man by meditation on virtue and constant practice of it. The position which they thus take up is vehemently assailed by the Peripatetics who trace themselves to Aristotle, and by the new Academics of whom Cicero is a disciple ; and these overthrow not the facts of their opponents—for they have no facts—but the shadows and wishes which do duty for them. To maintain such a doctrine is to take man's nature from him, to forget that he is constituted of body as well as soul, to substitute mere wishes for sound teaching.[2] For the apostle says :—"O wretched man that I am ! who shall deliver me from the body of this death ?"[3] But as I cannot say all that I wish in a short letter I will briefly touch on the points that you must avoid. Virgil writes :—

Thus mortals fear and hope, rejoice and grieve,
And shut in darkness have no sight of heaven.[4]

For who can escape these feelings? Must we not all clap our hands when we are joyful, and shrink at the approach of sorrow? Must not hope always animate us and fear put us in terror? So in one of his Satires the poet Horace, whose words are so weighty, writes :

From faults no mortal is completely free ;
He that has fewest is the perfect man.[5]

2. Well does one of our own writers[6] say: "the philosophers are the patriarchs of the

---

[1] Cf. Letter LII. §3.

[1] Isa. xiv. 13, 14. [2] Cf. Letter LXXIX. §9. [3] Rom. vii. 24.
[4] Virgil. Æneid. vi. 733, 734. [5] Horace, Sat. I. iii. 68, 69.
[6] Tertullian, against Hermogenes, c. ix.

heretics." It is they who have stained with their perverse doctrine the spotlessness of the Church, not knowing that of human weakness it is said: "Why is earth and ashes proud?"[1] So likewise the apostle: "I see another law in my members warring against the law of my mind and bringing me into captivity";[2] and again, "The good that I would I do not: but the evil which I would not that I do."[3] Now if Paul does what he wills not, what becomes of the assertion that a man may be without sin if he will? Given the will, how is it to have its way when the apostle tells us that he has no power to do what he wishes? Moreover if we ask them who the persons are whom they regard as sinless they seek to veil the truth by a new subterfuge. They do not, they say, profess that men are or have been without sin; all that they maintain is that it is possible for them to be so. Remarkable teachers truly, who maintain that a thing may be which, on their own shewing, never has been; whereas the scripture says:—"The thing which shall be, it is that which hath been already of old time."[4]

I need not go through the lives of the saints or call attention to the moles and spots which mark the fairest skins. Many of our writers, it is true, unwisely, take this course; however, a few sentences of scripture will dispose alike of the heretics and the philosophers. What says the chosen vessel? "God had concluded all in unbelief that he might have mercy upon all;[5] and in another place, "all have sinned and come short of the glory of God."[6] The preacher also who is the mouthpiece of the Divine Wisdom freely protests and says: "there is not a just man upon earth, that doeth good and sinneth not:"[7] and again, "if thy people sin against thee, for there is no man that sinneth not:"[8] and "who can say, I have made my heart clean?"[9] and "none is clean from stain, not even if his life on earth has been but for one day. David insists on the same thing when he says: "Behold, I was shapen in iniquity and in sin did my mother conceive me;"[10] and in another psalm, "in thy sight shall no man living be justified."[11] This last passage they try to explain away from motives of reverence, arguing that the meaning is that no man is perfect in comparison with God. Yet the scripture does not say: "in comparison with thee shall no man living be justified," but "in thy sight shall no man living be justified." And when it says "in thy sight" it means that those who seem holy to men to God in his fuller knowledge are by no means holy. For "man looketh on the outward appearance, but the Lord looketh on the heart."[1] But if in the sight of God who sees all things and to whom the secrets of the heart lie open[2] no man is just; then these heretics instead of adding to man's dignity, clearly take away from God's power. I might bring together many other passages of scripture of the same import; but were I to do so, I should exceed the limits I will not say of a letter but of a volume.

3. It is with no new doctrines that in their self-applauding perfidy they deceive the simple and untaught. They cannot, however, deceive theologians who meditate in the law of the Lord day and night.[3] Let those blush then for their leaders and companions who say that a man may be "without sin" if he will, or, as the Greeks term it $\alpha\nu\alpha\mu\acute{\alpha}\rho\tau\eta\tau os$, "sinless." As such a statement sounds intolerable to the Eastern churches, they profess indeed only to say that a man may be "without sin" and do not presume to allege that he may be "sinless" as well. As if, forsooth, "sinless" and "without sin" had different meanings; whereas the only difference between them is that Latin requires two words to express what Greek gives in one. If you adopt "without sin" and reject "sinless," then condemn the preachers of sinlessness. But this you cannot do. You know[4] very well what it is that you teach your pupils in private; and that while you say one thing with your lips you engrave another on your heart. To us, ignorant outsiders you speak in parables; but to your own followers you avow your secret meaning. And for this you claim the authority of scripture which says: "to the multitudes Jesus spake in parables;" but to his own disciples He said: "it is given unto you to know the mysteries of the kingdom of heaven, but to them it is not given."[5]

But to return; I will shortly set forth the names of your leaders and companions to shew you who those are of whose fellowship you make your boast. Manichæus says of his elect—whom he places among Plato's orbits in heaven—that they are free from all sin, and cannot sin even if they will. To so great heights have they attained in virtue that they laugh at the works of the flesh. Then there is Priscillian in Spain whose infamy makes him as bad as Manichæus, and whose disciples profess a high esteem for you. These are rash enough to claim for them-

---

[1] Ecclus. x. 9.   [2] Rom. vii. 23.   [3] Rom. vii. 19.
[4] Eccles. i. 9.   Jerome inverts the words of the Preacher.
[5] Rom. xi. 32.   [6] Rom. iii. 23.   [7] Eccles. vii. 20.
[8] 1 K. viii. 46.   [9] Prov. xx. 9.
[10] Ps. li. 5.   [11] Ps. cxliii. 2.

[1] 1 S. xvi. 7.   [2] Ps. xliv. 21: Heb. iv. 13.   [3] Ps. i. 2.
[4] Jerome here addresses Pelagius.   [5] Matt. xiii. 3, 11.

selves the twofold credit of perfection and wisdom. Yet they shut themselves up alone with women and justify their sinful embraces by quoting the lines :

> The almighty father takes the earth to wife ;
> Pouring upon her fertilizing rain,
> That from her womb new harvest he may reap.[1]

These heretics have affinities with Gnosticism which may be traced to the impious teaching of Basilides.[2] It is from him that you derive the assertion that without knowledge of the law it is impossible to avoid sin. But why do I speak of Priscillian who has been condemned by the whole world and put to death by the secular sword ?[3] Evagrius[4] of Ibera in Pontus who sends letters to virgins and monks and among others to her whose name bears witness to the blackness of her perfidy,[5] has published a book of maxims on apathy, or, as we should say, impassivity or imperturbability ; a state in which the mind ceases to be agitated and—to speak simply—becomes either a stone or a God. His work is widely read, in the East in Greek and in the West in a Latin translation made by his disciple Rufinus.[6] He has also written a book which professes to be about monks and includes in it many not monks at all whom he declares to have been Origenists, and who have certainly been condemned by the bishops. I mean Ammonius, Eusebius, Euthymius,[7] Evagrius himself, Horus,[8] Isidorus,[9] and many others whom it would be tedious to enumerate. He is careful, however, to do as the physicians, of whom Lucretius says :[10]

> To children bitter wormwood still they give
> In cups with juice of sweetest honey smeared.

That is to say, he has set in the forefront of his book John,[11] an undoubted Catholic and saint, by his means to introduce to the church the heretics mentioned farther on. But who can adequately characterize the rashness or madness which has led him to ascribe a book of the Pythagorean philosopher Xystus,[1] a heathen who knew nothing of Christ, to Sixtus[2] a martyr and bishop of the Roman church ? In this work the subject of perfection is discussed at length in the light of the Pythagorean doctrine which makes man equal with God and of one substance with Him. Thus many not knowing that its author was a philosopher and supposing that they are reading the words of a martyr, drink of the golden cup of Babylon. Moreover in its pages there is no mention of prophets, patriarchs, apostles, or of Christ ; so that according to Rufinus[3] there has been a bishop and a martyr who had nothing to do with Christ. Such is the book from which you and your followers quote passages against the church. In the same way he played fast and loose with the name of the holy martyr Pamphilus ascribing to him the first of the six books in defence of Origen written by Eusebius of Cæsarea[4] who is admitted by every body to have been an Arian. His object in doing so was of course to commend to Latin ears Origen's four wonderful books about First Principles.

Would you have me name another of your masters in heresy ? Much of your teaching is traceable to Origen. For, to give one instance only, when he comments on the psalmist's words : " My reins also instruct me in the night season,"[5] he maintains that when a holy man like yourself has reached perfection, he is free even at night from human infirmity and is not tempted by evil thoughts. You need not blush to avow yourself a follower of these men ; it is of no use to disclaim their names when you adopt their blasphemies. Moreover, your teaching

---

[1] Virgil, Georg. ii. 325-327.
[2] See note on Letter LXXV. §3.
[3] He was condemned by a council at Saragossa in 380-381 A.D. and was put to death by Maximus at Trêves in 385 A.D. at the instigation of the Spanish bishops. Martin of Tours tried to save his life in vain.
[4] According to Sozomen (H. E. vi. c. 30) Evagrius was in his youth befriended by Gregory of Nyssa, who left him in Constantinople to assist Nectarius in dealing with theological questions. Being in danger, both as to his chastity and as to his personal safety on account of an acquaintance he had formed with a lady of rank, he withdrew to Jerusalem, where he was nursed through a severe illness by Melanium. The rest of his life he spent as an ascetic in the Egyptian desert. See also Pallad. Hist. Laus., §lxxxvi.
[5] Viz., Melanium, who having sided with Rufinus in his controversy with Jerome, incurred the latter's displeasure. The name means ' black.' See Letter IV. § 2.
[6] Viz., Rufinus of Aquileia, Jerome's former friend.
[7] These three were known as ' the long brothers.' Their expulsion from Egypt by Theophilus was one of the causes which led to the downfall of John of Chrysostom.
[8] A contemporary Egyptian monk of great celebrity.
[9] See Letter XCII. and note.
[10] Lucretius, i. 935-937.
[11] Viz., John of Lycopolis, an Egyptian hermit of the latter half of the fourth century. His reputation for sanctity was only second to that of Antony. The book about monks here spoken of does not occur in the list of the writings of Evagrius in the Dict. of Chr. Biog., taken from Socrates, Gennadius and Palladius. Rufinus' History of the Monks bears a close affinity to the Historia Lausiaca of Palladius, who was closely allied to

Evagrius ; and it is possible that Jerome may have attributed Palladius' work to Evagrius. See Prolegomena to Rufinus, and comp. Ruf. Hist. Mon. i. with Pall. Hist. Laus., xliii.
[1] In his references (here and in his comm. on Jeremiah, book iv., ch. 22) to the Gnomes of Sixtus or Xystus, Jerome is both inaccurate and unfair. For Rufinus merely states that the author was traditionally identified with Sixtus, bishop of Rome and martyr ; and he does not endorse the statement. In its present form the book is so strongly Christian in tone and language that it is strange to find it described as Christless and heathen. Of its origin nothing certain is known, but probably it is " the production of an early Christian philosopher working up heathen material with a leaven of the Gospel " (Dict. Chr. Biog. s. v. Xystus).
[2] It is not clear which Sixtus is meant. Sixtus I. is not known to have been a martyr and Sixtus II. can hardly be intended. For though his claim to the title is undisputed he can scarcely have written what Origen already quotes as well known.
[3] Jerome elsewhere twits Rufinus with the same mistake (see Comm. on Jer., book iv., ch. 22). He was not, however, alone in making it, for even Augustine was for a time similarly deceived (see his Retractations, ii. 42).
[4] Cf. Against Rufinus, i. 8, 9. There is now no doubt that Jerome was wrong and Rufinus right as to the authorship of the book. See the article entitled " Eusebius " in the Dict. of Christian Biog. and the prolegomena to his works as issued in this series.
[5] Ps. xvi. 7 and Origen's Comm. ad loc.

corresponds to Jovinian's second position.[1] You must, therefore, take the answer which I have given to him as equally applicable to yourself. Where men's opinions are the same their destinies can hardly be different.

4. Such being the state of the case, what object is served by "silly women laden with sins, carried about with every wind of doctrine, ever learning and never able to come to the knowledge of the truth?"[2] Or how is the cause helped by the men who dance attendance upon these, men with itching ears[3] who know neither how to hear nor how to speak? They confound old mire with new cement and, as Ezekiel says, daub a wall with untempered mortar; so that, when the truth comes in a shower, they are brought to nought.[4] It was with the help of the harlot Helena that Simon Magus founded his sect.[5] Bands of women accompanied Nicolas of Antioch that deviser of all uncleanness.[6] Marcion sent a woman before him to Rome to prepare men's minds to fall into his snares.[7] Apelles possessed in Philumena an associate in his false doctrines.[8] Montanus, that mouthpiece of an unclean spirit, used two rich and high born ladies Prisca and Maximilla first to bribe and then to pervert many churches.[9] Leaving ancient history I will pass to times nearer to our own. Arius intent on leading the world astray began by misleading the Emperor's sister.[10] The resources of Lucilla helped Donatus to defile with his polluting baptism many unhappy persons throughout Africa.[11] In Spain the blind woman Agape led the blind man Elpidius into the ditch.[12] He was followed by Priscillian, an enthusiastic votary of Zoroaster and a magian before he became a bishop. A woman named Galla seconded his efforts and left a gadabout sister to perpetuate a second heresy of a kindred form.[13] Now also the mystery of iniquity is working.[14]

Men and women in turn lay snares for each other till we cannot but recall the prophet's words: "the partridge hath cried aloud, she hath gathered young which she hath not brought forth, she getteth riches and not by right; in the midst of her days she shall leave them, and at her end she shall be a fool."[1]

5. The better to deceive men they have added to the maxim given above[2] the saving clause "but not without the grace of God;" and this may at the first blush take in some readers. However, when it is carefully sifted and considered, it can deceive nobody. For while they acknowledge the grace of God, they tell us that our acts do not depend upon His help. Rather, they understand by the grace of God free will and the commandments of the Law. They quote Isaiah's words: "God hath given the law to aid men,"[3] and say that we ought to thank Him for having created us such that of our own free will we can choose the good and avoid the evil. Nor do they see that in alleging this the devil uses their lips to hiss out an intolerable blasphemy. For if God's grace is limited to this that He has formed us with wills of our own, and if we are to rest content with free will, not seeking the divine aid lest this should be impaired, we should cease to pray; for we cannot entreat God's mercy to give us daily what is already in our hands having been given to us once for all. Those who think thus make prayer impossible and boast that free will makes them not merely controllers of themselves but as powerful as God. For they need no external help. Away with fasting, away with every form of self-restraint! For why need I strive to win by toil what has once for all been placed within my reach? The argument that I am using is not mine; it is that put forward by a disciple of Pelagius, or rather one who is the teacher and commander of his whole army.[4] This man, who is the opposite of Paul for he is a vessel of perdition, roams through thickets—not, as his partisans say, of syllogisms, but of solecisms, and theorizes thus: "If I do nothing without the help of God and if all that I do is His act, I cease to labour and the crown that I shall win will belong not to me but to the grace of God. It is idle for Him to have given me the power of choice if I cannot use it without His constant help. For will that requires external support ceases to be will. God has given me freedom of

---

[1] See Against Jovinian, book ii. 1. His second position is that "persons baptized with water and the spirit cannot be tempted of the devil."
[2] Eph. iv. 14; 2 Tim. iii. 6, 7.   [3] 2 Tim. iv. 3.
[4] Ezek. xiii. 10–16.
[5] This legendary companion and disciple of Simon Magus is said to have been identified by him with Helen of Troy. According to Justin Martyr she had been a prostitute at Tyre.
[6] Cf. Epiphanius, Adv. Haer. lib. i. tom. ii, p. 76, ed. Migne.
[7] Jerome is alone in speaking of this emissary. It has been suggested that he may have had in mind the gnostic Marcellina, who came to Rome during the episcopate of Anicetus.
[8] Apelles, the most famous of the disciples of Marcion, lived and taught mainly at Rome. Philumena was a clairvoyante whose revelations he regarded as inspired.
[9] See Letter XLI.
[10] Constantia, sister of Constantine the Great.
[11] Lucilla, a wealthy lady of Carthage, having been condemned by its bishop Cæcilianus, is said to have procured his deposition by bribing his fellow-bishops.
[12] Agape, a Spanish lady, was a disciple of the gnostic Marcus of Memphis (cf. Letter LXXV. § 3). She was thus one of the links between the gnosticism of the East and the Priscillianism of Spain. Elpidius was a rhetorician who spread in Spain the Zoroastrian opinions which culminated in Priscillianism.
[13] Of these sisters nothing further is known.
[14] 2 Th. ii. 7.

[1] Jer. xvii. 11, Vulg.
[2] Viz., "A man may be without sin." See for this and the other statements of Pelagius, Aug. de Gestis Pelagii, esp. c. 2 and 6. Jerome's Anti-Pelagian Dialogue takes these words as containing the essence of Pelagianism.
[3] Isa. viii. 20, LXX.
[4] Celestius is meant, after Pelagius the principal champion of free will.

choice, but what becomes of this if I cannot do as I wish?" Accordingly he propounds the following dilemma: "Either once for all I use the power which is given to me, and so preserve the freedom of my will ; or I need the help of another, in which case the freedom of my will is wholly abrogated."

6. Surely the man who says this is no ordinary blasphemer ; the poison of his heresy is no common poison. Since our wills are free, they argue, we are no longer dependent upon God ; and they forget the Apostle's words : "what hast thou that thou didst not receive? Now if thou didst receive it why dost thou glory as if thou hadst not received it?"[1] A nice return, truly, does a man make to God when to assert the freedom of his will he rebels against Him ! For our parts we gladly embrace this freedom, but we never forget to thank the Giver ; knowing that we are powerless unless He continually preserves in us His own gift. As the apostle says, "it is not of him that willeth, nor of him that runneth, but of God that sheweth mercy."[2] To will and to run are mine, but they will cease to be mine unless God brings me His continual aid. For the same apostle says : "it is God which worketh in you both to will and to do."[3] And in the Gospel the Saviour says : "my Father worketh hitherto and I work."[4] He is always a giver, always a bestower. It is not enough for me that he has given me grace once ; He must give it me always. I seek that I may obtain, and when I have obtained I seek again. I am covetous of God's bounty ; and as He is never slack in giving, so I am never weary in receiving. The more I drink, the more I thirst. For I have read the song of the psalmist : "O taste and see that the Lord is good."[5] Every good thing that we have is a tasting of the Lord. When I fancy myself to have finished the book of virtue, I shall then only be at the beginning. For "the fear of the Lord is the beginning of wisdom,"[6] and this fear is in its turn cast out by love.[7] Men are only perfect so far as they know themselves to be imperfect. "So likewise ye," Christ says, "when ye shall have done all those things which are commanded you, say, We are unprofitable servants : we have done that which was our duty to do."[8] If he is unprofitable who has done all, what must we say of him who has failed to do so? This is why the Apostle declares that he has attained in part and apprehended in part, that he is not yet perfect, and that forgetting those things which are behind he reaches forth unto those things which are before.[1] Now he who always forgets the past and longs for the future shews that he is not content with the present.

They are for ever objecting to us that we destroy free will. Nay, we reply, it is you who destroy it ; for you use it amiss and disown the bounty of its Giver. Which really destroys freedom? the man who thanks God always and traces back his own tiny rill to its source in Him? or the man who says : "come not near to me, for I am holy ;[2] I have no need of Thee. Thou hast given me once for all freedom of choice to do as I wish. Why then dost Thou interfere again to prevent me from doing anything unless Thou Thyself first makest Thy gifts effective in me?" To such an one I would say : "your profession of belief in God's grace is insincere. For you explain this of the state in which man has been created and you do not look for God to help him in his actions. To do this, you argue, would be to surrender human freedom. Thus disdaining the aid of God you have to look to men for help."

7. Listen, only listen, to the blasphemer. "Suppose," he avers, "that I want to bend my finger or to move my hand, to sit, to stand, to walk, to run to and fro, to spit or to blow my nose, to perform the offices of nature ; must the help of God be always indispensable to me?" Thankless, nay blasphemous wretch, hear the apostle's declaration : "whether therefore ye eat or drink, or whatsoever ye do, do all to the glory of God."[3] Hear also the words of James : "go to now, ye that say, To-day or to-morrow we will go into such a city and continue there a year, and buy, and sell, and get gain. Whereas ye know not what shall be on the morrow : for what is your life? It is even a vapour that appeareth for a little time, and then vanisheth away. For that ye ought to say, If the Lord will, we shall live, and do this or that. But now ye rejoice in your boastings ; all such rejoicing is evil."[4] You fancy that a wrong is inflicted on you and your freedom of choice is destroyed if you are forced to fall back on God as the moving cause of all your actions, if you are made dependent on His Will, and if you have to echo the psalmist's words : "mine eyes are ever toward the Lord : for it is he that shall pluck my feet out of the net."[5] And so you presume rashly to maintain that each individual is governed by his own choice. But if he is governed by his own choice, what becomes of God's help? If he does not need Christ to rule him, why does Jeremiah write : "the way of man is not in himself"[6] and "the Lord directeth his steps."[7]

[1] 1 Cor. iv. 7.   [2] Rom. ix. 16.   [3] Phil. ii. 13.
[4] John v. 17.   [5] Ps. xxxiv. 8.   [6] Ps. cxi. 10.
[7] 1 Joh. iv. 18.   [8] Luke xvii. 10.

[1] Phil. iii. 12, 13.   [2] Isa. lxv. 5, LXX.   [3] 1 Cor. x. 31.
[4] Jas. iv. 13-16.   [5] Ps. xxv. 15.   [6] Jer. x. 23.   [7] Prov. xvi. 9.

You say that the commandments of God are easy, and yet you cannot produce any one who has fulfilled them all. Answer me this : are they easy or are they difficult ? If they are easy, then produce some one who has fulfilled them all. Explain also the words of the psalmist : "thou dost cause toil by thy law,"[1] and "because of the words of thy lips I have kept hard ways."[2] And make plain our Lord's sayings in the gospel : "enter ye in at the strait gate;"[3] and "love your enemies;" and "pray for them which persecute you."[4] If on the other hand the commandments are difficult and if no man has kept them all, how have you presumed to say that they are easy? Do not you see that you contradict yourself ? For either they are easy and countless numbers have kept them; or they are difficult and you have been too hasty in calling them easy.

8. It is a common argument with your party to say that God's commandments are either possible or impossible. So far as they are the former you admit that they are rightly laid upon us; but so far as they are the latter you allege that blame attaches not to us who have received them but to God who has imposed them on us. What ! has God commanded me to be what He is,[5] to put no difference between myself and my creator, to be greater than the greatest of the angels, to have a power which no angels possess ? Sinlessness is made a characteristic of Christ, "who did no sin neither was guile found in his mouth."[6] But if I am sinless as well as He, how is sinlessness any longer His distinguishing mark ? for if this distinction exists, your theory becomes fatal to itself.

You assert that a man may be without sin if he will; and then, as though awakening from a deep sleep, you try to deceive the unwary by adding the saving clause "yet not without the grace of God." For if by his own efforts a man can keep himself without sin, what need has he of God's grace ? If on the other hand he can do nothing without this, what is the use of saying that he can do what he cannot do? It is argued that a man may be without sin and perfect if he only wills it. What Christian is there who does not wish to be sinless or who would reject perfection if, as you say, it is to be had for the wishing, and if the will is sure to be followed by the power ? There is no Christian who does not wish to be sinless; wishing to be so, therefore, they all will be so. Whether you like it or not you will be caught in this dilemma, that you can produce nobody

or hardly anybody who is without sin, yet have to admit that everybody may be sinless if he likes. God's commandments, it is argued, are possible to keep. Who denies it ? But how this truth is to be understood the chosen vessel thus most clearly explains : "what the law could not do in that it was weak through the flesh, God, sending his own Son in the likeness of sinful flesh and for sin, condemned sin in the flesh;"[1] and again : "by the deeds of the law there shall no flesh be justified."[2] And to shew that it is not only the law of Moses that is meant or all those precepts which collectively are termed the law, the same apostle writes : "I delight in the law of God after the inward man. But I see another law in my members, warring against the law of my mind, and bringing me into captivity to the law of sin which is in my members. O wretched man that I am : who shall deliver me from the body of this death? The grace of God through Jesus Christ our Lord."[3] Other words of his further explain his meaning : "we know that the law is spiritual : but I am carnal, sold under sin. For that which I do I know[4] not : for what I would that do I not, but what I hate that do I. If then I do that which I would not, I consent unto the law that it is good. Now then it is no more I that do it : but sin that dwelleth in me. For I know that in me (that is, in my flesh) dwelleth no good thing. For to will is present with me : but how to perform that which is good I find not. For the good that I would, I do not : but the evil which I would not, that I do. Now if I do that I would not, it is no more I that do it, but sin that dwelleth in me."[5]

9. But you will demur to this and say that I follow the teaching[6] of the Manichæans and others who make war against the church's doctrine in the interest of their belief that there are two natures diverse from one another and that there is an evil nature which can in no wise be changed. But it is not against me that you must make this imputation but against the apostle who knows well that God is one thing and man another, that the flesh is weak and the spirit strong.[7] "The flesh lusteth against the spirit and the spirit against the flesh : and these are contrary the one to the other : so that ye cannot do the things that ye would."[8] But from me you will never hear that any nature is essentially evil. Let us learn then from him who tells us so in what sense the flesh is weak. Ask him why he has said :

---

[1] Ps. xciv. 20, LXX and Vulg. [2] Ps. xvii. 4, LXX.
[3] Matt. vii. 13. [4] Matt. v. 44.
[5] αὐταρκής, self-determined. [6] 1 Pet. ii. 22.

[1] Rom. viii. 3. [2] Rom. iii. 20.
[3] Rom. vii. 22-25. In the Latin as in the Greek one word does duty for 'grace' and 'thanks.'
[4] R. V. [5] Rom. vii. 14-20.
[6] This is the well known dualism of Manes (Manichæus), who held that the physical world and the human body are essentially evil. [7] cf. Matt. xxvi. 41. [8] Gal. ♀. 17.

"the good that I would, I do not; the evil which I would not, that I do."[1] What necessity fetters his will? What compulsion commands him to do what he dislikes? And why must he do not what he wishes but what he dislikes and does not wish? He will answer you thus: "nay, but, O man, who art thou that repliest against God? Shall the thing formed say unto him that formed it, Why hast thou made me thus? Hath not the potter power over the clay, of the same lump to make one vessel unto honour and another unto dishonour?"[2] Bring a yet graver charge against God and ask Him why, when Esau and Jacob were still in the womb, He said: "Jacob have I loved, but Esau have I hated."[3] Accuse Him of injustice because, when Achan the son of Carmi stole part of the spoil of Jericho, He butchered so many thousands for the fault of one.[4] Ask Him why for the sin of the sons of Eli the people were well-nigh annihilated and the ark captured.[5] And why, when David sinned by numbering the people, so many thousands lost their lives.[6] Or lastly make your own the favorite cavil of your associate Porphyry, and ask how God can be described as pitiful and of great mercy when from Adam to Moses and from Moses to the coming of Christ He has suffered all nations to die in ignorance of the Law and of His commandments.[7] For Britain, that province so fertile in despots, the Scottish tribes, and all the barbarians round about as far as the ocean were alike without knowledge of Moses and the prophets. Why should Christ's coming have been delayed to the last times? Why should He not have come before so vast a number had perished? Of this last question the blessed apostle in writing to the Romans most wisely disposes by admitting that he does not know and that only God does. Do you too, then, condescend to remain ignorant of that into which you inquire. Leave to God His power over what is His own; He does not need you to justify His actions. I am the hapless being against whom you ought to direct your insults, I who am for ever reading the words: "by grace ye are saved,"[8] and "blessed is he whose transgression is forgiven, whose sin is covered."[9] Yet, to lay bare my own weakness, I know that I wish to do many things which I ought to do and yet cannot. For while my spirit is strong and leads me to life my flesh is weak and draws me to death. And I have the warning of the Lord in my ears: "watch and pray that ye enter not into temptation. The spirit indeed is willing, but the flesh is weak."[1]

10. It is in vain that you misrepresent me and try to convince the ignorant that I condemn free will. Let him who condemns it be himself condemned. We have been created endowed with free will; still it is not this which distinguishes us from the brutes. For human free will, as I have said before, depends upon the help of God and needs His aid moment by moment, a thing which you and yours do not choose to admit. Your position is that, if a man once has free will, he no longer needs the help of God. It is true that freedom of the will brings with it freedom of decision. Still man does not act immediately on his free will, but requires God's aid who Himself needs no aid. You yourself boast that a man's righteousness may be perfect and equal to God's; yet you confess that you are a sinner. Answer me this, then; do you or do you not wish to be free from sin? If you do, why on your principle do you not carry out your desire? And if you do not, do you not prove yourself a despiser of God's commandments? If you are a despiser, then you are a sinner. And if you are a sinner, then the scripture says: "unto the wicked God saith, what hast thou to do to declare my statutes, or that thou shouldest take my covenant in thy mouth? seeing thou hatest instruction and castest my words behind thee."[2] So long as you are unwilling to do what God commands, so long do you cast His words behind you. And yet like a new apostle you lay down for the world what to do and what not to do. However, your words and your thoughts by no means correspond. For when you say that you are a sinner—yet that a man may be without sin if he will, you wish it to be understood that you are a saint and free from all sin. It is only out of humility[3] that you call yourself a sinner; to give you a chance of praising others while you depreciate yourself.

11. Another of your arguments is also intolerable, one which runs thus: "To be sinless is one thing, to be able to be so is another. The first is not in our power, the second generally is. For though none ever has been sinless, yet, if a man wills to be so, he can be so." What sort of reasoning, I ask, is this? that a man can be what a man never has been! that a thing is possible which according to your own admission, no man has yet achieved! You are predicating of man a quality which, for aught you know, he may never possess! and you are assigning to any chance person a grace which you cannot

---

[1] Rom. vii. 19. [2] Rom. ix. 20, 21. [3] Mal. i. 2, 3. Rom. ix. 13.
[4] Josh. vii. [5] 1 Sam. iv. [6] 2 Sam. xxiv.
[7] This objection is dealt with at length by Augustine (Letter CXI. §§ 8-15. See Vol. I. Series I. of this Library).
[8] Eph. ii. 5. [9] Ps. xxxii. 1.

[1] Matt. xxvi. 41. [2] Ps. l. 16, 17. [3] Or rather, mock humility.

shew to have marked patriarchs, prophets, or apostles. Listen to the Church's words, plain as they may seem to you or crude or ignorant. And speak what you think ; preach publicly what secretly you tell your disciples. You profess to have freedom of choice ; why do you not speak your thoughts freely ? Your secret chambers hear one doctrine, the crowd around the platform hear another. The uneducated throng, I suppose, is not able to digest your esoteric teaching. Satisfied with the milk-diet of an infant it cannot take solid food.[1]

I have written nothing yet, and still you menace me with the thunders of a reply ; hoping, I suppose, that I may be scared by your terrors and may not venture to open my mouth. You fail to see that my purpose in writing is to force you to answer and to commit yourself plainly to doctrines which at present you maintain or ignore, as time, place, and person require. One kind of freedom I must deny to you, the freedom to deny what you have once written. An open avowal on your part of the opinions that you hold will be a victory for the church. For either the language of your reply will correspond to mine, in which case I shall count you no longer as opponents but as friends ; or else you will gainsay my doctrine, in which case the making known of your opinion to all the churches will be a triumph for me. To have brought your tenets to light is to have overcome them. Blasphemy is written on the face of them, and a doctrine, which in its very statement is blasphemous, needs no refutation. You threaten me with a reply, but this nobody can escape except the man who does not write at all. How do you know what I am going to say that you talk of a reply ? Perhaps I shall take your view and then you will have sharpened your wits to no purpose. Eunomians, Arians, Macedonians — all these, unlike in name, alike in impiety, give me no trouble. For they say what they think. Yours is the only heresy which blushes openly to maintain what secretly it does not fear to teach. But the frenzy of the disciples exposes the silence of the masters ; for what they have heard from them in the closet they preach upon the housetop. If their auditors like what they say, their masters get the credit ; and if they dislike it, only the disciples are blamed, the masters go free. In this way your heresy has grown and you have deceived many ; especially those who cleave to women and are assured that they cannot sin. You are always teaching, you are always denying ;

you deserve to have the prophet's words applied to you : " give to them glory, O Lord, when they are in travail and in the throes of labour. Give them, O Lord ; what wilt thou give ? Give them a miscarrying womb and dry breasts." [1] My temper rises and I cannot check my words. The limits of a letter do not admit of a lengthy discussion. I assail nobody by name here. It is only against the teacher of perverse doctrine that I have spoken. If resentment shall induce him to reply, he will but betray himself like a mouse which always leaves traces of its presence ; and, when it comes to blows in earnest, will receive more serious wounds.

12. From my youth up until now I have spent many years in writing various works and have always tried to teach my hearers the doctrine that I have been taught publicly in church. I have not followed the philosophers in their discussions but have preferred to acquiesce in the plain words of the apostles. For I have known that it is written : " I will destroy the wisdom of the wise, and will bring to nothing the understanding of the prudent," [2] and " the foolishness of God is wiser than men." [3] This being the case, I challenge my opponents thoroughly to sift all my past writings and, if they can find anything that is faulty in them, to bring it to light. One of two things must happen. Either my works will be found edifying and I shall confute the false charges brought against me ; or they will be found blameworthy and I shall confess my error. For I would sooner correct an error than persevere in an opinion proved to be wrong. And as for you, illustrious doctor, go you and do likewise : either defend the statements that you have made, and support your clever theories with corresponding eloquence, and do not when the whim takes you disown your own words ; or if, as a man may do, you have made a mistake, confess it frankly and restore harmony where there has been disagreement. Recall to mind how even the soldiers did not rend the coat of the Saviour.[4] When you see brothers at strife you laugh ; and are glad that some are called by your name and others by that of Christ. Better would it be to imitate Jonah and say : " If it is for my sake that this great tempest is upon you, take me up and cast me forth into the sea." [5] He in his humility was thrown into the deep that he might rise again in glory to be a type of the Lord.[6] But you are lifted up in your pride to the stars, only that of you too Jesus may

---

[1] Hos. ix. 11, 14, partly after the LXX., partly from memory.
[2] Isa. xxix. 14, as quoted by Paul, 1 Cor. i. 19.
[3] 1 Cor. i. 25.   [4] Joh. xix. 23, 24.
[5] Jon. i. 12.   [6] Matt. xii. 39, 40.

say : "I beheld Satan as lightning fall from heaven." [1]

13. It is true that in the holy scriptures many are called righteous, as Zacharias and Elizabeth, Job, Jehosaphat, Josiah, and many others who are mentioned in the sacred writings. Of this fact I shall, if God gives me grace, give a full explanation in the work which I have promised [2] ; in this letter it must suffice to say that they are called righteous, not because they are faultless but because their faults are eclipsed by their virtues. [3] In fact Zacharias is punished with dumbness, [4] Job is condemned out of his own mouth, [5] and Jehoshaphat and Josiah who are beyond a doubt described as righteous are narrated to have done things displeasing to the Lord. The first leagued himself with the ungodly Ahab and brought upon himself the rebuke of Micaiah ; [6] and the second—though forbidden by the word of the Lord spoken by Jeremiah—went against Pharaoh-Nechoh, king of Egypt, and was slain by him. [7] Yet they are both called righteous. Of the rest this is not the time to write ; for you have asked me not for a treatise but for a letter. For a complete refutation I require leisure and then I hope to destroy all their cavils by the help of Christ. For this purpose I shall rely on the holy scriptures in which God every day speaks to those who believe. And this is the warning which I would give through you to all who are assembled within your holy and illustrious house, that they should not allow one or at the most three mannikins to taint them with the dregs of so many heresies and with the infamy—to say the least—attaching to them. A place once famous for virtue and holiness must not be defiled by the presumption of the devil and by unclean associations. And let those who supply money to such men know that they are adding to the ranks of the heretics, raising up enemies to Christ, and fostering his avowed opponents. It is idle for them to profess one thing with their lips when by their actions they are proved to think another.

LETTER CXXXIV.

TO AUGUSTINE.

Jerome acknowledges the receipt of Letters CXXXI. and CXXXII. and excuses himself from answering the questions raised in them on the twofold ground (1) that the times are evil and (2) that it is inexpedient that he should be supposed to differ from Augustine. He prays for the speedy extinction of Pelagianism, regrets that he cannot send Augustine a critical Latin text of the O.T., and concludes with a number of salutations from

himself and those with him. The date of the letter is 416 A.D. Its number in Augustine's Letters is CLXXII.

LETTER CXXXV.

FROM POPE INNOCENT TO AURELIUS.

Shortly after the synod of Diospolis the Pelagians exulting in their success made an attack upon Jerome's monasteries at Bethlehem which they pillaged and partially burned. This gained for him the sympathy of Innocent who now (A.D. 417) asks Aurelius to transmit to him the letter which follows this.

Innocent to his most esteemed friend and brother Aurelius. [1]

Our fellow-presbyter Jerome has informed us of your most dutiful desire to come to see us. We suffer with him as with a member of our own flock. We have been swift also to take such measures as have appeared to us expedient and practicable. As you count yourself one of us, most dear brother, make haste to transmit the following letter [2] to the aforesaid Jerome.

LETTER CXXXVI.

FROM POPE INNOCENT TO JEROME.

Innocent expresses his sympathy with Jerome and promises to take strong measures to punish his opponents if he will bring specific charges against them. The date of the letter is A.D. 417.

Innocent to his most esteemed son, the presbyter Jerome.

The apostle [3] bears witness that contention has never done good in the church ; and for this reason he gives direction that heretics should be admonished once or twice in the beginning of their heresy and not subjected to a long series of rebukes. Where this rule is negligently observed, the evil to be guarded against so far from being evaded is rather intensified.

Your grief and lamentation have so affected us that we can neither act nor advise.

To begin however, we commend you for the constancy of your faith. To quote your own words spoken many times in the ears of many, a man will gladly face misrepresentation or even personal danger on behalf of the truth ; if he is looking for the blessedness that is to come. We remind you of what you have yourself preached although we are sure that you need no reminder. The spectacle of these terrible evils has so thoroughly roused us that we have hastened to put forth the authority of the apostolic see to repress the plague in all its manifestations ; but as your letters name no individuals and bring no specific charges, there is no one at present against whom we can proceed. But we do

---

[1] Luke. x. 18.
[2] The Anti-Pelagian Dialogue, to which this letter is a kind of prelude.
[3] Cf. Letter CXXIII. §3.   [4] Luke i. 20-22.   [5] Job xlii. 6.
[6] 1 Kings xxii. 19.   [7] 2 Chr. xxxv. 20-24.

[1] At this time bishop of Carthage and a friend of Augustine.
[2] Letter CXXXVI.   [3] Tit. iii. 10, 11.

all that we can ; we sympathize deeply with you. And if you will lay a clear and unambiguous accusation against any persons in particular we will appoint suitable judges to try their cases ; or if you, our highly esteemed son, think that it is needful for us to take yet graver and more urgent action, we shall not be slow to do so. Meantime we have written to our brother bishop John [1] advising him to act more considerately, so that nothing may occur in the church committed to him which it is his duty to foresee and to prevent, and that nothing may happen which may subsequently prove a source of trouble to him.

LETTER CXXXVII.

FROM POPE INNOCENT TO JOHN, BISHOP OF JERUSALEM.

Innocent censures John for having allowed the Pelagians to cause the disturbance at Bethlehem mentioned in the two preceding letters and exhorts him to be more watchful over his diocese in future. The date of the letter is A.D. 417. This was the year of the death of both John and Innocent, and it is probable that John never received the letter.

Innocent to his most highly esteemed brother John.

The holy virgins Eustochium and Paula [2] have deplored to me the ravages, murders, fires and outrages of all kinds, which they say that the devil has perpetrated in the district belonging to their church ; for with wonderful clemency and generosity they have left untold the name and motive of his human agent. Now although there can be no doubt as to who is the guilty person ; [3] yet you, my brother, ought to have taken precautions and to have been more careful of your flock so that no disturbance of the kind might arise ; for others suffer by your negligence, and you encourage men by it to make havoc of the Lord's flock till His tender lambs, fleeced and weakened by fire, sword and persecution, their relations murdered and dead, are, as we are informed, themselves scarce alive. Does it not touch your sacred responsibility as a priest [4] that the devil has shewn himself so powerful against you and yours ? Against you, I say ; for surely it speaks ill of your capacity as a priest that a crime so terrible should have been committed in the pale of your church. Where were your precautions ? Where, after the blow had been struck, were your attempts at

relief ? Where too were your words of comfort ? These ladies tell me that up to the present they have been in a state of too great apprehension to complain of what they have already suffered. I should judge more gravely of the matter had they spoken to me concerning it more freely than they have. Beware then, brother, of the wiles of the old enemy, and in the spirit of a good ruler be vigilant either to correct or to repress such evils. For they have reached my ears in the shape of rumours rather than as specific accusations. If nothing is done, the law of the Church on the subject of injuries may compel the person who has failed to defend his flock to shew cause for his negligence.

LETTER CXXXVIII.

TO RIPARIUS.

Jerome praises Riparius for his zeal on behalf of the Catholic faith and for his efforts to put down the Pelagians. He then describes the attack made by these heretics upon the monasteries of Bethlehem. Now, he is glad to say, they have at last been driven from Palestine. Most of them, that is, for some still linger at Joppa including one of their chief leaders. The date is A.D. 417.

That you fight Christ's battles against the enemies of the Catholic Faith your own letters have informed me as well as the reports of many persons, but I am told that you find the winds contrary and that those who ought to have been the world's champions have backed the cause of perdition to each other's ruin. You are to know that in this part of the world, without any human help and merely by the decree of Christ, Catiline [1] has been driven not only from the capital but from the borders of Palestine. Lentulus, however, and many of his fellow-conspirators still linger to our sorrow in Joppa. I myself have thought it better to change my abode than to surrender the true faith ; and have chosen to leave my pleasant home rather than to suffer contamination from heresy. For I could not communicate with men who would either have insisted on my instant submission or would else have summoned me to support my opinions by the sword. A good many, I dare say, have told you the story of my sufferings and of the vengeance which Christ's uplifted hand has on my behalf taken upon my enemies. I would beg of you, therefore, to complete the task which you have taken up and not, while you are in it,

---

[1] i.e. John of Jerusalem. See the next letter.
[2] i.e. Paula the younger, Eustochium's niece, concerning whose education Jerome had written to her mother Læta (Letter CVII.).
[3] The attack was supposed to have been instigated by Pelagius.
[4] In Jerome's writings this title is often given to bishops. Presbyters are by him rarely so called.

[1] Pelagius would naturally be understood by Catiline, and Celestius by Lentulus, who was Catiline's lieutenant. But it is known that, after the Synod of Diospolis which acquitted them, Celestius went to Africa, Ephesus, Constantinople, and Rome, while Pelagius apparently remained in Palestine, where he died.

to leave Christ's church without a defender. Every one knows the weapons that must be used in this warfare; and you, I feel sure, will ask for no others. You must contend with all your might against the foe; but it must be not with physical force but with that spiritual charity which is never overcome. The reverend brothers who are with me, unworthy as I am, salute you warmly. The reverend brother, the deacon Alentius, is sure to give you, my worshipful friend, a faithful narrative of all the facts. May Christ our Lord, of His almighty power, keep you safe and mindful of me, truly reverend sir and esteemed brother.

LETTER CXXXIX.

TO APRONIUS.

Of Apronius nothing is known; but from the mention of Innocent (for whom see Letter CXLIII.) it seems a fair inference that he lived in the West. Jerome here congratulates him on his steadfastness in the faith and exhorts him to come to Bethlehem. He then touches on the mischief done by Pelagius and complains that his own monastery has been destroyed by him or by his partisans. The date of the letter is A. D. 417.

I know not by what wiles of the devil it has come to pass that all your toil and the efforts of the reverend presbyter Innocent [1] and my own prayers and wishes seem for the moment to produce no effect. God be thanked that you are well and that the fire of faith glows in you even when you are in the midst of the devil's wiles. My greatest joy is to hear that my spiritual sons are fighting in the cause of Christ; and assuredly He in whom we believe will so quicken this zeal of ours that we shall be glad freely to shed our blood in defence of His faith.

I grieve to hear that a noble family has been subverted,[2] for what reason I cannot learn; for the bearer of the letter could give me no information. We may well grieve over the loss of our common friends and ask Christ the only potentate and Lord [3] to have mercy upon them. At the same time we have deserved to receive punishment at God's hand, for we [4] have harboured the enemies of the Lord.

The best course you can take is to leave everything and to come to the East, before all to the holy places; for everything is now quiet here. The heretics have not, it is true, purged the venom from their breasts, but they do not venture to open their impious mouths. They are "like the deaf adder that stoppeth her ear." [1] Salute your reverend brothers on my behalf.

As for our house,[2] so far as fleshly wealth is concerned, it has been completely destroyed by the onslaughts of the heretics; but by the mercy of Christ it is still filled with spiritual riches. To live on bread is better than to lose the faith.

LETTER CXL.

TO CYPRIAN THE PRESBYTER.

Cyprian had visited Jerome at Bethlehem and had asked him to write an exposition of Psalm XC. in simple language such as might be readily understood. With this request Jerome now complies, giving a very full account of the psalm, verse by verse, and bringing the treasures of his learning and especially his knowledge of Hebrew to bear upon it. He asserts its Mosaic authorship but is careful to add that "the man of God" may have spoken not for himself but in the name of the Jewish people. He speaks of the five books into which the psalter is divisible and says that it is a mistake to ascribe all the psalms to David. An allusion to the doctrine of Pelagius shows that the letter must belong to Jerome's last years, and Vallarsi is probably right in assigning it to A. D. 418.

LETTER CXLI.

TO AUGUSTINE.

A short note in which Jerome praises Augustine for the determined stand which he has made against heresy and speaks of him as "the restorer of the ancient faith." The allusion seems to be to his action in the Pelagian controversy. If so, the date is probably 418 A.D. This letter is among those of Augustine, number 195.

LETTER CXLII.

TO AUGUSTINE.

There is good ground for supposing this to form part of the previous letter. If so, Jerome speaks in a figure of the success gained by Pelagianism in Palestine. "Jerusalem," he says, "is in the hands of Nebuchadnezzar and will not heed the voice of Jeremiah," that is, as the context shews, Jerome himself. This letter is among those of Augustine, number 123.

LETTER CXLIII.

TO ALYPIUS AND AUGUSTINE.

In this letter Jerome congratulates Alypius and Augustine on their success in strangling the heresy of Cælestius, the co-adjutor of Pelagius, and states that, if he can find time and secretaries, he hopes to write a refutation of the absurd errors of the Pelagian pseudo-deacon Annianus. The date is 419 A.D. This letter is among those of Augustine, number 202.

---

[1] At this time in Palestine whither he had come as the bearer of letters from Augustine to Jerome and others.
[2] The family meant is probably the one warned by Jerome in his letter to Ctesiphon (CXXXIII. § 13). In that case the troubler of its peace is of course Pelagius.
[3] 1 Tim. vi. 15.
[4] It would seem as if Jerome, like Augustine, had at first thought favourably of Pelagius.

---

[1] Ps. lviii. 4.
[2] i.e. the monastic establishment under Jerome's guidance at Bethlehem. See Letters CXXXV.–CXXXVII.

LETTER CXLIV.

FROM AUGUSTINE TO OPTATUS.

Augustine writes to Optatus, bishop of Milevis, to say that he cannot send him a copy of his letter to Jerome on the origin of the soul (Letter CXXXI.) as it is incomplete without Jerome's reply which he has not yet received. He then criticises the arguments with which Optatus combats traducianism and points out that his reasoning is inconclusive. The date of the letter is A. D. 420. The letter has been somewhat compressed in translation : the involved sentences of the original have been simplified and its redundancies curtailed.

To the blessed lord and brother, sincerely loved and longed-for, his fellow-bishop Optatus, Augustine [sends] greeting in the Lord.

1. By the hand of the reverend presbyter Saturninus I have received a letter from you, venerable sir, in which you earnestly ask me for what I have not yet got. You thus shew clearly your belief that I have already had a reply to my question on the subject. Would that I had ! Knowing the eagerness of your expectation, I should never have dreamed of keeping back from you your share in the gift ; but if you will believe me, dear brother, it is not so. Although five years have elapsed since I despatched to the East my letter (which was one of inquiry, not of assertion), I have so far received no reply, and am consequently unable to untie the knot as you wish me to do. Had I had both[1] letters, I should gladly have sent you both ; but I think it better not to circulate mine[2] by itself lest he to whom it is addressed and who may still answer me as I desire should prove displeased. If I were to publish so elaborate a treatise as mine without his reply to it, he might be justly indignant, and suppose me more intent on displaying my talents than on promoting some useful end. It would look as if I were bent on starting problems too hard for him to solve. It is better to wait for the answer which he probably means to send. For I am well aware that he has other subjects to occupy him which are more serious and urgent than this question of mine. Your holiness will readily understand this if you read what he wrote to me a year later when my messenger was returning. The following is an extract from his letter :[3]

"A most trying time has come upon us[4] in which I have found it better to hold my peace than to speak. Consequently my studies have ceased, that I may not give occasion to what Appius calls 'the eloquence of dogs.'[1] For this reason I have not been able to send any answer to your two learned and brilliant letters. Not, indeed, that I think anything in them needs correction, but that I recall the Apostle's words : ' One judges in this way, another in that ; let every man give full expression to his own opinion.'[2] All that a lofty intellect can draw from the well of holy scripture has been drawn by you. So much your reverence must allow me to say in praise of your ability. But though in any discussion between us our joint object is the advancement of learning, our rivals and especially the heretics will ascribe any difference of opinion between us to mutual jealousy. For my part, however, I am resolved to love you, to look up to you, to reverence and admire you, and to defend your opinions as my own. I have also in a dialogue which I have recently brought out made allusion to your holiness in suitable terms. Let us, rather, then, strain every nerve to banish from the churches that most pernicious heresy,[3] which feigns repentance that it may have liberty to teach in our churches. For were it to come out into the light of day, it would be expelled and die."

2. You can see, worshipful brother, from this reply that my friend does not refuse to answer my inquiry ; he postpones it because he is condemned to give his time to more urgent matters. Moreover, that he is well disposed towards me is clear from his friendly warning that a controversy between us begun in all charity and in the interests of learning may be misconstrued by jealous and heretical persons as due to mutual illfeeling. No ; it will be better for the public to have both together, his explanation as well as my inquiry. For, as I shall have to thank him for instructing me if he is able to explain the matter, the discussion will be of no small advantage when it comes to the knowledge of the world. Those who come after us will not only know what view they ought to take of a subject thus fully argued but will also learn how under the divine mercy brothers in affection may dispute a difficult question and yet preserve each other's esteem.

3. On the other hand, if I were to publish the letter in which I raise this obscure point without the reply in which it may be set at rest, it might circulate widely and reach men who " comparing themselves," as the Apostle says, "with themselves,"[4] would misconstrue a motive which they could not understand, and would explain my feeling towards one whom I love and esteem for his immense ser-

---

[1] That is Augustine's to Jerome and the expected answer.
[2] In Jerome's Letters, No. CXXXI. ; in Augustine's, No. CLXVI.
[3] In Jerome's Letters, No. CXXXIV. ; in Augustine's, No. CLXXII.
[4] After the Council of Diospolis Jerome suffered much from the violence of the Pelagians. See Letters CXXXVI.–CXXXIX.

[1] i.e. railing.
[2] Suo sensu abundet. Rom. xiv. 5, Vulg.
[3] i.e. Pelagianism.   [4] 2 Cor. x. 12.

vices not as it would appear to them (for it would be invisible to them) but as their own fancy and malice would dictate. Now this is a danger which, so far as in me lies, I am bound to guard against. But if a document which I am unwilling to publish is published without my consent and placed in hands from which I would withhold it, then I shall have to resign myself to the will of God. Indeed, had I wished to keep my words permanently undivulged I should never have sent them to any one. For if (though I hope it may not be so) chance or necessity shall prevent any reply being ever given me, my letter of inquiry is still bound sooner or later to come to light. Nor will it be useless to those who read it; for, although they will not find what they seek, they will learn how much better it is, when one is uninformed, to put questions than to make assertions; and in the meantime those whom they consult[1] will work out the points raised by me, laying aside contention and in the interests of learning and charity trying to obtain sound opinions about them. Thus they will either arrive at the solutions they desire, or their faculties will be quickened and they will learn from the investigation that farther inquiry is useless. At present, however, as I have no reason to despair of an answer from my friend I have decided not to publish the letter I have sent him, and I trust, my dear comrade, that this decision may commend itself to you. It should do so, for you have not asked for my letter so much as for the answer to it; and this I would gladly send you if I had it to send. It is true that in your epistle you speak of "the lucid demonstration of my wisdom which in virtue of my life the Giver of light has bestowed upon me"; and if by this you mean not the way in which I have stated the problem but a solution which I have obtained of the point in question, I should like to gratify your wish. But I must admit that I have so far failed to discover how the soul can derive its sin from Adam (a truth which it is unlawful to question) and yet not itself be derived from Adam. At present I think it better to sift the matter farther than to dogmatize rashly.

4. Your letter speaks of "many old men and persons educated by learned priests whom you have failed to recall to your modest way of thinking, and to a statement of the case which is truth itself." You do not, however, explain what this mode of expression is. If your old men hold fast what they have received from learned priests, how comes it that you are troubled by a boorish mob of unlettered clerics? On the other hand, if the old men and the unlettered clerics have wickedly departed from the priests' teachings, surely these latter are the persons to correct them and restrain them from controversial excesses. Again when you say that "you as a new-fledged and inexperienced teacher have been afraid to tamper with the doctrines handed down by great and famous bishops, and that you have been loth to draw men into a better path lest you should cast discredit on the dead," do you not imply that in refusing to agree with you the objects of your solicitude are but preferring the tradition of great and famous bishops to the views of a new-fledged and inexperienced teacher? Of their conduct in the matter I say nothing, but I am most anxious to learn that "mode of expression which is truth itself," not the thing expressed, but the mode of expression.

5. For you have made it sufficiently plain to me that you disapprove of those who assert that men's souls are derived from that of the protoplast[1] and propagated from one generation to another; but as your letter does not inform me, I have no means of knowing on what grounds and from what passages of scripture you have shewn this view to be false. What does commend itself to you is not clear either from your letter to the brothers at Cæsarea or from that which you have lately addressed to me. Only I see that you believe and write that "God has been, is, and will be the maker of men, and that there is nothing either in heaven or on earth which does not owe its existence wholly to Him." This is of course a truism which nobody can call in question. But as you affirm that souls are not propagated, you ought to explain out of what God makes them. Is it out of some preexisting material, or is it out of nothing? For it is impossible that you should hold the opinion of Origen, Priscillian, and other heretics *that* it is for deeds done in a former life that souls are confined in earthly and mortal bodies. This opinion is, indeed, flatly contradicted by the apostle who says of Jacob and Esau that before they were born they had done neither good nor evil.[2] Your view of the matter, then, is known to me though only partially, but of your reasons for supposing it to be true I know nothing. This was why in a former letter I asked you to send me your confession of faith, the one which you were vexed to find that one of your presbyters had signed dishonestly. I now again ask you for this, as well as for any passages of scripture which you have brought to bear on the question. For you say in your letter to the broth-

---

[1] At this point the text is obscure.

[1] i. e. Adam, "our first-formed father." (Wisd. x. 1.)
[2] Rom. ix. 11.

rs at Cæsarea that you "have resolved to have all definitions of dogma reviewed by lay judges, sitting by general invitation, and investigating all points touching the faith." And you continue : " the divine mercy has made it possible for them to put forward their views in a positive and definite form, which your modest ability has reinforced with a great weight of evidence." Now it is this " great weight of evidence" which I am so anxious to obtain. For, so far as I can see, your one aim has been to refute your opponents when they deny that our souls are the handiwork of God. If they hold such a view, you are right in thinking that it should be condemned. Were they to say the same thing of our bodies, they would be forced to retract it, or else be held up to execration. For what Christian can deny that every single human body is the work of God ? Yet when we admit that they are of divine origin we do not mean to deny that they are humanly engendered. When therefore it is asserted that our souls are procreated from a kind of immaterial seed, and that they, like our bodies, come to us from our parents, yet are made souls by the working of God, it is not by human guesses that the assertion is to be refuted, but by the witness of divine scripture. Numbers of passages may indeed be quoted from the sacred books which have canonical authority, to prove that our souls are God's handiwork. But such passages only refute those who deny that each several human soul is made by God ; not at all those who while they admit this contend that, like our bodies, they are formed by divine agency through the instrumentality of parents. To refute these you must look for unmistakable texts ; or, if you have already discovered such, shew your affection by communicating them to me. For though I seek them most diligently I fail to find them.

As stated shortly by yourself (at the end of your letter to the brothers at Cæsarea) our dilemma is as follows : " Inasmuch as I am your son and disciple and have but recently by God's help come to consider these mysteries, I beg you with your priestly wisdom to teach me which of two opposite views I ought to hold. Am I to maintain that souls are transmitted by generation, and that they are derived in some mysterious way from Adam our first-formed father ?[1] Or am I with your brothers and the priests who are here to hold that God has been, is, and will be the author and maker of all things and all men ? "

6. Of the two alternatives which you thus

put forward you wish to be urged to choose one or other ; and this would be the course of wisdom if your alternatives were so contrary that the choice of one would involve the rejection of the other. But as it is, instead of selecting one of them a man may say that they are both true. He may maintain that the souls of all mankind are derived from Adam our first-formed father, and yet believe and assert that God has been, is, and will be the author and maker of all things and all men. How on your principles is such a man to be confuted ? Shall we say : " If they are transmitted by generation God is not their author, for He does not make them ?" In that case he will reply : " Bodies too are engendered and not made by God ; on your shewing, then He is not their author." Will any one maintain that God is the maker of no bodies but Adam's which He made out of the dust and Eve's which He formed out of Adam's side ; and that other bodies are not made by Him because they are engendered by human parents ?

7. If your opponents go so far in maintaining the derivation of souls as to deny that they are made and formed by God, you may use this argument as a weapon to confute them so far as God's help enables you. But if, while they assert that the soul's beginnings come from Adam first and then from a man's parents, they at the same time hold that the soul in every man is created and formed by God the author of all things, they can only be confuted out of scripture. Search therefore till you find a passage that is neither obscure nor capable of a double meaning ; or if you have already found one, hand it on to me as I have begged you to do. But if, like myself, you have so far failed to discover any such passage, you must still strain every nerve to confute those who say that souls are in no sense God's handiwork. This seems to be your opponents' position, for in your first letter you write that " they have secretly whispered scandalous doctrines and have forsaken your communion and the obedience of the church on account of this foolish, nay impious opinion." Against such men defend and uphold by every possible expedient the doctrine you have laid down in the same letter, that God has been, is, and will be the maker of souls ; and that everything in heaven and on earth owes its existence wholly to Him. For this is true of every creature ; and as such is to be believed, asserted, defended, and proved. God has been, is, and will be the author and maker of all things and all men as you have told your fellow-bishops of the province of Cæsarea, exhorting them to adopt the doctrine by the ex-

---

[1] Wisdom x. 1.

ample of your brothers and fellow-priests. But there are two quite distinct dilemmas : (1) Is God the author and maker of all souls and bodies (the true view), or is there something in nature which He has not made (a view which is wholly erroneous)? (2) If souls are undoubtedly God's handiwork, does He make them directly, or indirectly by propagation? It is in dealing with this second dilemma that I would have you to be sober and vigilant. Else in refuting the propagation-theory you may fall incautiously into the heresy of Pelagius. Everybody knows that human bodies are propagated by generation ; yet if we are right in saying that all human souls—and not only those of Adam and Eve —are created by God, it is clear that to assert their transmission by generation is not to deny their divine origin. For in this view God makes the soul as He makes the body, indirectly by a process of generation. If the truth condemns this as an error, some fresh argument must be sought to confute it. No persons could better advise you on the point (if only they were within reach) than those dead worthies whom you feared to discredit by drawing men away from them into a better path. They were, you said, great and famous bishops while you were a new-fledged and inexperienced teacher ; thus you were loth to tamper with their doctrines. Would that I could know on what passages these great men rested their opinion that souls are transmitted ! For in your letter to the brothers at Cæsarea, you speak of their view with a total disregard of their authority, as a new invention, an unheard-of doctrine ; though we all know that, error as it may be, it is no novelty but old and of ancient date.

8. Now when we have reason to be doubtful about a point, we need not doubt that we are right in doubting. There is no doubt but that we ought to doubt things that are doubtful. For instance, the Apostle has no doubt about doubting whether he was in the body or out of the body when he was carried up into the third heaven.[1] Whether it was thus or thus, he says, I know not ; God knows. Why may not I, then, so long as I have no light, doubt whether my soul comes to me by generation or unengendered? Why may I not be doubtful about this, so long as I do not doubt that in either case it is the work of God most high? Why may I not say : "I know that my soul owes its existence to God and is altogether His handiwork ; but whether it comes by generation, as the body does, or unengendered, as was Adam's soul, I know not ; God knows." You wish me to assert

positively one view or the other. I might do so if I knew which was right. You may have some light on the point, and if so you will find me keener to learn what I know now than to teach what I know. But if, like myself, you are in the dark, you should pray as I do, that either through one of His servants, or with His own lips, He would teach us who said to His disciples : "Be not ye called masters ; for one is your master, even Christ."[1] Yet such knowledge is only expedient for us when He knows it to be expedient who knows both what He has to teach and what we ought to learn. Nevertheless to you, my dear friend, I confess my eagerness. Still much as I desire to know this after which you seek, I would sooner know when the desire of all nations shall come and when the kingdom of the saints will be set up, than how my soul has come to its earthly abode. But when His disciples (who are our apostles) put this question to the all-knowing Christ, they were told : "It is not yours to know the times or the seasons which the Father hath put in His own power."[2] What if Christ, who knows what is expedient for us, knows this knowledge not to be expedient? Through Him I know that it is not ours to know the times which God has placed in His own power ; but concerning the origin of souls, I am ignorant whether it is or is not ours to know. If I could be sure that such knowledge is not for us, I should cease not only to dogmatize, but even to inquire. As it is, though the subject is so deep and dark that my fear of becoming a rash teacher is almost greater than my eagerness to learn the truth, I still wish to know it if I can do so. It may be that the knowledge for which the psalmist prays : "Lord, make me to know mine end,"[3] is much more necessary ; yet I would that my beginning also might be revealed to me.

9. But even as touching this I must not be ungrateful to my Master. I know that the human soul is spiritual not corporeal, that it is endowed with reason and intelligence, and that it is not of God's essence but a thing created. It is both mortal and immortal : the first because it is subject to corruption and separable from the life of God in which it is alone blessed, the second because its consciousness must ever continue and form the source of its happiness or woe. It does not it is true, owe its immersion in the flesh to acts done before the flesh ; yet in man it is never without sin, not even when "its life has been but for one day."[4] Of those engendered of the seed of Adam no man is born without

[1] 2 Cor. xii. 4.

[1] Matt. xxiii. 10. [2] Acts i. 7.
[3] Ps. xxxix. 4. [4] Job xiv. 5, LXX.

in, and it is necessary even for babes to be born anew in Christ by the grace of regeneration. All this I know concerning the soul, and it is much; the greater part of it, indeed, is not only knowledge but matter of faith as well. I rejoice to have learned it all and I can truly say that I know it. If there are things of which I am still ignorant (as whether God creates souls by generation or apart from it—for that He does create them I have no doubt) I would sooner know the truth than be ignorant of it. But so long as I cannot know it I had rather suspend my judgment than assert what is plainly contrary to an indisputable truth.

10. You, my brother, ask me to decide for you whether men's souls as made by the Creator come like their bodies by generation from Adam, or whether like his soul they are made without generation and separately for each individual. For in one way or the other we both admit that they are God's handiwork. Suffer me then in turn to ask you a question. Can a soul derive original sin from a source from which it is not itself derived? For unless we are to fall into the detestable heresy of Pelagius, we must both of us allow that all souls do derive original sin from Adam. And if you cannot answer my question, pray give me leave to confess my ignorance alike of your question and of my own. But if you already know what I ask, teach me and then I will teach you what you wish to know. Pray do not be displeased with me for taking this line, for though I have given you no positive answer to your question, I have shewn you how you ought to put it. When once you are clear about that, you may be quite positive where you have been doubtful.[1]

This much I have thought it right to write to your holiness seeing that you are so sure that the transmission of souls is a doctrine to be rejected. Had I been writing to maintainers of the doctrine I might perhaps have shewn how ignorant they are of what they fancy they know and how cautious they should be not to make rash assertions.

It may perhaps perplex you that in my friend's answer as I have quoted it in this letter he mentions *two* letters of mine to which he has no time to reply. Only one of these deals with the problem of the soul;[2] in the other I have asked light on another difficulty.[3] Again when he urges me to take more pains for the removal from the church of a most pernicious heresy, he alludes to the error of the Pelagians which I earnestly beg you, my brother, at all hazards to avoid. In

speculating or arguing on the origin of the soul you must never give place to this heresy with its insidious suggestions. For there is no soul, save that of the one Mediator, which does not derive original sin from Adam. Original sin is that which is fastened on the soul at its birth and from which it can only be freed by being born again.

LETTER CXLV.

TO EXUPERANTIUS.

Jerome advises Exuperantius, a Roman soldier, to come to Bethlehem and with his brother Quintilian to become a monk. According to Palladius (H. L. c. lxxx.) Exuperantius came to Jerome but went away again 'unable to endure his violence and ill-will.' The date of the letter is unknown.

Among all the favours that my friendship with the reverend brother Quintilian has conferred upon me the greatest is this that he has introduced me in the spirit to you whom I do not know personally. Who can fail to love a man who, while he wears the cloak and uniform of a soldier does the work of a prophet, and while his outer man gives promise of quite a different character, overcomes this by the inner man which is formed after the image of the creator. I come forward therefore to challenge you to an interchange of letters and beg that you will often give me occasion to reply to you that I may for the future feel less constraint in writing.

For the present I will content myself by suggesting to your discretion that you should bear in mind the apostle's words: "Art thou bound unto a wife? Seek not to be loosed. Art thou loosed from a wife? Seek not a wife;"[1] that is, seek not that binding which is contrary to loosing. He who has contracted the obligations of marriage, is bound, and he who is bound is a slave; on the other hand he who is loosed is free. Since therefore you rejoice in the freedom of Christ, since your life is better than your profession, since you are all but on the housetop of which the Saviour speaks; you ought not to come down to take your clothes,[2] you ought not to look behind you, you ought not having put your hand to the plough, then to let it go.[3] Rather, if you can, imitate Joseph and leave your garment in the hand of your Egyptian mistress,[4] that naked you may follow your Lord and Saviour. For in the gospel He says: "Whosoever doth not leave all that he hath and bear his cross and come after me cannot be my disciple."[5] Cast from you the burthen of the things of this world, and seek not those riches which in the gospel are compared to the

---

[1] i.e. you may be quite sure that souls are created by God.
[2] Letter CXXXI., ante.   [3] Letter CXXXII., ante.

[1] 1 Cor. vii. 27.   [2] Matt. xxiv. 17, 18.   [3] Luke ix. 62.
[4] Gen. xxxix. 12.   [5] Luke xiv. 26, 27.

humps [1] of camels. Naked and unencumbered fly up to heaven ; masses of gold will but impede the wings of your virtue. I do not speak thus because I know you to be covetous, but because I have a notion that your object in remaining so long in the army is to fill that purse which the Lord has commanded you to empty. For they who have possessions and riches are bidden to sell all that they have and to give to the poor and then to follow the Saviour.[2] Thus if your worship is rich already you ought to fulfil the command and sell your riches ; or if you are still poor you ought not to amass what you will have to pay away. Christ accepts the sacrifices made for him [3] according as he who makes them has a willing mind. Never were any men poorer than the apostles ; yet never any left more for the Lord than they. The poor widow in the gospel who cast but two mites into the treasury was set before all the men of wealth because she gave all that she had.[4] So it should be with you. Seek not for wealth which you will have to pay away ; but rather give up that which you have already acquired that Christ may know his new recruit to be brave and resolute, and then when you are a great way off His Father will run with joy to meet you. He will give you a robe, will put a ring upon your finger, and will kill for you the fatted calf.[5] Then when you are freed from all encumbrances God will soon make a way for you to cross the sea to me with your reverend brother Quintilian. I have now knocked at the door of friendship : if you open it to me, you will find me a frequent visitor.

LETTER CXLVI.

TO EVANGELUS.

Jerome refutes the opinion of those who make deacons equal to presbyters, but in doing so himself makes presbyters equal to bishops.
The date of the letter is unknown.

1. We read in Isaiah the words, "the fool will speak folly," [6] and I am told that some one has been mad enough to put deacons before presbyters, that is, before bishops. For when the apostle clearly teaches that presbyters are the same as bishops, must not a mere server of tables and of widows [7] be insane to set himself up arrogantly over men through whose prayers the body and blood of Christ are produced ? [8] Do you ask for proof of what I say ? Listen to this passage : "Paul and Timotheus, the servants of Jesus Christ, to all the saints in Christ Jesus which are

at Philippi with the bishops and deacons." [1] Do you wish for another instance ? In the Acts of the Apostles Paul thus speaks to the priests [2] of a single church : "Take heed unto yourselves and to all the flock, in the which the Holy Ghost hath made you bishops, to feed the church of God which He purchased with His own blood." [3] And lest any should in a spirit of contention argue that there must then have been more bishops than one in a single church, there is the following passage which clearly proves a bishop and a presbyter to be the same. Writing to Titus the apostle says : "For this cause left I thee in Crete, that thou shouldest set in order the things that are wanting, and ordain presbyters [4] in every city, as I had appointed thee : if any be blameless, the husband of one wife, having faithful children not accused of riot or unruly. For a bishop must be blameless as the steward of God." [5] And to Timothy he says : "Neglect not the gift that is in thee, which was given thee by prophecy, with the laying on of the hands of the presbytery." [6] Peter also says in his first epistle : "The presbyters which are among you I exhort, who am your fellow-presbyter and a witness of the sufferings of Christ and also a partaker of the glory that shall be revealed : feed the flock of Christ [7] . . . taking the oversight thereof not by constraint but willingly, according unto God." [8] In the Greek the meaning is still plainer, for the word used is ἐπισκοποῦντες, that is to say, overseeing, and this is the origin of the name overseer or bishop. [9] But perhaps the testimony of these great men seems to you insufficient. If so, then listen to the blast of the gospel trumpet, that son of thunder,[10] the disciple whom Jesus loved [11] and who reclining on the Saviour's breast drank in the waters of sound doctrine. One of his letters begins thus : "The presbyter unto the elect lady and her children whom I love in the truth ; " [12] and another thus : "The presbyter unto the wellbeloved Gaius whom I love in the truth." [13] When subsequently one presbyter was chosen to preside over the rest, this was done to remedy schism and to prevent each individual from rending the church of Christ by drawing it to himself. For even at Alexandria from the time of Mark the Evangelist until the episcopates of Heraclas and Dionysius the presbyters always named as bishop one of their own number chosen by themselves and set in a more exalted position, just as an army elects a general, or as deacons appoint one of themselves whom they know to be diligent

---

[1] Pravitates, deformities. Matt. xix. 24. [2] Matt. xix. 21.
[3] 2 Cor. viii. 12. [4] Luke xxi. 1–4.
[5] Luke xv. 20–23. [6] Isa. xxxii. 6, RV. [7] Acts vi. 1, 2.
[8] Ad quorum preces Christi corpus sanguisque conficitur. Cp. Letter XIV. § 8.

[1] Ph. i. 1. [2] Sacerdotes. [3] Acts xx. 28, RV.
[4] A.V. ' elders.' [5] Tit. i. 5–7. [6] Tim. iv. 14.
[7] AV. ' of God.' [8] 1 Pet. v. 1, 2. The last clause from RV.
[9] ἐπίσκοπος. [10] Mark iii. 17.
[11] Joh. xiii. 23. [12] 2 Joh. 1. [13] 3 Joh. 1.

and call him archdeacon. For what function, excepting ordination, belongs to a bishop that does not also belong to a presbyter? It is not the case that there is one church at Rome and another in all the world beside. Gaul and Britain, Africa and Persia, India and the East worship one Christ and observe one rule of truth. If you ask for authority, the world outweighs its capital.[1] Wherever there is a bishop, whether it be at Rome or at Engubium, whether it be at Constantinople or at Rhegium, whether it be at Alexandria or at Zoan, his dignity is one and his priesthood is one. Neither the command of wealth nor the lowness of poverty makes him more a bishop or less a bishop. All alike are successors of the apostles.[2]

2. But you will say, how comes it then that at Rome a presbyter is only ordained on the recommendation of a deacon? To which I reply as follows. Why do you bring forward a custom which exists in one city only? Why do you oppose to the laws of the Church a paltry exception which has given rise to arrogance and pride? The rarer anything is the more it is sought after. In India pennyroyal is more costly than pepper. Their fewness makes deacons persons of consequence[3] while presbyters are less thought of owing to their great numbers. But even in the church of Rome the deacons stand while the presbyters seat themselves, although bad habits have by degrees so far crept in that I have seen a deacon, in the absence of the bishop, seat himself among the presbyters and at social gatherings give his blessing to them.[4] Those who act thus must learn that they are wrong and must give heed to the apostles' words: "it is not reason that we should leave the word of God and serve tables."[5] They must consider the reasons which led to the appointment of deacons at the beginning. They must read the Acts of the Apostles and bear in mind their true position.

Of the names presbyter and bishop the first denotes age, the second rank. In writing both to Titus and to Timothy the apostle speaks of the ordination of bishops and of deacons, but says not a word of the ordination of presbyters; for the fact is that the word bishops includes presbyters also. Again when a man is promoted it is from a lower place to a higher. Either then a presbyter should be ordained a deacon, from the lesser office, that

is, to the more important, to prove that a presbyter is inferior to a deacon; or if on the other hand it is the deacon that is ordained presbyter, this latter should recognize that, although he may be less highly paid than a deacon, he is superior to him in virtue of his priesthood. In fact as if to tell us that the traditions handed down by the apostles were taken by them from the old testament, bishops, presbyters and deacons occupy in the church the same positions as those which were occupied by Aaron, his sons, and the Levites in the temple.[1]

LETTER CXLVII.

TO SABINIANUS.

Jerome writes in severe but moderate language to Sabinianus, a deacon, calling on him to repent of his sins. Of these he recounts at length the two most serious, an act of adultery at Rome and an attempt to seduce a nun at Bethlehem. The date of the letter is uncertain.

1. Of old, when it had repented the Lord that he had anointed Saul to be king over Israel,[2] we are told that Samuel mourned for him; and again, when Paul heard that there was fornication among the Corinthians and such fornication as was not so much as named among the gentiles,[3] he besought them to repent with these tearful words: "lest, when I come again, my God will humble me among you and that I shall bewail many which have sinned already and have not repented of the uncleanness and fornication and lasciviousness which they have committed."[4] If an apostle or a prophet, themselves immaculate, could speak thus with a clemency embracing all, how much more earnestly should a sinner like you I plead with a sinner like you. You have fallen and refuse to rise; you do not so much as lift your eyes to heaven; having wasted your father's substance you take pleasure in the husks that the swine eat;[5] and climbing the precipice of pride you fall headlong into the deep. You make your belly your God instead of Christ; you are a slave to lust; your glory is in your shame;[6] you fatten yourself like a victim for the slaughter, and imitate the lives of the wicked, careless of their doom. "Thou knowest not that the goodness of God leadeth thee to repentance. But after thy hardness and impenitent heart thou treasurest up unto thyself wrath against the day of wrath."[7] Or is it that your heart is hardened, as Pharaoh's was, because your punishment is deferred and you are not smitten at the moment? The ten plagues were sent upon Pharaoh not as by an

---

[1] Orbis major est urbe.
[2] In this passage Jerome does his best to minimize the distinction between bishops and presbyters. Elsewhere also he stands up for the rights of the latter (see Letter LII. § 7).
[3] At Rome there were only seven, that having been the number of 'servers' appointed by the apostles. (See Acts vi. and Sozomen H. E. vii. 19.)
[4] Contrary to the eighteenth canon of Nicæa.
[5] Acts vi. 2.

[1] This analogy had become very common in Jerome's day. The germ of it is to be found in Clem. ad Cor. I. xl.
[2] 1 Sam. xv. 11, 17.   [3] 1 Cor. v. 1.   [4] 2 Cor. xii. 21.
[5] Luke xvi. 13. 16.   [6] Phil. iii. 19.   [7] Rom. ii. 4, 5.

angry God but as by a warning father, and his day of grace was prolonged until he repented of his repentance. Yet doom overtook him when he pursued through the wilderness the people whom he had previously let go and presumed to enter the very sea in the eagerness of his pursuit. For only in this one way could he learn the lesson that He is to be dreaded whom even the elements obey. He had said : " I know not the Lord, neither will I let Israel go ; " [1] and you imitate him when you say : " The vision that he seeth is for many days to come, and he prophesieth of the times that are far off." [2] Yet the same prophet confutes you with these words : " Thus saith the Lord God, There shall none of my words be prolonged any more, but the word which I have spoken shall be done." David too says of the godless (and of godlessness you have proved yourself not a slight but an eminent example), that in this world they rejoice in good fortune and say : " How doth God know? And is there knowledge in the Most High ? Behold these are the ungodly who prosper in the world ; they increase in riches." [3] Then almost losing his footing and staggering where he stands he complains, saying : " Verily I have cleansed my heart in vain, and washed my hands in innocency." [4] For he had previously said : " I was envious at the foolish, when I saw the prosperity of the wicked. For they have no regard for death,[1] but their strength is firm. They are not in trouble as other men are ; neither are they plagued like other men. Therefore pride compasseth them about as a chain; violence covereth them as a garment. Their eyes stand out with fatness : they have more than heart could wish. They are corrupt, and speak wickedly concerning oppression : they speak loftily. They set their mouth against the heavens, and their tongue walketh through the earth." [5]

2. Does not this whole psalm seem to you to be written of yourself? Certainly you are hale and strong ; and like a new apostle of Antichrist, when you are found out in one city, you pass to another.[6] You are in no need of money, no crushing blow strikes you down, neither are you plagued as other men who are not like you mere brute beasts. Therefore you are lifted up into pride, and lust covers you as a garment. Out of your fat and bloated carcass you breathe out words fraught with death. You never consider that you must some day die, nor feel the slightest repentance when you have satisfied your lust.

You have more than heart can wish ; and, not to be alone in your wrongdoing, you invent scandals concerning those who are God's servants. Though you know it not, it is against the most High that you are speaking iniquity and against the heavens that you are setting your mouth. It is no wonder that God's servants small and great are blasphemed by you, when your fathers did not scruple to call even the master of the house Beelzebub. " The disciple is not above his master nor the servant above his lord." [1] If they did this with the green tree, what will you do with me, the dry ? [2] Much in the same way also the offended believers in the book of Malachi gave expression to feelings like yours ; for they said, " It is vain to serve God : and what profit is it that we have kept his ordinance, and that we have walked mournfully before the Lord of Hosts ? And now we call the proud happy ; yea, they that work wickedness are set up ; yea, they that tempt God are even delivered." Yet the Lord afterwards threatens them with a day of judgment ; and announcing beforehand the distinction that shall then be made between the righteous and the unrighteous, speaks to them thus : " Return ye,[3] and discern between the righteous and the wicked, between him that serveth God and him that serveth him not." [4]

3. All this may perhaps seem to you matter for jesting, seeing that you take so much pleasure in comedies and lyrics and mimes like those of Lentulus ; [5] although so blunted is your wit that I am not disposed to allow that you can understand even language so simple. You may treat the words of prophets with contempt, but Amos will still make answer to you : " Thus saith the Lord, For three transgressions and for four shall I not turn away from him ? " [6] For inasmuch as Damascus, Gaza, Tyre, Edom, the Ammonites and the Moabites, the Jews also and the children of Israel, although God had often prophesied to them to turn and to repent, had refused to hear His voice, the Lord wishing to shew that He had most just cause for the wrath that he was going to bring upon them used the words already quoted, " For three transgressions and for four shall I not turn away from them ? " It is wicked, God says, to harbour evil thoughts; yet I have allowed them to do so. It is still more wicked to carry them out ; yet in My mercy and kindness I have permitted even this. But should the sinful thought have become the sinful deed ? Should men in their pride have trampled thus on my tenderness ?

---

[1] Ex. v. 2.   [2] Ezek. xii. 27, 28.
[3] Ps. lxxiii. 11, 12.   [4] Ps. lxxiii. 13.
[5] So the Vulgate, from which Jerome quotes.
[6] Ps. lxxiii. 3-9.   [7] Cf. Matt. x. 23.

[1] Matt. x. 24, 25.   [2] Luke xxiii. 31.
[3] So the Latin.   [4] Mal. iii. 14, 15, 18.
[5] A writer and actor of mimes, probably in the first century of the Empire.
[6] Am. i. 3, LXX.

Nevertheless "I have no pleasure in the death of the wicked, but that the wicked turn from his way and live;"[1] and as it is not they that are whole who need a physician but they that are sick,[2] even after his sin I hold out a hand to the prostrate sinner and exhort him, polluted as he is in his own blood,[3] to wash away his stains with tears of penitence. But if even then he shews himself unwilling to repent, and if, after he has suffered shipwreck, he refuses to clutch the plank which alone can save him, I am compelled at last to say : "Thus saith the Lord, For three transgressions and for four shall I not turn away from him?" For this "turning away" God accounts a punishment, inasmuch as the sinner is left to his own devices. It is thus that he visits the sins of the fathers upon the children unto the third and fourth generation ;[4] not punishing those who sin immediately but pardoning their first offences and only passing sentence on them for their last. For if it were otherwise and if God were to stand forth on the moment as the avenger of iniquity, the church would lose many of its saints ; and certainly would be deprived of the apostle Paul. The prophet Ezekiel, from whom we have quoted above, repeating God's words spoken to himself speaks thus : "Open thy mouth and eat what I shall give thee. And behold," he says, "an hand was sent unto me ; and, lo, a roll of a book was therein ; and he spread it before me ; and it was written within and without : and there was written therein lamentations, and a song, and woe."[5] The first of these three belongs to you if you prove willing, as a sinner, to repent of your sins. The second belongs to those who are holy, who are called upon to sing praises to God ; for praise does not become a sinner's mouth. And the third belongs to persons like you who in despair have given themselves over to uncleanness, to fornication, to the belly, and to the lowest lusts ; men who suppose that death ends all and that there is nothing beyond it ; who say : "When the overflowing scourge shall pass through it shall not come unto us."[6] The book which the prophet eats is the whole series of the Scriptures, which in turn bewail the penitent, celebrate the righteous, and curse the desperate. For nothing is so displeasing to God as an impenitent heart. Impenitence is the one sin for which there is no forgiveness. For if one who ceases to sin is pardoned even after he has sinned, and if prayer has power to bend the judge ; it follows that every impenitent sinner must provoke his judge to wrath. Thus despair is the one sin for which there is no remedy. By obstinate rejection of

God's grace men turn His mercy into sternness and severity. Yet, that you may know that God does every day call sinners to repentance, hear Isaiah's words : "In that day," he says, "did the Lord God of Hosts call to weeping and to mourning and to baldness and to girding with sackcloth : and behold joy and gladness, slaying oxen, and killing sheep, eating flesh, and drinking wine ; let us eat and drink, for to-morrow we shall die." After these words filled with the recklessness of despair the Scripture goes on to say : "And it was revealed in my ears by the Lord of Hosts, Surely this iniquity shall not be purged from you till ye die."[1] Only when they become dead to sin, will their sin be forgiven them. For, so long as they live in sin, it cannot be put away.

4. Have mercy I beseech you upon your soul. Consider that God's judgment will one day overtake you. Remember by what a bishop you were ordained. The holy man was mistaken in his choice ; but this he might well be. For even God repented that he had anointed Saul to be king.[2] Even among the twelve apostles Judas was found a traitor. And Nicolas of Antioch—a deacon like yourself[3]—disseminated the Nicolaitan heresy and all manner of uncleanness.[4] I do not now bring up to you the many virgins whom you are said to have seduced, or the noble matrons who have suffered death[5] because violated by you, or the greedy profligacy with which you have hied through dens of sin. For grave and serious as such sins are in themselves, they are trivial indeed when compared with those which I have now to narrate. How great must be the sin beside which seduction and adultery are insignificant ? Miserable wretch that you are ! when you enter the cave wherein the Son of God was born, where truth sprang out of the earth and the land did yield her increase,[6] it is to make an assignation. Have you no fear that the babe will cry from the manger, that the newly delivered virgin will see you, that the mother of the Lord will behold you ? The angels cry aloud, the shepherds run, the star shines down from heaven, the wise men worship, Herod is terrified, Jerusalem is in confusion, and meantime you creep into a virgin's cell to seduce the virgin to whom it belongs. I am filled with consternation and a shiver runs through me, soul and body, when I try to set before your eyes the deed that you have done. The whole church was keeping vigil by night and proclaiming Christ as its Lord ; in one spirit though in different tongues the

[1] Ezek. xxxiii. 11.
[2] Luke v. 31.
[3] Cf. Ezek. xvi. 6.
[4] Ex. xx. 5.
[5] Ezek. iii. 1 : ii. 9, 10, Vulg.
[6] Is. xxviii. 15.

[1] Isa. xxii. 12–14.
[2] 1 Sam. xv. 11.
[3] Acts vi. 5.
[4] Rev. ii. 6, 15.
[5] Women guilty of adultery were legally punishable with death until the time of Justinian.
[6] Ps. lxxxv. 11, 12.

praises of God were being sung. Yet you were squeezing your love-notes into the openings of what is now the altar, as it was once the manger, of the Lord, choosing this place in order that your unhappy victim might find and read them when she came to kneel and worship there. Then you took your place among the singers, and with impudent nods communicated your passion to her.

5. Oh! crying shame! I can go no farther. For sobs anticipate my words, and indignation and grief choke me in the act of utterance. Oh! for the sea of Tully's eloquence! Oh! for the impetuous current of the invective of Demosthenes! Yet in this case I am sure you would both be dumb; your eloquence would fail you. A deed has been disclosed which no rhetoric can explain; a crime has been discovered which no mime can represent, nor jester play, nor comedian describe.[1]

It is usual in the monasteries of Egypt and Syria for virgins and widows who have vowed themselves to God and have renounced the world and have trodden under foot its pleasures, to ask the mothers of their communities to cut their hair; not that afterwards they go about with heads uncovered in defiance of the apostle's command,[2] for they wear a close-fitting cap and a veil. No one knows of this in any single case except the shearers and the shorn, but as the practice is universal, it is almost universally known. The custom has in fact become a second nature. It is designed to save those who take no baths and whose heads and faces are strangers to all unguents, from accumulated dirt and from the tiny creatures which are sometimes generated about the roots of the hair.

6. Let us see then, my good friend, how you acted in these surroundings. You promised to marry your unhappy victim; and then in that venerable cave you took from her, either as securities for her fidelity or as a pledge of the engagement, some locks of hair, some handkerchiefs, and a girdle, swearing at the same time that you would never love another as you loved her. Then you ran to the place where the shepherds were watching their flocks when they heard the angels singing over head, and there again you plighted your troth. I say no more; I do not accuse you of kissing her or of embracing her. Although I believe that there is nothing of which you are not capable, still the sacred character of stable and field forbids me to suppose you guilty except in will and determination. Unhappy man! When you first stood beside the virgin in the cave, surely a mist must have dimmed your eyes,

your tongue must have been paralysed, your arms must have fallen to your sides, your chest must have heaved, your gait must have become unsteady. She had assumed the bridal-veil of Christ in the basilica of the apostle Peter and had vowed to live henceforth in the monastery, in the spots consecrated by the Lord's Cross, His Resurrection, and His Ascension; and yet after all this you dared to accept that hair, which at Christ's command she had cut off in the cave of His birth, as a token of her readiness to sleep with you. Again you used to sit beneath her window from the evening till the morning; and because owing to its height you could not come to close quarters with her, you conveyed things to her and she in her turn to you by the aid of a cord. How careful the lady superior must have been is shewn by the fact that you never saw the virgin except in church; and that, although both of you had the same inclination, you could find no means of conversing with each other except at a window under cover of night. As I was afterwards told you used to be quite sorry when the sun rose. Your face looked bloodless, shrunken, and pale; and to remove all suspicion, you used to be for ever reading Christ's gospel as if you were a deacon indeed.[1] I and others used to attribute your paleness to fasting, and to admire your bloodless lips—so unlike the brilliant colour which they generally shewed—in the belief that they were caused by frequent vigils. You were already preparing ladders to fetch the unhappy virgin from her cell; you had already arranged your route, ordered vessels, settled a day, and thought out the details of your flight, when, behold, the angel who kept the door of Mary's chamber, who watched over the cradle of the Lord and who bore in his arms the infant Christ, in whose presence you had committed these great sins, himself and none other, betrayed you.

7. Oh! my unlucky eyes! Oh! day worthy of the most solemn curse, on which with utter consternation I read your letters, the contents of which I am forced to remember still! What obscenities they contained! What blandishments! What exultant triumph in the prospect of the virgin's dishonour. A deacon should not have even known such things, much less should he have spoken of them. Unhappy man! where can you have learned them, you who used to boast that you had been reared in the church. It is true, however, that in these letters you swear that you have never led a chaste life and that you are not really a deacon. If you try to disown them your own handwriting will convict you, and the very

---

[1] Mimus, scurra, atellanus.   [2] 1 Cor. xi. 5, 6.

[1] At the Eucharistic service the gospel was commonly though not exclusively read by a deacon. (See Const. Apost. II. 57, 5, and Sozomen, H. C. VII. 19.)

letters will cry out against you. But meantime you may make what you can of your sin, for what you have written is so foul that I cannot bring it up as evidence against you.

8. You threw yourself down at my knees, you prostrated yourself, you begged me—I use your own words—to spare "your half-pint of blood." Oh! miserable wretch! you thought nothing of God's judgment, and feared no vengeance but mine. I forgave you, I admit; what else being a Christian could I do? I urged you to repent, to wear sackcloth, to roll in ashes, to seek seclusion, to live in a monastery, to implore God's mercy with constant tears. You however showed yourself a pillar of confidence, and excited as you were by the viper's sting you became to me a deceitful bow; you shot at me arrows of reviling. I am become your enemy because I tell you the truth.[1] I do not complain of your calumnies; everyone knows that you only praise men as infamous as yourself. What I lament is that you do not lament yourself, that you do not realize that you are dead, that, like a gladiator ready for Libitina,[2] you deck yourself out for your own funeral. You wear not sackcloth but linen, you load your fingers with rings, you use toothpowder for your teeth, you arrange the stray hairs on your brown skull to the best advantage. Your bull's neck bulges out with fat and droops no whit because it has given way to lust. Moreover you are redolent of perfume, you go from one bath to another, you wage war[3] against the hair that grows in spite of you, you walk through the forum and the streets a spruce and smooth-faced rake. Your face has become the face of a harlot: you know not how to blush.[4] Return, unhappy man, to the Lord, and He will return to you.[5] Repent, and He will repent of the evil that He has purposed to bring upon you.

9. Why is it that you disregard your own scars and try to defame others? Why is it that when I give you the best advice you attack me like a madman? It may be that I am as infamous as you publicly proclaim; in that case you can at least repent as heartily as I do. It may be that I am as great a sinner as you make me out; if so, you can at least imitate a sinner's tears. Are my sins your virtues? Or does it alleviate your misery that many are in the same plight as yourself? Let a few tears fall on the silk and fine linen which make you so resplendent. Realize that you are naked, torn, unclean, a beggar.[1] It is never too late to repent.[2] You may have gone down from Jerusalem and may have been wounded on the way; yet the Samaritan will set you upon his beast, and will bring you to the inn and will take care of you.[3] Even if you are lying in your grave, the Lord will raise you though your flesh may stink.[4] At least imitate those blind men for whose sake the Saviour left His home and heritage and came to Jericho. They were sitting in darkness and in the shadow of death when the light shone upon them.[5] For when they learned that it was the Lord who was passing by they began to cry out saying: "Thou Son of David, have mercy on us."[6] You too will have your sight restored; if you cry to Him, and cast away your filthy garments at His call.[7] "When thou shalt turn and bewail thyself then shalt thou be saved, and then shalt thou know where thou hast hitherto been."[8] Let Him but touch your scars and pass his hands over your eyeballs; and although you may have been born blind from the womb and although your mother may have conceived you. in sin, he will purge you with hyssop and you shall be clean, he will wash you and you shall be whiter than snow.[9] Why is it that you are bowed together and bent down to the ground, why is it that you are still prostrate in the mire? She whom Satan had bound for eighteen years came to the Saviour; and being cured by Him was made straight so that she could once more look up towards heaven.[10] God says to you what He said to Cain: "Thou hast sinned: hold thy peace."[11] Why do you flee from the face of God and dwell in the land of Nod? Why do you struggle in the waves[12] when you can plant your feet upon the rock? See to it that Phinehas does not thrust you through with his spear while you are committing fornication with the Midianitish woman.[13] Amnon did not spare Tamar,[14] and you her brother and kinsman in the faith have had no mercy upon this virgin. But why is it that when you have defiled her you change into an Absalom and desire to kill a David who mourns over your rebellion and spiritual death? The blood of Naboth[15] cries out against you. The vineyard also of

---

1 Gal. iv. 16.
2 The goddess who in the Roman pantheon presided over funerals. The gladiators meant are the so-called bustuarii who were engaged to fight at the funeral pile (bustum) in honour of the dead.
3 *i. e.* by the use of depilatories.
4 Jer. iii. 3.
5 Mal. iii. 7.

1 Rev. iii. 17.
2 Cf. Cyprian, Epist. ad Demet. xxv.
3 Luke x. 30-34.
4 Joh. xi. 39, 44.
5 Luke i. 79.
6 Matt. ix. 27: cf. Luke xviii. 35-38.
7 Mark x. 50.
8 Isa. xxx. 15, LXX.
9 Ps. li. 5, 7.
10 Luke xiii. 11-13.
11 Gen. iv. 7, LXX.
12 An etymological allusion. Nod='ebb and flow.'
13 Num. xxv. 6-8.
14 2 Sam. xiii. 14.
15 1 Kings xxi. 13.

Jezreel, that is, of God's seed, demands due vengeance upon you, seeing that you have turned it into a garden of pleasures and made it a seed-bed of lust. God sends you an Elijah to tell you of torment and of death. Bow yourself down therefore and put on sackcloth for a little while ; then perhaps the Lord will say of you what He said of Ahab : "Seest thou how Ahab humbleth himself before me? Because he humbleth himself before me,[1] I will not bring the evil in his days."

10. But possibly you flatter yourself that since the bishop who has made you a deacon is a holy man, his merits will atone for your transgressions. I have already told you that the father is not punished for the son nor the son for the father. "The soul that sinneth it shall die."[2] Samuel too had sons who forsook the fear of the Lord and "turned aside after lucre" and iniquity.[3] Eli also was a holy priest, but he had sons of whom we read in the Hebrew that they lay with the women that assembled at the door of the tabernacle of God, and that like you they shamelessly claimed for themselves the right to minister in His sanctuary.[4] Wherefore the tabernacle itself was overthrown and the holy place made desolate by reason of the sins of those who were God's priests. And even Eli himself offended God by shewing too great leniency to his sons ; therefore, so far from the righteousness of your bishop being able to deliver you, it is rather to be feared that your wickedness may hurl him from his seat and that falling on his back like Eli he may perish irretrievably.[5] If the Levite Uzzah was smitten merely because he tried to hold up from falling the ark which it was his special province to carry ;[6] what punishment, think you, will be inflicted upon you who have tried to overthrow the Lord's ark when standing firm? The more estimable the bishop is who ordained you, the more detestable are you who have disappointed the expectations of so good a man. His long ignorance of your misdoings is indeed easy to account for ; as it generally happens that we are the last to know the scandals which affect our homes, and are ignorant of the sins of our children and wives even when our neighbors talk of nothing else. At all events all Italy was aware of your evil life ; and it was everywhere a subject of lamentation that you should still stand before the altar of Christ. For you had neither the cunning nor the forethought to conceal your vices. So hot were you, so lecherous, and so wanton, so entirely under the sway of this and

that caprice of self-indulgence, that, not content with satisfying your passions, you gloried in each intrigue as a triumph and emerged from it bearing palms of victory.

11. Once more the fire of unchastity seized you, this time among savage swords and in the quarters of a married barbarian of great influence and power. You were not afraid to commit adultery in a house where the injured husband might have punished you without calling in a judge's aid. You found yourself attracted and drawn to suburban parks and gardens ; and, in the husband's absence behaved as boldly and madly as if you supposed your companion to be not your paramour but your wife. She was at last captured, but you escaped through an underground passage and secretly made your way to Rome. There you hid yourself among some Samnite robbers ; and on the first hint that the aggrieved husband was coming down from the Alps like a new Hannibal in search of you, you did not think yourself safe till you had taken refuge on shipboard. So hasty indeed was your flight that you chose to face a tempest at sea rather than take the consequences of remaining on shore. Somehow or other you reached Syria, and on arriving there professed a wish to go on to Jerusalem and there to serve the Lord. Who could refuse to welcome one who declared himself to be a monk ; especially if he were ignorant of your tragical career and had read the letters of commendation which your bishop had addressed to other prelates ?[1] Unhappy man ! you transformed yourself into an angel of light ;[2] and while you were in reality a minister of Satan, you pretended to be a minister of righteousness. You were only a wolf in sheep's clothing ;[3] and having played the adulterer once towards the wife of a man, you desired now to play the adulterer to the spouse of Christ.[4]

12. My design in recounting these events has been to sketch for you the picture of your evil life and to set your misdeeds plainly before your eyes. I have wished to prevent you from making God's mercy and His abundant tenderness an excuse for committing new sins and to save you from crucifying to yourself the son of God afresh and putting Him to an open shame. For you may do these things if you do not read the words which follow the passage to which I have alluded. They are these : " The earth which drinketh in the rain that cometh oft upon it, and bringeth forth herbs meet for them by whom it is dressed,

---

[1] 1 Kings xxi. 29.　　　　[2] Ezek. xviii. 4.
[3] 1 Sam. viii. 3.　　　　　[4] 1 Sam. ii. 12-17, 22.
[5] 1 Sam. iv. 18.　　　　　[6] 2 Sam. vi. 6, 7.

[1] Sacerdotes, lit. priests.
[2] 2 Cor. xi. 14, 15.
[3] Matt. vii. 15.
[4] i.e. to the church at large represented by individual virgins.

receiveth blessings from God : but that which beareth thorns and briers is rejected and is nigh unto cursing; whose end is to be burned."[1]

LETTER CXLVIII.

TO THE MATRON CELANTIA.

This is an interesting letter addressed to a lady of rank, on the principles and methods of a holy life. It is not, however, the work of Jerome, of whose style it shews few traces. It has been ascribed in turn to Paulinus of Nola and Sulpicius Severus.

[1] Heb. vi. 6, 7–8.

LETTER CXLIX.

ON THE JEWISH FESTIVALS.

The theme of this letter is the abrogation of the Jewish festivals by the evangelical law. It has no claim to be considered a work of Jerome.

LETTER CL.

FROM PROCOPIUS TO JEROME.

This letter is extant also among those of Procopius of Gaza, to whose works it properly belongs. As this Procopius flourished a century later than Jerome, the letter cannot be addressed to him.

TREATISES

THE LIFE OF PAULUS THE FIRST HERMIT

The Life of Paulus was written in the year 374 or 375 during Jerome's stay in the desert of Syria, as is seen from c. 6, and was dedicated to Paulus of Concordia as stated in Jerome's Ep. x. c. 3.

1. It has been a subject of wide-spread and frequent discussion what monk was the first to give a signal example of the hermit life. For some going back too far have found a beginning in those holy men Elias and John, of whom the former seems to have been more than a monk and the latter to have begun to prophesy before his birth. Others, and their opinion is that commonly received, maintain that Antony was the originator of this mode of life, which view is partly true. Partly I say, for the fact is not so much that he preceded the rest as that they all derived from him the necessary stimulus. But it is asserted even at the present day by Amathas and Macarius, two of Antony's disciples, the former of whom laid his master in the grave, that a certain Paul of Thebes was the leader in the movement, though not the first to bear the name, and this opinion has my approval also. Some as they think fit circulate stories such as this—that he was a man living in an underground cave with flowing hair down to his feet, and invent many incredible tales which it would be useless to detail. Nor does the opinion of men who lie without any sense of shame seem worthy of refutation. So then inasmuch as both Greek and Roman writers have handed down careful accounts of Antony, I have determined to write a short history of Paul's early and latter days, more because the thing has been passed over than from confidence in my own ability. What his middle life was like, and what snares of Satan he experienced, no man, it is thought, has yet discovered.

2. During the persecutions of Decius and Valerian, when Cornelius at Rome and Cyprian at Carthage shed their blood in blessed martyrdom, many churches in Egypt and the Thebaid were laid waste by the fury of the storm. At that time the Christians would often pray that they might be smitten with the sword for the name of Christ. But the desire of the crafty foe was to slay the soul, not the body; and this he did by searching diligently for slow but deadly tortures. In the words of Cyprian himself who suffered at his hands: they who wished to die were not suffered to be slain. We give two illustrations, both as specially noteworthy and to make the cruelty of the enemy better known.

3. A martyr, steadfast in faith, who stood fast as a conqueror amidst the racks and burning plates, was ordered by him to be smeared with honey and to be made to lie under a blazing sun with his hands tied behind his back, so that he who had already surmounted the heat of the frying-pan might be vanquished by the stings of flies. Another who was in the bloom of youth was taken by his command to some delightful pleasure gardens, and there amid white lilies and blushing roses, close by a gently murmuring stream, while overhead the soft whisper of the wind played among the leaves of the trees, was laid upon a deep luxurious feather-bed, bound with fetters of sweet garlands to prevent his escape. When all had withdrawn from him a harlot of great beauty drew near and began with voluptuous embrace to throw her arms around his neck, and, wicked even to relate! to handle his person, so that when once the lusts of the flesh were roused, she might accomplish her licentious purpose. What to do, and whither to turn, the soldier of Christ knew not. Unconquered by tortures he was being overcome by pleasure. At last with an inspiration from heaven he bit off the end of his tongue and spat it in her face as she kissed him. Thus the sensations of lust were subdued by the intense pain which followed.

4. While such enormities were being perpetrated in the lower part of the Thebaid, Paul and his newly married sister were bereaved of both their parents, he being about sixteen years of age. He was heir to a rich inheritance, highly skilled in both Greek and Egyptian learning, gifted with a gentle disposition and a deep love for God. Amid the thunders of persecution he retired to a house at a considerable distance and in a more secluded spot. But to what crimes does not the " accursed thirst for gold " impel the human heart? His brother-in-law conceived the thought of betraying the youth whom he was bound to conceal. Neither a wife's tears which so often prevail, nor the ties of blood, nor the all-seeing eye of God above him could turn the traitor from his wickedness. " He

¹ A.D. 249-260.

came, he was urgent, he acted with cruelty while seeming only to press the claims of affection."

5. The young man had the tact to understand this, and, conforming his will to the necessity, fled to the mountain wilds to wait for the end of the persecution. He began with easy stages, and repeated halts, to advance into the desert. At length he found a rocky mountain, at the foot of which, closed by a stone, was a cave of no great size. He removed the stone (so eager are men to learn what is hidden), made eager search, and saw within a large hall, open to the sky, but shaded by the wide-spread branches of an ancient palm. The tree, however, did not conceal a fountain of transparent clearness, the waters whereof no sooner gushed forth than the stream was swallowed up in a small opening of the same ground which gave it birth. There were besides in the mountain, which was full of cavities, many habitable places, in which were seen, now rough with rust, anvils and hammers for stamping money. The place, Egyptian writers relate, was a secret mint at the time of Antony's union with Cleopatra.

6. Accordingly, regarding his abode as a gift from God, he fell in love with it, and there in prayer and solitude spent all the rest of his life. The palm afforded him food and clothing. And, that no one may deem this impossible, I call to witness Jesus and His holy angels that I have seen and still see in that part of the desert which lies between Syria and the Saracens' country, monks of whom one was shut up for thirty years and lived on barley bread and muddy water, while another in an old cistern (called in the country dialect of Syria *Gubba*) kept himself alive on five dried figs a day. What I relate then is so strange that it will appear incredible to those who do not believe the words that "all things are possible to him that believeth."

7. But to return to the point at which I digressed. The blessed Paul had already lived on earth the life of heaven for a hundred and thirteen years, and Antony at the age of ninety was dwelling in another place of solitude (as he himself was wont to declare), when the thought occurred to the latter, that no monk more perfect than himself had settled in the desert. However, in the stillness of the night it was revealed to him that there was farther in the desert a much better man than he, and that he ought to go and visit him. So then at break of day the venerable old man, supporting and guiding his weak limbs with a staff, started to go : but what direction to choose he knew not. Scorching noontide came, with a broiling sun overhead, but still he did not

suffer himself to be turned from the journey he had begun. Said he, " I believe in my God : some time or other He will shew me the fellow-servant whom He promised me." He said no more. All at once he beholds a creature of mingled shape, half horse half man, called by the poets Hippo-centaur. At the sight of this he arms himself by making on his forehead the sign of salvation, and then exclaims, " Holloa ! Where in these parts is a servant of God living ? " The monster after gnashing out some kind of outlandish utterance, in words broken rather than spoken through his bristling lips, at length finds a friendly mode of communication, and extending his right hand points out the way desired. Then with swift flight he crosses the spreading plain and vanishes from the sight of his wondering companion. But whether the devil took this shape to terrify him, or whether it be that the desert which is known to abound in monstrous animals engenders that kind of creature also, we cannot decide.

8. Antony was amazed, and thinking over what he had seen went on his way. Before long in a small rocky valley shut in on all sides he sees a mannikin with hooked snout, horned forehead, and extremities like goats' feet. When he saw this, Antony like a good soldier seized the shield of faith and the helmet of hope : the creature none the less began to offer him the fruit of the palm-trees to support him on his journey and as it were pledges of peace. Antony perceiving this stopped and asked who he was. The answer he received from him was this : " I am a mortal being and one of those inhabitants of the desert whom the Gentiles deluded by various forms of error worship under the names of Fauns, Satyrs, and Incubi. I am sent to represent my tribe. We pray you in our behalf to entreat the favour of your Lord and ours, who, we have learnt, came once to save the world, and ' whose sound has gone forth into all the earth.' " As he uttered such words as these, the aged traveller's cheeks streamed with tears, the marks of his deep feeling, which he shed in the fulness of his joy. He rejoiced over the Glory of Christ and the destruction of Satan, and marvelling all the while that he could understand the Satyr's language, and striking the ground with his staff, he said, " Woe to thee, Alexandria, who instead of God worshippest monsters ! Woe to thee, harlot city, into which have flowed together the demons of the whole world ! What will you say now ? Beasts speak of Christ, and you instead of God worship monsters." He had not finished speaking when, as if on wings, the wild creature fled away. Let no one scruple to believe this incident ; its truth is

supported by what took place when Constantine was on the throne, a matter of which the whole world was witness. For a man of that kind was brought alive to Alexandria and shewn as a wonderful sight to the people. Afterwards his lifeless body, to prevent its decay through the summer heat, was preserved in salt and brought to Antioch that the Emperor might see it.

9. To pursue my proposed story. Antony traversed the region on which he had entered, seeing only the traces of wild beasts, and the wide waste of the desert. What to do, whither to wend his way, he knew not. Another day had now passed. One thing alone was left him, his confident belief that he could not be forsaken by Christ. The darkness of the second night he wore away in prayer. While it was still twilight, he saw not far away a she-wolf gasping with parching thirst and creeping to the foot of the mountain. He followed it with his eyes; and after the beast had disappeared in a cave he drew near and began to look within. His curiosity profited nothing: the darkness hindered vision. But, as the Scripture saith, perfect love casteth out fear. With halting step and bated breath he entered, carefully feeling his way; he advanced little by little and repeatedly listened for the sound. At length through the fearful midnight darkness a light appeared in the distance. In his eager haste he struck his foot against a stone and roused the echoes; whereupon the blessed Paul closed the open door and made it fast with a bar. Then Antony sank to the ground at the entrance and until the sixth hour or later craved admission, saying, "Who I am, whence, and why I have come, you know. I know I am not worthy to look upon you: yet unless I see you I will not go away. You welcome beasts: why not a man? I asked and I have found: I knock that it may be opened to me. But if I do not succeed, I will die here on your threshold. You will surely bury me when I am dead."

"Such was his constant cry; unmoved he stood.
To whom the hero thus brief answer made"[1]

"Prayers like these do not mean threats; there is no trickery in tears. Are you surprised at my not welcoming you when you have come here to die?" Thus with smiles Paul gave him access, and, the door being opened, they threw themselves into each other's arms, greeted one another by name, and joined in thanksgiving to God.

10 After the sacred kiss Paul sat down and thus began to address Antony. "Behold the man whom you have sought with so much toil, his limbs decayed with age, his gray hairs unkempt. You see before you a man who ere long will be dust. But love endures all things. Tell me therefore, I pray you, how fares the human race? Are new homes springing up in the ancient cities? What government directs the world? Are there still some remaining for the demons to carry away by their delusions?" Thus conversing they noticed with wonder a raven which had settled on the bough of a tree, and was then flying gently down till it came and laid a whole loaf of bread before them. They were astonished, and when it had gone, "See," said Paul, "the Lord truly loving, truly merciful, has sent us a meal. For the last sixty years I have always received half a loaf: but at your coming Christ has doubled his soldier's rations."

11. Accordingly, having returned thanks to the Lord, they sat down together on the brink of the glassy spring. At this point a dispute arose as to who should break the bread, and nearly the whole day until eventide was spent in the discussion. Paul urged in support of his view the rites of hospitality, Antony pleaded age. At length it was arranged that each should seize the loaf on the side nearest to himself, pull towards him, and keep for his own the part left in his hands. Then on hands and knees they drank a little water from the spring, and offering to God the sacrifice of praise passed the night in vigil. At the return of day the blessed Paul thus spoke to Antony: "I knew long since, brother, that you were dwelling in those parts: long ago God promised you to me for a fellow-servant; but the time of my falling asleep now draws nigh; I have always longed to be dissolved and to be with Christ; my course is finished, and there remains for me a crown of righteousness. Therefore you have been sent by the Lord to lay my poor body in the ground, yea to return earth to earth."

12. On hearing this Antony with tears and groans began to pray that he would not desert him, but would take him for a companion on that journey. His friend replied: "You ought not to seek your own, but another man's good. It is expedient for you to lay aside the burden of the flesh and to follow the Lamb; but it is expedient for the rest of the brethren to be trained by your example. Wherefore be so good as to go and fetch the cloak Bishop Athanasius gave you, to wrap my poor body in." The blessed Paul asked this favour not because he cared much whether his corpse when it decayed were clothed or naked (why should he indeed, when he had so long worn a garment of palm-leaves stitched together?); but that he might soften his friend's regrets at

---

[1] Virg. Æn. ii, 650, and vi, 672.

his decease. Antony was astonished to find Paul had heard of Athanasius and his cloak ; and, seeing as it were Christ Himself in him, he mentally worshipped God without venturing to add a single word ; then silently weeping he once more kissed his eyes and hands, and set out on his return to the monastery which was afterwards seized by the Saracens. His steps lagged behind his will. Yet, exhausted as he was with fasting and broken by age, his courage proved victorious over his years.

13. At last wearied and panting for breath he completed his journey and reached his little dwelling. Here he was met by two disciples who had begun to wait upon him in his advanced age. Said they, " Where have you stayed so long, father ? " He replied, " Woe to me a sinner ! I do not deserve the name of monk. I have seen Elias, I have seen John in the desert, and I have really seen Paul in Paradise." He then closed his lips, beat upon his breast, and brought out the cloak from his cell. When his disciples asked him to explain the matter somewhat more fully he said, " There is a time to keep silence, and a time to speak."

14. He then went out, and without taking so much as a morsel of food returned the same way he came, longing for him alone, thirsting to see him, having eyes and thought for none but him. For he was afraid, and the event proved his anticipations correct, that in his absence his friend might yield up his spirit to Christ. And now another day had dawned and a three hours' journey still remained, when he saw Paul in robes of snowy white ascending on high among the bands of angels, and the choirs of prophets and apostles. Immediately he fell on his face, and threw the coarse sand upon his head, weeping and wailing as he cried, " Why do you cast me from you, Paul ? Why go without one farewell ? Have you made yourself known so late only to depart so soon ? "

15. The blessed Antony used afterwards to relate that he traversed the rest of the distance at such speed that he flew along like a bird; and not without reason : for on entering the cave he saw the lifeless body in a kneeling attitude, with head erect and hands uplifted. The first thing he did, supposing him to be alive, was to pray by his side. But when he did not hear the sighs which usually come from one in prayer, he fell to kisses and tears, and he then understood that even the dead body of the saint with duteous gestures was praying to God unto whom all things live.

16. Then having wrapped up the body and carried it forth, all the while chanting hymns and psalms according to the Christian tradi-

tion, Antony began to lament that he had no implement for digging the ground. So in a surging sea of thought and pondering many plans he said : " If I return to the monastery, there is a four days' journey : if I stay here I shall do no good. I will die then, as is fitting, beside Thy warrior, O Christ, and will quickly breathe my last breath." While he turned these things over in his mind, behold, two lions from the recesses of the desert with manes flying on their necks came rushing along. At first he was horrified at the sight, but again turning his thoughts to God, he waited without alarm, as though they were doves that he saw. They came straight to the corpse of the blessed old man and there stopped, fawned upon it and lay down at its feet, roaring aloud as if to make it known that they were mourning in the only way possible to them. Then they began to paw the ground close by, and vie with one another in excavating the sand, until they dug out a place just large enough to hold a man. And immediately, as if demanding a reward for their work, pricking up their ears while they lowered their heads, they came to Antony and began to lick his hands and feet. He perceived that they were begging a blessing from him, and at once with an outburst of praise to Christ that even dumb animals felt His divinity, he said, " Lord, without whose command not a leaf drops from the tree, not a sparrow falls to the ground, grant them what thou knowest to be best." Then he waved his hand and bade them depart. When they were gone he bent his aged shoulders beneath the burden of the saint's body, laid it in the grave, covered it with the excavated soil, and raised over it the customary mound. Another day dawned, and then, that the affectionate heir might not be without something belonging to the intestate dead, he took for himself the tunic which after the manner of wicker-work the saint had woven out of palm-leaves. And so returning to the monastery he unfolded everything in order to his disciples, and on the feast-days of Easter and Pentecost he always wore Paul's tunic.

17. I may be permitted at the end of this little treatise to ask those who do not know the extent of their possessions, who adorn their homes with marble, who string house to house and field to field, what did this old man in his nakedness ever lack ? Your drinking vessels are of precious stones ; he satisfied his thirst with the hollow of his hand. Your tunics are of wrought gold ; he had not the raiment of the meanest of your slaves. But on the other hand, poor though he was, Paradise is open to him ; you with all your gold will be received into Gehenna. He though naked yet kept the robe of Christ ; you, clad

---

in your silks, have lost the vesture of Christ. Paul lies covered with worthless dust, but will rise again to glory ; over you are raised costly tombs, but both you and your wealth are doomed to the burning. Have a care, I pray you, at least have a care for the riches you love. Why are even the grave-clothes of your dead made of gold? Why does not your vaunting cease even amid mourning and tears ? Cannot the carcases of rich men decay except in silk ?

18. I beseech you, reader, whoever you may be, to remember Jerome the sinner. He, if God would give him his choice, would much sooner take Paul's tunic with his merits, than the purple of kings with their punishment.

THE LIFE OF S. HILARION

The life of Hilarion was written by Jerome in 390 at Bethlehem. Its object was to further the ascetic life to which he was devoted. It contains, amidst much that is legendary, some statements which attach it to genuine history, and is in any case a curious record of the state of the human mind in the 4th century. A theory started in Germany, that it was a sort of religious romance, seems destitute of foundation. It may possibly have been, in Jerome's intention, a contribution to the church history the writing of which he proposed but never executed. (See the Life of Malchus, c. 1.)

1. Before I begin to write the life of the blessed Hilarion I invoke the aid of the Holy Spirit who dwelt in him, that He who bestowed upon the saint his virtues may grant me such power of speech to relate them that my words may be adequate to his deeds. For the virtue of those who have done great deeds is esteemed in proportion to the ability with which it has been praised by men of genius. Alexander the Great of Macedon, who is spoken of by Daniel as the ram, or the panther, or the he-goat, on reaching the grave of Achilles exclaimed, "Happy Youth ! to have the privilege of a great herald of your worth," meaning, of course, Homer. I, however, have to tell the story of the life and conversation of a man so renowned that even Homer were he here would either envy me the theme or prove unequal to it. It is true that that holy man Epiphanius, bishop of Salamis in Cyprus, who had much intercourse with Hilarion, set forth his praises in a short but widely circulated letter. Yet it is one thing to praise the dead in general terms, another to relate their characteristic virtues. And so we in taking up the work begun by him do him service rather than wrong : we despise the abuse of some who as they once disparaged my hero Paulus,[1] will now perhaps disparage Hilarion ; the former they censured for his solitary life ; they may find fault with the latter for his intercourse with the world ; the one was always out of sight, therefore they think he had no existence ; the other was seen by many, therefore he is deemed of no account. It is just what their ancestors the Pharisees did of old ! they were not pleased with [2] John fasting in the desert,

nor with our Lord and Saviour in the busy throng, eating and drinking. But I will put my hand to the work on which I have resolved, and go on my way closing my ears to the barking of Scylla's hounds.

2. The birth place of Hilarion was the village Thabatha, situate about five miles to the south of Gaza, a city of Palestine. His parents were idolaters, and therefore, as the saying is, the rose blossomed on the thorn. By them he was committed to the charge of a Grammarian at Alexandria, where, so far as his age allowed, he gave proofs of remarkable ability and character : and in a short time endeared himself to all and became an accomplished speaker. More important than all this, he was a believer in the Lord Jesus, and took no delight in the madness of the circus, the blood of the arena, the excesses of the theatre : his whole pleasure was in the assemblies of the Church.

3. At that time he heard of the famous name of Antony, which was in the mouth of all the races of Egypt. He was fired with a desire to see him, and set out for the desert. He no sooner saw him than he changed his former mode of life and abode with him about two months, studying the method of his life and the gravity of his conduct : his assiduity in prayer, his humility in his dealings with the brethren, his severity in rebuke, his eagerness in exhortation. He noted too that the saint would never on account of bodily weakness break his rule of abstinence or deviate from the plainness of his food. At last, unable to endure any longer the crowds of those who visited the saint because of various afflictions or the assaults of demons, and deeming it a strange anomaly that he should have to bear in

---

[1] See life of Paulus above.   [2] Matt. xi. 18.

the desert the crowds of the cities, he thought it was better for him to begin as Antony had begun. Said he : "Antony is reaping the reward of victory like a hero who has proved his bravery. I have not entered on the soldier's career." He therefore returned with certain monks to his country, and, his parents being now dead, gave part of his property to his brothers, part to the poor, keeping nothing at all for himself, for he remembered with awe the passage in the Acts of the Apostles and dreaded the example and the punishment of Ananias and Sapphira ; above all he was mindful of the Lord's words,[1] "whosoever he be of you that renounceth not all that he hath, he cannot be my disciple." At this time he was about fifteen years old. Accordingly, stripped bare and armed with the weapons of Christ, he entered the wilderness which stretches to the left seven miles from Majoma, the port of Gaza, as you go along the coast to Egypt. And although the locality had a record of robbery and of blood, and his relatives and friends warned him of the danger he was incurring, he despised death that he might escape death.

4. His courage and tender years would have been a marvel to all, were it not that his heart was on fire and his eyes bright with the gleams and sparks of faith. His cheeks were smooth, his body thin and delicate, unfit to bear the slightest injury which cold or heat could inflict. What then ? With no other covering for his limbs but a shirt of sackcloth, and a cloak of skins which the blessed Antony had given him when he set out, and a blanket of the coarsest sort, he found pleasure in the vast and terrible wilderness with the sea on one side and the marshland on the other. His food was only fifteen dried figs after sunset. And because the district was notorious for brigandage, it was his practice never to abide long in the same place. What was the devil to do ? Whither could he turn ? He who once boasted and said,[2] "I will ascend into heaven, I will set my throne above the stars of the sky, I will be like the most High," saw himself conquered and trodden under foot by a boy whose years did not allow of sin.

5. Satan therefore tickled his senses and, as is his wont, lighted in his maturing body the fires of lust. This mere beginner in Christ's school was forced to think of what he knew not, and to revolve whole trains of thought concerning that of which he had no experience. Angry with himself and beating his bosom (as if with the blow of his hand he could shut out his thoughts) "Ass !" he exclaimed, " I'll stop your kicking, I will not feed you with barley, but with chaff. I will weaken you with hunger and thirst, I will lade you with heavy burdens, I will drive you through heat and cold, that you may think more of food than wantonness." So for three or four days afterwards he sustained his sinking spirit with the juice of herbs and a few dried figs, praying frequently and singing, and hoeing the ground that the suffering of fasting might be doubled by the pain of toil. At the same time he wove baskets of rushes and emulated the discipline of the Egyptian monks, and put into practice the Apostle's precept, [1] " If any will not work, neither let him eat." By these practices he became so enfeebled and his frame so wasted, that his bones scarcely held together.

6 One night he began to hear the wailing of infants, the bleating of flocks, the lowing of oxen, the lament of what seemed to be women, the roaring of lions, the noise of an army, and moreover various portentous cries which made him in alarm shrink from the sound ere he had the sight. He understood that the demons were disporting themselves, and falling on his knees he made the sign of the cross on his forehead. Thus armed as he lay he fought the more bravely, half longing to see those whom he shuddered to hear, and anxiously looking in every direction. Meanwhile all at once in the bright moonlight he saw a chariot with dashing steeds rushing upon him. He called upon Jesus, and suddenly before his eyes, the earth was opened and the whole array was swallowed up. Then he said, [2] " The horse and his rider hath He thrown into the sea." And,[3] " Some trust in chariots, and some in horses ; but we will triumph in the name of the Lord our God."

7. So many were his temptations and so various the snares of demons night and day, that if I wished to relate them, a volume would not suffice. How often when he lay down did naked women appear to him, how often sumptuous feasts when he was hungry ! Sometimes as he prayed a howling wolf sprang past or a snarling fox, and when he sang a gladiatorial show was before him, and a man newly slain would seem to fall at his feet and ask him for burial.

8. Once upon a time he was praying with his head upon the ground. As is the way with men, his attention was withdrawn from his devotions, and he was thinking of something else, when a tormentor sprang upon his back and driving his heels into his sides and beating him across the neck with a horse-whip

---

[1] Luke xiv. 33.   [2] Isa. xiv. 14.

[1] 2 Thess. iii. 10.   [2] Exod. xv. 1.   [3] Ps. xx. 7.

cried out "Come! why are you asleep?" Then with a loud laugh asked if he was tired and would like to have some barley.

9. From his sixteenth to his twentieth year he shielded himself from heat and rain in a little hut which he had constructed of reeds and sedge. Afterwards he built himself a small cell which remains to the present day, five feet in height, that is less than his own height, and only a little more in length. One might suppose it a tomb rather than a house.

10. He shaved his hair once a year on Easter Day, and until his death was accustomed to lie on the bare ground or on a bed of rushes. The sackcloth which he had once put on he never washed, and he used to say that it was going too far to look for cleanliness in goats' hair-cloth. Nor did he change his shirt unless the one he wore was almost in rags. He had committed the Sacred Writings to memory, and after prayer and singing was wont to recite them as if in the presence of God. It would be tedious to narrate singly the successive steps of his spiritual ascent; I will therefore set them in a summary way before my reader, and describe his mode of life at each stage, and will afterwards return to proper historical sequence.

11. From his twentieth to his twenty-seventh year, for three years his food was half a pint of lentils moistened with cold water, and for the next three dry bread with salt and water. From his twenty-seventh year onward to the thirtieth, he supported himself on wild herbs and the raw roots of certain shrubs. From his thirty-first to his thirty-fifth year, he had for food six ounces of barley bread, and vegetables slightly cooked without oil. But finding his eyes growing dim and his whole body shrivelled with a scabby eruption and dry mange, he added oil to his former food and up to the sixty-third year of his life followed this temperate course, tasting neither fruit nor pulse, nor anything whatsoever besides. Then when he saw that his bodily health was broken down, and thought death was near, from his sixty-fourth year to his eightieth he abstained from bread. The fervour of his spirit was so wonderful, that at times when others are wont to allow themselves some laxity of living he appeared to be entering like a novice on the service of the Lord. He made a sort of broth from meal and bruised herbs, food and drink together scarcely weighing six ounces, and, while obeying this rule of diet, he never broke his fast before sunset, not even on festivals nor in severe sickness. But it is now time to return to the course of events.

12. While still living in the hut, at the age of eighteen, robbers came to him by night, either supposing that he had something which they might carry off, or considering that they would be brought into contempt if a solitary boy felt no dread of their attacks. They searched up and down between the sea and the marsh from evening until daybreak without being able to find his resting place. Then, having discovered the boy by the light of day they asked him, half in jest, "What would you do if robbers came to you?" He replied, "He that has nothing does not fear robbers." Said they, "At all events, you might be killed." "I might," said he, "I might; and therefore I do not fear robbers because I am prepared to die." Then they marvelled at his firmness and faith, confessed how they had wandered about in the night, and how their eyes had been blinded, and promised to lead a stricter life in the future.

13. He had now spent twenty-two years in the wilderness and was the common theme in all the cities of Palestine, though everywhere known by repute only. The first person bold enough to break into the presence of the blessed Hilarion was a certain woman of Eleutheropolis who found that she was despised by her husband on account of her sterility (for in fifteen years she had borne no fruit of wedlock). He had no expectation of her coming when she suddenly threw herself at his feet. "Forgive my boldness," she said: "take pity on my necessity. Why do you turn away your eyes? Why shun my entreaties? Do not think of me as a woman, but as an object of compassion. It was my sex that bore the Saviour.[1] They that are whole have no need of a physician, but they that are sick." At length, after a long time he no longer turned away, but looked at the woman and asked the cause of her coming and of her tears. On learning this he raised his eyes to heaven and bade her have faith, then wept over her as she departed. Within a year he saw her with a son.

14. This his first miracle was succeeded by another still greater and more notable. Aristæneté the wife of Elpidius who was afterwards pretorian prefect, a woman well known among her own people, still better known among Christians, on her return with her husband, from visiting the blessed Antony, was delayed at Gaza by the sickness of her three children; for there, whether it was owing to the vitiated atmosphere, or whether it was, as afterwards became clear, for the glory of God's servant Hilarion, they were all alike seized by a semi-tertian ague and despaired of by the physicians. The mother lay wailing, or as one might say walked up and down between the corpses of her three

---

[1] Luke v. 31.

sons not knowing which she should first have to mourn for. When, however, she knew that there was a certain monk in the neighbouring wilderness, forgetting her matronly state (she only remembered she was a mother) she set out accompanied by her hand-maids and eunuchs, and was hardly persuaded by her husband to take an ass to ride upon. On reaching the saint she said, " I pray you by Jesus our most merciful God, I beseech you by His cross and blood, to restore to me my three sons, so that the name of our Lord and Saviour may be glorified in the city of the Gentiles. Then shall his servants enter Gaza and the idol Marnas shall fall to the ground." At first he refused and said that he never left his cell and was not accustomed to enter a house, much less the city; but she threw herself upon the ground and cried repeatedly, " Hilarion, servant of Christ, give me back my children: Antony kept them safe in Egypt, do you save them in Syria." All present were weeping, and the saint himself wept as he denied her. What need to say more? the woman did not leave him till he promised that he would enter Gaza after sunset. On coming thither he made the sign of the cross over the bed and fevered limbs of each, and called upon the name of Jesus. Marvellous efficacy of the Name! As if from three fountains the sweat burst forth at the same time: in that very hour they took food, recognized their mourning mother, and, with thanks to God, warmly kissed the saint's hands. When the matter was noised abroad, and the fame of it spread far and wide, the people flocked to him from Syria and Egypt, so that many believed in Christ and professed themselves monks. For as yet there were no monasteries in Palestine, nor had anyone known a monk in Syria before the saintly Hilarion. It was he who originated this mode of life and devotion, and who first trained men to it in that province. The Lord Jesus had in Egypt the aged Antony: in Palestine He had the youthful Hilarion.

15. Facidia is a hamlet belonging to Rhino-Corura, a city of Egypt. From this village a woman who had been blind for ten years was brought to the blessed Hilarion, and on being presented to him by the brethren (for there were now many monks with him) affirmed that she had spent all her substance on physicians. The saint replied: " If you had given to the poor what you have wasted on physicians, the true physician Jesus would have cured you." But when she cried aloud and entreated pity, he spat into her eyes, in imitation of the Saviour, and with similar instant effect.

16. A charioteer, also of Gaza, stricken by a demon in his chariot became perfectly stiff, so that he could neither move his hand nor bend his neck. He was brought on a litter, but could only signify his petition by moving his tongue; and was told that he could not be healed unless he first believed in Christ and promised to forsake his former occupation. He believed, he promised, and he was healed: and rejoiced more in the saving of the soul than in that of the body.

17. Again, a very powerful youth called Marsitas from the neighbourhood of Jerusalem plumed himself so highly on his strength that he carried fifteen bushels of grain for a long time and over a considerable distance, and considered it as his highest glory that he could beat the asses in endurance. This man was afflicted with a grievous demon and could not endure chains, or fetters, but broke even the bolts and bars of the doors. He had bitten off the noses and ears of many: had broken the feet of some, the legs of others. He had struck such terror of himself into everybody, that he was laden with chains and dragged by ropes on all sides like a wild bull to the monastery. As soon as the brethren saw him they were greatly alarmed (for the man was of gigantic size) and told the Father. He, seated as he was, commanded him to be brought to him and released. When he was free, " Bow your head," said he, " and come." The man began to tremble; he twisted his neck round and did not dare to look him in the face, but laid aside all his fierceness and began to lick his feet as he sat. At last the demon which had possessed the young man being tortured by the saint's adjurations came forth on the seventh day.

18. Nor must we omit to tell that Orion, a leading man and wealthy citizen of Aira, on the coast of the Red Sea, being possessed by a legion of demons was brought to him. Hands, neck, sides, feet were laden with iron, and his glaring eyes portended an access of raging madness. As the saint was walking with the brethren and expounding some passage of Scripture the man broke from the hands of his keepers, clasped him from behind and raised him aloft. There was a shout from all, for they feared lest he might crush his limbs wasted as they were with fasting. The saint smiled and said, " Be quiet, and let me have my rival in the wrestling match to myself." Then he bent back his hand over his shoulder till he touched the man's head, seized his hair and drew him round so as to be foot to foot with him; he then stretched both his hands in a straight line, and trod on his two feet with both his own, while he cried out again and again, " To torment with you! ye crowd of demons, to torment!" The sufferer shouted aloud

and bent back his neck till his head touched the ground, while the saint said, " Lord Jesus, release this wretched man, release this captive. Thine it is to conquer many, no less than one." What I now relate is unparalleled : from one man's lips were heard different voices and as it were the confused shouts of a multitude. Well, he too was cured, and not long after came with his wife and children to the monastery bringing many gifts expressive of his gratitude. The saint thus addressed him—" Have you not read what befell Gehazi and Simon, one of whom took a reward, the other offered it, the former in order to sell grace, the latter to buy it ?" And when Orion said with tears, " Take it and give it to the poor," he replied, " You can best distribute your own gifts, for you tread the streets of the cities and know the poor. Why should I who have forsaken my own seek another man's ? To many the name of the poor is a pretext for their avarice ; but compassion knows no artifices. No one better spends than he who keeps nothing for himself." The man was sad and lay upon the ground. " Be not sad, my son," he said ; " what I do for my own good I do also for yours. If I were to take these gifts I should myself offend God, and, moreover, the legion would return to you."

19. There is a story relating to Majomites of Gaza which it is impossible to pass over in silence. While quarrying building stones on the shore not far from the monastery he was helplessly paralysed, and after being carried to the saint by his fellow-workman immediately returned to his work in perfect health. I ought to explain that the shore of Palestine and Egypt naturally consists of soft sand and gravel which gradually becomes consolidated and hardens into rock ; and thus though to the eye it remains the same it is no longer the same to the touch.

20. Another story relates to Italicus, a citizen of the same town. He was a Christian and kept horses for the circus to contend against those of the Duumvir of Gaza who was a votary of the idol god Marnas. This custom at least in Roman cities was as old as the days of Romulus, and was instituted in commemoration of the successful seizure of the Sabine women. The chariots raced seven times round the circus in honour of Consus in his character of the God of Counsel.[1] Victory lay with the team which tired out the horses opposed to them. Now the rival of Italicus had in his pay a magician to incite his horses by certain demoniacal incantations, and keep back those of his opponent. Italicus there-

fore came to the blessed Hilarion and besought his aid not so much for the injury of his adversary as for protection for himself. It seemed absurd for the venerable old man to waste prayers on trifles of this sort. He therefore smiled and said, " Why do you not rather give the price of the horses to the poor for the salvation of your soul ?" His visitor replied that his office was a public duty, and that he acted not so much from choice as from compulsion, that no Christian man could employ magic, but would rather seek aid from a servant of Christ, especially against the people of Gaza who were enemies of God, and who would exult over the Church of Christ more than over him. At the request therefore of the brethren who were present he ordered an earthenware cup out of which he was wont to drink to be filled with water and given to Italicus. The latter took it and sprinkled it over his stable and horses, his charioteers and his chariot, and the barriers of the course. The crowd was in a marvellous state of excitement, for the enemy in derision had published the news of what was going to be done, and the backers of Italicus were in high spirits at the victory which they promised themselves. The signal is given ; the one team flies towards the goal, the other sticks fast : the wheels are glowing hot beneath the chariot of the one, while the other scarce catches a glimpse of their opponents' backs as they flit past. The shouts of the crowd swell to a roar, and the heathens themselves with one voice declare Marnas is conquered by Christ. After this the opponents in their rage demanded that Hilarion as a Christian magician should be dragged to execution. This decisive victory and several others which followed in successive games of the circus caused many to turn to the faith.

21. There was a youth in the neighbourhood of the same market-town of Gaza who was desperately in love with one of God's virgins. After he had tried again and again those touches, jests, nods, and whispers which so commonly lead to the destruction of virginity, but had made no progress by these means, he went to a magician at Memphis to whom he proposed to make known his wretched state, and then, fortified with his arts, to return to his assault upon the virgin. Accordingly after a year's instruction by the priest of Æsculapius, who does not heal souls but destroys them, he came full of the lust which he had previously allowed his mind to entertain, and buried beneath the threshold of the girl's house certain magical formulæ and revolting figures engraven on a plate of Cyprian brass. Thereupon the maid began to show signs of insanity, to throw away the covering of her

---

[1] He was also the god of agricultural fertility. The festival of the Consualia, supposed to have been instituted by Romulus, was on August 21.

head, tear her hair, gnash her teeth, and loudly call the youth by name. Her intense affection had become a frenzy. Her parents therefore brought her to the monastery and delivered her to the aged saint. No sooner was this done than the devil began to howl and confess. " I was compelled, I was carried off against my will. How happy I was when I used to beguile the men of Memphis in their dreams! What crosses, what torture I suffer! You force me to go out, and I am kept bound under the threshold. I cannot go out unless the young man who keeps me there lets me go." The old man answered, "Your strength must be great indeed, if a bit of thread and a plate can keep you bound. Tell me, how is it that you dared to enter into this maid who belongs to God?" "That I might preserve her as a virgin," said he. " You preserve her, betrayer of chastity! Why did you not rather enter into him who sent you?" "For what purpose," he answers, "should I enter into one who was in alliance with a comrade of my own, the demon of love?" But the saint would not command search to be made for either the young man or the charms till the maiden had undergone a process of purgation, for fear that it might be thought that the demon had been released by means of incantations, or that he himself had attached credit to what he said. He declared that demons are deceitful and well versed in dissimulation, and sharply rebuked the virgin when she had recovered her health for having by her conduct given an opportunity for the demon to enter.

22. It was not only in Palestine and the neighbouring cities of Egypt or Syria that he was in high repute, but his fame had reached distant provinces. An officer[1] of the Emperor Constantius whose golden hair and personal beauty revealed his country (it lay between the Saxons and the Alemanni, was of no great extent but powerful, and is known to historians as Germany, but is now called France), had long, that is to say from infancy, been pursued by a devil, who forced him in the night to howl, groan, and gnash his teeth. He therefore secretly asked the Emperor for a post-warrant, plainly telling him why he wanted it, and having also obtained letters to the legate at Palestine came with great pomp and a large retinue to Gaza. On his inquiring of the local senators where Hilarion the monk dwelt, the people of Gaza were much alarmed, and supposing that he had been sent by the Emperor, brought him to the monastery, that they might show respect to one so highly accredited, and that, if

any guilt had been incurred by them by injuries previously done by them to Hilarion it might be obliterated by their present dutifulness. The old man at the time was taking a walk on the soft sands and was humming some passage or other from the psalms. Seeing so great a company approaching he stopped, and having returned the salutes of all while he raised his hand and gave them his blessing, after an hour's interval he bade the rest withdraw, but would have his visitor together with servants and officers remain: for by the man's eyes and countenance he knew the cause of his coming. Immediately on being questioned by the servant of God the man sprang up on tiptoe, so as scarcely to touch the ground with his feet, and with a wild roar replied in Syriac in which language he had been interrogated. Pure Syriac was heard flowing from the lips of a barbarian who knew only French and Latin, and that without the absence of a sibilant, or an aspirate, or an idiom of the speech of Palestine. The demon then confessed by what means he had entered into him. Further, that his interpreters who knew only Greek and Latin might understand, Hilarion questioned him also in Greek, and when he gave the same answer in the same words and alleged in excuse many occasions on which spells had been laid upon him, and how he was bound to yield to magic arts, " I care not," said the saint, "how you came to enter, but I command you in the name of our Lord Jesus Christ to come out." The man, as soon as he was healed, with a rough simplicity offered him ten pounds of gold. But the saint took from him only bread, and told him that they who were nourished on such food regarded gold as mire.

23. It is not enough to speak of men; brute animals were also daily brought to him in a state of madness, and among them a Bactrian camel of enormous size amid the shouts of thirty men or more who held him tight with stout ropes. He had already injured many. His eyes were bloodshot, his mouth filled with foam, his rolling tongue swollen, and above every other source of terror was his loud and hideous roar. Well, the old man ordered him to be let go. At once those who brought him as well as the attendants of the saint fled away without exception. The saint went by himself to meet him, and addressing him in Syriac said, "You do not alarm me, devil, huge though your present body is. Whether in a fox or a camel you are just the same." Meanwhile he stood with outstretched hand. The brute raging and looking as if he would devour Hilarion came up to him, but immediately fell down, laid its head on the ground, and to the amazement of all present showed suddenly no

[1] Or secretary—Candidatus, a quæstor appointed by the Emperor to read his rescripts, etc.

ess tameness than it had exhibited ferocity before. But the old man declared to them how the devil, for men's sake, seizes even beasts of burden; that he is inflamed by such intense hatred for men that he desires to destroy not only them but what belongs to them. As an illustration of this he added the fact that before he was permitted to try the saintly Job, he made an end of all his substance. Nor ought it to disturb anyone that[1] by the Lord's command two thousand swine were slain by the agency of demons, since those who witnessed the miracle could not have believed that so great a multitude of demons had gone out of the man unless an equally vast number of swine had rushed to ruin, showing that it was a legion that impelled them.

24 Time would fail me if I wished to relate all the miracles which were wrought by him. For to such a pitch of glory was he raised by the Lord that the blessed Antony among the rest hearing of his life wrote to him and gladly received his letters. And if ever the sick from Syria came to him he would say to them, 'Why have you taken the trouble to come so far, when you have there my son Hilarion?" Following his example, however, innumerable monasteries sprang up throughout the whole of Palestine, and all the monks flocked to him. When he saw this he praised the Lord for His grace, and exhorted them individually to the profit of their souls, telling them that the fashion of this world passes away, and that the true life is that which is purchased by suffering in the present.

25. Wishing to set the monks an example of humility and of zeal he was accustomed on fixed days before the vintage to visit their cells. When the brethren knew this they would all come together to meet him, and in company with their distinguished leader go the round of the monasteries, taking with them provisions, because sometimes as many as two thousand men were assembled. But, as time went on, all the settlements round gladly gave food to the neighbouring monks for the entertainment of the saints. Moreover, the care he took to prevent any brother however humble or poor being passed over is evidenced by the journey which he once took into the desert of Cades to visit one of his disciples. With a great company of monks he reached Elusa, as it happened on the day when the annual festival had brought all the people together to the temple of Venus. This goddess is worshipped on account of Lucifer to whom the Saracen nation is devoted. The very town too is to a great extent semi-bar-

barous, owing to its situation. When therefore it was heard that Saint Hilarion was passing through (he had frequently healed many Saracens possessed by demons), they went to meet him in crowds with their wives and children, bending their heads and crying in the Syriac tongue *Barech*, that is, *Bless*. He received them with courtesy and humility, and prayed that they might worship God rather than stones; at the same time, weeping copiously, he looked up to heaven and promised that if they would believe in Christ he would visit them often. By the marvellous grace of God they did not suffer him to depart before he had drawn the outline of a church, and their priest with his garland upon his head had been signed with the sign of Christ.

26. Another year, again, when he was setting out to visit the monasteries and was drawing up a list of those with whom he must stay and whom he must see in passing, the monks knowing that one of their number was a niggard, and being at the same time desirous to cure his complaint, asked the saint to stay with him. He replied, " Do you wish me to inflict injury on you and annoyance on the brother?" The niggardly brother on hearing of this was ashamed, and with the strenuous support of all his brethren, at length obtained from the saint a reluctant promise to put his monastery on the roll of his resting places. Ten days after they came to him and found the keepers already on guard in the vineyard through which their course lay, to keep off all comers with stones and clods and slings. In the morning they all departed without having eaten a grape, while the old man smiled and pretended not to know what had happened.

27. Once when they were being entertained by another monk whose name was Sabus (we must not of course give the name of the niggard, we may tell that of this generous man), because it was the Lord's day, they were all invited by him into the vineyard so that before the hour for food came they might relieve the toil of the journey by a repast of grapes. Said the saint, " Cursed be he who looks for the refreshment of the body before that of the soul. Let us pray, let us sing, let us do our duty to God, and then we will hasten to the vineyard." When the service was over, he stood on an eminence and blessed the vineyard and let his own sheep go to their pasture. Now those who partook were not less than three thousand. And whereas the whole vineyard had been estimated at a hundred flagons, within thirty days he made it worth three hundred. The niggardly brother gathered much less than usual, and he was grieved to find that even what he had turned to vinegar. The old man had predicted this to many

---

[1] Matt. viii. and Mark v.

brethren before it happened. He particularly abhorred such monks as were led by their lack of faith to hoard for the future, and were careful about expense, or raiment, or some other of those things which pass away with the world.

28. Lastly he would not even look at one of the brethren who lived about five miles off because he ascertained that he very jealously guarded his bit of ground, and had a little money. The offender wishing to be reconciled to the old man often came to the brethren, and in particular to Hesychius who was specially dear to Hilarion. One day accordingly he brought a bundle of green chick-pea just as it had been gathered. Hesychius placed it on the table against the evening, whereupon the old man cried out that he could not bear the stench, and asked where it came from. Hesychius replied that a certain brother had sent the brethren the first fruits of his ground. "Don't you notice," said he, "the horrid stench, and detect the foul odour of avarice in the peas? Send it to the cattle, send to the brute-beasts and see whether they can eat it." No sooner was it in obedience to his command laid in the manger than the cattle in the wildest alarm and bellowing loudly broke their fastenings and fled in different directions. For the old man was enabled by grace to tell from the odour of bodies and garments, and the things which any one had touched, by what demon or with what vice the individual was distressed.

29. His sixty-third year found the old man at the head of a grand monastery and a multitude of resident brethren. There were such crowds of persons constantly bringing those who suffered from various kinds of sickness or were possessed of unclean spirits, that the whole circuit of the wilderness was full of all sorts of people. And as the saint saw all this he wept daily and called to mind with incredible regret his former mode of life. When one of the brethren asked him why he was so dejected he replied, "I have returned again to the world and have received my reward in my lifetime. The people of Palestine and the adjoining province think me of some importance, and under pretence of a monastery for the well-ordering of the brethren I have all the apparatus of a paltry life about me." The brethren, however, kept watch over him and in particular Hesychius, who had a marvellously devoted affection and veneration for the old man. After he had spent two years in these lamentations Aristæneté the lady of whom we made mention before, as being then the wife of a prefect though without any of a prefect's ostentation, came to him intending to pay a visit to Antony also. He said to her, "I should like to go myself too if I were not kept a prisoner in this monastery, and if my going could

be fruitful. For it is now two days since mankind was bereaved of him who was so truly a father to them all." She believed his word and stayed where she was: and after a few days the news came that Antony had fallen asleep.

30. Some may wonder at the miracles he worked, or his incredible fasting, knowledge and humility. Nothing so astonishes me as his power to tread under foot honour and glory. Bishops, presbyters, crowds of clergymen and monks, of Christian matrons even (a great temptation), and a rabble from all quarters in town and country were congregating about him, and even judges and others holding high positions, that they might receive at his hands the bread or oil which he had blessed. But he thought of nothing but solitude, so much so that one day he determined to be gone, and having procured an ass (he was almost exhausted with fasting and could scarcely walk) endeavoured to steal away. The news spread far and wide, and, just as if a public mourning for the desolation of Palestine were decreed, ten thousand people of various ages and both sexes came together to prevent his departure. He was unmoved by entreaties and striking the sand with his stick kept saying: "I will not make my Lord a deceiver I cannot look upon churches overthrown, Christ's altars trodden down, the blood of my sons poured out." All who were present began to understand that some secret had been revealed to him which he was unwilling to confess, but they none the less kept guard over him that he might not go. He therefore determined, and publicly called all to witness that he would take neither food nor drink unless he were released. Only after seven days was he relieved from his fasting; when having bidden farewell to numerous friends he came to Betilium attended by a countless multitude. There he prevailed upon the crowd to return and chose as his companions forty monks who had resources for the journey and were capable of travelling during fasting-time, that is, after sunset. He then visited the brethren who were in the neighbouring desert and sojourning at a place called Lychnos, and after three days came to the castle of Theubatus to see Dracontius, bishop and confessor, who was in exile there. The bishop was beyond measure cheered by the presence of so distinguished a man. At the end of another three days he set out for Babylon and arrived there after a hard journey. Then he visited Philo the bishop who was also a confessor; for the Emperor Constantius who favoured the Arian heresy had transported both of them to those parts Departing thence he came in three days t

he town Aphroditon. There he met with a leacon Baisanes who kept dromedaries which were hired, on account of the scarcity of water n the desert, to carry travellers who wished o visit Antony. He then made known to the brethren that the anniversary of the blessed Antony's decease was at hand, and that he must spend a whole night in vigil in the very place where the saint had died. So then after three days' journey through the waste and terrible desert they at length came to a very high mountain, and there found two monks, Isaac and Pelusianus, the former of whom had been one of Antony's attendants.[1]

31. The occasion seems a fitting one, since we are on the spot itself, to describe the abode of this great man. There is a high and rocky mountain extending for about a mile, with gushing springs amongst its spurs, the waters of which are partly absorbed by the sand, partly flow towards the plain and gradually form a stream shaded on either side by countless palms which lend much pleasantness and charm to the place. Here the old man might be seen pacing to and fro with the disciples of blessed Antony. Here, so they said, Antony himself used to sing, pray, work, and rest when weary. Those vines and shrubs were planted by his own hand: that garden bed was his own design. This pool for watering the garden was made by him after much toil. That hoe was handled by him for many years. Hilarion would lie upon the saint's bed and as though it were still warm would affectionately kiss it. The cell was square, its sides measuring no more than the length of a sleeping man. Moreover on the lofty mountain-top, the ascent of which was by a zig-zag path very difficult, were to be seen two cells of the same dimensions, in which he stayed when he escaped from the crowds of visitors or the company of his disciples. These were cut out of the live rock and were only furnished with doors. When they came to the garden, "You see," said Isaac, "this garden with its shrubs and green vegetables; about three years ago it was ravaged by a troop of wild asses. One of their leaders was bidden by Antony to stand still while he thrashed the animals' sides with a stick and wanted to know why they devoured what they had not sown. And ever afterwards, excepting the water which they were accustomed to come and drink, they never touched anything, not a bush or a vegetable." The old man further asked to be shown his burial place, and they thereupon took him aside ; but whether they showed him the tomb or not is unknown. It is related that the motive for secrecy was compliance

with Antony's orders and to prevent Pergamius, a very wealthy man of the district, from removing the saint's body to his house and erecting a shrine to his memory.

32. Having returned to Aphroditon and keeping with him only two of the brethren, he stayed in the neighbouring desert, and practised such rigid abstinence and silence that he felt that then for the first time he had begun to serve Christ. Three years had now elapsed since the heavens had been closed and the land had suffered from drought, and it was commonly said that even the elements were lamenting the death of Antony. Hilarion did not remain unknown to the inhabitants of that place any more than to others, but men and women with ghastly faces and wasted by hunger earnestly entreated the servant of Christ, as being the blessed Antony's successor, to give them rain. Hilarion when he saw them was strangely affected with compassion and, raising his eyes to heaven and lifting up both his hands, he at once obtained their petition. But, strange to say, that parched and sandy district, after the rain had fallen, unexpectedly produced such vast numbers of serpents and poisonous animals that many who would have been bitten would have died at once if they had not run to Hilarion. He therefore blessed some oil with which all the husbandmen and shepherds touched their wounds, and found an infallible cure.

33. Seeing that even there surprising respect was paid to him, he went to Alexandria, intending to cross from thence to the farther oasis of the desert. And because he had never stayed in cities since he entered on the monk's life, he turned aside to some brethren at Bruchium, not far from Alexandria, whom he knew, and who welcomed the old man with the greatest pleasure. It was now night when all at once they heard his disciples saddling the ass and making ready for the journey. They therefore threw themselves at his feet and besought him not to leave them ; they fell prostrate before the door, and declared they would rather die than lose such a guest. He answered : "My reason for hastening away is that I may not give you trouble. You will no doubt afterwards discover that I have not suddenly left without good cause." Next day the authorities of Gaza with the lictors of the prefect having heard of his arrival on the previous day, entered the monastery, and when they failed to find him anywhere they began to say to one another : "What we heard is true. He is a magician and knows the future." The fact was that the city of Gaza on Julian's accession to the throne, after the departure of Hilarion from Palestine and the destruction of his monastery, had pre-

[1] Interpres. Probably one who spoke for him to the people, as Elijah had Elisha as his attendant.

sented a petition to the Emperor requesting that both Hilarion and Hesychius might be put to death, and a proclamation had been published everywhere that search should be made for them.

34. Having then left Bruchium, he entered the oasis through the trackless desert, and there abode for a year, more or less. But, inasmuch as his fame had travelled thither also, he felt that he could not be hidden in the East, where he was known to many by report and by sight, and began to think of taking ship for some solitary island, so that having been exposed to public view by the land, he might at least find concealment in the sea. Just about that time Hadrian, his disciple, arrived from Palestine with information that Julian was slain and that a Christian emperor [1] had commenced his reign ; he ought therefore, it was said, to return to the relics of his monastery. But he, when he heard this, solemnly refused to return ; and hiring a camel crossed the desert waste and reached Paretonium, a city on the coast of Libya. There the ill-starred Hadrian wishing to return to Palestine and unwilling to part with the renown so long attaching to his master's name, heaped reproaches upon him, and at last having packed up the presents which he had brought him from the brethren, set out without the knowledge of Hilarion. As I shall have no further opportunity of referring to this man, I would only record, for the terror of those who despise their masters, that after a little while he was attacked by the king's-evil [2] and turned to a mass of corruption.

35. The old man accompanied by Gazanus went on board a ship which was sailing to Sicily. Half way across the Adriatic he was preparing to pay his fare by selling a copy of the Gospels which he had written with his own hand in his youth, when the son of the master of the ship seized by a demon began to cry out and say : " Hilarion, servant of God, why is it that through you we cannot be safe even on the sea ? Spare me a little until I reach land. Let me not be cast out here and thrown into the deep." The saint replied : " If my God permit you to remain, remain ; but if He casts you out, why bring odium upon me a sinner and a beggar ? " This he said that the sailors and merchants on board might not betray him on reaching shore. Not long after, the boy was cleansed, his father and the rest who were present having given their word that they would not reveal the name of the saint to any one.

36. On approaching Pachynus, a promontory of Sicily, he offered the master the Gospel for the passage of himself and Gazanus. The man was unwilling to take it, all the more because he saw that excepting that volume and the clothes they wore they had nothing, and at last he swore he would not take it. But the aged saint, ardent and confident in the consciousness of his poverty, rejoiced exceedingly that he had no worldly possessions and was accounted a beggar by the people of the place.

37. Once more, on thinking the matter over and fearing that merchants coming from the East might make him known, he fled to the interior, some twenty miles from the sea, and there on an abandoned piece of ground, every day tied up a bundle of firewood which he laid upon the back of his disciple, and sold at some neighbouring mansion. They thus supported themselves and were able to purchase a morsel of bread for any chance visitors. But that came exactly to pass which is written : [1] " a city set on a hill cannot be hid." It happened that one of the shields-men [2] who was vexed by a demon was in the basilica of the blessed Peter at Rome, when the unclean spirit within him cried out, " A few days ago Christ's servant Hilarion entered Sicily and no one knew him, and he thinks he is hidden. I will go and betray him." Immediately he embarked with his attendants in a ship lying in harbour sailed to Pachynus and, led by the demon to the old man's hut, there prostrated himself and was cured on the spot. This, his first miracle in Sicily, brought the sick to him in countless numbers (but it brought also a multitude of religious persons) ; insomuch that one of the leading men who was swollen with the dropsy was cured the same day that he came. He afterwards offered the saint gifts without end, but the saint replied to him in the words of the Saviour to his disciples : [3] " Freely ye received, freely give."

38. While this was going on in Sicily Hesychius his disciple was searching the world over for the old man, traversing the coast, penetrating deserts, clinging all the while to the belief that wherever he was he could not long be hidden. At the end of three years he heard at Methona from a certain Jew, who dealt in old-clothes, that a Christian prophet had appeared in Sicily, and was working such miracles and signs, one might think him one of the ancient saints. So he asked about his dress, gait and speech, and in particular his age, but could learn nothing. His informant merely

[1] Jovian, A. D., 363-4.
[2] Morbo regio. The dictionaries give " jaundice " as the meaning, but it is universally used in modern times for scrofula. Here it seems to mean leprosy.

[1] Matt. v. 14.
[2] Scutarius, one of a corps of guards, whose prominent weapons were shields.
[3] Matt. x. 8.

eclared that he had heard of the man by report. He therefore crossed the Adriatic and
after a prosperous voyage came to Pachynus, where he took up his abode in a cottage
on the shore of the bay, and, on inquiring for
tidings of the old man, discovered by the tale
which every one told him where he was, and
what he was doing. Nothing about him surprised them all so much as the fact that after
such great signs and wonders he had not
accepted even a crust of bread from any one
in the district. And, to cut my story short,
the holy man Hesychius fell down at his master's knees and bedewed his feet with tears;
at length he was gently raised by him, and
when two or three days had been spent in
talking over matters, he learned from Gazanus
that Hilarion no longer felt himself able to
live in those parts, but wanted to go to certain
barbarous races where his name and fame were
unknown.

39. He therefore brought him to Epidaurus,[1]
a town in Dalmatia, where he stayed for a few
days in the country near, but could not be
hid. An enormous serpent, of the sort which
the people of those parts call *boas*[2] because
they are so large that they often swallow oxen,
was ravaging the whole province far and wide,
and was devouring not only flocks and herds,
but husbandmen and shepherds who were
drawn in by the force of its breathing. He
ordered a pyre to be prepared for it, then
sent up a prayer to Christ, called forth the
reptile, bade it climb the pile of wood, and
then applied the fire. And so before all the
people he burnt the savage beast to ashes.
But now he began anxiously to ask what he
was to do, whither to betake himself. Once
more he prepared for flight, and in thought
ranged through solitary lands, grieving that
his miracles could speak of him though his
tongue was silent.

40. At that time there was an earthquake
over the whole world, following on the death
of Julian, which caused the sea to burst its
bounds, and left ships hanging on the edge of
mountain steeps. It seemed as though God were
threatening a second deluge, or all things were
returning to original chaos. When the people
of Epidaurus saw this, I mean the roaring
waves and heaving waters and the swirling
billows mountain-high dashing on the shore,
fearing that what they saw had happened elsewhere might befall them and their town be
utterly destroyed, they made their way to the
old man, and as if preparing for a battle
placed him on the shore. After making the
sign of the cross three times on the sand, he

faced the sea, stretched out his hands, and no
one would believe to what a height the swelling sea stood like a wall before him. It
roared for a long time as if indignant at the
barrier, then little by little sank to its level.
Epidaurus and all the region roundabout tell
the story to this day, and mothers teach their
children to hand down the remembrance of
it to posterity. Verily, what was said to the
Apostles,[1] "If ye have faith, ye shall say to this
mountain, Remove into the sea, and it shall be
done," may be even literally fulfilled, provided
one has such faith as the Lord commanded
the Apostles to have. For what difference
does it make whether a mountain descends
into the sea, or huge mountains of waters
everywhere else fluid suddenly become hard
as rock at the old man's feet?

41. The whole country marvelled and the
fame of the great miracle was in everyone's
mouth, even at Salonæ.[2] When the old man
knew this was the case he escaped secretly by
night in a small cutter, and finding a merchant
ship after two days came to Cyprus. Between
[3] Malea and [4] Cythera, the pirates, who had left
on the shore that part of their fleet which is
worked by poles instead of sails, bore down on
them with two light vessels of considerable
size; and besides this they were buffeted by
the waves on every side. All the rowers began
to be alarmed, to weep, to leave their places,
to get out their poles, and, as though one
message was not enough, again and again told
the old man that pirates were at hand. Looking at them in the distance he gently smiled,
then turned to his disciples and said,[5] "O ye
of little faith, wherefore do ye doubt? Are
these more than the army of Pharaoh? Yet
they were all drowned by the will of God."
Thus he spake, but none the less the enemy
with foaming prows kept drawing nearer and
were now only a stone's throw distant. He
stood upon the prow of the vessel facing them
with out-stretched hand, and said, "Thus far
and no farther." Marvellous to relate, the
boats at once bounded back, and though
urged forward by the oars fell farther and
farther astern. The pirates were astonished
to find themselves going back, and laboured
with all their strength to reach the vessel, but
were carried to the shore faster by far than
they came.

42. I pass by the rest for fear I should seem
in my history to be publishing a volume of
miracles. I will only say this, that when sailing
with a fair wind among the Cyclades he heard
the voices of unclean spirits shouting in all

---

[1] More properly in Argolis. It was the native town of Æscu-
apius, who was worshipped under the form of a serpent.
[2] *Boas* because they can swallow oxen (*boves*).

[1] Matt. xvii. 20 sq.
[2] In Dalmatia, three miles from Diocletian's great palace (Spa-
latro). [3] The southern promontory of Greece.
[4] Now Cerigo. [5] Matt. xiv. 32.

directions from towns and villages, and running in crowds to the shore. Having then entered Paphos, the city of Cyprus renowned in the songs of the poets, the ruins of whose temples after frequent earthquakes are the only evidences at the present day of its former grandeur, he began to live in obscurity about two miles from the city, and rejoiced in having a few days' rest. But not quite twenty days passed before throughout the whole island whoever had unclean spirits began to cry out that Hilarion Christ's servant had come, and that they must go to him with all speed. Salamis, Curium, Lapetha, and the other cities joined in the cry, while many declared that they knew Hilarion and that he was indeed the servant of Christ, but where he was they could not tell. So within a trifle more than thirty days, about two hundred people, both men and women, came together to him. When he saw them he lamented that they would not suffer him to be quiet, and thirsting in a kind of manner to avenge himself, he lashed them with such urgency of prayer that some immediately, others after two or three days, all within a week, were cured.

43. Here he stayed two years, always thinking of flight, and in the meantine sent Hesychius, who was to return in the spring, to Palestine to salute the brethren and visit the ashes of his monastery. When the latter returned he found Hilarion longing to sail again to Egypt, that is to the locality called [1] Bucolia ; but he persuaded him that, since there were no Christians there, but only a fierce and barbarous people, he should rather go to a spot in Cyprus itself which was higher up and more retired. After long and diligent search he found such a place twelve miles from the sea far off among the recesses of rugged mountains, the ascent to which could hardly be accomplished by creeping on hands and knees. Thither he conducted him. The old man entered and gazed around. It was indeed a lonely and terrible place ; for though surrounded by trees on every side, with water streaming from the brow of the hill, a delightful bit of garden, and fruit-trees in abundance (of which, however, he never ate), yet it had close by the ruins of an ancient temple from which, as he himself was wont to relate and his disciples testify, the voices of such countless demons re-echoed night and day, that you might have thought there was an army of them. He was highly pleased at the idea of having his opponents in the neighbourhood, and abode there five years, cheered in these his last days by the frequent visits of Hesychius, for owing to the

steep and rugged ascent, and the numerous ghosts (so the story ran), nobody or scarcely anybody either could or dared to go up to him. One day, however, as he was leaving his garden, he saw a man completely paralysed lying in front of the gates. He asked Hesychius who he was, or how he had been brought. Hesychius replied that he was the agent at the country-house to which the garden belonged in which they were located. Weeping much and stretching out his hand to the prostrate man he said, " I bid you in the name of our Lord Jesus Christ arise and walk." The words were still on the lips of the speaker, when, with miraculous speed, the limbs were strengthened and the man arose and stood firm. Once this was noised abroad the need of many overcame even the pathless journey and the dangers of the place. The occupants of all the houses round about had nothing so much in their thoughts as to prevent the possibility of his escape, a rumour having spread concerning him to the effect that he could not stay long in the same place. This habit of his was not due to levity or childishness, but to the fact that he shunned the worry of publicity and praise, and always longed for silence and a life of obscurity.

44. In his eightieth year, during the absence of Hesychius, he wrote by way of a will a short letter with his own hand, and left him all his riches (that is to say, a copy of the gospels, and his sack-cloth tunic, cowl and cloak), for his servant had died a few days before. Many devout men therefore came to the invalid from Paphos, and specially because they had heard of his saying that he must soon migrate to the Lord and must be liberated from the bonds of the body. There came also Constantia a holy woman whose son-in-law and daughter he had anointed with oil and saved from death. He earnestly entreated them all not to let him be kept even a moment of time after death, but to bury him immediately in the same garden, just as he was, clad in his goat-hair tunic, cowl, and his peasant's cloak.

45. His body was now all but cold, and nought was left of life but reason. Yet with eyes wide open he kept repeating, " Go forth, what do you fear ? Go forth, my soul, why do you hesitate ? You have served Christ nearly seventy years, and do you fear death ? " Thus saying he breathed his last. He was immediately buried before the city heard of his death.

46. When the holy man Hesychius heard of his decease, he went to Cyprus and, to lull the suspicions of the natives who were keeping strict guard, pretended that he wished to live in the same garden, and then in the course of about ten months, though at great peril to his

---

[1] Probably the place which gave its name to one of the mouths of the Nile (Bucolicum).

life, stole the saint's body. He carried it to Majuma ; and there all the monks and crowds of towns-folk going in procession laid it to rest in the ancient monastery. His tunic, cowl and cloak, were uninjured ; the whole body as perfect as if alive, and so fragrant with sweet odours that one might suppose it to have been embalmed.

47. In bringing my book to an end I think I ought not to omit to mention the devotion of the holy woman Constantia who, when a message was brought her that Hilarion's body was in Palestine, immediately died, proving even by death the sincerity of her love for the servant of God. For she was accustomed to spend whole nights in vigil at his tomb, and to converse with him as if he were present in order to stimulate her prayers. Even at the present day one may see a strange dispute between the people of Palestine and the Cypriotes, the one contending that they have the body, the other the spirit of Hilarion. And yet in both places great miracles are wrought daily, but to a greater extent in the garden of Cyprus, perhaps because that spot was dearest to him.

THE LIFE OF MALCHUS, THE CAPTIVE MONK

The life of Malchus was written at Bethlehem, A.D., 391. Its origin and purpose are sufficiently described in chapters 1 and 2.

---

1. They who have to fight a naval battle prepare for it in harbours and calm waters by adjusting the helm, plying the oars, and making ready the hooks and grappling irons. They draw up the soldiers on the decks and accustom them to stand steady with poised foot and on slippery ground ; so that they may not shrink from all this when the real encounter comes, because they have had experience of it in the sham fight. And so it is in my case. I have long held my peace, because silence was imposed on me by one to whom I give pain when I speak of him. But now, in preparing to write history on a wider scale I desire to practise myself by means of this little work, and as it were to wipe the rust from my tongue. For I have purposed (if God grant me life, and if my censurers will at length cease to persecute me, now that I am a fugitive and shut up in a monastery) to write a history of the church of Christ[1] from the advent of our Saviour up to our own age, that is from the apostles to the dregs of time in which we live, and to show by what means and through what agents it received its birth, and how, as it gained strength, it grew by persecution and was crowned with martyrdom ; and then, after reaching the Christian Emperors, how it increased in influence and in wealth but decreased in Christian virtues. But of this elsewhere. Now to the matter in hand.

2. Maronia is a little hamlet some thirty miles to the east of Antioch in Syria. After having many owners or landlords,[1] at the time when I was staying as a young man in Syria[2] it came into the possession of my intimate friend, the Bishop Evagrius,[3] whose name I now give in order to show the source of my information. Well, there was at the place at that time an old man by name Malchus, which we might render "king," a Syrian by race and speech, in fact a genuine son of the soil. His companion was an old woman very decrepit who seemed to be at death's door, both of them so zealously pious and such constant frequenters of the Church, they might have been taken for Zacharias and Elizabeth in the Gospel but for the fact that there was no John to be seen. With some curiosity I asked the neighbours what was the link between them ; was it marriage, or kindred, or the bond of the Spirit ? All with one accord replied that they were holy people, well pleasing to God, and gave me a strange account of them. Longing to know more I began to question the man with much eagerness about the truth of what I heard, and learnt as follows.

3. My son, said he, I used to farm a bit of ground at Nisibis[4] and was an only son. My parents regarding me as the heir and the only survivor of their race, wished to force me into marriage, but I said I would rather be a monk. How my father threatened and my mother coaxed me to betray my chastity requires no other proof than the fact that I fled from home and parents. I could not go to the East because Persia was close by and

---

[1] This purpose was never carried into effect. These Lives of the Monks may be regarded as a contribution towards it, and also the book *De Viris Illustribus* (translated in Vol. iii. of this series) which was written in the following year, 392.

[1] Patronos. Properly defenders or advocates, but passing into the sense of proprietor, as in the Italian padrone.
[2] In the year 374. [3] See Letters i. 15, iii. 3.
[4] A populous city in Mesopotamia.

the frontiers were guarded by the soldiers of Rome; I therefore turned my steps to the West, taking with me some little provision for the journey, but barely sufficient to ward off destitution. To be brief, I came at last to the desert of Chalcis[1] which is situate between Immæ and Beroa farther south. There, finding some monks, I placed myself under their direction, earning my livelihood by the labour of my hands, and curbing the wantonness of the flesh by fasting. After many years the desire came over me to return to my country, and stay with my mother and cheer her widowhood while she lived (for my father, as I had already learnt, was dead), and then to sell the little property and give part to the poor, settle part on the monasteries and (I blush to confess my faithlessness) keep some to spend in comforts for myself. My abbot began to cry out that it was a temptation of the devil, and that under fair pretexts some snare of the old enemy lay hid. It was, he declared, a case of the dog returning to his vomit. Many monks, he said, had been deceived by such suggestions, for the devil never showed himself openly. He set before me many examples from the Scriptures, and told me that even Adam and Eve in the beginning had been overthrown by him through the hope of becoming gods. When he failed to convince me he fell upon his knees and besought me not to forsake him, nor ruin myself by looking back after putting my hand to the plough. Unhappily for myself I had the misfortune to conquer my adviser. I thought he was seeking not my salvation but his own comfort. So he followed me from the monastery as if he had been going to a funeral, and at last bade me farewell, saying, " I see that you bear the brand of a son of Satan. I do not ask your reasons nor take your excuses. The sheep which forsakes its fellows is at once exposed to the jaws of the wolf."

4. On the road from Beroa to Edessa[2] adjoining the high-way is a waste over which the Saracens roam to and fro without having any fixed abode. Through fear of them travellers in those parts assemble in numbers, so that by mutual assistance they may escape impending danger. There were in my company men, women, old men, youths, children, altogether about seventy persons. All of a sudden the Ishmaelites on horses and camels made an assault upon us, with their flowing hair bound with fillets, their bodies half-naked, with their broad military boots, their cloaks streaming behind them, and their quivers slung upon the

shoulders. They carried their bows unstrung and brandished their long spears ; for they had come not to fight, but to plunder. We were seized, dispersed, and carried in different directions. I, meanwhile, repenting too late of the step I had taken, and far indeed from gaining possession of my inheritance, was assigned, along with another poor sufferer, a woman, to the service of one and the same owner. We were led, or rather carried, high upon the camel's back through a desert waste, every moment expecting destruction, and suspended, I may say, rather than seated. Flesh half raw was our food, camel's milk our drink.

5. At length, after crossing a great river we came to the interior of the desert, where, being commanded after the custom of the people to pay reverence to the mistress and her children, we bowed our heads. Here, as if I were a prisoner, I changed my dress, that is, learnt to go naked, the heat being so excessive as to allow of no clothing beyond a covering for the loins. Some sheep were given to me to tend, and, comparatively speaking, I found this occupation a comfort, for I seldom saw my masters or fellow slaves. My fate seemed to be like that of Jacob in sacred history, and reminded me also of Moses ; both of whom were once shepherds in the desert. I fed on fresh cheese and milk, prayed continually, and sang psalms which I had learnt in the monastery. I was delighted with my captivity, and thanked God because I had found in the desert the monk's estate which I was on the point of losing in my country.

6. But no condition can ever shut out the Devil. How manifold past expression are his snares ! Hid though I was, his malice found me out. My master seeing his flock increasing and finding no dishonesty in me (I knew that the Apostle has given command that master should be as faithfully served as God Himself) and wishing to reward me in order to secure my greater fidelity, gave me the woman who was once my fellow servant in captivity. On my refusing and saying I was a Christian, and that it was not lawful for me to take a woman to wife so long as her husband was alive (her husband had been captured with us, but carried off by another master), my owner was relentless in his rage, drew his sword and began to make at me. If I had not without delay stretched out my hand and taken possession of the woman, he would have slain me on the spot. Well ; by this time a darker night than usual had set in and, for me, all too soon. I led my bride into an old cave ; sorrow was bride's-maid ; we shrank from each other but did not confess it. Then I really felt my captivity ; I threw myself down on the ground and began to lament the monastic state which

[1] The desert in which Jerome spent the years 375-80. See Letters ii., v., xiv., xvii.
[2] A city of Mesopotamia, formerly the capital of Abgarus' kingdom : at this time a great centre of Syrian Christianity.

I had lost, and said : "Wretched man that I am ! have I been preserved for this ? has my wickedness brought me to this, that in my gray hairs I must lose my virgin state and become a married man ? What is the good of having despised parents, country, property, for the Lord's sake, if I do the thing I wished to avoid doing when I despised them ? And yet it may be perhaps the case that I am in this condition because I longed for home. What are we to do, my soul ? are we to perish, or conquer ? Are we to wait for the hand of the Lord, or pierce ourselves with our own sword ? Turn your weapon against yourself ; I must fear your death, my soul, more than the death of the body. Chastity preserved has its own martyrdom. Let the witness for Christ lie unburied in the desert ; I will be at once the persecutor and the martyr." Thus speaking I drew my sword which glittered even in the dark, and turning its point towards me said : 'Farewell, unhappy woman : receive me as a martyr not as a husband." She threw herself at my feet and exclaimed : "I pray you by Jesus Christ, and adjure you by this hour of trial, do not shed your blood and bring its guilt upon me. If you choose to die, first turn your sword against me. Let us rather be united upon these terms. Supposing my husband should return to me, I would preserve the chastity which I have learnt in captivity ; I would even die rather than lose it. Why should you die to prevent a union with me ? I would die if you desired it. Take me then as the partner of your chastity ; and love me more in this union of the spirit than you could in that of the body only. Let our master believe that you are my husband. Christ knows you are my brother. We shall easily convince them we are married when they see us so loving." I confess, I was astonished and, much as I had before admired the virtue of the woman, I now loved her as a wife still more. Yet I never gazed upon her naked person ; I never touched her flesh, for I was afraid of losing in peace what I had preserved in the conflict. In this strange wedlock many days passed away. Marriage had made us more pleasing to our masters, and there was no suspicion of our flight ; sometimes I was absent for even a whole month like a trusty shepherd traversing the wilderness.

7. After a long time as I sat one day by myself in the desert with nothing in sight save earth and sky, I began quickly to turn things over in my thoughts, and amongst others called to mind my friends the monks, and specially the look of the father who had instructed me, kept me, and lost me. While I was thus musing I saw a crowd of ants swarming over a narrow path. The loads they carried were clearly larger than their own bodies. Some with their forceps were dragging along the seeds of herbs : others were excavating the earth from pits and banking it up to keep out the water. One party, in view of approaching winter, and wishing to prevent their store from being converted into grass through the dampness of the ground, were cutting off the tips of the grains they had carried in ; another with solemn lamentation were removing the dead. And, what is stranger still in such a host, those coming out did not hinder those going in ; nay rather, if they saw one fall beneath his burden they would put their shoulders to the load and give him assistance. In short that day afforded me a delightful entertainment. So, remembering how Solomon sends us to the shrewdness of the ant and quickens our sluggish faculties by setting before us such an example, I began to tire of captivity, and to regret the monk's cell, and long to imitate those ants and their doings, where toil is for the community, and, since nothing belongs to any one, all things belong to all.

8. When I returned to my chamber, my wife met me. My looks betrayed the sadness of my heart. She asked why I was so dispirited. I told her the reasons, and exhorted her to escape. She did not reject the idea. I begged her to be silent on the matter. She pledged her word. We constantly spoke to one another in whispers ; and we floated in suspense betwixt hope and fear. I had in the flock two very fine he-goats : these I killed, made their skins into bottles, and from their flesh prepared food for the way. Then in the early evening when our masters thought we had retired to rest we began our journey, taking with us the bottles and part of the flesh. When we reached the river which was about ten miles off, having inflated the skins and got astride upon them, we intrusted ourselves to the water, slowly propelling ourselves with our feet, that we might be carried down by the stream to a point on the opposite bank much below that at which we embarked, and that thus the pursuers might lose the track. But meanwhile the flesh became sodden and partly lost, and we could not depend on it for more than three days' sustenance. We drank till we could drink no more by way of preparing for the thirst we expected to endure, then hastened away, constantly looking behind us, and advanced more by night than day, on account both of the ambushes of the roaming Saracens, and of the excessive heat of the sun. I grow terrified even as I relate what happened ; and, although my mind is perfectly at rest, yet my frame shudders from head to foot.

9. Three days after we saw in the dim

distance two men riding on camels approaching with all speed. At once foreboding ill I began to think my master purposed putting us to death, and our sun seemed to grow dark again. In the midst of our fear, and just as we realized that our footsteps on the sand had betrayed us, we found on our right hand a cave which extended far underground. Well, we entered the cave : but we were afraid of venomous beasts such as vipers, basilisks, scorpions, and other creatures of the kind, which often resort to such shady places so as to avoid the heat of the sun. We therefore barely went inside, and took shelter in a pit on the left, not venturing a step farther, lest in fleeing from death we should run into death. We thought thus within ourselves : If the Lord helps us in our misery we have found safety : if He rejects us for our sins, we have found our grave. What do you suppose were our feelings? What was our terror, when in front of the cave, close by, there stood our master and fellow-servant, brought by the evidence of our footsteps to our hiding place? How much worse is death expected than death inflicted! Again my tongue stammers with distress and fear ; it seems as if I heard my master's voice, and I hardly dare mutter a word. He sent his servant to drag us from the cavern while he himself held the camels, and, sword in hand, waited for us to come. Meanwhile the servant entered about three or four cubits, and we in our hiding place saw his back though he could not see us, for the nature of the eye is such that those who go into the shade out of the sunshine can see nothing. His voice echoed through the cave : "Come out, you felons ; come out and die ; why do you stay? Why do you delay? Come out, your master is calling and patiently waiting for you." He was still speaking when lo! through the gloom we saw a lioness seize the man, strangle him, and drag him, covered with blood, farther in. Good Jesus! how great was our terror now, how intense our joy! We beheld, though our master knew not of it, our enemy perish. He, when he saw that he was long in returning, supposed that the fugitives being two to one were offering resistance. Impatient in his rage, and sword still in hand, he came to the cavern, and shouted like a madman as he chided the slowness of his slave, but was seized upon by the wild beast before he reached our hiding place. Who ever would believe that before our eyes a brute would fight for us?

One cause of fear was removed, but there was the prospect of a similar death for ourselves, though the rage of the lion was not so bad to bear as the anger of the man. Our hearts failed for fear ; without venturing to stir a step we awaited the issue, having no wall of defence in the midst of so great dangers save the consciousness of our chastity ; when, early in the morning, the lioness, afraid of some snare and aware that she had been seen took up her cub in her teeth and carried it away leaving us in possession of our retreat. Our confidence was not restored all at once. We did not rush out, but waited for a long time for as often as we thought of coming out we pictured to ourselves the horror of falling in with her.

10. At last we got rid of our fright ; and when that day was spent, we sallied forth towards evening, and saw the camels, on account of their great speed called dromedaries, quietly chewing the cud. We mounted, and with the strength gained from the new supply of grain after ten days' travelling through the desert arrived at the Roman camp. After being presented to the tribune we told all, and from thence were sent to Sabianus, who commanded in Mesopotamia, where we sold our camels. My dear old abbot was now sleeping in the Lord ; I betook myself therefore to this place and returned to the monastic life, while entrusted my companion here to the care of the virgins ; for though I loved her as a sister I did not commit myself to her as if she were my sister.

Malchus was an old man, I a youth, when he told me these things. I who have related them to you am now old, and I have set them forth as a history of chastity for the chaste Virgins, I exhort you, guard your chastity Tell the story to them that come after, that they may realize that in the midst of swords and wild beasts of the desert, virtue is never a captive, and that he who is devoted to the service of Christ may die, but cannot be conquered.

THE DIALOGUE AGAINST THE LUCIFERIANS

Introduction.

This Dialogue was written about 379, seven years after the death of Lucifer, and very soon after Jerome's turn from his hermit life in the desert of Chalcis. Though he received ordination from Paulinus, who had ʋen consecrated by Lucifer, he had no sympathy with Lucifer's narrower views, as he shows plainly in this ialogue. Lucifer, who was bishop of Cagliari in Sardinia, first came into prominent notice about A. D. 354, hen great efforts were being made to procure a condemnation of S. Athanasius by the Western bishops. He ɪergetically took up the cause of the saint, and at his own request was sent by Liberius, bishop of Rome, in ›mpany with the priest Pancratius and the deacon Hilarius, on a mission to the Emperor Constantius. The ıperor granted a Council, which met at Milan in A. D. 354. Lucifer distinguished himself by resisting a ·oposition to condemn Athanasius, and did not hesitate to oppose the emperor with much violence. In conse- ɪence of this he was sent into exile from A. D. 355 to A. D. 361, the greater portion of which time was spent Eleutheropolis in Palestine, though he afterwards removed to the Thebaid. It was at this time that his ›lemical writings appeared, the tone and temper of which is indicated by the mere titles *De Regibus Apostaticis* ʃ Apostate Kings), *De non Conveniendo cum Hæreticis, etc.* (of not holding communion with heretics). On ɪe death of Constantius in 361, Julian permitted the exiled bishops to return ; but Lucifer instead of going to ɪexandria where a Council was to be held under the presidency of Athanasius for the healing of a schism in ɪe Catholic party at Antioch (some of which held to Meletius, while others followed Eustathius), preferred to go ·raight to Antioch. There he ordained Paulinus, the leader of the latter section, as bishop of the Church. ɪsebius of Vercellæ soon arrived with the synodal letters of the Council of Alexandria, but, finding himself ɪus anticipated, and shrinking from a collision with his friend, he retired immediately. Lucifer stayed, and declared that he would not hold communion with Eusebius or any who adopted the moderate policy of the ɪexandrian Council. By this Council it had been determined that actual Arians, if they renounced their ɪresy, should be pardoned, but not invested with ecclesiastical functions ; and that those bishops who had ɪerely consented to Arianism should remain undisturbed. It was this latter concession which offended Lucifer, ɪd he became henceforth the champion of the principle that no one who had yielded to any compromise what- ·er with Arianism should be allowed to hold an ecclesiastical office." He was thus brought into antagonism ɪth Athanasius himself, who, it has been seen, presided at Alexandria. Eventually he returned to his see in ɪrdinia where, according to Jerome's Chronicle, he died in 371. Luciferianism became extinct in the beginning the following century, if not earlier. It hardly appears to have been formed into a separate organization, ›ough an appeal was made to the emperor by some Luciferian presbyters about the year 384, and both Ambrose ɪd Augustine speak of him as having fallen into the schism.

The argument of the Dialogue may be thus stated. It has been pointed out above that Lucifer of ɪgliari, who had been banished from his see in the reign of Constantius because of his adherence to the cause Athanasius, had, on the announcement of toleration at the accession of Julian (361), gone to Antioch and ›nsecrated Paulinus a bishop. There were then three bishops of Antioch, Dorotheus the Arian (who had succeeded ɪzoius in 376), Meletius who, though an Athanasian in opinion, had been consecrated by Arians or Semi-Arians, ɪd Paulinus ; besides Vitalis, bishop of a congregation of Apollinarians. Lucifer, in the earnestness of his ɪti-Arian opinion, refused to acknowledge as bishops those who had come over from Arianism, though he ·cepted the laymen who had been baptized by Arian bishops. This opinion led to the Luciferian schism, ɪd forms the subject of the Dialogue.

The point urged by Orthodoxus throughout is that, since the Luciferian accepts as valid the baptism conferred ' Arian bishops, it is inconsistent in him not to acknowledge the bishops who have repented of their Arian opinions. ɪe Luciferian at first (2) in his eagerness, declares the Arians to be no better than heathen ; but he sees that he ɪs gone too far, and retracts this opinion. Still it is one thing, he says, (3) to admit a penitent neophyte, ɪother to admit a man to be bishop and celebrate the Eucharist. We do not wish, he says (4) to preclude ɪdividuals who have fallen from repentance. And we, replies Orthodoxus, by admitting the bishops save not ɪem only but their flocks also. "The salt," says the Luciferian (5), "which has lost its savour cannot be salted," ɪd, "What communion has Christ with Belial ?" But this, it is answered (6), would prove that Arians could ·t confer baptism at all. Yes, says the objector, they are like John the Baptist, whose baptism needed to be lowed by that of Christ. But, it is replied, the bishop gives Christ's baptism and confers the Holy Spirit. ɪe confirmation which follows (9) is rather a custom of the churches than the necessary means of grace.

The argument is felt to be approaching to a philosophical logomachy (10, 11), but it is resumed by the ɪciferian. There is a real difference, he says (12), between the man who in his simplicity accepts baptism from ɪ Arian bishop, and the bishop himself who understands the heresy. Yet both, it is replied (13), when they ɪe penitent, should be received.

At this point (14) the Luciferian yields. But he wishes to be assured that what Orthodoxus recommends ɪs been really the practice of the Church. This leads to a valuable chapter of Church history. Orthodoxus ɪ calls the victories of the Church, which the Luciferians speak of as corrupt (15). The shame is that, though ɪey have the true creed, they have too little faith. He then describes (17, 18) how the orthodox bishops ɪre beguiled into accepting the creed of Ariminum, but afterwards saw their error (19). "The world groaned find itself Arian." They did all that was possible to set things right. Why should they not be received, as ɪ but the authors of heresy had been received at Nicæa ? (20) Lucifer who was a good shepherd, and Hilary ɪe Deacon, in separating their own small body into a sect have left the rest a prey to the wolf (20, 21). The ɪeat and tares must grow together (22). This has been the principle of the Church (23), as shown by Scrip- ɪre (24) and Apostolic custom, and even Cyprian, when he wished penitent heretics to be re-baptized (25), could ·t prevail. Even Hilary by receiving baptism from the Church which always has re-admitted heretics in repent- ɪce (26, 27) acknowledges this principle. In that Church and its divisions and practice it is our duty to abide.

1. It happened not long ago that a follower of Lucifer had a dispute with a son of the Church. His loquacity was odious and the language he employed most abusive. For he declared that the world belonged to the devil, and, as is commonly said by them at the present day, that the Church was turned into a brothel. His opponent on the other hand, with reason indeed, but without due regard to time and place, urged that Christ did not die in vain, and that it was for something more than a Sardinian cloak of skins [1] that the Son of God came down from heaven. To be brief, the dispute was not settled when night interrupted the debate, and the lighting of the street-lamps gave the signal for the assembly to disperse. The combatants therefore withdrew, almost spitting in each other's faces, an arrangement having been previously made by the audience for a meeting in a quiet porch at daybreak. Thither, accordingly, they all came, and it was resolved that the words of both speakers should be taken down by reporters.

2. When all were seated, Helladius the Luciferian said, I want an answer first to my question. Are the Arians Christians or not?

Orthodoxus. I answer with another question, Are all heretics Christians?

L. If you call a man a heretic you deny that he is a Christian.

O. No heretics, then, are Christians.

L. I told you so before.

O. If they are not Christ's, they belong to the devil.

L. No one doubts that.

O. But if they belong to the devil, it makes no difference whether they are heretics or heathen.

L. I do not dispute the point.

O. We are then agreed that we must speak of a heretic as we would of a heathen.

L. Just so.

O. Now it is decided that heretics are heathen, put any question you please.

L. What I wanted to elicit by my question has been expressly stated, namely, that heretics are not Christians. Now comes the inference. If the Arians are heretics, and all heretics are heathen, the Arians are heathen too. But if the Arians are heathen and it is beyond dispute that the church has no communion with the Arians, that is with the heathen, it is clear that your church which welcomes bishops from the Arians, that is from the heathen, receives priests of the Capitol [2] rather than bishops, and accordingly it ought more cor-

rectly to be called the synagogue of Antichrist than the Church of Christ.

L. Lo! what the prophet said is fulfilled [1] "They have digged a pit before me, the have fallen into the midst thereof themselves.

L. How so?

O. If the Arians are, as you say, heathen and the assemblies of the Arians are the devil camp, how is it that you receive a person wh has been baptized in the devil's camp?

L. I do receive him, but as a penitent.

O. The fact is you don't know what you ar saying. Does any one receive a peniten heathen?

L. In my simplicity I replied when we begar that all heretics are heathen. But the ques tion was a captious one, and you shall hav the full credit of victory in the first point. I wil now proceed to the second and maintain tha a layman coming from the Arians ought to b received if penitent, but not a cleric.

O. And yet, if you concede me the firs point, the second is mine too.

L. Show me how it comes to be yours.

O. Don't you know that the clergy an laity have only one Christ, and that there i not one God of converts and another of bish ops? Why then should not he who receive laymen receive clerics also?

L. There is a difference between sheddin; tears for sin, and handling the body of Christ there is a difference between lying prostrat at the feet of the brethren, and from the higl altar administering the Eucharist to the people It is one thing to lament over the past another to abandon sin and live the glorifie life in the Church. You who yesterday im piously declared the Son of God to be creature, you who every day, worse than a Jew were wont to cast the stones of blasphemy a Christ, you whose hands are full of blood, whos pen was a soldier's spear, do you, the conver of a single hour, come into the Church as a adulterer might come to a virgin? If you re pent of your sin, abandon your priestly func tions: if you are shameless in your sin, remai what you were.

O. You are quite a rhetorician, and fly fror the thicket of controversy to the open field of declamation. But, I entreat you, refrai from common-places, and return to the groun and the lines marked out; afterwards, if yo like, we will take a wider range.

L. There is no declamation in the case; m indignation is more than I can bear. Mak what statements you please, argue as yo please, you will never convince me that a peni tent bishop should be treated like a peniten layman.

---

[1] The Sardinian cloak of skins is contrasted by Cicero (pro Scauro) with the Royal purple:—Quem purpura regalis non commovit, eum Sardorum mastruca mutavit. Jerome's meaning is that Christ came not to win the lowest place on earth, but the highest. The fact that Lucifer was Bishop of Cagliari in Sardinia gives point to the saying.

[2] That is, of Jupiter, whose temple was in the Capitol.

[1] Ps. lvii. 6.

O. Since you put the whole thing in a nut-shell and obstinately cling to your position, that the case of the bishop is different from that of the layman, I will do what you wish, and I shall not be sorry to avail myself of the opportunity you offer and come to close quarters. Explain why you receive a layman coming from the Arians, but do not receive a bishop.

L. I receive a layman who confesses that he has erred; and the Lord willeth not the death of a sinner, but rather that he should repent.

O. Receive then also a bishop who, as well as the layman, confesses that he has erred, and it still holds good that the Lord willeth not the death of a sinner, but rather that he should repent.

L. If he confesses his error why does he continue a bishop? Let him lay aside his episcopal functions, and I grant pardon to the penitent.

O. I will answer you in your own words. If a layman confesses his error, how is it he continues a layman? Let him lay aside his lay-priesthood, that is, his baptism, and I grant pardon to the penitent. For it is written [1] "He made us to be a kingdom, to be priests unto his God and Father." And again, [3] "A holy nation, a royal priesthood, an elect race." Everything which is forbidden to a Christian, is forbidden to both bishop and layman. He who does penance condemns his former life. If a penitent bishop may not continue what he was, neither may a penitent layman remain in that state on account of which he confesses himself a penitent.

L. We receive the laity, because no one will be induced to change, if he knows he must be baptized again. And then, if they are reject-ed, we become the cause of their destruction.

O. By receiving a layman you save a single soul: and I in receiving a bishop unite to the Church, I will not say the people of one city, but the whole [4] province of which he is the head; if I drive him away, he will drag down many with him to ruin. Wherefore I beseech you to apply the same reason which you think you have for receiving the few to the salva-tion of the whole world. But if you are not satisfied with this, if you are so hard, or rather so unreasonably unmerciful as to think him who gave baptism an enemy of Christ, though you account him who received it a son, we do not contradict ourselves: we either receive a bishop as well as the people which is con-stituted as a Christian people by him, or if we

do not receive a bishop, we know that we must also reject his people.

5. L. Pray, have you not read what is said concerning the bishops, [1] "Ye are the salt of the earth: but if the salt have lost its savour, wherewith shall it be salted? It is thence-forth good for nothing, but to be cast out and trodden under foot of man." And then there is the fact that the priest [2] intercedes with God for the sinful people, while there is no one to entreat for the priest. Now these two pas-sages of Scripture tend to the same conclu-sion. For as salt seasons all food and nothing is so pleasant as to please the palate without it: so the bishop is the seasoning of the whole world and of his own Church, and if he lose his savour through the denial of truth, or through heresy, or lust, or, to comprehend all in one word, through sin of any kind, by what other can he be seasoned, when he was the season-ing of all? The priest, we know, offers his oblation for the layman, lays his hand upon him when submissive, invokes the return of the Holy Spirit, and thus, after inviting the prayers of the people, reconciles to the altar him who had been delivered to Satan for the destruction of the flesh that the spirit might be saved; nor does he restore one member to health until all the members have wept to-gether with him. For a father easily pardons his son, when the mother entreats for her off-spring. If then it is by the priestly order that a penitent layman is restored to the Church, and pardon follows where sorrow has gone before, it is clear that a priest who has been removed from his order cannot be restored to the place he has forfeited, because either he will be a penitent and then he cannot be a priest, or if he continues to hold office he cannot be brought back to the Church by penitential discipline. Will you dare to spoil the savour of the Church with the salt which has lost its savour? Will you replace at the altar the man who having been cast out ought to lie in the mire and be trodden under foot by all men? What then will become of the Apostle's command, [3] "The bishop must be blameless as God's steward"? And again, [4] "But let a man prove himself, and so let him come." What becomes of our Lord's intima-tion, [5] "Neither cast your pearls before the swine"? But if you understand the words as a general admonition, how much more must care be exercised in the case of priests when so much precaution is taken where the laity are concerned? [6] "Depart, I pray you," says the Lord by Moses, "from the tents of these wicked men, and touch nothing of theirs, lest ye be consumed in all their sins." And

---

[1] Sacerdotium.   [2] Apoc. i. 6.   [3] 1 Pet. ii. 9.
[4] That is diocese. The word diocese was in early times the larger expression, and contained many provinces. See Can-on II of Constantinople, Bright's edition, and note.

[1] Matt. v. 13.   [2] Lev. ix. 7.   [3] Tit. i. 7.
[4] 1 Cor. xi. 28.   [5] Matt. vii. 6.   [6] Numb. xvi. 26.

again in the Minor Prophets, [1] " Their sacrifices shall be unto them as the bread of mourners ; all that eat thereof shall be polluted." And in the Gospel the Lord says, [2] " The lamp of the body is the eye : if therefore thine eye be single, thy whole body shall be full of light." For when the bishop preaches the true faith the darkness is scattered from the hearts of all. And he gives the reason, [3] " Neither do men light a lamp, and put it under the bushel, but on the stand; and it shineth unto all that are in the house." That is, God's motive for lighting the fire of His knowledge in the bishop is that he may not shine for himself only, but for the common benefit. And in the next sentence [4] " If," says he, " thine eye be evil, thy whole body shall be full of darkness. If therefore the light that is in thee be darkness, how great is the darkness ! " And rightly ; for since the bishop is appointed in the Church that he may restrain the people from error, how great will the error of the people be when he himself who teaches errs. How can he remit sins, who is himself a sinner ? How can an impious man make a man holy ? How shall the light enter into me, when my eye is blind ? O misery ! Antichrist's disciple governs the Church of Christ. And what are we to think of the words, [4] " No man can serve two masters " ? And that too [5] " What communion hath light and darkness ? And what concord hath Christ with Belial ? " In the old testament we read, [6] " No man that hath a blemish shall come nigh to offer the offerings of the Lord." And again, [7] " Let the priests who come nigh to the Lord their God be clean, lest haply the Lord forsake them." And in the same place, [7] " And when they draw nigh to minister in holy things, let them not bring sin upon themselves, lest they die." And there are many other passages which it would be an endless task to detail, and which I omit for the sake of brevity. For it is not the number of proofs that avails, but their weight. And all this proves that you with a little leaven have corrupted the whole lump of the Church, and receive the Eucharist to-day from the hand of one whom yesterday you loathed like an idol.

6. O. Your memory has served you, and you have certainly given us at great length many quotations from the sacred books : but after going all round the wood, you are caught in my hunting-nets. Let the case be as you would have it, that an Arian bishop is the enemy of Christ, let him be the salt that has lost its savour, let him be a lamp without flame, let him be an eye without a pupil : no doubt your argument will take you thus far—that he cannot salt another who himself ha no salt : a blind man cannot enlighten others nor set them on fire when his own light ha gone out. But why, when you swallow foo which he has seasoned, do you reproach th seasoned with being saltless ? Your Churc is bright with his flame, and do you accuse hi lamp of being extinguished ? He gives yo eyes, and are you blind ? Wherefore, I pra you, either give him the power of sacrificin since you approve his baptism, or reject hi baptism if you do not think him a priest. Fo it is impossible that he who is holy in baptisn should be a sinner at the altar.

L. But when I receive a lay penitent, it i with laying on of hands, and invocation of th Holy Spirit, for I know that the Holy Spiri cannot be given by heretics.

O. All the paths of your propositions lea to the same meeting-point, and it is with yo as with the frightened deer—while you fl from the feathers fluttering in the wind, yo become entangled in the strongest of net For seeing that a man, baptized in the nam of the Father and the Son and the Hol Ghost, becomes a temple of the Lord, and tha while the old abode is destroyed a new shrin is built for the Trinity, how can you say tha sins can be remitted among the Arians with out the coming of the Holy Ghost ? How i a soul purged from its former stains whicl has not the Holy Ghost ? For it is not mer water which washes the soul, but it is itsel first purified by the Spirit that it may be abl to spiritually wash the souls of men. [1] " Th Spirit of the Lord," says Moses, " move upon the face of the waters," from which i appears that there is no baptism without th Holy Ghost. Bethesda, the pool in Judea could not cure the limbs of those who suffere from bodily weakness without the advent o an angel,[2] and do you venture to bring me soul washed with simple water, as though i had just come from the bath ? Our Lor Jesus Christ Himself, of whom it is less correc to say that He was cleansed by washing that that by the washing of Himself He cleanse all waters, no sooner raised His head from th stream than He received the Holy Ghost Not that He ever was without the Hol Ghost, inasmuch as He was born in th flesh through the Holy Ghost ; but in orde to prove that to be the true baptism by whicl the Holy Ghost comes. So then if an Aria cannot give the Holy Spirit, he cannot eve baptize, because there is no baptism of th Church without the Holy Spirit. And you when you receive a person baptized by a

---

[1] Hos. ix. 4.   [2] Matt. vii. 22.   [3] Matt. v. 15.
[4] Matt. vi. 23-24. [5] 2 Cor. vi. 14, 15.   [6] Levit. xxi. 17.
[7] Quoted apparently from memory as giving the general sense of passages in Lev. xxi, xxii.

[1] Gen. i. 2.   [2] John v. 2 sq.

rian and afterwards invoke the Holy Ghost, ght either to baptize him, because without e Holy Ghost he could not be baptized, or, he was baptized in the Spirit, you must not voke the Holy Ghost for your convert who ceived Him at the time of baptism.

7. L. Pray tell me, have you not read[1] the Acts of the Apostles that those who d already been baptized by John, on their ying in reply to the Apostles' question that ey had not even heard what the Holy Ghost as, afterwards obtained the Holy Ghost? hence it is clear that it is possible to be ptized, and yet not to have the Holy Ghost. O. I do not think that those who form our dience are so ignorant of the sacred books at many words are needed to settle this little estion. But before I say anything in support of my assertion, listen while I point out hat confusion, upon your view, is introduced to Scripture. What do we mean by saying at John in his baptism could not give the oly Spirit to others, yet gave him to Christ? nd who is that John? [2] "The voice of one ying in the wilderness, Make ye ready the ay of the Lord, make his paths straight." He ho used to say, [3] "Behold the Lamb of God, hich taketh away the sins of the world": I y too little, he who from his mother's womb ied out, [4] "And whence is this to me that the other of my Lord should come unto me," d he not give the Holy Ghost? And did Ananias give him to Paul? It perhaps looks e boldness in me to prefer him to all other en. Hear then the words of our Lord, "Among them that are born of women there th not arisen a greater than John the Baptst." For no prophet had the good fortune th to announce the coming of Christ, and to int Him out with the finger. And what cessity is there for me to dwell upon the aises of so illustrious a man when God the ather even calls him an angel? [7] "Behold, send my messenger (angel) before thy face, ho shall prepare thy way before thee." He ust have been an angel who after lodging in s mother's womb at once began to frequent e desert wilds, and while still an infant ayed with serpents; who, when his eyes had ce gazed on Christ thought nothing else orth looking at; who exercised his voice, orthy of a messenger of God, in the words of e Lord, which are sweeter than honey and e honey-comb. And, to delay my question further, thus it behooved [8] the Forerunner the Lord to grow up. Now is it possible at a man of such character and renown did

not give the Holy Ghost, while Cornelius the centurion received Him before baptism? Tell me, pray, why could he not give Him? You don't know? Then listen to the teaching of Scripture: the baptism of John did not so much consist in the forgiveness of sins as in being a baptism of repentance for the remission of sins, that is, for a future remission, which was to follow through the sanctification of Christ. For it is written, [1] "John came, who baptized in the wilderness, and preached the baptism of repentance unto remission of sins." And soon after, [2] "And they were baptized of him in the river Jordan, confessing their sins." For as he himself preceded Christ as His forerunner, so also his baptism was the prelude to the Lord's baptism. [3] "He that is of the earth," he said, "speaketh of the earth; he that cometh from heaven is above all." And again, [4] "I indeed baptize you with water, he shall baptize you with the Holy Ghost." But if John, as he himself confessed, did not baptize with the Spirit, it follows that he did not forgive sins either, for no man has his sins remitted without the Holy Ghost. Or if you contentiously argue that, because the baptism of John was from heaven, therefore sins were forgiven by it, show me what more there is for us to get in Christ's baptism. Because it forgives sins, it releases from Gehenna. Because it releases from Gehenna, it is perfect. But no baptism can be called perfect except that which depends on the cross and resurrection of Christ. Thus, although John himself said, [5] "He must increase, but I must decrease," in your perverse scrupulosity you give more than is due to the baptism of the servant, and destroy that of the master to which you leave no more than to the other. What is the drift of your assertion? Just this—it does not strike you as strange that those who had been baptized by John, should afterwards by the laying on of hands receive the Holy Ghost, although it is evident that they did not obtain even remission of sins apart from the faith which was to follow. But you who receive a person baptized by the Arians and allow him to have perfect baptism, after that admission do you invoke the Holy Ghost as if this were still some slight defect, whereas there is no baptism of Christ without the Holy Ghost? But I have wandered too far, and when I might have met my opponent face to face and repelled his attack, I have only thrown a few light darts from a distance. The baptism of John was so far imperfect that it is plain they who had been baptized by him were afterwards baptized with the baptism of Christ. For thus the history relates, [6] "And it came to pass that while

---

[1] xix. 2.   [2] Is. xi. 3: Matt. iii. 3.   [3] John i. 29.
Luke i. 43.   [5] Acts ix. 17.
Matt. xi. 11.   [7] Matt. xi. 10.
We venture to read 'decebat' instead of 'dicebat.' Otherse, we may render 'Thus (the Scripture) said that,' etc.

[1] Mark i. 4.   [2] Mark i. 5.   [3] John iii. 31.
[4] Matt. iii. 11.   [5] John iii. 30.   [6] Acts xix. 1, sqq.

Apollos was at Corinth, Paul having passed through the upper country came to Ephesus, and found certain disciples : and he said unto them, Did ye receive the Holy Ghost when ye believed ? And they said unto him, Nay, we did not so much as hear whether the Holy Ghost was given. And he said, Into what then were ye baptized? And they said, Into John's baptism. And Paul said, John baptized with the baptism of repentance, saying unto the people, that they should believe on Him which should come after him, that is, on Jesus. And when they heard this, they were baptized into the name of the Lord Jesus : And when Paul had laid his hands upon them, immediately the Holy Ghost fell on them." If then they were baptized with the true and lawful baptism of the Church, and thus received the Holy Ghost : do you follow the apostles and baptize those who have not had Christian baptism, and you will be able to invoke the Holy Ghost.

8. L. Thirsty men in their dreams eagerly gulp down the water of the stream, and the more they drink the thirstier they are. In the same way you appear to me to have searched everywhere for arguments against the point I raised, and yet to be as far as ever from being satisfied. Don't you know that the laying on of hands after baptism and then the invocation of the Holy Spirit is a custom of the Churches? Do you demand Scripture proof? You may find it in the Acts of the Apostles. And even if it did not rest on the authority of Scripture the consensus of the whole world in this respect would have the force of a command. For many other observances of the Churches, which are due to tradition, have acquired the authority of the written law, as for instance [1] the practice of dipping the head three times in the laver, and then, after leaving the water, of [2] tasting mingled milk and honey in representation of infancy ;[3] and, again, the practices of standing up in worship on the Lord's day, and ceasing from fasting every Pentecost ; and there are many other unwritten practices which have won their place through reason and custom. So you see we follow the practice of the Church, although it

may be clear that a person was baptized befo the Spirit was invoked.

9. O. I do not deny that it is the practi of the Churches in the case of those w living far from the greater towns have be baptized by presbyters and deacons, for t bishop to visit them, and by the laying on hands to invoke the Holy Ghost upon the. But how shall I describe your habit of app ing the laws of the Church to heretics, and exposing the virgin entrusted to you in t brothels of harlots? If a bishop lays hands on men he lays them on those w have been baptized in the right faith, and w have believed that the Father, Son, and Ho Ghost, are three persons, but one essenc But an Arian has no faith but this (close yo ears, my hearers, that you may not be defil by words so grossly impious), that the Fath alone is very God, and that Jesus Christ o Saviour is a [1] creature, and [2] the Holy Gho the Servant of both. How can he th receive the Holy Ghost from the Church, wh has not yet obtained remission of sins ? F the Holy Ghost must have a clean abod nor will He become a dweller in that temp which has not for its chief priest the tr faith. But if you now ask how it is that person baptized in the Church does n receive the Holy Ghost, Whom we declare be given in true baptism, except by th hands of the bishop, let me tell you that o authority for the rule is the fact that aft our Lord's ascension the Holy Ghost d scended upon the Apostles. And in man places we find it the practice, more by way honouring the [3] episcopate than from any co pulsory law. Otherwise, if the Holy Gho descends only at the bishop's prayer, they a greatly to be pitied who in isolated houses, in forts, or retired places, after being baptiz by the presbyters and deacons have fall asleep before the bishop's visitation. T well-being of a Church depends upon th dignity of its chief-priest, and unless son extraordinary and unique functions be a signed to him, we shall have as many schisr in the Churches as there are priests. Hen it is that without ordination and the bisho license neither presbyter nor deacon has t power to baptize. And yet, if necessity be, we know that even laymen may, ar frequently do, baptize. For as a man r ceives, so too he can give ; for it will hard

---

[1] Triple immersion, that is, thrice dipping the head while standing in the water, was the all but universal rule of the Church in early times. There is proof of its existence in Africa, Palestine, Egypt, at Antioch and Constantinople, in Cappadocia and Rome. See Basil, On the H. Sp. § 66, and Apostolical Canons. Gregory the Great ruled that either form was allowable, the one symbolizing the Unity of the Godhead, the other the Trinity of Persons.

[2] This ceremony together with the kiss of peace and white robes probably dated from very early times. In the fourth century some new ceremonies were introduced, such as the use of lights and salt, the unction with oil before baptism in addition to that with chrism which continued to be administered after baptism.

[3] At Holy Communion the first prayer of the faithful was said by all kneeling. During the rest of the liturgy all stood. At other times of service the rule was for all to kneel in prayer except on Sundays and between Easter and Whitsuntide.

---

[1] The Arians said He was the creature (made out of nothi through whom the Father gave being to all other creatures.

[2] The Macedonians, who became nearly co-extensive v the Semi-Arians about 360, held that the Spirit not being ' ve God must be a creature and therefore a Servant of God.

[3] Sacerdotium—often used by Jerome in a special sense the Episcopate. He says of Pammachius and of himself (I ter xlv., 3) that many people thought them digni sacerdo meaning the Bishopric of Rome.

said that we must believe that the eunuch
om Philip[1] baptized lacked the Holy Spirit.
e Scripture thus speaks concerning him,
,nd they both went down into the water ;
1 Philip baptized him." And on leaving
: water, "The Holy Spirit fell upon the
uuch." You may perhaps think that we
ght to set against this the passage in which
read, "Now when the apostles which were
Jerusalem heard that Samaria had received
: word of God, they sent unto them Peter
d John : who, when they were come down,
iyed for them that they might receive the
ly Ghost : for as yet he was fallen upon
ne of them." But why this was, the context
ls us,—"Only they had been baptized into
: name of the Lord Jesus. Then laid they
:ir hands on them, and they received the
ly Ghost." And if you here say that you
 the same, because the heretics have not
ptized into the Holy Spirit, I must remind
u that Philip was not separated from the
ostles, but belonged to the same Church
d preached the same Lord Jesus Christ :
at he was without question a deacon of
ose who afterwards laid their hands on his
nverts. But when you say that the Arians
ve not a Church, but a synagogue, and that
eir clergy do not worship God but creatures
d idols, how can you maintain that you
ght to act upon the same principle in cases
totally different ?

L. You repel my attack in front with vigour
d firmness : but you are smitten in the
ar and leave your back exposed to the darts.
:t us even grant that the Arians have no
ptism, and therefore that the Holy Ghost can-
t be given by them, because they themselves
ve not yet received remission of sins ; this
ogether makes for victory on my side, and
 your argumentative wrestling is but labori-
s toil to give me the conqueror's palm. An
ian has no baptism ; how is it then that he
s the episcopate ? There is not even a lay-
an among them, how can there be a bishop ? I
ay not receive a beggar, do you receive a
ng ? You surrender your camp to the enemy,
d are we to reject one of their deserters ?

11. O. If you remember what has been said
u would know that you have been already
swered ; but in yielding to the love of con-
idiction you have wandered from the subject,
e those persons who are talkative rather
an eloquent, and who, when they cannot
gue, still continue to wrangle. On the pres-
t occasion it is not my aim to either accuse
defend the Arians, but rather to get safely
st the turning-post of the race, and to main-
in that we receive a bishop for the same

reason that you receive a layman. If you
grant forgiveness to the erring, I too pardon
the penitent. If he that baptizes a person into
our belief has had no injurious effect upon the
person baptized, it follows that he who con-
secrates a bishop in the same faith causes no
defilement to the person consecrated. Heresy
is subtle, and therefore the simple-minded are
easily deceived. To be deceived is the common lot of both layman and bishop. But you
say, a bishop could not have been mistaken.
The truth is, men are elected to the episcopate
who come from the bosom of Plato and Aristophanes. How many can you find among
them who are not fully instructed in these
writers ? Indeed all, whoever they may be, that
are ordained at the present day from among the
literate class make it their study not how to seek
out the marrow of Scripture, but how to tickle
the ears of the people with the flowers of
rhetoric. We must further add that the Arian
heresy goes hand in hand with the wisdom of
the world, and [1] borrows its streams of argument from the fountains of Aristotle. And so
we will act like children when they try to outdo
one another—whatever you say I will say : what
you assert, I will assert : whatever you deny,
I will deny. We allow that an Arian may
baptize ; then he must be a bishop.[2] If we
agree that Arian baptism is invalid, you must
reject the layman, and I must not accept the
bishop. I will follow you wherever you go ;
we shall either stick in the mud together, or
shall get out together.

12. L. We pardon a layman because, when
he was baptized, he had a sincere impression
that he was joining the Church. He believed
and was baptized in accordance with his faith.

O. That is something new for a man to be
made a Christian by one who is not a Christian. When he joined the Arians into what
faith was he baptized ? Of course into that
which the Arians held. If on the other hand
we are to suppose that his own faith was correct, but that he was knowingly baptized by
heretics, he does not deserve the indulgence
we grant to the erring. But it is quite absurd
to imagine that, going as a pupil to the master,
he understands his art before he has been
taught. Can you suppose that a man who has
just turned from worshipping idols knows
Christ better than his teacher does ? If you

---

[1] "The philosophical relations of Arianism have been differently stated. Baur, Newman (The Arians, p. 17), and others,
bring it into connection with Aristotle, and Athanasianism with
Plato ; Petavius, Ritter, and Voigt, on the contrary, derive the
Arian idea of God from Platonism and Neo-Platonism. The
empirical, rational, logical tendency of Arianism is certainly
more Aristotelian than Platonic, and so far Baur and Newman
are right ; but all depends on making either revelation and faith,
or philosophy and reason, the starting point and ruling power of
theology." Doctor Schaff in Dict. of Chris. Biog.

[2] Baptism was at this time, as a rule, administered by the
bishop alone.

[1] Acts viii. 26 sq.

say, he sincerely believed in the Father, and
the Son, and the Holy Ghost, and therefore
obtained baptism, what, let me ask, is the
meaning of being sincerely ignorant of what
one believes ? He sincerely believed. What
did he believe ? Surely when he heard the
three names, he believed in three Gods, and
was an idolater ; or by the three titles he was
led to believe in a God with three names, and
so fell into the [1] Sabellian heresy. Or he was
perhaps trained by the Arians to believe that
there is one true God, the Father, but that the
Son and the Holy Spirit are creatures. What
else he may have believed, I know not : for
we can hardly think that a man brought up in
the Capitol would have learnt the doctrine of
the co-essential Trinity. He would have
known in that case that the Father, Son, and
Holy Spirit are not divided in nature, but in
person. He would have known also that the
name of Son was implied in that of Father and
the name of Father in that of Son. It is ridiculous to assert that any one can dispute concerning the faith before he believes it ; that
he understands a mystery before he has been
initiated ; that the baptizer and the baptized
hold different views respecting God. Besides,
it is the custom at baptism to ask, after the
confession of faith in the Trinity, do you believe in Holy Church ? Do you believe in the
remission of sins ? What Church do you say he
believed in ? The Church of the Arians ? But
they have no Church. In ours ? But the man
was not baptized into it : he could not believe
in that whereof he was ignorant.

L. I see that you can prattle cleverly about
each point that I raise ; and when we let fly a
dart you elude it by a harangue which serves
you for a shield ; I will therefore hurl a single
spear which will be strong enough to pierce
your defences and the hail-storm of your
words. I won't allow strength any longer to
be overcome by artifice. Even a layman baptized without the Church, if he be baptized
according to the faith, is received only as a
penitent : but a bishop either does no penance
and remains a bishop, or, if he does penance
he ceases to be a bishop. Wherefore we do
right both in welcoming the penitent layman,
and in rejecting the bishop, if he wishes to
continue in his office.

O. An arrow which is discharged from the
tight-drawn bow is not easy to avoid, for it
reaches him at whom it was aimed before the
shield can be raised to stop it. On the other

hand your propositions are pointless and there
fore cannot pierce an opponent. The spear the
which you have hurled with all your might an
about which you speak such threatening word
I turn aside, as the saying is, with my litt
finger. The point in dispute is not mere
whether a bishop is incapable of penitence an
a layman capable, but whether a heretic ha
received valid baptism. If he has not (an
this follows from your position), how can t
be a penitent, before he is a Christian ? Sho
me that a layman coming from the Arians ha
valid baptism, and then I will not deny hir
penitence. But if he is not a Christian, if h
had no priest to make him a Christian, ho
can he do penance when he is not yet a be
liever ?

14. L. I beseech you lay aside the method
of the philosophers and let us talk with Chris
tian simplicity ; that is, if you are willing t
follow not the logicians, but the Galilea
fishermen. Does it seem right to you that a
Arian should be a bishop ?

O. You prove him a bishop becaus
you receive those he has baptized. An
it is here that you are to blame :—Wh
are there walls of separation between u
when we are at one in faith and in receivin
Arians ?

L. I asked you before not to talk like a ph
losopher, but like a Christian.

O. Do you wish to learn, or to argue ?

L. Of course I argue because I want t
know the reason for what you do.

O. If you argue, you have already had a
answer. I receive an Arian bishop for th
same reason that you receive a person who
only baptized. If you wish to learn, com
over to my side : for an opponent must b
overcome, it is only a disciple who can b
taught.

L. Before I can be a disciple, I must hea
one preach whom I feel to be my master.

O. You are not dealing quite fairly : yo
wish me to be your teacher on the terms tha
you may treat me as an opponent wheneve
you please. I will teach you therefore in th
same spirit. We agree in faith, we agree i
receiving heretics, let us also be at one in ou
terms of communion.

L. That is not teaching, but arguing.

O. As you ask for peace with a shield i
your hand, I also must carry my olive branc
with a sword grafted in it.

L. I drop my hands in token of submissior
You are conqueror. But in laying down m
arms, I ask the meaning of the oath you forc
me to take.

O. Certainly, but first I congratulate yo
and thank Christ my God for your good di
positions which have made you turn from th

---

[1] This was, approximately, the Patripassian form of the heresy,
according to which the person of the Father who is one with the
Son, was incarnate in Christ, and the Father might then be said
to have died upon the cross. The personality of the Holy Ghost
appears to have been denied. With varying shades of opinion
and modes of expression the doctrine was expounded by
Praxeas (circ. A. D. 200), Noetius (A. D. 220), Sabellius (A. D.
225), Beryllus and Paul of Samosata (circ. A. D. 250).

unsavoury teaching of the [1] Sardinians to that which the whole world approves as true ; and no longer say as some do, [2] "Help, Lord ; for the godly man ceaseth." By their impious words they make of none effect the cross of Christ, subject the Son of God to the devil, and would have us now understand the Lord's lamentation over sinners to apply to all men, "What profit is there in my blood, when I go down to the pit?" But God forbid that our Lord should have died in vain. [4] The strong man is bound, and his goods are spoiled. What the Father says is fulfilled, [5] "Ask of me, and I will give thee the nations for thine inheritance, and the uttermost parts of the earth for thy possession." [6] "Then the channels of water appeared, and the foundations of the world were laid bare." [7] "In them hath he set a tabernacle for the sun, and there is nothing hid from the heat thereof." The Psalmist fully possessed by God sings, [8] "The words of the enemy are come to an end, and the cities which thou hast overthrown."

15. And what is the position, I should like to know, of those excessively scrupulous, or rather excessively profane persons, who assert that there are more synagogues than Churches? How is it that the devil's kingdoms have been destroyed, and now at last in the consummation of the ages, the idols have fallen? If Christ has no Church, or if he has one only, in Sardinia, he has grown very poor. And if Satan owns Britain, Gaul, the East, the races of India, barbarous nations, and the whole world at the same time, how is it that the trophies of the cross have been collected in a mere corner of the earth? Christ's powerful opponent, forsooth, gave over to him the serpent of Spain: he disdained to own a poor province and its half-starved inhabitants. If they flatter themselves that they have on their side that verse of the gospel, [10] "Howbeit when the Son of man cometh, shall he find faith on the earth?" let me remind them that the faith in question is that of which the Lord himself said, [11] "Thy faith hath made thee whole." And elsewhere, of the centurion, [12] "I have not found so great faith, no, not in Israel." And again, to the Apostles, [13] "Why are ye fearful, O ye of little faith?" In another place also, [14] "If ye have faith as a grain of mustard seed, ye shall

say unto this mountain, Remove hence to yonder place, and it shall remove." For neither the centurion nor that poor woman who for twelve years was wasting away with a bloody flux, had believed in the mysteries of the Trinity, for these were revealed to the Apostles after the resurrection of Christ ; so that the faith of such as believe in the mystery of the Trinity might have its due pre-eminence: but it was her singleness of mind and her devotion to her God that met with our Lord's approval: [1] "For she said within herself, If I do but touch his garment, I shall be made whole." This is the faith which our Lord said was seldom found. This is the faith which even in the case of those who believe aright is hard to find in perfection. [2] "According to your faith, be it done unto you," says God. I do not, indeed, like the sound of those words. For if it be done unto me according to my faith, I shall perish. And yet I certainly believe in God the Father, I believe in God the Son, and I believe in God the Holy Ghost. I believe in one God ; nevertheless, I would not have it done unto me according to my faith. For the enemy often comes, and sows tares in the Lord's harvest. I do not mean to imply that anything is greater than the purity of heart which believes that mystery ; but undoubted faith towards God it is hard indeed to find. To make my meaning plain, let us suppose a case :—I stand to pray ; I could not pray, if I did not believe ; but if I really believed, I should cleanse that heart of mine with which God is seen, I should beat my hands upon my breast, the tears would stream down my cheeks, my body would shudder, my face grow pale, I should lie at my Lord's feet, weep over them, and wipe them with my hair, I should cling to the cross and not let go my hold until I obtained mercy. But, as it is, frequently in my prayers I am either walking in the arcades, or calculating my interest, or am carried away by base thoughts, so as to be occupied with things the mere mention of which makes me blush. Where is our faith ? Are we to suppose that it was thus that Jonah prayed? or the three youths? or Daniel in the lion's den? or the robber on the cross? I have given these illustrations that you may understand my meaning. But let every one commune with his own heart, and he will find throughout the whole of life how rare a thing it is to find a soul so faithful that it does nothing through the love of glory, nothing on account of the petty gossip of men. For he who fasts does not as an immediate consequence fast unto God, nor he who holds out his hand to a poor man, lend to the Lord.

---

[1] That is the followers of Lucifer, whose see was in Sardinia.
[2] Ps. xii. 1. The Luciferians believed that few or none outside their own sect could be saved.
[3] Ps. xxx. 9. [4] Mark iii. 27. [5] Ps. ii. 8. [6] Ps. xviii. 15.
[7] Lit. In the sun hath he placed his tabernacle, and there is none who can hide himself from the heat thereof. Ps. xix. 6.
[8] Ps. ix. 6. Sept. Vulg. Syr.
[9] The allusion is doubtful. It probably refers to some province of Spain (perhaps that of the Ibera or Ebro), in which the views of Lucifer prevailed and which his followers considered almost the sole land of the faithful. The expression, however, is used in a more general sense by Jerome, Letter VI.
[10] Luke xviii. 8. [11] Matt. ix. 22. [12] Matt. viii. 10.
[13] Matt. viii. 26. [14] Matt. xvii. 20.

---

[1] Matt. ix. 21. [2] Matt. ix. 29.

Vice is next-door neighbour to virtue. It is hard to rest content with God alone for judge.

16. L. I was reserving that passage until last, and you have anticipated my question about it. Almost all our party, or rather not mine any more, use it as a sort of controversial battering ram: as such I am exceedingly glad to see it broken to pieces and pulverized. But will you be so good as to fully explain to me, not in the character of an opponent but of a disciple, why it is that the Church receives those who come from the Arians? The truth is I am unable to answer you a word, but I do not yet give a hearty assent to what you say.

17. O. When Constantius was on the throne and Eusebius and Hypatius were Consuls, there was composed, under the pretext of unity and faith,[1] an unfaithful creed, as it is now acknowledged to have been. For at that time, nothing seemed so characteristic of piety, nothing so befitting a servant of God, as to follow after unity, and to shun separation from communion with the rest of the world. And all the more because the current profession of faith no longer exhibited on the face of it anything profane. "We believe," said they, "in one true God, the Father Almighty. This we also confess: We believe in the only begotten Son of God, who, before all worlds, and before all their origins,[2] was born of God. The only-begotten Son, moreover, we believe to be born alone of the Father alone, God of God, like to his Father who begot Him, according to the Scriptures; whose birth no one knows, but the Father alone who begot Him." Do we find any such words inserted here as [3] "There was a time, when he was not?" Or, "The Son of God is a creature though not made of things which exist." No. This is surely the perfection of faith to say we believe Him to be God of God. Moreover, they called Him the only begotten, "born alone of the Father." What is the meaning of *born?* Surely, *not made.* His birth removed all suspicion of His being a creature. They added further, "Who came down from heaven, was conceived of the Holy Ghost, born of the Virgin Mary, crucified by Pontius Pilate, rose again the third day from the dead, ascended into heaven, sitteth at the right hand of the Father, who will come to judge the quick and the dead." There was a ring of piety in the words, and no one thought

that poison was mingled with the honey of such a proclamation.

18. As regards the term [1]*Usia*, it was not rejected without a show of reason for so doing. [2] "Because it is not found in the Scriptures," they said, "and its novelty is a stumbling-block to many, we have thought it best to dispense with it." The bishops were not anxious about the name, so long as that which it implied was secured. Lastly, at the very time when rumour was rife that there had been some insincerity in the statement of the faith, Valens, bishop of Mursa, who had drawn it up, in the presence of Taurus the pretorian prefect who attended the Synod by imperial command, declared that he was not an Arian, and that he utterly abhorred their blasphemies. However, the thing had been done in secret, and it had not extinguished the general feeling. So on another day, when crowds of bishops and laymen came together in the Church at Ariminum, Muzonius, bishop of the province of Byzacena, to whom by reason of seniority the first rank was assigned by all, spoke as follows: "One of our number has been authorized to read to you, reverend fathers, what reports are being spread and have reached us, so that the evil opinions which ought to grate upon our ears and be banished from our hearts may be condemned with one voice by us all." The whole body of bishops replied, Agreed. And so when Claudius, bishop of the province of Picenum at the request of all present, began to read the blasphemies attributed to Valens, Valens denied they were his and cried aloud, "If any one denies Christ our Lord, the Son of God, begotten of the Father before the worlds, let him be anathema." There was a general chorus of approval, "Let him be anathema." [3] "If anyone denies that the Son is like the Father according to the Scriptures, let him be anathema." All replied, "Let him be anathema." "If anyone does not say that

---

[1] For an account of the "Dated Creed" here referred to, and of the Councils of Seleucia and Ariminum, A. D. 359. see Bright's History of the Church, A. D. 313–451, fourth edition, pp. 93–100.

[2] Principium, the equivalent of the Greek Ἀρχή, which means beginning, or principle, or power.

[3] These two propositions constituted the essence of the teaching of Arius.

---

[1] Usia (οὐσία) is defined by Cyril of Alexandria as that which has existence in itself, independent of everything else to constitute it. A discussion of both it and its companion term *hypostasis* may be found in Newman's Arians, Appendix p. 432. Around οὐσία, or some compound of the word, the great Arian controversy always raged. In asserting that the son was *homoousios* with the Father, i.e., consubstantial or co-essential, the Church affirmed the Godhead of the Son. But the formula experienced varying fortunes. It was disowned as savouring of heterodoxy by the Council of Antioch (264–269) which was held to decide upon the views of Paulus: was imposed at Nicæa (325): considered inexpedient by the great body of the episcopate in the next generation: was most cautiously put forward by Athanasius himself (see Stanley's Hist. of Eastern Church, 1883, p. 240): does not occur in the catecheses of S. Cyril of Jerusalem (347): was momentarily abandoned by 400 bishops at Ariminum who were "tricked and worried" into the act. "They had not," says Newman, "yet got it deeply fixed in their minds as a sort of first principle, that to abandon the formula was to betray the faith."

[2] The distinguishing principle of the doctrine of Acacius was adherence to Scriptural phraseology. See Bright's Hist., p. 69.

[3] The teaching of Aetius and Eunomius, the Anomœans, who were the extremists of the Arians. See Robertson's Hist. of Chris. Ch., fourth edition, pp. 236 237, etc. The other tenets anathematized are Arian or Semi-Arian.

he Son of God is co-eternal with the Father,
et him be anathema." There was again a
horus of approval, " Let him be anathema."
If anyone says that the Son of God is a
reature, like other creatures, let him be
nathema." The answer was the same, " Let
im be anathema." " If anyone says that the
Son was of no existing things, yet not of
God the Father, let him be anathema." All
houted together, " Let him be anathema."
If anyone says, There was a time when the
Son was not, let him be anathema." At this
point all the bishops and the whole Church
together received the words of Valens with
clapping of hands and stamping of feet. And
if anyone thinks we have invented the story
let him examine the public records. At all
events the muniment-boxes of the Churches
are full of it, and the circumstance is fresh in
men's memory. Some of those who took part
in the Synod are still alive, and the Arians
themselves (a fact which may put the truth
beyond dispute) do not deny the accuracy of
our account. When, therefore, all extolled
Valens to the sky and penitently condemned
themselves for having suspected him, the same
Claudius who before had begun to read, said
" There are still a few points which have
escaped the notice of my lord and brother
Valens ; if it seem good to you, let us, in
order to remove all scruples, pass a general
vote of censure upon them. If anyone says
that the Son of God was indeed before all
worlds but was by no means before all time,
so that he puts some thing before Him, let him
be anathema." And many other things which
had a suspicious look were condemned by
Valens when Claudius recited them. If anyone wishes to learn more about them he will
find the account in the acts of the Synod of
Ariminum, the source from which I have myself drawn them.

19. After these proceedings the Council was
dissolved. All returned in gladness to their
own provinces. For the Emperor and all
good men had one and the same aim, that the
East and West should be knit together by the
bond of fellowship. But wickedness does not
long lie hid, and the sore that is healed super-
ficially before the bad humour has been
worked off breaks out again. Valens and
[1] Ursacius and others associated with them in
their wickedness, eminent Christian bishops of
course, began to wave their palms, and to say
they had not denied that He was a creature,
but that He was like other creatures. At that
moment the term *Usia* was abolished : the

Nicene Faith stood condemned by acclamation. The whole world groaned, and was astonished to find itself Arian. Some, therefore,
remained in their own communion, others
began to send letters to those Confessors who
as adherents of Athanasius were in exile ;
several despairingly bewailed the better relations into which they had entered. But a few,
true to human nature, defended their mistake
as an exhibition of wisdom. The ship of the
Apostles was in peril, she was driven by the
wind, her sides beaten with the waves : no hope
was now left. But the Lord awoke and bade
the tempest cease ; the [1] beast died, and there
was a calm once again. To speak more
plainly, all the bishops who had been banished
from their sees, by the clemency of the new
[2] emperor returned to their Churches. Then
Egypt welcomed the [3] triumphant Athanasius ;
then [4] Hilary returned from the battle to the
embrace of the Church of Gaul ; then [5] Eusebius returned and Italy laid aside her mourning weeds. The bishops who had been caught
in the snare at Ariminum and had unwittingly
come to be reported of as heretics, began to
assemble, while they called the Body of our
Lord and all that is holy in the Church to
witness that they had not a suspicion of anything faulty in their own faith. We thought,
said they, the words were to be taken in their
natural meaning, and we had no suspicion that
in the Church of God, the very home of simplicity and sincerity in the confession of truth,
one thing could be kept secret in the heart,
another uttered by the lips. We thought too
well of bad men and were deceived. We did
not suppose that the bishops of Christ were fighting against Christ. There was much besides
which they said with tears, but I pass it over
for brevity's sake. They were ready to condemn their [6] former subscription as well as all
the blasphemies of the Arians. Here I ask
our excessively scrupulous friends what they
think ought to have been done with those who
made this Confession? Deprive the old bishops, they will say, and ordain new ones. The
plan was tried. But how many whose conscience does not condemn them will allow
themselves to be deprived. Particularly when
all the people who loved their bishops flocked
together, ready to stone and slay those who
attempted to deprive them. The bishops
should, it may be said, have kept to themselves

---

[1] Constantius.   [2] Julian.
[3] In August 362, " All Egypt seemed to assemble in the city
(Alexandria), which blazed with lights and rang with acclamations ; the air was fragrant with incense burnt in token of joy ;
men formed a choir to precede the Archbishop ; to hear his
voice, to catch a glimpse of his face, even to see his shadow, was
deemed happiness." Bright, p. 115.
[4] Bishop of Poictiers (A. D. 350). Died A. D. 368.
[5] Bishop of Vercellae in N. Italy. Died about A. D. 370. Both
he and Hilary had been sent into exile by Constantius for their
opposition to Arianism.
[6] That is, the creed of Ariminum.

---

[1] Bishop of Singedunum (Belgrade). " He and Valens, bishop
of Mursa (in Pannonia) appear at every Synod and Council from
330 till about 370, as leaders of the Arian party, both in the East
and West . . . They are described by Athanasius as the disciples
of Arius." Dict. of Chris. Biog.

within their own communion. That is to say, with senseless cruelty they would have surrendered the whole world to the devil. Why condemn those who were not Arians? Why rend the Church when it was continuing in the harmony of the faith? Lastly, were they by obstinacy to make Arians of orthodox believers? We know that at the Council of Nicæa, which was assembled on account of the Arian perfidy, eight Arian bishops were welcomed, and there is not a bishop in the world at the present day whose ordination is not dependent on that Council. This being so, how could they act in opposition to it, when their loyalty to it had cost them the pain of exile?

20. L. Were Arians really then received after all? Pray tell me who they were.

O. [1] Eusebius, bishop of Nicomedia, [2] Theognis, bishop of Nicæa, Saras, at the time presbyter of Libya, [3] Eusebius, bishop of Cæsarea in Palestine, and others whom it would be tedious to enumerate; Arius also, the presbyter, the original source of all the trouble; Euzoius the deacon, [4] who succeeded Eudoxius as bishop of Antioch, and Achillas, the reader. These three who were clerics of the Church of Alexandria were the originators of the heresy.

L. Suppose a person were to deny that they were welcomed back, how is he to be refuted?

O. There are men still living who took part in that Council. And if that is not enough, because owing to the time that has elapsed they are but few, and it is impossible for witnesses to be everywhere, if we read the acts and names of the bishops of the Council of Nicæa, we find that those who we saw just now were welcomed back, did subscribe the *homoousion* along with the rest.

L. Will you point out how, after the Council of Nicæa, they relapsed into their unfaithfulness?

O. A good suggestion, for unbelievers are in the habit of shutting their eyes and denying that things which they dislike ever happened. But how could they afterwards do anything but relapse, when it was owing to

them that the Council was convened, and their letters and impious treatises which were published before the Council, remain even to the present day? Seeing, therefore, that at that time three hundred bishops or more welcomed a few men whom they might have rejected without injury to the Church, I am surprised that certain persons, who are certainly upholders of the faith of Nicæa, are so harsh as to think that [1] three Confessors returning from exile were not bound in the interests of the world's salvation to do what so many illustrious men did of their own accord. But, to go back to our starting point, on the return of the Confessors it was determined, in a synod afterwards [2] held at Alexandria, that, the authors of the heresy excepted (who could not be excused on the ground of error), penitents should be admitted to communion with the Church: not that they who had been heretics could be bishops, but because it was clear that those who were received had not been heretics. The West assented to this decision, and it was through this conclusion, which the necessities of the times demanded, that the world was snatched from the jaws of Satan. I have reached a very difficult subject, where I am compelled against my wishes and my purpose, to think somewhat otherwise of that saintly man Lucifer than his merits demand, and my own courtesy requires. But what am I to do? Truth opens my mouth and urges my reluctant tongue to utter the thoughts of my heart. At such a crisis of the Church, when the wolves were wildly raging, he separated off a few sheep and abandoned the remnant of the flock. He himself was a good shepherd, but he was leaving a vast spoil to the beasts of prey. I take no notice of reports originating with certain evil speakers, though maintained by them to be authenticated facts; such as that he acted thus through the love of glory, and the desire of handing down his name to posterity; or again that he was influenced by the grudge he bore against Eusebius on account of the [3] quarrel at Antioch. I believe none of these reports in the case of such a man; and this I will constantly affirm even now—that the difference between us and him is one of words, not of things, if he really does receive those who have been baptized by the Arians.

21. L. The account I used before to hear given of these things was widely different, and, as I now think, better calculated to promote error than hope. But I thank Christ my God for pouring into my heart the light of truth, that I might no longer profanely call the

---

[1] Said to have been the "most prominent and most distinguished man of the entire movement." Athanasius suggested that he was the teacher rather than the disciple of Arius. He died A. D. 342.

[2] Regarded as one of the chief opponents of Athanasius. He and others it is said saved themselves from exile by secretly substituting ὁμοιούσιος for ὁμοούσιος in the sentence of the Council.

[3] Born, probably, about A. D. 260. He was made bishop of Cæsarea about 313 and lived to be eighty. At the time of the Council he was the most learned man and most famous living writer. He had great influence with Constantine, and was among the most moderate Arians.

[4] Eudoxius was deposed from the bishopric of Antioch by the Council of Seleucia, A. D. 359; but the immediate predecessor of Euzoius was Meletius, deposed A. D. 361. Baronius describes him as the worst of all the Arians. Euzoius had been the companion and intimate friend of Arius from an early age. Athanasius (Hist. Arian. p. 858) calls him the "Canaanite."

---

[1] Saints Athanasius, Hilary of Poictiers, and Eusebius of Vercellæ.
[2] A. D. 328, when Athanasius was consecrated bishop.
[3] See introduction.

Church, which is His Virgin, the harlot of the devil. There is one other point I should like you to explain. What are we to say about Hilary who does not receive even those who have been baptized by the Arians?

O. Since Hilary when he left the Church was only a deacon, and since the Church is to him, though to him alone, a mere worldly multitude, he can neither duly celebrate the Eucharist, for he has no bishops or priests, nor can he give baptism without the Eucharist. And since the man is now dead, inasmuch as he was a deacon and could ordain no one to follow him, his sect died with him. For there is no such thing as a Church without bishops. But passing over a few very insignificant persons who are in their own esteem both laymen and bishops, let me point out to you what views we should hold respecting the Church at large.

L. You have settled a great question in three words, as the saying is, and indeed while you speak, I feel that I am on your side. But when you stop, some old misgivings arise as to why we receive those who have been baptized by heretics.

O. That is just what I had in mind when I said I would point out what views we ought to hold concerning the Church at large. For many are exercised by the misgivings you speak of. I shall perhaps be tedious in my explanation, but it is worth while if the truth gains.

22. Noah's ark was a type of the Church, as the Apostle Peter says—[2] "In Noah's ark few, that is, eight souls, were saved through water: which also after a true likeness doth now save us, even baptism." As in the ark there were all kinds of animals, so also in the Church there are men of all races and characters. As in the one there was the leopard with the kids, the wolf with the lambs, so in the other there are found the righteous and sinners, that is,[3] vessels of gold and silver with those of wood and of earth. The ark had its rooms: the Church has many mansions. Eight souls were saved in Noah's ark. And [4] Ecclesiastes bids us "give a portion to seven, yea, even unto eight," that is to believe both Testaments. This is why some psalms bear the inscription[5] *for the octave*, and why the one hundred and nineteenth psalm is divided into portions of eight verses each beginning

with its own letter for the instruction of the righteous. The beatitudes which our Lord spoke to his disciples on the mountain, thereby delineating the Church, are eight. And Ezekiel for the building of the temple employs the number eight. And you will find many other things expressed in the same way in the Scriptures. The raven also is sent forth from the ark but does not return, and afterwards the dove announces peace to the earth. So also in the Church's baptism, that most unclean bird the devil is expelled, and the dove of the Holy Spirit announces peace to our earth. The construction of the ark was such that it began with being thirty cubits broad and gradually narrowed to one. Similarly the Church, consisting of many grades, ends in deacons, presbyters, and bishops. The ark was in peril in the flood, the Church is in peril in the world. When Noah left the ark he planted a vineyard, drank thereof, and was drunken. Christ also, born in the flesh, planted the Church and suffered. The elder son made sport of his father's nakedness, the younger covered it: and the Jews mocked God crucified, the Gentiles honoured Him. The daylight would fail me if I were to explain all the mysteries of the ark and compare them with the Church. Who are the eagles amongst us? Who the doves and lions, who the stags, who the worms and serpents? So far as our subject requires I will briefly show you. It is not the sheep only who abide in the Church, nor do clean birds only fly to and fro there; but amid the grain other seed is sown,[1] "amidst the neat corn-fields burrs and caltrops and barren oats lord it in the land." What is the husbandman to do? Root up the darnel? In that case the whole harvest is destroyed along with it. Every day the farmer diligently drives the birds away with strange noises, or frightens them with scarecrows: here he cracks a whip, there he spreads out some other object to terrify them. Nevertheless he suffers from the raids of nimble roes or the wantonness of the wild asses; here the mice convey the corn to their garners underground, there the ants crowd thickly in and ravage the corn-field. Thus the case stands. No one who has land is free from care. [2] While the householder slept the enemy sowed tares among the wheat, and when the servants proposed to go and root them up the master forbade them, reserving for himself the separation of the chaff and the grain. [3] There are vessels of wrath and of mercy which the Apostle speaks of in the house of God. The day then will come when the storehouses of the Church shall be opened and the Lord will

---

[1] This Hilary was a deacon of Rome, sent by Liberius the bishop with Lucifer and Pancratius to the Emperor Constantius. He joined the Luciferians, and wrote in their interest on the re-baptism of heretics. He appears, however, to have been reconciled before his death.
[2] 1 Pet. iii. 20.   [3] 2 Tim. ii. 20.   [4] Ecc. xi. 2.
[5] Vulg. for עַל שְׁשִׁינִית Pss. vi. xii. and 1 Chron. xv. 21, The meaning is ‏ ‎ probably " in a lower octave," or, "in the bass." According to others, an air, or key in which the psalm was to be sung, or a musical instrument with eight strings.

[1] Virg. Georg. i. 154.   [2] S. Matt. xiii. 24 sq.
[3] Rom. ix. 22, 23 : 2 Tim. ii. 20, 21.

bring forth the vessels of wrath ; and, as they depart, the saints will say,[1] "They went out from us, but they were not of us ; for if they had been of us, they would no doubt have continued with us." No one can take to himself the prerogative of Christ, no one before the day of judgment can pass judgment upon men. If the Church is already cleansed, what shall we reserve for the Lord ? [2] "There is a way which seemeth right unto a man, but the end thereof are the ways of death." When our judgment is so prone to error, upon whose opinion can we rely ?

23. Cyprian of blessed memory tried to avoid broken cisterns and not to drink of strange waters: and therefore, rejecting heretical baptism, he summoned his [3] African synod in opposition to Stephen,[4] who was the blessed Peter's twenty-second successor in the see of Rome. They met to discuss this matter ; but the attempt failed. At last those very bishops who had together with him determined that heretics must be re-baptized, reverted to the old custom and published a fresh decree. Do you ask what course we must pursue ? What we do our forefathers handed down to us as their forefathers to them. But why speak of later times ? When the blood of Christ was but lately shed and the apostles were still in Judæa, the Lord's body was asserted to be a phantom ; the Galatians had been led away to the observance of the law, and the Apostle was a second time in travail with them ; the Corinthians did not believe the resurrection of the flesh, and he endeavoured by many arguments to bring them back to the right path. Then came [5] Simon Magus and his disciple Menander. They asserted themselves to be [6] powers of God. Then [7] Basilides invented the most high god *Abraxas* and the three hundred and sixty-five manifestations of him. Then [8] Nicolas, one of the seven Deacons, and one whose lechery knew no rest by night or day, indulged in his filthy dreams. I say nothing of the Jewish heretics who before the coming of Christ destroyed the law delivered to them: of [9] Dositheus, the leader of the Samaritans

who rejected the prophets : of the Sadducees who sprang from his root and denied even the resurrection of the flesh: of the Pharisees who separated themselves from the Jews[1] on account of certain superfluous observances, and took their name from the fact of their dissent : of the Herodians who accepted Herod as the Christ. I come to those heretics who have mangled the Gospels, [2] Saturninus, and the [3] Ophites, [4] the Cainites and [5] Sethites, and [6] Carpocrates, and [7] Cerinthus, and his successor [8] Ebion, and the other pests, the most of which broke out while the apostle John was still alive, and yet we do not read that any of these men were re-baptized.

24. As we have made mention of that distinguished saint, let us show also from his Apocalypse that repentance unaccompanied by baptism ought to be allowed valid in the case of heretics. It is imputed (Rev. ii. 4) to the angel of Ephesus that he has forsaken his first love. In the angel of the Church of Pergamum the eating of idol-sacrifices is censured (Rev. ii. 14), and the doctrine of the Nicolaitans (ib. 15). Likewise the angel of Thyatira is rebuked (ib. 20) on account of Jezebel the prophetess, and the idol meats, and fornication. And yet the Lord encourages all these to repent, and adds a threat, moreover, of future punishment if they do not turn. Now he would not urge them to repent unless he intended to grant pardon

---

[1] I John ii. 19.   [2] Prov. xiv. 12.
[3] Stephen was willing to admit all heretical baptism, even that by Marcionites and Ophites ; Cyprian would admit none. The Council was held at Carthage A. D. 255, and was followed by two in the next year.
[4] Bishop of Rome from May 12, A. D. 254, to Aug. 2, A. D. 257. See note on ch. 25.
[5] The words of 1 John iv. 3 would appear to support Jerome's remark.
[6] Acts viii. 10. In the Clementine Homilies and Recognitions Simon is the constant opponent of St. Peter.
[7] Commonly regarded as the chief among the Egyptian Gnostics. The Basilidian system is described by Irenaeus (101f).
[8] Acts vi. 5. Rev. ii. 6, 15. As to how far Jerome's estimate of the character of Nicolas is correct, the article *Nicolas* in Smith's Dict. of Bible may be consulted.
[9] Jerome here reproduces almost exactly the remark of Pseudo-Tertullian. The Dositheans were probably a Jewish or Samaritan ascetic sect, something akin to the Essenes.

---

[1] The name Pharisee implies separation, but in the sense of dedication to God.
[2] Of Antioch. One of the earliest of the Gnostics (second century).
[3] The Ophites, whose name is derived from ὄφις, a serpent, were a sect which lasted from the second century to the sixth. Some of them believed that the serpent of Gen. iii. was either the Divine Wisdom, or the Christ himself, come to enlighten mankind. Their errors may in great measure, like those of the Cainites, be traced to the belief, common to all systems of Gnosticism, that the Creator of the world, who was the God of the Jews, was not the same as the Supreme Being, but was in antagonism to Him. They supposed that the Scriptures were written in the interest of the Demiurge or Creator, and that a false colouring being given to the story, the real worthies were those who are reprobated in the sacred writings.
[4] The Cainites regarded as saints, Cain, Korah, Dathan, the Sodomites, and even the traitor Judas.
[5] The Sethites are said to have looked upon Seth as the same person as Christ.
[6] Carpocrates, another Gnostic, held that our Lord was the son of Joseph and Mary, and was distinguished from other men by nothing except moral superiority. He also taught the indifference of actions in themselves, and maintained that they take their quality from opinion or from legislation ; he advocated community of goods and of wives, basing his views on the doctrine of natural rights. See Mosheim, Cent. ii.
[7] Cerinthus was a native of Judæa, and after having studied at Alexandria established himself as a teacher in his own country. He afterwards removed to Ephesus, and there became prominent. He held that Jesus and the Christ were not the same person ; Jesus was, he said, a real man, the son of Joseph and Mary ; the Christ was an emanation which descended upon Jesus at his baptism to reveal the Most High, but which forsook him before the Passion. S. John in his Gospel and Epistles combats this error. See Westcott's Introduction to 1 John, p. xxxiv. (second ed.) etc. Cerinthus is said to have been the heretic with whom S. John refused to be under the same roof at the bath. To him as author is also referred the doctrine of the Millennium.
[8] The Ebionites were mere humanitarians. Whether Ebion ever existed, or whether the sect took its name from the *beggarliness* of their doctrine, or their vow of *poverty*, or the *poorness of spirit* which they professed, is disputed.

to the penitents. Is there any indication of his having said, Let them be re-baptized who have been baptized in the faith of the Nicolaitans? or let hands be laid upon those of the people of Pergamum who at that time believed, having held the doctrine of Balaam? Nay, rather, "Repent therefore,"[1] he says, "or else I come to thee quickly, and I will make war against them with the sword of my mouth."

25. If, however, those men who were ordained by Hilary, and who have lately become sheep without a shepherd, are disposed to allege Scripture in support of what the blessed Cyprian[2] left in his letters advocating the rebaptization of heretics, I beg them to remember that he did not anathematize those who refused to follow him. At all events, he remained in communion with such as opposed his views. He was content with exhorting them, on account of [3]Novatus and the numerous other heretics then springing up, to receive no one who did not condemn his previous error. In fact, he thus concludes the discussion of the subject with Stephen, the Roman Pontiff : " These things, dearest brother, I have brought to your knowledge on account of our mutual respect and love unfeigned, believing, as I do, that from the sincerity of your piety and your faith you will approve such things as are alike consonant with piety and true in themselves. But I know that some persons are unwilling to abandon views which they have once entertained, and are averse to a change of purpose ; they would rather, without breaking the bond of peace and concord between colleagues, adhere to their own plans, when once they have been adopted. This is a matter in which we do not force anyone, or lay down a law for anyone ; let each follow his own free choice in the administration of the Church : let each be ruler in his own sphere since he must give account of his action to the Lord." In the letter also to Jubaianus on the re-baptization of heretics, towards the end, he says this : " I have written these few remarks, my dearest brother, to the best of my poor ability, without dictating to anyone, or prejudicing the case of anyone : I would not hinder a single bishop from doing what he thinks right with the full exercise of his own judgment. So far as is possible, we avoid disputes with colleagues and fellow-bishops about the heretics, and maintain with them a divine harmony and the Lord's peace, particularly since the Apostle says :[1] ' But if any man seem to be contentious, we have no such custom, neither the churches of God.' With patience and gentleness we preserve charity at heart, the honour of our order, the bond of faith, the harmony of the episcopate."

26. There is another argument which I shall adduce, and against that not even Hilary,[2] the modern Deucalion, will venture to mutter a syllable. If heretics are not baptized and must be re-baptized because they were not in the Church, Hilary himself also is not a Christian. For he was baptized in that Church which always allowed heretical baptism. Before the Synod of Ariminum was held, before Lucifer went into exile, Hilary when a deacon of the Roman Church welcomed those who came over from the heretics on account of the baptism which they had previously received. It can hardly be that Arians are the only heretics, and that we are to accept all but those whom they have baptized. You were a deacon, Hilary (the Church may say), and received those whom the Manichæans had baptized. You were a deacon, and acknowledged Ebion's baptism. All at once after Arius arose you began to be quite out of conceit with yourself. You and your household separated from us, and opened a new laver of your own. If some angel or apostle has re-baptized you, I will not disparage your procedure. But since you who raise your sword against me are the son of my womb, and nourished on the milk of my breasts, return to me what I gave you, and be, if you can, a Christian in some other way. Suppose I am a harlot, still I am your mother. You say, I do not keep the marriage bed undefiled : still what I am now I was when you were conceived. If I commit adultery with Arius, I did the same before with Praxias, with Ebion, with Cerinthus, and Novatus. You think much of them and welcome them, adulterers as they are, to your mother's home. I don't know why one adulterer more than others should offend you.

27. But if anyone thinks it open to question whether heretics were always welcomed by our ancestors, let him read the letters of the blessed Cyprian in which he applies the lash to Stephen, bishop of Rome, and his errors which had grown inveterate by usage.[3] Let

---

[1] Rev. ii. 16.
[2] Cyprian's opinion as stated in his reply to the Numidian and Mauritanian bishops (Ep. 71) was that converts must be baptized, unless they had received the regular baptism of the Church before falling into heresy or schism, in which case imposition of hands would suffice. The question was afterwards decided against Cyprian's views by the Council of Arles (A. D. 314), which ordered that if the baptism had been administered in the name of the Trinity, converts should be admitted to the Church by imposition of hands.
[3] For Novatus and an account of the dispute between Cyprian and Stephen, see Robertson's "Hist. of Christian Church," fourth ed., vol. i. pp. 120-127.

[1] 1 Cor. xi. 16.
[2] As Deucalion was left alone after the flood, so, Jerome implies, Hilary imagined himself the sole survivor after the flood of Arianism.
[3] The advocates on each side could plead immemorial local usage. If imposition of hands was the rule at Rome, synods held at Iconium and at Synnada had established the rule of re-baptism nearly throughout Asia Minor. In Africa the same practice had been sanctioned early in the third century, but it seems to have fallen into disuse long before Cyprian's time.

him also read the pamphlets of Hilary on the re-baptization of heretics which he published against us, and he will there find Hilary himself confessing that [1]Julius, Marcus, Sylvester, and the other bishops of old alike welcomed all heretics to repentance ; and, further, to shew that he could not justly claim possession of the true custom ; the Council of Nicæa also, to which we referred not long ago, welcomed all heretics with the exception of [2] the disciples of Paul of Samosata. And, what is more, it allows a Novatian bishop on conversion to have the rank of presbyter,[3] a decision which condemns both Lucifer and Hilary, since the same person who is ordained is also baptized.

28. I might spend the day in speaking to the same effect, and dry up all the streams of argument with the single Sun of the Church. But as we have already had a long discussion and the protracted controversy has wearied out the attention of our audience, I will tell you my opinion briefly and without reserve. We ought to remain in that Church which was founded by the Apostles and continues to this day. If ever you hear of any that are called Christians taking their name not from the Lord Jesus Christ, but from some other, for instance, Marcionites, Valentinians, Men of

the mountain or the plain,[1] you may be sure that you have there not the Church of Christ, but the synagogue of Antichrist. For the fact that they took their rise after the foundation of the Church is proof that they are those whose coming the Apostle foretold. And let them not flatter themselves if they think they have Scripture authority for their assertions, since the devil himself quoted Scripture, and the essence of the Scriptures is not the letter, but the meaning. Otherwise, if we follow the letter, we too can concoct a new dogma and assert that such persons as wear shoes and have two coats must not be received into the Church.

L. You must not suppose that victory rests with you only. We are both conquerors, and each of us carries off the palm,—you are victorious over me, and I over my error. May I always when I argue be so fortunate as to exchange wrong opinions for better ones. I must, however, make a confession, because I best know the character of my party, and own that they are more easily conquered than convinced.

---

[1] Bishops of Rome—Julius 337–352 ; Mark Jan. 18–Oct. 7, 336; Sylvester 314–335.
[2] Canon 19.
[3] Canon 8. The bishop might give him the nominal honour of a bishop.

[1] By the " men of the mountain or the plain," Jerome appears to contemptuously designate the Circumcellions who were an extreme section of the Donatists. They roamed about the country in bands of both sexes, and struck terror into the peaceable inhabitants. They were guilty of the grossest excesses, and no Catholic was safe except in the towns. Robertson's " Hist. of the Church," vol. i. fourth ed. pp. 200, 419, and the original authorities there referred to.

THE PERPETUAL VIRGINITY OF BLESSED MARY

Against Helvidius.

This tract appeared about A.D. 383. The question which gave occasion to it was whether the Mother of our Lord remained a Virgin after His birth. Helvidius maintained that the mention in the Gospels of the " sisters " and " brethren " of our Lord was proof that the Blessed Virgin had subsequent issue, and he supported his opinion by the writings of Tertullian and Victorinus. The outcome of his views was that virginity was ranked below matrimony. Jerome vigorously takes the other side, and tries to prove that the " sisters " and " brethren " spoken of, were either children of Joseph by a former marriage, or first cousins, children of the sister of the Virgin. A detailed account of the controversy will be found in Farrar's " Early Days of Christianity," pp. 124 sq. When Jerome wrote this treatise both he and Helvidius were at Rome, and Damasus was Pope. The only contemporary notice preserved of Helvidius is that by Jerome in the following pages.

Jerome maintains against Helvidius three propositions :—

1st. That Joseph was only putatively, not really, the husband of Mary.
2d. That the " brethren " of the Lord were his cousins, not his own brethren.
3d. That virginity is better than the married state.

1. The first of these occupies ch. 3-8. It turns upon the record in Matt. i. 18-25, and especially on the words, " Before they came together " (c. 4), " knew her not till, &c." (5-8).
2. The second (c. 9-17) turns upon the words " first-born son " (9, 10), which, Jerome argues, are applicable not only to the eldest of several, but also to an only son : and the mention of brothers and sisters, whom Jerome asserts to have been children of Mary the wife of Cleophas or Clopas (11-16); he appeals to many Church writers in support of this view (17).

3. In support of his preference of virginity to marriage, Jerome argues that not only Mary but Joseph also remained in the virgin state (19); that, though marriage may sometimes be a holy estate, it presents great hindrances to prayer (20), and the teaching of Scripture is that the states of virginity and continency are more accordant with God's will than that of marriage (21, 22).

1. I was requested by certain of the brethren not long ago to reply to a pamphlet written by one Helvidius. I have deferred doing so, not because it is a difficult matter to maintain the truth and refute an ignorant boor who has scarce known the first glimmer of learning, but because I was afraid my reply might make him appear worth defeating. There was the further consideration that a turbulent fellow, the only individual in the world who thinks himself both priest and layman, one who,[1] as has been said, thinks that eloquence consists in loquacity and considers speaking ill of anyone to be the witness of a good conscience, would begin to blaspheme worse than ever if opportunity of discussion were afforded him. He would stand as it were on a pedestal, and would publish his views far and wide. There was reason also to fear that when truth failed him he would assail his opponents with the weapon of abuse. But all these motives for silence, though just, have more justly ceased to influence me, because of the scandal caused to the brethren who were disgusted at his ravings. The axe of the Gospel must therefore be now laid to the root of the barren tree, and both it and its fruitless foliage cast into the fire, so that Helvidius who has never learnt to speak, may at length learn to hold his tongue.

2. I must call upon the Holy Spirit to express His meaning by my mouth and defend the virginity of the Blessed Mary. I must call upon the Lord Jesus to guard the sacred lodging of the womb in which He abode for ten months from all suspicion of sexual intercourse. And I must also entreat God the Father to show that the mother of His Son, who was a mother before she was a bride, continued a Virgin after her son was born. We have no desire to career over the fields of eloquence, we do not resort to the snares of the logicians or the thickets of Aristotle. We shall adduce the actual words of Scripture. Let him be refuted by the same proofs which he employed against us, so that he may see that it was possible for him to read what is written, and yet to be unable to discern the established conclusion of a sound faith.

3. His first statement was : "Matthew says,[2] Now the birth of Jesus Christ was on this wise : When his mother Mary had been betrothed to Joseph, before they came together she was found with child of the Holy Ghost. And

Joseph her husband, being a righteous man, and not willing to make her a public example, was minded to put her away privately. But when he thought on these things, behold, an angel of the Lord appeared unto him in a dream, saying, Joseph, thou son of David, fear not to take unto thee Mary thy wife : for that which is conceived in her is of the Holy Ghost." Notice, he says, that the word used is *betrothed*, not *intrusted* as you say, and of course the only reason why she was betrothed was that she might one day be married. And the Evangelist would not have said *before they came together* if they were not to come together, for no one would use the phrase *before he dined* of a man who was not going to dine. Then, again, the angel calls her *wife* and speaks of her as *united* to Joseph. We are next invited to listen to the declaration of Scripture :[1] "And Joseph arose from his sleep, and did as the angel of the Lord commanded him, and took unto him his wife ; and knew her not till she had brought forth her son."

4. Let us take the points one by one, and follow the tracks of this impiety that we may show that he has contradicted himself. He admits that she was betrothed, and in the next breath will have her to be a man's wife whom he has admitted to be his betrothed. Again, he calls her wife, and then says the only reason why she was betrothed was that she might one day be married. And, for fear we might not think that enough, "the word used," he says, "is *betrothed* and not *intrusted*, that is to say, not yet a wife, not yet united by the bond of wedlock." But when he continues, "the Evangelist would never have applied the words, *before they came together* to persons who were not to come together, any more than one says, before he dined, when the man is not going to dine," I know not whether to grieve or laugh. Shall I convict him of ignorance, or accuse him of rashness? Just as if, supposing a person to say, "Before dining in harbour I sailed to Africa," his words could not hold good unless he were compelled some day to dine in harbour. If I choose to say, "the apostle Paul before he went to Spain was put in fetters at Rome," or (as I certainly might) "Helvidius, before he repented, was cut off by death," must Paul on being released at once go to Spain, or must Helvidius repent after death, although the Scripture says[2] "In sheol who shall give thee thanks?" Must we not rather understand

---

[1] Ut ait ille. The sentiment, almost in the same words, is found in Tertullian against Hermogenes, ch. 1.
[2] i. 18 sq.

[1] S. Matt. i. 24, 25.   [2] Ps. vi. 5.

that the preposition *before*, although it frequently denotes order in time, yet sometimes refers only to order in thought? So that there is no necessity, if sufficient cause intervened to prevent it, for our thoughts to be realized. When, then, the Evangelist says *before they came together*, he indicates the time immediately preceding marriage, and shows that matters were so far advanced that she who had been betrothed was on the point of becoming a wife. As though he said, before they kissed and embraced, before the consummation of marriage, she was found to be with child. And she was found to be so by none other than Joseph, who watched the swelling womb of his betrothed with the anxious glances, and, at this time, almost the privilege, of a husband. Yet it does not follow, as the previous examples showed, that he had intercourse with Mary after her delivery, when his desires had been quenched by the fact that she had already conceived. And although we find it said to Joseph in a dream, "Fear not to take Mary thy wife"; and again, "Joseph arose from his sleep, and did as the angel of the Lord commanded him, and took unto him his wife," no one ought to be disturbed by this, as though, inasmuch as she is called *wife*, she ceases to be *betrothed*, for we know it is usual in Scripture to give the title to those who are betrothed. The following evidence from Deuteronomy establishes the point.[1] "If the man," says the writer, "find the damsel that is betrothed in the field, and the man force her, and lie with her, he shall surely die, because he hath humbled his neighbour's wife." And in another place,[2] "If there be a damsel that is a virgin betrothed unto an husband, and a man find her in the city, and lie with her; then ye shall bring them both out unto the gate of that city, and ye shall stone them with stones that they die; the damsel, because she cried not, being in the city; and the man, because he hath humbled his neighbour's wife: so thou shalt put away the evil from the midst of thee." Elsewhere also,[3] "And what man is there that hath betrothed a wife, and hath not taken her? let him go and return unto his house, lest he die in the battle, and another man take her." But if anyone feels a doubt as to why the Virgin conceived after she was betrothed rather than when she had no one betrothed to her, or, to use the Scripture phrase, no husband, let me explain that there were three reasons. First, that by the genealogy of Joseph, whose kinswoman Mary was, Mary's origin might also be shown. Secondly, that she might not in accordance with the law of Moses be stoned

as an adulteress. Thirdly, that in her flight to Egypt she might have some solace, though it was that of a guardian rather than a husband. For who at that time would have believed the Virgin's word that she had conceived of the Holy Ghost, and that the angel Gabriel had come and announced the purpose of God? and would not all have given their opinion against her as an adulteress, like Susanna? for at the present day, now that the whole world has embraced the faith, the Jews argue that when Isaiah says,[1] "Behold, a virgin shall conceive and bear a son," the Hebrew word denotes a young woman, not a virgin, that is to say, the word is ALMAH, not BETHULAH, a position which, farther on, we shall dispute more in detail. Lastly, excepting Joseph, and Elizabeth, and Mary herself, and some few others who, we may suppose, heard the truth from them, all considered Jesus to be the son of Joseph. And so far was this the case that even the Evangelists, expressing the prevailing opinion, which is the correct rule for a historian, call him the father of the Saviour, as, for instance,[2] "And he (that is, Simeon) came in the Spirit into the temple: and when the parents brought in the child Jesus, that they might do concerning him after the custom of the law;" and elsewhere,[3] "And his parents went every year to Jerusalem at the feast of the passover." And afterwards,[4] "And when they had fulfilled the days, as they were returning, the boy Jesus tarried behind in Jerusalem; and his parents knew not of it." Observe also what Mary herself, who had replied to Gabriel with the words,[5] "How shall this be, seeing I know not a man?" says concerning Joseph,[6] "Son, why hast thou thus dealt with us? behold, thy father and I sought thee sorrowing." We have not here, as many maintain, the utterance of Jews or of mockers. The Evangelists call Joseph father: Mary confesses he was father. Not (as I said before) that Joseph was really the father of the Saviour: but that, to preserve the reputation of Mary, he was regarded by all as his father, although, before he heard the admonition of the angel,[7] "Joseph, thou son of David, fear not to take unto thee Mary thy wife: for that which is conceived in her is of the Holy Ghost," he had thoughts of putting her away privily; which shows that he well knew that the child conceived was not his. But we have said enough, more with the aim of imparting instruction than of answering an opponent, to show why Joseph is called the father of our Lord, and why Mary is called Joseph's wife. This also

---

[1] Deut. xxii. 24, 25.   [2] Deut. xxii. 23, 24.   [3] Deut. xx. 7.

[1] Is. vii. 14. See Cheyne's Isaiah, and critical note.
[2] S. Luke ii. 27.   [3] S. Luke ii. 41.   [4] ib. ii. 43.
[5] ib. i. 34.   [6] S. Luke ii. 48.   [7] S. Matt. i. 20.

at once answers the question why certain persons are called his brethren.

5. This, however, is a point which will find its proper place further on. We must now hasten to other matters. The passage for discussion now is, " And Joseph arose from his sleep, and did as the angel of the Lord commanded him, and took unto him his wife, and knew her not till she had brought forth a son, and he called his name Jesus." Here, first of all, it is quite needless for our opponent to show so elaborately that the word *know* has reference to coition, rather than to intellectual apprehension : as though anyone denied it, or any person in his senses could ever imagine the folly which Helvidius takes pains to refute. Then he would teach us that the adverb *till* implies a fixed and definite time, and when that is fulfilled, he says the event takes place which previously did not take place, as in the case before us, " and knew her not till she had brought forth a son." It is clear, says he, that she was known after she brought forth, and that that knowledge was only delayed by her engendering a son. To defend his position he piles up text upon text, waves his sword like a blind-folded gladiator, rattles his noisy tongue, and ends with wounding no one but himself.

6. Our reply is briefly this,—the words *knew* and *till* in the language of Holy Scripture are capable of a double meaning. As to the former, he himself gave us a dissertation to show that it must be referred to sexual intercourse, and no one doubts that it is often used of the knowledge of the understanding, as, for instance, " the boy Jesus tarried behind in Jerusalem, and his parents knew it not." Now we have to prove that just as in the one case he has followed the usage of Scripture, so with regard to the word *till* he is utterly refuted by the authority of the same Scripture, which often denotes by its use a fixed time (he himself told us so), frequently time without limitation, as when God by the mouth of the prophet says to certain persons,[1] " Even to old age I am he." Will He cease to be God when they have grown old ? And the Saviour in the Gospel tells the Apostles,[2] " Lo, I am with you alway, even unto the end of the world." Will the Lord then after the end of the world has come forsake His disciples, and at the very time when seated on twelve thrones they are to judge the twelve tribes of Israel will they be bereft of the company of their Lord ? Again Paul the Apostle writing to the Corinthians[3] says, " Christ the first-fruits, afterward they that are Christ's, at his coming. Then cometh the end, when he shall have delivered up the kingdom to God, even the Father,

when he shall have put down all rule, and all authority and power. For he must reign, till he hath put all enemies under his feet." Granted that the passage relates to our Lord's human nature, we do not deny that the words are spoken of Him who endured the cross and is commanded to sit afterwards on the right hand. What does he mean then by saying, " for he must reign, till he hath put all enemies under his feet " ? Is the Lord to reign only until His enemies begin to be under His feet, and once they are under His feet will He cease to reign ? Of course His reign will then commence in its fulness when His enemies begin to be under His feet. David also in the fourth Song of Ascents[1] speaks thus, " Behold, as the eyes of servants look unto the hand of their master, as the eyes of a maiden unto the hand of her mistress, so our eyes look unto the Lord our God, until he have mercy upon us." Will the prophet, then, look unto the Lord until he obtain mercy, and when mercy is obtained will he turn his eyes down to the ground ? although elsewhere he says,[2] " Mine eyes fail for thy salvation, and for the word of thy righteousness." I could accumulate countless instances of this usage, and cover the verbosity of our assailant with a cloud of proofs ; I shall, however, add only a few, and leave the reader to discover like ones for himself.

7. The word of God says in Genesis,[3] "And they gave unto Jacob all the strange gods which were in their hand, and the rings which were in their ears ; and Jacob hid them under the oak which was by Shechem, and lost them until this day." Likewise at the end of Deuteronomy,[4] "So Moses the servant of the Lord died there in the land of Moab, according to the word of the Lord. And he buried him in the valley, in the land of Moab over against Beth-peor : but no man knoweth of his sepulchre unto this day." We must certainly understand by *this day* the time of the composition of the history, whether you prefer the view that Moses was the author of the Pentateuch or that Ezra re-edited it. In either case I make no objection. The question now is whether the words *unto this day* are to be referred to the time of publishing or writing the books, and if so it is for him to show, now that so many years have rolled away since that day, that either the idols hidden beneath the oak have been found, or the grave of Moses discovered; for he obstinately maintains that what does not happen so long as the point of time indicated by *until* and *unto* has not been attained, begins to be when that point

---

[1] Is. xlvi. 4.   [2] S. Matt. xxviii. 20.   [3] 1 Cor. xv. 23 sq.

[1] Ps. cxxiii. 2. The songs of the *up-goings* or ascents (τῶν ἀναβαθμῶν *Sept.*, graduum *Vulg.*), are the fifteen psalms cxx.– cxxxiv.
[2] Ps. cxix. 123.   [3] Gen. xxxv. 4, Sept.   [4] Deut. xxxiv. 5–6.

has been reached. He would do well to pay heed to the idiom of Holy Scripture, and understand with us, (it was here he stuck in the mud) that some things which might seem ambiguous if not expressed are plainly intimated, while others are left to the exercise of our intellect. For if, while the event was still fresh in memory and men were living who had seen Moses, it was possible for his grave to be unknown, much more may this be the case after the lapse of so many ages. And in the same way must we interpret what we are told concerning Joseph. The Evangelist pointed out a circumstance which might have given rise to some scandal, namely, that Mary was not known by her husband until she was delivered, and he did so that we might be the more certain that she from whom Joseph refrained while there was room to doubt the import of the vision was not known after her delivery.

8. In short, what I want to know is why Joseph refrained until the day of her delivery? Helvidius will of course reply, because he heard the angel say,[1] "that which is conceived in her is of the Holy Ghost." And in turn we rejoin that he had certainly heard him say,[2] "Joseph, thou son of David, fear not to take unto thee Mary thy wife." The reason why he was forbidden to forsake his wife was that he might not think her an adulteress. Is it true then, that he was ordered not to have intercourse with his wife? Is it not plain that the warning was given him that he might not be separated from her? And could the just man dare, he says, to think of approaching her, when he heard that the Son of God was in her womb? Excellent! We are to believe then that the same man who gave so much credit to a dream that he did not dare to touch his wife, yet afterwards, when he had learnt from the shepherds that the angel of the Lord had come from heaven and said to them,[3] "Be not afraid: for behold I bring you good tidings of great joy which shall be to all people, for there is born to you this day in the city of David a Saviour, which is Christ the Lord;" and when the heavenly host had joined with him in the chorus[4] "Glory to God in the highest, and on earth peace among men of good will;" and when he had seen just Simeon embrace the infant and exclaim,[5] "Now lettest thou thy servant depart, O Lord, according to thy word in peace: for mine eyes have seen thy salvation;" and when he had seen Anna the prophetess, the Magi, the Star, Herod, the angels; Helvidius, I say, would have us believe that Joseph, though well acquainted with such

surprising wonders, dared to touch the temple of God, the abode of the Holy Ghost, the mother of his Lord? Mary at all events "kep` all these sayings in her heart." You cannot for shame say Joseph did not know of them, for Luke tells us,[1] "His father and mother were marvelling at the things which were spoken concerning Him." And yet you with marvellous effrontery contend that the reading of the Greek manuscripts is corrupt, although it is that which nearly all the Greek writers have left us in their books, and not only so, but several of the Latin writers have taken the words the same way. Nor need we now consider the variations in the copies, since the whole record both of the Old and New Testament has since that time been[2] translated into Latin, and we must believe that the water of the fountain flows purer than that of the stream.

9. Helvidius will answer, "What you say, is in my opinion mere trifling. Your arguments are so much waste of time, and the discussion shows more subtlety than truth. Why could not Scripture say, as it said of Thamar and Judah,[3] 'And he took his wife, and knew her again no more'? Could not Matthew find words to express his meaning? 'He knew her not,' he says, 'until she brought forth a son.' He did then, after her delivery, know her, whom he had refrained from knowing until she was delivered."

10. If you are so contentious, your own thoughts shall now prove your master. You must not allow any time to intervene between delivery and intercourse. You must not say,[4] "If a woman conceive seed and bear a man child, then she shall be unclean seven days; as in the days of the separation of her sickness shall she be unclean. And in the eighth day the flesh of his foreskin shall be circumcised. And she shall continue in the blood of her purifying three and thirty days. She shall touch no hallowed thing," and so forth. On your showing, Joseph must at once approach her, and be subject to Jeremiah's[5] reproof, "They were as mad horses in respect of women: every one neighed after his neighbour's wife." Otherwise, how can the words stand good, "he knew her not, till she had brought forth a son," if he waits after the time of another purifying has expired, if his lust must brook another long delay of forty days? The mother must go unpurged from her child-bed taint, and the wailing infant be attended to by the midwives, while the husband clasps his exhausted wife. Thus for-

---

[1] S. Matt. i. 20.   [2] S. Matt. i. 20.
[3] S. Luke ii. 10 sq.   [4] S. Luke ii. 14.
[5] ib. ii. 29.

[1] S. Luke ii. 33.
[2] The allusion is to the Old Latin, the *Versio Itala*. The quotations which follow stand differently in Jerome's Vulgate, made subsequently (391-404). The argument is that, since the copies of the Latin version substantially agree in the present case, it is futile to suppose variations in the original.
[3] Gen. xxxviii. 26.   [4] Lev. xii. 2-3 margin.   [5] Jer. v. 8.

sooth must their married life begin so that the Evangelist may not be convicted of falsehood. But God forbid that we should think thus of the Saviour's mother and of a just man. No midwife assisted at His birth; no women's officiousness intervened. With her own hands she wrapped Him in the swaddling clothes, herself both mother and midwife,[1] "and laid Him," we are told, "in a manger, because there was no room for them in the inn"; a statement which, on the one hand, refutes the ravings of the apocryphal accounts, for Mary herself wrapped Him in the swaddling clothes, and on the other makes the voluptuous notion of Helvidius impossible, since there was no place suitable for married intercourse in the inn.

11. An ample reply has now been given to what he advanced respecting the words *before they came together*, and *he knew her not till she had brought forth a son*. I must now proceed, if my reply is to follow the order of his argument, to the third point. He will have it that Mary bore other sons, and he quotes the passage,[2] "And Joseph also went up to the city of David to enroll himself with Mary, who was betrothed to him, being great with child. And it came to pass, while they were there, the days were fulfilled that she should be delivered, and she brought forth her first-born son." From this he endeavours to show that the term *first-born* is inapplicable except to a person who has brothers, just as he is called *only begotten* who is the only son of his parents.

12. Our position is this: Every only begotten son is a first-born son, but not every first-born is an only begotten. By first-born we understand not only one who is succeeded by others, but one who has had no predecessor. [3] "Everything," says the Lord to Aaron, "that openeth the womb of all flesh which they offer unto the Lord, both of man and beast, shall be thine: nevertheless the first born of man shalt thou surely redeem, and the firstling of unclean beasts shalt thou redeem." The word of God defines *first-born* as everything that openeth the womb. Otherwise, if the title belongs to such only as have younger brothers, the priests cannot claim the firstlings until their successors have been begotten, lest, perchance, in case there were no subsequent delivery it should prove to be the first-born but not merely the only begotten.[4] "And those that are to be redeemed of them from a month old shalt thou redeem, according to thine estimation for the money of five shekels, after the shekel of the sanctuary (the same is twenty gerahs). But the firstling of an ox, or the firstling of a sheep, or the firstling of a goat, thou shalt not redeem;

they are holy." The word of God compels me to dedicate to God everything that openeth the womb if it be the firstling of clean beasts: if of unclean beasts, I must redeem it, and give the value to the priest. I might reply and say, Why do you tie me down to the short space of a month? Why do you speak of the first-born, when I cannot tell whether there are brothers to follow? Wait until the second is born. I owe nothing to the priest, unless the birth of a second should make the one I previously had the first-born. Will not the very points of the letters cry out against me and convict me of my folly, and declare that first-born is a title of him who opens the womb, and is not to be restricted to him who has brothers? And, then, to take the case of John: we are agreed that he was an only begotten son: I want to know if he was not also a first-born son, and whether he was not absolutely amenable to the law. There can be no doubt in the matter. At all events Scripture thus speaks of the Saviour,[1] "And when the days of her purification according to the law of Moses were fulfilled, they brought him up to Jerusalem, to present him to the Lord (as it is written in the law of the Lord, every male that openeth the womb shall be called holy to the Lord) and to offer a sacrifice according to that which is said in the law of the Lord, a pair of turtle-doves, or two young pigeons." If this law relates only to the first-born, and there can be no first-born unless there are successors, no one ought to be bound by the law of the first-born who cannot tell whether there will be successors. But inasmuch as he who has no younger brothers is bound by the law of the first-born, we gather that he is called the first-born who opens the womb and who has been preceded by none, not he whose birth is followed by that of a younger brother. Moses writes in Exodus,[2] "And it came to pass at midnight, that the Lord smote all the first-born in the land of Egypt, from the first-born of Pharaoh that sat on his throne unto the first-born of the captive that was in the dungeon: And all the first-born of cattle." Tell me, were they who then perished by the destroyer, only your first-born, or, something more, did they include the only begotten? If only they who have brothers are called first-born, the only begotten were saved from death. And if it be the fact that the only begotten were slain, it was contrary to the sentence pronounced, for the only begotten to die as well as the first-born. You must either release the only begotten from the penalty, and in that case you become ridiculous: or, if you allow that they were slain, we gain our point, though

[1] S. Luke ii. 7.   [2] S. Luke ii. 4 sq.
[3] Numb. xviii. 15.   [4] Numb. xviii. 16.

[1] S. Luke ii. 22 sq.   [2] Exod. xii. 29.

we have not to thank you for it, that only begotten sons also are called first-born.

13. The last proposition of Helvidius was this, and it is what he wished to show when he treated of the first-born, that brethren of the Lord are mentioned in the Gospels. For example,[1] "Behold, his mother and his brethren stood without, seeking to speak to him." And elsewhere,[2] "After this he went down to Capernaum, he, and his mother, and his brethren." And again,[3] "His brethren therefore said unto him, Depart hence, and go into Judæa, that thy disciples also may behold the works which thou doest. For no man doeth anything in secret, and himself seeketh to be known openly. If thou doest these things, manifest thyself to the world." And John adds,[4] "For even his brethren did not believe on him." Mark also and Matthew,[5] "And coming into his own country he taught them in their synagogues, insomuch that they were astonished, and said, Whence hath this man this wisdom, and mighty works? Is not this the carpenter's son? is not his mother called Mary? and his brethren James, and Joseph, and Simon, and Judas? And his sisters, are they not all with us?" Luke also in the Acts of the Apostles relates,[6] "These all with one accord continued stedfastly in prayer, with the women and Mary the mother of Jesus, and with his brethren." Paul the Apostle also is at one with them, and witnesses to their historical accuracy,[7] "And I went up by revelation, but other of the apostles saw I none, save Peter and James the Lord's brother." And again in another place,[8] "Have we no right to eat and drink? Have we no right to lead about wives even as the rest of the Apostles, and the brethren of the Lord, and Cephas?" And for fear any one should not allow the evidence of the Jews, since it was they from whose mouth we hear the name of His brothers, but should maintain that His countrymen were deceived by the same error in respect of the brothers into which they fell in their belief about the father, Helvidius utters a sharp note of warning and cries, "The same names are repeated by the Evangelists in another place, and the same persons are there brethren of the Lord and sons of Mary." Matthew says,[9] "And many women were there (doubtless at the Lord's cross) beholding from afar, which had followed Jesus from Galilee, ministering unto him: among whom was Mary Magdalene, and Mary the mother of James and Joses, and the mother of the sons of Zebedee." Mark also,[1] "And there were also women beholding from afar, among whom were both Mary Magdalene, and Mary the mother of James the less and of Joses, and Salome"; and in the same place shortly after, "And many other women which came up with him unto Jerusalem." Luke too,[2] "Now there were Mary Magdalene, and Joanna, and Mary the mother of James, and the other women with them."

14. My reason for repeating the same thing again and again is to prevent him from raising a false issue and crying out that I have withheld such passages as make for him, and that his view has been torn to shreds not by evidence of Scripture, but by evasive arguments. Observe, he says, James and Joses are sons of Mary, and the same persons who were called brethren by the Jews. Observe, Mary is the mother of James the less and of Joses. And James is called the less to distinguish him from James the greater, who was the son of Zebedee, as Mark elsewhere states,[3] "And Mary Magdalene and Mary the mother of Joses beheld where he was laid. And when the sabbath was past, they bought spices, that they might come and anoint him." And, as might be expected, he says: "What a poor and impious view we take of Mary, if we hold that when other women were concerned about the burial of Jesus, she His mother was absent; or if we invent some kind of a second Mary; and all the more because the Gospel of S. John testifies that she was there present, when the Lord upon the cross commended her, as His mother and now a widow, to the care of John. Or must we suppose that the Evangelists were so far mistaken and so far mislead us as to call Mary the mother of those who were known to the Jews as brethren of Jesus?"

15. What darkness, what raging madness rushing to its own destruction! You say that the mother of the Lord was present at the cross, you say that she was entrusted to the disciple John on account of her widowhood and solitary condition: as if upon your own showing, she had not four sons, and numerous daughters, with whose solace she might comfort herself? You also apply to her the name of widow which is not found in Scripture. And although you quote all instances in the Gospels, the words of John alone displease you. You say in passing that she was present at the cross, that you may not appear to have omitted it on purpose, and yet not a word about the women who were with her. I could pardon you if you were ignorant, but I

---

[1] S. Matt. xii. 46. [2] S. John ii. 12.
[3] S. John vii. 3, 4. [4] S. John vii. 5.
[5] S. Matt. xiii. 54, 55. S. Mark vi. 1-3.
[6] Acts i. 14. [7] Gal. ii. 2 ; i. 19.
[8] 1 Cor. ix. 4, 5.
[9] S. Matt. xxvii. 55, 56. For *Joses*, Jerome has *Joseph*.

[1] S. Marc. xv. 40, 41. For Joses, Jerome has Joseph.
[2] S. Luc. xxiv. 10. [3] S. Mark xv. 47 : xvi. 1.

see you have a reason for your silence. Let me point out then what John says,[1] "But there were standing by the cross of Jesus his mother, and his mother's sister, Mary the wife of Clopas, and Mary Magdalene." No one doubts that there were two apostles called by the name James, James the son of Zebedee, and James the son of Alphæus. Do you intend the comparatively unknown James the less, who is called in Scripture the son of Mary, not however of Mary the mother of our Lord, to be an apostle, or not? If he is an apostle, he must be the son of Alphæus and a believer in Jesus, "For neither did his brethren believe in him." If he is not an apostle, but a third James (who he can be I cannot tell), how can he be regarded as the Lord's brother, and how, being a third, can he be called *less* to distinguish him from *greater*, when *greater* and *less* are used to denote the relations existing, not between three, but between two? Notice, moreover, that the Lord's brother is an apostle, since Paul says,[2] "Then after three years I went up to Jerusalem to visit Cephas, and tarried with him fifteen days. But other of the Apostles saw I none, save James the Lord's brother." And in the same Epistle,[3] "And when they perceived the grace that was given unto me, James and Cephas and John, who were reputed to be pillars," etc. And that you may not suppose this James to be the son of Zebedee, you have only to read the Acts of the Apostles, and you will find that the latter had already been slain by Herod. The only conclusion is that the Mary who is described as the mother of James the less was the wife of Alphæus and sister of Mary the Lord's mother, the one who is called by John the Evangelist "Mary of Clopas," whether after her father, or kindred, or for some other reason. But if you think they are two persons because elsewhere we read, "Mary the mother of James the less," and here, "Mary of Clopas," you have still to learn that it is customary in Scripture for the same individual to bear different names. Raguel, Moses' father-in-law, is also called Jethro. Gedeon,[4] without any apparent reason for the change, all at once becomes Jerubbaal. Ozias, king of Judah, has an alternative, Azarias. Mount Tabor is called Itabyrium. Again Hermon is called by the Phenicians Sanior, and by the Amorites Sanir. The same tract of country is known by three names,[5] Negebh, Teman, and Darom in Ezekiel. Peter is also called Simon and Cephas. Judas the zealot

in another Gospel is called Thaddaeus. And there are numerous other examples which the reader will be able to collect for himself from every part of Scripture.

16. Now here we have the explanation of what I am endeavouring to show, how it is that the sons of Mary, the sister of our Lord's mother, who though not formerly believers afterwards did believe, can be called brethren of the Lord. Possibly the case might be that one of the brethren believed immediately while the others did not believe until long after, and that one Mary was the mother of James and Joses, namely, "Mary of Clopas," who is the same as the wife of Alphæus, the other, the mother of James the less. In any case, if she (the latter) had been the Lord's mother S. John would have allowed her the title, as everywhere else, and would not by calling her the mother of other sons have given a wrong impression. But at this stage I do not wish to argue for or against the supposition that Mary the wife of Clopas and Mary the mother of James and Joses were different women, provided it is clearly understood that Mary the mother of James and Joses was not the same person as the Lord's mother. How then, says Helvidius, do you make out that they were called the Lord's brethren who were not his brethren? I will show how that is. In Holy Scripture there are four kinds of brethren— by nature, race, kindred, love. Instances of brethren by nature are Esau and Jacob, the twelve patriarchs, Andrew and Peter, James and John. As to race, all Jews are called brethren of one another, as in Deuteronomy, [1] "If thy brother, an Hebrew man, or an Hebrew woman, be sold unto thee, and serve thee six years; then in the seventh year thou shalt let him go free from thee." And in the same book,[2] "Thou shalt in anywise set him king over thee, whom the Lord thy God shall choose: one from among thy brethren shalt thou set king over thee; thou mayest not put a foreigner over thee, which is not thy brother." And again,[3] "Thou shalt not see thy brother's ox or his sheep go astray, and hide thyself from them: thou shalt surely bring them again unto thy brother. And if thy brother be not nigh unto thee, or if thou know him not, then thou shalt bring it home to thine house, and it shall be with thee until thy brother seek after it, and thou shalt restore it to him again." And the Apostle Paul says, [4] "I could wish that I myself were anathema from Christ for my brethren's sake, my kinsmen according to the flesh: who are Israelites." Moreover they are called brethren by kindred who are of one family, that is πατρία,

---

[1] S. John xix. 25.
[3] Gal. ii. 9.
[5] The Heb. *Negebh* signifies *South*, and it is probable that the land of *Teman* was a southern portion of the land of Edom. If *Darom* be the right reading, it is, apparently, the same as Dedan (Ezek. xxv. 13, etc).
[2] Gal. i. 18, 19.
[4] But see Judges vi. 2.

[1] Deut. xv. 12.
[3] Deut. xxii. 1.
[2] Deut. xvii. 15.
[4] Rom. ix. 3, 4.

which corresponds to the Latin *paternitas*, because from a single root a numerous progeny proceeds. In Genesis [1] we read, "And Abram said unto Lot, Let there be no strife, I pray thee, between me and thee, and between my herdmen and thy herdmen ; for we are brethren." And again, "So Lot chose him all the plain of Jordan, and Lot journeyed east : and they separated each from his brother." Certainly Lot was not Abraham's brother, but the son of Abraham's brother Aram. For Terah begat Abraham and Nahor and Aram : and Aram begat Lot. Again we read,[2] "And Abram was seventy and five years old when he departed out of Haran. And Abram took Sarai his wife, and Lot his brother's son." But if you still doubt whether a nephew can be called a son, let me give you an instance.[3] "And when Abram heard that his brother was taken captive, he led forth his trained men, born in his house, three hundred and eighteen." And after describing the night attack and the slaughter, he adds, "And he brought back all the goods, and also brought again his brother Lot." Let this suffice by way of proof of my assertion. But for fear you may make some cavilling objection, and wriggle out of your difficulty like a snake, I must bind you fast with the bonds of proof to stop your hissing and complaining, for I know you would like to say you have been overcome not so much by Scripture truth as by intricate arguments. Jacob, the son of Isaac and Rebecca, when in fear of his brother's treachery he had gone to Mesopotamia, drew nigh and rolled away the stone from the mouth of the well, and watered the flocks of Laban, his mother's brother.[4] "And Jacob kissed Rachel, and lifted up his voice, and wept. And Jacob told Rachel that he was her father's brother, and that he was Rebekah's son." Here is an example of the rule already referred to, by which a nephew is called a brother. And again,[5] "Laban said unto Jacob. Because thou art my brother, shouldest thou therefore serve me for nought ? Tell me what shall thy wages be." And so, when, at the end of twenty years, without the knowledge of his father-in-law and accompanied by his wives and sons he was returning to his country, on Laban overtaking him in the mountain of Gilead and failing to find the idols which Rachel hid among the baggage, Jacob answered and said to Laban,[6] "What is my trespass ? What is my sin, that thou hast so hotly pursued after me ? Whereas thou hast felt all about my stuff, what hast thou found of all thy household stuff ? Set

it here before my brethren and thy brethren, that they may judge betwixt us two." Tell me who are those brothers of Jacob and Laban who were present there ? Esau, Jacob's brother, was certainly not there, and Laban, the son of Bethuel, had no brothers although he had a sister Rebecca.

17. Innumerable instances of the same kind are to be found in the sacred books. But, to be brief, I will return to the last of the four classes of brethren, those, namely, who are brethren by affection, and these again fall into two divisions, those of the spiritual and those of the general relationship. I say *spiritual* because all of us Christians are called brethren, as in the verse,[1] "Behold, how good and how pleasant it is for brethren to dwell together in unity." And in another psalm the Saviour says,[2] "I will declare thy name unto my brethren." And elsewhere,[3] "Go unto my brethren and say to them." I say also *general*, because we are all children of one Father, there is a like bond of brotherhood between us all.[4] "Tell these who hate you," says the prophet, "ye are our brethren." And the Apostle writing to the Corinthians : [5] "If any man that is named brother be a fornicator, or covetous, or an idolater, or a reviler, or a drunkard, or an extortioner : with such a one no, not to eat." I now ask to which class you consider the Lord's brethren in the Gospel must be assigned. They are brethren by nature, you say. But Scripture does not say so; it calls them neither sons of Mary, nor of Joseph. Shall we say they are brethren by race ? But it is absurd to suppose that a few Jews were called His brethren when all Jews of the time might upon this principle have borne the title. Were they brethren by virtue of close intimacy and the union of heart and mind ? If that were so, who were more truly His brethren than the apostles who received His private instruction and were called by Him His mother and His brethren ? Again, if all men, as such, were His brethren, it would have been foolish to deliver a special message, "Behold, thy brethren seek thee," for all men alike were entitled to the name. The only alternative is to adopt the previous explanation and understand them to be called brethren in virtue of the bond of kindred, not of love and sympathy, nor by prerogative of race, nor yet by nature. Just as Lot was called Abraham's brother, and Jacob Laban's, just as the daughters of Zelophehad received a lot among their brethren, just as Abraham himself had to wife Sarah his sister, for he says,[6] "She is in-

[1] Gen. xiii. 8, 11.
[2] Gen. xii. 4.
[3] Gen. xiv. 14.
[4] Gen. xxix. 11.
[5] Gen. xxix. 15.
[6] Gen. xxxi. 36, 37.

[1] Ps. cxxxiii. 1.
[2] Ps. xxii. 22.
[3] S. John xx. 17.
[4] Is. lxvi. 5.
[5] 1 Cor. v. 11.
[6] Gen. xx. 11.

deed my sister, on the father's side, not on the mother's," that is to say, she was the daughter of his brother, not of his sister. Otherwise, what are we to say of Abraham, a just man, taking to wife the daughter of his own father? Scripture, in relating the history of the men of early times, does not outrage our ears by speaking of the enormity in express terms, but prefers to leave it to be inferred by the reader : and God afterwards gives to the prohibition the sanction of the law, and threatens,[1] "He who takes his sister, born of his father, or of his mother, and beholds her nakedness, hath commited abomination, he shall be utterly destroyed. He hath uncovered his sister's nakedness, he shall bear his sin."

18. There are things which, in your extreme ignorance, you had never read, and therefore you neglected the whole range of Scripture and employed your madness in outraging the Virgin, like the man in the story who being unknown to everybody and finding that he could devise no good deed by which to gain renown, burned the temple of Diana : and when no one revealed the sacrilegious act, it is said that he himself went up and down proclaiming that he was the man who had applied the fire. The rulers of Ephesus were curious to know what made him do this thing, whereupon he replied that if he could not have fame for good deeds, all men should give him credit for bad ones. Grecian history relates the incident. But you do worse. You have set on fire the temple of the Lord's body, you have defiled the sanctuary of the Holy Spirit from which you are determined to make a team of four brethren and a heap of sisters come forth. In a word, joining in the chorus of the Jews you say,[2] "Is not this the carpenter's son? is not his mother called Mary? and his brethren James, and Joseph, and Simon, and Judas? and his sisters, are they not all with us?" The word all would not be used if there were not a crowd of them." Pray tell me, who, before you appeared, was acquainted with this blasphemy? who thought the theory worth twopence? You have gained your desire, and are become notorious by crime. For myself who am your opponent, although we live in the [3]same city, I don't know, as the saying is, whether you are white or black. I pass over faults of diction which abound in every book you write. I say not a word about your absurd introduction. Good heavens! I do not ask for eloquence, since, having none yourself, you applied for a supply of it to your brother Craterius. I do not ask for grace of style, I look for purity of soul : for with Christians it is

the greatest of solecisms and of vices of style to introduce anything base either in word or action. I am come to the conclusion of my argument. I will deal with you as though I had as yet prevailed nothing ; and you will find yourself on the horns of a dilemma. It is clear that our Lord's brethren bore the name in the same way that Joseph was called his father :[1] "I and thy father sought thee sorrowing." It was His mother who said this, not the Jews. The Evangelist himself relates that His father and His mother were marvelling at the things which were spoken concerning Him, and there are similar passages which we have already quoted in which Joseph and Mary are called his parents. Seeing that you have been foolish enough to persuade yourself that the Greek manuscripts are corrupt, you will perhaps plead the diversity of readings. I therefore come to the Gospel of John, and there it is plainly written,[2] "Philip findeth Nathanael, and saith unto him, We have found him of whom Moses in the law, and the prophets did write, Jesus of Nazareth, the son of Joseph." You will certainly find this in your manuscript. Now tell me, how is Jesus the son of Joseph when it is clear that He was begotten of the Holy Ghost? Was Joseph His true father? Dull as you are, you will not venture to say that. Was he His reputed father? If so, let the same rule be applied to them when they are called brethren, that you apply to Joseph when he is called father.

19. Now that I have cleared the rocks and shoals I must spread sail and make all speed to reach his epilogue. Feeling himself to be a smatterer, he there produces Tertullian as a witness and quotes the words of Victorinus bishop of [3]Petavium. Of Tertullian I say no more than that he did not belong to the Church. But as regards Victorinus, I assert what has already been proved from the Gospel —that he spoke of the brethren of the Lord not as being sons of Mary, but brethren in the sense I have explained, that is to say, brethren in point of kinship not by nature. We are, however, spending our strength on trifles, and, leaving the fountain of truth, are following the tiny streams of opinion. Might I not array against you the whole series of ancient writers? Ignatius, Polycarp, Irenæus, Justin Martyr, and many other apostolic and eloquent men, who against Ebion, Theodotus of Byzantium, and Valentinus, held these same views, and wrote volumes replete with wisdom. If you had ever read what they wrote, you would be a wiser man. But I think it better to reply

---

[1] Lev. xviii. 9.
[2] S. Matt. xiii. 55 : S. Mark vi. 3.
[3] That is, Rome.

[1] S. Luke i. 18.
[2] S. John i. 45.
[3] That is, Pettau in Upper Pannonia. See Jerome, *De Vir. Ill.*

briefly to each point than to linger any longer and extend my book to an undue length.

20. I now direct the attack against the passage in which, wishing to show your cleverness, you institute a comparison between virginity and marriage. I could not forbear smiling, and I thought of the proverb, *did you ever see a camel dance?* "Are virgins better," you ask, "than Abraham, Isaac, and Jacob, who were married men? Are not infants daily fashioned by the hands of God in the wombs of their mothers? And if so, are we bound to blush at the thought of Mary having a husband after she was delivered? If they find any disgrace in this, they ought not consistently even to believe that God was born of the Virgin by natural delivery. For according to them there is more dishonour in a virgin giving birth to God by the organs of generation, than in a virgin being joined to her own husband after she has been delivered." Add, if you like, Helvidius, the other humiliations of nature, the womb for nine months growing larger, the sickness, the delivery, the blood, the swaddling-clothes. Picture to yourself the infant in the enveloping membranes. Introduce into your picture the hard manger, the wailing of the infant, the circumcision on the eighth day, the time of purification, so that he may be proved to be unclean. We do not blush, we are not put to silence. The greater the humiliations He endured for me, the more I owe Him. And when you have given every detail, you will be able to produce nothing more shameful than the cross, which we confess, in which we believe, and by which we triumph over our enemies.

21. But as we do not deny what is written, so we do reject what is not written. We believe that God was born of the Virgin, because we read it. That Mary was married after she brought forth, we do not believe, because we do not read it. Nor do we say this to condemn marriage, for virginity itself is the fruit of marriage; but because when we are dealing with saints we must not judge rashly. If we adopt possibility as the standard of judgment, we might maintain that Joseph had several wives because Abraham had, and so had Jacob, and that the Lord's brethren were the issue of those wives, an invention which some hold with a rashness which springs from audacity not from piety. You say that Mary did not continue a virgin: I claim still more, that Joseph himself on account of Mary was a virgin, so that from a virgin wedlock a virgin son was born. For if as a holy man he does not come under the imputation of fornication, and it is nowhere written that he had another wife, but was the guardian of Mary whom he was supposed to have to wife rather than her

husband, the conclusion is that he who was thought worthy to be called father of the Lord, remained a virgin.

22. And now that I am about to institute a comparison between virginity and marriage, I beseech my readers not to suppose that in praising virginity I have in the least disparaged marriage, and separated the saints of the Old Testament from those of the New, that is to say, those who had wives and those who altogether refrained from the embraces of women : I rather think that in accordance with the difference in time and circumstance one rule applied to the former, another to us upon whom the ends of the world have come. So long as that law remained,[1] "Be fruitful, and multiply and replenish the earth"; and [2] "Cursed is the barren woman that beareth not seed in Israel," they all married and were given in marriage, left father and mother, and became one flesh. But once in tones of thunder the words were heard,[3] "The time is shortened, that henceforth those that have wives may be as though they had none" : cleaving to the Lord, we are made one spirit with Him. And why?[4] Because "He that is unmarried is careful for the things of the Lord, how he may please the Lord : but he that is married is careful for the things of the world, how he may please his wife. And there is a difference also between the wife and the virgin. She that is unmarried is careful for the things of the Lord, that she may be holy both in body and in spirit : but she that is married is careful for the things of the world, how she may please her husband." Why do you cavil? Why do you resist? The vessel of election says this ; he tells us that there is a difference between the wife and the virgin. Observe what the happiness of that state must be in which even the distinction of sex is lost. The virgin is no longer called a woman.[5] "She that is unmarried is careful for the things of the Lord, that she may be holy both in body and in spirit." A virgin is defined as she that is holy in body and in spirit, for it is no good to have virgin flesh if a woman be married in mind.

"But she that is married is careful for the things of the world, how she may please her husband." Do you think there is no difference between one who spends her time in prayer and fasting, and one who must, at her husband's approach, make up her countenance, walk with mincing gait, and feign a shew of endearment? The virgin's aim is to appear less comely ; she will wrong herself

1 Gen. i. 28.
2 Probably a mistranslation of Exod. xxiii. 26.
3 1 Cor. vii. 29.   4 ib. vii. 32, 33.
5 1 Cor. vii. 34.

so as to hide her natural attractions. The married woman has the paint laid on before her mirror, and, to the insult of her Maker, strives to acquire something more than her natural beauty. Then come the prattling of infants, the noisy household, children watching for her word and waiting for her kiss, the reckoning up of expenses, the preparation to meet the outlay. On one side you will see a company of cooks, girded for the onslaught and attacking the meat : there you may hear the hum of a multitude of weavers. Meanwhile a message is delivered that the husband and his friends have arrived. The wife, like a swallow, flies all over the house. "She has to see to everything. Is the sofa smooth ? Is the pavement swept ? Are the flowers in the cups ? Is dinner ready ?" Tell me, pray, where amid all this is there room for the thought of God ? Are these happy homes? Where there is the beating of drums, the noise and clatter of pipe and lute, the clanging of cymbals, can any fear of God be found ? The parasite is snubbed and feels proud of the honour. Enter next the half-naked victims of the passions, a mark for every lustful eye. The unhappy wife must either take pleasure in them, and perish, or be displeased, and provoke her husband. Hence arises discord, the seed-plot of divorce. Or suppose you find me a house where these things are unknown, which is a *rara avis* indeed ! yet even there the very management of the household, the education of the children, the wants of the husband, the correction of the servants, cannot fail to call away the mind from the thought of God. [1] "It had ceased to be with Sarah after the manner of women" : so the Scripture says, and afterwards Abraham received the command,[2] "In all that Sarah saith unto thee, hearken unto her voice." She who is not subject to the anxiety and pain of child-bearing and having passed the change of life has ceased to perform the functions of a woman, is freed from the curse of God : nor is her desire to her husband, but on the contrary her husband becomes subject to her, and the voice of the Lord commands him, "In all that Sarah saith unto thee, hearken unto her voice." Thus they begin to have time for prayer. For so long as the debt of marriage is paid, earnest prayer is neglected.

23. I do not deny that holy women are found both among widows and those who have husbands ; but they are such as have ceased to be wives, or such as, even in the close bond of marriage, imitate virgin chastity. The Apostle, Christ speaking in him, briefly bore witness to this when he said,

[1] "She that is unmarried is careful for the things of the Lord, how she may please the Lord : but she that is married is careful for the things of the world, how she may please her husband." He leaves us the free exercise of our reason in the matter. He lays no necessity upon anyone nor leads anyone into a snare : he only persuades to that which is proper when he wishes all men to be as himself. He had not, it is true, a commandment from the Lord respecting virginity, for that grace surpasses the unassisted power of man, and it would have worn an air of immodesty to force men to fly in the face of nature, and to say in other words, I want you to be what the angels are. It is this angelic purity which secures to virginity its highest reward, and the Apostle might have seemed to despise a course of life which involves no guilt. Nevertheless in the immediate context he adds,[2] "But I give my judgment, as one that hath obtained mercy of the Lord to be faithful. I think therefore that this is good by reason of the present distress, namely, that it is good for a man to be as he is." What is meant by *present distress ?* [3] "Woe unto them that are with child and to them that give suck in those days !" The reason why the wood grows up is that it may be cut down. The field is sown that it may be reaped. The world is already full, and the population is too large for the soil. Every day we are being cut down by war, snatched away by disease, swallowed up by shipwreck, although we go to law with one another about the fences of our property. It is only one addition to the general rule which is made by those who follow the Lamb, and who have not defiled their garments, for they have continued in their virgin state. Notice the meaning of *defiling*. I shall not venture to explain it, for fear Helvidius may be abusive. I agree with you, when you say, that some virgins are nothing but tavern women ; I say still more, that even adulteresses may be found among them, and, you will no doubt be still more surprised to hear, that some of the clergy are inn-keepers and some monks unchaste. Who does not at once understand that a tavern woman cannot be a virgin, nor an adulterer a monk, nor a clergyman a tavern-keeper ? Are we to blame virginity if its counterfeit is at fault ? For my part, to pass over other persons and come to the virgin, I maintain that she who is engaged in huckstering, though for anything I know she may be a virgin in body, is no longer one in spirit.

24. I have become rhetorical, and have disported myself a little like a platform orator.

---

[1] Gen. xviii. 11.   [2] Gen. xxi. 12.

[1] 1 Cor. vii. 34.   [2] 1 Cor. vii. 25.
[3] Matt. xxiv. 19 : S. Mark xiii. 17.

You compelled me, Helvidius ; for, brightly as the Gospel shines at the present day, you will have it that equal glory attaches to virginity and to the marriage state. And because I think that, finding the truth too strong for you, you will turn to disparaging my life and abusing my character (it is the way of weak women to talk tittle-tattle in corners when they have been put down by their masters), I shall anticipate you. I assure you that I shall regard your railing as a high distinction, since the same lips that assail me have disparaged Mary, and I, a servant of the Lord, am favoured with the same barking eloquence as His mother.

AGAINST JOVINIANUS

Book I.

Jovinianus, concerning whom we know little more than is to be found in the two following books, had published at Rome a Latin treatise containing all, or part of the opinions here controverted, viz. (1) "That a virgin is no better as such than a wife in the sight of God. (2) Abstinence is no better than a thankful partaking of food. (3) A person baptized with the Spirit as well as with water cannot sin. (4) All sins are equal. (5) There is but one grade of punishment and one of reward in the future state." In addition to this he held the birth of our Lord to have been by a "true parturition," and was thus at issue with the orthodoxy of the time, according to which the infant Jesus passed through the walls of the womb as His Resurrection body afterwards did out of the tomb or through the closed doors. Pammachius, Jerome's friend, brought Jovinian's book under the notice of Siricius, bishop of Rome, and it was shortly afterwards condemned in synods at that city and at Milan (about A.D. 390). He subsequently sent Jovinian's books to Jerome, who answered them in the present treatise in the year 393. Nothing more is known of Jovinian, but it has been conjectured from Jerome's remark in the treatise against Vigilantius, where Jovinian is said to have " amidst pheasants and pork rather belched out than breathed out his life," and by a kind of transmigration to have transmitted his opinions into Vigilantius, that he had died before 409, the date of that work.

The first book is wholly on the first proposition of Jovinianus, that relating to marriage and virginity. The first three chapters are introductory. The rest may be divided into three parts :

1 (ch. 4-13). An exposition, in Jerome's sense, of St. Paul's teaching in 1 Cor. vii.
2 (ch. 14-39). A statement of the teaching which Jerome derives from the various books of both the Old and the New Testaments.
3. A denunciation of Jovinianus (c. 40), and the praises of virginity and of single marriages derived from examples in the heathen world.

The treatise gives a remarkable specimen of Jerome's system of interpreting Scripture, and also of the methods by which asceticism was introduced into the Church, and marriage brought into disesteem.

1. Very few days have elapsed since the holy brethren of Rome sent to me the treatises of a certain Jovinian with the request that I would reply to the follies contained in them, and would crush with evangelical and apostolic vigour the [1] Epicurus of Christianity. I read but could not in the least comprehend them. I began therefore to give them closer attention, and to thoroughly sift not only words and sentences, but almost every single syllable ; for I wished first to ascertain his meaning, and then to approve, or refute what he had said. But the style is so barbarous, and the language so vile and such a heap of blunders, that I could neither understand what he was talking about, nor by what arguments he was trying to prove his points. At one moment he is all bombast, at another he grovels : from time to time he lifts himself up, and then like a wounded snake finds his own effort too much for him. Not satisfied with the language of men, he attempts something loftier.

[1] " The mountains labour ; a poor mouse is born."
[2] " That he's gone mad ev'n mad Orestes swears."

Moreover he involves everything in such inextricable confusion that the saying of [3] Plautus might be applied to him :—" This is what none but a Sibyl will ever read."

To understand him we must be prophets. We read Apollo's[4] raving prophetesses. We remember, too, what [5] Virgil says of senseless

---

[1] From this expression and that quoted in the notice above, it would be supposed that Jerome knew Jovinianus and his mode of life. But there is no reason to think that he had this knowledge ; and his imputations against his adversary must be taken as the inferences which he draws from his opinions.

[1] Hor. Ars Poet. 139.
[2] Pers. Sat. iii. 118.
[3] Plautus. Pseudolus, i. 1. 23.
       Has quidem, pol, credo, nisi Sibylla legerit,
       Interpretari alium potesse neminem.
[4] The allusion is probably to the Sybilline books.
[5] Æn. x. 640.

noise. [1] Heraclitus, also, surnamed the Obscure, the philosophers find hard to understand even with their utmost toil. But what are they compared with our riddle-maker, whose books are much more difficult to comprehend than to refute? Although (we must confess) the task of refuting them is no easy one. For how can you overcome a man when you are quite in the dark as to his meaning? But, not to be tedious to my reader, the introduction to his second book, of which he has discharged himself like a sot after a night's debauch, will show the character of his eloquence, and through what bright flowers of rhetoric he takes his stately course.

2. " I respond to your invitation, not that I may go through life with a high reputation, but may live free from idle rumour. I beseech the ground, the young shoots of our plantations, the plants and trees of tenderness snatched from the whirlpool of vice, to grant me audience and the support of many listeners. We know that the Church through hope, faith, charity, is inaccessible and impregnable. In it no one is immature : all are apt to learn : none can force a way into it by violence, or deceive it by craft."

3. What, I ask, is the meaning of these portentous words and of this grotesque description? Would you not think he was in a feverish dream, or that he was seized with madness and ought to be put into the strait jacket which Hippocrates prescribed? However often I read him, even till my heart sinks within me, I am still in uncertainty of his meaning.[2] Everything starts from, everything depends upon, something else. It is impossible to make out any connection; and, excepting the proofs from Scripture which he has not dared to exchange for his own lovely flowers of rhetoric, his words suit all matter equally well, because they suit no matter at all. This circumstance led me shrewdly to suspect that his object in proclaiming the excellence of marriage was only to disparage virginity. For when the less is put upon a level with the greater, the lower profits by comparison, but the higher suffers wrong. For ourselves, we do not follow the views of [3] Marcion and Manichæus, and disparage marriage; nor, deceived by the error of [4] Tatian,

the leader of the Encratites, do we think all intercourse impure; he condemns and rejects not only marriage but also food which God created for the use of man. We know that in a great house, there are not only vessels of gold and silver, but also of wood and earthenware. And that upon the foundation, Christ, which Paul the master-builder laid, some build gold, silver, precious stones : others, on the contrary, hay, wood, straw. We are not ignorant of the words, [1] " Marriage is honourable among all, and the bed undefiled." We have read God's first command,[2] " Be fruitful, and multiply, and replenish the earth " ; but while we honour marriage we prefer virginity which is the offspring of marriage. Will silver cease to be silver, if gold is more precious than silver? Or is despite done to tree and corn, if we prefer the fruit to root and foliage, or the grain to stalk and ear? Virginity is to marriage what fruit is to the tree, or grain to the straw. Although the hundred-fold, the sixty-fold, and the thirty-fold spring from one earth and from one sowing, yet there is a great difference in respect of number. The thirty-fold has reference to marriage. The very way the [3] fingers are combined—see how they seem to embrace, tenderly kiss, and pledge their troth either to other—is a picture of husband and wife. The sixty-fold applies to widows, because they are placed in a position of difficulty and distress. Hence the upper finger signifies their depression, and the greater the difficulty in resisting the allurements of pleasure once experienced, the greater the reward. Moreover (give good heed, my reader), to denote a hundred, the right hand is used instead of the left : a circle is made with the same fingers which on the left hand represented widowhood, and thus the crown of virginity is expressed. In saying this I have followed my own impatient spirit rather than the course of the argument. For I had scarcely left harbour, and had barely hoisted sail, when a swelling tide of words suddenly swept me into the depths of the discussion. I must stay my course, and take in canvas for a little while ; nor will I indulge my sword, anxious as it is to strike a blow for virginity. The farther back the catapult is drawn, the greater the force of the missile. To linger is not to lose, if by lingering victory is better assured. I will briefly set forth our adversary's views, and will drag them out from

---

[1] The philosopher of Ephesus. Flourished about B. C. 513.
[2] Ibi est distinctio. Instead of clearness we have to make a choice between possible meanings.
[3] Marcion lived about A.D.150,and was co-temporary with Polycarp, who is said to have had a personal encounter with him at Rome. Unlike other Gnostics he professed to be purely Christian in his doctrines. He is specially noted for his violent treatment of Scripture : he rejected the whole of the Old Testament, while of the New he acknowledged only the Gospel of S. Luke and ten of S. Paul's Epistles, and from these he expunged whatever he did not approve of. His sect lasted until the sixth century.
[4] By birth an Assyrian, and a pupil of Justin Martyr. His followers were called *Encratites*, or *Temperates*, from their great austerity. They also bore the names *Water-drinkers* and *Renouncers*.

[1] Heb. xiii. The Revised Ver. translates " let marriage be, etc." There is no verb in the original, the sentence being probably designed to be a Christian proverb, and capable of serving either as an *assertion* or as a precept. The revised rendering is preferred by the chief modern commentators.
[2] Gen. i. 28.
[3] For much interesting information relating to counting on the fingers, and for authorities on the subject, see Mayor's note on Juvenal x. 249.

his books like snakes from the holes where they hide, and will separate the venomous head from the writhing body. What is baneful shall be discovered, that, when we have the power, it may be crushed.

He says that "virgins, widows, and married women, who have been once passed through the laver of Christ, if they are on a par in other respects, are of equal merit."

He endeavours to show that "they who with full assurance of faith have been born again in baptism, cannot be overthrown by the devil."

His third point is "that there is no difference between abstinence from food, and its reception with thanksgiving."

The fourth and last is "that there is one reward in the kingdom of heaven for all who have kept their baptismal vow."

4. This is the hissing of the old serpent; by counsel such as this the dragon drove man from Paradise. For he promised that if they would prefer fulness to fasting they should be immortal, as though it were an impossibility for them to fall; and while he promises they shall be as Gods, he drives them from Paradise, with the result that they who, while naked and unhampered, and as virgins unspotted enjoyed the fellowship of the Lord, were cast down into the vale of tears, and sewed skins together to clothe themselves withal. But, not to detain the reader any longer, I will keep to the division given above, and taking his propositions one by one will rely chiefly on the evidence of Scripture to refute them, for fear he may chatter and complain that he was overcome by rhetorical skill rather than by force of truth. If I succeed in this and with the aid of a cloud of witnesses from both Testaments prove too strong for him, I will then accept his challenge, and adduce illustrations from secular literature. I will show that even among philosophers and distinguished statesmen, the virtuous are wont to be preferred by all to the voluptuous, that is to say men like [1] Pythagoras, [2] Plato and [3] Aristides, to [4] Aristippus, [5] Epicurus and

[1] Alcibiades. I entreat virgins of both sexes and all such as are continent, the married also and the twice married, to assist my efforts with their prayers. Jovinian is the common enemy. For he who maintains all to be of equal merit, does no less injury to virginity in comparing it with marriage than he does to marriage, when he allows it to be lawful, but to the same extent as second and third marriages. But to digamists and trigamists also he does wrong, for he places on a level with them whoremongers and the most licentious persons as soon as they have repented; but perhaps those who have been married twice or thrice ought not to complain, for the same whoremonger if penitent is made equal in the kingdom of heaven even to virgins. I will therefore explain more clearly and in proper sequence the arguments he employs and the illustrations he adduces respecting marriage, and will treat them in the order in which he states them. And I beg the reader not to be disturbed if he is compelled to read Jovinian's nauseating trash. He will all the more gladly drink Christ's antidote after the devil's poisonous concoction. Listen with patience, ye virgins; listen, I pray you, to the voice of the most voluptuous of preachers; nay rather close your ears, as you would to the Syren's fabled songs, and pass on. For a little while endure the wrongs you suffer: think you are crucified with Christ, and are listening to the blasphemies of the Pharisees.

5. First of all, he says, God declares that [2] "therefore shall a man leave his father and his mother, and shall cleave unto his wife: and they shall be one flesh." And lest we should say that this is a quotation from the Old Testament, he asserts that it has been [3] confirmed by the Lord in the Gospel—"What God hath joined together, let not man put asunder": and he immediately adds,[4] "Be fruitful, and multiply, and replenish the earth." He next repeats the names of Seth, Enos, Cainan, Mahalalel, Jared, Enoch, Methuselah, Lamech, Noah, and tells us that they all had wives and in accordance with the will of God begot sons, as though there could be any table of descent or any history of mankind without wives and children. "There," says he, "is Enoch, who walked with God and was carried up to heaven. There is Noah, the only person who, except his wife, and his sons and their wives, was saved at the deluge, although there must have been many persons not of marriageable age, and therefore presumably virgins. Again, after the deluge, when the human race started as it were anew men and women were paired together and a fresh blessing was pronounced on procreation,

---

[1] The philosopher of Crotona, in Italy, B. C. 580-510. See some of his sayings in Jerome's Apology, iii. 39-40.
[2] The great teacher of the Academy at Athens; lived B. C. 428-389.
[3] Surnamed the "Just." He was the opponent of Themistocles. He fought at Marathon (490), and although in exile did good service at Salamis (480). He was now recalled, and after commanding the Athenians at Plataea (479) died, probably in 468, so poor that he did not leave enough to pay for his funeral.
[4] Flourished about B. C. 370. A disciple of Socrates, and founder of the Cyrenaic School of Philosophy; he was luxurious in his life, and held pleasure to be the highest good.
[5] Epicurus (B. C. 342-270), though a disciple of Aristippus, does not appear to have deserved the odium attached to his name by Jerome and many others. "Pleasure with him was not a mere momentary and transitory sensation, but something lasting and imperishable, consisting in pure and noble enjoyments. that is, in ἀταραξία and ἀπονία, or the freedom from pain and from all influences which disturb the peace of our mind, and thereby our happiness which is the result of it." See Zeller's Socrates and the Socratic Schools (Reichel's translation), second ed., p. 337 sq.

[1] The famous Athenian, talented, reckless and unscrupulous born about B. C. 450, assassinated 404.
[2] Gen. ii. 24.   [3] Matt. xix. 5.   [4] Gen. i. 28; ix. 1.

" Be fruitful, and multiply, and replenish the earth." Moreover, free permission was given to eat flesh,[2] " Every moving thing that liveth shall be food for you ; as the green herb have I given you all." He then flies off to Abraham, Isaac, and Jacob, of whom the first had three wives, the second one, the third four, Leah, Rachel, Billah, and Zilpah, and he declares that Abraham by his faith merited the blessing which he received in begetting his son. Sarah, typifying the Church, when it had ceased to be with her after the manner of women, exchanged the curse of barrenness for the blessing of child-bearing. We are informed that Rebekah went like a prophet to inquire of the Lord, and was told,[3] " Two nations and two peoples are in thy womb," that Jacob served for his wife, and that when Rachel, thinking it was in the power of her husband to give her children, said,[4] " Give me children, or else I die," he replied,[5] " Am I in God's stead, who hath withheld from thee the fruit of the womb?" so well aware was he that the fruit of marriage cometh from the Lord and not from the husband. We next learn that Joseph, a holy man of spotless chastity, and all the patriarchs, had wives, and that God blessed them all alike through the lips of Moses. Judah also and Thamar are brought upon the scene, and he censures Onan, slain by the Lord, because he, grudging to raise up seed to his brother, marred the marriage rite. He refers to Moses and the leprosy of Miriam, who, because she chided her brother on account of his wife, was stricken by the avenging hand of God. He praises Samson, I may even say extravagantly panegyrizes the uxorious Nazarite. Deborah also and Barak are mentioned, because, although they had not the benefit of virginity, they were victorious over the iron chariots of Sisera and Jabin. He brings forward Jael, the wife of Heber the Kenite, and extols her for arming herself with the [6] stake. He says there was no difference between Jephthah and his virgin daughter, who was sacrificed to the Lord : nay, of the two, he prefers the faith of the father to that of the daughter who met death with grief and tears. He then comes to Samuel, another Nazarite of the Lord, who from infancy was brought up in the tabernacle and was clad in a linen ephod, or, as the words are rendered, in linen vestments : he, too, we are told, begot sons without a stain upon his priestly purity. He places Boaz and his wife Ruth side by side in his repository, and traces the descent of Jesse and David from them. He then points out how David himself, for the price of two hundred foreskins and at the peril of his life, was bedded

with the king's daughter. What shall I say of Solomon, whom he includes in the list of husbands, and represents as a type of the Saviour, maintaining that of him it was written,[1] " Give the king thy judgments, O God, and thy righteousness unto the king's son "? And[2] " To him shall be given of the gold of Sheba, and men shall pray for him continually." Then all at once he makes a jump to Elijah and Elisha, and tells us as a great secret that the spirit of Elijah rested on Elisha. Why he mentioned this he does not say. It can hardly be that he thinks Elijah and Elisha, like the rest, were married men. The next step is to Hezekiah, upon whose praises he dwells, and yet (I wonder why) forgets to mention that he said,[3] " Henceforth I will beget children." He relates that Josiah, a righteous man, in whose time the book of Deuteronomy was found in the temple, was instructed by Huldah, wife of Shallum. Daniel also and the three youths are classed by him with the married. Suddenly he betakes himself to the Gospel, and adduces Zachariah and Elizabeth, Peter and his father-in-law, and the rest of the Apostles. His inference is thus expressed : " If they idly urge in defence of themselves the plea that the world in its early stage needed to be replenished, let them listen to the words of Paul,[4] ' I desire therefore that the younger widows marry, bear children.' And[5] ' Marriage is honourable and the bed undefiled.' And[6] ' A wife is bound for so long time as her husband liveth ; but if the husband be dead, she is free to be married to whom she will ; only in the Lord.' And[7] ' Adam was not beguiled, but the woman being beguiled hath fallen into transgression : but she shall be saved through the child-bearing, if they continue in faith and love and sanctification with sobriety.' Surely we shall hear no more of the famous Apostolic utterance,[8] ' And they who have wives as though they had them not.' It can hardly be that you will say the reason why he wished them to be married was that some widows had already turned back after Satan : as though virgins never fell and their fall was not more ruinous. All this makes it clear that in forbidding to marry, and to eat food which God created for use, you have consciences seared as with a hot iron, and are followers of the Manichæans." Then comes much more which it would be unprofitable to discuss. At last he dashes into rhetoric and apostrophizes virginity thus : " I do you no wrong, Virgin : you have chosen a life of chastity on account of the present distress : you determined on

---

[1] Gen. ix. 1. [2] Gen. ix. 3. [3] Gen. xxv. 23.
[4] Gen. xxx. 1. [5] Gen. xxx. 2. [6] Palo. Rev. Vers. tent-pin.

[1] Ps. lxxii. 1. [2] Ps. lxxii. 15.
[3] Is. xxxviii. 19. Sept. [4] 1 Tim. v. 14.
[5] Hebr. xiii. 4. See note on sec. 3.
[6] 1 Cor. vii. 39. [7] 1 Tim. ii. 14.
[8] 1 Cor. vii. 29.

the course in order to be holy in body and spirit : be not proud : you and your married sisters are members of the same Church."

6. I have perhaps explained his position at too great a length, and become tedious to my reader ; but I thought it best to draw up in full array against myself all his efforts, and to muster all the forces of the enemy with their squadrons and generals, lest after an early victory there should spring up a series of other engagements. I will not therefore do battle with single foes, nor will I be satisfied with skirmishes in which I meet small detachments of my opponents. The battle must be fought with the whole army of the enemy, and the disorderly rabble, fighting more like brigands than soldiers, must be repulsed by the skill and method of regular warfare. In the front rank I will set the Apostle Paul, and, since he is the bravest of generals, will arm him with his own weapons, that is to say, his own statements. For the Corinthians asked many questions about this matter, and the doctor of the Gentiles and master of the Church gave full replies. What he decreed we may regard as the law of Christ speaking in him. At the same time, when we begin to refute the several arguments, I trust the reader will give me his attention even before the Apostle speaks, and will not, in his eagerness to discuss the most weighty points, neglect the premises, and rush at once to the conclusion.

7. Among other things the Corinthians asked in their letter whether after embracing the faith of Christ they ought to be unmarried, and for the sake of continence put away their wives, and whether believing virgins were at liberty to marry. And again, supposing that one of two Gentiles believed on Christ, whether the one that believed should leave the one that believed not ? And in case it were allowable to take wives, would the Apostle direct that only Christian wives, or Gentiles also, should be taken ? Let us then consider Paul's replies to these inquiries. [1] " Now concerning the things whereof ye wrote : It is good for a man not to touch a woman. But, because of fornications, let each man have his own wife, and let each woman have her own husband. Let the husband render unto the wife her due : and likewise also the wife unto the husband. The wife hath not power over her own body, but the husband : And likewise also the husband hath not power over his own body, but the wife. Defraud ye not one the other, except it be by consent for a season, that ye may give yourselves unto prayer, and may be together again, that Satan tempt you not because of your incontinency.

But this I say by way of permission not c commandment. Yet I would that all me were even as I myself. Howbeit each man hat his own gift from God, one after this manne and another after that. But I say to the ur married and to widows, it is good for them they abide even as I. But if they have nc continency, let them marry : for it is better t marry than to burn." Let us turn back t the chief point of the evidence : " It is good, he says, " for a man not to touch a woman. If it is good not to touch a woman, it is ba to touch one : for there is no opposite t goodness but badness. But if it be bad an the evil is pardoned, the reason for the cor cession is to prevent worse evil. But surely thing which is only allowed because there ma be something worse has only a slight degre of goodness. He would never have adde " let each man have his own wife," unless h had previously used the words " but, becaus of fornications." Do away with fornicatior and he will not say " let each man have hi own wife." Just as though one were to lay down : " It is good to feed on wheaten breac and to eat the finest wheat flour," and yet t prevent a person pressed by hunger from de vouring cow-dung, I may allow him to ea barley. Does it follow that the wheat wi not have its peculiar purity, because such a one prefers barley to excrement ? That naturally good which does not admit of com parison with what is bad, and is not eclipse because something else is preferred. At th same time we must notice the Apostle's pru dence. He did not say, it is good not to hav a wife : but, it is good not to touch a woman as though there were danger even in th touch : as though he who touched her, woul not escape from her who " hunteth for th precious life," who causeth the young man understanding to fly away. [1] " Can a ma take fire in his bosom, and his clothes not b burned ? Or can one walk upon hot coals, an his feet not be scorched ?" As then he wh touches fire is instantly burned, so by th mere touch the peculiar nature of man an woman is perceived, and the difference of se is understood. Heathen fables relate hov [2] Mithras and [3] Ericthonius were begotten c the soil, in stone or earth, by raging lus' Hence it was that our Joseph, because th Egyptian woman wished to touch him, fle from her hands, and, as if he had been bitte by a mad dog and feared the spreading poisor

---

[1] 1 Cor. vii. 1 sq.

[1] Prov. vi. 27, 28.
[2] Mithras was the God of the Sun among the Persians. H worship was introduced at Rome under the Emperors, ar thence spread over the empire.
[3] Son of Vulcan, king of Athens, and the first to drive a fou in-hand, Virg. G. iii. 113 : " First to the chariot, Ericthoni dared four steeds to join, and o'er the rapid wheels victoriou hang."

hrew away the cloak which she had touched. But, because of fornications let each man ave his own wife, and let each woman have er own husband." He did not say, because f fornication let each man marry a wife: therwise by this excuse he would have thrown he reins to lust, and whenever a man's wife .ied, he would have to marry another to pre- ent fornication, but "have his own wife." .et him he says have and use his own wife, vhom he had before he became a believer, nd whom it would have been good not to ouch, and, when once he became a follower of Christ, to know only as a sister, not as a wife, nless fornication should make it excusable to ouch her. "The wife hath not power over er own body, but the husband: and likewise lso the husband hath not power over his wn body, but the wife." The whole question ere concerns those who are married men. s it lawful for them to do what our Lord for- ade in the Gospel, and to put away their ives? Whence it is that the Apostle says, 'It is good for a man not to touch a woman." 3ut inasmuch as he who is once married has o power to abstain except by mutual consent, nd may not reject an unoffending partner, et the husband render unto the wife her due. Ie bound himself voluntarily that he might e under compulsion to render it. "Defraud e not one the other, except it be by consent or a season, that ye may give yourselves unto rayer." What, I pray you, is the quality of hat good thing which hinders prayer? which loes not allow the body of Christ to be re- eived? So long as I do the husband's part, fail in continency. The same Apostle in nother place commands us to pray always. f we are to pray always, it follows that we nust never be in the bondage of wedlock, for s often as I render my wife her due, I cannot ray. The Apostle Peter had experience of he bonds of marriage. See how he fashions he Church, and what lesson he teaches Chris- ians:[1] "Ye husbands in like manner dwell vith your wives according to knowledge, riving honour unto the woman, as unto the veaker vessel, as being also joint-heirs of the grace of life; to the end that your prayers be not hindered." Observe that, as S. Paul be- ore, because in both cases the spirit is the ame, so S. Peter now, says that prayers are indered by the performance of marriage duty. When he says "likewise," he challenges the usbands to imitate their wives, because he as already given them commandment:[2] "be- holding your chaste conversation coupled with ear. Whose adorning let it not be the outward dorning of plaiting the hair, and of wearing

jewels of gold, or of putting on apparel: but let it be the hidden man of the heart, in the incorruptible apparel of a meek and quiet spirit, which is in the sight of God of great price." You see what kind of wedlock he enjoins. Husbands and wives are to dwell together according to knowledge, so that they may know what God wishes and desires, and give honour to the weak vessel, woman. If we abstain from intercourse, we give honour to our wives: if we do not abstain, it is clear that insult is the opposite of honour. He also tells the wives to let their husbands "see their chaste behaviour, and the hidden man of the heart, in the incorruptible apparel of a meek and quiet spirit." Words truly worthy of an apostle, and of Christ's rock! He lays down the law for husbands and wives, condemns outward ornament, while he praises continence, which is the ornament of the inner man, as seen in the incorruptible apparel of a meek and quiet spirit. In effect he says this: Since your outer man is corrupt, and you have ceased to possess the blessing of incorruption character- istic of virgins, at least imitate the incorrup- tion of the spirit by subsequent abstinence, and what you cannot show in the body exhibit in the mind. For these are the riches, and these the ornaments of your union, which Christ seeks.

8. The words which follow, "that ye may give yourselves unto prayer, and may be to- gether again," might lead one to suppose that the Apostle was expressing a wish and not making a concession because of the danger of a greater fall. He therefore at once adds, "lest Satan tempt you for your incontinency." It is a fine permission which is conveyed in the words "be together again." What it was that he blushed to call by its own name, and thought only better than a temptation of Satan and the effect of incontinence, we take trouble to discuss as if it were obscure, although he has explained his meaning by saying, "this I say by way of permission, not by way of command." And do we still hesitate to speak of marriage as a concession to weakness, not a thing commanded, as though second and third marriages were not allowed on the same ground, as though the doors of the Church were not opened by repentance even to forni- cators, and what is more, to the incestuous? Take the case of the man who outraged his step-mother. Does not the Apostle, after de- livering him, in his first Epistle to the Corinth- ians, to Satan for the destruction of the flesh that his spirit might be saved, in the second Epistle take the offender back and strive to prevent a brother from being swallowed up by overmuch grief. The Apostle's wish is one thing, his pardon another. If a wish be ex-

---

[1] 1 Pet. iii. 7.   [2] 1 Pet. iii. 2, 3.

pressed, it confers a right ; if a thing is only called pardonable, we are wrong in using it. If you wish to know the Apostle's real mind, you must take in what follows : "but I would that all men were as I am." Happy is the man who is like Paul ! Fortunate is he who attends to the Apostle's command, not to his concession. This, says he, I wish, this I desire, that ye be imitators of me, as I also am of Christ, who was a Virgin born of a Virgin, uncorrupt of her who was uncorrupt. We, because we are men, cannot imitate our Lord's nativity ; but we may at least imitate His life. The former was the blessed prerogative of divinity, the latter belongs to our human condition and is part of human effort. I would that all men were like me, that while they are like me, they may also become like Christ, to whom I am like. For [1] "he that believeth in Christ ought himself also to walk even as He walked." [2] " Howbeit each man hath his own gift from God, one after this manner, and another after that." What I wish, he says, is clear. But since in the Church there is a diversity of gifts, I acquiesce in marriage, lest I should seem to condemn nature. At the same time consider, that the gift of virginity is one, that of marriage, another. For were the reward the same for the married and for virgins, he would never after enjoining continence have said : [3] " Each man hath his own gift from God, one after this manner, and another after that." Where there is a distinction in one particular, there is a diversity also in other points. I grant that even marriage is a gift of God, but between gift and gift there is great diversity. In fact the Apostle himself speaking of the same person who had repented of his incestuous conduct, says : [3] " so that contrariwise ye should rather forgive him and comfort him, and to whom ye forgive anything, I forgive also." And that we might not think a man's gift contemptible, he added, [4] " for what I also have forgiven, if I have forgiven anything, for your sakes have I forgiven it, in the presence of Christ." There is diversity in the gifts of Christ. Hence it is that by way of type Joseph has a coat of many colours. And in the forty-fifth psalm we read, [5] " at thy right hand doth stand the queen in a vesture of gold wrought about with divers colours." And the Apostle Peter says, [6] " as heirs together of the manifold grace of God," where the more expressive Greek word ποικίλης, i. e., *varied*, is used.

9. Then come the words [7] "But I say to the unmarried and to widows, it is good for them if they abide even as I. But if they have not

continency, let them marry : for it is better t marry than to burn." Having conceded t married persons the enjoyment of wedloc and pointed out his own wishes, he passes o to the unmarried and to widows, sets befor them his own practice for imitation, and call them happy if they so abide. " But if the have not continency, let them marry," just a he said before " But because of fornications, and " Lest Satan tempt you, because of you incontinency." And he gives a reason for say ing " If they have not continency, let ther marry," viz. " It is better to marry than t burn." The reason why it is better to marr is that it is worse to burn. Let burning lus be absent, and he will not say it is better t marry. The word *better* always implies a com parison with something worse, not a thing at solutely good and incapable of comparison. I is as though he said, it is better to have on eye than neither, it is better to stand on on foot and to support the rest of the body wit a stick, than to crawl with broken legs. Wha do you say, Apostle ? I do not believe yo when you say " Though I be rude in speecl yet am I not in knowledge." As humility i the source of the sayings " For I am no worthy to be called an Apostle," and " To m who am the least of the Apostles," and " A to one born out of due time," so here also w have an utterance of humility. You know th meaning of language, or you would not quot [1] Epimenides, [2] Menander, and [3] Aratus. Whe you are discussing continence and virginit you say, " It is good for a man not to touch woman." And, " It is good for them if the abide even as I." And, " I think that this i good by reason of the present distress." Anc " That it is good for a man so to be." Whe you come to marriage, you do not say it i good to marry, because you cannot then ad " *than to burn ;* " but you say, " It is better t marry than to burn." If marriage in itself b good, do not compare it with fire, but simpl say " It is good to marry." I suspect the good ness of that thing which is forced into th position of being only the lesser of two evils What I want is not a smaller evil, but a thing absolutely good.

10. So far the first section has been ex plained. Let us now come to those whicl follow. [4] " But unto the married I give charge yea not I, but the Lord. That the wife de part not from her husband (but and if sh depart, let her remain unmarried, or else b reconciled to her husband): and that the hus band leave not his wife. But to the rest sa I, not the Lord : If any brother hath an un believing wife, and she is content to dwe

---

[1] 1 John ii. 6.   [2] 1 Cor. vii. 7.   [3] 2 Cor. ii. 7.
[4] 2 Cor. ii. 10. Margin.   [5] Ps. xlv. 9, 13, 14.
[6] 1 Peter iii. 7, joined with 1 Peter iv. 10.
[7] 1 Cor. vii. 8.

[1] Tit. i. 12.   [2] 1 Cor. xv. 33.
[3] Acts xvii. 28.   [4] 1 Cor. vii. 10 sq.

ith him, let him not leave her," and so on the words "As God hath called each, so t him walk. And so ordain I in all the urches." This passage has no bearing on ir present controversy. For he ordains, according to the mind of the Lord, that excepting the cause of fornication, a wife must not put away, and that a wife who has been it away, may not, so long as her husband ves, be married to another, or at all events at her duty is to be reconciled to her husand. But in the case of those who are already married at the time of conversion, that to say, supposing one of the two were a liever, he enjoins that the believer shall not it away the unbeliever. And after stating his ason, *viz.*, that the unbeliever who is unwilling to leave the believer becomes thereby a andidate for the faith, he commands, on the her hand, that if the unbeliever reject the ithful one on account of the faith of Christ, e believer ought to depart, lest husband or ife be preferred to Christ, in comparison ith Whom we must hold even life itself eap. Yet at the present day many women espising the Apostle's command, are joined to eathen husbands, and prostitute the temples Christ to idols. They do not understand at they are part of His body though indeed ey are His ribs. The Apostle is lenient the union of unbelievers, who having (beeving) husbands, afterwards come to believe Christ. He does not extend his indulgence those women who, although Christians, have een married to heathen husbands. To these elsewhere says,[1] "Be not unequally yoked ith unbelievers: for what fellowship have ghteousness and iniquity? or what communn hath light with darkness? And what conord hath Christ with Belial? or what portion ith a believer with an unbeliever? And what greement hath a temple of God with idols? or we are a temple of the living God." Alough I know that crowds of matrons will furious against me: although I know that st as they have shamelessly despised the ord, so they will rave at me who am but a ea and the least of Christians: yet I will eak out what I think. I will say what the postle has taught me, that they are not on e side of righteousness, but of iniquity: not light, but of darkness: that they do not long to Christ, but to Belial: that they are t temples of the living God, but shrines d idols of the dead. And, if you wish to e more clearly how utterly unlawful it is for Christian woman to marry a Gentile, conder what the same Apostle says,[2] "A wife is und for so long time as her husband liveth: t if the husband be dead, she is free to be

married to whom she will; only in the Lord," that is, to a Christian. He who allows second and third marriages in the Lord, forbids first marriages with a Gentile. Whence Abraham also makes his servant swear upon his thigh, that is, on Christ, Who was to spring from his seed, that he would not bring an alien-born as a wife for his son Isaac. And Ezra checked an offence of this kind against God by making his countrymen put away their wives. And the prophet Malachi thus speaks,[1] "Judah hath dealt treacherously, and an abomination is committed in Israel and in Jerusalem; for Judah hath profaned the holiness of the Lord which he loveth, and hath married the daughter of a strange god. The Lord will cut off the man that doeth this,[2] him that teacheth and him that learneth, out of the tents of Jacob, and him that offers an offering unto the Lord of hosts." I have said this that they who compare marriage with virginity, may at least know that such marriages as these are on a lower level than digamy and trigamy.

11. In the above discussion the Apostle has taught that the believer ought not to depart from the unbeliever, but remain in marriage as the faith found them, and that each man whether married or single should continue as he was when baptized into Christ; and then he suddenly introduces the metaphors of circumcision and uncircumcision, of bond and free, and under those metaphors treats of the married and unmarried.[3] "Was any man called being circumcised? let him not become uncircumcised. Circumcision is nothing, and uncircumcision is nothing: but the keeping of the commandments of God. Let each man abide in that calling wherein he was called. Wast thou called being a bondservant? Care not for it: but even if thou canst become free, use it rather. For he that was called in the Lord being a bondservant, is the Lord's freedman; likewise he that was called, being free, is Christ's bondservant. Ye were bought with a price; become not bondservants of men. Brethren, let each man, wherein he was called, therein abide with God." Some, I suppose, will find fault with the Apostle's way of reasoning. I would therefore ask first, What we are to infer from his suddenly passing in a discussion concerning husbands and wives to a comparison of Jew and Gentile, bond and free, and then returning, when this point is settled, to the question about virgins, and telling us "Concerning virgins I have no commandment from the Lord"; what has a comparison of Jew and Gentile, bond and free, to do with wedlock and virginity? In the next

---

a Cor. vi. 14 sq.   [2] 1 Cor. vii. 39.

[1] Mal. ii. 11, 12.
[2] R. V. "To the man that doeth this, him that waketh and him that answereth."
[3] 1 Cor. vii. 18 sq.

place, how are we to understand the words "Hath any been called in uncircumcision, let him not be circumcised"?[1] Can a man who has lost his foreskin restore it again at his pleasure? Then, in what sense are we to explain "For he that was called in the Lord, being a bondservant, is the Lord's freedman: likewise he that was called, being free, is Christ's bondservant." Fourthly, how is it that he who commanded servants to obey their masters according to the flesh, now says, "Become not bondservants of men." Lastly, how are we to connect with slavery, or with circumcision, his saying "Brethren, let each man, wherein he was called, therein abide with God," which even contradicts his previous opinion. We heard him say "Become not bondservants of men." How can we then possibly abide in that vocation wherein we were called, when many at the time they became believers had masters according to the flesh, whose bondservants they are now forbidden to be? Moreover, what has the argument about our abiding in the vocation wherein we were called, to do with circumcision? for in another place the same Apostle cries aloud "Behold I Paul tell you that, if ye be circumcised, Christ shall profit you nothing"? We must conclude, therefore, that a higher meaning should be given to circumcision and uncircumcision, bond and free, and that these words must be taken in close connection with what has gone before. "Was anyone called being circumcised? let him not become uncircumcised." If, he says, at the time you were called and became a believer in Christ, if I say, you were called being circumcised from a wife, that is, unmarried, do not marry a wife, that is, do not become uncircumcised, lest you lay upon the freedom of circumcision and chastity the burden of marriage. Again, if anyone was called in uncircumcision, let him not be circumcised. You had a wife, he says, when you believed: do not think the faith of Christ a reason for disagreement, because God called us in peace. [2] "Circumcision is nothing, and uncircumcision is nothing; but the keeping of the commandments of God." For neither celibacy nor marriage availeth anything without works, since even faith, which is specially characteristic of Christians, if it have not works, is said to be dead, and vestal virgins and Juno's widows might upon these terms be numbered with the saints. "Let each man in the vocation wherein he was called, therein abide." Whether he had, or had not, a wife

when he believed, let him remain in that co dition in which he was when called. Accor ingly he does not so strongly urge virgins be married, as forbid divorce. And as he d bars those who have wives from putting the away, so he cuts off from virgins the power being married. "Thou wast called being slave, heed it not; but even if thou canst b come free, use it rather." Even if you have, says, a wife, and are bound to her, and pay h due, and have not power over your own body or if, to speak more clearly, you are the bon servant of your wife, be not sad upon that a count, nor sigh for the loss of your virginit But even if you can find some causes of di cord, do not, for the sake of thoroughly enjo ing the liberty of chastity, seek your own we fare by destroying another. Keep your wi awhile, and do not go too fast for her laggi footsteps: wait till she follows. If you a patient, your spouse will become a sister, "F he that was called in the Lord, being a bon servant, is the Lord's freedman: likewise, that was called being free, is Christ's bon servant." He gives his reasons for not wis ing wives to be forsaken. He therefore say I command that Gentiles who believe on Chri do not abandon the married state in whi they were before embracing the faith: for who had a wife when he became a believer, not so strictly devoted to the service of God virgins and unmarried persons. But, in a ma ner, he has more freedom, and the reins of b bondage are relaxed; and, while he is t bondservant of a wife, he is, so to speak, t freedman of the Lord. Moreover, he wh when called by the Lord had not a wife ar was free from the bondage of wedlock, he truly Christ's bondservant. What happiness be the bondservant, not of a wife but of Chri to serve not the flesh, but the spirit! [1] "F he who is joined unto the Lord is one spirit There was some fear that by saying "Wa thou called being a bondservant? Care not f it: but, even if thou canst become free, use rather," he might seem to have flouted cont nence, and to have given us up to the slavery marriage. He therefore makes a remark whi removes all cavil: "Ye were bought with price, become not servants of men." We ha been redeemed with the most precious blo of Christ: the Lamb was slain for us, and ha ing been sprinkled with hyssop and the war drops of His blood, we have rejected poiso ous pleasure. Why do we at whose baptis Pharaoh died and all his host was drowne again turn back in our hearts to Egypt, a after the manna, angels' food, sigh for the ga lic and the onions and the cucumbers, a Pharaoh's meat?

---

[1] But S. Paul hints at a surgical operation. See Josephus, *Antiq.* Bk. xii. c. v. sec. 1, where certain apostates from Judaism are said "to have hid their circumcision that even when they were naked [in the gymnasium] they might appear to be Greeks." See also Celsus, Bk. vii. c. xxv.
[2] Gal. v. 19.

[1] 1 Cor. vi. 17.

12. Having discussed marriage and continency he at length comes to virginity and says "Now concerning virgins I have no commandment of the Lord : but I give my judgement, as one that hath obtained mercy of the Lord to be faithful. I think therefore that this is good by reason of the present distress, namely, that it is good for a man to be as he" Here our opponent goes utterly wild with exultation : this is his strongest battering-ram with which he shakes the wall of virginity. "See," says he, "the Apostle confesses that as regards virgins he has no commandment of the Lord, and he who had with authority laid down the law respecting husbands and wives, does not dare to command what the Lord has not enjoined. And rightly so. For what is enjoined is commanded, that is commanded must be done, and that which must be done implies punishment if it be not done. For it is useless to order a thing to be done and yet leave the individual free to do it or not do it. If the Lord had commanded virginity He would have seemed to condemn marriage, and to do away with the seed-plot of mankind, of which virginity itself is a growth. If He had cut off the root, how was He to expect fruit ? If the foundations were not first laid, how was He to build the edifice, and put on the roof to cover all ! Excavators toil hard to remove mountains ; the bowels of the earth are pierced in the search for gold. And, when the tiny particles, first by the blast of the furnace, then by the hand of the cunning workman have been fashioned into an ornament, men do not call him blessed who has separated the gold from the dross, but him who wears the beautiful gold. Do not marvel then if, placed as we are, amid temptations of the flesh and incentives to vice, the angelic life be not exacted of us, but merely recommended. If advice be given, a man is free to proffer obedience; if there be a command, he is a servant bound to compliance. "I have no commandment," he says, "of the Lord : but I give my judgement, as he that hath obtained mercy of the Lord to be faithful." If you have no commandment of the Lord, how dare you give judgement without orders ? The Apostle will reply : Do you wish me to give orders where the Lord has offered a favour rather than laid down a law ? The great Creator and Fashioner, knowing the weakness of the vessel which he made, left virginity open to those whom He addressed ; and shall I, the teacher of the Gentiles, who have become all things to all men that I might gain all, shall I lay upon the necks of weak believers from the very first the burden of per-

petual chastity ? Let them [1] begin with short periods of release from the marriage bond, and give themselves unto prayer, that when they have tasted the sweets of chastity they may desire the perpetual possession of that wherewith they were temporarily delighted. The Lord, when tempted by the Pharisees, and asked whether according to the law of Moses it was permitted to put away a wife, forbade the practice altogether. After weighing His words the disciples said to Him : [2] "If the case of the man is so with his wife, it is not expedient to marry. But He said unto them, all men cannot receive this saying, but they to whom it is given. For there are eunuchs, which were so born from their mother's womb : and there are eunuchs, which were made eunuchs by men : and there are eunuchs, which made themselves eunuchs for the kingdom of heaven's sake. He that is able to receive it, let him receive it." The reason is plain why the Apostle said, "concerning virgins I have no commandment of the Lord." Surely ; because the Lord had previously said "All men cannot receive the word, but they to whom it is given," and "He that is able to receive it, let him receive it." [3] The Master of the Christian race offers the reward, invites candidates to the course, holds in His hand the prize of virginity, points to the fountain of purity, and cries aloud [4] "If any man thirst, let him come unto me and drink." "He that is able to receive it, let him receive it." He does not say, you must drink, you must run, willing or unwilling : but whoever is willing and able to run and to drink, he shall conquer, he shall be satisfied. And therefore Christ loves virgins more than others, because they willingly give what was not commanded them. And it indicates greater grace to offer what you are not bound to give, than to render what is exacted of you. The apostles, contemplating the burden of a wife, exclaimed, "If the case of the man is so with his wife, it is not expedient to marry." Our Lord thought well of their view. You rightly think, said He, that it is not expedient for a man who is hastening to the kingdom of heaven to take a wife : but it is a hard matter, and all men do not receive the saying, but they to whom it has been given. Some are eunuchs by nature, others by the violence of men. Those eunuchs please Me who are such not of necessity, but of free choice. Willingly do I take them into my bosom who have made themselves eunuchs for the kingdom of heaven's sake, and in order to worship Me

[1] Ferias nuptiarum. The reference is to 1 Cor. vii. 5.
[2] Matt. xix. 10 sq.
[3] Jerome uses the Greek word ἀγωνοθέτης—President of the Games.
[4] S. John vii. 37.

have renounced the condition of their birth. We must now explain the words, " Those who have made themselves eunuchs for the kingdom of heaven's sake." If they who have made themselves eunuchs have the reward of the kingdom of heaven, it follows that they who have not made themselves such cannot be placed with those who have. He who is able, he says, to receive it, let him receive it. It is a mark of great faith and of great virtue, to be the pure temple of God, to offer oneself a whole burnt-offering, and, according to the same apostle, to be holy both in body and in spirit. These are the eunuchs, who thinking themselves dry trees because of their impotence, hear by the mouth of [1] Isaiah that they have a place prepared in heaven for sons and daughters. Their type is [2] Ebed-melech the eunuch in Jeremiah, and the eunuch of Queen Candace in the [3] Acts of the Apostles, who on account of the strength of his faith gained the name of a *man*. These are they to whom Clement, who was the successor of the Apostle Peter, and of whom the Apostle Paul makes mention, wrote letters, directing almost the whole of his discourse to the subject of virgin purity. After them there is a long series of apostolic men, martyrs, and men illustrious no less for holiness than for eloquence, with whom we may very easily become acquainted through their own writings. [4] "I think, therefore," he says, "that this is good for the present distress." What is this distress which, in contempt of the marriage tie, longs for the liberty of virginity? [5] "Woe unto them that are with child and to them that give suck in those days." We have not here a condemnation of harlots and brothels, of whose damnation there is no doubt, but of the swelling womb, and wailing infancy, the fruit as well as the work of marriage. " For it is good for a man so to be." If it is good for a man so to be, it is bad for a man not so to be. [6] "Art thou bound unto a wife? Seek not to be loosed. Art thou loosed from a wife? Seek not a wife." Each one of us has his appointed bounds ; let me have what is mine, and keep your own. If thou art bound to a wife, give her not a bill of divorce. If I am loosed from a wife, I will not seek a wife. As I do not dissolve marriages once contracted : so you should not bind what is loosed. And at the same time the meaning of the words must be taken into account. He who has a wife is regarded as a debtor, and is said to be uncircumcised, to be the servant of his wife, and like bad servants to be *bound*. But he who has no wife, in the first place owes no man

anything, then is circumcised, thirdly is fr lastly, is loosed.

13. Let us run through the remaining poir for our author is so voluminous that we ca not linger over every detail. " But and thou marry, thou hast not sinned." It is c thing not to sin, another to do good. " A if a virgin marry, she hath not sinned." N that virgin who has once for all dedicated h self to the service of God : for, should one these marry, she will have damnation, becau she has made of no account her first fai But, if our adversary objects that this sayi relates to widows, we reply that it applies w still greater force to virgins, since marriage forbidden even to widows whose previc marriage had been lawful. For virgins w marry after consecration are rather incestuo than adulterous. And, for fear he should saying, " And if a virgin marry, she hath 1 sinned," again stimulate the unmarried to married, he immediately checks himself, a by introducing another consideration, inva dates his previous concession. " Yet," says l " such shall have tribulation in the flesl Who are they who shall have tribulation the flesh? They to whom he had before i dulgently said " But and if thou marry, th hast not sinned ; and if a virgin marry, s hath not sinned. Yet such shall have tribu tion in the flesh." We in our inexperien thought that marriage had at least the joys the flesh. But if they who are married ha tribulation even in the flesh, which is imagin to be the sole source of their pleasure, wh else is there to marry for, when in the spir and in the mind, and in the flesh itself the is tribulation. " But I would spare yoι Thus, he says, I allege tribulation as a moti∾ as though there were not greater obligatio to refrain. " But this I say, brethren, the tir is shortened, that henceforth both those th have wives may be as though they had none I am by no means now discussing virgins, whose happiness no one entertains a doubt. am coming to the married. The time is sho the Lord is at hand. Even though we liv nine hundred years, as did men of old, yet ∾ ought to think that short which must one d have an end, and cease to be. But, as thin are, and it is not so much the joy as the tri ulation of marriage that is short, why do ∾ take wives whom we shall soon be compell∾ to lose? [1] " And those that weep, and tho that rejoice, and those that buy, and tho that use the world, as though they wept n∾ as though they rejoiced not, as though th bought not, as though they did not use t world : for the fashion of this world passe

---

[1] Is. lvi. 3.   [2] Jer. xxxviii. 7.
[3] Acts viii. 27.   [4] 1 Cor. vii. 26.
[6] Matt. xxiv. 19, &c.   [6] 1 Cor. vii. 27.

[1] 1 Cor. vii. 30 sqq.

ay." If the world, which comprehends all
ings, passes away, yea if the fashion and
tercourse of the world vanishes like the
ouds, amongst the other works of the world,
arriage too will vanish away. For after the
surrection there will be no wedlock. But if
ath be the end of marriage, why do we not
oluntarily embrace the inevitable? And why
o we not, encouraged by the hope of the re-
ard, offer to God that which must be wrung
om us against our will. "He that is un-
arried is careful for the things of the Lord,
ow he may please the Lord: but he that is
arried is careful for the things of the world,
ow he may please his wife, and is [1] divided."
et us look at the difference between the cares
the virgin, and those of the married man.
he virgin longs to please the Lord, the hus-
and to please his wife, and that he may please
er he is careful for the things of the world,
hich will of course pass away with the world.
And he is divided," that is to say, is dis-
acted with manifold cares and miseries.
his is not the place to describe the difficulties
marriage, and to revel in rhetorical com-
onplaces. I think I delivered myself fully
regards this point in my argument against
Ielvidius, and in the book which I addressed
[3] Eustochium. At all events [4] Tertullian,
hile still a young man, gave himself full play
th this subject. And my teacher, [5] Gregory
Nazianzus, discussed virginity and marriage
some Greek verses. I now briefly beg my
ader to note that in the Latin manuscripts
e have the reading "there is a difference
so between the virgin and the wife." The
ords, it is true, have a meaning of their own,
d have by me, as well as by others, been so
plained as showing the bearing of the pas-
ge. Yet they lack apostolic authority, since
e Apostle's words are as we have translated
em—"He is careful for the things of the
orld, how he may please his wife, [6] and he is
vided." Having laid down this, he passes
the virgins and the continent, and says
he woman that is unmarried and a virgin
inks of the things of the Lord, that she may
holy in body and in spirit." Not every un-
arried woman is also a virgin. But every
rgin is of course unmarried. It may be, that
gard for elegance of expression led him to
peat the same idea by means of another

word and speak of "a woman unmarried and
a virgin"; or at least he may have wished to
give to "unmarried" the definite meaning
of "virgin," so that we might not suppose
him to include harlots, united to no one by
the fixed bonds of wedlock, among the "unmarried." Of what, then, does she that is unmarried and a virgin think? "The things of
the Lord, that she may be holy both in body
and in spirit." Supposing there were nothing else, and that no greater reward followed
virginity, this would be motive enough for her
choice, to think of the things of the Lord.
But he immediately points out the contents of
her thought—that she may be holy both in
body and spirit. For there are virgins in the
flesh, not in the spirit, whose body is intact,
their soul corrupt. But that virgin is a sacrifice to Christ, whose mind has not been defiled
by thought, nor her flesh by lust. On the
other hand, she who is married thinks of the
things of the world, how she may please her
husband. Just as the man who has a wife is
anxious for the things of the world, how he
may please his wife, so the married woman
thinks of the things of the world, how she
may please her husband. But we are not of
this world, which lieth in wickedness, the fashion of which passeth away, and concerning
which the Lord said to the Apostles, [1] "If ye
were of the world, the world would love its
own." And lest perchance someone might
suppose that he was laying the heavy burden
of chastity on unwilling shoulders, he at once
adds his reasons for persuading to it, and says:
[2] "And this I say for your profit; not that I
may cast a snare upon you, but for that which
is seemly, and that ye may attend upon the
Lord without distraction." The Latin words
do not convey the meaning of the Greek.
What words shall we use to render $\Pi\rho\grave{o}\varsigma\ \tau\grave{o}$
$\epsilon\ddot{v}\sigma\chi\eta\mu\nu\nu\ \varkappa\grave{\alpha}\iota\ \epsilon\dot{v}\pi\rho\acute{o}\sigma\epsilon\delta\rho\nu\nu\ \tau\hat{\omega}\ K\nu\rho\acute{\iota}\omega$
$\dot{\alpha}\pi\epsilon\rho\iota\sigma\pi\acute{\alpha}\sigma\tau\omega\varsigma$? The difficulty of transla-
tion accounts for the fact that the clause is
completely wanting in Latin manuscripts. Let
us, however, use the passage as we have translated it. The Apostle does not lay a snare
upon us, nor does he compel us to be what we
do not wish to be; but he gives his advice as
to what is fair and seemly, he would have us
attend upon the Lord and ever be anxious
about that service, and await the Lord's will,
so that like active and well-armed soldiers we
may obey orders, and may do so without distraction, which, according to [3] Ecclesiastes, is
given to the men of this world that they may
be exercised thereby. But if anyone considers that his virgin, that is, his flesh, is wanton and boiling with lust, and cannot be

---

See Rev. Ver. Margin.
See the treatise on the Perp. Virginity of the Blessed Vir-
Mary. Rome, 384.
Ep. xxii. on the guarding of virginity. Rome, 384.
Jerome apparently, here, alludes to some early work of Ter-
lian not now extant.
Jerome often alludes to his relation to Gregory, in the year
; he was present at the council of Constantinople, of which
egory was then the bishop.
This rendering supposes $\varkappa\alpha\grave{\iota}\ \mu\epsilon\mu\epsilon\rho\acute{\iota}\sigma\tau\alpha\iota$ to be joined to the
ceding sentence. The Vulgate has *et divisus est*, and so also
Æthiopic Version.

[1] S. John xv. 19.   [2] 1 Cor. vii. 35.   [3] iii. 10.

bridled, and he must do one of two things, either take a wife or fall, let him do what he will, he does not sin if he marry. Let him do, he says, what he will, not what he ought. He does not sin if he marry a wife; yet, he does not well if he marry :[1] "But he that standeth stedfast in his heart, having no necessity, but hath power as touching his own will, and hath determined this in his own heart, to keep his own virgin, shall do well. So then both he that giveth his own virgin in marriage doeth well; and he that giveth her not in marriage shall do better." With marked propriety he had previously said "He who marries a wife does not sin ": here he tells us "He that keepeth his own virgin doeth well." But it is one thing not to sin, another to do well. [2] "Depart from evil," he says, "and do good." The former we forsake, the latter we follow. In this last lies perfection. But whereas he says "and he that giveth his virgin in marriage doeth well," it might be supposed that our remark does not hold good; he therefore forthwith detracts from this seeming good and puts it in the shade by comparing it with another, and saying, "and he that giveth her not in marriage shall do better." If he had not intended to draw the inference of doing better, he would never have previously referred to doing well. But where there is something good and something better, the reward is not in both cases the same, and where the reward is not one and the same, there of course the gifts are different. The difference, then, between marriage and virginity is as great as that between not sinning and doing well; nay rather, to speak less harshly, as great as between good and better.

14. He has ended his discussion of wedlock and virginity, and has carefully steered between the two precepts without turning to the right hand or to the left. He has followed the royal road and fulfilled the command [3] not to be righteous over much. Now again he compares monogamy with digamy, and as he had subordinated marriage to virginity, so he makes second marriages inferior to first, and says,[4] "A wife is bound for so long time as her husband liveth; but if the husband be dead, she is free to be married to whom she will; only in the Lord. But she is happier if she abide as she is, after my judgement: and I think that I also have the Spirit of God." He allows second marriages, but to such persons as wish for them and are not able to contain; lest,[5] having "waxed wanton against Christ," they desire to marry, " having condemnation, because they have re-

jected their first faith;" and he makes the concession because many had already turned aside after Satan. [1] "But," says he, "the will be happier if they abide as they are," and he immediately adds the weight of Apostolic authority, "after my judgement." And that an Apostle's authority might not, like that of an ordinary man, be without weight, he added "and I think that I also have the Spirit of God." When he incites to continence, it is not by the judgement or spirit of man, but by the judgement and Spirit of God; when, however, he grants the indulgence of marriage he does not mention the Spirit of God, but weighs his judgement with wisdom, and adapts the severity of the strain to the weakness of the individual. In this sense we must take the whole of the following passage :[2] "For the woman that hath a husband is bound by law to the husband while he liveth; but if the husband die, she is discharged from the law of the husband. So then if, while the husband liveth, she be joined to another man, she shall be called an adulteress: but if the husband die, she is free from the law, so that she is no adulteress, though she be joined to another man." And similarly the words to Timothy [3] "I desire therefore that the younger widows marry, bear children, rule the household, give none occasion to the adversary for reviling for already some are turned aside after Satan," and so on. For as on account of the danger of fornication he allows virgins to marry, and makes that excusable which itself is not desirable, so to avoid this same fornication, he allows second marriages to widows. For it is better to know a single husband, though he be a second or third than to have many paramours: that is, it is more tolerable for a woman to prostitute herself to one man than to many. At all events this is so if the Samaritan woman in John's Gospel who said she had her sixth husband was reproved by the Lord because he was not her husband. For where there are more husbands than one the proper idea of a husband, who is a single person, is destroyed. At the beginning one rib was turned into one wife. "And they two," he says, "shall be one flesh" not three, or four; otherwise, how can they be any longer two, if they are several. Lamech a man of blood and a murderer, was the first who divided one flesh between two wives Fratricide and digamy were abolished by the same punishment—that of the deluge. The one was avenged seven times, the other seventy times seven. The guilt is as widely different as are the numbers. What the holiness of second marriage is, appears from this—that

[1] 1 Cor. vii. 37, 38.   [2] Ps. xxxvi. 27.
[3] Eccles. vii. 16.   [4] 1 Cor. vii. 39, 40.
[5] 1 Tim. v. 11, 15.

[1] 1 Cor. vii. 40.   [2] Rom. vii. 2, 3.   [3] 1 Tim. v. 14, 15

person twice married [1] cannot be enrolled in the ranks of the clergy, and so the Apostle tells Timothy,[2] " Let none be enrolled as a widow under threescore years old, having been the wife of one man." The whole command concerns those widows who are supported on the alms of the Church. The age is therefore limited, so that those only may receive the food of the poor who can no longer work. And at the same time, consider that she who has had two husbands, even though she be a widow, decrepit, and in want, is not a worthy recipient of the Church's funds. But if she be deprived of the bread of charity, how much more is she deprived of that bread which cometh down from heaven, and of which if a man eat unworthily, he shall be guilty of outrage offered to the body and the blood of Christ ?

15. The passages, however, which I have adduced in support of my position and in which it is permitted to widows, if they so desire, to marry again, are interpreted by some concerning those widows who had lost their husbands and were found in that condition when they became Christians. For, supposing a person baptized and her husband dead, it would not be consistent if the Apostle were to bid her marry another, when he enjoins even those who have wives to be as though they had them not. And this is why the number of wives which a man may take is not defined, because when Christian baptism has been received, even though a third or a fourth wife has been taken, she is reckoned as the first. Otherwise, if, after baptism and after the death of a first husband, a second is taken, why should not a sixth after the death of the second, third, fourth, and fifth, and so on ? For it is possible, that through some strange misfortune, or by the judgement of God cutting short repeated marriages, a young woman may have several husbands, while an old woman may be left a widow by her first husband in extreme age. The first Adam was married once : the second was unmarried. Let the supporters of second marriages shew us as their leader a third Adam who was twice married. But granted that Paul allowed second marriages : upon the same grounds it follows that he allows even third and fourth marriages, or a woman may marry as often as her husband dies. The Apostle was forced to choose many things which he did not like. He circumcised Timothy, and shaved his own head, practised

going barefoot, let his hair grow long, and cut it at Cenchrea. And he had certainly chastised the Galatians, and blamed Peter because for the sake of Jewish observances he separated himself from the Gentiles. As then in other points connected with the discipline of the Church he was a Jew to Jews, a Gentile to Gentiles, and was made all things to all men, that he might gain all : so too he allowed second marriages to incontinent persons, and did not limit the number of marriages, in order that women, although they saw themselves permitted to take a second husband, in the same way as a third or a fourth was allowed, might blush to take a second, lest they should be compared to those who were three or four times married. If more than one husband be allowed, it makes no difference whether he be a second or a third, because there is no longer a question of single marriage. [1] " All things are lawful, but not all things are expedient." I do not condemn second, nor third, nor, pardon the expression, eighth marriages : I will go still further and say that I welcome even a penitent whoremonger. Things that are equally lawful must be weighed in an even balance.

16. But he takes us to the Old Testament, and beginning with Adam goes on to Zacharias and Elizabeth. He next confronts us with Peter and the rest of the Apostles. We are therefore bound to traverse the same course of argument and show that chastity was always preferred to the condition of marriage. And as regards Adam and Eve we must maintain that before the fall they were virgins in Paradise : but after they sinned, and were cast out of Paradise, they were immediately married. Then we have the passage,[2] " For this cause shall a man leave his father and mother, and shall cleave to his wife, and the twain shall become one flesh," in explanation of which the Apostle straightway adds,[3] " This mystery is great, but I speak in regard of Christ, and of the Church." Christ in the flesh is a virgin, in the spirit he is once married. For he has one Church, concerning which the same Apostle says,[4] " Husbands, love your wives, even as Christ also loved the Church." If Christ loves the Church holily, chastely, and without spot, let husbands also love their wives in chastity. And let everyone know how to possess his vessel in sanctification and honour, not in the lust of concupiscence, as the Gentiles who know not God : [5] " For God called us not for uncleanness, but in sanctification : seeing that ye have put off the old man with his doings, and have

---

[1] See 1 Tim. iii. 12. Most ancient writers interpreted S. Paul's words as referring to second marriages after loss of first wife, however happening. And certain Councils decided in the same sense, e. g. Neocæsarea (A.D. 314). Ellicott's Pastoral Ep., 5th ed., p. 41.
[2] 1 Tim. v. 9. Other authorities, however, suppose the words to refer to an *order* of widows, and pertinently ask, would the Church thus limit her alms.

[1] 1 Cor. vi. 12.　　　　[2] Eph. v. 31 : Gen. ii.
[3] Eph. v. 32.　　　　　　[4] Eph. v. 25 : Col. iii. 9-11.
[5] 1 Thess. iv. 7.

put on the new man, which is being renewed unto knowledge after the image of him that created him: where there cannot be male and female, Greek and Jew, circumcision and uncumcision, barbarian, Scythian, bondman, freeman : but Christ is all, and in all." The link of marriage is not found in the image of the Creator. When difference of sex is done away, and we are putting off the old man, and putting on the new, then we are being born again into Christ a virgin, who was both born of a virgin, and is born again through [1] virginity. And whereas he says "Be fruitful, and multiply, and replenish the earth," it was necessary first to plant the wood and to let it grow, so that there might be an after-growth for cutting down. And at the same time we must bear in mind the meaning of the phrase, " replenish the earth." Marriage replenishes the earth, virginity fills Paradise. This too we must observe, at least if we would faithfully follow the Hebrew, that while Scripture on the first, third, fourth, fifth, and sixth days relates that, having finished the works of each, " God saw that it was good," on the second day it omitted this altogether, leaving us to understand that two is not a good number because it destroys unity, and prefigures the marriage compact. Hence 't was that all the animals which Noah took into the ark by pairs were unclean. Odd numbers denote cleanness. And yet by the double number is represented another mystery: that not even in beasts and unclean birds is second marriage approved. For unclean animals went in two and two, and clean ones by sevens, so that Noah after the flood might be able to immediately offer to God sacrifices from the latter.

17. But if Enoch was translated, and Noah was preserved at the deluge, I do not think that Enoch was translated because he had a wife, but because he was [2] the first to call upon God and to believe in the Creator ; and the Apostle Paul fully instructs us concerning him in the Epistle to the Hebrews. Noah, moreover, who was preserved as a kind of second root for the human race, must of course be preserved together with his wife and sons, although in this there is a Scripture mystery. The ark,[3] according to the Apostle Peter, was a type of the Church, in which eight souls were saved. When Noah entered into it, both he and his sons were separated from their wives ; but when he landed from it, they united in pairs, and what had been separated in the ark, that is, in the Church, was joined together in the intercourse of the world.

And at the same time if the ark had many compartments and little chambers, and was made with second and third stories, and was filled with different beasts, and was furnished with dwellings, great or small, according to the kind of animal, I think all this diversity in the compartments was a figure of the manifold character of the Church.

18. He raises the objection that when God gave his second blessing, permission was granted to eat flesh, which had not in the first benediction been allowed. He should know that just as divorce according to the Saviour's word was not permitted from the beginning, but on account of the hardness of our heart was a concession of Moses to the human race, so too the eating of flesh was unknown until the deluge. But after the deluge, like the quails given in the desert to the murmuring people, the poison of flesh-meat was offered to our teeth. The Apostle writing to the Ephesians teaches that God had purposed in the fulness of time to sum up and renew in Christ Jesus all things which are in heaven and in earth. Whence also the Saviour himself in the Revelation of John says,[2] " I am Alpha and Omega, the beginning and the ending." At the beginning of the human race we neither ate flesh, nor gave bills of divorce, nor suffered circumcision for a sign. Thus we reached the deluge. But after the deluge, together with the giving of the law which no one could fulfil, flesh was given for food, and divorce was allowed to hard-hearted men, and the knife of circumcision was applied, as though the hand of God had fashioned us with something superfluous. But once Christ has come in the end of time, and Omega passed into Alpha and turned the end into the beginning, we are no longer allowed divorce nor are we circumcised, nor do we eat flesh, for the Apostle says,[3] " It is good not to eat flesh, nor to drink wine." For wine as well as flesh was consecrated after the deluge.

19. What shall I say of Abraham who had three wives, as Jovinianus says, and received circumcision as a sign of his faith ? If we follow him in the number of his wives, let us also follow him in circumcision. We must not partly follow, partly reject him. Isaac, moreover, the husband of one wife, Rebecca, prefigures the Church of Christ, and reproves the wantonness of second marriage. And if Jacob had two pairs of wives and concubines, and our opponent will not admit that blear-eyed Leah, ugly and prolific, was a type of the synagogue, but that Rachel, beautiful and long barren, indicated the mystery of the Church, let me remind him that when Jacob did this

---

[1] Lit. through a virgin. The allusion is, probably, to his baptism by a virgin, i.e., John Baptist.
[2] But see Gen. iv. 26.   [3] 1 Pet. iii. 20.

[1] Eph. i. 10.   [2] Rev. i. 8 ; xxii. 13.
[3] Rom. xiv. 21.

hing he was among the Assyrians, and in Mesopotamia in bondage to a hard master. But when he wished to enter the holy land, he raised on Mount Galeed [1] the heap of witness, in token that the lord of Mesopotamia had failed to find anything among his baggage, and there swore that he would never return to the place of his bondage; and when, [2] after wrestling with the angel at the brook Jabbok, he began to limp, because the great muscle of his thigh was withered, he at once gained the name of Israel. [3] Then the wife whom he once loved, and for whom he had served, was slain by the son of sorrow near Bethlehem which was destined to be the birthplace of our Lord, the herald of virginity: and the intimacies of Mesopotamia died in the land of the Gospel.

20. But I wonder why he set [4] Judah and Tamar before us for an example, unless perchance even harlots give him pleasure; or Onan who was slain because he grudged his brother seed. Does he imagine that we approve of any sexual intercourse except for the procreation of children? As regards Moses, it is clear that he would have been in peril at the inn, if [6] Sephora which is by interpretation a bird, had not circumcised her son, and cut off the foreskin of marriage with the knife which prefigured the Gospel. This is that Moses who when he saw a great vision and heard an angel, or the Lord speaking in the bush, [7] could not by any means approach to him without first loosing the latchet of his shoe, that is, putting off the bonds of marriage. And we need not be surprised at this in the case of one who was a prophet, lawgiver, and the friend of God, seeing that all the people when about to draw nigh to Mount Sinai, and to hear the voice speaking to them, were commanded to sanctify themselves in three days, and keep themselves from their wives. I am out of order in violating historical sequence, but I may point out that the same thing was said by [8] Ahimelech the priest to David when he fled to Nob: "If only the young men have kept themselves from women." And David answered, "of a truth about these three days." For the shew-bread, like the body of Christ, might not be eaten by those who rose from the marriage bed. And in passing we ought to consider the words "if only the young men have kept themselves from women." The truth is that, in view of the purity of the body of Christ, all sexual intercourse is unclean. In the law also it is enjoined that the [9] high priest must not marry any but a virgin, nor must he take to wife a widow. If a virgin and a widow

are on the same level, how is it that one is taken, the other rejected? [1] And the widow of a priest is bidden abide in the house of her father, and not to contract a second marriage. [2] If the sister of a priest dies in virginity, just as the priest is commanded to go to the funeral of his father and mother, so must he go to hers. But if she be married, she is despised as though she belonged not to him. He who has [3] married a wife, and he who has planted a vineyard, an image of the propagation of children, is forbidden to go to the battle. For he who is the slave of his wife cannot be the Lord's soldier. And the laver in the tabernacle was cast from the mirrors of the women who [4] fasted, signifying the bodies of pure virgins: And within, [5] in the sanctuary, both cherubim, and mercy-seat, and the ark of the covenant, and the table of shew-bread, and the candle-stick, and the censer, were made of the purest gold. For silver might not be brought into the holy of holies.

21. I must not linger over Moses when my purpose is at full speed to lightly touch on each topic and to sketch the outline of a proper knowledge of my subject. I will pass to Joshua the son of Nun, who was previously called *Ause*, or better, as in the Hebrew, *Osee*, that is, *Saviour*. For he, [6] according to the epistle of Jude, saved the people of Israel and led them forth out of Egypt, and brought them into the land of promise. As soon as this Joshua [7] reached the Jordan, the waters of marriage, which had ever flowed in the land, dried up and stood in one heap; and the whole people, barefooted and on dry ground, crossed over, and came to Gilgal, and there was a second time circumcised. If we take this literally, it cannot possibly stand. For if we had two foreskins, or if another could grow after the first was cut off, there would be room for speaking of a second circumcision. But the meaning is that Joshua circumcised the people who had crossed the desert, with the Gospel knife, and he circumcised them with a stone

---

[1] The reference is, probably, to Levit. xxii. 13. But the second marriage is not there prohibited, and in the ideal polity of Ezekiel (xliv. 22) a priest might marry the widow of a priest.
[2] Levit. xxi. 3.
[3] Deut. xx. 6, 7, where an indulgence, not a prohibition, is clearly indicated.
[4] Ex. xxxviii. 8. Sept. Vulg. "who watched;" Onkelos' Targum "who assembled to pray," and so the Syriac Version. The Hebrew word signifies "to go forth to war," but is applied to the temple service, a sort of militia sacra (Gesenius). Hence Rev. Version. "the serving women which served at the door of the tent of meeting;" and Margin, "the women which assembled to minister." Comp. Numb. iv. 3, 23, 30, 35, 39; and 1 Sam. ii. 22.
[5] Ex. xxxvii.
[6] In Jude 5, instead of "the Lord," A. B. read *Jesus*, and this is accepted by many ancient authorities. Farrar observes ("Early Days of Christianity," pop. ed., p. 128) "Jesus" is the more difficult, and therefore more probable reading of A. B. It is explained by 1 Cor. x. 4, and the identification of the Messiah with the "Angel of the Lord" (Ex. xiv. 19, xxiii. 20, &c.) and with the Pillar of Fire in Philo.
[7] Josh. iii.

---

[1] Gen. xxxi. 46-49, where the heap itself is called Galeed.
[2] Gen. xxxii. 25, 28, 31. [3] Gen. xxxv. 16, 20.
[4] Gen. xxxviii. [5] Gen. xxxviii. 9.
[6] Ex. iv. 24-26. [7] Ex. iii. 5.
[8] 1 Sam. xxi. 4. [9] Levit. xxi. 13, 14.

knife, that what in the case of Moses' son was prefigured in a few might under Joshua be fulfilled in all. Moreover, the very foreskins were heaped together and buried, and covered with earth, and the fact that the reproach of Egypt was taken away, and the name of the place, *Gilgal*, which is by interpretation [1] *revelation*, show that while the people wandered in the desert uncircumcised their eyes were blinded. Let us see what follows. After this Gospel circumcision and the consecration of twelve stones at the place of revelation, the Passover was immediately celebrated, a lamb was slain for them, and they ate the food of the Holy Land. Joshua went forth, and was met by the Prince of the host, sword in hand, that is either to shew that he was ready to fight for the circumcised people, or to sever the tie of marriage. And in the same way that Moses was commanded, so was he : [2] "loose thy shoe, for the place whereon thou standest is holy ground." For if the armed host of the Lord was represented by the trumpets of the priests, we may see in Jericho a type of the overthrow of the world by the preaching of the Gospel. And to pass over endless details (for it is not my purpose now to unfold all the mysteries of the Old Testament), [3] five kings who previously reigned in the land of promise, and opposed the Gospel army, were overcome in battle with Joshua. I think it is clearly to be understood that before the Lord led his people from Egypt and circumcised them, sight, smell, taste, hearing, and touch had the dominion, and that to these, as to five princes, everything was subject. And when they [4] took refuge in the cave of the body and in a place of darkness, Jesus entered the body itself and slew them, that the source of their power might be the instrument of their death.

22. But it is now time for us to raise the standard of Joshua's chastity. It is written that Moses had a wife. Now Moses is interpreted both by our Lord and by the Apostle tó mean the law : [5] "They have Moses and the prophets." And [6] "Death reigned from Adam until Moses, even over them that had not sinned after the likeness of Adam's transgression." And no one doubts that in both passages Moses signifies the law. We read that Moses, that is the law, had a wife : shew me then in the same way that Joshua the son of Nun had either wife or children, and if you can do so, I will confess that I am beaten. He certainly received the fairest spot in the division of the land of Judah, and died, not in the *twenties*, which are ever unlucky in Scripture —by them are reckoned the years of [1] Jacob's service, [2] the price of Joseph, and [3] sundry presents which Esau who was fond of them received—but in the [4] *tens*, whose praises we have often sung ; and he was buried in [5] *Thamnath Sare*, that is, *most perfect sovereignty*, or among those *of a new covering*, to signify the crowds of virgins, covered by the Saviour's aid on Mount Ephraim, that is, the *fruitful mountain;* on the north of the Mountain of Gaash, which is, being interpreted, *disturbance:* for [6] "Mount Sion is on the sides of the north, the city of the Great King," is ever exposed to hatred, and in every trial says [7] "But my feet had well nigh slipped." The book which bears the name of Joshua ends with his burial. Again in the book of Judges we read of him as though he had risen and come to life again, and by way of summary his works are extolled. We read too [8] "So Joshua sent the people away, every man unto his inheritance, that they might possess the land." And "Israel served the Lord all the days of Joshua," and so on. There immediately follows : "And Joshua the son of Nun, the servant of the Lord, died, being an hundred and ten years old." Moses, moreover, only saw the land of promise ; he could not enter : and [9] "he died in the land of Moab, and the Lord buried him in the valley in the land of Moab over against Beth-peor: but no man knoweth of his sepulchre unto this day." Let us compare the burial of the two : Moses died in the land of Moab, Joshua in the land of Judæa. The former was buried in a valley over against the house of Phogor, which is, being interpreted, *reproach* (for the Hebrew Phogor corresponds to Priapus [10]); the latter in Mount Ephraim on the north of Mount Gaash. And in the simple expressions of the sacred Scriptures there is always a more subtle meaning. The Jews gloried in children and child-bearing ; and the barren woman, who had not offspring in Israel, was accursed ; but blessed was he whose seed was in Sion, and his family in Jerusalem ; and part of the highest blessing was, [11] "Thy wife shall be as a fruitful vine,

---

[1] Jerome derives *Gilgal* from גָּלָה to uncover: the accepted derivation is from גָּלַל to roll.   [2] Ex. iii. 5: Jos. v. 15.   [3] Josh. x. 3.   [4] Josh. x. 16.   [5] S. Luke xvi. 29.   [6] Rom. v. 14.

[1] Gen. xxxi. 41.   [2] Gen. xxxvii. 28.   [3] Gen. xxxii. 14.   [4] Joshua died at the age of 110 years. Josh. xxiv. 29.   [5] Timnath-Serah was the original name of Joshua's inheritance (Josh. xix. 50), but in Judges ii. 9, we find the name changed to Timnath-Heres. Timnath-Serah and the tomb of its illustrious owner were shown in the time of Jerome (Letter cviii. 13). "Paula wondered greatly that he who assigned men their possessions had chosen for himself a rough and rocky spot." Jerome is looking at the inheritance with the eyes of an ardent controversialist when he describes it as "the fairest spot in the land of Judah."   [6] Ps. xlviii. 2. The correct rendering of the Hebrew is much disputed.   [7] Ps. lxxiii. 2.   [8] Josh. xxiv. 28.   [9] Deut. xxxiv. 6.   [10] Worshipped more especially at Lampsacus on the Hellespont. He was regarded as the promoter of fertility in vegetables and animals.   [11] Ps. cxxviii. 3.

n the innermost parts of thy house, thy children like olive plants, round about thy table." Therefore his grave is described as placed in a valley over against the house of an idol which was in a special sense consecrated to lust. But we who fight under Joshua our leader, even to the present day know not where Moses was buried. For we despise Phogor, and all his shame, knowing that they who are in the flesh cannot please God. And the Lord before the flood had said [1] "My spirit shall not abide in man for ever, for that he also is flesh." Wherefore, when Moses died, the people of Israel mourned for him ; but Joshua like one on his way to victory was unmourned. For marriage ends at death ; virginity thereafter begins to wear the crown.

23. Next he brings forward Samson, and does not consider that the Lord's Nazarite was once shaven bald by a woman. And although Samson continues to be a type of the Saviour because he loved a harlot from among the Gentiles, which harlot corresponds to the Church, and because he slew more enemies in his death than he did in his life, yet he does not set an example of conjugal chastity. And he surely reminds us [2] of Jacob's prophecy —he was shaken by his runaway steed, bitten by an adder and fell backwards. But why he enumerated Deborah, and Barak, and the wife of Heber the Kenite, I am at a loss to understand. For it is one thing to draw up a list of military commanders in historical sequence, another to indicate certain figures of marriage which cannot be found in them. And whereas he prefers the fidelity of the father Jephthah to the tears of the virgin daughter, that makes for us. For we are not commending virgins of the world so much as those who are virgins for Christ's sake, and most Hebrews blame the father for the rash vow he made, [3] " If thou wilt indeed deliver the children of Ammon into mine hand, then it shall be, that whatsoever cometh forth of the doors of my house to meet me, when I return in peace from the children of Ammon, it shall be for the Lord's, and I will offer it up for a burnt offering." Supposing (they say) a dog or an ass had met him, what would he have done ? Their meaning is that God so ordered events that he who had improvidently made a vow, should learn his error by the death of his daughter. And if Samuel who was brought up in the tabernacle married a wife, how does that prejudice virginity ? As if at the present day also there were not many married priests, and as though the Apostle did not [4] describe a bishop as the husband of one wife, having

children with all purity. At the same time we must not forget that Samuel was a Levite, not a priest or high-priest. Hence it was that his mother made for him a linen ephod, that is, a linen garment to go over the shoulders, which was the proper dress of the Levites and of the inferior order. And so he is not named in the Psalms among the priests, but among those who call upon the name of the Lord : [1] " Moses and Aaron among his priests, and Samuel among those who call upon his name." For [2] Levi begat Kohath, Kohath begat Amminadab, Amminadab begat Korah, Korah begat Assir, Assir begat Elkanah, Elkanah begat Zuph, Zuph begat Tahath, Tahath begat Eliel, Eliel begat Jeroham, Jeroham begat Elkanah, Elkanah begat Samuel. And no one doubts that the priests sprang from the stock of Aaron, Eleazar, and Phinees. And seeing that they had wives, they would be rightly brought against us, if, led away by the error of the Encratites, we were to maintain that marriage deserved censure, and our high priest were not after the order of Melchizedek, without father, without mother, [3] $A'\gamma\varepsilon\nu\varepsilon\alpha\lambda\delta\gamma\eta\tau\sigma\varsigma$, that is, unmarried. And much fruit truly did Samuel reap from his children ! he himself pleased God, but [4] begat such children as displeased the Lord. But if in support of second marriage, he urges the instance of Boaz and Ruth, let him know that in the Gospel (S. Matt. i. 6) to typify the Church even Rahab the harlot is reckoned among our Lord's ancestors.

24. He boasts that David bought his wife for two hundred foreskins. But he should remember that David had numerous other wives, and afterwards received Michal, Saul's daughter, whom her father had delivered to another, and when he was old got heat from the embrace of the Shunammite maiden. And I do not say this because I am bold enough to disparage holy men, but because it is one thing to live under the law, another to live under the Gospel. David slew Uriah the Hittite and committed adultery with Bathsheba. And because he was a man of blood— the reference is not, as some think, to his wars, but to the [5] murder—he was not permitted to build a temple of the Lord. But as for us, [6] if we cause one of the least to stumble, and if we say to a brother [7] *Raca*, or [8] use our eyes improperly, it were good that a millstone

---

[1] Ps. xcix. 6. [2] See 1 Chron. vi. 34-38.
[3] Heb. vii. 3. The Greek word in the text (" without genealogy ") is unknown to secular writers, and occurs here only in the New Test. It cannot mean *without descent* (see verse 6). *Unmarried* appears to be a false inference from this supposed meaning. Ignatius also (Ep. ad. Philad.) reckoned Melchizedek among celibates. Rev. Version translates, " without genealogy," *i.e.*, his ancestry was *unrecorded*. See Farrar's " Early Days of Christianity," pop. ed., p. 221.
[4] 1 Sam. ii. 22. [5] See, however, 1 Chron. xxii. 8.
[6] S. Matt. xviii. 6. [7] S. Matt. v. 22.
[8] S. Matt. v. 27.

---

[1] Gen. vi. 3. R. V. *Strive* or *rule in.*
[2] Gen. xlix. 17. Samson was of the tribe of Dan.
[3] Judg. xi. 30, 31. [4] 1 Tim. iii. 2.

were hanged about our neck, we shall be in danger of Gehenna, and a mere glance will be reckoned to us for adultery. He passes on to Solomon, through whom wisdom itself sang its own praises. Seeing that not content with dwelling upon his praises, he calls him uxorious, I am surprised that he did not add the words of the Canticles : [1] "There are threescore queens, and fourscore concubines, and maidens without number," and those of the First Book of Kings ; [2] And he had seven hundred wives, princesses, and three hundred concubines, and others without number." These are they who turned away his heart from the Lord : and yet before he had many wives, and fell into sins of the flesh, at the beginning of his reign and in his early years he built a temple to the Lord. For every one is judged not for what he will be, but for what he is. But if Jovinianus approves the example of Solomon, he will no longer be in favour of second and third marriages only, but unless he has seven hundred wives and three hundred concubines, he cannot be the king's antitype or attain to his merit. I earnestly again and again remind you, my reader, that I am compelled to speak as I do, and that I do not disparage our predecessors under the law, but am well aware that they served their generation according to their circumstances, and fulfilled the Lord's command to increase, and multiply, and replenish the earth. And what is more they were figures of those that were to come. But we to whom it is said,[3] "The time is shortened, that henceforth those that have wives may be as though they had none," have a different command, and for us virginity is consecrated by the Virgin Saviour.

25. What folly it was to include Elijah and Elisha in a list of married men, is plain without a word from me. For, since John Baptist came in the spirit and power of Elijah, and John was a virgin, it is clear that he came not only in Elijah's spirit, but also in his bodily chastity. Then the passage relating to Hezekiah might be adduced (though Jovinianus with his wonted stupidity did not notice it), in which after his recovery and the addition of fifteen years to his life he said, "Now will I beget children." It must be remembered, however, that in the Hebrew texts the passage is not so, but runs thus : [4] "The father to the children shall make known thy faithfulness." Nor need we wonder that Huldah, the prophetess, and wife of Shallum, was [5] consulted by Josiah, King of Judah, when the captivity was approaching and the wrath of the Lord

was falling upon Jerusalem : since it is the rule of Scripture when holy men fail, to praise women to the reproach of men. And it is superfluous to speak of Daniel, for the Hebrews to the present day affirm that the three youths were eunuchs, in accordance with the declaration of God which Isaiah utters to Hezekiah : [1] "And of thy sons that shall issue from thee, which thou shalt beget, shall they take away : and they shall be eunuchs in the palace of the King of Babylon." And again in Daniel we read : [2] "And the king spake unto Ashpenaz the master of his eunuchs, that he should bring in certain of the children of Israel, even of the seed royal and of the nobles : youth in whom was no blemish, but well favoured, and skilful in all wisdom, and cunning in knowledge, and understanding science." The conclusion is that if Daniel and the three youths were chosen from the seed royal, and if Scripture foretold that that there should be eunuchs of the seed royal, these men were those who were made eunuchs. If he meets us with the argument that in Ezekiel [3] it is said that Noah, Daniel and Job in a sinful land could not free their sons and daughters, we reply that the words are used hypothetically. Noah and Job were not in existence at that time : we know that they lived many ages before. And the meaning is this : if there were such and such men in a sinful land, they shall not be able to save their own sons and daughters : because the righteousness of the father shall not save the son, nor shall the sin of one be imputed to another. [4] "For the soul that sinneth, it shall die." This, too, must be said, that Daniel, as the history of his book shows, was taken captive with King Jehoiakim at the same time that Ezekiel was also led into captivity. How then could he have sons who was still a youth ? And only three years had elapsed when he was brought in to wait upon the king. Let no one suppose that Ezekiel at this time remembers Daniel as a man, not as a youth ; for " It came to pass," he says,[5] " in the sixth year," that is of King Jehoiakim, " in the sixth month, in the fifth day of the month ;" and, " as I sat in my house, and the elders of Judah sat before me." Yet on that same day it was said to him,[6] " Though these three men, Noah, Daniel, and Job were in it." Daniel was therefore a youth, and known to the people, either on account of his interpretation of the king's dreams,[7] or on account of the release of Susannah, and the slaying of the elders. And it is clearly proved that at the time these

[1] Cant. vi. 8.   [2] 1 Kings xi. 3.
[3] 1 Cor. vii. 29.   [4] Is. xxxviii. 19.
[5] 2 Kings xxii. 14.

[1] 2 Kings xx. 18.   [2] Dan. i. 3, 4.
[3] Ezek. xiv. 14, 20.   [4] Ezek. xviii. 4.
[5] Ezek. viii. 1.   [6] Ezek. xiv. 14.
[7] Apocryphal additions to Daniel.

things were spoken of Noah, Daniel, and Job, Daniel was still a youth and could not have had sons and daughters, whom he might save by his righteousness. So far concerning the Law.

26. Coming to the Gospel he sets before us Zacharias and Elizabeth, Peter and his mother-in-law, and, with a shamelessness to which we have now grown accustomed, fails to understand that they, too, ought to have been reckoned among those who served the Law. For the Gospel had no being before the crucifixion of Christ—it was consecrated by His passion and by His blood. In accordance with this rule Peter and the other Apostles (I must give Jovinianus something now and then out of my abundance) had indeed wives, but those which they had taken before they knew the Gospel. But once they were received into the Apostolate, they forsook the offices of marriage. For when Peter, representing the Apostles, says to the Lord :[1] " Lo we have left all and followed thee," the Lord answered him,[2] "Verily I say unto you, there is no man that hath left house, or wife, or brethren, or parents, or children, for the kingdom of God's sake, who shall not receive manifold more in this time, and in the world to come eternal life." But if, in order to show that all the Apostles had wives, he meets us with the words[3] " Have we no right to lead about women or wives" (for $\gamma \nu \nu \dot{\eta}$ in Greek has both meanings) "even as the rest of the apostles, and Cephas, and the brethren of the Lord ? " let him add what is found in the Greek copies, " Have we no right to lead about women that are sisters, or wives ? " This makes it clear that the writer referred to other holy women, who, in accordance with Jewish custom, ministered to their teachers of their substance, as we read was the practice with even our Lord himself. Where there is a previous reference to eating and drinking, and the outlay of money, and mention is afterwards made of women that are sisters, it is quite clear, as we have said, that we must understand, not wives, but those women who ministered of their substance. And we read the same account in the Old Testament of the Shunammite who was wont to welcome Elisha, and to put for him a table, and bread, and a candlestick, and the rest. At all events if we take $\gamma \nu \nu \alpha \hat{\imath} \kappa \alpha \varsigma$ to mean wives, not women, the addition of the word sisters destroys the effect of the word wives, and shews that they were related in spirit, not by wedlock. Nevertheless, with the exception of the Apostle Peter, it is not openly stated that the Apostles had wives ; and since the statement is made of one while nothing is said about the rest, we must understand that those of whom Scripture gives no such description had no wives. Yet Jovinianus, who has arrayed against us Zacharias and Elizabeth, Peter and his wife's mother, should know, that John was the son of Zacharias and Elizabeth, that is, a virgin was the offspring of marriage, the Gospel of the law, chastity of matrimony ; so that by a virgin prophet the virgin Lord might be both announced and baptized. But we might say concerning Peter, that he had a mother-in-law when he believed, and no longer had a wife, although in the [1] "Sentences" we read of both his wife and daughter. But for the present our argument must be based wholly on Scripture. He has made his appeal to the Apostles, because he thinks that they, who hold the chief authority in our moral system and are the typical Christian teachers, were not virgins. If, then, we allow that they were not virgins (and, with the exception of Peter, the point cannot be proved), yet I must tell him that it is to the Apostles that the words of Isaiah relate :[2] " Except the Lord of hosts had left unto us a small remnant, we should have been as Sodom, we should have been like unto Gomorrah." So, then, they who were by birth Jews could not under the Gospel recover the virginity which they had lost in Judaism. And yet John, one of the disciples, who is related to have been the youngest of the Apostles, and who was a virgin when he embraced Christianity, remained a virgin, and on that account was more beloved by our Lord, and lay upon the breast of Jesus. And what Peter, who had had a wife, did not dare ask,[3] he requested John to ask. And after the resurrection, when Mary Magdalene told them that the Lord had risen,[4] they both ran to the sepulchre, but John outran Peter. And when they were fishing in the ship on the lake of Gennesaret, Jesus stood upon the shore, and the Apostles knew not who it was they saw ;[5] the virgin alone recognized a virgin, and said to Peter, "It is the Lord." Again, after hearing the prediction that he must be bound by another, and led whither he would not, and must suffer on the cross, Peter said, "Lord, what shall this man do ?" being unwilling to desert John, with whom he had always been

[1] Matt. xix. 27.   [2] Luke xviii. 29, 30.
[3] 1 Cor. ix. 5. The text has been much tampered with by the advocates or opponents of celibacy. The reading first quoted by Jerome is that of F, a manuscript of the eighth or ninth century, and is found in Tertullian ; the other chief readings introduce the Greek equivalent for sister, either in the sing. or plural. The Rev. Version renders, "have we no right to lead about a wife that is a believer" (or sister). Augustine, Tertullian, Theodoret, &c., together with Cornelius-a-Lapide and Estius among the moderns, agree with Jerome in referring the passage to holy women who ministered to the Apostles as they did to the Lord Himself. The third canon of Nicæa is supposed to be directed against the practice encouraged by this interpretation of the Apostle's words.

[1] Attributed to Clement by Jerome.
[2] Isa. i. 9.   [3] S. John xiii. 25.
[4] S. John xx. 4.   [5] S. John xxi. 7 sq.

united. Our Lord said to him, "What is that to thee if I wish him so to be?" Whence the saying went abroad among the brethren that that disciple should not die. Here we have a proof that virginity does not die, and that the defilement of marriage is not washed away by the blood of martyrdom, but virginity abides with Christ, and its sleep is not death but a passing to another state. If, however, Jovinianus should obstinately contend that John was not a virgin, (whereas we have maintained that his virginity was the cause of the special love our Lord bore to him), let him explain, if he was not a virgin, why it was that he was loved more than the other Apostles. But you say, [1] the Church was founded upon Peter: although [2] elsewhere the same is attributed to all the Apostles, and they all receive the keys of the kingdom of heaven, and the strength of the Church depends upon them all alike, yet one among the twelve is chosen so that when a head has been appointed, there may be no occasion for schism. But why was not John chosen, who was a virgin? Deference was paid to age, because Peter was the elder : one who was a youth, I may say almost a boy, could not be set over men of advanced age ; and a good master who was bound to remove every occasion of strife among his disciples, and who had said to them, [3] "Peace I leave with you, my peace I give unto you," and, [4] "He that is the greater among you, let him be the least of all," would not be thought to afford cause of envy against the youth whom he had loved. We may be sure that John was then a boy because ecclesiastical history most clearly proves that he lived to the reign of Trajan, that is, he fell asleep in the sixty-eighth year after our Lord's passion, as I have briefly noted in my treatise on *Illustrious Men.*[5] Peter is an Apostle, and John is an Apostle—the one a married man, the other a virgin ; but Peter is an Apostle only, John is both an Apostle and an Evangelist, and a prophet. An Apostle, because he wrote to the Churches as a master ; an Evangelist, because he composed a Gospel, a thing which no other of the Apostles, excepting Matthew, did ; a prophet, for he saw in the island of Patmos, to which he had been banished by the Emperor Domitian as a martyr for the Lord, an Apocalypse containing the boundless mysteries of the future. Tertullian, moreover, relates that he was sent to Rome, and that having been plunged into a jar of boiling oil he came out fresher and more active than when he went in. But his very

Gospel is widely different from the rest. Matthew as though he were writing of a man begins thus : "The book of the Generation of Jesus Christ, the son of David, the son of Abraham ; " Luke begins with the priesthood of Zacharias ; Mark with a prophecy of the prophets Malachi and Isaiah. The first has the face of a man, on account of the genealogical table ; the second, the face of a calf, on account of the priesthood ; the third, the face of a lion, on account of the voice of one crying in the desert, [1] "Prepare ye the way of the Lord, make His paths straight." But John like an eagle soars aloft, and reaches the Father Himself, and says, [2] "In the beginning was the Word, and the Word was with God, and the Word was God. The same was in the beginning with God," and so on. The virgin writer expounded mysteries which the married could not, and to briefly sum up all and show how great was the privilege of John, or rather of virginity in John, the Virgin Mother[3] was entrusted by the Virgin Lord to the Virgin disciple.

27. But we toil to no purpose. For our opponent urges against us the Apostolic sentence and says,[4] "Adam was first formed, then Eve ; and Adam was not beguiled, but the woman being beguiled hath fallen into transgression : but she shall be saved through the child-bearing, if they continue in faith and love and sanctification with sobriety." Let us consider what led the Apostle to make this declaration : [5] "I desire therefore that the men pray in every place, lifting up holy hands, without wrath and disputing." So in due course he lays down rules of life for the women and says "In like manner that women adorn themselves in modest apparel, with shamefacedness and sobriety ; not with braided hair, and gold or pearls or costly raiment ; but (which becometh women professing godliness) through good works. Let a woman learn in quietness with all subjection. But I permit not a woman to teach, nor to have dominion over a man, but to be in quietness." And that the lot of a woman might not seem a hard one, reducing her to the condition of a slave to her husband, the Apostle recalls the ancient law and goes back to the first example : that Adam was first made, then the woman out of his rib ; and that the Devil could not seduce Adam, but did seduce Eve ; and that after displeasing God she was immediately subjected to the man, and began to turn to her husband ; and he points out that she who was once tied with the bonds of marriage and was reduced to the condition of Eve, might blot out the [6] old transgression

---

[1] S. Matt. xvi. 18.
[2] S. Matt. xviii. 18 : S. John xx. 22, 23.
[3] S. John xiv. 27.
[4] S. Matt. xx. 27 : S. Luke xxii. 26.
[5] See this book in Vol. III. of this series.

[1] Is. xl. 3.   [2] S. John i. 1.   [3] S. John xix. 26, 27.
[4] 1 Tim. ii. 13, 15.   [5] 1 Tim. ii. 8 sqq.
[6] Apparently, Eve's transgression imputed to her descendants.

by the [1] procreation of children : provided, however, that she bring up the children themselves in the faith and love of Christ, and in sanctification and chastity ; for we must not adopt the faulty reading of the Latin texts, *sobrietas*, but *castitas*, that is, [2] σωφροσύνη. You see how you are mastered by the witness of this passage also, and cannot but be driven to admit that what you thought was on the side of marriage tells in favour of virginity. For if the woman is saved in child-bearing, and the more the children the greater the safety of the mothers, why did he add " if they continue in faith and love and sanctification with chastity " ? The woman will then be saved, if she bear not children who will remain virgins : if what she has herself lost, she attains in her children, and makes up for the loss and decay of the root by the excellence of the flower and fruit.

28. Above, in passing, when our opponent adduced Solomon, who, although he had many wives, nevertheless built the temple, I briefly replied that it was my intention to run over the remaining points. Now that he may not cry out that both Solomon and others under the law, prophets and holy men, have been dishonoured by us, let us show what this very man with his many wives and concubines thought of marriage. For no one can know better than he who suffered through them, what a wife or woman is. Well then, he says in the Proverbs: [3] " The foolish and bold woman comes to want bread." What bread ? Surely that bread which cometh down from heaven : and he immediately adds [4] " The earth-born perish in her house, rush into the depths of hell." Who are the earth-born that perish in her house ? They of course who follow the first Adam, who is of the earth, and not the second, who is from heaven. And again in another place: " Like a worm in wood, so a wicked woman destroyeth her husband." But if you assert that this was spoken of bad wives, I shall briefly answer : What necessity rests upon me to run the risk of the wife I marry proving good or bad ? [5] " It is better," he says, "to dwell in a desert land, than with a contentious and passionate woman in a wide house." How seldom we find a wife without these faults, he knows who is married. Hence that sublime orator, Varius Geminus,[6] says well " The man

who does not quarrel is a bachelor." [1] " It is better to dwell in the corner of the housetop, than with a contentious woman in a house in common." If a house common to husband and wife makes a wife proud and breeds contempt for the husband : how much more if the wife be the richer of the two, and the husband but a lodger in her house ! She begins to be not a wife, but mistress of the house ; and if she offend her husband, they must part. [2] "A continual dropping on a wintry day " turns a man out of doors, and so will a contentious woman drive a man from his own house. She floods his house with her constant nagging and daily chatter, and ousts him from his own home, that is the Church. Hence the same Solomon previously commands : [3] " My son flows forth beyond." And the Apostle, writing to the Hebrews, says " Therefore we ought to give the more earnest heed to the things spoken, lest haply we flow forth beyond." But who can hide from himself what is thus enigmatically expressed ? [4] " The horseleech had three daughters, dearly loved, but they satisfied her not, and a fourth is not satisfied when you say Enough ; the grave, and woman's love, and the earth that is not satisfied with water, and the fire that saith not, Enough." The horseleech is the devil, the daughters of the devil are dearly loved, and they cannot be satisfied with the blood of the slain : *the grave, and woman's love, and the earth dry and scorched with heat.* It is not the harlot, or the adulteress who is spoken of ; but woman's love in general is accused of ever being insatiable ; put it out, it bursts into flame ; give it plenty, it is again in need ; it enervates a man's mind, and engrosses all thought except for the passion which it feeds. What we read in the parable which follows is to the same effect : " For three things the earth doth tremble, and for four which it cannot bear : for a servant when he is king : and a fool when he is filled with meat : for an odious woman when she is married to a good husband : and an handmaid that is heir to her mistress." See how a wife is classed with the greatest evils. But if you reply that it is an *odious* wife, I will give you the same answer as before—the mere possibility of such danger is in itself no light matter. For he who marries a wife is uncertain whether he is marrying an odious woman or one worthy of his love. If she be odious, she is intolerable. If worthy of love, her love

---

[1] The original admits of the rendering " by means of *her* child-bearing." But Ellicott and others interpret of the Incarnation.
[2] Rev. Version, " sobriety." *Sobermindedness* or *discretion* are given by Ellicott (Notes on translation) as alternative renderings. The word cannot mean *chastity*, but rather " the well-balanced state of mind resulting from habitual self-restraint " in general.
[3] Prov. vi. 26?   [4] Prov. vii. 27 : ix. 18.
[5] Prov. xxi. 19.
[6] Often mentioned by Seneca. A saying is reported of him : " Ho, traveller, stop. There is a miracle here: a man and his wife not at strife."

---

[1] Prov. xxi. 9 ; xxv. 24.
[2] Prov. xxvii. 15.
[3] Superefflüas. Prov. iii. 21 Sept., Heb. ii. 1. The Greek word signifies to fall away like flowing water. See Schleusner on παραρρύωμαι. In Heb. ii. 1, Rev. V. translates " We drift away " Vaughan, " We be found to have leaked, or ebbed away."
[4] Prov. xxx. 15, 16.

is compared to the grave, to the parched earth, and to fire.

29. Let us come to Ecclesiastes and adduce a few corroborative passages from him also. [1] "To everything there is a season, and a time to every purpose under the heaven : a time to be born, and a time to die : a time to plant, and a time to pluck up that which is planted." We brought forth young under the law with Moses, let us die under the Gospel with Christ. We planted in marriage, let us by chastity pluck up that which was planted. "A time to embrace, and a time to refrain from embracing : a time to love, and a time to hate : a time for war, and a time for peace." And at the same time he warns us not to prefer the law to the Gospel; nor to think that virgin purity is to be placed on a level with marriage : [2] "Better," he says, "is the end of a thing than the beginning thereof." And he immediately adds : "Say not thou, what is the cause that the former days were better than these ? for thou dost not inquire wisely concerning this." And he gives the reason why the latter days are better than the former : [3] "For wisdom with an inheritance is good." Under the law carnal wisdom was followed by the sword of death ; under the Gospel an eternal inheritance awaits spiritual wisdom. "Behold, this have I found, [4] saith the Preacher, one man among a thousand have I found ; but a woman among all those have I not found. Behold this only have I found, that God made man upright ; but they have sought out many inventions." He says that he had found man upright. Consider the force of the words. The word *man* comprehends both male and female. "But a woman," he says, "among all these have I not found." Let us read the beginning of Genesis, and we shall find Adam, that is *man*, called both male and female. Having then been created by God good and upright, by our own fault we have fallen to a worse condition ; and that which in Paradise had been upright, when we left Paradise was corrupt. If you object that before they sinned there was a distinction in sex between male and female, and that they could without sin have come together, it is uncertain what might have happened. For we cannot know the judgements of God, and anticipate his sentence as we choose. What really happened is plain enough,—that they who in Paradise remained in perpetual virginity, when they were expelled from Paradise were joined together. Or if Paradise admits of marriage, and there

is no difference between marriage and virginity, what prevented their previous intercourse even in Paradise ? They are driven out of Paradise ; and what they did not there, they do on earth ; so that from the very earliest days of humanity virginity was consecrated by Paradise, and marriage by earth. [1] "Let thy garments be always white." The eternal whiteness of our garments is the purity of virginity. In the morning we sowed our seed, and in the evening let us not cease. Let us who served marriage under the law, serve virginity under the Gospel.

30. I pass to the Song of Songs, and whereas our opponent thinks it makes altogether for marriage, I shall show that it contains the mysteries of virginity. Let us hear what the bride says before that the bridegroom comes to earth, suffers, descends to the lower world, and rises again. [2] "We will make for thee likenesses of gold with ornaments of silver while the king sits at his table." Before the Lord rose again, and the Gospel shone, the bride had not gold, but likenesses of gold. As for the silver, however, which she professes to have at the marriage, she not only had silver ornaments, but she had them in variety—in widows, in the continent, and in the married. Then the bridegroom makes answer to the bride, and teaches her that the shadow of the old law has passed away, and the truth of the Gospel has come. [3] "Rise up, my love, my fair one, and come away, for lo, the winter is past, the rain is over and gone." This relates to the Old Testament. Once more he speaks of the Gospel and of virginity : "The flowers appear on the earth, the time of the pruning of vines has come." Does he not seem to you to say the very same thing that the Apostle says : [4] "The time is shortened that henceforth both those that have wives may be as though they had none"? And more plainly does he herald chastity : [5] "The voice," he says, "of the turtle is heard in our land." The turtle, the chastest of birds, always dwelling in lofty places, is a type of the Saviour. Let us read the works of naturalists and we shall find that it is the nature of the turtle-dove, if it lose its mate, not to take another ; and we shall understand that second marriage is repudiated even by dumb birds. And immediately the turtle says to its fellow : [6] "The fig tree hath put forth its green figs," that is, the commandments of the old law have fallen, and the blossoming vines of the Gospel give forth their fra-

[1] Eccles. iii. 1, 2, sqq. [2] Eccles. vii. 10.
[3] R.V. "Good as an inheritance." [4] Eccles. vii. 28, 29.

[1] Eccles. ix. 8.
[2] Cant. i. 10, 11. "Plaits of gold with studs of silver." R.V.
[3] Cant. ii. 1, 10–12. [4] 1 Cor. vii. 29.
[5] Cant. ii. 12. [6] Verse 13.

grance. Whence the Apostle also says,[1] "We are a sweet savour of Christ." [2] "Arise, my love, my fair one, and come away. O my dove, thou art in the clefts of the rock, in the covert of the steep place. Let me see thy countenance, let me hear thy voice; for sweet is thy voice, and thy countenance is comely." [3] Whilst thou coveredst thy countenance like Moses and the veil of the law remained, I neither saw thy face, nor did I condescend to hear thy voice. I said, [4] "Yea, when ye make many prayers, I will not hear." But now with unveiled face behold my glory, and shelter thyself in the cleft and steep places of the solid rock. On hearing this the bride disclosed the mysteries of chastity: [5] "My beloved is mine, and I am his: he feedeth his flock among the lilies," that is among the pure virgin bands. Would you know what sort of a throne our true Solomon, the Prince of Peace, has, and what his attendants are like? [6] "Behold," he says, "it is the litter of Solomon: threescore mighty men are about it, of the mighty men of Israel. They all handle the sword, and are expert in war: every man hath his sword upon his thigh." They who are about Solomon have their sword upon their thigh, like Ehud, the left-handed judge, who slew the fattest of foes, a man devoted to the flesh, and cut short all his pleasures. [7] "I will get me," he says, "to the mountain of myrrh;" to those, that is, who have mortified their bodies; "and to the hill of frankincense," to the crowds of pure virgins; "and I will say to my bride, thou art all fair, my love, and there is no spot in thee." Whence too the Apostle: [8] "That he might present the church to himself a glorious church, not having spot or wrinkle, or any such thing." [9] "Come with me from Lebanon, my bride, with me from Lebanon. Thou shalt come [10] and pass on from the beginning of faith, from the top of Sanir and Hermon, from the lions' dens, from the mountains of the leopards." Lebanon is, being interpreted, *whiteness*. Come then, fairest bride, concerning whom it is elsewhere said [11] "Who is she that cometh up, all in white?" and pass on by way of this world, from the beginning of faith, and from Sanir, which is by interpretation, *God of light*, as we read in the psalm: [12] "Thy word is a lantern unto my feet, and light unto my path;" and "from Hermon," that is, *consecration:* and "flee from the lions' dens, and the mountains of the leopards who cannot change their spots." Flee, he says, from the lions' dens, flee from the pride of devils, that when thou hast been consecrated to me, I may be able to say unto thee: [1] "Thou hast ravished my heart, my sister, my bride, thou hast ravished mine heart with one of thine eyes, with one chain of thy neck." What he says is something like this—I do not reject marriage: you have a second eye, the left, which I have given to you on account of the weakness of those who cannot see the right. But I am pleased with the right eye of virginity, and if it be blinded the whole body is in darkness. And that we might not think he had in view carnal love and bodily marriage, he at once excludes this meaning by saying [2] "Thou hast ravished my heart, my bride, my sister." The name sister excludes all suspicion of unhallowed love. "How fair are thy breasts with wine," those breasts concerning which he had said above, My beloved is mine, and I am his: "betwixt my breasts shall he lie," that is in the princely portion of the heart where the Word of God has its lodging. What wine is that which gives beauty to the breasts of the bride, and fills them with the milk of chastity? That, forsooth, of which the bridegroom goes on to speak: [3] "I have drunk my wine with my milk. Eat, O friends: yea, drink and be drunken, my brethren." Hence the Apostles also were said to be filled with new wine; with *new*, he says, not with *old* wine; because [4] new wine is put into fresh wine-skins, and they [5] did not walk in oldness of the letter, but in newness of the Spirit. This is wine wherewith when youths and maidens are intoxicated, they at once thirst for virginity; they are filled with the spirit of chastity, and the prophecy of Zechariah comes to pass, at least if we follow the Hebrew literally, for he prophesied concerning virgins: [6] "And the streets of the city shall be full of boys and girls playing in the streets thereof. For what is his goodness, and what is his beauty, but the corn of the elect, and wine that giveth birth to virgins?" They are virgins of whom it is written in the forty-fifth psalm: [7] "The virgins her companions that follow her shall be brought unto thee. With gladness and rejoicing shall they be led: they shall enter into the King's palace."

31. Then follows: [8] "A garden shut up is my

---

[1] 2 Cor. ii. 15.   [2] Cant. ii. 13, 14.
[3] Ex. xxxiv. 33, 35: 2 Cor. iii. 7 sq.
[4] Is. i. 15.   [5] Cant. ii. 16.
[6] Cant. iii. 7, 8.   [7] Cant. iv. 6.   [8] Eph. v. 27.
[9] Cant. iv. 8.
[10] Sept. R.V. "Look from the top of Amana."
[11] Cant. viii. 5.   [12] Ps. cxix. 105.

[1] Cant. iv. 9.   [2] Cant. iv. 9, 10.
[3] Cant. v. 1.   [4] S. Matt. ix. 17.   [5] Rom. vii. 6.
[6] Zech. viii. 5; ix. 17, R. V. "How great is his goodness, and how great is his beauty! Corn shall make the young men flourish, and new wine the maids."
[7] Ps. xlv. 16, 17.
[8] Cant. iv. 12, 13.

sister, my bride : a garden shut up, a fountain sealed." That which is shut up and sealed reminds us of the mother of our Lord who was a mother and a Virgin. Hence it was that no one before or after our Saviour, was laid in his new tomb, hewn in the solid rock. And yet she that was ever a Virgin is the mother of many virgins. For next we read : "Thy shoots are an orchard of pomegranates with precious fruits." By pomegranates and fruits is signified the blending of all virtues in virginity. [1] "My beloved is white and ruddy"; white in virginity, ruddy in martyrdom. And because He is white and ruddy, therefore it is immediately added [2] "His mouth is most sweet, yea, he is altogether lovely." The virgin bridegroom having been praised by the virgin bride, in turn praises the virgin bride, and says to her : [3] "How beautiful are thy feet in sandals, [4] O daughter of Aminadab," which is, being interpreted, *a people that offereth itself willingly*. For virginity is voluntary, and therefore the steps of the Church in the beauty of chastity are praised. This is not the time for me like a commentator to explain all the mysteries of virginity from the Song of Songs ; I have no doubt that the fastidious reader will turn up his nose at what has already been said.

32. Isaiah tells of the mystery of our faith and hope : [5] "Behold a virgin shall conceive, and bear a son, and shall call his name Emmanuel." I know that the Jews are accustomed to meet us with the objection that in Hebrew the word *Almah* does not mean a virgin, but *a young woman*. And, to speak truth, a virgin is properly called *Bethulah*, but a young woman, or a girl, is not *Almah*, but *Naarah!* [6] What then is the meaning of *Almah*? A hidden virgin, that is, not merely virgin, but a virgin and something more, because not every virgin is hidden, shut off from the occasional sight of men. Then again, Rebecca, on account of her extreme purity, and because she was a type of the Church which she represented in her own virginity, is described in Genesis as *Almah*, not *Bethulah*, as may clearly be proved from the words of Abraham's servant, spoken by him in Mesopotamia : [7] "And he said, O Lord, the God of my master Abraham, if now thou do prosper my way which I go : behold I stand by the fountain of water; and

let it come to pass, that the maiden which cometh forth to draw, to whom I shall say, Give me, I pray thee, a little water of this pitcher to drink ; and she shall say to me, Both drink thou, and I will also draw for thy camels : let the same be the woman whom the Lord hath appointed for my master's son." Where he speaks of the maiden coming forth to draw water, the Hebrew word is *Almah*, that is, a *virgin secluded*, and guarded by her parents with extreme care. Or, if if this be not so, let them at least show me where the word is applied to married women as well, and I will confess my ignorance. "Behold a virgin shall conceive and bear a son." If virginity be not preferred to marriage, why did not the Holy Spirit choose a married woman, or a widow? For at that time Anna the daughter of Phanuel, of the tribe of Aser, was alive, distinguished for purity, and always free to devote herself to prayers and fasting in the temple of God. If the life, and good works, and fasting without virginity can merit the advent of the Holy Spirit, she might well have been the mother of our Lord. Let us hasten to the rest : [1] "The virgin daughter of Zion hath despised thee and laughed thee to scorn." To her whom he called daughter the prophet also gave the title virgin, for fear that if he spoke only of a daughter, it might be supposed that she was married. This is the virgin daughter whom elsewhere he thus addresses : [2] "Sing, O barren, thou that dost not bear ; break forth into singing, and cry aloud, thou that didst not travail with child : for more are the children of the desolate, than the children of the married wife, saith the Lord." This is she of whom God by the mouth of Jeremiah speaks, saying : [3] "Can a maid forget her ornaments, or a bride her attire." Concerning her we read of a great miracle in the same prophecy [4]—that a woman should compass a man, and that the Father of all things should be contained in a virgin's womb.

33. "Granted," says Jovinianus, "that there is a difference between marriage and virginity, what have you to say to this,—Suppose a virgin and a widow were baptized, and continued as they were, what difference will there be between them?" What we have already said concerning Peter and John, Anna and Mary, may be of service here. For if there is no difference between a virgin and a widow, both being baptized, because baptism makes a new man, upon the same principle harlots and prostitutes, if they are baptized, will be equal to virgins. If previous marriage is no prejudice to a baptized widow, and past pleas-

[1] Cant. v. 10.　　　[2] Cant. v. 16.　　　[3] Cant. vii. 1.
[4] R. V. "O Prince's daughter!" Sept., also "daughter of Nadab."
[5] Is. vii. 14.
[6] Delitzsch remarks, "The assertion of Jerome is untenable." See Cheyne, critical note on Is. vii. 14. The word probably denotes a female, married or unmarried, just attaining maturity. But in every other passage, the context shows that the word is used of an unmarried woman.
[7] Gen. xxiv. 42 sq.

[1] Is. xxxvii. 22.　　　　　　[2] Is. liv. 1.
[3] Jerem. ii. 32.　　　　　　[4] Jer. xxxi. 22.

ures and the exposure of their bodies to public lust are no detriment in the case of harlots, once they have approached the laver they will gain the rewards of virginity. It is one thing to unite with God a mind pure and free from any stain of memory, another to remember the foul and forced embraces of a man, and in recollection to act a part which you do not in person. Jeremiah, who was [1] sanctified in the womb, and was known in his mother's belly, enjoyed the high privilege because he was predestined to the blessing of virginity. And when all were captured, and even the vessels of the temple were plundered by the King of Babylon, he alone was [2] liberated by the enemy, knew not the insults of captivity, and was supported by the conquerors; and Nebuchadnezzar, though he gave Nebuzaradan no charge concerning the Holy of Holies, did give him charge concerning Jeremiah. For that is the true temple of God, and that is the Holy of Holies, which is consecrated to the Lord by pure virginity. On the other hand, Ezekiel, who was kept captive in Babylon, who saw the [3] storm approaching from the north, and the whirlwind sweeping all before it, says,[4] "My wife died in the evening and I did in the morning as I was commanded." For the Lord had previously told him that in that day he should open his mouth, and speak, and no longer keep silence. Mark well, that while his wife was living he was not at liberty to admonish the people. His wife died, the bond of wedlock was broken, and without the least hesitation he constantly devoted himself to the prophetic office. For he who was called being free, is truly the Lord's bondservant. I do not deny the blessedness of widows who remain such after their baptism; nor do I disparage those wives who maintain their chastity in wedlock; but as they attain a greater reward with God than married women who pay the marriage due, let widows themselves be content to give the preference to virginity. For if a chastity which comes too late, when the glow of bodily pleasure is no longer felt, makes them feel superior to married women, why should they not acknowledge themselves inferior to perpetual virginity.

34. All that goes for nothing, says Jovinianus, because even bishops, priests, and deacons, husbands of one wife, and having children, were appointed by the Apostle. Just as the Apostle [5] says he has no commandment respecting virgins, and yet gives his advice, as one who had obtained mercy from the Lord, and is anxious throughout the whole discussion to give virginity the

preference over marriage, and advises what he does not venture to command, lest he seem to lay a snare, and to put a heavier burden upon man's nature than it can bear; so also in establishing the constitution of the Church, inasmuch as the elements of the early Church were drawn from the Gentiles, he made the rules for fresh believers somewhat lighter that they might not in alarm shrink from keeping them. Then, again, the Apostles and elders wrote [1] letters from Jerusalem that no heavier burden should be laid on Gentile believers than that they should keep themselves from idolatry, and from fornication, and from things strangled. As though they were providing for infant children, they gave them milk to drink, not solid food. Nor did they lay down rules for continence, nor hint at virginity, nor urge to fasting, nor repeat the directions [2] given in the Gospel to the Apostles, not to have two tunics, nor scrip, nor money in their girdles, nor staff in their hand, nor shoes on their feet. And they certainly did not bid them,[3] if they wished to be perfect, go and sell all that they had and give to the poor, and "come follow me." For if the young man who boasted of having done all that the law enjoins, when he heard this went away sorrowful, because he had great possessions, and the Pharisees derided an utterance such as this from our Lord's lips: how much more would the vast multitude of Gentiles, whose highest virtue consisted in not plundering another's goods, have repudiated the obligation of perpetual chastity and continence, when they were told in the letter to keep themselves from idols, and from fornication, seeing that fornication was heard of among them, and such fornication as was not "even among the Gentiles." But the very choice of a bishop makes for me. For he does not say: Let a bishop be chosen who marries one wife and begets children; but who marries one wife, and [4] has his children in subjection and well disciplined. You surely admit that he is no bishop who during his episcopate begets children. The reverse is the case—if he be discovered, he will not be bound by the ordinary obligations of a husband, but will be condemned as an adulterer. Either permit [5] priests to perform the work of marriage with the result that virginity and marriage are on a par: or if it is unlawful for priests to touch their wives, they are so far holy in that they imitate virgin chastity. But something more follows. A layman, or any believer, cannot pray unless he abstain from sexual intercourse. Now a

---

[1] Jer. i. 5. [2] Jer. xxxix. 11; xl. i. [3] Ezek. i. 4.
[4] Ezek. xxiv. 18. [5] 1 Cor. vii. 25.

[1] Acts xv. 28, 29. [2] S. Matt. x. 10: S. Luke x. 5.
[3] S. Matt. xix. 21. [4] 1 Tim. iii. 2, 4: Tit. i. 6.
[5] Sacerdotes: that is, bishops.

priest must always offer sacrifices for the people : he must therefore always pray. And if he must always pray, he must always be released from the duties of marriage. For even under the old law they who used to offer sacrifices for the people not only remained in their houses, but purified themselves for the occasion by separating from their wives, nor would they drink wine or strong drink which are wont to stimulate lust. That married men are elected to the priesthood, I do not deny : the number of virgins is not so great as that of the priests required. Does it follow that because all the strongest men are chosen for the army, weaker men should not be taken as well ? All cannot be strong. If an army were constituted of strength only, and numbers went for nothing, the feebler men might be rejected. As it is, men of second or third-rate strength are chosen, that the army may have its full numerical complement. How is it, then, you will say, that frequently at the ordination of priests a virgin is passed over, and a married man taken ? Perhaps because he lacks other qualifications in keeping with virginity, or it may be that he is thought a virgin, and is not : or there may be a stigma on his virginity, or at all events virginity itself makes him proud, and while he plumes himself on mere bodily chastity, he neglects other virtues ; he does not cherish the poor : he is too fond of money. ·It sometimes happens that a man has a gloomy visage, a frowning brow, a walk as though he were in a solemn procession, and so offends the people, who, because they have no fault to find with his life, hate his mere dress and gait. Many are chosen not out of affection for themselves, but out of hatred for another. In most cases the election is won by mere simplicity, while the shrewdness and discretion of another candidate elicit opposition as though they were evils. Sometimes the judgement of the commoner people is at fault, and in testing the qualities of the priesthood, the individual inclines to his own character, with the result that he looks not so much for a good candidate as for one like himself. Not unfrequently it happens that married men, who form the larger portion of the people, in approving married candidates seem to approve themselves, and it does not occur to them that the mere fact that they prefer a married person to a virgin is evidence of their inferiority to virgins. What I am going to say will perhaps offend many. Yet I will say it, and good men will not be angry with me, because they will not feel the sting of conscience. Sometimes it is the fault of the bishops, who choose into the

ranks of the clergy not the best, but the cleverest, men, and think the more simple as well as innocent ones incapable ; or, as though they were distributing the offices of an earthly service, they give posts to their kindred and relations ; or they listen to the dictates of wealth. And, worse than all, they give promotion to the clergy who besmear them with flattery. To take the other view, if the Apostle's meaning be that marriage is necessary in a bishop, the Apostle himself ought not to have been a bishop, for he said,[1] "Yet I would that all men were even as I myself." And John will be thought unworthy of this rank, and all the virgins, and the continent, the fairest gems that give grace and ornament to the Church. Bishop, priest, and deacon, are not honourable distinctions, but names of offices. And we do not read : [2] "If a man seeketh the office of a bishop, he desireth a good degree," but, "he desireth a good work," because by being placed in the higher order an opportunity is afforded him, if he choose to avail himself of it, for the practice of virtue.

35. "The bishop, then, must be without reproach, so that he is the slave of no vice : "the husband of one wife," that is, in the past, not in the present ; "sober," or [3] better, as it is in the Greek, "vigilant," that is *νηφάλεον;* "chaste," for that is the [4] meaning of *σώφρονα;* [5] "distinguished," both by chastity and conduct : "hospitable," so that he imitates Abraham, and with strangers, nay rather *in* strangers, entertains Christ; "apt to teach," for it profits nothing to enjoy the consciousness of virtue, unless a man be able to instruct the people intrusted to him, so that he can exhort in doctrine, and refute the gainsayers ; [6] "not a drunkard," for he who is constantly in the Holy of Holies and offers sacrifices, will not drink wine and strong drink, since wine is a luxury. If a bishop drink at all, let it be in such a way that no one will know whether he has drunk or not. "No striker," that is, [7] a striker of men's consciences, for the Apostle is not pointing out what a boxer, but a pontiff ought not to do. He directly teaches what he ought to do : "but gentle, not contentious, no lover of money, one that ruleth well his own house, having his children in

[1] 1 Cor. vii. 7. [2] 1 Tim. iii. 1.
[3] V. supra, c. 27. R. V. "temperate." Ellicott observes, "under any circumstances the derivative translation *Vigilant,* Auth., though possibly defensible in the verb, is a needless and doubtful extension of the primary meaning."
[4] R. V. "orderly." V. above, c. 27.
[5] *κόσμιον.* R. V. "orderly."
[6] Non vinolentum. R.V. "no brawler," *i.e.,* as the Margin explains, "not quarrelsome over wine." The original is not thus a mere synonym for *νηφάλιος* in v. 2.
[7] So Chrysostom and Theodoret. The simple meaning appears to suit the context better.

subjection with all chastity." See what chastity is required in a bishop ! If his child be unchaste, he himself cannot be a bishop, and he offends God in the same way as did [1] Eli the priest, who had indeed rebuked his sons, but because he had not put away the offenders, fell backwards and died before the lamp of God went out. [2] "Women in like manner must be chaste," and so on. In every grade, and in both sexes, chastity has the chief place. You see then that the blessedness of a bishop, priest, or deacon, does not lie in the fact that they are bishops, priests, or deacons, but in their having the virtues which their names and offices imply. Otherwise, if a deacon be holier than his bishop, his lower grade will not give him a worse standing with Christ. If it were so, Stephen the deacon, the first to wear the martyr's crown, would be less in the kingdom of heaven than many bishops, and than Timothy and Titus, whom I venture to make neither inferior nor yet superior to him. Just as in the legions of the army there are generals, tribunes, centurions, javelin-men, and light-armed troops, common soldiers, and companies, but once the battle begins, all distinctions of rank are dropped, and the one thing looked for is valour : so too in this camp and in this battle, in which we contend against devils, not names but deeds are needed : and under the true commander, Christ, not the man who has the highest title has the greatest fame, but he who is the bravest warrior.

36. But you will say : "If everybody were a virgin, what would become of the human race"? Like shall here beget like. If every-one were a widow, or continent in marriage, how will mortal men be propagated? Upon this principle there will be nothing at all for fear that something else may cease to exist. To put a case : if all men were philosophers, there would be no husbandmen. Why speak of husbandmen? there would be no orators, no lawyers, no teachers of the other professions. If all men were leaders, what would become of the soldiers? If all were the head, whose head would they be called, when there were no other members? You are afraid that if the desire for virginity were general there would be no prostitutes, no adulteresses, no wailing infants in town or country. Every day the blood of adulterers [3] is shed, adulterers are condemned, and lust is raging and rampant in the very presence of the laws and the symbols of authority and the courts of justice. Be not afraid that all will become

virgins : virginity is a hard matter, and therefore rare, because it is hard : "Many are called, few chosen." Many begin, few persevere. And so the reward is great for those who have persevered. If all were able to be virgins, our Lord would never have said : [1] "He that is able to receive it, let him receive it :" and the Apostle would not have hesitated to give his advice,—[2] "Now concerning virgins I have no commandment of the Lord." Why then, you will say, were the organs of generation created, and why were we so fashioned by the all-wise creator, that we burn for one another, and long for natural intercourse? To reply is to endanger our modesty : we are, as it were, between two rocks, the [3] Symplegades of necessity and virtue, on either side ; and must make shipwreck of either our sense of shame, or of the cause we defend. If we reply to your suggestions, shame covers our face. If shame secures silence, in a manner we seem to desert our post, and to leave the ground clear to the raging foe. Yet it is better, as the story goes, to shut our eyes and fight like the [4] blindfold gladiators, than not to repel with the shield of truth the darts aimed at us. I can indeed say : "Our hinder parts which are banished from sight, and the lower portions of the abdomen, which perform the functions of nature, are the Creator's work." But inasmuch as the physical conformation of the organs of generation testifies to difference of sex, I shall briefly reply : Are we never then to forego lust, for fear that we may have members of this kind for nothing? Why then should a husband keep himself from his wife? Why should a widow persevere in chastity, if we were only born to live like beasts? Or what harm does it do me if another man lies with my wife? For as the teeth were made for chewing, and the food masticated passes into the stomach, and a man is not blamed for giving my wife bread : similarly if it was intended that the organs of generation should always be performing their office, when my vigour is spent let another take my place, and, if I may so speak, let my wife quench her burning lust where she can. But what does the Apostle mean by exhorting to continence, if continence be contrary to nature? What does our Lord mean when He instructs us in the various kinds of eunuchs. [5] Surely [6] the Apostle who bids us emulate his own chastity, must be asked, if we are to be consistent, Why are you like other men, Paul? Why are

---

[1] i Sam. ii. and iv.   [2] i Tim. iii. 11.
[3] The Code of Constantine, following the Mosaic law, imposed the penalty of death for adultery. See Gibbon, ch. xliv.

[1] S. Matt. xix. 12.   [2] i Cor. vii. 25.
[3] "Two rocky islands in the Euxine, that, according to the fable, floated about, dashing against and rebounding from each other, until at length they became fixed on the passage of the Argo between them."
[4] Andabatæ.   [5] Matt. xix. 12.   [6] i Cor. vii. 7.

you distinguished from the female sex by a beard, hair, and other peculiarities of person? How is it that you have not swelling bosoms, and are not broad at the hips, narrow at the chest? Your voice is rugged, your speech rough, your eyebrows more shaggy. To no purpose you have all these manly qualities, if you forego the embraces of women. I am compelled to say something and become a fool: but you have forced me to dare to speak. Our Lord and Saviour,[1] Who though He was in the form of God, condescended to take the form of a servant, and became obedient to the Father even unto death, yea the death of the cross—what necessity was there for Him to be born with members which He was not going to use? He certainly was circumcised to manifest His sex. Why did he cause John the Apostle and John the Baptist to make themselves eunuchs through love of Him, after causing them to be born men? Let us then who believe in Christ follow His example. And if we knew Him after the flesh, let us no longer know Him according to the flesh. The substance of our resurrection bodies will certainly be the same as now, though of higher glory. For the Saviour after His descent into hell had so far the self-same body in which He was crucified, that[2] He showed the disciples the marks of the nails in His hands and the wound in His side. Moreover, if we deny the identity of His body because[3] He entered though the doors were shut, and this is not a property of human bodies, we must deny also that Peter and the Lord had real bodies because they[4] walked upon the water, which is contrary to nature. [5] "In the resurrection of the dead they will neither marry nor be given in marriage, but will be like the angels." What others will hereafter be in heaven, that virgins begin to be on earth. If likeness to the angels is promised us (and there is no difference of sex among the angels), we shall either be of no sex as are the angels, or at all events, which is clearly proved, though we rise from the dead in our own sex, we shall not perform the functions of sex.

37. But why do we argue, and why are we eager to frame a clever and victorious reply to our opponent?[6] "Old things have passed away, behold all things have become new." I will run through the utterances of the Apostles, and as to the instances afforded by Solomon I added short expositions to facilitate their being understood, so now I will go over the passages bearing on Christian purity and continence, and will make of many proofs a connected series. By this method I shall succeed in omitting nothing relating to chastity, and shall avoid being tediously long. Amongst other passages, Paul the Apostle writes to the Romans:[1] "What fruit then had ye at that time in the things whereof ye are now ashamed? for the end of those things is death. But now being made free from sin, and become servants to God, ye have your fruit unto sanctification, and the end eternal life." I suppose too that the end of marriage is death. But the compensating fruit of sanctification, fruit belonging either to virginity or to continence, is eternal life. And afterwards:[2] "Wherefore, my brethren, ye also were made dead to the law through the body of Christ; that ye should be joined to another, even to him who was raised from the dead, that we might bring forth fruit unto God. For when we were in the flesh, the sinful passions, which were through the law, wrought in our members to bring forth fruit unto death. But now we have been discharged from the law, having died to that wherein we were holden; so that we serve in newness of the Spirit, and not in oldness of the letter." "When," he says, "we were in the flesh, and not in the newness of the Spirit but in the oldness of the letter," we did those things which pertained to the flesh, and bore fruit unto death. But now because we are dead to the law, through the body of Christ, let us bear fruit to God, that we may belong to Him who rose from the dead. And elsewhere, having previously said,[3] "I know that the law is spiritual," and having discussed at some length the violence of the flesh which frequently drives us to do what we would not, he at last continues: "O wretched man that I am! who shall deliver me out of the body of this death? I thank God through Jesus Christ our Lord." And again, "So then I myself with the mind serve the law of God; but with the flesh the law of sin." And,[4] "There is therefore now no condemnation to them that are in Christ Jesus, who walk not after the flesh. For the law of the Spirit of life in Christ Jesus made me free from the law of sin and death." And more clearly in what follows he teaches that Christians do not walk according to the flesh but according to the Spirit:[5] "For they that are after the flesh do mind the things of the flesh; but they that are after the spirit the things of the spirit. For the mind of the flesh is death; but the mind of the spirit is life and peace: because the mind of the flesh is enmity against

[1] Phil. ii. 6-8.
[2] S. John xx. 20.
[3] S. John xx. 19.
[4] S. Matt. xiv. 28.
[5] S. Matt. xxii. 30.
[6] 2 Cor. v. 17.

[1] Rom. vi. 21, 22.
[2] Rom. vii. 4 sq.
[3] Rom. vii. 14, 24, 25.
[4] Rom. viii. 1, 2.
[5] Rom. viii. 5 sq.

God ; for it is not subject to the law of God, neither indeed can it be : and they that are in the flesh cannot please God. But ye are not in the flesh, but in the Spirit, if so be that the Spirit of God dwelleth in you," and so on to where he says,[1] "So then, brethren, we are debtors, not to the flesh, to live after the flesh : for if ye live after the flesh, ye must die ; but if by the spirit ye mortify the deeds of the body, ye shall live. For as many as are led by the Spirit of God, these are sons of God." If the[2] wisdom of the flesh is enmity against God, and they who are in the flesh cannot please God, I think that they who perform the functions of marriage love the wisdom of the flesh, and therefore are in the flesh. The Apostle being desirous to withdraw us from the flesh and to join us to the Spirit, says afterwards : [3] "I beseech you therefore, brethren, by the mercies of God, to present your bodies a living sacrifice, holy, acceptable to God, which is your reasonable service. And be not fashioned according to this world : but be ye transformed by the renewing of your mind, that ye may prove what is the good and acceptable and perfect will of God. For I say, through the grace that was given me, to every man that is among you, not to think of himself more highly than he ought to think; but to think according to chastity"[4] (not *soberly* as the Latin versions badly render), but "think," he says, "according to chastity," for the Greek words are ἐις τὸ σωφρονεῖν. Let us consider what the Apostle says : "Be ye transformed by the renewing of your mind, that ye may prove what is the good and acceptable and perfect will of God." What he says is something like this—God indeed permits marriage, He permits second marriages, and if necessary, prefers even third marriages to fornication and adultery. But we who ought to present our bodies a living sacrifice, holy, acceptable to God, which is our reasonable service, should consider, not what God permits, but what He wishes : that we may prove what is the good and acceptable and perfect will of God. It follows that what He merely permits is neither good, nor acceptable, nor perfect. And he gives his reasons for this advice : [5] "Knowing the season, that now it is high time for you to awake out of sleep : for now is salvation nearer to us than when we first believed. The night is far spent, and the day is at hand." And lastly : "Put ye on the Lord Jesus Christ, and make not provision for the flesh, to fulfil the lusts thereof." God's will

is one thing, His indulgence another. Whence, writing to the Corinthians, he says,[1] "I, brethren, could not speak unto you as unto spiritual, but as unto carnal, even as unto babes in Christ. I have fed you with milk, and not with meat : for hitherto ye were not able to bear it, neither yet now are ye able. For ye are yet carnal." He who[2] is in the merely animal state, and does not receive the things pertaining to the Spirit of God (for he is foolish, and cannot understand them, because they are spiritually discerned), he is not fed with the food of perfect chastity, but with the coarse milk of marriage. As through man came death, so also through man came the resurrection of the dead. As in Adam we all die, so in Christ we shall all be made alive. Under the law we served the old Adam, under the Gospel let us serve the new Adam. For the first man Adam was made a living soul, the last Adam was made a quickening spirit.[3] "The first man is of the earth, earthy : the second man is of heaven. As is the earthy, such are they also that are earthy : and as is the heavenly, such are they also that are heavenly. And as we have borne the image of the earthy, we shall also bear the image of the heavenly. Now this I say, brethren, that flesh and blood cannot inherit the Kingdom of God ; neither doth corruption inherit incorruption." This is so clear that no explanation can make it clearer : "Flesh and blood," he says, "cannot inherit the Kingdom of God, neither doth corruption inherit incorruption." If corruption attaches to all intercourse, and incorruption is characteristic of chastity, the rewards of chastity cannot belong to marriage.[4] "For we know that if the earthly house of this tabernacle be dissolved, we have a building from God, a house not made with hands, eternal, in the heavens. For verily in this we groan, longing to be clothed upon with our habitation which is from heaven. We are willing to be absent from the body, and to be at home with the Lord. Wherefore also we make it our aim, whether in the body, or out of the body, to be well-pleasing unto God." And by way of more fully explaining what he did not wish them to be he says elsewhere : [5] "I espoused you to one husband, that I might present you as a pure virgin to Christ." But if you choose to apply the words to the whole Assembly of believers, and in this betrothal to Christ include both married women, and the twice-

---

[1] Rom. viii. 11, 14.
[3] Rom. xii. 1-3.
[5] Rom. xiii. 11, 12, 14.

[2] R. V. " mind."
[4] See ch. 27.

[1] 1 Cor. iii. 1, 2, 3.
[2] That is, under the dominion of the *psyche*, or principle of life common to man and the beasts, hence, *natural*. Opposed to the psyche is the *pneuma*, capable of being influenced by the Spirit of God. A man thus influenced is pneumatikos or spiritual. See also 1 Cor. xv. 44.
[3] 1 Cor. xv. 47 sq.
[4] 2 Cor. v. 1 sq.
[5] 2 Cor. xi. 2.

married, and widows, and virgins, that also makes for us. For whilst he invites all to chastity and to the reward of virginity, he shows that virginity is more excellent than all these conditions. And again writing to the Galatians he says:[1] "Because by the works of the law shall no flesh be justified." Among the works of the law is marriage, and accordingly under it they are cursed who have no children. And if under the Gospel it is permitted to have children, it is one thing to make a concession to weakness, another to hold out rewards to virtue.

38. Something else I will say to my friends who marry and after long chastity and continence begin to burn and are as wanton as the brutes:[2] "Are ye so foolish? having begun in the Spirit, are ye now perfected in the flesh? Did ye suffer so many things in vain?" If the Apostle in the case of some persons loosens the cords of continence, and lets them have a slack rein, he does so on account of the infirmity of the flesh. This is the enemy he has in view when he once more says:[3] "Walk by the Spirit, and ye shall not fulfil the lust of the flesh. For the flesh lusteth against the Spirit, and the Spirit against the flesh." It is unnecessary now to speak of the works of the flesh: it would be tedious, and he who chooses can easily gather them from the letter of the Apostle. I will only speak of the Spirit and its fruits, love, joy, peace, long suffering, kindness, goodness, faithfulness, meekness,[4] continence. All the virtues of the Spirit are supported and protected by continence, which is as it were their solid foundation and crowning point. Against such there is no law. [5]"And they that are of Christ have crucified their flesh with the passions and the lusts thereof. If we live by the Spirit, by the Spirit let us also walk." Why do we who with Christ have crucified our flesh and its passions and desires again desire to do the things of the flesh?[6] "Whatsoever a man soweth, that shall he also reap. For he that soweth unto his own flesh, shall of the flesh reap corruption; but he that soweth unto the Spirit shall of the Spirit reap eternal life." I think that he who has a wife, so long as he reverts to the practice in question, that Satan may not tempt him, is sowing to the flesh and not to the Spirit. And he who sows to the flesh (the words are not mine, but the Apostle's) reaps corruption. God the Father chose us in Christ before the foundation of the world, that we might be holy and without spot before Him. [1]We walked in the lusts of the flesh, doing the desires of the flesh and of the thoughts, and were children of wrath, even as the rest. But now He has raised us up with Him, and made us to sit with Him in the heavenly places in Christ Jesus,[2] that we may put away according to our former manner of life the old man, which is corrupt according to the lusts of deceit, and that blessing may be applied to us which so finely concludes the mystical Epistle to the Ephesians: [3]"Grace be with all them that love our Lord Jesus Christ in uncorruptness." [4]"For our citizenship is in heaven; from whence also we wait for a Saviour, the Lord Jesus Christ: who shall fashion anew the body of our humiliation, that it may be conformed to the body of his glory. [5]Whatsoever things then are true, whatsoever are chaste, whatsoever things are just, whatsoever things pertain to purity, let us join ourselves to these, let us follow these.[6] Christ hath reconciled us in his body to God the Father through his death, and has presented us holy and without spot, and without blame before himself: in whom we have been also circumcised, not with the circumcision made with hands, to the spoiling of the body of the flesh, but with the circumcision of Christ, having been buried with him in baptism, wherein also we rose with him. If then we have risen with Christ, let us seek those things which are above, where Christ sitteth on the right hand of God; let us set our affections on things above, not upon the things that are upon the earth. For we are dead, and our life is hid with Christ in God. When Christ our life shall appear, then we also shall appear with him in glory. [7]No soldier on service entangleth himself in the affairs of this life; that he may please him who enrolled him as a soldier. [8]For the grace of God hath appeared, bringing salvation to all men, instructing us, to the intent that, denying ungodliness and worldly lusts, we should live purely and righteously and godly in this present world."

39. The day would not be long enough were I to attempt to relate all that the Apostle enjoins concerning purity. These things are those concerning which our Lord said to the Apostles:[9] "I have yet many things to say unto you, but ye cannot bear them now. Howbeit, when he, the Spirit of truth, is come, he shall guide you into all the truth." After the crucifixion of Christ, we find in the [10]Acts of the Apostles that one house, that of Philip

---

[1] Gal. ii. 16.   [2] Gal. iii. 3, 4.
[3] Gal. v. 16, 17.
[4] Properly, *self-control* in the wide sense.
[5] Gal. v. 24, 25.   [6] Gal. vi. 7, 8.

[1] Eph. ii. 3, 4.   [2] Eph. iv. 22.
[3] Eph. vi. 24.   [4] Phil. iii. 20, 21.
[5] Phil. iv. 8.   [6] Coloss. ii. 11; iii. 1 sq.
[7] 2 Tim. ii. 4.   [8] Titus ii. 11, 12.
[9] S. John xvi. 12, 13.   [10] xxi. 9.

the Evangelist, produced four virgin daughters, to the end that Cæsarea, where the Gentile Church had been consecrated in the person of Cornelius the centurion, might afford an illustration of virginity. And whereas our Lord said in the Gospel :[1] " The law and the prophets were until John," they because they were virgins are related to have prophesied even after John. For they could not be bound by the law of the Old Testament, who had shone with the brightness of virginity. Let us pass on to James, who was called the brother of the Lord, a man of such sanctity and righteousness, and distinguished by so rigid and perpetual a virginity, that even [2] Josephus, the Jewish historian, relates that the overthrow of Jerusalem was due to his death. He, the first bishop of the Church at Jerusalem, which was composed of Jewish believers, to whom Paul went, accompanied by Titus and Barnabas, says in his Epistle :[3] " Be not deceived, my beloved brethren. Every good gift and every perfect boon is from above, coming down from the Father of lights,[4] with whom there is no difference, neither shadow that is cast by turning. Of his own will he brought us forth by the word of truth, that we should be a kind of first-fruits of his creatures." Himself a virgin, he teaches virginity in a mystery. Every perfect gift cometh down from above, where marriage is unknown ; and it cometh down, not from any one you please, but from the Father of lights, Who says to the apostles, " Ye are the light of the world ; " with Whom there is no difference of Jew, or Gentile, nor does that shadow which was the companion of the law, trouble those who have believed from among the nations ; but with His word He begat us, and with the word of truth, because some shadow, image, and likeness of truth went before in the law, that we might be the first-fruits of His creatures. And as He who was Himself the [5] first begotten from the dead has raised all that have died in Him : so He who was a virgin, consecrated the first-fruits of His virgins in His own virgin self. Let us also consider what Peter thinks of the calling of the Gentiles : [6]" Blessed be the God and Father of our Lord Jesus Christ, who according to his great mercy begat us again unto a living hope by the resurrection of Jesus Christ from the dead, unto an inheritance incorruptible, and undefiled, and that fadeth not away, reserved in heaven for you, who by the power of God are guarded through

faith unto a salvation ready to be revealed in the last time." Where we read of an inheritance incorruptible, and undefiled, and that fadeth not away, prepared in heaven and reserved for the last time, and of the hope of eternal life when they will neither marry, nor be given in marriage, there, in other words, the privileges of virginity are described. For he shows as much in what follows :[1] " Wherefore girding up the loins of your mind, be sober and set your hope perfectly on the grace that is to be brought unto you at the revelation of Jesus Christ ; as children of obedience, not fashioning yourselves according to your former lusts in the time of your ignorance ; but like as he which called you is holy, be ye yourselves also holy in all manner of living ; because it is written, ye shall be holy ; for I am holy.[2] For we were not redeemed with contemptible things, with silver or gold ; but with the precious blood of a lamb without spot, Jesus Christ,[3] that we might purify our souls in obedience to the truth, having been begotten again not of corruptible seed, but of incorruptible, through the word of God,[4] who liveth and abideth. And as living stones let us be built up a spiritual house, an holy priesthood offering up spiritual sacrifices through Christ our Lord. [5] For we are an elect race, a royal priesthood, a holy nation, a people for God's own possession. [6] Christ died for us in the flesh. Let us arm ourselves with the same conversation as did Christ ; for he that hath suffered in the flesh hath ceased from sin ; that we should no longer live the rest of our time in the flesh to the lusts of men, but to the will of God. For the time past is sufficient for us when we walked in lasciviousness, lusts, and other vices. Great and precious are the promises attaching to virginity which He has given us, [7] that through it we may become partakers of the divine nature, having escaped from the corruption that is in the world through lust. [8] The Lord knoweth how to deliver the godly out of temptation, and to keep the unrighteous under punishment unto the day of judgement, but chiefly them that walk after the flesh in the lust of defilement, and despise dominion, daring, self-willed. For they, as beasts of burden, without reason, think only of their belly and their lusts, railers who shall in their corruption be destroyed, and shall receive the reward of iniquity : men that count unrighteousness delight, spots and blemishes, think-

[1] S. Matt. xi. 13.
[2] The passage is not found in existing copies of Josephus.
[3] S. James i. 16–18.
[4] R. V. " can be no variation." The word " difference," as used by Jerome, is explained by the context.
[5] Rev. i. 5.   [6] 1 Pet. i. 3–5.

[1] 1 Pet. i. 13–16.   [2] 1 Pet. i. 18, 19.   [3] 1 Pet. i. 22, 23.
[4] In Jerome's rendering ' living and abiding,' are attributes of God. But in the original the participles may be taken as predicates of either word or God. The R. V. refers them to the former.
[5] 1 Pet. ii. 9.   [6] 1 Pet. iv. 1 sq.
[7] 2 Pet. i. 4.   [8] 2 Pet. ii. 9 sq.

ing of nothing but their pleasures ; having eyes full of adultery and insatiable lust, deceiving souls not yet strengthened by the love of Christ. For they utter swelling words and easily snare the unlearned with the seduction of the flesh ; promising them liberty while they themselves are the slaves of vice, luxury, and corruption. For of what a man is overcome, of the same is he also brought into bondage. But if, after they had escaped the defilements of the world through the knowledge of our Saviour Jesus Christ, they are again overcome by that which they before overcame, the last state is become worse with them than the first. And it were better for them not to have known the way of righteousness, than, after knowing it, to turn back and forsake the holy commandment delivered unto them. And it has happened unto them according to the true proverb, the dog hath turned to his own vomit again, and the sow that had washed to wallowing in the mire." I have hesitated, for fear of being tedious, to quote the whole passage of the second Epistle of Peter, and have merely shown that the Holy Spirit in prophecy foretold the teachers of this time and their heresy. Lastly, he more clearly denotes them, saying,[1] "In the last days seducing mockers shall come, walking after their own lusts."

40. The Apostle has described Jovinianus speaking with swelling cheeks and nicely balancing his inflated utterances, promising heavenly liberty, when he himself is the slave of vice and self-indulgence, a dog returning to his vomit. For although he boasts of being a monk, he has exchanged his dirty tunic, bare feet, common bread, and drink of water, for a snowy dress, sleek skin, honey-wine and dainty dishes, for the sauces of [2] Apicius and [3] Paxamus, for baths and rubbings, and for the cook-shops. Is it not clear that he prefers his belly to Christ, and thinks his ruddy complexion worth the kingdom of heaven ? And yet that handsome monk so fat and sleek, and of bright appearance, who always walks with the air of a bridegroom, must either marry a wife if he is to show that virginity and marriage are equal : or if he does not marry one, it is useless for him to bandy words with us when his acts are on our side. And John agrees with this almost to the letter :[4] "Love not the world, neither the things that are in the world. If any man love the world, the love of the Father is not in him. For all that is in the world is the

lust of the flesh, and the lust of the eyes, and the pride of this life, which is not of the Father, but is of the world." And, "The world passeth away, and the lust thereof : but he that doeth the will of God abideth for ever. A new commandment have I written unto you, which thing is true both in Christ and in you ; because the darkness is passing away, and the true light already shineth." And again, [1] "Beloved, now are we the children of God, and it is not yet made manifest what we shall be. But we know that, if he shall be manifested, we shall be like him : for we shall see him even as he is. And every one that hath this hope purifieth himself, even as he is pure. [2] Herein is our love made perfect, if we have boldness in the day of judgement : that as he is, even so may we be in this world." The Epistle of Jude also expresses nearly the same :[3] "Hating even the garment spotted by the flesh." Let us read the Apocalypse of John, and we shall there find the Lamb upon Mount Sion,[4] and with Him "a hundred and forty-four thousand of them that were sealed, having His name and the name of His Father written in their foreheads, who sing a new song, and no one can sing that song save they who have been redeemed out of the earth. These are they who have not defiled themselves with women, for they continued virgins. These follow the Lamb whithersoever He goeth : for they were redeemed from among men, first-fruits to God and to the Lamb, and in their mouth was found no guile, and they are without spot." [5] Out of each tribe, the tribe of Dan excepted, the place of which is taken by the tribe of Levi, twelve thousand virgins who have been sealed are spoken of as future believers, who have not defiled themselves with women. And that we may not suppose the reference to be to those who know not harlots, he immediately added : "For they continued virgins." Whereby he shows that all who have not preserved their virginity, in comparison of pure and angelic chastity and of our Lord Jesus Christ Himself, are defiled. [6] "These are they who sing a new song which no man can sing except him that is a virgin. These are first-fruits unto God and unto the Lamb, and are without blemish." If virgins are first-fruits, it follows that widows and the continent in marriage, come after the first-fruits, that is, are in the second and third rank : nor can a lost people be saved unless it offer such sacrifices of chastity to God, and with pure victims reconcile the spotless Lamb.

---

[1] 2 Pet. iii. 3.
[2] The notorious epicure of the time of Augustus and Tiberius.
[3] Paxamus wrote a treatise on cooking, which, Suidas states, was arranged in alphabetical order.
[4] 1 John ii. 15 sq.

[1] 1 John iii. 2, 3.
[2] 1 John iv. 7. R. V. "that we may have."
[3] Jude, 23.
[4] xiv. 1 sq.
[5] Rev. vii. 5 sq.
[6] Apoc. xiv. 3, 4.

It would be endless work to explain the Gospel mystery of the ten virgins, five of whom were wise and five foolish. All I say now is, that as mere virginity without other works does not save, so all works without virginity, purity, continence, chastity, are imperfect. And we shall not be hindered in the least from taking this view by the objection of our opponent that our Lord was at Cana of Galilee, and joined in the marriage festivities when He turned water into wine. I shall very briefly reply, that He Who was circumcised on the eighth day, and for Whom a pair of turtle-doves and two young pigeons were offered on the day of purification, like others, before He suffered, shewed His approval of Jewish custom, that He might not seem to give His enemies just cause for putting Him to death on the pretext that He destroyed the law and condemned nature. And even this was done for our sakes. For by going once to a marriage, He taught that men should marry only once. Moreover, at that time it was possible to injure virginity if marriage were not placed next to it, and the purity of widowhood in the third rank. But now when heretics are condemning wedlock, and despise the ordinance of God, we gladly hear anything he [1] may say in praise of marriage. For the Church does not condemn marriage, but makes it subordinate; nor does she reject it, but regulates it; for she knows, as was said before, that [2] in a great house there are not only vessels of gold and silver, but also of wood and earthenware; and that some are to honour, some to dishonour; and that whoever cleanses himself will be a vessel of honour, necessary, prepared for every good work.

41. I have given enough and more than enough illustrations from the divine writings of Christian chastity and angelic virginity. But as I understand that our opponent in his commentaries summons us to the tribunal of worldly wisdom, and we are told that views of this kind are never accepted in the world, and that our religion has invented a dogma against nature, I will quickly run through Greek and Roman and Foreign History, and will show that virginity ever took the lead of chastity. Fable relates that Atalanta, the virgin of Calydonian fame, lived for the chase and dwelt always in the woods; in other words that she did not set her heart on marriage with its troubles of pregnancy and of sickness, but upon the nobler life of freedom and chastity. [3] Harpalyce too, a Thracian virgin, is described by the famous poet; and so is [4] Camilla, queen of the Volsci, on whom, when she came to his assistance,

Turnus had no higher praise which he could bestow than to call her a virgin. "O Virgin, Glory of Italy!" And that famous daughter of [1] Leos, the lady of the brazen house, ever a virgin, is related to have freed her country from pestilence by her voluntary death: and the blood of the virgin [2] Iphigenia is said to have calmed the stormy winds. What need to tell of the Sibyls of Erythræ and Cumæ, and the eight others? for Varro asserts there were ten whose ornament was virginity, and divination the reward of their virginity. But if in the Æolian dialect "Sibyl" is represented by Θεοβούλη, we must understand that a knowledge of the *Counsel of God* is rightly attributed to virginity alone. We read, too, that Cassandra and Chryseis, prophetesses of Apollo and Juno, were virgins. And there were innumerable priestesses of the Taurian Diana, and of Vesta. One of these, Munitia, being suspected of unchastity was [3] buried alive, which would be in my opinion an unjust punishment, unless the violation of virginity were considered a serious crime. At all events how highly the Romans always esteemed virgins is clear from the fact that consuls and generals even in their triumphal chariots and bringing home the spoils of conquered nations, were wont to make way for them to pass. And so did men of all ranks. When [4] Claudia, a Vestal Virgin, was suspected of unchastity, and a vessel containing the image of Cybele was aground in the Tiber, it is related that she, to prove her chastity, with her girdle drew the ship which a thousand men could not move. Yet, as [5] the uncle of Lucan the poet says, it would have been better if this circumstance had decorated a chastity tried and proved, and had not pleaded in defence of a chastity equivocal. No wonder that we read such things of human beings, when heathen error also invented the virgin goddesses Minerva and Diana, and placed the Virgin among the twelve signs of the Zodiac, by means of which, as they suppose, the world

---

[1] Leos was the hero from whom the tribe Leontis derived its name. Once when Athens was suffering from famine or plague, the oracle at Delphi demanded that his daughters should be sacrificed. The father complied. The shrine called *Leocorium* was erected by the Athenians to their honour.
[2] Jerome's memory appears to be at fault. When the Greek fleet was on its way to Troy, it was detained by a *calm* at Aulis. The seer Calchas advised that Iphigenia, daughter of Agamemnon, should be sacrificed. See Dict. of Ant.
[3] According to the law of Numa, the punishment of a Vestal Virgin for violating the vow of chastity was stoning to death. Tarquinius Priscus first enacted that the offender should be buried alive, after being stripped of her badges of office, scourged and attired like a corpse. "From the time of the triumvirs each [Vestal] was preceded by a lictor when she went abroad; consuls and prætors made way for them, and lowered their fasces; even the tribunes of the plebs respected their holy character, and if any one passed under their litter, he was put to death."
[4] It is said, however, that Claudia (Quinta) was a Roman matron, not a Vestal Virgin. The soothsayers announced that only a chaste woman could move the vessel referred to. Claudia, who had been accused of incontinence, took hold of the rope, and the vessel forthwith followed her. B. C. 204.
[5] Seneca.

---

[1] or they may say.   [2] 2 Tim. ii. 20, 21.
[3] Virg. Æn. i. 317.   [4] Virg. Æn. vii. 803 : id. xi. 535.

revolves. It is a proof of the little esteem in which they held marriage that they did not even among the scorpions, centaurs, crabs, fishes, and capricorn, thrust in a husband and wife. When the thirty tyrants of Athens had slain Phidon at the banquet, they commanded his virgin daughters to come to them, naked like harlots, and there upon the ground, red with their father's blood, to act the wanton. For a little while they hid their grief, and then when they saw the revellers were intoxicated, going out on the plea of easing nature, they embraced one another and threw themselves into a well, that by death they might save their virginity. The virgin daughter of Demotion, chief of the Areopagites, having heard of the death of her betrothed, [1] Leosthenes, who had originated the Lamian war, slew herself, for she declared that although in body she was a virgin, yet if she were compelled to accept another, she should regard him as her second husband, when she had given her heart to Leosthenes. So close a friendship long existed between Sparta and Messene that for the furtherance of certain religious rites they even exchanged virgins. Well, on one occasion when the men of Messene attempted to outrage fifty Lacedæmonian virgins, out of so many not one consented, but they all most gladly died in defence of their chastity. Whence there arose a long and grievous war, and in the long run [2] Mamertina was destroyed. Aristoclides, tyrant of Orchomenos, fell in love with a virgin of Stymphalus, and when after the death of her father she took refuge in the temple of Diana, and embraced the image of the goddess and could not be dragged thence by force, she was slain on the spot. Her death caused such intense grief throughout Arcadia that the people took up arms and avenged the virgin's death. [3] Aristomenes of Messene, a just man, at a time when the Lacedæmonians, whom he had conquered, were celebrating by night the festival called the [4] Hyacinthia, carried off from the sportive bands fifteen virgins, and fleeing all night at full speed got away from the Spartan territory. His companions wished to outrage them, but he admonished them to the best of his power not to do so, and when certain refused to

obey, he slew them, and restrained the rest by fear. The maidens were afterwards ransomed by their kinsmen, and on seeing Aristomenes condemned for murder would not return to their country until clasping the knees of the judges they beheld the protector of their chastity acquitted. How shall we sufficiently praise the daughters of Scedasus at Leuctra in Bœotia? It is related that in the absence of their father they hospitably entertained two youths who were passing by, and who having drunk to excess violated the virgins in the course of the night. Being unwilling to survive the loss of their virginity, the maidens inflicted deadly wounds on one another. Nor would it be right to omit mention of the Locrian virgins. They were sent to Ilium according to custom which had lasted for nearly a thousand years, and yet not one gave occasion to any idle tale or filthy rumour of virginity defiled. Could any one pass over in silence the seven virgins of Miletus who, when the Gauls spread desolation far and wide, that they might suffer no indignity at the hands of the enemy, escaped disgrace by death, and left to all virgins the lesson of their example—that noble minds care more for chastity than life? Nicanor having conquered and overthrown Thebes was himself overcome by a passion for one captive virgin, whose voluntary self-surrender he longed for. A captive maid, he thought, must be only too glad. But he found that virginity is dearer to the pure in heart than a kingdom, when with tears and grief he held her in his arms slain by her own hand. Greek writers tell also of another Theban virgin who had been deflowered by a Macedonian foe, and who, hiding her grief for a while, slew the violator of her virginity as he slept, and then killed herself with the sword, so that she would neither live when her chastity was lost, nor die before she had avenged herself.

42. To come to the Gymnosophists of India, the opinion is authoritatively handed down that Budda, the founder of their religion, had his birth through the side of a virgin. And we need not wonder at this in the case of Barbarians when cultured Greece supposed that Minerva at her birth sprang from the head of Jove, and Father Bacchus from his thigh. [1] Speusippus also, Plato's nephew, and [2] Clearchus in his eulogy of Plato, and [3] Anaxelides in the second book of his

---

[1] In the year after the death of Alexander (B. C. 323), Leosthenes defeated Alexander's general Antipater, near Thermopylæ. Antipater then threw himself into the town of Lamia (in Phthiotis in Thessaly) which thus gave its name to the war. Leosthenes pressed the siege with great vigour, but was killed by a blow from a stone.

[2] Another name for Messana (or Messene), derived from the Mamertini, a people of Campania, some of whom were mercenaries in the army of the tyrant Agathocles, and were quartered in the town. At his death (B. C. 282) they rose and gained possession of it.

[3] The semi-legendary hero of the second war between Sparta and Messene. He lived about B. C. 270.

[4] The spring festival held in honour of Hyacinthus, the beautiful youth accidentally slain by Apollo, and from whose blood was said to have sprung the flower of the same name.

---

[1] He succeeded Plato as president of the Academy (B. C. 347-339). His works are all lost.

[2] One of Aristotle's pupils, and author of a number of works, none of which are extant.

[3] Diogenes Laërtius (so named from Laërte in Cilicia), who probably lived in the 2nd century after Christ, in the Third Book of his "Lives of the Philosophers" refers to a treatise by Anaxelides on the same subject. It has therefore been conjectured that Jerome may have written *Philosophica Historia* for *philosophiae*.

hilosophy, relates that Perictione, the mother f Plato, was violated by an apparition of Apollo, and they agree in thinking that the rince of wisdom was born of a virgin. [1] Timæus writes that the [2] virgin daughter of Pythagoras was at the head of a band of irgins, and instructed them in chastity. [4] Diorus, the disciple of Socrates, is said to ave had five daughters skilled in dialectics nd distinguished for chastity, of whom a ull account is given by Philo the master of Carneades. And mighty Rome cannot taunt s as though we had invented the story of the irth of our Lord and Saviour from a virgin ; r the Romans believe that the founders of heir city and race were the offspring of the irgin [6] Ilia and of Mars.

43. Let these allusions to the virgins of the orld, brief and hastily gathered from many istories, now suffice. I will proceed to maried women who were reluctant to survive the ecease or violent death of their husbands for ear they might be forced into a second mariage, and who entertained a marvellous affecion for the only husbands they had. This nay teach us that second marriage was reudiated among the heathen. Dido, the sister f Pygmalion, having collected a vast amount f gold and silver, sailed to Africa, and there uilt Carthage. And when her hand was ought in marriage by Iarbas, king of Libya, he deferred the marriage for a while until her ountry was settled. Not long after, having aised a [7] funeral pyre to the memory of her ormer husband Sichæus, she preferred to burn rather than to marry." Carthage was uilt by a woman of chastity, and its end vas a tribute to the excellence of the virtue.

For the [1] wife of Hasdrubal, when the city was captured and set on fire, and she saw that she could not herself escape capture by the Romans, took her little children in either hand and leaped into the burning ruins of her house.

44. What need to tell of the wife of [2] Niceratus, who, not enduring to wrong her husband, inflicted death upon herself rather than subject herself to the lust of the thirty tyrants whom Lysander had set over conquered Athens? [3] Artemisia, also, wife of Mausolus, is related to have been distinguished for chastity. Though she was queen of Caria, and is extolled by great poets and historians, no higher praise is bestowed upon her than that when her husband was dead she loved him as much as when he was alive, and built a tomb so great that even to the present day all costly sepulchres are called after his name, *mausoleums.* [4] Teuta, queen of the Illyrians, owed her long sway over brave warriors, and her frequent victories over Rome, to her marvellous chastity. The Indians and almost all the Barbarians have a plurality of wives. It is a law with them that the favourite wife must be burned with her dead husband. The wives therefore vie with one another for the husband's love, and the highest ambition of the rivals, and the proof of chastity, is to be considered worthy of death. So then she that is victorious, having put on her former dress and ornaments, lies down beside the corpse, embracing and kissing it, and to the glory of chastity despises the flames which are burning beneath her. I suppose that she who dies thus, wants no second marriage. The famous Alcibiades, the friend of Socrates, when Athens was conquered, fled to Pharnabazus, who took a bribe from Lysander the Lacedæmonian leader and ordered him to be slain. He was strangled, and when his head had been cut off it was sent to Lysander as proof of the murder, but the rest of his body lay unburied. His concubine, therefore, all alone, in defiance of the command of the cruel enemy, in the midst of strangers, and in the face of peril, gave him due burial, for she was ready to die for the dead man whom she had loved when living. Let matrons, Christian matrons at all events, imitate the fidelity of concubines, and

---

[1] Timæus of Locri, in Italy, a Pythagorean philosopher, is aid to have been a teacher of Plato. There is an extant work earing his name ; but its genuineness is considered doubtful, nd it is in all probability only an abridgment of Plato's diaogue of *Timæus.*

[2] Damo. Pythagoras is said to have entrusted his writings to er, and to have forbidden her to give them to any one. She rictly observed the command, although she was in extreme overty, and received many requests to sell them. According some accounts Pythagoras had another daughter, Myia.

[3] Flourished about B.C. 540-510.

[4] Clement of Alexandria (died about A.D. 220) in his *Stroata (i.e.* literally, *patchwork)* or *Miscellanies,* Bk. iv., relates he same story and gives the names of the daughters. The iodorus referred to in the text lived at Alexandria in the reign f Ptolemy Soter (B. C. 323-285), by whom he was said to have een surnamed *Cronos* or *Saturn,* on account of his inability solve *at once* some dialectic problem when dining with the ng, perhaps with a play upon the word *chronos* (time), or with sarcastic allusion to Cronos as the introducer of the arts of vilized life. The philosopher is said to have taken the disrace so much to heart, that he wrote a treatise on the problem, nd then died in despair. Another account derives his name om his teacher Apollonius Cronus.

[5] Born about B.C. 213, died B.C. 129. He was the deterined opponent of the Stoics, and maintained that neither our enses nor our understanding gives us a safe criterion of truth. B.C. 146.

[6] The poetical name of Rhea Silvia, daughter of Numitor nd mother of Romulus and Remus.

[7] According to the legend she stabbed herself on the funeral yre. Jerome ignores the modifications introduced into the gend by Virgil, who, in defiance of the common chronology, akes Dido a contemporary of Æneas, and represents her as estroying herself when forsaken by the hero.

[1] Hasdrubal and his family, with 900 deserters and desperadoes, retired into the temple of Æsculapius, as if to make a brave defence. But the commandant's heart failed him ; and, slipping out alone, he threw himself at the feet of Scipio, and craved for pardon. His wife, standing on the base of the temple, was near enough to witness the sight, and reproaching her husband with cowardice, cast herself with her children into the flames which were now wrapping the Citadel round on all sides. B.C. 146.

[2] Son of Nicias the celebrated Athenian general.

[3] She succeeded Mausolus and reigned B.C. 352-350.

[4] She was the wife of Agron, and assumed the sovereign power on the death of her husband, B.C. 231. War was declared against her by Rome in consequence of her having caused the assassination of an ambassador, and in 228 she obtained peace at the cost of the greater part of her dominions.

exhibit in their freedom what she in her captivity preserved.

45. Strato, ruler of Sidon, thought of dying by his own hand, that he might not be the sport of the Persians, who were close by and whose alliance he had discarded for the friendship of the king of Egypt. But he drew back in terror, and eying the sword which he had seized, awaited in alarm the approach of the enemy. His wife, knowing that he must be immediately taken, wrested the weapon from his hand, and pierced his side. When the body was properly laid out she lay down upon it in the agony of death, that she might not violate her virgin troth in the embraces of another. [1] Xenophon, in describing the early years of the elder Cyrus, relates that when her husband Abradatas was slain, Panthea who had loved him intensely, placed herself beside the mangled body, then stabbed herself, and let her blood run into her husband's wounds. The [2] queen whom the king her husband had shewn naked and without her knowledge to his friend, thought she had good cause for slaying the king. She judged that she was not beloved if it was possible for her to be exhibited to another. Rhodogune, daughter of Darius, after the death of her husband, put to death the nurse who was trying to persuade her to marry again. [3] Alcestis is related in story to have voluntarily died for Admetus, and Penelope's chastity is the theme of Homer's song. Laodamia's praises are also sung by the poets, because, when [4] Protesilaus was slain at Troy, she refused to survive him.

46. I may pass on to Roman women; and the first that I shall mention is [5] Lucretia, who would not survive her violated chastity, but blotted out the stain upon her person with her own blood. Duilius, the first Roman who won a [6] naval triumph, took to wife a virgin, Bilia, of such extraordinary chastity that she was an example even to an age which held unchastity to be not merely vicious but monstrous. When he was grown old and feeble he was once in the course of a quarrel taunted with having bad breath. In dudgeon he betook himself home, and on complaining to his wife that she had never told him of it so that he might remedy

the fault, he received the reply that she would have done so, but she thought that all men had foul breath as he had. In either case this chaste and noble woman deserves praise, whether she was not aware there was anything wrong with her husband, or if she patiently endured and her husband discovered his unfortunate condition not by the disgust of a wife, but by the abuse of an enemy. At all events the woman who marries a second time cannot say this. Marcia, Cato's younger daughter, on being asked after the loss of her husband why she did not marry again, replied that she could not find a man who wanted her more than her money. Her words teach us that men in choosing their wives look for riches rather than for chastity, and that many in marrying use not their eyes but their fingers. That *must* be an excellent thing which is won by avarice! When the same lady was mourning the loss of her husband, and the matrons asked what day would terminate her grief, she replied, "The same that terminates my life." imagine that a woman who thus followed her husband in heart and mind had no thought of marrying again. Porcia, whom [1] Brutus took to wife, was a virgin; Cato's wife, [2] Marcia was not a virgin; but Marcia went to and fro between Hortensius and Cato, and was quite content to live without Cato; while [3] Porcia could not live without Brutus; for women attach themselves closely to particular men and to keep to one is a strong link in the chain of affection. When a relative urged Annia to marry again (she was of full age and a goodly person), she answered, "I shall certainly not do so. For, if I find a good man, I have no wish to be in fear of losing him: if a bad one why must I put up with a bad husband after having had a good one?" [4] Porcia the younger, on hearing a certain lady of good character, who had a second husband, praised in her house, replied, "A chaste and happy matron never marries more than once." Marcella the elder, on being asked by her mother if she was glad she was married, answered "So much so that I want nothing more." [5] Valeria, sister of the Messalas, when she lost her husband Servius, would marry no one else

---

[1] Cyropædeia, Book vii.
[2] The wife of Candaules, also called Myrsilus. She was exhibited to Gyges, who, after the murder of her husband, married her. Herod. B. i.
[3] The story, as is well known, formed the subject of the play by Euripides bearing the heroine's name, which was brought out about B.C. 438.
[4] Protesilaus was the first of the Greeks to fall at Troy. According to some accounts he was slain by Hector. When her husband was slain Laodamia begged the gods to allow her to converse with him for only 3 hours. The request having been granted, Hermes led Protesilaus back to the upper world, and when he died a second time, Laodamia died with him.
[5] The wife of L. Tarquinius Collatinus, whose rape by Sextus led to the dethronement of Tarquinius Superbus and the establishment of the republic.
[6] Over the Carthaginian fleet near Mylæ, 260 B.C.

[1] One of the assassins of Julius Cæsar. Jerome appears to be at fault here. *Porcia*, the daughter of Cato by his first wife Atilia, before marrying Brutus in 45 B.C., had been married to M. Bibulus and had borne him three children. He died in 48. After the death of Brutus in 42 she put an end to her own life probably by the fumes of a charcoal fire.
[2] Marcia is related to have been ceded by Cato to his friend Hortensius. She continued to live with the latter until his death, when she returned to Cato.
[3] It has been conjectured that instead of "Marcia, Cato's younger daughter," a few lines above, we should read *Porcia*.
[4] Probably the daughter of Cato by his second wife Marcia.
[5] Jerome, apparently, makes a mistake here. Valeria, sister of the Messalas, married Sulla towards the end of his life. Valeria, the widow of Galerius, after the death of her husband in 311, rejected the proposals of Maximinus. Her consequent sufferings are related by Gibbon in his fourteenth chapter.

On being asked why not, she said that to her, her husband Servius was ever alive.

47. I feel that in giving this list of women I have said far more than is customary in illustrating a point, and that I might be justly censured by my learned reader. But what am I to do when the women of our time press me with apostolic authority, and before the first husband is buried, repeat from morning to night the precepts which allow a second marriage? Seeing they despise the fidelity which Christian purity dictates, let them at least learn chastity from the heathen. A book *On Marriage*, worth its weight in gold, passes under the name of [1] Theophrastus. In it the author asks whether a wise man marries. And after laying down the conditions—that the wife must be fair, of good character, and honest parentage, the husband in good health and of ample means, and after saying that under these circumstances a wise man sometimes enters the state of matrimony, he immediately proceeds thus: "But all these conditions are seldom satisfied in marriage. A wise man therefore must not take a wife. For in the first place his study of philosophy will be hindered, and it is impossible for anyone to attend to his books and his wife. Matrons want many things, costly dresses, gold, jewels, great outlay, maid-servants, all kinds of furniture, litters and gilded coaches. Then come curtain-lectures the livelong night: she complains that one lady goes out better dressed than she: that another is looked up to by all: 'I am a poor despised nobody at the ladies' assemblies.' 'Why did you ogle that creature next door?' 'Why were you talking to the maid?' 'What did you bring from the market?' 'I am not allowed to have a single friend, or companion.' She suspects that her husband's love goes the same way as her hate. There may be in some neighbouring city the wisest of teachers; but if we have a wife we can neither leave her behind, nor take the burden with us. To support a poor wife, is hard: to put up with a rich one, is torture. Notice, too, that in the case of a wife you cannot pick and choose: you must take her as you find her. If she has a bad temper, or is a fool, if she has a blemish, or is proud, or has bad breath, whatever her fault may be—all this we learn after marriage. Horses, asses, cattle, even slaves of the smallest worth, clothes, kettles, wooden seats, cups, and earthenware pitchers, are first tried and then bought: a wife is the only thing that is not shown before she is married, for fear she may not give satisfaction.

Our gaze must always be directed to her face, and we must always praise her beauty: if you look at another woman, she thinks that she is out of favour. She must be called my lady, her birth-day must be kept, we must swear by her health and wish that she may survive us, respect must be paid to the nurse, to the nurse-maid, to the father's slave, to the foster-child, to the handsome hanger-on, to the curled darling who manages her affairs, and to the eunuch who ministers to the safe indulgence of her lust: names which are only a cloak for adultery. Upon whomsoever she sets her heart, they must have her love though they want her not. If you give her the management of the whole house, you must yourself be her slave. If you reserve something for yourself, she will not think you are loyal to her; but she will turn to strife and hatred, and unless you quickly take care, she will have the poison ready. If you introduce old women, and soothsayers, and prophets, and vendors of jewels and silken clothing, you imperil her chastity; if you shut the door upon them, she is injured and fancies you suspect her. But what is the good of even a careful guardian, when an unchaste wife cannot be watched, and a chaste one ought not to be? For necessity is but a faithless keeper of chastity, and she alone really deserves to be called pure, who is free to sin if she chooses. If a woman be fair, she soon finds lovers; if she be ugly, it is easy to be wanton. It is difficult to guard what many long for. It is annoying to have what no one thinks worth possessing. But the misery of having an ugly wife is less than that of watching a comely one. Nothing is safe, for which a whole people sighs and longs. One man entices with his figure, another with his brains, another with his wit, another with his open hand. Somehow, or sometime, the fortress is captured which is attacked on all sides. Men marry, indeed, so as to get a manager for the house, to solace weariness, to banish solitude; but a faithful slave is a far better manager, more submissive to the master, more observant of his ways, than a wife who thinks she proves herself mistress if she acts in opposition to her husband, that is, if she does what pleases her, not what she is commanded. But friends, and servants who are under the obligation of benefits received, are better able to wait upon us in sickness than a wife who makes us responsible for her tears (she will sell you enough to make a deluge for the hope of a legacy), boasts of her anxiety, but drives her sick husband to the distraction of despair. But if she herself is poorly, we must fall sick with her and never leave her bedside. Or if she be a good and agreeable wife (how rare a bird she is!), we have to share

---

[1] The Greek philosopher to whom Aristotle bequeathed his library and the originals of his own writings. He died B.C. 287, after being President of the Academy for 35 years. If he were the author of the book here referred to, it is not to be found among his extant writings.

her groans in childbirth, and suffer torture when she is in danger. A wise man can never be alone. He has with him the good men of all time, and turns his mind freely wherever he chooses. What is inaccessible to him in person he can embrace in thought. And, if men are scarce, he converses with God. [1] He is never less alone than when alone. Then again, to marry for the sake of children, so that our name may not perish, or that we may have support in old age, and leave our property without dispute, is the height of stupidity. For what is it to us when we are leaving the world if another bears our name, when even a son does not all at once take his father's title, and there are countless others who are called by the same name. Or what support in old age is he whom you bring up, and who may die before you, or turn out a reprobate? Or at all events when he reaches mature age, you may seem to him long in dying. Friends and relatives whom you can judiciously love are better and safer heirs than those whom you must make your heirs whether you like it or not. Indeed, the surest way of having a good heir is to ruin your fortune in a good cause while you live, not to leave the fruit of your labour to be used you know not how."

48. When Theophrastus thus discourses, are there any of us, Christians, whose conversation is in heaven and who daily say [2] "I long to be dissolved, and to be with Christ," whom he does not put to the blush? Shall a joint-heir of Christ really long for human heirs? And shall he desire children and delight himself in a long line of descendants, who will perhaps fall into the clutches of Antichrist, when we read that [3] Moses and [4] Samuel preferred other men to their own sons, and did not count as their children those whom they saw to be displeasing to God? When Cicero after [5] divorcing Terentia was requested by [6] Hirtius to marry his sister, he [7] set the matter

altogether on one side, and said that he coul[d] not possibly devote himself to a wife and t[o] philosophy. Meanwhile that excellent partne[r] who had herself drunk wisdom at Tully's foun[n]tains, married [1] Sallust his enemy, and took fo[r] her third husband Messala Corvinus, and thu[s] as it were, passed through three degrees o[f] eloquence. Socrates had two wives, Xantipp[e] and Myron, grand-daughter of Aristides[.] They frequently quarrelled, and he was ac[c]customed to banter them for disagreeing abou[t] him, he being the ugliest of men, with snu[b] nose, bald forehead, rough-haired, and bandy[-] legged. At last they planned an attack upo[n] him, and having punished him severely, an[d] put him to flight, vexed him for a long time[.] On one occasion when he opposed Xantipp[e] who from above was heaping abuse upon hi[m] the termagant soused him with dirty wate[r] but he only wiped his head and said, " [I] knew that a shower must follow such thunde[r] as that." [2] Metella, consort of L. Sulla th[e] [3] Fortunate (except in the matter of hi[s] wife) was [4] openly unchaste. It was th[e] common talk of Athens, as I learnt in m[y] youthful years when we soon pick up what i[s] bad, and yet Sulla was in the dark, and firs[t] got to know the secrets of his househol[d] through the abuse of his enemies. Cn. Pompe[y] had an impure wife [5] Mucia, who was sur[r]ounded by eunuchs from Pontus and troop[s] of the countrymen of Mithridates. Other[s] thought that he knew all and submitted to it[,] but a comrade told him during the campaig[n] and the conqueror of the whole world wa[s] dismayed at the sad intelligence. [6] M. Cat[o] the Censor, had a wife Actoria Paula, a woma[n] of low origin, fond of drink, violent, and (wh[o] would believe it?) haughty to Cato. I sa[y] this for fear anyone may suppose that in mar[r]ying a poor woman he has secured peac[e] When [7] Philip king of Macedon, against who[m] [8] Demosthenes thundered in his Philippic[s] was entering his bed-room as usual, his wif[e]

---

[1] Cicero at the beginning of the third book of the *De Officiis*, makes Cato quote this saying as one frequently in the mouth of Publius Scipio.

[2] Phil. i. 23.

[3] We hear very little of the two sons of Moses, Gershom and Eliezer. See Ex. iv. 20, xviii. 3, 1 Chron. xxiii. 14. Their promotion is nowhere recorded, and Moses appointed a person of another tribe to be his successor.

[4] See 1 Sam. viii. 1-4 and ch. ix.

[5] B.C. 46. "What grounds for displeasure she had given him besides her alleged extravagance it is hard to say. His letters to her during the previous year had been short and rather cold." Watson, Select Letters of Cicero, third ed. p. 397.

[6] Hirtius was the friend personal and political of Julius Cæsar, and during Cæsar's absence in Africa he lived principally at his Tusculan estate which adjoined Cicero's villa. Hirtius and Cicero though opposed to each other in politics were on good terms, and the former is said to have received lessons in oratory from the latter.

[7] But not long after divorcing Terentia he married Publilia, a young girl of whose property he had the management, in order to relieve himself from pecuniary difficulties. She seems to have received little affection from her husband. Watson, p. 397.

[1] This statement is without authority. See Long's Article o[n] Sallust in Smith's Dict. of Classical Biography.

[2] Cæcilia Metella, the third of Sulla's five wives, had pre[-]viously been married to M. Æmilius Scaurus, consul B.C. 11[5?] She fell ill during the celebration of Sulla's triumph on accoun[t] of his victory over Mithridates in 81; and as her recovery wa[s] hopeless, Sulla for religious reasons divorced her. She soo[n] afterwards died, and Sulla honoured her memory with a splendi[d] funeral.

[3] The famous dictator claimed the name *Felix* for himself i[n] a speech which he delivered to the people at the close of th[e] celebration of his triumph, because he attributed his success i[n] life to the favour of the gods.

[4] But Sulla's youth and manhood were disgraced by the mo[st] sensual vices. He was indebted for a considerable portion o[f] his wealth to a courtesan Nicopolis, and his death in B.C. 78 a[t] the age of 60 was hastened by his dissolute mode of life.

[5] Pompey, like Sulla, was married five times. Mucia, h[is] third wife, daughter of Q. Mucius Scævola, the augur, cons[ul] B.C. 95, was divorced by Pompey in 62, and afterwards marrie[d] M. Æmilius Scaurus, son of the consul by Cæcilia and th[e] stepson of Sulla.

[6] Born B.C. 234. died B.C. 149. He was the great-gran[d]father of Cato of Utica.

[7] B.C. 382-336.   [8] B.C. 385-322.

a passion shut him out. Finding himself excluded he held his tongue, and consoled himself for the insult by reading a tragic poem. Gorgias the Rhetorician recited his excellent treatise on Concord to the Greeks, then at variance among themselves, at Olympia. Thereupon [2] Melanthius his enemy observed: "Here is a man who teaches us concord, and yet could not make concord between himself, his wife, and maid-servant, three persons in one house." The truth was that his wife envied the beauty of the girl, and drove the purest of men wild with daily quarrels. Whole tragedies of Euripides are censures on women. Hence Hermione says,[3] "The counsels of evil omen have beguiled me." In the semi-barbarous and remote city [4] Leptis it is the custom for a daughter-in-law on [5] the second day to beg the loan of a jar from her mother-in-law. The latter at once denies the request, and we see how true was the remark of [6] Terence, ambiguously expressed on purpose: "How is this? do all mothers-in-law hate their daughters-in-law?" We read of a certain Roman noble who, when his friends found fault with him for having divorced a wife, beautiful, chaste, and rich, put out his foot and said to them, "And the shoe before you looks new and elegant, yet no one but myself knows where it pinches." Herodotus [7] tells us that a woman puts off her modesty with her clothes. And our own comic poet [8] thinks the man fortunate who has never been married. Why should I refer to Pasiphaë,[9] Clytemnestra, and Eriphyle, the first of whom, the wife of a king and swimming in pleasure, is said to have lusted for a bull, the second to have killed her husband for the sake of an adulterer, the third to have betrayed Amphiaraus, and to have preferred a gold necklace to the welfare of her husband. In all the bombast of tragedy and the overthrow of houses, cities, and kingdoms, it is the wives and concubines who stir up strife. Parents take up arms against their children: unspeakable banquets are served: and on account of the rape of one wretched woman Europe and Asia are involved in a ten

years' war. We read of some who were divorced the day after they were married, and immediately married again. Both husbands are to blame, both he who was so soon dissatisfied, and he who was so soon pleased. Epicurus the patron of pleasure (though [1] Metrodorus his disciple married Leontia) says that a wise man can seldom marry, because marriage has many drawbacks. And as riches, honours, bodily health, and other things which we call indifferent, are neither good nor bad, but stand as it were midway, and become good and bad according to the use and issue, so wives stand on the border line of good and ill. It is, moreover, a serious matter for a wise man to be in doubt whether he is going to marry a good or a bad woman. [2] Chrysippus ridiculously maintains that a wise man should marry, that he may not outrage Jupiter [3] Gamelius and Genethlius. For upon that principle the Latins would not marry at all, since they have no Jupiter who presides over marriage. But if, as he thinks, the life of men is determined by the names of gods, whoever chooses to sit will offend Jupiter [4] Stator.

49. Aristotle and Plutarch and our Seneca have written treatises on matrimony, out of which we have already made some extracts and now add a few more. "The love of beauty is the forgetting of reason and the near neighbour of madness; a foul blot little in keeping with a sound mind. It confuses counsel, breaks high and generous spirits, draws away men from great thoughts to mean ones; it makes men querulous, ill-tempered, foolhardy, cruelly imperious, servile flatterers, good for nothing, at last not even for love itself. For although in the intensity of passion it burns like a raging fire, it wastes much time through suspicions, tears, and complaints: it begets hatred of itself, and at last hates itself." The course of love is laid bare in Plato's Phædrus from beginning to end, and Lysias explains all its drawbacks—how it is led not by reason, but by frenzy, and in particular is a harsh gaoler over lovely wives. Seneca, too, relates that he knew an accomplished man who before going out used to tie

---

[1] Born about B.C. 480 at Leontini in Sicily. He is said to have lived 105, or even 109 years. He was held in high esteem at Athens, where he had numerous distinguished pupils and imitators.
[2] An Athenian tragic poet, celebrated for his wit.
[3] See the *Andromache*.
[4] There were two cities of this name, Leptis *Magna* and Leptis *Parva*, in N. Africa.
[5] Or "on another day," that is, than the marriage day implied in the context.
[6] Terence, Hecyra II. i. 4.
[7] Bk. I. ch. 8. "Candaules addressed Gyges as follows: Gyges, as I think you do not believe me when I speak of my wife's beauty (for the ears of men are naturally more incredulous than their eyes), you must contrive to see her naked.' But , exclaiming loudly, answered: 'Sire, what a shocking proposal do you make, bidding me behold my queen naked! With her clothes a woman puts off her modesty,' " etc.
[8] Perhaps Terence, Phormio I. iii. 21.
[9] For these legends, see Classical Dict.

[1] The most distinguished disciple and the intimate friend of Epicurus. His philosophy appears to have been of a more sensual kind than that of his master. He made perfect happiness to consist in having a well-constituted body. He died B.C. 277 in the 53rd year of his age, 7 years before Epicurus.
[2] Chrysippus (B.C. 280-207) the Stoic philosopher, born at Soli in Cilicia. He opposed the prevailing scepticism and maintained the possibility of attaining certain knowledge. It was said of him "that if Chrysippus had not existed the Porch (*i.e.,* Stoicism) could not have been." He is reported to have seldom written less than 500 lines a-day, and to have left behind him 705 works.
[3] That is Zeus, regarded as presiding over marriages and the tutelary god of races or families.
[4] Literally, "Jupiter who causes to stand": hence Jerome's play upon the word. Jupiter Stator was the god regarded as supporting, preserving, etc. Cic., Cat. I. 13, 31—" quem (sc. Jovem) statorem hujus urbis atque imperii vere nominamus."

his wife's garter upon his breast, and could not bear to be absent from her for a quarter of an hour; and this pair would never take a drink unless husband and wife alternately put their lips to the cup; and they did other things just as absurd in the extravagant outbursts of their warm but blind affection. Their love was of honourable birth, but it grew out of all proportion. And it makes no difference how honourable may be the cause of a man's insanity. Hence [1] Xystus in his Sentences tells us that "He who too ardently loves his own wife is an adulterer." It is disgraceful to love another man's wife at all, or one's own too much. A wise man ought to love his wife with judgment, not with passion. Let a man govern his voluptuous impulses, and not rush headlong into intercourse. There is nothing blacker than to love a wife as if she were an adulteress. Men who say they have contracted marriage and are bringing up children, for the good of their country and of the race, should at least imitate the brutes, and not destroy their offspring in the womb; nor should they appear in the character of lovers, but of husbands. In some cases marriage has grown out of adultery: and, shameful to relate! men have tried to teach their wives chastity after having taken their chastity away. Marriages of that sort are quickly dissolved when lust is satiated. The first allurement gone, the charm is lost. What shall I say, says Seneca, of the poor men who in numbers are bribed to take the name of husband in order to evade the laws promulgated against bachelors? How can he who is married under such conditions be a guide to morality, teach chastity, and maintain the authority of a husband? It is the saying of a very learned man, that chastity must be preserved at all costs, and that when it is lost all virtue falls to the ground. This holds the primacy of all virtues in woman. This it is that makes up for a wife's poverty, enhances her riches, redeems her deformity, gives grace to her beauty; it makes her act in a way worthy of her forefathers whose blood it does not taint with bastard offspring; of her children, who through it have no need to blush for their mother, or to be in doubt about their

father; and above all, of herself, since it defends her from external violation. There no greater calamity connected with captivi than to be the victim of another's lust. Th consulship sheds lustre upon men; eloquen gives eternal renown; military glory ar a triumph immortalise an obscure famil Many are the spheres ennobled by splend ability. The virtue of woman is, in a speci sense, purity. It was this that made [1] Lucret the equal of Brutus, if it did not make her h superior, since Brutus learnt from a woman th impossibility of being a slave. It was th that made [2] Cornelia a fit match for Gracchu and [3] Porcia for a second Brutus. [4] Tanaqu is better known than her husband. His nam like the names of many other kings, is lost the mists of antiquity. She, through a virtu rare among women, is too deeply rooted in th hearts of all ages for her memory ever perish. Let my married sisters copy the e. amples of [5] Theano, [6] Cleobuline, Gorgent [7] Timoclia, the [8] Claudias and Cornelias; ar when they find the Apostle conceding secon marriage to depraved women, they will rea that before the light of our religion sho upon the world wives of one husband ev held high rank among matrons, that by the hands the sacred rites of Fortuna [9] Muliebr were performed, that a priest or [10] Flame twice [11] married was unknown, that the hig priests of Athens to this day[12] emasculate ther selves by drinking hemlock, and once the have been drawn in to the pontificate, cea to be men.

---

[1] See note above, p. 382.
[2] Daughter of P. Scipio Africanus, and wife of Ti. Semproni Gracchus, censor B.C. 169. The people erected a statue to h with the inscription "Cornelia, mother of the Gracchi."
[3] See note p. 376.
[5] Theano was the most celebrated of the female philosophe of the Pythagorean school. According to some authorities s was the wife of Pythagoras.
[6] Cleobuline, or Cleobule, was celebrated for her riddles hexameter verse. One on the subject of the year runs thus "A father has 12 children, and each of these 30 daughters, one side white, and on the other side black, and though i mortal they all die."
[7] Timoclia was a woman of Thebes, whose house at the captu of the city in B.C. 335 was broken into and pillaged by t soldiery. She was herself violated by the commander, who she afterwards contrived to push into a well.
[8] A vestal virgin who proved her innocence of the unchasti imputed to her by setting free a stranded ship with her girdle
[9] The epithet is said to have been given to the goddess at t time when Coriolanus was prevented by the entreaties of t *women* from destroying Rome.
[10] The name for any Roman priest devoted to the service one particular god. He took his distinguishing title from t deity to whom he ministered, *e.g. Flamen Martialis.*
[11] Comp. Tertullian *De Monogamia*, last chapter—"F tunæ, inquit, muliebri coronam non imponit, nisi univira . Pontifex Maximus et Flaminica (the wife of a Flamen) nubu semel."
[12] See Origen, *Contra Celsum*, Bk. VII. The water hemloc or cowbane, is the variety referred to.

---

[1] The greater number of manuscripts read *Sextus*, an alternative name for the same person. Jerome in his version of the *Chronicon* of Eusebius speaks of "Xystus a Pythagorean philosopher" who flourished at the time of Christ's birth; but there is great difficulty in establishing the identity of the author of the "Sentences." See also the Prolegomena to Rufinus who translated the Sentences of Xystus, in Vol. III. of this Series.

Book II.

Jerome answers the second, third, and fourth propositions of Jovinianus.

I. (c. 1–4). That those who have become regenerate cannot be overthrown by the devil. Jerome (c. 1) puts it at they cannot be *tempted* by the devil. He quotes 1 John i. 8–ii. 2, as shewing that faithful men can be tempted d sin and need an advocate. The expressions (3) in Heb. vi. as to those who crucify the Son of God afresh not apply to ordinary sins after baptism, as supposed by Montanus and Novatus. The epistles to the Seven urches shew that the lapsed may return. The Angels, and even our Lord Himself, (4) could be tempted.

II. (c. 5–17). That there is no difference (morally) between one who fasts and one who takes food with anksgiving. Jovinian has quoted (5) many texts of Scripture to shew that God has made animals for men's d. But (6) there are many other uses of animals besides food. And there are many warnings like 1 Cor. vi. , as to the danger arising from food. There are among the heathen (7) many instances of abstinence. They ognize (8) the evil of sensual allurements, and often, like Crates the Theban, (9) have cast away what would npt them; the senses, they teach, (10) should be subject to reason; and, that (11) except for athletes (Chris- ns do not want to be like Milo of Crotona) bread and water suffice. Horace (12), Xenophon and other eminent eeks (13), the Essenes and the Brahmans (14), as well as philosophers like Diogenes, testify to the value of stinence. The Old Testament stories (15) of Esau's pottage, of the lusting of Israel for the flesh-pots of ypt, and those in the New Testament of Anna, Cornelius, &c., commend abstinence. If some heretics culcate fasting (16) in such a way as to despise the gifts of God, and weak Christians are not to be judged for eir use of flesh, those who seek the higher life (17) will find a help in abstinence.

III. (c. 18–34). The fourth proposition of Jovinianus, that all who are saved will have equal reward, is refuted) by the various yields of thirty, sixty, and a hundred fold in the parable of the sower, by (20) the "stars differ- g in glory" of 1 Cor. xv. 41. It is strange (21) to find the advocate of self-indulgence now claiming equality the saints. But (22) as there were differences in Ezekiel between cattle and cattle, so in St. Paul between ose who built gold or stubble on the one foundation. The differences of gifts (23), of punishments (24), of lt (25), as in Pilate and the Chief Priests, of the produce of the good seed (26), of the mansions promised heaven (27–29), of the judgment upon sins both in the church and in Scripture (30–31), of those called at ferent times to the vineyard (32) are arguments for the diversity of rewards. The parable of the talents (33) ds out as rewards differences of station, and so does the church (34) in its different orders.

Jerome now recapitulates (35) and appeals (36) against the licentious views of Jovinianus, which have already uced many virgins to break their vows; and which, as the new Roman heresy (37), he calls upon the Imperial ty (38) to reject.

1. The second proposition of Jovinianus is at the baptized cannot be tempted [1] by the vil. And to escape the imputation of folly saying this, he adds: "But if any are mpted, it only shows that they were baptized th water, not with the Spirit, as we read was e case with Simon Magus." Hence it is that hn says,[2] "Whosoever is begotten of God eth no sin, because his seed abideth in him : d he cannot sin, because he is begotten of od. In this the children of God are manifest, d the children of the Devil." And at the end the Epistle,[3] "Whosoever is begotten of God neth not; but his being begotten of God epeth him, and the evil one toucheth him t."

2. This would be a real difficulty and one ever incapable of solution were it not lved by the witness of John himself, who mediately goes on to say, [4] "My little chil- en, guard yourselves from idols." If every- e that is born of God sinneth not, and can- t be tempted by the devil, how is it that he ds them beware of temptation? Again in e same Epistle we read : [5] "If we say that have no sins, we deceive ourselves, and the th is not in us. If we confess our sins, he faithful and just to forgive us our sins, and to cleanse us from all unrighteousness. If we say that we have not sinned, we make him a liar, and his word is not in us." I suppose that John was baptized and was writing to the baptized : I imagine too that all sin is of the devil. Now John confesses himself a sinner, and hopes for forgiveness of sins after bap- tism. My friend Jovinianus says, [1] "Touch me not, for I am clean." What then? Does the Apostle contradict himself? By no means. In the same passage he gives his reason for thus speaking: [2] "My little children, these things write I unto you, that ye may not sin. But if any man sin, we have an advocate with the Father, Jesus Christ the righteous: and he is the propitiation for our sins; and not for ours only, but also for the whole world. And hereby know we that we know him, if we keep his commandments. He that saith, I know him, and keepeth not his command- ments, is a liar, and the truth is not in him. But whoso keepeth his word, in him verily hath the love of God been perfected. Hereby know we that we are in him : he that saith he abideth in him ought himself also to walk even as he walked." My reason for telling you, little children, that everyone who is born of God sinneth not, is that you may not sin, and

---

This, according to i. 3, is "cannot be overthrown."
1 John iii. 9, 10.   [3] 1 John v. 18.
1 John v. 21.   [5] 1 John i. 8, sq.

[1] Is. lxv. 5. Quoted from memory. The LXX. and Vulg. have like A. V. and Rev., "Come not near me."
[2] 1 John ii. 1.

that you may know that so long as you sin not you abide in the birth which God has given you. Yea, they who abide in that birth cannot sin. [1] "For what communion hath light with darkness? Or Christ with Belial?" As day is distinct from night, so righteousness and unrighteousness, sin and good works, Christ and Antichrist cannot blend. If we give Christ a lodging-place in our hearts, we banish the devil from thence. If we sin and the devil enter through the gate of sin, Christ will immediately withdraw. Hence David after sinning says: [2] "Restore unto me the joy of thy salvation," that is, the joy which he had lost by sinning. [3] "He who saith, I know him, and keepeth not his commandments, is a liar, and the truth is not in him." Christ is called the truth: [4] "I am the way, the truth, and the life." In vain do we make our boast in him whose commandments we keep not. To him that knoweth what is good, and doeth it not, it is sin. [5] "As the body apart from the spirit is dead, even so faith apart from works is dead." And we must not think it a great matter to know the only God, when even devils believe and tremble. "He that saith he abideth in him ought himself also to walk even as he walked." Our opponent may choose whichever of the two he likes; we give him his choice. Does he abide in Christ, or not? If he abide, let him then walk as Christ walked. But if there is [6] rashness in professing to copy the virtues of our Lord, he does not abide in Christ, for he does not walk as did Christ. [7] "He did not sin, neither was guile found in his mouth: when he was reviled, he reviled not again, and as a lamb is dumb before its shearer, so opened he not his mouth." To Him came the prince of this world, and found nothing in Him; although He had done no sin, God made Him sin for us. But we, according to the Epistle of James, [8] "all stumble in many things," and [9] "no one is pure from sin, no not if his life be but a day long." [10] For who will boast "that he has a clean heart? or who will be sure that he is pure from sin?" And we are held guilty after the similitude of Adam's transgression. Hence David says, [11] "Behold, I was shapen in iniquity, and in sin did my mother conceive me." And the blessed Job, [12] "Though I be righteous my mouth will speak wickedness, and though I be perfect, I shall be found perverse. If I wash myself with snow water and make my hands never so clean, yet wilt thou plunge me in the ditch and mine own clothes shall abhor me." But that we may not utterly despair and think that if we sin after baptism we cannot be saved, he immediately checks the tendency: [1] "And if any man sin, we have an advocate with the Father, Jesus Christ the righteous, and he is the propitiation for our sins. And not for ours only, but also for the whole world." He addresses this to baptized believers, and he promises them the Lord as an advocate for their offences. He does not say: If you fall into sin, you have an advocate with the Father, Christ, and He the propitiation for your sins: you might then say that he was addressing those whose baptism had been destitute of the true faith: but what he says is this, "We have an advocate with the Father, Jesus Christ, and he is the propitiation for our sins." And not only for the sins of John and his contemporaries, but for those of the whole world. Now in "the whole world" are included apostles and all the faithful, and a clear proof is established that sin after baptism is possible. It is useless for us to have an advocate Jesus Christ if sin be impossible.

3. The apostle Peter, to whom it was said [2] "He that is bathed needeth not to wash again," and [3] "Thou art Peter, and upon this rock I will build my Church," through fear of a maid-servant denied Him. Our Lord himself says, [4] "Simon, Simon, behold Satan asketh to have you, that he might sift you as wheat. But I made supplication for thee, that thy faith fail not." And in the same place, "Watch and pray, that ye enter not into temptation: the spirit indeed is willing, but the flesh is weak." If you reply that this was said before the Passion, we certainly say after the Passion, in the Lord's prayer, [5] "Forgive us our debts, as we also forgive our debtors and lead us not into temptation, but deliver us from the evil one." If we do not sin after baptism, why do we ask that we may be forgiven our sins, which were already forgiven in baptism? Why do we pray that we may not enter into temptation, and that we may be delivered from the evil one, if the devil cannot tempt those who are baptized? The case is different if this prayer belongs to the Catechumens and is not adapted to faithful Christians. Paul, the chosen vessel, [6] chastised his body and brought it into subjection, lest after preaching to others he himself should be found reprobate, and [7] he tells that there was given to him "a thorn in the flesh, a messenger

---

[1] 2 Cor. vi. 14, 15. [2] Ps. li. 12. [3] 1 John ii. 4.
[4] John xiv. 6. [5] James ii. 26.
[6] Jerome is perhaps hinting at the opinions of Jovinianus, that there was no other distinction between men than the grand division into righteous and wicked, and drawing from this the inference that whoever had been truly baptized had nothing further to gain by progress in the Christian life.
[7] 1 Peter ii. 22. [8] James iii. 2.
[9] Job xiv. 4, 5. Sept. [10] Prov. xx. 9.
[11] Ps. li. 5. [12] Job ix. 20, 30. Sept.

[1] 1 John ii. 1, 2. [2] S. John xiii. 10.
[3] S. Matt. xvi. 18. [4] S. Luke xxi. 31.
[5] S. Matt. vi. 12. [6] 1 Cor. ix. 27.
[7] 2 Cor. xii. 7.

...tan to buffet" him. And to the Corinthians
he writes: [1] "I fear, lest by any means, as the
serpent beguiled Eve in his craftiness, your
minds should be corrupted from the simplicity that is toward Christ." And elsewhere:
"But to whom ye forgive anything, I forgive
also: for what I also have forgiven, if I have
forgiven anything, for your sakes have I forgiven it in the person of Christ: that no advantage may be gained over us by Satan: for
we are not ignorant of his devices." And
again: [3] "There hath no temptation taken
you, but such as man can bear; but God is
faithful, who will not suffer you to be tempted
above that ye are able; but will with the
temptation make also the way of escape, that
ye may be able to endure it." And, [4] "Let
him that thinketh he standeth, take heed lest
he fall." And to the Galatians: [5] "Ye were
running well; who did hinder you that ye
should not obey the truth?" And elsewhere:
"We would fain have come unto you, I Paul
once and again; and Satan hindered us."
And to the married he says: [7] "Be together
again, that Satan tempt you not because of
your incontinency." And again: [8] "But I
say, walk by the Spirit and ye shall not fulfil
the lust of the flesh. For the flesh lusteth
against the Spirit, and the Spirit against the
flesh; for these are contrary the one to the
other: that ye may not do the things that ye
would." We are a compound of the two, and
must endure the strife of the two substances.
And to the Ephesians: [9] "Our wrestling is
not against flesh and blood, but against the
principalities, against the powers, against the
world-rulers of this darkness, against the spir-
tual hosts of wickedness in the heavenly
places." Does any one think that we are safe,
and that it is right to fall asleep when once we
have been baptized? And so, too, in the epistle
to the Hebrews: [10] "For as touching those who
were once enlightened and tasted of the heavenly gift, and were made partakers of the Holy
Ghost, and tasted the good word of God, and
the powers of the age to come, and then fell
away, it is impossible to renew them again
into repentance; seeing they crucify to themselves the Son of God afresh, and put him to
an open shame." Surely we cannot deny that
they have been baptized who have been illu-
minated, and have tasted the heavenly gift, and
have been made partakers of the Holy Spirit,
and have tasted the good word of God. But
if the baptized cannot sin, how is it now that
the Apostle says, "And have fallen away"?

[1] Montanus and [2] Novatus would smile at
this, for they contend that it is impossible to
renew again through repentance those who
have crucified to themselves the Son of God,
and put Him to an open shame. He therefore corrects this mistake by saying: [3] "But,
beloved, we are persuaded better things of
you, and things that accompany salvation,
though we thus speak; for God is not unrighteous to forget your work and the love
which ye shewed towards his name, in that ye
ministered unto the Saints, and still do minister." And truly the unrighteousness of God
would be great, if He merely punished sin,
and did not welcome good works. I have so
spoken, says the Apostle, to withdraw you
from your sins, and to make you more careful
through fear of despair. But, beloved, I am
persuaded better things of you, and things
that accompany salvation. For it is not accordant with the righteousness of God to forget good works, and the fact that you have
ministered and do minister to the Saints for
His name's sake, and to remember sins only.
The Apostle James also, knowing that the
baptized can be tempted, and fall of their own
free choice, says: [4] "Blessed is the man that
endureth temptation: for when he hath been
approved, he shall receive the crown of life,
which the Lord promised to them that love
him." And that we may not think that we
are tempted by God, as we read in Genesis
Abraham was, he adds: "Let no man say
when he is tempted, I am tempted of God:
for God cannot be tempted with evil, and He
Himself tempteth no man. But each man is
tempted when he is drawn away by his own lust
and enticed. Then the lust, when it hath conceived, beareth sin: and the sin, when it is
full grown, bringeth forth death." God created us with free will, and we are not forced
by necessity either to virtue or to vice. Otherwise, if there be necessity, there is no crown.
As in good works it is God who brings them
to perfection, for it is not of him that willeth,

[1] Various dates, ranging between A.D. 126 and A.D. 173, are
assigned to the origin of Montanism. In addition to the tenet, that
the church has no power to remit sin after baptism (though the
power was claimed for the Montanistic prophets) and that some
sins exclude for ever from the communion of the saints on earth,
although the mercy of God may be extended to them hereafter,
Montanus held second marriages to be no better than adultery,
proscribed military service and secular life in general, denounced profane learning and amusements of every kind, advocated extreme simplicity of female dress, practised frequent and
severe fasting, and inculcated the most rigorous asceticism. The
sect produced a great effect on the church and lasted until the
sixth century. As is well known, Tertullian in middle life
lapsed into Montanism, and he was the most distinguished of
its champions. Montanism has been described as an anticipation of the mediæval system of Rome.
[2] The *founder* of the schism which afterwards bore the
name of Novatian was Novatus, a presbyter of Carthage who
went to Rome (about A.D. 250) and there co-operated with No-
vatianus, one of the most distinguished of the clergy of that city.
The Novatianists, whose doctrines were near akin in many
respects to those of Montanists, assumed the name of *Cathari*,
or *Puritans*.
[3] Heb. vi. 9.   [4] James i. 12 sq.

[1] 2 Cor. xi. 3.   [2] 2 Cor. ii. 10, 11.
[3] 1 Cor. x. 13.   [4] 1 Cor. x. 12.
[5] Gal. v. 7.   [6] 1 Thess. ii. 18.
[7] 1 Cor. vii. 5.   [8] Gal. v. 16, 17.
[9] Eph. vi. 12.   [10] Heb. vi. 4 sq.

nor of him that runneth, but of God that piti-
eth and gives us help that we may be able to
reach the goal : so in things wicked and sinful, the seeds within us give the impulse, and
these are brought to maturity by the devil.
When he sees that we are building upon the
foundation of Christ, hay, wood, stubble, then
he applies the match. Let us then build gold,
silver, costly stones, and he will not venture
to tempt us : although even thus there is not
sure and safe possession. For the lion lurks
in ambush to slay the innocent. [1] "Potters'
vessels are proved by the furnace, and just
men by the trial of tribulation." And in another place it is written : [2] "My son, when
thou comest to serve the Lord, prepare thyself
for temptation." Again, the same James says :
[3] "Be ye doers of the word, and not hearers
only. For if any one is a hearer of the word,
and not a doer, he is like unto a man beholding his natural face in a mirror : for he beholdeth himself, and goeth away, and straightway forgetteth what manner of man he was."
It was useless to warn them to add works to
faith, if they could not sin after baptism. He
tells us that [4] "whosoever shall keep the whole
law, and yet stumble in one point, he is become guilty of all." Which of us is without
sin ? [5] "God hath shut up all unto disobedience, that he might have mercy upon all."
Peter also says : [6] "The Lord knows how to
deliver the godly out of temptation." And
concerning false teachers : [7] "These are
springs without water, and mists driven by a
storm ; for whom the blackness of darkness
hath been reserved. For, uttering proud words
of vanity, they entice in the lusts of the flesh,
by lasciviousness, those who had just escaped, and have turned back to error." Does
not the Apostle in these words seem to you to
have depicted the new party of ignorance?
For, as it were, they open the fountains of
knowledge and yet have no water : they
promise a shower of doctrine like prophetic
clouds which have been visited by the truth
of God, and are driven by the storms of devils
and vices. They speak great things, and their
talk is nothing but pride : [8] "But every one
is unclean with God who is lifted up in his
own heart." Like those who had just escaped
from their sins, they *return* to their own error,
and persuade men to luxury, and to the delights of eating and the gratification of the
flesh. For who is not glad to hear them say :
"Let us eat and drink, and reign for ever "?
The wise and prudent they call corrupt, but
pay more attention to the honey-tongued.

John the apostle, or rather the Saviour in t
person of John, writes thus to the angel of tl
Church of Ephesus : [1] "I know thy works a
thy toil and patience, and that thou didst be
for my name's sake, and hast not grown wear
But I have this against thee, that thou did
leave thy first love. Remember therefo
from whence thou art fallen, and repent, a
do the first works ; or else I will come
thee, and will move thy candlestick out of i
place, except thou repent." Similarly He urg
the other churches, Smyrna, Pergamos, Thy
tira, Sardis, Philadelphia, Laodicea, to repen
ance, and threatens them unless they retu
to the former works. And in Sardis He sa
He has a few who have not defiled their ga
ments, and they shall walk with Him in whit
for they are worthy. But they to whom H
says : "Remember from whence thou a
fallen"; and, "Behold the devil is about
cast some of you into prison, that ye may I
tried"; and, "I know where thou dwelles
even where Satan's throne is"; and, "Remem
ber how thou hast received, and didst hea
and keep it, and repent," and so on, we
of course believers, and baptized, who on
stood, but fell through sin.

4. I delayed for a little while the produ
tion of proofs from the Old Testament, b
cause, wherever the Old Testament is again
them they are accustomed to cry out that [2] tl
Law and the Prophets were until John. B
who does not know that under the other di
pensation of God all the saints of past tim
were of equal merit with Christians at tl
present day? As Abraham in days gone b
pleased God in wedlock, so virgins now pleas
him in perpetual virginity. He served tl
Law and his own times ; let us now serve tl
Gospel and our times, [3] upon whom the en
of the ages have come. David the chose
one, the man after God's own heart, who ha
performed all His pleasure, and who in a ce
tain psalm had said, [4] "Judge me, O Lord, f
I have walked in mine integrity : I hav
trusted also in the Lord and shall not slid
Examine me, O Lord, and prove me ; try m
reins and my heart," even he was afterwar
tempted by the devil ; and repenting of h
sin said, [5] "Have mercy upon me, O God, a
cording to thy loving-kindness." He wou
have a great sin blotted out by great lovin
kindness. Solomon, beloved of the Lord, an
to whom God had twice revealed Himself, be
cause he loved women forsook the love of Go
It is related in the [6] Book of Days that M
nasses the wicked king was restored after th
Babylonish captivity to his former rank. An

---

[1] Ecclus. xxvii. 5.   [2] Ecclus. ii. 1.
[3] James i. 22 sq.   [4] James ii. 10.
[5] Rom. xi. 32.   [6] 2 Pet. ii. 9.
[7] 2 Pet. ii. 17, 18.   [8] Prov. xvi. 5. Sept.

[1] Apoc. ii. 2 sq.   [2] Matt. xi. 13.
[3] 1 Cor. x. 11.   [4] Ps. xxvi. 1, 2.
[5] Ps. li. 1.   [6] 2 Chron. xxxiii. 12, 13.

ɔsiah, a holy man, [1] was slain by the king of gypt on the plain of Megiddo. [2] Joshua so, the son of Josedech and high-priest, al- though he was a type of our Saviour Who bore ur sins, and united to Himself a church of ien birth from among the Gentiles, is never- ɪeless, according to the letter of Scripture, ɛpresented in filthy garments after he attained ɔ the priesthood, and with the devil standing ʓ his right hand ; and white raiment is after- ɑards restored to him. It is needless to tell ow Moses and Aaron [3] offended God at the ater of strife, and did not enter the land of romise. For the blessed Job relates that ʋen the angels and every creature can sin. 'Shall mortal man," he says, "be just before ȝod ? Shall a man be spotless in his works ? ʄ he putteth no trust in his servants, and hargeth his angels with folly, how much more hem that dwell in houses of clay," amongst ʌhom are we, and made of the same clay too. "The life of man is a warfare upon earth." Lucifer fell who was sending to all nations, nd he who was nurtured in a paradise of de- ght as one of the twelve precious stones, was ʌounded and went down to hell from the ɪount of God. Hence the Saviour says in ɦe Gospel : [7] "I beheld Satan falling as light- ɪing from heaven." If he fell who stood on ɔ sublime a height, who may not fall ? If here are falls in heaven, how much more on arth ! And yet though Lucifer be fallen (the ld serpent after his fall), [8] "his strength is in is loins, and his force is in the muscles of his ɪelly. The great trees are overshadowed by ɪim, and he sleepeth beside the reed, the rush, nd the sedge." [9] He is king over all things hat are in the waters—that is to say in the eat of pleasure and luxury, of propagation of hildren, and of the fertilisation of the marriage ɪed [10] "For who can strip off his outer gar- ɪent ? Who can open the doors of his face ? ʃations fatten upon him, and the tribes of ʔhenicia divide him." And lest haply the eader in his secret thought might imagine that hose tribes of Phenicia and peoples of Ethiopia ɔnly are meant by those to whom the dragon ʋas given for food, we immediately find a ref- ɛrence to those who are crossing the sea of

this world, and are hastening to reach the haven of salvation : [1] "His head stands in the ships of the fishermen like an anvil that can- not be wearied : [2] he counteth iron as straw, and brass as rotten wood. And all the gold of the sea under him is as mire. He maketh the deep to boil like a pot : he values the sea like a pot of ointment, and the blackness of the deep as a captive. He beholdeth every- thing that is high." And my friend Jovini- anus thinks he can gain an easy mastery over him. Why speak of holy men and angels, who, being creatures of God, are of course capable of sin ? He dared to tempt the Son of God, and though smitten through and through with our Lord's first and second answer, nevertheless raised his head, and when thrice wounded, withdrew only for a time, and deferred rather than removed the temptation. And we flatter ourselves on the ground of our baptism, which though it put away the sins of the past, cannot keep us for the time to come, unless the baptized keep their hearts with all diligence.

5. At length we have arrived at the ques- tion of food, and are confronted by our third difficulty. "All things were created to serve for the use of mortal men.' And as man, a rational animal, in a sense the owner and ten- ant of the world, is subject to God, and wor- ships his Creator, so all things living were created either for the food of men, or for clothing, or for tilling the earth, or conveying the fruits thereof, or to be the companions of man, and hence, because they are man's [3] help- ers, they have their name *jumenta*. [4] "What is man,' says David, 'that thou art mindful of him ? And the son of man, that thou visitest him ? For thou hast made him but little lower than the angels, and crownest him with glory and honour. Thou madest him to have do- minion over the works of thine hands ; thou hast put all things under his feet : all sheep and oxen, yea, and the beasts of the field : the fowl of the air, and the fish of the sea, what- soever passeth through the paths of the seas.' Granted, he says, that the ox was created for ploughing, the horse for riding, the dog for watching, goats for their milk, sheep for their fleeces. What is the use of swine if we may not eat their flesh ? of roes, stags, fallow-deer, boars, hares, and such like game ? of geese, wild and tame ? of wild ducks and [5] fig-peckers ? of woodcocks ? of coots ? of thrushes ? Why do hens run about our houses ? If they are not eaten, all these creatures were created by

---

[1] 2 Kings xxiii. 29 sq. [2] Chron. xxxv. 20 sq.
[2] Zech. iii. 1 sq. [3] Numb. xx. 13. Ps. cvi. 32.
[4] Job v. 17. [5] Job vii. 1.
[6] Jerome blends two passages, Is. xiv. 12 (in which the Sept. ɾeading is "that sendest to;" R. V. "didst lay low") and Ezek. ҳxviii. 13 sq. In the passage from Isaiah the king of Babylon s compared to Lucifer, *i.e.* the shining one, the morning star, ʋhose movements the Babylonians had been the first to record. ҕee Sayce, *Fresh Light from the Ancient Monuments*, p. 178, ɑnd Cheyne's *Isaiah*. The subject of Ezekiel's prophecy is the Prince of Tyre.
[7] S. Luke x. 18.
[8] Job xl. 16, 21. R. V. "He lieth under the lotus trees, in the ɔovert of the reed and the fen."
[9] Job xli. 34. Sept. R. V. "King over the sons of pride."
[10] Job xli. 13 sq. R. V. for the latter part of the verse has 'Round about his teeth is terror, his strong scales are his ɔride." Jerome's words are not found in the existing Septuagint.

[1] The Septuagint omits much in this portion of the Book of Job.
[2] xli. 27.
[3] That is, deriving *jumenta* from *juvo*. The derivation, how- ever, is from *jungo*.
[4] Ps. viii. 5 sq. [5] The Italian beccafico.

God for nothing. But what need is there of argument when Scripture clearly teaches that every moving creature, like herbs and vegetables, were given to us for food, and the Apostle cries aloud [1] 'All things are clean to the clean, and nothing is to be rejected, if it be received with thanksgiving,' and [2] tells us that men will come in the last days, forbidding to marry, and to eat meats, which God created for use? The Lord himself was called by the Pharisees a wine-bibber and a glutton, the friend of publicans and sinners, because he did not decline the invitation of Zacchæus to dinner, and went to the marriage-feast. But it is a different matter if, as you may foolishly contend, he went to the dinner intending to fast, and after the manner of deceivers said, I eat this, not that; I do not drink the wine which I created out of water. He did not make water, but wine, the type of his blood. After the resurrection he ate a fish and part of a honey-comb, not sesame nuts and service-berries. The apostle, Peter, did not wait like a Jew for the stars to peep, but went upon the house-top to dine at the sixth hour. Paul in the ship broke bread, not dried figs. When Timothy's stomach was out of order, he advised him to drink wine, not perry. In abstaining from meats they please their own fancy: as though superstitious Gentiles did not observe the [3] rites of abstinence connected with the Mother of the Gods and with Isis."

6. I will follow in detail the views now expounded, and before I come to Scripture and show by it that fasting is pleasing to God, and chastity accepted by him, I will meet philosophic argument with argument, and will prove that we are not followers of Empedocles and Pythagoras, who on account of their doctrine of the transmigration of souls think nothing which lives and moves should be eaten, and look upon him who fells a fir-tree or an oak as equally guilty with the parricide or the poisoner: but that we worship our Creator Who made all things for the use of man. And as the ox was created for ploughing, the horse for riding, dogs for watching, goats for milk, sheep for their wool: so it was with swine and stags, and roes and hares, and other animals: but the immediate purpose of their creation was not that they might serve for food, but for other uses of men. For if everything that moves and lives was made for food, and prepared for the stomach, let my opponents tell me why elephants, lions, leopards, and wolves

were created; why vipers, scorpions, bugs, lice, and fleas; why the vulture, the eagle, the crow, the hawk; why whales, dolphins, seals, and small snails were created. Which of us ever eats the flesh of a lion, a viper, a vulture, a stork, a kite, or the worms that crawl upon our shores? As then these have their proper uses, so may we say that other beasts, fishes, birds, were created not for eating, but for medicine. In short, to how many uses the flesh of vipers, from which we make our antidotes against poison, may be applied, physicians know well. Ivory dust is an ingredient in many remedies. Hyena's gall restores brightness to the eyes, and its dung and that of dogs cures gangrenous wounds. And (it may seem strange to the reader) Galen asserts in his treatise on Simples, that human dung is of service in a multitude of cases. Naturalists say that snake-skin, boiled in oil, gives wonderful relief in ear-ache. What to the uninitiated seems so useless as a bug? Yet, suppose a leech to have fastened on the throat, as soon as the odour of a bug is inhaled the leech is vomited out, and difficulty in urinating is relieved by the same application. As for the fat of pigs, geese, fowls, and pheasants, how useful they are is told in all medical works, and if you read these books you will see there that the vulture has as many curative properties as it has limbs. Peacock's dung allays the inflammation of gout. Cranes, storks, eagle's gall, hawk's blood, the ostrich, frogs, chameleons, swallow's dung and flesh—in what diseases these are suitable remedies, I could tell if it were my purpose to discuss bodily ailments and their cure. If you think proper you may read Aristotle and [1] Theophrastus in prose, or [2] Marcellus of Side, and our [3] Flavius who discourse on these subjects in hexameter verse; the [4] second Pliny also, and [5] Dioscorides, and others, both naturalists and physicians, who assign to every herb, every stone, every animal whether reptile, bird, or fish, its own use in the art of which they treat. So then when you ask me why the pig was created, I immediately reply, as if two boys were disputing, by asking you why were vipers and scorpions? You must not judge that anything from the hand of God is superfluous, because

---

[1] Rom. xiv. 20: 1 Tim. iv. 5.　　　[2] 1 Tim. iv. 3.
[3] Castum. Another reading is Cossum i.e. wood-worms, which were considered a delicacy in Pontus and Phrygia. The reading Castum is supported by Tert., De Jejun. cap. 16 : In nostris xerophagiis blasphemias ingerens. Casto Isidis et Cybeles eos adæquas. Compare Arnob. Bk. V., and Jerome's Letter cvii. ad Lætam c. 10, and below c. 7.

[1] See note on p. 383.
[2] That is, of Side in Pamphylia. He lived in the reigns of Hadrian and Antoninus Pius, A.D. 117-161. Only two fragments remain of his Greek poem in forty-two books.
[3] He appears to be Flavius the Grammarian to whom reference is made in the Book on Illustrious Men, chap. 80 :—Firmianus, qui et Lactantius, Arnobii discipulus, sub Diocletiano principe accitus cum Flavio grammatico, cujus de Medicinalibus versu compositi extant libri, etc.
[4] Born A.D. 23. His Historia Naturalis embraces astronomy, meteorology, geography, mineralogy, zoölogy, and botany, and comprises according to the author's own account 20,000 matters of importance drawn from 2,000 volumes.
[5] A native of Cilicia, who probably lived in the second century of the Christian era. He was a Greek physician and wrote a treatise on Materia Medica, in 5 books, which is still extant.

here are many beasts and birds which your palate rejects. But this may perhaps look more like contentiousness and pugnacity than truth. Let me tell you therefore that pigs and wild-boars, and stags, and the rest of living creatures were created, that soldiers, athletes, sailors, rhetoricians, miners, and other slaves of hard toil, who need physical strength, might have food : and also those who carry arms and provisions, who wear themselves out with the work of hand or foot, who ply the oar, who need good lungs to shout and speak, who level mountains and sleep out rain or fair. But our religion does not train boxers, athletes, sailors, soldiers, or ditchers, but followers of wisdom, who devote themselves to the worship of God, and know why they were created and are in the world from which they are impatient to depart. Hence also the Apostle says : [1] "When I am weak, then am I strong." And, [2] "Though our outward man is decaying, yet our inward man is renewed day by day." And [3] "I have the desire to depart and be with Christ." And, [4] "Make not provision for the flesh to fulfil the lusts thereof." Are all commanded [5] not to have two coats, nor food in their scrip, money in their purse, a staff in the hand, shoes on the feet ? or to sell all they possess and give to the poor, and follow Jesus ? Of course not : but the command is for those who wish to be perfect. On the contrary John the Baptist lays down one rule for the soldiers, another for the publicans. But the Lord says in the Gospel to him who had boasted of having kept the whole law : [6] "If thou wilt be perfect, go and sell all that thou hast, and give to the poor, and come, follow me." That He might not seem to lay a heavy burden on unwilling shoulders, He sent His hearer away with full power to please himself, saying " If thou wilt be perfect." And so I too say to you : If you wish to be perfect, it is good not to drink wine, and eat flesh. If you wish to be perfect, it is better to enrich the mind than to stuff the body. But if you are an infant and fond of the cooks and their preparations, no one will snatch the dainties out of your mouth. Eat and drink, and, if you like, with Israel rise up and play, and sing [7] " Let us eat and drink, for to-morrow we shall die." Let him eat and drink, who looks for death when he has feasted, and who says with Epicurus, "There is nothing after death, and death itself is nothing." We believe Paul when he says in tones of thunder : [8] "Meats for the belly, and the belly for meats. But God will destroy both them and it."

7. I have quoted these few passages of Scripture to show that we are at one with the philosophers. But who does not know that no universal law of nature regulates the food of all nations, and that each eats those things of which it has abundance ? For instance, the Arabians and Saracens, and all the wild tribes of the desert live on camel's milk and flesh : for the camel, to suit the climate and barren soil of those regions, is easily bred and reared. They think it wicked to eat the flesh of swine. Why ? Because pigs which fatten on acorns, chestnuts, roots of ferns, and barley, are seldom or never found among them : and if they were found, they would not afford the nourishment of which we spoke just now. The exact opposite is the case with the northern peoples. If you were to force them to eat the flesh of asses and camels, they would think it the same as though they were compelled to devour a wolf or a crow. In Pontus and Phrygia a paterfamilias pays a good price for fat white worms with blackish heads, which breed in decayed wood. And as with us the woodcock and fig-pecker, the mullet and scar, are reputed delicacies, so with them it is a luxury to eat the [1] xylophagus. Again, because throughout the glowing wastes of the desert clouds of locusts are found, it is customary with the peoples of the East and of Libya to feed on locusts. John the Baptist proves the truth of this. Compel a Phrygian or a native of Pontus to eat a locust, and he will think it scandalous. Force a Syrian, an African, or Arabian to swallow worms, he will have the same contempt for them as for flies, millepedes, and lizards, although the Syrians are accustomed to eat land-crocodiles, and the Africans even green lizards. In Egypt and Palestine, owing to the scarcity of cattle no one eats beef, or makes the flesh of bulls or oxen, or calves, a portion of their food. Moreover, in my province [2] it is considered a crime to eat veal. Accordingly the Emperor Valens recently promulgated a law throughout the East, prohibiting the killing and eating of calves. He had in view the interests of agriculture, and wished to check the bad practice of the commoner sort of the people who imitated the Jews in devouring the flesh of calves, instead of fowls and sucking pigs. The Nomad tribes, and the [3] Troglodytes, and Scythians, and the barbarous [4] Huns with whom we have recently become acquainted,

---

[1] That is, the wood-worm just referred to.
[2] Pannonia, of which Valens also was a native.
[3] This name, which signifies *dwellers in caves*, was applied by Greek geographers to various peoples, but especially to the uncivilized inhabitants of the west coast of the Red Sea, along the shores of Upper Egypt and Æthiopia. The whole coast was called *Troglodytice*.
[4] In 376 the Goths were driven out of their country by the Huns. They were allowed by Valens to cross the Danube, but war soon broke out and the emperor was defeated with great slaughter on Aug. 9, 378.

---

[1] 2 Cor. xii. 14.   [2] 2 Cor. iv. 16.   [3] Phil. i. 23.
[4] Rom. xiii. 14.   [5] Matt. x. 9, xix. 21 : Mark vi. 8.
[6] Matt. xix. 21.   [7] 1 Cor. xv. 85.   [8] 1 Cor. vi. 13.

eat flesh half raw. Moreover the Icthyophagi, a wandering race on the shores of the Red Sea, broil fish on the stones made hot by the sun, and subsist on this poor food. The [1]Sarmatians, the [2]Chuadi, the [3]Vandals, and countless other races, delight in the flesh of horses and wolves. Why should I speak of other nations when I myself, a youth on a visit to Gaul, heard that the Atticoti, a British tribe, eat human flesh, and that although they find herds of swine, and droves of large or small cattle in the woods, it is their custom to cut off the buttocks of the shepherds and the breasts of their women, and to regard them as the greatest delicacies? The Scots have no wives of their own; as though they read Plato's Republic and took Cato for their leader, no man among them has his own wife, but like beasts they indulge their lust to their hearts' content. The Persians, Medes, Indians, and Ethiopians, peoples on a par with Rome itself, have intercourse with mothers and grandmothers, with daughters and granddaughters. The [4]Massagetæ and [5]Derbices think those persons most unhappy who die of sickness—and when parents, kindred, or friends reach old age, they are murdered and devoured. It is thought better that they should be eaten by the people themselves than by the worms. The [6]Tibareni crucify those whom they have loved before when they have grown old. The [7]Hyrcani throw them out half alive to the birds and dogs: the Caspians leave them dead for the same beasts. The Scythians bury alive with the remains of the dead those who were beloved of the deceased. The Bactrians throw their old men to dogs which they rear for the very purpose, and when Stasanor, Alexander's general, wished to correct the practice, he almost lost his province. Force an Egyptian to drink sheep's milk: drive, if you can, a Pelusiote to eat an onion. Almost every city in Egypt venerates its own beasts and monsters, and whatever be the object of worship, that they think inviolable and sacred. Hence it is that their towns also are named after animals: Leonto, Cyno, Lyco, Busyris, Thmuis, which is, being interpreted, a *he-goat*. And to make us understand what sort of gods Egypt always

welcomed, one of their cities was recently called [1]Antinous after Hadrian's favourite. You see clearly then that not only in eating, but also in burial, in wedlock, and in every department of life, each race follows its own practice and peculiar usages, and takes that for the law of nature which is most familiar to it. But suppose all nations alike ate flesh, and let that be everywhere lawful which the place produces. How does it concern us whose conversation is in heaven? who, as well as Pythagoras and Empedocles and all lovers of wisdom, are not bound to the circumstances of our birth, but of our new birth: who by abstinence subjugate our refractory flesh, eager to follow the allurements of lust? The eating of flesh, and drinking of wine, and fulness of stomach, is the seed-plot of lust. And so the comic poet says,[2] "Venus shivers unless Ceres and Bacchus be with her."

8. Through the five senses, as through open windows, vice has access to the soul. The metropolis and citadel of the mind cannot be taken unless the enemy have previously entered by its doors. The soul is distressed by the disorder they produce, and is led captive by sight, hearing, smell, taste, and touch. If any one delights in the sports of the circus, or the struggles of athletes, the versatility of actors, the figure of women, in splendid jewels, dress, silver and gold, and other things of the kind, the liberty of the soul is lost through the windows of the eyes, and the prophet's words are fulfilled: [3]"Death is come up into our windows." Again, our sense of hearing is flattered by the tones of various instruments and the modulations of the voice; and whatever enters the ear by the songs of poets and comedians, by the pleasantries and verses of pantomimic actors, weakens the manly fibre of the mind. Then, again, no one but a profligate denies that the profligate and licentious find a delight in sweet odours, different sorts of incense, fragrant balsam, [4]kuphi, [5]œnanthe, and musk, which is nothing but the skin of a foreign rat. And who does not know that gluttony is the mother of avarice, and, as it were, fetters the heart and keeps it pressed down upon the earth? For the sake of a temporary gratification of the appetite, land and sea are ransacked, and we toil and sweat our lives through, that we may send down our throats honey-wine and costly food. The desire to handle other men's persons, and the burning lust for women, is a passion bordering on

---

[1] The Sarmatians dwelt on the N. E. of the Sea of Azov, E. of the river Don.
[2] They were located in the S. E. of Germany.
[3] The name given to the great confederacy of German peoples who in A.D. 409 traversed Germany and Gaul, and invaded Spain. In 429 they conquered all the Roman dominions in Africa, and in 455 they plundered Rome. Their kingdom was destroyed by Belisarius in 535.
[4] A people of Central Asia. Cyrus the Great was slain in an expedition against them.
[5] On the Oxus near its entrance into the Caspian Sea.
[6] An agricultural people on the W. coast of Pontus.
[7] Hyrcania was a province of the Persian Empire, on the S. and S. E. shores of the Caspian or Hyrcanian Sea. Jerome draws many of these details from the treatise of Porphyry Περὶ ἀποχῆς ἐμψύχων.

---

[1] Antinous was drowned in the Nile, A.D. 122. The emperor's grief was so great that he enrolled his favourite amongst the gods, caused a temple to be erected to his honour at Mantinea, and founded the city of Antinoopolis.
[2] Ter. Eunuch. iv. 5, 6.
[3] Jer. ix. 21.
[4] An Egyptian perfuming powder.
[5] Probably an ointment made from the grape of the wild vine.

insanity. To gratify this sense we languish, grow angry, throw ourselves about with joy, indulge envy, engage in rivalry, are filled with anxiety, and when we have terminated the pleasure with more or less repentance, we once more take fire, and want to do that which we again regret doing. Where, then, that which we may call the thin edge of disturbance, has entered the citadel of the mind through these doors, what will become of its liberty, its endurance, its thought of God, particularly since the sense of touch can picture to itself even bygone pleasures, and through the recollection of vice forces the soul to take part in them, and after a manner to practice what it does not actually commit ?

9. At the call of reasoning such as this, many philosophers have forsaken the crowded cities, and their pleasure gardens in the suburbs with well-watered grounds, shady trees, twittering birds, crystal fountains, murmuring brooks, and many charms for eye and ear, lest through luxury and abundance of riches, the firmness of the mind should be enfeebled, and its purity debauched. For there is no good in frequently seeing objects which may one day lead to your captivity, or in making trial of things which you would find it hard to do without. Even the Pythagoreans shunned company of this kind and were wont to dwell in solitary places in the desert. The Platonists also and Stoics lived in the groves and porticos of temples, that, admonished by the sanctity of their restricted abode, they might think of nothing but virtue. Plato, moreover, himself, when [1] Diogenes trampled on his couches with muddy feet (he being a rich man), chose a house called [2] *Academia* at some distance from the city, in a spot not only lonely but unhealthy, so that he might have leisure for philosophy. His object was that by constant anxiety about sickness the assaults of lust might be defeated, and that his disciples might experience no pleasure but that afforded by the things they learned. We have read of some who took out their own eyes lest through sight they might lose the contemplation of philosophy. Hence it was that [3] Crates the famous Theban, after throwing into the sea a considerable weight of gold, exclaimed, " Go to the bottom, ye evil lusts : I will drown you that you may not drown me."

But if anyone thinks to enjoy keenly meat and drink in excess, and at the same time to devote himself to philosophy, that is to say, to live in luxury and yet not to be hampered by the vices attendant on luxury, he deceives himself. For if it be the case that even when far distant from them we are frequently caught in the snares of nature, and are compelled to desire those things of which we have a scant supply : what folly it is to think we are free when we are surrounded by the nets of pleasure ! We think of what we see, hear, smell, taste, handle, and are led to desire the thing which affords us pleasure. That the mind sees and hears, and that we can neither hear nor see anything unless our senses are fixed upon the objects of sight and hearing, is an old saw. It is difficult, or rather impossible, when we are swimming in luxury and pleasure not to think of what we are doing : and it is an idle pretence which some men put forward [1] that they can take their fill of pleasure with their faith and purity and mental uprightness unimpaired. It is a violation of nature to revel in pleasure, and the Apostle gives a caution against this very thing when he says, [2] " She that giveth herself to pleasure is dead while she liveth."

10. The bodily senses are like horses madly racing, but the soul like a charioteer holds the reins. And as horses without a driver go at break-neck speed, so the body if it be not governed by the reasonable soul rushes to its own destruction. The philosophers make use of another illustration of the relations between soul and body ; [3] they say the body is a boy, the soul his tutor. Hence the [4] historian tells us "that our soul directs, our body serves. The one we have in common with the gods, the other with the beasts." So then unless the vices of youth and boyhood are regulated by the wisdom of the tutor, every effort and every impulse sets strongly in the direction of wantonness. We might lose four of the senses and yet live,—that is we could do without sight, hearing, smell, and the pleasures of touch. But a human being cannot subsist without tasting food. It follows that reason must be present, that we may take food of such a kind and in such quantities as will not burden the body, or hinder the free movement of the soul : for it is the way with us that we eat, and walk, and sleep, and digest our food, and afterwards in the fulness of blood have to bear the spur of lust. [5] " Wine is a mocker, strong drink a brawler." Whosoever has much to do with these is not wise.

---

[1] The celebrated Cynic philosopher. He died at Corinth, at the age of nearly 90, B. C. 323.
[2] *Academia* was a piece of land on the Cephisus about three-quarters of a mile from Athens, originally belonging to the hero Academus. Here was a Gymnasium with plane and olive plantations, etc. Plato had a piece of land in the neighbourhood ; here he taught, and after him his followers, who were hence called *Academici*. Cicero called his villa Academia.
[3] Flourished about B. C. 320. Though heir to a large fortune, he renounced it all, and lived and died as a true Cynic. He was called the "door-opener," because it was his practice to visit every house at Athens and rebuke its inmates.

[1] A common form of Gnostic error revived many centuries afterwards by the Anabaptists.
[2] 1 Tim. v. 6.   [3] See Cicero, Repub. Bk. III.
[4] Sallust. *In Cat.* ch. 1.   [5] Prov. xx. 1.

And we should not take such food as is difficult of digestion, or such as when eaten will
give us reason to complain that we got it and
lost it with much effort. The preparation of
vegetables, fruit, and pulse is easy, and does
not require the skill of expensive cooks : our
bodies are nourished by them with little trouble on our part ; and, if taken in moderation, such food is easier to digest, and at less
cost, because it does not stimulate the appetite, and therefore is not devoured with
avidity. No one has his stomach inflated
or overloaded if he eats only one or two
dishes, and those inexpensive ones : such a
condition comes of pampering the taste with
a variety of meats. The smells of the kitchen
may induce us to eat, but when hunger is
satisfied, they make us their slaves. Hence
gorging gives rise to disease : and many persons find relief for the discomfort of gluttony
in emetics,—what they disgraced themselves
by putting in, they with still greater disgrace
put out.

11. [1] Hippocrates in his Aphorisms teaches
that stout persons of a coarse habit of body,
when once they have attained their full growth,
unless the plethora be quickly relieved by
blood-letting, develop tendencies to paraly-
sis and the worst forms of disease : they
must therefore be bled, that there may be
room for fresh growth. For it is not the
nature of our bodies to continue in one stay,
but go on either to increase or decrease,
and no animal can live which is incapable
of growth. Whence [2] Galen, a very learned
man and the commentator on Hippocrates,
says in his exhortation to the practice of
medicine that athletes whose whole life and
art consists in stuffing cannot live long, nor
be healthy : and that their souls enveloped
with superfluous blood and fat, and as it were
covered with mud, have no refined or heavenly thoughts, but are always intent upon
gluttonous and voracious feasting. Diogenes
maintains that tyrants do not bring about
revolutions in cities, and foment wars civil or
foreign for the sake of a simple diet of vegetables and fruits, but for costly meats and
the delicacies of the table. And, strange to
say, Epicurus, the defender of pleasure, in all
his books speaks of nothing but vegetables and
fruits ; and he says that we ought to live on
cheap food because the preparation of sumptuous banquets of flesh involves great care and
suffering, and greater pains attend the search
for such delicacies than pleasures the con-

sumption of them. Our bodies need only
something to eat and drink. Where there is
bread and water, and the like, nature is satisfied. Whatever more there may be does not
go to meet the wants of life, but are ministers
to vicious pleasure. Eating and drinking
does not quench the longing for luxuries, but
appeases hunger and thirst. Persons who
feed on flesh want also gratifications not
found in flesh. But they who adopt a simple
diet do not look for flesh. Further, we cannot devote ourselves to wisdom if our thoughts
are running on a well-laden table, the supply
of which requires an excess of work and
anxiety. The wants of nature are soon satisfied : cold and hunger can be banished with
simple food and clothing. Hence the Apostle
says : " Having food and clothing let us be
therewith content." Delicacies and the various
dishes of the feast are the nurses of avarice.
The soul greatly exults when you are content
with little : you have the world beneath your
feet, and can exchange all its power, its
feasts, and its lusts, the objects for which
men rake money together, for common food,
and make up for them all with a sack-cloth
shirt. Take away the luxurious feasting and
the gratification of lust, and no one will want
riches to be used either in the belly, or beneath
it. The invalid only regains his health by
diminishing and carefully selecting his food,
i.e., in medical phrase, by adopting a "slender diet." The same food that recovers
health, can preserve it, for no one can imagine vegetables to be the cause of disease.
And if vegetables do not give the strength of
Milo of Crotona—a strength supplied and
nourished by meat—what need has a wise
man and a Christian philosopher of such
strength as is required by athletes and soldiers, and which, if he had it, would only
stimulate to vice ? Let those persons deem
meat accordant with health who wish to gratify their lust, and who, sunk in filthy pleasure, are always at heat. What a Christian
wants is health, but not superfluous strength.
And it ought not to disturb us if we find but
few supporters ; for the pure and temperate
are as rare as good and faithful friends, and
virtue is always scarce. Study the temperance of [1] Fabricius, or the poverty of [2] Curius,
and in a great city you will find few worthy of
your imitation. You need not fear that if you
do not eat flesh, fowlers and hunters will have
learnt their craft in vain.

---

[1] The most celebrated physician of antiquity. Born about
B.C. 460, died about 357.
[2] Born at Pergamum A.D. 130, died probably in the year 200.
His writings are considered to have had a more extensive influence on medical science than even those of Hippocrates.

[1] Fabricius was censor in B.C. 275, and devoted himself to
repressing the prevalent taste for luxury. The story of his
expelling from the Senate P. Cornelius Rufinus because he possessed ten pounds' weight of silver-plate is well-known.
[2] Curius Dentatus, Consul B.C. 290 with P. Cornelius Rufinus
to whom allusion has just been made, was no less distinguished
for simplicity of life than was Fabricius. He was censor B.C.
272.

12. We have read that some who suffered with disease of the joints and with gouty humours recovered their health by proscribing delicacies, and coming down to a simple board and mean food. For they were then free from the worry of managing a house and from unlimited feasting. Horace [1] makes fun of the longing for food which when eaten leaves nothing but regret.

" Scorn pleasure ; she but hurts when bought with pain."

And when, in the delightful retirement of the country, by way of satirizing voluptuous men, he described himself as plump and fat, his sportive verse ran thus :

" Pay me a visit if you want to laugh,
You'll find me fat and sleek with well-dress'd hide,
Like any pig from Epicurus' sty."

But even if our food be the commonest, we must avoid repletion. For nothing is so destructive to the mind as a full belly, fermenting like a wine vat and giving forth its gases on all sides. What sort of fasting is it, or what refreshment is there after fasting, when we are blown out with yesterday's dinner, and our [2] stomach is made a factory for the closet? We wish to get credit for protracted abstinence, and all the while we devour so much that a day and a night can scarcely digest it. The proper name to give it is not fasting, but rather debauch and rank indigestion.

13. [3] Dicæarchus in his book of Antiquities, describing Greece, relates that under Saturn, that is in the Golden Age, when the ground brought forth all things abundantly, no one ate flesh, but every one lived on field produce and fruits which the earth bore of itself. Xenophon in eight books narrates the life of Cyrus, King of the Persians, and asserts that they supported life on barley, cress, salt, and black bread. Both the aforesaid Xenophon, Theophrastus, and almost all the Greek writers testify to the frugal diet of the Spartans. [4] Chæremon the Stoic, a man of great eloquence, has a treatise on the life of the ancient priests of Egypt, who, he says, laid aside all worldly business and cares, and were ever in the temple, studying nature and the regulating causes of the heavenly bodies ; they never had intercourse with women ; they never from the time they began to devote themselves to the divine service set eyes on their kindred and relations, nor even saw their children ; they always abstained

from flesh and wine, on account of the light-headedness and dizziness which a small quantity of food caused, and especially to avoid the stimulation of the lustful appetite engendered by this meat and drink. They seldom ate bread, that they might not load the stomach. And whenever they ate it, they mixed pounded hyssop with all that they took, so that the action of its warmth might diminish the weight of the heavier food. They used no oil except with vegetables, and then only in small quantities, to mitigate the unpalatable taste. What need, he says, to speak of birds, when they avoided even eggs and milk as flesh. The one, they said, was liquid flesh, the other was blood with the colour changed? Their bed was made of palm-leaves, called by them baiæ : a sloping foot-stool laid upon the ground served for a pillow, and they could go without food for two or three days. The humours of the body which arise from sedentary habits were dried up by reducing their diet to an extreme point.

14. [1] Josephus in the second book of the history of the Jewish captivity, and in the eighteenth book of the Antiquities, and the two treatises against Apion, describes three sects of the Jews, the Pharisees, Sadducees, and Essenes. On the last of these he bestows wondrous praise because they practised perpetual abstinence from wives, wine, and flesh, and made a second nature of their daily fast. [2] Philo, too, a man of great learning, published a treatise of his own on their mode of life. [3] Neanthes of Cizycus, and [4] Asclepiades of Cyprus, at the time when Pygmalion ruled over the East, relate that the eating of flesh was unknown. Eubulus, also, who wrote the history of [5] Mithras in many volumes, relates that among the Persians there are three kinds of Magi, the first of whom, those of greatest learning and eloquence, take no food except meal and vegetables. At Eleusis it is customary to abstain from fowls and fish and certain fruits. [6] Bardesanes, a Babylonian, divides the Gymnosophists of India into two classes, the one called Brahmans, the other Samaneans, who are so rigidly self-restrained

---

[1] Ep. Lib. I. ep. 2.
[2] Or, "an ante-room to the closet "—Meditatorium. Comp. Tertullian, Treatise on Fasting, ch. 6.
[3] The Peripatetic philosopher, geographer, and historian, a disciple of Aristotle and the friend of Theophrastus.
[4] Chæremon was chief librarian of the Alexandrian library. He afterwards became one of Nero's tutors.

[1] Wars, Book II., ch. viii. 2 sq. ; Antiquities, Bk. xviii. I. 2 sq. Josephus nowhere says that the Essenes abstained from flesh and wine, or fasted daily. Philo commends them for so doing. Jerome here, as above, borrows from Porphyry. The " Wars of the Jews or History of the Destruction of Jerusalem," are here called the " History of the Jewish Captivity."
[2] Philo the Jew. His exact date cannot be given ; but he was advanced in years when he went to Rome (A.D. 40) on his famous embassy in behalf of his countrymen.
[3] Neanthes lived about B.C. 241. He was a voluminous writer, chiefly on historical subjects.
[4] There were many physicians of this name.
[5] The sun-god of the Persians.
[6] Supposed to be the same as the Bardesanes born at Edessa in Mesopotamia, who flourished in the latter half of the second century. Jerome again refers to him in the book on Illustrious Men, c. 33.

that they support themselves either with the fruit of trees which grow on the banks of the Ganges, or with common food of rice or flour, and when the king visits them, he is wont to adore them, and thinks the peace of his country depends upon their prayers. Euripides relates that the prophets of Jupiter in Crete abstained not only from flesh, but also from cooked food. [1] Xenocrates the philosopher writes that at Athens out of all the laws of [2] Triptolemus only three precepts remain in the temple of Ceres : respect to parents, reverence for the gods, and abstinence from flesh. [3] Orpheus in his song utterly denounces the eating of flesh. I might speak of the frugality of Pythagoras, Socrates, and [4] Antisthenes to our confusion : but it would be tedious, and would require a work to itself. At all events this is the Antisthenes who, after teaching rhetoric with renown, on hearing Socrates, is related to have said to his disciples, " Go, and seek a master, for I have now found one." He immediately sold what he had, divided the proceeds among the people, and kept nothing for himself but a small cloak. Of his poverty and toil Xenophon in the Symposium is a witness, and so are his countless treatises, some philosophical, some rhetorical. His most famous follower was the great Diogenes, who was mightier than King Alexander in that he conquered human nature. For Antisthenes would not take a single pupil, and when he could not get rid of the persistent Diogenes he threatened him with a stick if he did not depart. The latter is said to have laid down his head and said, " No stick will be hard enough to prevent me from following you." [5] Satyrus, the biographer of illustrious men, relates that Diogenes to guard himself against the cold, folded his cloak double : his scrip was his pantry : and when aged he carried a stick to support his feeble frame, and was commonly called " Old Hand-to-mouth," because to that very hour he begged and received food from any one. His home was the gateways and city arcades. And when he wriggled into his tub, he would joke about his movable house that adapted itself to the seasons. For when the weather was cold he used to turn the mouth of the tub towards the south : in summer towards the north ; and whatever the direction of the sun might be, that way the palace of Diogenes was turned. He had a wooden dish for drinking ; but on one occasion seeing a boy drinking with the hollow of his hand he is related to have dashed the cup to the ground, saying that he did not know nature provided a cup. His virtue and self-restraint were proved even by his death. It is said that, now an old man, he was on his way to the Olympic games, which used to be attended by a great concourse of people from all parts of Greece, when he was overtaken by fever and lay down upon the bank by the road-side. And when his friends wished to place him on a beast or in a conveyance, he did not assent, but crossing to the shade of a tree said, " Go your way, I pray you, and see the games : this night will prove me either conquered or conqueror. If I conquer the fever, I shall go to the games : if the fever conquers me, I shall enter the unseen world." There through the night he lay gasping for breath and did not, as we are told, so much die as banish the fever by death. I have cited the example of only one philosopher, so that our fine, erect, muscular athletes, who hardly make a shadow of a footmark in their swift passage, whose words are in their fists and their reasoning in their heels, who either know nothing of apostolic poverty and the hardness of the cross, or despise it, may at least imitate Gentile moderation.

15. So far I have dealt with the arguments and examples of philosophers. Now I will pass on to the beginning of the human race, that is, to the sphere which belongs to us. I will first point out that Adam received a command in paradise to abstain from one tree though he might eat the other fruit. The blessedness of paradise could not be consecrated without abstinence from food. So long as he fasted, he remained in paradise ; he ate, and was cast out ; he was no sooner cast out than he married a wife. While he fasted in paradise he continued a virgin : when he filled himself with food in the earth, he bound himself with the tie of marriage. And yet though cast out he did not immediately receive permission to eat flesh ; but only the fruits of trees and the produce of the crops, and herbs and vegetables were given him for food, that even when an exile from paradise he might feed not upon flesh which was not to be found in paradise, but upon grain and fruit like that of paradise. But afterwards when [1] God saw that the heart of man from his youth was set on wickedness continually, and that His Spirit could not remain in them because they were

[1] Xenocrates was born B.C. 396, died B.C. 314.
[2] Triptolemus was the legendary inventor of the plough and of agriculture.
[3] Poems ascribed to the mythical Orpheus are quoted by Plato. The extant poems which bear his name are forgeries of Christian grammarians and philosophers of the Alexandrine school ; but some fragments of the old Orphic poetry are said to be remaining.
[4] Antisthenes was the founder of the Cynic philosophy. He was a devoted disciple of Socrates and flourished about B.C. 366.
[5] The distinguished Peripatetic philosopher and historian. He lived, probably, about the time of Ptolemy Philopator (B.C. 222-205).

[1] Gen. vi. 3, 5.

flesh, He by the deluge passed sentence on the works of the flesh, and, taking note of the extreme greediness of men, [1] gave them liberty to eat flesh : so that while understanding that all things were lawful for them, they might not greatly desire that which was allowed, lest they should turn a commandment into a cause of transgression. And yet even then, fasting was in part commanded. For, seeing that some animals are called clean, some unclean, and the unclean animals were taken into Noah's ark by pairs, the clean in uneven numbers (and of course the eating of the unclean was forbidden, otherwise the term un-clean would be unmeaning), fasting was in part consecrated : restraint in the use of all was taught by the prohibition of some. Why did Esau lose his birthright? Was it not on account of food? and he could not atone with tears for the impatience of his appetite. The people of Israel cast out from Egypt and on their way to the land of promise, the land flowing with milk and honey, longed for the flesh of Egypt, and the melons and garlic, saying : [2] "Would that we had died by the hand of the Lord in the land of Egypt, when we sat by the flesh pots." And again, [3] "Who shall give us flesh to eat? We remember the fish which we did eat in Egypt for nought ; the cucumbers, and the melons, and the leeks, and the onions, and the garlic : but now our soul is dried away : we have nought save this manna to look to."

They despised angels' food, and sighed for the flesh of Egypt. Moses for forty days and forty nights fasted on Mount Sinai, and showed even then that man does not live on bread alone, but on every word of God. He says to the Lord, "the people is full and maketh idols." Moses with empty stomach received the law written with the finger of God. The people that ate and drank and rose up to play fashioned a golden calf, and preferred an Egyptian ox to the majesty of the Lord. The toil of so many days perished through the fulness of a single hour. Moses boldly broke the tables : for he knew that drunkards cannot hear the word of God. [4] "The beloved grew thick, waxed fat, and became sleek : he kicked and forsook the Lord which made him, and departed from the God of his salvation." Hence also it is enjoined in the same Book of Deuteronomy : [5] "Beware, lest when thou hast eaten and drunk, and hast built goodly houses, and when thy herds and thy flocks multiply, and thy silver and gold is multiplied, then thine heart be lifted

up, and thou forget the Lord thy God." In short the people ate and their heart grew thick, lest they should see with their eyes, and hear with their ears, and understand with their heart : so the people well fed and fat-fleshed could not bear the countenance of Moses who fasted, for, to correctly render the Hebrew, it was [1] furnished with horns through his converse with God. And it was not, as some think, to show that there is no difference between virginity and marriage, but to assert his sympathy with severe fasting, that our Lord and Saviour when he was transfigured on the Mount revealed Moses and Elias with Himself in glory. Although Moses and Elias were properly types of the Law and the Prophets, as is clearly witnessed by the Gospel : [2] "They spake of his departure which he was about to accomplish at Jerusalem." For the passion of our Lord is declared not by virginity or marriage, but by the Law and the Prophets. If, however, any persons contentiously maintain that by Moses is signified marriage, by Elias virginity, let me tell them briefly that Moses died and was buried, but Elias was carried off in a chariot of fire and entered on immortality before he approached death. But the second writing of the tables could not be effected without fasting. What was lost by drunkenness was regained by abstinence, a proof that by fasting we can return to paradise, whence, though fulness, we have been expelled. In [3] Exodus we read that the battle was fought against Amalek while Moses prayed, and the whole people fasted until the evening. [4] Joshua, the son of Nun, bade sun and moon stand still, and the victorious army prolonged its fast for more than a day. [5] Saul, as it is written in the first book of Kings, pronounced a curse on him who ate bread before the evening, and until he had avenged himself upon his enemies. So none of his people tasted any food. And all they of the land took food. And so binding was a solemn fast once it was proclaimed to the Lord, that Jonathan, to whom the victory was due, was taken by lot, and [6] could not escape the charge of sinning in ignorance, and his father's hand was raised against him, and the prayers of the people scarce availed to save him. [7] Elijah after the preparation of a forty days' fast saw God on Mount Horeb, and heard from Him

---

[1] The curious custom of representing Moses with horns arose from a mistake in the Vulgate rendering. The Hebrew verb קָרַן, to emit rays, is derived from a word which, meaning mostly a *horn*, has in the dual the signification *rays of light*. See Hab. iii. 4.
[2] Luc. ix. 31.
[4] Josh. x. 13.
[5] 1 Sam. xiv. 24. Heb. "entered into the wood." The English version follows the Hebrew. The Sept. ἠρίστα (Jerome's prandebat) is perhaps only a repetition of the preceding thought. Another rendering inserts the negative, οὐκ ἠρίστα.
[6] 1 Sam. xiv. 24.
[7] 1 Kings xix. 8-11.

---

[1] Gen. viii. 21 : ix. 3.　　[2] Ex. xvi. 3.　　[3] Numb. xi. 4-6..
[4] Deut. xxxii. 15. "Beloved" (dilectus). Correctly Jeshurun, that is, the Upright, a name of Israel.
[5] Deut. viii. 12-14.

the words, "What doest thou here, Elijah?" There is much more familiarity in this than in the "Where art thou, Adam?" of Genesis. The latter was intended to excite the fears of one who had fed and was lost; the former was affectionately addressed to a fasting servant. [1] When the people were assembled in Mizpeh, Samuel proclaimed a fast, and so strengthened them, and thus made them prevail against the enemy. [2] The attack of the Assyrians was repulsed, and the might of Sennacherib utterly crushed, by the tears and sackcloth of King Hezekiah, and by his humbling himself with fasting. So also the city of Nineveh by fasting excited compassion and turned aside the threatening wrath of the Lord. And [3] Sodom and Gomorrha might have appeased it, had they been willing to repent, and through the aid of fasting gain for themselves tears of repentance. [4] Ahab, the most impious of kings, by fasting and wearing sackcloth, succeeded in escaping the sentence of God, and in deferring the overthrow of his house to the days of his posterity. [5] Hannah, the wife of Elkanah, by fasting won the gift of a son. [6] At Babylon the magicians came into peril, every interpreter of dreams, soothsayer, and diviner was slain. Daniel and the three youths gained a good report by fasting, and although they were fed on pulse, they were fairer and wiser than they who ate the flesh from the king's table. Then it is written that Daniel fasted for three weeks; he ate no pleasant bread; flesh and wine entered not his mouth; he was not anointed with oil; and the angel came to him saying, [7] "Daniel, thou art worthy of compassion." He who in the eyes of God was worthy of compassion, afterwards was an object of terror to the lions in their den. How fair a thing is that which propitiates God, tames lions, terrifies demons! Habakkuk (although we do not find this in the Hebrew Scriptures [8]) was sent to him with the reaper's meal, for by a week's abstinence he had merited so distinguished a server. David, when his son was in danger after his adultery, made confession in ashes and with fasting. [9] He tells us that he ate ashes like bread, and mingled his drink with weeping. [10] And that his knees became weak through fasting. Yet he had certainly heard from Nathan the words, [11] "The Lord also hath put away thy sin." Samson and Samuel drank neither wine nor strong drink, for they were children of promise, and conceived in abstinence and fasting. [1] Aaron and the other priests when about to enter the temple, refrained from all intoxicating drink for fear they should die. Whence we learn that they die who minister in the Church without sobriety. And hence it is a reproach against Israel: [2] "Ye gave my Nazarites wine to drink." Jonadab, the son of Rechab, commanded his sons to drink no wine for ever. And when Jeremiah offered them wine to drink, and they of their own accord refused it, the Lord spake by the prophet, saying: [3] "Because ye have obeyed the commandment of Jonadab your father, Jonadab the son of Rechab shall not want a man to stand before me for ever." On the [4] threshold of the Gospel appears Anna, the daughter of Phanuel, the wife of one husband, and a woman who was always fasting. Long-continued chastity and persistent fasting welcomed a Virgin Lord. His forerunner and herald, John, fed on locusts and wild honey, not on flesh; and the hermits of the desert and the monks in their cells, at first used the same sustenance. But the Lord Himself consecrated His baptism by a forty days' fast, and He taught us that the more violent devils [5] cannot be overcome, except by prayer and fasting. [6] Cornelius the centurion was found worthy through almsgiving and frequent fasts to receive the gift of the Holy Spirit before baptism. [7] The Apostle Paul, after speaking of hunger and thirst, and his other labours, perils from robbers, shipwrecks, loneliness, enumerates frequent fasts. And he [8] advises his disciple Timothy, who had a weak stomach, and was subject to many infirmities, to drink wine in moderation: "Drink no longer water," he says. The fact that he bids him *no longer* drink water shows that he had previously drunk water. The apostle would not have allowed this had not frequent infirmities and bodily pain demanded the concession.

16. The Apostle does indeed [9] blame those who forbade marriage, and commanded to abstain from food, which God created for use with thanksgiving. But he has in view Marcion, and Tatian, and other heretics, who inculcate perpetual abstinence, to destroy, and express their hatred and contempt for, the works of the Creator. But we praise every creature of God, and yet prefer leanness to corpulence, abstinence to luxury, fasting to fulness. [10] "He that laboureth laboureth for

---

[1] 1 Sam. vii. 7. [2] 2 Kings xviii.
[3] Gen. xviii. 23 sq. [4] 1 Kings xxi. 27-29.
[5] 1 Sam. i. 15, 17. [6] Dan. i and ii.
[7] Dan. ix. 23. Heb. A man of desires. A. V. greatly beloved.
[8] The story is in the apocryphal part of the book of Daniel.
[9] Ps. cii. 9. [10] Ps. cix. 24. [11] 2 Sam. xii. 13.

[1] Lev. x. 9. [2] Amos ii. 12.
[3] Jer. xxxv. 18. [4] S. Luke ii. 36.
[5] S. Jerome is in accord with the Vulgate, Peshito, and certain manuscripts, but the R. V. omits S. Matt. xvii. 21 (Howbeit this kind goeth not out but by prayer and fasting) and in S. Mark ix. 29 omits the words respecting fasting. S. Luke does not refer to our Lord's supposed remark.
[6] Acts x. 4. [7] 2 Cor. xi. 27. [8] 1 Tim. v. 23.
[9] 1 Tim. iv. 3. [10] Prov. xvi. 26. Sept.

himself, and he is eager to his own destruction." And,[1] "From the days of John the Baptist (who fasted and was a virgin) until now the kingdom of heaven suffereth violence, and men of violence take it by force." For we are afraid lest at the coming of the eternal judge we be caught, as in the days of the flood, and at the overthrow of Sodom and Gomorrha, eating and drinking, and marrying, and giving in marriage. For both the flood and the fire from heaven found fulness as well as marriage ready for destruction. Nor need we wonder if the Apostle commands that everything sold in the market be bought and eaten, since with idolaters, and with those who still ate in the temples of the idols meats offered to idols as such, it passed for the highest abstinence to abstain only from food eaten by the Gentiles. And if he says to the Romans: [2] "Let not him that eateth set at nought him that eateth not: and let not him that eateth not judge him that eateth," he does not make fasting and fulness of equal merit, but he is speaking against those believers in Christ who were still judaizing: and he warns Gentile believers, not to offend those by their food who were still too weak in faith. In brief this is clear enough in the sequel: [3] "I know and am persuaded in the Lord Jesus, that nothing is unclean of itself: save that to him who accounteth anything to be unclean, to him it is unclean. For if because of meat thy brother is grieved, thou walkest no longer in love. Destroy not with thy meat him for whom Christ died. Let not then your good be evil spoken of: for the Kingdom of God is not eating and drinking." And that no one may suppose he is referring to fasting and not to Jewish superstition, he immediately explains,[4] "One man hath faith to eat all things: but he that is weak eateth herbs." And again,[5] "One man esteemeth one day above another: another esteemeth every day alike. Let each man be fully assured in his own mind. He that regardeth the day, regardeth it unto the Lord: and he that eateth, eateth unto the Lord, for he giveth God thanks; and he that eateth not, unto the Lord he eateth not, and giveth God thanks." For they who were still weak in faith and thought some meats clean, some unclean: and supposed there was a difference between one day and another, for example, that the Sabbath, and the New Moons, and the Feast of Tabernacles were holier than other days, were commanded to eat herbs which are indifferently partaken of by all. But such as were of stronger faith believed all meats and all days to be alike.

17. My opponent has dared to maintain that our Lord was called by the Pharisees a wine-bibber and a glutton: and from the fact of His going to marriage feasts and from His not despising the banquets of sinners, I am to infer His wishes respecting ourselves. That Lord, so you suppose, is a glutton who fasted forty days to hallow Christian fasting; [1] who calls them blessed that hunger and thirst; [2] who says that He has food, not that which the disciples surmised, but such as would not perish for ever; [3] who forbids us to think of the morrow; who, though He is said to have hungered and thirsted, and to have gone frequently to various meals, except in celebrating the mystery whereby He represented His passion, or [4] in proving the reality of His body is nowhere described as ministering to His appetite; [5] who tells of purple-clad Dives in hell for his feasting, and says that poor Lazarus for his abstinence was in Abraham's bosom; who, when we fast, [6] bids us anoint our head and wash our face, that we fast not to gain glory from men, but praise from the Lord; who did indeed [7] after His resurrection eat part of a broiled fish and of a honey-comb, not to allay hunger and to gratify His palate, but to show the reality of His own body. For whenever He raised anyone from the dead He [8] ordered that food should be given him to eat, lest the resurrection should be thought a delusion. And this is why Lazarus after his resurrection is [9] described as being at the feast with our Lord. We do not deny that fish and other kinds of flesh, if we choose, may be taken as food; but as we prefer virginity to marriage, so do we esteem fasting and spirituality above meats and full-bloodedness. And if Peter [10] before dinner went to the supper chamber at the sixth hour, a chance fit of hunger does not prejudice fasting. For, if this were so, because our Lord [11] at the sixth hour sat weary on the well of Samaria and wished to drink, all must of necessity, whether they so desire or not, drink at that time. Possibly it was the Sabbath, or the Lord's day, and he hungered at the sixth hour after two or three days' fasting; for I could never believe that the Apostle, if he had eaten a dinner only one day previous and had been blown out with a great meal, would have been hungry by noon next day. But if he did dine the day pre-

[1] S. Matt. v. 6.　　[2] S. John iv. 32.
[3] S. Matt. v. 34. (Rather, not to be *anxious* about it.)
[4] S. Luke xxiv. 42: S. John xxi. 13.
[5] S. Luke xv. 19-31.
[6] S. Matt. xvi. 17, 18.　　[7] See above.
[8] S. Mark v. 43: S. Luke viii. 55. Our Lord is not related to have given the command in the case of the son of the widow of Nain, or in that of Lazarus.
[9] S. John xii. 2.
[10] Acts x. 10. In our version "the housetop."
[11] S. John iv. 6.

[1] S. Matt. xi. 12.　　[2] Rom. xiv. 3.　　[3] Rom. xiv. 14 sq.
[4] Rom. xiv. 2.　　[5] Rom. xiv. 5 sq.

vious, and was hungry next day before lunch-eon, I do not think that a man who was so soon hungry ate until he was satisfied. Again, God by the mouth of Isaiah says what fast He did not choose : [1] "In the day of your fast ye find pleasure, and afflict the lowly : ye fast for strife and debate, and to smite with the fist of wickedness. It is not such a fast that I have chosen, saith the Lord." What kind He has chosen He thus teaches : "Deal thy bread to the hungry, and bring the house-less poor into thy house. When thou seest the naked cover him, and hide not thyself from thine own flesh." He did not therefore reject fasting, but showed what He would have it to be : for that bodily hunger is not pleasing to God which is made null and void by strife, and plunder, and lust. If God does not desire fasting, how is it that in [2] Leviticus He commands the whole people in the seventh month, on the tenth day of the month, to fast until the evening, and threatens that he who does not afflict his soul shall die and be cut off from his people ? How is it that the [3] graves of lust where the people fell in their devotion to flesh remain even to this day in the wilderness? Do we not read that the stupid people gorged themselves with quails until the wrath of God came upon them? Why was the man of God at whose prophecy the hand of King Jeroboam withered, and who ate contrary to the command of God, [4] immediately smitten ? Strange that the lion which left the ass safe and sound should not spare the prophet just risen from his meal ! He who, while he was fasting, had wrought miracles, no sooner ate a meal than he paid the penalty for the gratification. Joel also cries aloud : [5] "Sanctify a fast, proclaim a time of healing," that it might appear that a fast is sanctified by other works, and that a holy fast avails for the cure of sin. Moreover, just as true virginity is not prejudiced by the counterfeit professions of the virgins of the devil, so neither is true fasting by the peri-odic fast and perpetual abstinence from cer-tain kinds of food on the part of the wor-shippers of Isis and Cybele, particularly when a fast from bread is made up for by feasting on flesh. And just as the signs of Moses were imitated by the signs of the Egyptians which were in reality no signs at all, for the rod of Moses swallowed up the rods of the magicians : so when the devil tries to be the rival of God this does not prove that our religion is superstitious, but that we are negli-gent, since we refuse to do what even men of the world see clearly to be good.

18. His fourth and last contention is that there are two classes, the sheep and the goats, the just and the unjust : that the just stand on the right hand, the other on the left : and that to the just the words are spoken : [1] "Come, ye blessed of my Father, and inherit the king-dom prepared for you from the foundation of the world." But that sinners are thus ad-dressed : [2] "Depart from me, ye cursed, into the eternal fire which is prepared for the devil and his angels." That a good tree cannot bring forth evil fruit, nor an evil tree good fruit. Hence it is that the Saviour says to the Jews : [3] "Ye are of your father the devil, and the lusts of your father it is your will to do." He quotes the parable of the ten virgins, the wise and the foolish, and shows that the five who had no oil remained outside, but that the other five who had gotten for themselves the light of good works went into the marriage with the bridegroom. He goes back to the flood, and tells us that they who were right-eous like Noah were saved, but that the sinners perished all together. We are informed that among the men of Sodom and Gomorrha no difference is made except between the two classes of the good and the bad. The right-eous are delivered, the sinners are consumed by the same fire. There is one salvation for those who are released, one destruction for those who stay behind. Lot's wife is a clear warning that we must not deviate a hair's breadth from right. If, however, he says, you object and ask me why the righteous toils in time of peace, or in the midst of persecution, if he is to gain nothing nor have a greater reward, I would assert that he does this, not that he may gain a further reward but that he may not lose what he has already received. In Egypt also the ten plagues fell with equal violence upon all that sinned, and the same darkness hung over master and slave, noble and ignoble, the king and the people. Again at the Red Sea the righteous all passed over, the sinners were all overwhelmed. Six hun-dred thousand men, besides those who were unfit for war through age or sex, all alike fell in the desert, and two who were alike in right-eousness are alike delivered. For forty years all Israel toiled and died alike. As regards food, an homer of manna was the measure for all ages : the clothes of all alike did not wear out : the hair of all alike did not grow, nor the beard increase : the shoes of all lasted the same time. Their feet grew not hard : the

---

[1] Isa. lviii. 5 sq.   [2] xvi. 29.
[3] Numb. xi. 34.   Tertullian also speaks of the graves re-maining.
[4] 1 Kings xiii. 24.
[5] Joel i. 14 : ii. 15.   Jerome agrees with the Sept. Θεραπεία. The Heb. root signifies to *close or bind ;* hence the meaning *healing.*   But others translate Θεραπεία by *worship,* or *service.* The correct rendering appears to be *a solemn assembly* as in A. V.

---

[1] S. Matt. xxv. 34.   [2] S. Matt. xxv. 41.   [3] S. John viii. 44.

food in the mouths of all had the same taste. They went on their way to one resting place with equal toil and equal reward. All Hebrews had the same Passover, the same Feast of Tabernacles, the same Sabbath, the same New Moons. In the seventh, the Sabbatical Year, all prisoners were released without distinction of persons, and in the year of Jubilee all debts were forgiven to all debtors, and he who had sold land returned to the inheritance of his fathers.

19. Then, again, as regards the parable of the sower in the Gospel, we read that the good ground brought forth fruit, some a hundred fold, some sixty fold, and some thirty fold ; and, on the other hand, that the bad ground admitted of three degrees of sterility : but Jovinianus makes only two classes, the good soil and the bad. [1] And as in one Gospel our Lord promises the Apostles a hundred fold, in another seven fold, for leaving children and wives, and in the world to come life eternal ; and the seven and the hundred mean the same thing : so, too, in the passage before us, the numbers describing the fertility of the soil need not create any difficulty, particularly when the Evangelist Mark gives the inverse order, thirty, sixty, and a hundred. The Lord says, [2] "He that eateth my flesh and drinketh my blood abideth in me, and I in him." As, then, there are not varying degrees of Christ's presence in us, so neither are there degrees of our abiding in Christ. [3] "Every one that loveth me will keep my word : and my Father will love him, and we will come unto him, and make our abode with him." He that is righteous, loves Christ : and if a man thus loves, the Father and the Son come to him, and make their abode with him. Now I suppose that when the guest is such as this the host cannot possibly lack anything. And if our Lord says, [4] "In my Father's house are many mansions," His meaning is not that there are different mansions in the kingdom of heaven, but He indicates the number of Churches in the whole world, for though the Church be seven-fold she is but one. "I go," He says, "to prepare a place for you," not places. If this promise is peculiar to the twelve apostles, then Paul is shut out from that place, and the chosen vessel will be thought superfluous and unworthy. John and James, because they asked more than the others, did not obtain it ; and yet their dignity is not diminished, because they were equal to the rest of the apostles. [5] "Know ye not that your bodies are a temple of the Holy Ghost ?" A temple, He says, not temples, in order to show that God dwells in all alike. [1] "Neither for these only do I pray, but for them also that believe on me through their word ; as thou, Father, in me, and I in thee, are one, so they may be all one in us. And the glory which thou hast given me I have given unto them. I have loved them, as thou hast loved me. And as we are Father, Son, and Holy Ghost, one God, so may they be one people in themselves, that is, like dear children, partakers of the divine nature." Call the Church what you will, bride, sister, mother, her assembly is but one and never lacks husband, brother, or son. Her faith is one, and she is not defiled by variety of doctrine, nor divided by heresies. She continues a virgin. Whithersoever the Lamb goeth, she follows Him : she alone knows the Song of Christ.

20. "If you tell me," says he, "that one star differeth from another star in glory, I reply, that one star does differ from another star ; that is, spiritual persons differ from carnal. We love all the members alike, and do not prefer the eye to the finger, nor the finger to the ear : but the loss of any one is attended by the sorrow of all the rest. We all alike come into this world, and we all alike depart from it. There is one Adam of the earth, and another from heaven. The earthly Adam is on the left hand, and will perish : the heavenly Adam is on the right hand, and will be saved. He who says to his brother, 'thou fool,' and 'raca,' will be in danger of Gehenna. And the murderer and the adulterer will likewise be sent into Gehenna. In times of persecution some are burnt, some strangled, some beheaded, some flee, or die within the walls of a prison : the struggle varies in kind, but the victors' crown is one. No difference was made between the son who had never left his father, and his brother who was welcomed as a returning penitent. To the labourers of the first hour, the third, the sixth, the ninth, and the eleventh, the same reward of a penny was given, and what may perhaps seem still more strange to you, the first to receive the reward were they who had toiled least in the vineyard."

21. Who is there even of God's elect that would not be disturbed at these and similar passages of Holy Scripture which our crafty opponent, with a perverse ingenuity, twists to the support of his own views ? The Apostle John says that many Antichrists had come, and to make no difference between John himself and the lowest penitent is the preaching of a real Antichrist. At the same time, I am amazed at the portentous forms which Jovi-

---

1 S. Matt. xix. 29 : S Mark x. 29, 30: S. Luke xviii. 29, 30.
2 S. John vi. 56.   3 S. John xiv. 23.
4 S. John xiv. 2.   5 1 Cor. iii. 16 : vi. 19.

1 S. John xvii. 20-23.

nianus, as slippery as a snake and like another Proteus, so rapidly assumes. In sexual intercourse and full feeding he is an Epicurean ; in the distribution of rewards and punishments he all at once becomes a Stoic. He exchanges Jerusalem for [1] Citium, Judæa for Cyprus, Christ for Zeno. If we may not depart a hair's breadth from virtue, and all sins are equal, and a man who in a fit of hunger steals a piece of bread is no less guilty than he who slays a man : you must, in your turn, be held guilty of the greatest crimes. The case is different if you say that you have no sin, not even the least, and if, although all apostles and prophets and all the saints (as I have maintained in dealing with [2] his second proposition) bewail their sinfulness, you alone boast of your righteousness. But a minute ago you were barefooted : now you not only wear shoes, but decorated ones. Just now you wore a rough coat and a dirty shirt, you were grimy, and haggard, and your hand was horny with toil : now you are clad in linen and silks, and strut like an exquisite in the fashions of the Atrebates and the Laodiceans. Your cheeks are ruddy, your skin sleek, your hair smoothed down in front and behind, your belly protrudes, your shoulders are little mountains, your neck full and so loaded with fat that the half-smothered words can scarce make their escape. Surely in such extremes of dress and mode of life there must be sin on the one side or the other. I will not assert that the sin lies in the food or clothing, but that such fickleness and changing for the worse is almost censurable in itself. And what we censure, is far removed from virtue ; and what is far from virtue becomes the property of vice ; and what is proved to be vicious is one with sin. Now sin, according to you, is placed on the left hand, and corresponds to the goats. You must, therefore, return to your old habits if you are to be a sheep on the right hand ; or, if you perversely repent of your former views and change them for others, whether you like it or not, and although you shave off your beard, you will be reckoned among the goats.

22. But what is the good of calling a [3] one-eyed man Old One-eye, and of showing the inconsistency of an assailant, when we have to refute a whole series of statements ? That the sheep and the goats on the right hand and on the left are the two classes of the righteous and the wicked, I do not deny. That a good tree does not bring forth evil fruit, nor an evil one good fruit, no one doubts. The ten virgins also, wise and foolish, we divide into good and bad. We are not ignorant that at the deluge the righteous were delivered, and sinners overwhelmed with the waters. That at Sodom and Gomorrha the just man was rescued, while the sinners were consumed by fire, is clear to everyone. We are also aware that Egypt was stricken with the ten plagues, and that Israel was saved. Even little children in our schools sing how the righteous passed through the Red Sea, and Pharaoh with his host was drowned. That six hundred thousand fell in the desert because they were unbelieving, and that two only entered the land of promise, is taught by Scripture ; and so is the rest of your description of the two classes, good and bad, down to the labourers in the vineyard. But what are we to think of your assertion, that because there is a division into good and bad, the good, or the bad it may be, are not distinguished one from another, and that it makes no difference whether one is a ram in the flock or a poor little sheep ? whether the sheep have the first or the second fleece ? whether the flock is diseased and covered with the scab, or full of life and vigour ?[1] especially when by the authoritative utterances of His own prophet Ezekiel God clearly points out the difference between flock and flock of His rational sheep, saying, " Behold I judge between cattle and cattle, and between the rams and the he-goats, and between the fat cattle and the lean. Because ye have thrust with side and with shoulder, and pushed all the diseased with your horns, until they were scattered abroad." And that we might know what the cattle were, He immediately added : [2] " Ye my flock, the flock of my pasture, are men." Will Paul and that penitent who had lain with his father's wife be on an equality, because the latter repented and was received into the Church : and shall the offender because he is with him on the right hand shine with the same glory as the Apostle ? How is it then that tares and wheat grow side by side in the same field until the harvest, that is the end of the world ? What is the significance of good and bad fish being contained in the Gospel net ? Why, in Noah's ark, the type of the Church, are there different animals with different abodes according to their rank ? Why standeth the queen upon the Lord's right hand, in raiment of wrought gold, in a vesture of gold ? Why had Joseph, representing Christ, a coat of many colours ? Why does the Apostle say to the Romans : [3] " According as God had dealt to each man a measure of faith. For even as we have

---

[1] In Cyprus, where Zeno the founder of the Stoic school was born.
[2] i.e., Jovinianus. Jerome for the moment addresses the reader.
[3] Persius I. 128, Conington's translation.

[1] Ezek. xxxiv. 17, 20, 21. [3] Rom. xii. 3 sq.
[2] Ezek. xxxiv. 31.

many members in one body, and all the members have not the same office : so we, who are many, are one body in Christ, and severally members one of another. And having gifts differing according to the grace that was given to us, whether prophecy, let us prophesy according to the proportion of our faith ; or ministry, let us give ourselves to our ministry ; or he that teacheth, to his teaching ; or he that exhorteth, to his exhorting : he that giveth, let him do it with liberality ; he that ruleth, with diligence," and so on. And elsewhere : [1] " One man esteemeth one day above another : another esteemeth every day alike. Let every man be fully persuaded in his own mind." To the Corinthians he says : [2] " I have planted, Apollos watered : but God gave the increase. So then, neither is he that planteth any thing, neither he that watereth : but God that giveth the increase. Now he that planteth and he that watereth are one : and every man shall receive his own reward according to his own labour. For we are labourers together with God, ye are God's husbandry, ye are God's building." And again elsewhere : [3] " According to the grace of God which is given unto me, as a wise master-builder I laid a foundation, and another buildeth thereon. But let each man take heed how he buildeth thereupon. For other foundation can no man lay, than that which is laid, which is Jesus Christ. But if any man buildeth on the foundation, gold, silver, costly stones, wood, hay, stubble : each man's work shall be made manifest : for the day shall reveal it, because it is revealed in fire : and the fire itself shall prove each man's work of what sort it is. If any man's work shall abide which he built thereon, he shall receive a reward. If any man's work shall be burned, he shall suffer loss : but he himself shall be saved ; yet so as through fire." If the man whose work is burnt and perishes, is to suffer the loss of his labour, while he himself is saved, yet not without proof of fire : it follows that if a man's work remains which he has built upon the foundation, he will be saved without probation by fire, and consequently a difference is established between one degree of salvation and another. Again in another place he says : [4] " Let a man so account of us, as of ministers of Christ, and stewards of the mysteries of God. Here, moreover, it is required in stewards, that a man be found faithful." Would you be assured that between one steward and another there is a great difference (I am not speaking of bad and good, but of the good themselves who stand

on the right hand) ? then listen to the sequel : [1] " Know ye not that they which minister about the sacrifices, eat of the sacrifices, and they which wait upon the altar have their portion with the altar ? Even so did the Lord ordain that they which proclaim the gospel should live of the gospel. But I have used none of these things : and I wrote not these things that it may be so done in my case : for it were good for me rather to die, than that any man should make my glorying void. For if I preach the gospel, I have nothing to glory of ; for necessity is laid upon me ; for woe is unto me if I preach not the gospel. For if I do this of mine own will, I have a reward : but if not of mine own will, I have a stewardship intrusted to me. What then is my reward ? That, when I preach the gospel, I may make the gospel without charge, so as not to use to the full my right in the gospel. For though I was free from all men, I brought myself under bondage to all, that I might gain the more." You surely cannot say that men commit sin by living by the Gospel, and partaking of the sacrifices. Of course not. The Lord himself made the rule that they who preach the Gospel, should live by the Gospel. But an Apostle who does not abuse this freedom, but labours with his hands that he may not be a burden to anyone, and toils night and day and ministers to his companions, of course does this, that for his greater toil he may receive a greater reward.

23. Let us hasten to what remains. [2] " There are diversities of gifts, but the same Spirit. And there are diversities of ministrations, and the same Lord. And there are diversities of operations, but the same God who worketh all things in all. But to each one is given the manifestation of the Spirit to profit withal." And again : [3] " As the body is one, and hath many members, and all the members of the body, being many, are one body : so also is Christ." But he precludes you from saying that the different members of the one body have the same rank ; for he immediately describes the orders of the Church, and says : [4] " And God hath set some in the Church, first, apostles ; secondly, prophets ; thirdly, teachers ; then miracles, then gifts of healings, helps, governments, divers kinds of tongues. Are all apostles? are all prophets ? are all teachers ? are all workers of miracles ? have all gifts of healings ? do all speak with tongues ? do all interpret ? But desire earnestly the greater gifts. And a still more excellent way shew I unto you." And after discoursing more in detail of the graces of

---

[1] Rom. xiv. 5.   [2] 1 Cor. iii. 6 sq.   [1] 1 Cor. ix. 13 sq.   [2] 1 Cor. xii. 4.
[3] 1 Cor. iii. 10 sq.   [4] 1 Cor. iv. 1, 2.   [3] 1 Cor. xii. 12.   [4] 1 Cor. xii. 28 sq.

charity, he added : [1] "Whether there be proph-ecies, they shall be done away ; whether there be tongues, they shall cease ; whether there be knowledge, it shall be done away. For we know in part, and we prophesy in part : but when that which is perfect is come, then that which is in part shall be done away." And afterwards we read : [2] "But now abideth faith, hope, love, these three ; and the greatest of these is love. Follow after love ; yet desire earnestly spiritual gifts, but rather that ye may prophesy." And again : [3] "I would have you all speak with tongues, but rather that ye should prophesy : and greater is he that prophesieth than he that speaketh with tongues." And again : [4] "I thank God, I speak with tongues more than you all." Where there are different gifts, and one man is greater, another less, and all are called spirit-ual, they are all certainly sheep, and they stand on the right hand ; but there is a differ-ence between one sheep and another. It is humility that leads the Apostle Paul to say : [5] "I am the least of the apostles, that am not meet to be called an apostle, because I perse-cuted the church of God. But by the grace of God I am what I am : and his grace which was bestowed upon me was not found vain : but I laboured more abundantly than they all : yet not I, but the grace of God which was with me." But the very fact of his thus hum-bling himself shows the possibility of there being apostles of higher or lower rank, and God is not unjust that He will forget the work of him who is called the chosen vessel of elec-tion, and who laboured more abundantly than they all, or assign equal rewards to unequal deserts. Afterwards we read, [6] "As in Adam all die, so also in Christ shall all be now alive. But each in his own order." If each is to rise in his own order, it follows that those who rise are of different degrees of merit. [7] "All flesh is not the same flesh ; but there is one flesh of men, and another flesh of beasts, and another flesh of birds, and another of fishes. There are also celestial bodies, and bodies terrestrial : but the glory of the celestial is one, and the glory of the terrestrial is another. There is one glory of the sun, and another glory of the moon, and another glory of the stars ; for one star differeth from another star in glory. So also is the resurrection of the dead." Like a learned commentator, you have explained this passage by saying that the spiritual differ from the carnal. It follows that in heaven there will be both spiritual and carnal persons, and not only will the sheep climb thither, but your

goats also. "One star," he says, "differeth from another star in glory": this is not the distinction of sheep and goat, but of sheep and sheep, star and star. Lastly, he says, "there is one glory of the sun, and another glory of the moon." But for this, you might maintain that the phrase *one star from another star* cov-ers the whole human race ; but he introduces the sun and moon, and you cannot possibly reckon them among the goats. "So," says he, "is also the resurrection of the dead"— the just will shine with the brightness of the sun, and those of the next rank will glow with the splendour of the moon, so that one will be a Lucifer, another an Arcturus, a third an Orion, another Mazzaroth, or some other of the stars whose names are hallowed in the book of Job. [1] [2] "For we all," he says, "must be made manifest before the judgment-seat of Christ ; that each one may receive the things done in the body, according to what he hath done, whether it be good or bad." And you cannot say that the mode of our manifestation before the judgment-seat of Christ is such that the good receive good things, the bad evil things ; for he [3] teaches us in the same epistle that he who soweth sparingly shall reap also sparingly, and he that soweth bountifully shall reap also bounti-fully. Surely he who sows more and he who sows less are both on the right side. And although they belong to the same class, that of the sower, yet they differ in respect of measure and number. The same Paul, writ-ing to the Ephesians, says : [4] "to the intent that now unto the principalities and the pow-ers in the heavenly places might be made known through the church the manifold wis-dom of God." You observe that it is a varied and manifold wisdom of God which is spoken of as existing in the different ranks of the church. And in the same epistle we read, [5] "Unto each one of us was the grace given according to the measure of the grace of Christ" : not that Christ's measure varies, but only that so much of His grace is poured out as we can receive.

24. In vain, therefore, do you multiply in-stances of sheep and goats, of the five wise and five foolish virgins, of Egyptians and Israelites, and so forth, because retribution is not in the present, but will be in the future. Hence we find that the day of judgment is promised at the end of all things, because the judgment is not now. For it would be ab-surd to call the last day the day of judgment, if God were judging at the present time. Now we sail the ship, wrestle, and fight, that at last

[1] 1 Cor. xiii. 8, 9, 10. [2] 1 Cor. xiii. 18 : xiv. 1.
[3] 1 Cor. xiv. 5. [4] 1 Cor. xiv. 18.
[5] 1 Cor. xv. 9, 10. [6] 1 Cor. xv. 22.
[7] 1 Cor. xv. 39.

[1] Job ix. 9 : xxxviii. 32. [2] 2 Cor. v. 10.
[3] 2 Cor. ix. 6. [4] Eph. iii. 10.
[5] Eph. iv. 7.

we may reach the haven, be crowned, and triumph. But you, with no less adroitness than perversity, make the life of this world illustrate that of the world to come, although we know full well that here unrighteousness prevails, there, righteousness : [1] "until we go into the sanctuary of God, and understand the end of those men." The saint does not die one way, the sinner another. Those who sail the same sea have the same calm and storm. A violent death is not one thing to the robber, another to the martyr. Children are not born one way of adultery and prostitution, in another of pure marriage. Certainly our Lord and the robbers incurred the same penalty of crucifixion. If the judgment of this world and of that which is to come be the same, it follows that they who were here crucified side by side, will also be esteemed of equal rank hereafter. Paul and they who bound him, sailed together, endured the same storm, escaped together to the shore when the ship was broken with the waves. You cannot deny that the prisoner and the keepers were of unequal merit. And what were the circumstances of that same shipwreck of the Apostle and the soldiers ? The Apostle Paul afterwards [2] related a vision, and said that they who were with him in the ship had been given to him by the Lord. Are we to suppose that he to whom they were given, and they who were given to him, were of one degree of merit ? Ten righteous men can save a sinful city. Lot together with his daughters was delivered from the fire : his sons-in-law would also have been saved, had they been willing to leave the city. Now there was surely a great difference between Lot and his sons-in-law. One city out of the five, [3] Zoar, was saved, and a place which lay under the same sentence as Sodom, Gomorrha, Admah, and Zeboiim, was preserved by the prayers of a holy man. Lot and Zoar were of different merit, but both of them escaped the fire. [4] The robbers who in the absence of David had laid waste Ziklag, and made a prey of the wives and children of the inhabitants were slain on the third day in the plain, but forty men mounted on camels fled. Will you maintain that there was some difference between those who were slain and those who made good their escape ? We read in the [5] Gospel that the tower of Siloam fell upon eighteen men who perished in the ruins. Certainly our Saviour did not regard them as the only sinners : but they were punished to terrify the rest : it was like scourging a pestilent fellow to teach fools wisdom. If all sinners are punished alike, it is unjust for one to be slain while another is admonished by his comrade's death.

25. You raise the objection that all Israelites had the same measure of manna, an homer, and were alike in respect of dress, and hair, and beard, and shoes ; as though we did not all alike partake of the body of Christ. In the Christian mysteries there is one means of sanctification for the master and the servant, the noble and the low-born, for the king and his soldiers, and yet, that which is one varies according to the merits of those who receive it. [1] "Whosoever shall eat or drink unworthily shall be guilty of the body and blood of the Lord." Does it follow that because Judas drank of the same cup as the rest of the apostles, that he and they are of equal merit ? But suppose that we do not choose to receive the sacrament, at all events we all have the same life, breathe the same air, have the same blood in our veins, are fed on the same food. Moreover, if our viands are improved by culinary skill and are made more palatable for the consumer, food of this kind does not satisfy nature, but tickles the appetite. We are all alike subject to hunger, all alike suffer with cold : we alike are shrivelled with the frost, or melted with the broiling heat. The sun and the moon, and all the company of the stars, the showers, the whole world run their course for us all alike, and, as the Gospel tells us, the same refreshing rain falls upon all, good and bad, just and unjust. If the present is a picture of the future, then the Sun of Righteousness will rise upon sinners as well as upon the righteous, upon the wicked and the holy, upon the heathen as well as upon Jews and Christians, though the Scripture says, [2] "Unto you that fear the Lord shall the Sun of Righteousness arise." If He will rise to those that fear, He will set to the despisers and the false prophets. The sheep which stand on the right hand will be brought into the kingdom of heaven, the goats will be thrust down to hell. The parable does not contrast the sheep one with another, or on the other hand the goats, but merely makes a difference between sheep and goats. The whole truth is not taught in a single passage : we must always bear in mind the exact point of an illustration. For instance, the ten virgins are not examples of the whole human race, but of the careful and the slothful : the former are ever anticipating the advent of our Lord, the latter abandon themselves to idle slumber without a thought of future judgment. And so at the end of the parable it is said, [3] "Watch, for ye know not the

---

[1] Ps. lxxiii. 17.
[2] See Acts xxvii. 23 and the context.
[3] Gen. xix. 18–21.　　　[4] 1 Sam. xxx. 1 sq.
[5] S. Luke xiii. 4.

[1] 1 Cor. xi. 27.　　　[2] Mal. iv. 2.
[3] S. Matt. xxv. 13.

day, nor the hour." If at the deluge Noah was delivered, and the whole world perished, all men were flesh, and therefore were destroyed. You must either say that the sons of Noah and Noah for whose sake they were delivered were of unequal merit, or you must place the accursed Ham in the same rank as his father because he was delivered with him from the flood. At the passion of Christ all wavered, all were unprofitable together : there was none that did good, no not one. Will you therefore dare to say that Peter and the rest of the Apostles who fled denied the Saviour in the same sense as Caiaphas and the Pharisees and the people who cried out, [1] " Crucify him, crucify him " ? And, to say no more about the Apostles, do you think Annas and Caiaphas, and Judas the traitor guilty of no greater crime than Pilate who was compelled against his will to give sentence against our Lord ? The guilt of Judas is proportioned to his former merit, and the greater the guilt, the greater the penalty too. [2] " For the *mighty* shall mightily suffer torment." An evil tree does not bear good fruit, nor a good tree evil fruit. If this be so, tell me how it was that Paul though he was an evil tree and persecuted the Church of Christ, afterwards bore good fruit ? And Judas, though he was a good tree and wrought miracles like the other Apostles, afterwards turned traitor and brought forth evil fruit ? The truth is that a good tree does not bear evil fruit, nor an evil tree good fruit, so long as they continue in their goodness, or badness. And if we read that every Hebrew keeps the same Passover, and that in [3] the seventh year every prisoner is set free, and that at Jubilee, that is the fiftieth year, [4] every possession returns to its owner, all this refers not to the present, but to the future ; for being in bondage during the six days of this world, on the seventh day, the true and eternal Sabbath, we shall be free, at any rate if we wish to be free while still in bondage in the world. If, however, we do not desire it, our ear will be bored in token of our disobedience, and together with our wives and children, whom we preferred to liberty, that is, with the flesh and its works, we shall be in perpetual slavery.

26. As for the parable of the sower which makes both good and bad ground bear a triple crop, and the passage from the apostle in which upon Christ as the foundation one man builds gold, silver, costly stones, another wood, hay, stubble, the meaning is perfectly clear. We know that in a great house there are different vessels, and to wish to contradict so

plain a truth would be sheer impudence. Yet that Jovinianus may not triumph in a lie and quote the instance of the apostles by way of discrediting the hundred fold, sixty fold, and thirty fold, let me inform him that in [1] Matthew and Mark a hundred fold is promised to the apostles who had left all. And I would tell him further, that in the Gospel of Luke we find *much more*, that is πολὺ πλείονα, and that there is absolutely no instance in the Gospels of a *hundred* standing for *seven ;* and that he is convicted either of forgery, or of ignorance ; and that our cause is not prejudiced by the fact that in one Gospel the enumeration begins at a hundred, in another at thirty, since it is a rule with all Scripture, and especially with the older writings, to put the lowest number first and so ascend by degrees to the higher. For instance, suppose one to say that so and so lived five and seventy and a hundred years, it does not follow that five and seventy are more than a hundred because they were first mentioned. If you do not on the side of good admit the difference between a hundred, sixty, and thirty, neither will you do so on the side of evil, and the seed which fell by the wayside, upon the rock, and among thorns, will be equally faulty. But if the former three, or the latter three, on the side of good, or on the side of evil respectively, are one and the same, it was foolish instead of speaking of two things to enumerate six kinds, and all the more because according to the account of the parable in Matthew, Mark, and Luke, the Saviour always added : "He that hath ears to hear, let him hear." Where there is no deep inner meaning, it is useless to draw our attention to the mystic sense.

27. You give it as your opinion that, since the Father and the Son make their abode with the faithful, and since Christ is their guest, nothing is lacking. I suppose, however, that Christ's abiding with the Corinthians was one thing, with the Ephesians another : it was one thing, I say, for Him to abide with those whom Paul blamed for many sins, another for Him to dwell with those to whom the apostle revealed mysteries hidden from the beginning of the world ; one thing for Him to be in Titus and Timothy, another in Paul. Certainly amongst them that have been born of women, there has not arisen a greater than John the Baptist. But the term greater implies others who are less. And [2] "he who is least in the kingdom of heaven is greater than he." You see then that in heaven one is greatest and another is least, and that among the angels and the

---

[1] S. John xix. 6.   [2] Wisd. vi. 7.
[3] Ex. xxi. 2.   [4] Lev. xxv. 13.

[1] S. Matt. xix. 29 : S. Mark x. 30 : S. Luke xviii. 30. In S. Matthew some authorities agree with S. Luke in reading " *manifold.*"
[2] Matt. xi. 11.

invisible creation there is a manifold and infinite diversity. Why do the apostles say: [1] "Lord, increase our faith," if there is one measure for all? And why did our Lord rebuke His disciple, saying: [2] "O thou of little faith, wherefore didst thou doubt?" In Jeremiah also we read concerning the future kingdom: [3] "Behold, the days come, saith the Lord, that I will make a new covenant with the house of Israel, and with the house of Judah: not according to the covenant that I made with their fathers." And soon after: [4] "I will put my law in their inward parts, and in their heart will I write it; and I will be their God and they shall be my people: and they shall teach no more every man his neighbour, and every man his brother, saying, Know the Lord: for they shall all know me, from the least of them unto the greatest of them." The context of this passage clearly shows that the prophet is describing the future kingdom, and how can there possibly be in it a least or greatest, if all are to be equal? The secret is disclosed in the Gospel: [5] "Whosoever shall do and teach, he shall be called great in the kingdom of heaven: but whosoever shall teach, and not do, shall be least." [6] The Saviour taught us at a feast to take the lowest place, lest, when one greater than us came, we should be thrust with disgrace from the higher place. If we cannot fall, but only raise ourselves by penitence, what is the meaning of the ladder at Bethel, on which the angels come from heaven to earth and descend as well as ascend? Surely while on that ladder they are reckoned among the sheep and stand on the right hand. There are angels who descend from heaven; but Jovinianus is sure that they retain their inheritance.

28. But when Jovinianus supposes that the many mansions in our Father's house are churches scattered throughout the world, who can refrain from laughing; since Scripture plainly teaches in John's Gospel that our Lord was discoursing not of the number of the churches, but of the heavenly mansions, and the eternal tabernacles for which the prophet longed? [7] "In my Father's house," He says, "are many mansions: if it were not so, I would have told you; for I go to prepare a place for you. And if I go and prepare a place for you I will come again, and will receive you unto myself, that where I am, there ye may·be also." The place and the mansions which Christ says He would prepare for the apostles are of course in the Father's house, that is, in the kingdom of heaven, not on

earth, where for the present He was leading the apostles. And at the same time regard must be had to the sense of Scripture: "I might tell you," He says, "that I go to prepare a place for you, if there were not many mansions in my Father's house, that is to say, if each individual did not prepare for himself a mansion through his own works rather than receive it through the bounty of God. The preparation is therefore not mine, but yours." This view is supported by the fact that it profited Judas nothing to have a place prepared, since he lost it by his own fault. And we must interpret in the same way what our Lord says to the sons of Zebedee, one of whom wished to sit on His left hand, the other on His right: [1] "My cup indeed ye shall drink: but to sit on my right hand, and on my left hand, is not mine to give, but it is for them for whom it hath been prepared of my Father." It is not the Son's to give; how then is it the Father's to prepare? There are, He says, prepared in heaven, many different mansions, destined for many different virtues, and they will be awarded not to persons, but to persons' works. In vain therefore do you ask of me what rests with yourselves, a reward which my Father has prepared for those whose virtues will entitle them to rise to such dignity. Again when He says: [2] "I will come again, and will receive you unto myself: that where I am, there ye may be also," He is speaking especially to the apostles, concerning whom it is elsewhere written, "That as I and thou, Father, are one, so they also may be one in us," inasmuch as they have believed, have been perfected, and can say, [3] "the Lord is my portion." If, however, there are not many mansions, how is it taught in the Old Testament correspondingly with the New, that the chief priest has one rank, the priests another, the Levites another, the door-keepers another, the sacristans another? How is it that in the [4] book of Ezekiel, where a description is given of the future Church and of the heavenly Jerusalem, the priests who have sinned are degraded to the rank of sacristans and door-keepers, and although they are in the temple of God, that is on the right hand, they are not among the rams, but among the poorest of the sheep? How again is it that in the river which flows from the temple, and replenishes the salt sea, and gives new life to everything, we read there are many kinds of fish? Why do we read that in the kingdom of heaven there are Archangels, Angels, Thrones, Dominions, Powers, Cherubim and Seraphim, and every name which is named, not only in this present world, but also that which is to come? A difference of

[1] S. Luke xvii. 5.
[2] Matt. xiv. 31.
[3] Jer. xxxi. 31.
[4] Jer. xxxi. 33, 34.
[5] S. Matt. v. 19.
[6] S. Luke xiv. 9.
[7] S. John xiv. 2, 3.

[1] S. Matt. xx . 23.
[2] S. John xiv. 3.
[3] Ps. lxxiii. 26.
[4] Ez. xliv. 10.

name is meaningless where there is not a difference of rank. An Archangel is of course an Archangel to other inferior angels, and Powers, and Dominions have other spheres over which they exercise authority. This is what we find in heaven and in the administration of God. You must not therefore smile and sneer at us, as is your wont, for making a graduated series of emperors, præfects and counts, tribunes and centurions, companies, and all the other steps in the service.

29. It is mere trifling to quote the passage : [1] " Know ye not that your bodies are a temple of the Holy Ghost," for it is customary in Holy Scripture to speak of a single object as though it were many, and of many as though they were one. And Jovinianus himself should know that even in a temple there are many divisions—the outer and the inner courts, the vestibules, the holy place, and the Holy of Holies. There are also in a temple kitchens, pantries, oil-cellars, and cupboards for the vessels. And so in the temple of our body there are different degrees of merit. God does not dwell in all alike, nor does He impart Himself to all in the same degree. A portion of the spirit of Moses was taken and given to the seventy elders. I suppose there is a difference between the abundance of the river, and that of the rivulets. [2] Elijah's spirit was given in double measure to Elisha, and thus double grace wrought greater miracles. Elijah while living restored a dead man to life ; Elisha after death did the same. Elijah invoked famine on the people ; Elisha in a single day put the enemy's forces in the power of the city which they besieged. No doubt the words, " Know ye not that your bodies are a temple of the Holy Ghost," refer to the whole assembly of the faithful, who, joined together, make up the one body of Christ. But the question now is, who in the body is worthy to be the feet of Christ, and who the head ? who is His eye, and who His hand ?—a distinction indicated by the [3] two women in the Gospel, the penitent and the holy woman, one of whom held His feet, the other His head. Some authorities, however, think there was only one woman, and that she who began at His feet gradually advanced to His head. Jovinianus further urges against us our Lord's words, [4] " I pray not for these only, but also for those who shall believe on me through their word : that as I, Father, in thee and thou in me are one, so they all may be one in us," and reminds us that the whole Christian people is one in God, and, as His well-beloved sons, are [5] " partakers of the

divine nature." We have already said, and the truth must now be inculcated more in detail, that we are not one in the Father and the Son according to nature, but according to grace. For the essence of the human soul and the essence of God are not the same, as the Manichæans constantly assert. But, says our Lord : [1] " Thou hast loved them as thou hast loved me." You see, then, that we are privileged to partake of His essence, not in the realm of nature, but of grace, and the reason why we are beloved of the Father is that He has loved the Son ; and the members are loved, those namely of the body. [2] " For as many as received Christ, to them gave He power to become sons of God, even to them that believe on His name : which were born not of blood, nor of the will of the flesh, nor of the will of man, but of God." The Word was made flesh that we might pass from the flesh into the Word. The Word did not cease to be what He had been ; nor did the human nature lose that which it was by birth. The glory was increased, the nature was not changed. Do you ask how we are made one body with Christ ? Your creator shall be your instructor : [3] " He that eateth my flesh and drinketh my blood abideth in me, and I in him. As the living Father sent me, and I live because of the Father, so he that eateth me, he also shall live because of me. This is the bread which came down out of heaven." But the Evangelist John, who had drunk in wisdom from the breast of Christ, agrees herewith, and says : [4] " Hereby know we that we abide in him, and he in us, because he hath given us of his Spirit. Whosoever shall confess that Jesus is the Son of God, God abideth in him, and he in God." If you believe in Christ, as the apostles believed, you shall be made one body with them in Christ. But, if it is rash for you to claim for yourself a faith and works like theirs when you have not the same faith and works, you cannot have the same place.

30. You repeat the words bride, sister, mother, and affirm that all these are titles of the one Church and names applied to all believers. The fact goes against you. For if the Church admits but one rank, and has not many members in one body, what necessity is there for calling her bride, sister, mother ? It must be that she is the bride of some, the sister of others, the mother of others. All indeed stand on the right hand, but one stands as a bridegroom, another as a brother, a third as a son. [5] " My little children," says the Apostle, " of whom I am again in travail

---

[1] 1 Cor. vi. 19.
[2] Correctly, a portion of two, *i.e.*, the portion of a first-born. Deut. xxi. 17.
[3] S. Luke vii., S. Matt. xxvi., S. Mark xiv., S. John xii.
[4] S. John xvii. 20, 21.   [5] 2 Pet. i. 4.

[1] S. John xvii. 23.   [2] S. John i. 12, 13.
[3] S. John vi. 57 sq.   [4] 1 John iv. 13, 15.
[5] Gal. iv. 19.

until Christ be formed in you." Do you think that the children who are being born and the apostle who is in travail are of equal rank? And the folly of your contention that we love all the members alike, and do not prefer the eye to the finger, nor the hand to the ear, but that if one be lost all mourn, is proved by the lesson which the apostle teaches the Corinthians: [1] "Some members are more honourable, others excite the sense of shame: and those parts to which shame attaches are clothed with more abundant honour; whereas our comely parts have no need of our care." Do you think that the mouth and the belly, the eyes and the outlets of the body are to be classed together as of equal merit? [2] "The lamp of thy body," he says, "is thine eye. If thine eye be blinded, thy whole body is in darkness." If you cut off a finger, or the tip of the ear, there is indeed pain, but the loss is not so great, nor is the disfigurement attended by so much pain as it would be were you to take out the eyes, mutilate the nose, or saw through a bone. Some members we can dispense with and yet live: without others life is an impossibility. Some offences are light, some heavy. It is one thing to owe ten thousand talents, another to owe a farthing. We shall have to give account of the idle word no less than of adultery; but it is not the same thing to be put to the blush, and to be put upon the rack, to grow red in the face and to ensure lasting torment. Do you think I am merely expressing my own views? Hear what the Apostle John says: [3] "He who knows that his brother sinneth a sin not unto death, let him ask, and he shall give him life, even to him that sinneth not unto death. But he that hath sinned unto death, who shall pray for him?" You observe that if we entreat for smaller offences, we obtain pardon: if for greater ones, it is difficult to obtain our request: and that there is a great difference between sins. And so with respect to the people of Israel who had sinned a sin unto death, it is said to Jeremiah: [4] "Pray not thou for this people, neither entreat for them, and do not withstand me, for I will not hear thee." Moreover, if it be true that we all alike enter the world and all alike leave it, and this is a precedent for the world to come, it follows that whether righteous or sinners we shall all be equally esteemed by God, because the conditions of our birth and death are now the same. And if you contend that there are two Adams, the one of the earth, the other from heaven; and that they who were in the earthly Adam stand on the left hand, those who were

in the heavenly are on the right hand, before we go further, let me ask you a question concerning two brothers: Was Esau in the earthly Adam, or in the heavenly? No one doubts that you will reply, he was in the earthly. In which was Jacob? Without hesitation you will say, in the heavenly. How then was he in the heavenly when Christ had not yet come in the flesh—Christ who is called the second Adam from heaven? You must either reckon all before the incarnation of Christ in the old Adam, and even the just in the man from the earth, and then they will be on the left among your goats; or, if it be impious to give Isaac the same place as Ishmael, Jacob as Esau, the saints as sinners, the last Adam will date from the time when Christ was born of a Virgin, and your argument from the two Adams will not benefit your sheep and goats, because we have proved that in the first Adam there were both sheep and goats, and that of those who were in one and the same man, some stood on the right hand of God, others on the left: [1] "For from Adam even until Moses death reigned over all, even over them that had not sinned after the likeness of Adam's transgression."

31. As regards your attempt to show that railing and murder, the use of the expression *raca* and adultery, the idle word and godlessness, are rewarded with the same punishment, I have already given you my reply, and will now briefly repeat it. You must either deny that you are a sinner if you are not to be in danger of Gehenna: or, if you are a sinner you will be sent to hell for even a light offence: [2] "The mouth that lieth," says one, "kills the soul." I suspect that you, like other men, have occasionally told a lie: [3] for all men are liars, that God alone may be true, [4] and that He may be justified in His words, and may prevail when He judges. It follows either that you will not be a man lest you be found a liar: or if you are a man and are consequently a liar, you will be punished with parricides and adulterers. For you admit no difference between sins, and the gratitude of those whom you raise from the mire and set on high will not equal the rage against you of those whom for the trifling offences of daily life you have thrust into utter darkness. And if it be so that in a persecution one is stifled, another beheaded, another flees, or the fourth dies within the walls of a prison, and one crown of victory awaits various kinds of struggle, the fact tells in our favour. For in martyrdom it is the will, which gives occasion to the death, that is crowned. My duty is to

---

[1] 1 Cor. xii. 22-24. [2] S. Luke xi. 34.
[3] 1 John v. 16. [4] Jer. vii. 16.

[1] Rom. v. 14. Wisd. i. 11.
[3] Ps. cxvi. 11. Rom. iii. 4. [4] Ps. li. 4.

resist the frenzy of the heathen, and not deny the Lord. It rests with them either to behead, or to burn, or to shut up in prison, or enforce various other penalties. But if I escape, and die in solitude, there will not at my death be the same crown for me as for them, because the confession of Christ will not have been to me as to them the cause of death. As for your remark that absolutely no difference was made between the brother who had always been with his father, and him who was afterwards welcomed as a penitent, I am willing to add, if you like, that the one drachma which was lost and was found was put with the others, and that the one sheep which the good shepherd, leaving the ninety and nine, sought and brought back, made up the full tale of a hundred. But it is one thing to be a penitent, and with tears sue for pardon, another to be always with the father. And so both the shepherd and the father say by the mouth of Ezekiel to the sheep that was carried back, and to the son that was lost, [1] "And I will establish my covenant with thee ; and thou shalt know that I am the Lord : that thou mayest remember, and be confounded, and never open thy mouth ever more, because of thy shame, when I have forgiven thee all that thou hast done." That penitents may have their due it is enough for them to feel shame instead of all other punishment. Hence in another place it is said to them, [2] " Then shall ye remember your evil ways, and all the crimes wherewith ye were defiled, and ye shall loathe yourselves in your own sight for all the wickedness that ye have done ; and ye shall know that I am the Lord, when I shall have done you good for my name's sake, and not according to your evil ways, nor according to your evil doings." The son, moreover, was reproved by his father for envying his brother's deliverance, and for being tormented by jealousy while the angels in heaven were rejoicing. The parallel, however, is not to be drawn between the merits of the two sons (one of whom was temperate, the other a prodigal) and those of the whole human race, but the characters depicted are either Jews and Christians, or saints and penitents. In the lifetime of Bishop Damasus I dedicated to him a small treatise upon this parable.[3]

32. And if a penny was given to all the labourers, those of the first, the third, the sixth, the ninth, and the eleventh hours, and they came first for the reward who were the last to work in the vineyard, even here the persons described do not belong to one time or one age, but from the beginning of the world to the end of it there are different calls and a special meaning attaches to each. Abel and Seth were called at the first hour : Enoch and Noah at the third : Abraham, Isaac, and Jacob at the sixth : Moses and the prophets at the ninth : at the eleventh the Gentiles, to whom the recompense was first given because they believed on the crucified Lord, and inasmuch as it was hard for them to believe they earned a great reward. Many kings and prophets have desired to see the things that we see, and have not seen them. But the one penny does not represent one reward, but one life, and one deliverance from Gehenna. And as by the favour of the sovereign those guilty of various crimes are released from prison, and each one, according to his toil and exertions, is in this or that condition of life, so too the penny, as it were by the favour of our Sovereign, is the discharge from prison of us all by baptism. Now our work is, according to our different virtues, to prepare for ourselves a different future.

33. So far I have replied to the separate portions of his argument ; I shall now address myself to the general question. Our Lord says to his disciples, [1] "Whosoever would become great among you, let him be least of all." If we are all to be equal in heaven, in vain do we humble ourselves here that we may be greater there. Of the two debtors who owed, one five hundred pence, the other fifty, he to whom most was forgiven loved most. And so the Saviour says, [2] "I say to you, her sins which are many are forgiven her, for she hath loved much. But to whom little is forgiven, the same loveth little." He who loves little, and has little forgiven, he will of course be of inferior rank. [3] The householder when he set out delivered to his servants his goods, to one five talents, to another two, to another one, to each according to his ability. Just as in another Gospel it is written that a nobleman setting out for a far country to receive for himself a kingdom and return, called the servants, and gave them each a sum of money, with which one gained ten pounds, another five, and they, each according to his ability and the gain he had made, received ten or five cities. But one who had received a talent, or a pound, buried it in the ground, or tied it up in a napkin, and kept it until his master's return. Our first thought is that if, according to the modern Zeno, the righteous do not toil in hope of reward, but to avoid the loss of what they already have, he who buried his pound or talent that he might not lose it, did no wrong,

---

[1] Ezek. xvi. 62, 63.   [2] Ezek. xxxvi. 31, 32.
[3] Letter XXI.

[1] S. Matt. xx. 26.   [2] S. Luke vii. 47.
[3] S. Matt. xxv. 15 sq.

nd the caution of him who kept his money s worthy of more praise than the fruitless oil of those who wore themselves out and yet eceived no reward for their labour. Then bserve that the very talent which was taken rom the timid or negligent servant, was not given to him who had the smaller profit, but o him who had gained the most, that is, to im who had been placed over ten cities. If difference of rank is not constituted by the difference in number, why did our Lord say, "He gave to everyone according to his bility"? If the gain of five talents and ten alents is the same, why were not ten cities given to him who gained the least, and five to im who gained the most? But that our Lord s not satisfied with what we have, but always desires more, He himself shows by saying, "Wherefore didst thou not give my money o the money-changers, that so when I came might have received it with usury?" The Apostle Paul understood this, and [1] forgetting hose things which were behind, reached forward to those things which were in front, that s, he made daily progress, and did not keep he grace given to him carefully wrapped up n a napkin, but his spirit, like the capital of keen man of business, was renewed from lay to day, and if he were not always growing larger, he thought himself growing less. ix cities of refuge are mentioned in the law, provided for fugitives who were involuntary omicides, and the cities themselves belonged o the priests. I should like to ask whether ou would put those fugitives among your goats, or among our sheep. If they were goats, they would be slain like other homicides, and would not enter the cities of God's ninisters. If you say they were sheep, they will not possibly be such sheep as can enjoy full liberty and feed without fear of wolves. And it will be plain to you that sheep indeed hey are, but wandering sheep: that they are n the right hand, but do not stand there: hey flee until the High Priest dies and descending into hell liberates their souls. The Gibeonites met the children of Israel, and lthough other nations were slaughtered, they were kept [2] for hewers of wood and drawers f water. [3] And of such value were they in God's eyes, that the family of Saul was destroyed for the wrong done to them. Where would you put them? Among the goats? But hey were not slain, and they were avenged y the determination of God. Among the heep? But holy Scripture says they were ot of the same merit as the Israelites. You ee then that they do indeed stand on the right hand, but are of a far inferior grade. Jonathan came between David, the holy man, and Saul, the worst of kings, and we can neither place him among the kids because he was worthy of a prophet's love, nor amongst the rams lest we make him equal to David, and particularly when we know that he was slain. He will, therefore, be among the sheep, but low down. And just as in the case of David and Jonathan, you will be bound to recognize differences between sheep and sheep. [1] "That servant, which knew his lord's will, and made not ready, nor did according to his will, shall be beaten with many stripes; but he that knew not, and did things worthy of stripes, shall be beaten with few stripes. And to whomsoever much is given, of him shall much be required: and to whom they commit much, of him will they ask the more." Lo! more or less is committed to different servants, and according to the nature of the trust, as well as of the sin, is the number of stripes inflicted.

34. The whole account of the land of Judah and of the tribes is typical of the church in heaven. Let us read Joshua, the son of Nun, or the concluding portions of Ezekiel, and we shall see that the historical division of the land as related by the one finds a counterpart in the spiritual and heavenly promises of the other. What is the meaning of the seven and eight steps in the description of the temple? or again, what significance attaches to the fact that in the Psalter, after being taught the mystic alphabet by the [2] one hundred and eighteenth psalm we arrive by fifteen steps at the point where we can sing: [3] "Behold, now bless the Lord, all ye servants of the Lord: ye who stand in the house of the Lord, in the courts of the house of our God." Why did [4] two tribes and a half dwell on the other side of Jordan, a district abounding in cattle, while the remaining nine tribes and a half either drove out the old inhabitants from their possessions, or dwelt with them? Why did the tribe of Levi [5] receive no portion in the land, but have the Lord for their portion? And how is it that of the priests and Levites, themselves, the [6] high priest alone entered the Holy of Holies where were the cherubim and the mercyseat? Why did the other priests wear [7] linen raiment only, and not have their clothing of

---

[1] S.Luke xii. 47, 48.
[2] Ps. cxix. in our arrangement of the Psalter. The psalm is divided into twenty-two portions, which begin with the successive letters of the Hebrew alphabet. The following fifteen psalms are called in our Authorized Version, Songs of Degrees (Vulgate, graduum, steps). For the origin of the title, Wordsworth, or Neal and Littledale on Ps. cxx. may be consulted.
[3] Ps. cxxxiv. 1.
[4] Numb. xxxiv. 15; Josh. xiv. 3.
[5] Numb. xviii. 20.
[6] Lev. xvi. 2; Heb. ix. 7.
[7] Ex. xxviii. etc.

[1] Phil. iii. 13.　　[2] Josh. ix. 27.
[3] 2 Sam. xxi. 1.

wrought gold, blue, scarlet, purple, and fine cloth? The priests and [1]Levites of the lower order took care of the oxen and wains : those of the higher order carried the ark of the Lord on their shoulders. If you do away with the gradations of the tabernacle, the temple, the Church, if, to use a common military phrase, all upon the right hand are to be "up to the same standard," bishops are to no purpose, priests in vain, deacons useless. Why do virgins persevere? widows toil? Why do married women practise continence? Let us all sin, and when once we have repented, we shall be on the same footing as the apostles.

35. But now we have just sighted land : the foaming billows have been rolling mountain-high : our ship has been borne aloft, or has rushed headlong into the depths beneath : little by little the haven opens to the view of the weary and exhausted sailors. We have discussed the married, widows, and virgins. We have preferred virginity to widowhood, widowhood to marriage. The passage of the apostle, in which he treats questions of this kind, has been expounded, and particular objections have been met. We also took a survey of secular literature, and inquired what was thought of virgins, and what of those who had one husband ; and by way of contrast we pointed out the cares which sometimes attend wedlock. Then we passed to the second division, in which our opponent denies the possibility of sinning to those who have been baptized with complete faith. And we showed that God alone is faultless, and every creature is at fault, not because all have sinned, but because all may sin, and those who stand have cause to fear when they see the fall of men like themselves. In the third place we came to fasting, and inasmuch as our opponent's argument fell under two heads, and he appealed either to philosophy, or to Holy Scripture, we also furnished a several reply. In the fourth, that is the last section, the sheep and goats on the right hand and the left, the righteous and the wicked, were distributed into two classes, the intention being to show that there is no difference between one just man and another, or between one sinner and another. To prove the point Jovinianus had accumulated countless instances from Scripture which apparently favoured his view, and this contention we rebutted both by arguments and illustrations from Scripture, and pulverized Zeno's old opinion no less with common sense than with the words of inspiration.

36. I must in conclusion say a few words to our modern Epicurus wantoning in his gardens with his favourites of both sexes. On your side are the fat and the sleek in their festal attire. I may mock like Socrates, add if you please all swine and dogs, and, since you like flesh so well, vultures too, eagles, hawks, and owls. We shall never be afraid of the host of [1]Aristippus. If ever I see a fine fellow, or a man who is no stranger to the curling-irons, with his hair nicely done and his cheeks all aglow, he belongs to your herd, or rather grunts in concert with your pigs. To our flock belong the sad, the pale, the meanly clad, who, like strangers in this world, though their tongues are silent, yet speak by their dress and bearing. [2] "Woe is me," say they, "that my sojourning is prolonged ! that I dwell among the tents of Kedar!" that is to say, in the darkness of this world, for the light shineth in the darkness, and the darkness comprehended it not. Boast not of having many disciples. The Son of God taught in Judæa and only twelve apostles followed Him. [3] " have trodden the wine-press alone," He says " and of the peoples there was no man with me." At the passion He was left alone, and even Peter's fidelity to Him wavered : on the other hand all the people applauded the doctrine of the Pharisees, saying, [4] " Crucify him, crucify him. We have no king but Cæsar," that is in effect, we follow vice, not virtue ; Epicurus, not Christ ; Jovinianus, not the Apostle Paul. If many assent to your views, that only indicates voluptuousness ; for they do not so much approve your utterance as favour their own vices. In our crowded thoroughfares a false prophet may be seen any day stick in hand belabouring the fools about him, and knocking out the teeth of those who offend him, and yet he never lacks constant followers. And do you regard it as a mark of great wisdom if you have a following of many pigs whom you are feeding to make pork for hell? Since you published your views, and set the mark of your approval on baths in which the sexes bathe together, the impatience which once threw over burning lust the semblance of a robe of modesty has been laid bare and exposed. What was once hidden is now open to the gaze of all. You have revealed your disciples, such as they are, not made them. One result of your teaching is that sin is no longer even repented of. Your virgins whom, with depth of wisdom never found before in speech or writing, you have taught the apostle's maxim that it is better to marry than to burn, have turned secret adulterers into acknowledged

---

usbands.[1] It was not the apostle, the chosen
essel, who gave this advice ; it was Virgil's
widow :

[2] " She calls it wedlock ; thus she veils her fault."

37. About four hundred years have passed
since the preaching of Christ flashed upon the
world, and during that time in which His robe
has been torn by countless heresies, almost
the whole body of error has been derived from
the Chaldæan, Syriac, and Greek languages.
Basilides, the master of licentiousness and
the grossest sensuality, after the lapse of so
many years, and like a second [3] Euphorbus,
was changed by transmigration into Jovinian,
o that the Latin tongue might have a heresy
f its own. Was there no other province
in the whole world to receive the gospel
of pleasure, and into which the serpent
might insinuate itself, except that which was
founded by the teaching of Peter, upon
the rock Christ ? Idol temples had fallen
before the standard of the Cross and the
severity of the Gospel : now on the contrary
ust and gluttony endeavour to overthrow the
olid structure of the Cross. And so God
says by Isaiah, [4] " O my people, they which
less you cause you to err, and trouble the
paths of your feet." Also by Jeremiah,[5] " Flee
out of the midst of Babylon, and save every
man his life, and believe not the false proph-
ts which say, Peace, peace, and there is no
peace ; " who are always repeating, [6] " The
emple of the Lord, the temple of the Lord."
Thy prophets have seen for thee false and
oolish things ; they have not laid bare thine
iniquity that they might call thee to repent-
nce : who devour God's people like bread :
hey have not called upon God." Jeremiah
announced the captivity and was stoned by
he people. [7] Hananiah, the son of Azzur,
broke the bars of wood for the present, but
was preparing bars of iron for the future.
False prophets always promise pleasant things,
and please for a time. Truth is bitter, and
hey who preach it are filled with bitterness.
For with the unleavened bread of sincerity
and truth the Lord's passover is kept, and it is
aten with bitter herbs. Admirable are your
tterances and worthy of the ears of the bride
of Christ standing in the midst of her virgins,
and widows, and celibates ! (their very name
s [8] derived from the fact that they who ab-
tain from intercourse are fit for heaven). This
s what you say : " Fast seldom, marry often.

You cannot do the work of marriage unless
you take mead, and flesh, and *solid food*. For
lust strength is required. Flesh is soon spent
and enervated. You need not be afraid of
fornication. He who has been once baptized
into Christ cannot fall, for he has the consolation of marriage to slake his lust. And if
you do fall, repentance will restore you, and
you who were hypocrites at baptism may have
a firm faith in your repentance. Be not disturbed by the thought of a difference between
the righteous and the penitent, and do not imagine that pardon even gives a lower place ;
rather believe that it takes away your crown.
For there is one reward : he who stands on the
right hand shall enter into the kingdom of
heaven." Through counsels such as these your
swine-herds are richer than our shepherds, and
the he-goats draw after them many of the other
sex : [1] " They were as fed horses : they were
mad after women " : they no sooner see a
woman than they neigh after her, and, shame
to say ! find scriptural authority for the consolation of their incontinence. But the very
women, unhappy creatures ! though they deserve no pity, who chant the words of their
instructor (for what does God require of them
but to become mothers ?), have lost not only
their chastity, but all sense of shame, and defend their licentious practices with an access
of impudence. You have, moreover, in your
army many subalterns, you have your guards-
men and your skirmishers at the outposts, the
round-bellied, the well-dressed, the exquisites,
and noisy orators, to defend you with tooth
and nail. The noble make way for you, the
wealthy print kisses on your face. For unless
you had come, the drunkard and the glutton
could not have entered paradise. All honor
to your virtue, or rather to your vices! You
have in your camp, even amazons with uncovered breasts, bare arms and knees, who
challenge the men who come against them to
a battle of lust. Your household is a large
one, and so in your aviaries not only turtle-
doves, but hoopoes are fed, which may wing
their flight over the whole field of rank debauchery. Pull me to pieces and scatter me
to the winds : tax me with what offences you
please : accuse me of luxurious and delicate
living : you would like me better if I were
guilty, for I should belong to your herd.

38. But I will now address myself to you,
great Rome, who with the confession of
Christ have blotted out the blasphemy written
on your forehead. Mighty city, mistress-city
of the world, city of the Apostle's praises, shew
the meaning of your name. *Rome* is either
strength in Greek, or *height* in Hebrew. Lose

---

[1] Jovinianus's doctrine is said to have influenced some who had
taken a vow of virginity, to marry.
[2] Virgil Æn. iv. 172.
[3] Pythagoras asserted that he had once been the Trojan Eu-
horbus.
[4] Is. iii. 16.
[5] Jer. li. 6 ; vi. 14.
[6] Jer. vii. 4 ; Ps. xiv. 4, liii. 4.
[7] Jer. xxviii. 13.
[8] That is, *cælebs* from *cælum.*

[1] Jer. v. 8.

not the excellence your name implies : let virtue lift you up on high, let not voluptuousness bring you low. By repentance, as the history of Nineveh proves, you may escape the curse wherewith the Saviour threatened you in the Apocalypse. Beware of the name of Jovinianus. It is derived from that of an idol.[1]

The Capitol is in ruins : the temples of Jove with their ceremonies have perished. Why should his name and vices flourish now in the midst of you, when even in the time of Numa Pompilius, even under the sway of kings, your ancestors gave a heartier welcome to the self-restraint of Pythagoras than they did under the consuls to the debauchery of Epicurus ?

---

[1] That is, Jove.

AGAINST VIGILANTIUS

Introduction.

Full details respecting Vigilantius, against whom this treatise, the result of a single night's labour, is directed, may be found in a work on "Vigilantius and His Times," published in 1844 by Dr. Gilly, canon of Durham. It will perhaps, however, assist the reader if we briefly remark that he was born about 370, at Calagurris, near Convenæ (Comminges), which was a station on the Roman road from Aquitaine to Spain. His father was probably the keeper of the inn, and Vigilantius appears to have been brought up to his father's business. He was of a studious character, and Sulpicius Severus, the ecclesiastical historian, who had estates in those parts, took him into his service, and, possibly, made him manager of his estates. Having been ordained he was introduced to Jerome (then living at Bethlehem, in 395) through Paulinus of Nola, who was the friend of Sulpicius Severus. After staying with Jerome for a considerable time he begged to be dismissed, and left in great haste without giving any reason. Returning to Gaul, he settled in his native country. Jerome hearing that he was spreading reports of him as favouring the views of Origen, and in other ways defaming him and his friends, wrote him a sharp letter of rebuke (Letter LXI.). The work of Vigilantius which drew from Jerome the following treatise was written in the year A.D. 406 ; not "hastily, under provocation such as he may have felt in leaving Bethlehem," but after the lapse of six or seven years. The points against which he argued as being superstitious are : (1) the reverence paid to the relics of holy men by carrying them round the church in costly vessels or silken wrappings to be kissed, and the prayers offered to the dead ; (2) the late watchings at the basilicas of the martyrs, with their attendant scandals, the burning of numerous tapers, alleged miracles, etc.; (3) the sending of alms to Jerusalem, which, Vigilantius urged, had better be spent among the poor in each separate diocese, and the monkish vow of poverty ; (4) the exaggerated estimate of virginity.

The bishop of the diocese, Exsuperius of Toulouse, was strongly in favour of the views of Vigilantius, and they began to spread widely. Complaints having reached Jerome through the presbyter Riparius, he at once expressed his indignation, and offered to answer in detail if the work of Vigilantius were sent to him. In 406 he received it through Sisinnius, who was bearing alms to the East. It has been truly said that this treatise has less of reason and more of abuse than any other which Jerome wrote. But in spite of this the author was followed by the chief ecclesiastics of the day, and the practices impugned by Vigilantius prevailed almost unchecked till the sixteenth century.

1. The world has given birth to many monsters ; in [1] Isaiah we read of centaurs and sirens, screech-owls and pelicans. Job, in mystic language, describes Leviathan and Behemoth ; Cerberus and the birds of Stymphalus, the Erymanthian boar and the Nemean lion, the Chimæra and the many-headed Hydra, are told of in poetic fables. Virgil describes Cacus. Spain has produced Geryon, with his three bodies. Gaul alone has had no monsters, but has ever been rich in men of courage and great eloquence. All at once Vigilantius, or, more correctly, Dormitantius, has arisen, animated by an unclean spirit, to fight against the Spirit of Christ, and to deny that religious reverence is to be paid to the tombs of the martyrs. Vigils, he says, are to be condemned ; Alleluia must never be sung except at Easter ; continence is a heresy ; chastity a hot-bed of lust. And as Euphorbus is said to have been born again in the person of Pythagoras, so in this fellow the corrupt mind of Jovinianus has arisen ; so that in him, no less than in his predecessor, we are bound to meet the snares of the devil. The words may be justly applied to him : [2] "Seed of evil-doers, prepare thy children for the slaughter because of the sins of thy father." Jovinianus, condemned by the authority of the Church of Rome, amidst pheasants and swine's flesh, breathed out, or rather belched out his spirit. And now this tavern-keeper of Calagurris, who, according to the name of his [1] native village is a Quintilian, only dumb instead of eloquent, is [2] mixing water with the wine. According to the trick which he knows of old, he is trying to blend his perfidious poison with the Catholic faith ; he assails virginity and hates chastity ; he revels with worldlings and declaims against the fasts of the saints ; he plays the philosopher over his cups, and soothes himself with the sweet strains of psalmody, while he smacks his lips over his cheese-cakes ; nor could he deign to listen to the songs of David and Jeduthun, and Asaph and the sons of Core, except at the banqueting table. This I have poured forth with more grief than amusement, for I cannot restrain myself and turn a deaf ear to the wrongs inflicted on apostles and martyrs.

2. Shameful to relate, there are bishops who are said to be associated with him in his wickedness—if at least they are to be called bishops—who ordain no deacons but such as have been previously married ; who credit no celibate with chastity—nay, rather, who show

---

[1] Is. xiii. 21, 22, and xxxiv. 14–16.   [2] Is. xix. 21. Sept.

clearly what measure of holiness of life they can claim by indulging in evil suspicions of all men, and, unless the candidates for ordination appear before them with pregnant wives, and infants wailing in the arms of their mothers, will not administer to them Christ's ordinance. What are the Churches of the East to do? What is to become of the Egyptian Churches and those belonging to the Apostolic Seat, which accept for the ministry only men who are virgins, or those who practice continency, or, if married, abandon their conjugal rights? Such is the teaching of Dormitantius, who throws the reins upon the neck of lust, and by his encouragement doubles the natural heat of the flesh, which in youth is mostly at boiling point, or rather slakes it by intercourse with women; so that there is nothing to separate us from swine, nothing wherein we differ from the brute creation, or from horses, respecting which it is written: [1] "They were toward women like raging horses; everyone neighed after his neighbour's wife." This is that which the Holy Spirit says by the mouth of David: [2] "Be ye not like horse and mule which have no understanding." And again respecting Dormitantius and his friends: [3] "Bind the jaws of them who draw not near unto thee with bit and bridle."

3. But it is now time for us to adduce his own words and answer him in detail. For, possibly, in his malice, he may choose once more to misrepresent me, and say that I have trumped up a case for the sake of showing off my rhetorical and declamatory powers in combating it, like the letter [4] which I wrote to Gaul, relating to a mother and daughter who were at variance. This little treatise, which I now dictate, is due to the reverend presbyters Riparius and Desiderius, who write that their parishes have been defiled by being in his neighbourhood, and have sent me, by our brother Sisinnius, the books which he vomited forth in a drunken fit. They also declare that some persons are found who, from their inclination to his vices, assent to his blasphemies. He is a barbarian both in speech and knowledge. His style is rude. He cannot defend even the truth; but, for the sake of laymen, and poor women, laden with sins, ever learning and never coming to a knowledge of the truth, I will spend upon his melancholy trifles a single night's labour, otherwise I shall seem to have treated with contempt the letters of the reverend persons who have entreated me to undertake the task.

4. He certainly well represents his race. Sprung from a set of brigands and persons collected together from all quarters (I mean those whom Cn. Pompey, after the conquest of Spain, when he was hastening to return for his triumph, brought down from the Pyrenees and gathered together into one town, whence the name of the city Convenæ[1]), he has carried on their brigand practices by his attack upon the Church of God. Like his ancestors the Vectones, the Arrabaci, and the Celtiberians, he makes his raids upon the churches of Gaul, not carrying the standard of the cross, but, on the contrary, the ensign of the devil. Pompey did just the same in the East. After overcoming the Cilician and Isaurian pirates and brigands, he founded a city, bearing his own name, between Cilicia and Isauria. That city, however, to this day, observes the ordinances of its ancestors, and no Dormitantius has arisen in it; but Gaul supports a native foe, and sees seated in the Church a man who has lost his head and who ought to be put in the strait-jacket which Hippocrates recommended. Among other blasphemies, he may be heard to say, "What need is there for you not only to pay such honour, not to say adoration, to the thing whatever it may be, which you carry about in a little vessel and worship?" And again, in the same book, "Why do you kiss and adore a bit of powder wrapped up in a cloth?" And again, in the same book, "Under the cloak of religion we see what is all but a heathen ceremony introduced into the churches: while the sun is still shining, heaps of tapers are lighted, and everywhere a paltry bit of powder, wrapped up in a costly cloth, is kissed and worshipped. Great honour do men of this sort pay to the blessed martyrs, who, they think, are to be made glorious by trumpery tapers, when the Lamb who is in the midst of the throne, with all the brightness of His majesty, gives them light?"

5. Madman, who in the world ever adored the martyrs? who ever thought man was God? Did not [2] Paul and Barnabas, when the people of Lycaonia thought them to be Jupiter and Mercury, and would have offered sacrifices to them, rend their clothes and declare they were men? Not that they were not better than Jupiter and Mercury, who were but men long ago dead, but because, under the mistaken ideas of the Gentiles, the honour due to God was being paid to them. And we read the same respecting Peter, who, when Cornelius wished to adore him, raised him by the hand and said, [3] "Stand up, for I also am a man." And have you the audacity to speak of "the mysterious something or other which you

[1] Jerem. v. 8.   [2] Ps. xxxii. 9.   [3] Ibid.   [4] Letter CXVII.
[1] From *convenio*, to come together.   [2] Acts xiv. 11.
[3] Acts x. 26.

carry about in a little vessel and worship?" I want to know what it is that you call "something or other." Tell us more clearly (that there may be no restraint on your blasphemy) what you mean by the phrase "a bit of powder wrapped up in a costly cloth in a tiny vessel." It is nothing less than the relics of the martyrs which he is vexed to see covered with a costly veil, and not bound up with rags or hair-cloth, or thrown on the midden, so that Vigilantius alone in his drunken slumber may be worshipped. Are we, therefore, guilty of sacrilege when we enter the basilicas of the Apostles? Was the Emperor Constantius I. guilty of sacrilege when he transferred the sacred relics of Andrew, Luke, and Timothy to Constantinople? In their presence the demons cry out, and the devils who dwell in Vigilantius confess that they feel the influence of the saints. And at the present day is the Emperor Arcadius guilty of sacrilege, who after so long a time has conveyed the bones of the blessed Samuel from Judea to Thrace? Are all the bishops to be considered not only sacrilegious, but silly into the bargain, because they carried that most worthless thing, dust and ashes, wrapped in silk in a golden vessel? Are the people of all the Churches fools, because they went to meet the sacred relics, and welcomed them with as much joy as if they beheld a living prophet in the midst of them, so that there was one great swarm of people from Palestine to Chalcedon with one voice re-echoing the praises of Christ? They were, forsooth, adoring Samuel and not Christ, whose Levite and prophet Samuel was. You show mistrust because you think only of the dead body, and therefore blaspheme. Read the Gospel—[1] "The God of Abraham, the God of Isaac, the God of Jacob: He is not the God of the dead, but of the living." If then they are alive, they are not, to use your expression, kept in honourable confinement.

6. For you say that the souls of Apostles and martyrs have their abode either in the bosom of Abraham, or in the place of refreshment, or under the altar of God, and that they cannot leave their own tombs, and be present where they will. They are, it seems, of senatorial rank, and are not subjected to the worst kind of prison and the society of murderers, but are kept apart in liberal and honourable custody in the isles of the blessed and the Elysian fields. Will you lay down the law for God? Will you put the Apostles into chains? So that to the day of judgment they are to be kept in confinement, and are not with their Lord, although it is written concerning them, [2] "They follow the Lamb, whither-

soever he goeth." If the Lamb is present everywhere, the same must be believed respecting those who are with the Lamb. And while the devil and the demons wander through the whole world, and with only too great speed present themselves everywhere; are martyrs, after the shedding of their blood, to be kept out of sight shut up in a [1] coffin, from whence they cannot escape? You say, in your pamphlet, that so long as we are alive we can pray for one another; but once we die, the prayer of no person for another can be heard, and all the more because the martyrs, though they [2] cry for the avenging of their blood, have never been able to obtain their request. If Apostles and martyrs while still in the body can pray for others, when they ought still to be anxious for themselves, how much more must they do so when once they have won their crowns, overcome, and triumphed? A single man, Moses, oft [3] wins pardon from God for six hundred thousand armed men; and [4] Stephen, the follower of his Lord and the first Christian martyr, entreats pardon for his persecutors; and when once they have entered on their life with Christ, shall they have less power than before? The Apostle Paul [5] says that two hundred and seventy-six souls were given to him in the ship; and when, after his dissolution, he has begun to be with Christ, must he shut his mouth, and be unable to say a word for those who throughout the whole world have believed in his Gospel? Shall Vigilantius the live dog be better than Paul the dead lion? I should be right in saying so after [6] Ecclesiastes, if I admitted that Paul is dead in spirit. The truth is that the saints are not called dead, but are said to be asleep. Wherefore [7] Lazarus, who was about to rise again, is said to have slept. And the Apostle [8] forbids the Thessalonians to be sorry for those who were asleep. As for you, when wide awake you are asleep, and asleep when you write, and you bring before me an apocryphal book which, under the name of Esdras, is read by you and those of your feather, and in this book it is [9] written that after death no one dares pray for others. I have never read the book: for what need is there to take up what the Church does not receive? It can hardly be your intention to confront me with Balsamus, and Barbelus, and the Thesaurus of Manichæus, and the ludicrous name of Leusiboras; though possibly because you live at the foot of the Pyrenees, and border on Iberia, you

---

[1] Another reading is, "Shut up in the altar."
[2] Apoc. vi. 10.
[3] Ex. xxxii. 30 sqq.   [4] Acts vii. 59, 60.
[5] Acts xxvii. 37.   [6] ix. 4.
[7] John xi. 11.   [8] 1 Thess. iv. 13.
[9] vii. 35 sq. The passage occurs in the Ethiopic and Arabic versions, not in the Latin. It was probably rejected in later times for dogmatic reasons.

follow the incredible marvels of the ancient heretic[1] Basilides and his so-called knowledge, which is mere ignorance, and set forth what is condemned by the authority of the whole world. I say this because in your short treatise you quote Solomon as if he were on your side, though Solomon never wrote the words in question at all ; so that, as you have a second Esdras you may have a second Solomon. And, if you like, you may read the imaginary revelations of all the patriarchs and prophets, and, when you have learned them, you may sing them among the women in their weaving-shops, or rather order them to be read in your taverns, the more easily by these melancholy ditties to stimulate the ignorant mob to replenish their cups.

7. As to the question of tapers, however, we do not, as you in vain misrepresent us, light them in the daytime, but by their solace we would cheer the darkness of the night, and watch for the dawn, lest we should be blind like you and sleep in darkness. And if some persons, being ignorant and simple minded laymen, or, at all events, religious women—of whom we can truly say,[2] "I allow that they have a zeal for God, but not according to knowledge"—adopt the practice in honour of the martyrs, what harm is thereby done to you ? Once upon a time even the Apostles [3] pleaded that the ointment was wasted, but they were rebuked by the voice of the Lord. Christ did not need the ointment, nor do martyrs need the light of tapers ; and yet that woman poured out the ointment in honour of Christ, and her heart's devotion was accepted. All those who light these tapers have their reward according to their faith, as the Apostle says : [4] "Let every one abound in his own meaning." Do you call men of this sort idolaters ? I do not deny that all of us who believe in Christ have passed from the error of idolatry. For we are not born Christians, but become Christians by being born again. And because we formerly worshipped idols, does it follow that we ought not now to worship God lest we seem to pay like honour to Him and to idols ? In the one case respect was paid to idols, and therefore the ceremony is to be abhorred ; in the other the martyrs are venerated, and the same ceremony is therefore to be allowed. Throughout the whole Eastern Church, even when there are no relics of the martyrs, whenever the Gospel is to be read the candles are lighted, although the dawn may be reddening the sky, not of course to scatter the darkness, but by way of evidencing our joy. [1] And accordingly the virgins in the Gospel always have their lamp lighted. And the Apostles are [2] told to have their loins girded, and their lamps burning in their hands. And of John Baptist we read [3] "He was the lamp that burneth and shineth " so that, under the figure of corporeal light that light is represented of which we read in the Psalter,[4] "Thy word is a lamp unto my feet, O Lord, and a light unto my paths."

8. Does the bishop of Rome do wrong when he offers sacrifices to the Lord over the venerable bones of the dead men Peter and Paul, as we should say, but according to you over a worthless bit of dust, and judges their tombs worthy to be Christ's altars ? And not only is the bishop of one city in error, but the bishops of the whole world, who, despite the tavern-keeper Vigilantius, enter the basilica of the dead, in which " a worthless bit of dust and ashes lies wrapped up in a cloth," defiled and defiling all else. Thus, according to you, the sacred buildings are like the sepulchres of the Pharisees, whitened without while within they have filthy remains, and are full of foul smells and uncleanliness. And then he dares to expectorate his filth upon the subject and to say : "Is it the case that the souls of the martyrs love their ashes, and hover round them, and are always present, lest haply if any one come to pray and they were absent, they could not hear ?" Oh, monster who ought to be banished to the ends of the earth ! do you laugh at the relics of the martyrs, and in company with Eunomius, the father of this heresy, slander the Churches of Christ ? Are you not afraid of being in such company, and of speaking against us the same things which he utters against the Church For all his followers refuse to enter the basilicas of Apostles and martyrs, so that, for sooth, they may worship the dead Eunomius whose books they consider are of more authority than the Gospels ; and they believe that the light of truth was in him, just as other heretics maintain that the Paraclete came into Montanus, and say that Manichæus himself was the Paraclete. You cannot find an occasion of boasting even in supposing that you are the inventor of a new kind of wickedness for your heresy long ago broke out against the Church. It found, however, an opponent in Tertullian, a very learned man, who wrote a famous treatise which he called most correctly Scorpiacum,[5] because, as the scorpion bends itself like a bow to inflict its wound, so what was formerly called the heresy of Cain pour poison into the body of the Church ; it ha

[1] The chief of the Egyptian Gnostics.
[2] Rom. x. 2.
[3] Matt. xxvi. 8 ; Mark xiv. 4.
[4] Rom. xiv. 5. Let each man be fully assured in his own mind. R. V.

[1] Matt. xxv. 1.   [2] Luke xii. 35.
[3] John v. 35.   [4] Ps. cxix. 105.
[5] i.e. antidote to the scorpion's bite.

lept or rather been buried for a long time, but has been now awakened by Dormitantius. I am surprised you do not tell us that there must upon no account be martyrdoms, inasmuch as God, who does not ask for the blood of goats and bulls, much less requires the blood of men. This is what you say, or rather, even if you do not say it, you are taken as meaning to assert it. For in maintaining that the relics of the martyrs are to be trodden under foot, you forbid the shedding of their blood as being worthy of no honour.

9. Respecting vigils and the frequent keeping of night-watches in the basilicas of the martyrs, I have given a brief reply in another letter [1] which, about two years ago, I wrote to the reverend presbyter Riparius. You argue that they ought to be abjured, lest we seem to be often keeping Easter, and appear not to observe the customary yearly vigils. If so, then sacrifices should not be offered to Christ on the Lord's day lest we frequently keep the Easter of our Lord's Resurrection, and introduce the custom of having many Easters instead of one. We must not, however, impute to pious men the faults and errors of youths and worthless women such as are often detected at night. It is true that, even at the Easter vigils, something of the kind usually comes to light ; but the faults of a few form no argument against religion in general, and such persons, without keeping vigil, can go wrong either in their own houses or in those of other people. The treachery of Judas did not annul the loyalty of the Apostles. And if others keep vigil badly, our vigils are not thereby to be stopped ; nay, rather let those who sleep to gratify their lust be compelled to watch that they may preserve their chastity. For if a thing once done be good, it cannot be bad if often done ; and if there is some fault to be avoided, the blame lies not in its being done often, but in its being done at all. And so we should not watch at Easter-tide, for fear that adulterers may satisfy their long pent-up desires, or that the wife may find an opportunity for sinning without having the key turned against her by her husband. The occasions which seldom recur are those which are most eagerly longed for.

10. I cannot traverse all the topics embraced in the letters of the reverend presbyters ; I will adduce a few points from the tracts of Vigilantius. He argues against the signs and miracles which are wrought in the basilicas of the martyrs, and says that they are of service to the unbelieving, not to believers, as though the question now were for whose advantage they occur, not by what power. Granted that signs belong to the faithless, who, because they would not obey the word and doctrine, are brought to believe by means of signs. Even our Lord wrought signs for the unbelieving, and yet our Lord's signs are not on that account to be impugned, because those people were faithless, but must be worthy of greater admiration because they were so powerful that they subdued even the hardest hearts, and compelled men to believe. And so I will not have you tell me that signs are for the unbelieving ; but answer my question—how is it that poor worthless dust and ashes are associated with this wondrous power of signs and miracles ? I see, I see, most unfortunate of mortals, why you are so sad and what causes your fear. That unclean spirit who forces you to write these things has often been tortured by this worthless dust, aye, and is being tortured at this moment, and though in your case he conceals his wounds, in others he makes confession. You will hardly follow the heathen and impious Porphyry and Eunomius, and pretend that these are the tricks of the demons, and that they do not really cry out, but feign their torments. Let me give you my advice : go to the basilicas of the martyrs, and some day you will be cleansed ; you will find there many in like case with yourself, and will be set on fire, not by the martyrs' tapers which offend you, but by invisible flames ; and you will then confess what you now deny, and will freely proclaim your name—that you who speak in the person of Vigilantius are really either Mercury, for greedy of gain was he ; or Nocturnus, who, according to Plautus's "Amphitryon," slept while Jupiter, two nights together, had his adulterous connection with Alcmena, and thus begat the mighty Hercules ; or at all events Father Bacchus, of drunken fame, with the tankard hanging from his shoulder, with his ever ruby face, foaming lips, and unbridled brawling.

11. Once, when a sudden earthquake in this province in the middle of the night awoke us all out of our sleep, you, the most prudent and the wisest of men, began to pray without putting your clothes on, and recalled to our minds the story of Adam and Eve in Paradise ; they, indeed, when their eyes were opened were ashamed, for they saw that they were naked, and covered their shame with the leaves of trees ; but you, who were stripped alike of your shirt and of your faith, in the sudden terror which overwhelmed you, and with the fumes of your last night's booze still hanging about you, showed your wisdom by exposing your nakedness in only too evident a manner to the eyes of the brethren. Such

---

[1] Letter CIX.

are the adversaries of the Church; these are the leaders who fight against the blood of the martyrs; here is a specimen of the orators who thunder against the Apostles, or, rather, such are the mad dogs which bark at the disciples of Christ.

12. I confess my own fear, for possibly it may be thought to spring from superstition. When I have been angry, or have had evil thoughts in my mind, or some phantom of the night has beguiled me, I do not dare to enter the basilicas of the martyrs, I shudder all over in body and soul. You may smile, perhaps, and deride this as on a level with the wild fancies of weak women. If it be so, I am not ashamed of having a faith like that of those who were the first to see the risen Lord; who were sent to the Apostles; who, in the person of the mother of our Lord and Saviour, were commended to the holy Apostles. Belch out your shame, if you will, with men of the world, I will fast with women; yea, with religious men whose looks witness to their chastity, and who, with the cheek pale from prolonged abstinence, show forth the chastity of Christ.

13. Something, also, appears to be troubling you. You are afraid that, if continence, sobriety, and fasting strike root among the people of Gaul, your taverns will not pay, and you will be unable to keep up through the night your diabolical vigils and drunken revels. Moreover, I have learnt from those same letters that, in defiance of the authority of Paul, nay, rather of Peter, John, and James, who gave the right hand of fellowship to Paul and Barnabas, and commanded them to remember the poor, you forbid any pecuniary relief to be sent to Jerusalem for the benefit of the saints. Now, if I reply to this, you will immediately give ·tongue and cry out that I am pleading my own cause. You, forsooth, were so generous to the whole community that if you had not come to Jerusalem, and lavished your own money or that of your patrons, we should all be on the verge of starvation. I say what the blessed Apostle Paul says in nearly all his Epistles; and he makes it a rule for the Churches of the Gentiles that, on the first day of the week, that is, on the Lord's day, contributions should be made by every one which should be sent up to Jerusalem for the relief of the saints, and that either by his own disciples, or by those whom they should themselves approve; and if it were thought fit, he would himself either send, or take what was collected. Also in the Acts of the Apostles, when speaking to the governor Felix, he says, [1] "After many years I went up to Jerusalem to bring alms to my nation and offerings, and to perform my vows, amidst which they found me purified in the temple.' Might he not have distributed in some other part of the world, and in the infant Churches which he was training in his own faith, the gifts he had received from others? But he longed to give to the poor of the holy places who, abandoning their own little possessions for the sake of Christ, turned with their whole heart to the service of the Lord. It would take too long now if I purposed to repeat all the passages from the whole range of his Epistles in which he advocates and urges with all his heart that money be sent to Jerusalem and to the holy places for the faithful; not to gratify avarice, but to give relief; not to accumulate wealth, but to support the weakness of the poor body, and to stave off cold and hunger. And this custom continues in Judea to the present day, not only among us, but also among the Hebrews, so that they who [1] meditate in the law of the Lord, day and night, and have [2] no father upon earth except the Lord alone, may be cherished by the aid of the synagogues and of the whole world; that there may be [3] equality—not that some may be refreshed while others are in distress, but that the abundance of some may support the need of others.

14. You will reply that every one can do this in his own country, and that there will never be wanting poor who ought to be supported with the resources of the Church. And we do not deny that doles should be distributed to all poor people, even to Jews and Samaritans, if the means will allow. But the Apostle teaches that alms should be given to all, indeed,[4] especially, however, to those who are of the household of faith. And respecting these the Saviour said in the Gospel,[5] "Make to yourselves friends of the mammon of unrighteousness, who may receive you into everlasting habitations." What! Can those poor creatures, with their rags and filth, lorded over, as they are, by raging lust, can they who own nothing, now or hereafter, have eternal habitations? No doubt it is not the poor simply, but the poor in spirit, who are called blessed; those of whom it is written, [6] "Blessed is he who gives his mind to the poor and needy; the Lord shall deliver him in the evil day." But the fact is, in supporting the poor of the common people, what is needed is not mind, but money. In the case of the saintly poor the mind has blessed exercises, since you give to one who receives with a blush, and when he has received is grieved,

---

[1] Acts xxiv. 17, 18.

[1] Ps. i. 2.
[2] Deut. xviii. 2 sq.
[3] 2 Cor. viii. 14.
[4] Gal. vi. 10.
[5] Luke xvi. 9.
[6] Ps. xli. 9.

hat while sowing spiritual things he must reap your carnal things. As for his argument that they who keep what they have, and distribute among the poor, little by little, the increase of their property, act more wisely than they who sell their possessions, and once for all give all away, not I but the Lord shall make answer : [1] "If thou wilt be perfect, go sell all that thou hast and give to the poor, and come, follow Me." He speaks to him who wishes to be perfect, who, with the Apostles, leaves father, ship, and net. The man whom you approve stands in the second or third rank ; yet we welcome him provided it be understood that the first is to be preferred to the second, and the second to the third.

15. Let me add that our monks are not to be deterred from their resolution by you with your viper's tongue and savage bite. Your argument respecting them runs thus : If all men were to seclude themselves and live in solitude, who is there to frequent the churches? Who will remain to win those engaged in secular pursuits? Who will be able to urge sinners to virtuous conduct? Similarly, if all were as silly as you, who could be wise? And, to follow out your argument, virginity would not deserve our approbation. For if all were virgins, we should have no marriages ; the race would perish ; infants would not cry in their cradles ; midwives would lose their pay and turn beggars ; and Dormitantius, all alone and shrivelled up with cold, would lie awake in his bed. The truth is, virtue is a rare thing and not eagerly sought after by the many. Would that all were as the few of whom it is said : [2] "Many are called, few are chosen." The prison would be empty. But, indeed, a monk's function is not to teach, but to lament ; to mourn either for himself or for the world, and with terror to anticipate our Lord's advent. Knowing his own weakness and the frailty of the vessel which he carries, he is afraid of stumbling, lest he strike against something, and it fall and be broken. Hence he shuns the sight of women, and particularly of young women, and so far chastens himself as to dread even what is safe.

16. Why, you will say, go to the desert? The reason is plain : That I may not hear or see you ; that I may not be disturbed by your madness ; that I may not be engaged in conflict with you ; that the eye of the harlot may not lead me captive ; that beauty may not lead me to unlawful embraces. You will reply : "This is not to fight, but to run away. Stand in line of battle, put on your armour and resist your foes, so that, having overcome, you may wear the crown." I confess my weakness. I would not fight in the hope of victory, lest some time or other I lose the victory. If I flee, I avoid the sword ; if I stand, I must either overcome or fall. But what need is there for me to let go certainties and follow after uncertainties? Either with my shield or with my feet I must shun death. You who fight may either be overcome or may overcome. I who fly do not overcome, inasmuch as I fly ; but I fly to make sure that I may not be overcome. There is no safety in sleep with a serpent beside you. Possibly he will not bite me, yet it is possible that after a time he may bite me. We call women mothers who are no older than sisters and daughters,[1] and we do not blush to cloak our vices with the names of piety. What business has a monk in the women's cells? What is the meaning of secret conversation and looks which shun the presence of witnesses? Holy love has no restless desire. Moreover, what we have said respecting lust we must apply to avarice, and to all vices which are avoided by solitude. We therefore keep clear of the crowded cities, that we may not be compelled to do what we are urged to do, not so much by nature as by choice.

17. At the request of the reverend presbyters, as I have said, I have devoted to the dictation of these remarks the labour of a single night, for my brother Sisinnius is hastening his departure for Egypt, where he has relief to give to the saints, and is impatient to be gone. If it were not so, however, the subject itself was so openly blasphemous as to call for the indignation of a writer rather than a multitude of proofs. But if Dormitantius wakes up that he may again abuse me, and if he thinks fit to disparage me with that same blasphemous mouth with which he pulls to pieces Apostles and martyrs, I will spend upon him something more than this short lucubration. I will keep vigil for a whole night in his behalf and in behalf of his companions, whether they be disciples or masters, who think no man to be worthy of Christ's ministry unless he is married and his wife is seen to be with child.

---

[1] Matt. xix. 21.   [2] Matt. xx. 16 : xxii. 14.

[1] He seems to mean that monks spoke of young ladies as Mothers of the Convents, so as to be able to frequent their society without reproach.

TO PAMMACHIUS AGAINST JOHN OF JERUSALEM

Introduction.

The letter against John of Jerusalem was written about the year 398 or 399, and was a product of the Origenistic controversy. Its immediate occasion was the visit of Epiphanius, bishop of Salamis in Cyprus, a Jerusalem, in 394. The bishop preached, in the Church of the Resurrection (§ 11), a pointed sermon agains Origenism, which was thought to be so directly aimed at John that the latter sent his archdeacon to remonstrate with the preacher (§ 14). After many unseemly scenes, Epiphanius advised Jerome and his friends to separate from their bishop (§ 39). But how were they to have the ministrations of the Church? This difficulty was sur mounted by Epiphanius, who took Jerome's brother to the monastery which he had founded at Ad. in the diocese of Eleutheropolis, and there ordained him against his will, even using force to overcome his opposition (Jerome Letter LI. 1). Epiphanius attempted to defend his action (Jerome, Letter LI. 2), but John, after some time, ap pealed to Alexandria against Jerome and his supporters as schismatics. The bishop, Theophilus, at once took the side of John; but a letter, written by his emissary Isidore and intended for John, fell into the hands of Jerome (§ 37). The letter showed that Isidore was coming as a mere partisan of John, and Jerome, therefore treated both it and the bearer with secret contempt. The dispute was thus prolonged for about four years, and, after some attempts at reconciliation, and the exhibition of much bitterness, amounting to the practical excom munication of Jerome and his friends, the dispute was stopped, perhaps by Theophilus, perhaps through the influence of Melania. The letter written to Pammachius at Rome, in 397 or 398, against John, was abruptly broken off, and it is almost certain that it was never published during Jerome's lifetime. Jerome afterwards had so much influence with Theophilus that we find him interceding for John, who had fallen under the Pontiff's displeasure (Letter LXXXVI. 1).

The date of this treatise is the subject of controversy. In § 1 Jerome says that he wrote "after three years," that is, three years from the visit of Epiphanius to Jerusalem, which was in 394. This would give the date 397. At § 14, also, he says that Epiphanius had been brooding over his wrongs for three years. Another note of time is found in the words of § 43, that John had "lately" sought to obtain a sentence of exile against Jerome from "that wild beast who threatened the necks of the whole world," that is, the Prefect Rufinus, who died at the end of 395. All these statements point to the year 397. On the other hand, at § 17, he speaks of his "Commen taries" on Ecclesiastes and Ephesians as having been written "about (*ferme*) ten years ago"; and the preface to Ecclesiastes says that he had read Ecclesiastes with Blesilla at Rome "about (*ferme*) five years ago," conse quently, fifteen years before the writing of this treatise. Blesilla's death was in 384. The reading of Ecclesiastes may, therefore, have been in 383. And the fifteen years would bring us to 398. Also, at § 41, Jerome says, addressing John, "You seem to have slept for thirteen years." implying that it was for thirteen years that the state of things complained of by John had existed, that is, the presence of the monks in his diocese, or, at least, their leaving their own dioceses. Jerome left Antioch, the diocese of his ordination, at the end of 385 or be ginning of 386; these thirteen years, therefore, bring us to 399, the date adopted by Vallarsi. There is, how ever, an intimation in "Pallad. Hist. Laus.," c. 117, that Melania, the friend of Rufinus, gave assistance in the matter of "the schism of nearly 400 monks who followed Paulinus," which is admitted to relate to the schism at Bethlehem, caused by the question of the ordination of Paulinianus. We know that Melania and Rufinus left Jerusalem early in 397, and that, before their departure, Jerome and Rufinus were reconciled. It would, there fore, seem most probable that the treatise, which is written with so much animosity against John, Rufinus's fellow-worker, and contains invidious allusions to Rufinus himself (§ 11, "your friends, who grin like dogs and turn up their noses," Jerome's constant description of Rufinus), was written before the reconciliation of Rufinus and Jerome, that is, in the end of 386 or the beginning of 387, and that it was broken off and kept unpublished because the situation had changed. Vallarsi places it in 399. He quotes the passages which make for the later date, but strangely omits the more definite statements which make for the earlier. It should be added that the letter of Jerome (LXXXII.) to Theophilus is evidently written at the same time, and under the same feelings, as this treatise. and, if the arguments above given are valid, that letter must be placed in 397, not in 399, as stated in the note prefixed to it. The short letter (LXXXVI.) to Theophilus is, in that case, probably to be placed in 398 or 399, rather than 401, as there stated.

The treatise is a letter to Pammachius, who had been disturbed by the complaints of Bishop John to Siricius, bishop of Rome, against Jerome. Jerome begins (1) by pleading necessity for his attack on the bishop. Epiphanius has accused him of heresy (2). Let him answer plainly (3), for it is pride alone (4) which pre vents this. It is said that John's letter of explanation or apology was approved by Theophilus (5); but it did not touch the point, that is, the accusation of Origenism. Only three points are treated (6), and Epiphanius adduced eight—namely (7) Origen's opinions (i.) that the Son does not see the Father; (ii.) that souls are con fined in earthly bodies, as in a prison; (iii.) that the devil may be saved; (iv.) that the skins with which God clothed Adam and Eve were human bodies; (v.) that the body in the resurrection will be without sex; (vi.) that the descriptions of Paradise are allegorical: trees meaning angels, and rivers the heavenly virtues: (vii.) that the waters above and below the firmament are angels and devils; (viii.) that the image of God was altogether lost at the Fall. John, instead of answering on the first head, merely expressed his faith in the Trinity (8, 9), and all through tries to make out (10) that the question between him and Epiphanius relates merely to the ordination of Paulini anus. Jerome then relates the extraordinary scenes of the altercation between Epiphanius and John (11–14). He then turns to the Origenistic notions that angels are cast down into human souls (15, 16), that men pass into the heavenly bodies (17), and that the souls of men had a previous existence (18), and pass up and down in the scale of creation (19, 20). John, instead of answering on these points, contents himself with protest ng against Manichæism (21). Jerome presses him on the question of the origin of souls (22), pronouncing rashly for creationism. He then passes to the question of the state of the body after the resurrection (23), asserting the restoration of the *flesh* as it now is (24–27), both in the case of Christ (28) and in our own, adducing testimonies from the Old Testament (29–32), and discussing the appearances of our Lord after His resurrection (34–36). He then passes to a detailed examination of John's letter or "Apology" to Theophilus (37), quoting its words, and telling the story of the mission of Isidore (37, 38), and the attempts of the Count Archelaus to make peace (39). The ordination of Paulinianus, on which John lays stress, is a subterfuge (40, 41). The schism is due to the heretical tendencies of the bishop, who is everywhere denounced by Epiphanius (42, 43).

The letter is, throughout, violent and contemptuous in its tone, with an arrogant assumption that the writer is in possession of the whole truth on the difficult subject on which he writes, and that he has a right to demand from his bishop a confession of faith on each point on which he chooses to catechise him. Its importance lies in the fact that it, to a large extent, fixed the belief of churchmen on the points it deals with, and the mode of dealing with supposed heresy, for more than a thousand years.

1. If, according to the [1] Apostle Paul, we cannot pray as we feel, and speech does not express the thoughts of our own minds, how much more dangerous is it to judge of another man's heart, and to trace and explain the meaning of the particular words and expressions which he uses? The nature of man is prone to mercy, and in considering another's sin, every one commiserates himself. Accordingly, if you blame one who offends in word, a man will say it was only simplicity; if you tax a man with craft, he to whom you speak will not admit that there is anything more in it than ignorance, so that he may avoid the suspicion of malice. And it will thus come to pass that you, the accuser, are made a slanderer, and the censured party is regarded, not as a heretic, but merely as a man without culture. You know, Pammachius, you know that it is not enmity or the lust of glory which leads me to engage in this work, but that I have been stimulated by your letters and that I act out of the fervour of my faith; and, if possible, I would have all understand that I cannot be blamed for impatience and rashness, seeing that I speak only after the lapse of three years. In fact, if you had not told me that the minds of many are troubled at the "Apology" which I am about to discuss, and are tossing to and fro on a sea of doubt, I had determined to persist in silence.

2. So away with [2] Novatus, who would not hold out a hand to the erring! perish [3] Montanus and his mad women! Montanus, who would hurl the fallen into the abyss that they may never rise again. Every day we all sin and make some slip or other. Being then merciful to ourselves, we are not rigorous towards others; nay, rather, we pray and beseech [4] him either to simply tell us our own faults, or to openly defend those of other men.

I dislike ambiguities; I dislike to be told what is capable of two meanings. Let us contemplate with [1] unveiled face the glory of the Lord. Once upon a time the people of Israel halted [2] between two opinions. But, said Elias, which is by interpretation *the strong one of the Lord*,[3] "How long halt ye between two opinions? If the Lord be God, go after him; but if Baal, follow him." And the Lord himself says concerning the Jews,[4] "The strange children lied unto me; the strange children became feeble, and limped out of their by-paths." If there really is no ground for suspecting him of heresy (as I wish and believe), why does he not speak out my opinion in my own words? He calls it simplicity; I interpret it as artfulness. He wishes to convince me that his belief is sound; let his speech, then, also be sound. And, indeed, if the ambiguity attached to a single word, or a single statement, or two or three, I could be indulgent on the score of ignorance; nor would I judge what is obscure or doubtful by the standard of what is certain and clear. But, as things are, this "simplicity" is nothing but a platform trick, like walking on tiptoe over eggs or standing corn; there is doubt and suspicion everywhere. You might suppose he was not writing an exposition of the faith, but was writing a disputation on some imaginary theme. What he is now so keen upon, we learnt long ago in the schools. He puts on our own armour to fight against us. Even if his faith be correct, and he speaks with circumspection and reserve, his extreme care rouses my suspicions. [5] "He that walketh uprightly, walketh boldly." It is folly to bear a bad name for nothing. A charge is brought against him of which he is not conscious. Let him confidently deny the charge which hangs upon a single word, and freely turn the tables against his adversary. Let the one exhibit the same boldness in repelling the charge which the other shows in advancing it. And when he

---

[1] Rom. viii. 26.
[2] Novatus the Carthaginian was the chief ally of Novatian, who, about the middle of the third century, founded the sect of the *Cathari*, or *pure*. The allusion is to the severity with which they treated the lapsed.
[3] Maximilla and Priscilla, who forsook their husbands and followed him, professing to be inspired prophetesses. Circ. A.D. 150. Montanus, like Novatian, refused to re-admit the lapsed.
[4] That is, John.

[1] 2 Cor. iii. 18.
[2] In Jerome's text, "limped in both its feet." It seemed better to give the accepted meaning.
[3] 1 Kings xviii. 21.   [4] Ps. xviii. 45.   [5] Prov. x. 9.

has said all that he wishes and purposes to say, and such things as are above suspicion, if his opponent persists in slander, let him try conclusions in open court. I wish no one to sit still under an imputation of heresy, lest, if he say nothing, his want of openness be interpreted, amongst those who are not aware of his innocence, as the consciousness of guilt, although there is no need to demand the presence of a man and to reduce him to silence when you have his letters in your possession.

3. We all know what[1] he wrote to you, what charge he brought against you, wherein (as you maintain) he has slandered you. Answer the points, one by one; follow the footsteps of this letter; leave not a single jot or tittle of the slander unnoticed. For if you are careless, and accidentally pass over anything as I believe you on your oath to have done, he will immediately cry out : "Now, now, you have got the worst of it, the whole thing turns upon this." Words do not sound the same in the ears of friends and enemies. An enemy looks for a knot even in a bulrush ; a friend judges even crooked to be straight. It is a saying of secular writers that lovers are blind in their judgments, though, perhaps, you are too busy with the sacred books to pay any attention to such literature. You should never boast of what your friends think of you. That is true testimony which comes from the lips of foes. On the contrary, if a friend speaks in your behalf he will be considered not as a witness but a judge or a partisan. This is the sort of thing your enemies will say, who perhaps give no credit to you, and only wish to vex you. But I, whom you say you have never willingly injured, yet whose name you are always bound to bandy about in your letters, advise you either to openly proclaim the faith of the Church, or to speak as you believe. For that cautious mincing and weighing of words may, no doubt, deceive the unlearned ; but a careful hearer and reader will quickly detect the snare, and will show in open daylight the subterranean mines by which truth is overthrown. The Arians (no one knows more about them than you) for a long time pretended that they condemned the [2]*Homoousion* on account of the offence it gave, and they besmeared poisonous error with honeyed words. But at last the snake uncoiled itself, and its deadly head, which lay concealed under all its folds, was pierced by the sword of the Spirit. The Church, as you know, welcomes penitents, and is so overwhelmed by the multitude of sinners that it is forced, in the interests of the misguided flocks, to be lenient to the wounds of the shepherds.[1] Ancient and modern heresy observes the same rule—the people hear one thing, the priests preach another.

4. And first, before I translate and insert in this book the letter which you wrote to Bishop Theophilus, and show you that I understand your excessive care and circumspection, I should like a word of expostulation with you. What is the meaning of this towering arrogance which makes you refuse to reply to those who question you respecting the faith ? How is it that you regard almost as public enemies the vast multitude of brethren, and the bands of monks, who refuse to communicate with you in Palestine ? The Son of God, for the sake of one sick sheep, leaving the ninety and nine on the mountains, endured the buffeting, the cross, the scourge ; He took up the burden, and patiently carried on His shoulders to heaven the voluptuous woman that was a sinner. Is it for you to act the "most reverend father in God," the fastidious prelate ; to stand apart in your wealth and wisdom, in your grandeur and your learning ; to frown superciliously upon your fellow servants, and scarce vouchsafe a glance to those who have been redeemed with the blood of your Lord ? Is this what you have learnt from the Apostles' precept to be [2]"ready always to give answer to every man that asketh you a reason concerning the hope that is in you "? Suppose we do, as you pretend, seek occasion, and that, under the pretext of zeal for the faith, we are sowing strife, framing a schism, and fomenting quarrels. Then take away the occasion from those who wish for an occasion ; so that having given satisfaction on the point of faith, and solved all the difficulties in which you are involved, you may show clearly to all that the dispute is not one of doctrine, but of [3]order. But perhaps when questioned concerning the faith, you say that it is from wise forethought that you hold your tongue, so that it may not be said that you have proved yourself a heretic—inasmuch as you make satisfaction to your accusers. If that be so, then men ought not to refute any charges of which they are accused, lest, having denied them, they may be held to be guilty. The accusations of the laity, deacons, and presbyters, are, I suppose, beneath your notice. For you can, as you are perpetually boast-

---

[1] That is, Epiphanius. See Jerome, Letter LI. c. 6. Epiphanius prays that God would free John and Rufinus and all their flock from all heresies.
[2] The doctrine that the Son is of "one substance with the Father." More correctly *of one essence*, etc.

[1] The meaning is that, where error is widespread, the Church authorities are forced to wink at speciously expressed error in the pastors.
[2] 1 Pet. iii. 15.
[3] John complained of the ordination of Paulinianus, Jerome's brother, to the priesthood by Epiphanius, for the monastery of Bethlehem.

ng, make a thousand clerics in an hour. But you have to answer Epiphanius, our father in God, who, in the letters which he sent, openly calls you a heretic. Certainly you are not his superior in respect of years, of learning, of his exemplary life, or of the judgment of the whole world. If it is a question of age, you are a young man writing to an old one. If it is one of knowledge, you are a person not so very accomplished writing to a learned man, although your partisans maintain that you are a more finished speaker than Demosthenes, more sharp-witted than Chrysippus, wiser than Plato, and perhaps have persuaded you that they are right. As regards his life and devotion to the faith, I will say no more, that I may not seem to be seeking to wound you. At the time when the whole East (except our fathers in God Athanasius and Paulinus) was overrun by the Arian and Eunomian heresies; when you did not hold communion with the Westerns; then, in the very worst of the exile which made them confessors, he, though a simple convent priest, gained the ear of Eutychius, and afterwards as bishop of Cyprus was unmolested by Valens. For he was always so highly venerated that heretics on the throne thought it would redound to their own disgrace if they persecuted such a man. Write therefore to him. Answer his letter. So let the rest understand your purpose and judge of your eloquence and wisdom; do not keep all your accomplishments to yourself. Why, when you are challenged, in one quarter, do you turn your arms towards another? A question is put to you in Palestine, your answer is given in Egypt. When some are blear-eyed, you anoint the eyes of others who are not affected. If you tell another what is meant to give us satisfaction, such action springs entirely from pride; if you tell him what we do not ask for, it is entirely uncalled for.

5. But you say "the bishop of Alexandria approved of my letter." What did he approve of? Your correct utterances against Arius, Photinus, and Manichæus. For who, at this time of day, accuses you of being an Arian? Who now fastens on you the guilt of Photinus and Manichæus? Those faults were long ago corrected, those enemies were shattered. You were not so foolish as to openly defend a heresy which you knew was offensive to the whole Church. You knew that if you had done this, you must have been immediately removed, and your heart was upon the pleasures of your episcopal throne. You so tuned your expressions as to neither displease the simple, nor offend your own incontestably marked by deceit and slipperi-

ness; what, then, are we to do with the remaining five, with regard to which, because no opportunity was afforded for ambiguity, supporters. You wrote well, but nothing to the purpose. How was the bishop of Alexandria to know of what you were accused, or what things they were of which a confession was demanded from you? You ought to have set forth in detail the charges brought against you, and then have met them one by one. There is an old story which tells how a certain man, who, when he was speaking fluently, was carried along by a torrent of words, without touching the question before the court, and thus drew the wise remark from the judge, "Excellent! excellent! but to what purpose is all this excellence?" Quacks have but one lotion for all affections of the eyes. He who is accused of many things, and in dissipating the charges passes over some, confesses all that he omits to mention. Did you not reply to the letter of Epiphanius, and yourself choose the points for refutation? No doubt, in replying, you rested on the axiom, that no man is so brave as to put the sword to his own throat. Choose which alternative you like. You shall have your choice: you either replied to the letter of Epiphanius, or you did not. If you did reply, why did you take no notice of the most important, and the most numerous, of the charges brought against you? If you did not reply, what becomes of your "Apology," of which you boast amongst the simple, and which you are scattering broadcast amongst those who do not understand the matter?

6. The questions for you to answer were arranged, as I shall presently show, under eight heads. You touch only three, and pass on. As regards the rest, you maintain a magnificent silence. If you had with perfect frankness replied to seven, I should still cling to the charge which remained; and what you said nothing about, that I should hold to be the truth. But as things are, you have caught the wolf by the ears; you can neither hold fast, nor dare let go. With a sort of careless security and an air of abstraction, you skim over and touch the surface of three in which there is nothing or but little of importance. And your procedure is so dark and close that you confess more by your silence than you rebut by your arguments. Every one has the right forthwith to say to you,[1] "If the light that is in thee be darkness, how great is the darkness." Even in answering three little questions, respecting which you seemed to say something, you are not clear from suspicion and from blame, but your replies are

---

[1] Matt. vi. 23.

and you were therefore unable to cheat your hearers, you preferred to maintain unbroken silence rather than openly confess what had been covered in obscurity?

7. The questions relate to the passages in the [1]Περὶ Ἀρχῶν. The first is this, "for as it is unfitting to say that the Son can see the Father, so neither is it meet to think that the Holy Spirit can see the Son." The second point is the statement that souls are tied up in the body as in a prison; and that before man was made in Paradise they dwelt amongst rational creatures in the heavens. Wherefore, afterwards to console itself, the soul says in the Psalms,[2] "Before I was humbled, I went wrong"; and [3]"Return, my soul, to thy rest"; and [4]"Lead my soul out of prison"; and similarly elsewhere. Thirdly, he says that both the devil and demons will some time or other repent, and ultimately reign with the saints. Fourthly, he interprets the coats of skin, with which Adam and Eve were clothed after their fall and ejection from Paradise, to be human bodies, and we are to suppose of course that previously, in Paradise, they had neither flesh, sinews, nor bones. Fifthly, he most openly denies the resurrection of the flesh and the bodily structure, and the distinction of senses, both in his explanation of the first Psalm, and in many other of his treatises. Sixthly, he so allegorises Paradise as to destroy historical truth, understanding angels instead of trees, heavenly virtues instead of rivers, and he overthrows all that is contained in the history of Paradise by his figurative interpretation. Seventhly, he thinks that the waters which are said in Scripture to be above the heavens are holy and supernal essences, while those which are above the earth and beneath the earth are, on the contrary, demoniacal essences. The eighth is Origen's cavil that the image and likeness of God, in which man was created, was lost, and was no longer in man after he was expelled from Paradise.

8. These are the arrows with which you are pierced; these the weapons with which throughout the whole letter you are wounded; or I should rather say Epiphanius throws himself as a suppliant at your knees, and casts his hoary locks beneath your feet, and, for a time laying aside his episcopal dignity, prays for your salvation in words such as these: "Grant to me and to yourself the favour of your salvation; save yourself, as it is written, from this crooked generation,[5] and forsake the heresy of Origen, and all heresies, dearly beloved." And lower down, "In the defence of heresy you kindle hatred against me, and destroy that love which I had towards you; insomuch that you would make us even repent of holding communion with you who so resolutely defend the errors and doctrines of Origen." Tell me, prince of arguers, to which, out of the eight sections, you have replied. For the present, I say nothing of the rest. Take the first blasphemy—that the Son cannot see the Father, nor the Holy Spirit the Son. By what weapons of yours has it been pierced? The answer we get is, "We believe that the Holy and Adorable Trinity are of the same substance; that they are co-eternal, and of the same glory and Godhead, and we anathematize those who say that there is any greatness, smallness, inequality, or aught that is visible in the Godhead of the Trinity. But as we say the Father is incorporeal, invisible, and eternal; so we say the Son and Holy Spirit are incorporeal, invisible, and eternal." If you did not say this, you would not hold to the Church. I do not ask whether there was not a time when you refused to say this. I will not discuss the question, whether you were fond of those who preached such doctrines; on whose side you were when, for expressing those sentiments, they underwent banishment; or who the man was that, when the presbyter Theo preached in the Church that the Holy Spirit is God, closed his ears, and excitedly rushed out of doors that he might not so much as hear the impiety. I recognize a man, as one may say, as one of the faithful, even though his repentance comes late. [1]That unhappy man Prætextatus, who died after he had been chosen consul, a profane person and an idolater, was wont in sport to say to blessed Pope Damascus, "Make me bishop of Rome, and I will at once be a Christian." Why do you, with many words and intricate periods, take the trouble to show me that you are not an Arian? Either deny that the accused said what is imputed to him, or, if he did give utterance to such sentiments, condemn him for so speaking. You have still to learn how intense is the zeal of the orthodox. Listen to the Apostle: [2]"If I or an angel from heaven bring you another gospel than that we have declared, let him be anathema." You would extenuate the fault and hide the name of the guilty party; as though everything were right and no one were accused of blasphemy, you frame, in artificial language, an uncalled-for profession of your faith. Speak out at once, and let

[1] Origen's great speculative work "On First Principles."
[2] Ps. cxix. 67.   [3] Ps. cxvi. 7.   [4] Ps. cxlii. 7.
[5] Acts ii. 40.

[1] Vettius Agorius Prætextatus, one of the most virtuous of the heathen. Jerome writes of him to Marcella (Letter XXIII. 2): "I wish you to know that the consul designate is now in Tartarus."
[2] Gal. i. 8.

your letter thus begin : "Let him be accursed who has dared to write such things." Pure faith is impatient of delay. As soon as the scorpion appears, he must be crushed under foot. David, who was proved to be a man after God's own heart, says : [1] "Do not I hate those that hate thee, O Lord, and did not I pine away over thine enemies? I hated them with a perfect hatred." Had I heard my father, or mother, or brother say such things against my Master Christ, I would have broken their blasphemous jaws like those of a mad dog, and my hand should have been amongst the first lifted up against them. They who said to father and mother,[2] "We know you not," these men fulfilled the will of the Lord. [3] He that loveth father or mother more than Christ, is not worthy of Him.

9. It is alleged that your master, whom you call a Catholic, and whom you resolutely defend, said, "the Son sees not the Father, and the Holy Spirit sees not the Son." And you tell me that the Father is invisible, the Son invisible, the Holy Ghost invisible, as though the angels, both cherubim and seraphim, were not also, in accordance with their nature, invisible to our eyes. David was certainly in doubt even as regards the appearance of the heavens : [4] "I shall see," he says, "the heavens, the works of Thy fingers." I shall see, not I see. I shall see when with unveiled face I shall behold the glory of the Lord : but [5] now we see in part, and we know in part. The question is whether the Son sees the Father, and you say "The Father is invisible." It is disputed whether the Holy Spirit sees the Son, and you answer "The Son is invisible." The point at issue is, whether the Trinity have mutually the vision of one another; human ears cannot endure such blasphemy, and you say the Trinity is invisible. You wander in the realms of praise in all other directions; you spend your eloquence on things which no one wants to hear about. You put your hearer off the scent, to avoid telling us what we ask for. But granted that all this is superfluous. We make you a present of the fact that you are not an Arian; nay, even more, that you never have been. We allow that in the explanation of the first section no suspicion rests upon you, and that all that you said was frank and free from error. We speak to you with equal frankness. Did our father in God, Epiphanius, accuse you of being an Arian? Did he fasten upon you the heresy of [6] Eunomius, the *Godless*, or that of [7] Aerius?

The point of the whole letter is that you follow the erroneous doctrines of Origen, and are associated with others in this heresy. Why, when a question is put to you on one point, do you give an answer about another; and, as if you were speaking to fools, hide the charges contained in the letters, and tell us what you said in the church in the presence of Epiphanius? A confession of faith is demanded of you, and you inflict upon us your very eloquent dissertations. I beseech my readers to remember the judgment seat of the Lord, and as you know that you must be judged for the judgment you give, favour neither me nor my opponent, and consider not the persons of the arguers, but the case itself. Let us then continue what we began.

10. You write in your letter that, before Paulinianus was made a presbyter, the pope Epiphanius never took you to task in connection with Origen's errors. To begin with, this is doubtful, and I have to consider which of the two men I should believe. He says that he did object, you deny it; he brings forward witnesses, you will not listen to them when they are produced; he even relates that [1] another besides yourself was arraigned by him : you refuse to admit this in the case of either; he sends a letter to you by one of his clergy, and demands an answer : you are silent, dare not open your lips, and, challenged in Palestine, speak at Alexandria. Which of you is to be believed is not for me to say. I suppose that you yourself would not, in the face of so distinguished a man, venture to claim truth for yourself, and impute falsehood to him. But it is possible that each speaks from his own point of view. I will call a witness against you, and that witness is yourself. For if there were no dispute about doctrines, if you had not roused the anger of an old man, if he had given you no reply, what need was there for you, who do not excel in gifts of speech, to discuss in a single sermon in the church the whole circle of doctrine—the Trinity, the assumption of our Lord's body, the cross, hell, the nature of angels, the condition of souls, the Saviour's resurrection and our own, and this as taking place on this earth (topics perhaps omitted in your manuscript) in the presence of the masses, in the presence, too, of a man of such distinction? and to gallop through it all without stopping to draw breath? What shall we say of the ancient writers of the Church, who were scarce able to explain single difficulties in many volumes? What of the vessel of election,

---

[1] Ps. cxxxix. 21, 22.   [2] Deut. xxxiii. 9.   [3] Matt. x. 37.
[4] Ps. viii. 3.   [5] 1 Cor. xiii. 9.
[6] Eunomius held that the Son "resembles the Father in nothing but his working," and similar doctrines.
[7] Of Sebaste, in the Lesser Armenia. Epiphanius described him as an Arian. He asserted that Bishops and Presbyters were equal.

[1] This probably relates to Rufinus, whose name was mentioned by Epiphanius in his letter to John.

the Gospel trumpet, the roaring of our lion, the thunderer of the Gentiles, the river of Christian eloquence, who, when confronted by the [1] mystery concealed from ages and generations, and by [2] the depth of the riches of the wisdom and knowledge of God, rather marvels at it than discusses it? What of Isaiah, who pointed beforehand to the Virgin? That single thing was too much for him, and he says, [3] "Who shall declare his generation?" In our age a poor mannikin has been found, who, with one turn of the tongue, and a brilliancy exceeding that of the sun, discourses on all ecclesiastical questions. If no one asked you for the display, and everything was quiet, you were foolish to enter voluntarily upon so hazardous a discussion. If, on the other hand, the object of your speaking was the satisfaction you owed to the faith, it follows that the cause of strife was not the ordination of a [4] priest, who, it is certain, was ordained long after. You have deceived only those who were not on the spot, and your letters flatter the ears of strangers only.

11. We were present (we know the whole case) when the bishop Epiphanius spoke against Origen in your church, and he was the ostensible, you the real object of attack. You and your crew grinned like dogs, drew in your nostrils, scratched your heads, nodded to one another, and talked of the "silly old man." Did you not, in front of the Lord's tomb, send your archdeacon to tell him to cease discussing such matters? What bishop ever gave such a command to one of his own presbyters in the presence of the people? When you were going from the Church of the Resurrection to the Church of the Holy Cross, and a crowd of all ages, and both sexes, was flowing to meet him, presenting to him their little ones, kissing his feet, plucking the fringes of his garments, and when he could not stir a step forward, and could hardly stand against the waves of the surging crowd, were not you so tortured by envy as to exclaim against "the vainglorious old man"? And you were not ashamed to tell him to his face that his stopping was of set purpose and design. Pray recall that day when the people who had been called together were kept waiting until the seventh hour by the mere hope of hearing Epiphanius, and the subject of the harangue you then delivered. You spoke, forsooth, with indignant rage against the Anthropomorphites, who, with rustic simplicity, think that God has actually the members of which we read in Scripture; and showed by your eyes, hands, and every gesture that you had the old man in view, and wished him to be suspected of that most foolish heresy. When through sheer fatigue, with dry mouth, head thrown back, and quivering lips, to the satisfaction of the whole people, who had longed for the end, you at last wound up, how did the crazy and "silly old man" treat you? He rose to indicate that he would say a few words, and after saluting the assembly with voice and hand proceeded thus: "All that has been said by one who is my brother in the episcopate, but my son in point of years, against the heresy of the Anthropomorphites, has been well and faithfully spoken, and my voice, too, condemns that heresy. But it is fair that, as we condemn this heresy so we should also condemn the perverse doctrines of Origen." You cannot, I think, have forgotten what a burst of laughter, what shouts of applause ensued. This is what you call in your letter his speaking to the people anything he chose, no matter what it might be. He, forsooth, was mad because he contradicted you in your own kingdom. "Anything he chose, no matter what." Either give him praise, or blame. Why, here as well as elsewhere, do you move with so uncertain a step? If what he said was good, why not openly proclaim it? if evil, why not boldly censure it? And yet, let us note with what wisdom, modesty, and humility this pillar of truth and faith, who dares to say that so illustrious a man speaks to the people what he chooses, alludes to himself. "One day I was speaking in his presence; and, taking occasion from some words in the lesson for the day, I expressed, in his hearing and in that of the whole Church, such views respecting the faith and all the doctrines of the Church as by the grace of God I unceasingly teach in the Church, and in my catechetical lectures."

12. What, I ask, is the meaning of this effrontery and bombast? All philosophers and orators attack Gorgias of Leontini for daring openly to pledge himself to answer any question which any person might choose to put to him. If the honour of the priesthood and respect for your title did not restrain me, and if I did not know what the Apostle says, [1] "I wist not, brethren, that he was the high priest: for it is written, Thou shalt not speak evil of the ruler of thy people," how loudly and indignantly might I complain of what you relate! You, on the contrary, disparage the dignity of your title by the contempt which you throw, both in word and deed, on one who is almost the father of the whole episcopate, and a monument of the sanctity of former days. You say that on a certain day, when something in the lesson for

---

[1] Col. i. 26.　　　[2] Rom. xi. 33.　　　[3] Is. liii. 8.
[4] Paulinianus.

[1] Acts xxiii. 5; Ex. xxii. 28.

the day stirred you up, you made a discourse in his hearing, and in that of the whole Church, concerning the faith and all the doctrines of the Church. After this we cannot but wonder at the weakness of Demosthenes; for we are told that he spent a long time in elaborating his splendid oration against Æschines. We are quite mistaken in looking up to Tully; for his merit, according to Cornelius Nepos, who was present, was nothing but this, that he delivered his famous defence of the seditious tribune Cornelius, almost word for word as it was published. Behold a Lysias [1] and a Gracchus raised up for us! or, to name one of more modern days, a Quintus Aterius, [2] the man who had all his powers at hand like a stock of ready money, so that he needed some one to tell him when to stop, and of whom Cæsar Augustus said very well, "Our friend Quintus must have the break put on."

13. Is there any man in his right senses who would declare that in a single sermon he had discussed the faith and all the doctrines of the Church? Pray show me what that lesson is which is so seasoned with the whole savour of Scripture that its occurrence in the service induced you to enter the arena and put your wit to the hazard. And if you had not been overwhelmed by the torrent of your eloquence, you might have been convinced that it was impossible for you to speak upon the whole circle of doctrines without any deliberation. But how stands the case? You promise one thing and present another. Our custom is, for the space of forty days, to deliver public lectures to those who are to be baptized on the doctrine of the Holy and Adorable Trinity. If the lesson for the day stimulated you to discuss all doctrines in a single hour, what necessity was there to repeat the instruction of the previous forty days? But if you meant to recapitulate what you had been saying during the whole of Lent, how could one lesson on a certain day "stir you up" to speak of all these doctrines? But even here his language is ambiguous; for possibly he took occasion, from the particular lesson, to go over summarily what he was accustomed to deliver in church to the candidates for baptism during the forty days of Lent. For it is eloquence all the same, whether few things are said in many words, or many things in few words. There is another permissible meaning, that, as soon as the one lesson gave him the spur, he was fired with such oratorical zeal that for forty days he never ceased speaking. But, then, even

the easy-going old man, who was hanging upon his lips, and longing to know what he had never heard before, must have almost fallen from his seat asleep. However, we must put up with it; perhaps this, also, is a case of the simplicity which we know to be his manner.

14. Let us quote the rest, in which, after the labyrinths of his perplexing discussion, he expresses himself by no means ambiguously but openly, and thus concludes his wonderful homilies: "When we had thus spoken in his presence, and when out of the extreme honour which we paid him we invited him to speak after us, he praised our preaching, and said that he marvelled at it, and declared to all that it was the Catholic faith." The extreme honour you paid him is evidenced by the extreme insults offered to him, when through the archdeacon you bade him be silent, and loudly proclaimed that it was the love of praise which made him linger among the crowd. The present is the key to the past. For three whole years from that time he has brooded in silence [1] over the wrongs he suffered, and, spurning all personal strife, has only asked for a more correct expression of your faith. You, with your endless resources, and making a profit out of the religion of the whole world, have been sending those very dignified envoys of yours hither and thither, and have been trying to awake the old man out of his sleep that he might answer you. And in truth it was right that as you had conferred such signal honour upon him he should praise your utterances, particularly such as were *ex tempore*. But as men have a way of sometimes praising what they do not approve, and of nourishing another's folly by meaningless commendation, he not only praised your utterances, but praised and marvelled at them as well; and what is more, to magnify the marvel, he declared to the whole people that they were in harmony with the Catholic faith. Whether he really said all this, we ourselves are witnesses. The fact is, he came to us half dead with dismay at your words, and saying that he had been too precipitate in communicating with you. And further, when he was much entreated by the whole monastery to return to you from Bethlehem, and was unable to resist the entreaties of so many, he did indeed return in the evening, but only to escape again at midnight. His letters to the pope Siricius prove the same thing, and if you read them you will see clearly in what sense he marvelled at your utterances and acknowledged them Catholic. But we are threshing chaff, and have spent

---

[1] A celebrated orator of Athens, many of whose orations are extant. B. 458, d. 378 B.C.
[2] This story is from the 4th Declamation of Seneca.

[1] Literally "devours his wrongs."

many words in refuting gratuitous nonsense and old wives' fables.

15. Let us pass on to the second point. Here, as though there were nothing for his consideration, he vapours, and vents himself unconcernedly, pretending to be asleep, so that he may lull his readers also into slumber. " But we were speaking of the other matters pertaining to the faith, that is to say, that all things visible and invisible, the heavenly powers and terrestrial creatures have one and the same creator, even God, that is, the Holy Trinity, as the blessed David says, [1] ' By the word of the Lord were the heavens established, and all the host of them by the breath of His mouth '; and the creation of man is a simple proof of the same; for it was God Himself who took slime from the earth, and through the grace of His own inspiration bestowed on it a reasonable soul, and one endowed with free will; not a part of His own nature (as some impiously teach), but His own workmanship. And concerning the holy angels, the belief of Christians similarly follows Holy Scripture, which says of God, [2] " Who maketh His angels spirits, and His ministers a flaming fire." Holy Scripture does not allow us to believe that their nature is unchangeable, for it says, [3] " And angels which kept not their own principality, but left their proper habitation, He hath kept in everlasting bonds under darkness unto the judgment of the great day "; we know, therefore, that they have changed, and having lost their own dignity and glory have become more like demons. But that the souls of men are caused by the fall of the angels, or by their conversion, we never believed, nor have we so taught (God forbid !), and we confess that the view is at variance with the teaching of the Church."

16. We want to know whether souls, before man was made in paradise, and Adam was fashioned out of the earth, were among reasonable creatures; whether they had their own rank, lived, continued, subsisted; and whether the doctrine of Origen is true, who said that all reasonable creatures, incorporeal and invisible, if they grow remiss, little by little sink to a lower level, and, according to the character of the places to which they descend, take to themselves bodies. (For instance, that they may be at first ethereal, afterward aërial.) And that when they reach the neighbourhood of earth they are invested with grosser bodies, and last of all are tied to human flesh; and that the demons themselves who, of their own choice, together with their leader the devil, have forsaken the service of

God, if they begin to amend a little, are clothed with human flesh, so that, when they have undergone a process of repentance after the resurrection, and after passing through the same circuit by which they reached the flesh, they may return to proximity to God, being released even from aërial and ethereal bodies; and that then every knee will bow to God, of things in heaven, and things on earth, and things under the earth, and that God may be all to all. When these are the real questions, why do you pass over the points at issue, and, leaving the arena, fix yourself in the region of remote and utterly irrelevant discussion ?

17. You believe that one God made all creatures, visible and invisible. Arius, who says that all things were created through the Son, would also confess this. If you had been accused of holding Marcion's heresy, which introduces two Gods, the one the God of goodness, the other of justice, and asserts that the former is the Creator of things invisible, the latter of things visible, your answer would have been well adapted to satisfy me on a question of that sort. You believe it is the Trinity which creates the universe. Arians and Semi-Arians deny that, blasphemously maintaining that the Holy Spirit is not the Creator, but is Himself created. But who now lays it to your charge that you are an Arian ? You say that the souls of men are not a part of the nature of God, as though you were now called a Manichæan by Epiphanius. You protest against those who assert that souls are made out of angels, and say that their nature, in its fall, becomes the substance of humanity. Don't conceal what you know, nor feign a simplicity which you do not possess. Origen never said that souls are made out of angels, since he teaches that the term *angels* describes an office, not a nature. For in his book Περὶ Ἀρχῶν he says that angels, and thrones, and dominions, powers and rulers of the world, and of darkness, and [1] every name which is named, not only in this world, but in that which is to come, become the souls of those bodies which they have taken on either through their own desire or for the sake of their appointed duties; that the sun also, himself, and the moon, and the company of all the stars, are the souls of what were once reasonable and incorporeal creatures; and that though now subject to vanity, that is to say, to fiery bodies which we, in our ignorance and inexperience, call luminaries of the world, they shall be delivered from the bondage of corruption and brought to the liberty of the glory of the sons of

[1] Ps. xxxiii. 6.   [2] Ps. civ. 4.   [3] Jude 6.   [1] Eph. i. 21.

God. Wherefore every creature groaneth and travaileth in pain together. And the Apostle laments, saying,[1] "Wretched man that I am! who shall deliver me from the body of this death?" This is not the time to controvert this doctrine, which is partly heathen, and partly Platonic. About ten years ago in my "Commentary" on Ecclesiastes, and in my explanation of the Epistle to the Ephesians, I think my own views were made clear to thoughtful men.

18. I now beg you, whose eloquence is so exuberant, and who expound the truth concerning all topics in the course of one sermon, to give an answer to your interrogators in concise and clear terms. When God formed man out of slime, and through the grace of His own inspiration gave him a soul, had that soul previously existed and subsisted which was afterwards bestowed by the inspiration of God, and where was it? or did it gain its capacity both to exist and to live from the power of God, on the sixth day, when the body was formed out of the slime? You are silent regarding this, and pretend you do not know what is wanted, and busy yourself with irrelevant questions. You leave Origen untouched, and rave against the absurdities of Marcion, Apollinaris, Eunomius, Manichæus, and the other heretics. You are asked for a hand and you put out a foot, and all the while covertly insinuate the doctrine to which you hold. You speak smooth things to plain men like us, but in such a way as in no degree to displease those of your own party.

19. You say that demons rather than souls are made out of angels, as though you did not know that, according to Origen, the demons themselves are souls belonging to aërial bodies, and, after being demons, destined to become human souls if they repent. You write that the angels are mutable; and, under cover of a pious opinion, introduce an impiety by maintaining that, after the lapse of many ages, souls are produced not from the angels, but from whatever it was into which the angels were first changed. I wish to make my meaning clearer; suppose a person of the rank of tribune to be degraded through his own misconduct, and to pass through the several steps of the cavalry service until he becomes a private, does he all at once cease to be a tribune [2] and become a recruit? No; but he is first colonel, then, successively, major, officer of two hundred, captain, commissary, patrol, trooper, and, lastly, a recruit; and although our tribune eventually becomes a common

soldier, still he did not pass from the rank of tribune to that of recruit, but to that of colonel. Origen uses Jacob's ladder to teach that reasonable creatures by slow degrees sink to the lowest step, that is to flesh and blood; and that it is impossible for any one to be suddenly precipitated from number one hundred to number one without reaching the last by passing through the successive numbers, as in descending the rounds of a ladder; and that they change their bodies as often as they change their resting-places in going from heaven to earth. These are the tricks and artifices by which you make us out to be [1] "Pelusiots" and "beasts of burden" and "animal men" who do "not receive the things pertaining to the Spirit."[2] You are the "people of Jerusalem," and can make a mock even of the angels. But your mysteries are being dragged into the light, and your doctrine, which is a mere conglomerate of heathen fables, is publicly exposed in the ears of Christians. What you so much admire we long ago despised when we found it in Plato. And we despised it because we received the foolishness of Christ. And we received the foolishness of Christ because[3] the weakness of God is wiser than men. And is it not a shame for us, who are Christians and priests of God, to entangle ourselves in words of doubtful meaning, as though we were merely jesting; to keep our phrases balanced between two meanings, in a way which deceives the speaker himself more than his hearers?

20. One of your company, when pressed by me to say what he thought concerning the soul, whether it had existed before the flesh, or not, replied that soul and body had existed together. I knew the man was a heretic, and was seeking to entangle me in my speech. At last I caught him saying that the soul gained that name from the time when it began to animate a body, whereas it was formerly called a demon, or angel of Satan, or spirit of fornication, or, on the other hand, dominion, power, agent of the spirit, or messenger. Well, but if the soul existed before Adam was made in Paradise (in any rank and condition), and lived and acted (for we cannot think that what is incorporeal and eternal is dull and torpid like a dormouse), there must have been some precedent cause to account for the soul, which at first had no body, being afterwards invested with a body. And if it is natural to the soul to be without a body, it must be contrary to nature for it to be in a body. If it is contrary to nature to be in a body, it follows that the resurrection of the body is contrary to nature. But the resurrection will not be contrary to

---

[1] Rom. vii. 24.
[2] The names of the officers of the Roman Legion (some of them of doubtful meaning), viz., tribunes, primicerius, senator, ducenarius, centenarius, biarchus, circitor, eques, have been rendered approximately by these English equivalents.

[1] That is, apparently, with a play upon the word, *Men of Mud.*
[2] Cor. ii. 14.   [3] 1 Cor. i. 25.

nature; therefore, according to you, the body, which is contrary to nature, when it rises again will be without a soul.

21. You say that the soul is not of the essence of God. Well! This is what we might expect, for you condemn the impious Manichæus, to make mention of whose name is pollution. You say that angels are not turned into souls. I agree to some extent, although I know what meaning you give to the words. But, now that we have learnt what you deny, we wish to know what you believe. "Having taken slime of the earth," you say, "God fashioned man, and through the grace of His own inbreathing bestowed upon him a rational soul, and through the grace of free will, not a portion of His own divine nature (as some impiously maintain), but His own handiwork." See how he goes out of his way to be eloquent about what we did not ask for. We know that God fashioned man out of the earth; we are aware that He breathed into his face, and man became a living soul; we are not ignorant that the soul is characterized by reason and free choice, and we know that it is the workmanship of God. No one doubts that Manichæus errs in saying that the soul is the essence of God. I now ask: When was that soul made, which is the work of God, which is distinguished by free will and reason, and is not of the essence of the Creator? Was it made at the same time that man was made out of the slime, and the breath of life was breathed into his face? Or, having previously existed, and having associated with reasonable and incorporeal creatures as well as lived, was it afterwards gifted with the inbreathing of God? Here you are silent; here you feign a rustic simplicity, and make scriptural words a cloak for unscriptural tenets. Where you affirm what no one wants to know, that the soul is not a part of God's own nature (as some impiously maintain), you ought rather to have declared (and this is what we all want to know) that it is not that which previously existed, which He had before created, which had long dwelt among rational, incorporeal, and invisible creatures. You say none of these things; you bring forward Manichæus, and keep Origen out of sight, and, just as when children ask for something to eat their nurse-maids put them off with some little joke, so you direct the thoughts of us poor rustics to other matters, so that we may be taken up with the fresh character on the stage, and may not ask for what we want.

22. But suppose the fact to be that you merely omit this, and that your simplicity does not mean something you are shrewd enough to conceal. Having once begun to speak of the soul, and to deduce arguments

on such an important topic from man's first creation, why do you leave the discussion in mid-air, and suddenly pass to the angels, and the conditions under which the body of our Lord existed? Why do you pass by such a vast slough of difficulty, and leave us to stick in the mire? If the inbreathing of God (a view for which you have no liking, and a point which you now leave unsettled) is the creating of the human soul; whence had Eve her soul, seeing that God did not breathe into her face? But I will not dwell upon Eve, since she, as a type of the Church, was made out of one of her husband's ribs, and ought not, after so many ages, to be subjected to the calumnies of her descendants. I ask whence Cain and Abel, who were the first-born of our first parents, had their souls? And the whole human race downwards, what, are we to think, was the origin of their souls? Did they come by propagation, like brute beasts? So that, as body springs from body, so soul from soul. Or is it the case that rational creatures, longing for bodily existence, sink by degrees to earth, and at last are tied even to human bodies? Surely (as the Church teaches in accordance with the Saviour's words,[1] "My Father worketh hitherto and I work"; and the passage in Isaiah,[2] "Who maketh the spirit of man in him"; and in the Psalms,[3] "Who fashioneth one by one the hearts of them") God is daily making souls— He, with whom to will is to do, and who never ceases to be a Creator. I know what you are accustomed to say in opposition to this, and how you confront us with adultery and incest. But the dispute about these is a tedious one, and would exceed the narrow limits of the time at our disposal. The same argument may be retorted upon you, and whatever seems unworthy in the Creator of the present dispensation is again not unworthy, since it is His gift. Birth from adultery imputes no blame to the child, but to the father. As in the case of seeds, the earth which cherishes does not sin, nor the seed which is thrown into the furrows, nor the heat and moisture, under whose influence the grain bursts into bud, but some man, as for example, the thief and robber, who, by fraud and violence, plucks up the seed: so in the begetting of men, the womb, which corresponds to the earth, receives its own, and nourishes what it has received, and then gives a body to that which it nourishes, and divides into the several members the body it has formed. And among those secret recesses of the belly the hand of God is always working, and there is the same Creator of body and soul. Do not despise

---

[1] John v. 17.   [2] That is, Zechariah xii. i.   [3] Ps. xxxiii. 15.

the goodness of your Maker, who fashioned you and made you as He chose. He Himself is the virtue of God and the wisdom of God, who, in the womb of the Virgin, built a house for Himself. Jephthah, who is reckoned by the Apostle among the saints, is the son of a harlot. But listen: Esau, born of Rebecca and Isaac, a "hairy man," both in mind and body, like good wheat, degenerates into darnel and wild oats; because the cause of vice and virtue does not lie in the seed, but in the will of him who is born. If it is an offence to be born with a human body, how is it that Isaac, Samson, John Baptist, are the children of promise? You see, I trust, what it is to have the courage of one's convictions. Suppose I am wrong, I openly say what I think. Do you, then, likewise either freely profess our opinions, or firmly maintain your own. Do not set yourself in my line of battle, so that, by feigning simplicity, you may be safe, and may be able, when you choose, to stab your opponent in the back. It is impossible for me, at the present moment, to write a book against the opinions of Origen. If Christ gives us life, we will devote another work to them. The point now is, whether the accused has answered the questions put to him, and whether his reply be clear and open.

23. Let us pass from this to the most notorious point, that relating to the resurrection of the flesh and of the body; and here, my reader, I would admonish you that you may know I speak under a sense of fear and of the judgment of God, and that you ought so to hear. For, if the pure faith is to be found in his exposition, and there is no suspicion of unfaithfulness, I am not so foolish as to seek an occasion of accusing him, and while I wish to censure another for his fault be myself censured as a slanderer. I will ask you, therefore, to read what follows on the resurrection of the flesh; and, having read it, if it satisfies you (I know it is well calculated to please the ignorant), suspend your judgment, wait a while, refrain from expressing an opinion until I have finished my reply; and if after that it satisfies you, then you shall fix on us the brand of slander. "His passion also on the cross, His death and burial, which was the saving of the world, and His resurrection in a true and not an imaginary sense, we confess; and that[1] being the firstborn from the dead, He conveyed to heaven the firstfruits of our bodily substance which, after being laid in the tomb, He raised to life, thus giving us the hope of resurrection in the resurrection of His own body; wherefore we all hope so to rise from the dead, as He rose again; not in any foreign and strange bodies, which are but phantom shapes assumed for the moment; but as He Himself rose again in that body which was laid in the holy sepulchre at our very doors, so we, in the very bodies with which we are now clothed, and in which we are now buried, hope to rise again for the same reason and by the same[1] command. For the bodies which, as the Apostle says, are sown in corruption, shall rise in incorruption; being sown in dishonour, they shall rise in glory.[2] 'It is sown an animal body, it shall rise a spiritual body'; and of them the Saviour said in his teaching: [3] 'For they who shall be worthy of that world, and of the resurrection from the dead, shall neither marry nor be given in marriage, for they can die no more, but shall be as the angels of God, since they are the sons of the resurrection.'"

24. Again, in another part of his letter, that is, towards the end of his own homilies, that he might cheat the ear of the ignorant, he makes a grand parade and noise about the Resurrection, but in ambiguous and balanced language. He says: "We have not omitted the second glorious advent of our Lord Jesus Christ, who shall come in His own glory to judge the quick and the dead; for He shall awake all the dead, and cause them to stand before His own judgment-seat; and shall render to every one according to what he has done in the body, whether it be good or bad; for every one shall either be crowned in the body because he lived a pure and righteous life, or be condemned, because he was the slave alike of pleasure and iniquity." What we read in the Gospel, that at the end of the world,[4] if it were possible, even the elect are to be seduced, we see verified in this passage. The ignorant crowd hears of the dead and buried, hears of the resurrection of the dead in a true and not an imaginary sense, hears that the firstfruits of our bodily substance in our Lord's body have reached the heavenly regions, hears that we shall rise again not in foreign and strange bodies, which are mere phantom shapes, but, as our Lord rose in the body which lay amongst us in the holy sepulchre, so we also in the very bodies with which we are now clothed and buried shall rise again in the day of judgment. And that no one might think this too little, he adds in the last section: "And He shall render to every one according to what he did in the body, whether it were good or bad: for every one shall either be crowned in the body for his pure and righteous life, or shall be condemned, be-

---

[1] Col. i. 18.

[1] Jussione. Another reading, "Eâdem ratione et visione," might be rendered, "In the same condition and the same appearance." [2] 1 Cor. xv. 44.   [3] Luke xx. 35, 36.   [4] Matt. xxiv. 24.

cause he was the slave of pleasure and iniquity." Hearing these things the ignorant crowd suspects no artifice, no snares in all this noise about the dead, the burial of the body, and the resurrection. It believes things are as they are said to be. For there is more devotion in the ears of the people than in the priest's heart.

25. Again and again, my reader, I admonish you to be patient, and to learn what I also have learnt through patience ; and yet, before I take the veil off the dragon's face, and briefly explain Origen's views respecting the resurrection (for you cannot know the efficacy of the antidote unless you see clearly what the poison is), I beg you to read his statements with caution, and to go over them again and again. Mark well that, though he nine times speaks of the resurrection of the body, he has not once introduced the resurrection of the flesh, and you may fairly suspect that he left it out on purpose. Well, Origen says in several places, and especially in his fourth book " Of the Resurrection," and in the "Exposition of the First Psalm," and in the "Miscellanies," that there is a double error common in the Church, in which both we and the heretics are implicated : " We, in our simplicity and fondness for the flesh, say that the same bones, and blood, and flesh, in a word, limbs and features, and the whole bodily structure, rise again at the last day : so that, forsooth, we shall walk with our feet, work with our hands, see with our eyes, hear with our ears, and carry about with us a belly never satisfied, and a stomach which digests our food. Consequently, believing this, we say that we must eat, drink, perform the offices of nature, marry wives, beget children. For what is the use of organs of generation, if there is to be no marriage ? For what purpose are teeth, if the food is not to be masticated ? What is the good of a belly and of meats, if, according to the Apostle, both it and they are to be destroyed ? And the same Apostle again exclaims,[1] 'Flesh and blood shall not inherit the Kingdom of God, nor shall corruption inherit incorruption.'" This, according to him, is what we in our rustic innocence maintain. But as for the heretics, amongst whom are Marcion, Apelles, Valentinus, Manes (a synomym for Mania), he says that they utterly deny the resurrection of the flesh and of the body, and allow salvation only to the soul, and hold that it is futile for us to say that we shall rise after the pattern of our Lord, since our Lord also Himself rose again in a phantom body, and not only His resurrection, but His very nativity was *docetic*

or imaginary ; that is, more apparent than real. Origen himself is dissatisfied with both opinions. He says that he shuns both errors, that of the flesh, which our party maintain, and that of the phantoms, maintained by the heretics, because both sides go to the opposite extremes, some wishing to be the same that they have been, others denying altogether the resurrection of the body. "There are four elements," he says, "known to philosophers and physicians : earth, water, air, and fire, and out of these all things and human bodies are compacted. We find earth in flesh, air in the breath, water in the moisture of the body, fire in its heat. When, then, the soul, at the command of God, lets go this perishing and feeble body, little by little all things return to their parent substances : flesh is again absorbed into the earth, the breath is mingled with the air, the moisture returns to the depths, the heat escapes to the ether. And as if you throw into the sea a pint of milk and wine, and wish again to separate what is mixed together, although the wine and milk which you threw in is not lost, and yet it is impossible to keep separate what was poured out ; so the substance of flesh and blood does not perish, indeed, so far as concerns the original matter, yet they cannot again become the former structure, nor can they be altogether the same that they were." Observe that when such things are said, the firmness of the flesh, the fluidity of the blood, the density of the sinews, the interlacing of the veins, and the hardness of the bones is denied.

26. "For another reason," he says, "we confess the resurrection of our bodies, those which have been laid in the grave and have turned to dust ; Paul's body will be that of Paul, Peter's that of Peter, and each will have his own ; for it is not right that souls should sin in one body and be tormented in another, nor is it worthy of the Righteous Judge that one body should shed its blood for Christ and another be crowned." Who, hearing this, would think he denied the resurrection of the flesh ? "And," he says, "every seed has its own law of being inherent in it by the gift of God, the Creator, which law contains in embryonic form the future growth. The bulky tree, with its trunk, boughs, fruit, leaves, is not seen in the seed, but nevertheless exists in the seed by implication or, according to the Greek expression, by the *spermatikos logos*.[1] There is within the grain of corn a marrow, or vein, which, when it has been dissolved in the earth, attracts to itself the surrounding materials, and rises again in

---

[1] 1 Cor. xv. 58.

[1] That is, the reason of the seed.

the shape of stalk, leaves, and ear ; and thus, while it is one thing when it dies, it is another thing when it rises from the dead ; for in the grain of wheat, roots, stalk, leaves, ears, trunk are as yet unseparated. In the same manner, in human bodies, according to the law of their being, certain original principles remain which ensure their resurrection, and a sort of marrow, that is a seed-plot of the dead, is fostered in the bosom of the earth. But when the day of judgment shall have come, and at the voice of the archangel, and the sound of the last trumpet, the earth shall totter, immediately the seeds will be instinct with life, and in a moment of time will cause the dead to burst into life ; yet the flesh which they will reconstitute will not be the same flesh, nor will it be in the old forms. To give you the assurance that we speak the truth, let me quote the words of the Apostle :[1] 'But some one says, How shall the dead rise ? and with what body will they come ? Thou fool, that which thou sowest, thou sowest not that body which shall be, but a bare grain, it may be of wheat, or the seed of a vine and a tree.' And as we have already made the grain of wheat, and to some extent the planting of trees, the subject of our reasoning, let us now take the grape-stone as an example. It is a mere granule, so small that you can scarcely hold it between your two fingers. Where are the roots ? where the tortuous interlacing of roots, of trunk and off-shoots ? where the shade of the leaves, and the lovely clusters teeming with coming wine ? What you have in your fingers is parched and scarcely discernible ; nevertheless, in that dry granule, by the power of God and the secret law of propagation, the foaming new wine must have its origin. You will allow all this in the case of a tree ; will you not admit such things to be possible in the case of a man ? The plant which perishes is thus decked with beauty ; why should we think that man, who abides, will receive back his former meanness ? Do you demand that there should be flesh, bones, blood, limbs, so that you must have the barber to cut your hair, that your nose may run, your nails must be trimmed, your lower parts may gender filth or minister to lust ? If you introduce these foolish and gross notions, you forget what is told us of the flesh, namely, that in it we cannot please God, and that it is an enemy ; you forget, also, what is told us of the resurrection of the dead :[2] 'It is sown in corruption, it shall rise in incorruption. It is sown in dishonour, it shall rise in glory. It is sown in weakness, it shall rise in power. It is sown a natural body, it shall rise a spiritual body.'

Now we see with our eyes, hear with our ears, act with our hands, walk with our feet. But in that spiritual body we shall be all sight, all hearing, all action, all movement. The Lord shall transfigure[1] the body of our humiliation and fashion it according to His own glorious body. In saying *transfigure* he affirms *identity* with the members which we now have. But a *different* body, spiritual and ethereal, is promised to us, which is neither tangible, nor perceptible to the eye, nor ponderable ; and the change it undergoes will be suitable to the difference in its future abode. Otherwise, if there is to be the same flesh and if our bodies are to be the same, there will again be males and females, there will again be marriage ; men will have the shaggy eyebrow and the flowing beard ; women will have their smooth cheeks and narrow chests, and their bodies must adapt themselves to conception and parturition. Even tiny infants will rise again ; old men will also rise ; the former to be nursed, the latter to be supported by the staff. And, simple ones, be not deceived by the resurrection of our Lord, because He showed His side and His hands, stood on the shore, went for a walk with Cleophas, and said that He had flesh and bones. That body, because it was not born of the seed of man and the pleasure of the flesh, has its peculiar prerogatives. He ate and drank after His resurrection, and appeared in clothing, and allowed Himself to be touched, that He might make His doubting Apostles believe in His resurrection. But still He does not fail to manifest the nature of an aërial and spiritual body. For He enters when the doors are shut, and in the breaking of bread vanishes out of sight. Does it follow then that after our resurrection we shall eat and drink, and perform the offices of nature ? If so, what becomes of the promise,[2] 'The mortal must put on immortality.' "

27. Here we have the complete explanation of the fact that in your exposition of the faith, to deceive the ears of the ignorant, you nine times make mention of the body, and not even once of the flesh, and all the while men think that you confess the body of flesh, and that the flesh is identical with the body. If it is the same as the body, it means nothing different. I say this, for I know your answer : "I thought the body was the same as the flesh ; I spoke with all simplicity." Why do you not rather call it flesh to signify the body, and speak indifferently at one time of the flesh, at another of the body, that the body may be shown to consist of flesh, and the flesh to be

[1] 1 Cor. xv. 35, 37.   [2] 1 Cor. xv. 42, 44.   [1] Phil. iii. 21.   [2] 1 Cor. xv. 53.

the body. But believe me, your silence is not the silence of simplicity. For flesh is defined one way, the body another; all flesh is body, but not every body is flesh. Flesh is properly what is comprised in blood, veins, bones, and sinews. Although the body is also called flesh, yet sometimes it is designated ethereal or aërial, because it is not subject to touch and sight; and yet it is frequently both visible and tangible. A wall is a body, but is not flesh; a stone is a body, but it is not said to be flesh. Wherefore the Apostle calls some bodies celestial, some terrestrial. A celestial body is that of the sun, moon, stars; a terrestrial body is that of fire, air, water, and the rest, which bodies being inanimate are known as consisting of material elements. You see we understand your subtleties, and publish abroad the mysteries which you utter in the bedchamber and amongst the perfect, mysteries which may not reach the ears of outsiders. You smile, and with hand uplifted and a snap of the fingers retort,[1] "All the glory of the king's daughter is within." And, [2] "The king led me into his bedchamber." It is clear why you spoke of the resurrection of the body and not of that of the flesh; of course it was that we in our ignorance might think that when body was spoken of flesh was meant; while yet the perfect would understand that, when body was spoken of, flesh was denied. Lastly, the Apostle, in his Epistle to the Colossians, wishing to show that the body of Christ was made of flesh, and was not spiritual, aërial, attenuated, said significantly,[3] "And you, when you were some time alienated from Christ and enemies of His spirit in evil works, He has reconciled in the body of His flesh through death." And again in the same Epistle: [4] "In whom ye were circumcised with a circumcision made without hands in the putting off of the body of the flesh." If by body is meant flesh only, and the word is not ambiguous, nor capable of diverse significations, it was quite superfluous to use both expressions—*bodily* and *of flesh*—as though body did not imply flesh.

28. In the symbol of our faith and hope, which was delivered by the Apostles, and is not written with paper and ink, but on fleshy tables of the heart, after the confession of the Trinity and the unity of the Church, the whole symbol of Christian dogma concludes with the resurrection of the flesh. You dwell so exclusively upon the subject of the body, harping upon it in your discourse, repeating first the body, and secondly the body, and again the body, and nine times over the body, that you do not even once name

the flesh; whereas they always speak of the flesh, but say nothing of the body. I would have you know that we see through what you craftily add, and with wise precaution seek to conceal. For you make use of the same passages to prove the reality of the resurrection by means of which Origen denies it; you support questionable positions with doubtful arguments, and thus raise a storm which in a moment overthrows the settled fabric of faith. You quote the words,[1] "It is sown an animal body: it shall rise a spiritual body." "For they shall neither marry, nor be given in marriage, but shall be as the angels in heaven." What other instances would you take if you were denying the resurrection? You intend to confess the resurrection of the flesh, you say, in a real and not an imaginary sense. After the remarks with which you smooth things over to the ears of the ignorant, to the effect that we rise again with the very bodies with which we died and were buried, why do you not go on and speak thus: "The Lord after His resurrection showed the prints of the nails in His hands, pointed to the wound of the spear in His side, and when the Apostles doubted because they thought they saw a phantom, gave them reply, [2] 'Handle Me and see, for a spirit hath not flesh and blood as ye see Me have'; and specially to Thomas,[3] 'Put thy finger into My hands, and thy hand into My side, and be not faithless, but believing.' Similarly after the resurrection we shall have the same members which we now use, the same flesh and blood and bones, for it is not the nature of these which is condemned in Holy Scripture, but their works. Then again, it is written in Genesis :[4] 'My Spirit shall not abide in those men, because they are flesh.' And the Apostle Paul, speaking of the corrupt doctrine and works of the Jews, says :[5] 'I rested not in flesh and blood.' And to the Saints, who, of course, were in the flesh, he says :[6] 'But ye are not in the flesh, but in the spirit, if the Spirit of God dwells in you.' For by denying that they were in the flesh who clearly were in the flesh, he condemned not the substance of the flesh but its sins."

29. The true confession of the resurrection declares that the flesh will be glorious, but without destroying its reality. And when the Apostle says, [7] "This is corruptible and mortal," his words denote *this very body*, that is to say, the flesh which was then seen. But when he adds that it puts on incorruption and immortality, he does not say that that which is put on, that is the clothing, does

---

[1] Ps. xlv. 13.   [2] Cant. i. 4.   [3] Col. i. 21, 22.   [4] Col. ii. 11.

[1] 1 Cor. xv. 44; Matt. xxii. 30; Luke xx. 35.
[2] Luke xxiv. 39.   [3] John xx. 27.   [4] Gen. vi. 3.
[5] Gal. i. 16.   [6] Rom. viii. 9.   [7] 1 Cor. xv. 53.

away with the body which it adorns in glory, but that it makes that body glorious, which before lacked glory ; so that the more worthless robe of mortality and weakness being laid aside, we may be clothed with the gold of immortality, and, so to speak, with the blessedness of strength as well as virtue ; since we wish not to be stripped of the flesh, but to put on over it the vesture of glory, and desire to be clothed upon with our house, which is from heaven, that mortality may be swallowed up by life. Certainly, no one is clothed upon who was not previously clothed. Accordingly, our Lord was not so transfigured on the mountain that He lost His hands and feet and other members, and suddenly began to roll along in a round shape like that of the sun or a ball; but the same members glowed with the brightness of the sun and blinded the eyes of the Apostles. Hence, also, His garments were changed, but so as to become white and glistening, not aërial, for I suppose you do not intend to maintain that His clothes also were spiritual. [1] The Evangelist adds that His face shone like the sun ; but when mention is made of His face, I reckon that His other members were beheld as well. Enoch was translated in the flesh ; Elias was carried up to heaven in the flesh. They are not dead, they are inhabitants of Paradise, and even there retain the members with which they were rapt away and translated. What we aim at in fasting, they have through fellowship with God. They feed on heavenly bread, and are satisfied with every word of God, having Him as their food who is also their Lord. Listen to the Saviour saying : [2] "And my flesh rests in hope." And elsewhere, [3] "His flesh saw not corruption." And again,[4] "All flesh shall see the salvation of God." And must you be for ever making the body a twofold thing ? Rather quote the vision of [5] Ezekiel, who joins bones to bones and brings them forth from their sepulchres, and then, making them to stand on their feet, binds them together with flesh and sinews, and clothes them with skin.

30. Listen to those words of thunder which fall from Job, the vanquisher of torments, who, as he scrapes away the filth of his decaying flesh with a potsherd, solaces his miseries with the hope and the reality of the resurrection : [6] "Oh, that," he says, "my words were written ! Oh, that they were inscribed in a book with an iron pen, and on a sheet of lead, that they were graven in the rock for ever ! For I know that my Redeemer liveth, and that in the last day I shall rise from the earth, and again be clothed with my skin, and in my flesh shall see God, Whom I shall see for myself, and my eyes shall behold, and not another. This my hope is laid up in my bosom." What can be clearer than this prophecy ? No one since the days of Christ speaks so openly concerning the resurrection as he did before Christ. He wishes his words to last for ever ; and that they might never be obliterated by age, he would have them inscribed on a sheet of lead, and graven on the rock. He hopes for a resurrection ; nay, rather he knew and saw that Christ, his Redeemer, was alive, and at the last day would rise again from the earth. The Lord had not yet died, and the athlete of the Church saw his Redeemer rising from the grave. When he says, "And I shall again be clothed with my skin, and in my flesh see God," I suppose he does not speak as if he loved his flesh, for it was decaying and putrifying before his eyes; but in the confidence of rising again, and through the consolation of the future, he makes light of his present misery. Again he says : "I shall be clothed with my skin." What mention do we find here of an ethereal body ? What of an aërial body, like to breath and wind ? Where there is skin and flesh, where there are bones and sinews, and blood and veins, there assuredly is fleshy tissue and distinction of sex. "And in my flesh," he says, "I shall see God." When all flesh shall see the salvation of God, and Jesus as God, then I, also, shall see the Redeemer and Saviour, and my God. But I shall see him in that flesh which now tortures me, which now melts away for pain. Therefore, in my flesh shall I behold God, because by His own resurrection He has healed all my infirmities." Does it not seem to you that Job was then writing against Origen, and was holding a controversy similar to ours against the heretics, for the reality of the flesh in which he underwent tortures ? For he could not bear to think that all his sufferings would be in vain ; while the flesh he actually bore was tortured as flesh indeed, it would be some other and spiritual kind of flesh that would rise again. Wherefore he presses home and emphasizes the truth, and puts a stop to all that might lie hid in an artful confession, by speaking out plainly : "Whom I shall see for myself and my eyes shall behold and not another." If he is not to rise again in his own sex, if he is not to have the same members which were then lying on the dunghill, if he does not open the same eyes to see God with which he was then looking at the worms, where will Job then be ? You do away with what constituted Job, and give me the hollow phrase, *Job shall rise again ;* it is as if you

---

[1] Matt. xvii. 2. [2] Ps. xvi. 9. [3] Acts ii. 31.
[4] Is. xl. 5. [5] xxxvii. 1 sqq. [6] Job xix. 23 sqq.

were to order a ship to be restored after ship-wreck, and then were to refuse each particular thing of which a ship is made.

31. I will speak freely, and although you screw your mouths, pull your hair, stamp your feet, and take up stones like the Jews, I will openly confess the faith of the Church. The reality of a resurrection without flesh and bones, without blood and members, is unintelligible. Where there are flesh and bones, where there are blood and members, there must of necessity be diversity of sex. Where there is diversity of sex, there John is John, Mary is Mary. You need not fear the marriage of those who, even before death, lived in their own sex without discharging the functions of sex. When it is said, "In that day they shall neither marry, nor be given in marriage," the words refer to those who can marry, and yet will not do so. For no one says of the angels, "They shall not marry, nor be given in marriage." I never heard of a marriage being celebrated among the spiritual virtues in heaven : but where there is sex, there you have man and woman. Hence it is that, although you were reluctant, you were compelled by the truth to confess that, "A man must either be crowned in the body because he lived a pure and upright life, or be condemned in the body, because he was the slave of pleasure and iniquity." Substitute *flesh* for *body*, and you have not denied the existence of male and female. Who can have any glory from a life of chastity if we have no sex which would make unchastity possible ? Who ever crowned a stone for continuing a virgin ? Likeness to the angels is promised us, that is, the blessedness of their angelic existence without flesh and sex will be bestowed on us in our flesh and with our sex. I am simple enough so to believe, and so know how to confess that sex can exist without the functions of the senses ; that it is thus that men rise, and that it is thus that they are made equal to the angels. Nor will the resurrection of the members all at once seem superfluous, because they are to have no office, since, while we are still in this life, we strive not to perform the works of the members. Moreover, likeness to the angels does not imply a changing of men into angels, but their growth in immortality and glory.

32. But as for the arguments drawn from boys, and infants, and old men, and meats, and excrements, which you employ against the Church, they are not your own ; they flow from a heathen source. For the heathen mock us with the same. You say you are a Christian ; lay aside the weapons of the heathen. It is for them to learn from you

to confess the resurrection of the dead, not for you to learn from them to deny it. Or if you belong to the enemy's camp, show yourself openly as an adversary, that you may share the wounds we inflict on the heathen. I will allow you your jest about the necessity of nursemaids to stop the infants from crying ; of the decrepit old men, who, you fear, would be shrivelled with winter's cold. I will admit also that the barbers have learnt their craft for nothing, for do we not know that the people of Israel for forty years experienced no growth of either nails or hair ; and, still more, their clothes were not worn out, nor did their shoes wax old ? Enoch and Elias, concerning whom we spoke a while ago, abide all this time in the same state in which they were carried away. They have teeth, belly, organs of generation, and yet have no need of meats, or wives. Why do you slander the power of God, who can from that [1]*marrow* and *seed-plot* of which you speak, not only produce flesh from flesh, but also make one body from another ; and change water, that is worthless flesh, into the precious wine of an aërial body ? the same power by which He created all things out of nothing can give back what has existed, because it is a much smaller thing to restore what has been, than to make what never was. Do you wonder that there is a resurrection from the condition of infancy and old age to that of mature manhood, seeing that a perfect man was made out of the slime of the earth without having gone through successive stages of growth ? A rib is changed into a woman ; and by the third mode of creating man, the poor elements of our birth which put us to the blush are changed into flesh, bound together by the members, run into veins, harden into bones. There is a fourth sort of human generation of which I can tell you. "The Holy Spirit shall come upon thee, and the power of the Highest shall overshadow thee. Wherefore that [2] holy thing which shall be born of thee shall be called the Son of God." Adam was created one way, Eve another, Abel another, the man Jesus Christ another. And yet, different as are all these beginnings, the nature of man remains one and the same.

33. If I wished to prove the resurrection of the flesh and of all the members, and to give the meaning of the several passages, many books would be, required ; but the matter in hand does not call for this. For I purposed not to reply to Origen in every detail, but to disclose the mysteries of your insincere "Apol-

---

[1] Besides *medulla* and *seminarium* Jerome has ἐντερίωνη = *inward part*, or *pith*.
[2] Luke i. 35.

ogy." I have, however, tarried long in maintaining the opposite to your position, and am afraid that, in my eagerness to expose fraud, I may leave a stumbling-block in the way of the reader. I will, therefore, mass together the evidence, and glance at the proofs in passing, so that we may bring all the weight of Scripture to bear upon your poisonous argument. He who has not a wedding garment, and has not kept that command,[1] "Let your garments be always white," is bound hand and foot that he may not recline at the banquet, or sit on a throne, or stand at the right hand of God ;[2] he is sent to Gehenna, where there is weeping and gnashing of teeth. [3] "The hairs of your head are numbered." If the hairs, I suppose the teeth would be more easily numbered. But there is no object in numbering them if they are some day to perish. [4] "The hour will come in which all who are in the tombs shall hear the voice of the Son of God, and shall come forth." They shall hear with ears, come forth with feet. This Lazarus had already done. They shall, moreover, come forth from the tombs ; that is, they who had been laid in the tombs, the dead, shall come, and shall rise again from their graves. For the dew which God gives is[5] healing to their bones. Then shall be fulfilled what God says by the prophet, [6] "Go, my people, into thy closets for a little while, until mine anger pass." The closets signify the graves, out of which that, of course, is brought forth which had been laid therein. And they shall come out of the graves like young mules free from the halter. Their heart shall rejoice, and their bones shall rise like the sun ; all flesh shall come into the presence of the Lord, and He shall command the fishes of the sea ; and they shall give up the bones which they had eaten ; and He shall bring joint to joint, and bone to bone ; and [7] they who slept in the dust of the earth shall arise, some to life eternal, others to shame and everlasting confusion. Then shall the just see the punishment and tortures of the wicked, for[8] their worm shall not die, and their fire shall not be extinguished, and they shall be beheld by all flesh. As many of us, therefore, as have this hope, as we have yielded our members servants to uncleanness, and to iniquity unto iniquity, so let us yield them servants to righteousness unto holiness, that[9] we may rise from the dead and walk in newness of life. As also the life of the Lord Jesus is manifested in our mortal body, so[10] also He who raised up Jesus Christ from the dead shall quicken our mortal bodies on account of His Spirit Who dwelleth in us. For it is right that as we have always borne about the putting to death of Christ in our body, so the life, also, of Jesus, should be manifested in our mortal body, that is, in our flesh, which is mortal according to nature, but eternal according to grace. Stephen also [1] saw Jesus standing on the right hand of the Father, and the [2] hand of Moses became snowy white, and was afterwards restored to its original colour. There was still a hand, though the two states were different. The potter in[3] Jeremiah, whose vessel, which he had made, was broken through the roughness of the stone, restored from the same lump and from the same clay that which had fallen to pieces ; and, if we look at the word *resurrection* itself, it does not mean that one thing is destroyed, another raised up ; and the addition of the word *dead*, points to our own flesh, for that which in man dies, that is also brought to life. [4] The wounded man on the road to Jericho is taken to the inn with all his limbs complete, and the stripes of his offences are healed with immortality.

34. Even the graves were opened[5] at our Lord's passion when the sun fled, the earth trembled, and many of the bodies of the saints arose, and were seen in the holy city. [6] "Who is this," says Isaiah, "that cometh up from Edom, with shining raiment from Bozrah, so beautiful in his glistening robe ?" Edom is by interpretation either *earthy* or *bloody ;* Bosor either *flesh*, or *in tribulation*. In few words he shows the whole mystery of the resurrection, that is, both the reality of the flesh and the growth in glory. And the meaning is : Who is he that cometh up from the earth, cometh up from blood ? According to the[7] prophecy of Jacob, He has bound His foal to the vine, and has trodden the wine-press alone, and His garments are red with new wine from Bosor, that is from flesh, or from the tribulation of the world : for He Himself[8] has conquered the world. And, therefore, His garments are red and shining, because He is[9] beauteous in form more than the sons of men, and on account of the glory of His triumph they have been changed into a white robe ; and then, in truth, as concerns Christ's flesh, were fulfilled the words, [10] "Who is this that cometh up all in white, leaning upon her beloved ?" And that which is written in the same book : [11] "My beloved is white and ruddy." These men are his true followers who have not[12] defiled their gar-

[1] Ecc. ix. 8.   [2] Matt. xxii. 13.   [3] Luke xii. 7.
[4] John v. 25.
[5] Sept. "The dew which comes from thee is healing to them."
[6] Is. xxvi. 20.   [7] Dan. xii 2.   [8] Is. lxvi. 24.
[9] Rom. vi. 4.   [10] Rom. viii. 11.

[1] Acts vii. 55.   [2] Ex. iv. 6.   [3] xviii. 3, 4. Sept.
[4] Luke x. 34.   [5] Matt. xxvii. 52.   [6] lxiii. 1 sq.
[7] Gen. xlix. 11.   [8] John xvi. 33.   [9] Ps. xlv. (?).
[10] Cant. viii. 5.   [11] Cant. v. 16.   [12] Apoc. xiv. 4.

ments with women, for they have continued virgins, who have made themselves eunuchs for the kingdom of heaven's sake. And so they shall be in white clothing. Then shall the saying of our Lord appear perfectly realised : [1] " All that my Father has given me, I shall not lose aught thereof, but I will raise it up again at the last day ;" the whole of His humanity, forsooth, which He had taken upon Him in its entirety at His birth. Then shall the sheep which was [2] lost, and was wandering in the lower world, be carried whole on the Saviour's shoulders, and the sheep which was sick with sin shall be supported by the mercy of the Judge. Then shall they see him who pierced Him, who shouted, [3] " Crucify Him, crucify Him." Again and again shall they beat their breasts, they and their women, those women to whom our Lord said, as He carried His cross, [4] " Ye daughters of Jerusalem, weep not for me but weep for yourselves, and for your children." Then shall be fulfilled the prophecy of the angels, who said to the stupefied Apostles, [5] " Ye men of Galilee, why stand ye looking with astonishment into heaven ? This Jesus who is taken from you into heaven, shall come in like manner as ye have seen Him go into heaven." But what are we to think of a man saying that our Lord [6] ate with the Apostles for forty days after His resurrection in order that they might not think Him to be a phantom, and then asserting that it was a phantom which did this very thing, which ate and which was seen by many in the flesh. That which was seen is either real, or false. If it is real, it follows that He really ate, and really had members. But if it is false, how could He be willing to give false impressions in order to prove the truth of His resurrection ? For no one proves what is true by means of what is false. You will say, are we then going to eat after our resurrection ? I know not. Scripture does not tell us ; and yet, if the question be asked, I do not think we shall eat. For I have read that the kingdom of God is not meat and drink, while it promises [7] such things as eye hath not seen, nor ear heard, nor have entered into the heart of man. Moses fasted forty days and forty nights. Human nature does not allow of this, but what is impossible with men is not impossible with God. Just as, in foretelling the future, it matters not whether a person announces what will take place after ten years or after a hundred, since the knowledge of futurity is all one ; so he who can fast for fórty days and yet live,— not, indeed, that he can of himself fast, but

that he lives by the power of God,—will also be able to live for ever without food and drink. Why did our Lord eat an honeycomb ? To prove the resurrection : not to give your palate the pleasure of tasting of honey. He asked for a fish broiled on the coals that He might [1] confirm the doubting Apostles, who did not dare approach Him because they thought they saw not a body, but a spirit. [2] The daughter of the ruler of the synagogue was raised to life and took food. [3] Lazarus, who had been four days dead, rose again, and comes before us at a dinner ; not because he was accustomed to eat in the lower world, but because a case which presented such difficulties challenged the believer's criticism. As He showed them real hands and a real side, so He really ate with His disciples ; really walked with Cleophas ; conversed with men with a real tongue ; really reclined at supper ; with real hands took bread, blessed and brake it, and was offering it to them. And as for His suddenly vanishing out of their sight, that is the power of God, not of a shadowy phantom. Besides, even before His resurrection, when they had led Him out from Nazareth that they might cast Him down headlong from the brow of the hill, He passed through the midst of them, that is, escaped out of their hands. Can we follow Marcion, and say that because, when He was held fast, He escaped in a manner contrary to nature, therefore His birth must have been only apparent ? Has not the Lord a privilege which is conceded to magicians ? It is related of Apollonius of Tyana that, when standing in court before Domitian, he all at once disappeared. Do not put the power of the Lord on a level with the tricks of magicians, so that He may appear to have been what He was not, and may be thought to have eaten without teeth, walked without feet, broken bread without hands, spoken without a tongue, and showed a side which had no ribs.

35. And how was it, you will say, that they did not recognize Him on the road if He had the same body which He had before ? Let me recall what Scripture says : [4] " Their eyes were holden, that they might not know Him." And again, " Their eyes were opened, and they knew Him." Was He one person when He was not known, and another when He was known ? He was surely one and the same. Whether, therefore, they knew Him, or not, depended on their sight ; it did not depend upon Him Who was seen ; and yet it did depend on Him in this sense, that He held their eyes that they might not know Him. Lastly, that you may see that the

---

[1] John vi. 39.   [2] Luke xv. 3 sq.   [3] John xix. 6.
[4] Luke xxiii. 28.   [5] Acts i. 11.   [6] Ib. 3.
[7] 1 Cor. ii. 9.

[1] John xxi. 9.   [2] Mark v.   [3] John xii.   [4] Luke xxiv. 16.

mistake which held them was not to be attributed to the Lord's body, but to the fact that
their eyes were closed, we are told : [1] " Their
eyes were opened, and they knew Him."
Wherefore, also, Mary Magdalene so long as
she did not recognize Jesus, and sought the
living among the dead, thought He was the
gardener. Afterwards she recognized Him
and then she called Him Lord. After His
resurrection Jesus was standing on the shore,
His disciples were in the ship. When the
others did not know Him, the disciple whom
Jesus loved [2] said to Peter, "It is the Lord."
For virginity is the first to recognize a virgin
body. He was the same, yet was not seen
alike by all as the same. And immediately it
is added, [3] "And no one durst ask Him, Who
art Thou ? for they knew that He was the
Lord." No one durst, because they knew
that He was God. They ate with Him at dinner because they saw He was a man and had
flesh ; not that He was one person as God,
another as man : but, being one and the same
Son of God, He was known as man, adored
as God. I suppose I must now air my philosophy, and say that our senses are not to be
relied on, and especially sight. A [4] Carneades
must be awaked from the dead to tell us the
truth—that an oar seems broken in the water,
porticos afar off look more magnificent, the
angles of towers seem rounded in the distance, that the backs of pigeons change their
colours with every movement. When Rhoda [5]
announced Peter, and told the Apostles, they
did not believe that he had escaped, on
account of the greatness of the danger, but
suspected it was a phantom. Moreover, in
passing through closed doors, He exhibited
the same power as in vanishing out of sight.
[6] Lynceus, as fable relates, used to see through
a wall. Could not the Lord enter when the
doors were shut, unless He were a phantom ?
Eagles and vultures perceive dead bodies
across the sea. Shall not the Saviour see
His Apostles without opening the door ? Tell
me, sharpest of disputants, which is greater,
to hang the vast weight of the earth on nothing, and to balance it on the changing surface of the waves ; or that God should pass
through a closed door, and the creature yield
to the Creator ? You allow the greater ; you
object to the less. Peter [7] walked upon the
waters with his heavy and solid body. The
soft water does not yield : his faith doubts a
little, and immediately his body understands
its own nature ; that we may know that it

was not his body that walked on the water,
but his faith.

36. I pray you, who use such elaborate
arguments against the resurrection, let us
have some simple talk together. Do you believe that our Lord really rose again in the
same body in which He died and was buried,
or do you not believe it ? If you believe it,
why do you make propositions which lead to
the denial of the resurrection ? If you do not
believe, you who thus try to deceive the minds
of the ignorant, and parade the word resurrection, though you mean nothing by it, listen to me. Not long ago, a certain disciple
of Marcion said : "Woe to him who rises again
with this flesh and these bones !" Our heart
at once with joy replied,[1] "We are buried together, and we shall rise together with Christ
through baptism." "Do you speak of the
resurrection of the soul, or of the flesh ?" I
answered, "Not that of the soul alone, but
that of the flesh, which, together with the soul,
is born again in the laver. And how shall
that perish which has been born again in
Christ ?" "Because it is written," said he,
[2] "'Flesh and blood shall not inherit the kingdom of God.'" "I intreat you to mind what is
said—'Flesh and blood shall not inherit the
kingdom of God.'" "It is said that they shall
not rise again." "Not at all, but only 'they
shall not inherit the kingdom.'" "How so ?"
"'Because,' it follows,[3] 'neither shall corruption inherit incorruption.' So long then as
they remain mere flesh and blood, they shall
not inherit the kingdom of God. But when
the [4]corruptible shall have put on incorruption, and the mortal shall have put on immortality, and the clay of the flesh shall have been
made into a vessel, then that flesh which was
formerly kept down by a heavy weight upon
the earth, when once it has received the wings
of the spirit—wings which imply its change,
not its destruction—shall fly with fresh glory
to heaven ; and then shall be fulfilled that
which is written, [5] 'Death is swallowed up
in victory. Where, O death, is thy boasting ?
O death, where is thy sting ?'"

37. Reversing the order, we have given our
answer respecting the state of souls and the
resurrection of the flesh ; and, leaving out
the opening portions of the letter, we have confined ourselves to the refutation of this most
remarkable treatise. For we preferred to speak
of the things of God rather than of our own
wrongs. [6] "If one man sin against another,
they shall pray for him to the Lord. But if
he sin against God, who shall pray for him ?"
In these days, on the contrary, we make it
our first business to pursue with undying

---

[1] John xx.   [2] John xxi. 7.   [3] Ib. 12.
[4] Born at Cyrene about B.C. 213. He maintained that we can
be sure of nothing, neither through the senses, nor through the
understanding.
[5] Acts xii.   [6] One of the Argonauts.   [7] Matt. xiv. 28.

[1] Rom. vi. 4.   [2] 1 Cor. xv. 50.   [3] Ib.
[4] Ib. 54.   [5] Ib. 55.   [6] 1 Sam. ii. 25.

hate those who have injured us—to those who blaspheme God we indulgently hold out the hand. John writes to Bishop Theophilus an apology, of which the introduction runs thus : "You, indeed, as a man of God, adorned with apostolic grace, have upon you the care of all the Churches, especially of that which is at Jerusalem, though you yourself are distracted with countless anxieties for the Church of God, which is under you." This is bare-faced adulation, and an attempt to concentrate[1] authority in the hands of an individual. You, who ask for ecclesiastical rules, and make use of the[2] canons of the Council of Nicæa, and claim authority over clerics who belong to another diocese and are [3] actually living with their own bishop, answer my question, What has Palestine to do with the bishop of Alexandria ? Unless I am deceived, it is decreed in those canons that Cæsarea is the metropolis of Palestine, and Antioch of the whole of the East. You ought therefore either to appeal to the bishop of Cæsarea, with whom you know that we have communion while we disdain to communicate with you, or, if judgment were to be sought at a distance, letters ought rather to be addressed to Antioch. But I know why you were unwilling to send to Cæsarea, or to Antioch. You knew what to flee from, what to avoid. You preferred to assail with your complaints ears that were preoccupied rather than pay due honour to your metropolitan. And I do not say this because I have anything to blame in the mission itself, except certain partialities which beget suspicion, but because you ought rather to clear yourself in the actual presence of your questioners. You begin with the words, "You have sent a most devoted servant of God, the presbyter Isidore, a man of influence no less from the dignity of his very gait and dress than from that of his divine understanding, to heal those whose souls are grievously sick ; would that they had any sense of their illness ! A man of God sends a man of God." No difference is made between a priest and a bishop ; the same dignity belongs to the sender and the sent ; this is lame enough ; the ship, as the saying goes, is wrecked in harbour. That Isidore, whom you extol to the sky by your

praises, lies under the same imputation of heresy[1] at Alexandria as you at Jerusalem ; wherefore he appears to have come to you not as an envoy, but as a confederate. Besides, the letters in his own handwriting, which, three months before the sending of the embassy, had been sent to us[2] through an error in the address, were delivered to the presbyter Vincentius, and to this day they are in his keeping. In these letters the writer encourages the leader of his army [3] to plant his foot firmly upon the rock of the faith, and not to be terrified by our Jeremiads. He promises, before we had any suspicion of his mission, that he will come to Jerusalem, and that on his arrival the ranks of his adversaries will be instantly crushed. And amongst the rest he uses these words : "As smoke vanishes in the air, and wax melts beside the fire, so shall they be scattered who are for ever resisting the faith of the Church, and are now through simple men endeavouring to disturb that faith."

38. I ask you, my reader, what does a man, who writes these things before he comes, appear to you to be ? An adversary, or an envoy ? This is the man whom we may, indeed, call most pious, or most religious, and, to give the exact equivalent of the word, one devoted to the worship of God. This is the man of divine understanding, so influential, and of such dignity in gait and dress, that, like a spiritual Hippocrates, he is able by his presence to relieve the sickness of our souls, provided, however, we are willing to submit to his treatment. If such is his medicine, let him heal himself, since he is accustomed to heal others. To us, that divine understanding of his is folly for the sake of Christ. We willingly remain in the sickness of our simplicity, rather than, by using your eye-salve, learn an impious abuse of sight. Next come the words : "The excellent intentions of your Holiness compel our prayers to the Lord night and day ; and, as though those intentions were already perfectly realised, we offer our prayers to Him in the holy places, that He may give you a perfect reward, and bestow on you the crown of life." You do right in giving thanks ; for, if Isidore had not come you would not now have found in the whole of Palestine such a faithful associate. If he had not brought you the aid he had promised beforehand, you would find yourself surrounded by a crowd of rustics incapable of

---

[1] Laudat faciem, ad personam principum trahit. Literally, He praises the face (*i.e.* the person of Theophilus) and draws him on to act the part of (only fit for) princes.
[2] Canon 6 says that the old customs are to hold good, that all Egypt is to be subject to the authority of the bishop of Alexandria, just as the custom holds at Rome ; and similarly that at Antioch, and in the other churches the authority of the churches should be preserved to them. Canon 7 says : "Since custom and ancient tradition has prevailed to cause honour to be given to the bishop of Aelia (Jerusalem), let him have the proper results of this honour ; saving, however, the proper authority due to the metropolis " (that is, Cæsarea).
[3] This relates to Paulinianus, who was ordained by Epiphanius, and was then living with him in Cyprus.

[1] Theophilus, whose sympathies had suddenly changed. turned violently against Isidore, who had previously been his confidential friend, accused him of Origenism, and; on his taking refuge with Chrysostom at Constantinople, pursued both him and Chrysostom with unrelenting animosity.
[2] Reading *portantes errorem*. Another reading is, "Through the error of the bearer."
[3] John, to whom the letters were really written.

nderstanding your wisdom. This very apology of which we are now speaking was dictated in the presence and, to a great extent, with the assistance of Isidore, so that the same person both composed the letter and carried it to its destination.

39. Your letter goes on to relate that "though he had come hither and had had three separate interviews with us, and had applied to the matter the healing language no less of our divine wisdom than of his own understanding, he found that he could be of no use to any one, nor could any one be of use to him." The fact is that he who is said to have had "three separate interviews with us," so that in his coming he might maintain the mystic number, and who talked to us about the command issued by Bishop Theophilus, did not choose to deliver the letters sent to us by him. And when we said : If you are an envoy, produce your credentials; if you have no letters, how can you prove to us that you are an envoy ? he replied that he had, indeed, letters to us, but he had been adjured by the bishop of Jerusalem not to give them to us. You see here the true envoy consistent with his proper character ; you see how impartial he shows himself to both sides, that he may make peace, and exclude the suspicion of favouring either party. At all events, he had come without plaster, and had not the physician's instruments at his command, and therefore his medicine was of no avail. "Jerome and those associated with him," you continue, "both secretly, and in the presence of all, again and again and with the attestation of an oath, satisfied him that they never had any doubts of our orthodoxy, saying : We have now just the same feeling toward him, as regards matters of faith, that we had when we used to communicate with him." See what dogmatic agreement can do. Isidore, in order that he might make such a report as this, is taken into close fellowship, and is spoken of as a man of God, and a most devout priest, a man of influence, of holy and venerable gait, and of divine understanding, the Hippocrates of the Christians. a poor wretch, hiding away in solitude, suddenly cut off by this mighty pontiff, have lost the name of priest. This "Jerome," then, with his ragged herd and shabby following, did he dare to give any answer to Isidore and his thunderbolts ? Of course not ; and doubtless for no other motive than fear that the envoy would never yield, and might overwhelm them by his presence and [1] gigantic stature. "Not once, nor thrice, but again and again [2] they

swore that they knew the individual in question to be orthodox, and that they had never suspected him of heresy." What undisguised and shameless lying ! A witness borne by a man to himself ! Such witness as is not believed even in the mouth of a Cato, for [1] in the mouth of two or three witnesses shall every word be established. Was there ever a word said, or a message sent to you, to the effect that, without being satisfied as to your orthodoxy, we would endure communion with you ? When, through the instrumentality of the Count Archelaus, a most accomplished as well as a most Christian man, who tried to negotiate a peace between us, a place had been appointed where we were to meet, was not one of the first things postulated that the faith should form the basis of future agreement ? He promised to come. Easter was approaching ; a great multitude of monks had assembled ; you were expected at the appointed place ; what to do you did not know. All at once you sent word that some one or other was sick, you could not come that day. Is it a stage-player or a bishop who thus speaks ? Suppose what you said was true, to suit the pleasure of one feeble woman who fears that she may have a headache, or may feel sick, or have a pain in the stomach, while you are away, do you neglect the interests of the Church ? Do you despise so many men, Christians and monks assembled together ? We were unwilling to give occasion for breaking off the negotiation ; we saw through the artifice of your procrastination, and sought to overcome the wrong you did us by patience. Archelaus wrote again, advising him that he was staying on for two days, in case he should be willing to come. But he was busy ; his dear little woman had not ceased to vomit, he could not bestow a thought upon us until she should have escaped from her nausea. Well, after two months, at last the long-looked for Isidore arrived, and what he heard from us was not, as you pretend, a testimony in your behalf, but the reason why we demanded satisfaction. For when he raised the point, "Why, if he were a heretic, did you communicate with him ? " he was answered by us all that we communicated without any suspicion of his heresy ; but that, after he had been summoned by the Most Reverend Epiphanius, both by word and by letter, and had disdained to answer, documents were addressed to the monks by Epiphanius himself, to the effect that, unless he gave satisfaction respecting the faith, no one should rashly communicate with him. The letters are in our hands ; there can be no doubt about the matter. This, then,

---

[1] Isidore was closely associated with the three brothers known as the Long Monks from their great size, and seems to have shared the appellation with them.
[2] i.e. Jerome and his friends. This was Isidore's report, incorporated probably into John's letter.

[1] Numb. xxxv. 30 ; Deut. xvii. 6 ; 2 Cor. xiii. 1.

was the reply made by the whole body of the brethren : not, as you maintain, that you were not an heretic, because at a former time you were not said to be one. For upon that showing, a man must be said not to be sick, because previous to his sickness he was in good health.

40. To proceed with the letter. "But when the ordination of Paulinianus, and the others associated with him, was brought forward, they began to feel that they themselves were in the wrong. For the sake of charity and concord every concession was made to them, and the only point insisted on was that, though they had been ordained contrary to the rules, yet they should be subject to the authority of the Church of God, that they should not rend it, and set up an authority of their own. But they, not agreeing to this, began to raise questions concerning the faith ; and thus they made it evident to all that if the presbyter Jerome and his friends were not accused, they had no charge to bring against us, but that they only betook themselves to doctrinal questions because, when charges of error and misconduct were brought against them, they were utterly unable to reply to us on matters of that sort, or to give any satisfactory explanation of their wrong-doing : not that they had any hope that we could be convicted of heresy, but they were striving to injure our reputation."

41. No one must blame the translator for this verbiage : the Greek is the same. Meanwhile I rejoice that whereas I thought I was beheaded I find my presbyterial head on my shoulders again. He says that we are utterly incapable of conviction, and he draws back from the encounter. If the cause of discord is not due to discussions about the faith, but springs from the ordination of Paulinianus, is it not the extreme of folly to give occasion to those who seek occasion by refusing to answer ? Confess the faith ; but do it so as to answer the question put to you, that it may be clear to all that the dispute is not one of faith, but of order. For so long as you are silent when questioned concerning the faith, your adversary has a right to say to you : "The matter is not one of order but of faith." If it is a question of order, you act foolishly in saying nothing when questioned concerning the faith. If it is one of faith, it is foolish of you to make a pretext of the question of order. Moreover, when you say your aim was that they might be subject to the Church, that they might not rend it, nor set up an authority of their own ; who they are of whom you speak I do not well understand. If you are speaking of me and the presbyter Vincentius, you have been asleep long enough,

if you only wake up now, after thirteen years[1] to say these things. For the reason why forsook Antioch and he Constantinople,[2] bot famous cities, was, not that we might prais your popular eloquence, but that, in th country and in solitude, we might weep ove the sins of our youth, and draw down upo us the mercy of Christ. But if Paulinianus the subject of your remarks, he, as you see is subject to his[3] bishop, and lives at Cyprus he sometimes comes to visit us, not as one o your clergy, but as another's, his, namely, b whom he was ordained. But if he wished eve to stay here, and to live a quiet, solitary lif sharing our exile, what does he owe you excep the respect which we owe to all bishops ? Sup pose that he had been ordained by you ; h would only tell you the same that I, a poo wretch of a man, told Bishop Paulinus o blessed memory. "Did I ask to be ordained b you ?" I said. "If in bestowing the rank o presbyter you do not strip us of the monasti state, you can bestow or withhold ordinatio as you think best. But if your intention i giving the name presbyter was to take fror me that for which I forsook the world, I must still claim to be what I always was ; yo have suffered no loss by ordaining me."[4]

42. "That they might not rend the Church, he says, "and set up an authority of their own. Who rends the Church ? Do we, who as complete household at Bethlehem communi cate in the Church ? Or is it you, wh either being orthodox refuse through prid to speak concerning the faith, or else bein heterodox are the real render of the Church Do we rend the Church, who, a few month ago, about the day of Pentecost, when th sun was darkened and all the world dreade the immediate coming of the Judge, presente forty candidates of different ages and sexe to your presbyter for baptism ? There wer certainly five presbyters in the monastery wh had the right to baptize ; but they wer unwilling to do anything to move you t anger, for fear you might make this a pretex for reticence concerning the faith. Is it no you, on the contrary, who rend the Church you who commanded your presbyters at Beth lehem not to give baptism to our candidate at Easter, so that we sent them to [5] Diospoli to the Confessor and Bishop Dionysius fo baptism ? Are we said to rend the Churcl who, outside our cells, hold no position in th Church ? Or do not you rather rend th Church, who issue an order to your clerg

<hr />

[1] Dating probably from Jerome's coming to Palestine. Se Prefatory Note.
[2] Jerome was ordained at Antioch, Vincentius at Constantinopl
[3] That is, Jerome argues, Epiphanius, who ordained him.
[4] This perhaps means, "No virtue has gone out of you—yo have conferred nothing upon me."
[5] Lydda.

hat if any one says Paulinianus was conse-rated presbyter by Epiphanius, he is to be orbidden to enter the Church. Ever since hat time to this day we can only look from without on the cave of the Saviour, and, while heretics enter, we stand afar off and sigh.

43. Are we schismatics? Is not he the chismatic who refuses a habitation to the living, a grave to the dead, and demands he exile of his brethren? Who was it that et at our throats, with special fury, that wild beast who constantly menaced the throats of he whole world?[1] Who is it that permits he rain to beat upon the bones of the saints, and their harmless ashes, up to the present hour? These are the endearments with which he good shepherd invites us to reconciliation, and at the same time accuses us of setting up n authority of our own—us who are united in ommunion and charity with all the bishops, so long, at least, as they are orthodox. Do you yourself constitute the Church, and is whosoever offends you shut out from Christ? f we defend our own authority—prove that we have a bishop in your diocese. The eason that we have not had communion with you is the question of faith; answer our ques-ions, and it will become one of order.

44. "They," you go on, "also take advantage of other letters which they say Epiphanius wrote o them. But he, too, shall give account for all his doings before the judgment seat of Christ, where great and small shall be judged without espect of persons. Still, how can they rely on his letter which he wrote only because we ook him to task on the matter of the unlaw-ul ordination of Paulinianus and his associ-tes; as in the opening of that very letter he ntimates?" What, I ask, is the meaning of his blindness? how is it that he is immersed, as the saying goes, in Cimmerian darkness? He says that we make a pretext, and that we have no letters from Epiphanius against him,

and he immediately adds, "How can they rely on his letter, which he only wrote because he was taken to task by us, in the matter of the unlawful ordination of Paulinianus and his associates; as in the opening of that very letter he intimates?" We have no such let-ter! And what letter then is that, which in its opening sentence speaks of Paulinianus? There is something in the body of the letter of which you are afraid to make mention. Well! He was taken to task, you say, by you because of the age of Paulinianus. But you yourself ordain a man presbyter, and send him out as an envoy and a colleague. You have the boldness falsely to call Paulinianus a boy, and then to send out your own boy presbyter. You likewise take Theoseca, a deacon of the church of Thiria, and make him presbyter, and put weapons into his hands against us, and make a misuse of his eloquence for our injury. You alone are at liberty to trample on the rights of the Church; whatever you do, is the standard of teaching; and you do not blush to challenge Epiphanius to stand with you before the judgment seat of Christ. The sequel of this passage is to the following effect: [1] he throws it in the teeth of Epiphanius that he was the partner of his table and an inmate of his house, and declares that they never had any talk together concerning the views of Origen, and he supports what he says with the attestation of an oath, saying: "He never showed, as God is witness, that he had even the suspicion that our faith was not correct?" I am unwilling to answer and argue acrimoni-ously, lest I seem to be convicting a bishop of perjury. There are several letters of Epi-phanius in our possession. One to John him-self, others to the bishops of Palestine, and one of recent date to the pontiff of Rome; and in these he speaks of himself as impugning his views in the presence of many, and says that he was not thought worthy of a reply, "and the whole Monastery," he says, "is witness to what we in our insignificance assert."

---

[1] The allusion is believed to be to the Prefect Rufinus, who was the head of the government under the young Arcadius, and those intrigues with Alaric with a view to obtain the empire for himself led to his death in the end of 395.—Comp. Letter XXXII. 10.

[1] See Letter LI., which begins as John says, though Jerome denies it.

AGAINST THE PELAGIANS

DIALOGUE BETWEEN ATTICUS, A CATHOLIC, AND CRITOBULUS, A HERETIC.

The anti-Pelagian Dialogue is the last of Jerome's controversial works, having been written in the year 417, within three years of his death. It shows no lack of his old vigour, though perhaps something of the prolixity in-uced by old age. He looks at the subject more calmly than those of the previous treatises, mainly because it lay somewhat outside the track of his own thoughts. He was induced to interest himself in it by his increasing regard for Augustin, and by the coming of the young Spaniard, Orosius, in 414, from Augustin to sit at his feet. Pelagius also had come to Palestine, and, after an investigation of his tenets, at a small council at Jerusalem, in

415, presided over by Bishop John, and a second, at Diospolis in 416, had been admitted to communion. Jerome appears to have taken no part in these proceedings, and having been at peace with Bishop John for nearly twenty years, was no doubt unwilling to act against him. But he had come to look upon Pelagius as infected with the heretical " impiety," which he looked upon (i. 28) as far worse than moral evil ; and connected him, as we see from his letter to Ctesiphon (CXXXIII.), with Origenism and Rufinus ; and he brings his great knowledge of Scripture to bear upon the controversy. He quotes a work of Pelagius, though giving only the headings, and the number of the chapters, up to 100 (i. 26–32) ; and, though at times his conviction appears weak, and there are passages (i. 5, ii. 6–30, iii. 1) which give occasion to the observation that he really, if unconsciously, inclined to the views of Pelagius, and that he is a " Synergist," not, like Augustin, a thorough predestinarian, the Dialogue, as a whole, is clear and forms a substantial contribution to our knowledge. Although its tone is less violent than that of his ascetic treatises, it appears to have stirred up the strongest animosity against him. The adherents of Pelagius attacked and burned the monasteries of Bethlehem, and Jerome himself only escaped by taking refuge in a tower. His sufferings, and the interference of Pope Innocentius in his behalf, may be seen by referring to Letters CXXXV.–CXXXVII., with the introductory notes prefixed to them.

The following is a summary of the argument : Atticus, the Augustinian, at once (c. 1) introduces the question, Do you affirm that, as Pelagius affirms, men can live without sin ? Yes, says the Pelagian Critobulus, but I do not add, as is imputed to us, " without the grace of God." Indeed, the fact that we have a free will is from grace. Yes, replies Atticus, but what is this grace ? Is it only our original nature, or is it needed in every act. In every act, is the reply (2) ; yet one would hardly say that we cannot mend a pen without grace (3), for, if so, where is our free will ? But, says Atticus (5), the Scriptures speak of our need of God's aid in everything. In that case, says Critobulus, the promised reward must be given not to us but to God, Who works in us. Reverting then to the first point stated, Atticus asks, does the possibility of sinlessness extend to single acts, or to the whole life ? Certainly to the whole as well as the part, is the answer. But we wish, or will to be sinless ; why then are we not actually sinless ? Because (8) we do not exert our will to the full. But (9) no one has ever lived without sin. Still, says the Pelagian, God commands us to be perfect, and he does not command impossibilities. Job, Zacharias, and Elizabeth are represented as perfectly righteous. No, it is answered (12), faults are attributed to each of them. John says, " He that is born of God sinneth not" (13) ; yet, " If we say we have no sin we deceive ourselves." The Apostles, though told to be perfect (14) were not perfect : and St. Paul says (14a), " I count not myself to have apprehended." Men are called just and perfect only in comparison of others (16), or because of general subjection to the will of God (18), or according to their special characteristics (19), as we may speak of a bishop as excellent in his office, though he may not fulfil the ideal of the pastoral epistles (22).

The discussion now turns to the words of Pelagius' book. " All are ruled by their own will " (27). No ; for Christ says, " I came not to do My own will." " The wicked shall not be spared in the judgment." But we must distinguish between the impious or heretics who will be destroyed (28) and Christian sinners who will be forgiven. Some of his sayings contradict each other or are trifling (29, 30). " The kingdom of heaven is promised in the Old Testament." Yes, but more fully in the New. Returning to the first thesis, " That a man can be without sin if he wills it," the Pelagian says, If things, like desires which arise spontaneously and have no issue, are reckoned blamable, we charge the sin on our Maker ; to which it is only answered that, though we cannot understand God's ways, we must not arraign His justice. In the rest of the book, Atticus alone speaks, going through the Old Testament, and showing that each of the saints falls into some sin, which, though done in ignorance or half-consciousness, yet brings condemnation with it.

Prologue.

---

1. After writing the [1] letter to Ctesiphon, in which I replied to the questions propounded, I received frequent expostulations from the brethren, who wanted to know why I any longer delayed the promised work in which I undertook to answer all the subtleties of the preachers of Impassibility. [2] For every one knows what was the contention of the Stoics and Peripatetics, that is, the old Academy, some of them asserted that the πάθη, which we may call emotions, such as sorrow, joy, hope, fear, can be thoroughly eradicated from the minds of men ; others that their power can be broken, that they can be governed and restrained, as unmanageable horses are held in check by peculiar kinds of bits. Their views have been explained by Tully in the " Tusculan Disputations," and Origen in his " Stromata " endeavours to blend them with ecclesiastical truth. I pass over

Manichæus,[1] Priscillianus,[2] Evagrius of Ibora, Jovinianus, and the heretics found throughout almost the whole of Syria, who, by perversion of the import of their name, are commonly called [3] Massalians, in Greek Euchites, all of whom hold that it is possible for human virtue and human knowledge to attain perfection, and arrive, I will not say merely at a likeness to, but an equality

---

[1] Priscillian was a Spaniard, who began to propagate his views, which were a mixture of various heresies, about the year 370. See Robertson, p. 295 sq., and Note on Jerome, Letter CXXXIII.

[2] Evagrius Iberita. The name is taken either from a town named Ibera or Ibora in Pontus, or from the province of Iberia. Jerome, in the letter to which he refers, styles Evagrius Hyperborita, but this is thought to be an error for Hyborita. It has been suggested that Jerome was playing on the word Iberita. He was born in 345. He wrote, amongst many other works, a treatise Περὶ ἀπαθείας (On Impassibility), and no doubt Jerome refers to this a few lines above. He was a zealous champion of Origen. See also Jerome, Letter CXXXIII. and note.

[3] The Massalians or Euchites derived their name from the habit of continual prayer. The words are etymologically equivalents (Massalians, from ‏מצלא‎ to pray). The perversity lay in the misinterpretation of such texts as Luke xviii. 1, and 1 Thess. v. 1

with God ; and who go the length of asserting that, when once they have reached the height of perfection, even sins of thought and ignorance are impossible for them. And although in my former letter addressed to Ctesiphon and aimed at their errors, so far as time permitted, I touched upon a few points in the book which I am now endeavouring to hammer out, I shall adhere to the method of Socrates. What can be said on both sides shall be stated ; and the truth will thus be clear when both sides express their opinions. Origen is peculiar in maintaining on the one hand that it is impossible for human nature to pass through life without sin, and on the other, that it is possible for a man, when he turns to better things, to become so strong that he sins no more.

2. I shall add a few words in answer to those who say that I am writing this work because I am inflamed with envy. I have never spared heretics, and I have done my best to make the enemies of the Church my own. Helvidius wrote against the perpetual virginity of Saint Mary. Was it envy that led me to answer him, whom I had never seen in the flesh ? [2] Jovinianus, whose heresy is now being fanned into flame, and who disturbed the faith of Rome in my absence, was so devoid of gifts of utterance, and had such a pestilent style that he was a fitter object for pity than for envy. So far as I could, I answered him also. [3] Rufinus did all in his power to circulate the blasphemies of Origen and the treatise " On First Principles " (Περὶ Ἀρχῶν), not in one city, but throughout the whole world. He even published the first book of [4]Eusebius' " Apology for Origen " under the name of [5]Pamphilus the martyr, and, as though Origen had not said enough,[6] vomited forth a fresh volume on his behalf. Am I to be accused of envy because I answered him ? and was his eloquence such a rushing torrent as to deter me through fear from writing or dictating anything in reply ? [7] Palladius, no better than a villainous slave, tried to impart energy to the same heresy, and to excite against me fresh prejudice on account of my translation of the Hebrew. Was I [1]envious of such distinguished ability and nobility ? Even now the [2]mystery of iniquity worketh, and every one chatters about his views : yet I, it seems, am the only one who is filled with envy at the glory of all the rest ; I am so poor a creature that I envy even those who do not deserve envy. And so, to prove to all that I do not hate the men but their errors, and that I do not wish to vilify any one, but rather lament the misfortune of men who are deceived by knowledge falsely so-called, I have made use of the names of Atticus and Critobulus in order to express our own views and those of our opponents. The truth is that all we who hold the Catholic faith, wish and long that, while the heresy is condemned, the men may be reformed. At all events, if they will continue in error, the blame does not attach to us who have written, but to them, since they have preferred a lie to the truth. And one short answer to our calumniators, whose curses fall upon their own heads, is this, that the Manichæan doctrine condemns the nature of man, destroys free will, and does away with the help of God. And again, that it is manifest madness for man to speak of himself as being what God alone is. Let us so walk along the royal road that we turn neither to the right hand nor to the left ; and let us always believe that the eagerness of our wills is governed by the help of God. Should any one cry out that he is slandered and boast that he thinks with us ; he will then show that he assents to the true faith, when he openly and sincerely condemns the opposite views. Otherwise his case will be that described by the prophet : [3] " And yet for all this her treacherous sister Judah hath not returned unto me with her whole heart, but feignedly." It is a smaller sin to follow evil which you think is good, than not to venture to defend what you know for certain is good. If we cannot endure threats, injustice, poverty, how shall we overcome the flames of Babylon ? Let us not lose by hollow peace what we have preserved by war. I should be sorry to allow my fears to teach me faithlessness, when Christ has put the true faith in the power of my choice.

---

[1] He was a Roman lawyer. His treatise was written about A.D. 23. See Jerome's treatise against him in this volume.

[2] See introduction to Jerome's treatise against Jovinianus in his volume.

[3] See Rufinus' works, especially the " Prolegomena," and Jerome's controversy with him in vol. iii. of this series.

[4] That is, Eusebius of Cæsarea (A.D. 267–338), who was called Pamphilus from his friendship with Pamphilus the martyr.

[5] Suffered martyrdom A.D. 309. He erected a library at Cæsarea of 30.000 volumes. See Rufinus' Preface to his Apology in this series, vol. iii., with introductory note.

[6] See Rufinus on the adulteration of the works of Origen, in this series, vol. iii. p. 421.

[7] Palladius, bishop of Hellenopolis, the biographer and trusted friend of Chrysostom, was born about 367. He visited Bethlehem about 387 and formed a very unfavourable opinion of Jerome. He highly commended Rufinus. According to Epiphanius, as well as Jerome, he was tainted with Origenism. Tillemont, however, thinks that another Palladius may be referred to in these passages. His accounts of Jerome and Rufinus are given in his " Historia Lausiaca," c. 78 and 118.

[1] Jerome was accused of envy or ill-will by Palladius. " Tanta fuit ejus invidia ut ab ea obrueretur virtus doctrinæ. Cum ergo multis diebus cum eo versatus esset sanctus Posidonius. dicit mihi in aurem. " Ingenua quidem Paula, quæ ejus curam gerit, præmorietur, liberata ab ejus invidia. Ut autem arbitror, propter hunc virum non habitabit vir sanctus in his locis, sed ejus pervadet invidia usque ad proprium fratrem."—Pallad. Hist. Laus., § 78, cf. § 82.

[2] 2 Thess. ii. 7.

[3] Jer. iii. 10.

Book I.

1. Atticus. I hear, Critobulus, that you have written that man can be without sin, if he chooses ; and that the commandments of God are easy. Tell me, is it true ?

Critobulus. It is true, Atticus ; but our rivals do not take the words in the sense I attached to them.

A. Are they then so ambiguous as to give rise to a difference as to their meaning ? I do not ask for an answer to two questions at once. You laid down two propositions ; the one, that [1] man can be without sin, if he chooses : the other, that God's commandments are easy. Although, therefore, they were uttered together, let them be discussed separately, so that, while our faith appears to be one, no strife may arise through our misunderstanding each other.

C. I said, Atticus, that man can be without sin, if he chooses ; not, as some maliciously make us say, without the grace of God (the very thought is impiety), but simply that he can, if he chooses ; the aid of the grace of God being presupposed.

A. Is God, then, the author of your evil works ?

C. By no means. But if there is any good in me, it is brought to perfection through His impulse and assistance.

A. My question does not refer to natural constitution, but to action. For who doubts that God is the Creator of all things ? I wish you would tell me this : the good you do, is it your's or God's ?

C. It is mine and God's : I work and He assists.

A. How is it then that everybody thinks you do away with the grace of God, and maintain that all our actions proceed from our own will ?

C. I am surprised, Atticus, at your asking me for the why and wherefore of other people's mistakes, and wanting to know what I did not write, when what I did write is perfectly clear. I said that man can be without sin, if he chooses. Did I add, *without the grace of God?*

A. No ; but the fact that you added nothing implies your denial of the need of grace.

C. Nay, rather, the fact that I have not denied grace should be regarded as tantamount to an assertion of it. It is unjust to suppose we deny whatever we do not assert.

A. You admit then that man can be sinless, if he chooses, but with the grace of God.

C. I not only admit it, but freely proclaim it

A. So then he who does away with the grace of God is in error.

C. Just so. Or rather, he ought to be thought impious, seeing that all things are governed by the pleasure of God, and that we owe our existence and the faculty of individual choice and desire to the goodness of God, the Creator. For that we have free will, and according to our own choice incline to good or evil, is part of His grace who made us what we are, in His own image and likeness.

2. A. No one doubts, Critobulus, that all things depend on the judgment of Him Who is Creator of all, and that whatever we have ought to be attributed to His goodness. But I should like to know respecting this faculty which you attribute to the grace of God, whether you reckon it as part of the gift bestowed in our creation, or suppose it energetic in our separate actions, so that we avail ourselves of its assistance continually ; or is the case that, having been once for all created and endowed with free will, we do what we choose by our own choice or strength ? For I know that very many of your party refer all things to the grace of God in such a sense that they understand the power of the will to be a gift not of a particular, but of a general character, that is to say, one which is bestowed not at each separate moment, but once for all at creation.

C. It is not as you affirm ; but I maintain both positions, that it is by the grace of God we were created such as we are, and also that in our several actions we are supported by His aid.

A. We are agreed, then, that in good work besides our own power of choice, we lean on the help of God ; in evil works we are prompted by the devil.

C. Quite so ; there is no difference of opinion on that point.

A. They are wrong, then, who strip us of the help of God in our separate actions. The Psalmist sings : [1] "Except the Lord build the house, they labour in vain who build it. Except the Lord keep the city, the watchman waketh but in vain ; " and there are similar passages. But these men endeavour by perverse, or rather ridiculous interpretations, to twist his words to a different meaning.

3. C. Am I bound to contradict others when you have my own answer ?

---

[1] See S. Aug. De Sp. et Lit., c. i.

[1] Ps. cxxvii. 1.

A. Your answer to what effect ? That they are right, or wrong ?

C. What necessity compels me to set my opinion against other men's ?

A. You are bound by the rules of discussion, and by respect for truth. Do you not know that every assertion either affirms, or denies, and that what is affirmed or denied ought to be reckoned among good or bad things ? You must, therefore, admit, and no thanks to you, that the statement to which my question relates is either a good thing or a bad.

C. If in particular actions we must have the help of God, does it follow that we are unable to make a pen, [1] or mend it when it is made ? Can we not fashion the letters, be silent or speak, sit, stand, walk or run, eat or fast, weep or laugh, and so on, without God's assistance ?

A. From my point of view it is clearly impossible.

C. How then have we free will, and how can we guard the grace of God towards us, if we cannot do even these things without God ?

4. A. The bestowal of the grace of free will is not such as to do away with the support of God in particular actions.

C. The help of God is not made of no account ; inasmuch as creatures are preserved through the grace of free will once for all given to them. For if without God, and except He assist me in every action, I can do nothing. He can neither with justice crown me for my good deeds, nor punish me for my evil ones, but in each case He will either receive His own or will condemn the assistance He gave.

A. Tell me, then, plainly, why you do away with the grace of God. For whatever you destroy in the parts you must of necessity deny in the whole.

C. I do not deny grace when I assert that I was so created by God, that by the grace of God it was put within the power of my choice either to do a thing or not to do it.

A. So God falls asleep over our good actions, when once the faculty of free will has been given ; and we need not pray to Him to assist us in our separate actions, since it depends upon our own choice and will either to do a thing if we choose, or not to do it if we do not choose.

5. C. As in the case of other creatures, the conditions of their creation are observed ; so, when once the power of free will was granted, everything was left to our own choice.

A. It follows, as I said, that I ought not to beg the assistance of God in the details of conduct, because I consider it was given once for all.

C. If He co-operates with me in everything the result is no longer mine, but His Who assists, or rather works in and with me ; and all the more because I can do nothing without Him.

A. Have you not read, pray, [1] "that it is not of him that willeth, nor of him that runneth, but of God that showeth mercy !" From this we understand that to will and to run is ours, but the carrying into effect our willing and running pertains to the mercy of God, and is so effected that on the one hand in willing and running free will is preserved ; and on the other, in consummating our willing and running, everything is left to the power of God. Of course, I ought now to adduce the frequent testimony of Scripture to show that in the details of conduct the saints intreat the help of God, and in their several actions desire to have Him for their helper and protector. Read through the Psalter, and all the utterances of the saints, and you will find their actions never unaccompanied by prayer to God. And this is a clear proof that you either deny the grace which you banish from the parts of life ; or if you concede its presence in the parts, a concession plainly much against your will, you must have come over to the views of us who preserve free will for man, but so limit it that we do not deny the assistance of God in each action.

6. C. That is a sophistical conclusion and a mere display of logical skill. No one can strip me of the power of free will ; otherwise, if God were really my helper in what I do, the reward would not be due to me, but to Him who wrought in me.

A. Make the most of your free will; arm your tongue against God, and therein prove yourself free, if you will, to blaspheme. But to go a step farther, there is no doubt as to your sentiments, and the delusions of your profession have become as clear as day. Now, let us turn back to the starting-point of our discussion. You said just now that, granted God's assistance, man may be sinless if he chooses. Tell me, please, for how long ? For ever, or only for a short time ?

C. Your question is unnecessary. If I say for a short time, for ever will none the less be implied. For whatever you allow for a short time, you will admit may last for ever.

A. I do not quite understand your meaning.

C. Are you so senseless that you do not recognize plain facts ?

7. A. I am not ashamed of my ignorance.

And both sides ought to be well agreed on a definition of the subject of dispute.

C. I maintain this: he who can keep himself from sin one day, may do so another day: if he can on two, he may on three; if on three, on thirty: and so on for three hundred, or three thousand, or as long as ever he chooses to do so.

A. Say then at once that a man may be without sin for ever, if he chooses. Can we do anything we like?

C. Certainly not, for I cannot do all I should like; but all I say is this, that a man can be without sin, if he chooses.

A. Be so good as to tell me this: do you think I am a man or a beast?

C. If I had any doubt as to whether you were a man, or a beast, I should confess myself to be the latter.

A. If then, as you say, I am a man, how is it that when I wish and earnestly desire not to sin, I do transgress?

C. Because your choice is imperfect. If you really wished not to sin, you really would not.

A. Well then, you who accuse me of not having a real desire, are you free from sin because you have a real desire?

C. As though I were talking of myself whom I admit to be a sinner, and not of the few exceptional ones, if any, who have resolved not to sin.

8. A. Still, I who question, and you who answer, both consider ourselves sinners.

C. But we are capable of not being so, if we please.

A. I said I did not wish to sin, and no doubt your feeling is the same. How is it then that what we both wish we can neither do?

C. Because we do not wish perfectly.

A. Show me any of our ancestors who had a perfect will and the power in perfection.

C. That is not easy. And when I say that a man may be without sin if he chooses, I do not contend that there ever have been such; I only maintain the abstract possibility—if he chooses. For *possibility of being* is one thing, and is expressed in Greek by τῇ δυνάμει (possibility); *being* is another, the equivalent for which is τῇ ἐνεργείᾳ (actuality). I can be a physician; but meanwhile I am not. I can be an artisan; but I have not yet learnt a trade. So, whatever I am able to be, though I am not that yet, I shall be if I choose.

9. A. Art is one thing, that which is [1] above art is another. Medical skill, craftsmanship, and so on, are found in many persons; but to be always without sin is a characteristic of the Divine power only. Therefore, either give me an instance of those who were for ever without sin; or, if you cannot find one, confess your impotence, lay aside bombast, and do not mock the ears of fools with the *being* and *possibility of being* of yours. For who will grant that a man can do what no man was ever able to do? You have not learnt even the rudiments of logic. For if a man is able, he is no longer unable. Either grant that some one was able to do what you maintain was possible to be done; or if no one has had the power, you must, though against your will, be held to this position, that no one is able to effect what yet you profess to be possible. That was the point at issue between the powerful logicians, [1] Diodorus and [2] Chrysippus, in their discussion of possibility. Diodorus says that alone can possibly happen which is either true or will be true. And whatever will be, that, he says, must of necessity happen. But whatever will not be, that cannot possibly happen. Chrysippus, however, says that things which will not be might happen; for instance, this pearl might be broken, even though it never will. They therefore, who say that a man can be without sin if he chooses, will not be able to prove the truth of the assertion, unless they show that it will come to pass. But whereas the whole future is uncertain, and especially such things as have never occurred, it is clear that they say something will be which will not be. And Ecclesiastes supports this decision " All that shall be, has already been in former ages."

10. C. Pray answer this question: has God given possible or impossible commands?

A. I see your drift. But I must discuss it later on, that we may not, by confusing different questions, leave our audience in a fog. I admit that God has given possible commands, for otherwise He would Himself be the author of injustice, were He to demand the doing of what cannot possibly be done. Reserving this until later, finish your argument that a man can be without sin, if he chooses. You will either give instances of such ability, or, if no one has had the power, you will clearly confess that a man cannot avoid sin always.

C. Since you press me to give what I am not bound to give, consider what our Lord says, [3] " That it is easier for a camel to go

---

[1] That is, Diodorus, surnamed Cronus, who lived at Alexandria in the reign of Ptolemy Soter (B.C. 323–285). He was the teacher of Philo. For his discussions *On the Possible*, Zeller " Socrates and the Socratic Schools," Reichel's translation, pp. 272, 273, and authorities there cited, may be consulted.
[2] Died B.C. 207, aged 73. He was the first to base the Stoic doctrine on something like systematic reasoning.
[3] S. Matt. xix. 24.

rough a needle's eye, than for a rich man enter into the kingdom of heaven." And et he said a thing might possibly happen, hich never has happened. For no camel as ever gone through a needle's eye.

A. I am surprised at a prudent man submitting evidence which goes against himself. 'or the passage in question does not speak f a possibility, but one impossibility is compared with another. As a camel cannot go rough a needle's eye, so neither will a rich man enter the kingdom of heaven. Or, if you hould be able to show that a rich man does nter the kingdom of heaven, it follows, also, hat a camel goes through a needle's eye. 'ou must not instance Abraham and other ich men, about whom we read in the Old 'estament, who, although they were rich, ntered the kingdom of heaven ; for, by spending their riches on good works, they ceased to e rich ; nay, rather, inasmuch as they were ich, not for themselves, but for others, they ught to be called God's stewards rather than ich men. But we must seek evangelical perfection, according to which there is the command,[1] " If thou wilt be perfect, go and sell ll that thou hast, and give to the poor, and ome, follow Me."

11. C. You are caught unawares in your wn snare.

A. How so ?

C. You quote our Lord's utterance to the ffect that a man can be perfect. For when Ie says, " If thou wilt be perfect, sell all that hou hast, and give to the poor, and come, ollow Me," He shows that a man, if he hooses, and if he does what is commanded, an be perfect ?

A. You have given me such a terrible blow hat I am almost dazed. But yet the very vords you quote, " If thou wilt be perfect," vere spoken to one who could not, or rather vould not, and, therefore, could not ; show ne now, as you promised, some one who vould and could.

C. Why am I compelled to produce instances of perfection, when it is clear from vhat the Saviour said to one, and through ne to all, " If thou wilt be perfect," that it is possible for men to be perfect ?

A. That is a mere shuffle. You still stick ast in the mire. For, either, if a thing is possible, it has occurred at some time or ther ; or, if it never has happened, grant hat it is impossible.

12. C. Why do I any longer delay ? You nust be vanquished by the authority of Scripure. To pass over other passages, you nust be silenced by the two in which we read

the praises of Job, and of Zacharias and Elizabeth. For, unless I am deceived, it is thus written in the book of Job :[1] " There was a man in the land of Uz, whose name was Job ; and that man was perfect and upright, a true worshipper of God, and one who kept himself from every evil thing." And again : [2] " Who is he that reproveth one that is righteous and free from sin, and speaketh words without knowledge ? " Also, in the Gospel according to Luke, we read : [3] " There was in the days of Herod, king of Judæa, a certain priest named Zacharias, of the course of Abijah : and he had a wife of the daughters of Aaron, and her name was Elizabeth. And they were both righteous before God, walking in all the commandments and ordinances of the Lord blameless." If a true worshipper of God is also without spot and without offence, and if those who walked in all the ordinances of the Lord are righteous before God, I suppose they are free from sin, and lack nothing that pertains to righteousness.

A. You have cited passages which have been detached not only from the rest of Scripture, but from the books in which they occur. For even Job, after he was stricken with the plague, is convicted of having spoken many things against the ruling of God, and to have summoned Him to the bar : [4] " Would that a man stood with God in the judgment as a son of man stands with his fellow." And again : [5] " Oh that I had one to hear me ! that the Almighty might hear my desire, and that the judge would himself write a book ! " And again : [6] " Though I be righteous, mine own mouth shall condemn me : though I be perfect, it shall prove me perverse. If I wash myself with snow-water, and make my hands never so clean, Thou hast dyed me again and again with filth. Mine own clothes have abhorred me." And of Zacharias it is written, that when the angel promised the birth of a son, he said : [7] " Whereby shall I know this ? for I am an old man, and my wife well stricken in years." For which answer he was at once condemned to silence : [8] " Thou shalt be silent, and not able to speak, until the day that these things shall come to pass, because thou believest not my words, which shall be fulfilled in their season." From this it is clear that men are called righteous, and said to be without fault ; but that, if negligence comes over

---

[1] Job i. 1.
[2] This appears to be an inaccurate quotation made from memory.
[3] S. Luke i. 5 sqq.
[4] Job xvi. 21. Vulg. R. V. Margin—" That one might plead for a man with God as a son of man pleadeth for his neighbour."
[5] Job xxxi. 35.   [6] Job ix. 20, 30, 31.
[7] S. Luke i. 18.   [8] Ib. 20.

them, they may fall; and that a man always occupies a middle place, so that he may slip from the height of virtue into vice, or may rise from vice to virtue; and that he is never safe, but must dread shipwreck even in fair weather; and, therefore, that a man cannot be without sin. Solomon says, [1] " There is not a righteous man upon earth that doeth good and sinneth not "; and likewise in the book of Kings: [2] " There is no man that sinneth not." So, also, the blessed David says: [3] " Who can understand his errors? Cleanse Thou me from hidden faults, and keep back Thy servant from presumptuous sins." And again: [4] " Enter not into judgment with Thy servant, for in Thy sight shall no man living be justified." Holy Scripture is full of passages to the same effect.

13. C. But what answer will you give to the famous declaration of John the Evangelist: [5] " We know that whosoever is begotten of God sinneth not; but the begetting of God keepeth him, and the evil one toucheth him not. We know that we are of God, and the whole world lieth in the evil one?"

A. I will requite like with like, and will show that, according to you, the little epistle of the Evangelist contradicts itself. For, if whosoever is begotten of God sinneth not because His seed abideth in him, and he cannot sin, because he is born of God, how is it that the writer says in the same place: [6] "If we say that we have no sin, we deceive ourselves, and the truth is not in us?" You cannot explain. You hesitate and are confused. Listen to the same Evangelist telling us that [7] " If we confess our sins, he is faithful and just to forgive us our sins, and to cleanse us from all unrighteousness." We are then righteous when we confess that we are sinners, and our righteousness depends not upon our own merits, but on the mercy of God, as the Holy Scripture says, [8] " The righteous man accuseth himself when he beginneth to speak," and elsewhere, [9] " Tell thy sins that thou mayest be justified." [10] " God hath shut up all under sin, that He may have mercy upon all." And the highest righteousness of man is this—whatever virtue he may be able to acquire, not to think it his own, but the gift of God. He then who is born of God does not sin, so long as the seed of God remains in him, and he cannot sin, because he is born of God. But seeing that, while the householder slept, an enemy sowed tares, and that when we know not, a sower by night scatters in the Lord's field darnel and

wild oats among the good corn, this parable of the householder in the Gospel should excite our fears. He cleanses his floor, and gathers the wheat into his garner, but leaves the chaff to be scattered by the winds, or burned by the fire. And so we read in Jeremiah,[1] " What is the chaff to the wheat? saith the Lord." The chaff, moreover, is separated from the wheat at the end of the world, a proof that, while we are in the mortal body, chaff is mixed with the wheat. But if you object, and ask why did the Apostle say " and he cannot sin, because he is born of God," I reply by asking you what becomes of the reward of his choice. For if a man does not sin because he cannot sin, free will is destroyed, and goodness cannot possibly be due to his efforts, but must be part of a nature unreceptive of evil.

14. C. The task I set you just now was an easy one by way of practice for something more difficult. What have you to say to my next argument? Clever as you are, all your skill will not avail to overthrow it. I shall first quote from the Old Testament, then from the New. Moses is the chief figure in the Old Testament, our Lord and Saviour in the New. Moses says to the people, [2] " Be perfect in the sight of the Lord your God." And the Saviour bids the Apostles [3] " Be perfect as your heavenly Father is perfect." Now it was either possible for the hearers to do what Moses and the Lord commanded, or, if it be impossible, the fault does not lie with them who cannot obey, but with Him who gave impossible commands.

A. This passage to the ignorant, and to those who are unaccustomed to meditate on Holy Scripture, and who neither know nor use it, does appear at first sight to favour your opinion. But when you look into it, the difficulty soon disappears. And when you compare passages of Scripture with others, that the Holy Spirit may not seem to contradict Himself with changing place and time, according to what is written, [4] " Deep calleth unto deep at the noise of thy water spouts," the truth will show itself, that is, that Christ did give a possible command when He said " Be ye perfect as your heavenly Father is perfect," and yet that the Apostles were not perfect.

C. I am not talking of what the Apostles did, but of what Christ commanded. And the fault does not lie with the giver of the command, but with the hearers of it, because we cannot admit the justice of him who commands without conceding the possibility of doing what is commanded.

A. Good! Don't tell me then that a man

[1] Eccles. vii. 21.   [2] 2 Chron. vi. 36.   [3] Ps. xix. 12, 13.
[4] Ps. cxliii. 2.   [5] 1 John v. 18, 19.   [6] 1 John i. 8.
[7] 1 John i. 9.   [8] Prov. xviii. 17, Vulg. nearly.
[9] Is. xliii. 26, Sept.   [10] Rom. xi. 32.

[1] Jer. xxiii. 28.   [2] Deut xviii. 13.
[3] S. Matt. v. 48.   [4] Ps. xli. 7.

an be without sin if he chooses, but that a man can be what the Apostles were not.

C. Do you think me fool enough to dare say such a thing?

A. Although you do not say it in so many words, however reluctant you may be to admit the fact, it follows by natural sequence from your proposition. For if a man can be without sin, and it is clear the Apostles were not without sin, a man can be higher than the Apostles: to say nothing of patriarchs and prophets whose righteousness under the law was not perfect, as the Apostle says,[1] "For all have sinned, and fall short of the glory of God: being justified freely by His grace through the redemption that is in Christ Jesus: whom God set forth to be a propitiator."

14a. C. This way of arguing is intricate and brings the simplicity which becomes the Church into the tangled thickets of philosophy. What has Paul to do with Aristotle? or Peter with Plato? For as the latter was the prince of philosophers, so was the former chief of the Apostles: on him the Lord's Church was firmly founded, and neither rushing flood nor storm can shake it.

A. Now you are rhetorical, and while you taunt me with philosophy, you yourself cross over to the camp of the orators. But listen to what your same favourite orator says: "Let us have no more commonplaces: we let them at home."

C. There is no eloquence in this, no bombast like that of the orators, who might be defined as persons whose object is to persuade, and who frame their language accordingly. We are seeking unadulterated truth, and use unsophisticated language. Either the Lord did not give impossible commands, so that they are to blame who did not do what was possible; or, if what is commanded cannot be done, then not they who do not things impossible are convicted of unrighteousness, but He Who commanded things impossible, and that is an impious statement.

A. I see you are much more disturbed than is your wont; so I will not ply you with arguments. But let me briefly ask what you think of the well-known passage of the Apostle when he wrote to the Philippians:[3] "Not that I have already obtained, or am already made perfect: but I press on, if so be that I may apprehend that for which also I was apprehended by Christ Jesus. Brethren, I count not myself to have yet apprehended: but one thing I do; forgetting the things which are behind, and stretching forward to the things which are before, I press on towards the goal unto the prize of the high calling of God in Christ Jesus. Let us, therefore, as many as be perfect, be thus minded: and if in anything ye are otherwise minded, even this shall God reveal unto you," and so on; no doubt you know the rest, which, in my desire to be brief, I omit. He says that he had not yet apprehended, and was by no means perfect; but, like an archer, aimed his arrows at the mark set up (more expressively called [1] σκοπός in Greek), lest the shaft, turning to one side or the other, might show the unskilfulness of the archer. He further declares that he always forgot the past, and ever stretched forward to the things in front, thus teaching that no heed should be paid to the past, but the future earnestly desired; so that what to-day he thought perfect, while he was stretching forward to better things and things in front, to-morrow proves to have been imperfect. And thus at every step, never standing still, but always running, he shows that to be imperfect which we men thought perfect, and teaches that our only perfection and true righteousness is that which is measured by the excellence of God. "I press on towards the goal," he says, "unto the prize of the high calling of God in Christ Jesus." Oh, blessed Apostle Paul, pardon me, a poor creature who confess my faults, if I venture to ask a question. You say that you had not yet obtained, nor yet apprehended, nor were yet perfect, and that you always forgot the things behind, and stretched forward to the things in front, if by any means you might have part in the resurrection of the dead, and win the prize of your high calling. How, then, is it that you immediately add, "As many therefore as are perfect, are thus minded"? (or, let us be thus minded, for the copies vary). And what mind is it that we have, or are to have? that we are perfect? that we have apprehended that which we have not apprehended, received what we have not received, are perfect who are not yet perfect? What mind then have we, or rather what mind ought we to have who are not perfect? To confess that we are imperfect, and have not yet apprehended, nor yet obtained, this is true wisdom in man: know thyself to be imperfect; and, if I may so speak, the perfection of all who are righteous, so long as they are in the flesh, is imperfect. Hence we read in Proverbs:[2] "To understand true righteousness." For if there were not also a false righteousness, the rightousness of God would never be called true. The Apostle continues: "and if ye are otherwise minded, God will also reveal that to you." This sounds strange

[1] Rom. iii. 23, 24. So R. V. Margin—"To be propitiatory."
[2] Cic. Lib. iv. Acad. Quæst.   [3] Phil. iii. 12-16.

[1] From σχέπτομαι, to keep watch.   [2] Prov. i. 3, Sept.?

to my ears. He who but just now said, "Not that I have already obtained, or am already perfect"; the chosen vessel, who was so confident of Christ's dwelling in him that he dared to say "Do ye seek a proof of Christ that speaketh in me?" and yet plainly confessed that he was not perfect; he now gives to the multitude what he denied to himself in particular, he unites himself with the rest and says, "As many of us as are perfect, let us be thus minded." But why he said this, he explains presently. Let us, he means, who wish to be perfect according to the poor measure of human frailty, think this, that we have not yet obtained, nor yet apprehended, nor are yet perfect, and, inasmuch as we are not yet perfect, and, perhaps, think otherwise than true and perfect perfection requires, if we are minded otherwise than is dictated by the full knowledge of God, God will also reveal this to us, so that we may pray with David and say,[1] "Open Thou mine eyes that I may behold wondrous things out of Thy law."

15. All this makes it clear that in Holy Scripture there are two sorts of perfection, two of righteousness, and two of fear. The first is that perfection, and incomparable truth, and perfect righteousness [2] and fear, which is the beginning of wisdom, and which we must measure by the excellence of God; the second, which is within the range not only of men, but of every creature, and is not inconsistent with our frailty, as we read in the Psalms:[3] "In Thy sight shall no man living be justified," is that righteousness which is said to be perfect, not in comparison with God, but as recognized by God. Job, and Zacharias, and Elizabeth, were called righteous, in respect of that righteousness which might some day turn to unrighteousness, and not in respect of that which is incapable of change, concerning which it is said, [4] "I am God, and change not." And this is that which the Apostle elsewhere writes:[5] "That which hath been made glorious hath not been made glorious in this respect, by reason of the glory that surpasseth"; because, that is, the righteousness of the law, in comparison of the grace of the Gospel, does not seem to be righteousness at all. [6] "For if," he says, that which passeth away was with glory, much more that which remaineth is in glory." [7] And again, "We know in part, and we prophesy in part; but when that which is perfect is come, that which is in part shall be done away." And, [8] "For now we see in a mirror, darkly; but then face to face: now I know

in part; but then shall I know even as also I have been known." And in the Psalms [1] "Such knowledge is too wonderful for me; it is high, I cannot attain unto it.' And again, [2] "When I thought how I might know this, it was too painful for me until I went into the sanctuary of God and considered their latter end." And in the same place,[3] "I was as a beast before thee: nevertheless I am continually with thee." And Jeremiah says, [4] "Every man is become brutish and without knowledge." And to return to the Apostle Paul, [5] "The foolishness of God is wiser than men." And much besides, which I omit for brevity's sake.

16. C. My dear Atticus, your speech is really a clever feat of memory. But the labour you have spent in mustering this host of authorities is to my advantage. For I do not any more than you compare man with God but with other men, in comparison with whom he who takes the trouble can be perfect And so, when we say that man, if he chooses, can be without sin, the standard is the measure of man, not the majesty of God, in comparison with Whom no creature can be perfect.

A. Critobulus, I am obliged to you for reminding me of the fact. For it is just my own view that no creature can be perfect in respect of true and finished righteousness. But that one differs from another, and that one man's righteousness is not the same as another's, no one doubts; nor again that one may be greater or less than another, and yet that, relatively to their own status and capacity, men may be called righteous who are not righteous when compared with others. For instance, the Apostle Paul, the chosen vessel who laboured more than all the Apostles, was, I suppose, righteous when he wrote to Timothy, [6] "I have fought the good fight, I have finished the course, I have kept the faith: henceforth there is laid up for me the crown of righteousness, which the Lord, the righteous judge, shall give to me at that day: and not only to me, but also to all them that love His appearing." Timothy, his disciple and imitator, whom he taught the rules of action and the limits of virtue, was also righteous. Are we to think there was one and the same righteousness in them both, and that he had not more merit who laboured more than all? "In my Father's house are many mansions." I suppose there are also different degrees of merit. "One star differeth from another star in glory," and in the one body of the Church there are different members. The sun has its own splendour, the moon

---

[1] Ps. cxix. 18.   [2] The reading is much disputed.
[3] Ps. cxliii. 2.   [4] Malach. iii. 6.   [5] 2 Cor. iii. 10.
[6] Ib. 11.   [7] 1 Cor. xiii. 9, 10.   [8] 1 Cor. xiii. 12.

[1] cxxxix. 6.   [2] Ps. lxxiii. 16, 17.   [3] Ibid. 22, 23.
[4] Jer. x. 14.   [5] 1 Cor. i. 25.   [6] 2 Tim. iv. 7, 8.

empers the darkness of the night; and the ive heavenly bodies which are called planets raverse the sky in different tracks and with lifferent degrees of luminousness. There are countless other stars whose movements we race in the firmament. Each has its own orightness, and though each in respect of its own is perfect, yet, in comparison with one of greater magnitude, it lacks perfection. In the body also with its different members, the eye has one function, the hand another, the foot another. Whence the Apostle says,[1] "The eye cannot say to the hand, I have no need of thee: or again the head to the feet, I have no need of you. Are all Apostles? are all prophets? are all teachers? are all workers of miracles? have all gifts of healing? do all speak with tongues? do all interpret? But desire earnestly the greater gifts. But all these worketh the one and the same Spirit, dividing to each one severally even as He will." And here mark carefully that he does not say, as each member desires, but as the Spirit Himself will. For the vessel cannot say to him that makes it,[2] "Why dost thou make me thus or thus? Hath not the potter a right over the clay, from the same lump to make one part a vessel unto honour, and another unto dishonour?" And so in close sequence he added, "Desire earnestly the greater gifts," so that, by the exercise of faith and diligence, we may win something in addition to other gifts, and may be superior to those who, compared with us, are in the second or third class. In a great house there are different vessels, some of gold, some of silver, brass, iron, wood. And yet while in its kind a vessel of brass is perfect, in comparison with one of silver it is called imperfect, and again one of silver, compared with one of gold, is inferior. And thus, when compared with one another, all things are imperfect and perfect. In a field of good soil, and from one sowing, there springs a crop thirty-fold, sixty-fold, or a hundred-fold. The very numbers show that there is disparity in the parts of the produce, and yet in its own kind each is perfect. Elizabeth and Zacharias, whom you adduce and with whom you cover yourself as with an impenetrable shield, may teach us how far they are beneath the holiness of blessed Mary, the Lord's Mother, who, conscious that God was dwelling in her, proclaims without reserve, [3] "Behold, from henceforth all generations shall call me blessed. For He that is mighty hath done to me great things; and holy is His name. And His mercy is unto generations and generations of them that fear Him. He hath showed

strength with His arm." Where, observe, she says she is blessed not by her own merit and virtue, but by the mercy of God dwelling in her. And John himself, a greater than whom has not arisen among the sons of men, is better than his parents. For not only does our Lord compare him with men, but with angels also. And yet he, who was greater on earth than all other men, is said to be less than the least in the kingdom of heaven.

17. Need we be surprised that, when saints are compared, some are better, some worse, since the same holds good in the comparison of sins? To Jerusalem, piecred and wounded with many sins, it is said, [1] "Sodom is justified by thee." It is not because Sodom, which has sunk for ever into ashes, is just in herself, that it is said by Ezekiel,[2] "Sodom shall be restored to her former estate"; but that, in comparison with the more accursed Jerusalem, she appears just. For Jerusalem killed the Son of God; Sodom through fulness of bread and excessive luxury carried her lust beyond all bounds. The publican in the Gospel who smote upon his breast as though it were a magazine of the worst thoughts, and, conscious of his offences, dared not lift up his eyes, is justified rather than the proud Pharisee. And Thamar in the guise of a harlot deceived Judah, and in the estimation of this man himself who was deceived, was worthy of the words,[3] "Thamar is more righteous than I." All this goes to prove that not only in comparison with Divine majesty are men far from perfection, but also when compared with angels, and other men who have climbed the heights of virtue. You may be superior to some one whom you have shown to be imperfect, and yet be outstripped by another; and consequently may not have true perfection, which, if it be perfect, is absolute.

18. C. How is it then, Atticus, that the Divine Word urges us to perfection?

A. I have already explained that in proportion to our strength each one, with all his power, must stretch forward, if by any means he may attain to, and apprehend the reward of his high calling. In short Almighty God, to whom, as the Apostle teaches, the Son must in accordance with the dispensation of the Incarnation be subjected, that [4] "God may be all in all," clearly shows that all things are by no means subject to Himself. Hence the prophet anticipates his own final subjection, saying,[5] "Shall not my soul be subject to God alone? for of Him cometh my salvation." And because in the body of the Church Christ is the head, and some of the members

---

[1] 1 Cor. xii. 21, 29, 11. [2] Rom. ix. 21.
[3] S. Luke i. 48 sq.

[1] Lam. iv. 6. [2] Ezek xvi. 55. [3] Gen. xxxviii. 26.
[4] 1 Cor. xv. 28. [5] Ps. lxii. 2.

still resist, the body does not appear to be subject even to the head. For if one member suffer, all the members suffer with it, and the whole body is tortured by the pain in one member. My meaning may be more clearly expressed thus. So long as we have the treasure in earthen vessels, and are clothed with frail flesh, or rather with mortal and corruptible flesh, we think ourselves fortunate if, in single virtues and separate portions of virtue, we are subject to God. But when this mortal shall have put on immortality, and this corruptible shall have put on incorruption, and death shall be swallowed up in the victory of Christ, then will God be all in all: and so there will not be merely wisdom in Solomon, sweetness in David, zeal in Elias and Phinees, faith in Abraham, perfect love in Peter, to whom it was said, [1] "Simon, son of John, lovest thou me?" zeal for preaching in the chosen vessel, and two or three virtues each in others, but God will be wholly in all, and the company of the saints will rejoice in the whole band of virtues, and God will be all in all.

19. C. Do I understand you to say that no saint, so long as he is in this poor body, can have all virtues?

A. Just so, because now we prophesy in part, and know in part. It is impossible for all things to be in all men, for no son of man is immortal.

C. How is it, then, that we read that he who has one virtue appears to have all?

A. By partaking of them, not possessing them, for individuals must excel in particular virtues. But I confess I don't know where to find what you say you have read.

C. Are you not aware that the philosophers take that view?

A. The philosophers may, but the Apostles do not. I heed not what Aristotle, but what Paul, teaches.

C. Pray does not James the Apostle [2] write that he who stumbles in one point is guilty of all?

A. The passage is its own interpreter. James did not say, as a starting-point for the discussion, he who prefers a rich man to a poor man in honour is guilty of adultery or murder. That is a delusion of the Stoics who maintain the equality of sins. But he proceeds thus: "He who said, Thou shalt not commit adultery, said also, Thou shalt not kill: but although thou dost not kill, yet, if thou commit adultery, thou art become a transgressor of the law." Light offences are compared with light ones, and heavy offences with heavy ones. A fault that deserves the rod must not

be avenged with the sword; nor must a crime worthy of the sword, be checked with the rod.

C. Suppose it true that no saint has all the virtues: you will surely grant that within the range of his ability, if a man do what he can, he is perfect.

A. Do you not remember what I said before?

C. What was it?

A. That a man is perfect in respect of what he has done, imperfect in respect of what he could not do.

C. But as he is perfect in respect of what he has done, because he willed to do it, so in respect of that which constitutes him imperfect, because he has not done it, he might have been perfect, had he willed to do it.

A. Who does not wish to do what is perfect? Or who does not long to grow vigorously in all virtue? If you look for all virtues in each individual, you do away with the distinctions of things, and the difference of graces, and the variety of the work of the Creator, whose prophet cries aloud in the sacred song: [1] "In wisdom hast thou made them all." Lucifer may be indignant because he has not the brightness of the moon. The moon may dispute over her eclipses and ceaseless toil, and ask why she must traverse every month the yearly orbit of the sun. The sun may complain and want to know what he has done that he travels more slowly than the moon. And we poor creatures may demand to know why it is that we were made men and not angels; although your teacher, [2]*the Ancient*, the fountain from which these streams flow, asserts that all rational creatures were created equal and started fairly, like charioteers, either to succumb halfway, or to pass on rapidly and reach the wished-for goal. Elephants, with their huge bulk, and griffins, might discuss their ponderous frames and ask why they must go on four feet, while flies, midges, and other creatures like them have six feet under their tiny wings, and there are some creeping things which have such an abundance of feet that the keenest vision cannot follow their countless and simultaneous movements. Marcion and all the heretics who denied the Creator's works might speak thus. Your principle goes so far that while its adherents attack particular points, they are laying hands on God; they are asking why He only is God, why He envies the creatures, and why they are not all endowed with the same power and impor-

---

[1] Ps. civ. 24.
[2] According to some. Plato: more probably. Origen, the word ἀρχαῖος being an allusion to the title of his chief work, Περὶ Ἀρχῶν.

---

[1] S. John xxi. 15-17.   [2] James ii. 10.

ance. You would not say so much (for you re not mad enough to openly fight against ;od), yet this is your meaning in other vords, when you give man an attribute of ;od, and make him to be without sin like ;od Himself. Hence the Apostle, with his oice of thunder, says, concerning different ;races : [1] "There are diversities of gifts, but he same spirit ; and differences of ministraions, but the same Lord ; and there are diversities of workings, but the same God, Who vorketh all things in all."

20. C. You push this one particular point oo far in seeking to convince me that a man cannot have all excellences at the same time. As though God were guilty of envy, or unable to bestow upon His image and likeness a correspondence in all things to his Creator.

A. Is it I or you who go too far ? You revive. questions already settled, and do not understand that likeness is one thing, equality another ; that the former is a painting, the latter, reality. A real horse courses over the plains; the painted one with his chariot does not leave the wall. The Arians do not allow to the Son of God what you give to every man. Some do not dare to confess the perfect humanity of Christ, lest they should be compelled to accept the belief that He had the sins of a man ; as though the Creator were unequal to the act of creating, and the title Son of Man were co-extensive with the title Son of God. So either set me something else to answer, or lay aside pride and give glory to God.

C. You forget a former answer of yours, and have been so busy forging your chain of argument, and careering through the wide fields of Scripture, like a horse that has slipped its bridle, that you have not said a single word about the main point. Your forgetfulness is a pretext for escaping the necessity of a reply. It was foolish in me to concede to you for the nonce what you asked, and to suppose that you would voluntarily give up what you had received, and would not need a reminder to make you pay what you owed.

A. If I mistake not, it was the question of possible commands of which I deferred the answer. Pray proceed as you think best.

21. C. The commands which God has given are either possible or impossible. If possible, it is in our power to do them, if we choose. If impossible, we cannot be held guilty for omitting duties which it is not given us to fufil. Hence it results that, whether God has given possible or impossible commands, a man can be without sin if he chooses.

A. I beg your patient attention, for what we seek is not victory over an opponent, but the triumph of truth over falsehood. God has put within the power of mankind all arts, for we see that a vast number of men have mastered them. To pass over those which the Greeks call [1]βάναυσοι, as we may say, the manual arts, I will instance grammar, rhetoric, the three sorts of philosophy— physics, ethics, logic—geometry also, and astronomy, astrology, arithmetic, music, which are also parts of philosophy ; medicine, too, in its threefold division—theory, investigation, practice ; a knowledge of law in general and of particular enactments. Which of us, however clever he may be, will be able to understand them all, when the most eloquent of orators, discussing rhetoric and jurisprudence, said : " A few may excel in one, in both no one can." You see, then, that God has commanded what is possible, and yet, that no one can by nature attain to what is possible. Similarly he has given different rules and various virtues, all of which we cannot possess at the same time. Hence it happens that a virtue which in one person takes the chief place, or is found in perfection, in another is but partial ; and yet, he is not to blame who has not all excellence, nor is he condemned for lacking that which he has not ; but he is justified through what he does possess. The Apostle described the character of a bishop when he wrote to Timothy, [2] " The bishop, therefore, must be without reproach, the husband of one wife, temperate, modest, orderly, given to hospitality, apt to teach ; no brawler, no striker ; but gentle, not contentious, no lover of money ; one that ruleth well his own house, having his children in subjection with all modesty." And again, "Not a novice, lest, being puffed up, he fall into the condemnation of the devil. Moreover, he must have good testimony from them that are without, lest he fall into reproach and the snare of the devil." Writing also to his disciple Titus, he briefly points out what sort of bishops he ought to ordain : [3] " For this cause left I thee in Crete, that thou shouldest set in order the things that were wanting, and appoint elders in every city, as I gave thee charge ; if any man is blameless, the husband of one wife, having children that believe, who are not accused of riot or unruly. For the bishop must be blameless (or free from accusation, for so much is conveyed by the original) as God's steward ; not self-willed, not soon angry, no brawler, no striker, not greedy of filthy lucre ; but given to hospitality, kind, modest, just,

---

[1] 1 Cor. xii. 4, 5.   [1] That is, mean.   [2] 1 Tim. iii. 2 sq.   [3] Titus i. 5 sq.

holy, temperate ; holding to the faithful word which is according to the teaching, that he may be able both to exhort in the sound doctrine, and to convict the gainsayers." I will not now say anything of the various rules relating to different persons, but will confine myself to the commands connected with the bishop.

22. God certainly wishes bishops or priests to be such as the chosen vessel teaches they should be. As to the first qualification it is seldom or never that one is found *without reproach ;* for who is it that has not some fault, like a mole or a wart on a lovely body ? If the Apostle himself says of Peter that he did not tread a straight path in the truth of the Gospel, and was so far to blame that even Barnabas was led away into the same dissimulation, who will be indignant if that is denied to him which the chief of the Apostles had not ? Then, supposing you find one, "the husband of one wife, sober-minded, orderly, given to hospitality," the next attribute—διδακτικόν, *apt to teach,* not merely as the Latin renders the word, *apt to be taught*—you will hardly find in company with the other virtues. A bishop or priest that is a brawler, or a striker, or a lover of money, the Apostle rejects, and in his stead would have one gentle, not contentious, free from avarice, one that rules well his own house, and what is very hard, one who has his children in subjection with all modesty, whether they be children of the flesh or children of the faith. "With all modesty," he says. It is not enough for him to have his own modesty unless it be enhanced by the modesty of his children, companions, and servants, as David says,[1] "He that walketh in a perfect way, he shall minister unto me." Let us consider, also, the emphasis laid on modesty by the addition of the words "having his children in subjection with all modesty." Not only in deed but in word and gesture must he hold aloof from immodesty, lest perchance the experience of Eli be his. Eli certainly rebuked his sons, saying,[2] "Nay, my sons, nay ; it is not a good report which I hear of you." He chided them, and yet was punished, because he should not have chided, but cast them off. What will he do who rejoices at vice or lacks the courage to correct it ? Who fears his own conscience, and therefore pretends to be ignorant of what is in everybody's mouth ? The next point is that the bishop must be free from accusation, that he have a good report from them who are without, that no reproaches of opponents be levelled at him, and that they who dislike his doctrine may be pleased with his life. I suppose it would not be easy to find all this, and particularly one "able to resist the gainsayers," to check and overcome erroneous opinions. He wishes no novice to be ordained bishop, and yet in our time we see the youthful novice sought after as though he represented the highest righteousness. If baptism immediately made a man righteous, and full of all righteousness, it was of course idle for the Apostle to repel a novice ; but baptism annuls old sins, does not bestow new virtues ; it looses from prison, and promises rewards to the released if he will work. Seldom or never, I say, is there a man who has all the virtues which a bishop should have. And yet if a bishop lacked one or two of the virtues in the list, it does not follow that he can no longer be called righteous, nor will he be condemned for his deficiencies, but will be crowned for what he has. For to have all and lack nothing is the virtue of Him[1] "Who did no sin ; neither was guile found in His mouth ; Who, when He was reviled, reviled not again ; " Who, confident in the consciousness of virtue, said,[2] "Behold the prince of this world cometh, and findeth nothing in me ; " [3] "Who, being in the form of God, thought it not robbery to be on an equality with God, but emptied Himself, taking the form of a servant, and became obedient unto death, even the death of the cross. Wherefore God gave Him the name which is above every name, that at the name of Jesus every knee should bow, of things in heaven, and things on earth, and things under the earth." If, then, in the person of a single bishop you will either not find at all, or with difficulty, even a few of the things commanded, how will you deal with the mass of men in general who are bound to fulfil all the commandments ?

23. Let us reason from things bodily to things spiritual. One man is swift-footed, but not strong-handed. That man's movements are slow, but he stands firm in battle. This man has a fine face, but a harsh voice : another is repulsive to look at, but sings sweetly and melodiously. There we see a man of great ability, but equally poor memory ; here is another whose memory serves him, but whose wits are slow. In the very discussions with which when we were boys we amused ourselves, all the disputants are not on a level, either in introducing a subject, or in narrative, or in digressions, or in wealth of illustration, and charm of peroration, but their various oratorical efforts exhibit different degrees of merit. Of churchmen I will say more. Many discourse well upon

---

[1] Ps. ci. 6.   [2] 1 Sam. ii. 24.   [1] 1 Pet. ii. 22.   [2] S. John xiv. 30.   [3] Phil. ii. 6 sq.

the Gospels, but in explaining an Apostle's meaning are unequal to themselves. Others, although most acute in the New Testament, are dumb in the Psalms and the Old Testament. I quite agree with Virgil—*Non omnia possumus omnes ;* and seldom or never is the rich man found who in the abundance of his wealth has everything in equal proportions. That God has given possible commands, I admit no less than you. But it is not for each one of us to make all these possible virtues our own, not because our nature is weak, for that is a slander upon God, but because our hearts and minds grow weary and cannot keep all virtues simultaneously and perpetually. And if you blame the Creator for having made you subject to weariness and failure, I shall reply, your censure would be still more severe if you thought proper to accuse Him of not having made you God. But you will say, if I have not the power, no sin attaches to me. You have sinned because you have not done what another could do. And again, he in comparison with whom you are inferior will be a sinner in respect of some other virtue, relatively to you or to another person ; and thus it happens that whoever is thought to be first, is inferior to him who is his superior in some other particular.

24. C. If it is impossible for man to be without sin, what does the Apostle Jude mean by writing,[1] " Now unto Him that is able to keep you without sin, and to set you before the presence of His glory without blemish " ? This is clear proof that it is possible to keep a man without sin and without blemish.

A. You do not understand the passage. We are not told that a man can be without sin, which is your view, but that God, if He chooses, can keep a man free from sin, and of His mercy guard him so that he may be without blemish. And I say that all things are possible with God ; but that everything which a man desires is not possible to him, and especially, an attribute which belongs to no created thing you ever read of.

C. I do not say that a man is without sin, which, perhaps, appears to you to be possible ; but that he may be, if he chooses. For actuality is one thing, possibility another. In the actual we look for an instance ; possibility implies that our power to act is real.

A. You are trifling, and forget the proverb, " Don't do what is done." You keep turning in the same mire,[2] and only make more dirt. I shall, therefore, tell you what is clear to all,

that you are trying to establish a thing that is not, never was, and, perhaps, never will be. To employ your own words, and show the folly and inconsistency of your argument, I say that you are maintaining an impossible possibility. For your proposition, that a man can be without sin if he chooses, is either true or false. If it be true, show me who the man is ; if it be false, whatever is false can never happen. But let us have no more of these notions. Hissed off the stage, and no longer daring to appear in public, they should stay on the book shelves, and not let themselves be heard.

25. Let us proceed to other matters. And here I must speak uninterruptedly, so far, at least, as is consistent with giving you an opportunity of refuting me, or asking any question you think fit.

C. I will listen patiently, though I cannot say gladly. The ability of your reasoning will strike me all the more, while I am amazed at its falsity.

A. Whether what I am going to say is true or false, you will be able to judge when you have heard it.

C. Follow your own method. I am resolved, if I am unable to answer, to hold my tongue rather than assent to a lie.

A. What difference does it make whether I defeat you speaking or silent, and, as it is in the [1] story of Proteus, catch you asleep or awake ?

C. When you have said what you like, you shall hear what you will certainly not like. For though truth may be put to hard shifts it cannot be subdued.

A. I want to sift your opinions a little, that your followers may know what an inspired genius you are. You say, " It is impossible for any but those who have the knowledge of the law to be without sin " ; and you, consequently, shut out from righteousness a large number of Christians, and, preacher of sinlessness though you are, declare nearly all to be sinners. For how many Christians have that knowledge of the law which you can find but seldom, or hardly at all, in many doctors of the Church ? But your liberality is so great that, in order to stand well with your Amazons, you have elsewhere written, " Even women ought to have a knowledge of the law," although the Apostle preaches that women ought to keep silence in the churches, and if they want to know anything consult their husbands at home. And you are not content with having given your cohort a knowledge of Scripture, but you must delight yourself with their songs and canticles, for

---

[1] Verse 24.
[2] Literally, wash a brick (that has not been burnt). Hence (1) labour in vain, or (2) make bad worse. The latter appears to be the meaning here.

[1] Virg. Georg., iv.

you have a heading to the effect that "Women also should sing unto God." Who does not know that women should sing in the privacy of their own rooms, away from the company of men and the crowded congregation? But you allow what is not lawful, and the consequence is, that, with the support of their master, they make an open show of that which should be done with modesty, and with no eye to witness.

26. You go on to say, "The servant of God should utter from his lips no bitterness, but ever that which is sweet and pleasant"; and as though a servant of God were one thing, a doctor and priest of the Church another, forgetting what was previously laid down, you say in another heading, "A priest or doctor ought to watch the actions of all, and confidently rebuke sinners, lest he be responsible for them and their blood be required at his hands." And, not satisfied with saying it once, you repeat it, and inculcate that, "A priest or doctor should flatter no one, but boldly rebuke all, lest he destroy both himself and those who hear him." Is there so little harmony in one and the same work that you do not know what you have previously said? For if the servant of God ought to utter no bitterness from his mouth, but always that which is sweet and pleasant, it follows either that a priest and doctor will not be servants of God who ought to confidently rebuke sinners, and flatter no one, but boldly reprove all: or, if a priest and a doctor are not only servants of God, but have the chief place among His servants, it is idle to reserve smooth and pleasant speeches for the servants of God, for these are characteristic of heretics and of them who wish to deceive; as the Apostle says,[1] "They that are such serve not our Lord Christ but their own belly, and by their smooth and fair speech they beguile the hearts of the innocent." Flattery is always insidious, crafty, and smooth. And the flatterer is well described by the philosophers as "*a pleasant enemy.*" Truth is bitter, of gloomy visage and wrinkled brow, and distasteful to those who are rebuked. Hence the Apostle says,[2] "Am I become your enemy, because I tell you the truth?" And the comic poet tells us that "Obsequiousness is the mother of friendship, truth of enmity." Wherefore we also eat the Passover with bitter herbs, and the chosen vessel teaches that the Passover should be kept with truth and sincerity. Let truth in our case be plain speaking, and bitterness will instantly follow.

27. In another place you maintain that "All are governed by their own free choice." What Christian can bear to hear this? For if not one, nor a few, nor many, but all of us are governed by our own free choice, what becomes of the help of God? And how do you explain the text,[1] "A man's goings are ordered by the Lord"? And [2] "A man's way is not in himself"; and [3] "No one can receive anything, unless it be given him from above"; and elsewhere,[4] "What hast thou which thou didst not receive? But if thou didst receive it, why dost thou glory as if thou hadst not received it?" Our Lord and Saviour says: [5] "I am come down from heaven not to do Mine own, will, but the will of the Father who sent Me." And in another place,[6] "Father, if it be possible, let this cup pass from Me; nevertheless not My will, but Thine be done." And in the Lord's prayer,[7] "Thy will be done as in heaven, so on earth." How is it that you are so rash as to do away with all God's help? Elsewhere, you make a vain attempt to append the words "not without the grace of God"; but in what sense you would have them understood is clear from this passage, for you do not admit His grace in separate actions, but connect it with our creation, the gift of the law, and the power of free will.

28. The argument of the next section is, "In the day of judgment, no mercy will be shown to the unjust and to sinners, but they must be consumed in eternal fire." Who can bear this, and suffer you to prohibit the mercy of God, and to sit in judgment on the sentence of the Judge before the day of judgment, so that, if He wished to show mercy to the unjust and the sinners, He must not, because you have given your veto? For you say it is written in the one hundred and fourth Psalm,[8] "Let sinners cease to be in the earth, and the wicked be no more." And in Isaiah, [9] "The wicked and sinners shall be burned up together, and they who forsake God shall be consumed." Do you not know that mercy is sometimes blended with the threatenings of God? He does not say that they must be burnt with eternal fires, but let them cease to be in the earth, and the wicked be no more. For it is one thing for them to desist from sin and wickedness, another for them to perish for ever and be burnt in eternal fire. And as for the passage which you quote from Isaiah, "Sinners and the wicked shall be burned up together," he does not add for ever. "And they who forsake God shall be consumed." This properly refers to heretics, who leave the straight path of the faith, and shall be consumed if they will not return to the Lord

---

[1] Rom. xvi. 18.   [2] Gal. iv. 16.

[1] Prov. xx. 24.   [2] Jer. x. 23.   [3] S. John xx. 11.
[4] 1 Cor. iv. 7.   [5] S. John vi. 38.   [6] S. Luke xxii. 42.
[7] S. Matt. vi. 10.   [8] Ps. civ. 35.   [9] Is. i. 28.

whom they have forsaken. And the same sentence is ready for you if you neglect to turn to better things. Again, is it not marvellous temerity to couple the wicked and sinners with the impious, for the distinction between them is great? Every impious person is wicked and a sinner; but we cannot conversely say every sinner and wicked person is also impious, for impiety properly belongs to those who have not the knowledge of God, or, if they have once had it, lose it by transgression. But the wounds of sin and wickedness, like faults in general, admit of healing. Hence, it is written, [1] "Many are the scourges of the sinner"; it is not said that he is eternally destroyed. And through all the scourging and torture the faults of Israel are corrected, [2] "For whom the Lord loveth He chasteneth, and scourgeth every son whom He receiveth." It is one thing to smite with the affection of a teacher and a parent; another to be madly cruel towards adversaries. Wherefore, we sing in the first Psalm, [3] "The impious do not rise in the judgment," for they are already sentenced to destruction; "nor sinners in the counsel of the just." To lose the glory of the resurrection is a different thing from perishing for ever. "The hour cometh," he says, [4] "In which all that are in the tombs shall hear His voice, and shall come forth: they that have done good unto the resurrection of life, and they that have done ill unto the resurrection of judgment." And so the Apostle, in the same sense, because in the same Spirit, says to the Romans, [5] "As many as have sinned without law shall also perish without law; and as many as have sinned under law, shall be judged by law." The man without law is the unbeliever who will perish for ever. Under the law is the sinner who believes in God, and who will be judged by the law, and will not perish. If the wicked and sinners are to be burned with everlasting fire, are you not afraid of the sentence you pass on yourself, seeing that you admit you are wicked and a sinner, while still you argue that a man is not without sin, but that he may be. It follows that the only person who can be saved is an individual who never existed, does not exist, and perhaps never will, and that all our predecessors of whom we read must perish. Take your own case. You are puffed up with all the pride of Cato, and have [6] Milo's giant shoulders; but is it not amazing temerity for you, who are a sinner, to take the name of a teacher? If you are righteous, and, with a false humility, say you are a sinner, we may be surprised, but we

shall rejoice at having so unique a treasure, and at reckoning amongst our friends a personage unknown to patriarch, prophet, and Apostle. And if Origen does maintain that no rational creatures ought to be lost, and allows repentance to the devil, what is that to us, who say that the devil and his attendants, and all impious persons and transgressors, perish eternally, and that [1] Christians, if they be overtaken by sin, must be saved after they have been punished?

29. [2] Besides all this you add two chapters which contradict one another, and which, if true, would effectually close your mouth. "Except a man have learned, he cannot be acquainted with wisdom and understand the Scriptures." And again, "He that has not been taught, ought not to assume that he knows the law." You must, then, either produce the master from whom you learned, if you are lawfully to claim the knowledge of the law; or, if your master is a person who never learned from any one else, and taught you what he did not know himself, it follows that you are not acting rightly in claiming a knowledge of Scripture, when you have not been taught, and in starting as a master before you have been a disciple. And yet, perhaps, with your customary humility, you make your boast that the Lord Himself, Who teaches all knowledge, was your master, and that, like Moses in the cloud and darkness, face to face, you hear the words of God, and so, with the [3] halo round your head, take the lead of us. And even this is not enough, but all at once you turn Stoic, and thunder in our ears Zeno's proud maxims. "A Christian ought to be so patient that if any one wished to take his property he would let it go with joy." Is it not enough for us patiently to lose what we have, without returning thanks to him who ill-treats and plunders us, and sending after him all blessings? The Gospel teaches that to him who would go to law with us, and by strife and litigation take away our coat, we must give our cloak also. It does not enjoin the giving of thanks and joy at the loss of our property. What I say is this, not that there is any enormity in your view, but that everywhere you are prone to exaggeration, and indulge in ambitious flights. This is why you add that "The bravery of dress and ornament is an enemy of God." What enmity, I should like to know, is there to-

---

[1] Ps. xxxii. 10.   [2] Heb. xii. 6.   [3] Verse 5. Sept.
[4] S. John v. 28, 29.   [5] Rom. ii. 12.
[6] The reference is to the stature of Pelagius.

[1] The sense of this passage is much disputed. St. Jerome was, possibly, speaking of persons who upon the whole are sincere and not merely covenanted Christians.
[2] Jerome seems here to speak in his own person and to address Pelagius directly.
[3] *Cornuta fronte.* Literally, "with horned brow." The allusion is to the rays of light which beamed from the face of Moses, the Hebrew word bearing both meanings, *ray* and *horn.* Hence the portraiture of him with horns.

wards God if my tunic is cleaner than usual, or if the bishop, priest, or deacon, or any other ecclesiastics, at the offering of the sacrifices walk in white? Beware, ye clergy; beware, ye monks; widows and virgins, you are in peril unless the people see you begrimed with dirt, and clad in rags. I say nothing of laymen, who proclaim open war and enmity against God if they wear costly and elegant apparel.

30. Let us hear the rest. "We must love our enemies as we do our neighbours"; and immediately, falling into a deep slumber, you lay down this proposition: "We must never believe an enemy." Not a word is needed from me to show the contradiction here. You will say that both propositions are found in Scripture, but you do not observe the particular connection in which the passages occur. I am told to love my enemies and pray for my persecutors. Am I bidden to love them as though they were my neighbours, kindred, and friends, and to make no difference between a rival and a relative? If I love my enemies as my neighbours, what more affection can I show to my friends? If you had maintained this position, you ought to have taken care not to contradict yourself by saying that we must never believe an enemy. But even the law teaches us how an enemy should be loved. [1] If an enemy's beast be fallen, we must raise it up. And the Apostle tells us, [2] "If thine enemy hunger, feed him; if he thirst, give him drink. For by so doing thou shalt heap coals of fire upon his head," not by way of curse and condemnation, as most people think, but to chasten and bring him to repentance, so that, overcome by kindness, and melted by the warmth of love, he may no longer be an enemy.

31. Your next point is that "the kingdom of heaven is promised even in the Old Testament," and you adduce evidence from the Apocrypha, although it is clear that the kingdom of heaven was first preached under the Gospel by John the Baptist, and our Lord and Saviour, and the Apostles. Read the Gospels. John the Baptist cries in the desert, [3] "Repent, for the kingdom of heaven is at hand"; and concerning the Saviour it is written, [4] "From that time He began to preach and to say, Repent, for the kingdom of heaven is at hand." And again, [5] "Jesus went round about the towns and villages, teaching in their synagogues, and preaching the kingdom of God." And He commanded His Apostles to [6] "go and preach, saying, the kingdom of heaven is at hand." But you call us Manichæans because we prefer the Gospel to the law, and

say that in the latter we have the shadow, in the former, the substance, and you do not see that your foolishness goes hand in hand with impudence. It is one thing to condemn the law, as Manichæus did; it is another to prefer the Gospel to the law, for this is in accordance with apostolic teaching. In the law the servants of the Lord speak, in the Gospel the Lord Himself; in the former are the promises, in the latter their fulfilment; there are the beginnings, here is perfection; in the law the foundations of works are laid; in the Gospel the edifice is crowned with the top-stone of faith and grace. I have mentioned this to show the character of the teaching given by our distinguished professor.

32. The hundredth heading runs thus: "A man can be without sin, and easily keep the commandments of God if he chooses," as to which enough has already been said. And although he professes to imitate, or rather complete the work of the blessed martyr Cyprian in the treatise which the latter wrote to [1]Quirinus, he does not perceive that he has said just the opposite in the work under discussion. Cyprian, in the fifty-fourth heading of the third book, lays it down that no one is free from stain and without sin, and he immediately gives proofs, among them the passage in Job, [2] "Who is cleansed from uncleanness? Not he who has lived but one day upon the earth." [3]And in the fifty-first Psalm, "Behold I was shapen in iniquity, and in sin did my mother conceive me." And in the Epistle of John, [4] "If we say that we have no sin, we deceive ourselves, and the truth is not in us." You, on the other hand, maintain that "A man can be without sin," and that you may give your words the semblance of truth, you immediately add, "And easily keep the commandments of God, if he chooses," and yet they have been seldom or never kept by any one. Now, if they were easy, they ought to have been kept by all. But if, to concede you a point, at rare intervals some one may be found able to keep them, it is clear that what is rare is difficult. And by way of supplementing this and displaying the greatness of your own virtues (we are to believe, forsooth, that you bring forth the sentiment out of the treasure of a good conscience), you have a heading to the effect that: "We ought not to commit even light offences." And for fear some one might think you had not explained in the work the meaning of *light*, you add that, "We must not even think an evil thought," forgetting the words, [5] "Who

---

[1] A Christian of Carthage who, together with Cyprian, sent relief to the bishops and martyrs in the Mines of Sigus, in Numidia, and elsewhere (A.D. 257).

[1] Deut. xxii. 4.   [2] Rom. xii. 20.   [3] S. Matt. iii. 2.   [4] iv. 17.   [5] iv. 23.   [6] x. 7.   [2] Job xiv. 4.   [3] Ps. li. 5.   [4] 1 John i. 8.   [5] Ps. xix. 12, 13.

understands his offences? Clear thou me from hidden faults, and keep back thy servant from presumptuous sins, O Lord." You should have known that the Church admits even failures through ignorance and sins of mere thought to be offences ; so much so that she bids sacrifices be offered for errors, and the high priest who makes intercession for the whole people previously offers victims for himself. Now, if he were not himself righteous, he would never be commanded to offer for others. Nor, again, would he offer for himself if he were free from sins of ignorance. If I were to attempt to show that error and ignorance is sin, I must roam at large over the wide fields of Scripture.

33. C. Pray have you not read that [1] " He who looks upon a woman to lust after her hath committed adultery with her already in his heart ? " It seems that not only are the look and the allurements to vice reckoned as sin, but whatever it be to which we give assent. For either we can avoid an evil thought, and consequently may be free from sin ; or, if we cannot avoid it, that is not reckoned as sin which cannot be avoided.

A. Your argument is ingenious, but you do not see that it goes against Holy Scripture, which declares that even ignorance is not without sin. Hence it was that Job offered sacrifices for his sons, lest, perchance, they had unwittingly sinned in thought. And if, when one is cutting wood, the axe-head flies from the handle and kills a man, the owner is [2] commanded to go to one of the cities of refuge and stay there until the high priest dies; that is to say, until he is redeemed by the Saviour's blood, either in the baptistery, or in penitence which is a copy of the grace

of baptism, through the ineffable mercy of the Saviour, who [3] would not have any one perish, nor delights in the death of sinners, but would rather that they should be converted and live.

C. It is surely strange justice to hold me guilty of a sin of error of which my conscience does not accuse itself. I am not aware that I have sinned, and am I to pay the penalty for an offence of which I am ignorant ? What more can I do, if I sin voluntarily ?

A. Do you expect me to explain the purposes and plans of God ? The Book of Wisdom gives an answer to your foolish question : [4] " Look not into things above thee, and search not things too mighty for thee." And elsewhere, [5] " Make not thyself overwise, and argue not more than is fitting." And in the same place, " In wisdom and simplicity of heart seek God." You will perhaps deny the authority of this book ; listen then to the Apostle blowing the Gospel trumpet : [6] " O the depth of the riches both of the wisdom and knowledge of God ! how unsearchable are His judgments, and His ways past tracing out ! For who hath known the mind of the Lord ? or who hath been His counsellor ?" Your questions are such as he elsewhere describes : [7] " But foolish and ignorant questioning avoid, knowing that they gender strifes." And in Ecclesiastes (a book concerning which there can be no doubt) we read, [8] " I said, I will be wise, but it was far from me. That which is exceeding deep, who can find it out ?" You ask me to tell you why the potter makes one vessel to honour, another to dishonour, and will not be satisfied with Paul, who replies on behalf of his Lord, [9] " O man, who art thou that repliest against God ?"

The remainder of this book is occupied by a series of quotations from the Old Testament, designed to show that it is not only the outer and conscious act which is reckoned sinful, but the opposition to the Divine will, which is often implicit and half-conscious. Occasionally, also, the speaker shows how the texts quoted enforce the argument which he has before used, that men may be spoken of as righteous in a general sense, yet by no means free from sins of thought or desire, if not of act.

The passages quoted are :

Gen. viii. 21. I will not curse the ground . . . . for the mind of man is set on evil from his youth.
    xvii. 17, xviii. 12. Abraham and Sarah laughing at the promise.
    xxxvii. 35. Jacob's excessive grief.
Exod. xxi. 12, 13. The guilt of one who slays another unawares.
Lev. iv. 2, 27. Offerings for sins of ignorance.
    v. 3. Offerings for ceremonial uncleanness.
    ix. 1. Offerings for Aaron at his consecration.
    xii. 6. Offerings for women after childbirth.
    xiv. 1, 6, xvi. 6, xii. 7. Offerings for the leper.
    xv. 31, xvi. 2. 5. Offerings for the people on the day of atonement.
    xxii. 14. Eating the hallowed things ignorantly ; compared with 1 Cor. xi. 27, 28, of careless participation
        in the Sacrament.
Numbers vi. 1. Offerings for the Nazarite.
    xiv. 7, vii. 28, 29. Offerings for imploring God's mercy.
    xxviii. 15, 22, xxix. 5, v. 11, 17. Offerings at the feasts.

---

[1] S. Matt. v. 28. [2] Numb. xxxv. 6. [3] Ezek. xviii. 23. [4] iii. 21. [5] Eccles. vii. 16. [6] Rom. xi. 33, 34.
[7] 2 Tim. ii. 23. [8] Eccles. vii. 24, 25. [9] Rom. ix. 20.

Numbers xxxv. 13. The cities of refuge provided for manslayers.
Deut. ix. 6, xviii. 13. Israel warned not to boast of righteousness.
    xviii. 9-12, v. 14, 15. Perfection used only of avoiding idolatry.
    xxii. 8. The housetop without a parapet makes a man guilty.
    xxiii. 2. Defilement from unconscious personal acts.
Josh. vii. 12. The people made guilty by the sin of Achan.
    xi. 19, 20. The racial guilt of the Canaanites.
1 Sam. xiv. 27. Jonathan made guilty by tasting the honey.
    xvi. 6. The Lord sees the heart, not the outward appearance.
2 Sam. iv. 11. Ishbosheth spoken of as righteous.
    vi. 7, 8. Uzzah smitten for carelessness.
    xxiv. 10. David's numbering the people.
1 Kings viii. 46. Solomon's prayer—There is none that sinneth not.
    xiv. 5. The prophet detecting the motive of Jeroboam's wife.
2 Kings iv. 27. Elijah seeing the Shunamite's heart.
1 Chron. ii. 32. Sept. Half-prophets.
Habakkuk iii. 1. Vulgate. A prayer " for sins of ignorance" (" upon Shigionoth "), supposed to be in recogni-
    tion of over-boldness in i. 2-4.
Ezek. xlvi. 20. The sacrifices of Ezekiel's restored temple.
Jer. x. 23. The way of man not in himself.
    xvii. 9. The heart deceitful.
Prov. xiv. 12. A way that seemeth right to a man.
    xix. 21. Many devices in a man's heart.
    xx. 9. Who can say, I have a clean heart ?
       17. Who will boast that he is clean ?
Eccl. vii. 16. The heart of man is full of wickedness.

Book II.

    This book can hardly be said to form part of a dialogue. It is rather an argument from Scripture to prove the point of the Augustinian arguer, Atticus. From the fourth chapter onwards it consists, like the last five chapters of Book I., of a chain of Scripture texts, taken from the New Testament and the Prophets, to show the universality of sin, and thus to refute the Pelagian assertion that a man can be without sin if he wills. We shall, therefore, give, as in the previous case, a list of the texts and the first words of them, only giving Jerome's words where he introduces some original remark of his own, or some noteworthy comment.

    The Pelagian begins by reiterating the dilemma : If the commandments are given to be obeyed, then man can be without sin ; if he is, by his creation, such that he must be a sinner, then God, not he, is the author of sin. To the argument that sacrifices are enjoined for sins of ignorance, he replies by appealing from the Old Testament to the New, which leads to a discussion (2, 3) on St. Paul's description of the conflict with sin, in Romans vii. Paul, it is argued, speaks not as a sinner, but as a *man*, and thus confesses the sinfulness of humanity. That men may be without ingrained vice is possible; that they can be without sin is not. This leads the Augustinian, Atticus, resuming his list of testimonies, to the fact that, though men are found who are righteous as avoiding wickedness (κακία), yet none is without sin (ἀναμάρτητος).

In Psalm xxxii. 5. One who speaks of himself as "holy," yet confesses his transgressions.
Prov. xxiv. 16. Explains this, " The righteous falls, but sins again."
    xviii. 17, LXX. and Vulgate. A righteous man accuses himself when he begins to speak.
Ps. lviii. 3. Sinners are estranged from the womb ; that is, either, as St. Paul says (Rom. v. 14), they sin " after
    the similitude of Adam "; or, " when Christ, as the firstborn, opened the Virgin's womb "(Exod. xiii.
    2). The heretics refused to acknowledge the mystery, which was prefigured by the Eastern door of the
    Temple (Ezek. xliv. 2), which closed again when once the High Priest had gone through it.[1]
Job iv. 17-21. Shall mortal man be just with God ?
    vii. 1. The life of man is temptation.
       20, 21. If I have sinned, what can I do ?
    ix. 15, 16. If I were righteous, he would not hear me.
       29-31. If I wash myself with snow water, etc.
    x. 15. If I be righteous, etc.
    xiv. 4, 5. Who will be free from uncleanness ? Not one.
Prov. xvi. 26, LXX. Man toileth in sorrow.
Job xl. 4. What shall I answer thee ?
Prov. xx. 9. " Who will boast that he has a clean heart ?" which shows at least that the commandments are
    not easy, as Pelagius says they are.
1 John v. 3. " His commandments are not grievous," and
Matt. xi. 30. " My yoke is easy," are true only in comparison with Judaism, and should be compared with
Acts xv. 10. A yoke . . . which neither our fathers nor we were able to bear.
James iv. 11. " Thou judgest the law," that is, if you say that the condemnation of sins of ignorance is un-
    reasonable. That we all sin in such ways is evident from

---

[1] There was an early and widespread belief, afterwards confirmed by a decree of the Council of Ephesus, that the birth of Christ was by miracle, not by a true and proper parturition.

James i. 20.   "The wrath of man worketh not the righteousness of God."   But anger is constantly condemned
          as in
Prov. xv. 1, LXX.   "Wrath destroys even wise men."
Eph. iv. 26.   Let not the sun go down upon your wrath.
Matt. v. 22.   He who is angry . . . shall be in danger of the council.
Eccles. xi. 19.   "I am the most foolish of all men."   This is said by Christ in the person of humanity.   So
Ps. lxix. 5.   "God, Thou knowest my foolishness."   But
1 Cor. i. 25.   The foolishness of God is wiser than men.
Ecclus. i. 18.   "In much wisdom is much grief," shows the wise man's sense of imperfection.   So
     viii. 7.   "I hated my life," and
        14.   "There be righteous men unto whom it happeneth according to the work of the wicked;" that is,
                God sees evil where we do not.
        17.   "However much a man may labour, yet he shall not find it ;" and
     ix. 2, 3.   There is one event to all.   The heart . . . is full of evil.
     x. 1.   "Dead flies cause the ointment to stink ;" that is, almost every one is defiled by heresy or other faults.
1 Pet. ii. 17, 18.   Judgment must begin at the house of God.

6. There are four emotions which agitate mankind, two relating to the present, two to the future; two to good, and two to evil. There is sorrow, called in Greek λύπη, and joy, in Greek χαρά or ἡδονή, although many translate the latter word by *voluptas*, pleasure ; the one of which is referred to evil, the other to good. And we go too far if we rejoice over such things as we ought not, as, for example, riches, power, distinctions, the bad fortune of enemies, or their death ; or, on the other hand, if we are tortured with grief on account of present evils, adversity, exile, poverty, weakness, and the death of kindred, all of which is forbidden by the Apostle. And again, if we covet those things which we consider good, inheritance, distinctions, unvaried prosperity, bodily health, and the like, in the possession of which we rejoice and find enjoyment ; or if we fear those things which we deem adverse. Now, according to the Stoics, Zeno that is to say and Chrysippus, it is possible for a perfect man to be free from these emotions ; according to the Peripatetics, it is difficult and even impossible, an opinion which has the constant support of all Scripture. Hence Josephus, the historian of the Maccabees, said that the emotions can be subdued and governed, not extirpated, and Cicero's five books of "Tusculan Disputations" are full of these discussions. [1]According to the Apostle, the weakness of the body and spiritual hosts of wickedness in the heavenly places fight against us. And the same writer [2] tells us that the works of the flesh and the works of the spirit are manifest, and these are contrary the one to the other, so that we do not the things that we would. If we do not what we would, but what we would not, how can you say that a man can be without sin if he chooses ? You see that neither an Apostle, nor any believer can perform what he wishes. [3]"Love covereth a multitude of sins," not so much sins of the past as sins of the present, that we may not sin any more while the love of God abideth in us. Wherefore it is said concerning the woman that was a sinner, [4]"Her sins which are many are forgiven her, for she loved much." And this shows us that the doing what we wish does not depend merely upon our own power, but upon the assistance which God in His mercy gives to our. will.

7. The quotations from Scripture are now continued :

In 1 John i. 5, John i. 7, 8, Matt. v. 14, Christ and the Apostles are called the Light of the world.   The world
          therefore is in darkness.
1 Tim. vi. 16.   God only hath immortality and is "only wise"; yet others, like the Prince of Tyre (Ezek.
          xxviii. 3), are wise derivatively.   So we are pure, but only by grace.   Thus
1 John i. 7.   The blood of Christ cleanses us.
Job xxv. 5, 6.   The stars are not pure in His sight.
Gal. ii. 16.   "By the law no flesh shall be justified ;" but
Rom. iii. 1, 24, 28, 30.   Being justified freely through His grace, etc.
     vi. 14.   Not under the law, but under grace.
     ix. 16.   Not of him that willeth, but of God which showeth mercy.
     ix. 30–32.   The Gentiles . . . attained to the righteousness by faith
     x. 2.   Christ is the end of the law to every one that believeth.

8. The Apostle confesses his need of this grace for his work.

1 Cor. i. 1–3.   Grace to you from God.
     7, 8.   That ye come behind in no gift—that no flesh may glory in His sight.
     iii. 6–10.   Paul planted . . . but God gave the increase.
        18, 19.   If any man thinketh himself to be wise, let him become a fool.
     iv. 4.   I know nothing against myself, yet am I not hereby justified.
        7.   What have ye that ye did not receive ?
        19.   I will come to you, *if the Lord will.*

9. The Apostle shows also his need of grace for himself.

---

[1] Eph. vi. 12.   [2] Gal. v. 19   [3] 1 Pet. iv. 8.   [4] Luke vii. 47.

1 Cor. xv. 9, 10. By the grace of God I am what I am, etc.
2 Cor. iii. 4–6. Our sufficiency is of God.
Gal. ii. 16. We have believed, that we might be justified by faith.
    ii. 21. If righteousness come by the law, Christ is dead for nought.
    iii. 10, 13. Christ hath redeemed us from the curse of the law.
        24. The law our teacher to bring us to Christ.
    v. 4. Ye are severed from Christ, ye that would be justified by the law.

    10.

Phil. ii. 13. It is God that worketh in you.
2 Thess. iii. 3. The Lord is faithful, He shall establish you.
1 Tim. vi. 20, 21. O Timothy, guard that which is committed unto thee.
Tit. iii. 4–7. The kindness and mercy of God our Saviour saved us.

    11. We now turn to the Gospels "and supplement the flickering flame of the Apostolic light with the brightness of the lamp of Christ."

Matt. v. 22. "Every man who is angry . . . shall be in danger of the council." Which of us is not here condemned?
    23, 24. "First be reconciled to thy brother." Who is there that finds this command easy?
    37. "Let your speech be Yea, yea, Nay, nay." Who has ever kept this commandment? The Psalmist says
Ps. cxvi. 11. All men are liars.

    12.

Matt. vi. 34. "Be not anxious for to-morrow." Do you fulfil this?
    vii. 14. "Narrow is the gate which leadeth to life." How can you say that the commandments are easy?
Luke ix. 58. "The Son of Man hath not where to lay His head." This is interpreted by
Is. xxviii. 12. "Receive him that is weary, and this is my rest ;" and
Is. lxvi. 1, 2. "On whom shall I rest but on him that is humble?" Christ finds few on whom to rest. How then can His commands be said to be easy?
Matt. ix. 12, 13. "I came not to call the righteous." "They that are whole need not the physician." Had the world not been full of sin, Christ would not have come. So
Ps. xii. 1. Help, Lord, for the godly man ceaseth.
    xiv. 1, 3. They are corrupt . . . none doeth good.
Matt. x. 9. "Get you no gold . . . nor shoes." Who has fulfilled this? Not even the Apostles, for
Acts xii. 8. The angel bids Peter to bind on his sandals.

    13.

Matt. x. 22–34. Describes the persecutions of Christ's followers, and gives the command to take up the cross. Are these easy?
    xiv. 31. Even Peter's faith fails, and he begins to sink.
    xv. 19, 20. Out of the heart came evil thoughts, etc.
    xvi. 25. Whosoever will lose his life will find it.
    xviii. 7. "Woe to the man through whom stumbling cometh." But
James iii. 2. In many things we all stumble or err.
Phil. ii. 21. All seek their own.
Matt. xix. 21. The young lawyer had kept all the law, yet failed.
    xxiii. 26–28. The woes on the Pharisees fall in their measure upon all.

    14.

Matt. xxvi. 39. "Not as I will, but as Thou will." Yet Critobulus says, by his own will he can do right.
Mark xiv. 37. "Could ye not watch with me one hour?" They could not.
    vi. 5. He could do no mighty works because of their unbelief.
    vii. 24. "He went into the borders of Tyre and Sidon." If Christ could not do as he wished, how can we?
    ix. 5. Peter's request at the Transfiguration shows his ignorance.
    xiii. 32. Even the Son knows not all things ; how then can we?
    xiv. 35. If it be possible. How can you say it is possible every hour to avoid sin?

    15.

Mark xvi. 14. Even the Apostles showed unbelief and hardness of heart.
1 John v. 19. The world lieth in the evil one.
Luke i. 20. Even Zacharias disbelieved God's message.
Matt. xvii. 15. The disciples could not relieve the lunatic, because of unbelief.
Mark iv. 34. The disciples' dispute about precedence.
Luke ix. 54. James and John show a vindictive spirit.
    xiv. 26, 27. The commands to forsake all and take up the cross are not easy.
    xvi. 15. That which is exalted among men is abomination in the sight of God.
    xvii. 1. It is impossible but that occasions of stumbling should come.
    xvii. 6. The Apostles' faith was not even like a grain of mustard seed.
James iii. 2.
Matt. xvii. 19.

    16.

Luke xviii. 1. We are always to pray. This shows our weakness.
    27. Who, then, can be saved? It is possible, but to God only.
    xxii. 24. The contest for precedence at the last supper.
    31, 32. Peter's faith almost overcome by Satan.

Luke xxii. 43.   Even Christ in his agony needs an angel to strengthen Him.
     46.   Pray that ye enter not into temptation.

17.

John v. 30.   Even Christ says, " I cannot do anything by myself "; and
   vii. 10.   Was irresolute about going up to the Feast of Tabernacles.
     19.   None of you doeth the law.
   viii. 3.   None of the accusers of the woman taken in adultery were without sin.   Christ wrote their names in the earth (Jerem. xvii. 13).
   x. 8.   All who came (not who were sent ; Jerem. xiv. 15) before Christ were robbers.
   xvii. 12.   I kept them—they did not keep themselves.
Acts xv. 39.   Paul and Barnabas quarrelled.
   xvi. 6, 7.   They were forbidden to preach where they chose.

18. Even the Apostles, with their full light, show their dependence on grace.

Acts xvii. 30.   The times before Christ were times of ignorance.
1 Cor. iv. 19.   I will come *if the Lord will.*
James ii. 10.   To stumble in one point is to be guilty of all.
   iii. 2.   In many things we all stumble.
     8.   The tongue is a deadly poison.

19.

James iv. 1.   Wars arise from our lust.   David indeed said,
Ps. xxvi. 2.   " Examine me and prove me," etc.   This self-confidence led to his fall.
   li. 1.   Have mercy on me, O God.
   lxxx. 5.   " Thou feedest us with the bread of tears."   Similarly
Ps. xxx. 6, 7.   I said I shall never be moved . . . Thou didst hide Thy face.
   xxxii. 5.   I said I will confess my sin,
   xxxvii. 5, 6.   *He* shall make thy righteousness as the light.
     39.   The salvation of the righteous *is of the Lord.*
   xxxviii. 7.   There is no soundness in my flesh.
Rom. vii. 18.   In my flesh dwelleth no good thing.
Ps. xxxviii. 8.   Vulgate. My loins are filled with deceits.
   xxxix. 5.   He hath made our days as handbreadths.
   lxix. 5.   My sins are not hid from thee.
   lxxvii. 2.   My soul refused to be comforted.
     10.   This is the changing of the right hand of the Most High.[1]

20.

Ps. lxxxix. 2.   Mercy shall be *built up* forever.
   xci. 6.   From " the thing [2] that walketh in darkness " who can be free ?   For
   xi. 2.   " The wicked bend their bow "—an image of the heretics.
   xcii. 14.   Those that are planted in the house of the Lord shall flourish.
   ciii. 8, 10.   The Lord is full of compassion.
2 Sam. viii. 13, 14.   David receives the promises with the humble confession of his weakness.   " Is this the law of man, O God ? "
   xvi. 10.   He humbles himself under Abishai's violence and Shimei's curse.
   xvii. 14.   And is delivered only by God's confounding the counsel of Ahithophel.
1 Kings xiv. 8.   It was God who gave Jeroboam the kingdom.

21.

1 Kings xv. 11.   Asa, though a good man, was faulty.
     xix. 4.   Elijah fled from Jezebel.
Ps. cxviii. 6.   The Lord is my keeper.
2 Chron. xvii. 3.   Jehoshaphat prospers because the Lord is with him.   Yet
   xix. 2.   He is rebuked for joining with Ahab.
2 Chron. xxii. 9.   Ahaziah received burial among kings because descended from righteous Jehoshaphat.
2 Kings xviii. 3. 4, 7.   Hezekiah did great things, but only through the Lord's help.
     14.   He gave the consecrated gold to the king of Assyria.

22. Even the best kings of Judah were imperfect.

2 Kings xx. 1, 5.   Hezekiah wept when death was at hand, and recovered through special mercy.
     13, 17.   But he sinned in receiving the Babylonian envoys.
2 Chron. xxxii. 26.   He fell by the lifting up of his heart.
   xxxiv. 2.   Josiah was a righteous man ; yet
     22, 23.   He needed the aid of Huldah ; and
   xxxv. 22.   He was slain through not heeding God's warning ; and

23. The prophets also are weak and sinful.

Lam. iv. 20.   Jeremiah [3] lamented his fall.
Numb. xx. 10, 12.   Moses is punished for his sin at Meribah.   This is the meaning of
Ps. cxli. 6.   Vulgate. Their judges were swallowed up, joined to the Rock, etc.

---

[1] Vulgate, Rev. V. I will remember the years, etc. Marg.—The right hand of the Most High doth change.
[2] LXX. A. V. Pestilence.   [3] The words of the Lamentations refer to Zedekiah.

Hosea ii. 19.   God in mercy forgives Israel's unfaithfulness.
     xi. 9.   " I will not enter into the city."   Only the Holy One is not joined to the mass of ungodliness.
Amos vi. 13.   We turn righteousness into wormwood.
Jonah i. 14.   The sailors confess that God is just in raising the storm.
Micah vii. 2.   The godly man is perished from the earth, etc.
     vi. 8.   The command of justice, mercy, and a humble walk with God is only possible to humble faith, for
Ps. cxl. 6.   " The wicked walk on every side," and
James iv. 6.   God giveth grace to the humble.

     24.

Habakkuk iii. 16.   Let rottenness enter into my bones, if only I may rest, etc.
Zech. iii. 1.   Joshua is represented as clothed in filthy garments, and is freed through God's mercy.

But Jovinian's heir says " I am quite free from sin, I have no filthy garments, I am governed by my own will, I am greater than an Apostle. The Apostle does what he would not, and what he would he does not ; but I do what I will, and what I would not I do not : the kingdom of heaven has been prepared for me, or rather I have by my virtuous life prepared it for myself. Adam was subject to punishment, and so are others who think themselves guilty after the similitude of Adam's transgressions ; I and my crew alone have nothing to fear. Other men shut up in their cells and who never see women, because, poor creatures ! they do not listen to my words, are tormented with desire : crowds of women may surround me, I feel no stirring of concupiscence. For to me may be applied the [1] words, ' Holy stones are rolled upon the ground,' and the reason why I am insensible to the attraction of sin is that in the power of free will I carry Christ's trophy about with me." But let us listen to God [2] proclaiming by the mouth of Isaiah : " O my people, they which call thee happy cause thee to err, and destroy the way of thy paths." Who is the greatest subverter of the people of God—he who, relying on the power of free choice, despises the help of the Creator, and is satisfied with following his own will, or he who dreads to be judged by the details of the Lord's commandments ? To men of this sort, God [3] says, " Woe unto you that are wise in your own eyes, and prudent in your own sight." Isaiah, if we follow the Hebrew, laments [4] and says, " Woe is me because I have been silent, because I am a man of unclean lips : and I dwell in the midst of a people of unclean lips, for mine eyes have seen the Lord of Hosts." He for his meritorious and virtuous life enjoyed the sight of God, and conscious of his sins confessed that he had unclean lips. Not that he had said anything repugnant to the will of God, but because, either from fear, or from a deep sense of shame, he had been [5] silent, and had not reproved the errors of the people so freely as a prophet should. When do we sinners rebuke offenders, we who flatter wealth and accept the persons of sinners for the sake of filthy lucre ? for we shall hardly say that we speak with perfect frankness to men of whose assistance we stand in need. Suppose that we do not such things as they, suppose we keep ourselves from every form of sin ; to refrain from speaking the truth is certainly sin. In the Septuagint, however, we do not find the words " because I have been silent," but " because I was pricked," that is with the consciousness of sin ; and thus the words of the [6]prophet are fulfilled. " My life was turned into misery while I was pierced by the thorn." He was pricked by the thorn of sin : you are decked with the flowers of virtue. [7] " The moon shall be ashamed, and the sun confounded, when the Lord shall punish the host of heaven on high." This is explained by another passage. [8] " Even the stars are unclean in His sight ;" and again, [9] " He chargeth His angels with folly." The moon is ashamed, the sun is confounded, and the sky covered with sackcloth, and shall we fearlessly and joyously, as though we were free from all sin, face the majesty of the Judge, when the mountains shall melt away, that is, all who are lifted up by pride, and all the host of the heavens, whether they be stars, or angelic powers, when the heavens shall be rolled together as a scroll, and all their host shall fade away like leaves ?

The argument is now carried on mostly by the quotation of passages from the prophets :

     25.

Is. xxxiv. 5.   " My sword hath drunk its fill in the heavens.   It will come down in Edom."   How much more
          is there wrath against sin on earth !   Edom means blood, which cannot inherit the kingdom (1 Cor. xv. 50).
     xlv. 9.   Woe unto him who striveth with his Maker.
     liii. 6.   We have all gone astray like sheep.
Ezek. xvi. 14.   Jerusalem is perfect in beauty ; yet

---

[1] Zech. ix. 16, Sept.   Correctly, they (God's people) shall be as the stones of a crown lifting themselves up (or glittering) upon His land.
[2] Is. iii. 12.   [3] v. 21.   [4] vi. 5.
[5] That is, according to Jerome's rendering of the Hebrew.   R. V. has " I am undone."   For the Sept. rendering see below.
[6] Ps. xxxii. 4.   [7] Is. xxiv. 21.   [8] Job xxv. 5.   [9] Job iv. 18.

Ezek. xvi. 60, 61. Her salvation is not of merit but of mercy.
Nahum i. 3. Though he cleanse,[1] yet will he not make thee innocent.
1 Cor. xv. 9. I am not worthy—because I persecuted.
Ezek. xx. 43, 44. When pardoned, Jerusalem will still remember her sin.

Let us confess with shame that these are the utterances of men who have already won their reward ; sinners upon earth, and still in our frail and mortal bodies let us adopt the language of the saints in heaven who have even been endowed with incorruption and immortality. [2] " And ye say the way of the Lord is not equal, when your ways are not equal." It is Pharisaic pride to attribute to the injustice of the Creator sins which are due to our own will, and to slander His righteousness. The sons of Zadok, the priests of the spiritual temple, that is the Church, [3] go not out to the people in their ministerial robes, lest by human intercourse they may lose their holiness and be defiled. And do you suppose that you, in the thick of the throng, and an ordinary individual, are pure ?

26. Let us hastily run through the prophet Jeremiah :

Jerem. v. 1, 2. Is there any that doeth justly, etc.
    vii. 21, 22. God rejects the sacrifices, because of the worshippers' evil lives.
    xiii. 23. Can the Ethiopian change his skin ?

27.

Jerem. xvii. 14. " Heal me, O Lord." Otherwise Jeremiah could only say, as in the text next quoted,
    xx. 14, 17, 18. Cursed be the day wherein I was born, etc.
    xxiii. 23. Am I a God at hand, etc. So conscious is he of God's power.
    xxiv. 6, 7. God, not they themselves, will plant them, etc.
    xxvi. 21-24. Jeremiah needed the help of Ahikam. How much more do we need that of God.

28.

Jerem. xxxi. 34. The promise of the new covenant.
    xxxii. 30. The children of Israel have perpetually done evil.
    xxxvii. 18, 19. Yet Jeremiah himself trembled before Zedekiah.
    xxx. 10, 11. Fear not, O Jacob, for *I am with thee.*

29.

Amos vi. 14. " We have taken us horns by our own strength." These are the boasts of heretics. But
Is. xvi. 6. His strength (Moab's) is by no means according to his arrogance.[4]
Jerem. i. 7, 20. Men's sin will only be abolished because God is gracious to them. If you will abandon your assertions of natural ability, I will concede that your whole contention stands good, but only by the gift of God.
Lam. iii. 26–42. It is good that a man should quietly wait for the salvation of the Lord.

30.

Dan. iv. 17. The Most High ruleth in the kingdom of men.
Ps. cxiii. 7. 8. He raiseth up the poor out of the dust.
Is. xl. 17. He doeth what He will in heaven and in earth.

The words of 2 Maccabees v. 17, which say that Antiochus Epiphanes had power to overthrow the Temple, " because of the multitude of sins," are quoted in connection with the confessions of Daniel.

Dan. ix. 5. " We have sinned and dealt perversely," which is shown by
    20. " While I was yet praying," etc., to be a personal, not only a national confession.
    24. The prophecy of the seventy weeks shows that the prophet looked to God alone for the establishment of righteousness.

So then, until that end shall come, and this corruptible and mortal shall put on incorruption and immortality, we must be liable to sin ; not, as you falsely say, owing to the fault of our nature and creation, but through the frailty and fickleness of human will, which varies from moment to moment ; because God alone changeth not. You ask in what respects Abel, Enoch, Joshua the son of Nun, or Elisha, and the rest of the saints have sinned. There is no need to look for a knot in a bulrush ; I freely confess I do not know ; and I only wish that, when sins are manifest, I might still be silent. [5] " I know nothing against myself," says St. Paul, " yet am I not hereby justified." [6] " Man looketh on the outward appearance, but the Lord looketh on the heart." Before Him no man is justified. And so Paul says confidently, [7] " All have sinned, and come short of the glory of God "; and [8] " God hath shut up all under sin that He may have mercy upon all "; and similarly in other passages which we have repeated again and again.

---

[1] *Mundans :* not in the Vulgate nor in A. V.
[2] Ezek. xxxii. 17.
[3] Ibid. xliv. 15, 16.
[4] This is the sense of the Vulgate, but not the exact words.
[5] 1 Cor. iv. 4.
[6] 1 Sam. xvi. 7.
[7] Rom. iii. 23.
[8] Gal. iii. 22.

Book III.

1. Critob. I am charmed with the exuberance of your eloquence, but at the same time I would remind you that,[1] "In the multitude of words there wanteth not transgression." And how does it bear upon the question before us? You will surely admit that those who have received Christian baptism are without sin. And that being free from sin they are righteous. And that once they are righteous, they can, if they take care, preserve their righteousness, and so through life avoid all sin.

Attic. Do you not blush to follow the opinion of Jovinian, which has been exploded and condemned? For he relies upon just the same proofs and arguments as you do; nay, rather, you are all eagerness for his inventions, and desire to preach in the East what was formerly[2] condemned at Rome, and not long ago in[3] Africa. Read then the reply which was given to him, and you will there find the answer to yourself. For in the discussion of doctrines and disputed points, we must have regard not to persons but to things. And yet let me tell you that baptism condones past offences, and does not preserve righteousness in the time to come; the keeping of that is dependent on toil and industry, as well as earnestness, and above all on the mercy of God. It is ours to ask, to Him it belongs to bestow what we ask; ours to begin, His it is to finish; ours to offer what we can, His to fulfil what we cannot perform. [4] "For except the Lord build the house, they labour in vain that build it. Except the Lord keep the city, the watchman waketh but in vain." Wherefore the Apostle[5] bids us so run that we may attain. All indeed run, but one receiveth the crown. And in the[6] Psalm it is written, "O Lord, thou hast crowned us with thy favour as with a shield." For our victory is won and the crown of our victory is gained by His protection and through His shield; and here we run that hereafter we may attain; there he shall receive the crown who in this world has proved the conqueror. And when we have been baptized we are told, [7] "Behold thou art made whole; sin no more lest a worse thing happen unto thee." And again, [8] "Know ye not that ye are a temple of God, and that the Spirit of God dwelleth in you? If any man profane the temple of God, him shall God destroy." And in another place,[1] "The Lord is with you so long as ye are with Him: if ye forsake Him, He will also forsake you." Where is the man, do you suppose, in whom as in a shrine and sanctuary the purity of Christ is permanent, and in whose case the serenity of the temple is saddened by no cloud of sin? We cannot always have the same countenance, though the philosophers falsely boast that this was the experience of Socrates; how much less can our minds be always the same! As men have many expressions of countenance, so also do the feelings of their hearts vary. If it were possible for us to be always immersed in the waters of baptism, sins would fly over our heads and leave us untouched. The Holy Spirit would protect us. But the enemy assails us, and when conquered does not depart, but is ever lying in ambush, that he may secretly shoot the upright in heart.

2. In the Gospel according to the Hebrews, which is written in the Chaldee and Syrian language, but in Hebrew characters, and is used by the Nazarenes to this day (I mean the Gospel according to the Apostles, or, as is generally maintained, the Gospel according to Matthew, a copy of which is in the library at Cæsarea), we find, "Behold, the mother of our Lord and His brethren said to Him, John Baptist baptizes for the remission of sins; let us go and be baptized by him. But He said to them, what sin have I committed that I should go and be baptized by him? Unless, haply, the very words which I have said are only ignorance." And in the same volume, "If thy brother sin against thee in word, and make amends to thee, receive him seven times in a day." Simon, His disciple, said to Him, "Seven times in a day?" The Lord answered and said to him, "I say unto thee until seventy times seven." Even the prophets, after they were anointed with the Holy Spirit, were guilty of sinful words. Ignatius, an apostolic man and a martyr, boldly writes,[2] "The Lord chose Apostles who were sinners above all men." It is of their speedy conversion that the Psalmist sings,[3] "Their infirmities were multiplied; afterwards they made haste." If you do not allow the authority of this evidence, at least admit its antiquity, and see what has been the opinion of all good churchmen. Suppose a person who has

---

[1] Prov. x. 19.
[2] By a Synod under Siricius in A.D. 390.
[3] The allusion is to the African Synod, held A.D. 412, at which Celestius was condemned and excommunicated.
[4] Ps. cxxvii. 1.　　[5] 1 Cor. ix. 24.　　[6] v. 12.
[7] John v. 14.　　[8] 1 Cor. iii. 16, 17.

[1] 2 Chron. xv. 2.
[2] The words are those of S. Barnabas. Possibly in Jerome's copy the passage may have been attributed to Ignatius.
[3] Ps. xvi. 4. Sept. and Vulgate.

been baptized to have been carried off by death either immediately, or on the very day of his baptism, and I will generously concede that he neither thought nor said anything whereby, through error and ignorance, he fell into sin. Does it follow that he will, therefore, be without sin, because he appears not to have overcome, but to have avoided sin? Is not the true reason rather that by the mercy of God he was released from the prison of sins and departed to the Lord? We also say this, that God can do what He wills; and that man of himself and by his own will cannot, as you maintain, be without sin. If he can, it is idle for you now to add the word grace, for, with such a power, he has no need of it. If, however, he cannot avoid sin without the grace of God, it is folly for you to attribute to him an ability which he does not possess. For whatever depends upon another's will, is not in the power of him whose ability you assert, but of him whose aid is clearly indispensable.

3. C. What do you mean by this perversity, or, rather, senseless contention? Will you not grant me even so much—that when a man leaves the waters of baptism he is free from sin?

A. Either I fail to express my meaning clearly, or you are slow of apprehension.

C. How so?

A. Remember both what you maintained and also what I say. You argued that a man can be free from sin if he chooses. I reply that it is an impossibility; not that we are to think that a man is not free from sin immediately after baptism, but that that time of sinlessness is by no means to be referred to human ability, but to the grace of God. Do not, therefore, claim the power for man, and I will admit the fact. For how can a man be able who is not able of himself? Or what is that sinlessness which is conditioned by the immediate death of the body? Should the man's life be prolonged, he will certainly be liable to sins and to ignorance.

C. Your logic stops my mouth. You do not speak with Christian simplicity, but entangle me in some fine distinctions between being and ability to be.

A. Is it I who play these tricks with words? The article came from your own workshop. For you say, not that a man is free from sin, but that he is able to be; I, on the other hand, will grant what you deny, that a man is free from sin by the grace of God, and yet will maintain that he is not able of himself.

C. It is useless to give commandments if we cannot keep them.

A. No one doubts that God commanded things possible. But because men do not what they might, therefore the whole world is subject to the judgment of God, and needs His mercy. On the other hand, if you can produce a man who has fulfilled the whole law, you will certainly be able to show that there is a man who does not need the mercy of God. For everything which can happen must either take place in the past, the present, or the future. As to your assertion that a man can be without sin if he chooses, show that it has happened in the past, or at all events that it does happen at the present day; the future will reveal itself. If, however, you can point to no one who either is, or has been, altogether free from sin, it remains for us to confine our discussion to the future. Meanwhile, you are vanquished and a captive as regards two out of three periods of time, the past and the present. If anyone hereafter shall be greater than patriarchs, prophets, apostles, inasmuch as he is without sin, then you may perhaps be able to convince future generations as to their time.

4. C. Talk as you like, argue as you please, you will never wrest from me free will, which God bestowed once for all, nor will you be able to deprive me of what God has given, the ability if I have the will.

A. By way of example let us take one proof: [1] "I have found David, the Son of Jesse, a man after Mine own heart, who shall do all My will." There is no doubt that David was a holy man, and yet he who was chosen that he might do all God's will is blamed for certain actions. Of course it was possible for him who was chosen for the purpose to do all God's will. Nor is God to blame Who beforehand spoke of his doing all His will as commanded, but blame does attach to him who did not what was foretold. For God did not say that He had found a man who would unfailingly do His bidding and fulfil His will, but only one who would do all His will. And we, too, say that a man can avoid sinning, if he chooses, according to his local and temporal circumstances and physical weakness, so long as his mind is set upon righteousness and the string is well stretched upon the lyre. But if a man grow a little remiss it is with him as with the boatman pulling against the stream, who finds that, if he slackens but for a moment, the craft glides back and he is carried by the flowing waters whither he would not. Such is the state of man; if we are a little careless we learn our weakness, and find that our power is limited. Do you suppose that the Apostle Paul, when he wrote[2] "the coat (or cloak) that I left at Troas with Carpus, bring when thou comest, and the books, especially

---

[1] Acts xiii. 32; Ps. lxxxviii. 21. [2] 2 Tim. iv. 13.

the parchments," was thinking of heavenly mysteries, and not of those things which are required for daily life and to satisfy our bodily necessities? Find me a man who is never hungry, thirsty, or cold, who knows nothing of pain, or fever, or the torture of strangury, and I will grant you that a man can think of nothing but virtue. When the Apostle was [1] struck by the servant, he delivered himself thus against the High Priest who commanded the blow to be given : " God shall strike thee, thou whited wall." We miss the patience of the Saviour Who was led as a lamb to the slaughter, and opened not His mouth, but mercifully said to the smiter, [2]"If I have spoken evil, bear witness of the evil ; but if well, why smitest thou Me ?" We do not disparage the Apostle, but declare the glory of God Who suffered in the flesh and overcame the evil inflicted on the flesh and the weakness of the flesh—to say nothing of what the Apostle says elsewhere : [3] "Alexander, the coppersmith, did me much evil ; the Lord, the righteous Judge, will recompense him in that day."

5. C. I have been longing to say something, but have checked the words as they were bursting from my lips. You compel me to say it.

A. Who hinders you from saying what you think ? Either what you are going to say is good—and you ought not to deprive us of what is good—or it is bad, and, therefore, it is not regard for us, but shame that keeps you silent.

C. I will say, I will say after all, what I think. Your whole argument tends to this : You accuse nature, and blame God for creating man such as he is.

A. Is this what you wished, and yet did not wish, to say ? Pray speak out, so that all may have the benefit of your wisdom. Are you censuring God because he made man to be man ? Let the angels also complain because they are angels: Let every creature discuss the question, Why it is as it was created ? and not what the Creator could have made it. I must now amuse myself with the rhetorical exercises of childhood, and passing from the gnat and the ant to cherubim and seraphim, inquire why each was not created with a happier lot. And when I reach the exalted powers, I will argue the point : Why God alone is only God, and did not make all things gods? For, according to you, He will either be unable to do so, or will be guilty of envy. Censure Him, and demand why He allows the devil to be in this world, and carry off the crown when you have won the victory.

C. I am not so senseless as to complain of the existence of the devil, through whose malice death entered into the world ; but what grieves me is this : that dignitaries of the Church, and those who usurp the title of master, destroy free will ; and once that is destroyed, the way is open for the Manichæans.

A. Am I the destroyer of free will because, throughout the discussion, my single aim has been to maintain the omnipotence of God as well as free will?

C. How can you have free will, and yet say that man can do nothing without God's assistance ?

A. If he is to be blamed who couples free will and God's help, it follows that we ought to praise him who does away with God's help.

C. I am not making God's help unnecessary, for to His grace we owe all our ability ; but I and those who think with me keep both within their own bounds. To God's grace we assign the gift of the power of free choice ; to our own will, the doing, or the not doing, of a thing ; and thus rewards and punishments for doing or not doing can be maintained.

6. A. You seem to me to be lost in forgetfulness, and to be going over the lines of argument already traversed as though not a word had been previously said. For, by this long discussion, it has been established that the Lord, by the same grace wherewith He bestowed upon us free choice, assists and supports us in our individual actions.

C. Why, then, does He crown and praise what He has Himself wrought in us ?

A. That is to say, our will which offered all it could, the toil which strove in action, and the humility which ever looked to the help of God.

C. So, then, if we have not done what He commanded, either God was willing to assist us, or He was not. If He was willing and did assist us, and yet we have not done what we wished, then He, and not we, has been overcome. But if He would not help, the man is not to be blamed who wished to do His will, but God, who was able to help, but would not.

A. Do you not see that your dilemma has landed you in a deep abyss of blasphemy ? Whichever way you take it, God is either weak or malevolent, and He is not so much praised because He is the author of good and gives His help, as abused for not restraining evil. Blame Him, then, because He allows the existence of the devil, and has suffered, and still suffers, evil to be done in the world. This is what Marcion asks, and the whole pack of heretics who mutilate the Old

[1] Acts xxiii. 2 sq.   [2] S. John xviii. 23.   [3] 2 Tim. iv. 14.

Testament, and have mostly spun an argument something like this : Either God knew that man, placed in Paradise, would transgress His command, or He did not know. If He knew, man is not to blame, who could not avoid God's foreknowledge, but He Who created him such that he could not escape the knowledge of God. If He did not know, in stripping Him of foreknowledge you also take away His divinity. Upon the same showing God will be deserving of blame for choosing Saul, who was to prove one of the worst of kings. And the Saviour must be convicted either of ignorance, or of unrighteousness, inasmuch as He said in the Gospel, [1] "Did I not choose you the twelve, and one of you is a devil?" Ask Him why He chose Judas, a traitor? Why He entrusted to him the bag when He knew that he was a thief? Shall I tell you the reason? God judges the present, not the future. He does not make use of His foreknowledge to condemn a man though He knows that he will hereafter displease Him; but such is His goodness and unspeakable mercy that He chooses a man who, He perceives, will meanwhile be good, and who, He knows, will turn out badly, thus giving him the opportunity of being converted and of repenting. This is the Apostle's meaning when he says,[2] "Dost thou not know that the goodness of God leadeth thee to repentance? but after thy hardness and impenitent heart treasurest up for thyself wrath in the day of wrath and revelation of the righteous judgment of God, Who will render to every man according to his works." For Adam did not sin because God knew that he would do so; but God, inasmuch as He is God, foreknew what Adam would do of his own free choice. You may as well accuse God of falsehood because He said by the mouth of Jonah : [3] "Yet three days, and Nineveh shall be overthrown." But God will reply by the mouth of Jeremiah, [4] "At what instant I shall speak concerning a nation, and concerning a kingdom, to pluck up, and to break down, and to destroy it; if that nation, concerning which I have spoken, turn from their evil, I will repent of the evil that I thought to do unto them. And at what instant I shall speak concerning a nation, and concerning a kingdom, to build and to plant it ; if it do evil in my sight, that it obey not my voice, then I will repent of the good, wherewith I said I would benefit them." Jonah, on a certain occasion, was indignant because, at God's command, he had spoken falsely ; but his sorrow was proved to be ill founded, since he would rather speak truth

and have a countless multitude perish, than speak falsely and have them saved. His position was thus illustrated : [1] "Thou grievest over the ivy (or gourd), for the which thou hast not laboured, neither madest it grow, which came up in a night, and perished in a night ; and should not I have pity on Nineveh, that great city, wherein are more than six score thousand persons that cannot discern between their right hand and their left hand?" If there was so vast a number of children and simple folk, whom you will never be able to prove sinners, what shall we say of those inhabitants of both sexes who were at different periods of life? According to Philo, and the wisest of philosophers, Plato (so the "Timæus" tells us), in passing from infancy to decrepit old age, we go through seven stages, which so gradually and so gently follow one another that we are quite insensible of the change.

C. The drift of your whole argument is this—what the Greeks call αὐτέξουσιον, and we free will, you admit in terms, but in effect destroy. For you make God the author of sin, in asserting that man can of himself do nothing, but that he must have the help of God to Whom is imputed all we do. But we say that, whether a man does good or evil, it is imputed to him on account of the faculty of free choice, inasmuch as he did what he chose, and not to Him Who once for all gave him free choice.

A. Your shuffling is to no purpose ; you are caught in the snares of truth. For upon this showing, even if He does not Himself assist, according to you He will be the author of evil, because He might have prevented it and did not. It is an old maxim that if a man can deliver another from death and does not, he is a homicide.

C. I withdraw and yield the point ; you have won ; provided, however, that victory is the subverting of the truth by specious words, that is to say, not by truth, but by falsehood. For I might make answer to you in the Apostle's words, [2] "Though I be rude in speech, yet not in knowledge." When you speak, your rhetorical tricks are too much for me, and I seem to agree with you ; but when you stop speaking, it all goes out of my head, and I see quite clearly that your argument does not flow from the fountains of truth and Christian simplicity, but rests on the laboured subtleties of the philosophers.

A. Do you wish me, then, once more to resort to the evidence of Scripture ? If so, what becomes of the boast of your disciples

---

[1] S. John vi. 70.   [2] Rom. ii. 4, 5.   [3] iii. 4.
[4] Jerem. xviii. 7, 8.

[1] Jonah iv. 10, 11.   [2] 1 Cor. xi. 6.

that no one can answer your arguments or solve the questions you raise ?

C. I not only wish, but am eager that you should do so. Show me any place in Holy Scripture where we find that, the power of free choice being lost, a man does what of himself he either would not, or could not do.

8. A. We must use the words of Scripture not as you propose, but as truth and reason demand. Jacob says in his prayer,[1] " If the Lord God will be with me, and will keep me in this way that I go, and will give me bread to eat, and raiment to put on, so that I come again to my father's house in peace, then shall the Lord be my God, and this stone, which I have set up for a token, shall be God's house ; and of all that Thou shalt give me I will surely give the tenth unto Thee." He did not say, If thou preserve my free choice, and I gain by my toil food and raiment, and return to my father's house. He refers everything to the will of God, that he may be found worthy to receive that for which he prays. On Jacob's return from Mesopotamia[2] an army of angels met him, who are called God's camp. He afterwards contended with an angel in the form of a man, and was strengthened by God ; whereupon, instead of Jacob, the *supplanter*, he received the name, *the most upright of God.* For he would not have dared to return to his cruel brother unless he had been strengthened and secured by the Lord's help. In the sequel we read, [3] " The sun rose upon him after he passed over Phanuel," which is, being interpreted, *the face of God.* Hence [4] Moses also says, " I have seen the Lord face to face, and my life is preserved," not by any natural quality—but by the condescension of God, Who had mercy. So then the Sun of Righteousness rises upon us when God makes His face to shine upon us and gives us strength. Joseph in Egypt was shut up in prison, and we next hear that the keeper of the prison, believing in his fidelity, committed everything to his hand. And the reason is given : [5] " Because the Lord was with him : and whatsoever he did, the Lord made it to prosper." Wherefore, also, dreams were suggested to Pharaoh's attendants, and Pharaoh had one which none could interpret, that so Joseph might be released, and his father and brethren fed, and Egypt saved in the time of famine. Moreover, God[6] said to Israel, in a vision of the night, " I am the God of thy fathers ; fear not to go down into Egypt ; for I will make of thee there a great nation, and I will go down with thee into

Egypt ; and I will also surely bring thee up again, and Joseph shall put his hand upon thine eyes." Where in this passage do we find the power of free choice ? Is not the whole circumstance that he ventured to go to his son, and entrust himself to a nation that knew not the Lord, due to the help of the God of his fathers ? The people was released from Egypt with a strong hand and an outstretched arm ; not the hand of Moses and Aaron, but of Him who set the people free by signs and wonders, and at last smote the first-born of Egypt, so that they who at [1]first were persistent in keeping the people, eagerly urged them to depart. Solomon[2] says, " Trust in the Lord with all thine heart, and lean not upon thine own understanding : in all thy ways acknowledge Him, and He shall direct thy paths." Understand what He says —that we must not trust in our wisdom, but in the Lord alone, by Whom the steps of a man are directed. Lastly, we are bidden to show Him our ways, and make them known, for they are not made straight by our own labour, but by His assistance and mercy. And so it is written, [3]"Make my way right before Thy face," so that what is right to Thee may seem also right to me. Solomon says the same— [4] " Commit thy works unto the Lord, and thy thoughts shall be established." Our thoughts are then established when we commit all we do to the Lord our helper, resting it, as it were, upon the firm and solid rock, and attribute everything to Him.

9. The Apostle Paul, rapidly recounting the benefits of God, ended with the words, [5] " And who is sufficient for these things ?" Wherefore, also, in another place he [6] says, "Such confidence have we through Christ to Godward ; not that we are sufficient of ourselves to think anything as of ourselves ; but our sufficiency is from God ; Who also made us sufficient as ministers of a new covenant ; not of the letter but of the spirit ; for the letter killeth, but the spirit giveth life." Do we still dare to pride ourselves on free will, and to abuse the benefits of God to the dishonour of the giver ? Whereas the same chosen vessel openly [7] writes, " We have this treasure in earthen vessels, that the exceeding greatness of the power may be of God, and not from ourselves." Therefore, also, in another place, checking the impudence of the heretics, he [8]says, " He that glorieth, let him glory in the Lord. For not he that commendeth himself is approved, but whom the Lord commendeth." And again, [9] " In nothing was I behind the very chiefest Apostles,

[1] Gen. xxviii. 20 sq.   [2] Gen. xxxii. 2.
[3] Gen. xxxii. 31. L. R. V. Penuel. Comp. Mt. xix. 4.
[4] Ib. 30. The words are Jacob's, but they are attributed to Moses as author.
[5] Gen. xxxix. 23.   [6] Gen. xlvi. 3, 4.

[1] Ex. xi. and xii.   [2] Prov. iii. 5, 6.   [3] Ps. v. 8.
[4] Prov. xvi. 3.   [5] 2 Cor. ii. 16.   [6] 2 Cor. iii. 4-6.
[7] 2 Cor. iv. 7.   [8] 2 Cor. x. 17, 18.   [9] 2 Cor. xii. 11.

hough I be nothing." Peter, disturbed by he greatness of the miracles he witnessed, aid to the Lord,[1] " Depart from me, for I am a sinful man." And the Lord said to His lisciples, [2] " I am the vine and ye are the branches : He that abideth in Me and I in him, the same beareth much fruit, for apart rom Me ye can do nothing." Just as the vine branches and shoots immediately decay when they are severed from the parent stem, o all the strength of men fades and perishes, if it be bereft of the help of God. " No one,"[3] He says, " can come unto Me except he Father Who sent Me draw him." When He says, " No one can come unto Me," He shatters the pride of free will ; because, even if a man will to go to Christ, except that be realized which follows—" unless My heavenly Father draw him"—desire is to no purpose, and effort is in vain. At the same time it is to be noted that he who is drawn does not run freely, but is led along either because he holds back and is sluggish, or because he is reluctant to go.

10. Now, how can a man who cannot by his own strength and labour come to Jesus, at the same time avoid all sins? and avoid them perpetually, and claim for himself a name which belongs to the might of God? For if He and I are both without sin, what difference is there between me and God? One more proof only I will adduce, that I may not weary you and my hearers. [4] Sleep was removed from the eyes of Ahasuerus, whom the Seventy call Artaxerxes, that he might turn over the memoirs of his faithful ministers and come upon Mordecai, by whose evidence he was delivered from a conspiracy ; and that thus Esther might be more acceptable, and the whole people of the Jews escape imminent death. There is no doubt that the mighty sovereign to whom belonged the whole East, from India to the North and to Ethiopia, after feasting sumptuously on delicacies gathered from every part of the world would have desired to sleep, and to take his rest, and to gratify his free choice of sleep, had not the Lord, the provider of all good things, hindered the course of nature, so that in defiance of nature the tyrant's cruelty might be overcome. If I were to attempt to produce all the instances in Holy Writ, I should be tedious. All that the saints say is a prayer to God ; their whole prayer and supplication a strong wrestling for the pity of God, so that we, who by our own strength and zeal cannot be saved, may be preserved by His mercy. But when we are concerned with grace and mercy, free will is in part void ;

in part, I say, for so much as this depends upon it, that we wish and desire, and give assent to the course we choose. But it depends on God whether we have the power in His strength and with His help to perform what we desire, and to bring to effect our toil and effort.

11. C. I simply said that we find the help of God not in our several actions, but in the grace of creation and of the law, that free will might not be destroyed. But there are many of us who maintain that all we do is done with the help of God.

A. Whoever says that must leave your party. Either, then, say the same yourself and join our side, or, if you refuse, you will be just as much our enemy as those who do not hold our views.

C. I shall be on your side if you speak my sentiments, or rather you will be on mine if you do not contradict them. You admit health of body, and deny health of the soul, which is stronger than the body. For sin is to the soul what disease or a wound is to the body. If then you admit that a man may be healthy so far as he is flesh, why do you not say he may be healthy so far as he is spirit?

A. I will follow in the line you point out,

" and you to-day
Shall ne'er escape ; where'er you call, I come."

C. I am ready to listen.

A. And I to speak to deaf ears. I will therefore reply to your argument. Made up of soul and body, we have the nature of both substances. As the body is said to be healthy if it is troubled with no weakness, so the soul is free from fault if it is unshaken and undisturbed. And yet, although the body may be healthy, sound, and active, with all the faculties in their full vigour, yet it suffers much from infirmities at more or less frequent intervals, and, however strong it may be, is sometimes distressed by various humours ; so the soul, bearing the onset of thoughts and agitations, even though it escape shipwreck, does not sail without danger, and remembering its weakness, is always anxious about death, according as it is written, [1] " What man is he that shall live and not see death ?"—death, which threatens all mortal men, not through the decay of nature, but through the death of sin, according to the prophet's words,[2] " The soul that sinneth, it shall die." Besides, we know that Enoch and Elias have not yet seen this death which is common to man and the brutes. Show me a body which is never sick, or which after sickness is ever safe and sound, and I will

---

[1] S. Luke v. 8.   [2] S. John xv. 5.   [3] S. John vi. 44.
[4] Esther vi. i.

[1] Ps. lxxxix. 48.   [2] Ezek. xviii. 4.

show you a soul which never sinned, and after acquiring virtues will never again sin. The thing is impossible, and all the more when we remember that vice borders on virtue, and that, if you deviate ever so little, you will either go astray or fall over a precipice. How small is the interval between obstinacy and perseverance, miserliness and frugality, liberality and extravagance, wisdom and craft, intrepidity and rashness, caution and timidity! some of which are classed as good, others as bad. And the same applies to bodies. If you take precautions against biliousness, the phlegm increases. If you dry up the humours too quickly, the blood becomes heated and vitiated with bile, and a sallow hue spreads over the countenance. Without question, however much we may exercise all the care of the physician, and regulate our diet, and be free from indigestion and whatever fosters disease, the causes of which are in some cases hidden from us and known to God alone, we shiver with cold, or burn with fever, or howl with colic, and implore the help of the true physician, our Saviour, and [1] say with the Apostles, "Master, save us, we perish"

12. C. Granted that no one could avoid all sin in boyhood, youth, and early manhood ; can you deny that very many righteous and holy men, after falling into vice, have heartily devoted themselves to the acquisition of virtue and through these have escaped sin ?

A. This is what I told you at the beginning—that it rests with ourselves either to sin or not to sin, and to put the hand either to good or evil ; and thus free will is preserved, but according to circumstances, time, and the state of human frailty ; we maintain, however, that perpetual freedom from sin is reserved for God only, and for Him Who being the Word was made flesh without incurring the defects and the sins of the flesh. And, because I am able to avoid sin for a short time, you cannot logically infer that I am able to do so continually. Can I fast, watch, walk, sing, sit, sleep perpetually ?

C. Why then in Holy Scripture are we stimulated to aim at perfect righteousness ? For example : [2] "Blessed are the pure in heart, for they shall see God," and [3] "Blessed are the undefiled in the way, who walk in the law of the Lord." And God says to Abraham, [4] "I am thy God, be thou pleasing in My sight, and be thou without spot, or blame, and I will make My covenant between Me and thee, and will multiply thee exceedingly."

If that is impossible which Scripture testifie it was useless to command it to be done.

A. You play upon Scripture until you wea a question threadbare, and remind me of th platform tricks of a conjurer who assumes variety of characters, and is now Mars, nex moment Venus ; so that he who was at first al sternness and ferocity is dissolved into fem nine softness. For the objection you no raise with an air of novelty—" Blessed are th pure in heart," " Blessed are the undefiled i the way," and " Be without spot," and so fort —is refuted when the Apostle replies, [1] " W know in part, and we prophesy in part," anc " Now we see through a mirror darkly, bu when that which is perfect is come, tha which is in part shall be done away." An therefore we have but the shadow and like ness of the pure heart, which hereafter is des tined to see God, and, free from spot or stain to live with Abraham. However great th patriarch, prophet, or Apostle may be, it [2] said to them, in the words of our Lord an Saviour, "If ye being evil, know how t give good gifts unto your children, how muc more shall your Father Which is in heave give good things to them which ask Him ? Then again even Abraham, to whom it wa said, [3] " Be thou without spot and blame, in the consciousness of his frailty fell upo his face to the earth. And when God ha spoken to Him, saying, " Thy wife Sarai sha no longer be called Sarai, but Sara shall he name be, and I will give thee a son by her, an I will bless him and he shall become a great na tion, and kings of nations shall spring fro him," the narrative at once proceeds to say " Abraham fell upon his face, and laughed, an said in his heart, Shall a child be born unto hi that is an hundred years old ? and shall Sara that is ninety years old, bear ?" And Abra ham said unto God, " Oh, that Ishmael migh live before thee ! " And God said, " Nay but Sarah thy wife shall bear thee a son, an thou shall call his name Isaac," and so on He certainly had heard the words of God " I am thy God, be thou pleasing in My sigh and without spot "; why then did he not be lieve what God promised, and why did h laugh in his heart, thinking that he escape the notice of God, and not daring to laug openly ? Moreover he gives the reasons fo his unbelief, and says, " How is it possible fo a man that is an hundred years old to beget son of a wife that is ninety years old ? " " O that Ishmael might live before thee," he says " Ishmael whom thou once gavest me. I d not ask a hard thing, I am content with th blessing I have received." God convince

---

[1] S. Matt. viii. 25. [2] S. Matt. v. 8. [3] Ps. cxix. 1.
[4] Gen. xvii. 1, 2.

[1] 1 Cor. xiii. 9, 10. [2] S. Matt. vii. 11. [3] Gen. xvii. 1 sq.

n by a mysterious reply. He said, " Yea."
e meaning is, that shall come to pass
ich you think shall not be. Your wife
ra shall bear you a son, and before she
nceives, before he is born, I will give the
y a name. For, from your error in secretly
ighing, your son shall be called Isaac, that
laughter. But if you think that God is
en by those who are pure in heart in this
rld, why did Moses, who had previously
d, " I have seen the Lord face to face, and
· life is preserved," afterwards entreat that
might see him distinctly? And because
said that he had seen God, the Lord told
n,[1] " Thou canst not see My face. For man
all not see My face, and live." Wherefore
o the Apostle [2] calls Him the only invisible
d, Who dwells in light unapproachable, and
hom no man hath seen, nor can see. And
e Evangelist John in holy accents testifies,
ving, [3] " No man hath at any time seen
d. The only begotten Son Who is in the
som of the Father, He hath declared Him."
e Who sees, also declares, not how great
e is Who is seen, nor how much He knows
ho declares ; but as much as the capacity
mortals can receive.

13. And whereas you think he is blessed
o is undefiled in the way, and walks in His
v, you must interpret the former clause by
e latter. From the many proofs I have
duced you have learnt that no one has been
le to fulfil the law. And if the Apostle,
comparison with the grace of Christ, reck-
ed those things as filth which formerly,
der the law, he counted gain, so that he
ght win Christ, how much more certain
ght we to be that the reason why the grace
Christ and of the Gospel has been added
that, under the law, no one could be justi-
d? Now if, under the law, no one is
stified, how is he perfectly undefiled in the
y who is still walking and hastening to
ach the goal? Surely, he who is in the
urse, and who is advancing on the road, is
ferior to him who has reached his journey's
d. If, then, he is undefiled and perfect
o is still walking in the way and advancing
the law, what more shall he have who has
rived at the end of life and of the law?
ence the Apostle, speaking of our Lord,
ys that, at the end of the world, when all
rtues shall receive their consummation, He
ll present His holy Church to Himself with-
t spot or wrinkle, and yet you think that
urch perfect, while yet in the flesh, which
subject to death and decay. You deserve
be told, with the Corinthians,[4] " Ye are
ready perfect, ye are already made rich :

ye reign without us, and I would that ye did
reign, that we might also reign with you "—
since true and stainless perfection belongs to
the inhabitants of heaven, and is reserved for
that day when the bridegroom shall say to
the bride, [1] " Thou art all fair, my love ; and
there is no spot in thee." And in this sense
we must understand the words : [2] " That ye
may be blameless and harmless, as children of
God, without blemish " ; for He did not say
ye are, but *may be.* He is contemplating the
future, not stating a case pertaining to the
present; so that here is toil and effort, in that
other world the rewards of labour and of
virtue. Lastly, John writes : [3] " Beloved, we
are sons of God, and it is not yet made
manifest what we shall be. We know that
when He shall be manifested, we shall be like
Him : for we shall see Him even as He is."
Although, then, we are sons of God, yet likeness to God, and the true contemplation of
God, is promised us then, when He shall
appear in His majesty.

14. From this swelling pride springs the
audacity in prayer which marks the directions
in your letter to a [4] certain widow as to how
the saints ought to pray. " He," you say,
[5]" rightly lifts up his hands to God ; he pours
out supplications with a good conscience who
can say, ' Thou knowest, Lord, how holy,
how innocent, how pure from all deceit,
wrong, and robbery are the hands which I
spread out unto Thee ; how righteous, how
spotless, and free from all falsehood are the
lips with which I pour forth my prayers unto
Thee, that Thou mayest pity me.' " Is this
the prayer of a Christian, or of a proud
Pharisee like him who [6] says in the Gospel,
" God, I thank Thee that I am not as other
men are, robbers, unjust, adulterers, or even
as this publican : I fast twice in the week, I
give tithes of all that I possess." Yet he
merely thanks God because, by His mercy, he
is not as other men : he execrates sin, and
does not claim his righteousness as his own.
But you say, " Now Thou knowest how holy,
how innocent, how pure from all deceit,
wrong, and robbery are the hands which I
spread out before Thee." He says that he
fasts twice in the week, that he may afflict his
vicious and wanton flesh, and he gives tithes

---

[1] Cant. iv. 7.   [2] Phil. ii. 15.   [3] 1 John iii. 2.
[4] See S. Aug. De Gest. Pelag. § 16. The widow was Juliana,
mother to Demetrias (to whom Jerome addressed his Letter CXXX.
"On the keeping of Virginity "). Pelagius' letter to Demetrias is
found in Jerome's works (Ed. Vall.), vol. xi. col. 15.
[5] The whole passage, as quoted by Augustin, runs as follows :
" May piety find with thee a place which it has never found elsewhere. May truth, which no one now knows, be thy household
friend ; and the law of God, which is despised by almost all men,
be honoured by thee alone." " How happy, how blessed art thou,
if that justice which we are to believe exists only in heaven is
found with thee alone upon earth." Then follow the words
quoted above.
[6] S. Luke xviii. 11.

Ex. xxxiii. 20.   [2] 1 Tim. i. 17, vi. 16.   [3] i. 18.
1 Cor. iv. 8.

of all his substance. For [1] "the ransom of a man's life is his riches." You join the devil in boasting,[2] "I will ascend above the stars, I will place my throne in heaven, and I will be like the Most High." David says,[3] "My loins are filled with illusions"; and [4] "My wounds stink and are corrupt because of my foolishness"; and [5] "Enter not into judgment with Thy servant"; and [6] "In Thy sight no man living shall be justified." You boast that you are holy, innocent, and pure, and spread out clean hands unto God. And you are not satisfied with glorying in all your works, unless you say that you are pure from all sins of speech; and you tell us how righteous, how spotless, how free from all falsehood your lips are. The Psalmist sings, [7] "Every man is a liar"; and this is supported by apostolical authority: "That God may be true," says St. Paul,[8] "and every man a liar"; and yet you have lips righteous, spotless, and free from all falsehood. Isaiah laments, saying,[9] "Woe is me! for I am undone, because I am a man of unclean lips, and I dwell in the midst of a people of unclean lips"; and afterwards one of the seraphim brings a hot coal, taken with the tongs, to purify the prophet's lips, for he was not, according to the tenor of your words, arrogant, but he confessed his own faults. Just as we read in the Psalms, [10] "What shall be due unto thee, and what shall be done more unto thee in respect of a deceitful tongue? Sharp arrows of the mighty, with coals that make desolate." And after all this swelling with pride, and boastfulness in prayer, and confidence in your holiness, like one fool trying to persuade another, you finish with the words "These lips with which I pour out my supplication that Thou mayest have pity on me." If you are holy, if you are innocent, if you are cleansed from all defilement, if you have sinned neither in word nor deed—although James says,[11] "He who offends not in word is a perfect man," and "No one can curb his tongue"—how is it that you sue for mercy? so that, forsooth, you bewail yourself, and pour out prayers because you are holy, pure, and innocent, a man of stainless lips, free from all falsehood, and endowed with a power like that of God. Christ prayed thus on the cross: [12] "My God, my God, why hast Thou forsaken Me? Why art Thou so far from helping Me?" And, again,[13] "Father, into Thy hands I commend My spirit," and [14] "Father, forgive them, for

they know not what they do." And this He, who, returning thanks for us, had s. [1] "I confess to Thee, O Father, Lord of hea and earth."

15. Our Lord so instructed His Apos that, daily at the sacrifice of His body, believ make bold to say, "Our Father, Which ar Heaven, hallowed be Thy name"; they ea estly desire the name of God, which in it is holy, to be hallowed in themselves; you s "Thou knowest, Lord, how holy, how in cent, and how pure are my hands." T they say; "Thy Kingdom come," anticip ing the hope of the future kingdom, so th when Christ reigns, sin may by no means re in their mortal body, and to this they cou the words, "Thy will be done in earth a is in Heaven"; so that human weakness n imitate the angels, and the will of our L may be fulfilled on earth; you say, "A n can, if he chooses, be free from all sin." Apostles prayed for the daily bread, or bread better than all food, which was to co so that they might be worthy to receive body of Christ; and you are led by your cess of holiness and well established rig eousness to boldly claim the heavenly g Next comes, "Forgive us our debts, as we a forgive our debtors." No sooner do they from the baptismal font, and by being b again and incorporated into our Lord Saviour thus fulfil what is written of th [2] "Blessed are they whose iniquities are given and whose sins are covered," than the first communion of the body of Christ th say, "Forgive us our debts," though th debts had been forgiven them at their c fession of Christ; but you in your arrog pride boast of the cleanness of your h hands and of the purity of your spee However thorough the conversion of a n may be, and however perfect his possess of virtue after a time of sins and failings, such persons be as free from fault as th who are just leaving the font of Chri And yet these latter are commanded to s "Forgive us our debts, as we also forg our debtors"; not in the spirit of a fa humility, but because they are afraid of hun frailty and dread their own conscience. Th say, "Lead us not into temptation"; you a Jovinian unite in saying that those who w a full faith have been baptized cannot be f ther tempted or sin. Lastly, they add, "1 deliver us from the evil one." Why do th beg from the Lord what they have alread the power of free will? Oh, man, now th hast been made clean in the laver, and thee it is said, "Who is this that cometh

[1] Prov. xiii. 8.
[2] Is. xiv. 13, 14. Spoken of the King of Babylon.
[3] Ps. xxxviii. 7. Vulg. [4] Ibid. 5. [5] Ps. cxliii. 2.
[6] Ibid. 4. [7] Ps. cxvi. 11. [8] Rom. iii. 4.
[9] Is. vi. 5. [10] Ps. cxx. 3. Vulg. [11] James iii. 2.
[12] Ps. xxii. 2; Sept. and Vulgate. S. Matt. xxvii. 46, R. V., "and from the words of my roaring."
[13] S. Luke xxiii. 46. [14] S. Luke xxiii. 34.

[1] S. Matt. xi. 25. [2] Ps. xxi. 1.

white, leaning upon her beloved?" The
...e, therefore, is washed, yet she cannot
...p her purity, unless she be supported by
...Lord. How is it that you long to be set
...e by the mercy of God, you who but a little
...le ago were released from your sins? The
...y explanation is the principle by which we
...ntain that, when we have done all, we must
...fess we are unprofitable.

6. So then your prayer outdoes the pride
...the Pharisee, and you are condemned
...en compared with the Publican. He,
...nding afar off, did not dare to lift up his
...s unto Heaven, but smote upon his breast,
...ing,[1] "God be merciful unto me a sinner."
...d on this is based our Lord's declaration,
...say unto you this man went down to his
...se justified rather than the other. For
...ry one that exalteth himself shall be abased,
...d he that humbleth himself shall be exalted."
...e Apostles are humbled that they may be
...lted. Your disciples are lifted up that
...y may fall. In your flattery of the widow
...viously mentioned you are not ashamed to
...that piety such as is found on earth, and
...th which is everywhere a stranger, had
...de their home with her in preference to all
...ers. You do not recollect the familiar
...rds,[2] "O my people, they which call thee
...ssed cause thee to err, and destroy the
...chs of thy feet"; and you expressly praise
...r and say, "Happy beyond all thought are
...u! how blessed! if righteousness, which is
...lieved to be now nowhere but in Heaven,
...found with you alone on earth." Is this
...ching or slaying? Is it raising from earth,
...casting down from heaven, to attribute that
...a poor creature of a woman, which angels
...uld not dare arrogate to themselves? If
...ety, truth, and righteousness are found on
...rth nowhere but in one woman, where shall
...e find your righteous followers, who, you
...ast, are sinless on earth? These two
...apters on prayer and praise you and your
...sciples are wont to swear are none of yours,
...d yet your brilliant style is so clearly seen
...them, and the elegance of your Ciceronian
...ction is so marked that, although you strut
...out with the slow pace of a tortoise, you
...ve not the courage to acknowledge what
...u teach in private and expose for sale.
...appy man! whose books no one writes out
...t your own disciples, so that whatever
...pears to be unacceptable, you may contend
...not your own but some one else's work.
...nd where is the man with ability enough to
...itate the charm of your language?

17. C. I can put it off no longer; my pa-
...ence is completely overcome by your iniqui-

tous words. Tell me, pray, what sin have little
infants committed. Neither the consciousness of wrong nor ignorance can be imputed
to those who, according to the prophet Jonah,
know not their right hand from their left.
They cannot sin, and they can perish; their
knees are too weak to walk, they utter inartic-
ulate cries; we laugh at their attempts to
speak; and, all the while, poor unfortunates!
the torments of eternal misery are prepared
for them.

A. Ah! now that your disciples have
turned masters you begin to be fluent, not
to say eloquent. Antony,[1] an excellent
orator, whose praises Tully loudly proclaims,
says that he had seen many fluent men, but
so far never an eloquent speaker; so don't
amuse me with flowers of oratory which have
not grown in your own garden, and with which
the ears of inexperience and of boyhood are
wont to be tickled, but plainly tell me what
you think.

C. What I say is this—you must at least
allow that they have no sin who cannot sin.

A. I will allow it, if they have been baptized
into Christ; and if you will not then immediately bind me to agree with your opinion
that a man can be without sin if he chooses;
for they neither have the power nor the will;
but they are free from all sin through the
grace of God, which they received in their
baptism.

C. You force me to make an invidious remark and ask, Why, what sin have they committed? that you may immediately have me
stoned in some popular tumult. You have
not the power to kill me, but you certainly
have the will.

A. He slays a heretic who allows him to
be a heretic. But when we rebuke him we
give him life; you may die to your heresy,
and live to the Catholic faith.

C. If you know us to be heretics, why do
you not accuse us?

A. Because the[2] Apostle teaches me to
avoid a heretic after the first and second
admonition, not to accuse him. The Apostle
knew that such an one is perverse and self-
condemned. Besides, it would be the height
of folly to make my faith depend on another man's judgment. For supposing some
one were to call you a Catholic, am I to immediately give assent? Whoever defends
you, and says that you rightly hold your perverse opinions, does not succeed in rescuing
you from infamy, but charges himself with
perfidy. Your numerous supporters will
never prove you to be a Catholic, but will

---

[1] The grandfather of the Triumvir, born B.C. 142, died in the civil conflict excited by Marius, B.C. 87.

[1] S. Luke xviii. 13.   [2] Is. iii. 12.   [2] Tit. iii. 10.

show that you are a heretic. But I would have such opinions as these suppressed by ecclesiastical authority ; otherwise we shall be in the case of those who show some dreadful picture to a crying child. May the fear of God grant us this—to despise all other fears. Therefore, either defend your opinions, or abandon what you are unable to defend. Whoever may be called in to defend you must be enrolled as a partisan, not as a patron.

18. C. Tell me, pray, and rid me of all doubts, why little children are baptized.

A. That their sins may be forgiven them in baptism.

C. What sin are they guilty of ? How can any one be set free who is not bound ?

A. You ask me ! The Gospel trumpet will reply, the teacher of the Gentiles, the golden vessel shining throughout the world:[1] " Death reigned from Adam even unto Moses : even over those who did not sin after the likeness of the transgression of Adam, who is a figure of Him that was to come." And if you object that some are spoken of who did not sin, you must understand that they did not sin in the same way as Adam did by transgressing God's command in Paradise. But all men are held liable either on account of their ancient forefather Adam, or on their own account. He that is an infant is released in baptism from the chain which bound his father. He who is old enough to have discernment is set free from the chain of his own or another's sin by the blood of Christ. You must not think me a heretic because I take this view, for the blessed martyr Cyprian, whose rival you boast of being in the classification of Scripture proofs, in the [2]epistle addressed to Bishop Fidus on the Baptism of Infants speaks thus : " Moreover, if even the worst offenders, and those who previous to baptism sin much against God, once they believe have the gift of remission of sins, and no one is kept from baptism and from grace, how much more ought not an infant to be kept from baptism seeing that, being only just born, he has committed no sin ? He has only, being born according to the flesh among Adam's sons, incurred the taint of ancient death by his first birth. And he is the more easily admitted to remission of sins because of the very fact that not his own sins but those of another are remitted to him. And so, dearest brother, it was our decision in council that no one ought to be kept by us from baptism and from the grace of God,

Who is merciful to all, and kind, and go⟨ And whereas this rule ought to be observ⟨ and kept with reference to all, bear in mi⟨ that it ought so much the more to be observ⟨ with regard to infants themselves and th⟨ just born, for they have the greater clai⟨ on our assistance in order to obtain Divi⟨ mercy, because their cries and tears fr⟨ the very birth are one perpetual prayer."

19. That holy man and eloquent bish⟨ Augustin not long ago wrote to [1]Marc⟨ linus (the same that was afterwards, thou⟨ innocent, put to death by heretics on the p⟨ text of his taking part in the tyranny of H⟨ aclian[2]) two treatises on infant baptism, opposition to your heresy which maintai⟨ that infants are baptized not for remission sins, but for admission to the kingdom heaven, according as it is written in t⟨ Gospel,[3] " Except a man be born again water and of the Spirit, he cannot enter into t⟨ kingdom of heaven." He addressed a [4]thi⟨ moreover, to the same Marcellinus, agai⟨ those who say as do you, that a man can free from sin, if he chooses, without the h⟨ of God. And, recently, a [5]fourth to Hila⟨ against this doctrine of yours, which is full perversity. And he is said to have others the anvil with special regard to you, whi⟨ have not yet come to hand. Wherefore, think I must abandon my task, for fe⟨ Horace's words may be thrown at n⟨ [6]" Don't carry firewood into a forest." F⟨ we must either say the same as he does, a⟨ that would be superfluous ; or, if we wished say something fresh, we should[7] find our b⟨ points anticipated by that splendid geni⟨ One thing I will say and so end my discour⟨ that you ought either to give us a new cree⟨ so that, after baptizing children into the nar⟨ of the Father, Son, and Holy Spirit, you m⟨ baptize them into the kingdom of heaven ; ⟨ if you have one baptism both for infants a⟨ for persons of mature age, it follows that infar⟨ also should be baptized for the remission sins after the likeness of the transgressi⟨ of Adam. But if you think the remission

---

[1] Rom. v 14.
[2] Cyp. Ep. 64 (al. 59). S. Augustine preaching at Carthage on June 27, 413, quoted the same letter, which was a Synodical letter of A.D. 253. See Bright's Anti-Pelagian Treatises, Introduction, p. xxi.

---

[1] Marcellinus was the lay imperial commissioner appointed⟨ superintend the discussion between the Catholics and Donatist⟨ the Council of Carthage, A.D. 411. In 413 Heraclian, gover⟨ of Africa, revolted against Honorius, the Emperor, and inva⟨ Italy. The enterprise failed, and on his return to Africa the p⟨ moter of it was put to death. The Donatists, called by Jer⟨ " heretics," are supposed to have accused Marcellinus of tak⟨ part in the rebellion. He was executed in 414.
[2] " On the Deserts and Remission of Sins, and the Baptism Infants," in three books, the earliest of S. Augustin's Anti-Pe⟨ gian treatises. It was composed in reply to a letter from his frie⟨ Marcellinus, who was harassed by Pelagianising disputants. S. Aug. " De Gest. Pel." § 25.
[3] S. John iii. 3.
[4] The " De Spiritu et Littera." Marcellinus found a difficu⟨ in Augustin's view of the question of sinlessness. See Brig⟨ Anti-Pelagian Treatises, Introduction, p. xix.
[5] Whether he who was made Bishop of Arles, in 429, is dispu⟨ The treatise was the " De Natura et Gratia," written early in a⟨
[6] Sat. i. 10.
[7] Or, better positions have been occupied.

nother's sins implies injustice, and that he
as no need of it who could not sin, cross
ver to Origen, your special favourite, who
ays that ancient offences [1] committed long

before in the heavens are loosed in baptism.
You will then be not only led by his authority
in other matters, but will be following his
error in this also.

---

[1] Origen held the pre-existence of souls, endowed with free will, and supposed their condition in this world to be the result of their conduct in their previous state of probation.

PREFACES

The Prefaces to Jerome's works have in many cases a special value. This value is sometimes personal ;
hey are the free expressions of his feelings to those whom he trusts. Sometimes it lies in the mention of par-
icular events ; sometimes in showing the special difficulties he encountered as a translator, or the state of mind
f those for whom he wrote ; sometimes in making us understand the extent and limits of his own knowledge,
nd the views on points such as the inspiration of Scripture which actuated him as a translator or commentator ;
ometimes, again, in the particular interpretations which he gives. These things gain a great importance from
he fact that Jerome's influence and that of his Vulgate was preponderant in Western Europe for more than a
housand years.

We have had to make a selection, not only from want of space, but also because the Prefaces are of very
nequal value, and sometimes are mere repetitions of previous statements. We have therefore given specimens
f each class of Preface ; we have given also all which bears on the better understanding of the life and views of
erome ; but where a Preface repeats what has been said before, or where it gives facts or interpretations which
re well known or of no particular value, we have contented ourselves with a short statement of its contents.

The Prefaces fall under three heads : 1st. Those prefixed to Jerome's early works bearing on Church history
r Scripture. 2d. The Prefaces to the Vulgate translation. 3d. Those prefixed to the Commentaries.

PREFACES TO JEROME'S EARLY WORKS.

PREFACE TO THE CHRONICLE OF EUSEBIUS.

The " Chronicle " is a book of universal history, giving
he dates from the call of Abraham, and the Olympiads.
'or an account of it the reader is referred to the article
f Dr. Salmon in the " Dictionary of Christian Antiqui-
ies." It was translated by Jerome in the years 381–82,
This Preface shows that Jerome was already becoming
ware of the difficulties arising from the various versions
f the Old Testament, and of the necessity of going back
o the Hebrew.

Jerome to his friends [1] *Vincentius and Gallienus,
Greeting :*

1. It has long been the practice of learned
men to exercise their minds by rendering
nto Latin the works of Greek writers, and,
what is more difficult, to translate the
poems of illustrious authors though
rammelled by the farther requirements of
verse. It was thus that our Tully literally
translated whole books of Plato; and after
publishing an edition of [2] Aratus (who may
now be considered a Roman) in hexameter
verse, he amused himself with the econo-
mics of Xenophon. In this latter work the
golden river of eloquence again and again

meets with obstacles, around which its waters
break and foam to such an extent that persons
unacquainted with the original would not believe they were reading Cicero's words. And
no wonder! It is hard to follow another
man s lines and everywhere keep within
bounds. It is an arduous task to preserve
felicity and grace unimpaired in a translation.
Some word has forcibly expressed a given
thought ; I have no word of my own to convey the meaning; and while I am seeking
to satisfy the sense I may go a long way
round and accomplish but a small distance
of my journey. Then we must take into account the ins and outs of transposition, the
variations in cases, the diversity of figures,
and, lastly, the peculiar and, so to speak,
the native idiom of the language. A literal
translation sounds absurd; if, on the other
hand, I am obliged to change either the
order or the words themselves, I shall
appear to have forsaken the duty of a translator.

2. So, my dear Vincentius, and you, Gallienus, whom I love as my own soul, I beseech
you, whatever may be the value of this hurried
piece of work, to read it with the feelings of
a friend rather than with those of a critic.
And I ask this all the more earnestly because,
as you know, I dictated with great rapidity
to my amanuensis; and how difficult the task

---

[1] Vincentius appears to have attached himself to Jerome at Con-
tantinople and remained with him till the end of the century.
Jerome, Against John of Jerusalem, 41 ; Apol., iii. 22 ; Letter
LXXXVIII.) Nothing is known of Gallienus.
[2] Flourished B.C. 270.

is, the sacred records testify; for the old flavour is not preserved in the Greek version by the Seventy. It was this that stimulated Aquila, Symmachus, and Theodotion; and the result of their labors was to impart a totally different character to one and the same work; one strove to give word for word, another the general meaning, while the third desired to avoid any great divergency from the ancients. A fifth, sixth, and seventh edition, though no one knows to what authors they are to be attributed, exhibit so pleasing a variety of their own that, in spite of their being anonymous, they have won an authoritative position. Hence, some go so far as to consider the sacred writings somewhat harsh and grating to the ear; which arises from the fact that the persons of whom I speak are not aware that the writings in question are a translation from the Hebrew, and therefore, looking at the surface not at the substance, they shudder at the squalid dress before they discover the fair body which the language clothes. In fact, what can be more musical than the Psalter? Like the writings of our own [1] Flaccus and the Grecian Pindar it now trips along in iambics, now flows in sonorous alcaics, now swells into sapphics, now [2] marches in half-foot metre. What can be more lovely than the strains of Deuteronomy and Isaiah? What more grave than Solomon's words? What more finished than Job? All these, as Josephus and Origen tell us, were composed in hexameters and pentameters, and so circulated amongst their own people. When we read these in Greek they have *some* meaning; when in Latin they are utterly incoherent. But if any one thinks that the grace of language does not suffer through translation, let him render Homer word for word into Latin. I will go farther and say that, if he will translate this author into the prose of his own language, the order of the words will seem ridiculous, and the most eloquent of poets almost dumb.

3. What is the drift of all this? I would not have you think it strange if here and there we stumble; if the language lag; if it bristle with consonants or present gaping chasms of vowels; or be cramped by condensation of the narrative. The most learned among men have toiled at the same task; and in addition to the· difficulty which all experience, and which we have alleged to attend all translation, it must not be forgotten that a peculiar difficulty besets us, inasmuch as the history is manifold, is full of barbarous names, circumstances of which the Latins know nothing, dates which are tangled

knots, critical marks blended alike with the events and the numbers, so that it is almost harder to discern the sequence of the words than to come to a knowledge of what is related.

[Here follows a long passage showing an arrangement according to which the dates are distinguished by certain colours as belonging to one or another of the kingdoms, the history of which is dealt with. This passage seems unintelligible in the absence of the coloured figures, and would be of no use unless the book with its original arrangement were being studied.]

I am well aware that there will be many who, with their customary fondness for universal detraction (from which the only escape is by writing nothing at all), will drive their fangs into this volume. They will cavil at the dates, change the order, impugn the accuracy of events, winnow the syllables, and, as is very frequently the case, will impute the negligence of copyists to the authors. I should be within my right if I were to rebut them by saying that they need not read unless they choose; but I would rather send them away in a calm state of mind, so that they may attribute to the Greek author the credit which is his due, and may recognize that any insertions for which we are responsible have been taken from other men of the highest repute. The truth is that I have partly discharged the office of a translator and partly that of a writer. I have with the utmost fidelity rendered the Greek portion, and at the same time have added certain things which appeared to me to have been allowed to slip, particularly in the Roman history, which Eusebius, the author of this book, as it seems to me, only glanced at; not so much because of ignorance, for he was a learned man, as because, writing in Greek, he thought them of slight importance to his countrymen. So again from Ninus and Abraham, right up to the captivity of Troy, the translation is from the Greek only. From Troy to the twentieth year of Constantine there is much, at one time separately added, at another intermingled, which I have gleaned with great diligence from Tranquillus and other famous historians. Moreover, the portion from the aforesaid year of Constantine to the sixth consulship of the Emperor Valens and the second of Valentinianus is entirely my own. Content to end here, I have reserved the remaining period, that of Gratianus and Theodosius, for a wider historical survey; not that I am afraid to discuss the living freely and truthfully, for the fear of God banishes the fear of man; but because while our country is still exposed to the fury of the barbarians everything is in confusion.

---

[1] That is, Horace.
[2] Sublimia debent ingredi.—Quint, 9, 4 fin.

PREFACE TO THE TRANSLATION OF ORIGEN'S TWO HOMILIES ON THE SONG OF SONGS.

Written at Rome, A.D. 383.

Jerome to the most holy Pope Damasus :

Origen, whilst in his other books he has surpassed all others, has in the Song of Songs surpassed himself. He wrote ten volumes upon it, which amount to almost twenty thousand lines, and in these he discussed, first the version of the Seventy Translators, then those of Aquila, Symmachus, and Theodotion, and lastly, a fifth version which he states that he found on the coast of Actium, with such magnificence and fulness, that he appears to me to have realized what is said in the poem : "The king brought me into his chamber." I have left that work on one side, since it would require almost boundless leisure and labour and money to translate so great a work into Latin, even if it could be worthily done ; and I have translated these two short treatises, which he composed in the form of daily lectures for those who were still like babes and sucklings, and I have studied faithfulness rather than elegance. You can conceive how great a value the larger work possesses, when the smaller gives you such satisfaction.

PREFACE TO THE BOOK ON HEBREW NAMES.

The origin and scope of this book is described in the Preface itself. It was written in the year 388, two years after Jerome had settled at Bethlehem. He had, immediately on arriving in Palestine, three years previously, set to work to improve his knowledge of Hebrew, with a view to his translation of the Old Testament, which was begun in 391. This book, therefore, and the two which follow, may be taken as records of studies preparatory to the Vulgate.

Philo, the most erudite man among the Jews, is declared by Origen to have done what I am now doing ; he set forth a book of Hebrew Names, classing them under their initial letters, and placing the etymology of each at the side. This work I originally proposed to translate into Latin. It is well known in the Greek world, and is to be found in all libraries. But I found that the copies were so discordant to one another, and the order so confused, that I judged it to be better to say nothing, rather than to write what would justly be condemned. A work of this kind, however, appeared likely to be of use ; and my friends Lupulianus and Valerianus[1] urged me to attempt it, because, as they thought, I had made some progress in the knowledge of

---

[1] Nothing is known of these men. It is very improbable that this Valerianus was the bishop of Apuleia, who must, however, have been known to Jerome.

Hebrew. I, therefore, went through all the books of Scripture in order, and in the restoration which I have now made of the ancient fabric, I think that I have produced a work which may be found valuable by Greeks as well as Latins.

I here in the Preface beg the reader to take notice that, if he finds anything omitted in this work, it is reserved for mention in another. I have at this moment on hand a book of Hebrew Questions, an undertaking of a new kind such as has never until now been heard of amongst either the Greeks or the Latins. I say this, not with a view of arrogantly puffing up my own work, but because I know how much labour I have spent on it, and wish to provoke those whose knowledge is deficient to read it. I recommend all those who wish to possess both that work and the present one, and also the book of Hebrew Places, which I am about to publish, to make no account of the Jews and all their ebullitions of vexation. Moreover, I have added the meaning of the words and names in the New Testament, so that the fabric might receive its last touch and might stand complete. I wished also in this to imitate Origen, whom all but the ignorant acknowledge as the greatest teacher of the Churches next to the Apostles ; for in this work, which stands among the noblest monuments of his genius, he endeavoured as a Christian to supply what Philo, as a Jew, had omitted.

PREFACE TO THE BOOK ON THE SITES AND NAMES OF HEBREW PLACES.

For the scope and value of this book see Prolegomena. It was written A.D. 388.

Eusebius, who took his second name from the blessed Martyr Pamphilus, after he had written the ten books of his "Ecclesiastical History," the Chronicle of Dates, of which I published a Latin version, the book in which he set forth the names of the different nations and those given to them of old by the Jews and by those of the present day, the topography of the land of Judæa and the portions allotted to the tribes, together with a representation of Jerusalem itself and its temple, which he accompanied with a very short explanation, bestowed his labour at the end of his life upon this little work, of which the design is to gather for us out of the Holy Scriptures the names of almost all the cities, mountains, rivers, hamlets, and other places, whether they remain the same or have since been changed or in some degree corrupted. I have taken up the work of this admirable man, and have translated it, following the arrangement of the Greeks, and taking the words in the order of their initial letters, but leaving out those names which did not seem worthy of mention, and making a considerable number of alterations. I have explained my method once for all in the Preface to my translation of the Chronicle, where I said that I might be called at once a translator and the composer of a new work; but I repeat this especially because one who had hardly the first tincture of letters has ventured upon a translation of this very book into Latin, though his language is hardly to be called Latin. His lack of scholarship will be seen by the observant reader as soon as he compares it with my translation. I do not pretend to a style which soars to the skies; but I hope that I can rise above one which grovels on the earth.

PREFACE TO THE BOOK OF HEBREW QUESTIONS.

Written A.D. 388. For the scope and character of this work, see Prolegomena.

The object of the Preface to a book is to set forth the argument of the work which follows; but I am compelled to begin by answering what has been said against me. My case is somewhat like that of Terence, who turned the scenic prologues of his plays into a defence of himself. We have a [1] Luscius Lanuvinus, like the one who worried him, and who brought charges against the poet as if he had been a plunderer of the treasury. The bard of Mantua suffered in the same way; he had translated a few verses of Homer very exactly, and they said that he was nothing but a plagiarist from the ancients. But he answered them that it was no small proof of strength to wrest the club of Hercules from his hands. Why, even Tully, who stands on the pinnacle of Roman eloquence, that king of orators and glory of the Latin tongue, has actions for embezzlement[2] brought against him by the Greeks. I cannot, therefore, be surprised if a poor little fellow like me is exposed to the gruntings of vile swine who trample our pearls under their feet, when some of the most learned of men, men whose glory ought to have hushed the voice of ill will, have felt the flames of envy. It is true, this happened by a kind of justice to men whose eloquence had filled with its resonance the theatres and the senate, the public assembly and the rostra; hardihood always courts detraction, and (as Horace says):

> "The [3] highest peaks invoke
> The lightning's stroke."

But I am in a corner, remote from the city and the forum, and the wranglings of crowded courts; yet, even so (as Quintilian says) ill-will has sought me out. Therefore, I beseech the reader,

> "If [1] one there be, if one,
> Who, rapt by strong desire, these lines shall read,"

not to expect eloquence or oratorical grace in those Books of Hebrew Questions, which I propose to write on all the sacred books; but rather, that he should himself answer my detractors for me, and tell them that a work of a new kind can claim some indulgence. I am poor and of low estate; I neither possess riches nor do I think it right to accept them if they are offered me; and, similarly, let me tell them that it is impossible for them to have the riches of Christ, that is, the knowledge of the Scriptures, and the world's riches as well. It will be my simple aim, therefore, first, to point out the mistakes of those who suspect some fault in the Hebrew Scriptures, and, secondly, to correct the faults, which evidently teem in the Greek and Latin copies, by a reference to the original authority; and, further, to explain the etymology of things, names, and countries, when it is not apparent from the sound of the Latin words, by giving a paraphrase in the vulgar tongue. To enable the student more easily to take note of these emendations, I propose, in the first place, to set out the true[2] reading itself, as I am now able to do, and then, by bringing the later readings into comparison with it, to [3]indicate what has been omitted or added or altered. It is not my purpose, as snarling ill-will pretends, to convict the LXX. of error, nor do I look upon my own labour as a disparagement of theirs. The fact is that they, since their work was undertaken for King Ptolemy of Alexandria, did not choose to bring to light all the mysteries which the sacred writings contain, and especially those which give the promise of the advent of Christ, for fear that he who held the Jews in esteem because they were believed to worship one God, would come to think that they worshipped a second. But we find that the Evangelists, and even our Lord and Saviour, and the Apostle Paul, also, bring forward many citations as coming from the Old Testament which are not contained in our copies; and on these I shall dilate more fully in their proper

---

[1] Terence's rival, to whom he makes allusions in the Prologi to the Eunuchus, Heoutontimoroumenos and Phormio.
[2] *Repetundarum.* Properly an action to compel one who has left office to restore public money which he had embezzled.
[3] Hor. Odes II., x. 19, 20.

[1] Virgil, Ec., vi. 10.
[2] *Ipsa testimonia.* This is what he calls in other places Hebraica veritas. Jerome was right in the main in correcting the LXX. and other Greek versions by the Hebrew. He was not aware (as has been since made clear) that there are various readings in the Hebrew itself, and that these may sometimes be corrected by the LXX., which was made from older MSS.
[3] That is, by the obeli (†), to show what has been left out, and the asterisk (*), to show what has been inserted.

places. But it is clear from this fact that those are the best MSS. which most correspond with the authoritative words of the New Testament. Add to this that Josephus, who gives the story of the Seventy Translators, reports them as translating only the five books of Moses ; and we also acknowledge that these are more in harmony with the Hebrew than the rest. And, further, those who afterward came into the field as translators—I mean Aquila and Symmachus and Theodotion—give a version very different from that which we use.[1]

I have but one word more to say, and it may calm my detractors. Foreign goods are to be imported only to the regions where there is a demand for them. Country people are not obliged to buy balsam, pepper, and dates. As to Origen, I say nothing. His name (if I may compare small things with great) is even more than my own the object of ill-will, because, though following the common version in his Homilies, which were spoken to common people, yet, in his Tomes,[2] that is, in his fuller discussion of Scripture, he yields to the Hebrew as the truth, and, though surrounded by his own forces, occasionally seeks the foreign tongue as his ally. I will only say this about him : that I should gladly have his knowledge of the Scriptures, even if accompanied with all the ill-will which clings to his name, and that I do not care a straw for these shades and spectral ghosts, whose nature is said to be to chatter in dark corners and be a terror to babies.

[1] That is, from the copies of the LXX. commonly used in the fourth century.
[2] Larger Commentaries.

PREFACE TO THE COMMENTARY ON ECCLESIASTES.

Addressed to Paula and Eustochium, Bethlehem, A.D. 388.

I remember that, about five years ago, when I was still living at Rome, I read Ecclesiastes to the saintly Blesilla,[1] so that I might provoke her to the contempt of this earthly scene, and to count as nothing all that she saw in the world ; and that she asked me to throw my remarks upon all the more obscure passages into the form of a short commentary, so that, when I was absent, she might still understand what she read. She was withdrawn from us by her sudden death, while girding herself for our work ; we were not counted worthy to have such an one as the partner of our life ; and, therefore, Paula and Eustochium, I kept silence under the stroke of such a wound. But now, living as I do in the smaller community of Bethlehem, I pay what I owe to her memory and to you. I would only point out this, that I have followed no one's authority. I have translated direct from the Hebrew, adapting my words as much as possible to the form of the Septuagint, but only in those places in which they did not diverge far from the Hebrew. I have occasionally referred also to the versions of Aquila, Symmachus, and Theodotion, but so as not to alarm the zealous student by too many novelties, nor yet to let my commentary follow the side streams of opinion, turning aside, against my conscientious conviction, from the fountainhead of truth.

[1] Daughter of Paula. See Letter XXXIX.

PREFACES TO THE VULGATE VERSION OF THE NEW TESTAMENT.

This version was made at Rome between the years 382 and 385. The only Preface remaining is that to the translation of the Gospels, but Jerome speaks of, and quotes from, his version of the other parts also. The work was undertaken at the request and under the sanction of Pope Damasus, who had consulted Jerome in A.D. 383 on certain points of Scriptural criticism, and apparently in the same year urged him to revise the current Latin version by help of the Greek original. It is to be observed that Jerome's aim was " to revise the old Latin, and not to make a new version. When Augustin expressed to him his gratitude for ' his *translation* of the Gospels,' he tacitly corrected him by substituting for this phrase ' the *correction* of the New Testament.' Yet, although he proposed to himself this limited object, the various forms of corruption which had been introduced were, as he describes, so numerous that the difference of the old and revised (Hieronymian) text is throughout clear and striking." See article by Westcott in " Dictionary of Bible," on the Vulgate, and Fremantle's article on Jerome in " Dictionary of Christian Biography."

THE FOUR GOSPELS.

Addressed to Pope[1] Damasus, A.D. 383.

You urge me to revise the old Latin version, and, as it were, to sit in judgment on the copies of the Scriptures which are now scattered throughout the whole world ; and, inasmuch as they differ from one another, you would have me decide which of them agree with the Greek original. The labour is one of love, but at the same time both perilous and presumptuous ; for in judging others I must be content to be judged by all ; and how can I dare to change the language of the world in its hoary old age, and carry it back to the early days of its infancy ? Is there a man, learned or unlearned, who will not, when he

[1] Made pope 366, died 384. Jerome had been his secretary at the Council held at Rome in 382, and continued his literary services till the pope's death, in 385.

takes the volume into his hands, and perceives that what he reads does not suit his settled tastes, break out immediately into violent language, and call me a forger and a profane person for having the audacity to add anything to the ancient books, or to make any changes or corrections therein? Now there are two consoling reflections which enable me to bear the odium—in the first place, the command is given by you who are the supreme bishop; and secondly, even on the showing of those who revile us, readings at variance with the early copies cannot be right. For if we are to pin our faith to the Latin texts, it is for our opponents to tell us *which*; for there are almost as many forms of texts as there are copies. If, on the other hand, we are to glean the truth from a comparison of *many*, why not go back to the original Greek and correct the mistakes introduced by inaccurate translators, and the blundering alterations of confident but ignorant critics, and, further, all that has been inserted or changed by copyists more asleep than awake? I am not discussing the Old Testament, which was turned into Greek by the Seventy elders, and[1] has reached us by a descent of three steps. I do not ask what [2]Aquila and [3]Symmachus think, or why [4]Theodotion takes a middle course between the

ancients and the moderns. I am willing to let that be the true translation which had apostolic approval. I am now speaking of the New Testament. This was undoubtedly composed in Greek, with the exception of the work of Matthew the Apostle, who was the first to commit to writing the Gospel of Christ, and who published his work in Judæa in Hebrew characters. We must confess that as we have it in our language it is marked by discrepancies, and now that the stream is distributed into different channels we must go back to the fountainhead. I pass over those manuscripts which are associated with the names of [1]Lucian and Hesychius, and the authority of which is perversely maintained by a handful of disputatious persons. It is obvious that these writers could not amend anything in the Old Testament after the labours of the Seventy; and it was useless to correct the New, for versions of Scripture which already exist in the languages of many nations show that their additions are false. I therefore promise in this short Preface the four Gospels only, which are to be taken in the following order, Matthew, Mark, Luke, John, as they have been revised by a comparison of the Greek manuscripts. Only early ones have been used. But to avoid any great divergences from the Latin which we are accustomed to read, I have used my pen with some restraint, and while I have corrected only such passages as seemed to convey a different meaning, I have allowed the rest to remain as they are.

The Preface concludes with a description of lists of words made by Eusebius and translated by Jerome, designed to show what passages occur in two or more of the Gospels.

---

[1] That is, after being translated from Hebrew into Greek, and from Greek into Latin.

[2] Aquila belonged to the second century, but whether to the first half, or to the early part of the second half, cannot be determined. He was a Jewish proselyte, of Sinope in Pontus, and is supposed to have translated the books of the Old Testament into Greek in order to assist the Hellenistic Jews in their controversies with Christians. Jerome's estimate of him varied from time to time. In his commentary on Hos. ii., Is. xlix., and Letter XXVIII., etc., he treats him as worthy of credit. On the other hand, in the letter to Pammachius, *De Opt. Gen. Interp.* (LVII. 11), he describes him as *contentiosus;* but in Letter XXXVI. 12, he denies that he is such. In the preface to Job he speaks of Aquila, Symmachus, and Theodotion as "Judaising heretics, who by their deceitful translation have concealed many mysteries of salvation." The second edition of Aquila's version, which was extremely literal, was highly esteemed by the Jews, and was called by them *the Hebrew verity.* See Davidson's "Biblical Criticism," p. 215, etc.

[3] Symmachus was the author of the third Greek version. He is said to have been a Samaritan by birth. The date of his version cannot be accurately fixed; but, apparently, it appeared after Theodotion's. "He does not adhere to the text so closely as to render it verbatim into Greek; but chooses to express the same in perspicuous and intelligible language."—Davidson.

[4] Theodotion, the author of the second Greek version, was a native of Ephesus. His version is thought to have been made before 160. "The mode of translation adopted by him holds an in-

termediate place between the scrupulous literality of Aquila and the free interpretation of Symmachus," and his work was more highly valued by Christians than that of either Aquila or Symmachus. Daniel was read in his version in the churches (Pref. to Joshua).

[1] Lucian in Syria and Hesychius in Egypt attempted their recensions about the middle of the third century, the time when Origen also began to labour in the same direction. Lucian's recension, also called the Constantinopolitan, and to which the Slavonian and Gothic versions belong, spread over Asia Minor and Thrace. See the Preface to the Chronicles. It was decreed by a council held under Pope Gelasius, A.D. 494, that "the Gospels which Lucian and Hesychius falsified are apocryphal."

PREFACES TO THE BOOKS OF THE VULGATE VERSION OF THE OLD TESTAMENT.

This version was not undertaken with ecclesiastical sanction as was the case with the Gospels, but at the request of private friends, or from Jerome's "own sense of the imperious necessity of the work." It was wholly made at Bethlehem, and was begun about A.D. 391, and finished about A.D. 404. The approximate dates of the several books are given before each Preface in the following pages.

PREFACE TO GENESIS.

This Preface was addressed to Desiderius, but which of the three correspondents of Jerome who bore this name is uncertain (See Article Desiderius in Smith and Wace's "Dictionary of Christian Biography"). We do not give

it because it has been given at length as a specimen of the rest, in Jerome's "Apology," book ii., vol. iii. of this series, pp. 515–516). Jerome in it complains that he is accused of forging a new version. He justifies his undertaking by showing that in the versions then current many passages were left out (though they exist in our copies of the LXX.), such as "Out of Egypt" (Hos. xi. 1); "They shall look on him whom they pierced" (Zech. xii. 10), etc., which are quoted in the New Testament and are found in the Hebrew. He accounts for these omissions by the suggestion that the LXX. were afraid of offending Ptolemy Lagus for whom they worked, and who was a Platonist. He rejects the fable of the LXX. being shut up in separate cells and producing an identical version, and protests against the notion that they were inspired, and he urges his calumniators, by applying to those who knew Hebrew, to test the correctness of his version.

There is no Preface to the other books of the Pentateuch. From the allusion to the work on the Pentateuch as lately finished, in the Preface to Joshua, which was published in 404, it is presumed that the date of the translation of the Pentateuch is 403.

JOSHUA, JUDGES, AND RUTH.

The Preface to these books was written A.D. 404 ; Jerome speaks of the death of Paula, which took place in that year, and the work is addressed to Eustochium alone. The Preface is chiefly occupied with a defence of his translation. He tells those who carp at it that they are not bound to read it, and mentions that the Church had given no final sanction to the LXX., but read the book of Daniel in Theodotion's version. The books of Joshua, Judges, and Ruth, were probably the last of the Vulgate translation ; the Preface declares Jerome's intention of devoting himself henceforward to the Commentaries on the Prophets, a work which took up the remainder of his life.

THE BOOKS OF SAMUEL AND KINGS.

This Preface was the first in order of publication. It was set forth as an exposition of the principles adopted by Jerome in all his translations from the Hebrew—the "Helmeted Preface," as he calls it in the beginning of the last paragraph, with which he was prepared to do battle against all who impugn his design and methods. It was addressed to Paula and Eustochium, and published about A.D. 391.

That the Hebrews have twenty-two letters is testified by the Syrian and Chaldæan languages which are nearly related to the Hebrew, for they have twenty-two elementary sounds which are pronounced the same way, but are differently written. The Samaritans also employ just the same number of letters in their copies of the Pentateuch of Moses, and differ only in the shape and outline of the letters. And it is certain that Esdras, the scribe and teacher of the law, after the capture of Jerusalem and the restoration of the temple by Zerubbabel, invented [1]other letters which we now use, although up to that time the Samaritan and Hebrew characters were the same. In the [2] book of Numbers, also, where we have the census of the Levites and priests, the mystic teaching of Scripture conducts us to the same result. And we find the four-lettered name of the Lord in certain

Greek books written to this day in the ancient characters. The thirty-seventh Psalm, moreover, the one hundred and eleventh, the one hundred and twelfth, the one hundred and nineteenth, and the one hundred and forty-fifth, although they are written in different metres, have for their [1] acrostic framework an alphabet of the same number of letters. The Lamentations of Jeremiah, and his Prayer, the Proverbs of Solomon also, towards the end, from the place where we read "Who will find a brave woman ?" are instances of the same number of letters forming the division into sections. And, again, five are double letters, viz., *Caph, Mem, Nun, Phe, Sade*, for at the beginning and in the middle of words they are written one way, and at the end another way. Whence it happens that, by most people, five of the books are reckoned as double, viz., Samuel, Kings, Chronicles, Ezra, Jeremiah, with *Kinoth, i.e.*, his Lamentations. As, then, there are twenty-two elementary characters by means of which we write in Hebrew all we say, and the compass of the human voice is contained within their limits, so we reckon twenty-two books, by which, as by the alphabet of the doctrine of God, a righteous man is instructed in tender infancy, and, as it were, while still at the breast.

The first of these books is called *Bresith*, to which we give the name Genesis. The second, *Elle Smoth*, which bears the name Exodus ; the third, *Vaiecra*, that is Leviticus ; the fourth, *Vaiedabber*, which we call Numbers ; the fifth, *Elle Addabarim*, which is entitled Deuteronomy. These are the five books of Moses, which they properly call [2] *Thorath*, that is *law*.

The second class is composed of the Prophets, and they begin with *Jesus* the son of Nave, who among them is called Joshua the son of Nun. Next in the series is *Sophtim*, that is the book of Judges ; and in the same book they include Ruth, because the events narrated occurred in the days of the Judges. Then comes Samuel, which we call First and Second Kings. The fourth is *Malachim*, that is, Kings, which is contained in the third and fourth volumes of Kings. And it is far better to say *Malachim*, that is Kings, than *Malachoth*, that is Kingdoms. For the author does not describe the Kingdoms of many nations, but that of one people, the people of Israel, which is comprised in the twelve tribes. The fifth is Isaiah, the sixth,

---

[1] That is, the square character which was of Assyrian origin. As to how far the tradition is true, see Davidson's "Biblical Criticisms" (1854), p. 22, and the authorities there referred to.
[2] iii. 39. All the males from a month old and upwards are said to have been *twenty-two* thousand.

[1] These are the alphabetical Psalms which, being mainly didactic, were written acrostically to assist the memory. Others partially acrostic are ix., x., xxv., xxxiv., to make the alphabet complete in xxxvii. ע in verse 28 must be supposed to be represented by לְעַרְלָם, and ת in verse 39 by רְתִשְׁהֵיח.
[2] More correctly *Torah*.

Jeremiah, the seventh, Ezekiel, the eighth is the book of the Twelve Prophets, which is called among the Jews [1] *Thare Asra*.

To the third class belong the *Hagiographa*, of which the first book begins with Job, the second with David, whose writings they divide into five parts and comprise in one volume of Psalms; the third is Solomon, in three books, Proverbs, which they call *Parables*, that is *Masaloth*, Ecclesiastes, that is *Coeleth*, the Song of Songs, which they denote by the title *Sir Assirim;* the sixth is Daniel; the seventh, *Dabre Aiamim*, that is, *Words of Days*, which we may more expressively call a chronicle of the whole of the sacred history, the book that amongst us is called First and Second [2] Chronicles; the eighth, Ezra, which itself is likewise divided amongst Greeks and Latins into [3] two books; the ninth is Esther.

And so there are also twenty-two books of the Old Testament; that is, five of Moses, eight of the prophets, nine of the Hagiographa, though some include Ruth and Kinoth (Lamentations) amongst the Hagiographa, and think that these books ought to be reckoned separately; we should thus have twenty-four books of the old law. And these the Apocalypse of the John represents by the twenty-four elders, who adore the Lamb, and with downcast looks offer their crowns, while in their presence stand the four living creatures with eyes before and behind, that is, looking to the past and the future, and with unwearied voice crying, Holy, Holy, Holy, Lord God Almighty, who wast, and art, and art to come.

This preface to the Scriptures may serve as a "helmeted" introduction to all the books which we turn from Hebrew into Latin, so that we may be assured that what is not found in our list must be placed amongst the Apocryphal writings. Wisdom, therefore, which generally bears the name of Solomon, and the book of Jesus, the Son of Sirach, and Judith, and Tobias, and the Shepherd are not in the canon. The first book of Maccabees I have found to be Hebrew, the second is Greek, as can be proved from the very style. Seeing that all this is so, I beseech you, my reader, not to think that my labours are in any sense intended to disparage the old translators. For the service of the tabernacle of God each one offers what he can; some gold and silver and precious stones, others linen and blue and purple and scarlet; we shall do well if we offer skins and goats' hair. And yet the Apostle pronounces our more contemptible parts more necessary than others. Accordingly, the beauty of the tabernacle as a whole and in its several kinds (and the ornaments of the church present and future) was covered with skins and goats'-hair cloths, and the heat of the sun and the injurious rain were warded off by those things which are of less account. First read, then, my Samuel and Kings; mine, I say, mine. For whatever by diligent translation and by anxious emendation we have learnt and made our own, is ours. And when you understand that whereof you were before ignorant, either, if you are grateful, reckon me a translator, or, if ungrateful, a paraphraser, albeit I am not in the least conscious of having deviated from the Hebrew original. At all events, if you are incredulous, read the Greek and Latin manuscripts and compare them with these poor efforts of mine, and wherever you see they disagree, ask some Hebrew (though you ought rather to place confidence in me), and if he confirm our view, I suppose you will not think him a soothsayer and suppose that he and I have, in rendering the same passage, divined alike. But I ask you also, the [1] handmaidens of Christ, who anoint the head of your reclining Lord with the most precious ointment of faith, who by no means seek the Saviour in the tomb, for whom Christ has long since ascended to the Father—I beg you to confront with the shields of your prayers the mad dogs who bark and rage against me, and go about the city, and think themselves learned if they disparage others. I, knowing my lowliness, will always remember what we are told. [2] "I said, I will take heed to my ways that I offend not in my tongue. I have set a guard upon my mouth while the sinner standeth against me. I became dumb, and was humbled, and kept silence from good words."

CHRONICLES.

This Preface is almost wholly a repetition of the arguments adduced in the Preface to Genesis. It is addressed to Chromatius, bishop of Aquileia, who took great interest in the work and provided funds for its continuance. The date is A.D. 395.

EZRA AND NEHEMIAH.

This Preface is addressed to Domnio (a Roman presbyter. See Letters L., and XLVII. 3, Paulinus, Ep. 3) and Rogatianus, of whom nothing is known. It was written A.D. 394. It is a repetition of his constant ground of self-defence, and contains a noble expression of his determination to carry the work through. "The serpent may hiss, and

" 'Victorious Sinon hurl his brand of fire,'

---

[1] The laws or instructions of Ezra. By many of the Jews Ezra was regarded as the author of the Twelve Prophets.
[2] Jerome has in the text the Greek equivalent παραλειπομένων.
[3] That is, Ezra and Nehemiah.

[1] Paula and Eustochium.   [2] Ps. xxxix. 2 sq.

but never shall my mouth be closed. Cut off my tongue ; it will still stammer out something."

ESTHER.

To Paula and Eustochium, early in 404. Merely assures them that he is acting as a faithful translator, adding nothing of his own ; whereas in the version then in common use (vulgata), "the book is drawn out into all kinds of perplexing entanglements of language."

JOB.

This was put into circulation about the same time as the sixteen prophets, that is, about the year 393. It was written in 392. It has no dedication, but is full of personal interest, and shows the deplorable state in which the text of many parts of Scripture was before his time, thus justifying his boast, "I have rescued Job from the dunghill."

I am compelled at every step in my treatment of the books of Holy Scripture to reply to the abuse of my opponents, who charge my translation with being a censure of the Seventy ; as though Aquila among Greek authors, and Symmachus and Theodotion, had not rendered word for word, or paraphrased, or combined the two methods in a sort of translation which is neither the one nor the other ; and as though Origen had not marked all the books of the Old Testament with obeli and asterisks, which he either introduced or adopted from Theodotion, and inserted in the old translation, thus showing that what he added was deficient in the older version. My detractors must therefore learn either to receive altogether what they have in part admitted, or they must erase my translation and at the same time their own asterisks. For they must allow that those translators, who it is clear have left out numerous details, have erred in some points ; especially in the book of Job, where, if you withdraw such passages as have been added and marked with asterisks, the greater part of the book will be cut away. This, at all events, will be so in Greek. On the other hand, previous to the publication of our recent translation with asterisks and obeli, about seven or eight hundred lines were missing in the Latin, so that the book, mutilated, torn, and disintegrated, exhibits its deformity to those who publicly read it. The present translation follows no ancient translator, but will be found to reproduce now the exact words, now the meaning, now both together of the original Hebrew, Arabic, and occasionally the Syriac. For an indirectness and a slipperiness attaches to the whole book, even in the Hebrew ; and, as orators say in Greek, it [1] is tricked out with figures of speech, and while it says one thing, it does another ; just as if you close your hand to hold an eel or a little

[1] muræna, the more you squeeze it, the sooner it escapes. I remember that in order to understand this volume, I paid a not inconsiderable sum for the services of a teacher, a native of Lydda, who was amongst the Hebrews reckoned to be in the front rank ; whether I profited at all by his teaching, I do not know ; of this one thing I am sure, that I could translate only that which I previously understood. Well, then, from the beginning of the book to the words of Job, the Hebrew version is in prose. Further, from the words of Job where he says, [2] "May the day perish wherein I was born, and the night in which it was said, a man-child is conceived," to the place where before the close of the book it is written [3] "Therefore I blame myself and repent in dust and ashes," we have hexameter verses running in dactyl and spondee : and owing to the idiom of the language other feet are frequently introduced not containing the same number of syllables, but the same quantities. Sometimes, also, a sweet and musical rhythm is produced by the breaking up of the verses in accordance with the laws of metre, a fact better known to prosodists than to the ordinary reader. But from the aforesaid verse to the end of the book the small remaining section is a prose composition. And if it seem incredible to any one that the Hebrews really have metres, and that, whether we consider the Psalter or the Lamentations of Jeremiah, or almost all the songs of Scripture, they bear a resemblance to our Flaccus, and the Greek Pindar, and Alcæus, and Sappho, let him read Philo, Josephus, Origen, Eusebius of Cæsarea, and with the aid of their testimony he will find that I speak the truth. Wherefore, let my barking critics listen as I tell them that my motive in toiling at this book was not to censure the ancient translation, but that those passages in it which are obscure, or those which have been omitted, or at all events, through the fault of copyists have been corrupted, might have light thrown upon them by our translation ; for we have some slight knowledge of Hebrew, and, as regards Latin, my life, almost from the cradle, has been spent in the company of grammarians, rhetoricians, and philosophers. But if, since the version of the Seventy was published, and even now, when the Gospel of Christ is beaming forth, the Jewish Aquila, Symmachus, and Theodotion, judaising heretics, have been welcomed amongst the Greeks —heretics, who, by their deceitful translation, have concealed many mysteries of salvation, and yet, in the Hexapla are found in the

---

[1] A small fish well known to the ancients, but apparently not identified with any species known to us.
[2] Job iii. 3.   [3] xlii. 6.

[1] ἐσχηματισμένος.

Churches and are expounded by churchmen; ought not I, a Christian, born of Christian parents, and who carry the standard of the cross on my brow, and am zealous to recover what is lost, to correct what is corrupt, and to disclose in pure and faithful language the mysteries of the Church, ought not I, let me, ask, much more to escape the reprobation of fastidious or malicious readers? Let those who will keep the old books with their gold and silver letters on purple skins, or, to follow the ordinary phrase, in "uncial characters," loads of writing rather than manuscripts, if only they will leave for me and mine, our poor pages and copies which are less remarkable for beauty than for accuracy. I have toiled to translate both the Greek versions of the Seventy, and the Hebrew which is the basis of my own, into Latin. Let every one choose which he likes, and [1] he will find out that what he objects to in me, is the result of sound learning, not of malice.

PSALMS.

Dedicated to Sophronius about the year 392. Jerome had, while at Rome, made a translation of the Psalms from the LXX., which he had afterwards corrected by collation with the Hebrew text (see the Preface addressed to Paula and Eustochium, *infra*). His friend Sophronius, in quoting the Psalms to the Jews, was constantly met with the reply, " It does not so stand in the Hebrew." He, therefore, urged Jerome to translate them direct from the original. Jerome, in presenting the translation to his friend, records the intention which he had expressed of translating the new Latin version into Greek. This we know was done by Sophronius, not only for the Psalms, but also for the rest of the Vulgate, and was valued by the Greeks (Apol. ii. 24, vol. iii. of this series, p. 515).

PROVERBS, ECCLESIASTES, AND THE SONG OF SONGS.

Dedicated to Chromatius and Heliodorus, A.D. 393. The Preface is important as showing the help given to Jerome by his friends, the rapidity of his work, and his view of the Apocrypha. We give the two chief passages.

It is well that my letter should couple those who are coupled in the episcopate ; and that I should not separate on paper those who are bound in one by the law of Christ. I would have written the commentaries on Hosea, Amos, Zechariah, and the Kings, which you ask of me, if I had not been prevented by illness. You give me comfort by the supplies you send me ; you support my secretaries and copyists, so that the efforts of all my powers may be given to you. And then all at once comes a thick crowd of people with all sorts of demands, as if it was just that I should neglect your hunger and work for others, or

as if, in the matter of giving and receiving, I had a debt to any one but you. And so, though I am broken by a long illness, yet, not to be altogether silent and dumb amongst you this year, I have dedicated to you three days' work, that is to say, the translation of the three books of Solomon.

After speaking of the books of the Wisdom of Solomon and Ecclesiasticus, which were sent at the same time, the Preface continues :

As, then, the Church reads Judith, Tobit, and the books of Maccabees, but does not admit them among the canonical Scriptures, so let it read these two volumes for the edification of the people, not to give authority to doctrines of the Church. If any one is better pleased with the edition of the Seventy, there it is, long since corrected by me. For it is not our aim in producing the new to destroy the old. And yet if our friend reads carefully, he will find that our version is the more intelligible, for it has not turned sour by being poured three times over into different vessels, but has been drawn straight from the press, and stored in a clean jar, and has thus preserved its own flavour.

ISAIAH.

Addressed to Paula and Eustochium, about A.D. 393. This Preface speaks of Isaiah as using the polished diction natural to a man of rank and refinement, as an Evangelist more than a prophet, and a poet rather than a prose writer. He then reiterates his defence of his translation, saying that now, " The Jews can no longer scoff at our Churches because of the falsity of our Scriptures."

JEREMIAH AND EZEKIEL.

Short Prefaces without dedication, but probably addressed to Paula and Eustochium, about A.D. 393.

DANIEL.

The Preface is interesting as showing the difficulties caused by the incorporation of apocryphal matter into this book, the fact that Theodotion's version, not the LXX., was read in the Churches, and that the book was reckoned by the Jews not among the prophets but among the Hagiographa. It was addressed to Paula and Eustochium about A.D. 392.

The Septuagint version of Daniel the prophet is not read by the Churches of our Lord and Saviour. They use Theodotion's version, but how this came to pass I cannot tell. Whether it be that the language is Chaldee, which differs in certain peculiarities from our speech, and the Seventy were unwilling to follow those deviations in a translation ; or that the book was published in the name of the Seventy, by some one or other not familiar with Chaldee, or if there be some other reason, I know not ; this one thing I can affirm—that it differs widely from the original, and is rightly rejected. For we

---

[1] Reading *studiosum me magis quam malevolum probet.* Substituting *se* for *me*, according to some manuscripts, we must translate "and thus show that he is actuated more by a love of learning than by malice."

ust bear in mind that Daniel and Ezra, the
rmer especially, were written in Hebrew
tters, but in the Chaldee language, as was
ne section of Jeremiah; and, further, that
b has much affinity with Arabic. As for
yself, when, in my youth, after reading the
wery rhetoric of Quintilian and Tully, I
tered on the vigorous study of this lan-
uage, the expenditure of much time and
ergy barely enabled me to utter the puffing
d hissing words; I seemed to be walking
a sort of underground chamber with a few
attered rays of light shining down upon me;
d when at last I met with Daniel, such a
nse of weariness came over me that, in a fit
despair, I could have counted all my former
il as useless. But there was a certain He-
rew who encouraged me, and was for ever quot-
g for my benefit the saying that "Persist-
t labour conquers all things"; and so, con-
ious that among Hebrews I was only a smat-
rer, I once more began to study Chaldee.
nd, to confess the truth, to this day I can
ad and understand Chaldee better than I
n pronounce it. I say this to show you how
ard it is to master the book of Daniel, which
Hebrew contains neither the history of
usanna, nor the hymn of the three youths,
r the fables of Bel and the Dragon; be-
use, however, they are to be found every-
here, we have formed them into an appendix,
refixing to them an obelus, and thus making
end of them, so as not to seem to the
ninformed to have cut off a large portion of
e volume. I heard a certain Jewish teacher,
hen mocking at the history of Susanna,
ying that it was the fiction of some Greek
other, raise the same objection which Afri-
nus brought against Origen—that these
ymologies of $^2 \sigma\chi\acute{\iota}\sigma\alpha\iota$ from $^3 \sigma\chi\tilde{\iota}\nu o\varsigma$, and
$\pi\rho\acute{\iota}\sigma\alpha\iota$ from $^5 \pi\rho\tilde{\iota}\nu o\varsigma$, are to be traced to
e Greek. To make the point clear to
atin readers: It is as if he were to say,
laying upon the word *ilex*, *illico pereas*; or
pon *lentiscus*, may the angel make a *lentil*
you, or may you perish *non lente*, or may
u *lentus* (that is pliant or compliant) be led
death, or anything else suiting the name of
e tree. Then he would captiously main-
in that the three youths in the furnace of
ging fire had leisure enough to amuse
emselves with making poetry, and to sum-
on all the elements in turn to praise God.
r what was there miraculous, he would say,
what indication of divine inspiration, in the
aying of the dragon with a lump of pitch,

or in frustrating the schemes of the priests of
Bel? Such deeds were more the results of
an able man's forethought than of a prophetic
spirit. But when he came to [1] Habakkuk and
read that he was carried from Judæa into
Chaldæa to bring a dish of food to Daniel,
he asked where we found an instance in the
whole of the Old Testament of any saint with
an ordinary body flying through the air, and
in a quarter of an hour traversing vast tracts
of country. And when one of us who was
rather too ready to speak adduced the instance of Ezekiel, and said that he was transported from Chaldæa into Judæa, he derided
the man and proved from the book itself that
Ezekiel, in spirit, saw himself carried over.
And he argued that even our own Apostle,
being an accomplished man and one who had
been taught the law by Hebrews, had not
dared to affirm that he was bodily rapt away,
but had said: [2] "Whether in the body, or out
of the body, I know not; God knoweth."
By these and similar arguments he used to
refute the apocryphal fables in the Church's
book. Leaving this for the reader to pronounce upon as he may think fit, I give
warning that Daniel in Hebrew is not found
among the prophets, but amongst the writers
of the Hagiographa; for all Scripture is by
them divided into three parts: the law, the
Prophets, and the Hagiographa, which have
respectively five, eight, and eleven books, a
point which we cannot now discuss. But as to
the objections which [3] Porphyry raises against
this prophet, or rather brings against the
book, [4] Methodius, Eusebius, and Apollinaris
may be cited as witnesses, for they replied
to his folly in many thousand lines of writing,
whether with satisfaction to the curious
reader I know not. Therefore, I beseech
you, Paula and Eustochium, to pour out your
supplications for me to the Lord, that so
long as I am in this poor body, I may write
something pleasing to you, useful to the
Church, worthy of posterity. As for my contemporaries, I am indifferent to their opinions, for they pass from side to side as they
are moved by love or hatred.

THE TWELVE MINOR PROPHETS.

This Preface, dedicated to Paula and Eustochium in
A.D. 392, contains nothing of importance, merely mentioning the dates of a few of the prophets, and the
fact that the Twelve Prophets were counted by the
Hebrews as forming a single book.

---

[1] In the LXX. the story of Bel and the Dragon bears a special
heading as "part of the prophecy of Habakkuk."—Westcott. The
angel is said to have carried Habakkuk with a dish of food in his
hand for Daniel from Judæa to Babylon.
[2] 2 Cor. xii. 2.
[3] The bitter enemy of the Christian faith. Born at Tyre 223.
Died at Rome about 304.
[4] Bishop of Patara in Lycia, and afterwards of Tyre. Suffered
martyrdom 302 or 303.

---

x. 11.
To split. The word has no sort of etymological connection
th σχῖνος. Susanna, 54, 55, 58, 59. When the first elder says
e crime was committed under a mastich tree (schinos), Daniel
swers, "God shall cut thee in two" (schisei).
The mastich tree. [4] To saw. [5] The holm-oak.

TRANSLATIONS FROM THE SEPTUAGINT AND CHALDEE.

There are three stages of Jerome's work of Scripture Translation. The first is during his stay at Rome, A. 382–385, when he translated only from the Greek—the New Testament from the Greek MSS., and the Book Psalms from the LXX. The second is the period immediately after his settlement at Bethlehem, when translated still from the LXX., but marked with obeli and asterisks the passages in which that version diffe from the Hebrew ; the third from A.D. 390-404, in which he translated directly from the Hebrew. The we of the second period is that which is now before us. The whole of the Old Testament was translated from LXX. (see his "Apology," book ii. c. 24), but most of it was lost during his lifetime (see Letters CXXX) (end) and CXVI. 34 (in Augustin Letter, 62)). What remains is the Book of Job, the Psalms, Chronicles, Books of Solomon, and Tobit and Judith.

CHRONICLES.

This book was dedicated to [1]Domnion and Rogatianus, about A.D. 388. Jerome points out the advantages he enjoyed, in living in Palestine, for obtaining correct information on matters illustrative of Scripture, especially the names of places. The MSS. of the LXX. on such points were so corrupt that occasionally three names were run into one, and "you would think that you had before you, not a heap of Hebrew names, but those of some foreign and Sarmatian tribe." Jerome had sent for a Jew, highly esteemed among his brethren, from Tiberias, and, after "examining him from top to toe," had, by his aid, emended the text and made the translation. But he had not the critical knowledge to guard him against supposing that the Books of Chronicles are "the Book of the Chronicles of the Kings of Judah," referred to in the Books of Kings.

BOOK OF JOB.

This translation was dedicated to Paula and Eustochium, about the year 388. He complains that even the revision he was now making was the subject of many cavils. Men prefer ancient faults to new truths, and would rather have handsome copies than correct ones ; but he boasts that "the blessed Job, who, as far as the Latins are concerned, was till now lying amidst filth and swarming with the worms of error, is now whole and free from stain."

THE PSALMS.

Jerome first undertook a revision of the Psalter with the help of the Septuagint about the year 383, when living at Rome. This revision, which obtained the name of the *Roman* Psalter "probably because it was made for the use of the Roman Church at the request of Damasus," was retained until the pontificate of Pius V. (A.D. 1566). Before long "the old error prevailed over the new correction," the faults of the old version crept in again through the negligence of copyists ; and at the request of Paula and Eustochium, Jerome commenced a new and more thorough revision. The exact date is not known ; the work was in all probability done at Bethlehem in the years 387 and 388. This edition, which soon became popular, was introduced by Gregory of Tours into the services of the Church of France, and thus obtained the name of the *Gallican* Psalter. In 1566 it superseded the *Roman* in all churches except those of the Vatican, Milan, and St. Mark's, Venice.

Long ago, when I was living at Rome, I revised the Psalter, and corrected it in a great measure, though but cursorily, in accordance with the Septuagint version. You now find it, Paula and Eustochium, again

[1] See Preface to Ezra (Vulgate).

corrupted through the fault of copyists, a realise the fact that ancient error is mc powerful than modern correction ; and y therefore urge me, as it were, to cross-plou the land which has already been broken up, ar by means of the transverse furrows, to rc out the thorns which are beginning to spri again ; it is only right, you say, that rank a noxious growths should be cut down as oft as they appear. And so I issue my custo ary admonition by way of preface both you, for whom it happens that I am und taking the labour, and to those persons w desire to have copies such as I descril Pray see that what I have carefully revis be transcribed with similar painstaki care. Every reader can observe for hims where there is placed either a horizontal line mark issuing from the centre, that is, eith an obelus (†) or an asterisk (*). And wh ever he sees the former, he is to understa that between this mark and the two stops which I have introduced, the Septuag translation contains superfluous matter. B where he sees the asterisk (*), an additi to the Hebrew books is indicated, which a goes as far as the two stops.

BOOKS OF SOLOMON.

This is addressed to Paula and Eustochium. Jero describes the numerous emendations he has had to ma in what was then the received Latin text, but says has not found the same necessity in dealing with Eccle asticus. He adds, "All I aim at is to give you a revis edition of the Canonical Scriptures, and to employ Latin on what is certain rather than on what is dou ful."

TOBIT AND JUDITH.

The Preface is to Chromatius and Heliodorus. recognizes that the books are apocryphal. After usual complaints of "the Pharisees" who impugned translations, he says : "Inasmuch as the Chaldee closely allied to the Hebrew, I procured the help of most skilful speaker of both languages I could fir and gave to the subject one day's hasty labour, method being to explain in Latin, with the aid of secretary, whatever an interpreter expressed to me Hebrew words."

As to Judith, he notes that the Council of Nicæa ha contrary to the Hebrew tradition, included it in Canon of Scripture, and this, with his friends' reques had induced him to undertake the labour of emendati and translation.

THE COMMENTARIES.

The extant commentaries by Jerome on the books of Holy Scripture may be arranged thus, chronological ?quence being observed as far as possible :
A. New Testament :
    The Epistles to Philemon, Galatians, Ephesians, Titus. A.D. 387.
    Origen on St. Luke. A.D. 389.
    St. Matthew. A.D. 398.
B. Old Testament :
    Ecclesiastes. A.D. 388.
    1. The Twelve Minor Prophets :
        Nahum. Michah, Zephaniah, Haggai, Habakkuk. A.D. 392.
        Jonah. Begun three years after the foregoing (Preface). Finished between A.D. 395 and A.D. 397.
        Obadiah. A.D. 403.
        Zechariah, Malachi, Hosea, Joel, Amos. Finished by A.D. 406.
    2. The Four Greater Prophets :
        Daniel. A.D. 407.
        Isaiah. A.D. 408–410.
        Ezekiel. A.D. 410–414.
        Jeremiah. Commenced after the death of Eustochium in A.D. 418. The commentary on this book, which stops short at chapter xxxii., was therefore written in A.D. 419, the year which intervened between Eustochium's death and Jerome's own.

We have thought it best to give the Prefaces, as in those to the Vulgate, in the order of the books as they and in our Bible, not in the order in which they were written.

MATTHEW.

The Preface, addressed to Eusebius of Cremona, was ritten A.D. 398. Eusebius was at this time starting ?r Rome, and he was charged to give a copy of this ?mmentary to Principia, the friend of Marcella, for ?hom he had been unable through sickness to write on ?e Song of Songs as he had wished. Jerome begins ? distinguishing the Canonical from the Apocryphal ?spels, quoting the words of St. Luke, that many had ?ken in hand to write the life of Christ. He gives his ?ew of the origin of the Gospels as follows :

The first evangelist is Matthew, the pub??an, who was surnamed Levi. He published ?s Gospel in Judæa in the Hebrew language, ?iefly for the sake of Jewish believers in ?hrist, who adhered in vain to the shadow ?f the law, although the substance of the ?ospel had come. The second is Mark, the ?manuensis of the Apostle Peter, and first ?ishop of the Church of Alexandria. He ?id not himself see our Lord and Saviour, ?ıt he related the matter of his Master's ?eaching with more regard to minute detail ?an to historical sequence. The third is ?uke, the physician, by birth a native of ?ntioch, in Syria, whose praise is in the ?ospel. He was himself a disciple of the ?postle Paul, and composed his book in ?chaia and Bœotia. He thoroughly inves?gates certain particulars and, as he himself ?nfesses in the preface, describes what he ?ad heard rather than what he had seen. ?he last is John, the Apostle and Evangelist, ?hom Jesus loved most, who, reclining on ?e Lord's bosom, drank the purest streams ?f doctrine, and was the only one thought ?orthy of the words from the cross, " Behold ! ?y mother." When he was in Asia, at the

time when the seeds of heresy were springing up (I refer to Cerinthus, Ebion, and the rest who say that Christ has not come in the flesh, whom he in his own epistle calls Antichrists, and whom the Apostle Paul frequently assails), he was urged by almost all the bishops of Asia then living, and by deputations from many Churches, to write more profoundly concerning the divinity of the Saviour, and to break through all obstacles so as to attain to the very Word of God (if I may so speak) with a boldness as successful as it appears audacious. Ecclesiastical history relates that, when he was urged by the brethren to write, he replied that he would do so if a general fast were proclaimed and all would offer up prayer to God ; and when the fast was over, the narrative goes on to say, being filled with revelation, he burst into the heaven-sent Preface : " In the beginning was the Word, and the Word was with God, and the Word was God : this was in the beginning with God."

Jerome then applies the four symbolical figures of Ezekiel to the Gospels : the Man is Matthew, the Lion, Mark, the Calf, Luke, " because he began with Zacharias the priest," and the Eagle, John. He then describes the works of his predecessors : Origen with his twenty-five volumes, Theophilus of Antioch, Hippolytus the martyr, Theodorus of Heraclea, Apollinaris of Laodicæa, Didymus of Alexandria, and of the Latins, Hilary, Victorinus, and Fortunatianus ; from these last, he says, he had gained but little. He continues as follows :

But you urge me to finish the composition in a fortnight, when Easter is now rapidly approaching, and the spring breezes are blowing ; you do not consider when the short-hand writers are to take notes, when the sheets are to be written, when corrected, how long it takes to make a really accurate copy ; and this is the more surprising, since you

---

¹ Interpres.

know that for the last three months I have
been so ill that I am now hardly beginning
to walk ; and I could not adequately perform so great a task in so short a time.
Therefore, neglecting the authority of ancient writers, since I have no opportunity of
reading or following them, I have confined
myself to the brief exposition and translation
of the narrative which you particularly requested ; and I have sometimes thrown in a
few of the flowers of the ¹spiritual interpretation, while I reserve the perfect work for a
future day.

PREFACE TO TRANSLATION OF ORIGEN ON ST. LUKE.

Addressed to Paula and Eustochium, A.D. 388.

A few days ago you told me that you had
read some commentaries on Matthew and
Luke, of which one was equally dull in perception and expression, the other frivolous in
expression, sleepy in sense. Accordingly you
requested me to translate, without regarding
such rubbish, our Adamantius' thirty-nine
"homilies" on Luke, just as they are found
in the original Greek ; I replied that it was an
irksome task and a mental torment to write,
as Cicero phrases it, with another man's heart²
not one's own ; but yet I will undertake it, as
your requests reach no higher than this.
The demand which the sainted Blesilla once
made, at Rome, that I should translate into
our language his twenty-five volumes on
Matthew, five on Luke, and thirty-two on
John is beyond my powers, my leisure, and
my energy. You see what weight your influence and wishes have with me. I have
laid aside for a time my books on Hebrew
Questions because you think my labour will
not be in vain, and turn to the translation of
these commentaries, which, good or bad, are
his work and not mine. I do this all the
more readily because I hear on the left
of me the raven—that ominous bird—
croaking and mocking in an extraordinary
way at the colours of all the other birds,
though he himself is nothing if not a bird of
gloom. And so, before he change his note,
I confess that in these treatises Origen is
like a boy amusing himself with the dice-box ;
there is a wide difference between his mature
efforts and the serious studies of his old
age. If my proposal meet with your approbation, if I am still able to undertake the task,
and if the Lord grant me opportunity to
translate them into Latin after completing the
work I have now deferred, you will then be

able to see—aye, and all who speak Latin w
learn through you—how much good th
knew not, and how much they have n
begun to know. Besides this, I have arrang
to send you shortly the Commentaries
Hilary, that master of eloquence, and of t
blessed martyr Victorinus, on the Gospel
Matthew. Their style is different, but t
grace of the Spirit which wrought in the
is one. These will give you some idea
the study which our Latins also have,
former days, bestowed upon the Holy Scri
tures.

GALATIANS.

The Commentary is in three books, with full Preface
Book I., Ch. i. 1–iii. 9.
Addressed to Paula and Eustochium, A.D. 387.
The Preface to this book begins with a striki
description of the noble Roman lady Albina, which
as follows :

Only a few days have elapsed since, havi
finished my exposition of the Epistle of Pa
to Philemon, I had passed to Galatians, tur
ing my course backwards and passing ov
many intervening subjects. But all at on
letters unexpectedly arrived from Rome wi
the news that the venerable Albina has bee
recalled to the presence of the Lord, ar
that the saintly Marcella, bereft of the com
pany of her mother, demands more than ev
such solace as you can give, my dear Pau
and Eustochium. This for the present
impossible on account of the great distan
to be traversed by sea and land, and I coul
therefore, wish to apply to the wound so su
denly inflicted at least the healing virtue
Scripture. I know full well her zeal an
faith ; I know how brightly the fire burns
her bosom, how she rises superior to her se
and soars so far above human nature itsel
that she crosses the Red Sea of this worl
sounding the loud timbrel of the inspire
volumes. Certainly, when I was at Rom
she never saw me for ever so short a tim
without putting some question to me respec
ing the Scriptures, and she did not, like th
Pythagoreans, accept the "Ipse dixit" of h
teacher, nor did authority, unsupported k
the verdict of reason, influence her ; b
she tested all things, and weighed the who
matter so sagaciously that I perceived I ha
not a disciple so much as a judge. And s
believing that my labours would be mo
acceptable to her who is at a distance, an
profitable for you who are with me here,
will approach a work unattempted by an
writers in our language before me, and whic
scarcely any of the Greeks themselves hav
handled in a manner worthy of the dignity
the subject.

---

¹ That is, the allegorical or mystical sense.
² Alieno stomacho.

Jerome then speaks of Victorinus, who had published a commentary on St. Paul, but "was busily engaged with secular literature and knew nothing of the Scriptures," and of the great Greek writers, Origen, [1] Didymus, and [2] Appolinaris, Eusebius of Emesa, and Theodorus of Heraclea, and says he has plucked flowers out of their gardens, so that the Commentary is more theirs than his. The expository part of the Preface is chiefly remarkable as giving the view of St. Paul's rebuke of St. Peter in Galatians ii., which occasioned the controversy between Jerome and Augustin. Jerome says:

Paul does not go straight to the point, but is like a man walking in secret passages: his object is to exhibit Peter as doing what was expedient for the people of the circumcision committed to him, since, if a too sudden revolt took place from their ancient mode of life, they might be offended and not believe in the Cross; he wished, moreover, to show, inasmuch as the evangelisation of the Gentiles had been entrusted to himself, that he had justice on his side in defending as true that which another only pretended was a dispensation. That wretch Porphyry [3] Bataneotes by no means understood this, and, therefore, in the first book of the work which he wrote against us, he raised the objection that Peter was rebuked by Paul for not walking uprightly as an evangelical teacher. His desire was to brand the former with error and the latter with impudence, and to bring against us as a body the charge of erroneous notions and false doctrine, on the ground that the leaders of the Churches are at variance among themselves.

In the Preface to Book II. Jerome describes the origin of the Galatians as a Gaulish tribe settled in Asia; but he takes them as slow of understanding, and says that the Gauls still preserve this character, just as the Roman Church preserves the character for which it was praised by St. Paul, for it still has crowds frequenting its churches and the tombs of its martyrs, and "nowhere else does the Amen resound so loudly, like spiritual thunder, and shake the temples of the idols"; and similarly the traits of the churches of Corinth and Thessalonica are still preserved; in the first, the looseness of behaviour and of doctrine, and the conceit of worldly knowledge; in the second, the love of the brethren side by side with the disorderly conduct of busybodies. And he speaks of the condition of Galatia in his own day as follows:

Any one who has seen by how many schisms Ancyra, the metropolis of Galatia, is rent and torn, and by how many differences and false doctrines the place is debauched, knows this as well as I do. I say nothing of [4] Cataphrygians,

[1] Didymus, the blind teacher of Alexandria.
[2] He became bishop of Laodicea about 362. About 376 his followers became a sect, and about the same time he set up bishops of his own at Antioch and elsewhere.
[3] Probably from Batanea, the ancient Bashan, where Porphyry is said to have been born.
[4] "The patriarch (of the Montanists) resided at Pepuza, a small town or village in Phrygia, to which the sectaries gave the mystical name of Jerusalem, as believing that it would be the seat of the Millennial Kingdom, which was the chief subject of their hopes. Hence they derived the names of Pepuzians and Cataphrygians."—Robertson, Ch. Hist., vol. i. p. 76.

[1] Ophites, Borborites, and Manichæans; for these are familiar names of human woe. Who ever heard of Passaloryncitæ, and [2] Ascodrobi, and [3] Artotyritæ, and other portents—I can hardly call them names—in any part of the Roman Empire? The traces of the ancient foolishness remain to this day. One remark I must make, and so fulfil the promise with which I started. While the Galatians, in common with the whole East, speak Greek, their own language is almost identical with that of the [4] Treviri; and if through contact with the Greek they have acquired a few corruptions, it is a matter of no moment. The Africans have to some extent changed the Phenician language, and Latin itself is daily undergoing changes through differences of place and time.

The Preface to Book III. opens with the following passage, describing, in contrast with his own simple exposition, the arts of the preachers of his day.

We are now busily occupied with our third book on Galatians, and, my friends, Paula and Eustochium, we are well aware of our weakness, and are conscious that our slender ability flows in but a small stream and makes little roar and rattle. For these are the qualities (to such a pass have we come) which are now expected even in the Churches; the simplicity and purity of apostolic language is neglected; we meet as if we were in the [5] Athenæum, or the lecture rooms, to kindle the applause of the bystanders; what is now required is a discourse painted and tricked out with spurious rhetorical skill, and which, like a strumpet in the streets, does not aim at instructing the public, but at winning their favour; like a psaltery or a sweet-sounding lute, it must soothe the ears of the audience; and the passage of the prophet Ezekiel is suitable for our times, where the Lord says to him, "Thou art become unto them as the sound of a pleasant lute which is well made, for they hear thy words but do them not."

Jerome then speaks of the composition of his commentaries as follows:

How far I have profited by my unflagging study of Hebrew I leave to others to decide;

[1] The Ophites, who took their name from ὄφις, a serpent, supposed the serpent of Genesis iii. to have been either the Divine Wisdom or the Christ Himself, come to set men free from the ignorance in which the Demiurge wished to keep them. The sect began in the second century and lasted until the sixth.
[2] The Ben. editor prefers the form Tascodrogi, and states that it is the Phrygian or Galatian equivalent for Passaloryncitæ. The sect is said to have been so called from their habit of putting the finger to the nose when praying.
[3] Heretics who made offerings of bread and cheese (ἀρτό-τυρος. Arto-tyros).—Aug. de Hæres, No. 28.
[4] The people who lived between the Moselle and the Forest of Ardennes in and about the modern Treves.
[5] The Athenæum was the name specially given to a school founded by the Emperor Hadrian at Rome, about A.D. 133, for the promotion of literary and scientific studies. The word denoted in general any place consecrated to the goddess Athena.

what I have lost in my own language, I can tell. In addition to this, on account of the weakness of my eyes and bodily infirmity generally, I do not write with my own hand ; and I cannot make up for my slowness of utterance by greater pains and diligence, as is said to have been the case with Virgil, of whom it is related that he treated his books as a bear treats her cubs, and licked them into shape. I must summon a secretary, and either say whatever comes uppermost ; or, if I wish to think a little and hope to produce something superior, my helper silently reproves me, clenches his fist, wrinkles his brow, and plainly declares by his whole bearing that he has come for nothing.

He then points out how the Scriptures have dispossessed the great writers of the pre-Christian world.

How few there are who now read Aristotle. How many are there who know the books, or even the name of Plato ? You may find here and there a few old men, who have nothing else to do, who study them in a corner.[1] But the whole world speaks the language of our Christian peasants and fishermen, the whole world re-echoes their words. And so their simple words must be set forth with simplicity of style ; for the word *simple* applies to their *words*, not their meaning. But if, in response to your prayers, I could, in expounding their epistles, have the same spirit which they had when they dictated them, you would then see in the Apostles as much majesty and breadth of true wisdom as there is arrogance and vanity in the learned men of the world. To make a brief confession of the secrets of my heart, I should not like any one who wished to understand the Apostle to find a difficulty in understanding my writings, and so be compelled to find some one to interpret the interpreter.

EPHESIANS.

This Commentary was specially prized by Jerome as exhibiting his true views (Letter LXXXIV. 2), and they became in consequence one of the chief subjects of controversy between him and Rufinus, who traced in them, not unjustly, the influence of Origen. It was written immediately after that on the Epistle to the Galatians, in A.D. 387, and, like that, addressed to Paula and Eustochium. In the Preface to Book i. Jerome defends himself against various accusations. He declares that he has been, in the main, his own instructor, but yet that he has constantly consulted others as to Scriptural difficulties, and that he had, not long before, been to Alexandria to consult, Didymus. "I questioned him about everything which was not clear to me in the whole range of Scripture." As to his indebtedness to Origen, he speaks as follows, certainly not blaming his doctrines : "I remark in the Prefaces, for your information, that Origen composed three volumes on this Epistle, and I have partly followed him. Apollinaris

_____
[1] Angulis. So. Cic. Rep. i. 2.

and Didymus also published some commentaries, and though we have gleaned a few things from them, w have added or omitted such as we thought fit. Th studious reader will, therefore, understand at the outse that this work is partly my own, and that I am in par indebted to others."

The Preface to Books ii. and iii. is short. It speak in praise of Marcella, who had invited him to his task, an declares that he in his monastery could not accomplis as much as that noble woman amidst the cares of he household. "I beseech you," he says, "to bear i mind that the language of this publication has not bee long thought over or highly polished. In revealing th mysteries of Scripture I use almost the language of th street, and sometimes get through a thousand lines day, in order that the explanation of the Apostle whic I have begun may be completed with the aid of th prayers of Paul himself, whose Epistles I am endeavour ing to explain."

PHILEMON.

Written for Paula and Eustochium, A.D. 387 The Preface is a defence of the genuineness of th Epistle against those who thought its subject beneat the dignity of inspiration. "There are many degrees o inspiration," Jerome says, "though in Christ alone it i seen in its fulness." Many of the other Epistles touc upon small affairs of life, like the cloak left at Troas To suppose that common life is separate from God i Manichæanism. Jerome mentions that Marcion, wh altered many of the Epistles, did not touch that t Philemon; and brevity in a document which has in i so much of the beauty of the Gospel is a mark of it inspiration.

TITUS.

Addressed to Paula and Eustochium, A.D. 387 The Preface speaks of the rejection of the Epistle b Marcion and Basilides, its acceptance by Tatius, bu without assigning reasons. It ought, Jerome says, t be of special interest to Paula and Eustochium, a being written from Nicopolis, near Actium, where thei property lay.

ISAIAH.

The Commentary in eighteen books, each with it Preface. It was written in the years 404–410, and addressed to Eustochium alone, her mother Paula having died in 404.

The Preface to Book i. touches generally upon the character and contents of Isaiah, asserting that many of the prophecies are directly applicable to Christ, and that the nations who are dealt with have a spiritual meaning. Those to the following books mostly give a short statement of the contents of the chapters commented on, and entreat the prayers of Eustochium for the work. The Fifth Book (or chapters xiii. to xxiii.) had been published before by itself, at the instance of a bishop named Amabilis, but he says he must add the metaphorical and spiritual meaning of the Visions of the various nations, which is done in Books vi. and vii. The Preface to Book x. contains a bitter allusion to Rufinus, "the Scorpion, a dumb and poisonous brute, still grumbling over my former reply," and speaks of Pammachius as joining in the request for the continuation of the Commentaries.

The Preface to Book xi. intimates that his commentary upon Daniel, which expounded the statue with feet of iron and clay as the Roman Empire, and announced its fall, had been known at the court and resented by Stilicho, but that all danger from that source had been removed by the judgment of God, that is, through the death of Stilicho by the command of his son-in-law Honorius.

The Preface to Book xiii. records a severe illness which had stopped his work, though he was restored to health suddenly; and that to Book xiv. thanks Eustochium for her kind offices during this illness. The remaining Prefaces, though they have occasionally some interest in the history of the interpretation of Scripture, need not delay us.

JEREMIAH.

The Commentary on Jeremiah is in six books; but Jerome did not live to finish it. It was written between the years 317 and 319, but only extends to chapter xxxii. It was dedicated to Eusebius of Cremona. The Prefaces, which are full of vigour, contain many allusions to the events and controversies of the last years of Jerome's life. In the Preface to Book i., after speaking of the Book of Daniel and the apocryphal Letter of Jeremiah as not belonging to the prophet's writings, he continues:

I pay little heed to the ravings of disparaging critics who revile not only my words, but the very syllables of my words, and suppose they give evidence of some little knowledge if they discredit another man's work, as was exemplified in that[1] ignorant traducer who lately broke out, and thought it worth his while to censure my commentaries on Paul's Epistle to the Ephesians. He does not understand the rules of commenting (for he is more asleep than awake and seems utterly dazed), and is not aware that in our books we give the opinions of many different writers, the authors' names being either expressed or understood, so that it is open to the reader to decide which he may prefer to adopt; although I must add that, in my Preface to the First Book of that work, I gave fair notice that my remarks would be partly my own, partly those of other commentators, and that thus the commentary would be the work conjointly of the ancient writers and of myself. [2]Grunnius, his precursor, overlooked the same fact, and once upon a time did his best to cavil. I replied to him in two books, and there I cleared away the objections which he adduced in his own name, though the real traducer was some one else; to say nothing of my treatises against Jovinianus where, you may remember, I show that he (Jovinianus) laments that virginity is preferred to marriage, single marriage to digamy, digamy to polygamy. The stupid fool,[3] labouring under his load of Scotch porridge, does not recollect that we said, in that very work, "I do not condemn the twice married, nor the thrice married, and, if it so be, the

eight times married; I will go a step farther, and say that I welcome even a penitent whoremonger; for things equally lawful must be weighed in an even balance." Let him read the Apology[1] for the same work which was directed against his[2] master, and was received by Rome with acclamation many years ago. He will then observe that his revilings are but the echoes of other men's voices, and that his ignorance is so deep that even his abuse is not his own, but that he employs against us the ravings of foes long since dead and buried.

The Preface to Book ii. is short and contains nothing of special importance. In that to Book iii. Jerome declares that he will, like Ulysses with the Sirens, close his ears to the adversary. The devil, who once spoke through Jovinianus, "now barks through the hound of Albion (Pelagius), who is like a mountain of fat, and whose fury is more in his heels than in his teeth; for his offspring is among the Scots, in the neighbourhood of Britain; and, according to the fables of the poet, he must, like Cerberus, be smitten to death with a spiritual club, that, in company with his master Pluto, he may forever hold his peace."

In the Preface to Book iv. Jerome says he has been hindered in his work by the harassing of the Pelagian controversy. He regards Pelagius as reproducing the doctrines of impassibility and sinlessness taught by Pythagoras and Zeno, and revived by Origen, Rufinus, Evagrius Ponticus, and Jovinian. Their doctrines, he says, were promulgated chiefly in Sicily, Rhodes, and other islands; they were propagated secretly, and denied in public. They were full of malice, but were but dumb dogs, and were refuted in "certain writings," probably those of Augustin; but he declares his intention of writing against them, which he did in his anti-Pelagian Dialogue.

The Prefaces to Books v. and vi. contain nothing noteworthy.

EZEKIEL.

The Commentary on Ezekiel is in fourteen Books. It was dedicated to Eustochium, and was written between the years 410 and 414. The Prefaces gain a special interest from their descriptions of the sack of Rome by Alaric and the consequent immigration into Palestine. We give several passages.

In Preface to Book i.

Having completed the eighteen books of the exposition of Isaiah, I was very desirous, Eustochium, Christ's virgin, to go on to Ezekiel, in accordance with my frequent promises to you and your mother Paula, of saintly memory, and thus, as the saying is, put the finishing touches to the work on the prophets; but alas! intelligence was suddenly brought me of the death of Pammachius and [3]Marcella, [4]the siege of Rome, and the falling asleep of many of my brethren and sisters. I

---

[1] Pelagius.
[2] That is, Rufinus. See Preface to Book xii. of Isaiah, where Rufinus is called Grunnius Corocotta Porcellus, and Preface to Book iv. of Jeremiah.
[3] Scotorum pultibus prægravatus. The words have been translated "made fat with Scotch flummery" (Stillingfleet). Another rendering is, "having his belly filled and his head bedulled with Scotch porridge" (Wall on Infant Baptism, pt. i. c. 19, § 3). Some think the words refer to Celestius, Pelagius' supporter.

[1] The letter to Pammachius (Jer. Letter XLVIII.) in defence of the book against Jovinianus.
[2] Jovinian was condemned in a Synod at Rome about 390. Thirty years had thus passed since the events occurred to which Jerome refers. See Preface to the treatise against Jovinian.
[3] Under whose care Eustochium had been trained.
[4] By the Goths under Alaric. The city was taken in A.D. 410.

was so stupefied and dismayed that day and night I could think of nothing but the welfare of the community; it seemed as though I was sharing the captivity of the saints, and I could not open my lips until I knew something more definite; and all the while, full of anxiety, I was wavering between hope and despair, and was torturing myself with the misfortunes of other people. But when the bright light of all the world was put out, or, rather, when the Roman Empire was decapitated, and, to speak more correctly, the whole world perished in one city,[1] "I became dumb and humbled myself, and kept silence from good words, but my grief broke out afresh, my heart glowed within me, and while I meditated the fire was kindled;" and I thought I ought not to disregard the saying,[2] "An untimely story is like music in a time of grief." But seeing that you persist in making this request, and a wound, though deep, heals by degrees; and [3]the scorpion lies beneath the ground with [4]Enceladus and Porphyrion, and the many-headed Hydra has at length ceased to hiss at us; and since opportunity has been given me which I ought to use, not for replying to insidious heretics, but for devoting myself to the exposition of Scripture, I will resume my work upon the prophet Ezekiel.

Book ii. has, instead of a Preface, merely a line calling the attention of Eustochium to its opening words.

The Preface to Book iii. has a noteworthy passage on the sack of Rome and its results.

Who would believe that Rome, built up by the conquest of the whole world, had collapsed, that the mother of nations had become also their tomb; that the shores of the whole East, of Egypt, of Africa, which once belonged to the imperial city, were filled with the hosts of her men-servants and maid-servants, that we should every day be receiving in this holy Bethlehem men and women who once were noble and abounding in every kind of wealth, but are now reduced to poverty? We cannot relieve these sufferers: all we can do is to sympathise with them, and unite our tears with theirs. The burden of this holy work was as much as we could carry; the sight of the wanderers, coming in crowds, caused us deep pain; and we therefore abandoned the exposition of Ezekiel, and almost all study, and were filled with a longing to turn the words of Scripture into action, and not to say holy things but to do them. Now, however, in response to your

admonition, Eustochium, Christ's virgin, w[e] resume the interrupted labour, and approac[h] our third Book.

The Prefaces to Books iv., v., and vi. contain not[h]ing remarkable. The following is the important pa[rt] of the Preface to Book vii.

There is not a single hour, nor a sing[le] moment, in which we are not relieving crowd[s] of brethren, and the quiet of the monaster[y] has been changed into the bustle of a gue[st] house. And so much is this the case tha[t] we must either close our doors, or abando[n] the study of the Scriptures on which we de[-] pend for keeping the doors open. And s[o] turning to profit, or rather stealing the hou[rs] of the nights, which, now that winter is ap[-] proaching, begin to lengthen somewhat, [I] am endeavouring by the light of the lamp t[o] dictate these comments, whatever they may b[e] worth, and am trying to mitigate with exposi[-] tion the weariness of a mind which is a strange[r] to rest. I am not boasting, as some perhap[s] suspect, of the welcome given to the brethre[n] but I am simply confessing the causes of th[e] delay. Who could boast when the flight o[f] the people of the West, and the holy place[s] crowded as they are with penniless fugitives[,] naked and wounded, plainly reveal the ravage[s] of the Barbarians? We cannot see what ha[s] occurred, without tears and moans. Wh[o] would have believed that mighty Rome, with it[s] careless security of wealth, would be reduce[d] to such extremities as to need shelter, food, an[d] clothing? And yet, some are so hard-hearte[d] and cruel that, instead of showing compassio[n] they break up the rags and bundles of th[e] captives, and expect to find gold about thos[e] who are nothing than prisoners. In additio[n] to this hindrance to my dictating, my eyes ar[e] growing dim with age and to some extent share the suffering of the saintly Isaac: I a[m] quite unable to go through the Hebrew book[s] with such light as I have at night, for eve[n] in the full light of day they are hidden from m[y] eyes owing to the smallness of the letters. I[n] fact, it is only the voice of the brethren whic[h] enables me to master the commentaries o[f] Greek writers.

The Prefaces to Books viii. to xiv. contain nothing o[f] special interest.

DANIEL.

The Commentary on Daniel was dedicated to Pam[-] machius and Marcella in the year 407. It is in a singl[e] book, and is aimed at the criticisms of Porphyry, who[,] like most modern critics, took the predictions in th[e] Book of Daniel as relating to the time of Antiochu[s] Epiphanes and the Maccabees, and written near tha[t] date. The Preface is very similar to that prefixed t[o] the Vulgate translation of Daniel.

---

[1] Ps. xxxix. 3, 4.　　　[2] Ecclus. xxii. 6.
[3] Rufinus, who died A.D. 410, in Sicily, on his way to the Holy Land from Aquileia and Rome, whence he had been driven by the troubles in Italy.
[4] The giants who bore those names. See Hor. III. od. 4.

PREFACES TO THE COMMENTARIES ON THE MINOR PROPHETS.

For the order and date of writing of these Commentaries see the Preface to Amos, Book iii., and the note there.

HOSEA.

This Commentary was dedicated to Pammachius, A.D. 406 (sixth consulate of Arcadius—Preface to Amos, Book iii.). The Preface to Book i. is chiefly taken up with a discussion on Hosea's "wife of whoredoms." He takes the story as allegorical; it cannot be literal, for "God commands nothing but what is honourable, or does he, by bidding men do disgraceful things, make that conduct honourable which is disgraceful." Jerome then describes, as in former Prefaces, the chief Greek commentators, of whom Apollinaris and Origen had written very shortly on Hosea, Pierius at great length, but to little purpose ; and says that he had himself obtained from Didymus of Alexandria that he should complete the Commentary of Origen. He had himself often judged independently, though with little knowledge of Hebrew, but he had been in earnest, while most scholars were "more concerned for their bellies than their hearts, and thought themselves learned if in the doctors' waiting rooms they could disparage other men's works."

In the Preface to Book ii. Jerome complains of his detractors, and appeals from the present favour of high-placed men to the posthumous authority of sound ability.

In Book iii. he claims Pammachius as his defender, though he fears the judgment of his great learning.

JOEL.

This Commentary also is addressed to Pammachius, A.D. 406. It is in one book. It gives the order of the Twelve Prophets adopted by the LXX. and the Hebrew respectively, the Hebrew order being that now in use. It also gives the etymological meaning of their names.

AMOS.

In three books, addressed also to Pammachius, A.D. 406 (Preface to Amos, Book iii.). The Preface to Book i. merely gives a description of Tekoa, Amos' birthplace. That to Book ii. speaks of old age, with its advantages for self-control and its trials in various infirmities, such as phlegm, dim eyesight, loosened teeth, colic, and gout. That to Book iii. contains the passage several times referred to for the order of these Commentaries, which is as follows :

We have not discussed them in regular sequence from the first to the ninth, as they are read, but as we have been able, and in accordance with requests made to us. Nahum, Micah, Zephaniah, Haggai, [1] I first addressed to Paula and Eustochium, her daughter, who are never weary ; I next dedicated two books on Habakkuk to Chromatius, bishop of Aquileia ; I then proceeded to explain, at your command, Pammachius, and after a long interval of silence, Obadiah and Jonah.[1] In the [2]present year, which bears in the calendar the name of the sixth consulate of Arcadius Augustus and Anitius Probus, I interpreted Malachi for Exsuperius, bishop of Toulouse, and Minervius and Alexander, monks of that city. Unable to refuse your request I immediately went back to the beginning of the volume, and expounded Hosea, Joel, and Amos. A severe sickness followed, and I showed my rashness in resuming the dictation of this work too hastily ; and, whereas others hesitate to write and frequently correct their work, I entrusted mine to the fortune which attends those who employ a secretary, and hazarded my reputation for ability and orthodoxy ; for, as I have often testified, I cannot endure the toil of writing with my own hand ; and, in expounding the Holy Scriptures, what we want is not a polished style and oratorical flourishes, but learning and simple truth.

OBADIAH.

Addressed to Pammachius A.D. 403. The Preface records how in early youth (some thirty years before), he had attempted an allegorical commentary of Obadiah, of which he was now ashamed, though it has lately been praised by a youth of similar years.

JONAH.

This was addressed to Chromatius,[3] but belongs to the year 395. It is said in the Preface to be three years after the commentary on Micah, Nahum, etc. The Preface merely touches on the various places of Scripture in which Jonah is named.

MICAH.

Addressed to Paula and Eustochium, A.D. 392. It is in two books. In the Preface to Book ii., Jerome vindicates himself against the charge of making mere compilations from Origen. He confesses, however, his great admiration for him. "What they consider a reproach," he says, " I regard as the highest praise, since I desire to imitate him who, I doubt not, is acceptable to all wise men, and to you."

NAHUM.

Also to Paula and Eustochium, A.D. 392. The Preface contains little of importance. Jerome mentions that the village of Elkosh, Nahum's birthplace, was pointed out to him by a guide in Galilee.

HABAKKUK.

Addressed to Chromatius, A.D. 392. The commentary is in two books. The Preface to Book i. is long, but merely describes the contents of the book. That to Book ii. mentions among his adversaries, "The Serpent, and Sardanapalus, whose character is worse than his

---

[1] These four and Habakkuk are mentioned in the De Vir. Ill. (A.D. 492), and were written about that date, Jonah three years after, but Obadiah probably not till 403. The rest are fixed to the Sixth Consulate of Arcadius, 406.

[1] But see Preface to Jonah, which is addressed to Chromatius.
[2] The year A.D. 406.
[3] Chromatius is named in this Preface distinctly. But see Preface to Amos, Book iii., which says that the Commentaries to Obadiah and Jonah were written at the request of Pammachius.

name"—expressions which have been referred to Rufinus; but the enmity between Jerome and Rufinus had not broken out in 392.

ZEPHANIAH.

Addressed to Paula and Eustochium, A.D. 392. In the Preface Jerome defends himself for writing for women, bringing many examples from Scripture and from classical writers to show the capacity of women.

HAGGAI.

Also to Paula and Eustochium, A.D. 392. The preface merely describes the occasion of the book, but says that Haggai's prophecy was contemporary with the reign of Tarquinius Superbus (B.C. 535–510).

ZECHARIAH.

Addressed to Exsuperius, bishop of Toulouse, A.D 406, in three books, and sent, "in the closing days of autumn, by the monk, Sisinnius, who had been sent with presents for the poor saints at Jerusalem, and was hastening to Egypt on a similar errand." The Prefaces to the three books mention these facts, but have nothing in them of note which has not been said before.

MALACHI.

Addressed, A.D. 406, to Minervius and Alexander, presbyters of the diocese of Toulouse. The Jews, the Preface says, believe Malachi to be a name for Ezra. Origen and his followers believe that (according to his name) he was an angel. But we reject this view altogether, lest we be compelled to accept the doctrine of the fall of souls from heaven.

INDICES

JEROME

INDEX OF SUBJECTS

JEROME

INDEX OF TEXTS